'The scope and coverage of contemporary marketing issues with different perspectives makes the *Handbook* very unique in that it crosses not only disciplinary boundaries with critical and latest thinking but also links theory to the practical process of marketing applications and strategies. It is an excellent addition to the scholarly tourism marketing literature. It is a must have book for anyone who is involved in tourism and destination marketing.'

Muzaffer Uysal, Professor of Hospitality and Tourism,
Virginia Polytechnic Institute and State University

'This is an excellent text which offers a challenging and well-structured collection of practical and critical perspectives. Scott McCabe has orchestrated a comprehensive array of contributions by renowned experts to produce what is sure to become the core text for students of tourism marketing.'

John Tribe, Professor of Tourism, University of Surrey

'*The Routledge Handbook of Tourism Marketing* represents a considerable effort by leading researchers in the field to present a comprehensive overview of the subject. Tourism marketing covers a broad range of activities, and this book neatly organises chapters into themes, progressing from macro issues of the tourism environment to micro issues of tourists' individual decision making. A strength of the book is the breadth of knowledge of the contributing authors and their authoritative writing style which makes this a truly comprehensive handbook of tourism marketing. As well as providing historical perspectives, the *Handbook* is right up to date with coverage of social media.'

Adrian Palmer, Professor of Marketing, Swansea University

The Routledge Handbook of Tourism Marketing

Tourism has often been described as being about 'selling dreams', tourist experiences being conceptualized as purely a marketing confection, a socially constructed need. However, the reality is that travel for leisure, business, meetings, sports or visiting loved ones has grown to be a very real sector of the global economy, requiring sophisticated business and marketing practices.

The Routledge Handbook of Tourism Marketing explores and critically evaluates the current debates and controversies inherent to the theoretical, methodological and practical processes of marketing within this complex and multi-sector industry. It brings together leading specialists from a range of disciplinary backgrounds and geographical regions to provide reflection and empirical research. The *Handbook* is divided into nine inter-related sections: Part 1 deals with shifts in the context of marketing practice and our understanding of what constitutes value for tourists; Part 2 explores macromarketing and tourism; Part 3 deals with strategic issues; Part 4 addresses recent advances in research; Part 5 focuses on developments in tourist consumer behaviour; Part 6 looks at micromarketing; Part 7 moves on to destination marketing and branding issues; Part 8 looks at the influence of technological change on tourism marketing; and Part 9 explores future directions.

This timely book offers the reader a comprehensive synthesis of this sub-discipline, conveying the latest thinking and research. It will provide an invaluable resource for all those with an interest in tourism and marketing, encouraging dialogue across disciplinary boundaries and areas of study.

This is essential reading for Tourism students, researchers and academics as well as those of Marketing, Business, Events Management and Hospitality Management.

Scott McCabe is Associate Professor of Tourism Management/Marketing at Nottingham University Business School. His research focuses on theorizations of tourist experience, social tourism, and marketing communications and branding. He writes on qualitative methods, particularly socio-linguistics.

The Routledge Handbook of Tourism Marketing

Edited by Scott McCabe

Routledge
Taylor & Francis Group
LONDON AND NEW YORK

First published 2014
by Routledge
2 Park Square, Milton Park, Abingdon, Oxon OX14 4RN

and by Routledge
711 Third Avenue, New York, NY 10017

Routledge is an imprint of the Taylor & Francis Group, an informa business

British Library Cataloguing in Publication Data
A catalogue record for this book is available from the British Library

Library of Congress Cataloging in Publication Data
The Routledge handbook of tourism marketing / [edited by] Scott McCabe.
pages cm
Includes bibliographical references and index.
1. Tourism–Marketing–Handbooks, manuals, etc. I. McCabe, Scott.
G155.A1R69 2014
910.68'8–dc23

2013021847

ISBN: 978-0-415-59703-6 (hbk)
ISBN: 978-1-315-85826-5 (ebk)

Typeset in Bembo
by RefineCatch Limited, Bungay, Suffolk

MIX
Paper from responsible sources
FSC® C013056

Printed and bound in Great Britain by
TJ International Ltd, Padstow, Cornwall

Contents

PART 9
Reflections 547

Figures

Tables

Contributors

Ronnie Ballantyne is Lecturer in Marketing at Glasgow Caledonian University; Adjunct Professor of Marketing at the University of Nice and Adjunct Professor of Marketing University of Da'Nang Vietnam. His specialist area of research is branding and consumer behaviour – his previous research has been published in *The Journal of Brand Management* and several chapters on tourism marketing.

Stewart Barr obtained his PhD from the University of Exeter in 2001 and is now Associate Professor in the Geography Department at the University. His research interests focus on how environmental social science can lead academic discussions on social transformation in an age of accelerated environmental change.

Wided Batat is Associate Professor of Marketing at the University of Lyon 2 and a United Nations Representative of the International Federation for Home Economics IFHE at the UNESCO in Paris. Her research is in the area of experiential consumption and tourism.

Carmela Bosangit received her PhD in Business and Management from the University of Nottingham. Her research interests include social media, consumer-generated content, travel narratives, experience marketing and destination place/marketing. She has joined Coventry University Business School as a research assistant in the Marketing and Advertising Department.

Amy Bourke is a former postgraduate student and researcher in the Department of Marketing at the University of Otago. Her research interests include tourism destination marketing.

Dimitrios Buhalis is an internationally renowned researcher, who specialises in e-Tourism and advises on the use of information and communication technology (ICT) in the tourism business. He is Director of the eTourism Lab at the School of Tourism, Bournemouth University and is responsible for driving forward a cross-university initiative to pioneer collaborative research within the theme of the creative and digital economy.

Robert Caruana is Assistant Professor in Business Ethics at the International Centre for Corporate Social Responsibility of Nottingham University Business School. His current research interests include responsibility, independence, freedom and discourse in tourism markets, and he has published in journals such as *Organisation Studies*, *European Journal of Marketing* and *Annals of Tourism Research*.

Yeongbae Choe is a PhD student in the Fox School of Business and the School of Tourism and Hospitality Management and works as a research assistant at the National Laboratory for Tourism and eCommerce, Temple University. His research interests include online tourism information, tourists' decision-making process, and tourist information behaviour.

Jackie Clarke is Reader in Marketing at the Faculty of Business, Oxford Brookes University. Her research interests include tourism and services marketing, sustainability, consumer behaviour in service environments and gift giving behaviour for tourism.

Antónia Correia is a member of the editorial board of the *Journal of Travel Research* and acts as a reviewer for most of the tourism journals. She has received international awards and published in high-ranking journals. Her main interests are consumer behaviour, prestige and tourism.

Alain Decrop is Dean (and full Professor) of the Faculty of Economics, Social Sciences and Business Administration at the University of Namur, Belgium. His research interests include consumer behaviour, interpretive consumer research (CCT), qualitative methods and tourism marketing. He is author of *Vacation Decision Making* and co-editor of the *Handbook of Tourist Behavior* and has published many journal articles.

Sara Dolnicar is a professor of Marketing at the University of Wollongong. Sara's key areas of research interests are measurement in the social sciences and market segmentation methodology, primarily applied to tourism and social marketing.

John Fahy is Professor of Marketing at the University of Limerick and Adjunct Professor of Marketing at the University of Adelaide. His research interests are in the areas of customer value, evolutionary perspectives on marketing and strategic decision making.

Shelagh Ferguson is a lecturer in Consumer Behaviour at the University of Otago, New Zealand. Her research interests include adventure tourism, consumer theory and culture, and consumption communities within society.

Anita Fernandez-Young has spent half her professional life in business and half in research and teaching. She has taught tourism management and marketing with a special interest in the marketing of culture and heritage.

Daniel R. Fesenmaier is a professor in the School of Tourism and Hospitality Management and Director of the National Laboratory for Tourism and eCommerce, Temple University. His research focuses on tourism marketing, advertising evaluation and information technology.

Anthony Foley is a lecturer at the School of Business at Waterford Institute of Technology. His research interests are in marketing strategy, branding and tourism marketing.

Clare Foster is a lecturer in Marketing at Keele University Management School. Her main research interests are consumer behaviour in tourism, including tourist complaints and atrocity stories, tourist performances and participation, and tourism discourse.

Isabelle Frochot completed her PhD at Manchester Metropolitan University and then worked as a lecturer in Scotland. Since returning to France, Isabelle has moved her research focus to mountain tourism, conducting various studies on its image and exploring customer experience design and the complexity of satisfaction in an experiential context.

Alan Fyall is Professor, Rosen College of Hospitality Management, University of Central Florida. He is co-editor of the *Journal of Destination Marketing & Management* and serves on many editorial boards including *Annals of Tourism Research*.

Ulrike Gretzel is Associate Professor of Marketing at the University of Wollongong. She has a PhD in Communication. Her research focuses on persuasion in human–technology interaction and adoption and use of social media and mobile technologies.

Rebecca Hawkins is Research and Consultancy Fellow at the Oxford School of Hospitality Management; Visiting Professor, International Centre for Responsible Tourism at Leeds Metropolitan University; and Director of the Responsible Hospitality Partnership.

Sameer Hosany is Senior Lecturer in Marketing at Royal Holloway, University of London. His research interests include consumer emotions, luxury consumption, brand experience, tourist behaviour and destination marketing. He has published in leading tourism and marketing journals.

Simon Hudson is Endowed Chair for the Center of Economic Excellence in Tourism and Economic Development at the University of South Carolina. Prior to working in academia, he worked in the tourism industry in Europe. Simon is a leading expert in tourism research and development, has written six books and over 50 research articles, many on tourism marketing.

Anne Marie Ivers is a postdoctoral researcher at DCU Business School, Dublin City University. Her research interests are in marketing strategy, entrepreneurial marketing and research commercialisation.

Metin Kozak is co-editor of *Anatolia* and acts as an editorial board member of over 25 journals. He has received both national and international research awards to mark his achievements. His main research interests entail consumer behaviour, benchmarking and competitiveness.

Jacquie L'Etang is Professor of Public Relations and Applied Communication at Queen Margaret University, Scotland and is founding and lead editor of *Public Relations Inquiry*. Her writing on public relations encompasses history, ethics, public diplomacy, sport and anthropology.

Chunxiao Li is Lecturer in Tourism at the College of Tourism and Service Management, Nankai University, China. Her research interests include tourism decision making, choice heuristic and destination marketing.

Xiang (Robert) Li, PhD, is an associate professor in the School of Hotel, Restaurant, and Tourism Management at the University of South Carolina, Columbia. His research interests include tourist behaviour and psychology, and destination marketing.

Jairo Lugo-Ocando, PhD is a lecturer in Journalism Studies at the University of Sheffield in the United Kingdom. He has been a visiting research fellow at the Universidad de Málaga (Spain), Universidad Católica Andrés Bello (Venezuela) and the National University of Singapore.

Scott McCabe is Associate Professor of Tourism Management/Marketing at Nottingham University Business School. His research focuses on theorizations of tourist experience, social tourism and marketing communications and branding. He writes on qualitative methods, particularly socio-linguistics.

Una McMahon-Beattie has a PhD in the area of revenue management, relationship marketing and consumer trust. She is deputy editor for the *Journal of Revenue and Pricing Management* and is the author/editor of a number of revenue management books.

Judith Mair is a senior lecturer in Tourism and Events at Monash University, Australia. Her research interests include climate change, sustainability and post-disaster recovery for both tourism and events.

Josef Mazanec is Professor of Business Administration in Tourism. His research interests are in tourism management, consumer behaviour, strategic marketing, multivariate methods, decision-support systems and management science applications in leisure, hospitality and tourism.

Nigel Morgan is Adjunct Professor at the University of Tromsø – Norwegian Arctic University (and shortly to join the University of Surrey). He teaches and writes about the connections between tourism, identity, citizenship and place.

Luiz Moutinho is the Foundation Chair of Marketing at the Adam Smith Business School, University of Glasgow, Scotland. He has held academic positions in California, Arizona and Ohio. Luiz was appointed to his first Chair in Marketing in 1989 at Cardiff Business School and to his current Chair in 1996. He has published 25 books and more than 120 refereed articles in leading journals.

Karlan Muniz graduated in advertising and marketing from ESPM-SP and is currently a doctoral student in Business Administration at PUC/PR. Karlan's research is on marketing, consumer behaviour, brand management and communication. Besides academic activities, and performing work in support of market orientation to business, he is a frequent speaker on topics of branding and consumer behaviour.

Bhanu Nanda is Business Development Manager at Supreme Airways, New Delhi, India. His role is promoting responsible tourism while offering exciting and unique packages across the globe. He helps guests to use the right technology to make their travel experience a memorable one.

Barbara Neuhofer is a PhD researcher at the eTourismLab and the John Kent Institute in Tourism at Bournemouth University. Her research interests regard eTourism and the role of ICTs in the enhancement of tourism experiences.

Michael O'Regan has worked alongside the National Tourism Development Authority of Ireland with Gulliver and for Wicklow County Tourism as Marketing Executive before his PhD at the University of Brighton. He is Assistant Professor at the Institute for Tourism Studies, Macao. His research interests are on tourist, urban, historic, future, alternative, slow and cultural mobilities.

Bing Pan is Associate Professor in the Department of Hospitality and Tourism Management, School of Business, College of Charleston. His research interests include online behaviour, destination marketing, search engine marketing and social media.

Stephen Pratt is Assistant Professor at the School of Hotel and Tourism Management at the Hong Kong Polytechnic University. His research interests include the impacts of tourism and destination marketing.

Girish Prayag is a lecturer in Marketing in the Department of Management Marketing and Entrepreneurship, at the University of Canterbury, New Zealand. His research interests include consumer experiences, airline marketing and destination marketing. His research has appeared in leading tourism and marketing journals.

Nina K. Prebensen is a professor of marketing at Tromsø University Business School, Norway. Her current research focus is on experience value. She is part of the research programme 'Service Innovation and Tourist Experiences in the High North'.

Annette Pritchard is Professor of Tourism and Director of Cardiff Metropolitan University's Welsh Centre for Tourism Research. Annette has a long-standing interest in places, representations and identities and has published widely on their connectivities.

Shirley Rate is a senior lecturer at Glasgow Caledonian University and Subject Group Leader in Fashion, Marketing and Retailing. Previously, Shirley was a member of staff at the University of Dundee as a lecturer in Marketing delivering management and marketing education to an array of programmes in the School of Management.

Amata Ring is a research fellow at the University of Wollongong funded by an Australian Research Council grant. Her research interests include tourism destination competitiveness, (international) market segmentation, emotions in marketing and advertising, and intercultural service encounters.

Pisuda Sangsue is currently a lecturer in Tourism and Hospitality Management. She has recently completed a PhD in Tourism Marketing at the University of Nottingham, UK. Her major research interests include destination marketing, tourist behaviour and qualitative interpretive methods.

Gareth Shaw is Professor of Retail and Tourism Management and Associate Dean of Research in the University of Exeter Business School. He researches both in retail management and tourism and has held research grants from ESRC, British Academy, AHRC, Leverhulme, Defra and ESRC–AIM. He is currently leading a four-year EU project on Tourism and Wellbeing.

Suresh Sood is a key instigator leading the embracement of new technologies in business curriculum development at the University of Technology in Sydney (UTS) since 1995.

He writes numerous thought leadership articles and presents at a variety of local and global conferences. His PhD converges on storytelling, social media interactions and marketing.

Andrew J. Spencer is a lecturer in Tourism Management at the University of the West Indies, Mona and holds a PhD from the School of Tourism at Bournemouth University. His research focuses on the determinants of technology adoption for travel retailers with particular emphasis on the strategic management implications and leadership imperatives for owner-managers.

Brigitte Stangl is a lecturer in Tourism at the School of Hospitality and Tourism Management at the University of Surrey. Her research interests are in the fields of tourism, information systems and consumer behaviour.

Marc Stickdorn lectures service design at the Management Center Innsbruck in Austria. As a co-founder of *smaply* and associate of various design agencies, he develops new tools and methods and provides consultancy for many public and private organizations.

Rosemary Stockdale is Associate Professor in the Information Systems Group at Swinburne University, Victoria. Her research interests focus on topics related to how information technology affects organisational relationships. She has published widely on topics such as online communities and social networking in tourism and health.

Manuel Tão is a researcher at the University of the Algarve. He has published research in tourism journals. His main research interests are in economics, transport and tourism.

Karin Teichmann is Assistant Professor at the Department of Strategic Management, Marketing and Tourism at the University of Innsbruck. Her research interests are in the fields of consumer behaviour and service research.

Richard Tresidder is a senior lecturer in Marketing at the Sheffield Business School. He holds a PhD in the Social Anthropology of Tourism Marketing and he has a particular interest in the semiotics of tourism and hospitality and critical marketing.

Iis Tussyadiah is Associate Clinical Professor with the School of Hospitality Business Management, College of Business, Washington State University, Vancouver. Her research interest is at the intersection of digital technology and human experiences, which include a broad topic within consumer behaviour and mobility in the context of travel and tourism.

Victoria Waligo is a lecturer in Tourism at Middlesex University Business School. Her key research interests include sustainable tourism management, stakeholder engagement and social entrepreneurship with a focus on processes and implementation.

Gabby Walters is a lecturer in Tourism at the University of Queensland, Australia. Her research interests include disaster recovery, destination marketing and visitor behaviour.

Arch G. Woodside is Professor of Marketing, Boston College. He is a member and Fellow of the International Academy for the Study of Tourism, Royal Society of Canada, American Psychological Association, Association of Psychological Science, Society for Marketing Advances and the Global Innovation and Knowledge Academy. He is the Founder of the

International Academy of Culture, Tourism and Hospitality Research, and Founding Editor of the Academy's journal.

Julie Wooler is currently a PhD student at Exeter University undertaking an ESRC CASE award project on Social Marketing. Her research is supervised by Jeff French, Stewart Barr and Gareth Shaw, and concerns a destination-based approach to sustainable tourist behaviour in Devon.

Zheng Xiang is an assistant professor in the Department of Hospitality and Tourism Management at Virginia Tech. His research interests lie in information systems, hospitality and tourism marketing, and emergent technologies.

Ian Yeoman is the founding editor of the *Journal of Revenue and Pricing Management* and author of numerous publications in this field.

Kyung-Hyan Yoo is Assistant Professor of Communication at William Paterson University. She has a PhD in Tourism and focuses her research on online tourist information search and decision-making behaviour, online trust and electronic word-of-mouth.

Florian Zach is Tod and Maxine McClaskey Faculty Fellow with the School of Hospitality Business Management, College of Business, Washington State University, Vancouver. His main research interests include innovation in tourism destinations, focusing on the importance of collaboration in destinations to foster and to disseminate innovation in an effort to create sustainable and competitive destinations.

Acknowledgements

Editing this handbook has been an immense and complex challenge, but one which was made light-work turning the seemingly impossible possible, through the generosity of spirit, collegiality, goodwill, patience and obliging hard work given by all the contributors to this volume. I owe them a huge debt of gratitude. They responded to my requests and comments and demands for timeliness with enthusiasm and good heart at every point. It is very heartening indeed to be an academic in this field, with such an enormous range of talented professionals. I would also like to thank those people whom I pestered to contribute but who could not provide material. A special debt of honour must be paid to Dan Fesenmaier and Alan Fyall on whom I placed even further demands for advice and on whose sound counsel I relied so much. Further thanks are due to Andreas Zins. I would also like to thank all the team at Taylor and Francis, Emma Travis, Emily Davies and especially Pippa Mullins for all their support and help. Finally, thanks to Lisa, Kieran and Harry for putting up with me over all the weekends and evenings this has taken out of the last two years, we should now practice some tourism!

1
Introduction

Scott McCabe

> A few years ago, many tourism developers might have been pardoned for thinking that tourism demand was likely to grow almost continuously and that all they had to do was provide the facilities and tourists would flock in... Today, the stagnant world economy, the hugely increased price of energy and fluctuating exchange rates mean that there are no longer any certainties about tourism's growth. Countries, tourism resorts and individual hotels are having to work much harder to fill their beds.
>
> Does this mean that new tourism developments should be discouraged? No, it does not! But it does mean that more resources will be needed for marketing the development throughout its life. If a project is sensibly conceived and adequate marketing budgets are provided, I firmly believe new tourism projects can gain a share of the tourism pie, because marketing works!
>
> *(Bonnett 1982: 242)*

Introduction

Reading this quote now, it is hard to believe that Bonnett was not writing in the present. Not only does the global context outlined resonate so clearly with the current challenges of the global economy, but also, the marketing sentiments don't appear so much different from those that continue to drive the tourism industry. What Bonnett's article does not capture is the sense of flux that pervades the field of marketing theory and practice in the current era. Marketing is undergoing a period of great transformation in thought and practice and tourism marketing shares this sense of uncertainty about its future.

Tourists are becoming increasingly sophisticated and knowledgeable. They seem perfectly happy and capable of creating their own itineraries and managing their own tourist experiences. Technology has rendered information search and travel booking processes convenient, cheap and flexible. The digital era has transformed social relations, making it simple for people to create and maintain social bonds with strangers and friends in far-away places. Media habits are also being transformed, to the extent that it is no longer clear whether marketing is having any effects on consumers at all. The old certainties are peeling away one by one. Marketing is in danger of losing its way, senior executives are asking about marketing's relevance to the bottom line, when budgets are being squeezed from every direction.

This begs the question about the purpose of tourism marketing. What are the distinctive features of tourism that differentiate it from other service sectors or product marketing? What does tourism marketing contribute to our understanding of marketing issues? In order to answer some of these questions it is perhaps necessary to understand the context in which tourism marketing developed as a field. It would be facile to try to map the development of the field of tourism marketing from its early beginnings to the current time. However, it is also difficult not to place tourism marketing within a broad historical context.

From an early focus on understanding tourism as a phenomenon of consumer activity from the 1960s onwards, the marketing approach began to take hold, particularly in the American market where marketing issues were addressed even in the earliest issues of the *Journal of Travel Research* (e.g. Peattie 1968). Early research sought to identify the main sources of available data on travel markets, in an effort to enable better informed marketing strategies to be developed. Many researchers were oriented towards understanding motivations and tourist behaviour (Crompton 1979; Dann 1981; Pearce 1982). In the 1990s dedicated textbooks began to appear, some of which are still available and in print after many editions (e.g. Witt and Moutinho 1994; Middleton 1994). Research became more sophisticated and diffuse. During the 1990s, following the paradigmatic changes in the field of marketing, tourism researchers began to focus on the need for a market orientation, a recognition that marketing should try to understand customer needs and develop meaningful relationships that would drive loyalty.

In the following 20 years to the current time, tourism marketing has become a widely established field of research and scholarly activity with specialist journals such as the *Journal of Travel and Tourism Marketing*, *Journal of Vacation Marketing*, with continued developments such as the recent addition of the *Journal of Destination Marketing and Management*. Whilst generically, it may argued that tourism marketing remains an applied field of research, it is also true that it forms a very sophisticated body of knowledge. This makes the task of compiling a handbook of tourism marketing a very difficult one indeed. The vast wealth of research and the very broad coverage of issues mean that in many ways the choice of topics is in some sense arbitrary.

What I have attempted to do in this work is to focus in on foundational issues that, together with emerging and future research challenges, are important to understand current and future trends, challenges and opportunities, and to try to encourage a critical examination of marketing's role in the wider context of tourism and wider society. Whilst there are a large number of textbooks and other monographs devoted to various aspects of tourism marketing, and an emerging number of handbooks dealing with marketing strategy in tourism for example, there are fewer works that have tried to locate tourism marketing within a scientific context, and position tourism marketing in terms of its distinctive conceptual features, the characteristic methods and frameworks, and to link its main contributions to disciplines and fields. This was the main underpinning aim for this book.

At a very generic level, tourism marketing research can be best described as distorted in terms of its coverage of marketing concepts and fields, often with little emphasis on core marketing topics such as marketing communications. And yet in other aspects, tourism marketing research and scholarship are quite well integrated; place branding is one example. Similarly, tourism marketing academicians have made great strides in some areas, consumer research for example, but it is less obvious that this knowledge has impacted on theorizations of consumer behaviour more widely. Research methods have also been adopted by tourism marketing scholars, but there is often a lag in their uptake, thus it was important to understand how tourism research methods or contexts are useful to theory and method development. Therefore it seemed useful to try to engage with these contributions and gaps. Finally, it was important to address where tourism marketing has come from and where it is going.

Tourism marketing foundations

The handbook is structured into nine sections. The first and last sections each contain two chapters. The introductory part deals with fundamental paradigmatic issues that reflect both shifts in the context of marketing practice (Chapter 2) and our understanding of what constitutes value for tourists (Chapter 3). Xiang (Robert) Li begins by situating the current state of upheaval within the field of marketing within a historical context in Chapter 2. Marketing, born out of classical economic theory, initially concerned with understanding the functions of markets and the nature of value in exchange relationships, has evolved over the last century to become an established socio-economic process. The continued unfolding of technological developments has accelerated change in business innovation and consumer markets, the knowledge economy. The consequential structural changes to social relationships brought about by Internet and digital technology adoption has forced a radical shift in thinking about the function of marketing, taking us back to almost fundamental principles.

These can be summarized firstly, as the general shift in thinking about the role of marketing in this new knowledge economy, that firms should focus their energies on bringing together dynamic, specialized competences, knowledge and skills to create and deliver service, which should be the basis for all business activity, the new service-dominant logic (SDL) (Vargo and Lusch 2004). Secondly, a fundamental principle of SDL is that customers should also be treated as operant resources, bringing their skills, experience and knowledge into the relationship with firms, and it is through this process and only through this process that value can be created, in use. Value is co-created jointly and contextually by the company and the customer (Prahalad and Ramaswamy 2004). The first part of the book examines how these fundamental ideas in marketing have been and can be related to tourism. This is critical because intuitively and fundamentally tourism is a consumer experience that is primarily based on simultaneous production and consumption, context-specific and collaboratively produced by tourists and service employees.

In Chapter 2, Li outlines the main propositions of SDL, and discusses the links between this and related marketing concepts. He highlights some of the criticisms placed on this emerging set of ideas, and goes on to assess the implications within the context of destination marketing, arguing that DMOs have to reorient their thinking and activity to meet the demands of consumers in the future. However, these implications have resonance for all sectors of tourism marketing. In Chapter 3, Prebensen examines the basis of tourist experience to understand how value is conceived and perceived by tourists through their interactions with people and places. Thinking about tourists as active agents, rather than the passive receptors of actions provided by companies has a crucial consequence for tourism marketing research and yet there has been limited attention from the tourism marketing academy on the value creation process. However, this is dramatically changing with a slew of new studies emerging in the literature. Prebensen defines and outlines the literature in value co-creation and discusses critical issues such as the degree of involvement between the actors, the nature of tourist value as autotelic, and driven by intrinsic goals. She argues that firms should understand the types of core values desired by tourists from their experiences, and dramatize their service offers to meet those value expectations.

The themes explored in the two chapters in Part 1 resonate throughout the other parts and chapters in this volume. This indicates both the desire for tourism researchers to engage with foundational marketing theory and practice, and also a sense of the applicability of these ideas to tourism marketing contexts. Tourists are knowledgeable actors, who, particularly in the developed world, are eminently capable of deploying their skills to use technology to create their own travel experiences. Tourism firms must look beyond the marketing management perspective to establish what types of resources they can bring to facilitate experience value for consumers. This will require a more critical engagement with conceptual and broader scale issues relating to tourism marketing's effects on society and or social processes.

The last section, Part 9, also contains two chapters under the umbrella of 'reflections'. In the first Fesenmaier and Zheng Xiang (Chapter 40) plot the fundamental shifts in marketing thought and practice over the last two decades, a period of frenetic growth in marketing research amidst the context of deep socio-cultural change. Fesenmaier and Xiang identify key issues that will drive future marketing research such as the need for measurement and evaluation in the era of big data, what travel in the network does to transform tourist experience, and customized marketing. This is followed by the final chapter, Moutinho, Ballantyne and Rate (Chapter 41), that looks forward to assess how futurecast can help tourism marketers and researchers to understand key issues for the future. The authors reiterate some key themes expressed both in the first part of the book, such as prosumption, and the imperative to co-create tourism experiences to maximize consumer value. They emphasize the shifting power dynamics between consumers and firms and stress the diminishing impact of brands and conventional marketing. In many ways, these four chapters provide a critical lens which frames the issues discussed in the following parts.

The macromarketing perspective

Part 2 of this book explores macromarketing issues and tourism. Macromarketing is used here to mean the impacts of marketing on society, and the consequences of society on marketing systems in tourism (Schulz 2007). These issues raised in the chapters in Part 2 are fundamental to understanding how tourism marketing might be more successful in the future, and also from the perspective of research, how the context of tourism marketing might influence or otherwise relate to the main scientific community of marketing. Marketers in the future must act responsibly and demonstrate those actions to their stakeholders and the wider community. In tourism it is accepted that the industry depends on finite cultural and natural resources for its success, and that in terms of selling tourism experiences, there is a need to represent services appropriately, since the consequences of not acting responsibly are very high. Yet the highly competitive and fragmented business environment of the sector, the perishable nature of the product and fickle consumer demand perhaps dictates an orientation to short-termism and profit today mentality. Conterminously, the actions of the tourism industry are inseparably bound to wider socio-political forces of power. Hence there is a need to try to understand how and what tourism marketing contributes to the wider debates about marketing's role in society. The chapters in Part 2 aim to explore these issues.

Firstly, in Chapter 4, Clarke, Hawkins and Waligo interleave ideas from marketing, sustainable development, tourism studies, and sustainable marketing to debate the relationships between marketing, sustainability and responsible tourism. They outline the reasons why firms become involved in responsible tourism and contextualize their discussion in the dominant social paradigm of the 'West', a culture of consumerism, individualism and anthropocentrism that constrains the actions of sustainable marketers to merely reproducing rather than challenging the established norms. However the authors go on to provide examples from the micromarketing perspective and highlight new directions and strategies to challenge the status quo.

In Chapter 5, Shaw, Barr and Wooler pick up one of the themes mentioned in Chapter 4, that of social marketing. The tourism industry often generates a rhetoric of being fixated on second guessing next trends, and justifying this as providing what consumers want, and yet this stance overlooks the powerful role the industry plays in generating these appetites in the first place and in encouraging behaviour that might best be characterized as self-indulgent. Social marketing has rarely been applied to tourism, and yet offers potential to understand how consumers' attitudes, desires and behaviours might be 'nudged' into more positive directions. Shaw and colleagues discuss the political and practical issues surrounding this approach. Chapter 6 continues this theme in the context of the complexities of the relationships between public relations (PR) and tourism.

L'Etang and Lugo-Ocando (Chapter 6) argue for the fundamental dependency between tourism and reputation, implicitly linked to the importance of image, and in particular the organic forms of image production. L'Etang and Lugo-Ocando outline the main debates surrounding PR and explain how it has evolved into a broader strategic function from its earlier context as a function of micromarketing. However, the inclusion of this chapter in relation to tourism macromarketing is due to the positioning of the discussion of the ethicality of tourism-reputation systems, as they have developed into complex networks of actors and socio-political dynamics that orchestrate media information in an effort to attract tourists through reputation management, largely incorporating varying levels of government. Similarly, the authors argue that the emergence of digital media and social networks create a need for PR to rethink its research approaches and conceptual frameworks to develop multidisciplinary understandings and approaches to reputation management in the future that have critical implications for tourism firms and destination managers. What this chapter ably demonstrates is that communication is inextricably linked to power. This theme is the main focus of Chapter 7.

Caruana (Chapter 7) examines the role of marketing communications in producing discourses, and shows how tourism marketing has been directed towards the reproduction of power dynamics. Tourism marketing communications are social constructions, and as such they shape information in particular ways. This has been recognized as one of the main contributions of tourism social science within a marketing context, since tourism marketing texts and images have been shown to actively constitute broader social discourses of hedonism, alterity, authenticity, mythological places and post-colonial power relations for example. Caruana goes on to discuss how these cultural texts produce sets of power relationships between tourists and hosts which creates implications for marketing practice. In the last chapter of this section (Chapter 8), Tresidder takes the analysis of tourism marketing texts to a different level to explore how semiotics can be used to understand how marketing texts communicate to tourists through signs.

Tresidder argues that there is a discrete semiotic language of tourism, one that we would perhaps all recognize ('escape' for example is a trope discussed in Chapter 7). Signs and images act as a sort of prism through which meaning and value is connoted. As such, an understanding of the principles and practices of semiotics will enable a better understanding of how marketing functions at a symbolic level in the minds of consumers. The application of semiotics to tourism is significant, and has attracted social anthropologists, experts in communications and socio-linguistics, and cultural and media studies over many decades (e.g. MacCannell 1975; Culler 1981), and yet the links between these disciplines and tourism marketing has been limited. Tresidder highlights that in an increasingly mediated world, semiotics offers real insights into marketing theory and practice.

Strategic issues in tourism marketing

Having set the paradigmatic and broader socio-political context, Part 3 presents five chapters dealing with strategic issues in tourism. It is quite incredible to think that 'experience marketing' has only recently become a prevailing force in tourism marketing perspectives. Despite the experiential nature of tourism, a main criticism of tourism marketing until recent times can be that it has focused too much on the technical aspects of service delivery and not enough on the psychological environment of tourists in terms of what they seek from the experience of travel. The first chapter in this section moves us some way towards an understanding of what an experiential approach to tourism marketing might entail. Batat and Frochot develop a new framework for an experiential perspective to tourism marketing (Chapter 9). Whilst Neuhofer and Buhalis (Chapter 10) connect ideas about experience co-creation and experience marketing to technology enhanced tourism experiences, 'Experience 3.0'. Recognizing the importance of brands as mediators of all our lives, Foley, Fahy and Ivers outline the concept of brand experience and relate this to tourism marketing contexts (Chapter 11). The final two chapters in this section deal with some perennial strategic issues, collaboration and customer satisfaction.

Fyall (Chapter 12) outlines how the new marketing realities outlined in earlier chapters are pushing firms towards greater levels of collaboration. He provides the example of collaboration in the airline sector as one of the most successful and yet most complex forms of collaboration, which provides a useful illustration of issues and lessons for the broader sector. Whilst Foster (Chapter 13) debates the approaches taken to understanding satisfaction in tourism. She explains that if the tourism industry really wants to understand what makes customers satisfied, it needs to reconfigure the ways we conceptualize customer satisfaction studies. She argues that tourists evaluate their travel experiences in a socially constructed and co-created way through interactions with industry representatives, locals (hosts) and other tourists. The performative approach advocated by Foster chimes with the appeal made by Prebensen in Chapter 2 for a more considered engagement between the industry and tourists to understand the process of value co-creation.

New approaches and critical developments in the conceptualization of tourism from a marketing perspective require an examination of marketing research methodologies and research issues. Part 4 addresses recent advances and developments in research. The majority of marketing research comes from the quantitative perspective, and in tourism as with the main marketing field, there is a plethora of analytic techniques, challenges posed by tourism marketing research problems and new metrics being developed constantly.

Tourism marketing research

The issue of marketing metrics in the digital era is particularly relevant given the potential opportunities provided by 'big data' and the need to understand how to evaluate social media marketing activity. The section opens with a review of quantitative methods in tourism marketing research (Chapter 14). Mazanec, Ring, Stangl and Teichmann begin by reviewing the main techniques used in tourism marketing research. They argue that in general there is a lag in methods being adopted in tourism research from the main marketing field. Examples such as Principal Component Analysis and social and semantic network analysis are provided. The authors deal with foundational issues such as critical factors underpinning knowledge drawn from scales; a range of issues relating to assumptions underpinning Structural Equation Modelling; segmentation and clustering techniques and discrete choice modelling. The chapter synthesizes the main methodological issues facing quantitative marketing analysts in tourism and provides new avenues for future research that promise to overcome current challenges.

Identifying that segmentation research has formed a very important strand of tourism marketing research, Sara Dolnicar provides a focused discussion on the methods and issue in Chapter 15. Dolnicar first outlines the role of market segmentation in marketing planning before discussing the disconnect between academic research on market segmentation and the practices of the tourism industry. Industry often uses naïve or basic approaches to segment their markets, yet there are sophisticated approaches being used in academic research. However, these are not without their challenges, particularly the basic assumptions upon which segments are identified, either as natural (differences in market characteristics exist) or as exploratory (research process identifies and creates segments). Of course, each may have their use for the industry and Dolnicar points to the potential that segmentation methods offer in the future for this key aspect of tourism marketing research.

Much of the research on marketing evaluation has been undertaken from the perspective of destination marketing campaigns. This is a key weakness of tourism marketing research as highlighted elsewhere in this volume. Destination Marketing Organizations (DMOs) are often at least part-funded by public money and so there is a need for good quality evaluation of the success or otherwise of public investment in marketing activities. This is not the case with the tourism industry, where there is little evidence of the relative effectiveness of different marketing activities. Chapter 16 takes up the issues to discuss what works and what doesn't in destination marketing campaigns. This is a complex issue as Pratt outlines, since it is difficult to attribute destination visitation decisions to a particular stimulus and the complexity of the destination system. Pratt negotiates these complexities and presents a clear review of evaluation methods including combined and online evaluation techniques, and concludes that in the future doing nothing just won't be an option.

The need for novel solutions to help counteract the challenges posed by an increasingly digitally mediated world lead us on to the potential offered by combinations of positivistic approaches to qualitative data. In Chapter 17 Woodside, Muniz and Sood relate how narratives that tourists produce online during or after their travel experiences can be linked to psychological archetypes, and thus inform place branding strategies and consumer behaviour. They outline the use of degrees-of-freedom analysis (DFA) and visual narrative art (VNA) can be used to reveal narrative archetypes. These archetypes can be matched against destination branding, to feed into strategies and to understanding how consumers create value and attach meaning to their tourist experiences.

The final chapter in this part of the book continues with methods relating to destination image and branding, however from a qualitative perspective. Sangsue (Chapter 18) addresses the issue of brand confusion. Tourists, faced with an overwhelming mass of information from an increasing range of media channels, have difficulty in processing images and thus can become confused. However, the focus of this chapter is on how Sangsue used photo-elicitation as a stimulus to create confusion in her respondents. Visual methods have been used frequently in tourism sociology and cultural studies, but less so in the context of tourism marketing. Sangsue demonstrates the effectiveness of this approach to deal with marketing problems and outlines its potential for tourism marketing and destination branding.

The tourist consumer

Part 5 moves to focus on the tourist as consumer. The section begins with a review of recent theorizations of tourist behaviour by Decrop (Chapter 19). Linking back to previous chapters on the changing context of experience marketing and the tourist experience, Decrop argues that the changing consumer context makes it even more critical that tourism marketing understands the complex preference structures and decision patterns underpinning tourists' choice and consumption processes. Theory in tourist consumer behaviour is both rich and influenced by multi-disciplinary perspectives. Decrop outlines these underpinning paradigms, and shows how they have informed theory on tourist decision making process. This links to the experience concepts of Consumer Culture Theory (CCT) (Arnould and Price 1995) outlined in Chapter 9 by Batat and Frochot and the experience value concepts outlined by Prebensen in Chapter 3 and

Neuhofer and Buhalis in Chapter 10. Decrop argues that holistic approaches are required to develop more complete and nuanced understandings of tourist behaviour in the future.

Tourists are not an homogenous group and yet tourism marketing has applied a fairly standardized set of marketing practices. In Chapter 20, O'Regan interrogates the demand and supply relationships that have resulted in a highly fragmented marketplace on the one hand, but a largely undifferentiated set of marketing activities on the other. Whilst technologies offer marketing opportunities to engage with niche segments more from the bottom up, there are also challenges, which O'Regan outlines. One of the most important aspects of tourist decision making is the information search process. Travellers seek information as an essential element of their trip experience. Therefore the range, type and channels or sources of information are particularly relevant for successful outcomes for travellers. Information holds the key to success for tourism businesses. The ubiquitous-ness of the Internet, both in fixed locations and through mobile devices, has meant that information search processes are becoming more flexible and fluid. This is the essential argument proposed by Zheng Xiang, Choe and Fesemaier in Chapter 21. They synthesize a review of literature on information search in tourism, including the factors that influence search behaviour, and online information search. The authors provide a comprehensive analysis of the implications of this paradigm shift in information processes for tourism marketing in the future.

Focusing in on decision processes in detail, Correia, Kozak and Tão (Chapter 22) hone in on a critical discussion of decision making models and research. Despite decades of research and the development of complex models of tourist decisions, from a fundamental perspective, these efforts can be criticized since they do not include psychological factors. This is a crucial problem since, as many chapters in this volume mention, tourism involves emotion as well as cognition. Affect, alongside intuition and perception, has a role to play in decision making for tourism and Correia, Kozak and Tão outline the main aspects of prospect theory, and explain how it complements, and yet extends the ability of classical models of tourist decision-making. They argue that prospect theory offers a great deal of potential for tourism marketing research. Tourist decision making models should acknowledge that decisions are dynamic and risky, constrained by individual and social contexts of tourists, from which emotional and cognitive factors play a role in the final choice.

Chapter 23 focuses on destination choice and selection, particularly to advanced methods for estimating preferences in selection processes. Chunxiao Li, in agreement with Correia, Kozak and Tão, identifies that there has been little consideration in the tourism literature for the conceptual foundation on which decision making research is based. She reviews the literature on different methodological assumptions through a focus on destination decision making. In addressing the issue of the question of the importance of different destination attributes, Li reviews simple and multiple regression approaches with Analytic Hierarchy Process (AHP), which allow paired comparisons of attributes that more closely matches consumer's processes. However, these methods are only useful to a certain extent and in order to understand how attributes are considered, we need to understand the choice heuristics applied in the process. To do that, Li compares conjoint approaches with a novel approach called greedoid methods. This can be used to explore lexicographic choice heuristics and offers potential to understand tourist choice processes.

Micromarketing perspectives

Part 6 of the book focuses on micromarketing issues. In this section there are six chapters. Firstly, in Chapter 24, Stickdorn returns us to the co-creation of experience. Customer experience is often the decisive factor for the success of brands, products and services. It is in this sense that services must be designed based on a clear understanding of what and how customers value from their journey through the service experience, the touchpoints. This can only be achieved through the adoption of design principles, which Stickdorn defines as an ecosystem. He argues that service design is an iterative process, which must involve customers at each stage. He outlines the main principles of design thinking and shows how these can be applied in tourism. Chapter 25 centres on tourism distribution contexts and future strategic issues. Whilst technological change has been a driver behind many of the issues covered in the dynamic context of tourism marketing outlined thus far in the book, nowhere has that been more apparent than in the context of distribution and the mediation of travel services. Spencer and Buhalis describe the context of those debates, the history of information and communication technology (ICT) adoption and diffusion and acceptance, relating them to two key issues for the future, the digital divide and the imperative for leadership in driving forward technology adoption across the industry.

The following two chapters deal with pricing and revenue functions. Firstly Fernandez-Young argues that despite its positioning as an aspect of the marketing mix, it is essential that marketing recognizes the strategic role that price setting plays in the organizational strategy. Price setting is fundamental to tourism marketing and decision making, because it is often only by the price that consumers can judge the quality of the product. Fernandez-Young outlines the different mechanisms that can be used and relates these approaches to price discrimination methods. Helpfully, this chapter discusses pricing decisions in the context of a number of different sector examples. The following chapter (Chapter 27) takes up the issue of revenue management (RM) as a strategic tool. McMahon-Beattie and Yeoman provide an overview of development and use of RM in tourism. They relate RM to economic theory and to perceived value and highlight the challenges and potential conflicts between RM and customer relationship management (CRM) before discussing the implications of dynamic pricing and ethical issues relating to trust and fairness in the context of RM strategies.

CRM has often been cited as a key driver behind tourism marketing practice. Customer loyalty and retention is crucial to success of tourism businesses and tourism is often constructed as being a 'people' industry, based on face-to-face interaction. Yet technological change and competitive pressures have challenged businesses to focus on processes that increase efficiencies. Some of those efficiency gains have been brought about by the adoption of self-service technologies (SSTs). Tourists can now book, pay for and use a service without any contact with personnel. Often, tourists actually desire this minimal level of interaction. So, a challenge is to build long lasting relationships whilst at the same time encouraging them to be autonomous. Chapter 28 provides a critical analysis of the use of SSTs in tourism and how they can be used alongside CRM strategies. Stockdale develops and presents a framework to show how relationships and brand loyalty can be established in an SST environment and links these to outcomes for customers and firms. Finally in this section, McCabe and Foster (Chapter 29) review the literature on marketing communications in tourism. They show how tourism marketing research has approached communications issues in a rather limited and atomistic sense. The chapter outlines communications theory as a context for discussing the need for a more integrated approach to research on understanding the effects of marketing promotions and campaigns across different media channels.

Destination marketing

Part 7 moves on to focus on destination marketing and branding issues. This section begins with Morgan and Pritchard, who set the context for this section with a review of destination branding literature (Chapter 30). Destination marketing and branding seems to have had most impact in the main field of marketing research and practice. The concept of place branding has emerged alongside destination branding in recent years and offers a good opportunity for tourism destination marketing researchers to integrate tourism marketing into wider city and nation branding concepts (Papadopoulos 2004). This also shows how tourism development has become embedded into the wider planning and political processes underpinning competitiveness between places. Morgan and Pritchard review these debates and discuss avenues for future research. Returning to themes of value co-creation once more, Tussyadiah and Zach present findings from a study on DMO's capacity for value co-creation in Chapter 31. Their research highlights the specific characteristics of DMOs as aiming to represent a broad range of stakeholders across the destination and therefore constrained by the need for impartiality and broad representation. Organizational structures and processes play a role in facilitation and/or creating barriers to developing co-creation and these issues are teased out through the analysis to draw conclusions for future developments.

Taking the perspective of brand cultures and communities, Ferguson and Bourke (Chapter 32) show how destination brand experiences are created not solely by DMOs but also by employees in the resort. Taking the example of seasonal snowsport workers, their study reveals how important employees are in representing and co-creating destination brand experiences for tourists. Their investment in their sport and the destination it represents is based on an affective commitment to a particular way of life. In addition, a number of previous chapters highlighted the need to understand how affect influences tourist behaviours and the consequences for tourism brands.

In Chapter 33, Hosany and Prayag present a cross-disciplinary review of the literature on emotion in tourism and extend their previous work on the development of a scale that shows determinants and outcomes of tourists' emotional responses to destination brands. In order for tourism businesses and destination brands to succeed in the future, marketers will need to understand tourists' psychological environment much more effectively and understanding tourists' emotional responses will enable them to engineer positive enjoyable experiences and employ imagery more effectively in advertising.

Finally in this section, Walters and Mair (Chapter 34) present examples of post-disaster marketing strategies for tourism destinations. A basic issue underpinning tourism marketing is its vulnerability to external events. The need for effective communications strategies at the destination level is important to enable destinations to cope with unknown and unplanned events. The case studies outlined provide clear steps that destinations can embed into marketing strategies.

The digital media landscape

An underlying theme throughout the book up to this point has been the influence of technological change on the business and consumer environment of tourism. The Internet and web 2.0 technology, wifi-enabled mobile Internet access has effected the most widespread and fundamental changes to the business and practice of tourism. Part 8 places these technological changes at the heart of the discussion of tourism marketing issues. The section begins with an overview of the challenges brought about by digital technologies to tourism marketing in the global economy presented by Hudson (Chapter 35). Hudson first outlines the digital marketing environment, focusing on ICTs and their influence in bringing about critical changes in marketing, opening up opportunities for closer engagement, one-to-one marketing and more connective relationships. On the other hand, the Internet has also had a profound effect on consumer behaviour and processes. Hudson outlines these changes, particularly relating them to social media and how these can be leveraged in tourism marketing communications. There are some really pertinent practical examples of strategies being used by tourism organizations and destinations, which provides a useful context to discuss future potentials, particularly in terms of smartphones.

Social media applications and marketing potentials are the subject of closer scrutiny in Chapter 36. Social media can provide an effective platform to develop viral marketing campaigns, and this has proven a very attractive proposition for tourism marketers. Gretzel and Yoo outline the main principals of social media marketing strategies, arguing that some of the main premises of social media belie a lack of understanding of the costs and/or potential pitfalls in terms of customer reaction or engagement. Therefore careful design and management of social media strategies is essential as well as an understanding of the ways customers engage with social media. Gretzek and Yoo argue that because this field is evolving so rapidly, there is an urgent need for more research on how customers react to social media marketing and what they value from the relationships with tourism firms or destinations.

The most important source of online advertising revenue is in search engine marketing (SEM) and so it is fitting that Chapter 37 presents a detailed analysis of the dynamic relationships between the tourism firm, the user and the search engine, which have not been well documented and which need to be understood in order to address the potentials that search marketing plays in tourism marketing strategies. Zheng Xiang, Pan and Fesenmaier begin by reviewing the literature on search engine marketing in order to develop a framework to explain how tourists use search engines in travel planning. Pre-search considerations and search processes form frames through which post-search evaluation of information is cognitively organized. From this model, the authors develop six key lessons to guide effective strategies in search engine marketing in tourism.

Chapter 38 examines the role of travel blogs as communication vehicles and their applications for tourism marketing. Bosangit argues that there has been an expansion in research on the application of blogs in marketing and yet there have been limited analyses of their use in tourism contexts. She outlines how travel blogs serve as a great source of naturalistic data, upon which she performs powerful discourse analysis to demonstrate what travel blogs reveal about tourist experiences. Bosangit outlines the implications for tourism marketers. McCabe, Foster, Chunxiao Li and Nanda (Chapter 39) provide evidence form a study comparing UK smartphone users with non-users to provide empirical evidence on how travel experiences are becoming increasingly mediated by smartphone applications. This is a fitting end to the substantive chapters as the mobile marketing research agenda signals a new dimension to tourism marketing research and one that will take the subject into new, unchartered territories.

References

Bonnett, J. (1982) 'Implications of marketing and promotion for the development of tourism', *Tourism Management*, 3(4): 242–47.

Calantone, R.J. and Mazanec, J.A. (1991) 'Marketing management and tourism', *Annals of Tourism Research*, 18(1): 101–19.

Crompton, J.L. (1979) 'Motivations for pleasure vacations', *Annals of Tourism Research*, 6(4): 408–24.

Culler, J. (1981) 'Semiotics of tourism', *American Journal of Semiotics*, 1: 127–40.

Dann, G.M.S. (1981) 'Tourist motivation: an appraisal', *Annals of Tourism Research*, 8(2): 187–219.

MacCannell, D. (1999) *The Tourist: A New Theory of the Leisure Class*. Los Angeles: University of California Press.

Middleton, V.T.C. (1994) *Marketing in Travel and Tourism*. Oxford: Butterworth-Heinemann.

Papadopoulos, N. (2004) 'Place branding: evolution, meaning and implications', *Place Branding*, 1(1): 36–49.

Pearce, P.L. (1982) *The Social Psychology of Tourist Behaviour.* Wallingford: CABI.
Peattie, R.A. Jr. (1968) 'Tourism advertising', *Journal of Travel Research*, 7(1): 1–6.
Prahalad, C.K. and Ramaswamy, V. (2004) *The Future of Competition: Co-Creating Unique Value with Customers*. Boston: Harvard Business School Press.
Shultz, Clifford J. II. (2007) 'Marketing as constructive engagement', *Journal of Public Policy & Marketing*, 26(2): 293–301.
Vargo, S.L. and Lusch, R.F. (2004) 'Evolving to a new dominant logic for marketing', *Journal of Marketing*, 68: 1–17.
Witt, S.F. and Moutinho, L. (1994) *Tourism Marketing and Management Handbook*. London: Prentice Hall.

Part 1

Tourism marketing theory

Paradigms and perspectives

2

Linking service-dominant logic to destination marketing

Xiang (Robert) Li

Introduction

It has been widely suggested that the field of marketing, both its practice and research, is facing great challenges, which call for a major transition or paradigm shift (Achrol and Kotler 1999; Bolton 2005; Gummersson 2002; Vargo and Lusch 2004a). While some suggest evolutionary changes in reforming marketing's mental model (Wind 2009), others consider it necessary to take a more revolutionary approach, a 'process of de-programming' in terms of building fresh marketing theory foundation, creating alternative research methods, and inventing new pedagogical approaches (Gummersson 2002: 585). One line of thought which has drawn much attention lately is the service-dominant logic (SDL) (Vargo and Lusch 2004a, 2004b).

Vargo and Lusch (2004a) contended that marketing is evolving from the conventional 'goods-dominant' (G-D) logic toward a logic centring on service provision, which highlights intangible resources, co-created value, process orientation, and relationships. Their article ignited a heated debate and international discussion about the future of marketing and the role of service (Grönroos 2008). Increasingly, marketing researchers have agreed that SDL may be instrumental in providing an overarching framework, or at least a useful perspective unifying the seemingly fragmented marketing ideas. In the tourism literature, SDL has also drawn some attention (Li and Petrick 2008; Saraniemi and Kylänen 2011). Although most tourism scholars welcome and appreciate the intellectual challenges SDL presents to the field, some could argue that SDL is a moot point for tourism, a service-driven industry (Li and Petrick 2008).

This chapter attempts to continue what Li and Petrick (2008) have started, and further explores the relevance of SDL to destination marketing. To do so, this chapter will start with a review of the development of marketing, and external forces that may influence the future of marketing. While understandably for many this review is common knowledge, it is pertinent to be reminded where we have come from, to better understand where we should go. After that, the chapter will provide a brief overview of SDL, its latest development, as well as its criticisms. Finally, the chapter will conclude with a number of connections and implications of SDL in the destination marketing context.

The evolution of marketing thoughts

Over a century has passed since the formal study of marketing emerged as a separate field from economics. Marketing took shape as a recognized discipline by the mid-twentieth century (Bartels 1983). The growth of marketing as a discipline corresponds to the development of marketing as a business function and philosophy. Early efforts to track the evolution of marketing concept documented that marketing scholars used to view marketing as a simple activity, as the coordination of a group of activities, as a business process undertaken from the customer's point of view, as an economic function of production, but have increasingly viewed marketing as a social phenomenon (Bartels 1965).

In a similar vein, Kotler (1972) suggested that the focal point of marketing progressed from a commodity focus (e.g. farm products, manufactured goods, services), an institutional focus (e.g. producers, wholesalers, retailers, agents), a functional focus (e.g. buying, selling, promoting, transporting, storing, pricing), a managerial focus (e.g. analysis, planning, organization, control), to a social focus (e.g. marketing efficiency, product quality, and social impact). Correspondingly, Kotler and Amstrong (1999) concluded that the practice of marketing management has gone through five generations of philosophies, evolving from focusing on the improvement of production and distribution efficiency (the product concept) in early days, to now delivering 'superior value to consumers in a way that maintains or improves the consumer's and the society's well-being' (1999: 20). From the marketing function perspective, Sheth *et al.* (2000) proposed that the second half of the twentieth century has witnessed a shift from mass marketing to segmented marketing, with a further movement toward customer-centric marketing (i.e. serving the needs of each individual customer) on the way.

As for research, marketing studies have gone through at least four phases (Vargo and Lusch 2004a). The origins of marketing can be traced back to classical and neoclassical economics, as it was initially founded as a branch of applied economics studying distribution channels (Kotler 1972). In its formative period, owing to a traditional 'concern for agricultural markets and the processes by which products were brought to market and prices determined' (Webster 1992: 1–2), early marketing scholars focused on commodities exchange, the role that marketing institutions played, and functions these institutions performed. Starting in the 1950s, the marketing management school dominated the field, 'which was characterized by a decision-making approach to managing the marketing functions and an overarching focus on the customer' (Vargo and Lusch 2004a: 1). The well-known marketing mix model (or, 4Ps) also appeared during this period. New marketing theories surfaced in the 1980s, which broke free from the traditional 4Ps framework and challenged the dominant microeconomic profit-maximization worldview (Webster 1992). During the process of unifying these separate theoretical streams, a new paradigm was estimated to be emerging, characterized by the belief in marketing as a social and economic process (Vargo and Lusch 2004a; Webster 1992).

Changing environment

For an applied discipline boasting a traditional emphasis on 'empirical research', 'applied thought development', and 'occupational concern' (Bartels 1983: 33), external environment is critical in directing its future. The recent emergence of new marketing thoughts has been externally determined by demographic changes, technological development, as well as dissatisfaction with existing marketing productivity (Sheth, Sisodia and Sharma 2000). Thus, the on-going discussion on marketing's future direction should be regarded as a response to the changing environment, rather than a conceptual artefact.

At the macro level, the most pressing environmental condition that marketers are facing is the 'new economy', which is commonly labelled as the 'service economy', the 'knowledge society', and the 'information era' (Gummersson 2002: 587). Day and Montgomery (1999: 6) suggested that five emerging themes in the 'new economy' are shaping the future direction of marketing, including:

- the connected knowledge economy;
- globalizing, converging, and consolidating industries;
- fragmenting and frictionless markets;
- demanding customers and consumers and their empowered behaviour; and
- adaptive organizations.

The connected knowledge economy

In the connected knowledge economy, intellectual capabilities, or 'operant resources' (Constantin and Lusch 1994), become the key resource for wealth creating (Achrol 1991; Achrol and Kotler 1999) and productivity improvement (Powell and Snellman 2004). People are increasingly connected through networks, in which information and knowledge flow in a more free (low cost) and frequent (low barrier) manner – clearly, in recent years the ubiquity of social media has further reinforced this trend. For the knowledge-based industries – those focusing on 'the development, application, and diffusion of new knowledge' (Day and Montgomery 1999: 7) – the traditional assumption of diminishing returns (scale economy is eventually constrained by the upward marginal cost curve) may no longer hold true (Arthur 1996; Berthon and Hulbert 2003). Customers may be locked into the system, procedure, or protocol they are familiar with, due to the complexity of those information-intensive products, which makes the market a 'winner-take-all' (Frank and Cook 1995) or 'tippy' (Varadarajan and Yadav 2002) one. For destination marketing, travel today is less about location and more about experiences, and natural resource endowment alone can hardly make a place attractive any more. Experience providers' intellectual capital embedded in product offering is making a big difference.

Globalizing, converging and consolidating industries

The worldwide globalization process was caused by and has caused 'the homogenization of customer needs, gradual liberalization of trade, and the recognition of the competitive advantages of a global presence' (Day and Montgomery 1999: 7). International organizations and treaties such as WTO, NAFTA, and the EU, help extend market areas beyond national boundaries (Berthon and Hulbert 2003). Technology advancement has to a great extent eliminated the conventional spatial and temporal constraints and barriers of marketing. Market structures and boundaries, classification of industry and product, role of competitors and partners are increasingly blurring and undetermined. In the tourism context, globalization has created unprecedented convenience for destinations to access their target market, but this very accessibility could very well dilute a destination's novelty/exoticness, which is one fundamental driver of travel (Lee and Crompton 1992). Further, globalization has also presented major challenges to small, local tourism business when competing with multinational corporations.

Fragmenting and frictionless markets

As indicated, globalization, industrialization, and modernity have on the one hand led to a homogenized world (Franklin 2003), which features the confluence of demographic characteristics and the 'convergence of consumer needs and preference' (Ohmae 1989: 144), i.e. a frictionless market. Paradoxically, on the other hand, there has also been an obvious trend of increasing market diversity in household (due to lifestyle, ethnic, income, and age diversity) and business (due to size, locations, and type of business) markets (Sheth, Sisodia and Sharma 2000). The fragmented market is characterized by more porous segments, which may ultimately result in individual customers being targeted (Oliver, Rust and Varki 1998; Varadarajan and Yadav 2002). The strategic advantage of mass production has been overshadowed by that of mass customization (Kotha 1995); correspondingly, it has been suggested that what marketers offer today should not be merely 'products' but 'solutions' (Ettenson, Conrado and Knowles 2013; Tuli, Kohli and Bharadwaj 2007). Tourists worldwide are developing more diversified needs and tastes. Notably, tourists from emerging markets are going through the same, yet much accelerated transition as their counterparts in industrialized countries, from preferring conventional, mass-tourism products to more unique, individualized travel experiences (Li *et al.* 2011; Ryan and Chen 2012).

Demanding customers and consumers and their empowered behaviour

Customers (both in B-to-B and household contexts) nowadays are facing a plethora of choices, and have easy access and improved capability to acquire their choices. As a result, they 'are demonstrating a keen interest in developing and exercising greater control over the communication they receive and generate' (Varadarajan and Yadav 2002: 308). Traditional intermediaries, without whom transaction used to be impossible, get bypassed because direct transaction usually means a better value proposition (Buhalis and Licata 2002; Sheth and Parvatiyar 1995). Today's tourists, empowered by improved technology in an unprecedentedly transparent marketing environment, are expecting better efficiency and effectiveness brought by customer centric marketing (Niininen, Buhalis and March 2007).

Adaptive organizations

Market organizations today are forced to be more market-driven and more agile and capable of processing information (Achrol 1991). This is mainly due to changes in three dimensions (Day and Montgomery 1999):

1 fewer broadcast and more interactive strategies, i.e. firms need to interactively address individual needs and personalize the communication process;
2 more competition and more collaboration – a shift in mind-set is needed from transactional to relationship exchanges. Moreover, in order to be successful in competition, an organization needs to be a reliable co-operator first (Morgan and Hunt 1994; Varadarajan and Cunningham 1995);
3 more facts and less conjecture – information about market structure, market responses, and market economics is of vital importance in decision-making. Consequently, never has market information and strategy performance research been so important for destinations marketing and management organizations as today (Williams, Stewart and Larsen 2012).

While Vargo and Lusch (2008a) argued that the emergence of SDL is not justified by the service economy (and they claim 'all economies are service economies'), the abovementioned environmental changes have clearly made the inadequacy of the goods-based conceptualization more explicit, hence calling for a new frame of reference. Next the author turns to a brief synthesis of the SDL.

The service-dominant logic

Vargo and Lusch (Lusch and Vargo 2006; 2004a; 2005) reflect on the development of economic activity and argue that marketing inherited a goods-centred view from economics, which emphasized producing tangible outputs, completing transactions, and maximizing profits. They argue that marketing is evolving toward a service-centred logic, which:

1 views service as the common denominator of exchange;
2 focuses on process rather than output;
3 argues value is not embedded in product or unilaterally defined by manufacturer, but co-created with customers (Merz, He and Vargo 2009: 328).

After multiple rounds of revision (Lusch and Vargo 2006; Vargo and Lusch 2004a, 2006), Vargo and Lusch concluded that SDL involves a total of ten foundational premises (FPs), including:

> FP1: Service is the fundamental basis of exchange
> FP2: Indirect exchange masks the fundamental basis of exchange
> FP3: Goods are a distribution mechanism for service provision
> FP4: Operant resources are the fundamental source of competitive advantage
> FP5: All economies are service economies
> FP6: The customer is always a cocreator of value
> FP7: The enterprise cannot deliver value, but only offer value propositions
> FP8: A service-centred view is inherently customer oriented and relational
> FP9: All social and economic actors are resource integrators
> FP10: Value is always uniquely and phenomenologically determined by the beneficiary.
> *(2008a: 7)*

At the core of this view is service, which is defined as 'the application of specialized competences (knowledge and skills) through deeds, processes, and performances for the benefit of another entity or the entity itself' (Vargo and Lusch 2004a: 2). Note that, to emphasize the focus of SDL being the process rather than a special type of output, Vargo and Lusch (2008a, 2008b) switched from using the plural term 'services', to the singular term 'service'. Service is considered the basis for all exchanges, whereas goods are identified as vehicles for service provision (FP1 and 3) (Merz, He and Vargo 2009). However, because service provision usually involves complex combination of goods, money, and institutions, the service basis of exchange is not always evident (FP2). Organizations engage in and win competition by their knowledge and skills (FP4). Because ultimately value is idiosyncratically and experientially determined by the beneficiary (i.e. clients or customers in most cases) (FP10), firms cannot independently create or deliver value (FP7). Instead, they may offer value propositions for customers' consideration. The value creation process is interactional and collaborative (FP6), and the co-creation process implies that SDL is inevitably customer-oriented and relational (FP8).

Finally, Lusch and colleagues (Lusch, Vargo and Malter 2006; Lusch, Vargo and Tanniru 2010) suggest that SDL implies eight shifts in thinking, including:

> (1) a shift to a focus on the process of serving rather than the creation of goods; (2) a shift to the primacy of intangibles rather than tangibles in the firm's marketplace offering, (3) a shift to a focus on the creation and use of dynamic operant resources as opposed to the consumption and depletion of static operand resources, (4) a recognition of the strategic

> advantage of symmetric rather than asymmetric information, (5) a shift to conversation and dialog as opposed to propaganda, (6) an understanding that the firm can only make and follow through on value propositions rather than create or add value, (7) a shift in focus to relational rather than transactional exchange, and (8) a shift to an emphasis on financial performance for information feedback and learning rather than a goal of profit maximization.
>
> *(Lusch, Vargo and Tanniru 2010: 22)*

Collectively, these eight shifts direct organizations to be more sensitive to customer needs and wants, more adaptive to environment changes, and more capable of learning.

Granted, some of the specific ideas and propositions tackled by SDL are not necessarily new. For instance, manufacturing strategy researchers have long pleaded for 'servitization' (Baines *et al.* 2009; Vandermerwe and Rada 1988; Voss 2005), i.e. 'the innovation of an organization's capabilities and processes to shift from selling products to selling integrated products and services that deliver value in use' (Baines *et al.* 2009: 547). They argue that an organization's service capabilities, which allow it to add service components to goods manufacturing and create additional value to customers, may help it gain a competitive edge over rivals focusing only on manufacturing capabilities. A major contribution of SDL is it proposes a perspective bring related ideas together.

Since its introduction in 2004, SDL has found much resonance but also drawn criticisms. For a new perspective still largely lacking empirical evidence, it is understandable some researchers express criticism of SDL being just a smart way of repackaging or rebranding old ideas (Cova, Ford and Salle 2009; Grönroos and Voima 2013). Some issues, such as fuzzy definitions and misleading terminologies, or whether 'service' is the proper concept capturing the essence of the new logic, have at least been partly addressed by Vargo and Lusch (2008a, 2008b). Some other issues could only be resolved at the philosophical level after researchers agree upon fundamental issues such as what defines service (Grönroos 2006, 2008). Still, key issues remain including the testability (i.e. whether there is empirical evidence to support the logic and whether the logic is testable at all), normative power (i.e. whether firms should adopt the SDL for better performance) of SDL (Wright and Russell 2012), and the role of natural (operand) resources in an era of resource scarcity (Campbell, O'Driscoll and Saren 2012).

Despite these criticisms, by raising some fundamental questions such as what resource is and who defines value, SDL sparks attention to the inadequacy of the current marketing paradigm and the need to break free from conventional mentality. As Cova, Ford, and Salle (2009: 572) argue, 'SDL represents an opportunity for a huge amount of new work to be done once the service orientation is taken.'

Implications for destination marketing

Destination marketing organizations (DMOs) are usually government or non-profit organizations engaging in public–private partnerships. Destination marketers hence need to practice a different set of rules, wherein the concern for social equity transcends destination marketing (or marketing in public sectors in general) from for-profit, economic behaviour to a social function with complicated political and sociological implications (Novatorov and Crompton 2001a, 2001b). Unlike their private-sector counterparts who prioritize service as a key product differentiator and/or competitive advantage, destination marketers need to focus more on satisfying many disparate stakeholders with competing priorities in the marketing process, occasionally at the expense of service quality and customer involvement. Adopting SDL has some important implications to destination marketers and destination marketing research. For instance, although tourism is not traditionally viewed as a knowledge-intensive industry, it becomes clear that the information-intensive nature of tourism puts it at the forefront of adopting knowledge-based operation and practices. Destinations are hence not just competing with each other based on natural resource endowment, but operant resources and network.

The following paragraphs elaborate on three major implications this author deems important to tourism marketing, particularly destination marketing practices.

Service is not inferior to goods

Conventional wisdom of services marketing suggests that services are uniquely different from goods for at least four characteristics, i.e. intangibility (service is impalpable), heterogeneity (service production cannot be standardized), inseparability (service production and consumption is simultaneous, whereas goods production, purchase, and consumption is sequential), and perishability (service cannot be inventoried after production) (Zeithaml, Parasuraman and Berry 1985). These four features, collectively termed the IHIP characteristics by Lovelock and Gummesson (2004), are considered limitations or shortcomings of services that service marketers need to work exceptionally hard to make up for. Both Vargo and Lusch (2004b) and Lovelock and Gummesson (2004) argued that these four characteristics do not necessarily differentiate services from goods. Most importantly, the complaints about the IHIP characteristics of service reflect a goods- and manufacturing-based mentality, i.e. the G-D logic (Vargo and Lusch 2004a).

SDL instead calls for a new mindset, and suggests service marketers make no apologies for what service is about. In today's market environment, competence in customization, co-creation, and providing solutions, as opposed to standardization, scale of economy, and tangible outputs, are likely to bring marketers a competitive edge. The IHIP characteristics of service will be more desirable because fundamentally 'value is always intangible, heterogeneously experienced, co-created, and potentially perishable' (Vargo and Lusch 2008b: 28). Thus, one may argue that instead of making service more 'goods-like', goods should be marketed more like service (Grönroos 2006). Further, the traditional goods–service distinction is getting blurred, and service appears to be the more encompassing idea because ultimately, 'manufacturing is a service, and its output is part of the service-provision process' (Vargo and Lusch 2004b: 334). No longer do destination marketers need to be ashamed of the heterogeneity of their offerings, as designing and promoting highly customized travel experiences will become a norm rather than an exception. Put differently, SDL directs destination marketers to actively customize travel experiences and pursue tourists' involvement in product design and innovation (Lee, Tussyadiah and Zach 2010).

Tourists as co-creators and operant resources

Marketers used to view customers as white rats in labs or fish in ponds, i.e. objects to be observed, analyzed, and taken advantage of (AMA Task Force 1988; Li and Petrick 2008). Much has been said about the empowerment of customers in recent decades, mainly owing to the development of the information technology (Chen and Popovich 2003; Cova and Pace 2006). SDL goes one step further and emphasizes the idea of value-in-use, and the role and activities performed by customers to achieve their goal in the experiential value creation process (FP10) (Payne, Storbacka and Frow 2008; Vargo and Lusch 2004a). During this process, customers contribute their knowledge and skills to co-create value of their experiences with service providers. Customer value is created and determined by their total experience of all service elements. Thus, a tourism destination or service provider gains its competitive advantage by better understanding a tourist's values and needs (e.g. goals in life), by providing better solutions and resources to tourists during the entire co-creation process, and by optimizing tourists' value creation process (e.g. improving the process' efficiency) (FP4, 6, 7, and 8) (Payne, Storbacka and Frow 2008).

In the tourism literature, the idea of tourists being involved in defining and creating their own tourism experience is not necessarily new (Jackson, White and Schmierer 1996; Wang 1999), but an explicit recognition of tourism experience co-creation is fairly recent (Binkhorst and Dekker 2009; Prebensen and Foss 2011; Scott, Laws and Boksberger 2009). In addition to SDL, research interests on tourism experience co-creation seem to result partly from renewed attention to studying quality or memorable tourism experiences (Jennings, Lee and Ayling 2009; Jennings and Nickerson 2006; Ritchie and Hudson 2009; Tung and Ritchie 2011). Experience co-creation in tourism seems to include at least three types: tourist–tourist interaction/co-creation (e.g. the behaviour of fellow tourists in a theme park could substantially affect one's experience), tourist–service provider co-creation (see Lee and colleagues (2010) for an example of travel product innovation driven by tourists), and visitor–local co-creation (Binkhorst and Dekker 2009). Notably, one rather unique characteristic of experience co-creation in tourism is the high level of interaction with other tourists and local residents, as most other categories of services are catered either without other customers' involvement or with such involvement minimized.

Destination as a service system and resource integrator

In the past, most tourism scholars viewed destinations as places people travel to and stay for experiences unavailable at their home environment, as objective backdrops against which tourism development simply occurs and impacts upon (Bærenholdt *et al.* 2004; Leiper 1995), and as 'taken-for-granted resources and as fixed territorial entities where faceless tourist masses come and go via different routes' (Saraniemi and Kylänen 2011: 135). Put differently, they conceptualize destinations as *operand resources*, or 'resources on which an operation or act is performed to produce an effect' (Vargo and Lusch 2004a: 2). Saraniemi and Kylänen (2011), obviously impacted by SDL, recommend defining destinations as 'a set of institutions and actors located in a physical or a virtual space where marketing-related transactions and activities take place' (2011: 133). In essence, they view destinations more as operant resources – resources 'employed to act on operand resources (and other operant resources)' (Vargo and Lusch 2004a: 2).

This author concurs with Saraniemi and Kylänen (2011). Moreover, from a service science perspective, this author suggests viewing destinations as dynamic service systems that integrate resources (FP9). SDL researchers define service system as 'an arrangement of resources (including people, technology, information, etc.) connected to other systems by value propositions' (Vargo, Maglio and Akaka 2008: 149). Entities within a service system exchange competence by sharing information, work, risk, and goods (Maglio and Spohrer 2008). In the tourism destination context, because of the highly fragmented nature of tourism product offerings – multiple different service providers are involved in providing tourists' holistic travel experiences – destination marketing organizations (DMOs) today need to play a role in integrating localized, specialized skills and resources and transforming them into higher-order competences (FP9) (Lusch, Vargo and O'Brien 2007). To survive in today's environment, a destination needs to constantly enhance its competences, build relationships, and capture and process information (Lusch, Vargo and Tanniru 2010).

A destination's competitiveness thus comes from its ability to understand and co-create value with its clients (e.g. tour operators) and customers (e.g. tourists), its ability to empower and educate institutions and individuals in the value co-creation process, its ability to build relationships with other destinations and service systems, and its ability to optimize competence distribution and value propositions among entities involved to sustain the synergy. In short, for a destination to enhance its competitiveness, it needs to engage in knowledge-based interactions within itself, with other destinations (competitors or allies), and with its (potential) tourists. This is why DMOs need to evolve from 'marketing to' to 'marketing with' its (potential) tourists (Lusch, Vargo and O'Brien 2007; Saraniemi and Kylänen 2011). It calls for more knowledge-intensive tourism operation and the development of SMART tourism destinations or destination intelligence systems (Wang, Li and Li 2013; Gretzel 2011). Further, following the Nordic School of service marketing thoughts, the author believes many aspects of contemporary destination marketing are beyond the responsibility of DMOs, because all aspects of tourists' consumption 'that has an impact on customers' perception of quality and support their value creation' should be handled as part of destination marketing (Grönroos 2006: 328).

The global market is undergoing fast and profound changes, which call for new ways to understand and explain the world. For the first time, the idea of a more service-oriented logic is presented in front of the whole field of marketing, not just service marketing (Cova, Ford and Salle 2009; Grönroos 2008). SDL is clearly not a theory, but a mindset and increasingly a fertile ground for new ideas, conceptualizations, even theories (Vargo and Lusch 2008a). How destination marketers can take advantage of this transition of mindsets remains to be seen. This chapter aimed to present a more tourism-grounded understanding of SDL, as well as a more SDL-grounded understanding of destination marketing. It is hoped SDL provides a refreshing theoretical lens to destination marketing research as well as new strategies in destination marketing practices.

References

Achrol, R.S. (1991) 'Evolution of the marketing organization: new forms for turbulent environments', *Journal of Marketing*, 55 (October): 77–93.

Achrol, R.S. and Kotler, P. (1999) 'Marketing in the network economy', *Journal of Marketing*, 63: 146–63.

AMA Task Force (1988) 'Developing, disseminating, and utilizing marketing knowledge', *Journal of Marketing*, 52: 1–25.

Arthur, W.B. (1996) 'Increasing returns and the new world of business', *Harvard Business Review*, 74(4): 100–9.

Bærenholdt, J.O., Haldrup, M., Larsen, J. and Urry, J. (2004) *Performing Tourist Places: New Directions in Tourism Analysis Series*. Aldershot: Ashgate.

Baines, T.S., Lightfoot, H.W., Benedettini, O. and Kay, J.M. (2009) 'The servitization of manufacturing: a review of literature and reflection on future challenges', *Journal of Manufacturing Technology Management*, 20(5): 547–67.

Bartels, R. (1965) 'Development of marketing thoughts: a brief history', in G. Schwartz (ed.) *Science in Marketing*. New York: John Wiley and Sons, pp. 47–69.

— (1983) 'Is marketing defaulting its responsibilities?', *Journal of Marketing*, 47(4): 32–35.

Berthon, P. and Hulbert, J.M. (2003) 'Marketing in metamorphosis: breaking boundaries', *Business Horizons*, 46(3): 31–40.

Binkhorst, E. and Dekker, T.D. (2009) 'Agenda for co-creation tourism experience research', *Journal of Hospitality Marketing and Management*, 18(2–3): 311–27.

Bolton, R. (2005) 'Marketing renaissance: opportunities and imperatives for improving marketing thought, practice, and infrastructure', *Journal of Marketing*, 69: 1–25.

Buhalis, D. and Licata, M.C. (2002) 'The future eTourism intermediaries', *Tourism Management*, 23(3): 207–20.

Campbell, N., O'Driscoll, A. and Saren, M. (2012) 'Reconcepualizing resources: a critique of service-dominant logic', paper presented at the *37th Annual Macromarketing Conference*, Berlin.

Chen, I.J. and Popovich, K. (2003) 'Understanding customer relationship management (CRM): people, process and technology', *Business Process Management Journal*, 9(5): 672–88.

Constantin, J.A. and Lusch, R.F. (1994) *Understanding Resource Management*. Oxford, OH: The Planning Forum.

Cova, B. and Pace, S. (2006) 'Brand community of convenience products: new forms of customer empowerment – the case "my Nutella the community"', *European Journal of Marketing*, 40(9/10): 1087–095.
Cova, B., Ford, D. and Salle, R. (2009) 'Academic brands and their impact on scientific endeavour: the case of business market research and researchers', *Industrial Marketing Management*, 38: 570–76.
Day, G.S. and Montgomery, D.B. (1999) 'Charting New Directions for Marketing', *Journal of Marketing*, 63: 3–13.
Ettenson, R., Conrado, E. and Knowles, J. (2013) 'Rethinking the 4 P's', *Harvard Business Review*, 91(1): 26.
Frank, R.H. and Cook, P.J. (1995) *The Winner-Take-All Society*. New York: Free Press.
Franklin, A. (2003) *Tourism: An Introduction*. London: Sage Publications.
Gretzel, U. (2011) 'Intelligent systems in tourism: a social science perspective', *Annals of Tourism Research*, 38(3): 757–79.
Grönroos, C. (2006) 'Adopting a service logic for marketing', *Marketing Theory*, 6(3): 317–33.
— (2008) 'Service logic revisited: who creates value? And who co-creates?', *European Business Review*, 20(4): 298–314.
Grönroos, C. and Voima, P. (2013) 'Critical service logic: making sense of value creation and co-creation', *Journal of the Academy of Marketing Science*, 41(2): 133–50.
Gummersson, E. (2002) 'Relationship marketing and a new economy: it's time for deprogramming', *Journal of Services Marketing*, 16(7): 585–89.
Jackson, M.S., White, G.N. and Schmierer, C.L. (1996) 'Tourism experiences within an attributional framework', *Annals of Tourism Research*, 23(4): 798–810.
Jennings, G., Lee, Y. and Ayling, A. (2009) 'Quality tourism experiences: reviews, reflections, research agendas', *Journal of Hospitality Marketing and Management*, 18: 294–310.
Jennings, G.R. and Nickerson, N. (2006) *Quality Tourism Experiences*. Burlington, MA: Elsevier.
Kotha, S. (1995) 'Mass customization: implementing the emerging paradigm for competitive advantage', *Strategic Management Journal*, 16: 21–42.
Kotler, P. (1972) 'A generic concept of marketing', *Journal of Marketing*, 36: 46–54.
Kotler, P. and Armstrong, G. (1999) *Principles of Marketing*. Upper Saddle River, NJ: Prentice–Hall.
Lee, G., Tussyadiah, I.P. and Zach, F. (2010) 'A visitor-focused assessment of new product launch: the case of Quilt Gardens Tour in Northern Indiana's Amish Country', *Journal of Travel and Tourism Marketing*, 27: 723–35.
Lee, T.H. and Crompton, J. (1992) 'Measuring novelty seeking in tourism', *Annals of Tourism Research*, 19(4): 732–51.
Leiper, N. (1995) *Tourism Management*. Melbourne, Australia: RMIT Press.
Li, X. and Petrick, J. (2008) 'Tourism marketing in an era of paradigm shift', *Journal of Travel Research*, 46(3): 235–44.
Li, X., Lai, C., Harrill, R., Kline, S. and Wang, L. (2011) 'When East meets West: an exploratory study on Chinese outbound tourists' travel expectations', *Tourism Management*, 32(4): 741–9.
Lovelock, C. and Gummesson, E. (2004) 'Whither services marketing? In search of a new paradigm and fresh perspectives', *Journal of Service Research*, 7(1): 20–41.
Lusch, R.F. and Vargo, S.L. (2006) 'Service-dominant logic: reactions, reflections and refinements', *Marketing Theory*, 6(3): 281–8.
Lusch, R.F., Vargo, S.L. and Malter, A. (2006) 'Marketing as service exchange: taking a leadership role in global marketing management', *Organizational Dynamics*, 35(3): 264–78.
Lusch, R.F., Vargo, S.L. and O'Brien, M. (2007) 'Competing through service: insights from service-dominant logic', *Journal of Retailing*, 83(1): 5–18.
Lusch, R.F., Vargo, S.L. and Tanniru, M. (2010) 'Service, value networks and learning', *Journal of the Academy of Marketing Science*, 38: 19–31.
Maglio, P.P. and Spohrer, J. (2008) 'Fundamentals of service science', *Journal of Academy of Marketing Science*, 36(1): 18–20.
Merz, M.A., He, Y. and Vargo, S.L. (2009) 'The evolving brand logic: a service-dominant logic perspective', *Journal of the Academy of Marketing Science*, 37(3): 328–44.
Morgan, R.M. and Hunt, S.D. (1994) 'The commitment-trust theory of relationship marketing', *Journal of Marketing*, 58(3): 20–38.
Niininen, O., Buhalis, D. and March, R. (2007) 'Customer empowerment in tourism through consumer centric marketing (CCM)', *Qualitative Market Research: An International Journal*, 10(3): 265–81.

Novatorov, E.V. and Crompton, J.L. (2001a) 'Reformulating the conceptualization of marketing in the context of public leisure services', *Leisure Studies*, 20: 61–75.
— (2001b) 'A revised conceptualization of marketing in the context of public leisure services', *Journal of Leisure Research*, 33(2): 160–85.
Ohmae, K. (1989) 'The global logic of strategic alliances', *Harvard Business Review*, 67: 143–54.
Oliver, R.W., Rust, R.T. and Varki, S. (1998) 'Real-time marketing', *Marketing Management*, Fall/Winter: 29–37.
Payne, A.F., Storbacka, K. and Frow, P. (2008) 'Managing the co-creation of value', *Journal of the Academy of Marketing Science*, 36(1): 83–96.
Powell, W.W. and Snellman, K. (2004) 'The knowledge economy', *Annual Review of Sociology*, 30: 199–220.
Prebensen, N.K. and Foss, L. (2011) 'Coping and co-creating in tourist experiences', *International Journal of Tourism Research*, 13(1): 54–67.
Ritchie, J.R.B. and Hudson, S. (2009) 'Understanding and meeting the challenges of consumer/tourist experience research', *International Journal of Tourism Research*, 11(2): 111–26.
Ryan, C. and Chen, H. (2012) 'Tourism – trends and tensions to 2050', *Human Geography (China)*, 27(4): 109–14.
Saraniemi, S. and Kylänen, M. (2011) 'Problematizing the concept of tourism destination: an analysis of different theoretical approaches', *Journal of Travel Research*, 50(2): 133–43.
Scott, N., Laws, E. and Boksberger, P. (2009) 'The marketing of hospitality and leisure experiences', *Journal of Hospitality Marketing and Management*, 18: 99–110.
Sheth, J.N. and Parvatiyar, A. (1995) 'The evolution of relationship marketing', *International Business Review*, 4(4): 397–418.
Sheth, J.N., Sisodia, R.S. and Sharma, A. (2000) 'The antecedents and consequences of customer-centric marketing', *Journal of the Academy Marketing Science*, 28: 55–66.
Tuli, K.R., Kohli, A.K. and Bharadwaj, S.G. (2007) 'Rethinking customer solutions: from product bundles to relational processes', *Journal of Marketing*, 71(3): 1–17.
Tung, V.W.S. and Ritchie, J.R.B. (2011) 'Exploring the essence of memorable tourism experiences', *Annals of Tourism Research*, 38(4): 1367–386.
Vandermerwe, S. and Rada, J. (1988) 'Servitization of business: adding value by adding services', *European Management Journal*, 6(4): 314–24.
Varadarajan, P.R. and Cunningham, M.H. (1995) 'Strategic alliances: a synthesis of conceptual foundations', *Journal of the Academy of Marketing Science*, 23: 282–96.
Varadarajan, P.R. and Yadav, M.S. (2002) 'Marketing strategy and the Internet: an organizing framework', *Journal of the Academy of Marketing Science*, 30: 296–312.
Vargo, S.L. and Lusch, R.F. (2004a) 'Evolving to a new dominant logic for marketing', *Journal of Marketing*, 68: 1–17.
—(2004b) 'The four service marketing myths: remnants of a goods-based, manufacturing model', *Journal of Service Research*, 6(4): 324–35.
— (2006) 'Service-dominant logic: what it is, what it is not, what it might be', in R.F. Lusch and S.L. Vargo (eds) *The Service-Dominant Logic of Marketing: Dialog, Debate, and Directions.* Armonk, NY: ME Sharpe, pp. 43–56.
— (2008a) 'Service-dominant logic: continuing the evolution', *Journal of the Academy of Marketing Science*, 36(1): 1–10.
— (2008b) 'Why "service"?', *Journal of the Academy of Marketing Science*, 36(1): 25–38.
Vargo, S.L. and Morgan, F.W. (2005) 'An historical reexamination of the nature of exchange: the service-dominant perspective', *Journal of Macromarketing*, 25(1): 42–53.
Vargo, S.L., Maglio, P.P. and Akaka, M.A. (2008), 'On value and value co-creation: a service systems and service logic perspective', *European Management Journal*, 26(3): 145–52.
Voss, C.A. (2005) 'Paradigms of manufacturing strategy re-visited', *International Journal of Operations and Production Management*, 25(12): 1223–227.
Wang, D., Li, X. and Li, Y. (2013) 'China's "smart tourism destination" initiative: a taste of the service-dominant logic', *Journal of Destination Marketing and Management*, 2(2): 59–71.
Wang, N. (1999) 'Rethinking authenticity in tourism experience', *Annals of Tourism Research*, 26(2): 349–70.
Webster, F. (1992) 'The changing role of marketing in the corporation', *Journal of Marketing*, 56(4): 1–17.
Williams, P.W., Stewart, K. and Larsen, D. (2012) 'Toward an agenda of high-priority tourism research', *Journal of Travel Research*, 51(1): 3–11.

Wind, J.Y. (2009) 'Rethinking marketing: Peter Drucker's challenge', *Journal of the Academy of Marketing Science*, 37: 28–34.

Wright, M. and Russell, D. (2012) 'Some philosophical problems for service-dominant logic in marketing', *Australasian Marketing Journal*, 20: 218–23.

Zeithaml, V.A., Parasuraman, A. and Berry, L.L. (1985) 'Problems and strategies in services marketing', *Journal of Marketing*, 49: 33–46.

3

A framework for dramatizing interactions for enhanced tourist experience value

Nina K. Prebensen

Introduction

Tourists interact with people and natural or man-made elements. Consequently, interactions are core mediators of (and thus create an imperative for acknowledging) experience value in tourism. Interaction has traditionally been considered a core characteristic of tourism as a result of simultaneous production and consumption, described as 'prosumption' by Toffler (1967). Despite the importance of acknowledging how and why consumers visit places and exploring interactions between people including tourists, hosts and locals, the issue of interaction has scarcely been researched in tourism contexts. In tourism, interactions are more often performed for social and pleasure-seeking reasons affecting autotelic actions, i.e. actions performed here and now for instant enjoyment (Holt 1995), such as appreciating learning at a museum or having fun with fellow travellers. Interactions may, however, also reflect other goals or motives, e.g. instrumental, such as ordering a meal or questioning a guide to get information, with the aim of fulfilling other needs.

This chapter focuses on tourist interaction practices during a vacation journey and further indicates how these practices improve experience value for the tourists. The chapter ends with proposals for how a firm may facilitate, develop and motivate tourists to enhance experience value through interaction practices. Consumer practices (Holt 1995), customers' value perceptions (Holbrook 1999; Sheth *et al.* 1991) and the dramaturgy metaphor (Goffman 1959) are utilized as theoretical frameworks to delineate the relationship between what tourists do and value and how interaction practices may be stimulated through staging, storytelling and involvement.

Tourism research has adopted theories from the service field, defining services as 'a deed, a performance, and an effort' (Rathmell 1966: 33). In doing so, tourism has more or less focused on the service provider as someone who produces valuable offers for the tourists to favour and buy in order to use and enjoy after the transactions. In the last decade, this perspective, separating the producers and the consumers, has been strongly debated and as discussed in the previous chapter, has resulted in the development of a new service-dominant logic (SDL) (e.g. Vargo and Lusch 2004, 2008). This logic conjectures that 'co-creation is about joint creation of value by the company and the consumer' (Prahalad and Ramaswamy 2004: 8). SDL holds that value cannot be extracted without customer interaction. The value for the tourist then lies in being at the destination and partaking in and enjoying various experiences while staying there (Sandström *et al.* 2008).

The paradigm shift, from the customer as a passive receiver to an active agent in creating value, calls for a fundamental understanding of the customer's role in partaking in value creation processes. Although S-D logic in marketing (Vargo and Lusch 2004, 2008) argues for a customer-centric perspective, as opposed to a product-centric perspective, few studies have empirically explored value creation processes from the customer's perspective. An active patron needs knowledge and skills to partake in creating experience value. A journey cannot be undertaken (consumed as a product) or enjoyed if the customer chooses to stay at home, and tourists inevitably interact with numerous people, situations and places. Thus, tourism is an excellent example in terms of exploring value creation as part of interaction practices.

The level of perceived value depends to a great extent on the tourist's need and ability to partake in the interactive creation process; this points to the importance of considering interaction practices before, during and even after the journey. Experience value is defined by Prebensen *et al.* (2013a: 5) as '. . . comprised of the benefits the tourist perceives from a journey and stay in a destination, including those assets or resources that the tourist, other tourists and the host bring to the process of co-creating experiences'. The present work adopts this definition and explores interaction processes from a value perspective, which is why and how customers interact. Further, in line with Moiso and Arnould's (2005) research extending the dramaturgical framework, this work employs the components of a drama, namely the structure, interaction and content, in relation to tourist experiences. Then, the chapter sets out the process of interaction – before, during and after the journey – and suggests possibilities for enhancing value for the customer and the firm through facilitating, developing and staging the experience drama. Furthermore, examples are outlined.

Interaction and value co-creation in tourism

Interaction is about contact and participation which may be of a direct or indirect nature. Direct participation is when the individual is in immediate contact with another person or an object. Indirect interaction is when the individual is in contact with a person or an object through another party, such as a tour operator, or medium, such as the Internet. Bolton and Saxena-Iyer (2009: 92) define interactive services as 'services that have some form of customer–firm interaction in an environment . . .'. A service experience is further delineated as comprising four components (Fisk *et al.* 2013: 21):

1 the service worker;
2 the service setting;
3 the service customer; and
4 the service process.

In tourist consumption, the customer interacts with a host, often represented by the service worker, in addition to other guests and physical elements within a firm or as part of a destination. These interactions happen because they are valued or expected to provide future value (or hinder events, thereby diminishing value) for the customer. The actors in the service encounter, i.e. the participants in value creation, include all the individuals involved, whether customers or workers (Booms and Bitner 1981). The environment includes all aspects that facilitate or communicate the nature of the experience, before, during or after its performance. Subsequently, tourists and hosts are part of an experience process in which both parties – more or less willingly and actively – partake for the purpose of creating value (experience value for the customers, economic value for the firm, and social, economic and sustainable value for the destination).

The level of interaction, i.e. interactivity, is described by Bolton and Saxena-Iyer (2009) in terms of two dimensions, namely the extent of customer participation and the extent to which the service is technology enabled or delivered, which points to the idea of service as instrumental (solving a problem for the customer). Other researchers suggest that the dimensions of interactive experiences include passive versus active participation and absorption versus immersion (Pine and Gilmore 1999), and suggest four realms of experience: entertainment, educational, aesthetic and escapist. This perspective reflects the notion of actions as autotelic, indicating that the customer values being present and enjoying the moment. Despite these efforts to acknowledge interactive experiences, few studies have actually explored interaction from the customers' viewpoint, which is tourist participation as a resource in enhancing value for the tourist and the firms in the service encounter. As Ramirez (1999: 49) puts it:

> ... value co-produced by two or more actors, with and for each other, with and for yet other actors, invites us to rethink organizational structures and managerial arrangements for value creation inherited from the industrial era. But it also invites us to rethink value creation itself.

Hence, interaction practices can be inputs for firms to develop and facilitate enhanced value for the various interaction parties.

Hedonism is a foundational idea for tourist travel whatever the underlying motivations are, i.e. relaxation, learning, or socializing. Tourist travel is thus fundamentally different from traditional services purchased to solve a problem, e.g. due to lack of knowledge or because one does not have the time, energy or desire to perform the activity oneself. Tourists visit other places, events and people because they want to be present during the production, and more or less actively involved in the production or creation of the experience. Consequently, tourist experiences may differ from other services bought because of lack of motivation, time or knowledge to perform the service oneself. Research shows that tourists who are more motivated are more involved in the tourist trip (Prebensen *et al.* 2012). Prebensen *et al.*'s study also shows that both motivation and involvement positively affect tourists' perceived value of the trip experience. In a follow-up study, Prebensen *et al.* (2013b) show that tourists' knowledge, in addition to motivation and involvement, also affects the customers' perceptions of value, which in turn has a positive effect on evaluation and future intentions, such as word-of-mouth recommendations and intention to return to the destination. Thus, tourist motivation, involvement and knowledge are vital antecedents in value creation processes.

S-D logic embodies a move in the logic of exchange signifying a shift from a focus on products and results to a process and service-centric orientation (Vargo and Lusch 2008). The dichotomy between co-creation versus co-production is outlined in a tourist context by Chathoth *et al.* (2013), where the degree of involvement defines customization and co-creation. Co-production is delineated as comprising lower and more sporadic involvement, whereas co-creation is described in terms of a higher degree of involvement from both host and guests and being a continuous process. Further, the literature describes co-production as focusing on how to make the customers become 'partial employees' (e.g. Wickström 1996) and thus the firm should aim to co-opt customer competence (e.g. Prahalad and Ramaswamy 2004). In contrast, co-creation always considers the consumer as a vital agent in value creation processes; 'value can only be created with and determined by the user in the consumption process and through use or what is referred to as value-in-use' (Lusch and Vargo 2006: 284).

By partaking in value creation, the tourists' capabilities are converted into value for both parties (guest and host). Woodruff (1997) claims that consumers' perceptions of value are based on an evaluation of the trade-off between 'what they get' (perceived benefits, quality and performance) and 'what they give'. Value is not what the firm produces, but the perceived benefits over the costs, i.e. perceived benefits over sacrifices (Eggert and Ulaga 2002). However, a recent study by Prebensen *et al.* (2013b) contends that sacrifices and costs, such as time and effort, within one empirical setting (visiting a dentist or a lawyer) may be viewed as a benefit in other settings, e.g. a tourist trip. Their study outlines and tests various experience-relevant resources, such as service quality, price, effort, time spent and customer involvement, on overall experience evaluation. The study shows that the time spent and effort made, normally viewed as costs or sacrifices in the consumer behaviour literature, have a positive effect on overall experience value. Therefore, resources such as time and effort should not only be treated as costs for the customer, but as providing value through partaking in value creation.

How people interact

In order to understand consumption practices, Holt (1995: 1) asks 'what do people do when they consume?' Founded on participant observation at baseball games, Holt explores and classifies consumption practices based on the structure (how) and the purpose (why) of actions. Holt's (1995) model has been discussed in other empirical settings, e.g. investments (Allen and McGoun 2000; Prebensen 2007) and in networks (Prebensen 2012). Viewed from the perspective of these works and in relation to the theoretical discussion above regarding customer participation in creating value, Holt's (1995) model provides a framework for analysing tourist interaction activities and processes. The focus is on the action of the actors in creating experience value. The Holt (1995: 3) model includes a typology of consumption practices, labelled as 'experiencing, integration, play and classification', which are based on the purpose and the structure of the action. The purpose of the action deals with 'autotelic' and 'instrumental' actions, while the structure of the action includes actions towards objects (object actions) or people (interdependent actions).

The model can be described within a tourism framework. When tourists make sense of and respond to an object at the destination or the destination in itself (autotelic/object action), Holt describes them using a 'consuming-as-experience' metaphor. The tourists use various interpretive frameworks to experience a certain object at the destination, through accounting, i.e. summing up incidences, evaluating and appreciating the object or event. In contrast with consuming-as-experience, 'consuming-as-integration' (instrumental/object action) is about the spectators' use of the object as an instrument to enhance their identity. Integrating practices, i.e. assimilation, production and personalization, are used to break down distances between the consumer and the object. When an object at the destination is used as a resource to interact with fellow tourists, the metaphor 'consuming-as-play' (interpersonal/autotelic) is utilized. Among tourists, two types of play are prevalent, that is communing and socializing. The fourth metaphor, 'consuming-as-classification' (interpersonal/instrumental), refers to situations in which the tourists use the object to classify themselves. Classifying practices provide the means to build affiliation and to enhance distinction, and the tourists do so through objects or through actions. Tourists often use symbols, e.g. clothing and stories, in order to classify themselves.

Tourists represent their own (and maybe their family's) goals and purposes (e.g. learning about and experiencing novel places, socializing, enjoying life, gaining friends and acquaintances, relaxing). Discovering why and how tourists act in the way they do would generate new knowledge in relation to value creation theories and practices. Literature on customer participation focuses on the activities of customers during service delivery and the customer experiences in relation to these activities (e.g. Bendapudi and Leone 2003). This way of thinking reflects a traditional perspective on value. In tourist experiences, other types of value may readily come to mind, e.g. mental activities such as thinking, identity building and dreaming (Belk 1988). Consequently, combining customers' structure and purpose of travel in relation to their vacations with the firm's potential in dramatizing experiences, the present work suggests a framework to understand and enhance experience value through interactions during the whole experience process.

What people value in tourist settings

Customer perception of value is viewed as interactive between customer and offering, relativistic between people and situations, preferential and based on a holistic experience (Holbrook, 1999). Bradley and Sparks (2012) follow the lead of Holbrook (1999) and Woodall (2003) in perceiving value as a benefit or advantage, something consumers regard above other things. Based on similar ideas, Vargo and Lusch (2004) highlight the interactive, relativistic and experiential nature of customer value in relation to the topic of value co-creation, and further the concept of value propositions. Ballantyne and Varey (2006) note that value propositions are reciprocal promises of value, operating to and from suppliers and customers seeking an equitable exchange.

Perceived value has previously been operationalized using a single item scale such as 'value for money'; however, a single item scale does not address the whole concept of perceived value (Gallarza and Saura 2006; Sweeney *et al.* 1999). Bolton and Drew (1991: 377) draw on social judgment theory (e.g. Brunswick 1952) when they propose that value is the key link between the cognitive elements of perceived quality or performance, perceived monetary sacrifice and behavioural intentions, in that they claim that perceived value is a 'richer measure of customers' overall evaluation of a service than perceived service quality'. Measuring multiple components of perceived value has therefore been recommended by many researchers (e.g. Gallarza and Saura 2006; Sweeney and Soutar 2001). A comprehensive theoretical framework of perceived value has been developed by Sheth *et al.* (1991). Sweeney and Soutar (2001) utilize Sheth *et al.*'s (1991) framework in studying retail purchasing. To measure the on-site perceived value, the researchers proposed four distinct dimensions: emotional, social, quality/performance and price/value for money. The results indicated that these multiple value dimensions perform better than a single value item such as 'value for money'.

Holbrook (1994) employs the traditional extrinsic–intrinsic conceptualization of experiences as a foundation for his work on value perception and additionally includes a dimension of activity in the concept. As the consumer is assumed to be more or less active (active versus passive) in the experience, Holbrook supports the idea of the consumer as a participant in co-creating experience value. Based on the dichotomy between intrinsic/extrinsic and active/passive behaviour, Holbrook (1994) recommends that value elements include efficiency, excellence, status, esteem, play, aesthetics, ethics and spirituality. Gallarza and Saura (2006) use Holbrook's scale, adding time and effort spent (as costs for the tourist), and test the relationships between value perception, satisfaction and loyalty in tourism. Sweeney and Soutar (2001) base their work on Holbrook and Hirschman (1982) and further on the framework delineated by Sheth *et al.* (1991). Sweeney and Soutar (2001) view the consumer as a participant in creating experience value – both hedonic and utilitarian – for the customer.

Within this perspective, the consumer makes a choice based on many value dimensions dependent on the choice situation (Sheth *et al.* 1991). Functional value is defined as the 'perceived utility acquired from an alternative's capacity for functional, utilitarian or physical performance' (Sheth *et al.* 1991: 160). These authors assess the functional value as the primary driver of consumer choice and as more often including value for money, quality, reliability, durability and price. The emotional value echoes the product's ability to arouse feelings or affective states (Sheth *et al.* 1991) and is of particular interest in tourist experience settings (Williams and Soutar 2009) in that emotions to a great extent affect satisfaction evaluations (Otto and Ritchie 1996). A social value is defined as 'perceived utility acquired from an alternative's association with one or more specific groups' (Sheth *et al.* 1991: 161), which not only reflects conspicuous consumption (e.g. Bagwell and Bernheim 1996) but also reflects the need to bond and socialize (Arnould *et al.* 2002). Epistemic value, reflecting novelty and learning, is of great importance in experience-related consumption (Weber 2001) and mirrors consumers' curiosity and the need to learn and to experience variety within consumption (Sheth *et al.* 1991). This value scale has been tested in tourism contexts, such as adventure tourist experiences (e.g. Williams and Soutar 2009) and special interest tourism/historical sites, e.g. war-related sites (Lee *et al.* 2007), and in tourist experience settings (Gallarza and Saura 2006; Prebensen *et al.* 2012, 2013; Sànchez *et al.* 2006; Williams and Soutar 2009). The results from these studies reveal slightly different support for the value scale, indicating that further testing should be performed in a tourist experience setting.

Dramatizing for enhanced experience value

Goffman (1959) employed a theatrical metaphor in studying individual behaviour in public settings resulting in a theory of impression management. The theatrical metaphors, i.e. staging, roles and play, have been adopted in consumer research and the literature. Impression management is about the presentation of self or management of the impression of oneself. The fundamental idea is that the individual wants to develop congruence between his or her self-concept and feedback from the social groups to which he or she belongs. Impression management theory describes the process of forming and stabilizing one's identity. People participate in this process of identity building when they enter a social setting.

Bitner's (1992) servicescape framework, demonstrating the atmospherics in service encounters, articulates the effects of the servicescape – or service setting – on customers' behavioural responses, such as approach/avoidance, spending money and repatronage intentions, etc. In tourism research, the interaction between the servicescape provided by the management and the personal drama in the dining room, and the 'superobjectives' of the customers is discussed (Morgan *et al.* 2008). From this perspective, the tourist becomes an actor on or off stage, and the firm and service provider's roles become that of providing the space in which the experience is co-created (Morgan *et al.* 2008).

The company can thus only facilitate tourists' experience value. However, the planning, enabling and dramatizing of the interaction scenes are of vital importance for the customer to be motivated, involved and informed to partake in value creation processes. The change in focus on production and consumption practices from exchange to use includes acknowledging that the customer has valuable resources in partaking in the value creation process. Not only does the customer have a chance to partake in the value creation process, but also the host depends on the customer to partake in order to create value. Partaking in value creation not only requires motivation and drive to be present in the situation, it also requires some sort of knowledge and skills, defined as operant resources (Vargo and Lusch 2004). These resources are considered capable of 'purposefully' acting on other resources (Vargo and Lusch 2008: 257). Viewing beautiful scenery or hiking includes the customer in terms of using his or her senses and/or physical resources in order to enjoy the experience. Consequently, it is the application of resources that enables exchange. Furthermore, it is the benefits that the actors experience in partaking in co-creation that determine the level of value achievement.

The ultimate tourist experience happens on site, in a specific situation often together with other tourists and hosts. However, parts of the tourist experience start before and end after the journey takes place, often enabled by technology (Kohli and Grover 2008). Before the journey, the tourists talk to friends and family, and learn from them what to experience and which places to visit. The company should therefore ensure that existing customers bring home a toolkit (e.g. von Hippel and Katz 2002) of experiences promoting their destination and firm, as well as providing attractive and manageable homepages linked to various social media. Staging and dramaturgy is thus of great importance before the journey. However, the experience starts when people arrive at the experience scene, although the transportation from home to the destination also has an impact on the tourists' mood, energy and motivation. The tourist experience is filled with numerous minor experiences adding up to an overall experience, affecting evaluations and future intentions. The experience could therefore be compared to a theatre and a play, where the tourists are introduced to, involved and immersed in the drama (Goffman 1959).

Moiso and Arnould (2005) used the dramaturgical framework to explore shopping experiences, distinguishing between *drama structure*, *drama interaction* and *drama content*. The extended dramaturgical framework provided a more comprehensive understanding of the ways in which cultural resources, active consumer agency and the formal components of performances in consumption situations contribute to customer experiences. The components of the framework, i.e. the drama (drama structure), the narrative resources that organize performances in shopping contexts (drama content) and the active roles that consumers can take in drama performances (drama interaction), are outlined in Table 3.1 below. Drama structure denotes the set of theatrical components: setting, actors/audience and performance, or the formal components of drama (Grove and Fisk 1992). Drama interaction denotes the level of consumer involvement or activities, ranging from active to passive, which can shape, redirect and structure the unfolding of the drama performance (Firat 1977), thus focusing on customer involvement experiences. The drama content denotes the cultural resources that 'infuse ... activity with signs which dramatically highlight and portray confirmatory facts that might otherwise remain unapparent or obscure' (Goffman 1959: 30).

Based on an idea of what constitute core customer values, i.e. functional, social, emotional and/or epistemic, the message and the content should be founded on these premises. Tourists attracted by functional value should receive information regarding standards of quality and value for money, perhaps even compared to other facilities. If the core segment is more concerned about social experiences, the firm may promote and facilitate elements augmenting the customers' positive feeling of self and social acceptance, for instance focusing on a certain type of customer and fitting their own lifestyle or the lifestyle they seek. Customers seeking emotional value should receive information about and experience the sensations and emotions of the experience, e.g. excitement and enjoyment. For risk-takers climbing mountains, a film produced to evoke the emotions of experiencing heights would probably be of significance, while a person in need of relaxation would be more likely to appreciate calm and tranquil environments. For those tourists who value epistemic qualities, promotion material and actual experiences focusing on authentic stories and learning might be expected to be more effective in attracting tourists to search for more information and to choose the actual destination and activities. In these situations, the guide is often a key player in communicating and co-creating valuable experiences for the customers (Arnould *et al.* 2002). Below, Table 3.1 outlines the dramaturgy (structure, interaction and content) of a tourist experience and what the tourist values during an experience process. The table exemplifies how the firm may facilitate enhanced value creation processes by dramatizing a range of experience value elements.

Table 3.1 Dramatizing for enhanced experience value through interactions

Experience value	*Dramaturgy*		
	Structure (staging)	*Interaction (co-creation)*	*Content (involvement story)*
Emotional	Introduction: welcome – focusing on good feelings	Relationships: host and guest, and between guests, socialization	Involvement to boost excitement and other valued feelings
Social	Facilitating: ensuring the right atmosphere, valued encounters, group activities	Linking customers in networks and loyalty programmes	Partaking, interest, involvement and surprises – focusing on the tourist as part of a certain group
Quality/ facilitation	Control, quality and systems	Follow up, controls, asking for feedback	Ensuring standards, information and comparing quality levels
Price/value for money	Comparing and relating information	Loyalty programmes, price policy, guarantees, self-service	Value for money, comparing prices
Epistemic value	Presenting news, focus on learning activities	Communicating authentic and learning activities – the newness	Learning something new, authenticity and novelty – focus on tourist knowledge and skills

Interaction and value creation in tourism are core issues in terms of attracting the right customers and making their trip valuable and worthwhile. Thus, the focus of interaction in tourism is gradually shifting towards integrating the tourist as a co-creator to build value-in-use, before, during and after a journey. The tourism companies and destinations therefore have to put their efforts into attracting, facilitating and involving tourists in partaking in value creation in the whole process of a tourist experience. In particular, the firm needs to be active and creative in order to motivate the customer to engage in value creation before the journey takes place. A particular challenge is the fact that the destination, the place of enjoyment, cannot physically be transported to the customer. Accordingly, the firm has to propose value enhancement situations, i.e. staging value propositions, not only during the trip, but also before and after the journey. The tourist continues to evaluate and remember the experience after the journey, sometimes for a very long time. The company should therefore ensure that the customer has something valuable to recall and remember, and to tell others when arriving back home. People tend to travel for a variety of motives (body- and mind-related motives), but it seems that they are more likely to tell others about their mind-related experiences, such as learning and authentic experiences (Prebensen *et al.* 2010).

Based on theoretical frameworks, such as customers' actions (Holt 1995), customers' value perceptions (Holbrook 1999; Sheth *et al.* 1991) and the dramaturgy metaphor (Goffman 1959), the present work focuses on how tourism firms, by acknowledging what tourists value before, during and after a journey, may develop, facilitate and accommodate processes for the tourist to partake in value creation and co-creation processes through dramatizing interaction processes. Consequently, a dramaturgical framework is used to help firms provide tourists with the right motivation, involvement and skills to partake in and create valuable experiences in the tourism drama. The chapter outlines and exemplifies how tourist companies can enhance experience value for the tourist by dramatizing the experience value throughout the whole experience. As researchers outline (e.g. Vargo and Lusch 2004; Grönroos 2008) customers are the real creators of value because by combining different resources, such as goods, services or skills, they alter the firms' value propositions into real value (value-in-use; partake in fishing activities, showing the catch, taking pictures of the fish, telling others about the fishing trip etc.). Hence, a tourist buys into a potential value which will come to existence thorough being present (on or off stage), taking or adopting roles (more or less given to them), within a certain environment. The action or behaviour in the tourist experience will be different based on what the tourist value, i.e. quality standards, degree of socialising, learning orientation, search for passion etc. Further, the tourist acts differently at the destination or within a tourist activity framework based on their motivation (purposes) and with whom or what they interact (structure) of the action (Holt 1995).

In managerial terms, the chapter offers a framework for tourist companies to facilitate enhanced value creation through motivating, involving and teaching the customer to partake in value creation processes before, during and after the journey through employing the dramatizing framework. Based on what and the level of experience value the tourist prefer, the tourist company may develop value propositions for the tourist to realize. They will do so dependent of the purpose of why they participate, i.e. sunbathing to have a good time here and now, or if they act for instrumental reasons, i.e. get in shape or nice tan to show friends back home. The structure of the action, i.e. alone with an object such as enjoying a nice beach or being together with friends, family, other tourists or the host will also influence on the way experience value is created and co-created (Prebensen and Foss 2011). For tourist firms then to fulfil the tourist needs in a satisfactory way is through acknowledging and dramatizing for the right experience dimension to be fulfilled.

Theoretically, the chapter supports existing conceptualizations of the value-in-use perspectives by integrating various theoretical perspectives, i.e. consumption practices, consumer value perceptions and the dramaturgical metaphor. As research has acknowledged the perceived value as the leading predictor of satisfaction and behavioural intention (Cronin *et al.* 2000; Parasuraman and Grewal 2000; Woodruff 1997), further research on the imperative of the conceptualization, measurement and application of tourist value is needed. Additionally, due to the importance of servicescape (Bitner 1992) and dramaturgy (Goffman 1959) on consumption practices, different special dramaturgy effects, e.g. storytelling, role-play, acting, sound, smell etc., effects on motivation, involvement and partaking in value co-creation, should be further studied. Drawing upon the perspectives, the chapter suggests a new framework to acknowledge, structure and support interaction processes in order to enhance tourist experience value.

Acknowledgement

This research is a part of the research programme 'Service Innovation and Tourist Experiences in the High North: The Co-Creation of Values for Consumers, Firms and the Tourism Industry', financed by the Norwegian Research Association, Project No.: 195306/140.

References

Allen, D.E. and McGoun, E.G. (2000) 'Hedonic investment', *Financial Services Review*, 9: 389–403.

Arnould, E., Price, L. and Zinkhan, G. (2002) 'River magic: extraordinary experience and the extended service encounter', *Journal of Consumer Research*, 20(June): 24–45.

Bagweil, L.S. and Bernheim, D.B. (1996) 'Veblen effects in a theory of conspicuous consumption', *American Economic Review*, 86: 349–73.

Ballantyne, D. and Varey, R.J. (2006) 'Creating value-in-use through marketing interaction: the exchange logic of relating, communicating and knowing', *Marketing Theory*, 6(3): 335–48.

Belk, R. (1988) 'Possessions and the extended self', *Journal of Consumer Research*, 15: 139–68.

Benapudi, N. and Leone, R.P. (2003) 'Psychological implications of customer participation in co-production', *Journal of Marketing*, 67 (January): 14–28.
Bitner, M.J. (1992) 'Servicescapes: the impact of physical surroundings on customers and employees', *Journal of Marketing*, 56: 57–71.
Bolton, R.N. and Drew, J.H. (1991) 'A multistage model of customers' assessments of service quality and value', *Journal of Consumer Research*, 17(4): 375–84.
Bolton, R. and Saxena-Iyer, S. (2009) 'Interactive services: a framework, synthesis and research directions', *Journal of Interactive Marketing*, 23: 91–104.
Booms, B.H. and Bitner, M.J. (1981) 'Marketing strategies and organizational structures for service firms', in J.H. Donnelly and W.R. George (eds) *Marketing of Services.* Chicago: American Marketing Association.
Bradley, G.L. and Sparks, B.A. (2012) 'Antecedents and consequences of consumer value: a longitudinal study of timeshare owners', *Journal of Travel Research*, 51(2): 191–204.
Brunswick, E. (1952) *Conceptual Framework of Psychology.* Chicago, IL: University of Chicago Press.
Chathoth, P.K., Altinay, L., Harrington, R.J., Okumus, F. and Chan, E.S.W. (2013) 'Co-production versus co-creation: a process based continuum in the hotel service context', *International Journal of Hospitality Management*, 32(1): 11–20.
Cronin, J.J., Brady, M.K. and Hult, G.T.M. (2000) 'Assessing the effects of quality, value, and customer satisfaction on consumer behavioral intentions in service environments', *Journal of Retailing*, 76(2): 193–218.
Eggert, A. and Ulaga, W. (2002) 'Customer-perceived value: a substitute for satisfaction in business markets?', *Journal of Business and Industrial Marketing*, 17(2/3): 107–18.
Firat, A.F. (1977) 'Consumption patterns and macromarketing: a radical perspective', *European Journal of Marketing*, 11(4/5): 291–98.
Fisk, R., Grove, S.J. and Joby, J. (2013) *Services Marketing. An Interactive Approach*, 4th edn. Mason, OH: South-Western, Cengage Learning.
Gallarza, M.G. and Saura, I.G. (2006) 'Value dimensions, perceived value, satisfaction and loyalty: an investigation of university students' travel behavior', *Tourism Management*, 27(3): 437–52.
Goffman, E. (1959) *The Presentation of Self in Everyday Life.* Garden City, NY: Doubleday.
Grönroos, C. (2008) 'Service logic revisited: who creates value? And who co-creates?', *European Business Review*, 20(4): 298–314.
Grove, S.J. and Fisk, R.P. (1992) 'The service experience as theater', in John Sherry and Brian Stemhal (eds) *Advances in Consumer Research*, Vol. 19. Provo, UT: Association for Consumer Research, pp. 455–61.
Holbrook, M.B. (1994) 'The nature of consumer value: an axiology of services in the consumption experience', in R.T. Rust and R.L. Oliver (eds) *Service Quality: New Directions in Theory and Practice.* Thousand Oaks, CA: Sage.
Holbrook, M.B. (1999) *Consumer Value. A Framework for Analysis and Research.* London: Routledge.
Holbrook, M.B. and Hirschman, E.C. (1982) 'The experiential aspects of consumption: fantasies, feelings and fun', *Journal of Consumer Research*, 9(2): 132–39.
Holt, D.B. (1995) 'How consumers consume: a typology of consumption practices', *Journal of Consumer Research*, 22: 1–16.
Kohli, R. and Grover, V. (2008) 'Business value of IT: an essay on expanding research directions to keep up with the times', *Journal of the Association of Information Systems*, 28(12): 1187–212.
Lusch, R.F. and Vargo, S.L. (2006) 'Service-dominant logic: reactions, reflections and refinements', *Marketing Theory*, 6(3): 281–288.
Moisio, R. and Arnould, E.J. (2005) 'Extending the dramaturgical framework in marketing: drama structure, drama interaction and drama content in shopping experiences', *Journal of Consumer Behaviour*, 4: 1–11.
Morgan, M., Watson, P. and Hemmington, N. (2008) 'Drama in the dining room: theatrical perspectives on the foodservice encounter', *Journal of Foodservice*, 19: 111–18.
Otto, J.E. and Ritchie, J.R.B. (1996) 'The service experience in tourism', *Tourism Management*, 17(3): 165–74.
Pine, II, B.J. and Gilmore, J.H. (1999) *The Experience Economy.* Boston: Harvard Business School Press.
Prahalad, C.K. and Ramaswamy, V. (2004) 'Co-creation experiences: the next practice in value creation', *Journal of Interactive Marketing*, 18(3): 5–14.
Prebensen, N.K. (2007) 'Investing in an event: the case of a sledge dog race in Norway "The Finnmarksløpet"', *Event Management*, 11(3): 99–108.

Prebensen, N.K. (2012). 'Value creation in experience based networks: a case study of sport-events in Europe', in M. Kasimoglu (ed.) *Strategies for Tourism Industry – Micro and Macro Perspectives.* http://www.intechopen.com/books/strategies-for-tourism-industry-micro-and-macro-perspectives/value-creation-in-experience-based-networks-a-case-study-of-sport-events-in-europe.
Prebensen, N., Skallerud, K. and Chen, J.S. (2010) 'Tourist motivation with sun and sand destinations: satisfaction and the WOM-effect', *Journal of Travel and Tourism Marketing*, 27(8): 858–73.
Prebensen, N.K., Woo, E. and Uysal, M. (2012) 'Experience value. antecedents and consequences', *Current Issues in Tourism.* http://www.tandfonline.com/doi/pdf/10.1080/13683500.2013.770451.
Prebensen, N.K., Woo, E., Chen, J. and Uysal, M. (2013a) 'Motivation and involvement as antecedents of the perceived value of the destination experience', *Journal of Travel Research*, (5)2: 253–64.
Prebensen, N.K., Dahl, T. and Vittersø, J. (2013b) 'Value co-creation. Significance of tourist resources', *Annals of Tourism Research*, 42: 240–61.
Ramirez, R. (1999) 'Value co-production: intellectual origins and implications for practice and research', *Strategic Management Journal*, 20: 49–65.
Rathmel, J.M. (1966) 'What is meant by services?', *Journal of Marketing*, 30(April): 73–80.
Sánchez, J., Callarisa, L.J., Rodríguez, R.M. and Moliner, M.A. (2006) 'Perceived value of the purchase of a tourism product', *Tourism Management*, 27(4): 394–409.
Sandström, S., Edvardsson, B., Kristensson, P. and Magnusson, P. (2008) 'Value in use through service experience', *Managing Service Quality*, 18(2): 112–26.
Sheth, J.N., Newman, B.I. and Gross, B.L. (1991) *Consumption Values and Market Choice.* Cincinnati, OH: South Western Publishing.
Sweeney, J. and Soutar, G. (2001) 'Consumer perceived value: the development of a multiple item scale', *Journal of Retailing*, 77(2): 203–07.
Sweeney, J.C., Soutar, G.N. and Johnson, L.W. (1999) 'The role of perceived risk in the quality value relationship: a study in a retail environment', *Journal of Retailing*, 75(1): 77–105.
Toffler, A. (1980) *The Third Wave.* New York, NJ: Bantam Books.
Vargo, S.L. and Lusch, R.F. (2004) 'Evolving to a new dominant logic for marketing', *Journal of Marketing*, 68: 1–17.
— (2008) 'Service dominant logic: continuing the evolution', *Journal of Academy of Marketing Science*, 36(1): 1–11.
Von Hippel, E. and Katz, R. (2002) 'Shifting innovation to users via toolkits', *Management Science*, 48(7): 821–33.
Weber, K. (2001). 'Outdoor adventure tourism: a review of research approach', *Annals of Tourism Research*, 28(2): 363–80.
Wikström, S. (1996) 'Value creation by company–consumer interaction', *Journal of Marketing Management*, 12: 359–74.
Williams, P. and Soutar, G.N. (2009) 'Value, satisfaction and behavioral intentions in an adventure tourism context', *Annals of Tourism Research*, 36(3): 413–38.
Woodall, T. (2003) 'Conceptualising value for the customer: an attributional, structural and dispositional analysis', *Academy of Marketing Science Review*, 12: 1–42.
Woodruff, R.B. (1997) 'Customer value: the next source of competitive advantage', *The Journal of the Academy of Marketing Science*, 25(2): 139–53.

Part 2
Macromarketing and tourism

4

Sustainability and marketing for responsible tourism

Jackie Clarke, Rebecca Hawkins and Victoria Waligo

Introduction

Tourism is an amalgam of different interests weaving together both private sector and public sector organizations and initiatives. It is a criss-cross of sector businesses and organizations (attractions, accommodation, hospitality, activities, events, aviation, other modes of transport such as trains, ferries, hire car services etc.), of scales of businesses from the micro-enterprises of families to the big multinationals, and of levels of destination from local areas of distinctive character to national countries and cross-border regions. Tourism relies on an integration of resources, built, natural, cultural and human (as hosts or residents) in a way not paralleled in non-tourism products, and the costs of these resources are largely not shouldered by its tourists or users. This fundamental nature of tourism – its intrinsic interdependence and its external costs – has ensured that sustainability has long been debated and practical action sought through the lens of different disciplines and stakeholder groups. For example, tourism planners have long recognised the positive and negative impacts of tourism on the social, physical and economic systems (see, for example, de Kadt 1979; Mathieson and Wall 1982) and the stakeholder approach of community-based planning as championed by Murphy (1985).

An appreciation of tourism as perceived by different disciplines enriches the discussion of the interface between sustainability and marketing for responsible tourism. Tourism has been criticized for taking too narrow and introverted a view of sustainable development (e.g. Hall, 2005) and marketing has been criticized for being 'functionalist, anthropocentric and consumerist' in failing to respond to the wider goals of society (Varey 2010: 120). Tourism has been portrayed as both part problem and part solution, as both vector and victim (United Nations World Tourism Organization [UNWTO] 2007), in this bigger picture of sustainable development.

This chapter draws on contributions from marketing, tourism studies, tourism marketing, sustainable development and sustainable marketing (plus other related nomenclatures) and from the reports of practitioners and Non-Governmental Organizations (NGOs). It cannot be comprehensive nor delineate the numerous controversies, but draws attention to their existence within a chapter that seeks to be an introduction to this far reaching and argumentative topic. Within this proviso, the chapter sets out the language, issues and conceptualization of sustainability and the reasons for business involvement in responsible tourism before moving on to examine the macromarketing perspective, the behaviour of tourists as responsible consumers, and marketing theory and practice for responsible tourism.

Two revered commentators outside of tourism marketing provide memorable and thought-provoking insights to form part of the bigger picture on which this chapter relies. Their contribution is brought to the fore in a tourism and hospitality context by Hawkins and Bohdanowicz (2012) to draw attention to the immensity of the global challenge within which tourism plays its part. The first commentator, Pulitzer Prize winner Thomas Friedman (2008), drew three parallels between the current economic crisis and the impending environmental crisis. Friedman highlighted the common characteristics of a huge increase in debt (in the case of the environmental crisis, the drawdown of natural capital), an over-confidence in the ability of markets and regulatory systems to both identify and to alleviate risks, and the dominance of incentives driving individuals and organizations to pursue short-term benefits irrespective of the long term implications. The second commentator, scientist James Lovelock (2010) and originator of the Gaia theory in the 1960s, highlighted the importance of complexity in the environmental crisis and the role of 'good' sceptics in holding scientific research to account. Lovelock emphasized his belief that human society and humanity itself had not yet 'evolved' to a level clever enough to successfully manage a situation so complex as climate change. Such contributions from Friedman and Lovelock bring to life for the reader the limitations of too parochial a view of sustainability, marketing and responsible tourism.

There has been a proliferation of terminology for both tourism and marketing in the context of sustainability. There is variety in nuance, in accepted usage, and in the time period during which these terms were favoured and subsequently critiqued. Even implicit ownership of the terms varied. For example, the rise of alternative tourism, green tourism and ecotourism were associated with small and medium sized enterprises (SMEs) and predominantly positioned in opposition to mass tourism (Clarke 1997), a now largely historic view as sustainability is generally agreed to be the aspirational goal for all forms of tourism. Thus the lexicon includes alternative tourism, community-based tourism, ecotourism, fair trade tourism, green tourism, pro-poor tourism, responsible tourism, sustainable tourism and more recently (Hall 2011) de-growth tourism, slow tourism and steady-state tourism. Marketing too has generated terminology from ecological marketing in the early 1970s (see Van Dam and Apeldorm 1996) and then in very approximate succession and amongst others to green marketing (e.g. Charter 1992; Peattie 1992), environmental marketing (e.g. Coddington 1993), societal marketing, sustainable marketing (e.g. Fuller 1999; Van Dam and Apeldorm 1996), responsible marketing (e.g. Hudson and Miller 2005), quality of life marketing, social marketing as applied to sustainability (Peattie and Peattie 2009), welfare marketing (Varey 2010) and the emergence of the transformative consumer research (TCR) movement.

The position taken in this chapter inclines towards the language of responsibility; responsible business, responsible tourism and responsible marketing, without jettisoning the language of sustainability which provides its context. The term 'sustainability' has been critiqued for poor translation in the marketplace as being too overwhelming for individuals to act on, inducing numbness and inactivity and a sense of inevitability. Conversely, it is argued that the term 'responsibility' implies a sense of ownership of sustainability that stimulates ability, motivation and action towards better lifestyle choices. It is currently a term under the favoured spotlight although, like its forerunners, there is no blueprint for its success.

Synopsis of issues and conceptualization

The issues encompassed by sustainability are remorseless in number and interlocking, and as presented here, illustrative rather than comprehensive. Included are poverty, inequality (both inter-generational and intra-generational), disparities and growth in ecological footprint, environmental degradation and depletion and damage to finite or fragile resources, climate change, accumulation of chemicals and waste disposal. For example, Middleton and Hawkins (1998) highlighted the specifics of population growth, global warming and the greenhouse effect, ozone layer depletion, acid rain, deforestation, desertification, and the pollution and depletion of water resources. Porritt (2005) draws our attention to the depletion of fossil fuels, extreme climatic events, damage to coral reefs and wetlands, soil erosion and the salinization of agricultural land and the loss of biodiversity; also the disparities in access across the world to resources such as clean water, food, fuel and the provision of health care. These latter issues are captured at the higher level by notions of distributive and social justice. An examination of world maps (www.worldmapper.org, a collaborative project based at the University of Sheffield) vividly demonstrates the disparities amongst the global population in any number of categories, for example, in terms of purchasing power, production of greenhouse gases, pollution and hazardous waste, or ecological footprint. The maps displaying tourism such as the origin of tourists, tourism expenditures and tourism profit illustrate the inequalities across the global population in the rights, access and ability to travel for leisure purposes. In all cases, the shape of countries and regions appear grossly distorted to our eyes accustomed and attuned to seeing maps of the world presented according to land mass.

This jumble of illustrative issues can be subordinated into the three pillars of sustainable development, namely the environmental pillar, the social pillar and the economic pillar. These three pillars of sustainable development also underpin the thinking behind corporate social responsibility (CSR) and the so-called Triple Bottom Line. Many landmark events and conference reports have moulded our understanding of sustainable development and responsibility from the initial wake-up calls (e.g. Rachel Carson's *Silent Spring* in 1962) through the well-embedded contributions of the Brundtland Report (1987) 'Our Common Future' and United Nations Conference on Environment and Development (UNCED) or the Earth Summit (1992) to, say, the International Conference on Responsible Tourism in Destinations in Cape Town 2002 which examined the guiding principles for economic responsibility, social responsibility and for environmental responsibility, the Copenhagen Earth Summit in 2009 and the Rio+20 United Nations Conference on Sustainable Development in June 2012. In recognition of this improvement in understanding and call for action, professional marketing bodies such as the UK's Chartered Institute of Marketing and the American Marketing Association have also sought to realign marketing to the Triple Bottom Line approach.

Why do businesses buy into responsible tourism?

The reasons why businesses buy into responsible tourism gives insight into the potential gap between the conceptualisation, international agreements and documentation of sustainability, and the on-the-ground marketing practice of specific tourism businesses across the different industry sectors. Towards the end of the 1990s, Middleton and Hawkins (1998) discussed ten reasons for business involvement with sustainability. They gave consideration to legal compliance and the advantages to businesses of moving ahead of statutory requirements, the reduction of operational costs through the implementation of effective environmental management systems (a popular argument with businesses to 'sell' more responsible practice), and compliance with investors' funding criteria and investment risk reduction. From a communications angle, legal compliance and anticipatory developments in environmental performance enabled businesses to minimize and even avoid negative PR and the accompanying damage to brand, goodwill and reputation. Strong performance in sustainability also yielded benefits for strategic competitive advantage over others in the marketplace; marketing advantage could also be achieved through recognition in, or membership of, various green award schemes. In line with marketing as a consumer-focused management practice, business commitment to sustainability was also seen as meeting changing customer expectations and demands regarding improvements in an organization's environmental and social performance.

Aside from consumers, the interdependence of tourism at destination level also encouraged businesses to maintain good-neighbourhood policies with other stakeholder groups, such as residents and local non-tourism businesses; another reason highlighted by Middleton and Hawkins (1998) for business engagement with sustainability. The final three reasons comprised ensuring compliance with business to business procurement policies (for example, for an hotel, ensuring that the hotel met the responsible business criteria of a specific tour operator in order to become one of its preferred suppliers), meeting responsible membership criteria to join trade associations and tourist boards, and finally, the better conservation of business assets and resources over the longer term. Some 15 years later, the ten reasons proposed by Middleton and Hawkins (1998) still resonate, with Goodwin (2011) emphasising the building of trust, reputation and customer loyalty, and the lifting of employee morale amidst similar reasons for business engagement with the sustainability agenda.

The macromarketing perspective

It is also important to move beyond the managerial perspective of marketing to better challenge its precepts and conduct. For example, social marketing claims 'a grander vision' for what marketing is about than the classic generation of transactions by placing the quest for behavioural change at the heart of marketing (Andreasen 2003: 299). In this section we examine the contribution of macromarketing to our knowledge of sustainability and marketing for responsible tourism. Macromarketing addresses how micromarketing – or managerial level marketing – impacts on society, how society influences the broader macro-system and how these two systems interact. On this basis, sustainability becomes very much part of the macromarketing territory and ripe for investigation.

At the core of this way of thinking about marketing is the concept of the dominant social paradigm (DSP). The DSP is the set of norms, values, beliefs and behaviours that form the most commonly held world view or mindset within a culture. It is pervasive to the point that people scarcely notice or query the influence of the DSP on their daily lives. The DSP within which our lives are organized in Western societies is one driven by the imperatives of capitalism, economic growth and the accumulation of wealth, and the values of consumerism, individualism and dominance over nature in an anthropocentric value system (Emery 2012; Kilbourne 1998; Kilbourne, McDonagh and Prothero 1997; Varey 2010). It is argued that the reinventions of marketing for sustainability have operated within this DSP even if the intention was to make 'sweeping and substantive changes' (Kilbourne 2010: 109). Recently experts in consumer behaviour have written of consumerism experiencing 'a period of well-earned malaise' and that 'the future of global consumption must remain the object of questioning on economic, cultural, environmental and moral grounds' (Gabriel and Lang 2006: 5). Despite the debates, calls to action and minority alternative lifestyles, consumption as a way of life remains the driving principle of the Western DSP (Varey 2010: 115).

Thomas Friedman as cited in our opening salvo referred to the prevalence of short-term incentives driving people and businesses towards short-term benefits to the detriment of the longer term. This touches on Hardin's (1968) classic tragedy of the commons as iterated in the tourism (e.g. Goodwin 2011) and the marketing (e.g. Polonsky 2011) literature. Because no-one owns the shared communal space (i.e. the commons – for example the quality of the natural environment in all its aspects), no individual is motivated to protect it. Every individual behaves according to their personal interests and benefits, yet these personal interests and benefits may be in opposition to the wider interests of society. For example, it may be in the interests of the individual to take a short haul flight for a weekend break (rest, relaxation, sense of adventure, exploration, self-development, time out with the family etc.) but not for society and the natural environment (fuel emissions, air quality, noise pollution, waste generation at the destination, fresh water consumption etc.). The problem lies not with the behaviour of a solitary individual but in the multiplication of these individuals in their thousands and millions. Thus the tragedy of the commons draws attention to the calamity of the accumulation of self-interested individual behaviour and its inherent destruction of the value of shared resources, spaces and environments. It highlights the inherent conflict between benefits for the individual (person or business) and the wider goals of society including those for the natural environment (Polonsky 2011). Over time we have evolved to see ourselves as a consumer society, and with individual identities as consumers rather than as citizens. But consumers, unlike citizens, hold no obligations to other consumers (Varey 2010) and there is no intrinsic collective responsibility so that the sense of unity is eroded. Hall and Brown (2006: 62) contend that the morality of self-interest has acquired considerable social legitimacy in our way of living today and that this is reflected in the decline of once strong moral authorities such as church, community, family and State.

The macromarketing commentary on sustainability is one that largely rejects change within the current systems and seeks transformative change – to the DSP and its systems, norms and values, and to the behaviour of individuals and businesses within this new order. In doing so, it questions the degree to which sustainability can be achieved within existing Western mindsets and behaviours, both for consumers and for businesses. The commentators on macromarketing are unafraid to illuminate the essential quarrels between consumption, marketing and the quest for sustainability; an illumination of importance that extends to tourism as much as to any other product category. Our DSP is rooted in unremitting consumption (the imperative for continuous economic growth) and marketing has evolved as one of society's mechanisms for delivering this. Thus for marketing academics and practitioners, sustainability becomes 'the elephant in the marketing living room' (Kilbourne 2010: 110). This thinking within tourism is echoed in the emergence of de-growth tourism (Hall 2011) and its ilk (the slow tourism movement; steady-state tourism; and proposals for no tourism). These, in essence, argue for an alternative interpretation of sustainable development from the balancing of environmental, social and economic concerns to one insistent on prioritizing the need to conserve natural capital (Hall 2011), a seismic shift to a new order.

The behaviour of tourists as responsible consumers

The behaviour of tourists in the context of sustainability extends beyond the consumption practice of buying greener tourism products to behaviours relating to responsible consumption, consumption reduction (fewer tourist trips), voluntary simplicity and sustainable lifestyles. A review of consumer behaviour and demand responses of tourists to climate change noted the large adaptive capacity of tourists as consumers to substitute destination, timing and type of holiday, creating shifts in macro-demand for different destinations and patterns of tourist migration flows between countries as tempered by varying cultural perceptions of climatic attractiveness (Gossling, Scott, Hall, Ceron and Dubois 2012). For example, British tourists are drawn towards climates with average daytime temperatures of about 29°C (Benfield UCL Hazard Research Centre 2007) so by 2030 the level of physical comfort for British tourists in

Southern Europe will be a problem. How will such climate change impact on the traditional North–South flow of tourism for European summer holiday destinations? How will tourists alter their behaviour and patterns of movement?

Three trends are suggested by the Benfield UCL Hazard Research Centre (2007). Firstly, that there will be a switch in the timing of Mediterranean holidays from the hot summer months to the winter and shoulder months of autumn and spring. This change in pattern will call into question the structures of Northern European societies with regard to educational cycles and the timings of breaks in the educational and working calendar. Secondly, that tourists will increasingly choose not to visit the large Mediterranean cities so as to avoid both the 'heat island' effect (such cities are typically 1–2^{0}C hotter than the surrounding countryside) and the deteriorating air quality. Thirdly, that there will be greater flows of summer tourists to mountains and other more temperate destinations. This European example is but one illustration. Other regions of the world face other and related challenges. India and islands such as Goa, Maldives and the Seychelles benefit economically from tourism yet confront the problems of potentially more powerful cyclones, erosion and loss of beaches, flooding of coastal zones and inland areas, damage and loss of coral reefs, and even perhaps evacuation of some islands (Maldives) because of saltwater penetrating the aquifers and freshwater supplies (Benfield UCL Hazard Research Centre 2007). As yet, the adaptive capacity of tourists in response to climate change and the challenges it poses across the globe is insufficiently understood (Gossling *et al.* 2012).

At a micro-level, the complexities of tourism compared to many other common product categories make responsible choices difficult for the would-be tourist. This section pinpoints some of these tensions. It is also useful to note at this point Peattie and Crane's (2005) warning of the problems of sustainability research based on hypothetical situations. The use of hypothetical scenarios (such as hypothetical statements of responsible tourism and the respondent's 'intention/likelihood to purchase' in relation to price of the holiday) which typically are designed into questionnaire instruments or experiments create opportunities for unrealistic yet socially desirable responses. A respondent might claim that they would pay a higher price for a responsible tourism product because this is the 'feel good' answer. The reality – as evidenced by other data – suggests a different pattern of actual tourist behaviour. The cautionary note on such methodological weaknesses helps prevent naïve interpretation of the findings.

On the positive side, consumer empowerment enabled by Web 2.0 technologies, social media and mobile technologies have given impetus to the ability of consumers to act together to drive the sustainability agenda. Such collective behaviour gives new energy to boycotts of tourism brands or destinations perceived as falling short on responsibility (the 'stick') and to 'buycotts' for those perceived as deserving of encouragement (the 'carrot'). Flashmobs were used by consumers as part of the mass demonstrations in 2008 against the expansion of Heathrow Terminal Five. Conversely, the aptly named carrotmob.org which started in America harnesses the power of collective spend to reward businesses (such as local restaurants) for their actual or promised environmental performance. However, making good responsible choices in tourism is difficult even for those with the time and inclination to try. We have encapsulated this problem of consumer behaviour as 'tourist confusion'.

Tourist confusion

There are three components (complexity, certification, cynicism) that contribute to tourist confusion in respect of sustainability and responsible choices. Firstly, there is the complexity of tourism itself and how individuals 'trade-off' one sub-decision against another. It is in the nature of tourism that tourists seeking responsible choices have to trade-off sub-decisions about accommodation, attractions and activities, restaurants, excursion providers, perhaps inclusive tour providers (and other service providers that contribute to the total tourism experience such as car hire, financial services and so forth), as well as decisions about destination and mode of travel for arrival and departure. To do so with any accuracy requires knowledge about the respective corporate social responsibility, certification schemes or equivalent programmes. There might also be comparisons to be made between the respective environmental impacts, social impacts and economic impacts. Is it better to fly to a long haul ecotourism destination where you have close economic and social contact with the host community, or is it better to take the train and stay in locally owned accommodation within your own country (domestic tourism)? How does the intended length of stay affect the consequences of the decision? Even with the inclination, ability and access to all the required information for a responsible choice (a doubtful proposition) and assuming a rational decision process (also a doubtful proposition), making a robust decision for sustainability is a taxing task (Bowen and Clarke 2009). Even the 'most dedicated green consumer' is likely to be 'confused and disempowered' by the complexity of information to be considered (Sustainable Development Commission 2006: 15). To compound the problem, the level of environmental literacy amongst most consumers is low (Peattie and Crane 2005) and has been described as ill-informed and highly polarized (Gossling *et al.* 2012).

Secondly, the proliferation of ecolabels and tourism certification schemes designed to guide responsible tourism decisions aids and abets the confusion. Better established examples of these schemes include Blue Flag (international; beaches and marinas), Green Globe (international), Green Tourism Business Scheme (UK), Legambiente Tourismo (Italy), Certification for Sustainable Tourism (Costa Rica) and the Nature and Ecotourism Accreditation Program (NEAP; Australia). However, poor consumer recognition of many ecolabels and tourism certification schemes, in particular, what they stand for, and whether they are based on self-certification or independent verification, suggests such schemes currently do not deliver strong and unambiguous market value.

Thirdly, there is the prevailing and long standing sense of consumer cynicism and distrust of green claims across all product categories (National Consumer Council 1996; Peattie and Crane 2005), from which tourism is not exempt. In the United Kingdom, around 90 per cent of consumers distrust the green information communicated by businesses and government (Futerra 2008). Greenwashing, consisting of unsubstantiated or irrelevant environmental claims made by organizations, gives rise to consumer complaints. As an illustration, in the United Kingdom in 2007, holiday and travel companies totalled 9.5 per cent of the greenwash complaints made by consumers to the UK Advertising Standards Authority (Futerra 2008). Part of the problem may lie with the complex nature of tourism itself. A tourism business might be very active in marketing for responsible tourism but the trade-offs between environmental, social and economic concerns at different levels (local, regional, national), for different components (the business location and departure points, during travel, at the destination) and for the wider supplier and distributor networks means that it is easy to criticise a tourism business for things that it hasn't got right rather than acknowledging the many things that it has achieved. This is especially true when you consider the wide range of consumer views and stances held on what sustainability and its implementation really means. Highlighting the negative may serve to fuel overall consumer cynicism and distrust.

The value-action gap

Labelled the value-action gap by the Sustainable Development Commission (SDC 2006) and as the attitude-behaviour gap by the Worldwide Fund for Nature (WWF) (2008), this discrepancy between behavioural inclination and reality is a recognized phenomenon for sustainability and consumer behaviour. Hall and Brown (2006) allude to the gap when discussing the rhetoric of buying responsible tourism products set against the common desire for low prices and convenience. A UK research study found the majority of respondents willing to pay more for a holiday if the money went to responsible initiatives; however, the co-authors noted that the views were aspirational rather than concrete behaviours (Goodwin and Francis 2003). Research by the British Air Transport Association found 56 per cent of people claimed concern about the environmental impacts of air travel, but only 13 per cent had changed their travel behaviours to reflect these concerns (Sustainable Aviation Council 2006). There is complementary industry evidence to suggest that sustainable and responsible holidays make up a small percentage of total sales (Bowen and Clarke 2009; Thomson Future Holiday Forum 2004).

Of the pro-environmental consumer behaviours sought by the UK government, the avoidance of unnecessary short haul flights has been highlighted as one type of behaviour characterized by limited adoption amongst the UK population yet of significant CO_2 impact (Department for Environment, Food and Rural Affairs 2008). Since the widespread availability and growth of flights to holiday and short break destinations in the post-war era for developed country populations (in itself raising issues of equity across the global population), such tourists have come to regard flying as part of their lifestyles and normal behaviour patterns and this behaviour is entrenched. Research by Target Group Index (2008) found that although 2 per cent of the population of France, America and the UK could be labelled as 'eco-adopters' exhibiting many pro-environmental behaviours and values, for personal travel these eco-adopters had personal carbon footprints larger than the average. For example, French eco-adopters were 63 per cent more likely than average to have taken three or four flights a year, whilst American eco-adopters were 122 per cent more likely to be members of a frequent flier scheme (TGI 2008).

There is some criticism of endorsing strategies for behavioural transformation based on encouragement of small changes in behaviour (recycling, re-using, adoption of energy efficient products etc.) which have some track record of success with an accompanying belief in the overspill effect into larger and more difficult changes such as reduction in flight consumption (WWF 2008). The criticism runs that in reality there is less of an overspill effect and more of a compensation effect. The rationale for the individual follows the line that because as an individual they engage with recycling, re-using and using energy efficient products in and around their home, they can continue to fly because this is supposedly counterbalanced by their environmental behaviour in their home environment. This is the compensation effect but consumer belief in its efficacy is misplaced. It is apparent that motivation, or the driving force behind behaviour, is an important factor to take into account for sustainability and marketing for responsible tourism.

The question of motivation

A distinction is drawn between intrinsic motivation and extrinsic motivation for more sustainable consumption. Intrinsic motivation aligning behaviour with affiliation, community feeling, emotional intimacy and personally held pro-environmental values is argued to be a more powerful driver than extrinsic motivation with its emphasis on social recognition, self-interest, materialism and financial gain (Common Cause Research 2012; WWF 2008). If consumers change their behaviours on a cost-saving appeal (for example, the savings on home insulation or energy efficient bulbs), the evidence suggests they are less likely to switch, for example, from a low cost flight to the Mediterranean to taking the more expensive option of the train. If changes in behaviour stem from intrinsic motivation and the belief in doing environmental good, then the flight-to-train switch becomes more likely. This argument suggests that the motivation that lies behind the behaviour is important and that responsible tourist behaviour is best encouraged through developing pro-environmental values as part of intrinsic motivation.

Common motivators for pro-environmental behaviour stressed by Defra (2008) and covering both extrinsic and intrinsic motivation included the 'feel good' factor, individual benefits such as health or financial outlay, ease of behaviour, social norms and being 'part of something bigger'. A sense of equity and fairness felt by individuals comparing themselves to other members of society has been shown to be important (National Endowment for Science Technology and Arts [NESTA] 2008; Sustainable Development Commission 2006). Individual tourists are more likely to change their behaviours to more responsible choices if they believe others to be doing the same, a spirit of collective behavioural change eventually embedding in the social norm. Common barriers to behavioural change are also insightful, including external constraints such as working patterns and demands on time, but also ingrained behavioural habit, consumer scepticism and feelings of disempowerment (Defra 2008).

Marketing for responsible tourism

Having discussed the controversies of marketing at the macro-level, we focus here on marketing at the micro-level, as a management discipline and as practised by marketing professionals within tourism organizations. The strategic case for destinations to use marketing to spatially and temporally spread and disperse tourists, their associated benefits, and to mitigate their negative impacts, to increase length of stay as opposed to driving up trip numbers, to inform segmentation decisions according to responsible behaviour patterns and to encourage domestic tourism is well documented across both the tourism planning and tourism marketing literature. De-marketing has also received attention as a strategic tool to relieve detrimental pressure on the environmental capacity at honeypot or otherwise fragile destinations (e.g. Beeton 2003).

For tourism businesses, much of the attention has been on the 'greening' (or similar terminology) of the tourism product offer across all stages of the product life cycle, often through engagement with certification schemes, CSR and different types of partnerships. For example, the responsibility credentials of suppliers and supplier procurement policies as 'inputs' to the finished product are important decisions at the front end of the product life cycle (e.g. Schwartz, Tapper and Font 2008; Travelwatch 2006). At the opposite end of the product lifecycle, waste management and disposal are also integrated into the systems designed to engineer more responsible tourism products (e.g. Dileep 2007). There is now considerable expertise and specialism afforded to the different environmental components that could be said to contribute to 'greening' the tourism product offer (e.g. the three Rs, energy efficiency, fresh water management, waste disposal, research and development into technological solutions such as biofuels etc.) so that they are rarely identified in the literature as directly of marketing concern. Nonetheless the fact is that taken together they build the sustainability agenda for marketing.

Some effort has been made by tourism marketing academics to organize responsible activities in other ways. Pomering, Noble and Johnson (2011) cross-referenced an expanded marketing mix that absorbed the work of services marketers Booms and Bitner (participants, process and physical evidence) and tourism marketer Morrison (partnership, packaging and programming) against the Triple Bottom Line of sustainable development (environmental, economic and social). Hudson and Miller (2005) in their examination of responsible tourism marketing referred to tourism businesses as inactive, reactive, exploitative (associated with greenwashing practices) or proactive according to their distribution along the two dimensions of environmentally responsible action (waste management, fuel management, community relations etc.) and environmental communications (brochures, websites, press releases and – in today's currency – social media).

The position of a tourism business within the resulting matrix was seen as dynamic rather than fixed, with businesses able to move between cells over time.

Interdependency between tourism businesses and others involved in tourism provision is an accepted characteristic of tourism marketing (e.g. the 'composite product' of Burkart and Medlik 1981: 195; Middleton 1994: 31). Marketers need to manage their supplier networks who produce the different elements of the tourism product (for example, the food suppliers to the hotel restaurant; the hotel rooms and self-catering units to the tour operator) and for the business investing in sustainability, this means using suppliers meeting certain sustainability criteria and standards. Under the auspices of social marketing, Polonsky, Carlson and Fry (2003) have proposed the 'harm chain' concept as a way of bringing together networks of stakeholders with Porter's value chain as embedded in standard marketing practice to address 'harm' or negative consequences arising from both direct and indirect (externalities) exchanges amongst stakeholders. Types of 'harm' might include carbon dioxide emissions, poor living standards of tourism and hospitality workers, or inequities in fresh water supplies. Identification of 'harm' is the first step in developing a harm chain, and subsequent steps include resolving where the harm originated, how it might be prevented and who is being harmed (Polonsky *et al.* 2003). The harm chain is based on four exchange-oriented stages where harm may happen, namely pre-production, production, consumption and post-consumption. The harm chain also categorizes stakeholders using the criteria of those who cause or bring about the harm, those who are harmed, and those who help in alleviating the harm. The four stages and the three stakeholder types are brought together as a matrix, the harm table (Polonsky *et al.* 2003). From a tourism perspective, given the inseparability of production and consumption, it may be useful to merge the stages of production and consumption to produce a harm table that is a three by three matrix.

Communication has long been the preserve of the marketing practitioner and communication for responsible behaviour is an obvious area of engagement. Alongside criticism of using cost-saving messages as habituating the wrong behaviours for responsible choices in more complex product categories (e.g. flying) are criticisms of fear appeals (e.g. Futerra 2005; Obermiller 1995). The argument is that fear appeals in sustainable communications results in consumer apathy, an overwhelming feeling that little can be done, and is particularly unsuited under circumstances where the supporting infrastructure for pro-environmental behaviour (e.g. recycling facilities) are poor (Futerra 2005). Conversely, recent arguments have been made for appeals that prompt target audiences to reflect on the importance they attach as individual consumers to intrinsic values, even if they are naturally extrinsically-oriented (Common Cause Research 2012). This appeal for reflection is argued as being more effective than communicating systemic concern about big environmental and social issues and is partly predicated on the notion that individuals possess a greater mix of extrinsic and intrinsic values than originally believed (Common Cause Research 2012). Within communication research and the quest for responsible consumer behaviour, the rise of Web 2.0, mobile technologies and the power of social media merits attention. For example, tourism businesses devising social media network strategies and content strategies could experiment with social influence scores (e.g. Klout scores) for bringing on-side influential bloggers with expertise on sustainability, responsibility or on pro-environmental consumer behaviours.

Governments, regulatory bodies, retailers (travel agents) and tourism businesses have the strategic option of practising choice editing for responsible tourism. Choice editing is the pre-selection of products offered to consumers – under these circumstances according to sustainability criteria – and has success in various product categories (Sustainable Development Commission 2006). Applied to tourism, the goal would be to remove less responsible tourism from the possible choice sets of consumers, leaving the would-be tourist with a selection of possible tourism products meeting a minimum sustainability threshold. In doing so, the consumer drawbacks of information overload, possible misinformation and confusion are arguably reduced in the decision making process. A further option for tourism products with high negative impacts and long time horizons for product development (e.g. airplanes, cars, the search for alternative fuels and storage and delivery systems) is that of product roadmapping (Sustainable Development Commission 2006) led by government with a series of staged targets, timetabled interventions and incentives to push for better performing environmental products over a longer time period. A policy of product roadmapping supports technological innovation for sustainability in research and development for costly or complex products.

Conclusion

Sustainability and marketing for responsible tourism is the most pressing and intricate of tourism marketing problems. It requires both the development of specialist and technical expertise (e.g. waste management, biofuel research, energy efficiency etc.) in concentrated silos and the coordination and management of these silos to ensure effective across-the-board implementation. It can be approached from the perspective of managerial marketing and the individual firm and consumer, yet it operates in a context far greater than the concern of the individual tourism business. Both the tourism and the marketing literature in the context of sustainability pose questions for the very nature of the dominant social paradigm (limitless growth, continuous consumption, value of the natural environment), questions that translate for the individual tourism business with some awkwardness and discomfort. Thus, marketing decisions around greening the product, segmenting the tourist, communicating the brand and so forth are commonly open to criticism, cynicism or distrust from different consumer and stakeholder groups.

The directions for future academic research in sustainability and marketing for responsible tourism will depend on the researcher's or group of researchers' position and perspective that they hold in the sustainability debate. For example, do they position themselves as anthropocentric, placing people of central importance, or as ecocentric, placing nature of central importance? Do they perceive themselves as reformists and working within the dominant social paradigm or as radicals seeking to overthrow the dominant social paradigm (Kilbourne 1995) with a new order?

Stemming from this chapter, we would argue for more academic research using methodologies rooted in real life consumer behaviour rather than relying on hypothetical or experimental behaviour in relation to sustainability in tourism. For example, netnography may have a role to this end. There is scope to research the value-action gap in the context of tourism and how this might be mitigated, and to examine the issue of intrinsic motivation and how it best might be enhanced for pro-environmental behaviours in different consumer segments. Research could also address strategies for transforming behaviour for the big environmental decisions so often associated with tourism as a sector (e.g. flight reduction), given the evidence that confidence in an overspill effect from everyday consumer decisions (e.g. recycling) appears to be misdirected. Application of the harm chain as impinging on tourism organizations and associated stakeholders might strengthen the literature on tourism stakeholders in sustainability, supply chain management and impact identification and alleviation (with tourism as both vector and as victim as highlighted by the UNWTO). There is also scope for academic–practitioner collaboration for marketing research into the demand for, and development of, new more responsible tourism products and marketing practices. Finally, a large and relatively untapped area for academic research would be the role of online-communities, consumer e-tribes, and the use of social media in shifting travel and tourist behaviours and decision processes towards more responsible choices and behaviour patterns.

References

Andreasen, A.R. (2003) 'The life trajectory of social marketing', *Marketing Theory*, 3(3): 293–303.

Beeton, S. (2003) 'Swimming against the tide – integrating marketing with environmental management via demarketing', *Journal of Hospitality & Tourism Management*, 10(2): 95–107.

Benfield UCL Hazard Research Centre (2007) *Holiday 2030*, London: Benfield UCL Hazard Research Centre. Online. Available: <http://www.benfieldhrc.org/activities/misc_papers/Holiday.2030.pdf> (accessed 18 June 2008).

Bowen, D. and Clarke, J. (2009) *Contemporary Tourist Behaviour. Yourself and Others as Tourists*. Wallingford: CABI.

Burkart, A.J. and Medlik, S. (1981) *Tourism. Past, Present and Future*, 2nd edn. London: Heinemann.

Burroughs, J.E. (2010) 'Can consumer culture be contained? Comment on "marketing means and ends for a sustainable society"', *Journal of Macromarketing*, 30(2): 127–32.

Charter, M. (1992) *Greener Marketing – a Responsible Approach to Business*. Sheffield: Greenleaf.

Clarke, J. (1997) 'A framework of approaches to sustainable tourism', *Journal of Sustainable Tourism*, 5(3): 224–33.

Coddington, W. (1993) *Environmental Marketing. Positive Strategies for Reaching the Green Consumer*. London: McGraw-Hill.

Common Cause Research (2012) *Communicating Bigger-than-self Problems to Extrinsically-oriented Audiences*. London: COIN, CPRE, Friends of the Earth, Oxfam, WWF-UK. Online. Available: <http://www.wwf.org.uk/research_centre/research_centre_results.cfm?uNewsID=5641> (accessed 24 April 2012).

De Kadt, E. (1979) *Tourism. Passport to Development. Perspectives on the Social and Cultural Effects of Tourism in Developing Countries*. Oxford: Oxford University Press.

Department for Environment, Food and Rural Affairs (2008) *A Framework for Pro-environmental Behaviours*, London: Defra. Online. Available: <http://www.defra.gov.uk/publications/files/pb13574-behaviours-report-080110.pdf> (accessed 14 April 2010).

Dileep, M.R. (2007) 'Tourism and waste management: a review of implementation of "zero waste" at Kovalam', *Asia Pacific Journal of Tourism Research*, 12(4): 377–92.

Emery, B. (2012) *Sustainable Marketing*. Harlow: Pearson.

Friedman, T. (2008) *Hot, Flat and Crowded – Why We Need a Green Revolution and How It Can Renew America*. New York: Farrar, Strauss and Giroux.

Fuller, D.A. (1999) *Sustainable Marketing. Managerial – Ecological Issues*. London: Sage.

Futerra Sustainability Communications (2008) *The Greenwash Guide*. Online. Available: <http://www.futerra.co.uk/downloads/Greenwash_Guide.pdf> (accessed 3 March 2009).

Futerra and United Nations Environment Programme (2005) *Communicating Sustainability. How to Produce Effective Public Campaigns*. Online. Available: <http://www.futerra.co.uk/wp-content/uploads/2011/09/Communicating_Sustainability.pdf> (accessed 17 April 2012).

Gabriel, Y. and Lang, T. (2006) *The Unmanageable Consumer*, 2nd edn. London: Sage.

Goodwin, H. (2011) *Taking Responsibility for Tourism. Responsible Tourism Management*. Oxford: Goodfellow.

Goodwin, H. and Francis, J. (2003) 'Ethical and responsible tourism: consumer trends in the UK', *Journal of Vacation Marketing*, 9(3): 271–84.

Gossling, S., Scott, D., Hall, C.M., Ceron, J.-P. and Dubois, G. (2012) 'Consumer behaviour and demand response of tourists to climate change', *Annals of Tourism Research*, 39(1): 36–58.

Hall, C.M. (2005) *Sustainable Tourism and Tourism and Global Environmental Change*, TRINET. Online posting. Available e-mail: TRINET-L@lists.hawaii.edu (29 November 2005).

Hall, C.M. (2011) 'Policy learning and policy failure in sustainable tourism governance: from first- and second-order to third-order change?', *Journal of Sustainable Tourism*, 19(4-3): 649–71.

Hall, D. and Brown, F. (2006) *Tourism and Welfare: Ethics, Responsibility and Sustained Well-Being*. Wallingford: CABI.

Hawkins, R. and Bohdanowicz, P. (2012) *Responsible Hospitality. Theory and Practice*. Oxford: Goodfellow.

Hudson, S. and Miller, G.A. (2005) 'The responsible marketing of tourism: the case of Canadian Mountain Holidays', *Tourism Management*, 26(2): 133–42.

Kilbourne, W.E. (1995) 'Green advertising: salvation or oxymoron?', *Journal of Advertising*, 24(2): 7–19.

Kilbourne, W.E. (1998) 'Green marketing: a theoretical perspective', *Journal of Marketing Management*, 14(6): 641–55.

Kilbourne, W.E. (2010) 'Facing the challenge of sustainability in a changing world: an introduction to the special issue', *Journal of Macromarketing*, 30(2): 109–11.

Kilbourne, W.E., McDonagh, P. and Prothero, A. (1997) 'Sustainable consumption and the quality of life: a macromarketing challenge to the dominant social paradigm', *Journal of Macromarketing*, 17(1): 4–24.

Lovelock, J. (2010) 'Fudging data is a sin against science', *The Guardian*, 29 March.

Mathieson, A. and Wall, G. (1982) *Tourism. Economic, Physical and Social Impacts*. Harlow: Longman.

Middleton, V.T.C. (1994) *Marketing in Travel and Tourism*, 2nd edn. Oxford: Butterworth-Heinemann.

Middleton, V.T.C. with Hawkins, R. (1998) *Sustainable Tourism. A Marketing Perspective*. Oxford: Butterworth-Heinemann.

Murphy, P.E. (1985) *Tourism. A Community Approach*. London: Methuen.

National Consumer Council (1996) *Green Claims. A Consumer Investigation into Marketing Claims about the Environment*. London: NCC.

NESTA (2008) *Selling Sustainability. Seven Lessons from Advertising and Marketing to Sell Low-carbon Living*. London: NESTA.

Obermiller, C. (1995) 'The baby is sick/the baby is well: a test of environmental communication appeals', *Journal of Advertising*, 24(2): 55–71.

Parsons, E. and Maclaran, P. (2009) *Contemporary Issues in Marketing and Consumer Behaviour*. London: Routledge.

Peattie, K. (1992) *Green Marketing*. London: Pitman Publishing.

Peattie, K. and Crane, A. (2005) 'Green marketing: legend, myth, farce or prophesy?', *Qualitative Market Research*, 8(4): 357–70.

Peattie, K. and Peattie, S. (2009) 'Social marketing: a pathway to consumption reduction?', *Journal of Business Research*, 62(2): 260–68.

Polonsky, M.J. (2011) 'Transformative green marketing: impediments and opportunities', *Journal of Business Research*, 64(12): 1311–319.

Polonsky, M.J., Carlson, L. and Fry, M.-L. (2003) 'The harm chain: a public policy development and stakeholder perspective', *Marketing Theory*, 3(3): 345–64.

Pomering, A., Noble, G. and Johnson, L.W. (2011) 'Conceptualising a contemporary marketing mix for sustainable tourism', *Journal of Sustainable Tourism*, 19(8): 953–69.

Porritt, J. (2005) 'How capitalism can save the world', *The Independent Extra*, 4 November, 1–8.

Schwartz, K., Tapper, R. and Font, X. (2008) 'A sustainable supply chain management framework for tour operators', *Journal of Sustainable Tourism*, 16(3): 298–314.

Sustainable Aviation Council (2006) *Sustainable Aviation Progress Report 2006*, UK: Sustainable Aviation Council. Online. Available: <http://www.sustainableaviation.co.uk/images/stories/key%20documents/report06final.pdf> (accessed 29 March 2008).

Sustainable Development Commission (2006) *I Will if You Will: Towards Sustainable Consumption*, London: SDC and NCC. Online. Available: <http://www.sd-commission.org.uk/publications/downloads/I_Will_If_You_Will.pdf> (accessed 24 March 2008).

Target Group Index (2008) *Green Values. Consumers and Branding. Global Marketing Insights from TGI*, London: TGI in association with The CarbonNeutral Company. Online. Available: <http://www.tgisurveys.com> (accessed 12 February 2009).

Thomson Future Holiday Forum (2004) *A Future-gazing Study of How Holidays Are Set to Change over the Next Twenty Years*. Online. Available: <http://www.lexispr.com/thomson> (accessed 22 March 2007).

Travelwatch (2006) *Increasing Local Economic Benefits from the Accommodation Sector in the Eastern Caribbean*. London: Travelwatch for The Travel Foundation.

UNWTO (2007) *Tourism Can Help in Global Action on Climate Change and Poverty*, Media release, 13 December. Online. Available: <http://www.unwto.org/media/news/en/press_det.php?id=1581> (accessed 24 February 2008).

Van Dam, Y.K. and Apeldoorn, P.A.C. (1996) 'Sustainable marketing', *Journal of Macromarketing*, 16(2): 45–56.

Varey, R.J. (2010) 'Marketing means and ends for a sustainable society: a welfare agenda for transformative change', *Journal of Macromarketing*, 30(2): 112–26.

WWF (2008) *Weathercocks and Signposts. The Environment Movement at a Crossroads*. Online. Available: <http://assets.panda.org/downlaods/weathercocks_report2.pdf> (accessed 12 February 2009).

5
The application of social marketing to tourism

Gareth Shaw, Stewart Barr and Julie Wooler

The evolution of social marketing

For a subject that is only just over 40 years in the making social marketing has attracted a considerable amount of controversy and confusion over its actual definition. As a term social marketing appears to have been formally used for the first time by Kotler and Zaltmann (1971) who viewed marketing as a technological process which in turn was to have implications for how they viewed social marketing. As Andreasen (2003) argues, the initial views of social marketing culminating in the definition in 1971 grew from early post-war ideas in the USA which saw the birth of marketing as a professional activity as a response to a growing consumer market (Truss *et al.* 2009). Social scientists such as Wiebe (1952) whilst acknowledging the power and effectiveness of marketing saw other opportunities for shifting such techniques from the selling of commodities through to the domain of social change. He went on to propose a series of processes and social mechanisms which would be required to mount a successful programme of social change via marketing.

Wiebe (1952) identified the following key processes: force, direction, social mechanism, adequacy and compatibility, along with compatibility and distance. The first mechanism of 'force' was needed and referred to there being sufficient motivation from an individual to give attention to information being provided and equally to be strong enough to carry through to an action. The idea of 'direction' concerns how the individual could achieve the desired outcome, i.e. what type of behaviour was needed. 'Social mechanism' is that which needs to be put into place to achieve the outcome. This relates to perhaps structural changes to facilitate change, whilst 'adequacy and compatibility' relate to whether existing structures are sufficient enough to deal with the processes of change. Finally, 'distance' was defined by Wiebe (1952) as the physical or psychological distance from one type of behaviour to another. He concluded that it should be possible to 'market' social goals since principles are similar to those used to change consumer purchasing habits.

It was these ideas that Kotler and Zaltman (1971) extended into the notion of social marketing which they saw as a framework or structure. Their work opened up a debate about not only the definition of social marketing but also its legitimacy as a distinct discipline. Thus, Luck (1974) argued that social marketing would struggle to be recognized as a discipline whilst its definition and semantics remained blurred and imprecise. The debates and discussions from the 1960s through to the 1970s, according to Andreasen (2003), caused confusion on two fronts. First confusion grew over uses and the terminology of practice with 'social marketing', 'not for profit marketing' and 'responsible marketing' all being considered similar. Second, there was a tendency to confuse social marketing 'with just plain social advertising, public relations or most simply, mere education' (Andreasen 2003: 295).

It was only during the 1990s that social marketing overcame its identity crises when as a subject it became more focussed on one of its key defining features, that of behaviour change (Andreasen 1999; 2003; Hornik 2002). This aspect of behaviour change in turn encouraged links with the theoretical work on change behaviour, whilst at the same time such perspectives led to the recognition of the key features of social marketing (Stead *et al.* 2007). Table 5.1 highlights four of these key characteristics and in doing so draws attention to the essence of social marketing as used in this chapter.

Table 5.1 Key principles of social marketing

Principle	*Description*
1. Customer or consumer placed at the centre	All interventions are based around and directly respond to the needs and wants of the person, rather than the person having to fit around the needs of the service or intervention. Social marketing seeks to understand 'where the person is now' rather than 'where someone might think they are or should be'.
2. Clear behavioural goals	Social marketing aims to achieve measurable impacts on what people actually do, not just their knowledge, awareness or beliefs about an issue.
3. Developing 'insight'	Social marketing is driven by '*actionable insights*' that are able to provide a practical steer for the selection and development of interventions. This means moving beyond demographic or epidemiological data to ask *why* people behave in the way that they do.
4. 'The exchange'	Social marketing aims to maximize the potential 'offer' of a behavioural intervention, and its value to the audience, while minimizing all the 'costs' of adopting, maintaining or changing a particular behaviour. This involves considering ways to increase incentives and remove barriers to the positive behaviour, while doing the opposite for the negative or problematic behaviour.
5. 'The competition'	Social marketing uses the concept of 'competition' to examine all the factors that compete for people's attention and willingness or ability to adopt a desired behaviour.
6. Segmentation	Social marketing uses a 'segmentation' approach that ensures interventions can be tailored to people's different needs. In particular it looks at how different people are responding to an issue, and what motivates them.
7. The 'marketing mix'	Single interventions are generally less effective than multi-interventions, although multi-interventions are more time consuming and effortful. It is important to consider the relative mix between interventions selected.

Source: French *et al.* (2010) and Corner and Randall (2011)

This chapter explores a number of key aspects of social marketing starting with the relationships with behaviour change within the context of more policy driven agendas, before going on to explore its application to aspects of tourism. In this latter context we examine the growing applications of social marketing to behaviour change within a tourism context using a case study example based on holiday travel and conclude by considering future research opportunities that this aspect of marketing presents.

Social marketing, behaviour change and the emergence of the concept of 'nudge'

Whilst many of the early developments were in America with an emphasis on health and issues of increasing lifestyle choices (CDC 2005), there has in recent years been a widening of the social marketing agenda. Part of this unfolding research agenda has seen social marketing as a policy led tool for state campaigns on health, such as lowering alcohol consumption and stopping smoking (Gordon *et al.* 2006; Hastings 2007; National Social Marketing Centre 2006). In this context government policy has very often tended to use social marketing in terms of what Thaler and Sunstein (2008) describe as value-neutral approaches. Their influence has been significant on both the US and the UK governments according to Corner and Randall (2011) with the value-neutral approach of social marketing, where the 'characteristics of the audience and the social context determine' the most effective approach, being taken up by UK government policy (2011: 1010).

This was most evident in the establishment of the 'Behavioural Insight Team' or what became known as the so-called nudge unit in 2010. The notion of nudge behaviour was central to the ideas at the heart of Thaler and Sunstein's thesis. The basis of the ideas and their attractiveness to the UK government is in large part summed up by the following description, 'A nudge, as we will use the term, is any aspect of choice architecture that alters people's behaviour in a predictable way without forbidding any options or significantly changing their economic incentives. To count as a mere nudge, the intervention must be easy and cheap to avoid' (Thaler and Sunstein 2008: 6). The key aspects of this approach are first it is value-neutral as previously mentioned and second it assumes interventions can be made easy. Both of which are politically attractive to central government.

Whilst their approach has moved social marketing into a different way of approaching behaviour change its basis in behavioural economics has been seen by some as being rather too simplified. This view is supported by Hauseman and Welch (2010) who argued for a definition of nudge that recognised the flaws in individual decision-making, thereby calling for nudges as 'ways of influencing choice without limiting the choice set on making alternatives more costly in terms of time, trouble [and] social solutions' (2010: 126). However, at a wider level the use of the nudge approach has also been questioned by other UK policy makers in the form of the Science and Technology Committee (2011). This in part called for more research and a greater understanding as well as criticizing the application of nudge tactics in isolation. Eagle *et al.* (2012) have widened this debate to call for a more critical evaluation of social marketing and the use of behaviour change theories, following critiques from a range of academics.

These have not dismissed the concept of nudge but rather sought to draw attention to some potential limitations. For example, Avineri and Goodwin (2010) argue that nudge is best applied to unintentional or automatic behaviours but tends not to work as effectively on knowledge and attitudes and as a consequence is less sustainable over the longer term. Similarly, Sugden (2009) and Marteau *et al.* (2009) contest the notion of nudge since what may be a nudge to some policy makers may be seen by the individual recipients as a distinct 'shove'. Within the context of food policy and consumption patterns relating to healthy eating, there are mixed messages on the idea of using nudge theory (Food Ethics Council 2011). Thus, Warde (2011) suggests that 'nudging will probably be ineffective in situations of intense market competition' (2011: 21) such as in food retailing. As such the nudge mechanism on its own will struggle to overcome the commercial advertising of large supermarket organizations and food companies.

However, in spite of these concerns and possible limitations nudge is increasingly part of the UK policy landscape and attracting more interest from a wide range of academics. More recently the concepts of nudge and indeed the attempts to change behaviour using social marketing have been focussed on aspects of sustainable behaviour both in general terms and specifically in the context of travel. The latter has been firmly linked to the agenda of mitigating climate change (Corner and Randall 2011; Sussman 2010; Barr *et al.* 2011a). Social marketing has been used as one way of promoting sustainable lifestyles however slippery and ill defined this lifestyle concept is (Jackson 2005). Indeed the UK's Department for Environment, Food and Rural Affairs (Defra) commissioned research under the leading 'Promoting Sustainable Lifestyles: a social marketing approach' in 2006, which included some work on holiday travel (Barr *et al.* 2006).

Predating the so-called nudge unit the National Social Marketing Centre applied campaigns promoting pro-environmental behaviour (Corner and Randall 2011; Peattie and Peattie 2009). Such campaigns involved the 'de-marketing' of particular types of behaviours as well as promoting others. Such ideas were based on the notions of social marketing using in turn a number of underlying principles (Table 5.1). Of key importance is the idea of market segmentation and fitting campaigns to particular segments of the market. As a comparison the Community Based Social Marketing programme in the USA (McKenzie Mohr 2000; Corner and Randall 2011) has also demonstrated in part the effectiveness of social marketing in terms of encouraging pro-environmental behaviour at the community level.

One of the central parts of Defra's pro-environmental behaviour strategy is the development and application of a market segmentation policy. This embraces seven types of groups characterized by such criteria as environmental attitudes, socio-demographic variables and motivations. Such segments are based on the UK population relating to their propensity to undertake 12 key behaviours (Defra 2008). Clearly by using this approach behaviour change policy can be guided by social marketing techniques. As French *et al.* (2009) explain, social marketing for sustainability has emerged as both a major policy initiative and an academic area of research.

These are two key areas of academic concern relating to this social marketing approach; first, the underlying concepts of behaviour research and second, the importance of 'sites of practice'. As we shall see the latter is of particular importance to enacting behaviour change in the context of sustainable practices on holiday.

In terms of behaviour research there are two broad perspectives we need to note (Barr *et al.* 2011a). One concerns the more social-psychological theories that use a range of models and seek to understand the influences on environmental behaviour. These include Fishbein and Ajzen's (1975) 'Theory of Reasoned Action' and Ajzen's (1991) 'Theory of Planned Behaviour'. Such ideas have been criticized on the grounds that they tend to over-rationalize behaviour and more specifically simplify the debates concerning environmental practices. More significantly Eden (1993) argued that these rationalistic models are too linear in their approaches to decision making, and knowledge is often assumed to be a barrier to behaviour change. This forms the basis of the second main approach relating to the ideas of Shove (2003) with a perspective on social practices (Verbeck and Mommass 2008). In this context pro-environmental behaviour, 'in its conventional setting is framed by and within the daily practices of individuals and the interactions with different social, political and material cultures' (Barr *et al.* 2011b: 1235).

The second major area of interest concerns the notion of 'sites of practice', which are of particular significance to enacting behaviour change relative to tourism consumption. Barr *et al.*

(2011b) argue that there is a need to focus on different sites of practice as a way of understanding and questioning sustainable lifestyles. We can recognize two significant sites of practice in this context: the 'home' and the 'holiday'. Increasingly the home is seen as a site of practice to engage in sustainable behaviour through energy savings and recycling. By comparison the holiday destination as a site of practice shifts the boundaries of sustainable action, and research by Barr *et al.* (2011c) has demonstrated that there is a need to recognize such 'spaces of liminality', leisure practices and the home. These are important complications for the application of social marketing in terms of sustainable behaviour and will be considered in the following section.

We started this section by highlighting the increasing attention given by policy makers to the ideas relating to nudge theory along with recent criticisms. In terms of promoting and enacting pro-environmental behaviour a consensus seems to be emerging that nudge will not provide a single way forward but rather needs to form part of a range of social marketing strategies. This was the clear message from the House of Lords Report (Science and Technology Committee 2011). Young and Middlemiss (2012) go further and suggest 'a package of measures that impact on the individual, community and the wider context'. In these terms nudge strategies fit by providing a range of choice architecture. Here choice architecture refers to the means by which decisions are influenced and by how such choices are presented to people. Nudge ideas involve arranging the choice architecture in such a way that may nudge individuals to a certain pattern of behaviour but at the same time not taking away any freedom of choice. This approach therefore is very different from ideas of interventions such as fiscal incentives. Young and Middlemiss (2012) have demonstrated in their review of different social marketing approaches and environmental behaviour the importance of using a package of incentives and penalties along with nudge actions. This to some extent contradicts some of the basic ideas associated with nudge strategies which do not embrace direct incentives but at the same time appears to offer a potentially effective strategy.

The ideas of social marketing therefore are centred on some key principles (Table 5.1) but in addition to these Ong and Blair-Stevens (2010) have also outlined the intervention process in terms of a 'total process planning' framework. This is based on a series of phases or stages (Table 5.2) that embrace the more practical aspects of social marketing. Using these basic ideas gives the social marketing process a clear set of bench marks to develop the key interventions.

Social marketing approaches to tourism and travel

The application of social marketing techniques to tourism and travel is a relatively new phenomenon and in large part intersects with the growing agenda on pro-environmental

Table 5.2 Key stages in the total process planning framework for a social marketing campaign

Stage	*Aspects*
'Scoping'	– Examining issues and challenges, gaining detail understanding of the lives and behaviours associated with main problem
'Developing'	– Designing and developing behavioural goals into an intervention. Pre-test ideas to see which interventions likely to be most effective
'Implementation'	– Rolling out the intervention and monitoring its progress
'Evaluation'	– Receiving and reassessing the cost effectiveness of the campaign

Source: Ong and Blair-Stevens (2010)

behaviour and issues of climate change. Early inroads were made by tourism researchers seeking to explore the concepts and techniques of social marketing in the context of sustainable tourism. For example Dinan and Sargeant (2000) published one of the earliest papers which applied some basic ideas of social marketing, including the social marketing mix, to a survey of 540 visitors to three attractions in Devon (UK). This focussed on attempting to identify those market segments that had visitors willing to follow a responsible code of conduct. They concluded that, 'social marketing may have much to offer those responsible for the management of tourism products' (Dinan and Sargeant 2000: 11). In effect one part of the study was suggestive of the possible development of promotional marketing campaigns that focussed potentially on those individuals who had 'expressed a willingness to change'. The intervention part of social marketing was therefore limited.

Surprisingly this early study did not spark wider scale interest in social marketing, in part because it did not engage with the underlying theories of behaviour change. At the same time Bright (2000) argued for the use of the practices of social marketing to market the quality of life benefits of tourism and recreation – seeing a strong link between social marketing and recreational tourism. Hall (2013) has provided a discussion of the interests in social marketing by tourism researchers using a range of examples. However, he also admits that 'direct tourism related research on social marketing is still very limited' (Hall 2013: 5). He sees this in part as a matter of labelling given the growing interest in sustainability research and climate change being undertaken within tourism. Whilst much of this work may use the ideas of social marketing the authors do not label their projects as such (Hall 2013). Table 5.3 gives a short summary of selected social marketing approaches within tourism and in part illustrates the issues associated with both labelling as well as the actual use of social marketing processes.

We would add to Hall's view by returning to the 'sites of practice' discussion and argue the difficulties of spill-over sustainable behaviour between say home and holiday sites of practice. Our research on the use of air travel for holiday use has shown that even committed environmentalists within a domestic site of practice may very well not follow such pro-environmental behaviours when it comes to holidays (Barr *et al.* 2011a, 2011b, 2011c). Under these circumstances changing behaviour in terms of both social practices and sites of practice presents a more challenging set of circumstances for social marketing. One of the accepted social practices for holiday makers is the use of air travel and increasingly low cost carriers for short haul flights. Cohen *et al.* (2011) have discussed the so-called addiction some consumers have with a behavioural addiction to air travel. Such social practices are behavioural tendencies that contribute to climate change and lead to unsustainable patterns of behaviour. The issue is whether a social

Table 5.3 Selected examples of social marketing and tourist behaviour

Authors	*Context*
Dinan and Sargeant (2000)	Social marketing applied to visitor attractions, review of marketing mix
Bright (2000)	General review but applications to healthy lifestyles and social welfare
Beeton (2001)	Ideas of de-marketing of gambling holidays
Beeton and Benfield (2012)	De-marketing to control demand in environmental sensitive areas
Wearing *et al.* (2007)	Developing target marketing messages for national parks
Kim *et al.* (2006)	Use of films promoting pro-environmental behaviour. Limited use of social marketing methods

Source: Authors and modified from Hall (2013)

marketing campaign can be used to change such behaviour. To explore these ideas we have presented a case study based on a recent research project working jointly with two social marketing companies. The purpose of the case study is to highlight the key processes of a social marketing campaign.

We do this to move beyond many of the more general ideas of social marketing that are presented and also to show the nature of the stages involved in this context and as a form of action research in the social marketing of holiday travel behaviour.

Approaches to social marketing and sustainable travel behaviour: a case study

The case study formed part of a project entitled 'Social marketing for sustainability: developing a community of practice for co-creating behavioural change campaigns' (ESRC 2012). This project aimed to explore the potential of establishing a collaborative 'community of practice' between academics and practitioners to in turn develop a series of applications using existing technology platforms (for promoting responsible environmental behaviour). The focus was on reducing travel and tourism's impact on climate change. This in itself has been a rich source of potential for social marketing within tourism but few projects have actually tackled in detail the idea and more importantly the steps towards enacting behaviour change using social marketing strategies. The project had a number of research objectives but the two of most relevance to this case study are:

1. To co-create with practitioners an approach towards developing social marketing strategies relating to sustainable holiday travel.
2. To co-create a platform of products using social marketing for promoting responsible travel amongst key market segments.

The starting point for any social marketing strategy is indentifying the key behavioural goal. This is something that has to be achievable and again it is important that targets are not set too ambitiously. In our case our goal was 'to reduce so-called "aspiring green travellers" who fly short haul in the UK and Europe by 5 per cent by 2015'. However, our key focus was to switch travellers from plane to train on selected European routes.

Flying was chosen as it is the fastest growing source of greenhouse gas emissions and it accounts for 7 per cent of UK carbon emissions. In addition it is often at odds with the political agenda so there is no government policy to counteract the increasing demand for air travel. Finally, it appeared possible to reduce flying in certain circumstances as a potential behaviour change.

The main stages of research associated with the process of social marketing are shown in Table 5.4. As can be seen most effort was devoted to considering who were the key market segments and also what were the key challenges in attempting to change attitudes and hence behaviour. These are both critical starting points in the development of any social marketing strategy.

In terms of flying habits the highest number of users is in the socio-economic groups ABC1 and certainly in the first two of these. Using a desk based study, data from Mosaic identified three very general groups (Mosaic UK 2009), namely: 'Liberal opinions' (young professionals); 'Suburban mindsets' (mainly married middle aged people); and 'Professional Rewards' (managerial classes, 40+ years old with considerable spending power). Working in partnership with a social marketing company 'Uscreates' along with two other such organizations as stakeholders (Jeff French and Hyder Consultancy), more market segmentation analysis was undertaken and

Table 5.4 Key phases in a social marketing strategy

Phase 1
• Identifying the behaviour change target • Identifying the main market segments • Identifying key issues regarding attitudes/behaviours • What trends/themes can be used • Recruiting consumers within the selected market segments
Phase 2
• Development of co-creation workshops • Key topics for discussion/operation within the workshops, namely i. Green attitudes and behaviours ii. Flying: attitudes/behaviours iii. Rail travel: attitudes/behaviours iv. The decision making process v. Switching triggers/ideas
Phase 3
• Experimental marketing • Developing and launching the social marketing interventions

Source: Authors and Uscreates

mapped onto the Defra sustainable behaviour segments (Defra 2006). Two of these segments had positive attitudes towards sustainable behaviour: 'Positive Greens' (approximately 18 per cent of the population) and 'Concerned Consumers' (14 per cent of the population). From further market research analysis two key market segments were identified: 'Generation Y' (Liberal Opinions) and 'Empty Nesters' (Professional Rewards). These were to form the focus of co-creation workshops which were undertaken in a second phase of the research (Table 5.5).

The challenges to behaviour change are associated with the key motivations for flying, including – it's quicker, cheaper, easier and more convenient than other alternatives in most cases. It is also one of the last actions that many individuals are willing to reduce of all environmentally friendly behaviours. However, social market strategies also seek to identify those positive ideas/attitudes that exist to help change behaviour – in a way this can link with the notions of nudge

Table 5.5 Market segments identified in social marketing exercise

Group	*Age range*	*Characteristics*
½	25–early 30s	'Generation Y' – Young professionals engaging in environmental behaviour but reluctant to give up regular travel, seeking new experiences, individual income £40k, couple £80k+. ABC1
3	30–55 yrs	'Suburban families', married, unpretentious, engaged in environmental behaviour, car dependent household, income £80k+. ABC1
4	Over 55 yrs	'Empty nesters', married, grey gappers, environmentally aware, no guilt on environment – doing enough, income £80k+ (individual) ABC1

Source: Survey data collected in London (2012) for co-creation workshops

discussed earlier. These are associated with changing habits in gradual ways rather than stopping flying. Some sustainable travel companies already promote around savouring the journey (see for example Snowcarbon 2012). The ideas that our strategy attempted to harness embraced: a focus on values rather than actions, small changes rather than stopping flying, links with pro-environmental attitudes and to develop positive networks around such pro-environmental behaviour.

Individuals were recruited via on-street surveys in parts of London (Islington, Dulwich and Surbiton) during 2012. The recruitment questionnaire along with so-called 'vox-pops' video interviews were aimed at the high end of four market segments along with flying habits (on average most groups identified in Table 5.4 made three or more short haul flights per year).

In phase 2 of the research (Table 5.4) a key component was the use of co-creation workshops undertaken by the social marketing company Uscreates. These workshops were held for each of the four segments and contained six respondents per segment selected from the on-street interviews. The workshops differed from normal focus groups in that attendees were presented with the problem of how to change holiday travel behaviour from plane to train for certain short haul flights. This followed a citizen-central approach to social marketing as suggested by French *et al.* (2010). This argues that citizen consumers are not passive, calling for a more pragmatic and insight driven approach. Our use of co-creation workshops was therefore developed to serve such a strategy.

The workshops were used in two ways to inform the project on key aspects of behaviour change and to help co-create a behavioural change campaign. The workshops were designed to open up discussions in a playful way and in turn create opportunities for new ideas. Topics discussed within the workshops included: attitudes to climate change and sustainability, notions of environmental cynicism, attitudes and behaviour to flying, rail travel, switching triggers and ideas. It is not possible to present all the results here but we focus on the key points regarding plane and train travel along with switching triggers and related ideas. At this stage in the analysis our key market segments had been reduced to two core groups, 'Generation Y' and 'Empty Nesters'.

As expected plane travel was favoured for costs and time in the early stages of decision making, but few actually enjoyed the experience of flying. A frequently used statement in the workshops was plane travel 'was a necessary evil' with the whole process 'being fairly unpleasant' (quotes from 'Empty Nesters'). However, the workshops highlighted the obstacles to behavioural change. These were that flying was the social norm as illustrated by the following quotes: 'We are used to the plane, it's a habit' ('Generation Y'), and 'I guess I do it because everybody does. I just don't think about it' ('Generation Y').

In terms of the environmental impacts of flying in all the workshops few people had very little knowledge, with levels of understanding ranging from confusion, scepticism, powerlessness to transferral of blame.

In contrast, the attitudes towards rail travel were rooted in a great many negatives, associated with costs, time and the problems of getting to the station. Typical views were: 'The train is so much more expensive than getting on a plane' ('Generation Y'), 'Carrying a heavy case on public transport is difficult' ('Empty Nesters'). In terms of continental travel there were lots of positive experiences of using the Eurostar but people were more uncertain of continental sleeper trains. Comments such as 'I don't consider it safe on trains, if they are sleeper trains' ('Empty Nesters'), 'It can be unsafe. I don't know if I'd take one' ('Empty Nesters') were common. However, in general terms people spoke more passionately about continental train travel in terms of comfort, relaxation, 'quality time' and enjoyment.

A significant part of the workshops focussed on ideas for enabling switching from plane to train. These involved service changes (better online booking), incentivizing more frequent user schemes similar to AIRMILES, combination journeys – train out, plane back for example, social marketing to change the perceptions of time and price together with carbon emissions, easier more direct routes from the UK with Eurostar going to more continental destinations. Clearly these ideas depend not just on using social marketing to change the behaviour of certain market segments but also the willingness of rail providers and related enterprises to make changes. To explore some of these ideas a final part of the project involved holding a stakeholder workshop between the research team and the service providers. This provides a range of potential avenues for exploration for longer term aspects of social marketing.

In terms of this more limited project in phase 3 (Table 5.4) a number of main interventions were considered. To this end a decision was made to launch a social marketing intervention based on 'Generation Y' located within London. This will take the form of an App that will give direct route comparisons for selected destinations in Europe. It will provide a range of booking facilities, including hotels if breaks in the journey are required, and is being developed by a commercial sustainable travel operator (loco2). The purpose of presenting the case study was not to look at all the outcomes but rather to examine in more detail the key stages in a social marketing campaign.

Conclusions

Social marketing is a process that uses a range of related techniques. Its appeal and application has largely been to intervene in health issues but increasingly it is being seen as a means of changing other types of behaviour. Of growing importance is its use to promote environmental behaviour. In this context the concepts of behaviour change need to be considered in terms of both social practices and norms (as in the case for example of flying as a social norm), and also sites of practices. The latter hold particular importance when trying to apply aspects of social marketing to tourism. Whilst there is a growing recognition of social marketing's use with tourism (Hall 2013) the problems associated with social practices and certainly sites of practices have not yet been fully recognised. These not only present more complex issues but exciting opportunities for further research on many of the issues associated with changing tourist behaviour. To date most of the applications have related to pro-environmental behaviour and even here, as our case study illustrates, there are many more avenues to explore.

References

Aijen, I. (1991) 'The theory of planned behaviour', *Organisational Behaviour and Human Decision Processes*, 50: 179–211.

Andreasen, A.R. (2003), 'The life trajectory of social marketing: some implications', *Marketing Theory*, 3(3): 293–303.

Avineri, E. and Goodwin, P. (eds) (2010) *Individual Behaviour Change: Evidence in Transport and Public Health*. Department for Transport, London.

Barr, S., Gilg, A. and Shaw, G. (2011a) 'Helping people make better choices: exploring the behaviour change agenda for environmental sustainability', *Applied Geography*, 31: 712–20.

Barr, S., Shaw, G. and Coles, T. (2011b) 'Times for (un)sustainability? Challenges and opportunities for developing behaviour change policy: a case study of consumers at home and away', *Global Environmental Change*, 21: 1234–244.

— (2011c) 'Sustainable lifestyles: sites, practices and policy', *Environment and Planning A*, 43: 3011–029.

Beeton, S. (2001) 'Cyclops and sirens – demarketing as a proactive response to negative consequences of one-eyed competitive marketing', *Travel and Tourism Research Association 32nd Annual Conference Proceedings*, 125–36.

Beeton, S. and Benfield, R. (2002) 'Demand control: the case for demarketing as a visitor and environmental management tool', *Journal of Sustainable Tourism*, 10: 497–513.

Bright, A.D. (2000), 'The role of social marketing in leisure and recreation management', *Journal of Leisure Research*, 32(1): 12–17.

Centers for Disease Control and Prevention (CDC) (2005) *Communication at CDC, Practice Areas: Social Marketing* available on http://www.cdc.gov/communication/practice/socialmarketing.htm (accessed 5 November 2013).

Cohen, S., Higham, J.E.S. and Cavalier, C.T. (2011), 'Binge flying: behavioural addition and climate change', *Annals of Tourism Research*, 38(3): 1070–1089.

Corner, A. and Randall, A. (2001), 'Selling climate change? The limitations of social marketing as a strategy for climate change public engagement', *Global Environmental Change*, 21: 1005–014.

Department for the Environment and Rural Affairs (Defra) (2005), *Securing the Future*, London: Defra. See also Barr, S., Gilg, A. and Shaw, G. (2006) 'Promoting sustainable lifestyles: a social marketing approach', London: Defra available on http://randd.defra.gov.uk/Document.aspx?Document+SD14005_3524_FRP.doc (accessed 15 July 2011).

— (2008) *Framework for Environmental Behaviours*. London: Defra.

Dinan, C. and Sargeant, A. (2000), 'Social marketing and sustainable tourism: is there a match?', *International Journal of Tourism Research*, 2: 2–14.

Eagle, L., Dahl, S., Low, D.R. and Case, P. (2012) *Behaviour Change Tools: Soft Versus Hard Options*. School of Business James Cook University, Australia.

Eden, S. (1993) 'Individual environmental responsibility and its role in public environmentalism', *Environment and Planning A*, 25: 1743–758.

ESRC (2013) 'Social marketing for sustainability: developing a community of practice for co-creating behaviour change campaigns', End of Award Report REF ES/J10001007/1.

Fishbein, M. and Aijen, I. (1975) *Belief, Attitude, Intention and Behaviour: An Introduction to Theory and Research*. Addison-Wesley, MA.

Food Ethics Council (2011) Special edition 'Nudge politics', *Food Ethics*, 6(1).

French, J., Blair-Stevens, C., McVey, D. and Merritt, R. (2010) *Social Marketing and Public Health, Theory and Practice*. Oxford University Press, Oxford.

Gordon, R., McDermott, L., Stead, M. and Angus, K. (2006), 'The effectiveness of social marketing interventions for health improvement: what's the evidence?', *Public Health*, 120(12): 1133–139.

Hall, C.M. (2013) 'Social marketing and tourism: what is the evidence?', http://www.academia.edu/2924276/Socialmarketingandtourismwhatistheevidence?

Hastings, C. (2007) *Social Marketing: Why Should the Devil Have All the Best Tunes?* Elsevier, Oxford.

Hausman, D.M. and Welch, B. (2010), 'Debate: to nudge or not to nudge', *Journal of Political Philosopy*, 18(1): 123–36.

Hornik, R. (ed), *Public Health Communication: Evidence for Behaviour Change*. Lawrence Erlbaum Ass, NJ.

Jackson, T. (2005) *Motivating Sustainable Consumption*. SDRN, Surrey.

Kim, H., Borges, M.C. and Chon, J. (2006) 'Impacts of environmental values on tourism motivation: the case FICA, Brazil', *Tourism Management*, 27: 957–67.

Kotler, P. and Zaltman, G. (1971) 'Social marketing: an approach to planned social change', *Journal of Marketing*, 35: 3–12.

Luck, D.J. (1974), 'Social marketing: confusion compounded', *Journal of Marketing*, 38(4): 70–2.

McKenzie Mohr, D. (2000), 'Promoting sustainable behaviour: an introduction to community based social marketing', *Journal of Social Issues*, 56(3): 543–54.

Martineau, T.M., Oliver, A. and Ashcroft, R.E. (2009), 'Changing behaviour through state intervention', *British Medical Journal*, 337(12): 2543.

National Social Marketing Centre (2006) *It's Our Health! Realising the Potential of Effective Social Marketing*. N.S.M.C, London.

Ong, D. and Blair-Stevens, C. (2010) 'The total process planning (TPP) framework', in French, J., Blair-Stevens, C., McVey, D. and Mervitt, R. (eds) *Social Marketing and Public Health: Theory and Practice*. Oxford University Press, Oxford.

Peatie, S. and Peatie, K. (2009) 'Social marketing: a pathway to consumption reduction', *Journal of Business Research*, 62(2): 260–68.

Rainford, P. and Tinkler, J. (2010–11), 'Designing for nudge effects: how behaviour management can ease public sector problems', Seminar No 4, The Design Council, London.

Science and Technology Select Committee (2011) *Behaviour Change*. House of Lords Report, London.

Shove, E. (2003) *Comfort, Cleanliness and Convenience: The Social Organization of Normality.* Berg, London.

Snowcarbon (2012) http://www.snowcarbon.co.uk/ (accessed 2013).

Stead, M., Gordon, R., Angus, K. and McDermott, L. (2007) 'A systematic review of social marketing effectiveness', *Health Education*, 107(2), 126–91.

Sugden, R. (2009) 'On nudging: a review of nudge: improving decisions about health, wealth and happiness by R. Thaler and C.R. Sunstein', *International Journal of Business Economics*, 16(3): 365–73.

Sussman, E. (2010), 'Climate change framing and social marketing: the influences that persuade', *Pace Environmental Law Review*, 27 (special edition) article 9.

Thaler, R. and Sunstein, C. (2008) *Nudge: Improving Decisions about Health, Wealth and Happiness.* Yale University Press, Yale.

Verbeek, D. and Mommaas, H. (2008) 'Transitions to sustainable tourism mobility: the social practices approach', *Journal of Sustainable Tourism*, 16: 629–44.

Warde, A. (2011) 'The power of nudge', *Food Ethics*, 6(1): 20–1.

Wearing, S., Archer, D. and Beeton, S. (2007) 'The sustainable marketing of tourism in protected areas'. Gold Coast: Sustainable Tourism Co-operative Research, Research Centre.

Wiebe, G.D. (1951–52) 'Merchandising commodities and citizenship on television', *Public Opinion Quarterly*, 15: 679–91.

Young, W. and Middlemiss, L. (2012) 'A rethink of how policy and social science approach changing individuals' actions on greenhouse gas emissions', *Energy Policy*, 41: 742–47.

6

Tourism and public relations

A complex relationship?

Jacquie L'Etang and Jairo Lugo-Ocando

Introduction

No other economic activity is perhaps as dependent on reputation as tourism. Even after a year of the so-called Arab Spring and the overthrow of Hosni Mubarak, the city of Cairo was already showing a US$3bn decrease in tourism revenue alongside 32 per cent fewer visitors (Shenker 2012). The effects on employment, family life and even politics have been devastating considering the fact that tourism had become over the past few decades one of the most important streams of income for that country. However, Egypt is not alone in facing collateral effects from political turmoil and social upheaval; many places around the world have also seen important changes in their own tourism flows due to news affecting the reputation of these places. The Swiss tourist who was gang-raped in India in 2013, China's regular outbreaks of avian flu cases and crime in New York and Miami, all made for issues that at some point deterred tourists from visiting those places.

On the other side of the spectrum, some destinations have done remarkably well in turning around their reputation as a tourism destination after years of civil wars, terrorism or cataclysmic events. Colombia, Indonesia, Cambodia and Rwanda have many lessons to teach the world about how to change impressions and perceptions regarding a tourism destination. In the past few years, all of these places have managed to convince the public, or at least part of the public, that they are safe, attractive and interesting to visit. Even war-torn and still very dangerous Afghanistan has managed to attract a few tourists from the wealthy West (Nordland 2013). In all these cases, the concentrated effort to re-direct tourist flows back into these places by changing their tourism-reputation has required actions that go beyond marketing and advertising.

Public relations strategies to turn around the reputation in these places/destinations have included lobbying, public diplomacy, media relations and the management of relational networks. These efforts are set to foster and support tourism flows back, which has been achieved by articulating a variety of individual actors, organizations and institutions in order to orchestrate resources, efforts and set in motion certain dynamics. This is done despite the fact that sometimes these actors and organisations not only do not have anything in common but that in some cases they even represent competing or antagonistic interests. Under these circumstances, it takes a comprehensive series of PR strategies and actions to put these actors together and orchestrate their resources and actions towards attracting tourism flows.

In this context, we need to remind ourselves that public relations and related terms such as communication management, corporate communications, public affairs and integrated communications are twentieth-century terms associated with an occupation that has its roots in a variety of historical public communication practices. The idea of 'relating to the public', meaning the general public, has developed into more focused 'stakeholder relations/management'. That is not to say that media relations and publicity are not still important, particularly in certain contexts such as marketing communications, but increasingly practitioners and academics advocate a 'strategic' role for public relations whereby public relations activities are closely linked to organizational strategy and objectives and operations such as intelligence gathering, issues and risk management as well as crisis handling and day-to-day media relations and event management.

In thinking about definitions it is important to understand that:

1. The term 'public relations' connotes different meanings in different cultural contexts (in some parts of the world it means 'guest relations' or hospitality, in others it means 'working with publics and public opinion' or 'reputation management'; the terms 'public relations', 'communication management', 'corporate communications', 'public affairs' overlap even though a term may connote a particular emphasis, for example, 'public affairs' may imply work in a more political context, working with governmental publics (civil service and politicians).
2. The term 'public relations' has fallen into some disrepute in some cultures such as the UK, partly through its historical connections with propaganda and because more recently it has become associated with 'spin doctoring'. For this reason, alternative terms for the occupation have become more common.
3. In some cultural contexts the term 'public relations' has become a term that is interchangeable with 'media relations'.
4. Definitions need to be understood in terms of the specific cultural context since the term 'public relations' is not a neutral technical term but a concept that has historical and cultural baggage that varies from context to context – and therefore is of central importance to tourism.

Tourism, on the other hand, although a more established practice than public relations has nevertheless evolved in a parallel way, making use of public relations, marketing and promotional tactics since the second industrial revolution. Indeed, organized mass tourism evolved from the need to commodify the industrial workers' free time and appropriate/alienate it in terms of capital and reproduction of social capital that could foster and help sustain social cohesion. Over the years tourism has become a complex social phenomenon difficult to describe succinctly, which is why some authors have called for 'tourism systems' in order to explain its dynamics (Goeldner and Ritchie 2009). We have our own reservations in using the notion of systems as explanatory frameworks for both tourism and PR as they are positivist-functionalistic interpretations that tend to exclude materialistic relations of power. Nonetheless, these systems are useful to explain certain dynamics and the orchestration of resources and actions with regards to PR and tourism.

Overall, tourism systems' ability to attract tourism flows depend largely on their ability to present themselves and be perceived/understood by potential audiences as places of leisure, devotion and engagement with experiences of fulfilment (encompassing the full range of human emotions including empathy, pain, pleasure, solidarity). In so doing, they rely on reputation(s) that can articulate among the wider public a sense of what they are in terms of the touristic expectations and experiences. This is where public relations largely intersects with tourism. This because despite its functional role as part of marketing and promotion, public relations also makes strategic claims to be responsible for reputation, risk and relationship management, issues and crisis management, public affairs and lobbying, and corporate social responsibility. Therefore, PR plays more broadly in the relationships within tourism and between tourism, its stakeholders and the wider global societies and cultural contexts. Consequently, over the years, the tourism-reputation systems to which we refer here have become increasingly complex, incorporating a diversity of new actors and social dynamics.

Taking all this into consideration, it is surprising how little we know about the way reputation in particular and public relations in general relate to tourism as an economic activity and the role that is played in the development of international networks (L'Etang *et al.* 2007). This chapter therefore explores the relationship between public relations and tourism. In so doing, it tries to highlight the challenges of multi-cultural communication, ethics, safety, social responsibility and globalization in the extensive range of tourism contexts that includes business tourism, spiritual tourism, eco-tourism, city tourism, wildlife tourism, adventure tourism, sex tourism.

We locate public relations as a central feature of organizational strategy that is fuelled by political and economic imperatives rather than being only considered as a set of communications tactics in relation to tourism as an economic activity and sociological phenomenon. We have used complexity as a conceptual framework that can help explore the articulation of relational networks and the articulation of media narratives that affects reputation. Complexity has already been deployed in tourism (Faulkner and Russell 1997: 93) and public relations literatures (Lauzen and Dozier 1994; Murphy 2000) and permits nuanced understandings of the way in which different parts of tourist-reputation systems react and adapt to environmental changes. We understand tourist-reputation systems as networks made up by a diversity of individuals, organizations and institutions that orchestrate – although not necessarily in an intentionally or coordinated manner – efforts to attract tourist flows to a country, region or place at regional, national or international levels.

Although the state remains the main orchestrator of these efforts and does so from a geo-political stance and in terms of its own needs and aspiration for economic growth and development, the different actions are nonetheless carried out in a multi-level manner by a diversity of actors even within the state itself. In fact, as we will argue here, the tourism industry intersects and interpenetrates government in relation to heritage, nation-building and national identity and programmes of public and cultural diplomacy as well as public events.

Hence, while a campaign from the Turkish government to attract tourists from the US would have to promote the country as an attractive and secure place to visit, diplomatic efforts would also be required to minimize sensibilities and issues in relation to its Muslim identity and the positions taken by its post-9/11 government. These same efforts would need to be complemented directly or indirectly by a variety of actions performed by international individuals and networks that set the reputation of Turkey as a tourist destination. Within a complexity framework, we can understand that the small travel agent in a suburb of Milwaukee (USA) would not only play a role in the establishment of the reputation of Turkey as a tourist destination but s/he would also have influence in the ability for the tourism-reputation system to adapt and survive post-9/11 challenges. One of the few works in public relations that has explored such issues is Lisa Fall (2004) who researched the increasing role of public relations as a crisis management function by examining the efforts among destination organization managers in the wake of 11 September 2001.

Nevertheless, further empirical work of this nature is required in order to understand how tourist-reputation systems react and adapt to environmental changes. This is especially true in a time in which the relational networks and media ecologies that surround and shape reputation are undergoing important changes both in terms of inter-institutional relations as well as power-structures. By this, we do not only mean the emergence of digital media and social networks that facilitate active reconfigurations, the hyper-fragmentation of audience and the digitalization of information, but the over-arching process of globalization and interactivity that now frames all of the former. In this context, public relations needs to re-think and adapt its traditional research approaches and incorporate multi-disciplinary understandings if it is to explain fully the changing nature of tourism-reputation systems.

We have also linked this perspective in the broader context of the ethics of public relations and reputation because it is impossible to assess these tourism-reputation systems outside the ethical prerogatives that derive from tourism as economic activity. In so doing, the public relations field needs to raise questions regarding tourism-reputation systems and the economical sustainability of tourism in the face of commercial fairness, environmental issues and national/local politics. Is it ethical that tourism-reputation systems are designed and implemented only to attract touristic flows primarily for economic reasons while disregarding ethical considerations? What do tourism flows to Egypt under Mubarak tell us about reputation systems in terms of their ethical responsibilities? What can we say in relation to the politics of public relations and tourism visiting places under authoritarian and oppressing regimes? What can we learn about promoting touristic flows, the increasing pollution of beaches in the south of Spain and the financial crisis? This is indeed an overdue discussion in the public relations field; in particular in relation to the massive social, political and environmental impacts of tourism globally, nationally and locally and the issues that this raises for the PR industry in relation to risk, crisis, community relations and social responsibility.

Configuring public relations and tourism

The impact of strategic managed communication and relational activities in tourism has not received much attention even within public relations (Kang and Mastin 2008; Fall, 2004; L'Etang *et al.* 2007; Tilson and Stacks 1997). There has been some engagement within media and cultural studies, but the notion of public relations as a source for the media or as an occupation that is one of the cultural intermediaries in the touristic activities is still largely under-explored by scholars. Exceptions to this include of course the work of Crouch *et al.* (2005) and Long and Robinson (2009) and Pike (2005), the last of whom has influenced our approach in highlighting complexity as a useful metaphor for understanding the complex relationship between tourism and public relations.

However, the management disciplines (that have been highly influential on the public relations discipline even if it is largely understood as a communications discipline) have taken mostly a functional approach, while reducing communication to messaging and output-production rather than meaning-making; as consumer, rather than stakeholder and public focused. While we acknowledge the opaque boundaries and overlaps between public relations and marketing in many contexts, and the jurisdictional struggle between these aspiring semi-professions, our analysis is informed nevertheless from critical communications studies and our view that public relations plays an influential role in cultural intermediation and articulation of tourism-reputation systems. In this context we acknowledge the contribution made by the instrumental dominant paradigm in the use of systems theory as an explanatory framework to understand how PR in general creates reputation systems (Hazleton 1992; Hazleton and Botan 1989). Nevertheless, as indicated before, we believe that this functionalistic-system is overall unable to provide a comprehensive explanatory framework for the relationship between public relations and tourism. This is because it excludes, for example, the type of power relations and political issues that set in motion the orchestration of dynamics and actors that make tourism flows happen on a local and international level.

Indeed, the international dimension is also central to our approach and the concept of intercultural communication has become synonymous with global communications, diasporas and multiple intersectional identity formations. It is only through this international approach that the tourism-reputation systems can be understood as systems of meaning and mediation of perceived and real experiences. This applies to the individual-local level where reputation systems provide meaning to the tourists during their experience as well as to the collective-global level where public relations mediates culture in global tourism flows. This ability to address the different levels has become increasingly important in times in which 'the global–local tension [of globalization] has disrupted the traditional notion of geographically situated audiences contained within isolated national boundaries and identified by a set of permanent characteristics' (Pal and Dutta 2008: 164).

Consequently, if we seek to understand how tourism-reputation system mediate and create reality, we need to undertake a social-interpretive approach. This in the sense that our notion of 'reality is socially constructed, not objective; that knowing and acting are made possible through symbols and codes; that communicative action has a moral dimension and implications for self- and group identities since communication always conveys both explicit information about a topic and information that proposes "a definition of the participants and their relationship"' (Banks 1995: 36–7).

On this account, tourism is a socially constructed reality, which is culturally mediated by public relations in order to articulate symbolic systems of understanding, experience and satisfaction, which in itself can only be understood in relation to expectations created by propagation of ideas about the event-place. As such, public relations – underpinned by values of commodification and ideology of neo-liberal capitalism – helps to construct the tourism-reputation systems as a cluster of expectations to which stakeholders refer when tourism takes place as an action of performance. The parents visiting a theme-park not only expect their children to be safe and have fun because they think that that is the purpose of parenthood in general but also expect to consume these leisure activities as a necessary ritual of validation of their own parenthood; users of a hotel expect the people to speak their language (or at least be able to communicate with them) even if it is in a foreign place because for them globalization is in a tangible sense an extension of their own reality to other places and the ability to access these event-places on their own terms; visitors to a rainforest expect to see wild animals even if that is unlikely to happen, because their whole experiences have been mediated in anticipation by expectations disseminated by mainstream media programmes of natural history and environmental propaganda.

Tourists, who are of course at the centre of the tourism systems, also perform individually and collectively rituals that bring together expectations and experiences in new ways by evoking different times. The parents who only enjoy Disney World through the enjoyment of their sons and daughters; the Jews, Muslims and Christians who re-live the suffering of the ancestors in their pilgrimages to historic or religious sites; the WWII or Vietnam War veterans and their families who re-visit their own or parental memories by visiting Normandy or Ho-Chi-Min City; the British family who despite having the resources to go somewhere else decide for the rainy Blackpool sea resort because it reminds them of the past; the couple who live in the beautiful South of France but decide to visit Sydney or New York to fulfil their aspirations of modernity and future.

The performance of travelling rituals happens because the tourism-reputation systems create expectations while mediating the overall experience of reality; going to a resort in Punta Cana (which creates an artificial and secluded micro-environment for the tourist) and fulfilling all expectation becomes – as artificial as it might seem to some – a legitimate visit to the Dominican Republic and it will be recounted over and over again as (socially constructed) reality. This is equally true for third and fourth generation Ashkenazi Jews visiting the Auschwitz concentration camp as they will re-live the suffering of their parents and grandparents in their minds throughout the mediated construction of regimes of pity (Boltanski 1999) which lead to solidarity and empathy (by now many descendants of Ashkenazi Jews have only heard the stories of the Holocaust through the media, their schools and third parties). This is applicable too to the relatives and descendants of The Great War (World War I) soldiers killed at the Battle of the Somme or for Australians in Gallipoli or those descended from World War II soldiers who perished in the battle of Ardennes – all re-tracing their steps, paying homage, identifying with a past era or with nationalism. While presented as historical tours, there are also deeper anthropological and cultural issues in relation to ancestor worship and national neuroses (of lost global influence) to which public relations studies need to pay more attention.

Indeed, these examples illustrate the deeper meaning making with which public relations is entailed in the articulation of tourism-reputation systems and particularly about its ability to produce and re-create 'special events' that can evoke past, present and future among potential tourism flows. This is because tourism itself has never been only about geography but also about time as a socially constructed reality. Public relations as a political activity is able to bring together cultural references, relational networks and mediated realities in order to build an expectation-experience for the tourism flows in terms of particular event-places. Some of the event-places are very special, singular in their global scope; for example, places marked by the tourist systems as genocide-holocaust experiences. In these cases, PR sets tourist experiences by means of media-created expectations that refer directly or indirectly to the event-place, while promoting tourist flows globally in relation to the tourism-reputation system. This guarantees both that the tourism flow is not exclusively limited to those who directly are related to the event-place (hence safeguarding its commercial viability) and that the resources to mobilize those flows are more abundant as they come therefore from a diversity of sources.

For us a quintessential example of the former is the Martin Luther King Memorial in Atlanta (USA), where the set of distinctive landmarks such as the memorial, Reverend King's house and the Ebenezer Baptist Church are all brought together by a connected imagery articulated by a complexity of factors that operate individually but in an orchestrated manner to attract tourism flows. There is no tangible-centralized PR machinery in operation to bring all this together, rather it happens in terms of orchestrated complexity, allowing for tourist flows to visit the places despite vicissitudes and apparent disconnections among the different elements of the tourism-reputation system that encompasses the whole of the Martin Luther King Memorial. What does bring people to this place? Well a reputation system that allows among many other things African Americans to re-live the struggle of civil rights and white Americans and Europeans to exculpate their perceived sins by performing this pilgrimage. Such historical cases are particularly fascinating for public relations scholars because they are simultaneously part of public relations history (for example in terms of social movements or propaganda) so there is a double-layered meaning to this type of tourism and its rhetorical presentation.

This is why we do not think that what is often referred to as organized and disorganized complexity is able to explain wholly the way public relations as a communicative action tends to set in motion the different dynamics that allow tourism-reputation systems to promote tourism flows and adapt to challenges in changes. We suggest instead the concept of 'orchestrated complexity' – or 'concerted complexity' – is more useful here as an explanatory framework. We do acknowledge of course the risks and potential pitfalls when one translates these types of concepts into the sociology of public relations, but we find it relevant to the discussion that takes place in relation to tourism; moreover, the type of complexity that applies to these public relations systems is only partially organized/disorganized and partially intentional. For example, it would be impossible that the Holocaust Educational Trust in the UK would be able to fund or let alone know about all the trips from school children in Britain that go to Auschwitz. Nevertheless, these school trips occur more often than not because the tourism-reputation system sets in motion, by means of the reputation of the event-place, a series of dynamics that integrate a variety of actors-elements that bring about tourism-flows as an unintended consequence.

In the context of the relationship between public relations and tourism, orchestrated complexity describes the dynamics and process that take place among a diversity of individual actors, organizations and institutions in order to adapt to change and direct or re-direct tourism flows. These actions and dynamics affect directly and indirectly the reputation of the place-destination, but they are not necessarily set in motion intentionally or in a coordinated manner. These actions happen in some cases in a chaotic way that manages to achieve orchestration by means of probability and interactivity among the different elements of the tourism-reputation. Indeed, orchestrated complexity is made possible because developmental processes are interactive (Crawford and Kerbs 2008: 184).

Therefore, orchestrated complexity can also help us to understand how PR allows tourism-reputation systems to overcome and adapt to particular situations/challenges that arise from global risks and their impact on the reputation of the event or place that otherwise would have traditionally brought about tourism flows but that now is threatened by new situations and changes to the environment. The volcanic eruptions can be a very disruptive phenomenon for tourism as in the case of the Eyjafjallajokull volcano in Iceland in 2010, which provoked the cancellation of hundreds of flights and million dollar losses because of the interruption of tourism flows. Yet volcanic eruptions in the Northern hemisphere (and many in the South too) have overall become one of the most cherished tourist attractions by means of worldwide networks of scientists and amateur observers who are more than willing to pay good money to observe first hand these phenomena because such chaotic events may at one level be uncontrollable yet managed.

The notion of orchestrated complexity could be also used to explore responses to communication crises that threaten reputation, allowing the real possibility of modelling communication strategies to mitigate collateral damage. Indeed, by learning from complexity, PR can offer tourism-reputation systems the ability to predict scenarios of chaos, while identifying the key dynamics that enable adaptation and survival to change. In a way, eco-tourism is already in most cases a product of the inter-play between mixed imperatives of economics, development, public relations, tourism and corporate social responsibility. As such, eco-tourism is a properly contentious subject (Higham 2007: 2) and thus far sadly neglected from a public relations perspective.

Functional and critical perspectives

Public relations activity, whether it is conducted by 'professionals' or 'amateurs', by corporations or by activists, is present at all political, economic, socio-cultural and technological change in contemporary, post-modern promotional cultures. In this sense, it relates to tourism as a sociological phenomenon because it engages with cultural beliefs and practices, communicative action, discourse ethics, organizational cultures and climates, formation of public agendas and debates and of course with interest-group activism.

Public relations practitioners in tourism or related economic activities work on behalf of many different types of organizations, institutions and individuals to engage with multiple stakeholders and to act on their behalf as an advocate to attract and preserve tourism flows. In this context, public relations activity is integral to tourism at many levels. In addressing tourism flows, its concerns are central to public diplomacy, to international relations and state diplomacy, public and cultural diplomacy, corporate diplomacy and to inter-cultural communication as part of the political, economic and socio-cultural fabric, not solely management technocracy. More important in terms of tourism flows and as a consequence of a socio-cultural 'turn' (Edwards and Hodges 2011), it is becoming more common for public relations to be understood as a dynamic societal process or even, drawing on Appadurai's notion of cultural flows, as 'flow' (Edwards 2012). If that is the case, then it is possible to argue that PR and tourism not only are interlinked but are in many ways intrinsic to each other.

Therefore, if we assume that public relations and tourism are indeed intrinsic, then we need to understand the nature of this relationship by exploring what public relations theory has to say about tourism. In this sense, public relations literature can be roughly divided into two main approaches along a continuum: work that focuses on improving the effectiveness of practice and work that pursues interpretive and exploratory themes. A functional approach to tourism public relations will likely focus on the way in which public relations supports a variety of tourism clients. Functional definitions may describe public relations as an adjunct of organizational management, a defender and protector of organizational reputation, a risk manager, a nurturer of relationships, and a producer of communication outputs. Functional approaches tend to assume a benign and rather ideologically neutral approach to public relations, but the main thing that they have in common is their organizational rather than a societal focus. Non-functional approaches, on the other hand, might explore, for example, the way in which power, enacted through communication and discourse, shapes tourism interactions at local, regional, national and global levels; the way the tourism industry promotes a consumerist discourse that disguises underlying political issues; hegemonic relations within the supply chain; exploitative practices promoted by sex tourism; industry evasion of negative tourism side-effects and efforts to ameliorate reputation through corporate social responsibility. Thus non-functional approaches will tend to take a societal or cultural approach to public relations.

Johansson and Heide (2008) identified three key approaches within the public relations literature: communication as a tool; communication as a socially constructed process; communication as social transformation. 'Tool' literature focuses on persuasive/education approaches to increase effectiveness by aligning organizational members' views and behaviours with management goals. Some literature has suggested that communication during change needs to focus on the management of expectations in the context of uncertainty, to create readiness for change and to reduce resistance and dependence on rumour and grapevine. Literature pursuing this approach is functional and technical but does not engage with 'the fundamental relationship between communication and organization that organizations are produced, maintained and reproduced through communication' (Johnasson and Heide 2008: 293). The exploration of the communications function as a socially constructed process focuses on understanding and sense-making processes so that planned change communication programmes can be seen necessarily to alter the communication and organizational context and the relationships within it. Although change processes are often presented as linear they are in fact non-linear, unpredictable and haphazard because all the time multiple interpretations are being formed and preformed within multiple relational contexts and communication dimensions constantly reinterpreted, reconfigured and re-mediated in digital space. Managers can initiate change processes and associated communications, but they do not necessarily control interpretations or responses to the discourse of change they set in motion. There will always be multiple narratives, there will be discourses that are more dominant and 'communication managers' (one of many terms used to describe public relations) will seek to create a dominant discourse that may be transformative, that is, managers' discourses are reproduced in the discursive practices of organizational members (Johansson and Heide 2007: 297). This is more evident in the area of tourism where the ability to establish or not a dominant discourse and derivate from it a series of hegemonic narratives that frame and provides meaning to the expectation-experience of an event-place depends on the level of orchestrated complexity that a tourism-reputation system is able to achieve.

Tourism, events and public relations

Setting aside unplanned events such as natural and human disasters (that also impact the tourism industry with regard to its investment in intelligence and surveillance services, risk and crisis management) public relations motivations lie behind created events – 'they exhibit many elements of religious evangelism and old style salvationism' (Rojek 2013: ix). Information regarding these events is tightly controlled and advance information may be restricted, for example, at the Beijing and London Olympics, where the nature and contents of the opening ceremonies were kept a close secret despite the making distinctive claims of openness. In the case of London this had the advantage in terms of media handling because broadcast journalists, who were apparently unable to describe the unfolding episodic fantasy in front of them, appeared extremely reliant on a script that necessarily incorporated positive interpretations. Consequently, live media presented an uncritical view and much of the media discourse was around issues of national pride and historical achievement.

In the case of the London Olympics of 2012, part of the opening ceremony was used to promote the National Health Service – only a couple of weeks after the Olympics it was announced that the NHS 'brand' was to be marketed internationally, so the reason for its inclusion in the opening ceremony appeared to be driven by a marketing tactic. While mega-events (such as those for good causes) offer apparent transformative potential they operate within a status quo and may simply distract from more fundamental questions of social justice and structural change. The best example of this is the celebrity-led media event (sometimes defined as 'celebrity activism') to collect funding for foreign aid, which despite successfully raising important resources obviates a series of questions in relation to the nature of aid, the political regimes which will access those resources or the disparity and inequality in the comparative lifestyles between the celebrities promoting the event and those whom the event claims to favour.

We can claim that these constructed media events (Dayan 1994; Marriott 2007) are the catalyst to activate the different components of the tourism-reputation systems by creating a sense of community. These events – which are now devised specifically for the mass media – have been part of human history for millennia, a form of communication that performs and celebrates collective identifications through shared meanings of values and ideologies. Examples include the Roman Games, vast political rallies such as those conducted by the Nazis at Nuremburg or more recently mass weddings conducted by the Moonies. While all event-places have personal and cultural significance of some scale, some event-places in touristic terms are globally iconic and the focus of massive formal and informal media comment, social media, rumour, gossip and speculation. The Diana and Dodi Memorial located at the Harrods store in London became a main tourism attraction created by social networking rather than by any type of formal promotion.

As suggested earlier, historically, event-places have had a propaganda purpose as they propagate a particular ideology. Cuba, for example, besides the natural beauties, also attracts tourism flows thanks to the reputation-system that presents the island as a benign socialist experiment and nowadays as a historic relic of the Soviet era that still has resonance among some liberal and left-wing intellectuals. The fact that they are linked with business, trade and globalization makes no difference to this. The same can be said, however, of places such as New York and how it connects with the imaginary of 'America' as a society, created by a complexity of sub-systems of reputation that include films, oral family traditions, advertising campaigns and literature. Indeed, the emergence of international Expos, for example, and the provision of entrepreneurial and investment opportunities at a particular time and place that is reconstructed (and subsequently re-marketed) as a destination event play a crucial role in terms of propagating the idea of an event-place as a secure place to do business, while selling the notion of open market and globalization. Those who visit these expos perform as businesspeople looking for connections and to take advantage of commercial networks established in those event-places. However, those who visit the Expos also do this as tourists, whose experience will be defined by their expectations, which is why we need to study the interrelation between tourism and PR in more critical terms (Lee *et al.* 2008).

In the United Kingdom, royal event-places such as weddings, jubilees, coronations are all public events that are the focus of inward tourism to the UK and 'mega-media events' (Roche 2000). Royal funerals are the object of thanatourism, probably the most famous example being Princess Diana (Marriott 2007). The fact that the costs of such events are paid from the public purse is often justified on the basis of tourism and national promotion. However, these are seen as centrally organized by the state and fundamental to establish discourses of social cohesion; tourism in these cases is understood only as a by-product but not as a main objective. Nonetheless, let us reiterate that these events are only catalysts; none of these media-events operate in a vacuum nor are able to establish dominant discourses in their own. To do that, they need orchestrated complexity; one that can mobilize, activate or relate to a variety of elements encompassed within the tourism-reputation systems by evoking time and connexion in a way in which the different parts of the system feel willing and able to be involved as a community of stakeholders (such as the community celebrations of the Queen's Jubilee).

Globalization: risk, crisis and CSR

Tourism necessarily impacts upon natural, socio-cultural, economic and political environments and some of its side-effects are controversial and contested. For example, sports tourism has become a focus for inquiry into its relationship with a variety of issues such as sex tourism and disinvestment in local communities (one of the main criticisms of the Commonwealth Games in Manchester 2002 was that several local sport amenities were closed down in order to fund and sustain the main facilities of these games), highlighting it as both a reputational risk and a policy issue for future host cities (Matheson and Finkel 2012).

Indeed, tourism-reputation systems are vulnerable to risk partly because of their intangibility and complexity; therefore they are highly dependent on public relations and media discourses. As well as studying tourism, public relations assesses from a communicative action point of view the diversity of threats to safety and security such as crime, illness or kidnapping which is endemic in some locations such as Brazil and South Africa or terrorism threats in London or New York. It also needs to examine its impact in terms of local politics and culture. For example, tourism impacts on the natural environment, particularly in sensitive areas, and may threaten the very object of tourism or its authenticity. Adventure tourism results in human waste in remote locations, damaged coral reefs from recreational diving, rock faces damaged with permanent metal pegs, noise pollution (jetboating and speedboats). As much as we want to think of these activities as low impact because they are practised by few or because they are imagined to be 'clean and neat', the truth is that taking into account displacement, waste left behind and usage in general of the environment, these events can be as bad as the overuse of beaches in the south of Portugal. The effects at the end upon the tourism-reputation system can be devastating once a particular catalytic event is set in motion.

Corporate social responsibility (CSR) has become the response by default from the tourist operators and key stakeholders involved in attracting tourism flows. It is, however, a complex concept that can be viewed from a variety of perspectives but that in practice is more often than not misunderstood and badly implemented. It is a culturally specific topic that has links with a variety of practices around the globe, thus it is important to be sensitive to local conditions and traditions. In relation to tourism, CSR is a global practice that given its nature and history raises constantly questions of corporate colonialism and patronage; which means that for PR scholars and practitioners it is crucially important to maintain a critical awareness concerning strategic intentions and its viability as a unique response to the challenges posed by tourism-reputation systems.

CSR may be defined as the corporate/company practice which, so it is claimed, recognizes a societal obligation above and beyond existing legal obligations and economic contributions and consequently develops programmes to respond to societal needs. CSR may also be defined as a concept of social obligation, which recognizes corporate/company impacts (this connects the concept to issues/crisis management) but also celebrates the power of corporations/companies to facilitate and catalyze positive change and outcomes in otherwise under-resourced communities. CSR may respond to ongoing social issues or focus on programmes that address the side-effects of corporate/company production e.g. environmental side effects. In other words CSR programmes may respond to a general societal problem or a specific response to address a corporate/company impact.

Since CSR programmes tend to be directed towards identified needs in specific communities, it is logical to assume that the implementation and strict monitoring of these programmes would be an ideal tool for public relations to deal with tourism-reputation systems. They could be used to explore response scenarios and model complexity of a potential crisis. However, the problem for PR practitioners is that overall CSR activities have a wider political impact, beyond corporate/company stakeholders. They are primarily and strategically concerned with anticipating and impeding possible regulation/legislation while guaranteeing growth and profit. This presents enormous ethical limitations for those trying to deal with the complexity of the tourism-reputation systems from a public relations perspective.

If well managed, CSR programmes represent a diversity of actions, encompassing youth programmes, community programmes, financial information/training, skills transfer, technology transfer and arts sponsorship. Trying to centralize a response is a non-starter, in our view, to deal with the complexity of challenges posed by the tourism-reputation systems. CSR may be posited as a response to ongoing social and political issues, but it is not a motivation, and the intentionality behind such programmes is as important as what they do (L'Etang *et al.* 2011). According to Kantian deontology, should motivation for an action be anything other than to meet a duty or obligation, then the action cannot be judged as moral. This means that we have to ask questions of programmes which are designed primarily to address issues with a view to an organization's reputation. Likewise, publicizing CSR tourism programmes may be criticized because it suggests that the motivation behind such programmes is not to meet a moral obligation but to reap publicity (either through the media or personal networks) (L'Etang 1994, 1995, 1996, 2006). Others, however, take the view that communicating CSR is important in terms of accountability:

> CSR can be better understood as a means of reinforcing both reputation and legitimacy, as it provides an opportunity to communicate to stakeholders the congruence of the organization with societal concerns.
>
> *(Farache and Perks 2009: 237)*

In practice, however, there is little indication that in the tourism sector these programmes can be used as a measure of ethics or to contend the excess of the activity itself. In a study prepared for the CSR Practice Foreign Investment Advisory Service Investment Climate Department in Romania the authors recommend that 'to ensure that a more sustainable form of tourism is pursued, there is a need for stricter legislation coupled with joined-up government' (Dodds and Joppe 2005: 35). To hope therefore that CSR in itself can guarantee transparency, accountability and good behaviour is rather naïve or irresponsible.

Government, international relations and public diplomacy

As we claimed before, the state is central when dealing with tourism reputation systems. Although tourism is a global industry, it is still largely shaped, funded and constrained by nation-states and public money. Tourism is often seen as a major plank in economic policy and an element in the international positioning of a state. The nation-state and its cultural and historical heritage shape its tourism offerings, and the nation-state is a central sponsor and promoter in terms of marketing the destination and portraying the cultural identity; this by providing the regulatory framework for investment and resources in the face of subsidies, which are still key and largely present in the sector.

For the state, tourism is about more than attracting visitors and foreign capital, it is also about image-management, public and cultural diplomacy and development that together build the international status of a nation; thus tourism is a plank in political public relations and propaganda. Again the Beijing and London Olympics served to illustrate the intention of one country to portray itself as an emerging power and another as a still-wannabe world contender. Because of this, a tourism-reputation system makes use of public diplomacy aimed at foreign publics and aims to advance the nation's interests by achieving understanding of, 'its ideas and ideals, its institutions and culture, as well as its national goals and policies' (Melissen 2007: 11–12).

There has been renewed interest in public diplomacy since 9/11, reflected in the literature on public diplomacy, particularly in its communicative and relational aspects (Cowan 2008; Jonsson and Hall 2003; Kelley 2009; Wye 2008; Ronfledt and Acquila 2009; Snow and Taylor 2009; Zaharna 2009; L'Etang 2009), for example:

> Public diplomacy is part of a newly emerging paradigm of collaborative diplomacy, which requires an approach that is fundamentally dialogue-based ... nation-building and the struggle against international terrorism are two prime examples where such an approach has the potential to contribute to international stability ... new public diplomacy is increasingly about ideas and values, and involving non-governmental agents is seen as one of the most effective ways of promoting and developing it.
>
> *(Melissen 2007: xxi)*

We believe that public relations approaches to tourism need to incorporate cultural diplomacy perspectives within their ambit. Cultural access to the language, literature, music, art, history, film and media, science and technology, medical sciences, are all ways of engaging with the nation's values as a crucial aspect of the orchestrated complexity that takes place within tourism-reputation systems. Because of this, these same components are central to marketing the tourism potential of an event-place. There are some difficult communication challenges, however, since:

> Cultures exist in continuous flux, continuously interpreted and reinterpreted through human interactions, and embedded within the context of the lives of the members of the

> cultures. Culture is both a carrier of traditions and a site of transformation. It is within this dialectical tension between tradition and transformation that identities and relationships become meaningful, suggesting the necessity of conceptualizing public relations within an organic framework of evolving relationships rather than within a simplistic modernist frame that seeks to develop the best strategy for a national culture based on predefined markers.
>
> *(Pal and Dutta 2008: 167–68)*

The key example of this are the difficulties and struggles which places such as the United Arab Emirates (UEA) face to attract, deal with and retain tourism flows into their countries. The responses of the UEA have been as complex as the challenge: by creating a diversity of options for expectation-experiences, such 'reproductive tourism' is designed to attract parents looking for less expensive and high quality fertility treatment (Inhorn and Shrivastav 2010: 685).

Conclusions

Tourism is largely sponsored by governments and commercial enterprise that use public relations concepts and approaches to facilitate the expansion of markets. However, as we see here it is a far from centralized activity. Because of this, those studying public relations need to understand tourism as a series of reputation systems that are based on a complex set of elements, institutions and actors that are not only directly and indirectly interlinked but that also act, intentionally or not, in an orchestrated manner. It is our view that by bringing about this perspective, public relations scholars can be better placed to interpret and analyze the field and especially the relationship between public relations and tourism. We do not think, however, that this approach is sufficient to solve all the questions posed here. What we can assuredly state is that insufficient research in this field has been done. At a time where the research councils in the UK and in Europe in general are looking for ideas for growth and recovery – with this being the main theme of the new research funding scheme Horizon 2020 of the European Research Council – public relations scholars are faced with a unique opportunity to develop groundbreaking knowledge with high impact for our communities by exploring the complex relationship between tourism and public relations.

References

Banks, S. (1995) *Multicultural Public Relations: A Social-interpretive Approach*. Thousand Oaks, CA: Sage.

Bardhan, N. (2003) 'Rupturing public relations metanarratives: the example of India', *Journal of Public Relations Research*, 15: 225–48.

Boltanski, L. (1999) *Distant Suffering. Politics, Morality and the Media*. Cambridge: Cambridge University Press.

Couldry, Nick, Hepp, Andreas and Krotz, Friedrich (eds) (2009) *Media Events in a Global Age*. London: Routledge.

Crawford, Charles and Kerbs, Dennis (eds) (2008) *Foundation of Evolutionary Psychology*. New York: Lawrence Erlbaum Associates.

Crouch, D., Jackson, R. and Thompson, F. (2005) *The Media and the Tourist Imagination: Converging Cultures*. London: Routledge.

Curtin, P. and Gaither, K. (2005) 'Privileging identity, difference, and power: the circuit of culture as a basis for public relations theory', *Journal of Public Relations Research*, 17(2): 91–115.

— (2007) *International Public Relations: Negotiating Culture, Identity and Power*. London: Sage.

Dayan, Daniel (1994) *Media Events: Live Broadcasting of History*. Cambridge, MA: Harvard University Press.

Dodds, Rachel and Joppe, Marion (2005) *CSR in the Tourism Industry? The Status of and Potential for Certification, Codes of Conduct and Guidelines*. Study prepared for the CSR Practice Foreign Investment Advisory Service Investment Climate Department. http://www.turismdurabil.ro/literatura/csr/

additional_documents/I-CSR+in+the+Tourism+Industry%20-%20study.pdf (accessed on 12 March 2012).

Edwards, L. (2012) 'Defining the "object" of public relations research: a new starting point', *Public Relations Inquiry*, 1(1): 7–30.

Edwards, L. and Hodges, C.E.M. (2011) 'Introduction: implications of a (radical) socio-cultural "turn" in public relations scholarship'. In Edwards, L. and Hodges, C.E.M. (eds) *Public Relations, Society and Culture: Theoretical and Empirical Explorations*. Abingdon: Routledge, pp. 1–14.

Fall, Lisa T. (July 2004). 'The increasing role of public relations as a crisis management function: an empirical examination of communication restrategising efforts among destination organisation managers in the wake of 11th September', *Journal of Vacation Marketing*, 10(3): 238–52.

Faulkner, B. and Russell, R. (1997) 'Chaos and complexity in tourism: in search of a new perspective', *Pacific Tourism Review*, 1(2): 93–102.

Goeldner, Charles R. and Ritchie, J.R. Brent (2009) *Tourism: Principles, Practices, Philosophies*. New York: Wiley.

Hazleton, Vincent (1992) 'Toward a systems theory of public relations'. In Avenarius, Horst and Armbrecht, Wolfgang (eds) *Ist Public Relations eine Wissenschaft?* Preis für Großbritannien, Berlin: Springer-Verlag, pp. 33–45.

Hazleton, V. Jr. and Botan, C. (1989) 'The role of theory in public relations'. In Botan, C. and Hazleton, Jr., V. (eds) *Public Relations Theory*. Hillsdale, NJ: Lawrence Erlbaum Associates, pp. 3–15.

Higham, James (2007). 'Ecotourism: competing and conflicting schools of thought'. In Higham, James (ed.) *Critical Issues in Ecotourism: Understanding a Complex Tourism Phenomenon*. London: Elsevier.

Inhorn, Marcia C. and Shrivastav, Pankaj (2010). 'Globalization and reproductive tourism in the United Arab Emirates', *Asia Pacific Journal of Public Health*, 22(3): 68S–74S.

Johansson, C. and Heide, M. (2008) 'Speaking of change: three communication approaches in studies or organizational change', *Corporate Communications: An International Journal*, 13(3): 288–306.

Kang, Doo Syen and Mastin, Teresa (2008) 'How cultural difference affects international tourism public relations websites: a comparative analysis using Hofstede's cultural dimensions', *Public Relations Review*, 34(1): 54–6.

Lauzen, Martha M. and Dozier, David M. (1994) 'Issues management mediation of linkages between environmental complexity and management of the public relations function', *Journal of Public Relations Research*, 6(3): 163–84.

Lee, Choong-Ki, Songb, Hak-Jun and Mjeldec, James W. (2008) *Tourism Management*, 29(6): 1084–98.

L'Etang, J. (2009) 'Public relations and diplomacy in a globalised world', *American Behavioral Scientist*, 53(4): 607–26.

— (2011), 'Public relations and marketing: ethical issues and professional practice in society'. In Cheney, G., May, S. and Munchi, D. (eds) *The Handbook of Communication Ethics*. ICA Handbook series. New York: Routledge, pp. 221–41.

L'Etang, J., Falkheimer, J. and Lugo, J. (2007) 'Public relations and tourism: critical reflections and a research agenda', *Public Relations Review*, 33(1): 68–76.

L'Etang, J., Lugo-Ocando, J. and Ahmed, Z. (2011) 'Ethics, CSR, power and strategic communication'. In Ihlen, O., Bartlett, J. and May, S. (eds) *Handbook of Communication and Corporate Social Responsibility*. Chichester: Wiley-Blackwell.

Long, P. and Robinson, M. (2009) 'Tourism, popular culture and the media'. In Jamal, T. and Robinson, M. (eds) *The Sage Handbook of Tourism Studies*. London: Sage.

Matheson, C. and Finkel, R. (2012) 'Sex trafficking and the Vancouver Oympic Games: perceptions and preventative measures', *Tourism Management*, 1–16.

Munshi, D. and Kurian, P. (2005) 'Imperializing spin cycles: a postcolonial look at public relations, greenwashing and the separation of publics', *Public Relations Review*, 31(4): 513–20.

Murphy, Priscilla (Winter 2000). 'Symmetry, contingency, complexity: accommodating uncertainty in public relations theory', *Public Relations Review*, 26(4): 447–62.

Nordland, Rod (12 January 2013) 'Despite Taliban threat, Afghanistan manages to entice some tourists', *The New York Times Online*. http://www.nytimes.com/2013/01/13/world/asia/taliban-targets-tourists-but-some-still-visit-afghanistan.html?_r=0 (accessed on 28 February 2013).

Pal, M. and Dutta, M. (2008) 'Public relations in a global context: the relevance of critical modernism as a theoretical lens', *Journal of Public Relations Research*, 20: 159–79.

Pike, Steven (2005) 'Tourism destination branding complexity', *Journal of Product & Brand Management*, 14(4): 258–59.

Rojek, C. (2013) *Event Power: How Global Events Manage and Manipulate.* Los Angeles: Sage.
Shenker, Jack (19 January 2012) 'Egyptian frustration as tourists stay away', *The Guardian Online.* http://www.guardian.co.uk/world/2012/jan/19/egypt-tourism-visitor-numbers-collapse (accessed on 1 March 2013).
Szondi, G. (2009) 'Central and Eastern European public diplomacy: a transitional perspective on national reputation management'. In Snow, N. and Taylor, P. (eds) *Public Diplomacy.* London: Routledge, pp. 292–313.
Taylor, P. (1997) *Global Communications, International Affairs and the Media since 1945.* London: Routledge.

7

Discourse and power in tourism communications

Robert Caruana

Introduction

Understanding tourism as a marketing process is a matter of perspective (Tribe 2009). A common, if not *the* common view, tends to think of marketing communications as *information* about attributes of the 'tour product' such as price, quality, luxury, location etc., which are integrated into tourism choices. In this psychological view of tourism (Mannell and Iso-Ahola 1987), the nature of marketing communications is information. The process is a cognitive one, based on stimulus and response. And the role of marketers herein is to channel the information to the correct tourist segment as effectively and efficiently as possible. The key purpose of marketing communications is to connect to salient tourist motivations and enhance their *propensity to choose* between products, brands or destinations across the tourism market (Smith 1994).

Though evidently practical for marketers, this view of communications obscures certain assumptions about the nature of tourism as well as the role of tourists and marketers. How, for example, do tourists come to know what a certain category of tourism means in the first instance? How are they able to establish one meaningful choice context from another? How do they come to an understanding of the very different social practices that one type of tourism (e.g. luxury cruise) involves when compared to others (e.g. backpacker)? Is the only outcome of communications a marketing one – consumer choice – or are there wider social implications? Attempting to answer some of these questions requires an alternative way of conceiving the nature and role of marketing communications. Adopting a *discursive* perspective (Dann 1996; Matthews 2009) on tourism, this chapter illuminates the socially constitutive nature of communications in tourism markets, the role of communications in shaping knowledge for tourists and the role of marketers in mediating this process. The chapter will also give special consideration to how a discursive perspective illuminates relations of power between tourists, markets and other constituents represented in the 'tourism product' (Morgan and Pritchard 1998).

Tourism communications as a discourse

Central to the ideas discussed in this chapter is that discourse, as the purposive use of language in constituting social reality (Berger and Luckmann 1966; Fairclough 1995), plays a key role in organizing the ways in which tourism can be interpreted as a social practice. At its core, this perspective acknowledges a conceptual link between language, knowledge and social practices – of which tourism is one discursive domain. In a Foucauldian vein, how we know/interpret/conceptualize social subjects (tourists) and social practices (tourism) is organized in discourse. Discourse is able to do this because it is more than just a technical device – i.e. it is not just a collection of words that carry practical instructions. Discourse carries, conceals and (re)constitutes socio-cultural and ideological conventions which frame not only how a certain social practice is organized but who is involved, what roles they can take up as well as what actions can be done by and to them. Taking marketing communications as constitutive of social knowledge about tourism raises a number of pertinent questions; *how* does tourism discourse 'operate' in marketing communications? Through what social mechanisms does this occur? What role do marketers assume in this process? What are the (un)intended outcomes of this? This chapter will attempt to engage with these questions, pointing to potential research agendas for tourism scholars. A sensible starting point is to consider marketing communications as a tourism discourse.

Marketing communications as tourism discourse

Tourism is not an a priori category. The form that tourism takes, how tourists conceptualize different types of holiday and how they interpret themselves as subjects of them, is fundamentally entangled in *tourism discourse* (Matthews 2009; Norton 1996). Tourism discourse doesn't 'reflect' this process. It *is* this process. It is actively constitutive of the possible types of tourism available, the spaces where it can (and can't) occur, the categories of people who can (and can't) take part and the kinds of relations through which tourism is practised. In this sense, marketing communications doesn't merely point to the menu of available holiday choices. It is a social practice that plays an active, formative role in *defining* and mediating choices for tourists in the first place. As Caruana and Crane (2008) illustrate, marketing communications actively construct, organize and manage 'choice arenas' for the tourist, providing socially meaningful forms of knowledge that helps tourists adopt identity-positions in the tourism market. So what exactly is discourse then? What discursive properties enable interpretations of tourism choice? And where does discourse occur?

It is probably best to think of discourse as the process of 'meaning-making' – or knowledge-construction – that occurs in tourism text(s). This conceptualizes marketing communications – not as flows of information but as a socially constituting 'cultural text'. This textual process of meaning-making happens through the interaction of linguistic, discursive and socio-ideological practices (Fairclough 1995), in which tourists and marketers are both involved. At the *linguistic* level, we observe the role of formal textual features such as tourism metaphors, narratives, juxtapositions and myths (Johns and Clarke 2001) that make up the 'texture' of marketing communications. It is the operation of these textual features of tourism discourse that, in turn, organize *discursive* processes that create subjects (identities), practices and relations that might be adopted by tourists. Much of this dimension of discourse involves creating identity positions, practices and relationships that tourists can (dis)identify with (e.g. defining the category 'independent traveller' as someone who acts autonomously, engaging in tourist relations that appear authentic, whilst avoiding ostensibly 'commercial' ones). Finally, that tourism discourse contains *socio-ideological* features acknowledges that discourse doesn't occur in isolation from wider social conventions.

Discourse doesn't just appear either in an advert or in the tourist's own mind. Crucially, the process of producing and interpreting tourism discourse is facilitated by its '*interdiscursive*' nature (Fairclough 1995). Tourism discourse is woven into local tourism texts (e.g. travel guidebooks, adverts etc.) from wider social discourses. These wider *macro*-social discourses (e.g. hedonism, nature, otherness, authenticity, autonomy, gender or independence) are drawn upon by marketers (and tourists alike) in the process of establishing tourist meaning/s in local texts. In this vein, Johns and Clarke's (2001) study of boating holidays revealed how tourist narratives (linguistic), created 'liberated' identities (discursive), by drawing upon wider discourses (socio-ideological) that were re-worked into personal accounts of their holiday experiences:

> The myths used by respondents in this study derive from popular and commonsense sources, but were sometimes intensely personal in their interpretation. They included forms from postmodern society, such as 'nature' 'adventure' and 'good fun for adults and kids', but also concepts such as 'otherness' and 'activity'.
>
> *(Johns and Clarke 2001: 356)*

That the study involved the analysis of *photographs* as part of the tourist's discourse, points to another core feature of this discursive view of marketing communications – the centrality of the *text*.

Marketing communications as a tourism text

Knowledge of tourism is produced, mediated and disseminated through texts. Texts, then, are the central subject of analysis (not the subjective minds of tourists, agents or marketers). Here, postcards, tourists' diaries, travel fiction, corporate as well as tourist-board adverts, brochures, photographs and websites are broadly conceived of as textual sites (Ateljevic and Doorne 2002; Bhattacharyya 1997; Caruana *et al.* 2008; Caruana and Crane 2011; Markwick 2001; Salazar 2006; Urry 1990). Taken in their broadest sense, even tourists' verbal accounts can be considered as texts in the sense that they utilize textual devices such as narratives, metaphors and myths (Johns and Clarke 2001) in rendering the holiday experience meaningful. Crucially, these texts are sites of cultural production and meaning-making, in which tourism is defined and created as a certain kind of social practice. In the context of this chapter then *marketing communications are cultural texts* that constitute the social meanings of tourism. The advertising campaigns of National Tourist Boards are littered with such cultural texts, attempting to infuse a given country with cultural meanings appealing to the international tourist imaginary (exotic, adventure, cultural, primitive, erotic, untouched etc.) (Ateljevic and Doorne 2002; Borgerson and Schroeder 2002). Websites too are considered as texts in which cultural meanings create interpretations for specific market segments (Caruana and Crane 2008) whilst signifying differences between other segments. Texts not only produce cultural meanings but they are responsible for disseminating them throughout tourism markets and reinforcing, as well as transforming them, over time.

The dominant interpretation of *tourism as freedom* is the cumulative outcome of a history of tourism texts that have normalised tourism as the social practice of 'being away', 'escape' and 'getting away from it all'. Of the most iconic tourism text – the postcard – Urry (1990) notes how they traditionally drew upon other popular discursive critiques of work, city life and economic labour. Postcards (re-)constructed work and city life as the negatively motivating 'social toils' to which beach holidays were presented as the fun, healthy and above all liberating tonic. These textually situated cultural meanings are rarely fixed or uniform, highlighting the dynamic nature of discourse in texts. The meaning of freedom, for instance, has been found to vary across tourism markets, such that freedom is constructed for 'hedonist tourists' as avoiding work, for 'independent travellers' ('backpackers') as evading inauthentic, commercial tourists and for 'ethical tourists' as avoiding harmful tourism choices (Caruana and Crane 2011). In this sense tourism texts can re-work discourses (e.g. on freedom) into specific local contexts reflective of particular tourist groups that marketers want to communicate with. When we begin to think about tourism in this way, we acknowledge the 'situatedness' of tourism texts and the role of marketing communications in mediating potential interpretations of tourism practice through discourse.

'Cultural brokers' and the 'situated text'

Earlier in this chapter it was noted that conceptualizing marketing communications as a discourse had various implications, including, as discussed now, how we think about the role of marketers. A fundamental facet of discourse is that it produces intended or ideal interpretations for particular audiences (Fairclough 1995). More than just a text about tourism meanings, tourism texts are thus both 'purposive' and 'situated' – they are cultural repositories of meaning that are organized with a specific audience and ideal interpretation in mind. One tourist may produce a text (e.g. postcard or narrative) for interpretation by another tourist (Johns and Clarke 2001). A local guide may reproduce a text (e.g. about authenticity or tradition) for a foreign tourist to interpret (Salazar 2006). A tourist board or travel agent may produce a text for the international tourist (Ateljevic and Doorne 2002). That we consider marketing communications to be a kind of 'situated text' – produced to be read in a certain way by a particular audience – radically transforms our understanding of tourism marketers and the mediating role of their communications with tourists. More than just informing an audience about the attributes of a given tour product, marketers become influential cultural mediators over tourism knowledge and practice for that audience, rendering the 'choice arena' for a given tour product culturally relevant, plausible and desirable (Caruana and Crane 2008).

Thinking in line with Cheong and Miller (2000), it is thus possible to consider the role of tourism marketers as 'cultural brokers' (rather than product informers). This implies that marketers have some kind of authority in defining how, where, why and by whom tourism is practiced by tourists and others. Bhattacharyya (1997) evidenced how writers of the popular tourism publication *Lonely Planet* played a key role in mediating the 'backpacker' tourist's interpretation of India, providing guidance on what subjects and objects are of value to the tourist, how tourists should interact with local communities and (of some controversy) how to behave as an 'independent' category of tourist: 'In this regard, the analysis concludes that this guidebook serves a primary function as mediating tourists' experiences in India in ways that reinforce both certain images of India and certain relationships with indigenous inhabitants' (Bhattacharyya 1997: 371).

This implies that such forms of marketing communications are not just about where to go, what to see and do when on holiday, but, more fundamentally, *how* to go, how to see and do tourism, and indeed how to interact with other constituents of the tour product (guides, reps, local people, as well as other tourists). Travel writing, as a genre of tourism texts, becomes a powerful representational space for tourist knowledge of social practices and relationships (Santos and Rozier 2009). As an author of this tourist knowledge, marketing practitioners can (unwittingly) become powerful 'cultural brokers', authorizing legitimate social practices and relationships that tourists and others can have.

Crucially, this 'cultural authority' over tourist practices and relationships has *impacts* that extend beyond the creation of a particular travel ethos for the tourist to interpret. This brings us to the second major component of this chapter: considering the *relations of power* produced in tourism discourse. For as Bhattacharyya (1997: 388) goes on to show, in defining an 'independent' travel ethos for backpacker tourists, guidebooks represent local people in coercive practices and relations, often being 'portrayed as a passive, non-participating, non-autonomous object of observation . . . where their "unique human qualities and agency are not represented"'. Consequently, whilst a discursive approach to marketing communications reveals how cultural knowledge is produced for tourism markets, it also illuminates how they are implicated in relations of power between various constituents of the tour product. This suggests that marketing communications can be 'read' in ways that privilege certain tourism constituents (e.g. tourist) whilst marginalising, subverting or excluding others (e.g. workers or local communities), thus opening up tourism discourse to critical research agendas with a focus on *power*.

Tourism communications as a discourse of power

Notwithstanding the various conceptions in socio-political theory, it is necessary here to provide a summary outline of the notion of *power* and what this means for understanding marketing communications in tourism. In more 'structuralist' views, power has been thought of as a dialectic system of domination (e.g. Karl Marx), in which the choices and actions of one group are invariably limited by another dominant group within a hegemonic system. Here the system (e.g. capital) subjects the individual to alienating forms of incarceration, fixing them into positions of disempowerment that they cannot readily shake off (e.g. proletariat). In this view, power is seen as an omnipresent structural feature of social systems such as tourism markets, rendering marketing communications a social mechanism that reflects an entrenched touristic system of control and domination. Other 'post-structuralist' views do not take power as a given, *structural* axis of 'the system' but as a *process* or 'negotiated order' of (dis)empowerment. In particular, the process of creating social identities, practices and relations for tourist interpretations is seen to allocate privileges, resources and freedoms to some agents that are denied to others (Thurot and Thurot 1983). Crucially, in this view, marketing communications is seen as a discursive process that transforms relations of power in the process of constructing tourism knowledge. In the remainder of this chapter, we will consider the role of marketing communications in the allocation of social identities, relations and practices through tourism discourse that has both enabling and 'limiting effects' for tourism constituents.

Norton (1996) shows how marketing communications represent an ideal version of Africa for the tourist – as exotic and primitive – but in quite restricted ways that distort and confine how tourists might otherwise interpret their relationships with cultural and natural entities:

> Although the accounts of East Africa developed by tourists are rich in aesthetic detail compared with the archetypes promoted in tourism marketing, they are partial accounts which are unable to draw on discourses which are hidden from them, such as the history of civilisation and slavery in East Africa, economic and political differences between ethnic groups, and historical and contemporary struggles against the expropriation of park land.
>
> *(Norton 1996: 369)*

Thus, by augmenting knowledge of tourism, the discourse of marketing communications precipitates 'masking effects'. By creating an ideal representation of a holiday and the identities and relations operating in it, other (perhaps more candid if less appealing) versions are hidden, restricted or altogether expunged from it. However, whilst marketing communications precipitates relations of power, it is not necessary to conclude that these are fixed, absolute or immovable. Power is not (as in the Marxian view) unidirectional or totalizing. Under a broad discursive view, it is organized in ways that negotiate, but not dictate, relative power for agents to exercise certain choices. Tourists, locals and other constituents may contest, reject, negotiate and even transform the discourse of marketing communications (rather than enact it mechanistically!). In this sense it is better to speak of marketing communications as a process of 'discursive struggle' (Livesey 2001) between various tourism agents represented in the discourse. In the remainder of this chapter we highlight two axial relationships that might prove fruitful for tourism researchers with critical research agendas: relations of power between *tourists–markets* and between *tourists–others*.

Power in tourist–market relations

Of the research that has been undertaken in this area, there has tended to be a focus upon how tourism constrains *others*, principally local people, guides and the environment. This section considers the less frequently debated power relations to which the tourist is subjected. For, whilst Cheong and Miller (2000: 371) suggest power relations are 'omnipresent in a tripartite system of tourists, locals, and brokers', they note that the tourist is 'frequently vulnerable'. To what, though, are they vulnerable and how does a discursive perspective on marketing communications help illuminate this 'vulnerability'? In the context of the ideas forwarded in this chapter, two key, connected points can be illustrated here. Firstly, tourists themselves can be subjected to power relations, which though varied in source, often stem from the market and potentiate certain limiting effects on them. Secondly, in the process of constituting tourism knowledge, the discourse of marketing communications both contributes to and obscures these constraints.

As a social practice tourism is uniquely promoted as a form of freedom. Yet you only have to sit in a crowded airport, watch an episode of *Holidays from Hell* or read a travel magazine deriding the package tourist, locked away in their mainstream hotel, enclave or tour bus, to recognise that tourism is also a potentially constraining activity. Scholarly research is beginning to reveal a paradox between the liberatory, transcendental properties presented within the tourism view (gaze) and the potentially incarcerating and alienating realities hidden within (Bruner 1991; Caruana *et al.* 2008). An interesting case in point is the 'Independent Traveller'. As an icon of travel heroism, autonomy and adventure, this segment of the tourism market is often promoted as being one of the most liberating, least institutionalized, forms of tourism. A whole range of travel texts from postcards to diaries to billboards and certainly guidebooks (e.g. *Rough Guide, Lonely Planet, Fodors, Footprints*) will attest to this. However, whilst texts promoting this type of tourism often frame Independence in terms of freedom from institutional environments such as home, work and/or classically, from commercial tourists, they may conceal new forms of coercion for the tourist, 'Though the backpackers repeatedly express a desire to distance themselves from fellow Israelis and from state-related organizations, they routinely follow similar itineraries during the trip, find themselves in, or seek, the company of other Israelis, and spend a good deal of their time in Israeli "enclaves"' (Noy 2004: 81).

Whilst 'independent travel' – like other forms – is promoted as a practice about shaking off institutional constraints, this suggests the mere substitution of one set of institutional constraints for another. It is not uncommon, according to Huxley (2005), to find backpackers hanging out in 'backpacker ghettos' reproducing backpacker culture, visiting the same places, doing the same things and sharing the same commoditized cultural stories about their 'off-the-beaten track', 'on-a-shoestring' experiences. In sum, actual tourism realities deviate from tourism representations of tourism discourse promoted through marketing communications. How though are these contradictions and constraints not problematic for the tourist?

Bruner (1991) points to a discrepancy between representations of tourism in discourse and the reality of the tourist experience:

> Tourist discourse promises the tourist a total transformation of self, but the native is described as untouched by civilization and as frozen in time. The hypothesis here is that

> despite these claims, the very opposite occurs in experience, that the tourist self is changed very little by the tour, while the consequences of tourism for the native self are profound.
> *(Bruner 1991: 238)*

Marketing communications can promote knowledge of tourism as radically self-transforming and liberating for the tourist, whilst simultaneously concealing its profound lack of it. This masking effect of tourism discourse is interpretively developed by Caruana *et al.* (2008) who perform a critical discourse analysis of the guidebook *The Rough Guide to Spain*. In their close reading of the text they identify three persistent themes of independent travel that the book communicates uniformly to the reader as 'value for money', 'inaccessibility' and 'inauthenticity'. The text promotes a powerful cultural myth of the Independent Travel identity as someone who assertively avoids inauthentic people and places, defies inaccessible spaces and hunts for bargains. They go on to argue that this *myth of independence* obscures the role of the guidebook (and by proxy the market) in engendering *dependency* upon it – i.e. as a 'toolkit' for how to be independent. Thus tourism discourse present in marketing communications is capable of foregrounding a strongly autonomous perspective on tourism (for interpretation by tourists) whilst concealing the paradoxically mediating role of the market in facilitating this. This is not only relevant to the Independent Travel market.

Marketing communications both create and obscure power effects on tourists across different segments of the market, though according to Caruana and Crane (2011), these play out in different ways, take varied forms and are connected to specific contexts. For marketing communications promoting hedonistic tourism (they analyze a '*Club 18–30* youth holiday' brochure) the discourse foregrounds the tourist in a set of cultural practices that liberate them from coercive institutions of work and enable them to 'party' with other hedonists. Yet the view on hedonism promoted is very specific and is found to narrowly define what hedonism means (sex), who is involved in it (only other 'hedonic' tourists) and importantly how it can be achieved (drinking in nightclubs or 'playing' by the swimming pool). Here marketing communications idealizes a *version of* hedonism as a basis for tourism knowledge which actively encourages (and even requires for its success) that the tourists gather *only* in prescribed places and subscribe to predefined modes of practice with other tourists. The potential content, location and mode of other forms of hedonism are largely closed-off from the tourist's interpretation by the discourse. How do these issues carry across to the question of power relations between tourists and others?

Power in tourist–other relations

In light of the centrality of 'otherness' to tourism (Cave 2005), it is no surprise that marketing communications influence relations of power between tourists and other constituents involved in the tour product. Urry (1990) argues that one feature of modern tourism markets, fuelled by the growing desire for authentication, is for the tourist gaze to increasingly fall onto the backstage lives of other people (workers, locals, families etc.). Tourists don't just want to visit a destination; they want to immerse themselves in it as cultural participants in the lives and ways of others. The emergence of community, volunteer and cultural holidays, factory, plantation, 'backwater' tours and 'homestays' are reflections of this more intimate encounter with others. As modern tourism markets continue moving in this way (from viewing to participating), the potentiality for relations of power is likely to intensify. This final section outlines how marketing communications play an important representational as well as concealing role in shaping power relations in tourism discourse.

As a constituter of social knowledge about subjects and relations, discourse 'hails to us' as certain kinds of subjects (Parker 1998) to adopt certain practices and relationships with others.

For as Mellinger (1994: 756) points out, marketing communications enables subjects to be positioned in tourism discourse in different ways, creating negative representations of some subjects and empowered ones by others: 'Analysis of these photographic images reveals that specific iconographic strategies were employed by postcard photographers to culturally inscribe black bodies with "Otherness." ... These images positioned black subjects in a racist regime of representation that constructed subjectivities for those depicted and identities for their viewers' (Mellinger 1994: 756).

A similar observation is offered by Schroeder and Borgerson (2002: 578), who identify the role of marketing communications in constructing 'the other' within 'typified representations, especially those that are racist or sexist'. In later work they trace the historical construction of sexist categories in the marketing of Hawaii to North American tourists. Relations of power were organized within a 'paradisal' discourse used consistently in marketing communications about Hawaii. Images invariably depicted young, beautiful, semi-naked indigenous females lying pensively (and always unaccompanied) on a beach. In many, but not all cases, the empowered subject is implied as the (viewing) young white American male, looking for romantic relationships with their submissive indigenous female subjects. Other images were more explicit, placing the intended viewer in the 'paradisal' images, perhaps holding a surf board or a local woman's hand. Whilst marketing communications have the capacity to represent subjects and relations in a particular way within a (e.g. 'paradisal') discourse, they can also hide subjects and relations (especially those incongruous with the ideal image). Schroeder and Borgerson (2005) underline the importance of 'absent subjects' in this 'paradisal' discourse, such as the lack of children, elderly, families, local communities and crucially, Hawaiian males. They conclude that these absent subjects reinforced the tourist's interpretation of the sexual availability of indigenous women and the economic and cultural disempowerment of (invisible) Hawaiian men as well as others (families etc.).

Much research into power in tourism–other relations tends to take wealth disparity and cultural distance as a proxy for power asymmetry, such that studies often favour investigations of rich 'Western tourist's' and foreign 'third world' others. Power, though, is everywhere being shaped in a wide range of marketing communications, and often in the least obvious places. Returning to Caruana and Crane's (2011) study of tourism freedom, one of their case studies explores relations of power where 'the other' can equally be thought of as a tourist or even a working tour representative (i.e. not a classically 'vulnerable' indigenous population). Their case study of hedonistic tourism discourse (marketed in a brochure) observes the construction of a highly liberated self who, freed from the 'slave-like' incarceration of work, is able to engage in unencumbered sexual relationships with other 'like-minded' hedonists (other tourists). On one relational axis, the care-free, sexually-charged ethos promulgated in the brochure potentially disobliges tourists from moral responsibilities towards sexual partners, rendering other tourists vulnerable (e.g. to abuse, violence and/or sexual disease). The relations through which freedom is portrayed elevates one tourist's sexual licence (*freedom to* have sex) over another's liberty (*freedom from* sexual harm). On another relational axis, the ardent anti-work ethos that anchors the 'hedonic myth' co-opts tour reps into the sexualized relations being celebrated. The postures, expressions, clothing and activities of this (working) subject group are almost indistinguishable from the tourist subject, thus the interpretation 'we're all hedonists!'. Why, you might well ask, is this a problem? Despite being on low pay, short-term contracts and deployed in highly-charged emotional labour and tasked into humiliating 'performances' (e.g. 'striptease'), tour reps, argue Caruana and Crane (2011), are the subject of a double-incarceration, required to act as 'sexually available hedonists' whilst also carrying the implicit tag of 'enslaved worker' so derided by the hedonist ethos. How though do these tensions and contradictions in tourist–other relations not destabilise the tourist's interpretation?

By constructing a particular view of tourism with endorsed social practices, the idealized version, perhaps unwittingly and implicitly, comes to represent *the* version offered to the tourist's interpretive repertoire. One depicted reality hides another. A place, event or people that becomes marked out as a sign of tourism interest becomes the subject of a fixed, legitimate and eventually 'normal view'; even to the extent that tourists are more engaged with the 'paradisal reality' of Hawaii than with the actual place itself. This ideal view, as a basis for the appropriation of the tourist's cultural knowledge, potentially marginalizes other interpretations of a destination. As a result, marketing communications may construct a discourse of freedom and transcendence to represent a space where there is also coercion and constraint of others (Coles and Church 2007). More than this though, items, events and subjects that don't fit the construction privileged in marketing communications are extricated (sometimes very explicitly) from the tourist's gaze. In the texts employed by travel agent marketers, guidebooks, guides and even tourists themselves, certain subjects and relations are selectively edited out – being replaced by the idealized representation. Tourist boards, seeking to present their country's touristic assets in the best possible light to an international tourist audience, may well (mis)represent subject relations in this way:

> The relationships between the two cultures in New Zealand are represented as trouble free: 'like two distinct wines, the cultures co-mingle while retaining their individual distinctiveness' (NZTB 1996:8). The reality of Maori as largely urbanized people suffering high levels of intergenerational unemployment, poverty, and incarceration rates are carefully avoided by the contemporary tourism discourse.
>
> *(Ateljevic and Doorne 2002: 662)*

In this sense tourism discourses employed in marketing communications are only ever partial and incomplete representations (Norton 1996), whilst often claiming quite the opposite, i.e. to be an authority on how things *really* are (e.g. 'see the real Spain' or 'meet authentic local people and their traditions' etc.). Is misrepresenting subjects and relations the only issue here? Is the only outcome at issue here an *interpretive* one?

In the broad conception of discourse outlined here, there are important connections between the knowledge, identity and *practice* of tourism. In short, how a place comes to be commonly known, frames what kinds of subjects tourists can become in that space and accordingly, how they should act in the other's regard. Thus the knowledge of tourism that is represented in a given tourism text has the capacity to influence how tourists then do things to/with/for/against others on holiday. Various authors have made this connection between tourism discourse and knowledge/practice. Revisiting Bhattacharyya (1997) above, the Indian travel guidebook influenced the traveller's view of what is of value and significance, what can and should be done and how travellers should interact in regard to local populations, to the extent that it places the traveller above important moral conventions and rules that local people are strongly subject to. Thus marketing communications can place tourists above important socio-moral sanctions that would otherwise govern behaviour in those spaces – they can be *amoralizing*: 'Engendered by spatial discourses, the dominant tourism culture is essentialized and marked as a neutral activity, hardly ever questioned, yet assumes a distinct set of values and expectations' (Ateljevic and Doorne 2002: 663).

Discourse employed through marketing communications can be argued to disempower not only human others but ecological others too. As Johns and Clarke (2001) observe, tourists discursively construct emancipatory boating identities whilst readily overlooking the environmental destruction and water pollution caused by their 'free roaming' diesel boats. Once again, the tourist's interpretation of holiday implicates certain absences and marketing communications can play a key role in creating and managing these. The recent growth of the ethical travel market, for instance, has seen marketers employing pictures of tourism spaces that appear empty, wild, untrammelled, pristine etc. Despite marketing holidays to tourists, in these representations there are no tourists or locals depicted and certainly no groups – just 'untouched, pure' nature. This effectively idealizes the absence of the tourist (and thus tourist impacts), contributing to the popular 'tread lightly' view of this 'ethical' tourism practice (Shepherd 2003). Similarly, Caruana and Crane (2008) find that in the marketing of 'responsible tourism' the potential impacts (e.g. of long-haul flights) are easily hidden within a discourse that is promoted as self-evidently harmless and vehemently morally self-affirming. In sum, across a wide range of tourism products marketing communications enable tourists to understand their holiday but, because they can only ever 'stand in' for reality, they may well subvert fuller interpretations of tourist–other relations.

Conclusion

This chapter has adopted a discursive perspective in order to understand how marketing communications influence tourists' knowledge of their holiday. Rather than informing tourists of what attributes are involved in their tour product, this lens suggests marketing communications actually organize the meanings of tourism. Taking the tourism 'text' (brochure, postcard, advert, guidebook, diary etc.) as the culturally constructive sites where these meanings are produced and interpreted, elaborates on how tourism subjects – tourist, locals, guides, communities – are organized around sets of identities and relationships that culminate in ideal representations of tourism practice. On the one hand, these ideal interpretations provide a plausible and desirable view of the tourist's cultural milieu and the position(s) that they can adopt within it. In particular, a discursive lens helps demonstrate *how* these interpretations operate within these key texts, allowing researchers to see how marketing communications define 'how to be' and 'how to do tourism' for different tourist audiences.

On the other hand, this process engenders implicit relations of power between subjects included and excluded from the tourism discourse being promoted. These power relations implicate tourists' relations with the market, with other tourists and with other constituents involved more or less directly in the tour product. Specifically, in seeking to create a certain representation for the tourist (e.g. 'authentic' Silver 1993), marketing communications displace a fuller set of discourses that a destination may be subject to (e.g. poverty, war, exclusion, slavery), limiting the potential interpretive repertoire of the tourist. Whilst it is arguably the case that tourists themselves want idealized representations of escape, rather than more candid depictions of reality, it is still worth considering some reflexive points provoked by a discursive approach to marketing communications.

Implications for marketers

Marketing practitioners have traditionally been concerned with issues of honesty and accuracy in the representations of places and experiences. This has essentially framed tourists' concern with marketing communications as one of tourist trust in marketers' representation of the product offering. This has tended to limit representational concerns not only to tourist–market relations (despite other relational agents), but also to issues fairly limited in scope (i.e. consumer rights, deception, sovereignty). As has been identified, a potentially far wider range of constraints upon the tourist may well be engendered, and indeed subverted, in representations of tourism.

Questions that might be asked here are how do the tourism practices promoted by marketers expose tourists to risk, exploitation, violence and other forms of vulnerability. This might well be applicable, for example, in the promotion of hedonistic ('youth/pleasure') holidays where risk-taking, promiscuity and heavy drinking are key features of the hedonic ethos being promoted.

In addition to concerns in tourist–market relations, tourist relations with other human and ecological constituents represent new avenues of reflection and critique. Marketers may consider how alluring representations of 'pristine', 'unspoilt' and 'wilderness' destinations (e.g. Galapagos or Maldives) provoke high demands for such spaces which may, paradoxically, pressurize and destroy them. Equally, marketers may reflect upon the ways in which marketing communications misrepresent human subjects and relationships, for example, by subverting poor labour practices or promoting exploitation of local communities. Framed in this broader way, tourists may increasingly view marketing communications not only in terms of personal trust and deception (their consumer rights) but in terms of how marketers can be trusted to represent a destination's broader socio-political and environmental characteristics in ways that sustain and protect them.

This last point may encourage a heightened discourse in the industry concerning an ethics of representation. One obvious area of focus here would involve ethical issues surrounding representations of the other (Cave 2005), given the potential to render them vulnerable to forms of exploitation, risk and harm. Akin to arguments set out above, Borgerson and Schroeder (2002) have suggested ethical issues arise when 'representations of subordinate groups facilitate the erasure of identity and domination of that group' (2002: 584). They recommend critical reflection by marketers upon how their representations contribute to the creation and sustaining of domination (e.g. sexual, racial and colonial) of one group over another (e.g. male/female, black/white, civilized/native, Western/non-Western). Here, marketers might usefully consider not only how their representations dominate others but also how others lack the resources and/or access to media and advertising through which to control how they are represented. Such introspection is also important in representations of non-human 'others' such as the natural environment whose continued exploitation is partly facilitated through touristic representations. Here, marketers are urged to consider the potential risks to the ecosystems of their representations to tourists (e.g. of 'the wild', 'untamed nature', 'unspoilt' or 'virgin territory'). Whether tourism marketers will do this voluntarily and altruistically or for more instrumental reasons (i.e. because their customers support sustainability and good labour practices or merely want a clean, pristine destination and a 'service with a smile') remains to be seen.

Implications for tourists

It can, of course, be argued that the tourist doesn't have to accept the representations offered to them in marketing communications and indeed, some have argued that in practice tourists (and locals) can challenge or rework them (Norton 1996). However, as key (and sometimes sole) repositories of cultural meaning for tourist knowledge, marketing communications play a significant role in mediating how a tourist understands a place, a group of people and their relations to both. A critical, discursive perspective enables tourists and other tourist constituents (e.g. labour) to reflect upon the mediated nature of their taken-for-granted realities, offering a resource for responding to (Bramwell 2003), contesting and reconstructing prevailing identities, relations and practices circulated in tourism discourse.

A discursive perspective on marketing communications is of increasing importance in contemporary tourism, not least because of the continued global tensions around issues such as climate change, labour relations, poverty, pollution and the like but due to the accelerating 'textualization' of tourism practice. Facebook, twitter, Google Earth, travel agent websites, direct (Internet) marketing, online reviews, travel and mainstream media all represent the broadening of textual spaces where tourism can be communicated about by a range of actors. Knowledge of tourism is no longer so easily mediated by 'cultural brokers' but is opened up to a wider range of influences by various stakeholders, offering huge potential for the engagement in and transformation of relations of power. For marketing managers, policy makers and academics this represents new opportunities as well as threats. At the time of drafting this chapter, *The Guardian* ran an article entitled 'Maldives tourism campaign backfires as Twitter shows darker side of island life'. The initiative of the tourism authority to redefine the Maldives as a paradise island used twitter as a powerful marketing communications force to promote the island's credentials for love, romance and the exotic. Their campaign became hijacked by 'tweets about police brutality, coups d'état and political illegitimacy', bringing attention to the tourist audience, a range of power struggles, violence, political unrest and oppression commonly concealed within the 'paradisal' view of the island. Whilst these outcomes may be illuminating and instructive for tourists, locals and policy-makers, they offer something of a cautionary note to tourism marketers in terms of how they contribute to, as well as manage, the tourist's interpretation of holiday.

References

Ateljevic, I. and Doorne, S. (2002) 'Representing New Zealand: Tourism Imagery and Ideology', *Annals of Tourism Research*, 29: 648–67.

Berger, P.L. and Luckmann, T. (1966) *The Social Construction of Reality: A Treatise in the Sociology of Knowledge*. London: Penguin.

Bhattacharyya, D.P. (1997) 'Mediating India: An Analysis of a Guidebook', *Annals of Tourism Research*, 24: 371–89.

Borgerson, J. and Schroeder, J. (2002) 'Ethical Issues of Global Marketing: Avoiding Bad Faith in Visual Representation', *European Journal of Marketing*, 36(5/6): 570–94.

Bramwell, B. (2003) 'Maltese Responses to Tourism', *Annals of Tourism Research*, 30(3): 581–605.

Bruner, E.M. (1991) 'The Transformation of Self in Tourism', *Annals of Tourism Research*, 18(2): 238–50.

Caruana, R. and Crane, A. (2008) 'Constructing Consumer Responsibility: Exploring the Role of Corporate Communications', *Organization Studies*, 29: 1495–519.

— (2011) 'Getting Away from it All: Exploring Freedom in Tourism', *Annals of Tourism Research*, 38(4): 1495–151.

Caruana, R., Crane, A. and Fitchett, J. (2008) 'Paradoxes of Consumer Independence: A Critical Discourse Analysis of the Independent Traveller', *Marketing Theory*, 8: 254–72.

Caton, K. and Santos, C.A. (2009) 'Images of the Other: Selling Study Abroad in a Postcolonial World', *Journal of Travel Research*, 48(2): 191–204.

Cave, J. (2005) 'Conceptualising "Otherness" as a Management Framework for Tourism Enterprise', in C. Ryan and M. Aicken (eds) *Indigenous Tourism – The Commodification and Management of Culture*. Oxford: Pergamon.

Cheong, S.-M. and Miller, M.-L. (2000) 'Power and Tourism: A Foucauldian Observation', *Annals of Tourism Research*, 27: 371–90.

Coles, T. and Church, A. (2007) 'Tourism, Politics, and the Forgotten Entanglements of Power', in A. Church and T. Coles (eds) *Tourism, Power, and Space*. Abingdon: Routledge, pp. 1–40.

Dann, G. (1996) *The Language of Tourism. A Sociolinguistic Perspective*. Wallingford, UK: CAB International.

Fairclough, N. (1992) *Discourse and Social Change*. Cambridge: Polity.

— (1995) *Critical Discourse Analysis: The Critical Study of Language*. London: Longman.

Holt, D. (2002) 'Why do Brands Cause Trouble? A Dialectical Theory of Consumer Culture and Branding', *Journal of Consumer Research*, 29(1): 70–91.

Huxley, L. (2005) 'Western Backpackers and the Global Experience. An Exploration of Young People's Interaction with Local People', *Tourism, Culture and Communication*, 51: 37–44.

Johns, N. and Clarke, V. (2001) 'Mythological Analysis of Boating Tourism', *Annals of Tourism Research*, 28: 334–59.

Livesey, S. (2001) 'Eco-identity as Discursive Struggle: Royal Dutch Shell, Brent Spar, and Nigeria', *The Journal of Business Communication*, 38: 58–91.
Mannell, R. and Iso-Ahola, S.E. (1987) 'Psychological Nature of Leisure and Tourism Experience', *Annals of Tourism Research*, 14: 314–31.
Markwick, M. (2001) 'Postcards from Malta: Image, Consumption, Context', *Annals of Tourism Research*, 28(2): 417–38.
Matthews, A. (2009) 'Living Paradoxically: Understanding the Discourse of Authentic Freedom as it Emerges in the Travel Space', *Tourism Analysis*, 14: 165–74.
Mellinger, W.M. (1994) 'Toward a Critical Analysis of Tourism Representations', *Annals of Tourism Research*, 21(4): 756–79.
Morgan, N. and Pritchard, A. (1998) *Tourism Promotion and Power: Creating Images, Creating Identities.* Chichester: John Wiley.
Norton, A. (1996) 'Experiencing Nature: The Reproduction of Environmental Discourse Through Safari Tourism in East Africa', *Geoforum*, 27: 355–73.
Noy, C. (2004) 'This Trip Really Changed Me: Backpackers' Narratives of Self-Change', *Annals of Tourism Research*, 31: 78–102.
Parker, I. (1998) *Social Constructionism, Discourse and Realism.* London: Sage.
Salazar, N.B. (2006) 'Touristifying Tanzania: Local Guides, Global Discourse', *Annals of Tourism Research*, 33: 833–52.
Santos, C.A. and Rozier, S. (2009) 'Travel Writing as a Representational Space. "Doing Deviance"', *Tourism, Culture and Communication*, 9(3): 137–50.
Schroeder, J.E. and Borgerson, J. (2005) 'Packaging Paradise: Organising Representations of Hawaii', *Critical Management Studies Conference*, Cambridge.
Shepherd, R. (2003) 'Fieldwork Without Remorse: Travel Desires in a Tourist World', *Consumption, Markets and Culture*, 6: 133–44.
Silver, I. (1993) 'Marketing Authenticity in Third World Countries', *Annals of Tourism Research*, 20: 302–18.
Smith, S. (1994) 'The Tourism Product', *Annals of Tourism Research*, 3: 582–95.
Thurot, J.M. and Thurot, G. (1983) 'The Ideology of Class and Tourism: Confronting the Discourse of Advertising', *Annals of Tourism Research*, 10: 173–89.
Tribe, J. (2009) *Philosophical Issues in Tourism.* Bristol: Channel View Publications.
Urry, J. (1990) *The Tourist Gaze.* London: Sage.

8
The semiotics of tourism marketing

Richard Tresidder

Introduction

This chapter explores the relationship between the study of semiotics and the marketing of tourism experiences and products. Communication remains one of the most significant areas of marketing theory and practice, however the major emphasis of this theme within marketing studies focuses upon the mechanism of communication, and the means by which marketing communications are transmitted; resultantly, little reference is made to how the signs and images of tourism marketing are identified, constructed and utilized. It can be argued that there is a semiotic language of tourism that consists of a set of conventions, words, images and experiences that signpost the experience of tourism to the consumer, and that subsequently can be seen to underpin all tourism marketing. This chapter explores how signs and images used in tourism marketing bestow meaning and value to tourism products, activities and experiences. The production of meaning has its foundations in the structural linguistic science and philosophy of semiotics, and has been identified as a fundamental aspect of marketing practice (for a good discussion of semiotics within mainstream marketing see McCracken 1986; Mick, Burroughs, Hetzel and Brannen 2004; Mick and Oswald 2006; Oswald, 2012).

Semiotics is central to the marketing communication process, whereby, the meaning of tourism products and destination branding, are formed by utilizing codes that are understood, and whose significance is recognized by particular segments or consumer groups who possess similar levels of knowledge and cultural capital. Therefore the use of different images, words or experiences that convey the essence of meaning of tourism, enables the marketer to position the tourism product, experience, 'servicescape' and the host/guest relationship within focused marketing communications. By exploring the semiotic structure, or conceptual framework that informs tourism marketing practice, it is possible to identify a semiotic language, or code, that is used by marketers and frames tourism marketing systems. These meanings are generated within tourism marketing texts and are intended to be read and understood by the consumer. The semiotics of marketing is not external to the marketing practice, but is central to the communication process and it must be recognized that consumers exist within a semiotic system of signs, they are essential actors within the marketing system and are induced into thinking and behaving symbolically: 'That is they (*tourists*) symbolically interact in the world socially and experientially, they interact with symbolic products, engage in symbolic activities and engage in symbolic experiences' (Tresidder and Hirst 2012: 153).

Semiotics and the significance of signs

Before we can develop a semiotics of tourism marketing it is important to explore the meaning and significance of semiotics as an area of practice. Semiotics is very simply the study of signs and systems of representation. 'Signs are simply anything that stands for something (its object/referent), to somebody (interpreter), in some respect (its context, i.e. in an advert, label, package, servicescape or retail environment)' (Mick 1986: 198), therefore, as potential tourists or consumers we are all amateur semioticians. Signs surround our world, signs essentially make the world understandable and meaningful to us, they tell us when we can cross the road, which door to use and the way to the departure lounge. We all understand the global meaning of these signs, as we read, interpret and comprehend them; this is made possible from belonging to a shared cultural context and system of meaning that frames and guides our reading and understanding; in the literature this context is sometimes defined as a code (see Alexander 2000; McCracken and Roth 1989; Holt and Cameron 2010) or 'cultural template' (Arsel and Thompson 2011). Essentially these codes or templates provide a framework through which signs make sense and are interpreted by the individual tourist. A good example of this is to think about a set of traffic lights (Tresidder 2011; Tresidder and Hirst 2012); we all recognize and understand their role, this recognition is developed through historical conventions and experience whereby we equate the colour red with danger so we stop, and green with safety so know we can cross the road safely. Therefore, these rule based systems or organizing frameworks allows us to make sense of everyday reality and navigate our experience in the world, thus the images utilized in tourism marketing enable us to make sense of the tourism experience.

As codes are gathered and made sense of through our 'lived experience' and interactions with material and social reality, they are not always universally interpreted in the same way. That is to say, they may vary between individual consumers and particularly across different market segments, such as age, social background, geographical demographics or lifestyle sub-cultures. In this regard where we are unacquainted with the rules or do not understand the code, for example a 50 year old may not understand the codes represented within 18–30 marketing literature, as they do not belong to the age demographic, or possess the knowledge of contemporary clubbing culture to make sense of the experience being communicated. The signs and images contained and communicated with tourism marketing texts, direct our behaviour, expectations and perceptions of place, culture and heritage; thus signs place a significant role in promoting the tourist experience and engaging the potential tourist in the discourse of tourism.

The order of signs

What is a sign? Signs are more than words or images, pretty much anything and everything can be treated as a sign and can be seen to hold semiotic meaning and value. In this way, the world and all its components can be treated as text or narrative, they are read for meaning, and as such, they have discursive significance. Clothing for example has textual properties, and is often read in this way (McCracken and Roth 2003), this does not just work in terms of branded clothing but also the souvenir t-shirt purchased from a destination or an event. Both are read by the consumer, but are also read by people passing us by, through their reading they make all sorts of assumptions about the wearer, in terms of their experiences, background and cultural capital. As such, tourism products and activities carry and communicate meaning, as do the systems and styles of consumption adopted by consumers in their endeavour to gain value and meaning from using and interacting with them (Holt 1998). Thus, the meaning and significance of tourism products and experiences semiotically structure reality and our experiences of, and in, the world.

The signs contained within tourism marketing texts can be classified into three general categories, these are symbols, icons and indexes. What marks these categories out from each other is the difference in the relationship between the sign and what the sign signifies. The sign can be defined as the actual image or word, for example the word or image of a beach may equate to notions of warmth, escape or childhood etc. The result of this is that in order to understand the significance and meaning of the sign used in tourism marketing texts we need to classify its status as a symbol, icon or index as this will directly define and contextualize its meaning (see Tresidder and Hirst 2012).

Firstly, a symbol in tourism marketing is a sign that has an association to its object that works through processes of social and cultural convention, these come to define and underpin contemporary tourism (see Tresidder 2010) marketing and how as consumers we understand it. The use of a particular set of symbols in tourism marketing is one of the major conventions. For example one of the dominant semiotic conventions utilized within tourism brochures is the use of the deserted swimming pool or beach. The use of such images not only visually demonstrates the destination we may be visiting, but also through its denotative contents signifies various potential experiences such as escape, luxury or romance. In this way these images signify something to each individual consumer, it is not just a swimming pool or beach, but it defines the experience of being a holidaymaker, it creates desires and expectations. What is important to note is that, although these images are a dominant convention, they still possess individual connotative associations and are individually defined by the individual tourist's biography.

Secondly is the icon, this is a sign that has a close correspondence to its object, in short an iconic signifier could therefore look, sound, smell, taste, or feel like that which it signifies. According to Tresidder and Hirst (2012: 157):

> ... iconic signs that may be found in THEF (Tourism, Hospitality, Events and Food) marketing materials or contexts could include amongst others: the sound of gun shots or explosions in battlefield recreations; the smell of the everyday lived experience of our ancestors at the Jorvik Viking Centre in York, or the spritzed essence of the seashore that may accompany your fish supper at Heston Blumenthal's restaurant the Fat Duck. They could also be; a cartoon representation of a patriarchal Italian family in a pasta sauce advert; a performer adorned in a Roman Centurion uniform or staged as a male mine worker at an heritage center or within an advertisement for a living museum; or the plastic lemon shaped packaging that contains Jif lemon juice.

Such signs and images are central to tourism marketing as they enable the tourist or potential tourist to find something tangible in an intangible experience. They underpin the communicative staging of 'servicescapes' (Arnould, Price and Tierney 1998: 90). A very good example of this is Disney's World Showcase Area at the EPCOT centre in Florida, the area contains various international Pavilions including a French, Chinese, German and British Pavilion. Each Pavilion provides the tourist with a glimpse into the culture of the country with hyper-real sets containing iconic buildings such as the Eiffel Tower, heavily country specific accented workers and the opportunity to consume indigenous food such as Beer and Fish and Chips in the British Pavilion or Sausages and Pretzels in the German Pavilion. The Showcase area enables the tourist to be transported semiotically to a bucolic context and setting (Arnould, Price and Tierney 1998) in which the essence of a country may be consumed.

Finally, is the use of indexical signs, these in a way represent the result of engaging in tourism, the use of romance (couples wandering down the deserted beach hand in hand for example) may be defined as an indexical sign as the romance or space for romance is the result of entering into the physical, environmental and liminality of the destination. This differs from the previous two categories by focusing on the relationship between an object and an indexical sign, this difference is marked out by a causal relationship between destination etc. and result. For example the convention of locating healthy and tanned tourists within tourism marketing materials demonstrates the causal link between the climate, the sun, the water and their health giving properties. Thus what we can see is that signs and images can take on differing meanings according to their context and purpose, for example the picture of a cake in a cooking book would generate meanings of luxury and indulgence, yet if the same picture was placed in a book aimed to help dieting, then the meaning would change completely.

The semiotics of tourism

The semiotics of tourism is not a new subject area, it has been developed and discussed by a number of authors who have identified its application within tourism studies (see Dann 1996; Echtner 1999; Jenkins 2003; Berger 2007; Thurlow and Aiello 2007) while Crick (1989) defined 'the semiology of tourism' as one of the three main strands of tourism research. The significance of the semiotics of tourism is recognised by MacCannell (1999: 3) who considers that '... there is a privileged relationship between tourism and semiotics'. This opinion is reinforced by Dann who comments, 'Nowhere ... is a semiotics perspective considered more appropriate than in the analysis of tourism advertising with its culture coded covert connotations, in the study of tourism imagery and in treatment of tourism communication as a discourse of myth' (1996: 6).

The representations of tourism within marketing utilize a semiotic language that has been formulated and embedded in contemporary travel writing and marketing texts, the language draws from a set of myths about the experience of tourism, the nature of destinations and the impact the activity may have on the individual. Therefore, it is important that we think about the relationship between tourism marketing, the discourse that underpins this and how the individual interacts and negotiates marketing communications.

Although the area of semiotics has not been fully developed in mainstream tourism studies or marketing, the significance of semiotics in understanding and communicating of the touristic experience cannot be denied. In a famous quote Urry (2001: 139) states that: 'One learns that a thatched cottage with roses around the door represents "ye olde England", or the waves crashing on to rocks signifies "wild, untamed nature"; or especially, that a person with a camera draped around his/her neck is clearly a tourist'. In the same vein Culler (1981: 158) observes that, 'All over the world the unsung armies of semioticians, the tourists, are fanning out in search of the signs of Frenchness, typical Italian behaviour, exemplary Oriental scenes ...'.

We cannot ignore the significance of semiotics and their construction of the tourism experience. However, one of the reasons why semiotics has not been fully developed is that it is categorized as an interpretative methodology, and as such it is difficult to utilize in a commercial environment, as it does not produce replicable or objective readings of texts. What we end up with, is multiple semiotic readings with each individual creating and negotiating their own understanding of the messages communicated within marketing texts, this information is difficult to incorporate into mass marketing communications. As such, what we see is the semiotic language of tourism achieving in marketing texts the 'signposting' of experience (Jenkins 2003), whereby, the individual tourist's interpretation is guided to a set of experiences in the forms of icons, symbols and indexical signs that make the link between marketing communications and the individually negotiated experience of tourism.

The semiotic language of tourism marketing

Through the analysis of various tourism marketing texts including brochures, websites and television adverts, it is unmistakable that tourism marketing both relies upon, and creates, what may be termed a semiotic language of marketing (Tresidder 2010; Tresidder and Hirst 2012). This language of tourism marketing is formed by a number of reoccurring conventions, themes, images and words, which signpost a comprehensible and appreciated contemporary experience of tourism. These conventions include various discourses that revolve around escape, authenticity, luxury, freedom, experience, play and time (Tresidder 2010). These may be divided into a number of pervasive categories the most dominant of these being time and authenticity.

The semiotic time and space of tourism

This operates at a number of levels, the purpose of focusing on time and space has two purposes, the first purpose is to elevate the experience to that of the extraordinary and secondly the difference between time and space as a part of everyday lived experience and touristic time and space.

Time as extraordinary: There is a clear convention that there is a clear division between the extraordinary nature of touristic time and the stress, monotony of everyday lived experiences such as sitting in a traffic jam or doing your washing. This is demonstrated in the use of time to set up the experience of tourism. For example we will witness discussion about 'not enough time in the week' or 'everyone wants a part of you'. In the recent Baz Luhrmann television and cinema advertisement for Australia, the extraordinary nature of the Australian Outback was set against the dark, rainy, stressful urban environment of New York, whereby the executive was stressed and arguing with her partner. This was used as juxtaposition against the un-spoilt, light, sunny undeveloped Australian landscape in which it became possible to relax and find peace in both life and her relationship. Time becomes used as a means of both fixing everyday lived experience and release into a reflexive and therapeutic space. A very good example of this is the 2010 Thompson 'Time for a Holiday' campaign, the dialogue which accompanied moving images of a family being together, swimming, having fun on the beach, hugging each other and playing, expressed the significance of time in our lives and the relationship between tourism and time, its constraints and the blurring between work and play time. What this advert does, and others like it, is to provide us with an alternative conception of time that is removed from the stress of everyday life, it becomes an extraordinary place of escape for two weeks each year, the chance to take stock of your lives, find meaning. What it also accomplishes is the identification of a type or form of emotional authenticity of feeling and experience. This is reinforced by the use of words such as timeless, luxury, escape and freedom.

The semiotics of authenticity

The notion of authenticity has always been identified as an important theme in tourism studies (MacCannell 1999) and is often seen as a reaction to post-industrial society or part of the individual's search for meaning. It is also an important convention for tourism marketing as it adds another level of significance to the tourism experience.

Experiences as authentic: The notion of authenticity works at a number of levels within tourism marketing, but it can broadly be broken down into a cultural lens and an experiential lens. The utilization of culture in tourism marketing remains a significant and reoccurring theme, the representation of culture may be seen both in terms of attractions, and also as representing the tourist having access to a more authentic and real world. These representations can take two forms. Cultural representations provide the opportunity for the potential to gaze upon traditional cultures and cultural artifacts, the immersion into these as a tourist enables them to participate (even if this is only as a voyeur) vicariously in these cultures. The recent 'Incredible India' advertisement uses this convention, it shows the tourist as an interactive participant, who is both watching and physically participating in cultural festivals and rituals. This provides an oppositional world in which to escape the inauthentic post-modern media led world of the West. Authenticity also operates at the level of the emotional in which it becomes possible to find meaningful authentic time with your loved ones, family and friends (as seen in the 2010 Thompson 'Time for a Holiday' campaign). This theme of authenticity of emotions is a recurring theme with a couple being represented sitting alone at a table or walking hand in hand down a beach or, in the case of Luhrmann's advertisement, swimming in a deserted pool. The idea of authenticity of emotion and family is heavily used in family orientated marketing communications and is reinforced by phrases such as 'What would you like your children to inherit, a house, a clock, the family silver or something a little more valuable ... memories start here' ('Center Parcs Memories Start Here!' campaign 2013).

The semiotic language of tourism is specific to the subject area, as it draws from the complex discourse of tourism that is constructed at the historical, social, cultural and individual level. What is also important within the semiotic language of tourism is to recognize what is left out or missing from representations of the tourism experience, the sanitization of landscapes (clean beaches, or, no traffic or tourists at attractions), and is a significant convention in tourism marketing. If we are trying to escape, or find authenticity within the tourism experience, it is important that we do not get distracted by the reality and technology of modern life. So if we return again to the Luhrmann Australia advertisement, during all of the images of Australia used in the production, we do not see any other people, telephone poles, cars, technology etc. just an empty pure un-spoilt timeless environment. If any of these elements of modern life were included then the message and significance of the campaign would be lost. Through the development of a conceptual framework it is possible to clearly identify and classify the semiotic themes that are contained within tourism marketing communications. However, it is more difficult to chart how the individual finds meaning and negotiates the marketing landscapes of tourism.

Interpreting tourism texts

The interpretation of marketing texts is an individual reflexive process, although we can state that marketing communications signpost or direct interpretation of the tourism experience, much of the interpretation process is reliant upon the individual's personal biography, view of the world and their value systems. This biography is formed by the reader's social and cultural background, gender, educational background and geographical awareness of place. In other words the interpretation of marketing texts is a direct consequence of their epistemological, ontological and axiological influences (for good general discussion of these aspects see Bryman 2004: 21–4), it is these areas of the individual's experience or personality that define the way in which they relate to the marketing process and the product or service being sold. Each of these three areas contributes to the individual's interpretation process in a different way, and is summarized in Table 8.1 below.

Table 8.1 Epistemological, ontological and axiological influences

Influences that structure the individual's interpretation of tourism marketing texts		
Epistemological foundations (knowledge base)	*Ontological foundations (position in world)*	*Axiological foundations (value systems)*
Tourist's knowledge How tourism materials produced Status of materials Individual tourist's perception Individual tourist's memory Individual tourist's consciousness Individual tourist's reason	Individual tourist's reality and influences Tourist's social and cultural background • Class • Education • Religion • Race • Geographical roots	Tourist's values systems Tourist's moral code Informed by ontology and epistemology

Source: Adapted from Tresidder and Hirst (2012): 131

The inference of this is that each individual tourist, producer and marketer's production and interpretation of marketing texts will be influenced by their individual set of 'knowledges', lived experience and values. Therefore as marketers we need to acknowledge that there are multiple worldviews or realities.

Although the interpretation of tourism marketing texts is a personal and reflexive activity in which tourists will find their own meaning, it is possible to recognize how epistemological, ontological and axiological influences induce certain meanings. It is also possible to recognize that there are certain themes or messages that transcend individual resistance, these include authenticity of emotions and the need to escape (see Phillimore and Goodson 2004 for discussion on epistemological, ontological and axiological in tourism). Therefore, tourism marketing texts signpost experience, they direct us, influence our perceptions of place, people and experience and ultimately inform our purchasing behavior. The signposting of experience within marketing texts leads the tourist on a journey in which they traverse the communication by extracting knowledge from their depository of experiences and worldview, the role of the marketer is to influence the way in which the tourist negotiates these signs and images by signposting and encouraging the tourist to find their own individual meaning within the text. This is supported by the convention of using empty landscapes within tourism marketing, the deserted beach or table at a restaurant, the image is empty, free from other people thus creating a sterile space in which tourists can invest their emotions, experiences and values and find their own meaning within the text unhindered by external influences such as other diners, families etc.

The method of semiotics

There are various traditions of semiotics that have led to various approaches to the application of a semiotic methodology, the adoption of a social semiotic approach enables us to identify both the relationship between interpretation, and the individual and the significance of tourism as a social and cultural activity. The signs and images used in tourism marketing communications can be separated into two components, the 'narrative' and the 'conceptual' (Kress and Van Leeuwen 1996: 56). Narrative structures always have a line of communication that directs the consumer to the message being presented within the communication. Conversely, conceptual representations do not rely on vectors to transmit meaning as the conceptual aspect belongs to the culture in which they are generated, for example the significance of tourism as an activity in contemporary society. Vectors are established by lines of vision across the screen or image, these vectors connect the text to the author, and as a consequence, an image can be both a participant and a vector (Kress and Van Leeuwen 1996: 59). A vector affords a connection or method of realization between the consumer and the text, once this connection is made initial interpretation is achieved. The vector guides the consumer and emphasizes the importance of the representation, critically, the 'means of realisation produce quite similar semantic relations' (Kress and Van Leeuwen 2001: 44), whereby, the relationship between the marketing text and the tourist is supported. Resultantly, enabling the communication of meaning to be identified and espoused by the consumer in terms of collective hegemonic definitions of tourism and destinations etc. However, not all visual or textual elements on the website maintain universal forms of interpretation:

> Rather, a given culture has a range of general, possible relations which is not tied to expression in any particular semiotic code . . . This distribution of realisation possibilities across the semiotic codes is itself determined historically and socially.
>
> *(Kress and Van Leeuwen 2001: 44)*

Therefore, the representations in the three websites are mediated by a historical and cultural discourse (see Artbury 2005; O'Connor 2005; O'Gorman 2007), that are contextualized by a language of tourism. According to Kress and Van Leeuwen, this mediation challenges notions of reality, as they state:

> Pictorial structures do not simply reproduce the structure of reality. On the contrary, they produce images of reality which are bound up with the interests of the social institutions within which the pictures are produced, circulated and read. They are ideological.
>
> *(Kress and Van Leeuwen 1996: 45)*

Therefore semiotically, destination marketing websites can be seen to have both an objective and ideological purpose (Ferguson 1998) in that they represent a number of commercial or capitalist discourses that exclude the negative impacts that tourism has on the environment and indigenous culture.

The reactional process the tourist enters into when reading tourism marketing texts observes the actors within the site also becoming reactors, while the goals become phenomena (Kress and Van Leeuwen 2001: 64). The reactor is the participant who does the looking or gazing while the phenomenon element is shaped by alternative participants at whom the reactor is looking, or by a whole visual proposition. Therefore, the images become the actor as they are non-transactional, while representing a phenomenon of tourism by virtue that it is located or contained for example in a tourism brochure. While the texts or words that accompany pictures in brochures become a reactor, a transactional response is then devised by the reader as the 'text directs perception' and interpretation, through reinforcing 'signposts' of tourism experience. Critically, the written textual element of the tourism marketing texts guides perception and underlines the significance of the images used, this results in a conversion activity taking place that is guided by techniques such as the use of text (Davis 2005), and changes in written context and the represented meaning of the tourism experience (Marshall 2005). Kress and van Leeuwen (2001: 67) call this process 'participant relay'. This relay demonstrates a text-image association in which text extends or re-conceptualizes the visual information about the nature of the experience being offered by the restaurants. A good example of this is the use of a landscape in marketing materials, the picture of a deserted coastline, could almost be anywhere, however the text gives ownership of the image to the place or destination being marketed.

The interpretation of narrative images in tourism marketing texts is additionally directed by the presence of what Kress and van Leeuwen define as 'secondary participants' (1996: 67). These participants are not related via vectors but become linked in other contexts (2001: 71) within the 'setting' of the narrative images. For example, if an image of a tourist is contained within an advertisement, they create a vector that defines their role and status within the service context, while waiting staff in the background emphasize the nature of the relationship between the host and guest and status of the guest within the service relationship as they are demonstrating their subservience and cannot be separated from the power and ideological relations that underpin both the promotion and interpretation process.

The first stage of the tourist's interpretation places the experience of tourism within the numerous cultural and historical discourses that define hospitality (see Tresidder and Hirst 2012). These discourses are supported by narrative and conceptual structures utilized within marketing texts. The recognition of these structures both locates and signposts experience of tourism and is represented in the semiotic language of tourism marketing. The use of hegemonic representations of tourism within marketing texts creates what Jenkins (2003) calls 'expected places', these places reflect the ordering of images by providing representations of all of the aspects of tourism we would expect to see, or in other words, the foundations of the language of tourism. Therefore, 'time' as discussed above, represents a semiotic convention in tourism marketing that unifies the past, present and future into a temporal malaise that is expressed by Jameson (1991: 67) as, 'a series of pure and unrelated presents in time'. Although the language of tourism within marketing communications offers countless escape attempts in which the consumer can find significance and escape, the experience of hospitality becomes '. . . dominated by a consciousness which emphasizes the discontinuity of experience' (Harvey 1993: 157). Nevertheless, the representations of destinations and experiences of tourism proffer a delineated tourism space in which experience may be semiotically consumed in a tangible ontological way.

Semiotics and power

As stated previously, semiotics and semiosis as a process of signification cannot be separated from ideological discourses of power, as the images utilized in tourism marketing can often be seen to be the result of an expression of cultural dominance, and for some, the exploitation of indigenous peoples and culture. Additionally we must remember that tourism marketing is a commercial activity that is motivated by the requirement to generate income. Consequently, the signs and images and their meanings have been adopted as they will generate the most economically beneficial result at the expense of those that are not, this is often achieved by offering access to fragile environments as part of the 'extraordinariness' of the destination while ignoring the fragile nature of many of these environments. Resultantly, all tourism marketing texts can be scrutinized for asymmetric power relations and power consequences. For example Dann's (1996) study of how indigenous people are signified within tourism brochures illustrates the means by which hosts are represented within marketing texts (see also Nelson 2005) as either providing entertainment in the form of 'communicative staging', or service, rather than being represented or characterized as social, economic or cultural equals. Dann's work provides an insight into the way in which tourism marketing creates and reinforces definitions of subordination and power relations between the host and guest in terms of composition, the position of the host is also reinforced by the angle, position or size of represented participants.

The elevation of the guest's status is an important convention as it reinforces the extraordinary nature of the tourism experience, and is part of offering an escape even if temporary from the role they may have in the home society, it provides tourists with the opportunity for a temporary period to be a King or Queen, or to take on the role of Master. This process is plainly demonstrated in SAGA Travellers World Brochure where the guest is transported to a rarified world of formal service, luxury and chauffeurs, the tourist's status is reinforced by their relationship to the indigenous people, who again are only seen in the service or entertainment context. The representations of people or cultural manifestations that have the utmost attractive assets and economic value are accentuated in the foreground while those that are not linger in the background. In this sense, marketing maintains and replicates cultural and social myths of people, places, and cultures by commodifying, packaging and selling them to potential tourists. It is interesting to note that SAGA, and in particular SAGA Cruises, are targeting a particular segment that has become known as the SKIER (Spend Kids' Inheritance in Early Retirement).

This offers a very different experience from the idea of the semiotics of authenticity, by offering a more individualistic form of experience where meaning can be found through adoption of status and membership to a particular social or cultural group or tribe. The SAGA example is archetypal of a number of host/guest semiotic conventions and power relationships that are contained within tourism marketing texts. It is important to remember that Kress and Van Leeuwen see general 'signs and images' and other representational customs such as communicative staging, as (re)producing 'hierarchies of social power' (1996: 83), these concerns are not merely associated with the marketing of tourism, but involve the use of signs and images. Thus, many of the semiotic structures and material practices identified in tourism marketing 'represent the world in hierarchical order' (1996: 85) and essentially in which the connection between the host (be it the culture, population or service personnel) and the guest or tourist is identified. In a way the host is often represented as a servant or a cultural attraction and the visitor is consuming this through the marketing process and their experience.

Conclusion

Semiotics provides an alternative approach to understanding the relationship between the tourism product and the end consumer. Understanding how images are formulated and read or interpreted by tourists provides an insight into how marketing campaigns can be built, formulated and staged. The semiotics of tourism marketing should not sit in isolation, but should be used to enhance marketing practices and to understand how particular market segment groups find and generate meaning through the interpretation process. It can also be argued that the tourism experience does not start and finish when we get on or off a plane, but the benefits we feel in terms of escape and longing start the minute we begin to plan and research our holiday choices. This chapter explores the semiotic language and experience of tourism and outlines a general theory of the semiotics of tourism, we live in an increasingly visually orientated world and as such, semiotics is increasingly being recognized as performing an important role in contemporary marketing practice. Semiotics, as an approach, supports the marketing and promotion of tourism as it raises practical and ethical issues as to how tourism, and the subjects of tourism, are presented and consumed within both contemporary marketing texts and represented servicescapes.

Often we do not question the meaning or purpose of the signs and images we are presented with on a daily basis, neither do we take the time to understand the signs that are put in front of us. Is the traffic light just a means of ensuring the orderly flow of traffic, or is it an ideological and political construct that ensures citizens behave in a particular way? Such questions can also be asked of the signs and images utilized in tourism marketing and it is important that we understand the meanings, the foundation of these meanings, and the power relations that underpin them. By taking the time to explore and analyze what images and other signifiers are being used in the staging of tourism experiences within marketing texts, and what they signify, marketers will be better informed about how the messages we communicate are received and understood by consumers. By undertaking this, we can start to make sense of what tourists are looking for, or alternatively are seeking to circumvent, in the sense of what motivates them or turns them off and what fuels and frames their desires and interactions with the marketplace.

Understanding how the language of tourism is constructed within marketing texts and how it is used enables us to tailor marketing communications to reflect the very individualistic and specialist nature of tourism as a subject area, thus ensuring that the message communicated by marketers is understood and recognized by the potential tourist. The semiotics of tourism is a multi-disciplinary approach that enables us to understand how the message and meaning of tourism is communicated. The discipline of semiotics and to a certain degree tourism marketing has to not only draw from marketing or business practices and theory but also to be informed by the social, cultural and economic debates that allow us to understand and embed the meaning of tourism within a practical and tangible semiotic framework. Additionally, it is important that we recognize that the tourist or consumer is an individual who will reflexively find and negotiate their own meaning and find their individual significance within the marketing text. It is dangerous to make the assumption that everyone, even every member of an identified segment group, will think and behave in the same way. With the rise of new technology and the introduction of technology such as Web 3.0 and the focus on the personalization ability of the platform, the ability to identify individual consumption trends becomes even more significant for the contemporary tourism marketer and as such semiotics becomes another tool that they can draw from.

References

Alexander, A. (2000) 'Codes and Contexts: Practical Semiotics for the Qualitative Researcher', *Market Research Society Annual Conference*, 9: 2.

Arnould, E., Price, L. and Tierney, P. (1998) 'Communicative Staging of the Wilderness Servicescape', *Service Industries Journal*, 18(3): 90–115.

Arsel, Z. and Thompson, C.J. (2011) 'Demythologizing Consumption Practices: How Consumers Protect their Field-dependent Identity Investments from Devaluing Marketplace Myths', *Journal of Consumer Research*, 37(5): 791–806.

Artbury, A. (2005) *Entertaining Angels*. Sheffield: Sheffield Phoenix Press.

Berger, A.A. (2007) *Thailand Tourism*. Philadelphia: Haworth Press.

Bryman, A. (2004) *Social Research Methods*, 2nd edn. New York: Oxford University Press.

Crick, M. (1989) 'Representations of Sun, Sex, Sights, Savings and Servility: International Tourism in the Social Sciences', *Annual Review of Anthropology*, 18: 307–44.

Culler, J. (1981) 'Semiotics of Tourism', *American Journal of Semiotics*, 1: 127–40.

— (1988) *Framing the Sign: Criticism and its Institutions*. Oxford: Basil Blackwell.

Dann, G. (1996) 'The People of Tourist Brochures', in Selwyn, T. (ed.) *The Tourist Image: Myths and Myth Making in Tourism*. West Sussex: Wiley, pp. 61–82.

Davis, J.S. (2005) 'Representing Place: Deserted Islands and the Reproduction of Bikini Atoll', *Annals of the Association of American Geographers*, 93(3): 607–25.

Echtner, C.M. (1999) 'The Semiotic Paradigm: Implications For Tourism Research', *Tourism Management*, 20(1): 47–57.

Ferguson, P. (1998) 'A Cultural Field in the Making: Gastronomy in 19th Century France', *American Journal of Sociology*, 104(3): 597–641.

Harvey, D. (1993) 'From Space to Place and Back Again: Reflections on the Condition of Postmodernity', in Bird. J. *et al.* (eds) *Mapping the Futures Local Cultures, Global Change*. London: Routledge, pp. 3–39.

Holt, D. (1998) 'Does Cultural Capital Structure American Consumption?', *Journal of Consumer Research*, 25(June).

Holt, D.B. and Cameron, D. (2010) *Cultural Strategy: Using Innovative Ideologies To Build Breakthrough Brands*. Oxford: Oxford University Press.

Jameson, F. (1991) *Postmodernism or the Cultural Logic of Late Capitalism*. London: Verso.

Jenkins, O. (2003) 'Photography and Travel Brochures: The Circle of Representation', *Tourism Geographies*, 5(3): 305–28.

Kress, G. and Van Leeuwen, T. (1996) *Reading Images: The Grammar of Visual Design*. London: Routledge.

— (2001) *Multimodal Discourse: The Modes and Media of Contemporary Communication*. London: Arnold.

MacCannell, D. (1999) *The Tourist: A New Theory of the Leisure Class*. Los Angeles: University of California Press.

McCracken, G. (1986) 'Culture and Consumption: A Theoretical Account of the Structure and Movement of the Cultural Meaning of Consumer Goods', *Journal of Consumer Research*, 13(1): 71–84.

McCracken, G.D. and Roth, V.J. (1989) 'Does Clothing Have A Code? Empirical Findings and Theoretical Implications in the Study of Clothing as a Means of Communication', *International Journal of Research in Marketing*, 6(1): 13–33.

Marshall, D. (2005) 'Food as Ritual, Routine or Convention; Consumption', *Markets and Culture*, 8(1): 69–85.

Mick, D.G. (1986) 'Consumer Research and Semiotics: Exploring the Morphology of Signs, Symbols, and Significance', *Journal of Consumer Research*, 13(2): 196–213.

Mick, D.G. and Oswald, L.R. (2006) 'The Semiotic Paradigm on Meaning in the Marketplace', in Belk, R.W. (ed.) *Handbook of Qualitative Research Methods in Marketing*. Northampton: Edward Elgar Publishing, pp. 31–45.

Mick, D.G., Burroughs, J.E., Hetzel, P. and Brannen, M.Y. (2004) 'Pursuing the Meaning of Meaning in the Commercial World: An International Review of Marketing and Consumer Research Founded on Semiotics', *Semiotica*, 152(1–4): 1–74.

Nelson, V. (2005) 'Representation and Images of People, Place and Nature in Grenada's Tourism', *Geografiska Annaler B*, 87(2): 131–43.

O'Connor, D. (2005) 'Towards a New Interpretation of Hospitality', *International Journal of Hospitality Management*, 17(3): 267–71.

O'Gorman, K. (2007) 'Dimensions of Hospitality: Exploring Ancient Origins', in Lashley, C., Lynch, P.A. and Morrison, A. (eds) *Hospitality: A Social Lens*. Oxford: Elsevier.

Oswald, L.R. (2012) *Marketing Semiotics: Signs, Strategies, and Brand Value*. Oxford: Oxford University Press.

Phillimore, J. and Goodson, L. (2004) *Qualitative Research in Tourism: Ontologies, Epistemologies and Methodologies*. London: Routledge.

Thurlow, C. and Aiello, G. (2007) 'National Pride, Global Capital: A Social Semiotic Analysis of Transnational Visual Branding in the Airline Industry', *Visual Communication*, 6(3): 305–44.

Tresidder, R. (2010) 'What No Pasties!? Reading the Cornish Tourism Brochure', *Journal of Travel and Tourism Marketing*, 27(6): 596–611.

— (2011) 'Reading Hospitality: The Semiotics of Le Manoir aux Quat'Saisons', *Hospitality and Society*, 1(1): 67–84.

Tresidder, R. and Hirst, C. (2012) *Marketing in Food, Hospitality, Tourism and Events: A Critical Approach*. Oxford: Goodfellows.

Urry, J. (2001) *The Tourist Gaze: Leisure and Travel in Contemporary Society*. London: Sage.

Part 3

Strategic issues in tourism

9

Towards an experiential approach in tourism studies

Wided Batat and Isabelle Frochot

Introduction

Research in tourism has a long established interest in the study of tourist behaviour. Marketers, sociologists, psychologists, human geographers and other disciplines have all contributed over 50 years towards better understandings of tourist experience and behaviour. However, consumer experience is a fairly recent field of interest for marketing scholars and yet has produced a complex and fascinating array of conceptualizations. This interest stems from the recognition that the consumption of services such as art, leisure or tourism necessitates the development of new theoretical frameworks due to the specificities of these consumption contexts (irrational behaviour, symbolic and esthetical criteria, emotional benefits maximisation, importance of pleasure and memorability of the experience). This approach, the experiential marketing perspective, can be tremendously useful to enhancing understanding of tourist behaviour.

The objective of this chapter is then to provide a comprehensive and critical overview of the theoretical, methodological and practical issues in tourism marketing. The chapter shows that the experience marketing literature almost totally overlooks one of the most highly experiential consumption contexts, tourism. Indeed, the focus on product marketing contexts seems to underplay the contribution that analyses of tourism consumption could offer to this literature. Thus greater links between experience marketing and tourism marketing research could assist tourism professionals to develop strategies to better engage consumers' emotional and hedonic responses. Through the application of Consumer Culture Theory (CCT), this chapter offers new directions and approaches to inform tourism marketing, highlighting the key debates and issues related to consumer experiences in the tourism sector.

This chapter first discusses the evolution from traditional marketing to experiential marketing and details the key principles of the experiential perspective. It then addresses the particularities of tourism to establish how experiential tourism can be defined and conceptualized. The last part of the chapter expands on this by integrating a vision of Consumer Culture Theory, since it provides a useful guide to the evolution observed in tourist consumer behaviour and offers indications about future changes to tourist experiences.

From a traditional marketing to an experiential marketing

For several decades, marketing and consumer researchers have conceived the consumer as a rational economic actor, the "homo economicus" philosophy. As a result, the cognitive and behaviourist models have dominated marketing research for decades (Batat 2011). Schmitt (1999) uses the term "traditional marketing" to refer to these cognitive approaches, which views consumers as rational decision makers who are mostly concerned with functional features of products and services and maximising the utility gained from consumption. However, this conception has been criticized, for instance human beings' rational behaviour has been fiercely questioned (Holbrook and Hirschman 1982). Another frustration with those theories has been their lack of consideration for the psychological dimensions of experiences. In 1970, Baudrillard had already exposed that consumption practices are social activities in which consumers produce meanings and exchange symbols. Since Baudrillard's work, marketing and consumer behaviour researchers have developed a rich research stream on aspects of aestheticism, symbolism and hedonism in everyday life (c.f. Levy 1959; Sheth 1980; Westbrook 1987; Lipovetsky 2003).

In 1982, Holbrook and Hirschman produced a new approach that revolutionized academic approaches within consumer research. The authors theorized the consumer experience as subjective and personal, often emotionally charged. They introduced the concept of hedonic consumption, which was defined as designating 'those facets of consumer behaviour that relate to the multi-sensory, fantasy and emotive aspects of one's experience with products' (Holbrook and Hirschman 1982: 92). In this perspective, the utilitarian functions of products were not denied but the symbolic meanings and emotions were also established as important dimensions of product evaluation.

Holbrook and Hirschman (1982) consequently proposed that considerations of the hedonic component would provide a better understanding of consumers that traditional consumer behaviour models had yet not addressed. This aspect was portrayed as particularly important in products for which 'the symbolic role is especially rich and salient: for example, entertainment, arts, and leisure activities encompass symbolic aspects of consumption behaviour that make them particularly fertile ground for research' (Holbrook and Hirschman 1982: 134).

In their original article Holbrook and Hirschman (1982) suggested that most variables used in traditional marketing should be reconsidered to establish the grounds of an experiential perspective (see Table 9.1).

According to the experiential perspective, the consumer becomes an active economic actor involved with his consumption experiences. The role of companies is to assist their customers in the production and the achievement of their experiences. O'Sullivan and Spangler (1998) proposed that the key concepts of the experiential marketing approach could be categorized as:

1 the nature of user involvement (physical, mental, emotional, social and spiritual);
2 the extent of user's co-participation in the product's offer;
3 the relevance of the product or service's symbolic values;
4 the product or service's multi-functionality; and
5 the central role placed on the experience.

The consumer tends to immerse him/herself and explore a multiplicity of new meanings of his/her life (Firat and Dholakia 1998). It is this full immersion within an original experience that provides unique unforgettable pleasure for consumers (Carù and Cova 2006).

Table 9.1 Variables used in traditional marketing theories compared to the experiential approach

	Traditional approaches	*Experiential approach*
Stimuli	Verbal	Non-verbal
	Tangible	Sensorial
Consumer objective	Maximize utility	Experience lived
	Extrinsic objectives (to consume in order to achieve an objective)	Intrinsic objective (product consumed for itself)
	Utilitarian criteria	Esthetical and symbolical criteria
Goal	Maximize utility and value	Maximize emotional benefits
Decision	Formulate preferences with multi attributes comparisons	Holistic perception and difficulty to elaborate concise expectations
Mediating variables	Attitudes	Emotions, feelings
Post-purchase evaluation	Satisfaction	Pleasure, memory
Involvement	Level of involvement (high/low)	Involvement type (portion of the hedonic component)

Source: Adapted from Bourgeon and Filser (1995)

Since the consumption experience extends over a period of time, Arnould and Price (1993) have identified four major stages:

- The pre-consumption experience, which involves searching for, planning, day-dreaming about, foreseeing or imagining the experience.
- The purchase experience, which encompasses choice, payment, packaging, the encounter with the service and the environment.
- The core consumption experience including sensation, satiety, satisfaction/dissatisfaction, irritation or flow, and transformation.
- The remembered consumption experience and the nostalgia for previously lived experiences that reactivates consumption through the use of photographs to re-live past experiences for example. This is also based on accounts of stories and on discussions or arguments with friends about the past, which contributes to the classification of memories.

Thirty years later, the experiential perspective has gained ground to be recognized as an essential approach in consumer behaviour. Pine and Gilmore (1998) argue that companies or destinations, to achieve competitive advantages, should produce experiences, as a kind of new category of offer that can be launched on the market. The staged experience is then the ultimate category of the company's offer as opposed to the goods, services and ideas produced (Hetzel 2002; Schmitt 1999).

Over the years the experience literature has taken two directions. On one side, practitioners have produced a series of books that have become useful guides to assist managers in designing the experience (Pine and Gilmore 1998; Schmitt 1999, etc.). Whilst those contributions are valuable, they have also been criticized for their lack of consideration of value creation, especially in the pre-purchase and post-purchase consumptions steps (Tynan and McKechnie 2009). They also tend to lack theoretical grounding that would provide more power to the practical applications they describe. On the other side, academics have produced theoretical contributions that bring more depth to the understanding of the consumer experience such as the service dominant logic and the notion of co-construction (Vargo and Lusch 2004; Carù and Cova 2006; Edvardsson, Tronvoll and Cruger 2011; etc.), and the understanding of emotions in the experience (Oliver 1980; Westbrook 1987; Richins 1997; etc.), which are discussed in other chapters in this volume.

The experiential approach in the tourism context

Surprisingly, despite the relevance of tourism consumption contexts as exemplary to study experiential consumption theory and practice, tourism has rarely been the object of experiential marketing studies in the mainstream marketing field. In contrast tourism marketing and consumer behaviour researchers have been slow to embrace experience marketing theory and practice, despite the fact that many tourism and leisure researchers have provided very interesting insights into behavioural processes associated with the distinctive characteristics of tourism experiences. Indeed, tourism embraces such a vast array of experiences, ranging from a short weekend visiting family to a world tour that might last a year that it may impede the application of experience marketing concepts. Everything about tourism consumption is different from other forms of services: it involves multiple encounters and staying in a different place and culture for a relatively long length of time (longer than any other service experiences studied apart from perhaps hospital stays). It often takes place in locations where tourists would not necessarily wish to live on a daily basis (coastal areas, islands, countryside, high up mountain resorts, developing countries . . .) but that are prized for their resources (space available, activities, weather, 'exoticism' of the location, etc.). In order to explicate the tourist experience, the following section addresses two main components of tourist behaviour: motivations and, the different experiences that tourists seek at the destination.

The specificities of the tourist experience: motivation to escape

To understand fully tourist behaviour it is important to understand what drives tourists to consumer vacation experiences, since this dictates what types of experiences they seek from a tourism product or destination. The first and most important motivation expressed by tourists is that of getting away from their daily life: a priori to the idea of travelling is the identification of need to escape the usual environment. The strength of this motivation is associated to the fact that getting away represents a facilitating factor to an achievement of other motivations that will be experienced at the destination. For instance, to be in a different location allows tourists to forget about their daily burdens (stressful urban environments but also simple everyday burdens such as the pile of washing up or the DIY that needs to be done around the house). The only way to detach from those daily burdens is to physically get away, this then allows tourists to free their time and spirit to immerse themselves fully in their holiday experience. This element has strong implications in terms of managing the experience as tourists on vacation seek freedom from elements that remind them of the negative aspects of their daily life (long commuting, crowded and noisy environments, pollution, excessive noise, queuing, imposed rhythms, lack of space, etc.).

The specificities of the tourist experience: what tourists seek

The second dimension to the tourist experience lies with what tourists seek while at the destination. One of the most frequently cited studies of motivations was that by Crompton in 1979 that investigated travel motives of a small sample of tourists. This study identified eight major travel motives: escape from a perceived mundane environment, exploration, evaluation of self, relaxation, prestige, regression, enhancement of kinship relationships and facilitation of social interactions. Other researchers have presented classifications of motivations, which added to our understanding of the diversity of motivations for travelling (Krippendorf 1987; Moutinho 1987; Mcintosh and Goeldner 1990; Crompton and McKay 1997). Overall, most studies identified as key vacation motivations: getting away, relaxing, social connections, learning, and improving one's own capabilities. Those motivations are directly connected to the experience tourists expect while at the destination, and therefore they are central to the understanding of the tourist experience.

Successful tourism products are those that achieve satisfaction for these motivations. However, very different types of experience exist depending on the strength of intervention from the tourism industry and the strength and direction of tourists' motivations.

- On a first level, various forms of connections with the tourism industry can be sought. For instance, tourists travelling independently perhaps wish to immerse themselves in the culture of a new country (particularly if they decide to stay with local people, share eating experiences, etc.). Therefore they may seek limited contacts with the tourism industry. On the other side of the spectrum, consumers may prefer tourist experiences within holiday resorts or cruise ships where everything is planned for the consumer (especially within an all-inclusive offer). Often, even the burden of making daily decisions is removed from consumers, allowing them another form of total immersion with their holiday. Between those two extremes, various other forms of tourist experience exist especially since over the years consumers have evolved towards more alternative forms of tourism (Stamboulis and Skayannis 2009).
- On a second level, it is important to understand the extent to which tourists might require home comforts, familiar cultural environments while at the destination, or whether they want to immerse themselves fully in the culture/country visited and escape familiar cultural norms. In other terms, consumers might travel thousands of miles only to stay very much in their own socio-cultural environmental bubble (Cohen 1979). Typically, mass Mediterranean packaged resort destinations can reproduce the cultural environment of British tourists (food, drinks, pubs, newspapers, satellite television, language, etc.) and only a few of the visited destination assets (sea, sand and sun and goods at a lower price than at home) are required.

Pine and Gilmore (1998) argued that companies could gain competitive advantage by differentiating experiences according to the degree of active or passive participation of individuals with the service environment. The relation with the environment could either be one of immersion (the individual is fully immersed in the experience, living the experience through all senses and often in communion with others) or absorption (the individual becomes absorbed by what he sees/does, but this implication does not necessarily involve other processes). Pine and Gilmore advocated that the more the four realms were present in an encounter, the richer the experience would be.

The approach adopted by Pine and Gilmore can be satisfying for leisure/entertainment experiences but is insufficient to translate the variety of experiences observed in the tourism world. Underneath, the four realms proposed by Pine and Gilmore have been revisited to take on board existing knowledge from the tourism field (Figure 9.1). The first axis is inspired by Cohen's work on the environmental bubble (1979) that views tourists as ranging from individuals who seek total immersion with the country visited (non-institutionalized tourists) to tourists who prefer to stay in their own environmental bubble (institutionalized tourists). The other axis

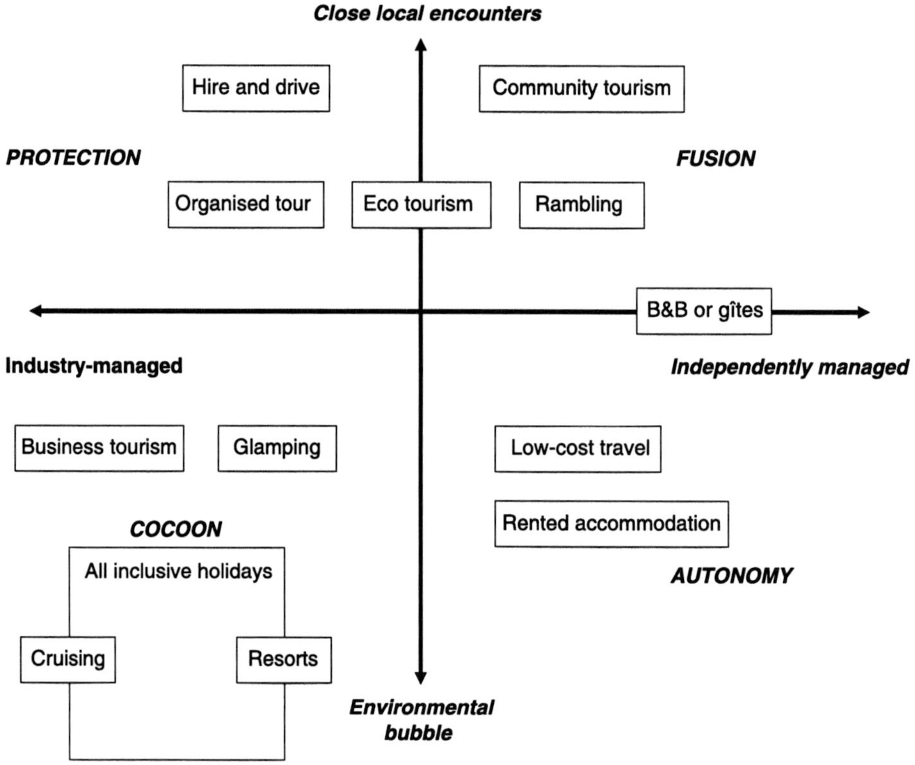

Figure 9.1 Classifying tourist experiences (adapted from Morgan *et al.* 2012).

is then composed of the willingness or not, from tourists, to purchase a product managed for them by the tourism industry or whether they want to undertake their travel independently from this industry.

By using both these axes, all of the tourists' experiences can be portrayed and the figure gives a good indication of the level and type of intervention from the tourism industry in that process. As an example, several tourist products have been placed on the map, however the sizes of the boxes are not indicative of market shares.

The first category, **COCOON,** refers to experiences where consumers seek total disconnection from everyday life and pressures. Those consumers do not necessarily want to discover the country, they will tend to stay within a known environment, with other tourists of the same nationality, a known level of comfort and references to their own culture (language, food, etc.). They seek total immersion in the holiday mood but not necessarily with the country visited. The types of products that correspond to this category are for instance integrated resorts, cruise ships, all-inclusive offers or business tourism.

The second category, **AUTONOMY**, groups consumers who seek an experience that remains close to their environmental bubble but do not rely totally on the tourism industry to organize their experience. In other words, those consumers will wish to stay within their environmental bubble but organize their holiday themselves (often for financial reasons). For instance with the advent of the Internet and low-cost airlines, consumers can organize a holiday with the same characteristics as a basic packaged product.

The third category, **FUSION**, groups experiences whereby consumers are both involved in its organization and aim to immerse themselves within the destination. This immersion can be linked to an interest in the destination's culture, natural elements and/or local inhabitants. Tourists have the need to 'feel' the destination through different senses: see, try, taste, smell, feel, etc. They appreciate the possibility to organize their own travel and seek authenticity and real connections with the destination. Products which fall in that category are varied and numerous: a hiking trip in a national park or staying with local inhabitants (*gîtes*, bed & breakfast, couch surfing, etc.).

The fourth category, **PROTECTION**, groups consumers who are in need for connections with the destination visited but who want to stay within the safety net of the tourism industry. Their experience mixes a need or some degree of discovery but the experience is partly managed by the tourism industry since consumers have some degree of fear for unknown settings. This category can group vacations such as an organized holiday led by a guide or a hire and drive holiday. The following part of the chapter will address how this variety of experiences can translate into a list of experience standards and attributes that can be considered by practitioners and academics.

Tourist experience and experiential tourism

The tourist experience is the locus of value creation within the tourism sector. Studies show that the tourism industry is based on creating unforgettable experiences (Prentice, Witt and Hamer 1998; Buhalis 2000). Offering high quality services and unforgettable experiences is then the focus of the tourist industry. Tourists travel to different places, interact with people from different cultural backgrounds, and bring back travel memories, and these travel activities become embedded within the totality of lived experiences (McCabe and Foster 2006). Thus, the tourist experience is a socially constructed term whereby the meaning of the tourist experience is associated with multiple interpretations from social, environmental, and activity components of the overall experience (Tussyadiah and Fesenmaier 2009). The attributes of socially constructed tourist experiences encompass a set of qualities such as symbolism (meaning, feelings and emotion), socialization (meeting the locals, participation), immersion, memories, etc. These qualities may be used by tourism professionals to enhance tourist experiences and immersion within the destination.

Based on a review of the tourism literature, a set of attributes can be considered by tourism professionals to define experiential tourism. This list of standards has been adapted from the works of Haugen and Erffmeyer (2004) and Hedin, Barnes and Chen (2005), and might be used as either a checklist, with a simple check to point out presence or absence of the standard, or as an evaluation form, rating each standard, for example, on a scale of one (little or none of the attribute) to five (full compliance with the standard):

- People create meaning through direct experience.
- The experience includes the people met, the places visited and the activities participated in.
- Experiential tourism can draw people into local nature, culture and history.
- Experiences can also take place in closed environments (resorts) with little contacts with local culture/nature.
- The experience includes pre-departure trip planning and post-trip follow-up, including memories.
- Experiential tourism is very personal, individual and perceived as unique for each visitor.
- Quality, memorable visitor experiences are a shared outcome between the visitor and the experience provider, but some experiences can take place independently from the provider (auto-creation).

- Experiential tourism opportunities allow for personal growth and reflect the values and interests of the individual visitor.
- Experiential tourism provides diverse experiences that match the visitor's interests and provide a sense of personal accomplishment, thereby creating their own unique memories.
- The desired outcome of experiential tourism is to achieve a complete participatory experience that provides new knowledge and experiences.
- Experiential tourism opportunities can encourage the meeting and coming together of different cultures, their problems and potential.
- Cultural elements are shared in an atmosphere of traditional or non-traditional ways of life.
- Experiential tourism involves visitors in what is being experienced rather than merely describing.
- Experiential tourism opportunities expand personal horizons.
- Experiential tourism opportunities should provide personal enrichment, enlightenment, stimulation and engagement as motivators.
- Experiential tourism attracts people to destinations and attractions.
- Experiential tourism attracts markets to merchandise.
- Experiential tourism engages all five senses.
- Experiential tourism will be laden with strong emotions and will most probably be a transformative experience.
- Experiential tourism opportunities include learning a new skill, engaging in a new activity or experiencing an existing activity differently.
- Experiential tourism includes the story of a place/person/culture.

These attributes serve as a framework for managers of service providers as they adjust and grow their enterprises in the twenty-first century. Each comparison will provide some opportunities to make small or large adjustments in current practices in order to provide more meaningful and memorable experiences for customers.The next section will go beyond the experience standards by providing a deeper theoretical context to the discussion of tourist experiences. In this part authors will include issues of a new theoretical approach, Consumer Culture Theory (CCT) to better understand the characteristics of the 'new tourist' behaviours.

The definition of the 'new tourist' through the multidisciplinary paradigm of CCT

As discussed earlier in the chapter, marketing and consumer researchers such as Arnould and Thompson (2005) and Belk and Sherry (2007) have placed the concept of 'experience' at the heart of an emerging paradigm through the philosophy of CCT. It is a multidisciplinary approach based on the works of some French sociologists such as Baudrillard (1970), Bourdieu (1980) and Certeau (1990), which are partly responsible for the emergence of a cultural and a symbolic approach in the consumption field. In consumer research, Belk and Sherry (2007: xiii) in the first conference dedicated to CCT, defined it as 'an interdisciplinary fieldencompassing macro approaches, interpretative and critical perspective of the consumer behaviour'. Following this perspective, CCT researchers take into account the social representations and the cultural practices when studying the complex behaviour of the consumer/tourist. The main objective is then to study each cultural group in relation to the meanings he provides to his consumption practices and the symbolic dimensions he expects within his experiences. Thus, adopting a cultural consumption posture through a CCT perspective, allows researchers to rethink the act of consumption as a consumer or a group participation in the identity construction process.

Therefore, aspects such as: ideology, culture, symbolism and experience are all an integral part of the individual behaviour and can't be isolated when studying consumption activities in different contexts. Since the consolidation of the multidisciplinary current of CCT, the research in the consumer field has taken a major socio-cultural and experiential turn, which requires a new analytical approach. In contrast to tourism studies, CCT has contributed to the enrichment of research methodologies in the consumption field and led researchers to overcome the cognitive and rational approaches so far applied in consumer and tourism studies by focusing on the interpretative approaches that give a central place to the individual's experience and his feelings. The following section will highlight the use of CCT as a conceptual framework to explain the main characteristics of tourist behaviours by taking into account cultural, symbolic, experiential and ideological aspects related to his tourism and consumption experiences.

The starting point of the first reflections is none other than *the tourist* who has changed status and even multiplied his functions and roles in relation to the meanings he assigns to his consumption. The underlying idea is that the Western consumer society has changed over the past decades. This has contributed to the emergence of a tourist/consumer who has new expectations and may be qualified as emotional, active, digital, experiential, etc. Thus, new consumption paradoxes and trends related to the hyperconsumption society and the omnipresence of social media have influenced the shift in market segmentation from market/product logic to a more consumer/tourist centric approach.

Following the CCT paradigm, the main characteristics of the 'new tourist' may reflect different behaviours:

1 responsible and ethical;
2 paradoxical;
3 experiential and hedonistic;
4 empowered and competent;
5 co-producing; and
6 seeking intermediation.

These characteristics have been inspired by the works of Batat (2011) who identified the main consumption patterns of the new consumer.

A *new tourist* who is responsible and ethical

The *new tourist* is very critical towards marketing discourses and particularly advertising. He expresses a responsible behaviour and engages himself within his consumption practices since he is aware of the impact of his consumption acts. This kind of responsible behaviours reflects the fact that the *new tourist* who becomes aware of his economic power, decides to consume and act with respect to his values. His main ideology is to consume and purchase consumption items only if it fits his ethical value system. The reasons that justify tourist motivations to be responsible might be: product safety, environmental impact or employees' welfare (Crane 2001). These reasons are all conscious or unconscious ways to reveal the ideological dimension of goods (Chessel and Cochoy 2004) and build a set of ethical propositions around consumption (Smith 1990). The responsible consumer acts then as a citizen who wants to learn more about the company political engagement and the fairness of its brand and/ or product.

While small-scale sustainable tourist products have developed successfully, most major actors now have some ecological/social orientations in their corporate policy even if those actions are relatively greenwashing. Recently, new forms of mass-scale tourism products have been developed or re-developed to include a stronger ecological and/or social welfare content (such as the nature village that is currently being built by Disney in Marne la Vallée: tourist accommodation in the form of a sustainable resort with a sustainable (geothermique) water park (*DLRP Times* 2011)). This evolution shows that there is now a real and significant consumer demand for sustainable products that can be compatible with commercialized, large-scale tourism products.

A *new tourist* who displays paradoxical behaviour

Some consumer researchers have been influenced by postmodern sociological analyses, which offer a different perspective on the rather paradoxical behaviour of *the new consumer*. Based on the works of the French sociologist Lyotard on the postmodern society and its paradoxes, Decrop (2008) identifies some postmodern paradoxes of consumer behaviour according to six characteristics:

1 the desire to be alone and together;
2 masculine and feminine;
3 nomadic and sedentary;
4 Kairos and Kronos;
5 real and virtual; and
6 the quest for old and new.

The first characteristic is closely related to the information and communication era where Internet, social media and mobile phones are an integral part of the consumer daily lives. These tools enable the consumer to stay permanently connected with friends and colleagues, and at the same time increase his isolation and the dehumanization of human relations. The second characteristic shows that the erosion of boundaries between masculine values (bravery, power, etc.) and feminine values (peace, kindness, etc.) enhances the paradoxical behaviour of the postmodern individual. Therefore, more and more women become independent and adopt masculine behaviours; men in turn are feminized.

The third characteristic reflects the need to be nomadic and sedentary at the same time. Indeed, the postmodern consumer is behaving in a non-rational way such as seeking for somewhere else but like at home. The fourth paradox is related to our relationship to time where kairos means the real time and the instant transformed into action while kronos refers to the measurable time flowing linearly. The fifth paradox 'real and virtual' is based on the idea of 'hyperreality' defined by the erosion of boundaries between real and virtual worlds thanks to online dating websites and realistic video games. Finally, the last paradox shows that the new consumer requires 'old' and nostalgic consumption items and experiences, but should be updated and improved by including technologies and modern comfort.

Therefore, the postmodern consumer/tourist is non-rational and may behave in very paradoxical ways (as previously discussed). It is then difficult to apply rational models of decision making because of the multiple identities of tourists as well as their paradoxical behaviours. In this sense, tourism is not only used as a form of conspicuous consumption but also as a way to perform different identities through different experiences: to be a good parent, to excel at sport, to portray oneself as a playful and fun person, to maintain or develop kinship and friendship relations, etc.

Furthermore, contemporary tourists can change the type of products consumed regularly. For instance, a family might book a two-week cultural trip in Malaysia but later on in the year will purchase a cheaper summer sun holiday based in a resort. This paradoxical behaviour can add to the complexity of tourism marketing and management, making tourism segments more amorphous perhaps, and highlighting the importance of building longer relationships between travel firms and customers, based on customer value cycles.

A *new tourist* who is emotionally and hedonically engaged

Today's tourists are in search of experiences that dazzle their senses, engage them personally, touch their hearts and stimulate their minds (Schmitt 1999), whilst indulging in fantasies, feelings and fun (Holbrook and Hirschman 1982). Consumer experiences are subjective, personal, constructed over time, and involve multiple sensations and meanings. Therefore, for the *new tourist*, hedonism and emotion are at the heart of his/her consumption and tourism experiences.

Hedonism is considered as a source of happiness and reflects different dimensions such as: playfulness, enjoyment and fun. In the recent works in the human science disciplines, academic consideration of the measuring and understanding human happiness has been the focus of various consumer and tourism studies (Holbrook and Hirschman 1982; Nicolao, Irwin and Goodman 2009; Nawijn *et al.* 2010; McCabe and Johnson 2013). Whereas some authors argue that absolute wealth and consumption level are important determinants of happiness, others hold the view that happiness depends primarily on wealth and consumption level relative to others (Hsee, Yangjie and Chen 2009). However, there is no doubt that people often use consumption experiences and purchase products to make themselves feel better or to reassure themselves of their identity. This shows that emotion and symbolic consumption are an integral part of today's consumer and tourist experiences. Gilbert and Abddullah (2004) demonstrated that tourists experience a higher sense of well-being before and after a holiday. In their study conducted in 2009 among 1,530 Dutch vacationers, Nawijn and colleagues (2010) examined the difference between vacationers and non-vacationers and the association between vacation and happiness before and after a holiday trip. The conclusions of their work show that vacationers demonstrated a higher degree of pre-trip happiness, compared to non-vacationers. Memories of holidays have also been shown to contribute to individuals' happiness through reminiscent memories (Morgan and Xu 2009) and affect different life domains such as family and social lives (Sirgy, Phillips and Rahtz 2011).

A *new tourist* who is competent and empowered

The *new tourist* is also a competent consumer because (s)he engages knowledge and skills actively to shape and determine the outcomes of their tourism experiences. This presupposes that (s)he knows how to select, organize, combine and use this set of knowledge within an environment that presents constraints and resources. The competent tourist is the one who, having constructed knowledge and competencies through his own experiences in a specific area such as tourism, is able to use them in other situations of consumption to satisfy his needs. The competent tourist thus combines knowledge, know-how and social skills that are essential to make choices and value judgments. Denegri-Knott, Zwick and Schroeder (2006) utilize the concept of the consumer/tourist empowerment to underline the ability of consumers to control choices and understand the power they hold in their relationships with travel companies. Furthermore, the consumers use the knowledge, skills and power to inform other consumers about issues they feel are important through social media.

Other authors talk about the consumer agency (Arnould and Thompson 2005), which is related to value creation and consumer/tourist performance that requires competencies and ability to create a sense of consumption activity and generate creative knowledge. This creative learning through the diversion offers a source of innovation and sustainable competitive advantage for the company.

A *new tourist* who is a co-producer

The *new tourist* becomes a producer able to create a new meaning of the company's offer (Certeau 1990) to fit with his needs. The joint production of goods and services between the company and the customer is not a new idea; for example fast food or supermarkets have gained some of their success through customer participation in order to reduce production costs. Historically, consumer participation in service production was first studied as a strategy to improve productivity by using the client as a source of free labour, thereby achieving a lower price (Fitzsimmons 1985; Mills and Morris 1986). In the CCT perspective, a number of authors have proposed to expand the notion of consumer/tourist participation to the experiential domain, as it helps to guide the consumer towards a consumption experience related or not to the marketplace, which may bring him satisfaction (Ladwein 2004). In this sense, co-production is related to active participation that reflects the consumer/tourist involvement in shaping the company's offer (Cermak, File and Price 1994).

Authors such as Cova and Dalli (2009) and Dujarier (2008) show in their works that the co-producer status of the modern consumer is a direct consequence of consumer empowerment thanks to the use of digital technology as well as ICTs and Internet as a source of information. Indeed, with the democratization of the use of digital technologies, new consumption knowledge in terms of creation and sharing information on consumption have emerged through online communities.

The *new tourist* who is seeking intermediation

New tourists have also evolved drastically in the way they relate to information provided within a service context. Indeed, contemporary tourists are still keen to learn from a destination/culture/attraction, but in a lot of instances the transmission of knowledge has taken new modes of interpretation. The dominating vision now is to provide information mixed with entertainment, an approach also known as edutainment (Hertzman, Anderson and Rowley 2008). This can take different forms: smartphone applications, interactive devices, serious games, cultural treasure hunts, live interpretation, historical re-enactments, story-telling, etc. Those new forms of interpretation respond to a need from visitors to engage with local history and culture but in a lighter approach: they want to know what is essential and important about a place but not in a detailed and formal way.

To summarize, the six characteristics of the new tourist/consumer identified through the use of a CCT perspective as a conceptual framework may open up discussions and simulate debate among consumer and tourism researchers by thinking around a number of theoretical aspects and related marketing implications. Therefore, researchers and marketers should go beyond the tangible and the cognitive side and focus more on the dimensions described above when studying consumer/tourist behaviours. This will help professionals to adapt their offers as well as co-create and share values with a consumer/tourist who is paradoxical, emotional, empowered, well informed, competent, ethical and responsible.

Conclusion

The present chapter has aimed to set the theoretical basis of experiential consumption and has investigated its applications in the specific context of tourism. The last part especially sets out to identify the main characteristics of the new tourist. Contemporary tourists belong to the fourth generation of mass tourists and they have accumulated, through individual experience and through their socialization process, an extensive experience in tourism consumption. At the start of the twenty-first century, we have recognized that tourist demand has evolved drastically, not only sustainable principles are blossoming but tourists have become more and more involved in the production and diffusion of services (co-creation, customer empowerment, etc.). Tourists also appear to be more confident in terms of what they expect out of a tourist experience. For instance, their search for highly hedonic experiences seems to be increasingly important and stronger as they have realized the necessity and benefits to their quality of life of a successful vacation.

Experiential marketing concepts have been very useful in bringing a theoretical structure to the understanding of the tourist experience. The six characteristics identified via a CCT perspective appreciate the nuances and textures of the contemporary tourist landscape and thus do not try to generalize the 'new tourist' paradigm. Indeed, these characteristics are more likely to be related to 'a' new tourist/consumer among a large variety of segments of tourists/consumers. While there are certainly consumers who are 'responsible and ethical', there are certainly large and possibility even majority segments who care little about corporate responsibility practices. For example, the emergence of a postmodern tourist with paradoxical behaviours, who subsists along with other types of tourists such as the family tourist and the traditional and the modern tourist leads tourism researchers and marketers to explore the values and desires within a consumption context where juxtaposition, fragmentation, and individualisation are an integral part of tourist behaviours and experiences.

The study of tourist behaviour also benefits from several decades of research in tourism and leisure consumption, which complements this theoretical knowledge. As a result, the understanding of the specificities of tourism consumption and of the behaviour associated with its consumption has proved to be better understood over the years. Yet, there is a need for further research on tourist experience itself and of the emotional processes at stake during the experience. The current state of the literature shows some great knowledge developments, both from a service quality point of view and also from an experiential perspective; but the years to come should provide some even more interesting research project that will benefit the understanding of experiential consumption, and especially in a tourism context.

References

Arnould, E.J. and Price, L. (1993) 'River Magic: Extraordinary Experience and the Extended Service Encounter', *Journal of Consumer Research*, 20(June): 24–5.

Arnould, E.J. and Thompson, C.J. (2005) 'Consumer Culture Theory (CCT): Twenty Years of Research', *Journal of Consumer Research*, 31(March): 868–82.

Batat, W. (2011) 'An Overview of Postmodern Research in the Consumer Behaviour Field: Towards the "New Consumer" Paradigm', *Asia-Pacific Advances in Consumer Research*, in Yi, Z., Xiao, J-J., Cotte, J. and Price, L. (eds), Vol. 9, Duluth, MN: Association for Consumer Research, pp. 304–12.

Baudrillard, J. (1970) *La Société de Consommation*. Paris: Denoël.

Belk, R.W. and Sherry, J.F. (eds) (2007) *Consumer Culture Theory*. UK: Elsevier.

Bourdieu, P. (1980) *Le Sens Pratique*. Paris: Edition de Minuit.

Bourgeon, D. and Filser, M. (1995) 'Les Apports du Modèle de Recherches d'Expériences à l'Analyse du Comportement Dans le Domaine Culturel: Une Exploration Conceptuelle et Méthodologique', *Recherche et Applications en Marketing*, 4(10): 5–25.

Buhalis, D. (2000) 'Marketing the Competitive Destination of the Future', *Tourism Management*, 21(1): 97–116.

Carù, A. and Cova, B. (2006) 'Expériences de Consommation et Marketing Expérientiel', *Revue Française de Gestion*, 162: 99–113.

Cermak, D., File, K. and Price. R. (1994) 'Customer Participation in Service Specification and Delivery', *Journal of Applied Business Research*, 10(2): 90–8.

Certeau (De), M. (1990) *L'invention du Quotidien. Arts de Faire*. Paris: Gallimard.

Chessel, M.E. and Cochoy, F. (2004) 'Autour de la Consommation Engagée: Enjeux Historiques et Politiques', *Sciences de la Société*, 62(May): 3–14.

Cohen, E. (1979) 'Rethinking the Sociology of Tourism', *Annals of Tourism Research*, 6(1): 18–35.

Cova, B. and Dalli, D. (2009) 'Working Consumers: The Next Step in Marketing Theory?', *Marketing Theory*, 9(3): 315–39.

Crane, A. (2001) 'Unpacking the Ethical Product', *Journal of Business Ethics*, 30(4): 361–73.

Crompton, J.L. (1979) 'Motivations for Pleasure Vacations', *Annals of Tourism Research*, 6(4): 408–24.

Crompton, J.L. and MacKay, S.L. (1997) 'Motives of Visitors Attending Festival Events', *Annals of Tourism Research*, 24(2): 425–39.

Decrop, A. (2008) 'Les Paradoxes du Consommateur Postmoderne', *Reflets et Perspectives de la Vie Economique*, 47(2): 85–93.

Denegri-Knott, J., Zwick, D. and Schroeder, J.E. (2006) 'Mapping Consumer Power: An Integrative Framework for Marketing and Consumer Research', *European Journal of Marketing*, 40(9–10): 950–71.

DRLP Times (2011) *Villages Nature*. Online. Available at http://dlrptimes.over-blog.fr/article-villages-nat-66938169.html.

Dujarier, M.A. (2008) *Le Travail du Consommateur. De McDo a EBay: Comment Nous Coproduisons Ce Que Nous Achetons*. Paris: La Découverte.

Edvardsson, B., Tronvoll, B. and Gruber. T. (2011) 'Expanding Understanding of Service Exchange and Value Co-Creation: A Social Construction Approach', *Journal of the Academy of Marketing Science*, 39(2): 327–39.

Firat, A.F. and Dholakia, N. (1998) *Consuming People: From Political Economy to Theatres of Consumption*. London: Sage.

Fitzsimmons, J. (1985) 'Consumer Participation and Productivity in Service Operations', *Interfaces*, 15(3): 60–7.

Gilbert, D. and Abdullah, J. (2004) 'Holiday Taking and the Sense of Well-being', *Annals of Tourism Research*, 31(1): 103–21.

Haugen, S., Becker, D. and Erffmeyer. R. (2004) 'Standards for Determining the Quality of Online MBA Education: A Survey of Accredited Programmes', *International Journal of Services and Standards*, 1(2): 193–205.

Hedin, S.R., Barnes, C.H. and Chen. J.C.H. (2005) 'AACSB 2003 Accreditation Standards: Impact on Continuous Quality Improvement', *International Journal of Services and Standards*, 1(3): 358–78.

Hertzman, E., Anderson, D. and Rowley. S. (2008) 'Edutainment Heritage Tourist Attractions: A Portrait of Visitors' Experiences at Storyeum', *Museum Management and Curatorship*, 23(2): 155–75.

Hetzel, P. (2002) *Planète Conso, Marketing Expérientiel et Nouveaux Univers de Consommation*. Paris: P.U.F.

Holbrook, M.B. and Hirschman, E.C. (1982) 'The Experiential Aspects of Consumption: Consumer Fantasy, Feelings and Fun', *Journal of Consumer Research*, 9(2): 132–40.

Hsee, C.K., Yangjie-Gu, Y.Y. and Chen. J. (2009) 'Specification Seeking: How Product Specifications Influence Consumer Preference', *Journal of Consumer Research*, 35(April): 952–66.

Krippendorf, J. (1987) *The Holiday Makers. Understanding the Impact of Leisure and Travel*. Wallingford: CABI Publishing.

Ladwein, R. (2004) 'L'expérience de Consommation et la Mise en Récit de Soi: Le Cas du Trekking', Actes des 9ème Journées de Recherche en Marketing de Bourgogne, Bourgogne.

Levy, S.J. (1959) 'Symbols for Sale', *Harvard Business Review*, 37(July): 117–24.

Lipovetsky, G. (2003) 'La Société d'Hyperconsommation', *Le Débat* no 124.

Lyotard, J.F. (1979) *La Condition Postmoderne*. Paris: Les Éditions de Minuit.

McCabe, S. and Foster, C. (2006) 'The Role and Function of Narrative in Tourist Interaction', *Journal of Tourism and Cultural Change*, 4(3): 194–215.

McCabe, S. and Johnson, S. (2013) 'The Happiness Factor in Tourism: Subjective Well-being and Social Tourism', *Annals of Tourism Research*, 41: 42–65.

Mcintosh, R.W., Goeldner, C.R. and Ritchie. J.R.B. (1995) 'Pleasure Travel Motivations', *Tourism: Principles, Practices and Philosophies*, 167–90.

Mills, P.K. and Morris, J.H. (1986) 'Clients as "Partial" Employer of Service Organizations: Role Development in Client Participation', *Academy of Management Review*, 11(4): 726–35.
Morgan, N. and Pritchard, A. (1998) *Tourism Promotion and Power: Creating Images, Creating Identities*. New York: Wiley.
Moutinho, L. (1987) 'Consumer Behaviour in Tourism', *European Journal of Marketing*, 21(10): 5–44.
Nawijn, J., Marchand, M.A., Veenhoven, R. and Vingerhoets, A.J. (2010) 'Vacationers Happier, but Most not Happier After a Holiday', *Applied Research Quality Life*, 5: 35–47.
Nicolao, L., Irwin, J.R. and Goodman. J.K. (2009) 'Happiness for Sale: Do Experiential Purchases Make Consumers Happier than Material Purchases?', *Journal of Consumer Research*, 36 (August): 188–98.
Oliver, R.L. (1980) 'A Cognitive Model of the Antecedents and Consequences of Customer Satisfaction', *Journal of Marketing Research*, 17(November): 460–69.
O'Sullivan, E. L. and Spangler, K. (1998) *Experience Marketing: Strategies for the New Millennium*. State College (PA): Venture Publishing.
Pine, B.J. and Gilmore, J.H. (1998) 'Welcome to the Experience Economy', *Harvard Business Review*, July–August: 97–105.
Prahalad, C.K. and Ramaswamy, V. (2003) 'The New Frontier of Experience Innovation', *Sloan Management Review*, Summer: 12–18.
Prentice, R.C., Witt, S.F. and Hamer, C. (1998) 'Tourism as an Experience: The Case of Heritage Parks', *Annals of Tourism Research*, 25(1): 1–24.
Richins, M.L. (1997) 'Measuring Emotions in the Consumption Experience', *Journal of Consumer Research*, 24(2): 127–46.
Schmitt, B. H. (1999) *Experiential Marketing: How to Get Customers to Sense, Feel, Think, Act, and Relate to Your Company and Brands*. New York: Free Press.
Sheth, J.N. (1980) 'The Surpluses and Shortages in Consumer Behavior Theory and Research', *Journal of the Academy of Marketing Science*, 7(4): 414–27.
Sirgy, M., Phillips, R. and Rahtz, D. (2011) *Community Quality-of-Life Indicators: Best Cases III*. Netherlands: Springer Publishers Dordrechet.
Smith, N.C. (1990) *Morality and the Market – Consumer Pressure for Corporate Accountability*. London: Routledge.
Stamboulis, Y. and Skayannis, P. (2003) 'Innovation Strategies and Technology for Experience-Based Tourism', *Tourism Management*, 24: 35–47.
Tussyadiah, I.P. and Fesenmaier, D.R. (2009) 'Mediating Tourist Experiences: Access to Places via Shared Videos', *Annals of Tourism Research*, 36(1): 24–40.
Tynan, C. and McKennie, S. (2009) 'Experience Marketing: A Review and Assessment', *Journal of Marketing Management*, 25(5-6): 501–17.
United Nations World Tourism Organization (1995) *UNWTO Technical Manual: Collection of Tourism Expenditure Statistics*. Online. Available: <http://pub.unwto.org/WebRoot/Store/Shops/Infoshop/Products/1034/1034-1.pdf> (accessed 24 July 2012).
Vargo, S.L. and Lusch, R.F. (2004) 'Evolving to a New Dominant Logic for Marketing', *Journal of Marketing*, 68: 1–17.
Westbrook, R.A. (1987) 'Product/Consumption-Based Affective Responses and Post Purchase Processes', *Journal of Marketing Research*, 25(August): 258–70.

10

Experience, co-creation and technology

Issues, challenges and trends for technology enhanced tourism experiences

Barbara Neuhofer and Dimitrios Buhalis

Introduction

Consumers are increasingly striving for experiences. As products and services have become interchangeable and replicated, the search for unique, compelling and memorable experiences in the context of tourism has become a key notion. In tourism marketing, the concept of the experience economy has long provided a valuable vehicle to design, stage and deliver experiences to consumers and gain competitive advantage. In the past years, the advent of two major shifts to the field of marketing has challenged the current understanding of tourism experiences. The concept of the experience economy has evolved, as consumers have become more active and empowered in playing a part in co-creating their own experiences in quest for personal growth (Prahalad and Ramaswamy 2004).

In addition to the development of the notion of co-creation, a second major change has taken place. With the advances in the field of technology, tourism experiences are not only co-created but more than ever technology-mediated (Tussyadiah and Fesenmaier 2009). The proliferation of recent information and communication technologies (ICTs) has had a great influence on society and people's everyday lives and has implied new challenges for the creation of experiences. With the dynamics of empowered consumers adopting emerging technologies for travel, traditional roles and processes of experiences creation have changed. These recent developments have led to the discussion of a new paradigm in the field of marketing, moving from Experience 1.0 (the experience economy) to the Experience 2.0 (co-creation experiences), towards a new era of experiences, namely Experience 3.0 technology enhanced tourism experiences. A rethinking in marketing to reflect upon possible potentials, issues, challenges and future trends of tourism experiences is needed.

In this light, this chapter has the aim, by drawing upon experience, co-creation and technology literature, to provide a discussion of the issues, challenges and trends for the creation of technology enhanced tourism experiences. The chapter is divided into three main sections. The first part reviews the theoretical development of tourism experiences in the field of marketing, by briefly covering its definitional basis, historical evolution and emergence of latest concepts. The evolution in the experience economy, from the staging of experiences *for* the consumer to co-creating experiences *with* the consumer is discussed subsequently. The second part reviews the dynamic technological advances, with particular emphasis on the mobile sector, and provides new insights into their role in enhancing the co-creation of tourism experiences. The section highlights a paradigm shift in marketing and introduces the concept of technology enhanced tourism experiences. It outlines how tourism organizations can exploit the full potential of the plethora of ICTs to enhance the tourism experience co-creation process throughout all stages of the travel. The third and final part of this chapter discusses practical implications of this development for tourism marketing and provides an outlook on the future agenda for tourism marketing research.

Tourism experiences: theoretical developments

Definitions of tourism experiences

What are technology enhanced tourism experiences? To answer this question for the purpose of this chapter, as the underlying concept, it is crucial to start with understanding the origins and the evolution of the notion of tourism experiences. Experience, first noted in the 1960s, has been defined as a vague and highly ambiguous term, which encompasses a specific occurrence that a person would have in everyday life. In the domain of marketing, the notion of experiences emerged with Holbrook and Hirschman's (1982) seminal work postulating that consumer behaviour is not mere information processing but constitutes an active engagement in an emotional consumption experience. Succeeding this revolution, experiences have become a key concept in numerous fields including consumer behaviour, marketing and the experience economy. In the specific context of tourism, experiences have initially been portrayed as a quest for novelty and a reversal of everyday life (Cohen 1979). These early attempts were followed by a stream of literature focusing on capturing single elements, typologies, dimensions and chronological stages to develop a more holistic understanding of the tourism experience construct (Killion 1992, Otto and Ritchie 1996). Despite the numerous approaches having integrated perspectives from different social sciences, there is no consensus to date on a single definition of the tourism experience. Instead, it needs to be recognized in its full complexity with various influences, stages, elements, outcomes and types, all shaping and contributing to its current understanding (Jennings *et al.* 2009).

Experiences have always played a primary role in both tourism research and practice. The ongoing theoretical progress in the area underpins its importance and unabated relevance. In recent years, the study of experiences has received a revived interest, which is reflected in the amount of state-of-the-art literature discussing the concept (e.g. Cutler and Carmichael 2010; Morgan *et al.* 2010; Darmer and Sundbo 2008; Tung and Ritchie 2011; McCabe *et al.* 2012). With the tourism industry being subject to constant change, the nature of experiences is evolving alike, requiring new ways for understanding the design and the creation of successful experiences. For tourism marketing it is paramount to appraise the key developments forming the theoretical and practical understanding to date as well as to capture the latest changes, trends and challenges. For this purpose, the subsequent section provides a progress of *experience generations* that both encompasses a synthesis of the major theoretical milestones of the past and sheds light on some of the latest advances in the area.

Experience 1.0: the experience economy

In the course of the past decades, society has undergone several fundamental shifts. People have abandoned the idea of buying simple products and services and started to seek experiences by consuming products and services instead (Morgan *et al.* 2010). In the 1990s, this growing trend led to the emergence of a number of different key concepts, including the dream society (Jensen 1999), the entertainment economy (Wolf 1999) and the experience economy (Pine and Gilmore 1999). Pine and Gilmore (1999), in coining the renowned term experience economy, provided one of the most seminal contributions marking a new era in marketing. Their core proposition is the consumers' pursuit of memorable experiences in the context of consumption and the progression of economic value. In a market characterized by globalization, deregulation, advances in technologies and intensified competition, companies were forced to find new ways to differentiate their offers (Prahalad and Ramaswamy 2004).

The experience economy hit the zeitgeist of the time as a key instrument to yield differentiation, added value and competitive advantage. In practice, the principal idea for businesses was to no longer compete in terms of price but in terms of the distinctive value of the experience provided. For the years to follow, the experience economy has provided an unprecedented guide for strategic staging, managing and delivering experiences to consumers among a variety of contexts and industries. Particularly fostered by the adoption of emerging technologies, such as interactive games, online spaces and virtual reality, it was possible to meet the demand and create ever-more immersive consumer experiences (Pine and Gilmore 1998). Despite its perpetual popularity in both marketing theory and practice, the experience economy has however received critique due to its capitalist thinking (Boswijk *et al.* 2007) and the company's prominent role in initiating and producing experiences (Binkhorst *et al.* 2010).

Experience 2.0: co-creation experiences

With an evolution in society, characterized by consumers being active, powerful and connected, thanks to social information and communication technologies, there has been a transformation in the traditional company–consumer power relationship (Ramaswamy 2009). Subsequently, the orchestrated design of experiences has been considered no longer suitable to reflect the needs, wants and roles of contemporary consumers. With technologies allowing for multiple stakeholders to be connected more than ever before, the consumer has assumed a much bigger role as an active prosumer of the experience. In recognizing this change, Prahalad and Ramaswamy (2004) propose a balance between companies and consumers as equal partners in co-creating the experience. This milestone has advanced the notion of the experience economy and introduced its successor generation. Co-creation represents a new paradigm for marketing. In widely replacing the pre-existing service-dominant views it has marked the beginning of a novel understanding of *how* and *by whom* services and experiences are created. The consumer has become the central element in both the experience production and consumption process, which implied that the first point of interaction is no longer to be found at the end of the value chain. Rather, it is framed as a collective and collaborative process of interactions between individuals and companies. Co-creation manifests itself as a convergence of production and consumption and represents an encounter in which consumer experiences are co-created and unique value is extracted (Prahalad and Ramaswamy 2004).

The notion of value creation *with* the consumer rather than *for* the consumer has been particularly advanced by Vargo and Lusch (2004) who introduced the concept of value-in-use in service-dominant logic (S-D logic). Whilst historically value has always been co-produced, it was viewed as a give and get dichotomy of benefits and sacrifices (Zeithaml *et al.* 1988), neglecting the role of the consumer in the co-creation of value (Sandström *et al.* 2008). Value however is not inherently existent, but for value to emerge, the experience needs to be co-created by the consumer. In ascribing the consumer the role of a collaborator, this perspective highlights two main arguments suggesting that it a) involves the consumer's participation in the creation of the core offering itself and b) 'value can only be created with and determined by the user in the "consumption" process and through use' (Vargo and Lusch 2006: 284). Accordingly, this argument links back to the earlier raised criticism of the experience economy, i.e. that experiences cannot be simply designed and delivered. What can be created instead are the necessary prerequisites and a value proposition, as an intermediary connection of companies towards consumers generating their own value (Vargo *et al.* 2008). For marketing, the opportunities subsequently lie in recognising this fundamental shift and adapting the experience and value creation to these new assumptions. The locus of experience co-creation is to acknowledge the tourist as the central point embodying multiple roles as:

1 the consumer of the service and experience;
2 the co-creator of the experience and value;
3 the co-creator of the experience space; and
4 the extractor and judge of the value at the same time.

The key principle therefore is to recognize the individual tourist as the dynamic hub, around which companies, stakeholders and other consumers orbit. In advancing the theoretical argument, recent literature suggests a myriad of possibilities of interactions, as consumers not only co-create with companies but also among each other (Baron and Harris 2010; Baron and Warnaby 2011; Huang and Hsu 2010). Organizations thus need to nurture an environment that facilitates not only its interactions *with* consumers (B2C), but allows for interactions *among* consumers and consumer communities (C2C). Accordingly, the tourism industry has unprecedented opportunities to facilitate co-created experiences and value on multiple levels of engagement and spaces. As consumers are in a constant search for experiences, co-creation represents a unique source of added value, innovation and competitive advantage (*Shaw et al.* 2011). While it is still fairly novel, Neuhofer *et al.* (2012) however urge that the tourism industry needs to strategically innovate and identify new sources to add value to co-creation experiences by means of instrumentalising technologies. With a plethora of ICTs available, consumers are always connected, which unfolds new possibilities for tourists to proactively co-create experiences and value in every step of the consumption process. The co-creation environment must therefore embrace the potential brought by emerging ICTs (van Limburg 2012). This chapter, in having reviewed the developments until the point of co-creation, now turns to introducing technologies as a strategic means for the creation of technology enhanced tourism experiences, marking a novel era for tourism marketing.

Experience 3.0: technology enhanced tourism experiences – a new paradigm for tourism marketing

In recent years it has become evident that consumer empowerment and co-creation have been particularly fostered by one factor, namely technology. ICTs have caused a drastic impact by changing not only society and industries but by transforming the nature of service and experience provision. In light of this evolution, we need to understand how to exploit the full potential of ICTs, as an integral part for the creation of contemporary tourism experiences and value. The following section aims to shed light on this issue by conceptually integrating experience, co-creation and technology within the concept of technology enhanced tourism experiences. For this purpose, it assesses the most recent developments of ICTs within the tourism industry. While reviewing emerging technologies, such as the Web 2.0, social media and a range of social networking sites (covered in Part 8 of this book), this chapter places particular emphasis on mobile technologies for the creation of tourism experiences.

It tackles the advancements of mobile services and the mobile tourist and its implications for tourism experiences, co-creation and value. In introducing the notion of Experiences 3.0: technology enhanced tourism experiences, the chapter discusses a paradigm shift in tourism marketing, the factors contributing towards this shift and offers a juxtaposition of the characteristics of Experiences 1.0/2.0/3.0 underlining this evolution. To allow for a better practical understanding, the chapter takes a closer look at novel experience creation processes with respect to the individuals involved (*who*) and the travel stages comprised (*where/when*). The discussion is supported by a range of best-practice examples demonstrating its current realization and highlighting its potential for future experience creation.

ICTs' impact on the tourism industry

In the twenty-first century, society has been undergoing a number of fundamental changes. One of the most far-reaching shifts regards the adoption of technologies in people's everyday lives. The proliferation of ICTs, such as computers and the Internet gave rise to the knowledge-based economy, characterized by new ways in which information has become available. The importance of information and communication is not only prevalent in society but across various industries, including tourism. As a dynamically developing sector, the tourism industry has always been in the forefront of technology (Sheldon 1997). With information being the so-called lifeblood of the travel industry (Sheldon 1997), technologies have induced an information revolution that has caused entire tourism structures to change.

In allowing for better access and transparency of information (Hall 2005), ICTs have fostered an increasing consumer independence to access information online (Buhalis and Licata 2002) and at the same time induced a decreasing importance of traditional travel distributions. Due to the intangible, heterogeneous and perishable nature of the tourism product (Buhalis and Jun 2011), information and communication tools have become essential for presentation and description of information, prices, reviews and opinions online. Despite allowing for information, ICTs have become instrumental in interacting and engaging with consumers more effectively. In particular, the emergence of social consumer-oriented technologies has revolutionized tourism. The Internet and its successive advances in the Web 2.0 have represented one of the most critical technological developments over the past years (Dwivedi *et al.* 2012; Hays *et al.* 2013; Xiang and Gretzel 2010) by turning the Internet into an immense space of networking and collaboration (Sigala 2009). A wide range of social media, such as networking sites, blogs or wikis, have enabled consumers to interact, collaborate and share content, opinions and experiences to an unprecedented scale. In addition to the Web 2.0, a further development has implied one of the most significant changes to tourism, namely mobile technologies.

Mobile ICTs and mobile tourists

Mobility has been identified as one of the four mega trends next to globalization, communication and virtuality, as identified by Egger and Buhalis (2008). The rapid technological development has led to a massive mobility in terms of the physical movement of products, services and people and at the same time encouraged the mobility and ubiquity of technological artifacts themselves (Gretzel and Jamal 2009). Society is characterized by a 'mobilities paradigm', reflected in the increasingly mobile nature of people, travel and tourism (Sheller and Urry 2006). People travel more often for work, study or leisure, rendering tourism a simple extension of the mobile everyday life. As a result, the advances in the mobile market are highly relevant to tourism, as one of the industries that can use the advantages of the mobile information medium most (Brown and Chalmer 2003).

Mobile devices function as 'transportable smart computers' that can be accessed almost without limit (Wang *et al.* 2012) causing a transformation in travel. By being implemented on the move (Schmidt-Belz *et al.* 2002), stationary access has been widely replaced and information has become accessible anywhere and anytime (Balasubramanian *et al.* 2002). This resulted in a gradual revolution of tourist behaviour in shifting from a simple 'sit and search' to a dynamic 'roam and receive' behaviour (Pihlström 2008). Moreover, the integration of technological prerequisites, including GPS, compass and maps, gave rise to numerous services, such as location based services (LBS), context based services (CBS) and augmented reality (AR).

In allowing for geographical positioning and access to location and context relevant information, these services have become a key tool of the mobile twenty-first century and particularly the tourism industry (Egger and Jooss 2010). As tourists are connected to their mobile device, traditional tourism services, such as information, entertainment, shopping or navigation have become amplified, as tourism providers and consumers are able to dynamically connect, exchange and engage through the mobile device online (Green 2002). Thus, with a plethora of mobile services at the tourist's disposal which are accessible almost *anywhere* and *anytime*, it is now possible to connect with *anyone* at *any stage* of travel, opening up new opportunities for multiplied levels of co-creation of experiences and value. Given the advancements of the Internet, the Web 2.0 and the mobile sector, ICTs represent the key instrument of change by transforming the way travel experiences are created. Due to their increasing mobility and ubiquitousness, ICTs are an essential part of the entire travel experience, as the mobile tourist is empowered to use ICTs to create more participatory and personalized technology-enabled experiences. With these prospects in mind, this chapter now turns to introduce the latest experience generation, namely technology enhanced tourism experiences.

Paradigm shift towards technology enhanced tourism experiences

To understand this new generation of experiences for tourism marketing, it is crucial to capture the most fundamental changes, whereby it is not technology on functional terms but rather its implementation into experiences which is of relevance. Synthesizing the developments within society, tourism and the field of technology, it appears that four main factors have contributed towards the paradigm shift of technology enhanced tourism experiences. These include consumer empowerment, a dynamic market environment, information and communication technologies revolution and competitive companies. Figure 10.1 below presents a graphical overview highlighting the key components and influences which have been touched upon in this chapter so far.

In its core Figure 10.1 represents three major components conceptually framing technology enhanced tourism experiences. First, it constitutes the tourist's personal subjective *experience* (Larsen 2007) at the moment of value creation (Andersson 2007) occurring before, during and after the travel (Aho 2001). The second component is *co-creation* describing the process that tourism experiences and value are conjointly created between the tourist, the provider and co-consumers involved in the particular context of consumption (Prahalad and Ramaswamy

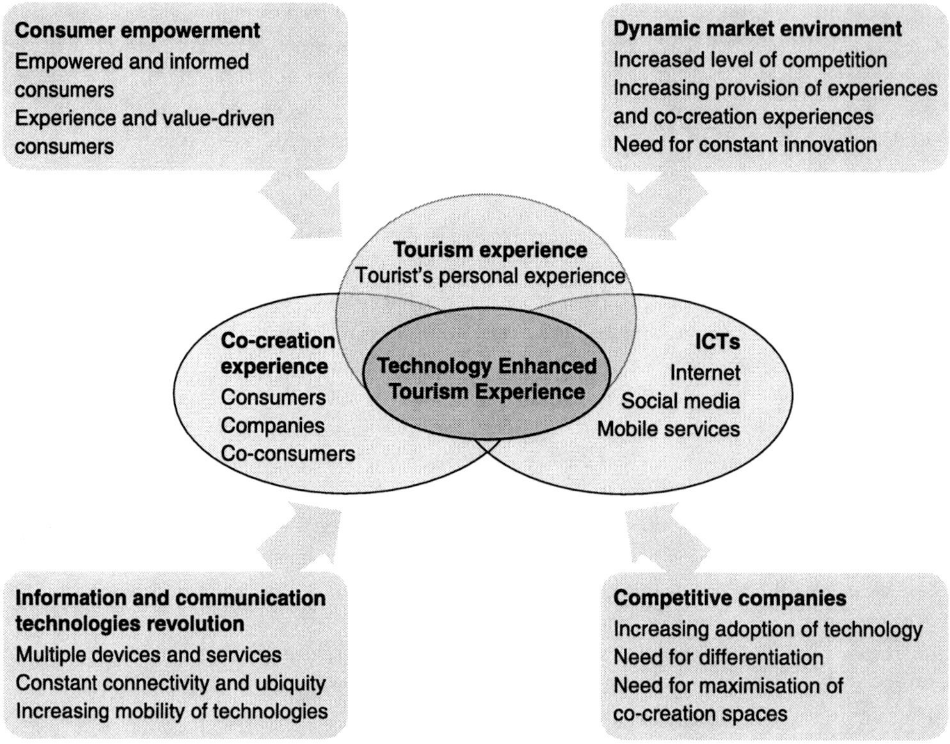

Figure 10.1 Paradigm shift towards technology enhanced tourism experiences.

2004). The third component represents *ICTs*, which in different manifestations, such as the Internet, social media or mobile services, facilitate the co-creation of enhanced tourism experiences and value (Neuhofer *et al.* 2012).

Surrounding the inner circle, four factors were critical in allowing for an emergence of technology enhanced tourism experiences. *Consumer empowerment* is characterized by the shift from passive to active consumers driven by their search for more meaningful experiences. With a dynamic *market environment*, characterized by increased competition, need for constant innovation and creation of compelling experiences, businesses are faced with ever-more competitiveness. In a response to this market force, companies have become highly *competitive* in order to reduce commodification and differentiate themselves by creating more valuable experiences and maximizing the opportunities for co-creation. In this respect, ICTs have been suggested as key instrument to facilitate and enrich this process. By exploiting its full potential, companies have taken advantage of the range of services available to engage with consumers, not only online in the pre/post stage of travel, but due to the mobility of devices, on the move along every step of the journey.

Having outlined the elements framing technology enhanced tourism experiences, it is equally important to take a closer inspection at the differences that make this type distinct from previous experience generations. Table 10.1 presents the theoretical development of tourism experiences and offers an overview in juxtapositioning the advancements from Experience 1.0 (the experience economy), Experience 2.0 (co-creation experiences) to the latest paradigm of Experience 3.0 (technology enhanced tourism experiences). While prior experiences were characterized by company-focused approaches, we have now moved towards an active,

Table 10.1 Comparison of experiences

Experience 1.0	*Experience 2.0*	*Experience 3.0*
Passive provision	Active co-creation	Holistic technology enhanced co-creation
Physical staging	Physical co-creation	Physical and virtual co-creation
Experience on-site	Experience on-site	Extended experience in the pre-travel, on-site and post-travel stage
Company staging	Company engaging and co-creating	Company co-creating and technology-enhancing
Standardized, mass produced experience	Customized co-creation experience	Rich, personalized, connected, co-constructed experience
One-way delivery (company to consumer)	Two-way engagement (company and consumer)	Multi-level engagement (company, consumer and surrounding connected network of providers, co-consumers, and social networks)
Innovation by transforming services into experiences	Innovation by transforming experiences into co-creation experiences	Innovation by transforming co-creation experiences into rich technology enhanced tourism experiences

participatory approach of experience creation. Facilitated by ICTs, experiences have become multiplied in terms of consumer participation, engagement and spaces, resulting in a connected, rich and more personalized experience and value extraction.

Elaborating on the notion that ICTs constitute an integral part of tourism experiences, a change of perspective in marketing is needed. Co-creation needs to be open for the potential inherent in technology. To take the lead in creating more compelling experiences, it is therefore not sufficient for tourism marketing and organizations to only allow for co-creation but it is paramount that they uncover the potential of ICTs for experience creation (Neuhofer *et al.* 2012). Innovation is one of the biggest decommoditizers to create something new, differentiated and valuable (Pine and Korn 2011). In this particular respect, this means to exploit one of the most decisive resources of innovation, namely technology to generate Experience 3.0: technology enhanced tourism experiences offering a new point of departure for innovative experience creation. Only those making the shift to instrumentalize ICTs for enhanced co-creation will be able to increase their value proposition, reduce commodification and gain competitive advantage. The future success of companies will therefore lie with those who are able to realize technology enhanced tourism experiences.

Realizing technology enhanced tourism experiences in practice

To most effectively implement this concept in tourism practice, it is necessary to fully understand the processes involved in this endeavour on a practical level. For this purpose, this chapter continues by breaking down the experience creation process and taking a closer look at the single components involved. Figure 10.2 provides a graphical overview, representing the components involved in the dynamic multi-stage and multi-individual co-creation process of technology enhanced tourism experiences.

This chapter now seeks to assess the following elements in detail, namely:

- *Individuals*: who is involved in the co-creation of technology enhanced tourism experiences?
- *Stages*: where/when are technology enhanced tourism experiences created?

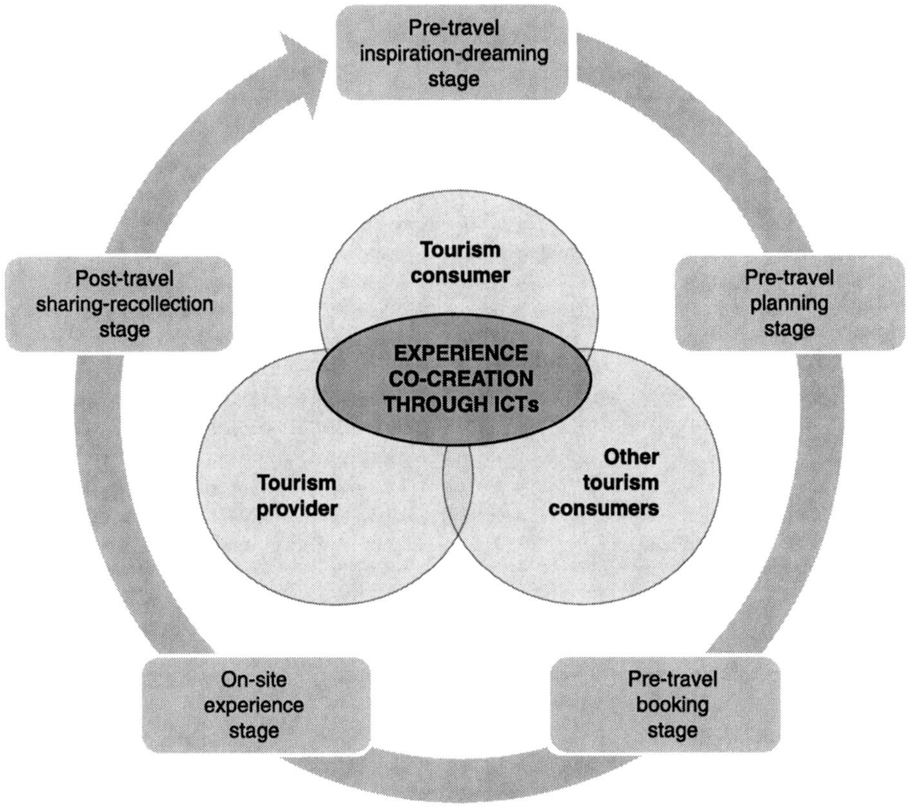

Figure 10.2 Co-creation process: technology enhanced tourism experiences.

Individuals: tourists, consumers, tourism providers and co-consumers

Technology enhanced tourism experiences imply new ways of how consumers interact with companies and consumer communities. ICTs have fostered a transformation towards inter-connected and co-creating prosumers in a technology enabled experience environment. Recent literature confirms that the range of ICTs available support co-creation experiences in a number of different ways (Gretzel and Jamal 2009; Tussyadiah and Fesenmaier 2007; Tussyadiah and Fesenmaier 2009). The Internet, for instance, provides a valuable platform for the interaction of suppliers and consumers. It represents a multi-purpose medium that:

1 gives consumers more control;
2 empowers them to establish closer relationships with the company; and
3 encourages them to actively co-create their experiences.

This active role of the tourist has been particularly fostered by the collective and collaborative space of Web 2.0 technologies. The Web 2.0 is one of the most relevant technological developments that reflect the paradigm shift towards technology enhanced tourism experiences. It enables consumers to become 'co-marketers, co-producers and co-designers of their service experiences by providing them a wide spectrum of value' (Sigala 2009: 1345). The plethora of social interaction tools in the Web 2.0, including blogs, videos, wikis, fora, chat rooms and podcasts, have encouraged individuals to generate content and share their experiences online at home or through mobile devices while being on the move and in turn co-create their experiences more than ever before (Ramaswamy 2009).

Due to the proliferation of the Internet, constant connectivity of mobile technologies, and engaging nature of social media tools, co-creation experiences between individuals are maximized. In fact, there is evidence that interactions between individuals have 'exploded on an unprecedented scale everywhere in the value creation system' (Ramaswamy 2009: 17).

This means that through ICTs, co-creation is no longer only occurring between companies and consumers (B2C) but increasingly among other consumers and the social network which enforces consumer-to-consumer (C2C) co-creation on all levels. As a result, with new forms of social technologies continuing to emerge over the next years, experience co-creation is expected to flourish even more. It will become crucial that tourism marketers exploit the tools of the Web 2.0 to allow for more meaningful interrelations with tourists and among tourists by building platforms and spaces to interact, comment and share experiences.

Stages: multiple stages of the travel process

By integrating ICTs, co-creation experiences are taken to a whole new level in terms of temporal and geographical dimensions of when/where experiences can be created. ICTs surround the tourist anywhere, at any time in any travel stage. This leads to unprecedented opportunities to co-create experiences everywhere along the value creation system, i.e. the whole customer journey. The tourism experience has been recognized as a multi-phase phenomenon in the past (Clawson and Knetch 1966; Craig-Smith and French 1994). However, ICTs enforce these dimensions by facilitating experience creation long before the actual service encounter, on-site and after the tourist's return to his/her home environment (Fotis *et al.* 2011; Huang *et al.* 2010; Tussyadiah and Fesenmaier 2009). Thereby, ICTs are adopted for information search, comparison, decision making, travel planning, booking, communication, and sharing of experiences. Depending on the specific task, a wide range of tools is used to facilitate and enhance the experience (Buhalis and Law 2008; Gretzel *et al.* 2006), including the Internet, virtual communities or Second Life (Binkhorst and Den Dekker 2009), social networking platforms, blogs or micro-blogging, such as Twitter (Wang and Fesenmaier 2004), virtual worlds or social networking sites (Shaw *et al.* 2011), Facebook, YouTube or Wikipedia (Ramaswamy 2009). Businesses across all sectors of the travel and tourism industry therefore need to capture their own peculiarities and resources and assess where they can best implement technology to facilitate experience co-creation, not only on-site but in all stages of the travel.

Pre-Travel Stage: Getting inspired, planning, decision-making, booking. With the emergence of the Internet, social media and virtual worlds, tourists are now empowered to experience tourism destinations before the physical travel. By using ICTs, the pre-travel phase has a high potential for enhancing co-creation distinctively. Tourists start dreaming, seek for inspiration and information and look for opinions and advice from others (Xiang 2011). The range of social media tools available, such as Facebook, Twitter, YouTube, TripAdvisor and more recently Pinterest, assist tourists to experience potential hotels, destinations and attractions prior to travelling. In these online environments, some destinations, such as Sweden, Thailand and Puerto Rico have already successfully demonstrated co-creation by encouraging users to upload and share images, stories and videos with the travel community (Buhalis and Wagner 2013). This underlines the importance to not only provide tourist consumers with information, but actively connect and engage to enhance their pre-holiday experience by co-creating with them in the available spaces online (Huang *et al.* 2010). Moreover, virtual realities, such as Second

Life, by offering an immersive computer-generated tourism environment, have particularly fostered interaction and co-creation experiences through avatars online (Guttentag 2010; Kohler *et al.* 2011).

On-Site Travel Stage: Experiencing the tourism destination. The on-site travel phase is the most intensive phase with the highest potential for the co-creation of experience and value (Neuhofer *et al.* 2012). In this phase, different technologies can enhance the experience while moving through the physical space. Mobile technologies play a key role (Egger and Jooss 2010), by allowing for information retrieval anywhere and at any time (Wang *et al.* 2012). Emerging mobile services, such as location based and context based services, gamification or augmented reality apps (Buhalis and Wagner 2013) all contribute to enhance the tourist's place experience on-site (Tussyadiah and Zach 2011). It allows them to access information, media, booking sites and recommendations, which are relevant to the tourist's current geographical location and context, including season, weather, time of the day, situation and preferences. Furthermore, the use of augmented reality applications enables tourists to overlay reality with virtual spatial information and points of interests to enhance the tourist's entire travel experience in the physical world (Yovcheva *et al.* 2013).

The role of ICTs during the holiday is thus to support tourists in the physical environment and stay connected in the online space at the same time. By being interconnected to social networking sites, such as Facebook or Twitter, tourists can share, comment and co-create with friends, peers, tourism providers, and other consumers while being immersed in the tourism destination (Tussyadiah and Fesenmaier 2009). This means that tourists no longer only co-create with their physical surrounding, e.g. destination, hotels, attractions or other tourists but are now empowered to co-create with their entire network in a virtual co-creation space (Neuhofer *et al.* 2012). Thus, tourism providers need to make use of technologies in order to fully exploit co-creation with the tourist both in the physical and virtual space.

Post-Travel Stage: Remembering, sharing, recollecting. Besides their integration in the pre- and during travel stage, ICTs play an important role after the tourist's return to the home environment. In the post-travel stage ICTs principally serve to engage, recollect, remember and share experiences with destinations, users worldwide and their social network alike (Fotis *et al.* 2011). For instance, tourists can post pictures on Facebook, share videos on YouTube or write reviews and recommendations on TripAdvisor, which provides major opportunities for destinations to engage, build trust and more long-lasting relationships (Buhalis and Wagner 2013).

It is evident that by integrating ICTs, tourism providers, tourists and other consumers are able to co-create experiences and value throughout all stages of travel, including the pre-travel inspiration, planning, booking stages, during the on-site destination stage and in the post-travel recollection stage. Mobile technologies particularly benefit tourists to be constantly connected and co-create experiences and value with a multiplicity of individuals and places. In this vein, technology enhanced tourism experiences can be considered a new paradigm for marketing that maximizes levels of engagement and co-creation with multiple individuals in physical, online and virtual spaces throughout all stages of travel. In the field of tourism marketing, ICTs will be the decisive elements for differentiation, innovation and future competitiveness of experiences. In order for marketers to develop a better understanding of how to create this new type of experiences, insights can be gained by exploring how these experiences are currently realized across the tourism industry. For this purpose, Table 10.2 provides an overview of a number of best-practice industry examples from which marketers could learn how to successfully create technology enhanced tourism experiences in practice.

In outlining these diverse use scenarios of organizations from a variety of industries, including the tourism, hospitality, cruise and aviation sector, it becomes evident that not one single but a

Table 10.2 Industry examples of technology enhanced tourism experiences

Industry examples	*Technology enhanced tourism experience*
Hospitality experiences	
Inamo Restaurant London	Enhanced dining experience through eTable technology
Sol Melia Hotels	Enhanced guest experience through social media person-to-person interaction between staff and guests
Destination experiences	
Visit Britain	Enhanced co-creation and engagement; mobile, user-generated application Love UK
Thailand	Enhanced pre-destination experience through websites featuring videos, images and user-generated stories
New Zealand	Enhanced pre-travel experience through interactive trip planner with integrated maps, price range and activities
Hong Kong	Enhanced destination navigation through augmented reality applications for more space information
Cruise experience	
Royal Caribbean	Enhanced on-board experience through digital signage to get directions, restaurant options, events, guest service etc.
Norwegian	Enhanced cruise experience through Norwegian iConcierge app to make reservations and check activities and communicate with other smart phone users
Airline experiences	
British Airways	Enhanced in-flight customer experience through mobile technology use for cabin crew
KLM	Enhanced co-creation through social media engagement; facilitate pre-travel C2C co-creation through social seating programme

whole spectrum of technology enhanced tourism experiences can be created. Whether it is co-creation with consumers through social media engagement (Visit Britain), interactive travel planners and platforms (Thailand, New Zealand) or the facilitation of customer-to-customer co-creation (KLM), the potential use applications for ICTs are manifold. Whatever type of experience is created, the industry needs to follow the underlying principles, which are:

1 to put the tourist consumer and his/her needs first;
2 allow for an active involvement in the co-creation process; and
3 understand, based on the particularities of the sector, how to implement ICTs to enhance this process best.

Conclusions and outlook on the future

The developments of experiences, consumer co-creation and technologies have caused a significant impact on tourism marketing in offering both unprecedented opportunities and at the same time rising challenges for experience creation in the future. This chapter had the aim to critically reflect upon the advances up to date and discuss a paradigm shift towards the creation of technology enhanced tourism experiences. It has first provided a review of the theoretical developments of experiences and discussed that the biggest challenge, and at the same time, opportunity is to abandon dated company-led experience creation approaches and keep up with the current movement towards consumer empowerment and emergences in the field of technology. To do so, tourism marketing will need to adapt to:

1 the changing nature of experiences;
2 new implications for co-creation; and
3 the need to exploit the potential of technologies for the enhancement of experiences.

To put the changed paradigm into practice, it is necessary for marketers to consider collaboration with consumers and their use of ICTs as the key to a successful creation of innovative experiences, added value and competitive advantage.

Being on the forefront of technology in a dynamic tourism environment thus means to capture cutting-edge technologies and pioneer in using them as tools for innovation and strategic competitive advantage in the marketing and management of experiences. As the understanding and implementation of co-creation in tourism (Binkhorst and Den Dekker 2009), let alone the realization of technology enhanced tourism experiences is still in its infancy (Neuhofer *et al.* 2012), there will be great potential in this area in the near future. With emerging technologies and the dynamics of the tourism industry, tourism experiences are equally exposed to constant change, which renders the evolution of tourism experiences far from completed. It will be an on-going and transformational process with new opportunities for experiences unfolding over the coming years. With continuous innovations in the IT sector, we can foresee opportunities in social media engagement and the role of real time service delivery, location and context based services, augmented reality applications and social gaming. Thus, research is never-ending and continuous efforts in exploring new and reappraising the existing understanding of tourism experiences are needed. Subsequently, this chapter concludes by setting out an agenda for tourism practice and research alike to highlight the need to conceptually and practically advance knowledge of innovating and creating competitive experiences.

For tourism marketing and management, numerous practical implications become evident. It is necessary to constantly monitor current trends and emerging technologies in order to explore the potential of their implementation for the enhancement of tourism experiences. In doing so, it is paramount for marketers to create strategic innovations by using the latest technologies available to maximize co-creation, create added value with consumers and generate competitive advantage. By using social technologies, such as social media, interactive platforms or mobile applications, there is great potential to intensify the levels of co-creation and value extraction and create fully enhanced experiences throughout multiple touch points and stages, including pre/during/post stage of travel. Future research on multiple levels is needed to advance our understanding of tourism experience creation. For instance, company-centric studies are required to investigate provider and stakeholder involvement in the facilitation and co-creation of successful technology enhanced tourism experiences. To complement this perspective, studies focusing on the consumer are essential in better understanding the tourists' roles in, needs and perceptions regarding experiences. Research investigating value perspectives needs to be encouraged to understand how value propositions can be maximized through the use of ICTs. Moreover, research, in exploring these current issues and challenges, should exploit the potential of technology as a research instrument, by using online, virtual and mobile spaces and applying technology-led methods to develop a better understanding of technology enhanced tourism experiences. While these recommendations only provide a snapshot of the status quo, many questions undoubtedly remain open and much more research is needed for understanding future developments in the creation of experiences in tourism marketing theory and practice.

References

Aho, S.K. (2001) 'Towards a general theory of touristic experiences: modelling experience process in tourism', *Tourism Review*, 56(3/4): 33–7.

Andersson, T.D. (2007) 'The tourist in the experience economy', *Scandinavian Journal of Hospitality and Tourism*, 7(1): 46–58.

Balasubramanian, S., Peterson, R.A. and Jarvenpaa, S.L. (2002) 'Exploring the implications of m-commerce for markets and marketing', *Journal of the Academy of Marketing Science*, 30(4): 348–61.

Baron, S. and Harris, K. (2010) 'Toward an understanding of consumer perspectives on experiences', *Journal of Services Marketing*, 24(7): 518–31.

Baron, S. and Warnaby, G. (2011) 'Individual customers' use and integration of resources: empirical findings and organizational implications in the context of value co-creation', *Industrial Marketing Management*, 40(2): 211–18.

Binkhorst, E. and Den Dekker, T. (2009) 'Agenda for co-creation tourism experience research', *Journal of Hospitality Marketing & Management*, 18(2/3): 311–27.

Binkhorst, E., Den Dekker, T. and Melkert, M. (2010) 'Blurring boundaries in cultural tourism research', in G. Richards and W. Munsters (eds) *Cultural Toruism Research Methods*. Wallingford: CABI.

Boswijk, A., Thijssen, T. and Peelen, E. (2007) *The Experience Economy: A New Perspective*. Amsterdam: Pearson Education.

Brown, B. and Chalmers, M. (2003) 'Tourism and mobile technology', in K. Kutti, E. Karsten, G. Fitzpatrick, P. Dourish and K. Schmidt (eds) *Proceedings of the Eighth European Conference on Computer Supported Cooperative Work*. Dordrecht: Kluwer Academic Publishers, 335–54.

Buhalis, D. and Jun, S.H. (2011) 'E-tourism', *Contemporary Tourism Reviews* [Online]. Available: http://www.goodfellowpublishers.com/free_files/fileEtourism.pdf (accessed 10 October 2012).

Buhalis, D. and Law, R. (2008) 'Progress in information technology and tourism management. 20 years on and 10 years after the Internet. The state of eTourism research', *Tourism Management*, 29(4): 609–23.

Buhalis, D. and Licata, M.C. (2002) 'The future eTourism intermediaries', *Tourism Management*, 23(3): 207–20.

Buhalis, D. and Wagner, R. (2013) 'E-destinations: global best practice in tourism technologies and application', in L. Cantoni and Z. Xiang (eds) *Information and Communication Technologies in Tourism 2012*. Austria: Springer Verlag.

Clawson, M. and Knetch, J.L. (1966) *Economics of Outdoor Recreation*. Baltimore: Johns Hopkins.

Cohen, E. (1979) 'A phenomenology of tourist experiences', *Sociology*, 13(2): 179–201.

Craig-Smith, S. and French, C. (1994) *Learning to Live with Tourism*. Melbourne: Pitman.

Cutler, S.Q. and Carmichael, B. (2010) 'The dimensions of the tourist experience', in M. Morgan, P. Lugosi and J.R.B. Ritchie (eds) *The Tourism and Leisure Experience: Consumer and Managerial Perspectives*. Bristol: Channel View Publications.

Darmer, P. and Sundbo, J. (2008) 'Introduction to experience creation', in J. Sundbo and P. Darmer (eds) *Creating Experiences in the Experience Economy*. Cheltenham: Edward Elgar.

Dwivedi, M., Yadav, A. and Venkatesh, U. (2012) 'Use of social media by national tourism organizations: a preliminary analysis', *Information Technology and Tourism*, 13(2): 93–103.

Egger, R. and Buhalis, D. (2008) *eTourism Case Studies: Management and Marketing Issues*. Burlington: Elsevier Ltd.

Egger, R. and Jooss, M. (2010) 'Die Zukunft im mTourism: Ausblick auf Technologie- und Dienstentwicklung', in R. Egger and M. Jooss (eds) *mTourism: Mobile Dienste im Tourismus*. Wiesbaden: Gabler Verlag.

Fotis, J., Buhalis, D. and Rossides, N. (2011) 'Social media impact on holiday travel planning: the case of the Russian and the FSU markets', *International Journal of Online Marketing*, 1(4): 1–19.

Green, N. (2002) 'On the move: technology, mobility, and the mediation of social time and space', *The Information Society*, 18(4): 281–92.

Gretzel, U. and Jamal, T. (2009) 'Conceptualizing the creative tourist class: technology, mobility, and tourism experiences', *Tourism Analysis*, 14(4): 471–81.

Gretzel, U., Fesenmaier, D.R. and O'Leary, J.T. (2006) 'The transformation of consumer behaviour', in D. Buhalis and C. Costa (eds) *Tourism Business Frontiers: Consumers, Products and Industry*. Oxford: Elsevier.

Guttentag, D. (2010) 'Virtual reality: appplications and implication for tourism', *Tourism Management*, 31(5): 637–51.

Hall, C.M. (2005) *Tourism: Rethinking the Social Science of Mobility*. London: Pearson Education.

Hays, S., Page, S.J. and Buhalis, D. (2013) 'Social media as a destination marketing tool: its use by national tourism organisations', *Current Issues in Tourism*, 16(3): 211–39.

Holbrook, M.B. and Hirschman, E.C. (1982) 'The experiential aspects of consumption – consumer fantasies, feelings, and fun', *Journal of Consumer Research*, 9(2): 132–40.

Huang, J. and Hsu, C.H.C. (2010) 'The impact of customer-to-customer interaction on cruise experience and vacation satisfaction', *Journal of Travel Research*, 49(1): 79–92.

Huang, Y.C., Backman, S.J. and Backman, K.F. (2010) 'The impacts of virtual experiences on people's travel intentions', in U. Gretzel, R. Law and M. Fuchs (eds) *ENTER 2010*. Lugano, Switzerland: Springer-Verlag.

Jennings, G., Lee, Y.S., Ayling, A., Lunny, B., Cater, C. and Ollenburg, C. (2009) 'Quality tourism experiences: reviews, reflections, research agendas', *Journal of Hospitality Marketing & Management*, 18(2–3): 294–310.

Jensen, R. (1999) *The Dream Society: How the Coming Shift from Information to Imagination will Transform Your Business*. New York: McGraw-Hill.

Killion, G.L. (1992) *Understanding Tourism. Study Guide*. Rockhampton: Central Queensland University.

Kohler, T., Fueller, J., Stieger, D. and Matzler, K. (2011) 'Avatar-based innovation: consequences of the virtual co-creation experience', *Computers in Human Behavior*, 27: 160–68.

Larsen, S. (2007) 'Aspects of a psychology of the tourist experience', *Journal of Hospitality and Tourism*, 7(1): 7–18.

McCabe, S., Sharples, M. and Foster, C. (2012) 'Stakeholder engagement in the design of scenarios of technology-enhanced tourism services', *Tourism Management Perspectives*, 4(October): 36–44.

Morgan, M., Lugosi, P. and Ritchie, J.R.B. (2010) *The Tourism and Leisure Experience: Consumer and Managerial Perspectives*. Bristol: Channel View.

Neuhofer, B., Buhalis, D. and Ladkin, A. (2012) 'Conceptualising technology enhanced destination experiences', *Journal of Destination Marketing & Management*, 1(1–2): 36–46.

Otto, J. E. and Ritchie, J.R.B. (1996) 'The service experience in tourism', *Tourism Management*, 17(3): 165–74.

Pihlström, M. (2008) *Perceived Value of Mobile Service Use and Its Consequences*. Swedish School of Economics and Business Administration.

Pine, J.B. and Gilmore, J.H. (1998) 'Welcome to the experience economy', *Harvard Business Review*, 76(4): 97.

— (1999) *The Experience Economy: Work is a Theatre and Every Business a Stage*. Cambridge: Harvard Business School.

Pine, J.B. and Korn, K. (2011) *Infinite Possibility: Creating Customer Value on the Digital Frontier*. San Francisco: Berrett-Koehler Publishers.

Prahalad, C.K. and Ramaswamy, V. (2004) 'Co-creation experiences: the next practice in value creation', *Journal of Interactive Marketing*, 18(3): 5–14.

Ramaswamy, V. (2009) 'Co-creation of value – towards an expanded paradigm of value creation', *Marketing Review St. Gallen*, 6: 11–17.

Sandström, S., Edvardsson, B., Kristensson, P. and Magnusson, P. (2008) 'Value in use through service experience', *Managing Service Quality*, 18(2): 112–26.

Schmidt-Belz, B., Nick, A., Poslad, S. and Zipf, A. (2002) 'Personalized and location-based mobile tourism services', *Proceedings from the Workshop on Mobile Tourism Support Systems*.

Shaw, G., Bailey, A. and Williams, A.M. (2011) 'Service dominant logic and its implications for tourism management: the co-production of innovation in the hotel industry', *Tourism Management*, 32(2): 207–14.

Sheldon, P. (1997) *Tourism Information Technologies*. Wallingford: CABI.

Sheller, M. and Urry, J. (2006) 'The new mobilities paradigm', *Environment and Planning A*, 38(2): 207–26.

Sigala, M. (2009) 'E-service quality and Web 2.0: expanding quality models to include customer participation and inter-customer support', *The Service Industries Journal*, 29(10): 1341–358.

Tung, V.W.S. and Ritchie, J.R.B. (2011) 'Exploring the essence of memorable tourism experiences', *Annals of Tourism Research*, 38(4): 1367–386.

Tussyadiah, I.P. and Fesenmaier, D.R. (2007) 'Interpreting tourist experiences from first-person stories: a foundation for mobile guides', paper presented at the *15th European Conference on Information Systems*. St. Gallen, Switzerland.

— (2009) 'Mediating the tourist experiences: access to places via shared videos', *Annals of Tourism Research*, 36(1): 24–40.

Tussyadiah, I.P. and Zach, F.J. (2011) 'The role of geo-based technology in place experiences', *Annals of Tourism Research*, 39(2): 780–800.

Van Limburg, B. (2012) 'Visiting Suriname, using DART to analyze a visitor's perspective in a cocreation enviornment', *Information Technology and Tourism*, 13(2): 119–32.
Vargo, S.L. and Lusch, R.F. (2004) 'Evolving to a new dominant logic for marketing', *Journal of Marketing*, 68(January): 1–17.
— (2006) 'Service-dominant logic: reactions, reflections and refinements', *Marketing Theory*, 6(3): 281–88.
Vargo, S.L., Maglio, P.P. and Archpru-Akaka, M. (2008) 'On value and value co-creation: a service systems and service logic perspective', *European Management Journal*, 26: 145–52.
Wang, D., Park, S. and Fesenmaier, D.R. (2012) 'The role of smartphones in mediating the touristic experience', *Journal of Travel Research*, 51(4): 371–87.
Wang, Y. and Fesenmaier, D.R. (2004) 'Towards understanding members' general participation in and active contribution to an online travel community', *Tourism Management*, 25(6): 709–22.
Wolf, M.J. (1999) *The Entertainment Economy – How Mega-media Forces are Transforming our Lives*. New York: Times Books, Random House.
Xiang, Z. (2011) 'Dynamic social media in online travel information search: a preliminary analysis', in R. Law, M. Fuchs and F. Ricci (eds) *ENTER 2011*. Innsbruck, Austria: Springer.
Xiang, Z. and Gretzel, U. (2010) 'Role of social media in online travel information search', *Tourism Management*, 31(2): 179–88.
Yovcheva, Z., Buhalis, D. and Gatzidis, C. (2013) 'Engineering augmented tourism experiences', in L. Cantoni Z. and Xiang (eds) *Information and Communication Technologies in Tourism 2012*. Austria: Springer Verlag.
Zeithaml, V., Berry, L.L. and Parasuraman, A. (1988) 'Communication and control processes in the delivery of service quality', *Journal of Marketing*, 52: 35–48.

11

Brand experience in tourism in the Internet age

Anthony Foley, John Fahy and Anne-Marie Ivers

Introduction

Tourism is a major world industry and very broad in its scope – including the travel trade (retail and wholesale), accommodation, transport, activities, heritage and attractions, retail and food, media, state and industry destination management organizations (DMOs) (McKercher, Denizci-Guillet and Ng 2011). Tourism is experiential in nature, and whether linked to business or pleasure, is characterized by sustained consumer interaction with tourism service providers and the destination. The Internet has had a transformational effect on how these consumer interactions take place. This is primarily due to the shift in the power relationship between the firm and the consumer, with the Internet providing the information and communications potential to fuel this empowerment (Urban 2005; Pires, Stanton and Rita 2006). Tourists or potential tourists routinely refer to the Web for information on travel propositions, and importantly, consult with other tourists online to establish their experiences and opinions of the tourism service before reservation. It is particularly interesting to reflect on the influence of the Internet on the brand.

The brand is very much about personal experience, so different consumers will interpret the brand in different ways; indeed the same person can interpret different meanings of the brand over time (Allen, Fournier and Miller 2008). Technologies facilitate online communities of consumers to share and review information on tourism brands, and to 'co-construct' an individualised and unique experience (Muniz and O'Guinn 2001; Bengtsson 2003; Prahalad and Ramaswamy 2004). This co-creation experience can be seen *as* the brand (Prahalad and Ramaswamy 2004). Therefore, it is no longer the sole responsibility of the marketing department to construct the brand meaning – the consumer is a key partner in this process (Brown, Kozinets and Sherry 2003; Coupland 2005). Internet technologies expose the tourist to the brand offering before, during and after the actual consumption of the experience. This chapter will investigate the various web applications which influence the tourist brand experience, at the different stages of brand consumption. We will also draw out conclusions and implications for tourism firms wishing to enhance the brand experience for the tourist, through the Internet.

Co-creation of the tourism brand experience

A brand is the name or symbol or design or other characterizing feature of a product or service which differentiates it from competing offerings, and which represents all of the consumer goodwill built up towards the brand (Kotler, Keller, Brady, Goodman and Hansen 2009). It is possible to brand anything, goods, services, ideas, organizations – and of course, destinations (Kotler *et al.* 2009). In order to provide a rationale for discussing brand 'meaning', it is pertinent to focus on the belief that a brand can have a personality; essentially 'human characteristics associated with the brand' (Aaker 1997: 347). Consumers effectively humanize brands by translating the brand into personality traits (Aaker 1997). Brand meaning is therefore complex as brands can have different meaning for consumers over time (Allen *et al.* 2006). Organizations therefore need to consider the role of both brand managers and consumers in the brand co-creation process (Brown, Kozinets and Sherry 2003; Coupland 2005).

Consumers do not have to be necessarily excited or engaged by the brand, they simply project certain personality traits onto the brand (Brakus, Schmitt and Zarantonello 2009) as part of the brand experience co-creation process. If a brand can take on human personality characteristics it also follows that a consumer can form a relationship with a brand (Allen *et al.* 2008). This separate identity of the brand from the company which created or managed it removes the brand from the realm of total control by the brand promoter. This was something that was brought forcibly to the attention of Coca Cola in 1985, with the response to its ill-judged decision to change the formulation of Coke, in response to the growing threat of its main competitor, Pepsi Cola. The launch of 'New Coke' created a tidal wave of protest, including the formation of adhoc groups such as the 'Old Cola Drinkers of America', claiming 10,000 members, established to vocalize opposition to the interloper (Coca Cola 2012). This phenomenon of consumer loyalty to the brand and in opposition to the firm, possibly the most successful brand promoter in marketing history, marked one of the first signals that the company no longer has a monopoly on brand management, and even less on the values of the brand, particularly consumers' identification with the brand. One clear message is that stronger brands result from greater involvement with the brand by consumers – but also effective brand management involvement (Coupland 2005). It is possibly less likely that the Coke marketing debacle would happen now, as the marketing manager can more tangibly hear the voice of the customer, through the various social media available. Therefore, while social media raises many challenges for the tourism and hospitality firm, it importantly acts as a conduit to what the customer is thinking.

The centrality of experience is captured by Gilmore and Pine (2002) where they equate the experience with effective marketing: 'the way to reach your customers is to create an experience with them' (Gilmore and Pine 2002: 3). Tourism experience can be defined as 'an individual's subjective evaluation and undergoing (i.e. affective, cognitive, and behavioural) of events related to his/her tourist activities which begins before (i.e. planning and preparation), during (i.e. at the destination), and after the trip (i.e. recollection)' (Tung and Ritchie 2011: 1369). The focus on stages of experience (pre, during and after) in this definition will be echoed later in this chapter, when we investigate the impact of various Internet applications on the tourism brand experience at different stages of consumption.

While brand involvement presumes a consumer need, brand experience is independent of motivation, interest or involvement, and can also be differentiated from customer satisfaction or delight, which occurs after consumption, unlike brand experience, which happens whenever there is brand interaction (Brakus *et al.* 2009). The implication of the subjective and individual nature of experience from a firm or destination perspective is that the tourism experience cannot be directly manufactured or delivered (Tung and Ritchie 2011). The tourism brand experience, as with any service experience is personally and individually constructed, as reflected in the nature of brand experience as 'actual sensations, feelings, cognitions, and behavioural responses' (Brakus *et al.* 2009: 54), and indeed, '(t)he experience is the brand. The brand is co-created and evolves with experiences' (Prahalad and Ramaswamy 2004: 136). This is reflected in a paradigmatic change in the way that value is created; no longer by the firm, but jointly by consumers and the firm, with the co-creation of the experience providing this value (Vargo and Lusch 2004; Prahalad and Ramaswamy 2004).

The experience environment is composed not only of the firm and its employees, channels, products and services, but also the consumer community – and the consumer co-creates his/her individual and unique experience, within this environment (Muniz and O'Guinn 2001; Bengtsson 2003; Prahalad and Ramaswamy 2004). Essentially, the individualized brand meaning emerges – not from the brand communications of the firm (though this is of course significant) – but through the social interaction of the members of the brand community 'with brand meaning being socially negotiated, rather than delivered unaltered and in toto from context to context, consumer to consumer' (Muniz and O'Guinn 2001: 414). Significantly, this does not have to involve physical interactions with other brand users, but can involve online social interaction through such means as forums or blogs, or even be characterized by a psychological sense of brand community, where brand users do not necessarily interact socially with others (Carlson, Sutter and Brown 2008).

Tourism and the social media challenge

The term 'social media' can be used to represent all of the various Internet based applications that influence the tourism brand, based on Web 2.0, and using user generated content (UGC) (Kaplan and Haenlein 2010). A noticeable feature of social media is their role in extending traditional consumer word-of-mouth (WOM) into an online space (Mangold and Faulds 2009), becoming eWOM (Hennig-Thurau and Walsh 2004). Positive eWOM has been found to produce a more favourable attitude towards the brand (Jones, Aiken and Bousch 2009). Web 2.0 represents a later incarnation of the Internet marked by collaboration and content sharing, facilitated by technological functionality, provided by applications such as Adobe Flash (which enhances web pages with animation and interactivity), and RSS (Really Simple Syndication), which provides frequently updated web feed content (Kaplan and Haenlein 2010).

UGC represents online content provided by consumers on publicly available websites, facilitated in latter years by technological advances, and a more technology and media savvy younger generation (Kaplan and Haenlein 2010). An integrative definition of social media is 'a group of Internet-based applications that build on the ideological and technological foundations of Web 2.0, and that allow the creation and exchange of User Generated Content' (Kaplan and Haenlein 2010: 61). These applications include company and user blogs, email, consumer feedback websites, online discussion forums, social networking websites, virtual worlds, and content (video, image, music ...) sharing websites (Mangold and Faulds 2009). Specific attention in this chapter will be given to a number of social media that are increasingly influential on the brand strategy of the tourism firm, and the tourist experience, including user generated content; tourism communities; tourism firm websites; destination brand online promotion; intermediary websites; social networks; virtual environments; and blogs.

User generated content shared by individuals can be in the form of e.g. video (YouTube), text (Wikipedia) or other content such as photos (Flickr). YouTube has become an incredibly successful and prolific medium. Almost eight years of content is uploaded daily (70 per cent from outside the USA), and nearly 17 million people have linked YouTube to at least one social medium, while 98 of Ad Age Top 100 advertisers have had campaigns on YouTube (YouTube 2012). The *brand community* plays a critical role in providing a social context for understanding development of brand meaning (Muniz and O'Guinn 2001; McAlexander, Schouten and Koenig 2002). The brand community is not limited by the physical realm; apart from the social brand community, which involves consumers interacting face to face or within virtual worlds, there may also be a psychological sense of brand community, which does not involve any social interaction but where consumers have a perceived connection to other users of the brand (Carlson, Sutter, and Brown 2008). The communal interaction within the brand community can have a significant impact on how the individual's personalized brand meaning is created (Patterson and O'Malley 2006). Within the tourism industry, travellers can exchange experiences, information and recommendations in the *online communities* (Buhalis and Law 2008; Sanchez-Franco and Rondan-Cataluna 2010), which are more likely to be trusted by tourists than corporate communications (Buhalis and Law 2008). Tourism communities include *virtualtourist.com* and *tripadvisor.com*. TripAdvisor provides an opportunity for guests to post reviews of tourism services providers such as hotels, and is very influential as a first point of contact for travellers. Tourism can be perceived to be high involvement and high risk, exacerbated by the absence of the personal touch of the travel agent, and online reviews address these issues (Papathanassis and Knolle 2011). While negative reviews can be traumatic for the tourism firm, there is evidence that improvements in service quality can be linked to TripAdvisor (Cunningham, Smyth, Wu and Greene 2010).

The *tourism firm website* is the electronic shop window, and by the use of virtual tours can provide a more meaningful taste of the experience awaiting the tourist. The corporate site needs to be engaging and yet informative. Many tourism firms now have booking engines embedded in their websites. Tourism firms can obtain valuable information about visitors to their website by tracking their identity and their activity on the site, and also develop potential customer databases by inviting enquiries and registration (Buhalis 2011). At the destination level, *online brand communication and promotions* are critical. DMOs are the public or private agencies responsible for management and marketing of branded destinations, and the tourism stakeholders, enterprises, local authorities etc., e.g. England Tourist Board, Destination Bristol. DMOs have become alert to the opportunities for more effective marketing presented by the Internet. This can be done through various means such as driving traffic by linking to suitable sites, sending virtual cards to visitors to the destination with a link to the site, and also importantly, facilitating visitors to make online bookings for accommodation or other services, or at least to link to these suppliers (Raventos 2006).

Intermediary websites such as Expedia, Travelocity, Venere, Hotels.com, Booking.com are highly visible portal sites which have become mainstream in a relatively short time period (Buhalis 2011) and are likely to be among the first sites the consumer will see on a search engine when seeking accommodation or other tourist services. Indeed, 'mega travel e-mediaries ... established as internet brands' have become dominant in tourism ecommerce at the expense of DMOs (Hyun and Cai 2009: 38). These intermediaries provide a useful service to the consumer in aggregating details and facilitating the user in identifying accommodation that meets the time, location, benefits and price requested. Many of these sites also incorporate user reviews, and are forcing tourism firms to re-evaluate their value chains (Buhalis and Law 2008).

Social networking sites facilitate users in creating an online profile, to invite friends to their page, to share all types of content including text, images, audio, blogs (Kaplan and Haenlin 2010). Facebook is the dominant social network, with 845 million active subscribers at the end of 2011, 80 per cent of whom are outside North America (Facebook 2012). Virtual reality is the 'use of a computer-generated 3D environment – called a "virtual environment" – that one can navigate and possibly interact with, resulting in real-time simulation of one or more of the user's five senses' (Guttentag 2010: 638). These virtual experiences can seem to be quite close to real life (Buhalis and Law 2008). The most well-known virtual environment is Second Life, where the user can explore a virtual world, represented by an avatar (Guttentag 2010). Users in Second Life can do pretty much a lot of what they can do in the non-virtual world, speaking, creating content, and even selling using Linden dollars (Kaplan and Haenlein 2010). Tourism themes are apparent in Second Life, and the Dresden Old Masters Picture Gallery was the first to have a virtual representation of a museum on Second Life (Guttentag 2010).

Blogs are essentially personal web pages, mainly text based where the blog owner posts personal commentary, and there may also be a response feature (Kaplan and Haenlein 2010). Blogs are increasingly used by companies to inform employees and customers, but have the risk of facilitating comment from employees and customers which may not be favourable to the firm (Kaplan and Haenlein 2010). Consumers are increasingly going online to record their views and experiences on blogs.

Implications of Internet for tourism brand experience at different stages of consumption

The Internet is particularly important in tourism, which relies on description and also representation, as it facilitates communication of tourism offerings and transactions (Buhalis 2011). The Internet has had major benefits for the sector, allowing tourism firms to communicate their offerings at much lower cost, bypassing intermediaries such as travel agencies and also critically functioning as a distribution channel, allowing tourists to reserve beds or flights directly (Raventos 2006). All consumer interactions with the brand comprise the brand experience (Prahalad and Ramaswamy 2004; Brakus *et al.* 2009). Brand experience does not necessarily have to involve consumption; it can be indirect exposure through brand communications (Brakus *et al.* 2009). Therefore, it is problematic to associate the brand experience exclusively with the actual consumption of the service. If the tourist is browsing the Web looking at various hotel bedroom offerings and settles on a particular one, perhaps using a virtual tour or online user review to inform the decision, the brand experience has already started. When the tourist arrives at the hotel, and the holiday or business stay commences, the brand experience is intensified. The tourist may also blog his/her experience while staying. Subsequent to the stay, the tourist may post a review online, or join a virtual community. Therefore, it is useful from a management perspective to investigate the different stages of brand experience prior to consumption, at consumption, and post consumption, and this is consistent with the definition of tourist experience by Tung and Ritchie (2011). In particular, this will allow analysis of the influence of the Internet on the brand experience of the consumer from first awareness of the brand through to post consumption reflection. Figure 11.1 illustrates the different stages of brand experience, and the social media which can influence the brand experience at each stage. It also highlights the co-creation by the tourism firm/DMO and consumer of the tourist brand experience. The increasing engagement by DMOs with visitors in the tourism brand experience is apparent from the Experience Nottinghamshire website web page, 'Your Experience', where the DMO is explicit about how it intends to use social media to involve the visitor (Experience Nottinghamshire 2012).

Pre-consumption brand experience

The tourist brand experience begins in advance of the actual consumption of the service. A consumer investigating a potential holiday experience in France becomes exposed to commercial

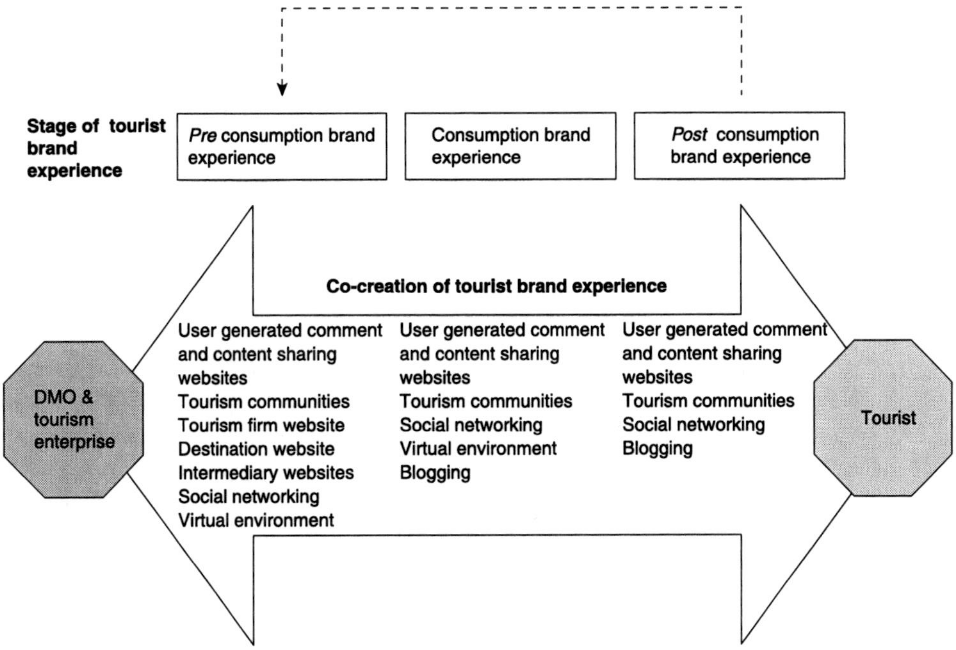

Figure 11.1 Stages of tourist brand experience and the Internet.

communications from French tourism and travel companies, at the destination and service provider level. The Internet introduces a whole range of other tourist experiences and comments, images, video, and communities which will also influence this pre-consumption experience, and which will influence where this consumption experience happens. UGC and content sharing websites are very influential at this stage. The evolution of technology in wireless technologies and smart phones allows the tourist to upload images, text, video and audio to the Internet, to sites such as YouTube and Virtual Tourist (Buhalis and Law 2008; Munar 2009). These communications can be compelling as they are from other consumers and not the tourism firm (Buhalis and Law 2008).

DMOs and tourism firms can influence this process by encouraging travellers to post videos and images of their trips, perhaps through competitions or other incentives. Online tourist networks and communities provide probably the most influential Internet generated phenomena on tourism brand experience. This is because of the considerable influence that online consumer review has on tourist decision making (Papathassis and Knolle 2011; Sparks and Browning 2011). Negative reviews can be magnified in impact on the tourist evaluations of the tourist service (Sparks and Browning 2011). TripAdvisor has emerged as a dominant online community where consumers can share travel experiences. It has been established that for hotels benefiting from TripAdvisor reviews, that these reviews were prominent in online searches of the hotel name (Cunningham *et al.* 2010).

The firm website is the shop window for the tourism services provider, and acts as an important source of practical information on the tourism offering. Importantly, it has the power to produce a positive or negative influence on the brand experience. Search engine optimization (SEO) presents the tourism firm with the opportunity to promote its ranking in enquiries on search engines, which is critical in exposing the tourism offering to the tourist. Tourists are not just consuming a tourism offering such as accommodation, dining or activity. They are also consuming a destination. Therefore, the brand experience communicated by the DMO is critically important. The functionality of DMO websites appears on a continuum from ones which are effectively just online versions of the brochure to fully interactive portal sites, where visitors can make reservations and even take a virtual tour (Hyun and Cai 2009). However, destinations have substantially failed to engage with consumer net communities, not taking the opportunity to develop virtual brands, and in many cases just digitising existing offline logos and brand communications (Hyun and Cai 2009).

It is important also for tourism organizations to note that communications and media messages may have a significant impact upon an individual's sense of being in a community and their perceptions of the brand community (Carlson *et al.* 2008). Intermediaries (such as Expedia) are also emerging as critical influences on pre-consumption behaviour, acting as 'one-stop-shop' vehicles where visitors can reserve all travel needs including accommodation, transport, car rental etc. (Buhalis 2011). Tourism firms and DMOs need to be aware of their capability to communicate effectively with the target audience through an engaging web presence. The tourist may also be able to experience the tourism brand virtually through a virtual tour in advance of consumption of the service. Virtual reality is particularly useful in tourism, providing a taste of the service prior to booking; a virtual environment allows the consumer to make a more informed decision (Guttentag 2010).

Consumption brand experience

Brand experience is created individually by the consumer, whenever there is interaction with the brand (Prahalad and Ramaswamy 2004). However, one would expect the actual physical consumption of the brand experience, such as the overnight hotel accommodation, to make the strongest impression on the brand experience. When tourists are immersed in the experience, they may wish to share this with their friends through posting video, text and images to content sharing websites, and social networks. Mobile based systems like Foursquare allow tourists to tweet, share information, upload videos and other content, and encourage their friends to get involved in the tourist experience (e.g. a festival). Virtual reality has much potential to enhance the entertainment and educational value of the experience, as in the *Futuroscope* theme park in France where a real setting is enhanced with projection of futuristic animals, or the *Foundation of the Hellenic World* in Greece, where visitors can travel through the ancient city of Miletus (Guttentag 2010). Augmented reality (AR), where computer generated images are merged with real world view (Guttentag 2010), is also used effectively for tourism attractions. Tourists are also increasingly using blogs as online diaries, which can be distributed to friends and personal networks (Munar 2009). Smartphones and Wi-Fi make it very easy for tourists to post to online communities such as TripAdvisor or Wayn.com during their stay. A strong influence on the content disseminated through social media by the tourist will be the quality of the service experience.

Post-consumption brand experience

The brand experience lives on after the core consumption experience, when the tourist can upload video, images and text to various content sharing websites, coloured by the individual recollection of the experience. Online tourist networks and communities impact significantly on the tourism brand experience, because of the considerable influence that online consumer review has on tourist decision making (Papathassis and Knolle 2011), and so positive reviews of the tourist experience are very desirable. Once the tourist has experienced the consumption of

The Gathering: Developing an integrated Brand Proposition for Destination Ireland in 2013 through the Internet

The Gathering is an Irish government initiative, in conjunction with the tourism support agencies, Tourism Ireland, and Fáilte Ireland. The intention of the initiative is to encourage some of the 70 million people living outside Ireland, claiming Irish ancestry, to visit their ancestral land, during 2013 (The Gathering. 2012). A distinctive aspect of this brand experience is the fostering of community involvement in Ireland, with local communities encouraged to arrange any type of 'gathering', which could be a clan gathering (e.g. meeting of the O'Connor clan), or class reunion. Apart from the core 'gatherings', a second strand is composed of festivals and events. Enterprises and community groups can register to get brand support through templates, and tourism images – and branding guidelines are used to support co-branding. Individuals and groups can create their own gatherings, through registering details on the website. The Gathering is using social media extensively, including Facebook, LinkedIn and Twitter, to facilitate host community development and communication of activities, and online communications by potential visitor/visitors, essentially to develop the destination Ireland brand. A Global Community page on the website (http:/www.thegatheringireland.com) teases out the nature of being Irish, building on the community of the Irish diaspora, now able through a digital platform to express this identity. The website uses videos (one featuring the US talk-show host, Conan O'Brien), links, news, stories and thought pieces to generate a brand narrative. As the gatherings are taking place in 2013,tourists report on their experiences and positively promote the Irish brand to the world. Ireland as a destination will be depicted through the user generated content as local communities, potential visitors and visitors share their experiences with others through each of the consumption phases.

Figure 11.2 The Gathering: example of tourism brand experience creation through an Internet platform.

the holiday experience, and if this has been positive, the tourist may be open to joining tourism destination/firm sponsored social network, such as a Facebook site. This then operates as a virtual community where the tourist can post content, and continue to interact with the tourism organization. Tourists may also take the opportunity to reflect on their experience, once the trip is over, through online blogging. Again, all of these online conversations and interactions contribute towards consumer co-creation of the tourist brand experience (Muniz and O'Guinn 2001; McAlexander, Schouten and Koenig 2002; Prahalad and Ramaswamy 2004; Brakus *et al.* 2009).

Conclusions

The Internet presents a major challenge to attempts to control tourism brand image (Munar 2009). But is there any point in the DMO or tourism firm attempting to exclusively control image? Tourism destinations and firms must engage with the newly empowered tourist, and respond to the desire and ability of the tourist to co-create the tourism brand experience through social media. This chapter has highlighted the importance for tourism firms and DMOs of being aware of the impact of social media on the tourism brand experience. The consumer co-creation of the experience effectively is the brand (Brakus *et al.* 2009), and the brand experience happens at pre-consumption, consumption and post-consumption stages. Tourism authorities must develop strategies to positively influence the influence of social media on this brand experience, at each stage. At the *pre-consumption stage*, social media provides a first exposure to the tourism brand experience through UGC. Therefore, it is important that tourists are encouraged to upload to content sharing sites such as YouTube, and also to firm/destination sponsored social networking sites. Virtual tourism communities such as TripAdvisor are enormously influential in representing the first exposure to the tourism firm brand experience for the consumer. The most effective way for the hotel or other tourism firm to get positive reviews on TripAdvisor is through service quality. Consistency between employee and customer understanding of the service brand, and commitment by managers to employee development is critical (De Chernatony and Segal-Horn 2003) as employees are at the critical interface with the customer, and it is vital to remember the critical role of tourism employees in driving positive eWOM.

DMOs and tourism entrepreneurs must facilitate the development of online communities through engaging with tourists on online blogs, discussion groups and social network groups, and incentivizing tourist participation – as these are seen to be critical in the consumer co-creation of the brand (Muniz and O'Guinn 2001; Prahalad and Ramaswamy 2004). The websites of the tourism firm and the DMO are also important in allowing the tourist to embrace the brand experience, particularly if enhanced by features such as a virtual tour (Hyun and Cai 2009). The Internet presents the opportunity to present customized multi-component offerings to the tourist (Buhalis 2011). Employing rich multimedia in the firm or destination website can create a 'telepresence' for the tourist, and this can simulate the experience of interaction with tourism products and destinations (Buhalis and Law 2008). Intermediary websites (such as Expedia) are increasingly dominant as aggregators and portals, and so DMOs and tourism firms need to be very conscious of the efficacy of their own corporate web presence. Similarly, at the *consumption stage*, when tourists are actively engaging with the physical brand experience, it can be of benefit to encourage them to upload content, which shows how they are enjoying the experience.

Tourism communities offer the potential for tourism firms to better understand the needs and the motivations of tourists, therefore informing more consumer focused marketing (Buhalis and Law 2008). As yet, tourism firms and DMOs have been slow to engage with this potential (Hyun and Cai 2009). This is important because the visitor may have a vertical relationship, e.g. not being loyal to an airline, but staying true to the destination (McKercher *et al.* 2011). Timing is also important for tourists contributing to online communities such as TripAdvisor – if the experience is good, tourists should be encouraged to share this knowledge through a community or social network, or blog – at the point of consumption. Virtual reality also can enhance the tourist brand experience consumption, particularly in education and heritage sites (Guttentag 2010).

In the *post-consumption stage*, the tourism brand experience lives on through the sharing of text, videos, images and other content by tourists in social media. Again, DMOs and tourism firms can influence this process by encouraging tourists to disseminate, and by promoting corporate sponsored social networking sites and blogs where customers can continue to engage with the brand through interaction with other tourists, and the firm. The ability to integrate positive eWOM with online advertising, particularly on third party managed sites, is also likely to have a significant positive impact for the firm (Jones *et al.* 2009). There is a substantial benefit to the tourism firm and to the DMO in harnessing the information available on the Internet from tourist enquiries, and the online chatter and comment in a multitude of Internet chatrooms and communities, to provide valuable market data (see Buhalis 2011). These market insights can be of immense value in informing modification and redesign of the tourism offering, and helping to ensure that the tourism brand experience is compelling for the visitor.

Above all, it is critical to remember that the individual tourist co-creates and forms a unique personalized brand experience (Prahalad and Ramaswamy 2004). It has been highlighted that stronger brands are created as a result of including both brand managers and consumers in the co-creation of the brand (Brown *et al.* 2003; Coupland *et al.* 2005). Maintaining quality customer experience and facilitating the consumer co-creation experience is critical (Prahalad and Ramaswamy 2004). Therefore, tourism authorities and enterprises should provide compelling and quality experiences, informed by the wealth of tourist market information on the Internet, and facilitate the tourist in co-creating compelling brand experiences through social media. Initiatives such as 'The Gathering' (see Figure 11.2) highlight how by simply providing an idea, and a digital platform, consumers are facilitated to co-create, and communicate a compelling a tourism brand experience. More research is required on destination brand strategy using social media (Goldsmith and Tsiotsou 2012). While there has been attention in the literature to tourism branding at the individual enterprise, and destination level, and to visitor experience; there has been a marked lack of investigation of the impact of digital platforms on tourism branding and experience.

A challenge for academic research is to integrate examination of the tourism brand experience with tourist self-concept, and in particular, how tourists use social media to co-create the tourism experience. This requires an adjustment from the traditional destination management framework, with the DMO in control, creating and communicating a tourism experience, to a consumer driven paradigm. This will involve a multi-disciplinary lens from scholars, on destination management, marketing, branding, and digital marketing, to consumer psychology, self-image and consumer community.

References

Aaker, L.J. (1997) 'Dimensions of brand personality', *Journal of Marketing Research*, 34: 347–56.

Allen, T.C., Fournier, S. and Miller, F. (2008) 'Brands and their meaning makers', in C. Haugtvedt, P. Herr and F. Kardes (eds) *Handbook of Consumer Psychology*. Mahwah, NJ: Lawrence Earlbaum Associates, pp. 781–822.

Bengtsson, A. (2003) 'Towards a critique of brand relationships', *Advances in Consumer Research*, 30: 154–58.

Brakus, J.J., Schmitt, B.H. and Zarantonello, L. (2009) 'Brand experience: what is it? How is it measured? Does it affect loyalty?', *Journal of Marketing*, 73: 52–68.

Brown, S., Kozinets, V.R. and Sherry, F.J. (2003) 'Teaching old brands new tricks: retro branding and the revival of brand meaning', *Journal of Marketing*, 67: 19–38.

Buhalis, D. (2011) 'eTourism Strategy', in L. Moutinho (ed.) *Strategic Management in Tourism*, 2nd edn. Wallingford: CABI, pp. 262–73.

Buhalis, D. and Law, R. (2008) 'Progress in information technology and tourism management: 20 years on and 10 years after the Internet – the state of eTourism research', *Tourism Management*, 29: 609–23.

Carlson, D.B., Sutter, A.T. and Brown, J.T. (2008) 'Social versus psychological brand community: the role of psychological sense of brand community', *Journal of Business Research*, 61: 284–91.

Coca-Cola (2012) online. Available: http://www.thecocacolacompany.com/heritage/cokelore_newcoke.html (accessed 20 November 2012).

Coupland, C.J. (2005) 'Invisible brands: an ethnography of households and the brands in their kitchen pantries', *Journal of Consumer Research*, 32: 106–18.

Cunningham, P., Smyth, B., Wu, G. and Greene, D. (2010) 'Does TripAdvisor make hotels better?', *Technical Report UCD*, University College Dublin, December: 1–11.

De Chernatony, L. and Segal Horn, S. (2003) 'The criteria for successful services brands', *European Journal of Marketing*, 37: 1095–118.

Experience Nottinghamshire (2012) Online. Available: http://www.experiencenottinghamshire.com (accessed 3 December 2012).

Facebook (2012) Online. Available: http://newsroom.fb.com/content/default.aspx?NewsAreaId=22 (accessed 24 February 2012).

Gilmore, J.H. and Pine, B.J.P (2002) 'The experience is the marketing'. Online. Available: http://www.soloseo.com/blog/files/experience-is-the-marketing.pdf (accessed 26 February 2012).

Goldsmith, R.E. and Tsiotsou, R.K. (eds) (2012) *Strategic Marketing in Tourism Services*. Bingley, UK: Emerald.

Guttentag, D.A. (2010) 'Virtual reality: applications and implications for tourism', *Tourism Management*, 31: 637–51.

Hennig-Thurau, T. and Walsh, G. (2004) 'Electronic word-of-mouth for and consequences of reading customer articulations on the Internet', *International Journal of Electronic Commerce*, 8: 51–74.

Hyun, M.Y. and Cai, L.A. (2009) 'A model of virtual destination branding', in L.A. Cai, W.C. Gartner and A.M. Munar, (eds) *Tourism Branding: Communities in Action, Bridging Theory and Practice Volume 1*. Bingley, UK: Emerald, pp. 37–50.

Jones, S.A., Aiken, K.D. and Boush, D.M. (2009) 'Integrating experience, advertising, and electronic word-of-mouth', *Journal of Internet Commerce*, 8: 246–67.

Kaplan, A.M. and Haenlein, M. (2010) 'Users of the world, unite! The challenges and opportunities of Social Media', *Business Horizons*, 53: 59–68.

Kotler, P., Keller, K.L., Brady, M., Goodman, M. and Hansen, T. (2009) *Marketing Management*. Essex: Pearson.

McAlexander, H.J., Schouten, W.J. and Koenig, F.H. (2002) 'Building brand community', *Journal of Marketing*, 66: 38–54.

McKercher, B., Denizci-Guillet, B. and Ng, E. (2011) 'Rethinking loyalty', *Annals of Tourism Research*, 39: 708–34.

Mangold, W. and Faulds, D. (2009) 'Social media: the new hybrid element of the promotion mix', *Business Horizons*, 52: 357–65.

Munar, A.M. (2009) 'Challenging the brand', in L.A. Cai, W.C. Gartner and A.M. Munar, *Tourism Branding: Communities in Action, Bridging Theory and Practice Volume 1*. Bingley: Emerald.

Muniz, M.A. and O'Guinn, C.T. (2001) 'Brand community', *Journal of Consumer Research*, 27: 412–32.

Papathassis, A. and Knolle, F. (2011) 'Exploring the adoption and processing of online holiday reviews: a grounded theory approach', *Tourism Management*, 32: 215–24.

Patterson, M and O'Malley, L. (2006) 'Brands, consumers and relationships: a review', *Irish Marketing Review*, 18: 10–20.

Pires, G.D., Stanton, J. and Rita, P. (2006) 'The Internet, consumer empowerment and marketing strategies', *European Journal of Marketing*, 40: 936–49.

Prahalad, C.K. and Ramaswamy, V. (2004) *The Future of Competition: Co-Creating Unique Value with Customers*. Boston: Harvard Business School Press.

Raventos, P. (2006) 'The Internet strategy of the Costa Rican Tourism Board', *Journal of Business Research*, 59: 375–86.

Sanchez-Franco, M.J. and Rondan-Cataluna, F.J. (2009) 'Virtual travel communities and customer loyalty: customer purchase involvement and web site design', *Electronic Commerce Research and Applications*, 9: 171–82.

Sparks, B.A. and Browning V. (2011) 'The impact of online reviews on hotel booking intentions and perception of trust', *Tourism Management*, 32: 1310–323.

The Gathering (2012) Online. Available: https://www.thegatheringireland.com (accessed 23 November 2012).

Tung, V.W.S. and Ritchie, J.R.B. (2011) 'Exploring the essence of memorable tourism experiences', *Annals of Tourism Research*, 38: 1367–386.

United Nations World Tourism Organisation (UNWTO) (2012) Online. Available: http://media.unwto.org/en/press-release/2012-01-16/international-tourism-reach-one-billion-2012 (accessed 3 March 2012).

Urban, G. (2004) 'The emerging era of customer advocacy', *MIT Sloan Management Review*, Winter 45: 77–82.

Vargo, L.S. and Lusch, F.R. (2004) 'Evolving to a new dominant logic for marketing', *Journal of Marketing*, 68: 1–17.

You Tube (2012) Online. Available: http://www.youtube.com/t/press_statistics (accessed 1 March 2012).

12
Collaboration marketing

Alan Fyall

Introduction

Although collaboration is often advanced as a new and innovative marketing approach for organizations seeking to achieve competitive advantage, the wider management literature suggests that collaboration has been omnipresent across many industries for many decades. Initial studies by Emery and Trist (1965) set the early foundations for the study of collaboration with contributions from Gray (1985, 1989), Waddock (1989), Terpstra and Simonin (1993), Kanter (1995) and Palmer (1996) further developing the subject throughout the 1980s and 1990s. More recently, Christopher, Payne and Ballantyne (2002: 129) introduced the concept of 'network competition' where rewards go to those organizations that are able to best 'structure, co-ordinate and manage relationships with their partners in a network committed to creating customer and consumer value through collaboration'. This would certainly seem to be the case for international airlines, the case focus of this chapter, although Selin (1993) is one of many who argue that collaboration now represents a strategic necessity in tourism more broadly due to the interdependencies of its predominantly large number of small actors and widespread market fragmentation.

Despite the widespread adoption of collaborative strategies across many industries and sectors, it is, thus, somewhat surprising that no generally accepted definition of collaboration exists. One of the biggest hurdles for those attempting to define collaboration is the multitude of similar, but different, terms that on the surface appear to be used interchangeably. One interesting dimension of collaboration is that there is a tendency for particular terms to be used in different contexts, especially in tourism. For example, while the airline industry refers to collaboration as 'alliances' (Morley 2003), hotels and restaurants prefer the term 'consortia' (Spyriadis and Fyall, 2003). Public-sector organizations, attractions and destinations, meanwhile, appear to be more comfortable with the term 'partnership' (Hill and Shaw 1995; Bramwell and Lane 2000; Augustyn and Knowles 2000).

The definition that best underpins the above interpretations is that of Gray (1989) who identified five key components of the collaboration process. To meet conditions of collaboration, Gray (1989) argued that: stakeholders need to be independent; they need to assume joint responsibility for the outcomes of collaboration; solutions will only be achieved through stakeholders constructively dealing with differences; the ownership of decisions is shared; and that collaboration, ultimately, is an emergent process. Wood and Gray (1991: 146) advanced the debate further in advocating collaboration occurring as when a 'group of autonomous stakeholders of a problem domain engage in an interactive process, using shared rules, norms, and structures, to act or decide on issues related to that domain'. Although somewhat generic in nature, this is the definition to be used in this chapter as it provides sufficient breadth for the inclusion of variants to be subsumed within.

Perhaps more significant than a definition of collaboration, is that of collaborative advantage which has been described as when 'something unusually creative is produced – perhaps an objective is met – which no organization could have produced on its own and when each organization, through the collaboration, is able to achieve its own objectives better than it could alone' (Huxham 1993: 603). Hence, rather than focusing on the process of collaboration, collaborative advantage focuses on the synergistic outcomes of collaboration in that organizations that fail to demonstrate competitive advantage independently may be able through collaboration to achieve collaborative advantage which, in turn, then potentially leads to a competitive advantage.

This chapter, therefore, seeks to synthesize the theoretical explanations that underpin our understanding of collaboration, clarify the different types of collaboration that exist in the context of marketing, and identify those criteria that contribute to collaborative success. To illustrate the above, the chapter includes a case study on international airline alliances. The chapter concludes by suggesting that although not always an easy strategic choice, collaboration is particularly relevant in times of market turbulence despite its dynamic and emergent, rather than more predictable and prescriptive, characteristics. The following section provides a brief overview of collaboration in the context of international airline alliances. The section that follows then provides a thorough introduction to the various theoretical approaches that underpin our understanding of collaboration and which serve as a vehicle to understand the complexities of international airline collaboration in the second half of the chapter.

Collaboration and international airline alliances

Defined as a an important form of collaboration between two or more organizations (Zhang and Zhang 2006), a strategic alliance enables 'firms to achieve increased economies of scale, and scope through joint operations, asset specialization, knowledge acquisition, and access to resources' (Oum *et al.* 2004: 844). The adoption of such a strategy is widely believed to contribute to enhanced profitability gains for the firm due to greater levels of efficiency and a strong and strengthened competitive position. Consistent with the broader definition of collaboration, those partnering in strategic alliances remain separate entities and retain their decision-making autonomy with firms interacting with their 'social environments' to secure scarce resources (Pfeffer and Salancik 1978), resources which more often than not include access to key markets. Strategic alliances are highly prevalent in network-oriented industries such as shipping, telecommunications and logistics with international air travel that sector within the wider tourism industry which has perhaps most fully embraced collaboration in a strategic sense over the past two decades (Holtbrügge, Wilson and Berg 2006; Goertz and Shapiro 2012). Notwithstanding, international airline alliances have served as a rich area of research scrutiny with a number of studies exploring the various dimensions of collaboration in this domain including the forms and extent of collaboration between partners (Mountford and Tacoun 2004), the impact of alliances on competition (Wang *et al.* 2004), policy and consumer issues (Gudmundsson 1999) and the impact on productivity and profitability (Oum *et al.* 2000) and human resource management (Holtbrügge *et al.* 2006).

Driven by regulatory restrictions on market access, ownership and control, and the deregulation and liberalisation of air travel markets in the late 1970s and early 1980s, membership of an international airline alliance has today become a 'key component of business strategy for many airlines, and a means of differentiating member airlines from low-cost competitors in terms of the quality of service offered' (Tiernan, Rhoades and Waguespack 2008: 99). In essence, international airline alliances have further consolidated the industry and have served to centralise the balance of power into a relatively small number of airlines who dominate the three most significant international airline alliances, namely Oneworld, Star Alliance and Sky Team. The following section now provides an overview of theoretical explanations that underpin the development of such collaborative forms.

Theoretical explanations of collaboration

Although a large number of theories exist that help clarify understanding of collaboration, Wood and Gray (1991) share the view that nearly all such theories acknowledge the contribution of environmental complexity, uncertainty, and turbulence as common problems faced by organizations of all shapes and sizes. As such, collaboration is believed to be that vehicle most suited to reducing these common problems to manageable levels. Such a view, however, does tend to fuel the debate that collaboration is a secondary-reactive rather than a primary-proactive strategy with it being viewed more as a 'next-best alternative' rather than as a strategy of choice. This is certainly a question worthy of asking those airlines that are already members of international airline alliances as well as those that have yet to join. Accepting that collaboration can, however, be explained by a variety of theoretical perspectives and that no single perspective predominates, two recent reviews in the context of tourist destinations, seek to synthesize the multitude of theoretical explanations in the wider literature. The first by Beritelli (2011) studies cooperation at different levels and identifies six approaches: game theory; rational choice theory; institutional analysis; resource dependence theory; transaction cost economics; social exchange theory. The second, by Fyall, Garrod and Wang (2012), refers to similar studies but identifies five theoretical groupings: resource-based theories; relationship-based theories; politics-based theories; process-based theories; chaos-based theories. Each theory is introduced below with questions raised as to the potential contribution of each in explaining the emergence of international airline alliances.

Resource-based theories

Resource-based theories are dominated by resource dependency theory which is built upon two assumptions: the first that resources are scarce and the second that organizations have sufficient power to leverage such resources (see Emerson 1962; Ulrich and Barney 1984; Barney 1991; Hamel and Prahalad 1994; Faulkner and de Rond 2000; Donaldson and O'Toole 2002). In other words, organizations rely on each other due to their endowments and their differing contextual environments (Beritelli 2011) where power-conflict assessment is a key determinant as to whether organizations compete or collaborate with others (Fyall *et al.* 2012). One of the considerations for organizations contemplating collaboration, therefore, is the extent to which they are prepared to concede autonomy as there are instances where collaboration may increase levels of uncertainty due to new inter-organizational relationships and dependencies (Wood and Gray 1991). The desire by many airlines to attain global market reach coupled with their insufficient resource endowments to achieve such a goal have historically been the main drivers of collaboration to the extent that a certain loss of autonomy has been a price worth paying, to date at least.

Interestingly, strategic management theory, which focuses on the long-term activities and structure of the organization, is also based on scarcity and shared problems serving as the basis for collaboration. In the wider context of strategic management and the collective achievement of long-term, strategic goals, Gulati (1998) highlights a number of collaboration issues of relevance, namely:

1 their formation;
2 their governance structure;
3 their dynamic evolution;
4 their performance; and
5 consequences for the performance of new entrants to such arrangements.

The emphasis of a strategic management approach to collaboration is primarily long term with the commitment of management resources and capital invested in search of collaborative advantage to achieve competitive positioning. At the outset, one has to question to what extent any airline, or any organization for that matter, fully thinks through the longer-term consequences of their decision to collaborate, or not as the case may be. The emergent nature of collaboration and the turbulence of the external environment are such that predicting competitive, let alone collaborative, outcomes is beset with problems. That said, the appeal of global reach appears sufficient in the context of most airlines to limit such concerns of the future direction of international airline alliances.

The third resource-based view of collaboration is that of microeconomic theory generally and transaction cost economics in particular which is underpinned by organizations seeking to minimize costs incurred in economic exchanges generally and collaboration processes in particular (Ross 1973; Williamson 1975, 1985; Barney and Ouchi 1986; Weaver 2009). Underpinning this approach is the concept of the value chain whereby the various components of organizations are broken up and reconfigured in new relational forms to the benefit of the organization, its costs and outputs. Although the desire to achieve transaction cost efficiencies is not doubted, the main driver for membership of international airline alliances is value added with the considerable benefits for both airlines and their passengers of global connectivity. One issue here, however, is the view that rather than being bi-lateral in nature, transaction cost economics needs to recognize the multi-lateral nature of tourism and the complexity and interdependence of the wider system as compared to other industries. One of the negative outcomes of collaboration in a multi-lateral context is the issue of 'free-rider' effects, this being where one partner or stakeholder is not contributing to the collective good (Long 1997). If not contained, such behaviour can lead to the dissolution of the collaborative arrangement which frequently is to the detriment of all participants. One further issue with transaction cost economics is its focus on the costs of collaboration rather than the benefits to be achieved. With all forms of collaboration fundamentally dynamic in nature, the more rigid interpretation of transaction cost economics does not ideally fit the more dynamic phenomenon of collaboration. For example, collaboration in the context of international airlines is continually shaped by a fast-changing market environment, crises of a natural and man-made nature and a whole host of diverse organizational dynamics that include labour relations, contractual legalities, financial reporting, and the measurement and management of performance.

Relationship-based theories

The second theoretical approach advocated by Fyall *et al.* (2012) is relationship-based theories where collaboration is explained by the search for, and acceptance of mutual dependency, and the need for reciprocity in the search for joint benefits (Macaulay 1963; Dwyer, Shurr and Oh 1987). The main contrasting feature between relational and resource-based approaches is that they are built on the formation of social and interpersonal relationships rather than the conduct of transactions, a scenario which makes self-serving behaviour more transparent and, therefore, less likely. One challenging outcome of such an approach, however, is the extent to which organizational boundaries become blurred. Although a particular challenge for destinations, boundary-creep is also an issue for other sectors of the tourism industry with notable issues for strategic international airline alliances as to what systems, policies, marketing and brands are adopted for the collaborative good.

One of the key relational-based theories is stakeholder theory which is predicated on organizations having a range of stakeholders which can affect or be affected by the achievement of an organization's objectives (Freeman 1984). With its focus on management decision making, stakeholder theory advocates that stakeholder relationships in part determine outcomes for both the organization and its stakeholders with the interests of all stakeholder groups demonstrating equal value. Two issues of relevance here though are those of salience and legitimacy. While the first relates to all stakeholders being treated equally, the latter relates to how a particular stakeholder is able to impact the organization's decision-making, much of which will depend on their power within the group (Friedman and Miles 2002).

Although also relational in nature, network theory explores the complexity of relationships between individuals, groups and organizations in a designated space such as a destination or airline alliance (Mouge and Contractor 2003). Emphasis here is primarily on information flows and what Christopher, Payne and Ballantyne (2002) refer to as 'network competition', whereby organizations compete through relational networks rather than as stand-alone organizations in search of customer 'value'. As such, the 'value' for passengers travelling with an international airline alliance may include seamless service, connectivity and pricing convergence along with the considerable benefits to be achieved from an alliance-wide frequent flyer programme. As with all relational approaches to collaboration, trust is a critical component as advocated recently by Erkuz-Ozturk and Eraydin (2010). One relational approach gaining credence as an explanatory theory in the wider literature is that of game theory whereby a 'set of players carries out a set of moves and attains payoffs for each combination of moves' (Beritelli 2011: 4). The purpose of such a theory is to gain an improved understanding of both organizational and human behaviour with the success of one component dependent on the choices of another (Jafari 2000; Fennell 2006; Zhang, Song, Huang and Chen 2010). Of relevance to international airline alliances is the potential for one airline to cut or change its route network to the detriment of others in the collaborative grouping. Game theory would thus serve as an ideal means by which to understand the potential implications of such a unilateral action and the consequent reshaping of the collaborative relationships of existing, and potentially new members.

Politics-based theories

Politics-based theories, meanwhile, demonstrate a slightly different focus in that the balance of power among individuals and organizations is key to understanding their collaborative motivations and dynamics and the consequent distribution, or uneven distribution, of collaboration benefits (Keohane and Nye 1977; Gray and Wood 1991; Kelly 2006). The theory of power relations is viewed as integral to the understanding of collaborative efforts (Reed 1997) while Jamal and Getz (1995) believe that issues of power and authority need to be considered at each stage of collaboration as a means to ensure equity and fairness. One legitimate concern with political theories in general, however, is the view that governance institutions always have, and always will have, their own agendas to follow in formulating and implementing policy and as such collaboration strategies need to be adopted with caution (Hollinshead 1990). There is also the issue in the context of international airline alliances that member size, reach and impact on decision making varies with power not always equally shared.

Other politics-based theoretical explanations of collaboration include theories of corporate social performance and institutional theory. While Wood (1991) highlights the former as being of benefit in assessing the extent to which principles of social responsibility motivate collaborative behaviour, Clarkson (1995) suggests that collaborating stakeholders need to perceive fairness and equity in the distribution of the wealth and value created through collaboration. With an increasing need for organizations to be accountable for their actions, closer scrutiny of collaborating partners is a natural reaction with scrutiny now going well beyond traditional market and financial performance (Boesso and Kumar 2007) with social contracts not now uncommon between organizations and society (Lieberman and Nissen 2008). Although true for international airline alliances, and possibly a feature of longer-term maturity of the key alliances, such ambitions were not integral to the early stages of development. Along similar lines, institutional theory and negotiated order theory both seek to explain processes of change as well as the symbolic and perceptual aspects of collaboration and collaborative relationships (Strauss 1978; Modell 2006). Although maybe less significant in the past, such approaches are gaining traction as the need to adhere to regulation and the need to demonstrate a sense of duty or 'moral obligation' to stakeholders becomes more apparent (Vargas-Sanchez and Riquel-Ligero 2010). The need to reduce carbon emissions is perhaps the most obvious issue facing airlines with collaborative efforts integral to a more effective and efficient international airline industry.

Process-based theories

While process-based theories are dominated by the need to understand how collaborative arrangements emerge, evolve, decline and disappear over time, they also focus on the need to determine common features in their dynamics and evolution (Ring and van de Ven 1994; Jap and Anderson 2007). Although there is an emerging corpus of research in this field, there is a surprising paucity of consensus as to the exact number of phases, their duration and what constitutes collaborative success (Wang and Fesenmaier 2007). One of the impediments to consensus is the number of macro and micro environmental factors at play that can impact, both positively and negatively, the collaboration process and in turn impact the performance and effectiveness of the collaboration. Despite the complexity of the issues at hand, the models advocated by Gray (1985, 1989), Selin and Chavez (1995) and Caffyn (2000) are widely referred to in the literature with a synthesis provided in Fyall and Garrod (2005). Although each vary, they all seek: identification of the problem domain and key stakeholders; agreement as to the common sense of purpose and how and when it is to be achieved; the effective management of the collaborative process in a systematic manner and one in which evolutionary behaviour is encouraged which, ultimately, may lead to termination, dissolution or reformulation of the collaborative arrangement. This latter point is a particular feature of the study by Caffyn (2000) in that it includes an 'after-life' component where the actual purpose of the collaboration is implicitly or explicitly re-evaluated. Interestingly, this is not an option that has surfaced to date with the three major international airline alliances. That said, the time will surface when for reasons of cost, changing ownership or changing strategic direction individual airlines will begin to question their member benefits and begin to confront the need to either remain collaborative or seek a more individual competitive route.

Chaos-based theories

Although much of the above furthers our understanding of collaboration and the collaborative process, Wang and Fesenmaier (2007) conclude that in most cases collaboration has to be viewed on a case-by-case and highly context-specific basis, a view that in part justifies the increasing prevalence of chaos-based theories as a suitable vehicle to explain collaborative behaviour. Defined by Seeger (2002: 239) as a 'broad set of loosely related theoretical and meta-theoretical orientations to the behaviour of complex non-linear systems', chaos theory is based on the premise that predictable linear relationships rarely exist in reality. Non-linear, highly complex systems are the norm with them being subject to random occurrences and highly susceptible to their operating conditions. Similar to elements of process-based theories chaos theory explores the dissolution and regrouping of individual elements of the wider 'system' and the means by which a new sense of order re-establishes itself (Russell and Faulkner 2004; Zahra and Ryan 2007). The focus on self-organization and self-renewal are commonplace for many collaborative arrangements as the highly case-specific context of collaboration affirms itself. As discussed previously, although this has yet to happen in the context of international airline alliances, the current economic challenges around the world are such that many of the smaller airlines are beginning to be severely challenged by threats in the external environment.

Despite what on the surface appears to be limited opportunity for learning, the complexity, dynamism, significance and reach of collaboration across the wider tourism industry is such that there remains much scope for the further scrutiny of collaboration and its raft of theoretical explanations. Where there is more consensus, however, is in our understanding of the process of collaboration generally, and in the motives for and various types and stages of collaboration as discussed in the section that follows.

Motivations and typologies of collaboration

In exploring the process of collaboration, the logical starting point rests with an exploration of the motives that drive individuals and organizations to collaborate in the first place. The study undertaken by Beverland and Brotherton (2001) still carries considerable weight with the motivations for inter-organizational collaboration being broken down into eight groupings, namely: market entry and market position-related motives; product-related motives; product/market-related motives; market structure modification-related motives; market entry timing-related motives; resource use efficiency-related motives; resource extension and risk reduction-related motives; skills enhancement-related motives. Although comprehensive, their study possibly underscores the predominance of market-related motivations evident across the tourism industry. In addition to its inherent complexity, fragmentation and high levels of interdependency, and the turbulence evident in the external environment (particularly with regard to crises and disasters that are now seemingly omnipresent across tourism), it is perhaps no surprise that collaboration is such a strong feature of tourism. What is a surprise perhaps is the increase in market-related motivations where collaboration is proving to be a valuable strategy for market access, especially in international markets, allowing firms to build and expand customer bases for purposes of relationship marketing, defending existing market positioning and enhancing future market positioning (Fyall and Garrod 2005). For many organizations with limited resources, collaboration often represents a more cost-effective way of progressing rather than seeking finance for organic growth. That said, for most organizations, and especially airlines, preference would still be to 'go it alone', resource endowments permitting.

However, rather than talking purely of collaboration in a generic sense, it is important to outline the various types of collaborative arrangements that exist. For example, collaborations can be directional in that they can be 'horizontal', 'vertical' or 'diagonal' in nature. While horizontal collaboration relates to collaboration between two 'competitors' at the same level (the primary collaborative from of international airline alliances) vertical collaboration relates to collaboration between suppliers of a product and its buyers. Diagonal, or external, collaboration, meanwhile, refers to collaboration between organizations in different sectors or industries. An alternative way of describing different forms of collaboration is by comparing them to personal relationships. Dev and Klein (1993), for example, compare collaborative arrangements to short-term, opportunistic 'one night stands', medium-term and tactical collaborations with a sense of self-protection as 'affairs' with long-term relationships, involving continuity and a high degree of commitment as marriages. Fyall and Garrod (2005) provide a summary of other, more complex typologies which are all designed to take the form of a continuum or hierarchy, with 'simpler' forms of collaboration at one end of the scale and more 'complex' types at the other.

The first, which originates from Kanter (1994), presents a continuum of collaboration ranging from 'weak and distant' at one end to 'strong and close' at the other. In contrast, Walker and Johannes (2003), drawing on the original work of Segil (1996), focus on risk as the predominant distinguishing feature of different types of collaborative arrangements. Child and Faulkner (1998), meanwhile, present a simple typology of collaborative 'alliances' based on three dimensions: scope (whether it is 'complex' or 'focused'); the number of participants (whether there are two or several partners in the collaboration); and the legal nature of collaboration (whether it is a 'joint venture' or simply a 'collaboration'). One of the limitations of this framework is that it allows for only two categories along each dimension where in reality collaboration can, and often does, involve more than two partners. One particularly useful typological framework is that proposed by Terpstra and Simonin (1993) whereby four principal features are identified to distinguish between different types of collaboration, namely: coverage, mode, form and motive (1993). While 'motive' has been discussed earlier, the extensiveness of a collaboration vis-à-vis markets and geographical reach is referred to as 'coverage' while 'mode' refers to the intrinsic nature of relationship among the members involved which can be either of a personal or cultural nature (Palmer and Bejou 1995). 'Form', meanwhile refers to the constitutional characteristics of the collaboration with the governance style adopted normally sitting on a continuum between loose (less formal) governance styles at one end and tight (more formal) governance styles at the other. While trust is critical in the establishment and implementation of loose governance styles, as styles become tighter, there is a greater need for more concrete systems or rules to be in place, most probably endorsed by some form of legal intervention.

Collaboration effectiveness

One of the perennial challenges for all forms of collaboration is in determining how best to measure their performance (Donaldson and O'Toole 2002). Over the years a number of approaches have been advocated that include forms of economic measurement (Goodman 1970), behavioural measurement vis-à-vis trust and commitment (Bucklin and Sengupta 1993), perceived success (Kanter 1994) and propensity (Gulati 1995). It is interesting to note that where studies have sought to examine collaboration effectiveness, in most cases it is not effectiveness that has been examined rather the reasons behind termination of the collaboration which clearly is not the same thing (Gulati 1998).

In spite of such problems, however, a variety of studies have attempted to shed light on those factors that contribute to collaborative effectiveness. One of the earlier studies, albeit in the context of social, public–private sector partnerships was that conducted by Waddock and Bannister (1991) who concluded that effectiveness was ultimately determined by: participant trust; adequate flexibility and power to make decisions; inclusion of key participants in the collaboration; fair and equitable distribution of benefits; recognition of interdependency; balance of power; clarification of objectives; clarity of vision; and strong leadership. As with personal relationships, finding suitably like-minded partners is a particularly noteworthy contributor to collaboration effectiveness, while the role of convenor is widely regarded as an underestimated variable in the equation. The role of the convenor is critical to success with the convenor requiring a high degree of empathy with the collaborative domain, credibility among all partners as well as the ability to stay neutral and not take sides, an ability to filter out the essential and non-essential items of collaborative arrangements and to manage expectations. Clearly patience is a virtue for such a role while the ability to bring all parties together in a constructive and forward-looking manner is critical.

International airline alliances – a collaborative success story?

From humble resource-based 'codesharing' beginnings in the early 1960s, where two or more airlines agreed to use the same designator code (flight number) for connecting services and so benefit from an extension of their respective networks, the three largest international airline alliances today together employ just under 1.2 million people, operate nearly 40,000 daily flights and span the global through an extensive truly-global route network. With most of the major international airlines now members of either Oneworld, Star Alliance or Sky Team, only those airlines that have considerable resources at their disposal such as Emirates, Etihad or Qatar, or those that differentiate themselves through splendid isolation, such as Virgin, are able to survive outside of the 'big three' multi-product international airline alliances (Tiernan *et al.* 2008). With so much market turbulence over the past decade commencing with the aviation aftermath of 9/11 in the USA, many airlines which otherwise might not have survived have developed and grown as a result of their collaborative membership of alliances. Zhang and Zhang (2006), for example, stress that alliance members are able to maximize their own profit as at the same time expand the share of its partner's profit, a successful outcome from their resource-based origins.

Although reasons for joining vary slightly the majority of airlines have joined one of the 'big three' alliances as a means to access global markets which, in turn, confers on them a significant market advantage. Iatrou and Alamdari (2005: 128), for example, stress that a strategic alliance is one involving 'strategic commitment by top management to link up a substantial part of their respective route networks as well as collaborating on some key areas of airline business'. Collaborating airlines are thus sharing resources, including brand assets and market access capability as a means to expand their market reach and networks, strengthen their market positioning, reduce costs, benefit from economies of scale and scope which in turn increases productivity and profitability. Although there is some dispute as to what transaction costs really are saved due to the complexity of alliance formation, most airlines remain confident that the benefits outweigh costs with considerable opportunity for organizational learning a key benefit (Inkpen 1995).

With the exponential growth of low-cost airlines in North America, Europe and Asia, international airline alliances also serve as highly effective means of product differentiation for traditional 'flag-carrier' airlines due to the aggressive price-competitive nature of domestic markets where low-cost carriers increasingly dominate with their particularly strong regional airport presence. One aspect of international airline alliances that remains inconclusive, however, is their ability to improve product quality and customer service with a number of inconsistencies still evident where American airlines tend to lag behind the superior service levels offered by European and especially Asian airlines (Weber and Sparks 2004). Although passengers are able to benefit from access to multiple lounges and seamless frequent flyer programmes, to date there is limited evidence of a single check-in on the horizon; while talk of the 'global consumer' and 'global traveller' abounds, integration to date primarily relates to standardization or procurement, IT systems, facilities and marketing with pressure, especially in the area of HRM to maintain differentiated strategies. Thus, although considerable benefits are to be achieved via economies of scale and reduced costs through global co-ordination, there remains a reluctance to deviate too much from the respective political forces of each airline, their governmental demands and individual cultural needs (Holtbrügge *et al.* 2006). One wonders also whether trust is as widespread across all alliances as one would have us believe with the constant fear of competitive individual actions always at the back of one's mind.

One notable impact of the development and continued growth of international airline alliances is on the changing relationship between airlines and airports (Dennis 2005). Whereas 'point-to-point' route networks used to dominate, 'hub-and-spoke' networks represent the engines that drive the alliances with the major hubs critical in feeding long-haul flights as well as leveraging considerable competitive advantage to those airports that serve as the major hubs (Albers, Koch and Ruff 2005). In fact, the vast majority of the increased traffic generated by international airline alliances is on hub-to-hub routes with these routes contributing significantly to increased load factors, revenue and profit. Although of great benefit to 'hub' airports, such rationalization brings with it severe consequences for those marginalized non-hub airports (Dennis 2005).

As with collaboration generally, vertical and technology-based alliances also exist. In the context of international airline alliances, these include vertical linkages with companies in the supply chain (such as car rental companies, hotels and financial services providers) and technology-driven relationships with providers of maintenance and safety products and services. Hence, in addition to codesharing, other alliance forms include blocked-space agreements, leasing and franchising, computerized reservation systems, insurance and airline pooling, joint services, baggage handling, ground maintenance and facilities sharing, and joint-marketing activity (Fyall and Garrod 2005). The latter is particularly noteworthy as the three leading international airline alliances have adopted different branding strategies over the years with regard to the extent to which they market themselves as either individual airlines which are part of a globalized network (such as in the case of Oneworld) or as a collaborative entity made up of individual airlines (as in the case of Star Alliance). There is also the issue of multiple alliance membership with relationship-based theories well placed to explain the network consequences of such behaviour.

Although continually lauded as highly successful, the three largest international airline alliances represent highly complex collaborative arrangements and remain highly emergent in nature in that lessons are continually being learned. To some commentators, the three largest alliances serve as highly defensive and potentially damaging competitive tools to restrict market entry (Iatrou and Alamdari 2005; Goertz and Shapiro 2012) with the benefits seemingly disproportionate to the larger airlines in the collaborative groupings. The authorities are thus continually looking at the potential elimination of fair competition across the industry while the health of non-allied airlines is of concern in some parts of the world as the industry, through collaboration, concentrates even further. In addition, although there are obvious cost advantages to be gained from such collaboration, there is little evidence to suggest that cost savings are always being passed on in the form of cheaper fares to passengers. Pitfield (2007: 201) is also of the view that 'fluctuations in traffic and traffic shares have more to do with the *ceteris paribus* conditions than with alliance formation and development, despite the expectations of airlines'.

With regard to the future, two interesting threats loom on the horizon for international airline alliances. Although each of the 'big three' have grown consistently over a number of years, the first issue of concern ahead relates to airlines beginning to switch alliances, partly through choice, but also in response to changing patterns of ownership where the new owners are allied to 'competing' alliances. This will naturally impact on alliance choice and begin to create some instability in a phenomenon which to date has simply grown with limited attrition and withdrawal. International airline alliances represent complex collaborative arrangements but one anticipates that they are soon to become even more complex. The second issue is perhaps even more troubling in that the market is becoming increasingly more able, and willing, to seek cheaper fares elsewhere through the Internet facilitated to a great degree by the speed and ease with which individuals can now create, book and pay for their own itinerary online. Although this has been a strong feature of domestic and short-haul flights for some time, and which has served as the catalyst for the exponential growth of low-cost airlines across Europe, the USA and Asia, only recently has it started to make inroads into the highly lucrative long-haul market. For the future, therefore, it may in fact be external technological advances driven by the Internet that represent the greatest threat to existing collaborative arrangements in the domain of international airline alliances rather than internal migrations between existing alliances.

Conclusion

Although far from being a new phenomenon, collaboration continues to represent a significant strategic choice for many industries with collaboration widespread across travel and tourism. The example of international airline alliances is indicative of many of the issues such collaborative arrangements face with the emergent nature of collaboration particularly noteworthy. It is ironic, perhaps, that collaboration has served as an ideal strategy for international airlines to enhance their market reach and overall marketing appeal while it is the very dynamic nature of the market, and technological advances at their disposal, which may yet serve as the greatest threat to their long-term survival in the years ahead. That said, to date Zhang and Zhang (2006: 298) conclude that the 'rivalry between complementary alliances tends to enhance economic welfare, because the strategic effort results in a higher degree of alliance, and hence greater output levels, than would be the case in the absence of such rivalry' (Zhang and Zhang 2006: 298).

As with nearly all forms of collaboration, however, it is interesting to reflect on the thoughts of Fyall and Garrod (2005: 219) who conclude that 'when the organization – or more precisely the individuals making decisions on behalf of the organization – begin to recognize that they can do better by collaborating with other organizations in their problem domain rather than competing against them, the collaborative efforts in which they are participating will likely begin to flourish'. By the same token, 'collaboration among those still deeply wed to the competition paradigm is more likely to meet with failure, or partial performance, than it is with unqualified success'. As such, although there are multiple rationales for the adoption of collaboration strategies with numerous benefits and drawbacks arising, it is more often than not the mindset and collaborative orientations of those contemplating collaboration that are likely to continue to represent the key drivers of collaborative success.

Ultimately, to succeed through collaboration there is a genuine need to believe in it and not view such an approach as 'second best'. As with international airline alliances, all those entering into collaborative alliances need to fully recognize the benefits to be achieved, the challenges they introduce and the timescale that best fit their individual objectives. More importantly, perhaps, there is also the need to recognize the temporary nature of collaboration as all collaborative forms are emergent in nature with the vast majority coming to some form of closure or realignment in what Caffyn (2000) describes as their 'after life' options. As such, one can guarantee that the future for international airline alliances will continue to remain emergent with further collaboration potentially being that strategy best suited to accommodate the turbulent times ahead.

References

Albers, S., Koch, B. and Ruff, C. (2005) 'Strategic alliances between airlines and airports: Theoretical assessment and practical evidence', *Journal of Air Transport Management*, 11: 49–58.

Augustyn, M.M. and Knowles, T. (2000) 'Performance of tourism partnerships: A focus on York', *Tourism Management*, 21: 341–51.

Barney, J. (1991) 'Firm resources and sustained competitive advantage', *Journal of Management*, 17(1): 99–119.

Barney, J. and Ouchi, W. (1986) *Organizational Economics*. San Francisco: Jossey Bass.

Benson, J.K. (1975) 'The interorganizational network as a political economy', *Administrative Science Quarterly*, 20: 229–49.

Beritelli, P. (2011) 'Cooperation among prominent actors in a tourist destination', *Annals of Tourism Research*, 38(2): 607–29.

Beverland, M. and Brotherton, P. (2001) 'The uncertain search for opportunities: Determinants of strategic partnerships', *Qualitative Market Research: An International Journal*, 4(2): 88–99.

Boesso, G. and Kumar, K. (2007) 'Drivers of corporate voluntary disclosure: A framework and empirical evidence from Italy and the United States', *Accounting, Auditing and Accountability Journal*, 20(2): 269–96.

Bramwell, B. and Lane, B. (2000) *Tourism Collaboration and Partnerships: Politics, Practice and Sustainability*. Clevedon: Channel View Publications.

Bucklin, L.P. and Sengupta, S. (1993) 'Organizing successful co-marketing alliances', *Journal of Marketing*, 57: 32–46.

Caffyn, A. (2000) 'Is there a tourism partnership life cycle?', in B. Bramwell and B. Lane (eds) *Tourism Collaboration and Partnerships: Politics, Practice and Sustainability*. Clevedon: Channel View Publications.

Child, J. and Faulkner, D. (1998) *Strategies of Co-operation: Managing Alliances, Networks and Joint Ventures*. Oxford: Oxford University Press.

Christopher, M., Payne, A. and Ballantyne, D. (2002) *Relationship Marketing: Creating Stakeholder Value*. Oxford: Butterworth Heinemann.

Clarkson, M.B.E. (1995) 'A stakeholder framework for analyzing and evaluating corporate social performance', *The Academy of Management Review*, 20(1): 92–117.

Dennis, N. (2005) 'Industry consolidation and future airline network structures in Europe', *Journal of Air Transport Management*, 11: 175–83.

Dev, C.S. and Klein, S. (1993) 'Strategic alliances in the hotel industry', *The Cornell Hotel and Restaurant Administration Quarterly*, 34(1): 42–5.

Donaldson, B. and O'Toole, T. (2002) *Strategic Marketing Relationships: From Strategy to Implementation*. Chichester: John Wiley & Sons.

Dwyer, F.R., Shurr, P.H. and Oh, S. (1987) 'Developing buyer–seller relationships', *Journal of Marketing*, 51(2): 11–27.

Emerson, K.M. (1962) 'Power-dependence relations', *American Sociological Review*, 27(1): 31–41.

Emery, F. and Trist, E. (1965) 'The causal texture of organizational environments', *Human Relations*, 18(1): 21–35.

Erkuz-Ozturk, H. and Eraydin, A. (2010) 'Environmental governance for sustainable tourism development: Collaborative networks and organization building in the Antalya tourism region', *Tourism Management*, 31(1): 113–24.

Faulkner, D.O. and de Rond, M. (2000) *Cooperative Strategy: Economic, Business and Organizational Issues*. New York: Oxford University Press.

Fennell, D.A. (2006) *Tourism Ethics*. Clevedon: Channel View Publications.

Freeman, R.E. (1984) *Strategic Management: A Stakeholder Approach*. Boston: Pitman.

Friedman, A.L. and Miles, S. (2002) 'Developing stakeholder theory', *Journal of Management Studies*, 39(1): 1–21.

Fyall, A. and Garrod, B. (2005) *Tourism Marketing: A Collaborative Approach*. Clevedon: Channel View Publications.

Fyall, A., Garrod, B. and Wang, Y. (2012) 'Destination collaboration: A critical review of theoretical approaches to a multi-dimensional phenomenon', *Journal of Destination Marketing & Management*, 1(1-2): 10–26.

Goertz, C.F. and Shapiro, A.H. (2012) 'Strategic alliance as a response to the threat of entry: Evidence from airline codesharing', *International Journal of Industrial Organization*, 30: 735–47.

Goodman, S.R. (1970) *Techniques of Profitability Analysis*. New York: Wiley & Sons.

Gray, B. (1985) 'Conditions facilitating interorganizational collaboration', *Human Relations*, 38(10): 911–36.

— (1989) *Collaborating: Finding Common Ground for Multiparty Problems*. San Francisco: Jossey Bass.

Gray, B. and Wood, D.J. (1991) 'Collaborative alliances: Moving from theory to practice', *Journal of Applied Behavioural Science*, 27(1): 3–22.

Gudmundsson, S.V. (1999) 'Airline alliances: Consumer and policy issues', *European Business Journal*, 11: 139–45.

Gulati, R. (1995) 'Social structure and alliance formation patterns: A longitudinal analysis', *Administrative Science Quarterly*, 40: 619–52.

— (1998) 'Alliances and networks', *Strategic Management Journal*, 19(4): 293–317.

Hamel, G. and Prahalad, C.K. (1994) *Competing For the Future*. Boston: Harvard Business School Press.

Hill, T. and Shaw, R.N. (1995) 'Co-marketing tourism internationally: Bases for strategic alliances', *Journal of Travel Research*, 34(1): 25–32.

Hollinshead, K. (1990) 'The powers behind play: The political environments for recreation and tourism', *Australia Journal of Park and Recreation Administration*, 8(1): 35–50.

Holtbrügge, D., Wilson, S. and Berg, N. (2006) 'Human resource management at Star Alliance: Pressures for standardization and differentiation', *Journal of Air Transport Management*, 12: 306–12.

Huxham, C. (1993) 'Pursuing collaborative advantage', *Journal of the Operational Research Society*, 44(6): 599–611.

Iatrou, K. and Alamdari, F. (2005) 'The empirical analysis of the impact of alliances on airline operations', *Journal of Air Transport Management*, 11: 127–34.

Inkpen, A. (1995) *The Management of International Joint Ventures: An Organizational Learning Perspective*. London: Routledge.

Jafari, J. (2000) *Encyclopedia of Tourism*. Oxford: Routledge.

Jamal, T.B. and Getz, D. (1995) 'Collaboration theory and community tourism planning', *Annals of Tourism Research*, 22(1): 186–204.

Jap, S.D. and Anderson, E. (2007) 'Testing a life-cycle theory of cooperative interorganizational relationships movement across stages and performance', *Management Science*, 53(2): 260–75.

Kanter, R.M. (1994) 'Collaborative advantage: The art of alliances', *Harvard Business Review*, (July–August): 96–108.

— (1995) 'Thinking locally in the global economy', *Harvard Business Review*, (September–October): 151–60.

Kelly, P. (2006) 'Political theory: The state of the art', *Politics*, 26(1): 47–53.

Keohane, R. and Nye, J.S. (1977) *Power and Interdependence*. Oxford: Longman.

Levine, S. and White, P.E. (1961) 'Exchange as a conceptual framework for the study of interorganizational relationships', *Administrative Science Quarterly*, 5(4): 583–601.

Lieberman, K. and Nissen, B. (2008) *Ethics in the Hospitality and Tourism Industry*, 2nd edn. Orlando: American Hotel & Motel Association.

Long, P. (1997) 'Researching tourism partnership organizations: From practice to theory to methodology', in P. Murphy (ed.) *Quality Management in Urban Tourism*. Chichester: Wiley.

Macaulay, S. (1963) 'Non-contractual relations in business: A preliminary study', *American Sociological Review*, 28: 55–67.

Modell, S. (2006) 'Institutional and negotiated order perspectives on cost allocations: The case of the Swedish University sector', *European Accounting Review*, 15(2): 219–251.

Morley, C.L. (2003) 'Impacts of international airline alliances on tourism', *Tourism Economics*, 9(1): 31–51.

Mouge, P.R. and Contractor, N.S. (2003) *Theories of Communication Networks*. New York: Oxford University Press.

Mountford, T. and Tacoun, F. (2004) 'Airline alliance survey 2004', *Airline Business*, 20: 53.

Oneworld (2012) www.oneworld.com (accessed 28 October 2012).

Oum, T.H., Park, J.H., Kim, K. and Yu, C. (2004) 'The effect of horizontal alliances on firm productivity and profitability: Evidence from the global airline industry', *Journal of Business Research*, 57: 844–53.

Palmer, A. (1996) 'Relationship marketing: A universal paradigm or management fad?', *The Learning Organization*, 3(3): 18–25.

Palmer, A. and Bejou, D. (1995) 'Tourism destination marketing alliances', *Annals of Tourism Research*, 22(3): 616–29.

Pfeffer, J. and Salancik, G. (1978) *The External Control of Organizations: A Resource Dependence Perspective.* New York: Harper & Row.
Pitfield, D.E. (2007) 'The impact on traffic, market shares and concentration of airline alliances on selected European–US routes', *Journal of Air Transport Management*, 13: 192–202.
Reed, M.G. (1997) 'Power relations and community-based tourism planning', *Annals of Tourism Research*, 24(3): 566–91.
Ring, P.S. and van de Ven, A.H. (1994) 'Developmental processes of cooperative interorganizational relationships', *The Academy of Management Review*, 19(1): 90–118.
Ross, S. (1973) 'The economic theory of agency: The principal's problem', *American Economic Review*, 63: 134–39.
Russell, R. and Faulkner, B. (2004) 'Entrepreneurship, chaos and the tourism area lifecycle', *Annals of Tourism Research*, 31(3): 556–79.
Seeger, M.W. (2002) 'Chaos and crisis: Propositions for a general theory of crisis communication', *Public Relations Review*, 28(4): 329–37.
Segil, L. (1996) *Intelligent Business Alliances.* London: Random House.
Selin, S. (1993) 'Collaborative alliances: New interorganizational forms in tourism', *Journal of Travel and Tourism Marketing*, 2(2/3): 217–27.
Selin, S. and Chavez, D. (1995) 'Developing an evolutionary tourism partnership model', *Annals of Tourism Research*, 22(4): 844–56.
Sky Team (2012) www.skyteam.com (accessed 28 October 2012).
Spyriadis, A. and Fyall, A. (2003) 'Collaborating for growth: The international hotel industry', *Journal of Hospitality and Tourism Management*, 10(2): 108–23.
Star Alliance (2012) www.staralliance.com (accessed 28 October 2012).
Strauss, A.L. (1978) *Negotiations: Varieties, Contexts, Processes, and Social Order.* San Francisco: Jossey Bass.
Terpstra, V. and Simonin, B. (1993) 'Strategic alliances in the triad: An exploratory study', *Journal of International Marketing*, 1(1): 4–25.
Tiernan, S., Rhoades, D. and Waguespack, B. (2008) 'Airline alliance service quality performance: An analysis of US and EU member airlines', *Journal of Air Transport Management*, 14: 99–102.
Ulrich, D. and Barney, J.B. (1984) 'Perspectives in organizations: Resource dependency, efficiency and population', *The Academy of Management Review*, 9(3): 471–81.
Vargas-Sanchez, A. and Riquel-Ligero, F. (2010) 'An institutional approach to the environmental management systems of golf courses in Andalusia', *European Journal of Tourism, Hospitality and Recreation*, 1(1): 24–38.
Waddock, S.A. (1989) 'Understanding social partnerships', *Administration and Society*, 21(2): 78–100.
Waddock, S.A. and Bannister, B.D. (1991) 'Correlates of effectiveness and partner satisfaction in social partnerships', *Journal of Organizational Change Management*, 4(2): 64–79.
Walker, D.H.T. and Johannes, D.S. (2003) 'Construction industry joint venture behaviour in Hong Kong: Designed for collaborative results?', *International Journal of Project Management*, 21(1): 39–49.
Wang, Y. and Fesenmaier, D.R. (2007) 'Collaborative destination marketing: A case study of Elkhart county, Indiana', *Tourism Management*, 28(3): 863–75.
Wang, Z.H., Evans, M. and Turner, L. (2004) 'Effects of strategic airline alliances on air transport market competition: An empirical analysis', *Tourism Economics*, 10: 23–43.
Weaver, R.D. (2009) 'Microeconomics of collaboration and network configuration', *British Food Journal*, 111(8): 746–61.
Weber, K. and Sparks, B. (2004) 'Consumer attributions and behavioural responses to service failures in strategic airline alliance settings', *Journal of Air Transport Management*, 10: 362–67.
Williamson, O. (1975) *Markets and Hierarchies.* New York: The Free Press.
— (1985) *The Economic Institutions of Capitalism.* New York: Free Press.
Wood, D.J. (1991) 'Corporate social performance revisited', *The Academy of Management Review*, 16(4): 691–718.
Wood, D.J. and Gray, B. (1991) 'Towards a comprehensive theory of collaboration', *Journal of Applied Behavioural Science*, 27(2): 139–62.
Zahra, A. and Ryan, C. (2007) 'From chaos to cohesion: Complexity in tourism structures – an analysis of New Zealand's regional tourism organizations', *Tourism Management*, 28(3): 854–62.
Zhang, A. and Zhang, Y. (2006) 'Rivalry between strategic alliances', *International Journal of Industrial Organization*, 24: 287–301.
Zhang, X., Song, H., Huang, G.Q. and Chen, W. (2010) 'Game-theoretic approach to tourism supply chain coordination under demand uncertainty for package holidays', *Tourism Analysis*, 15(3): 287–98.

13

Customer satisfaction in tourism

The search for the Holy Grail

Clare Foster

Introduction

In some respects, the concept of customer satisfaction in tourism can be likened to the search for the Holy Grail. It is highly revered and sought after by the industry, but remains an elusive concept methodologically. There is in fact little consensus as to 'what' satisfaction actually is despite exhaustive attention given to the subject over recent decades. To provide a comprehensive review of the literature on the subject, therefore, is not an easy task as one is immediately faced with a plethora of research from different approaches, spanning decades. And yet despite all this research, and despite customer satisfaction being the ultimate goal of tourism marketing, it seems we are still no closer to understanding what satisfaction actually *means* to people.

The quest to understand customer satisfaction from a marketing perspective has so far been led by approaches taking a psychological perspective. Satisfaction is perceived as a cognitive process and as the outcome of a '*post consumption evaluative judgement*'. Although there have been numerous iterations and variations, Kozak (2001) argues these approaches are in fact a family of mini-theories and conceptual schemes, which share a number of theoretical and methodological assumptions. Based on this understanding in the first section of the chapter an overview of these approaches is provided rather than a review of specific models and subsequent variants. The studies that are featured in this section are representative examples from within this tradition.

Partly as a result of increasing criticism of the cognitive approaches but also partly due to the evolution of tourism studies generally, a number of alternative approaches to customer satisfaction have emerged. For convenience, rather than any unifying theoretical basis or conceptual scheme, these approaches have been grouped together and are reviewed in the second section of the chapter. They include studies, which aim to understand satisfaction within the totality of tourist experience rather than specific attributes. These approaches often recognize the importance of consumers' emotional responses and the meanings of experience. Tourism is understood as an embodied experience, whereby tourists are contributors or co-producers of the experience and therefore have an input into satisfactory outcomes. These approaches often also highlight the importance of the social aspects of tourist experiences and recognize the influence and contribution of other people to satisfactory experiences.

The final section will turn to more emergent approaches to understanding satisfaction. These build on approaches which position the tourist as an active agent 'doing tourism' (Crouch *et al.*

2001). However, further evidence is drawn from ethnomethodology and discursive psychology, which places greater emphasis on the interactions of tourists, conceives evaluations as constitutive actions and thus satisfaction as something that is constructed in and through social interaction.

The process of satisfaction

Pearce (2005) argues satisfaction is simply a post-experience attitude, a cognitive process and the outcome of a '*post-consumption evaluative judgment*'. Research in this tradition has attempted to understand this individual cognitive process and the ways that tourists process experiences into subjective evaluations (Decrop 1999: 103). By looking at satisfaction as a process, these approaches concentrate on the antecedents to satisfaction rather than the construction of satisfaction itself.

At the core of this approach is the assumption that tourists make a rational cognitive evaluation by comparing the evaluative object or experience with some absolute or relative standard. Evaluations, for the most part, are treated as part of the individual cognitive process; they are the internal assessment procedure that individuals undertake to judge their levels of (dis)satisfaction. Customers use these evaluative judgments to inform future purchases. Satisfied consumers will engage in positive word-of-mouth behaviour and may remain loyal to the company. Dissatisfied consumers may engage in negative word-of-mouth, they may complain to the company and may ultimately choose not to use that company again.The link between attitudes and behavioural intentions is in the treatment of (dis)satisfaction as an attitude on the assumption that by understanding (dis)satisfaction, predictions can be made about future behaviour. Customer satisfaction is therefore a relative concept, which is always judged in relation to a standard. However, as Ekinci (2003) notes, although the use of a comparison standard is central to the measurement of customer satisfaction the choice of standard remains a key issue.

Historically, amongst the 'process' approaches to satisfaction, the 'disconfirmations approach' prevails and it forms the basis for numerous models used in tourism studies. Expectancy disconfirmation models assume that consumers purchase services with pre-purchase expectations about anticipated performance. Tourists evaluate their current experience based on these prior expectations and thus, the expectation level becomes a standard against which the service is judged. The theory works on the premise that confirmation occurs where customer perceptions of performance match expectations. Disconfirmation occurs where perceptions of performance deviate from expectations and this can be positive (perception of performance better than expectations), or negative (perception of performance worse than expectations). By measuring the difference between expectations and perceptions of performance, a 'gap-analysis' can be taken to judge the levels of satisfaction. Thus, satisfaction is related to the size of the disconfirmation experience, where disconfirmation is related to the person's initial expectations (Johnson 1995).

Despite on-going debate in relation to whether expectations are based on what consumers believe will happen or should happen, and whether consumers compare performance to expectations or norms, researchers generally agree that unfulfilled expectations can be an important source of consumer dissatisfaction. Alternative comparison standards also based on the 'disconfirmations approach' include 'experience based norms' where comparisons are made against previous experience. Similarly, 'equity theory' is posited as a comparison standard where satisfaction is judged in terms of the costs associated with the purchase (price, time, effort) and the rewards or benefits anticipated. If the rewards exceed the costs then tourists will be satisfied. However, some researchers (see for example Spreng *et al.* 1996; Bowen 2001; Decrop 2001;

Ekinci 2003) question the use of a single comparison standard and have instead called for recognition that tourists might use multiple comparison standards at any point in time.

The basic expectancy disconfirmation model has undergone various adaptations and it also forms the basis for the popular SERVQUAL model (Zeithaml *et al.* 1990). This model assumes that customers have expectations of service quality and any deviations result in disconfirmations of expectations. It operates under the assumption that gaps between customers' expected and perceived service are not only a measure of the quality of the service but also a determinant of customer (dis)satisfaction (Pizam and Ellis 1999). Therefore, although service quality and (dis) satisfaction are not the same thing, they are linked in that customers perceiving poor service quality for example, are unlikely to be satisfied. The SERVQUAL scale remains one of the most popular models in tourism and it has been used in various studies including: alpine resorts (Weiermair and Fuchs 1999), airlines (Robledo 2001; Gilbert and Wong 2003) and specific destinations (Pawitra and Tan 2003; Lee *et al.* 2004) among many others. Furthermore, Laws (1991) notes that many more researchers also refer their work to the SERVQUAL model either by using some of its constructs, or by differentiating their analyses from it.

The disconfirmations approach also forms the basis of Importance-performance models. These models stem from decision making models as discussed in part five of this volume, and they recognize that all attributes of the experience may not be of equal value to the consumer and hence satisfaction levels will vary accordingly. Based on this approach, compensatory models presume that customers make trade-offs of satisfaction of one attribute for another. Weighted compensatory models operate in the same way except they assume that each attribute has an importance weight relative to other attributes. On the other hand, non-compensatory models posit that tourism products consist of both core (the taken for granted elements) and peripheral attributes (the secondary features that differentiate the product) and whilst failure in the core elements is likely to cause dissatisfaction, positive evaluations are not reflected in a commensurately positive evaluation overall.

The disconfirmations approach assumes satisfaction to be mainly based on expectations. Yet for first time users, expectations are often vague or non-existent (Arnold and Price 1993; Obenour *et al.* 2006; Yuskal and Yuksal 2001) and people may update their expectations where there are delays between purchase and consumption or where they obtain additional information (Kozak 2001). Furthermore the most memorable and satisfying experiences can often be the most unexpected (Botterill 1987; Curtin 2005). These difficulties with using expectations as a comparison standard, amongst others, led to the development of 'performance only' approaches, which position evaluative judgements as made solely against the performance of the product or experience, and thus tourists are likely to be satisfied when performance is at a desired level (see for example Qu and Li 1997; Kozak and Rimmington 2000; Robledo 2001).

Despite numerous variations there remain some common assumptions inherent in process approaches that are worth highlighting. Regardless of the comparison standard used, process approaches assume satisfaction to be the outcome of a rational cognitive process and despite the assumption of an evaluative process the focal point is always the post-consumption assessment. Satisfaction is treated as an abstract and theoretical phenomenon (Kozak 2001) measurable through quantifiable methods, using indicators defined by the researcher. Tourists are required to rate their level of satisfaction against the standards determined by the researcher. Furthermore, there is also an assumption that satisfaction is individually interpreted and independent of other individuals. However, there are also differences, most specifically in relation to the most appropriate comparative standard, the role of expectations, the relationship between quality and satisfaction and the relative importance of various attributes. This has resulted in an increasing level of complexity in process models and context-dependency of findings of studies in an attempt to overcome shortcomings (Callahan and Elliott 1996).

Despite their continued popularity, process approaches using quantitative methods are not without criticism. Stewart and Hull (1996) highlight the growing body of literature which has begun to question the degree of cognitive processing implicit in these models. They argue that they characterise 'the human mind as having memory and computational abilities similar to the processing of a computer' (1996: 10). Others argue against the treatment of tourists as 'information processors' (Obenour *et al.* 2006; Callahan and Elliott 1996) whilst Otto and Ritchie (1996: 169) note that 'rational information processing schemes which focus on functional or purely attribute-based elements are incommensurate with tourism' (Otto and Ritchie 1996: 168). Additionally, Yi (1990 cited in Boote 1998) argues that dissatisfaction is an affective or emotional state, which can bypass any cognitive process of evaluation. Also, the emphasis in process approaches is on the individual cognitive judgement which leads Swan and Bowers (1998) to argue against individuals being treated as though they are in 'solitary confinement', in that they assume a complete absence of consumer interactions with other tourists or service delivery personnel in attempts to understand satisfaction (1998: 60). As Carey and Gountas argue 'satisfaction levels and perception of a situation are likely to be influenced not only by our personal evaluation but also by those who are closely participating in our experience' (2000: 65).

When satisfaction is calculated using specific attributes, the outcome depends on the choice of attributes included. Changing the selection of attributes affects the level of satisfaction accordingly, even though the level of overall satisfaction of the individual may not alter (Dmitrović *et al.* 2009). Similarly, Obenour *et al.* (2006) argue that disconfirmation models measure satisfaction with narrowly defined functions and attributes which ultimately creates a fragmented rather than holistic characterisation of the service experience. Yet as Palmer (2011) notes in the context of theatre performance evaluations, a musical cannot be assessed by judging each individual chord, but only by the way that they are performed together. Criticism is also directed to the fact that whilst outcomes (satisfaction) may be similar, the meanings of satisfactory experience are likely to be fundamentally different. As Ryan warns, 'the apparent ease of satisfaction measurement makes us blind to the real nature of the experience tourists seek and often find' (1999: 267).

Danaher and Hadrell (1996: 11) note 'the emerging consensus appears to be that performance drives disconfirmation, which in turn drives satisfaction'. However, Ryan (1995b: 52) argues that holidays are chosen with a goal in mind and any model of tourist behaviour must thus include consideration of tourists' predisposition to certain actions. Holidays ought to be successful since they are generally carefully chosen by individuals, who work towards them with considerable anticipation all year, investing in substantial time, effort and expense, and to admit that they were less than wonderful would be tantamount to social failure (Krippendorf 1987).

Concepts such as cognitive dissonance and behaviour adaptation whereby tourists re-evaluate the sources of disappointment as being unimportant, in order to achieve 'a fulfilling and satisfactory holiday' have been highlighted (Pearce 1988), which 'casts a shadow on the traditional method of tourism research' (Stewart and Hull 1996: 11). Tourists may be predisposed towards satisfaction, which in turn positively affects disconfirmation evaluations and thus, the perception of the overall experience or performance. In such a reverse causal sequence, a predisposition toward satisfaction may drive tourists to perform in such a way so as to achieve satisfaction. Essentially therefore, whilst satisfaction is posited as an outcome of an evaluative process, by focusing on the outcome, the process through which the outcome is achieved is often overlooked.

Alternative approaches

The experience of satisfaction

In cognitive models satisfaction is defined by the degree the experience has met expected outcomes, rather than on the actual experience itself. In alternative approaches the focus is on understanding tourism as an experience and thus attention is placed on the experiential benefits of tourism as an important factor in tourist satisfaction and in understanding the contribution of consumption experiences. They advocate that understanding customer experiences and benefits is critical for suppliers since customers perceive these experiences to be the core product (the bundle of memories they take away with them) (Slatten *et al.* 2011). Focusing on experiences leads to an emphasis on the emotional aspects of consumers' evaluations rather than rational cognition for as Otto and Ritchie (1996: 168) observe 'perhaps more than any other service, tourism holds the potential to elicit strong emotional and experiential reactions'. Emotional reactions and subjective responses are therefore seen as fundamental determinants of tourist satisfaction and post-consumption behaviour (McIntosh and Siggs 2005: 74).

In most cases, priority is given to a contextual understanding of the experience and to reconstructing the actor's own world-view in a way that is faithful to their everyday life (Rock 2001). The practical knowledge that people employ to guide their own actions is also important since individuals are interpretive beings that construct their lives purposefully and practically, creating meaning from their interactions with their environment (Rock ibid.). From an experiential perspective, focus is shifted away from the product to the perceptions or the meaning that the experience has for the individual. Tourists constantly construct their experiences in relation to their cultural context and the meaning of the experience to them as members of their culture. They are active agents and co-producers and to some extent 'responsible for creating their own satisfaction' (Slatten *et al.* 2011: 87).

By adopting an experiential, meaning-based approach, in-depth insights of the wider factors which contribute to satisfaction can be gleaned. For example Otto and Ritchie (1996) identified six dimensions in the tourism experience: hedonic, novelty, comfort, safety, stimulation and interaction, whilst Obenour *et al.* (2006) highlighted the importance of social interaction, independence and the symbols of distinctive accommodation for backpackers. Bitner (1992) and Swan and Trawick (1999) have shown that elements of the physical environment elicit strong emotional and subjective reactions and, as a consequence, influence satisfaction. Through gaining insights pertaining to the holistic perspective, suggestions can be made to improve satisfaction most notably through improvements in service design.

Others have noted the important contribution of service personnel such as tour leaders (Swan and Bowers 1998) and guides (Arnould *et al.* 1999) to satisfaction. Similarly Jennings and Weiler (2006) refer to the role of both formal (guides, representatives, service personnel) and informal (other tourists, host population) 'brokers' in mediating the experience. Arnould and Price (1993) found that the interaction with others sharing the journey had a profound effect upon tourists' satisfaction with the trip and the importance of this social aspect is a theme which recurs in a number of studies (Obenour *et al.* 2006; Murphy 2001; Andereck *et al.* 2006; Yarnal and Kerstetter 2005). However, such is the importance of social interaction to certain tourists that a service provider and/or product may be judged on the degree to which the provider/product offers a suitable venue or 'space' to facilitate social interaction (Obenour *et al.* 2006; Murphy 2001; Yarnal and Kerstetter 2005). Furthermore Gainer (1995) argues that by shifting the focus of inquiry to the relationship among consumers, a company may be evaluated not only in terms of its own performance but also in terms of its ability to provide a venue for the enactment of consumers' own performances.

The social experience of satisfaction

The importance of the social aspect of the tourism experience has been highlighted by experiential approaches. However, there are differences between studies and approaches in terms of how such social aspects are framed. At the fundamental level, the 'presence' of others has been identified as a factor contributing to the satisfaction of the experience (see for example Quiroga 1990). Tourism is, after all, largely an activity that people experience together. This is the 'collective gaze' (Urry 1990) where social sharing of tourist experiences with like-minded others is an enhancer of satisfaction.

At another level, is the 'influence' of others in producing satisfactory outcomes. Research gathered over several decades indicates that individuals can frequently be induced to alter their attitudes, feelings, or behaviour as a result of social influences (Baron 1977) and 'it is known that interpersonal influence on the evaluation of a product can stem from the beliefs one person conveys to another' (Howard and Gengler 2001: 12). For example, some researchers suggest that emotional contagion influences other customers' emotional states (Howard and Gengler 2001; Gountas and Gountas 2004) resulting in a convergence of emotions and, where the emotion is positive, more favourable product evaluations result. Conversely, Kowalski (1996) highlights the 'contagion of complaints', whereby the hearers of complaints often respond with complaints of their own. Research has also found that customer-to-customer relationships increase perceptions of satisfaction (Arnould and Price 1993; Harris and Baron 2004; Guenzi and Pelloni 2004; Wu 2007) and may positively contribute to the development of long-term relations with the company.

In the context of service encounters it is common to see people doing things together and so 'recognition of the simple fact of the group as the service user could be an important sensitising concept for many services' (Swan and Bowers 1998: 62). Yet tourists not only do things together, they also have ample opportunity to discuss their experiences throughout the holiday, and such discussions may potentially influence their subsequent evaluations (Laws 1991; Ryan 1995; Kozak 2001). From this perspective research on group interactions could be significant to understanding tourist satisfaction. Baron *et al.* (1992) note that in experimental situations individuals can be strongly influenced by the opinions of others. Furthermore, opinions are maintained for subsequent judgements even in the absence of a group. Ekinci and Riley (1998) argue that our social identity leads us to affiliate with groups and consequently towards consensual judgements.

Furthermore, the more intangible the object to be evaluated, the more the individual relies on consensus. The need for consensual judgements which affect evaluations can have a powerful influence even in the absence of other members of the group (Friedman and Fireworker 1977). Understanding satisfaction from a group, rather than an individual perspective remains under-researched in tourism. Exceptions include Swan and Bowers' (1998: 67) study of tourists of a bird-watching trip where they concluded that satisfaction was determined by factors other than product attributes and 'the concept of social norms may prove to be a significant determinant of service satisfaction because services take place in a social context'. Others call for tourists to be treated as a type of 'visitor community' (Levy and Hassay 2005) as members of a 'short-lived society' (Foster 1986), or as 'co-tourists' (Cheyenne Harvey and Lorenzen 2006), whilst Brown (2007) argues for the collaborative nature of tourist experience to be more widely recognized.

The performance of satisfaction

Performative approaches are predicated on the 'social' aspects of experiences, the co-production perspective. Drawing on the work of Goffman (1959) and the idea that social life can be likened to drama, performative approaches acknowledge that tourist experiences are carried out upon particular stages or settings. Edensor (2001) notes these settings are distinguished by boundedness, whether physical or symbolic, and although these do not determine the kinds of performance which occur, they provide and sustain common-sense understandings about what activities should take place. Within these settings we acquire the competence to reproduce recognizable performative conventions (Goffman 1959) and hence a key component of performative approaches is the concept of 'roles'. Rather than tourists holding expectations merely of the product, Goossens (2000) suggests they also have expectations of the 'role' they anticipate performing; an 'enactive imagery', which is described as 'a kind of imagined action or role play . . . an anticipating and motivating force that mediates emotional experiences, affective appraisals, evaluations, and behavioural intentions' (2000: 308). Bowen (2001a) found the performance of the individual was deemed more important than that of the product to long-haul passengers. Similarly Gyimothy's (2000) study of island visitors suggested that people interpret events according to the role perspective in which they identify themselves and, furthermore, that service providers were assessed according to the supporting or adversary role they occupied in tourists' personal discourses.

Another element is the concept of scripts. These are not rigid rules that limit behaviour but a set of guiding principles. Scripts denote what 'should' happen in the enactment of any performance: the form that the drama should take, what should be seen, what should be done and what actions are inappropriate (Edensor 2001). On a similar note MacCannell (1999: 25) argues 'each production (of tourism) is assembled from available cultural elements and it remains somewhat faithful to the other cultural models for the same experience'. Tourists may hold expectations of the overall script and as George and Mekoth (2004) found in a study of international tourists to India, an important source of dissatisfaction was when the expected scripts and events could not be observed. Unscripted events were similarly found to be a cause for complaint. According to Shoemaker (1996) satisfaction can best be achieved when companies possess an understanding of their customers' scripts.

Performative approaches recognize that tourists produce the experience through the practice of tourism and a degree of 'work' is involved for the experience to be realized. Tourism work is seen 'not in terms of paid employment but in the form of the organized purposeful activities which are part of tourism' (Brown 2007: 365). Yet, 'work' may also be undertaken by tourists in how experiences and activities are evaluated. Kennedy (2005) argues that there is a societal obligation to provide an assessment of the on-going experience, and Bowen (2001) found evaluations were made throughout the experience and with 'unanticipated frequency' (2001: 55). Evaluative work may therefore form a crucial part of the overall 'work' of 'being a tourist'. In this case, satisfaction is not simply realized, it is 'worked at' and actively achieved within the overall process and performance of being a tourist.

Performative approaches are useful in that they simultaneously acknowledge the importance of the context of the experience, the 'role' of the individual, the 'role' of others, and the role that both play in the overall production of the experience. It is possible therefore to understand satisfaction from a performative approach not as an outcome of the evaluation of an experience but as a performance enacted in the role of a tourist. Each experience is produced and reproduced in an ongoing interactive process and the success of the performance is determined according to the skill of the actors (Edensor 2001). In the co-constructed and interactional setting where there is concern for 'impression management' (Goffman 1959), tourists have to be accountable for their performances and they need to enact them in such a way that they will be acceptable to the recipient audiences. In other words, the audience needs to recognize and understand what is being performed. The way in which evaluations and satisfaction are socially constructed, negotiated and performed within the interaction with other members forms the focus of the final section of this chapter.

The evaluative process and the social construction of satisfaction

The most recent and emergent approaches present the possibility of understanding satisfaction as a social construction. Building on the understanding of tourists 'doing tourism' (Crouch *et al.* 2001:254) and on the importance of understanding the 'social' aspect of the experience these approaches do not necessarily attempt to question the psychological notion of satisfaction itself, but rather its treatment as readily accessible and measurable through quantitative approaches. Instead an alternative frame is presented where psychological concepts are considered in sociological terms and particular attention is placed on the social context in which people attach meaning to experiences. This perspective aims to understand tourists as members of society and therefore tourism experiences are not differentiated from the everyday context which shapes the way tourists associate meaning from their experiences.

Tourists are viewed as actively constructing their experiences through interactions with other people they encounter (Moore 2002) and these approaches seek to understand how the meaning of satisfaction is accomplished collectively and socially through a continuous process of social interaction. From this perspective expressing an evaluation is a social action (rather than an internal cognitive process) with an emphasis on the construction of evaluations as interactional practices (Wiggins 2001). Although evaluative expressions are a common feature of interaction (Pomerantz 1984) and the process of evaluation forms the basis for understanding satisfaction, evaluations per se have rarely been studied (Wiggins and Potter 2003).

However, drawing on ethnomethodology and discursive psychology Foster (2010) explored tourists' evaluations of their package holiday experiences. The study highlighted the strategies used in the accomplishment of evaluations and thus in part, how tourists negotiate the task of being a tourist. This study demonstrated the way in which evaluations and (dis)satisfaction are locally occasioned, managed and accomplished and highlighted the methods and procedures through which descriptions of good and bad holiday experiences are made sensible and understandable. In this type of approach (dis)satisfaction becomes a social accomplishment which is achieved through evaluative practices. The study presented the possibility that (dis)satisfaction can be treated as a culturally constructed phenomenon that cannot be separated from its social and interactional context.

Tourists were found to use devices such as 'scenic framing' and 'breach formulations' in evaluative talk of experiences. These devices draw on the 'known in common' spatial and social organization of the experience and become a resource to justify positive and negative evaluations and a way to communicate the shared meaning of good and bad experiences.

The meaning of good and bad holidays and (dis)satisfaction with such is therefore a participants' concern that is produced, formulated and negotiated in interaction. The social and local orientation to the meaning of evaluations and (dis)satisfaction was further demonstrated in tourists' frequent use of 'one-up-man-ship' strategies in response to other's negative evaluations. By responding to negative evaluations with descriptions of more extreme circumstances tourists display an intersubjectively shared understanding of the meaning of the evaluation. However, by positing alternative situations as being worse, the initial negative evaluation is downgraded.

Dissatisfaction, or at least the degree of dissatisfaction, can therefore be understood as socially constructed and negotiated within interactional practices.

Where satisfaction is understood as possessing an affective component, then the relevance of the social construction of emotions and the appropriate socially sanctioned response is also pertinent. Laurier (1999: 204) argues that 'leisure is constructed around notions of appropriate emotions, having a bad time is the ultimate failure of precious investment given over to leisure' and in his study of yacht cruising he noted the considerable amount of effort required to keep up the appearance of having a good time, to maintain a sense of a defined situation and to 'fit' within the constructed boundaries of appropriate behaviour. Similarly, from a constructionist perspective Stearns (1995: 37) argues that emotional reactions change according to cultural requirements and in relation to anger, 'people to an extent select how angry they will become and certainly how much anger they will display, not in spontaneous response to the magnitude of the stimulus but in keeping with the social setting'.

Stemming from the seminal work of Hochschild (1983) the concept of 'emotional labour' has increasingly become an area of interest. The work of exotic dancers (Montemurro 2001; Wood 2000), restaurant servers (Paules 1991) and adventure guides (Holyfield 1999; Sharpe 2005) has been explored, all of whom must display good cheer even when they are otherwise frustrated, bored, or angry. Sharpe argues that adventure provides a setting for a character contest and central to displaying the appropriate style of conduct is maintaining control over one's emotions. As a consequence, being able to control one's emotions in adventure has become a valued trait in our culture. Laurier's study is important in terms of highlighting the 'emotional work' involved in leisure experiences. Yet, the study refers to the work that he himself undertook as a participant. With the exception of Foster (2010) the work that tourists in general undertake is as yet unknown.

However, Foster demonstrated the way in which tourists work to readjust their evaluations in order to maintain a positive response to the experience and how notions of dissatisfaction are 'worked up' in negative accounts of holiday experiences. Sources of dissatisfaction were routinely re-evaluated as being unimportant or presented in a way to limit their impact on satisfaction. Additionally tourists also worked to demonstrate their ability to cope with negative elements of the experience and they presented themselves as competent, discerning customers. In the same way that emotional control is code for being 'professional' for airline stewards (Hochchild 1983), appropriate control of one's emotions is a key element of the performance in the role of a tourist.

Conclusion

Customer satisfaction remains an important element of any organization's strategy and in a competitive market the ability to assess levels of customer satisfaction is crucial to survival. This situation has led to a quest to find 'instrumentally useful' frameworks for the measurement of customer satisfaction and it is these approaches which currently dominate the field. From these perspectives tourists are considered rational consumers that undertake a 'post consumption evaluative judgement' frequently in relation to some standard. As yet, there remains no agreement as to which standard should be used, nor of the attributes against which the experience should be assessed. The product is placed at the centre of these approaches and concern turns to the methods to measure tourist satisfaction as it pertains to performance of the product. These approaches may be useful in terms of assessing specific elements of the experience, yet they also attract much criticism.

Whilst the focus of process approaches tends to be either transactional or attribute based, experiential approaches explore the more holistic, dynamic and less tangible features (Pearce

2005) along with the emotional responses they elicit. Furthermore, a priority is placed on understanding context and the meaning of experience to those involved. However, whilst the importance of social sharing and the influence of others is highlighted, most studies predominately retain the notion of the judgement of satisfaction as pertaining to the individual.

Yet, tourists are not isolated from society, they are fully participating members. Therefore, as Williams and Buswell (2003: 75) note, 'it is not enough to interpret the individual's thoughts and impressions as self-centred acts; the experience in which the tourism meaning is formed should also be studied'. This chapter explored approaches that place more emphasis on the collective nature of tourist experience and the social context in which they occur. These share with experiential approaches the goal of understanding the complex world of lived experience from the point of view of those concerned and an understanding that the lived world of reality (and meaning) is constructed by social actors (Schwandt 1998). However, rather than focus on the matter of individuals' inner states, attention is turned to how reality is intersubjectively shared, and thus socially constructed.

This view is predicated on the assumption that the terms by which the world is understood are social artefacts and products of historically situated interchanges among people (Gergen 1985 cited in Schwandt, ibid.). As Wang (2000) argues, it is actually expected that people will designate some of their resources in order to acquire new experiences geographically remote from their daily life as part of their leisure time. Similarly Krippendorf (1987: 18) argues that going on holiday is something taken for granted as normal behaviour: 'We don't ask "what are you doing during the holidays?" but "where are you going?"'. Each holiday can therefore be understood not only as a holistic experience but also within the wider cultural 'practice' of taking holidays. The emphasis from a social constructionist perspective is therefore on the collective generation of meaning as shaped by conventions of language and other social processes.

As Curtin (2005: 2) notes 'there are few major purchasing decisions which are based on a mere promise, a notion, and a socially constructed image of what constitutes an interesting or appealing experience'. Similarly, Smith (1995: 3) states 'tourism is an activity that individuals enjoy'. This statement is not disputed. Rather it is repeated here as a way to draw attention to a fundamental, yet neglected assumption. That is, discourses of tourism regularly construct holidays as enjoyable experiences. Ryan (1997) argues that holiday-making is a goal driven activity whereby the goal is 'to have a good time'. Krippendorf (1987: 38) similarly identifies the 'have a good time' ideology, which sets the tone for holidays. The social construction of holidays as good and, or, positive experiences, may therefore be more of an influence on satisfaction than the actual experience itself.

Research that explores the collectively held beliefs and values in the tourists' community may be of use in developing the understanding of satisfaction with that specific consumption experience. More than simply touching on a different level of analysis, emergent approaches therefore reframe satisfaction from approaches that emphasize the individual psychological notion of the concept to one involving collective intersubjective meaning. The plethora of research which has been conducted in an attempt to understand tourist satisfaction has undoubtedly contributed to our knowledge of the subject. However, as Pearce (2005: 173) notes, 'there is still much to be done to develop satisfaction studies specifically in the tourism context'. The quest for the Holy Grail therefore continues.

References

Andereck, K., Bricker, K.S., Kerstetter, D. and Polovitz Nickerson, N. (2006) 'Connecting Experiences to Quality: Understanding the Meanings behind Visitors' Experiences', in G. Jennings, and N. Polovitz Nickerson (eds) *Quality Tourism Experiences*. Oxford: Elsevier Butterworth-Heinemann.

Arnould, E.J. and Price, L.L. (1993) 'River Magic: Hedonic Consumption and the Extended Service Encounter', *Journal of Consumer Research*, 20: 24–45.
Arnould, E.J., Price, L.L. and Otnes, C. (1999) 'Making Magic Consumption. A Study of White-water River Rafting', *Journal of Contemporary Ethnography*, 28(1): 33–68.
Baron, R.A. (1977) *Human Aggression*. New York: Plenum Press.
Baron, R.S., Kerr, N.L. and Miller, N. (1992) *Group Process, Group Decision, Group Action*. Buckingham: Open University Press.
Bitner, M.J. (1992) 'Servicescapes: The Impact of Physical Surroundings on Customers and Employees', *Journal of Marketing*, 56(2): 57–71.
Boote, J. (1998) 'Towards a Comprehensive Taxonomy and Model of Consumer Complaining Behaviour', *Journal of Consumer Satisfaction, Dissatisfaction and Complaining Behaviour*, 11: 140–51.
Botterill, D. (1987) 'Dissatisfaction with a Construction of Satisfaction', *Annals of Tourism Research*, 14: 139–41.
Bowen, D. (2001) 'Antecedents of Consumer Satisfaction and Dissatisfaction on Long-haul Inclusive Tours – A Reality Check on Theoretical Considerations', *Tourism Management*, 22: 49–61.
Brown, B. (2007) 'Working the Problems of Tourism', *Annals of Tourism Research*, 34(2): 364–83.
Callahan, C. and Elliott, C.S. (1996) 'Listening: A Narrative Approach to Everyday Understandings and Behaviour', *Journal of Economic Psychology*, 17: 79–114.
Carey, S. and Gountas, J.Y. (2000) 'Tourism Satisfaction and Service Evaluation', in M. Robinson, P. Long, N. Evans, R. Sharpley and J. Swarbrooke (eds) *Motivations, Behaviour and Tourist Types*. Sunderland: Business Education Publishers Ltd, pp. 55–74.
Cheyenne Harvey D. and Lorenzen J. (2006) 'Signifying Practices and the Co-Tourist', *Tourismos: An International Multidisciplinary Journal of Tourism*, 1(1): 11–28.
Crouch, D., Aronsson, L. and Wahlstrom, L. (2001) 'Tourist Encounters', *Tourist Studies*, 1(3): 253–70.
Curtin, S. (2005) 'Nature, Wild Animals and Tourism: An Experiential View', *Journal of Ecotourism*, 4(1): 1–15.
Danaher, P.J. and Haddrell, V. (1996) 'A Comparison of Question Scales Used for Measuring Customer Satisfaction', *International Journal of Service Industry Management*, 7(4): 4–26.
Decrop, A. (1999) 'Tourists' Decision Making and Behaviour Processes', in A. Pizam and Y. Mansfield (eds) *Consumer Behaviour in Travel and Tourism*. New York: The Haworth Press.
— (2001) 'The Antecedents and Consequences of Vacationers' Dis/satisfaction: Tales from the Field', in J.A. Mazanec, A.G. Woodside, G.I. Crouch and J.R. Brent Ritchie (eds) *Consumer Psychology of Tourism, Hospitality and Leisure*, Volume 2. Oxon: CABI Publishing, pp. 333–47.
Dmitrović, T., Knežević Cvelbar, L., Kolar, T., Makovec Brenčič, M., Ograjenšell, I. and Žabkav, V. (2009) 'Conceptualizing Tourist Satisfaction at the Destination Level', *International Journal of Culture, Tourism and Hospitality Research*, 3(2): 116–26.
Edensor, T. (2001) 'Performing Tourism, Staging Tourism', *Tourist Studies*, 1(1): 59–81.
Ekinci, Y. (2003) 'Which Comparison Standard Should be Used for Service Quality and Customer Satisfaction?', in J.A. Williams and M. Uysal (eds) *Current Issues and Developments in Hospitality and Tourism Satisfaction*. Binghamton, NY: The Haworth Press, pp. 61–76.
Ekinci, Y. and Riley, M. (1998) 'A Critique of the Issues and Theoretical Assumptions in Service Quality Measurement in the Lodging Industry: Time to Move the Goal-posts?', *Hospitality Management*, 17: 349–62.
Foster, C. (2010) 'Tourists' Evaluations of their Package Holiday Experiences', unpublished Doctoral thesis, University of Nottingham.
Foster, G.M. (1986) 'South Seas Cruise. A Case Study of a Short-lived Society', *Annals of Tourism Research*, 13: 215–38.
Friedman, H.H. and Fireworker, R.B. (1977) 'The Susceptibility of Consumers to Unseen Group Influence', *The Journal of Social Psychology*, 102: 155–56.
Gainer, B. (1995) 'Ritual and Relationships: Interpersonal Influences on Shared Consumption', *Journal of Business Research*, 32: 253–60.
George, B.P. and Mekoth, N. (2004), 'Self-Monitoring as a Key to the Tourist: Potential Scenarios and Some Propositions', *International Journal of Hospitality and Tourism Administration*, 5(2): 25–41.
Gilbert, D. and Wong, R.K.C. (2003) 'Passenger Expectations and Airline Services: A Hong Kong Based Study', *Tourism Management*, 24(5): 519–532.
Goffman, E. (1959) *The Presentation of Self in Everyday Life*. London: Penguin.
Goossens, C. (2000) 'Tourism Information and Pleasure Motivation', *Annals of Tourism Research*, 27(2): 301–21.

Gountas, S. and Gountas, J.Y. (2004) 'The Influence of Consumers' Emotions on their Service Product Evaluations', in G.I. Crouch, R.R. Perdue, H.J.P. Timmermans and M. Uysal (eds) *Consumer Psychology of Tourism, Hospitality and Leisure*, Volume 3. Wallingford: CAB International.
Guenzi, P. and Pelloni, O. (2004) 'The Impact of Interpersonal Relationships on Customer Satisfaction and Loyalty to the Service Provider', *International Journal of Service Industry Management*, 15(4): 365–84.
Gyimothy, S. (2000) 'Odysseys: Analysing Service Journeys from the Customer's Perspective', *Managing Service Quality*, 10(6): 389–96.
Harris, K. and Baron, S. (2004) 'Consumer-to-Consumer Conversations in Service Settings', *Journal of Service Research*, 6(3): 287–303.
Hochschild, A.R. (1983) *The Managed Heart: Commercialisation of Human Feeling*. Berkeley, CA: University of California Press.
Holyfield, L. (1999) 'Manufacturing Adventure: The Buying and Selling of Emotions', *Journal of Contemporary Ethnography*, 29(1): 3–32.
Howard, D.J. and Gengler, C. (2001) 'Emotional Contagion Effects on Product Attitudes', *Journal of Consumer Research*, 28(2): 189–201.
Jennings, G. and Weiler, B. (2006) 'Mediating Meaning: Perspectives on Brokering Quality Tourist Experiences', in G. Jennings and N. Nickerson (eds) *Quality Tourism Experiences*. Oxford: Butterworth-Heinemann, pp. 55–75.
Johnson, R. (1995) 'The Zone of Tolerance: Exploring the Relationship between Service Transactions and Satisfaction with the Overall Service', *International Journal of Service Industry Management*, 6(2): 46–61.
Kennedy, C. (2005) 'Just Perfect! The Pragmatics of Evaluation in Holiday Postcards', in A. Jaworski and A. Pritchard (eds) *Discourse, Communication and Tourism*. Clevedon: Channel View Publications, pp. 223–46.
Kowalski, R.M. (1996) 'Complaints and Complaining: Functions, Antecedents, and Consequences', *Psychological Bulletin*, 119(2): 179–96.
Kozak, M. (2001) 'A Critical Review of Approaches to Measure Satisfaction with Tourist Destinations', in J.A. Mazanec, G.I. Crouch, J.R. Brent Ritchie and A.G. Woodside (eds) *Consumer Psychology of Tourism, Hospitality and Leisure*, Volume 2. Oxon: CABI Publishing, pp. 303–20.
Kozak, M. and Rimmington, M. (2000) 'Tourist Satisfaction with Mallorca, Spain as an Off-season Holiday Destination', *Journal of Travel Research*, 38: 260–69.
Krippendorf, J. (1987) *The Holidaymakers: Understanding the Impact of Leisure and Travel*. Oxford: Butterworth-Heinemann Ltd.
Laurier, E. (1999) 'That Sinking Feeling: Elitism, Working, Leisure, and Yachting', in D. Crouch (ed.) *Leisure Practices and Geographical Knowledge*. London: Routledge, pp.195–213.
Laws, E. (1991) *Tourism Marketing: Service and Quality Management Perspectives*. Cheltenham: Stanley Thornes.
Lee, J., Graefe, A.R. and Burns, R.C. (2004) 'Service Quality, Satisfaction and Behavioural Intention among Forest Visitors', *Journal of Travel and Tourism Marketing*, 17(1): 73–82.
Levy, S. and Hassay, D. (2005) 'Visitor Communities', *Journal of Hospitality and Leisure Marketing*, 12(4): 57–72.
MacCannell, D. (1999) *The Tourist. A New Theory of the Leisure Class*, (3rd edn). Berkeley, CA: University of California Press.
McIntosh, A.J. and Siggs, A. (2005) 'An Exploration of the Experiential Nature of Boutique Accommodation', *Journal of Travel Research*, 44: 74–81.
Montemurro, B. (2001) 'Strippers and Screamers: The Emergence of Social Control in a Non-institutionalised Setting', *Journal of Contemporary Ethnography*, 30(3): 275–304.
Moore, K. (2002) 'The Discursive Tourist', in G.M.S. Dann (ed.) *The Tourist as a Metaphor of the Social World*. Oxon: CABI Publishing, pp. 41–69.
Murphy, L. (2001) 'Exploring Social Interactions of Backpackers', *Annals of Tourism Research*, 28(1): 50–67.
Obenour, W., Patterson, M., Pederson, P. and Pearson, L. (2006) 'Conceptualisation of a Meaning-based Approach for Tourism Service Experiences', *Tourism Management*, 34: 34–41.
Otto, J.E. and Ritchie, J.R.B. (1996) 'The Service Experience in Tourism', *Tourism Management*, 17(3): 165–74.
Palmer, A. (2011) *Principles of Services Marketing*, (6th edn). Maidenhead: McGraw-Hill Education.
Paules, G.F. (1991) *Dishing It Out: Power and Resistance among Waitresses in a New Jersey Restaurant*. Philadelphia: Temple University Press.
Pawitra, T.A. and Tan, K.C. (2003) 'Tourist Satisfaction in Singapore – A Perspective from Indonesian Tourists', *Managing Service Quality*, 13(5): 399–411.
Pearce, P.L. (1988) *The Ulysses Factor: Evaluating Visitors in Tourist Settings*. New York: Springer Verlag.

— (2005) *Tourist Behaviour: Themes and Conceptual Schemes.* Bristol: Channel View Publications.
Pomerantz, A. (1984) 'Agreeing and Disagreeing with Assessments: Some Features of Preferred/Dispreferred Turn Shapes', in J.M. Atkinson and J. Heritage (eds) *Structures of Social Action: Studies in Conversation Analysis.* Cambridge: Cambridge University Press, pp. 57–101.
Qu, H. and Li, I. (1997) 'The Characteristics and Satisfaction of Mainland Chinese Visitors to Hong Kong', *Journal of Travel Research*, 36: 37–41.
Quiroga, I. (1990) 'Characteristics of Package Tours in Europe', *Annals of Tourism Research*, 17: 185–207.
Robledo, M.A. (2001) 'Measuring and Managing Service Quality: Integrating Customer Expectations', *Managing Service Quality*, 11(1): 22–31.
Rock, P. (2001) 'Symbolic Interactionism and Ethnography', in P. Atkinson, A. Coffey, S. Delamont, J. Lofland and L. Lofland (eds) *Handbook of Ethnography.* London: Sage, pp. 26–38.
Ryan, C. (1995) *Researching Tourist Satisfaction: Issues, Concepts, Problems.* London: Routledge.
— (ed.) (1997) *The Tourist Experience: A New Introduction.* London: Cassell.
— (1999) 'From the Psychometrics of SERVQUAL to Sex: Measurements of Tourist Satisfaction', in A. Pizam and Y. Mansfield (eds) *Consumer Behaviour in Travel and Tourism.* New York: The Haworth Press, pp. 267–86.
Schwandt, T.A. (1998) 'Constructivist, Interpretivist Approaches to Human Inquiry', in N.K. Denzin and Y.S. Lincoln (eds) *The Landscape of Qualitative Research.* London: Sage Publications, pp. 292–331.
Sharpe, E.K. (2005) '"Going Above and Beyond": The Emotional Labour of Adventure Guides', *Journal of Leisure Research*, 37(1): 29–50.
Shoemaker, S. (1996) 'Scripts: Precursor of Consumer Expectations', *Cornell Hotel and Restaurant Administration Quarterly*, 37: 42–53.
Slatten, V., Krogh, C. and Connolley, S. (2011) 'Make it Memorable: Customer Experiences in Winter Amusement Parks', *International Journal of Culture, Tourism and Hospitality Research*, 5(1): 80–91.
Smith, S.L.J. (1995) *Tourism Analysis. A Handbook*, (2nd edn). Harlow: Addison Wesley Longman Ltd.
Spreng, R.A., MacKenzie, S.B. and Olshavsky, R.W. (1996) 'A Re-examination of the Determinants of Consumer Satisfaction', *Journal of Marketing*, 60: 15–32.
Stearns, P. (1995) 'Emotion', in R. Harre and P. Stearns (eds) *Discursive Psychology in Practice.* London: Sage, pp. 37–54.
Stewart, W.P. and Hull, R.B. IV. (1996) 'Capturing the Moments: Concerns of In Situ Research', *Journal of Travel and Tourism Marketing*, 5(1/2): 3–20.
Swan, J.E. and Bowers, M.R. (1998) 'Service Quality and Satisfaction: The Process of People Doing Things Together', *Journal of Services Marketing*, 12(1): 59–72.
Swan, J.E. and Trawick, I.F. (1999) 'Delight on the Nile: An Ethnography of Experiences that Produce Delight', *Journal of Consumer Satisfaction, Dissatisfaction and Complaining Behaviour*, 12: 64–70.
Urry, J. (1990) *The Tourist Gaze: Leisure and Travel in Contemporary Societies.* London: Sage.
Wang, N. (2000) *Tourism and Modernity: A Sociological Analysis.* Oxford: Pergamon Press.
Weiermair, K. and Fuchs, M. (1999) 'Measuring Tourist Judgment on Service Quality', *Annals of Tourism Research*, 26(4): 1004–21.
Wiggins, S. (2001) 'Construction and Action in Food Evaluation', *Journal of Language and Social Psychology*, 20(4): 445–63.
Wiggins, S. and Potter, J. (2003) 'Attitudes and Evaluative Practices: Category vs Item and Subjective vs Objective Constructions in Everyday Food Assessments', *British Journal of Social Psychology*, 42: 513–31.
Williams, C. and Buswell, J. (2003) *Service Quality in Leisure and Tourism.* Oxon: CABI Publishing.
Wood, E.A. (2000) 'Working in the Fantasy Factory: The Attention Hypothesis and the Enacting of Masculine Power in Strip Clubs', *Journal of Contemporary Ethnography*, 29(1): 5–31.
Wu, C.H. (2007) 'The Impact of Customer-to-customer Interaction and Customer Homogeneity on Customer Satisfaction in Tourism Service – The Service Encounter Prospective', *Tourism Management*, 28: 1518–528.
Yarnal, C.M. and Kerstetter, D. (2005) 'Casting Off. An Exploration of Cruise Ship Space, Group Tour Behaviour, and Social Interaction', *Journal of Travel Research*, 43: 368–79.
Yuksel, A. and Yuksel, F. (2001) 'The Expectancy–Disconfirmation Paradigm: A Critique', *Journal of Hospitality and Tourism Research*, 25: 107–31.
Zeithaml, V.A., Parasuraman, A. and Berry, L.L. (1990) *Delivering Service Quality.* New York: Free Press.

Part 4

Advances in tourism marketing research

14

Advanced analytical methods in tourism marketing research

Usage patterns and recommendations

Josef Mazanec, Amata Ring, Brigitte Stangl and Karin Teichmann

Usage and application patterns

When the American Marketing Association launched its *Journal of Marketing Research* in 1963, it triggered off what is nowadays called the 'multivariate revolution' in marketing. It took about a decade for marketing researchers to discover the intriguing application area of tourism that poses plenty of challenges for advanced analytical methods. Table 14.1 highlights the most prominent analytical tasks together with conventional and nonstandard methods encountered in these fields of marketing decision making. Nontrivial methods are instrumental for decision-support since the analyst must come to terms with problems such as data reduction for purifying redundant observations, qualitative variables, latent constructs and multiple indicators, ambiguity in the direction of causality, unobserved heterogeneity, nonlinearity or multicollinearity. Given these intricacies the need for advanced analytical methods is apparent and the investigation may proceed with highlighting the actual method use in tourism marketing research.

The usage frequency of advanced analytical methods in tourism research was analyzed in a survey article by Mazanec *et al.* (2010). The following text is based on this article (by courtesy of Cognizant Communication Corp.). The survey covers six journals (*Annals of Tourism Research, Journal of Information Technology and Tourism, Journal of Travel Research, Journal of Travel and Tourism Marketing, Tourism Analysis* and *Tourism Management*) during the time period 1988–2008. If tourist behaviour research is considered a key element of tourism marketing one may safely assume that the six-journal findings are representative of empirical studies with a marketing background. Under this assumption linear and nonlinear regression methods along with Exploratory Factor Analysis (EFA) were heading the frequency list of popular methods (23 per cent each; see also Lee and Law 2012). Confirmatory Factor Analysis (CFA) was far less frequent as a stand-alone technique (3 per cent), but necessarily features in a fast growing number of Structural Equation Models (SEMs) with latent variables (7 per cent). Advanced Time Series Models (5 per cent) were relatively rare compared to the regression-based econometric models. Hierarchical and Partitioning Clustering methods put together attained an application frequency of almost 10 per cent.

Multivariate Analysis of (Co-)Variance (MAN(C)OVA; 5 per cent) and Multiple Discriminant Analysis (MDA; 3 per cent) were among the more popular techniques from the traditional

Table 14.1 Analytical methods employed in marketing research

Decision domains of strategic tourism marketing	*Research aim in a nutshell*	*Conventional methods*	*Recent developments*
Market response models (aggregate and disaggregate)	Explain and predict consumer response to marketing action of tourism businesses and DMOs	Linear and nonlinear regression; Discrete choice models; Time series models	Computer simulation models; Agent-based modelling
Brand positioning (BP)	Uncover tourists' perceptions of and preferences for competing choice alternatives	Exploratory and confirmatory factor analysis; (Non)metric multidimensional scaling and unfolding; Correspondence analysis	Semantic networks; Item response theory; *for BP and MS*: vector quantization (self-organizing maps and topology representing networks)
Market segmentation (MS)	Generate market segments that react homogeneously to tailor-made offerings and targeting	partitioning and hierarchical cluster analysis; Automatic interaction detection; Discriminant analysis; Latent class analysis; Covariance-based SEM and partial least squares path models	Classification and decision trees; Feedforward neural networks; Sequence alignment method; Nonlinear structural equation models *for MS and BP*: joint positioning/ segmentation with finite mixture models
New product planning and interactive travel recommender systems	Develop and examine product/service bundles capable of building market share	Conjoint analysis; Expert systems; Analytical hierarchy process	fuzzy set theory; Genetic algorithms; adaptive (self-learning) models

multivariate toolkit. Correspondence Analysis and Conjoint Analysis exhibited a disappointing number of applications (less than 2 per cent each). While Conjoint Analysis was introduced into marketing research as early as 1971 by Green and Rao in a famous *Journal of Marketing Research* article, the first application in tourism marketing research appeared much later (Bojamic and Calantone 1990). Despite its resourcefulness this study could not trigger off a research tradition within tourism marketing comparable to the wealth of conjoint applications in core marketing.

(Nonmetric) Multidimensional Scaling ((N)MDS, less than 2 per cent) is not a homogeneous class of methods but offers a variety of approaches to analyzing direct or attribute-based proximity and preference data. (N)MDS has been a standard analytical instrument for perceptual mapping in marketing research from the early 1970s on. In tourism research Fenton and Pearce (1988) presented a comprehensive overview of MDS techniques. One of the typical applications related to tourism market segmentation was Yiannakis and Gibson's (1992) attempt of typifying tourist roles.

Discrete Choice Models (2 per cent) were not considered in the 1988–2008 survey unless they explicitly dealt with tourists' or managers' individual choice alternatives and decisions. Choice Models on individual level were addressed as early as 1993 in a purely theoretical paper (Wie and Choy 1993) and in an empirical study on modal choice (Winzar, Pidcock and Johnson 1993). After a first empirical application to modelling destination choice (Morley 1994) it took tourism research quite a while to adopt random coefficient specifications of choice models (Nicolau and Más 2005).

Despite their long tradition and their unmistakable merits in handling the qualitative (less than interval-scaled) data that abound in tourist behaviour research some methods are extremely sparse. Examples are Latent Class Analysis (LCA), Canonical Correlation, Log-Linear Models or the Analytical Hierarchy Process (AHP, introduced by Thomas Saaty in 1977). Saaty's eigenvector method got mentioned in an *Annals* paper (Calantone and Mazanec 1991) but had been practically applied by the Austrian National Tourism Organization as early as 1984 (with a little help from their friends in academia).

Applications of Expert Systems are rare. After the early example of an application to computer-assisted travel counselling (Hruschka and Mazanec 1990) there was a fairly long period of silence until the advent of trip recommender systems became fashionable. Other examples of neglected fields with a promising problem-solving potential are Fuzzy Set Theory or Classification and Decision Trees.

Tourism marketing research was fairly quick in embracing Neural Networks. Among the early adopters Mazanec (1992) and Pattie and Snyder (1996) used a feedforward network with backpropagation learning to classify tourists into market segments and to forecast visiting behaviour. Other neural network architectures such as the Self-Organizing Map (SOM) and its descendants in the field ofVector Quantization (VQ) must be taken into account to portray the full picture of neurocomputing methodology. Genetic Algorithms (GA) were not quite as prolific though their 'tourism' history began no later than 1997 when Taplin and Qiu decided to use GA methodology for estimating the parameters of a route choice model. A little later Hurley, Moutinho and Witt (1998) published a 'stand-alone' genetic application.

A method such as (non-naïve) Meta-Analysis is still under-utilized in tourism marketing research. An early example such as Geoff Crouch's (1995) analysis of tourism demand models would have deserved a larger number of followers. Several other methods were subject to very late detection by tourism marketing. Social and Semantic Network Analysis is one of them and does not yet enjoy a long tradition of tourism marketing applications. Interestingly, the first example found in the 1988–2008 period did not analyze sociometric or semantic data but tourists' drive patterns (Shih 2006). Shortly after, the 'ordinary' applications to social or semantic networks follow suit (Pan and Fesenmaier 2006).

Judging the frequency of usage over time the number of SEMs, and to a lesser extent, of CFAs has risen exponentially. These two categories will be examined more closely to verify whether the enormous gain in popularity also implies qualitative improvement and has contributed to advancement in theory building. CFA, besides its natural role within SEM, has also been instrumental as a routine method in scale construction and validation. Both aspects will be considered in a separate evaluation section.

Clustering methods show a persistent record of applications over the years. This prompts the question whether there is a discernible improvement of how the various decisions an analyst has to make during a cluster analysis are justified and substantiated. Hierarchical and partitioning methods will be explored later.

The lower than average usage frequency of Choice Modelling does not correspond to the success story apparent in core marketing. However, choice models tend to appear in tandem with other advanced analytical methods and examples will be mentioned in the next section.

There are typical examples of how to combine analytical methods in tourism marketing research. Regression techniques and Exploratory Factor Analysis are the methods to enter into such combinations most frequently. EFA lets the analyst condense a number of observables into 'factors' (or principal components) and benefit from their orthogonality in subsequent regression runs. Such two-step setups are still in use. As a typical example see Molina and Esteban (2006) who apply PCA and logistic regression. However, with the advent of SEMs there is no more need for proceeding in a stepwise manner when analyzing cause–effect relationships among a set of hypothetical constructs. Single-step methods are not just superior because of statistical reasons. They enforce a unified view of theory building acknowledging that the measurement and structural submodels are constituents of an integral theory and must not be tested and adjusted separately in an incremental approach to model fitting.

Classification procedures are common in method combinations. For example, Bargeman, Timmermans and Van der Waerden (1999) search for profiling criteria of tourist segments. The tourist clusters are derived out of panel data with the Sequence Alignment Method and the correlates of segment membership are detected with a double-application of decision-tree analysis (CHAID) and a loglinear model. Further processing a cluster structure of tourists is not limited to simple profiling with passive variables. As Jang, Morrison and O'Leary (2004) demonstrate, the selection of target segments may be optimized in terms of receipts and seasonal stability by means of Quadratic Programming.

Multiple uses of methods are sometimes driven by the analysts' desire to cross-validate empirical findings. This is particularly helpful where a method does not include statistical significance testing. For example, Fodness and Milner (1992) run a connected sequence of four analytical steps:

1 aggregating theme park visitation patterns into a 'visitor interchange matrix';
2 processing these park similarity data with MDS;
3 clustering visitors by their individual visitation history into market segments; and
4 testing a number of demographic and socio-economic variables for profiling the visitor segments.

Dale Fodness in a 1994 article moves from MDS to PCA and on to a Partitioning Clustering method when measuring tourist motivation. Molera and Albaladejo (2007) make joint use of factorization of perceived benefit items with principal components, hierarchical and partitioning clustering, ANOVA testing of cluster differences, and multinomial logit regression for segment profiling.

Smart combinations of methods are not limited to the traditional toolkit. Tsaur, Tzeng and Wang (1997) worked on assessing tourist risks. These authors relied on Fuzzy Set Theory, but facing a situation of multi-criteria decision making elegantly linked it to the Analytical Hierarchy Process. Doing this they avoided the artificial accuracy of crisp measurements while aggregating the tourists' risk evaluation criteria. As tourism has begun uniting forces with Information Technology new opportunities for incorporating Artificial Intelligence methodology have opened. A promising field is the development and refinement of travel recommender systems. Fuzzy Reasoning is one of the instruments for making these systems smarter (Franke 2003). There is an ample field of incorporating analytical methods in travel counselling systems. As an example consider Wallace *et al.*'s (2004) proposal of feeding hierarchically clustered trip plans into a Radial Base Function Neural Network for achieving rapid online response. Chen and Wang

(2007) succeeded in optimizing the parameter settings of a Support Vector Machine with a Genetic Algorithm. Their SVM-GA results turned out to be superior to the demand forecasts of an ARIMA model and an ordinary neural network with standard backpropagation learning.

Assessment and recommendations

Three classes of analytical methods and application areas are chosen for further treatment: Scale Development, Structural Equation Modelling and Classification Techniques. These selected fields and method classes have been gaining top awareness among the research community, and they exhibit a problem-solving potential for tourism marketing intelligence not yet fully exploited. When drafting recommendations for tourism marketing proper attention is paid to the development in core marketing.

Scale development

Marketing research in any sector of industry, like all empirical sciences, depends on observation and measurement. In the social sciences the aim of attaining standardized measuring instruments is not fundamentally different from the situation in the natural sciences. However, Bond and Fox (2001) argue that quantitative researchers in the human sciences merely focus on data analysis while neglecting the development of criteria for measurement quality.

Measurement issues

More than 30 years ago, Jacoby (1978) criticized the market researchers' blind acceptance of measures while ignoring quality criteria such as reliability or validity. One year later, Churchill (1979) published a seminal paper on developing measures for behavioural constructs and proposed a procedure for gaining reliable and valid measures. In doing so, he discusses a series of steps starting from the specification of the construct's domain to the development of norms. A vital point Churchill (1979) raises is the suggestion to use a new sample of data for confirming the dimensional structures that emerged from preceding Exploratory Factor Analysis. The claim of having confirmed relevant dimensions cannot be made if exploratory and confirmatory factor analyses are applied to the same data set. Interestingly, up to now it seems that few tourism researchers have become aware of this requirement.

Churchill (1979) outlines the superiority of multi-item measures compared to single-item measures. He argues that single items only imperfectly capture a concept. Rossiter (2002), on the contrary, holds that single items which have content validity are capable of properly representing the construct of interest. He argues that in most cases multi-items are misused as these items are inappropriately pre-tested. Rossiter (2002) specifies his C-OAR-SE procedure and contends that content validity is the sole reasonable and necessary quality criterion for scale measures. More specifically, he states that '[. . .] construct validity and predictive validity are inappropriate for scale evaluation, and [. . .] reliability should be regarded only as a precision-of-score estimate for a particular application' (2000: 308). However, he admits that until now, no empirical proof has yet been found for his assumption. Rossiter's focus on content validity is in contrast with Churchill's argument that face or content validity is a first step but '[. . .] not the whole story' (2000: 69). According to Bagozzi (1984) and Rigdon *et al.* (2011) theory-building research requires involving both the conceptual and the empirical domain as well as correspondence rules as the latter offer valuable information on the measure's reliability and validity.

Diamantopoulos and Winklhofer (2001) lament that constructs are often mis-specified. The authors provide examples of multi-item measures where a formative perspective appears more valid than reflective measures. The differences between reflective and formative measurement models become apparent in issues such as interchangeability, item correlation, internal consistency, error and disturbance terms, and model identification (Diamantopoulos and Winklhofer 2001). However, assessing formative constructs in terms of reliability and validity is not as straightforward as for reflective measurement models. Rossiter (2002) claims that formative constructs cannot lack reliability or validity due to reasons he insufficiently justifies. This assertion has been challenged by Diamantopoulos, Riefler and Roth (2008) who provide guidelines for assessing formative constructs in terms of reliability and validity while emphasizing the need for further research on methodology to evaluate formative constructs.

An alternative measurement theory

The bulk of research in the social sciences measurement has been based on classical test theory (CTT). From time to time, attempts were made to challenge the paradigm of classical test theory in the discipline of marketing. Diamantopoulos and Winklhofer (2001), with their discussion of formative indicators, and Rossiter (2002), with his C-OAR-SE procedure, point to alternatives to the classical principles of scale construction (see Salzberger 2009). An alternative measurement framework that has been developed in parallel to classical test theory since the 1960s (Rasch 1960) originates from psychometrics and educational psychology. This measurement theory is known as probabilistic test theory or as Item Response Theory (IRT). IRT has long recognized the measurement problems that CTT is confronted with. According to the literature survey of Salzberger (2009) the first application of Rasch modelling in marketing science dates back to 1979, written in German and hence invisible internationally (Mazanec 1979). Only recently and still reluctantly, IRT has gained acceptance in research areas such as business, marketing or tourism.

Similar to factor-analytic models, IRT models assume that observable responses are based on underlying interval-scaled latent variables. However, while the first analyze responses on an aggregate level such as calculating variances, covariances and means, IRT models directly analyze the individual response in a probabilistic manner. In CTT, rating scales are treated as interval-scaled without testing if this assumption is valid at all. By contrast, the Rasch model – a basic type of probabilistic measurement models – converts raw data into equal-interval data through logit transformation (Bond and Fox 2001). Therefore, data for IRT models need not exhibit interval properties. Rather, the data for IRT models may have any kind of measurement level (e.g. ordinal, categorical, dichotomous data). In a nutshell, CTT draws correspondence rules between observable and latent variables which are interval-scaled, while IRT maps non-interval-scaled observables onto interval-scaled latent variables (Singh 2004). Concerning the mathematical model that specifies the relationship between observables and latent variables CTT thus hypothesizes a linear and IRT a non-linear relationship.

To date, classical test theory is still the predominant paradigm in tourism and marketing research. However, according to the adepts of IRT, Rasch modelling provides more profound insights into measurement characteristics of items, scales and constructs than CTT. IRT respects the requirements of rigorous measurement, investigates the quality of measurement instruments, examines the distribution of persons and items, and provides directions for improving the measurement instruments. Despite the numerous advantages of Item Response Theory for scale construction, IRT has only been scarcely used in tourism research. If tourism researchers are prepared to take a self-critical stance they may not fully agree with a remark by Singh (2004).

He points out that '[. . .] IRT is not a panacea for all measurement woes [. . .] rather, IRT is just another approach that rests on different assumptions than CTT and, as a consequence, allows researchers to tackle measurement issues differently' (2004: 185). Seeking a stronger link between CTT and IRT would certainly improve the quality of measurement scales while taking into account each paradigm's strengths and weaknesses.

Structural Equation Modelling

From the mid-1990s onwards, applications of SEM have experienced a tremendous upswing. Implementations embrace a variety of themes; for a comprehensive overview and a discussion of critical issues in the modelling process the reader is referred to Reisinger and Mavondo (2006). The first article published in the field of tourism research is a JTTM paper by Bartkus (1995). He assesses a mediation model where expertise acts as a mediator for the effect of work experience on travel agents' sale performance.

In early occurrences of SEM in tourism marketing, authors praise SEM's methodological usefulness, explain the basics and objectives of this method, give advice on what and how to report and encourage applications in tourism research. This effort culminates in Reisinger and Turner's (1999) paper providing a step-by-step guidebook to SEM based on the mainstream software known as LISREL. They clearly point to the necessity of cross-validating one's results if the model has been modified and suggest using comparisons of competing or nested models in order to strive for sound theory building and testing (Steenkamp and Baumgartner 2000). Even though the paper is frequently cited (169 times, or 12.1 times per year according to Google Scholar, July 2012) this advice does not seem to have become second nature to tourism researchers.

Some general issues that have been critically noted by a number of authors deserve closer attention.

Exploratory versus confirmatory analysis

A perennial problem is the heavy reliance on a single cross-sectional data set for testing a hypothesized model that is then repeatedly calibrated on the same data to arrive at a final model with good fit. Clearly, this approach is prone to suffer from sample idiosyncrasies (Baumgartner and Homburg 1996). Nevertheless, the vast majority of papers rely on a single sample. Authors should at least admit that once the originally hypothesized model gets modified (to increase its fit) SEM loses its confirmatory character. While the most desirable approach to deal with this problem is testing the fitted model on a fresh sample, this is often not possible. A random sample split is advisable. For a recent sample application, see Hallak, Brown and Lindsay (2012).

Multinormality assumption

The most frequently applied estimation procedure is Maximum Likelihood (ML), due to its default status in standard software packages. This method is based on multinormally distributed data (Reinartz, Haenlein and Henseler 2009). Unsurprisingly, given the ordinal and categorical data prevailing in most SEM applications in tourism research, this assumption is quite often not met (Mazanec 2000). Even though a recent simulation study shows that ML estimation is fairly robust against violations of the multinormality assumption (Reinartz *et al.* 2009), researchers should be aware of this deficiency and cross-validate with second-generation estimation software (e.g. *Mplus*; Muthén and Muthén 2007) that allows for sound statistical modelling of ordered categorical indicators.

Equivalent models

Very few applications consider equivalent models. Even when a hypothesized model fits the data well, it is likely that the same variance-covariance matrix may be reproduced by a variety of alternative models 'that are indistinguishable from the original model in terms of goodness-of-fit to sample data' (MacCallum *et al.* 1993: 185). Consequently, a satisfactory goodness of fit does not automatically prove that a model is correct. Therefore, a theory-guided approach comparing competing and theoretically justified models and cross-validating the findings is essential.

Multiple items

Although assuming that multi-item constructs outstrip single items is true with regard to measurement error (Steenkamp and Baumgartner 2000), it often urges the analyst to invent largely redundant items for a variable that might easily be measured directly. An example of a reasonably directly measured variable can be found in Oh (2003). The author operationalizes price unfairness by the difference between the reference and the actual price.

Reflective or formative indicators

In most SEM studies constructs are implicitly declared as reflective, even though this may not be theoretically sound in every instance (Diamantopoulos and Winklhofer 2001). Only recently (Murphy, Olaru and Hofacker 2009), a research note has called for rigour regarding the specification of reflective and formative constructs and authors have started to incorporate formative constructs into their models, e.g. Song, van der Veen, Li and Chen (2011) who develop a formative satisfaction index.

Alternatives to covariance-based modelling

One such alternative that has recently recaptured attention is PLS Path Modelling (PLSPM). First applications in tourism marketing date back to the early 2000s and have experienced growth in the last four to five years. A recent simulation study demonstrates that, whereas covariance-based SEM (CBSEM) outperforms PLS in terms of consistency, PLSPM is clearly preferable for small sample sizes. Additionally, PLSPM is superior when it comes to statistical power, which makes PLSPM attractive where the research goal is identifying rather than confirming relationships (Reinartz *et al.* 2009). PLSPM may be complemented by covariance-based latent variable modelling when analyzing secondary data on tourism destination competitiveness (Mazanec and Ring 2011).

Unobserved heterogeneity

Another often neglected issue in SEM is unobserved heterogeneity. The adjective 'unobserved' points to lacking prior knowledge about the causes of heterogeneity forcing the analyst into a data-driven method. Usually, authors first segment respondents and then apply multi-group analysis to test for differences between these segments (see e.g. Barroso Castro, Martín Armario and Martín Ruiz (2007) for a combination of Latent Class and subsequent Path Analysis). In their seminal marketing research paper introducing heterogeneity into SEM, Jedidi, Jagpal and DeSarbo (1997) argue that though a step-by-step approach is useful if segments can be identified a priori, it is not satisfactory for detecting unobserved heterogeneity. The frequent habit of considering data collected for the purpose of testing a model to be drawn from one single population may produce misleading results. Additionally, standard goodness-of-fit measures cannot detect unobserved heterogeneity. They propose a finite mixture structural equation model where path estimates and unobserved heterogeneity are treated simultaneously. Accordingly, probabilistic clusters are formed and cluster-specific estimates for the structural and the measurement models are obtained in parallel. Finite mixture modelling should be used 'when substantive theory supports the structural equation model, a priori segmentation is infeasible, and theory suggests that the data are heterogeneous and belong to a finite number of unobserved groups' (Jedidi *et al.* 1997: 39). This approach has not yet been widely applied, even though it has been identified to be promising for market segmentation (Steenkamp and Baumgartner 2000).

New methodology for treating heterogeneity non-parametrically is waiting for applications, too. A non-parametric approach is often more appropriate due to the rarely met distributional assumption of parametric analysis. A combined Latent Class and Vector Quantization approach to perceptions-based market segmentation is discussed in Mazanec and Strasser (2007).

Within SEM, nonlinear relationships and tackling the intricate problem of causality with novel instruments of inferred causation theory are promising areas for future applications (Mazanec 2007a). Reaching out into the bigger latent variable family, Latent Class Analysis and Latent Growth Models hold promise as well. Latent Growth Models have only recently found their way into the tourism field, however, not yet into tourism marketing research. Consequently, tourism research has just scratched the surface of latent variable analysis. Readers interested in an overview of latent variable modelling that exceeds ordinary SEMs are referred to Muthén (2002).

Classification techniques

Marketing strives to classify market segments to be capable of catering to the needs of homogenous groups more precisely. The ultimate goal of segmentation and accordingly customized tourist products, services and marketing mix actions is gaining competitive advantage.

Classification approaches

Two basic approaches of classification have been used (Bailey, 1994). The first a priori (Smith 1989: 46ff.) or common-sense segmentation (Dolnicar 2004a) is theory driven, meaning segments are known in advance. The second a posteriori (Mazanec and Strasser 2000) or data-driven approach (Dolnicar 2004a) is explorative; no prior information about segments is available. Among the most popular methods for a posteriori classification is cluster analysis. Cluster analysis groups individuals based on the similarity of response patterns regarding selected variables by minimizing within-group variance and maximizing between-group variance (Wedel and Kamakura 2000).

Cluster analysis methods

The family of methods used for performing a posteriori segmentation comprises hierarchical clustering (agglomerative or divisive), iterative partitioning clustering, density search, factor-analytic procedures, clumping (permitting overlapping clusters), graph theoretic algorithms and probabilistic models such as Latent Class Analysis. Generally, the technique selected depends on the classification goals, the metric properties of the underlying variables and on the similarity or density measure (Aldenderfer and Blashfield 1984). In tourism marketing hierarchical and partitioning segmentations are most common (Dolnicar 2002).

The decision regarding the similarity measure (i.e. correlation coefficients, distance measures, association coefficients and probabilistic similarity measures) is imperative, but the algorithm for creating clusters usually attracts greater attention (Aldenderfer and Blashfield 1984). With respect to hierarchical cluster analysis the most prominent algorithms are single linkage (Sneath 1957), complete linkage (Sokal and Michener 1958) and Ward's method (Ward 1963). In tourism about half of all clustering studies are hierarchical; about one third of these fail to specify the linkage algorithm; Ward's method is used most often followed by complete linkage (Mazanec *et al.* 2010). Tkaczynski *et al.* (2010) suggest a two-step analysis where the hierarchical clustering is preceded by a grouping of cases into pre-clusters. As with hierarchical cluster analysis heuristics for partitioning methods are available for choosing the number of clusters or seed points, types of pass (i.e. ways in which cases are allocated to groups) and statistical criteria (for determining how to compute homogeneity). The most prominent are k-means and hill climbing pass. Partitioning methods cannot guarantee globally optimal solutions. Non-hierarchical procedures are favoured with binary data and large data sets (Hair *et al.*, 1998). Tourism studies also apply the so called two-stage clustering procedure where the hierarchical primer is used to define the number of clusters; then k-means is applied for generating a partition (Punj and Stewart 1983).

Segmentation base and data preprocessing

For all a posteriori segmentation methods a base of variables has to be defined. In tourism marketing clustering is most often based on motives or needs, activities, followed by benefits sought and attitudes. Regrettably, there are also segmentation studies which do base the classification on a seemingly arbitrary mixture of different variables rather than on one well defined behavioural concept (for more elaborate criticism see Mazanec *et al.* 2010). Tourism researchers often choose large numbers of variables to capture the scope of a concept, but manage to collect only small numbers of survey respondents which leads to methodological problems (Dolnicar and Leisch 2010). To overcome this problem many researchers condense data before the actual segmentation by applying Correspondence Analysis (e.g. Arimond and Elfessi 2001), Conjoint Analysis (e.g. Sedmak and Michalic 2008) and most often PCA (e.g. Decrop and Zidda 2006). These methods are also used to improve the level of scaling. Within tourism research, pre-processing measures as well as data standardization are heavily criticized (Dolnicar and Grün 2008). Sheppard (1996) demonstrates the differences between using raw data and factor scores by means of artificial data. He shows consequences for the segment structure, variation of dimensionality across segments and problems with items that would be discarded due to prior factoring. In spite of these findings, there are still publications featuring factor-cluster analysis in top tourism journals (e.g. Suni and Komppula 2012). Recently, improvements in handling cluster procedure drawbacks have found entrance into tourism marketing and authors also propose statistically sound ways to overcome data dimensionality problems.

Recent developments

When dealing with high-dimensional data Dolnicar *et al.* (2012) suggest either collecting large samples, including only most managerially relevant items based on a series of pretests, or applying Biclustering. This procedure providing algorithms for all scale levels simultaneously classifies variables and cases. For each segment only relevant subgroups of variables are used while invalid ones are ignored. Analysts may choose whether they want to generate overlapping or non-overlapping clusters, and they can trust that repeated computation runs lead to identical results. Dolnicar *et al.* (2012) provide empirical evidence for the superiority of Biclustering by comparing leisure activity segmentation results with results using k-means and Ward's method.

Since k-means may not result in a global optimum several extensions such as fuzzy k-means or overlapping k-centroids clustering (Chaturvedi *et al.* 1997) were introduced but have not yet become popular in tourism marketing. Other extensions of partitioning approaches have found their way into tourism research. Examples are Bagged Clustering (Dolnicar and Leisch 2000; Leisch 1999), Vector Quantization techniques and other fuzzy or probabilistic algorithms (e.g. Rough Set Theory Fuzzy Set Theory or Latent Class Analysis).

Vector Quantization procedures such as the Topology Representing Network (TRN) and Kohonen's Self Organizing Map (SOM) produce more stable results than ordinary k-means clustering. According to Martinez *et al.* (1993) TRN is faster and achieves smaller distortion error than both SOM and k-means. SOM is for instance used by Rong *et al.* (2012) to identify segments among online users of hotel websites. TRN is a nonparametric method applying the 'neural gas' algorithm (Martinetz and Schulten 1994). It is particularly useful for condensing three-way data (respondents, objects and their attributes); offers heuristics for interpretive assistance (Mazanec 2001); and provides methods for estimating the stability of results (see e.g. Ganglmair and Wooliscroft 2000, who report on a comparison of k-means and TRN proving that k-means is very sensitive to changes in the order of input data). Lately, TRN got applied to cluster ranking data concerning quality of life domains (Dolnicar *et al.* 2012).

Tourism research has begun experimenting with probabilistic classification approaches such as Latent Class Analysis or methods based on Rough Set Theory. Rough set classification handles non-numeric classification replacing incomplete or imprecise data with precise lower and upper approximations (Pawlak 1984). Rough set classification was applied in tourism to induce decision rules which were then used to forecast dining behaviour (Au and Law 2002). Voges (2006) introduced an evolutionary algorithm based on rough clustering which overcomes the dependence of k-means on seed points. The algorithm allows objects to be a member of several clusters. Another approach capable of dealing with vague data is Fuzzy Set Theory (Zadeh 1965). A fuzzy set implies a function of membership which allocates to each object a membership grade between 0 and 1. Hsu and Lin (2006) apply this technique for classifying travellers' risk perceptions.

Validation and replication

External validity may be tested by randomly splitting one's sample and using the first half for the segmentation and the second half for testing the results (e.g. Tkaczynski and Prebensen 2012). Several clustering methods may be compared, or differences in cluster characteristics/profiles can be examined statistically (e.g. Spotts and Mahoney 1993). Reliability can be tested by repeating a clustering procedure and judging the stability of results (Dolnicar 2002). The development of segments may also be monitored over time by investigating a priori segments or by tracking changes of a posteriori segments over time emerging from repetitive surveys (Dolnicar 2004b). Reference examples for repetitive surveys are rare; however, Shoemaker (2000) shows how a mature market has changed in the course of a ten-year time period.

Conclusions

If tourism marketing research were deprived of Regression-Based models and Exploratory Factor Analysis, about half of the applications of advanced analytical methods would vanish. Heavy usage of regression and related methods is easily explained by convenient access to secondary data describing international tourist flows, and demand modellers loving their favourite pet of forecasting. With EFA the situation is different. The large majority of EFA, or actually PCA, are fed with cross-sectional primary data. EFA/PCA typically serves as a precursor for later confirmatory analysis. As a deterministic method of tentative data reduction it is clearly focused on definition and concept formation and thus signals an infant stage of theory development. A similar diagnosis pertains to the highly popular method class of clustering procedures (accumulating hierarchical and partitioning routines). Classification results per se explain nothing unless they become building blocks in subsequent cause–effect hypothesizing. Nevertheless, classification for its own sake remains attractive for tourism marketing, which shares problems such as the 'curse of dimensionality' with most other applications of marketing segmentation. Hence, new approaches such as Biclustering are highly welcome (Dolnicar *et al.* 2012).

Tourism marketing research has caught up with other social science disciplines as far as SEMs are concerned. In relative terms, this method class has grown most rapidly and this exerts a beneficial influence. While the best-practice requirements of methodologically sound SEM are not always strictly met, the quest for specifying cause–effect relationships on structural level strengthens explanatory power in the long run. Tourism marketing research has already begun to climb next levels of SEM, e.g. accounting for unobserved heterogeneity and nonlinear relationships (Mazanec 2007b). Discrete heterogeneity has been tapped with SEM-LCA models; managing continuous heterogeneity with Bayes models and Markov-Chain-Monte-Carlo estimation are being discovered.

Regarding Discrete Choice Modelling tourism marketing is lagging behind core marketing where it has been an avenue for mainstream research for more than three decades, strongly driven by an abundance of scanner panel data. Unfortunately, tourist panels are rare. On the other hand, the repeated measurements collected with longitudinal data are necessary to guarantee that an up-to-date specification of an advanced choice model, say, a finite mixture multinomial logit model, is identified and can be safely estimated. At least, there are encouraging developments such as the choice experiment of Chaminuka *et al.* (2012) or Huang and Pengs's (2012) ingenious combination of Fuzzy Sets and Item Response Theory.

Several of the methods yet rarely encountered in tourism marketing research bear a promising potential. A prominent example is nontrivial (i.e. based on Graph Theory) Social and Semantic Network Analysis which offers a variety of application opportunities for marketing intelligence. Information exchange networks emergent in Internet communities are a natural field of application becoming more widely acknowledged.

Some new analytical methods have received quick acceptance in tourism marketing, though the absolute number of applications is still small. For example, the various methods of Vector Quantization and Topology Representing Networks are likely to survive and expand as researchers realize that they produce a meaningful partition where traditional clustering may detect nothing (see the recent example of a quality of live segmentation by Dolnicar, Yanamandram and Cliff (2012). Considering optimization procedures Data Envelopment Analysis comes to mind. When economics re-discovered this method (originally developed in the 1970s) a couple of years ago it became quickly adopted for efficiency measurement of tourism businesses and destinations.

Method combinations are ambiguous. As indicated above, they may originate from obsolete usage of methods. A striking example is data reduction with Principal Components and subsequent Regression Analysis (better replaced by SEM, Path Modelling or Graphical Models). Another example is Cluster Analysis with subsequent model estimation (nowadays replaced by Finite Mixture Modelling). Method combinations are valuable as long as a single-step procedure is unavailable. In this case they may serve as forerunners for elaborating more general models and methods. But, of course, there are no limits to resourcefulness and ingenuity in proposing joint usage of methods seemingly unrelated before.

References

Aldenderfer, M.E. and Blashfield, R.K. (1984) *Cluster Analysis. Paper Series on Quantitative Applications in the Social Sciences, 07-044.* Beverly Hills, CA: Sage.

Arimond, G. and Elfessi, A. (2001) 'A Clustering Method for Categorical Data in Tourism Market Segmentation Research', *Journal of Travel Research*, 39: 391–97.

Au, N. and Law, R. (2002) 'Categorical Classification of Tourism Dining', *Annals of Tourism Research*, 29: 819–33.

Bagozzi, R.P. (1984) 'A Prospectus for Theory Construction in Marketing', *Journal of Marketing*, 48: 11–29.

Bailey, K.D. (1994) *Typologies and Taxonomies: An Introduction to Classification Techniques.* Thousand Oaks: Sage.

Bargeman, B., Joh, Ch.-H., Timmermans, H. and Van der Waerden, P. (1999) 'Correlates of Tourist Vacation Behavior: A Combination of CHAID and Loglinear Logit Analysis', *Tourism Analysis*, 4: 83–93.

Barroso Castro, C., Martín Armario, E. and Martín Ruiz, D. (2007) 'The Influence of Market Heterogeneity on the Relationship between a Destination's Image and Tourists' Future Behaviour', *Tourism Management*, 28: 175–87.

Bartkus, K.R. (1995) 'An Expanded Model of the Experience/Performance Relationship in Travel Service Selling', *Journal of Travel and Tourism Marketing*, 4(2): 51–63.

Baumgartner, H. and Homburg, C. (1996) 'Applications of Structural Equation Modeling in Marketing and Consumer Research: A Review', *International Journal of Research in Marketing*, 13: 139–61.

Bojamic, D.C. and Calantone, R. (1990) 'A Contribution Approach to Price Bundling in Tourism', *Annals of Tourism Research*, 17: 528–40.

Bond, T.G. and Fox, C.M. (2001) *Applying the Rasch Model: Fundamental Measurement in the Human Sciences.* Mahwah, NJ: Erlbaum.

Calantone, R.J. and Mazanec, J.A. (1991) 'Marketing Management and Tourism', *Annals of Tourism Research*, 18: 101–19.

Chaminuka , P., Groeneveld, R.A., Selomane, A.O. and van Ierland, E.C. (2012) 'Tourist Preferences for Ecotourism in Rural Communities Adjacent to Kruger National Park: A Choice Experiment Approach', *Tourism Management*, 33: 168–76.

Chaturvedi, A., Carroll, J.D., Green, P.E. and Rotondo, J.A. (1997) 'A Feature-based Approach to Market Segmentation via Overlapping k-Centroids Clustering', *Journal of Marketing Research*, 34: 370–77.

Chen, K.-Y. and Wang, C.-H. (2007) 'Support Vector Regression With Genetic Algorithms in Forecasting Tourism Demand', *Tourism Management*, 28: 215–26.

Churchill, G.A. (1979) 'A Paradigm for Developing Better Measures of Marketing Constructs', *Journal of Marketing Research*, 16(1): 64–73.

Crouch, G.I. (1995) 'A Meta-Analysis of Tourism Demand', *Annals of Tourism Research*, 22: 103–18.

Decrop, A. and Zidda, P. (2006) 'Typology of Vacation Decision-Making Modes', *Tourism Analysis*, 11: 189–97.

Diamantopoulos, A. and Winklhofer, H.M. (2001) 'Index Construction with Formative Indicators: An Alternative to Scale Development', *Journal of Marketing Research*, 38: 269–77.

Diamantopoulos, A., Riefler, P. and Roth, K.P. (2008) 'Advancing Formative Measurement Models', *Journal of Business Research*, 61: 1203–218.

Dolnicar, S. (2002) 'A Review of Data-driven Market Segmentation in Tourism', *Journal of Travel and Tourism Marketing*, 12: 1–22.

— (2004a) 'Beyond "Commonsense Segmentation": A Systematics of Segmentation Approaches in Tourism', *Journal of Travel Research*, 42: 244–50.

— (2004b) 'Tracking Data-driven Market Segmentation', *Tourism Analysis*, 8: 227–32.

Dolnicar, S. and Grün, B. (2008) 'Challenging "Factor Cluster Segmentation"', *Journal of Travel Research*, 47: 63–71.

Dolnicar, S. and Leisch, F. (2000) 'Behavioral Market Segmentation Using the Bagged Clustering Approach Based on Binary Guest Survey Data: Exploring and Visualizing Unobserved Heterogeneity', *Tourism Analysis*, 5: 163–70.

— (2010) 'Evaluation of Structure and Reproducibility of Cluster Solutions Using the Bootstrap', *Marketing Letters*, 21: 83–101.

Dolnicar, S., Kaiser, S., Lazarevski, K. and Leisch, F. (2012) 'Biclustering: Overcoming Data Dimensionality Problems in Market Segmentation', *Journal of Travel Research*, 51: 41–9.

Dolnicar, S., Yanamandram, V. and Cliff, K. (2012) 'The Contribution of Vacations to Quality of Life', *Annals of Tourism Research*, 39: 59–83.

Fenton, M. and Pearce, Ph. (1988) 'Multidimensional Scaling and Tourism Research', *Annals of Tourism Research*, 15: 236–54.

Fodness, D. (1994) 'Measuring Tourist Motivation', *Annals of Tourism Research*, 21: 555–81.

Fodness, D. and Milner, L.M. (1992) 'A Perceptual Mapping Approach to Theme Park Visitor Segmentation', *Tourism Management*, 13: 95–101.

Franke, Th. (2003) 'Enhancing an Online Regional Tourism Consulting System with Extended Personalized Services', *Information Technology and Tourism*, 5: 135–50.

Ganglmair, A. and Wooliscroft, B. (2000) 'K-means vs. Topology Representing Networks, Comparing Ease of Use for Gaining Optimal Results with Reference to Data Input Order', *Tourism Analysis*, 5: 157–62.

Green, P.E. and Rao, V.R. (1971) 'Conjoint Measurement for Quantifying Judgmental Data', *Journal of Marketing Research*, 8: 355–63.

Hair, J., Anderson, R., Tatham, R. and Black, M. (1998) *Multivariate Data Analysis.* Upper Saddle River: Prentice Hall.

Hallak, R., Brown, G. and Lindsay, N.J. (2012) 'The Place Identity – Performance Relationship Among Tourism Entrepreneurs: A Structural Equation Modeling Analysis', *Tourism Management*, 33: 143–54.

Hruschka, H. and Mazanec, J.A. (1990) 'Computer-Assisted Travel Counseling', *Annals of Tourism Research*, 17: 208–27.

Hsu, T.-H. and Lin, L.-Z. (2006) 'Using Fuzzy Set Theoretic Techniques to Analyze Travel Risk: An Empirical Study', *Tourism Management*, 27: 968–81.

Huang, J.-H. and Peng, K.-H. (2012) 'Fuzzy Rasch Model in TOPSIS: A New Approach for Generating Fuzzy Numbers to Assess the Competitiveness of the Tourism Industries in Asian Countries', *Tourism Management*, 33: 456–65.

Hurley, St., Moutinho, L. and Witt, St.F. (1998) 'Genetic Algorithms for Tourism Marketing', *Annals of Tourism Research*, 25: 498–514.

Jacoby, J. (1978) 'Consumer Research: A State of the Art Review', *Journal of Marketing*, 42: 87–96.

Jang, S.-Ch., Morrison, A.M. and O'Leary, J.T. (2004) 'The Tourism Efficient Frontier: An Approach to Selecting the Most Efficient Travel Segment Mixes', *Journal of Travel and Tourism Marketing*, 16: 33–46.

Jedidi, K., Jagpal, H. and DeSarbo, W. (1997) 'Finite-mixture Structural Equation Models for Response-based Segmentation and Unobserved Heterogeneity', *Marketing Science*, 16: 39–59.

Lee, H.A. and Law, R. (2012) 'Diversity in Statistical Research Techniques: An Analysis of Referred Research Articles in the *Journal of Travel & Tourism Marketing*', *Journal of Travel and Tourism Marketing*, 29: 1–17.

Leisch, F. (1999) *Bagged Clustering*, Working Papers 51, SFB Adaptive Information Systems and Modelling in Economics and Management Science, WU. Vienna: Vienna University of Economics and Business (http://epub.wu.ac.at/1272/).

MacCallum, R.C., Wegener, D.T., Uchino, B.N. and Fabrigar, L.R. (1993) 'The Problem of Equivalent Models in Applications of Covariance Structure Analysis', *Psychological Bulletin*, 114: 185–99.

Martinetz, T. and Schulten, K.J. (1994) 'Topology Representing Networks', *Neural Networks*, 7: 507–22.

Martinetz, T.M., Berkovich, S.G. and Schulten, K.J. (1993) '"Neural Gas" Network for Vector Quantization and its Application to Time Series Prediction', *IEEE Transactions on Neural Networks*, 4: 558–69.

Mazanec, J.A. (1979) 'Probabilistische Messverfahren in der Marketingforschung: Ein empirischer Anwendungsversuch zur Planung absatzwirtschaftlicher Strategien des Imagetransfers', *Marketing – Zeitschrift für Forschung und Praxis*, 1(3): 174–86.

— (1992) 'Classifying Tourists into Market Segments: A Neural Network Approach', *Journal of Travel and Tourism Marketing*, 1: 39–59.

— (2000) 'Mastering Unobserved Heterogeneity in Tourist Behavior Research', *Tourism Analysis*, 5: 171–6.

— (2001) 'Neural Market Structure Analysis: Novel Topology-Sensitive Methodology', *European Journal of Marketing*, 35: 894–916.

— (2007a) 'Exploring Tourist Satisfaction with Nonlinear Structural Equation Modeling and Inferred Causation Theory', *Journal of Travel and Tourism Marketing*, 21: 73–90.
— (2007b) 'New Frontiers in Tourist Behavior Research: Steps Toward Causal Inference from Non-experimental Data', *Asia Pacific Journal of Tourism Research*, 12: 223–35.
Mazanec, J.A. and Ring, A. (2011) 'Tourism Destination Competitiveness: Second Thoughts on the World Economic Forum Reports', *Tourism Economics*, 17: 725–75.
Mazanec, J.A. and Strasser, H. (2000) *A Nonparametric Approach to Perceptions-Based Market Segmentation: Foundations*. Vienna–New York: Springer.
Mazanec, J.A., Ring, A., Stangl, B. and Teichmann, K. (2010) 'Usage Patterns of Advanced Analytical Methods in Tourism Research 1988–2008: A Six Journal Survey', *Information Technology and Tourism*, 12: 17–46.
Molera, L. and Albaladejo, I.P. (2007) 'Profiling Segments of Tourists in Rural Areas of South-Eastern Spain', *Tourism Management*, 28: 757–67.
Molina, A. and Esteban, Á. (2006) 'Tourism Brochures, Usefulness and Image', *Annals of Tourism Research*, 33: 1036–056.
Morley, C.L. (1994) 'Experimental Destination Choice Analysis', *Annals of Tourism Research*, 21: 780–91.
Murphy, J., Olaru, D. and Hofacker, C.F. (2009) 'Rigor in Tourism Research. Formative and Reflective Constructs', *Annals of Tourism Research*, 36: 730–4.
Muthén, B. (2002) 'Beyond SEM: General Latent Variable Modeling', *Behaviormetrika*, 29: 81–117.
Muthén, L.K. and Muthén, B.O. (2007) *Mplus User's Guide*, 5th edn. Los Angeles: Muthén & Muthén.
Nicolau, J.L. and Más, F.J. (2005) 'Stochastic Modeling, A Three-Stage Tourist Choice Process', *Annals of Tourism Research*, 32: 49–69.
Oh, H. (2003) 'Price Fairness and its Asymmetric Effects on Overall Price, Quality and Value Judgments: The Case of an Upscale Hotel', *Tourism Management*, 24: 387–99.
Pan, B. and Fesenmaier, D.R. (2006) 'Online Information Search: Vacation Planning Process', *Annals of Tourism Research*, 33: 809–32.
Pattie, D.C. and Snyder, J. (1996) 'Using a Neural Network to Forecast Visitor Behavior', *Annals of Tourism Research*, 23: 151–64.
Pawlak, Z. (1984) 'Rough Classification', *International Journal of Man-Machine Studies*, 20: 469–83.
Punj, G. and Stewart, D.W. (1983) 'Cluster Analysis in Marketing Research: Review and Suggestions for Application', *Journal of Marketing Research*, 20: 134–48.
Rasch, G. (1960) *Probabilistic Models for Some Intelligence and Attainment Tests*. Copenhagen: Danish Institute for Educational Research.
Reinartz, W., Haenlein, M. and Henseler, J. (2009) 'An Empirical Comparison of the Efficacy of Covariance-based and Variance-based SEM', *International Journal of Research in Marketing*, 26: 332–44.
Reisinger, Y. and Mavondo, F. (2006) 'Structural Equation Modelling: Critical Issues and New Developments', *Journal of Travel & Tourism Marketing*, 21(4): 41–71.
Reisinger, Y. and Turner, L. (1999) 'Structural Equation Modeling with LISREL: Application in Tourism', *Tourism Management*, 20: 71–88.
Rigdon, E.E., Preacher, K.J., Lee, N., Howell, R.D., Franke, G.R. and Borsboom, D. (2011) 'Avoiding Measurement Dogma: A Response to Rossiter', *European Journal of Marketing*, 45(11/12): 1589–600.
Rong, J., Vu, H.Q., Law, R. and Li, G. (2012) 'A Behavioral Analysis of Web Sharers and Browsers in Hong Kong Using Targeted Association Rule Mining', *Tourism Management*, 33: 731–40.
Rossiter, J.R. (2002) 'The C-OAR-SE Procedure for Scale Development in Marketing', *International Journal of Research in Marketing*, 19: 305–35.
Saaty, T.L. (1977) 'A Scaling Method for Priorities in Hierarchical Structures', *Journal of Mathematical Psychology*, 15: 234–81.
Salzberger, Th. (2009) *Measurement in Marketing Research – An Alternative Framework*. Cheltenham: Elgar.
Sedmak, G. and Michalic, T. (2008) 'Authenticity in Mature Seaside Resorts', *Annals of Tourism Research*, 35: 1007–31.
Sheppard, A.G. (1996) 'The Sequence of Factor Analysis and Cluster Analysis: Differences in Segmentation and Dimensionality Through the Use of Raw and Factor Scores', *Tourism Analysis*, 1: 49–57.
Shih, H. -Y. (2006) 'Network Characteristics of Drive Tourism Destinations: An Application of Network Analysis in Tourism', *Tourism Management*, 27: 1029–39.
Shoemaker, S. (2000) 'Segmenting the Mature Market 10 Years Later', *Journal of Travel Research*, 39: 11–26.
Singh, J. (2004) 'Tackling Measurement Problems with Item Response Theory: Principles, Characteristics, and Assessment, with an Illustrative Example', *Journal of Business Research*, 57: 184–208.

Smith, S.L.J. (1989) *Tourism Analysis*. New York: Wiley.
Sneath, P. (1957) 'The Application of Computers to Taxonomy', *Journal of General Microbiology*, 17: 201–26.
Sokal, R. and Michener, C.D. (1958) 'A Statistical Method for Evaluating Systematic Relationships', *University of Kansas Scientific Bulletin*, 38: 1409–38.
Song, H., van der Veen, R., Li, G. and Chen, J.L. (2011) 'The Hong Kong Tourist Satisfaction Index', *Annals of Tourism Research*, 39: 459–79.
Spotts, D.M. and Mahoney, E.M. (1993) 'Understanding the Fall Tourism Market', *Journal of Travel Research*, 32: 3–15.
Steenkamp, J.-B. and Baumgartner, H. (2000) 'On the Use of Structural Equation Models for Marketing Modeling', *International Journal of Research in Marketing*, 17: 195–202.
Suni, J. and Komppula, R. (2012) 'SF-Filmvillage as a Movie Tourism Destination – A Case Study of Movie Tourist Push Motivations', *Journal of Travel & Tourism Marketing*, 29: 460–71.
Taplin, J.H.E. and Qiu, M. (1997) 'Car Trip Attraction and Route Choice in Australia', *Annals of Tourism Research*, 24: 624–37.
Tkaczynski, A. and Prebensen, N.K. (2012) 'French Nature-based Tourist Potentials to Norway: Who are They?', *Tourism Analysis*, 17: 181–93.
Tkaczynski, A., Rundle-Thiele, S. and Beaumont, N. (2010) 'Destination Segmentation: A Recommended Two-Step Approach', *Journal of Travel Research*, 49: 139–52.
Tsaur, S.-H., Tzeng, G.-H. and Wang, K.-C. (1997) 'Evaluating Tourist Risks from Fuzzy Perspectives', *Annals of Tourism Research*, 24: 796–812.
Voges, K.E. (2006) 'Rough Clustering of Destination Image Data Using an Evolutionary Algorithm', *Journal of Travel and Tourism Marketing*, 21: 121–37.
Wallace, M., Maglogiannis, I., Karpouzis, K., Kormentzas, G. and Kollias, St. (2004) 'Intelligent One-Stop-Shop Travel Recommendations Using an Adaptive Neural Network and Clustering of History', *Information Technology and Tourism*, 6: 1–13.
Ward, J. (1963) 'Hierarchical Grouping to Optimize an Objective Function', *Journal of the American Statistical Association*, 58: 236–44.
Wedel, M. and Kamakura, W. (2000) *Market Segmentation – Conceptual and Methodological Foundations*, 2nd edn. Dordrecht: Kluwer Academic Publishers.
Wie, B.-W. and Choy, D.J.L. (1993) 'Traffic Impact Analysis of Tourism Development', *Annals of Tourism Research*, 20: 505–18.
Winzar, H., Pidcock, P. and Johnson, L. (1993) 'Modelling Long Distance Pleasure Travel Mode using Perceived Modal Attributes', *Journal of Travel and Tourism Marketing*, 2: 53–67.
Yiannakis, A. and Gibson, H. (1992) 'Roles Tourists Play', *Annals of Tourism Research*, 19: 287–303.
Zadeh, L. (1965) 'Fuzzy Sets', *Information and Control*, 8: 338–53.

15

Market segmentation approaches in tourism

Sara Dolnicar

The role of market segmentation in marketing planning

Marketing planning is widely acknowledged as critical to the success of organizations.

Marketing planning is a process organizations go through which follows a logical sequence and leads to the formulation of objectives, strategies and tactics (McDonald 1982). Denison and McDonald (1995) showed that marketing planning in outstanding organizations occurs at three levels: the cultural level which reflects an organization's values and benefits, the strategic level which includes decisions about long-term directions and typically involves the use of tools such as market segmentation and product positioning and the tactical level at which the organization plans how to best use the marketing toolbox (product, price, promotion and place) to achieve their strategic aims (McDonald 1996).

The marketing planning process is illustrated in Figure 15.1. It is critical to understand that culture sets the basis for any subsequent strategic marketing planning which, in turn, sets the basis for tactical marketing planning. In practice this is often forgotten and organizations busily prepare tactical marketing plans (where to advertise, what promotions to offer etc.) without knowing what exactly they are aiming for in the long term. This is highly inefficient because products and services are being developed, but it is unclear which tourists they should be customized to, advertisements are being aired, but it is unclear who they are targeted at, which image of the destination they should be conveying and how they should be differentiating the destination from other destinations.

Tactical marketing efforts are much more effective if based on strategy. If a destination, for example, chooses to target families as their key segment, and comes to the conclusion during the strategic planning process that it is uniquely suited to serve this segment because of the many attractions available for children, most tactical marketing decisions follow logically (packages could be developed for families including entry to attractions of interest to children, accommodation in child friendly hotels, advertisements are likely to emphasize how much fun a family would have at the destination, pricing would reflect family package deals and media planning would ensure that families would be exposed to advertisements). Such targeted tactical marketing means that marketing activities 'wasted' on tourists who are unlikely to visit the destination can be avoided, while at the same time communicating a perfectly customized product at the right price using the right communication channels with the right advertising

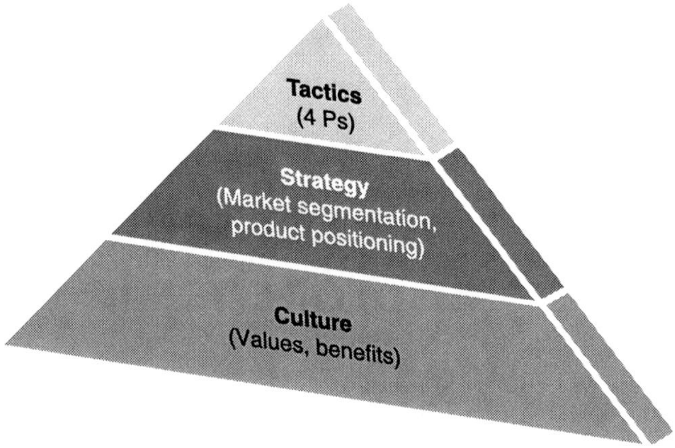

Figure 15.1 Levels of marketing planning.

message to the chosen target segment, thus increasing the probability of this segment visiting the destination.

Market segmentation 'consists of viewing a heterogeneous market . . . as a number of smaller homogeneous markets' (Smith 1956: 6) and forms an integral part of the overall marketing planning process, specifically part of the strategic marketing planning process. It is critical to the successful implementation of tactical marketing and therefore it is of utmost importance that market segmentation analyses are conducted correctly by data analysts and understood well by managers. But are they?

Market segmentation in practice

Market segmentation analysis is commonly used in academic tourism research. Zins (2008) for example, notes that 5 per cent of articles published in seven key tourism journals between 1986 and 2005 were related to market segmentation. However, a number of authors have noted that there is a substantial theory–practice divide in market segmentation (Dibb 2005; Greenberg and McDonald 1989): academic research on market segmentation and the practical use of market segmentation in industry have little in common. Academic research focuses mainly on the improvement of algorithms at a level of sophistication rarely used by industry, and often ignores key conceptual and practical challenges segmentation data analysts and users in industry face. Users of segmentation studies, on the other hand, appear to blindly trust consulting companies who conduct segmentation studies for them and then report very basic results without any warnings about how segmentation results should be interpreted, and perhaps more importantly, *should not* be interpreted. As a consequence, suboptimal segmentation studies are regularly used as the strategic basis for marketing.

Empirical evidence for the problems with the use of market segmentation in practice has been provided by Dolnicar and Lazarevski (2009) in an empirical study of 167 Australian marketing managers who stated that they deal with issues of market segmentation in their day to day business. The following key insights are derived from this snapshot of industry practice with respect to market segmentation:

- 40 per cent of participating marketing managers believe that market segmentation is a computation which follows clear, pre-specified rules. This is incorrect. Rather, market segmentation is exploratory by very nature, requiring the data analyst to make a number of crucial decisions in the process (e.g. how many variables are in the segmentation base, which algorithm is used, which distance measure is used, how many segments are created etc.), which have a major impact on the resulting segments.

- 65 per cent of marketing managers surveyed believe that market segmentation only leads to segments if they are actually present in the data. This is also incorrect. The job of a segmentation algorithm is to split objects contained in a data set into groups. The segmentation algorithm will obediently do so, whether or not segments actually exist in the data.
- 70 per cent of managers state that market segmentation reveals naturally existing groupings of consumers. Whilst it is correct that segmentation algorithms will find naturally occurring market segments in the data, such cases are extremely rare in consumer data. More typically no segments exist. If no segments exist, the segmentation algorithm will create some.
- 30 per cent of marketing managers either believe that the number of segments chosen when the market segmentation task was performed does not affect the nature of the segments or are unsure about this. Although this is a minority belief among marketing managers, it is troubling: if the same data set is used to create either five or ten segments, it will clearly have a major impact on the results, making the decision on how many segments to create highly critical to the outcomes of the process.
- 30 per cent of managers either believe that the age of the data does not affect the nature of the segments or are unsure about this. In addition, 27 per cent believe that market segments stay the same over time. Both age and quality of data are critical to a good market segmentation solution. A market segmentation solution aims to provide a snapshot of the market at the time of analysis. Typically, given the time it takes to collect and analyze data, segmentation solutions are already outdated when first presented. Optimally, new data should be collected regularly to ensure no major structural changes have taken place with respect to the targeted segment or segments.
- About one third of marketing managers believe that, if a segmentation analysis is repeated, it leads to the same solution. This is incorrect. All segmentation algorithms contain random components and will therefore very likely lead to different results if recalculated.
- Finally, 30 per cent of surveyed marketing managers state that segmentation is independent of positioning and competition, the other two key considerations of the strategic marketing planning phase. This is a matter for concern because optimal segments can only be selected when the positioning or intended positioning of the organization or destination is known, and when it is clear what the competitive pressures are for the segments under consideration for targeting.

It is also interesting that 38 per cent of the surveyed marketing managers report that they use external consultants to run their segmentation studies, and only 32 per cent run their own segmentation analyses. This may well be due to the fact that 20 per cent admit that they do not actually feel that they understand the technical details of the market segmentation solution which was used to derive segments for targeting.

It has to be concluded that nothing much has changed since McDonald's case study of organizations revealed 'inadequate understanding and inappropriate use of SWOT analyses, the directional policy matrix, market segmentation, and objective and strategy setting' (1996: 22–3). There is indeed a substantial theory–practice divide in market segmentation. While the above findings are a result of surveying marketing managers more broadly, not specifically tourism marketing managers, there is no reason to believe that the situation would be any different among marketing managers given that segmentation analyses are a commonly used strategic marketing tool in most industries.

Approaches to market segmentation

Market segmentation is the process of identifying or creating groups of similar consumers for the purpose of:

1 developing the most suited product or service for them; and
2 communicating and selling it to them in the most effective manner.

Consumers can be similar in many different ways, all of which can be used to conduct market segmentation. For example, if a tourist destination decides to target families and deliberately not to target retired people, the chosen criterion for the similarity (also referred to as a *segmentation base*) is socio-demographics. A large number of segmentation bases can and have been used to conduct market segmentation in tourism in the past; they can roughly be grouped into the following categories:

- tourists' socio-demographic characteristics such as age (Reece 2004), gender (Hudson 2000), disabled versus non-disabled tourists (Israeli 2002), or international versus domestic student travellers (Field 1999);
- geographic characteristics such as tourists' country of origin, which is the single most common segmentation undertaken by national tourism organizations because geographical segments are easy to target practically;
- tourists' psychographic characteristics such as travel motivations (Bieger and Laesser 2002) or perceptions of tourist destinations (Dolnicar *et al.*1999); and
- tourist behaviour. For example, many studies have investigated the differences between people who differ in their frequency of using products or visiting destinations (so called heavy versus light users, Goldsmith 1999). Others have investigated heterogeneity with respect to product choice (Arimond and Lethlean 1996), actual visitation to certain attractions, such as wineries (Dodd and Bigotte 1997), engagement in winter holiday activities (Dolnicar and Leisch 2003), visitation of rural areas (Kastenholz *et al.* 1999), patterns of expenditure of discretionary income derived from a choice task (Dolnicar *et al.* 2008), or movement patterns (Xia *et al.* 2010).

The assumption underlying market segmentation is that – because consumers are different in many ways – it is difficult for a business, an organization or a tourism destination to satisfy the needs of all consumers with the same product or service. If, however, a group of tourists (or *market segment*) can be identified which is particularly interested in the product or service a business or organization of destination has to offer, it is easier and more cost-effective to develop a customized marketing mix which will appeal to tourists in that market segment.

The original conceptual assumption about market segmentation was that natural groups of tourists exist in the data (Frank *et al.* 1972; Myers and Tauber 1977). This is certainly the case with very distinct criteria, such as family status, because people can either be single, or partnered or a family with children; there is nothing 'fuzzy' about such a classification. But in the case of most segmentation criteria, such clear natural groups rarely exist and this is increasingly acknowledged among segmentation experts (Mazanec *et al.* 1997; Wedel and Kamakura 1998). As a consequence of this new understanding of what market segmentation can and cannot achieve, Dolnicar and Leisch (2010) introduce the terms 'natural', 'reproducible' and 'constructive clustering/segmentation':

- Natural segments are in line with the traditional conceptualization of market segmentation, which is that groups of tourists exist and that the role of segmentation is to *identify* them.
- Reproducible segments result from a segmentation exercise which, if calculated multiple times, leads to similar (not identical) segments. This indicates that there is some structure in the data, but distinct natural segments do not exist.
- Finally, constructive clustering is the process which can be applied to data which neither contains density clusters, nor any other data structure which would allow arriving at the same result repeatedly. Instead, this approach implies that artificial segments are created in line with management needs. At first glance this appears like a sub-optimal outcome, but this is not the case. Imagine a situation as illustrated in Figure 15.2: tourists have been asked how important the natural beauty of a tourist destination is and how important man-made attractions are. As can be seen from the illustration, there are no distinct segments in this data. Following the classical paradigm of market segmentation this would be the end of the segmentation exercise (because no natural segments exist) and the logical consequence would be to try mass marketing. But would that be the best option? Clearly not. A natural heritage site which is of outstanding natural beauty but not permitted to develop any man-made attractions would be best off developing offers for and marketing them to people in the right bottom corner of Figure 15.2 (shaded area); those who want natural beauty but do not care about man-made attractions. The situation is the same at the other extreme: a theme park would be inclined to focus their attention on people who are located in the top left corner of Figure 15.2; those to whom man-made attractions matter, but for whom natural beauty of the tourist destination is not of importance.

In situations where only two pieces of information are used, as in Figure 15.2, no segmentation analysis is required, but when the number of pieces of information increases, the use of segmentation algorithms is unavoidable. However, the basic principle does not change: if no distinct segments exist, it still makes sense to divide the market into groups rather than mass market and data analysts and managers have to work together to identify the groups of tourists who best match what they as a provider are good at.

It should also be noted that the concept of market segmentation is independent of the size of segments or the avenues by which they are communicated to. The current level of sophistication of online tools makes it possible to work with segments which contain only single individuals. Think of amazon.com. The moment a user stars shopping, amazon 'learns' about the person's preference and, treating them as a segment of one, offers other products which may also be of interest to this person. This offers great new opportunities for micro-marketing segmentation. Such micro-segmentation, however, is not applicable to all problems. For example, brand image campaigns cannot be individualized (how could you convince one potential tourist that a destination is perfect for motorcycle groups and another that it is a relaxing retreat for the retired?), so more conventional market segmentation approaches will continue to be required.

Market segments can be identified or created using a range of procedures and algorithms. In terms of procedures, the two extreme options are referred to as a priori (Mazanec 2000) or commonsense segmentation (Dolnicar 2003) and data-driven approaches (Dolnicar 2003), also known as a posteriori (Mazanec 2000) or post-hoc segmentation (Myers and Tauber 1977); both will be discussed in detail in the following sections.

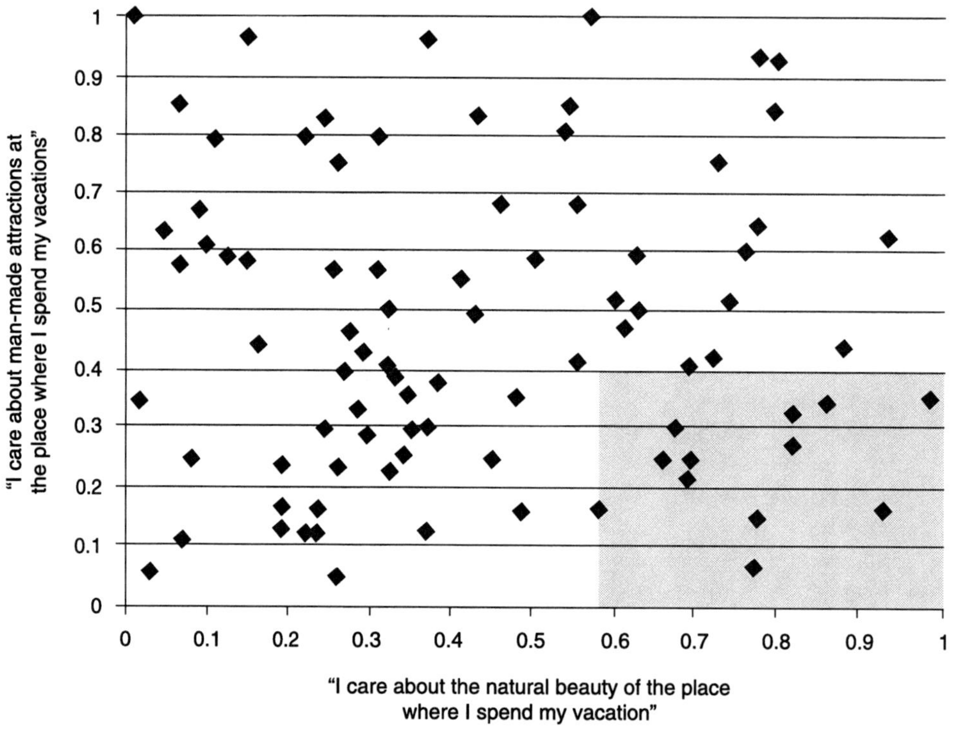

Figure 15.2 Illustration of the usefulness of artificially constructed segments.

Commonsense segmentation refers to the case where management thinks about which characteristics of tourists may be relevant for a segmentation to be useful to them. For example, for a natural heritage site at least one segmentation criterion is obvious: people's interest in the natural beauty of the destination. It may even be that this is the only criterion of interest, in which case the segmentation study design is very simple and consists of three steps only.

Commonsense segmentation step #1: Data collection

The key information required from respondents is whether or not natural beauty of a destination matters to them. In addition, other personal characteristic as well as behavioural and psychographic information could be collected. Such additional information should only be collected if it is important to be able to describe and thus better understand the resulting market segments. It should be noted that it is not advisable to use 'any old guest survey data'. It is critical that the data is recent – because market segments are dynamic, they change all the time, just as the market itself does. It is also important that the key questions required for the segmentation exercise are asked in a valid way. It is unlikely that a 'second hand data set' which has been collected for a different purpose will contain the exact measure that is required.

Commonsense segmentation step #2: Forming of segments

Respondents are split into groups based on their response to the key question of interest, in our example their interest in the natural beauty of the destination. Note that, as also visible in

Figure 15.2, the splitting task may require the data analysts to make a decision about which level of interest is deemed as high or low. If, for example, respondents are offered ten options with higher numbers indicating higher levels of interest, then a decision needs to be made whether only people above, say, seven are included in the high interest group or if anyone above five is included or if the median response is chosen as the splitting point. The only way to avoid this decision is to offer respondents two options to answer the question: Yes and No.

Commonsense segmentation step #3: Description of segments

Once the segments have been constructed, they need to be described in detail to enable management to best develop a customized marketing mix. Information that might be useful at this stage of the analysis ranges from socio-demographic information (for example, are those interested in nature younger?), over psychographic information (for example, is their key motivation to relax or is their key motivation to learn about fauna and flora with the help of experts?) to behavioural information (for example, do those interested in nature like to go out to eat or do they prefer self-catering arrangements? Do they like to take their vacations during school holidays or off-season? Which sources of information do they use to choose their next travel destination?). It is important that the description of segments is made relative to other segments. If only one segment is picked and described it is not clear if the other characteristics are actually typical for that segment or not.

Data-driven segmentation is required when a set of information (multiple variables) is used to identify or create segments. Examples include behavioural segmentation where respondents

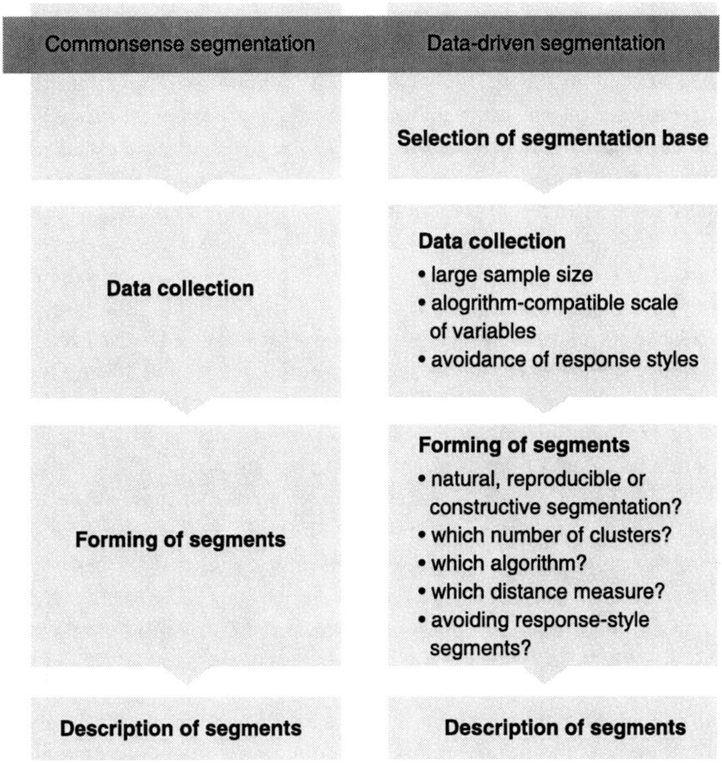

Figure 15.3 Comparison of the steps required in commonsense and data-driven segmentation.

are grouped based on their participation in each one of, say, ten vacation activities or benefit segmentation, where respondents have stated the importance of, say, seven key benefits people may seek when going on a vacation and resulting segments include people who have similar sets of benefits sought. The data-driven segmentation process requires a number of additional steps as well as a number of additional methodological decisions to be made. As a consequence it is often perceived as being 'more sophisticated'. The problem is that the greater number of steps and methodological decisions can also lead to an increasing number of mistakes in the process. Below is an outline of the key steps in this process including key methodological understanding that is required and the type of decisions that are necessary.

Data-driven segmentation step #1: Choice of segmentation base

Just as management needs to decide which single criterion may be relevant to determine useful segments, a decision about the set of questions to be used as a segmentation base in the data-driven segmentation process is required before data is collected. This is critical to ensure that the questions asked in the survey capture exactly what management believes are the key dimensions by which tourists should be grouped.

Data-driven segmentation step #2: Data collection

This first stage does not differ much from the commonsense approach. However, two key decisions need to be made at this stage of the process which has implications later in the data analysis step.

The first is the number of questions (or items or variables) included which are intended to be used as the segmentation base. So, for example, in case of a behavioural segmentation: how many behaviours will be included? This is a critical decision because the number of variables that can be used later in data analysis is not unlimited. A rule of thumb provided by Formann (1984) in the context of latent class analysis, is that sample size needs to be 2^k, where k indicates the number of variables used in the segmentation base. So, according to Formann's rule, if the number of behaviours included in the questionnaire is 15, the sample size required would be higher than 32,768. At first glance this appears to be a significant restriction imposed on the data analyst, but usually it only requires careful choice of survey questions, so rather than randomly inserting a list of 30 behaviours in the questionnaire, managers should make considered decisions as to which behaviours are actually relevant for the segmentation task at hand. If, indeed, it is impossible to restrict the number of questions so as to be suitably low given the sample size, an alternative is to select a subset of those questions (the most different ones) for the segmentation analysis and then use the other questions when segments are described.

The second critical decision in the data collection stage is the choice of answer formats (Dolnicar 2013). The vast majority of academic survey studies in tourism use so-called five or seven point Likert scales that ask respondents to indicate their level of agreement with a statement in the questionnaire. This answer format is particularly tricky in the context of data-driven market segmentation for two reasons:

1 It is prone to capturing response styles, such as respondents' tendencies to use the middle ('neither agree/nor disagree') or extreme options ('strongly agree', 'strongly disagree'). Such tendencies contaminate the data set and can lead to artificial segments which are meaningless in content; they actually just capture the response style. One such example is a segment which has extremely high agreement with all statements.

2 Likert scales are ordinally scaled. The distance between answer options is not defined, as is the case with metric data. Most segmentation algorithms are based on distance computations, but distance cannot easily be measured at ordinal level.

One way of avoiding both problems above is to use full binary answer formats (where respondents are asked to answer with a Yes or a No). The full binary answer format does not capture response styles and distance can easily be computed. This approach has been recommended a long time ago by Cronbach (1950) because the use of binary or dichotomous scales addresses the problem of response styles at its very source and does not give respondents the opportunity to display them. Cronbach's suggestion has not been taken up, instead multi-category answer formats, mostly the five and seven point Likert scale, still dominate survey research in tourism.

Data-driven segmentation step #3: Forming of segments

After the data is collected a segmentation algorithm is used to identify or create market segments based on the segmentation base. A number of critical decisions are made during this step.

First, it has to be assessed whether the exercise of forming segments is likely to reveal natural, reproducible or constructed segments. The implication is that where natural segments exist, the aim of the analysis is to identify the true segmentation solution. If, however, and this is the trickiest case, clusters cannot be reproduced when the analysis is repeated and thus constructed segments will be formed, the responsibility of the data analysts shifts to presenting a range of interesting solutions to management and letting management choose which is most strategically useful to them.

Second, and related to the first point: a decision about the number of clusters needs to be made (this is also true for the case of hierarchical clustering although the dendrogram may offer some guidance). Obviously, the number of clusters will hugely influence the final segmentation result. If, for example, two segments are chosen, it is likely that one will simply contain respondents who tended to say Yes to questions and another will contain respondents who tend to say No. Typically, this is not very informative for management. If, however, the same respondents are grouped into a larger number of clusters, more distinct patterns will start to emerge.

One way that can help resolve both issues discussed above is to simply repeat the segmentation analysis multiple times for a range of numbers of clusters (for example, ten calculations with four segments, ten calculations with five segments . . . and ten calculations with ten segments) and compare the resulting segments. This procedure has been proposed and illustrated by Dolnicar and Leisch (2010) using R code which runs the repeat analysis automatically, but can be reproduced with other statistical packages. If the exact same segments emerge from repeated computations it can be assumed that natural segments exist, if similar segments emerge the segments are likely to be reproducible, and if segments are different every single time, then segments need to be constructed artificially. In terms of decisions on the number of clusters chosen, the number of clusters which leads to most stable results (meaning that similar segments result from repeated computations) is preferable.

Other, less critical decisions at this stage include the choice of algorithm. Some algorithms have known tendencies of creating clusters of certain shapes, but our research has shown over the years that the algorithm is only critical in the case of constructive clustering (Buchta *et al.* 1997). If there is sufficient structure in the data, most algorithms will lead to similar solutions. Another decision is the choice of distance measure which needs to be suitable for the scale of the data.

Data-driven segmentation step #4: Description of segments

The description stage is identical to that in the commonsense approach: segments are compared to each other with respect to other relevant personal characteristics, which enables management to get a full picture of the segments which they then select one or more target segments from. A common mistake made in tourism segmentation research, is to conduct an analysis of variance using the segmentation base and then arguing that significant differences between segments in the segmentation base provide evidence of the fact that the segments are distinctly different. This approach is acceptable for any variables *except* the segmentation base for the following reason: any algorithm that is used to group respondents using the segmentation base, does this in a way which maximizes the differences between segments. A significance test determines whether relationships observed between variables are random. Clearly, after running an algorithm, the aim of which is to achieve maximum difference between segments, the relationship of variables between segments is no longer random and cannot be tested. Rather, it is the default expectation that resulting segments differ significantly in the segmentation base. Tests of differences are, however, critical for other variables, those not included in the segmentation base, like other travel behaviours, beliefs or socio-demographics.

Conclusion

Market segmentation is a central part of marketing strategy for businesses, organizations and tourism destinations. Market segmentation studies are not only popular in academic publications where they are conducted for the purpose of knowledge development, they are also very popular and commonly used in the tourism industry with the aim of gaining market intelligence to ensure future organizational success.

A comparison of current state of the art methods in both the conceptualisation of market segmentation as well as the methods used to conduct segmentation analysis indicates that there indeed is a significant gap in both the understanding of what market segmentation can and cannot achieve, as well as the methods used to actually conduct segmentation studies.

To close this gap it is important for both data analysts and managers involved in segmentation analyses to understand that, conceptually, market segmentation is an exploratory exercise and that one single computation is nothing more than one random grouping of many possible alternatives, and most likely not the best one of them. Once the notion of the exploratory nature of segmentation is accepted, it is clear that an assessment is needed of the nature of the segmentation study: is the aim to reveal true segments; identify reproducible segments; or construct artificial segments? This can be achieved by repeating computations a number of times with different numbers of clusters to determine the level of stability of results across replications. Low levels of stability puts pressure on decision makers because it is entirely up to them which of many possible segmentation solutions to choose.

A second key success factor in market segmentation studies goes beyond what is traditionally understood as segmentation analysis and includes critical steps before and after the actual analysis. These steps include: a thorough assessment of the constructs which will form the segmentation base; careful questionnaire design in order to capture the construct under study validly and avoid data analysis problems further down the marketing decision process; and use of recent data (collected from a sample that is suitable to the research question at hand, rather than a convenience sample).

Reports describing segmentation studies should disclose the full details of how the study was conducted and how all critical conceptual and methodological decisions have been made.

This is the case for both academic and industry studies and would greatly contribute to increasing the general understanding of market segmentation and enable users to assess its quality and managerial usefulness.

Many areas of market segmentation which are highly relevant to its correct use by both academics and industry require further research, for example: sample size requirements for market segmentation studies need to be determined, recommendations for data collection should be developed, which ensure that data of the most suitable nature for subsequent market segmentation analysis is collected. In addition, approaches are required which will enable data analysts to segment respondents based on typical ordinal survey data (data resulting from the popular Likert scale) while avoiding bias through response styles, and ways of assessing which of the resulting segments or which combination of resulting segments should be selected as a target segment.

In terms of the practical application of market segmentation in the tourism industry: it is still surprisingly simple. Most national tourism organizations still use basic commonsense approaches, such as using country of origin of tourists as the splitting criterion. There is nothing wrong with this approach. More complicated approaches are not necessarily the best. On the other hand, having used a simple commonsense segmentation for decades does not necessarily mean that it is the most promising segmentation strategy today. Tourism managers should continuously monitor possibilities for interesting segmentation analysis, after all they are exploratory. And, maybe most importantly: tourism managers should never let a data analyst produce a segmentation solution, just like data analysts should never run a segmentation analysis if the user refuses to be involved in every step of the process. The best segmentation solutions results from a team approach where tourism manager and data analyst work together from day one. Day one is not the day the data analysis starts, rather it is the day the tourism organization decides to undertake a segmentation study, well before the collection of data. An integrated team approach starting before data collection and ending with the joint interpretation of segment is not currently the most common approach to market segmentation in tourism, but it is the most promising approach which prevents any theory–practice divide from occurring, trains the data analyst to understand the key aims of the user and trains the tourism manager to understand what actually happens when data is segmented, thus allowing managers to have a more realistic assessment of what implications can be drawn from segmentation solutions for marketing strategy and, equally importantly, what implications cannot be drawn.

References

Arimond, G. and Lethlean, S. (1996) 'Profit Center Analysis within Private Campgrounds', *Journal of Travel Research*, 34: 52–8.

Bieger, T. and Laesser, C. (2002) 'Market Segmentation by Motivation: The Case of Switzerland', *Journal of Travel Research*, 41: 68–76.

Buchta, C., Dimitriadou, E., Dolnicar, S., Leisch, F. and Weingessel, A. (1997) *A Comparison of Several Cluster Algorithms on Artificial Binary Data Scenarios from Travel Market Segmentation*, Working Paper # 7. Vienna: Centre of Excellence Adaptive Information Systems and Modelling in Economics and Management Science.

Cronbach, L.J. (1950) 'Further Evidence on Response Sets and Test Design', *Educational and Psychological Measurement*, 10(1): 3–31.

Denison, T. and McDonald, M.H.B. (1995) 'The Role of Marketing Past, Present and Future', *Journal of Marketing Practice*, 1(1), Spring: 54–76.

Dibb, S. (2005) 'Market Segmentation Implementation Barriers and How to Overcome Them', *The Marketing Review*, 5: 13–30.

Dodd, T. and Bigotte, V. (1997) 'Perceptual Differences among Visitor Groups to Wineries', *Journal of Travel Research*, 35: 46–51.

Dolnicar, S. (2004) 'Beyond "Commonsense Segmentation" – A Systematics of Segmentation Approaches in Tourism', *Journal of Travel Research*, 42: 244–50.
Dolnicar, S. (2013) 'Asking Good Survey Questions', *Journal of Travel Research*, 52(5): 551–74.
Dolnicar, S. and Grün, B. (2013) 'Validity Measuring Destination Images in Survey Studies', *Journal of Travel Research*, 52(1): 3–13
Dolnicar, S. and Lazarevski, K. (2009) 'Methodological Reasons for the Theory/Practice Divide in Market Segmentation', *Journal of Marketing Management*, 25: 357–74.
Dolnicar, S. and Leisch, F. (2003) 'Winter Tourist Segments in Austria – Identifying Stable Vacation Styles for Target Marketing Action', *Journal of Travel Research*, 41: 281–93.
— (2010) 'Evaluation of Structure and Reproducibility of Cluster Solutions Using the Bootstrap', *Marketing Letters*, 21: 83–101.
Dolnicar, S., Crouch, G.I., Devinney, T., Huybers, T., Louviere, J.J. and Oppewal, H. (2008) 'Tourism and Discretionary Income Allocation – Heterogeneity Among Households', *Tourism Management*, 29: 44–52.
Dolnicar, S., Grabler, K. and Mazanec, J.A. (1999) 'Analysing Destination Images: A Perceptual Charting Approach', *Journal of Travel & Tourism Marketing*, 8: 43–57.
Field, A.M. (1999) 'The College Student Market Segment: A Comparative Study of Travel Behaviors of International and Domestic Students at a Southeastern University', *Journal of Travel Research*, 37: 375–81.
Formann, A.K. (1984) *Die Latent-Class-Analyse: Einführung in die Theorie und Anwendung*. Weinheim: Beltz.
Frank, R.E., Massy, W.F. and Wind, Y. (1972) *Market Segmentation*. Englewood Cliffs, NJ: Prentice Hall.
Goldsmith, R.E. and Litvin, S.W. (1999) 'Heavy Users of Travel Agents: A Segmentation Analysis of Vacation Travelers', *Journal of Travel Research*, 38: 127–33.
Greenberg, M. and McDonald, S.S. (1989) 'Successful Needs/Benefits Segmentation: A User's Guide', *The Journal of Consumer Marketing*, 6: 29–36.
Hudson, S. (2000) 'The Segmentation of Potential Tourists: Constraint Differences between Men and Women', *Journal of Travel Research*, 38: 363–68.
Israeli, A.A. (2002) 'A Preliminary Investigation of the Importance of Site Accessibility Factors for Disabled Tourists', *Journal of Travel Research*, 41: 101–4.
Kastenholz, E., Davis, D. and Paul G. (1999) 'Segmenting Tourism in Rural Areas: The Case of North and Central Portugal', *Journal of Travel Research*, 37: 353–63.
McDonald, M.H.B. (1982) 'The Theory and Practice of Marketing Planning for Industrial Goods in International Markets', Bedford UK: Cranfield Institute of Technology PhD.
McDonald, M. (1996) 'Strategic Marketing Planning: Theory, Practice and Research Agendas', *Journal of Marketing Management*, 12(1-3): 4–27.
Mazanec, J.A. (2000) 'Market Segmentation', in: J. Jafari (ed.), *Encyclopedia of Tourism*. London: Routledge.
Mazanec, J.A., Grabler, K. and Maier, G. (1997) *International City Tourism: Analysis and Strategy*. London: Pinter/Cassell.
Myers, J.H. and Tauber, E. (1977) *Market Structure Analysis*. Chicago: American Marketing.
Reece, W.S. (2004) 'Are Senior Leisure Travelers Different?', *Journal of Travel Research*, 43: 11–18.
Smith, W. (1956) 'Product Differentiation and Market Segmentation as Alternative Marketing Strategies', *Journal of Marketing*, 21: 3–8.
Wedel, M. and Kamakura, W.A. (1998) *Market Segmentation – Conceptual and Methodological Foundations*. Boston: Kluwer.
Xia, J., Evans, F.H., Spilsbury, K., Ciesielski, V., Arrowsmith, C. and Wright, G. (2010) 'Market Segments Based on the Dominant Movement Patterns of Tourists', *Tourism Management*, 31: 464–9.
Zins, A. (2008) 'Market Segmentation in Tourism: A Critical Review of 20 Years' Research Efforts', in S.M.C. Kronenberg, M. Peters, B. Pikkemaat and K. Weiermair (eds), *From the "OLD" to the "NEW" Tourism: Managing Change in the Tourism Industry*. Berlin: Erich Schmidt Verlag, pp. 289–301.

16

Determining what works, what doesn't and why

Evaluating tourism marketing campaigns

Stephen Pratt

Introduction

Destination Marketing Organizations (DMOs) face threats, both external and internal (Gretzel *et al.* 2006). Stakeholders of DMOs are demanding more accountability than ever before from their colleagues (Gretzel *et al.* 2006). Increasingly, DMOs have to justify their marketing budgets to their funding organizations. The funding organizations want clear evidence that the funds they provide for marketing are achieving their objectives. Tourism marketing campaign objectives need to be quantifiable, realistic, achievable, relevant and time specific. A critical factor in determining the success or otherwise of DMOs' marketing campaigns is deciding what the key performance indicators (KPI) should be, finding the right benchmarks and deciding on what techniques or methods should be used in their evaluation. A recent study by Williams *et al.* (2012) among Travel and Tourism Research Association (TTRA) members found that the performance of destination marketing/management strategies ranked second as a research priority area. Both academics and practitioners want to identify the strategies and programs that contribute to long term sustainable growth of tourism destinations. In terms of research into evaluation methods, the study by Williams and colleagues found the second-most priority area for a better understanding was return-on-investment. For practitioners, this area had the highest ranking. There is a clear desire to estimate the (predominantly economic) benefits of a marketing campaign and compare them with the costs of implementing the campaign.

The systematic evaluation of marketing campaigns assists DMOs determine what works and what doesn't, leading to a more efficient use of marketing resources. Despite 'marketing control' being a necessary element of every marketing plan (Kotler *et al.* 2009), this component is often overlooked so that, in reality, DMOs are unable to determine the success or otherwise of their marketing. Several approaches have been proposed to evaluate tourism marketing campaigns in the tourism research literature. These approaches include conversion studies, advertising tracking studies, quasi-experiments and cross-sectional analysis. The following section discusses some of the difficulties in deciding what to measure before reviewing the most common evaluation methods. For each evaluation method, advantages and disadvantages of each evaluation method are highlighted. Further, with increasing use of online marketing, a new set of marketing metrics have arisen that have been used to assess the success of DMOs' websites. These Internet marketing metrics will be reviewed. However, the real test of what works and what doesn't in terms of tourism marketing, both for online and more traditional marketing campaigns, is whether the marketing drives potential tourists to visit and spend at the destination.

Deciding what to measure

DMOs tend to be funded by the public sector and hence ultimately answer to resident taxpayers. In the United States for example, some State Governments impose hotel/bed taxes where the tax revenue gained is earmarked for the marketing activities of DMOs, signalling a direct link between the DMO, tourists and the public. They are often quasi public organizations and need to justify their public funding (Morgan *et al.* 2012). DMOs increasingly have a coordinating role and facilitate private sector tourism operators to market their products. They are only partly responsible for marketing the destination, since the private sector also advertise and market their individual products. So attributing destination success as a result of a DMO marketing strategies becomes even more complicated. Yet evaluating DMO effectiveness is important because it is more difficult to attribute consumer decisions to marketing actions vis-à-vis alternative information sources.

In contrast to the publically funded DMOs, the private sector tourism operations, such as hotels, resorts and airlines generally have better access to sales and performance data internally. They are able to directly isolate the success of the marketing campaigns in influencing occupancy rates/passenger load factors and sales. Alternatively, some of these operations will outsource the implementation of their marketing campaigns to third party organizations or marketing intermediaries who may include an evaluation component that is built into the marketing programme. For example, hotels will often use Online Travel Agents (OTA) to help sell their rooms (Anderson 2011; Page and Connell 2009). Examples of some of the more well-known international OTAs are Expedia.com, Travelocity.com and Orbitz.com. Even though the hotel would prefer to sell the rooms directly through their own website, so they can retain a higher proportion of the sale, OTAs are an important distribution channel. Based on where the hotel guest made the booking, the hotel or airline then pays commission to the OTA. Hence, within the private sector, there may be fewer marketing research or evaluation projects needed.

Tasci and Williams (2007) argue that the ultimate goal of destination marketing is to attract tourists by influencing their travel decision-making and choice to travel to the destination. Yet before tourists travel to a destination, there is a process of consumer decision making. Different consumers will be at different stages of buyer readiness. Kotler *et al.* (2009) list these buyer readiness states as: awareness; knowledge; liking; preference; conviction; and purchase. Often, tourism marketing objectives seek to address different stages of buyer readiness, that is, they seek to raise awareness of the destination, increase potential tourists' knowledge of the destination, create a favourable impression of the destination in the mind of potential tourists, build destination preference or ultimately convert the potential tourists to a visitor to the destination. For each target group, DMOs ought to evaluate the effectiveness of their marketing to push the potential tourists further toward visiting the destination. Both the intermediate objectives of the buyer readiness state and the ultimate objective of increased tourist visits need to be evaluated. The decision on what criteria or KPIs that DMOs will be assessed and evaluated on and which evaluation instrument will be used should encompass both.

Measuring the effectiveness of destination marketing campaigns is complex (Morgan *et al.* 2012). The reasons for this are numerous and have been highlighted previously in the literature. One of the reasons for the complexity is that destinations comprise numerous stakeholders including private and public sector organizations, each with their own objectives and different level of resources (Pike 2005). In most destinations, destination level marketing is undertaken by the respective DMO, a public sector or semi-autonomous authority. The delivery of tourism services, on the whole, is undertaken by the private sector. DMOs then, while competing in the global market place, need to operate in a resource poor and highly politicised environment (Fyall *et al.* 2003). Some marketing objectives have short-term goals and are more tactical by nature while other marketing objectives are more strategic, with expected benefits not being realized for several years. The difficulty then arises as to how to attribute the achievement of a KPI to an individual campaign.

The tourist decision-making process further complicates the evaluation of the effectiveness of destination marketing campaigns as there are many factors that can affect tourist decision making as outlined by Sairakaya and Woodside (2005). Complicating factors include limitations on destination choice sets (Um and Crompton 1990), the influence of other household members and friends on travel decisions (Currie *et al.* 2008; Gitelson and Kerstetter 1994) and the recognition that factors that influence destination choice can be interactive (Woodside and King 2001).

The Internet has played a key role in the travel information perspective of tourism. Xiang *et al.* (2008) group this information search into three phases. Noting their potentially different information needs, the pre-travel stage is where tourists seek information to be used for planning, decision making and expectation formation; the consumption stage is where information is sought establishing connections and relationships with tourism and travel service providers, to aid short term decision making and conduct at-destination transactions; and the third post-consumption stage is where information about the trips is generated, recorded and shared with others. At all these stages, there is an opportunity to evaluate the effectiveness of different elements of the marketing strategies. Given online information seekers will not typically examine more than the first three pages of search results, it is important for DMOs to have their web link rank highly in the search engine. Hence, the ranking and position of the DMO website on popular search engines can be a key measure of online marketing effectiveness (Xiang and Fesenmaier 2005).

Review of evaluation methods

Various evaluation methods have been used to assess the effectiveness of tourism marketing campaigns. These different evaluation techniques include conversion studies (Burke and Gitelson 1990; Woodside and Reid 1974; Pratt *et al.*; 2009), advertising tracking studies (Siegel and Ziff-Levine 1990), experiments (Woodside and Sakai 2001) and quasi-experiments (Mok 1990), and cross-sectional analysis (Silberman and Klock 1986). With the growth of Internet marketing and social media, additional methods of evaluation have been created to assess the effectiveness of the new media to achieve tourism marketing goals. The evaluation of websites has been undertaken using five approaches: counting, automated, numerical computation, user judgement and combined methods (Law *et al.* 2010).

Advertising tracking studies generally seek to capture information relating to the intermediate marketing objectives and KPIs. By collecting data on spontaneous and aided destination awareness and destination advertising awareness, as well as destination preference and destination image attributes, advertising tracking studies measure shifts in cognitive knowledge and attitudes and travel intent toward a destination. Although it is important for marketers to understand what works and what doesn't, this type of evaluation falls short of assessing whether tourists have travelled to the destination as a result of being exposed to destination marketing. An evaluation of South Australia's direct marketing campaign is described in Trembath (1999). The research used Computer Assisted Telephone Interviews among households in the campaign distribution areas in the other Australian cities of Sydney and Melbourne. It involved a pre-distribution and post-distribution survey that captured prompted and unprompted advertising recall, travel intentions, destination image and perceptions of the direct marketing material but stopped short of attempting any measurement of conversion. Trembath found that the campaign increased advertising recall and stimulated interest in visiting the destination yet could not determine whether the campaign actually drove consumers to the destination. Advertising tracking studies are generally more expensive than other types of evaluation methods and their long-term impact is difficult to separate out of other environmental impacts. This is problematic as it is difficult to attribute tourist arrivals or tourist expenditure directly to a specific marketing campaign (Morgan *et al.* 2012). If the advertising tracking is conducted using face-to-face omnibus surveys, this can be expensive. Advertising tracking studies are useful if the goal is to evaluate cognitive knowledge about the destination and travel intent toward a destination (Siegel and Ziff-Levine 1990)

Historically, conversion studies have been the most common method of destination marketing campaign effectiveness, comparing relative performance of one campaign over another (Woodside 1981). Conversion studies tend to be generally well-understood and relatively inexpensive to implement which may be a reason for their popularity (Silberman and Klock 1986; Woodside 1990). USA State DMOs have used conversion studies quite extensively to evaluate their campaigns. For example, conversion studies have been used to evaluate marketing campaigns in Arkansas (McLemore and Mitchell 2001), Montana (TravelMontana 1998), Vermont (Kuentzel 1993a; Kuentzel 1993b) and Virginia (VTC 2001). Conversion studies can also assess the effectiveness of DMO marketing campaigns implemented via different channels and visitor markets. Examples in the literature of assessing the effectiveness of marketing campaigns using different media include magazine advertising (TravelMontana, 1998), telephone inquiries (Messmer and Johnson 1993) and websites (McLemore and Mitchell 2001; Tierney 2000).

Conversion studies usually involve assessing whether recipients of destination marketing visit the destination (become converted) as a result of being exposed to destination advertising or a promotion (Pratt *et al.* 2009). These types of studies are usually implemented through questionnaire surveys. The common metrics of conversion studies include gross and net conversion rates, costs per inquiry, revenue per inquiry and return on investment generated in different media or target markets. The conversion rates express the proportion of enquirers who visit the destination after being exposed to the destination marketing campaign. The number of visitors and the amount they spend in the destination is then used to estimate cost efficiency indices, expenditure impacts and return on investment figures (Burke and Lindblom 1989). Although used extensively, conversion studies have some limitations. Early iterations of conversion studies failed to correct for non-response bias, used incorrect sampling techniques (Butterfield *et al.* 1998; Silberman and Klock 1986) or failed to take into account multiple trips (Perdue and Gustke 1992). Woodside and Dubelaar (2003) also found that response rates for conversion studies vary depending on whether the sponsor for the survey was identified or not.

Pratt *et al.* (2009) seek to overcome some of the shortfalls of conversion studies. They do this by adjusting downward the proportion of respondents estimated to visit the destination as a result of the marketing campaign to calculate at a net conversion rate. This net conversion rate weighs the proportion of visitors who visit the destination by the degree to which the marketing campaign influenced their decision to visit (Ballman *et al.* 1984; Burke and Gitelson 1990). Further, the researchers only attribute the incremental expenditure of those visitors who had already booked or planned their trip to the destination and were motivated to stay as a result of the marketing campaign. Lastly, previous research found that respondents differed in their travel patterns and reaction to marketing stimuli compared to non-respondents (Ellerbrock 1981) so

Pratt and colleagues adjusted the incremental expenditure estimates down by 20 per cent to allow for non-response bias. This technique has been used in previous research (Hunt and Dalton 1983; Woodside and Ronkainen 1984).

Conversion studies make a strong underlying assumption of a direct, causal relationship between a destination visit and the requested marketing material. This might not necessarily be the case. Destination visitors draw from a wide range of information sources. By making that direct assumption, conversion studies cannot evaluate a range of psychological and cognitive or underlying behaviour motivation from the marketing (Pratt *et al.* 2009).

Woodside and Sakai (2001) undertake a meta-evaluation, that is, an assessment of evaluation practices across government tourism marketing programmes in the USA. The authors categorize the evaluations into four efficiency factors and six indices of effectiveness. Effectiveness indicators included such measurements as: revenues generated by the tourism marketing programmes; revenue per inquiry (RPI) using conversion studies; taxes generated from tourism expenditures; tourist visits, tourism awareness, attitudes and intentions to visit; likelihood of return visits and likelihood to recommend. Efficiency indicators include return on investment (ROI), cost–benefit analysis, cost per inquiry (CPI) and constructed metrics, such as ratio comparisons (e.g. CPI/RPI).

Experimental design methodology, it is argued, is able to test causation rather than merely correlation. The process involves testing possible combinations of different attributes in a marketing strategy across a sample using a fractional factorial design method. A logistic regression model is then used to analyze the impact of each stimulus in the experiment (Almquist and Wyner 2001). Woodside and Sakai (2001) argue for experiential design techniques though they cite several reasons why the adoption of true experiments has not been taken up. These obstacles include lack of training and knowledge of evaluation literature; arguments that research costs would be excessive; comfort with conversion studies and advertising effectiveness studies; and perceived risk of using alternative evaluation methods. The limitations of the experimental design technique are that the marketers need extensive knowledge in framing the research, application of theoretically sound methods and that experimental designs rely on 'main effects', that is, they do not take into account the impact of one variable on another, through a third variable.

An alternative measurement of campaign effectiveness is Data Envelopment Analysis (DEA) is used by Wöber and Fesemaier to evaluate the inefficiencies of tourism advertising programmes and consequently to DMOs to benchmark against (Wöber and Fesenmaier 2004). The DEA method can incorporate multiple inputs and outputs and uses a linear optimization technique. For example, Wöber and Fesenmaier evaluate the performance of US state DMOs using such variables as their advertising budgets, the allocation of marketing budgets for both international and domestic markets and the number of visitors and expenditures generated. Proponents of the DEA method note that this method does not require any formal system of hypothesis testing and it requires no a priori information regarding which inputs and outputs are most important in the evaluation procedure. A drawback with this technique is that the method is largely dependent on the definition of input and outputs and does not provide DMOs with detailed recommendations concerning a particular marketing strategy.

Morgan and colleagues (2012) propose an integrated approach to evaluation that seeks to link different elements of buyer readiness states. The four elements they propose include a panel survey to monitor advertising awareness of marketing campaigns. The second element is a DMO contact survey similar to traditional conversion research but implemented on a continuous basis. The third element of their framework is a re-contact survey. The re-contact survey, conducted online, follows up those who responded to the contact survey and seeks to correlate advertising awareness with visitation as well as probing those who did not visit the destination.

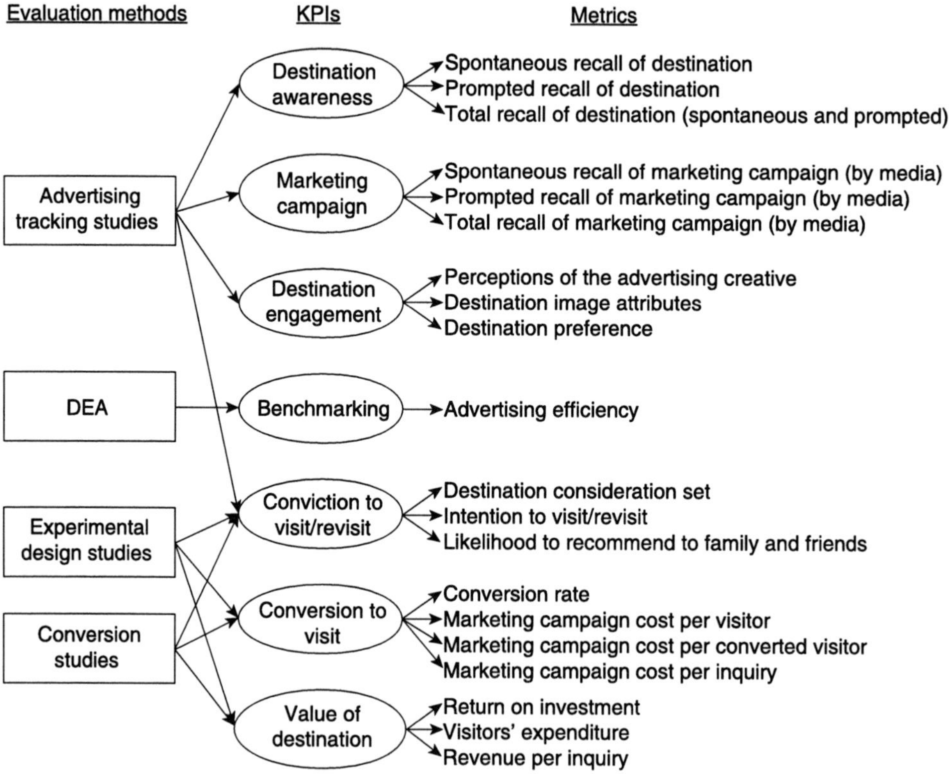

Figure 16.1 Evaluation method, KPIs and metrics.

The last element in their framework seeks to evaluate the DMO website through an online survey, asking the DMO website visitors the sources of information used to direct them to the DMO website and the extent to which these DMO website visitors were motivated to visit the destination as a result of visiting the website.

Figure 16.1, adapted from Morgan *et al.* (2012), displays a common set of KPIs, their evaluation methods and specific metrics associated with each evaluation method. The figure provides a graphical representation of review discussed above. Which KPIs the DMO are focussing and being assessed on will determine the appropriate evaluation method to use.

Internet marketing metrics

Just as more marketing strategies implemented through traditional channels have become subject to evaluation and measured for their effectiveness, so too, new media channels and marketing strategies and programs implemented using social media and the Internet are also being evaluated. The evaluation of Internet-based marketing campaigns and websites has grown in recent years. Morrison *et al.* provide one of the earlier reviews on website evaluation (Morrison *et al.* 2004). Law *et al.* (2010) provide a comprehensive review of website evaluation in tourism research. These authors categorize website evaluation into five approaches: counting, user judgement, automated, numerical computation and combined methods.

Counting methods involve constructing a checklist of website attributes that a website should have and evaluating different websites against this checklist. Those assessing the website, as Law *et al.* surveyed in the literature have been tourists, practitioners, policymakers, researchers and students. One example of this is Morrison *et al.* (2004) who advocate a Balanced Scorecard (BSC) approach which seeks to measure website performance on a range of factors including: customer, financial, learning and growth, and internal business processes. They provide a standardized form to evaluate DMO websites, which comprises technical aspects, user friendliness, site attractiveness, marketing effectiveness, link popularity, trip planner assistance and legal compliance. As with the BSC approach, these areas are then weighted to give an overall score so that comparisons can be made across time and with competitors (Morrison *et al.* 2004).

User judgement methods involve different cohorts (students, tourists, researchers, policy makers) evaluating user satisfaction or perceptions of a particular website. These studies tend to evaluate the websites using modified SERVQUAL-type survey instruments. Numerical computation evaluation methods use mathematical functions to compute tourism website performance based on a number of factors.

Automated methods use information technology software to evaluate the success of websites. The advantages of these techniques include their consistency in evaluation and greater objectivity compared to human-based evaluations. Technical indices of website usage have been used to evaluate the effectiveness of DMO websites (Sterne 2002). These indices include such metrics as average time spent on a particular page, cost per click, click-through rate. These metrics can then determine key performance indicators for websites, such as ROI on a website by comparing website sales versus costs. As with the evaluation techniques of marketing strategies implemented through traditional channels, determining what works and what doesn't for DMOs is more difficult because DMOs do not have the ability to control tourist travel, like a private sector hotel or airline would (Middleton and Clarke 2001). They can only influence travel decisions. There are many external and internal factors that influence tourist decision-making (Papatheodorou 2001; Seddighi and Theocharous 2002).

By analyzing these web metrics, DMOs can see at what stage of the website browsing visitors are navigating away (Hieggelke, n.d.). However as many DMOs are public entities, they may generate little or no revenue of their own. Their objective, then, is to pull tourists to the destination. One popular tool for measuring website performance is through the automated method of Google Analytics. This web analyzer provides easy to understand statistics concerning the website (Plaza 2011). Google Analytics is a free service, offered by Google, which can answer such questions marketers might be interested in, such as 'how deep do visitors navigate into the website? Are search engines more effective than referring site entries?' (Plaza 2011). Some of the common metrics associated with Google Analytics and other web analyzers that can assist DMOs to evaluate their websites include visits to the webpage, page views, pages viewed per website visit, bounce rate and average time on site. The tool can track website visitors from different referrers, such as highlighting those who came from search engines, display advertising, pay-per-click networks, e-mail marketing or links within PDF documents.

Combined methods, as the name suggests, use a combination of different methods to evaluate websites. Clearly, it is difficult for any one method or even a combination of methods to capture a single criterion for website evaluation. Hence, there is no absolute right or wrong methodological paradigm – one size doesn't fit all.

The importance of websites has developed as Internet-based marketing can offer the destination for unique opportunities over and above traditional marketing. It can provide potential tourists with up-to-date and accurate information on tourism products and services; it can offer potential tourists the opportunity to develop an immediate and constant conversation with the DMO; it can provide potential tourists with the opportunity to purchase tourism products and services online; and it can enhance the marketing relationship as marketers can identify attractive market segments and offer tailored value-added services (Wang and Russo 2007).

Li and Wang (2010) state that US travellers commence their search for a destination using an Internet search engine, such as Google or Yahoo, with the DMOs' websites being the next most common Internet search. Not surprisingly, several models have been developed by scholars to evaluate website effectiveness. Li and Wang (2010) argue a website should be evaluated on five dimensions: information, communication, transaction, relationship and technical merit. Chiou *et al.* (2011) propose a model, 4PsC, encompassing the 4Ps of marketing (Product, Price, Place and Promotion) plus Customer Relationship.

As with the evaluation of more traditional marketing channels, there is no consensus on the best way to evaluate DMO websites. In terms of who actually determines website effectiveness, several studies use travel and tourism experts to evaluate website effectiveness (Li and Wang 2011; Chiou *et al.* 2011). Other studies use tourists to evaluate website effectiveness. Financial returns, customer satisfaction and purchase intention are frequently used as indicators of website effectiveness (Schmidt *et al.* 2008). Chiou *et al.* (2011) use gap analysis to evaluate two Taiwanese travel websites against a weighted criterion.

Social media allows tourism businesses to interact directly with tourists and potential tourists via various Internet platforms and to monitor and interact with opinions and evaluations of services. Hvass and Munar (2012) evaluate the Facebook and Twitter communication between 42 different airlines and their online audiences using online ethnographic research and content analysis. They find that these airlines communicate traditional advertising messages and fail to take advantage of the interconnectivity of user generated content that social media can harness.

As a summary of the above section, Table 16.1 shows the more common evaluation methods that have been used to assess the efficiency and effectiveness of travel and tourism websites. For each evaluation method, the KPIs and the individual metrics in assessing the success criteria are shown. Different stakeholders will have different priorities in terms of what the DMO websites can and should do. As with off-line marketing, no one evaluation technique can achieve every marketing objective the DMO might set. As with marketing through off-line methods, deciding what is important and the definition of success (KPIs) and how to measure success (metrics) determines what evaluation technique is most appropriate. An attractive, logical and focussed DMO website will be one component in the marketing mix.

Table 16.1 Internet evaluation methods, KPIs and metrics

Evaluation method	*KPI*	*Metrics*
Counting	Website quality	Checklist of attributes
user judgement	Website user satisfaction	Perceptions of information quality; perceived usefulness; perceived ease of use; perceived accessibility; attitude
	Website strength and weaknesses	Balanced scorecard
Automated	Website effectiveness	Visits to the webpage; page views; pages viewed per website visit; average time on website; Tracking of different referrers
Numerical computation	Website performance	Mathematical functions

Source: Morrison *et al.* (2004) and Law *et al.* (2010)

Conclusions

There is a growing need to standardize marketing strategy evaluations and provide more robust assessments in comparing ROIs for different marketing campaigns (Williams *et al.* 2012). This chapter seeks to review the most common marketing evaluation tools used to date to measure the effectiveness of DMO marketing campaigns. Learning and adapting from previous research, more recent conversion studies have found that marketing campaign evaluations undertaken using experimental design also have value. For several reasons, this type of evaluation has not been as widely implemented as conversion studies. Both conversion studies and experimental design studies seek to capture the incidence of those exposed to the marketing campaigns who are then been converted to visitors. DMOs should desire to quantify these KPIs as they estimate the ultimate goal for DMOs – to drive potential tourists to visit their destination.

Nevertheless, intermediate goals, such as destination awareness, destination preference and intention to visit, as well as potential tourists' perception of the advertising creative, are equally important to DMOs. Where sufficient resources are available, marketing evaluations carried out in a holistic framework, as suggested by Morgan *et al.* (2012) would be ideal. This applies to marketing campaigns undertaken through traditional media as well as web-based and Internet marketing campaigns. Yet, the current funding environment for many DMOs means they need to do more with less. The funds that they are given will come under more and more scrutiny and need to be justified. The lack of resources will drive DMOs to use more creative (and free) marketing tools, such as Facebook and Twitter. Undertaking comprehensive and holistic methods as outlined above or undertaking data mining procedures to assess the effectiveness of online marketing may be too expensive or too difficult for many DMOs. Consequently, rigorous evaluations are not completed and DMOs are back to wondering which marketing campaigns work and which don't.

As mentioned by Li and Wang (2011), there is a need to go beyond merely evaluating destination websites. Evaluations of websites need to link their effectiveness with visitation and expenditure statistics if they are to be seen as truly effective. Hence, using a combination of methods for website evaluations seems most prudent. Regardless of the marketing channel, DMOs need to pay more attention to quality rather than the quantity of their marketing strategies (Li and Wang 2011).

Current performance measurement and benchmarking approaches have several shortcomings. As highlighted by Gretzel *et al.* (2006), to adequately measure the effectiveness of all the marketing activities, both above and below the line, offline and online can be time consuming and expensive. There is a need to evaluate internal marketing efforts, partnering initiatives and community outreach, long term and short term marketing activities as well as strategies using traditional and new channels and technologies.

Almquist and Wyner (2001) argue that the medium of evaluation should match the medium of the marketing program so that Internet-based marketing strategies should be evaluated with Internet-based evaluation techniques. Further, the evaluation process needs to be built into the planning process. Evaluating marketing campaigns and strategies should not be conducted in an ad hoc manner (Hieggelke n.d.) if DMOs are to determine what works, what doesn't and why.

Considering how marketing evaluations might develop in the future, the challenges DMOs face will become exacerbated in the next few years. Potential tourists are exposed to an increasing number of tourism marketing stimuli, especially with the emergence of new media (Xiang and Gretzel 2010). The pre-decision stage of the travel decision is influenced by multiple factors. Distinguishing which marketing execution motivated the tourists to visit the destination may be beyond the capability of DMOs, even if they have the resources to undertake evaluation. Tourists themselves may not know or be able to articulate which marketing campaign or tools motivated them to choose that particular destination to visit. Yet, to do nothing and undertake no assessment is not an option.

References

Almquist, E. and Wyner, G. (2001) 'Boost Your Marketing ROI with Experimental Design', *Harvard Business Review*, October: 5–11.

Anderson, C. (2011) 'Search, OTAs, and Online Booking: An Expanded Analysis of the Billboard Effect', *Cornell Hospitality Report*, 11: 4–10.

Ballman, G., Burke, J., Blank, U. and Korte, D. (1984) 'Towards Higher Quality Conversion Studies: Refining the Numbers Game', *Journal of Travel Research*, 22: 28–33.

Burke, J. and Lindblom, L.A. (1989) 'Strategies for Evaluating Direct Response Tourism Marketing', *Journal of Travel Research*, 28: 33–7.

Burke, J.F. and Gitelson, R. (1990) 'Conversion Studies: Assumptions, Accuracy and Abuse', *Journal of Travel Research*, 28: 46–51.

Butterfield, D.W., Deal, K.R. and Kubursi, A.A. (1998) 'Measuring the Returns to Tourism Advertising', *Journal of Travel Research*, 37: 12–20.

Chiou, W.-C., Lin, C.-C. and Perng, C. (2011) 'A Strategic Website Evaluation of Online Travel Agencies', *Tourism Management*, 32: 1463–73.

Currie, R.R., Wesley, F. and Sutherland, P. (2008) 'Going Where the Joneses Go: Understanding How Others Influence Travel Decision-making', *International Journal of Culture, Tourism and Hospitality Research*, 2: 12–24.

Ellerbrock, M. (1981) 'Improving Coupon Conversion Studies: A Comment', *Journal of Travel Research*, 19: 37–8.

Fyall, A., Callod, C. and Edwards, B. (2003) 'Relationship Marketing: The Challenge for Destinations', *Annals of Tourism Research*, 30: 644–59.

Gitelson, R. and Kerstetter, D. (1994) 'The Influence of Friends and Relatives in Travel Decision-Making', *Journal of Travel and Tourism Marketing*, 3: 59–68.

Gretzel, U., Fesenmaier, D.R., Formica, S. and O'Leary, J.T. (2006) 'Searching for the Future: Challenges Faced by Destination Marketing Organizations', *Journal of Travel Research*, 45: 116–26.

Hieggelke, B. (n.d.) 'Marketing ROI – Learn It, Love It, Act On It', *Industry Insights from WebTrends*.

Hunt, J.D. and Dalton, M.J. (1983) 'Comparing Mail and Telephone for Conducting Coupon Conversion Studies', *Journal of Travel Research*, 21: 16.

Hvass, K.A. and Munar, A.M. (2012) 'The Takeoff of Social Media in Tourism', *Journal of Vacation Marketing*, 18: 93–103.

Kotler, P., Bowen, J.T. and Makens, J.C. (2009) *Marketing for Hospitality and Tourism*. New Jersey: Pearson Education Inc.

Kuentzel, W.F. (1993a) '1992 Summer/Fall Conversion Study: Comparing the Effectiveness of Four Media Promotions', in: Vermont Department of Travel and Tourism (ed.). Burlington, Vermont. Available from tourismresearch@uvm.edu.

— (1993b) '1994 Winter Conversion Study: Media Effectiveness, Travel Planning and 1-800-VERMONT', in: Vermont Department of Travel and Tourism (ed.). Burlington, Vermont. Available from tourismresearch@uvm.edu.

Law, R., Qi, S. and Buhalis, D. (2010) 'Progress in Tourism Managment: A Review of Website Evaluation', *Tourism Management*, 31: 297–313.

Li, X. and Wang, Y. (2010) 'Evaluating the Effectiveness of Destination Marketing Organizations' Websites: Evidence from China', *International Journal of Tourism Research*, 12: 536–49.

— (2011) 'Measuring the Effectiveness of US Official State Tourist Websites', *Journal of Vacation Marketing*, 17: 287–302.

Mclemore, C. and Mitchell, N. (2001) 'An Internet Conversion Study of www.arkansas.com – A State Tourism Website', *Journal of Vacation Marketing*, 7: 268–74.

Messmer, D.J. and Johnson, R.R. (1993) 'Inquiry Conversion and Travel Advertising Effectiveness', *Journal of Travel Research*, 31: 14–21.

Middleton, V. and Clarke, J. (2001) *Marketing in Travel and Tourism*. Oxford: Butterworth-Heinemann.

Mok, H.M. (1990) 'A Quasi-experimental Measure of Effectiveness of Destination Advertising: Some Evidence from Hawaii', *Journal of Travel Research*, 29: 30–4.

Morgan, N., Hastings, E. and Pritchard, A. (2012) 'Developing a New DMO Marketing Evaluation Framework: The Case of Visit Wales', *Journal of Vacation Marketing*, 18: 73–89.

Morrison, A., Taylor, S. and Douglas, A. (2004) 'Website Evaluation in Tourism and Hospitality', *Journal of Travel and Tourism Marketing*, 17: 233–51.

Page, S. and Connell, J. (2009) *Tourism: A Modern Synthesis*. Andover, Hampshire, UK: Cengage Learning EMEA.

Papatheodorou, A. (2001) 'Why People Travel to Different Places', *Annals of Tourism Research*, 28: 164–79.

Perdue, R.R. and Gustke, L.D. (1992) 'The Influence of Multiple Trips on Inquiry Conversion Research Results', *Journal of Travel Research*, 30: 27–30.

Pike, S. (2005) 'Tourism Destination Branding Complexity', *Journal of Product and Brand Management*, 14: 258–9.

Plaza, B. (2011) 'Google Analytics for Measuring Website Performance', *Tourism Management*, 32 : 477–81.

Pratt, S., McCabe, S., Cortes-Jimenez, I. and Blake, A. (2009) 'Measuring the Effectiveness of Destination Marketing Campaigns: Comparative Analysis of Conversion Studies', *Journal of Travel Research*, 49: 179–90.

Schmidt, S., Cantallops, A.S. and dos Santos, C.P. (2008) 'The Characteristics of Hotel Websites and their Implications for Website Effectiveness', *International Journal of Hospitality Management*, 27: 504–16.

Seddighi, H.R. and Theocharous, A.L. (2002) 'A Model of Tourism Destination Choice: A Theoretical and Empirical Analysis', *Tourism Management*, 23: 475–87.

Siegel, W. and Ziff-Levine, W. (1990) 'Evaluating Tourism Advertising Campaigns: Conversion vs Advertising Tracking Studies', *Journal of Travel Research*, 29(3): 51–5.

Silberman, J. and Klock, M. (1986) 'Alternative to Conversion Studies for Measuring the Impact of Travel Ads', *Journal of Travel Research*, 24: 12–16.

Sirakaya, E. and Woodside, A. (2005) 'Building and Testing Theories of Decision Making by Travellers', *Tourism Management*, 26: 815–32.

Sterne, E. (2002) *Web Metrics. Proven Methods for Measuring Web Site Success*. New York: Wiley Publishing.

Tasci, A.D.A. and Gartner, W. (2007) 'Destination Image and its Functional Relationship', *Journal of Travel Research*, 45: 413–25.

Tierney, P. (2000) 'Internet-based Evaluation of Tourism Web Site Effectiveness: Methodological Issues and Survey Results', *Journal of Travel Research*, 39: 212–19.

Travelmontana (1998) 'Magazine Travel Conversion Study', Online. Available at http://travelmontana.state.mt.us/research/Magazineconversionstudy98.pdf.

Trembath, R. (1999) 'Best Kept Secrets: An Evaluation of South Australia's Direct Marketing Campaign', *Journal of Vacation Marketing*, 6: 76–85.

Um, S. and Crompton, J.L. (1990) 'Attitude Determinants in Tourism Destination Choice', *Annals of Tourism Research*, 17: 432–48.

V.T.C. (2001) 'German Conversion Study Results', in: Virginia Tourism Corporation (ed.). Online. Available at http://www.vatc.org/research/2001GermanWriteup.htm.

Wang, Y. and Russo, S.M. (2007) 'Conceptualizing and Evaluating the Functions of Destination Marketing Systems', *Journal of Vacation Marketing*, 13: 187–203.

Williams, P.W., Stewart, K. and Larsen, D. (2012) 'Toward an Agenda of High-Priority Tourism Research', *Journal of Travel Research*, 51: 3–11.

Wöber, K. and Fesenmaier, D.R. (2004) 'A Multi-Criteria Approach to Destination Benchmarking', *Journal of Travel and Tourism Marketing*, 16: 1–18.

Woodside, A. and King, R. (2001) 'Tourism Consumption Systems: Theory and Empirical Research', *Journal of Travel and Tourism Marketing*, 10: 3–27.

Woodside, A. and Sakai, M.Y. (2001) 'Meta-Evaluations of Performance Audits of Government Tourism-Marketing Programs', *Journal of Travel Research*, 39: 369–79.

Woodside, A.G. (1981) 'Measuring the Conversion of Advertising Coupon Inquirers into Visitors', *Journal of Travel Research*, 19(4): 381–9.

— (1990) 'Measuring Advertising Effectiveness in Destination Marketing Strategies', *Journal of Travel Research*, 29: 3–8.

Woodside, A.G. and Dubelaar, C. (2003) 'Increasing Quality in Measuring Advertising Effectiveness: A Meta-Analysis of Question Framing in Conversion Studies', *Journal of Advertising Research*, 43: 78–85.

Woodside, A.G. and Reid, D.M. (1974) 'Tourism Profiles versus Audience Profiles: Are Upscale Magazines Really Upscale?', *Journal of Travel Research*, 12: 17–23.

Woodside, A.G. and Ronkainen, I.A. (1984) 'How Serious is Nonresponse Bias in Advertising Conversion Research', *Journal of Travel Research*, 22: 36.

Xiang, Z. and Fesenmaier, D. R. (2005) 'An Analysis of Two Search Engine Interface Metaphors for Trip Planning', *Information Technology and Tourism*, 7: 103–17.
Xiang, Z. and Gretzel, U. (2010) 'Role of Social Media in Online Travel Information Search', *Tourism Management*, 31: 179–88.
Xiang, Z., Wöber, K. and Fesenmaier, D. (2008) 'Representation of the Online Tourism Domain in Search Engines', *Journal of Travel Research*, 47: 137–50.

17

Archetype enactments in travellers' stories about places

Theory and advances in positivistic and qualitative methods

Arch G. Woodside, Karlan Muniz and Suresh Sood

Introduction

This chapter provides theory for and shows how to examine the stories consumers tell in natural contexts involving brands (in this study, place brands) in ways relevant for psychological archetypes, brand strategies and consumer behaviour. Consumers mention place brands as actors that play roles in the consumers' lives and that help them (consumers as protagonists) to experience roles that give them the feelings of achievement, well-being and/or excitement. In order to identify and interpret the archetypal themes in stories told by the consumer, this study advances the use of degrees-of-freedom analysis (DFA) and creating visual narrative art (VNA) as useful steps for confirming or disconfirming whether or not the stories consumers tell have themes, events and outcomes that match with the core storylines told by brands. The chapter includes a review of work on archetypal theory, DFA and VNA. The study's theory, method and findings provide useful tools for managers and researchers on issues that relate to tourism and marketing.

Consumers may tell stories involving buying and experiencing brands, in part, to relive archetypal experiences and to clarify the meaning for themselves about these experiences. 'Archetypes' are collective, mostly unconscious, primal forces according to Jung (1959); these forces are strong motivational stimuli that compel action. The ABCs of desire are the conjoining of archetypes, brands (i.e. alternative objects, services and ideas) and consumers. This chapter presents theory and tools of analysis that are may be useful for interpreting the ABCs of desire appearing in the stories consumers tell about their life experiences – stories consumers tell to each other and to themselves in naturally-occurring reports rather than as responses to survey questions.

The discussion supports the expansion of the ABC domain with theory and an analysis of the archetypes appearing in stories that consumers tell in everyday life. The chapter offers an analysis and an empirical positivistic method for examining archetypes enacted in stories told by consumers by proposing the use of degree-of-freedom analysis (Wilson and Wilson 1988) as a means for decoding stories that include the presence of brands. This data analysis method for archetypes appearing in stories, in addition to creating panels of visual narrative art (VNA, see Megehee and Woodside 2010), provides a rigorous method for analyzing meaning in the stories consumers tell – stories involving using brands to enable experiencing archetypal primal forces.

Some scholars discuss brand construction from the viewpoint of strategic narratives that create meaning for consumers (Allen, Fournier and Miller 2008; Holt 2004; Padgett and Allen 1997), indicating that this field includes more than one theoretical base relevant for understanding brand construction and meaning. Allen, Fournier and Miller (2008) describe the challenge that this poses, 'If a brand is first and foremost a repository of meanings for consumers to use in living their own lives (Fournier 1998; McCracken 1986), then today's challenge is to understand more deeply the multiple sources and dynamic nature of that meaning.'

The insertion/use of archetypes and myths as platforms to support brand construction is a proposition arising in recent research. Research informs this view in both the academic context, analyzing the relationship between consumers and brands (Holt 2004; Veen 1994; Woodside, Sood and Miller 2008; Zaltman 2003), and in the marketing context as guidelines for marketing professionals (Mark and Pearson 2001; Vincent 2002; Wertime 2002).

This chapter includes a brief explanation of the function of archetypes in human behaviour. It also discusses the importance of narratives in human behaviour and the materialization of archetypal themes. The study presents degrees-of-freedom (DFA) and visual narrative art (VNA) as possible ways of identifying the archetypes adopted and the role of the destination brand in the narrative projection of the consumer, and two examples of stories, taken from blogs, illustrate how brands of services, products, people and places are positioned in order to support the experience of these roles by the consumer. Finally, the discussion concludes with theoretical and managerial implications of this approach.

Archetypes and the self-fulfilment of the consumers' need to experience primal forces

According to Jung (1959) human beings, at all times and in all places, are under the influence of dominating unconscious thoughts. Jung's greatest contributions to psychology may include the concepts of the collective unconscious and the archetypes from which they are constituted (Gray 1996). Jung (1959) proposes that the accumulated experiences of past generations influence who we are today. The collective unconscious is a deposit of memories that humans inherit from their ancestors and which influence their current lives (Jung 1959). Within this deposit archetypes are stored; symbols, images and representations capture the essential and universal communalities (Zaltman 2003).

Archetypes are also known as elementary ideas (Campbell 1988). Indeed, as Gray (1996) states, archetypal imagery finds its external referents in the common themes of myths, dreams and folklores. According to Gray (1996) (and the study by Campbell 1988) the same themes and imagery, with minor variations, appear in each individual, culture and race, over and over. According to Jung (1959), myths and fairytales are forms of archetypes that receive a specific identification mark (symbol, stamp), while an archetype is essentially unconscious in content which, despite belonging to the collective, adapts itself to the individual less intelligibly. Archetypes are stored iconic images and impulses, whereas myths are discourses or vehicles that carry encoded meaning (cf. Zehnder and Calvert 2004). Studying the use of archetypes in the stories produced for the cinema, Vogler (2007: xxvii) states, 'All stories consist of a few common structural elements found universally in myths, fairy tales, dreams, and movies.' In Vogler's (2007) view, stories have healing power, helping human beings deal with difficult emotional situations by giving examples of human behaviour, which might inspire for a different strategy of living, responding to human emotions and wishes.

Brand stories as vehicles for communicating archetypal themes

The psychology literature shows that narratives serve the cognitive organization processes of consumers (Polkinghorne 1991). Much of the information and many social experiences that the consumer acquires in life are transmitted in the form of narratives (Adaval and Wyer 1998). Escalas and Bettman (2000) describe consumers as builders of stories, whose major focus makes sense when it comes to saying who they are and what they consume. Based on a review of the literature, Woodside *et al.* (2008) provide propositions useful for supporting the importance of stories in consumer psychology; first, people reason through narration rather than using argumentative tools. Second, information is stored and retrieved from memory in episodes. Third, people seek clarity in their experiences and results automatically by organizing experiences in the form of stories. Fourth, people feel pleasure when reliving or retelling stories in order to experience archetypal myths, albeit unconsciously. Finally, brands and products play important roles in enabling consumers to achieve their results and live the roles that bring them pleasure and happiness. The informants in a study by Fournier (1998) also describe the roles brands play in their relationships with them in the form of stories relating to their daily lives.

In general, the brand communication process through brand narratives, rather than the traditional reasons-to-buy lecture, continues to gain attention. Studies both in the field of consumer research and other fields demonstrate the impact of narratives in altering beliefs and attitudes in individuals (Green and Brock 2000; Escalas 2004a; Escalas 2007); outcomes of this impact include increases in empathy and in emotional responses from listeners (Adaval and Wyer 1998; Deighton *et al.* 1989; Escalas, Moore and Britton 2004). Narratives had a more positive impact on the evaluations of consumers than lecture formatted messages (Adaval and Wyer 1998), showing the benefits of services more significantly (Padgett and Allen 1997; Matilla 2000) and strengthened the self-connection between consumer and brand (Escalas 2004b).

Figure 17.1 is a visual summary of the model. Based on an archetypal theme that has consumer appeal (line 1) and makes sense for the brand (line 2), the manager develops a story for the brand (line 3) that essentially transmits the archetype in question (line 4), enabling the consumer to experience that archetype (line 5), thereby strengthening attachment to the brand (line 6). Building a brand strategy based on appealing via a primal force requires first identifying a relevant archetype that prime users of the brand unconsciously (and possibly consciously) desire to experience. Line 1 represents the association of archetypal force and consumer desire.

DFA as a method for scoring and confirming archetype embeds

Campbell (1975) outlines degrees-of-freedom analysis (DFA) in case study research as, 'Pattern-matching' between the theoretical propositions and observations in a set of data is the essence of DFA' (Woodside 2010b). DFA compares propositions or ingredients from a separate theory or a 'theory-in-use' to check how well the case under analysis matches one or two or more competing theories. As Campbell (1975) states, keeping a record of all theories considered in the puzzle-solving process is important, and this method represents the degrees-of-freedom from multiple implications and can be useful for the creation of a box score of hits and misses to test which theory is relevant to a specific case. Although used little and mentioned only in passing in the literature (Yin 1994), this technique has the potential for research in the field of marketing

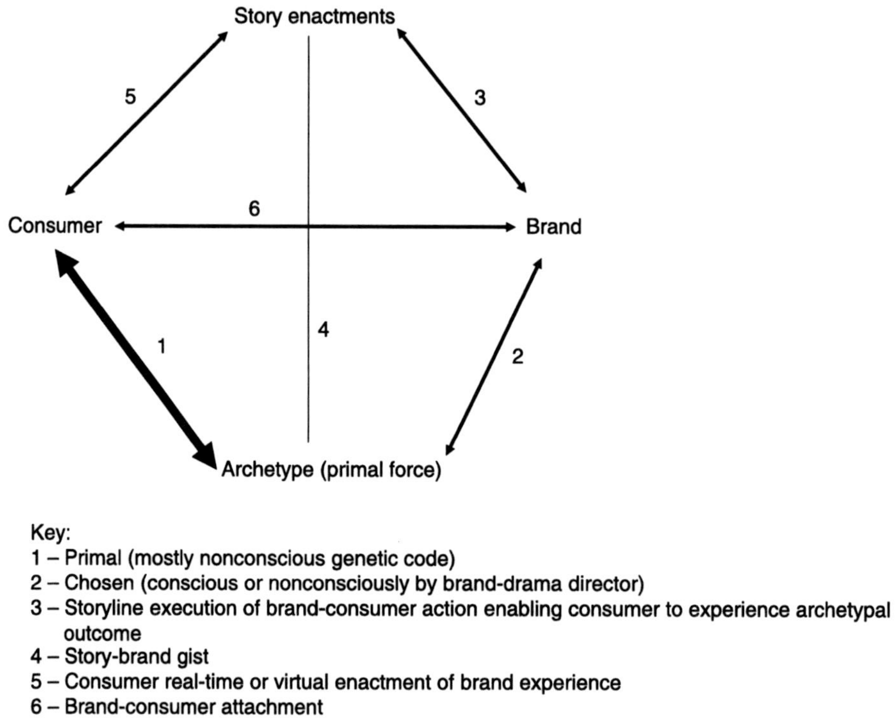

Figure 17.1 Archetypes, brands and consumer enactments: Diamond Core Theory.

(Woodside 2010b). To see examples of this technique being used in the marketing field, see Wilson and Vlosky (1997) and Wilson and Wilson (1988).

Woodside (2010b) suggests that other approaches for analyzing case data, such as content analysis, seek to express counts, means and frequencies of the phenomenon, and that the DFA goes one step further by subjecting the counts and patterns in a qualitative dataset to an a priori set of predictions, as hypothesis, propositions and conjectures, helping in testing, comparing and building a theory in accordance with the purpose of the study.

Visual narrative art as a means of mapping (and deepening understanding) stories

When dealing with the mapping of metaphors of organizations for the purpose of identifying the meanings that professionals give to their experiences in the working environment, Stein (2003) suggests using art to access thoughts and feelings in order to connect unconscious images and bring them to light. Stein (2003: 92) states, 'Certainly narrative science and social science can do this, and increasing access to the inner life is, after all, one of the central tasks of therapy.' In the field of marketing, some researchers defend the idea that consumers are incapable of reporting all relevant causes for their actions and that some memories, emotions and other cognitive processes lie in the unconscious (Zaltman 2003), and that a multiple-methods approach is necessary to explain this amount of information (Woodside 2004).

Visual narrative art (VNA) utilizes one or more types of illustrations (paintings, sculpture, photographs, physical movements, film, or other media beyond verbal reporting) that create a story formed by scenes or episodes in which people, animals, objects and symbols interact while the narrative unfolds (Megehee and Woodside 2010). Art as a means for telling a story non-verbally is one of the oldest forms in which human beings tell a story, since the days when the cavemen painted on the walls of caves, and remains one of the most modern forms of communication in the twenty-first century (Megehee and Spake 2012).

In consumer behaviour research, creating and interpreting a VNA helps to make explicit unconscious thinking and emotion-based associations, and helps to clarify the role of a brand in consumers' stories and consumers' lives. VNA can increase accuracy (and find different insights concerning) of how archetype enactments in consumer stories about buying/using a brand.

The use ofVNA in research is based on the theory of dual processing accounts of reasoning, emotions, judgment and social recognition (Evans 2008), where there occurs on the one hand unconscious, holistic and associative thought processes that are common to all animals irrespective of intelligence, while on the other there is also a parallel process that is conscious, analytical, based on rules and solely human, pertaining to intelligence and limited to the capacity of a working memory. As individuals use both types of mental processing, researchers can make use of reports that reflect on the two processes, creating verbal reports of the concepts and results, but also VNA enhances data interpretation (Megehee and Woodside 2010).

Method

Two stories by consumers were collected from blogs on the Internet, both of which involve place brands. Both stories appear in Appendix 17.1 and Appendix 17.3. The stories were analyzed using the DFA method, using an instrument created for each archetype. A total of 13 archetypal themes were used, all of which had previously been classified in the literature (Mark and Pearson 2001). Two themes appear. The first example of a consumer story is compatible with the innocent archetype. The story describes two sisters who travel to New York City. The second narrative involves the magician archetype and includes the adventures of a protagonist and her 'labmates'.

Example 1: The innocent archetype

In general, human beings dream of the triumph of good over evil and happiness resulting from the ideation of purity and kindness in the world. This utopian and somewhat naïve view is the essence of the innocent archetype (Mark and Pearson 2001). Sood (2010) uses the story of Daphne (Hamilton 1942) to illustrate this archetype. Daphne is a nymph who wanders freely and happily through the forest, which she has made her playground. The Greek god Apollo falls in love with her and becomes besotted with her as she runs through the forest. Apollo gives chase and Daphne asks her father, the river god Peneus, for help. She is turned into a laurel tree, no longer free to roam the forest and fields. To show his love for Daphne, Apollo presents winners at the Delphi games with laurel wreaths.

According to Pearson (1998), the image of innocence is usually one of youth filled with hope and expectation, without having experienced any disappointment, rejection or betrayal. But at a higher level, the innocent archetype is one of simplicity and optimism, with emphasis on values and integrity (Mark and Pearson 2001), leading human beings to live freely and 'be' rather than 'have'.

Classic brands such as Ivory Soap and Coca-Cola use this archetype (Mark and Pearson 2001). The 1970s campaign, 'I'd Like to Buy the World a Coke', is a good example of optimism and viable happiness here and now. Mark and Pearson (2001) state that consumers who respond to the appeal of the innocent archetype are likely to be loyal to a brand provided their experience is positive, because they like predictability more than novelty.

Enacting the innocent archetype

Appendix 17.1 is a story in which it is possible to visualize the components of the innocent archetype. This text represents the emic interpretation and contains an entire blog story. Appendix 17.2 is a prediction matrix of the innocent archetype, developed using the literature on the archetype (Hamilton 1942; Mark and Pearson 2001).

Kit, the protagonist, describes a journey in New York as an adventure in an ideal setting, be it at the museum or in restaurants and cafes. The city becomes one huge playground for the sisters and, like Daphne in Greek mythology (Hamilton 1942), they wander around happily and freely. Optimism and contemplation run throughout the story, and the sisters are satisfied with the solution that they find for Erin to have contact with and photograph the work of the architect Hector Guimard at the Museum of Modern Art, with the added benefit of being able to visit a place with many restaurants. Like Alice in Wonderland (Carroll 1992), the sisters take a hint that they are given at the museum and discover that they are near this place, with many fun and high quality opportunities. In the end, as when Daphne is turned into a tree, the sisters also have their bad moments when they have their final meal at the train station.

The story portrays an idealized view of New York as the place to experience freedom, wonderful possibilities and enjoy life by adopting the idealism (and to a certain extent naivety) of the innocent archetype.

When the Innocent's 'Archetypal Story Pattern Instrument (ASPI)', proposed and described in Appendix 17.2, is applied to analyze the consumer's story, the result is that all 16 theoretical propositions match with the observed features in the story. The DFA approach and the prediction matrix can confirm or disconfirm the theory based on case data, in this case the story nuances and details. This perfect level of matching occurred independently for two judges trained in psychology but who were unfamiliar with the relevant literature on storytelling.

The DFA may represent, therefore, a flexible and objective approach for examining the consumer's discourse in search of patterns that confirm (or disconfirm) a specific archetypal theme.

Example 2: The magician archetype

Making the dream a reality occurs through moments of magical transformations. That is the mission of the magician archetype. One of the most representative characters of this archetype is Merlin (Mark and Pearson 2001). In the foreword to *Merlin through the Ages*, Spangler (1995: 12) claims that Merlin is not only a character with power but 'someone who uses any power or resource available to bring something new into being, and to guard and nourish it until it is able and in its rightful place in the scheme of things, whether it is a baby, an idea or a civilization.' Thus, his power is at the service of a new vision and new possibilities.

Therefore, progress and happiness are the goals of the magician, for himself and for others, to develop a vision and make it come true. According to Pearson (1998), when the magician archetype is activated, the person feels confident that he knows what must be done to transform his life and his world, including in this 'vision' the will to run some risks, if required. Every culture pays attention to this type of character, beginning with a shaman, medicine man or alchemist and in modern times as the central figures in many religions (Mark and Pearson 2001). Campbell (1988) goes as far as saying that these characters may represent the way in which some religions are constructed. In most religions there are stories of holy figures doing miraculous things (Pearson 1998).

In the field of marketing, the magician involves fostering 'magical moments' that are based on products, services, experiences or people with the power to change people and their destiny (Mark and Pearson 2001), such as technological products, political candidates or places that afford people some type of personal or professional improvement.

Enacting the magician archetype

Appendix 17.3 is an abstract of a story in which the components of the magician archetype are observable. This text represents the emic interpretation and contains an entire blog story. Appendix 17.4 shows a prediction matrix of the magician archetype, developed using literature on the archetype (Eliot 1990; Mark and Pearson 2001).

An analysis of the consumer's magician storyline

The story recounts experiences of the protagonist and her colleagues in Tokyo while spending most of her time working in a laboratory. There are many references to the magician theme, beginning with her work in the lab, which has a connotation of a quest for knowledge and mastery in her field of study. Knowledge of the laws of the universe is one of the desires of the magician (Pearson and Mark 2001). The experience of buying clothes, eating, playing a sport and the positive results of her lab work portray magic moments and times of transformation. In the final story, where the protagonist in the consumer story ascribes magical powers to the stick at the temple guarded by the God of Thunder, she feels she has control of the luck and good fortune she and her labmates intend to inherit in the forthcoming year. The protagonist believes that magic can control future events. Spangler (1995) claims that if figures like Merlin have such Power in our collective imagination, it is because we intuitively know that we are all potential magicians.

In order to use the DFA as the approach to test the consistency of the story as an example of the magician archetype, the 'Magician's Archetypal Story Pattern Instrument' (Appendix 17.4) was applied to the Tokyo story, resulting in 100 per cent matches with the 16 theoretical propositions stated.

Conclusions

In his study on the contemplative look and behaviour of tourists, Urry (1992) proposes that how a tourist faces an experience of this kind involves placing himself within a historical process and consuming signs or markers that represent stories in particular, and that how different tourists face a particular process (and in relation to a specific place, city or country) is influenced by the way that the collective memory of society is organized and reproduced.

Archetypal themes are bridges that connect consumers and places, not only from the viewpoint of marketing managers that use the 'mask' of myth, but also from consumers' unconscious perspectives. Through experiencing stories and daily interaction with places, the tourist can enact and enjoy archetypal themes. According to Jung (1959), archetypal ideas or themes are part of the unconscious system that works in the present to compensate for or correct the extravagances of the conscious mind. The conscious mind desires clarity and to work with a handful of content at a time, while archetypes help a human being not to forget his roots and seek a synthesis of his self (Jung 1959).

The present study offers a useful method for analyzing the theme of archetypes in stories told by consumers about (or including) brands, using DFA that results in a prediction matrix. Applying the prediction matrix verifies or disconfirms the pattern, based on the theory, to confirm or not the presence of an archetype in a story. This study might prove useful to researchers who aim to further their studies of consumer-brand relationships and to practitioners who might find in this tool a powerful support for developing and auditing the effects of their actions in terms of brand construction.

As Veen (1994) suggests, the research here follows a branch of humanistic inquiry in order to provide insights into consumer behaviour (Holbrook 1987; Stern 1989) and as a way to identify templates that govern the relationship between consumers and brands (Fournier 1998). Fournier (2009) admits that the study of the consumer-brand relationship also requires research into how these relationships come about, but she concludes that their essential purpose is to provide meaning for consumers when engaging in brands. The present study deals with the question of 'why', using the psychology of archetypes and proposes the use of DFA and VNA as a means for verifying the presence of archetypal forces.

References

Adaval, R. and Wyer Jr, R. (1998) 'The role of narratives in consumer information processing', *Journal of Consumer Psychology*, 7: 207–45.

Ahuvia, A.C. (2005) 'Beyond the extended self: loved objects and consumers' identity narratives', *Journal of Consumer Research*, 32: 171–84.

Allen, C.T., Fournier, S. and Miller, F. (2008) 'Brands and their meaning makers', in C.P. Haugtvedt, P.M. Herr and F.R. Kardes (eds) *Handbook of Consumer Psychology*. New York: Taylor and Francis Group, pp. 781–822.

Belk, R.W. (1988) 'Possessions and the extended self', *Journal of Consumer Research*, 15: 139–68.

Brasel, S.A. and Gips, J. (2011) 'Red Bull "Gives You Wings" for better or worse: a double-edged impact of brand exposure on consumer performance', *Journal of Consumer Psychology*, 21: 57–64.

Bruner, J. (2004) 'Life as a narrative', *Social Research*, 71: 691–710.

Caldwell, M., Henry, P. and Alman, A. (2010) 'Constructing audio-visual representations of consumer archetypes', *Qualitative Market Research: An International Journal*, 13: 84–96.

Campbell, D.T. (1975) 'Degrees of freedom in the case study', *Comparative Political Studies*, 8: 178–93.

Campbell, J. (1988) *The Power of Myth, with Bill Moyers*. New York: Doubleday.

Carroll, L. (1992) *Alice's Adventures in Wonderland*. New York: Book of Wonders.

Christensen, G.L. and Olson, J.C. (2002) 'Mapping consumers' mental models with ZMET', *Psychology and Marketing*, 19: 477–502.

Deighton, J., Romer, D. and McQueen, J. (1989) 'Using drama to persuade', *Journal of Consumer Research*, 16: 335–43.

Eliot, A. (1990) *The Universal Myths: Heroes, Gods, Tricksters, and Others*. England: Penguin Books.

Escalas, J.E. (2004a) 'Imagine yourself in the product', *Journal of Advertising*, 33: 37–48.

— (2004b) 'Narrative processing: building consumer connections to brands', *Journal of Consumer Psychology*, 14: 168–80.

— (2007) 'Narrative versus analytical self-referencing and persuasion', *Journal of Consumer Research*, 34: 421–9.

Escalas, J.E. and Bettman, J.R. (2000) 'Using narratives and autobiographical memories to discern motives', in S. Ratneshwar, D.G. Mick and C. Huffman (eds) *The Why of Consumption: Perspectives on Consumer Motives, Goals, and Desires*. New York: Routledge, pp. 236–56.

Escalas, J.E., Moore, M.C. and Britton, J.E. (2004) 'Fishing for feelings? Hooking viewers helps!', *Journal of Consumer Psychology*, 14: 105–14.

Evans, J.S. (2008) 'Dual-processing accounts of reasoning, judgment and social recognition', *Annual Review of Psychology*, 255–78.

Faber, M.A. and Mayer, J.D. (2009) 'Resonance to archetypes in media: there's some accounting for taste', *Journal of Research in Personality*, 43: 307–22.

Fournier, S. (1998) 'Consumers and their brands: developing relationship theory in consumer research', *Journal of Consumer Research*, 24: 343–73.
Gray, R.M. (1996) *Archetypal Explorations: Towards an Archetypal Sociology*. New York: Routledge.
Green, M.C. and Brock, T.C. (2000) 'The role of transportation in the persuasiveness of public narratives', *Journal of Personality and Social Psychology*, 79: 701–21.
Hall, S. (1997) 'Introduction', in S. Hall (ed.) *Representation: Cultural Representations and Signifying Practices.* London: Sage.
Hamilton, E. (1942) *Mythology: Timeless Tales of Gods and Heroes*. London: Penguin Group.
Hirschman, E.C. (2010) 'Evolutionary branding', *Psychology and Marketing*, 27: 568–83.
Holbrook, M. B. (1987) 'What is consumer research?', *Journal of Consumer Research*, 14: 128–32.
Holt, D.B. (2003) 'What becomes an icon most?', *Harvard Business Review*, 81: 43–9.
— (2004) *How Brands become Icons: The Principles of Cultural Branding*. Boston: Harvard Business School Press.
Holt, D.B. and Thompson, C.J. (2004) 'Man-of-action heroes: the pursuit of heroic masculinity in everyday consumption', *Journal of Consumer Research*, 31: 425–40.
Jung, C.G. (1959) *The Archetypes and the Collective Unconscious*. New York: Pantheon Books.
Kotler, P. and Keller, K.L. (2012) *Marketing Management*. New Jersey: Prentice Hall.
McAdams, D.P. (1993) *The Stories we Live By: Personal Myths and the Making of the Self.* New York: William Morrow and Company.
McCracken, G. (1986) 'Culture and consumption: a theoretical account of the structure and movement of the cultural meaning of consumer goods', *Journal of Consumer Research*, 13: 71–84.
Mark, M. and Pearson, C.S. (2001) *The Hero and the Outlaw: Building Extraordinary Brands through the Power of Archetypes.* New York: McGraw-Hill.
Mattila, A.S. (2000) 'The role of narratives in the advertising of experiential services', *Journal of Service Research*, 3: 35–45.
Megehee C.M. and Spake D.F. (2012) 'Consumer enactments of archetypes using luxury brands', *Journal of Business Research*, 65(10): 1434–42.
Megehee, C.M. and Woodside, A.G. (2010) 'Creating visual narrative art for decoding stories that consumers and brands tell', *Psychology and Marketing*, 27: 603–22.
Padgett, D. and Allen, D. (1997) 'Communicating experiences: a narrative approach to creating service brand image', *Journal of Advertising*, 26: 49–62.
Padulo, M.K. and Rees, A.M. (2006) 'Motivating women with disordered eating towards empowerment and change using narratives of archetypal metaphor', *Women and Therapy*, 29: 63–81.
Pearson, C.S. (1998) *The Hero Within: Six Archetypes we Live By*. New York: HarperCollins.
Polkinghorne, D.E. (1991) 'Narrative and self-concept', *Journal of Narrative and Life History*, 1: 135–53.
Randazzo, S. (2006) 'Subaru: the emotional myths behind brand's growth', *Journal of Advertising Research*, 46: 11–17.
Shankar, A., Elliott, R. and Goulding, C. (2001) 'Understanding consumption: contributions from a narrative perspective', *Journal of Marketing Management*, 17: 429–53.
Shiv, B., Carmon, Z. and Ariely, D. (2005) 'Placebo effects of marketing actions: consumers may get what they pay for', *Journal of Marketing Research*, 42: 383–93.
Solomon, M.R. (2013) *Consumer Behaviour*. New Jersey: Pearson.
Sood, S.C. (2010) 'Consumer archetype brand stories: theory and research on consumers' reports of interactions with brands and experiencing primal forces', unpublished dissertation. University of Technology, Sydney.
Spangler, D. (1995). 'The once and future Merlin' (foreword) in R.J. Stewart and J. Matthews, *Merlin through the Ages*. London: Blandford.
Stein, H.F. (2003) 'The inner world of workplaces: accessing this world through poetry, narrative literature, music, and visual art', *Consulting Psychology Journal: Practice and Research*, 55: 84–93.
Stern, B. (1989) 'Literary criticism and consumer research: overview and illustrative analysis', *Journal of Consumer Research*, 16: 322–44.
Urry, J. (1992) 'The tourist gaze "revisited"', *American Behavioural Scientist*, 36: 172–86.
Veen, S.V. (1994) 'The consumption of heroes and the hero hierarchy of effects', in C.T. Allen and D.R. John (eds) *Advances in Consumer Research*, 21, Provo, UT, pp. 332–36.
Vincent, L. (2002) *Legendary Brand: Unleashing the Power of Storytelling to Create a Winning Market Strategy*. Chicago: Kaplan Business.
Vogler, C. (2007) *The Writer's Journey: Mythic Structure for Writers*. Studio City, CA: Michael Wiese Productions.

Wertime, K. (2002) *Building Brands and Believers: How to Connect with Consumers using Archetypes.* Singapore: Wiley.
Wilson, E.J. and Vlosky, R.P. (1997) 'Partnership relationship activities: building theory from case study research', *Journal of Business Research*, 39: 59–70.
Wilson, E.J. and Wilson, D.T. (1988) 'Degrees of freedom in case study research of behavioural theories of group buying', *Advances in Consumer Research*, 15: 587–94.
Woodside, A.G. (2004) 'Advancing from subjective to confirmatory personal introspection in consumer research', *Psychology and Marketing*, 21: 987–1010.
— (2008) 'Using the forced metaphor-elicitation technique (FMET) to meet animal companions within self', *Journal of Business Research*, 61: 280–7.
— (2010a) 'Brand-consumer storytelling theory and research', *Psychology and Marketing*, 27: 531–40.
— (2010b) *Case Study Research: Theory, Methods and Practice.* Bingley: Emerald.
Woodside, A.G. and Chebat, J.-C. (2001) 'Updating Heider's balance theory in consumer behaviour: a Jewish couple buys a German car and additional buying–consuming transformation stories', *Psychology and Marketing*, 18: 475–95.
Woodside, A.G., Sood, S. and Miller, K.E. (2008) 'When consumers and brands talk: storytelling theory and research in psychology and marketing', *Psychology and Marketing*, 25: 97–145.
Woodside, A.G., Megehee, C.M. and Sood, S. (2011) 'Conversations with(in) the collective unconscious by consumers, brands and relevant others', *Journal of Business Research*, 65: 594–602.
Zaltman, G. (2003) *How Consumers Think: Essential Insights into the Mind of the Marketer.* Boston: Harvard Business School Press.
Zehnder, S.M. and Calvert, S.L. (2004) 'Between the hero and the shadow: developmental differences in adolescents' perceptions and understanding of mythic themes in film', *Journal of Communication Inquiry*, 28: 122–37.

Appendix 17.1

Text from blog: two sisters eating in NYC

Eating in NYC

Thursday, 29 December 2005

As I mentioned, my sister and I spent Tuesday traipsing around New York, where the sky was blue and the air was not freezing. We were very happy. It was Erin's first visit to NYC since eighth grade (she's now a senior in college) and my first in just over a year. And, as the saying goes, I love New York. I'd never want to actually live there, but it's a great place to visit. The official purpose of our visit was research-oriented. Erin's writing her senior thesis on the Guimard metro entrances in Paris, and she needed to actually see one up close, and photograph it. Last fall, when I was in Paris, I took a few pics for her. Unfortunately, I am a miserable photographer. She really needed to see one for herself. We tossed around the idea of taking a quick trip to Paris, but between the cost and the scheduling (her Christmas break is only two weeks long), that just wasn't going to happen.

But, when she discovered that one of the original entrances was transplanted from Paris to the MOMA sculpture garden, we made plans to get to New York, tout de suite. It's only a two and a half hour train ride from Baltimore – child's play. Once we arrived, we dispensed with the 'work' part of the trip immediately. We both love modern art, so we spent a very enjoyable several hours touring the MOMA galleries and gift shops, where I picked up this super cool bowl.

After our visit to the MOMA, we were starving. Several hours of expressionism and beyond will do that to you. New York is an amazing town for restaurants. However, the neighborhood immediately surrounding the MOMA is not exactly representative of the melting pot of restaurant fabulousness the city is famous for being. We were a little lost. But not for long! As our stomachs growled in the gift shop, Erin looked at me and said, 'I know you're going to hate this, but Rachael Ray would ask the guy behind the counter where to go.' As much as I do hate supporting anything Rachael Ray, I knew she was right, so I asked. And thank God I did. We were only a few short blocks away from Hell's Kitchen, and the culinary wonderland I was looking for.

Once we hit 9th Street, we were totally overwhelmed. How to decide where to eat when we have, literally, 20 choices in two blocks? And choices of every type imaginable? I wanted to cry ... mostly because there were more restaurants in those two blocks than there are in my entire zip code. And I knew that almost every one of them would be fantastic. In the end, we played it safe and went with Thai. Can't go wrong with Thai in my family. We decided that a restaurant called Chanpen was cute enough on the outside to earn our business. It was a good call. The place wasn't super busy, but it was also almost 2 pm on a Tuesday. The service was good and the menu was, well, everything we were looking for in a Thai place. And cheap. The decor was ... Thai. The requisite shrine to the Queen, some gold elephants, lots of pink. Standard stuff. I don't go to Thai places for their minimalist design.

And the food was great. Standard Thai fare – nothing fancy or unexpected. Which was perfect? We each chose one dish to share. I, not surprisingly, ordered the panang curry, which was darker than what I'm used to, but tasted *exactly the same* as my hometown panang (and that is a good thing). After stuffing ourselves full of Thai, we walked around for a looong time, eventually (after a cab ride) ending up in Soho. After a few hours, we'd both reached the point of complete exhaustion and just needed to sit down and have a glass of wine. We chose the first bar we saw – which turned out to not really be a bar at all, but more of a chocolate cafe. Mariebelle's Cacao Bar is a little jewel box of a tea room, cozy and very inviting, especially after walking around for hours. The tables are charmingly tight, the walls are mirrored and girly, and silent movies play near the ceiling. It was perfect. We each got a glass of wine, and Erin ordered a pain au chocolate: she'd been complaining, just the day before, that after visiting France, she'd been spoiled forever by 'real' croissants, and that simply nothing in the US would do. This did. It was so buttery and so perfectly chocolatey. Not too sweet, not too bitter. Flaky and smooth. Delicious!

After finishing our wine and croissant (we shared a little more than she might have liked), we dragged ourselves back out to the street, where we eventually found a cab to take us back to the train station. I won't torture you with tales of the miserable spinach dip we had while waiting for our train. I do mean miserable. And expensive. I'd recommend staying away from Houlihan's in Penn Station – at all costs. But despite the sucky spin dip, overall, our big day in the big city couldn't have been better. Or more nourishing.

And, with that, I'm starving. Must go fix a snack!

(Source: http://mangoandginger.blogspot.com/2005/12/eating-in-nyc.html)

Appendix 17.2

Innocent archetype for eating in NYC

The archetypal story pattern instrument

Please circle N = No; ? = Not sure; Y = Yes for each item below.

Blog: mango and ginger

Title of Blog Entry: Eating in NYC

1. Does the story convey happiness? N ? Y
   If yes, discuss evidence: **The sisters are happy to be together and after the research is over enjoy eating at nearby restaurants.**
2. Does the protagonist avoid problems? N ? Y
   Evidence: **They ask advice of where to eat rather than getting lost.**
3. Is the story inspirational? N ? Y
   Evidence: **The story covers how two sisters in middle age and younger can enjoy themselves at work and play.**
4. Does the story take a simplistic perspective? N ? Y
   Evidence: **A lot of details at the MOMA regarding the thesis are left out of the story.**
5. Is the protagonist a positive thinker? N ? Y
   Evidence: **Kit wraps up the story with a gloss, 'But despite the sucky spin dip, overall, our big day in the big city couldn't have been better. Or more nourishing.'**
6. Protagonist is trustworthy? N ? Y
   Evidence: **Nothing to suggest otherwise.**
7. Is the story optimistic? N ? Y
   Evidence: **The story ends with how successful the trip has been.**
8. Is 'nice' a term that connects with the protagonist? N ? Y
   Evidence: **Both sisters come across as 'nice' people.**
9. Is perseverance an important aspect of the story? N ? Y
   Evidence: **Several hours at the MOMA for research qualifies.**

10. Does the story highlight fairness? N ? Y
    Evidence: **Both sisters are at different stages of life yet each enjoy the company of one another.**
11. Is the protagonist dependable? N ? Y
    Evidence: **The trip has been a long time in preparation and could not have gone better without the protagonist involvement.**
12. Protagonist is naïve? N ? Y
    Evidence: **Naïve in relation to knowledge of NYC.**
13. Does faith have any association with the story? N ? Y
    Evidence: **The trip is planned to allow Erin to complete her thesis.**
14. Is goodness an outcome of the protagonist's actions? N ? Y
    Evidence: **The trip ends well with both research completed and restaurants visited.**
15. Any areas where story depicts an optimistic protagonist? N ? Y
    Evidence: **The protagonist loves New York and finds the city a great place to visit.**
16. Any comments regarding the parents of protagonist? N ? Y
    Evidence: **The sisters do not discuss family matters in accordance with story as reported.**

Appendix 17.3

Emic interpretation of a tour of Tokyo with my labmates in Tokyo, Japan Tuesday, 10 June 2008

So many things have happened since the last entry that I don't know where to start. Of course I spend the vast majority of my time in the laboratory. The resources and the environment in the laboratory are so very good for me that it is hard to pass up.

June 30th, 2 Sundays ago, I went to Shibuya a second time; this time a bit more prepared for what I was to see and of course I didn't forget my camera ... The place was so full of people I could hardly believe it. While there, I bought some tights, and these interesting slipper things women put under dress shoes. I love them. Makes wearing dress shoes so much more comfortable.

More Shibuya

That following Tuesday, my labmates had a welcome party for me. It was great. We went to a barbeque restaurant, which was essentially a heavy woodblock table with a fire in the middle of it. Individual fume hoods were above each table to remove the smoke. Most of the barbeque was amazing, all different cuts of beef, chicken and pork. I would say the one thing I did not like was 'cow tongue'. It was such a hard piece of meat, one could not chew it at all. The party was an evening affair, starting around 7.30 and proceeding until after 10. They order food and it is brought out continuously throughout the night.

The rest of the week was a lot of work, and I performed my very first animal study on Saturday. I'm not sure how I felt about it other than emotionally drained, but the results turned out good so far so I was relieved.

Yesterday, the post-doc Tetsu arranged soccer. Apparently, the Peppas lab had left a soccer legacy (Kristy and Nikhil are both excellent soccer players). I was able to hold my own; so that was good. I scored 3 or 4 goals and assisted several as well. The group was about 10 people from the lab plus a few outside friends. The soccer place is like every other place in Tokyo. Tall.

Afterwards, several members of the lab including Nunchan (who I will call Apollo), Uniquo, and Tetsu (who I will call Arizona) met me. We went to lunch in Asakusa; a traditional district in Tokyo. We went to this very inexpensive diner where we were served a rather large piece of fish.

Afterwards we went to a Buddhist temple in Asakusa. There was this mile-long line of little shops leading up to the place, mostly selling trinkets, good luck charms and candy; one could not get to the temple without walking past maybe 200 of them. This area was crowded with people.

Temple – with Apollo and Uniquo

Once we reached the temple proper, we crossed under a gate guarded by the God of Thunder.

God of Thunder

There is a large open square where people buy incense, light it and then fan the smoke over themselves. Then they proceed to drink from a special fountain. This is supposed to bring luck. Once a year, you pay for this stick that comes out of a metal box with a small hole in the bottom. The stick has a number of Japanese characters that indicate which fortune that you have. You remove this fortune from a drawer and that is it for the year . . . Apparently I'm going to be rich, famous and have good luck with children and marriage all this year. My labmates told me I had the very best fortune. To the left of the open area, there is this several-story tall cool looking building; assumedly where the leaders live.

What is he wearing?

Outside of the gardens were still more stands of people selling their wares, home-made carvings, all kinds of food and more trinkets. Once we finished at the temple, we visited Roppongi; this absolutely wonderful area of town that had great gardens, great shopping and beautiful buildings. One of the shopping centers had a viewing deck that is quite popular; there we went to view the Tokyo Tower and I was given an 'aerial tour'.

A great view of Tokyo

I think all of the foreigners live in this area, because for the first time since I left Detroit, I finally fit in. We ended the evening by eating dinner in this cool little restaurant. The restaurant was in the basement of a building; and the opening in the door was so small one had to crawl to get inside (even me). I was incredulous about such a place; didn't seem very inviting to me. But the place was packed!! It was very traditional Japanese, no shoes, sit on little mats, and the restaurant is comprised of large tables where the dinner tables are divided using large mats. We ate for a long time; like the French, dinner for them is a very long affair. By this time, it was after 10 and we went home exhausted.

(Source: http://www.travelpod.ca/travel-blog-entries/melkanz/1/1213111260/tpod.html)

Appendix 17.4

Magician archetype for Tokyo with labmates

Magician (MA) – archetypal story pattern instrument

Please circle N = No; ? = Not sure; Y = Yes for each item below.

Blog: http://www.travelpod.com/travel-blog-entries/melkanz/

Title of Blog Entry: A tour of Tokyo with my labmates

1. Does protagonist inspire and communicate transforming vision? N ? Y
   If yes, discuss evidence: **The protagonist shows willingness to visit temple.**
2. Protagonist has props to help magical powers (e.g. robe)? N ? Y
   Evidence: **Protagonist is pleased to eat eel and has access to laboratory equipment.**
3. Does the story contain any miracles (e.g. rabbit out of hat)? N ? Y
   Evidence: **Melkanz is convinced she will be rich, famous and have luck with the temple stick in a box ceremony.**
4. Is the protagonist charismatic? N ? Y
   Evidence: **She is well respected by team members and holds her own in soccer.**
5. Is the protagonist a catalyst for change? N ? Y
   Evidence: **As a foreigner in Tokyo she is perfectly positioned for changes in the lab.**
6. Story is about a transforming event e.g. misfortune to opportunity? N ? Y
   Evidence: **the protagonist looks forward to the transforming event to find fame and fortune as conveyed to her at the temple with the stick in a box.**
7. Protagonist is involved with science? N ? Y
   Evidence: **The protagonist works in the laboratory.**
8. The story is action orientated? N ? Y
   Evidence: **The tour of Tokyo includes a game of soccer, visit to the temple and eating.**

9. Protagonist inner thoughts linked to changes in physical world? N ? Y
   Evidence: **The protagonist notices the foreigners in Roppongi.**
10. The protagonist uses meditation or chanting to improve thinking? N ? Y
    Evidence: **Protagonist has spent time in the Buddhist temple.**
11. Does the story highlight serendipity and synchronicity? N ? Y
    Evidence: **The members of the lab eat and play together.**
12. The story is mysterious? N ? Y
    Evidence: **The description of the Buddhist temple, gate guard statues and prayer/clapping ritual makes the story mysterious.**
13. The protagonist uses intuition? N ? Y
    Evidence: **In areas which she does not understand, the protagonist uses intuition.**
14. Spiritual help plays a part in the story? N ? Y
    Evidence: **The temple adds a strong spiritual component to the story.**
15. Any areas where a presentation is made? N ? Y
    Evidence: **A presentation is possible on top of the viewing deck in Tokyo Tower.**
16. Any sign of a transformation? N ? Y
    Evidence: **The stick at the temple is supposed to bring luck and much more in the coming year for the protagonist.**

18

Destination confusion

A photo elicitation study on brand confusion in tourism destinations

Pisuda Sangsue

Introduction

Travel and tourism has become a global industry which forces destinations to develop their brand in order to compete on the global stage. Tourism is about moving people away from home, and so destinations must try to attract people based on the creation and promotion of positive images (Prebensen 2007). Thus in a tourism environment, destination branding and image creation has become one of the most powerful tools in tourism marketing, as outlined in Chapter 30 of this volume. Major objectives of any destination branding strategy are to emphasize positive images that are already held by target travellers, to correct negative images, or to create awareness through the creation of favourable images targeted to potential tourists (Pike and Ryan 2004). In recent years, the variety of available information sources has rapidly increased and fragmented, to include not only official tourism marketing communications, but also online and offline media and word-of-mouth, and this plethora of communication channels poses a potential threat to tourist destinations in their efforts to attract visitors because of the lack of control DMOs have over the images produced through them. The aim of this chapter is to explore the concept of brand confusion in tourist destinations through its branding and image.

The concept of brand confusion is relevant in a tourism context because of the multiple communication channels available and the potential they have to present consumers with ambiguous and often conflicting information, and also because consumers use different interpretive strategies, which calls for an examination of the role of confusion in destination branding and image processes as well as tourists' choice processes. Destination brand confusion takes place when a person perceives a particular destination, referred to by its attributes, image and branding, as an alternative destination. Brand confusion was originally applied in tangible product selection processes where confusion resulted in significant lost sales and an impact on the legal status of original brands. The examination of brand confusion, especially in tourism marketing, which is generally a high-cost, high involvement and high risk decision (Cai 2002), becomes very relevant. This is mainly due to the importance of branding within service marketing in general, and tourism marketing in particular, where strong and clearly defined brands offer consumers a promise of future satisfaction, leading to increased customer trust in relation to an ostensibly intangible service purchase.

Destination brand and image vs brand confusion

In a travel and tourism context, tourists are faced with a great deal of information when selecting a holiday destination and, like services in general, tourists are unable to test destinations before visiting and so have limited knowledge about destination experiences before their actual visit. Correspondingly, information that potential tourists acquire before a visit is generally concerned with the concept of destination branding and images. Since the development of the tourism industry, many countries have combined the concept of branding to promote a positive image in order to make their destinations stand out. Customers have limited knowledge of destinations based on their experience, hence image is believed to represent the destination and influence tourists' decision-making (Tasci and Gartner 2007). Understanding the image formation process could help to improve marketing strategy for the tourist destinations, especially in terms of their attractiveness and competitiveness (San Martin and Rodriguez del Bosque 2008).

Court and Lupton (1997) argue that tourists' perceptions of a destination are based on different sources of information gathered over time. There are three main types of information that form a destination image. According to Gunn's articulation (1997), destination image formation is constructed by organic (non-tourist information) and induced (marketing information) images. Destination image affects choice criteria in tourists' selection process due to this slow agglomeration of image development based on organic and induced sources, such as books, exposure to news media, TV documentaries, travel brochures and word-of-mouth. Andreu *et al.* (2000) explain that image is the mental representation that forms a product/brand in consumers' minds. Moreover, as Kotler *et al.* (1999) specified, the image of a place is people's total impression of various elements and attributions connected with places. Their definition emphasizes the role of the visitor's mental processing required to pick out essential information from large amounts of data about a destination.

Therefore, images of places are commonly used as short-cuts for information processing and consumer decisions. Even though a place might not consciously manage its name as a brand, people still have images of places that can be activated and associated with brands, often simply the place name (Kotler and Gertner 2002). Similar to product and service brands, destination brands generate sets of expectations or experiences of a place prior to a visit. Image is important and how a place is represented can inspire people to visit and revisit (Coshall 2000). Therefore, building a strong brand image means that companies can position their product image (and communications appeals) directly to a target market. Consequently, destination image plays an important role in marketing related variables, especially positioning and promotions (Tasci and Gartner 2007). Applying a place-branding strategy, researchers concur that promotional materials are used in order to establish, reinforce, or even change the image of a destination (Mackay and Fesenmaier 1997; Reilly 1990; and Young 1999). Promotional materials present destination images which become much more important because those materials speak for the tourism product until the destination is visited (Mackay and Fesenmaier 1997).

In managing a destination brand of a country, marketers need to understand that different places attract different tourists. Cai (2002) suggests that image is becoming very important to destination branding, since it generates affective associations in the minds of consumers. Riezebos (2003) also clarifies that brand images are networks of knowledge elements stored in long-term memory; a network such as brand name is linked to other knowledge elements. Moreover, Cai (2002) claimed that destination branding included a consistent mix of brand elements to identify and distinguish a destination, so that differences in meaning and dimensions may occur. However, certain destination attributes can contribute to how destination promotions are perceived

(Mackay and Fesenmaier 1997). This also endorses the importance of confusion that might arise from the different dimensions of destination information held by travellers.

The more positive the image, the more likely potential tourists will visit the destination (Rittichainuwat *et al.* 2001). Hence this stage of pre-consumption search behaviour has been an important component in tourists' decision-making processes in selecting holiday destinations (Gursoy and McCleary 2004). The studies of information overload in the marketing literature reveal that increasing amounts of information tend to cause problems for customers in making brand choices (Jacoby 1977; Malhotra 1982). Jacoby (1977) adds that when the information provided exceeds certain limits, information overload results in confused, less accurate, less effective decision making of customers. According to Um and Crompton (1990), tourists will select a destination from a set of alternatives in the consideration set. At this point, the brand of a particular destination plays an important role in consumers' considerations, since when tourists search for a destination to visit, they are exposed to various destination brand-related stimuli. These elements include terms, names, signs, logos, designs, symbols, slogans, colour, packages, architecture, typography, photographic styles, as well as heritage, language, myths and legends (Cai 2002).

Therefore, numerous elements have been associated with how people picture the destination. As a result, a mass of information and choices of destination brands are competing in consumers' minds which could lead them to a state of confusion.

Brand confusion

Brand confusion refers to a state of mind which affects information processing and decision-making (Mitchell and Papavassiliou 1999). The brand confusion concept originated as a result of brand imitation strategies by companies, which aimed to emulate a successful product, and which usually consisted of imitation of packaging and positioning of the new product next to the better-known brand (Foxman *et al.* 1990). Initially, consumer brand confusion occurs when the customer buys the imitation brand thinking it is a real one (Loken *et al.* 1986). The most common form of brand confusion takes place when a person perceives brand X as a different brand Y (Foxman *et al.* 1990; Poiesz and Verhallen 1989; Kapferer 1995). Foxman *et al.* (1992) concur that the complicated nature of products can lead to information overload and consequently confusion. Foxman *et al.* (1992: 125) define brand confusion as:

> Consumer brand confusion consists of one or more errors in inferential processing that lead a consumer to unknowingly form inaccurate beliefs about the attributions or performance of a less-known brand based on a more familiar brand's attributes or performance.

The concept of brand confusion itself is still very limited in the literature. A review of the previous studies on brand confusion reveals few areas of research that have applied brand confusion, including: consumer behaviour, retailing, advertising, and judicial research. To date, many major works on brand confusion have examined confusion in the context of visual appearance of the brand product and package (Foxman *et al.* 1990). Some studies have focused on how confusion might harm firms. However, Foxman *et al.* (1990) argue that confusion can also harm customers themselves. The term confusion is used to describe a disturbance of awareness that can cause an individual to be restless and careless, to misjudge the environment and to act ineffectively (Walsh *et al.* 2007).

Moreover, Foxman *et al.* (1992) explain that brand confusion must involve consumers' unaware error(s) due to an incorrect belief about the brand attributes or performances which will be a continuum of error and hence can lead to a possible alteration of consumers' choice of brands. Mitchell and Papavassiliou (1999) also add that confusion arises from stimulus overload, stimulus similarity and conflicting, misleading, ambiguous or even inadequate information. They explain that when consumers are exposed to excessive choice and excessive product-related information, they can become confused and react with feelings of stress, frustration and sub-optimal decision-making (Mitchell and Papavassiliou 1999).

The main factors that have been identified to impact on brand confusion are: product category related factors, consumer characteristics and message characteristics (Christou 2009; Brengman *et al.* 2001; Poiesz and Verhallen 1989). Leek and Kun (2006) state that consumer confusion is a mental state characterized by a lack of clear and orderly thought and behaviour. Thus, there is the possibility that confusion is not purely caused by an information overload, but also confusion may be due to consumers' lack of information about the product/destination. Matzler *et al.* (2007) concur that consumers who have little product-related knowledge will get confused more easily than consumers with extensive product knowledge.

Brand confusion can then lead to sales loss, as confused consumers are more likely to abandon or postpone the purchase of a product/a tourist destination, or switch to another destination (Mitchell and Papavassiliou 1999). Furthermore, increased levels of dissatisfaction and decreased tendency to purchase have been found to be a consequence of confusion (Foxman *et al.* 1990; Mitchell and Papavassiliou 1999). Shukla *et al.* (2008) have claimed that confusion has a direct impact on satisfaction and final purchase decision. Confused consumers also find it difficult to select, interpret and evaluate stimuli (Mitchell *et al.* 2005) and so potential tourists may unintentionally choose to visit one place instead of the one intended.

Taking into account that tourism destinations are considered as brands, this study investigated the problem of brand confusion amongst travellers. Many scholars concur that, by the use of a place-branding strategy, promotional materials are used in order to establish, reinforce, or even change the image of a destination (Reilly 1990; Mackay and Fesenmaier 1997; Young 1999). Mackay and Fesenmaier (1997) claim that, due to the intangible nature of tourism products, promotional materials become much more important when they represent the tourism product, the destination under consideration, up until an actual visit, as they assist in creating awareness, generating interest, and stimulating desire which results in action (Selby and Morgan 1996). Moreover, tourist destinations have to recognize the importance of consumers' perceptions, which are not only based on visual or verbal information. Those perceptions include biases, histories, assumptions, fantasies, prejudices, and factual stories as well as socio-demographic and culture characteristics. These affect needs, preferences, interests, and motivations which in turn determine what they select to see, hear, read, think and pay attention to, and importantly how they interpret a destination (Tasci and Gartner 2007).

Research methodology

The purpose of this study was to explore the issue of brand confusion in tourism destination branding and images, specifically in the early consideration stage of tourists' image formation processes. The chosen context for this study was Thailand and its recent marketing brand campaign 'Amazing Thailand'. Thailand is a suitable location for this study because it offers a broad variety of interests to visitors from cultural and historical to fun and entertainment venues, while it has repeatedly attracted media attention in contentious positive and negative issues such as political riots, sex tourism and Buddhism festivals. Also, the competition in the region is quite fierce due to a region-emphasis on tourism development as a driver of economic modernization and some quite generic aspects of tourism product and service, particularly in countries which share particular geographical characteristics such as sun, sand, beach, and jungles and wildlife. Some countries in the South East Asian region also share similar culture and history. To explore destination brand confusion a qualitative methodology was chosen to facilitate in-depth understanding. The main reason for using a qualitative approach is the relatively new and therefore still under-researched concept of brand confusion, especially in the tourism context. Moreover, the method employed is an in-depth interview with a photo elicitation technique in order to gain a deeper understanding of the occurrence of brand confusion of potential tourists during their early stage decision processes, which provides a quite novel approach within tourism marketing research.

Photo elicitation approach

Photo elicitation is the process of using photographs in an interview to act as a stimulus to the questions (Harper 2002). Photographs used in this study were researcher-assembled as a tool for framing questions to allow respondents to reflect upon their feelings and thoughts about the photographs (Scarles 2010). Albers and James (1988) also claim that photographs in tourism are used to gain understanding of the tourist experience and the process of representing the tourist destination. The use of photos might be the best way to communicate the concept of destination branding and any possible confusion. Scarles (2010) concludes that visual research could become a platform for sharing encounters and facilitating mutual exchange that 'ignites' tourism experiences.

Since tourism is uniquely visual, photographs are a key successful agent in creating and communicating an image of a destination (Mackay and Fesenmaier 1997). Also a destination brand itself is an abstract notion that comprises different attributes and images of the destination. Moreover, the concept of brand confusion is referred to as an emotional state of mind which is difficult to capture through words alone, as people who are in a state of confusion may not want to share their frustration or mistaken beliefs with others, as this could cause them embarrassment (Walsh and Mitchell 2010). However, Harper (2002) argues that photo elicitation during conversation offers comfort, security and contemplation to respondents through a focus on the photographs. Moreover, Scarles (2010) also claims that the use of the visual can facilitate rapport, as participants reach out, touch or hold the photograph around which conversations develop; thus, within a photo elicitation interview, a mutual vulnerability that emerges as both researcher and participant open themselves to each other. The versions of photo elicitations adopted in this research are to provide visual stimuli to encourage participants to reveal their conscious and unconscious feelings, their views and their thoughts.

The intangible aspect of confusion, therefore, is depicted through the use of a visual technique that would otherwise be excluded from the conversation. The images of the destination applied were represented by the destination attributes which aimed to investigate the sources and types of confusion that affect tourists' decision-making and the possible consequences this confusion holds for destination branding. With the use of this method, this study attempted to obtain participants' perspectives in terms of destination image, information search and sources and to present them with a range of stimulus material to inform a discussion on how destination branding is linked to brand confusion (Patton 1990).

This qualitative approach, especially the photo elicitation technique, aimed to create conversation and elicit meanings, opinions, perceptions and behaviour. In terms of sample, the selected participants were potential tourists to Thailand who were in an early stage of decision-making and had never been to Thailand before. By selecting these groups, the intention was to minimize the influence of previous knowledge and direct experience of Thailand prior to the interview. It was assumed that at the early decision-making stage, confusion about destination branding and images was likely to occur as at this stage a tourist would have limited knowledge compared with a tourist who is at a later stage of decision-making. The assumption was that tourists who were at later stages of decision-making would exhibit different types of confusion, such as travel choice, rather than destination brand/image issues.

A total of 52 images were used during the photo elicitation interview. The major destination attributes of Thailand that are most cited in the literature were selected. All attributes, including negative attributes, influencing the image assessments of Thailand were integrated into the interview protocol of the study. These images represented the country's attributes from both marketing (induced image) sources such as advertisements and the promotional campaign from DMO and non-marketing (organic image) sources such as books, TV, documentary, news, film and word-of-mouth. Both stereotypes and lesser-known images were included. Importantly, some images which are not from Thailand were also included, so as to challenge and generate conversation related to confusion regarding the typical view that participants held of Thailand. This also helped to trigger thoughts and feelings tourists held towards the destination brand and to understand the consumer's behaviour when they were confused. The use of a mixture of destination images from a variety of sources during the photo elicitation process was found to be very useful in generating a discussion on the confusion of the potential tourists.

After the data collection process, thematic analysis was used to analyze the interview transcriptions using an inductive approach. The analysis focused around three main areas of destination brand confusion: the visitors' pre-conception of destination image; the experience, which referred to the emotions and attitudes of potential tourists toward Thailand; and the factors contributing to destination brand confusion. Destination brand confusion is considered upon a potential tourist's false identification of the original destination during the photo elicitation interview, which will be discussed in the following section.

Results and discussion

In this section, the most important findings on brand confusion that emerged from the data are summarized. The findings suggested that an individual tourist can experience more than one type of confusion, as different types of confusion resulted from different factors. Moreover, the study revealed that travellers who were highly involved with their travel intention were more likely to be in a stage of destination brand confusion than travellers who had less immediate travel intention. This also shows a significant role of brand confusion during the early decision-making stage of tourists. Different types of confusion through destination brand and image were found. Emotion-related brand confusion towards the destination was also discovered.

One type of destination confusion found, *Destination Similarity Confusion*, refers to the situation where potential tourists perceive one destination as another without knowing their mistake. This similarity confusion arose when respondents selected images which were based on generic attributes, such as beaches and seaside, which Thailand shares with other countries of South East Asia. Here consumers selected images based on their assumption that each scene was in Thailand. This referred to the most common forms of similarity confusion when consumers think that one product is the same as another (Foxman *et al.* 1992). In the study, potential tourists were prone to similarity confusion when they were faced with similar-looking stimuli of a destination which made them think that all of the attributions were from the original destination. This concurs with Walsh and Mitchell (2010), who suggest that similarity confusion can be caused by stimuli that are similar to those that individuals learned in the past. Loken *et al.* (1986)

recommend that physical similarities between products (destinations) may result in the misattribution of the identity of the product. This means that confused tourists assumed that destination attributes from the competing destination have similar characteristics that made them think of the original one.

Moreover, the study also discovered that similarity confusion is likely to occur when tourists had an emotional attachment to the unvisited destination; since misattribution of the identity of the product leading to similarity confusion usually occurred. The antecedent of confusion in tourist destinations was found to be influenced by affective and cognitive evaluations which related to the destination image components suggested by Baloglu (1999). An affective evaluation toward a particular destination was also found to influence similarity confusion in the travel and tourism context. Drawing on the study by Baloglu (1999), an affective component of a destination image deals with emotional responses to a place. This emotional response was influenced from the affective experience they had with the destination through destination information including its image and branding. The work in consumer confusion by Loken, Ross and Hinkle (1986) also discussed that consumers may form their impressions about the functions of a product or service knowing nothing else about it but the way it looks. Impressions about the destination refer to the affective experience with destinations as it is relates to an emotional response toward the destination. One interpretation is that tourists may form their impressions of the destination from its attributes knowing nothing else about it but the way it is supposed to look, in other words the destination image from their perceptions. Therefore an emotional response toward a particular destination could lead a traveller into a state of confusion between the original and other destinations. This affective reaction generated emotional attachment to the destination, which appears to present a great difficulty for the potential tourist to differentiate between the destinations, leading to a confused state. The study found that when positive emotions were evoked by the destination, confusion tended to occur when tourists faced similar-looking destinations.

With the complex nature of the tourism product, it has been proposed that the outcomes of brand confusion in a tourism context would be different from those of a tangible product. The findings were opposite to the result of confusion in tangible products, as the behavioural outcome of brand confusion would lead to delay, altered choice or even abandonment of the product purchase (Foxman *et al.* 1992; Dhar 1997; Walsh *et al.* 2007). This study found that potential tourists who were in a state of confusion evoked by destination image and branding still had an intention to visit Thailand. However, the study found that emotion-related confusion played an important role in brand confusion in tourist destinations, revealed through some of the negative experiences elicited during the interview. Confused tourists referred to embarrassment when they were informed about their confusion; feeling 'silly' and 'disappointed' were also mentioned. At the same time, ambiguity-confused tourists referred to doubt, which led to them losing confidence. As a result, most of the confused participants would prefer to search for more information.

It could be understood that purchasing a holiday is not an immediate decision, hence tourists have time to search for more information and evaluate their destination choices. As can be seen, the results of the study also emphasized the significance of information search activity amongst confused travellers. In selecting a holiday destination tourists are often involved in a more complicated process than in ordinary buying contexts. Therefore confusion between destinations found in this particular study does not affect traveller intention but rather triggers an additional search for information about the destination in order to lessen their confusion. In the last section, the marketing implications of this current concept of brand confusion will be discussed.

Implications for tourism marketing

The study provided an alternative method to understand destination image issues, which scholars agree are important, difficult to measure and related to individuals' subjective and emotional feelings. The qualitative interview with the photo elicitation approach applied in this study allowed an in-depth investigation of the formation of pre-visitors' destination image and their information sources leading to destination brand confusion. The results suggest several managerial policies and individual implications. It provides useful insights into the factors that influence the occurrence of brand confusion for tourist destinations through image and branding.

The study discussed different types of destination brand confusion which are useful to DMOs to determine the different factors that contribute to different types of confusion. In addition to the key results on brand confusion, the image of a destination that tourists hold prior to visiting revealed interesting aspects for destination marketers to address in communications strategies. It is also important to understand how potential tourists perceived unvisited destinations, in order to communicate the right message to travellers. The results also revealed that the occurrence of brand confusion was more likely to affect travellers who were highly involved and intend to visit, which shows the significant consequences of brand confusion during the early consideration stage of decision making. This indicates the need for tourism marketers to examine more closely the factors that affect brand confusion in a tourist destination, as this stage of decision making would greatly affect an alternative choice of destination. Therefore the results of brand confusion suggest DMOs need to design effective marketing strategies for potential tourists at the early stage of decision making, especially during information search processing stages. Different types of information sources also provided a better understanding of how they influence destination image. This also refers to information search as a method to reduce confusion, which could suggest to destination marketers the importance of providing a trustworthy information source to avoid confusion.

Despite the different sources/types that have an influence on the occurrence of brand confusion, this study also highlights the importance of the emotional attachment consumers displayed toward the unvisited destination, which related to the occurrence of brand confusion. An important aspect of brand experience of an unvisited destination shows how potential tourists hold strong destination images based on a narrow set of considerations of positive attributes. This emphasizes the benefits of positive and affective images in destination marketing. Those positive aspects were primarily brought into the consideration set when potential tourists evaluated their choice of destinations. Even though confusion was found, positive images still attract travellers to visit a destination. The study found that confusion was usually counteracted by positive destination attributes due to the pleasurable and hedonic experiences of a tourism product that most tourists are looking for. Therefore, the results reiterate that DMOs should develop and promote a strong destination brand at all stages of destination awareness formation and destination selection.

Moreover, the importance in promoting positive images of a tourist destination was found to play a significant role in attracting potential tourists to a destination. Promoting the unique image of a destination is suggested to destination marketers as this would help in reducing confusion among destinations. A related outcome of brand confusion about a tourist destination also provides an in-depth understanding of the concept of confusion which can help DMOs to adopt a suitable marketing strategy in order to promote the destination as well as reduce confusion among potential tourists. The concept of destination brand confusion provides practical and useful strategies for further development in destination marketing practices and to academics in terms of theory development.

References

Albers, P. and James, W. (1988) 'Travel photography: A methodological approach', *Annals of Tourism Research*, 15: 134–58.

Andreu, L., Bigne, J.E. and Cooper, C. (2000) 'Projected and perceived image of Spain as a tourist destination for British travellers', *Journal of Travel & Tourism Marketing*, 9: 47–67.

Baloglu, S. (1999) 'A path analytic model of visitation intention involving information sources, socio-psychological motivations, and destination image', *Journal of Travel & Tourism Marketing*, 8: 81–90.

Brengman, M., Geuens, M. and De Pelsmacker, P. (2001) 'The impact of consumer characteristics and campaign related factors on brand confusion in print advertising', *Journal of Marketing Communications*, 7: 231–43.

Cai, L.A. (2002) 'Cooperative branding for rural destinations', *Annals of Tourism Research*, 29: 720–42.

Christou, E. 'Advertising mass tourism destinations: Mediterranean brand confusion', paper presented at International CHRIE Conference, Massachusetts, July 2009.

Coshall, J.T. (2000) 'Measurement of tourists' images: the repertory grid approach', *Journal of Travel Research*, 39: 85–9.

Court, B. and Lupton, R.A. (1997) 'Customer portfolio development: Modeling destination adopters, inactives, and rejecters', *Journal of Travel Research*, 36: 35–43.

Dhar, R. (1997) 'Consumer preference for a no-choice option', *Journal of Consumer Research*, 24: 215–31.

Foxman, E., Berger, P. and Cote, J. (1992) 'Consumer brand confusion: a conceptual framework', *Psychology and Marketing*, 9: 123–41.

Gunn, C. (1997) *Vacationscape: Developing Tourist Areas*. Washington: Taylor & Francis.

Gursoy, D. and McCleary, K. (2004) 'An integrative model of tourists' information search behavior', *Annals of Tourism Research*, 31: 353–73.

Harper, D. (2002) 'Talking about pictures: A case for photo elicitation', *Visual Studies*, 17: 13–26.

Jacoby, J. (1977) 'Information load and decision quality: Some contested issues', *Journal of Marketing Research*, 14: 569–73.

Kapferer, J. (1995) 'Brand confusion: Empirical study of a legal concept', *Psychology and Marketing*, 12: 551–68.

Kotler, P. and Gertner, D. (2002) 'Country as brand, product, and beyond: A place marketing and brand management perspective', *The Journal of Brand Management*, 19: 24–32.

Kotler, P., Asplund, C., Rein, I. and Haider, D.H. (1999) 'Marketing places Europe: How to attract investments, industries, residents and visitors to cities, communities, regions and nations in Europe', *Financial Times*, Prentice Hall.

Leek, S. and Kun, D. (2006) 'Consumer confusion in the Chinese personal computer market', *Journal of Product and Brand Management*, 15: 184–93.

Loken, B., Ross, I. and Hinkle, R.L. (1986) 'Consumer "confusion" of origin and brand similarity perceptions', *Journal of Public Policy & Marketing*, 195–211.

MacKay, K. and Fesenmaier, D. (1997) 'Pictorial element of destination in image formation', *Annals of Tourism Research*, 24: 537–65.

Malhotra, N. (1982) 'Information load and consumer decision making', *Journal of Consumer Research*, 8: 419–30.

Matzler, K., Waiguny, M. and Fueller, H. (2007) 'Spoiled for choice: Consumer confusion in Internet-based mass customization', *Innovative Marketing*, 3: 7–20.

Mitchell, V. and Papavassiliou, V. (1999) 'Marketing causes and implications of consumer confusion', *Journal of Product & Brand Management*, 8: 319–42.

Mitchell, V., Walsh, G. and Yamin, M. (2005) 'Towards a conceptual model of consumer confusion', *Advances in Consumer Research*, 32: 143–50.

Patton, M. (1990) *Qualitative Evaluation and Research Methods: A Systematic Approach*, 2nd edn. Newbury Park, CA: Sage.

Pike, S. and Ryan, C. (2004) 'Destination positioning analysis through a comparison of cognitive, affective, and conative perceptions', *Journal of Travel Research*, 42: 333–42.

Poiesz, T. and Verhallen, T. (1989) 'Brand confusion in advertising', *International Journal of Advertising*, 23: 231–44.

Prebensen, N. (2007) 'Exploring tourists' images of a distant destination', *Tourism Management*, 28: 747–56.

Reilly, M. (1990) 'Free elicitation of descriptive adjectives for tourism image assessment', *Journal of Travel Research*, 28: 21–6.

Riezebos, R. (2003) *Brand Management: A Theoretical and Practical Approach*. Harlow: Prentice Hall.
Rittichainuwat, B., Qu, H. and Brown, T. (2001) 'Thailand's international travel image: mostly favorable', *The Cornell Hotel and Restaurant Administration Quarterly*, 42: 82–95.
San Martin, H. and Rodriguez Dei Bosque, I.A. (2008) 'Exploring the cognitive-affective nature of destination image and the role of psychological factors in its formation', *Tourism Management*, 29: 263–77.
Scarles, C. (2010) 'Where words fail, visuals ignite: Opportunities for visual autoethnography in tourism research', *Annals of Tourism Research*, 37: 905–26.
Selby, M. and Morgan, N. (1996) 'Reconstruing place image: A case study of its role in destination market research', *Tourism Management*, 17: 287–94.
Shukla, P., Perks, K. and Achakobe, N. (2008) 'A study measuring the impact of integrated technologies on consumer confusion in the mobile phone market', paper presented at Academy of Marketing Annual Conference, Aberdeen, July 2008.
Tasci, A. and Gartner, W. (2007) 'Destination image and its functional relationships', *Journal of Travel Research*, 45: 413–25.
Um, S. and Crompton, J.L. (1990) 'Attitude determinants in tourism destination choice', *Annals of Tourism Research*, 17: 432–48.
Walsh, G. and Mitchell, V. (2010) 'The effect of consumer confusion proneness on word-of-mouth, trust, and customer satisfaction', *European Journal of Marketing*, 44: 838–59.
Walsh, G., Hennig-Thurau, T. and Mitchell, V. (2007) 'Consumer confusion proneness: scale development, validation, and application', *Journal of Marketing Management*, 23: 697–721.
Young, M. (1999) 'The social construction of tourist places', *Australian Geographer*, 30: 373–89.

Part 5

Tourist consumer behaviour

19
Theorizing tourist behaviour

Alain Decrop

Introduction

In today's highly competitive and global economy, understanding tourist behaviour and consumption is crucial both for private companies, public operators and citizens. First, leisure and travel companies have to narrowly understand the needs and desires of their target customers as a key aim and critical success factor. Designing, communicating, and selling a product or service is difficult if it does not match consumers' expectations. Understanding tourist behaviour is important for public operators as well in order to effectively address consumers' wishes and to develop relevant laws and policies for informing and protecting them. Finally, understanding behaviour and consumption is also useful for tourists and travellers themselves. It may help them to make 'good' decisions or to be more critical towards commercial information sources that are likely to influence their preferences and choices.

Understanding tourists is even more critical today as they appear to be more demanding and changeable, and they show complex preference structures and decision patterns. Choosing, buying and consuming tourism/travel products and services involves a range of psycho-social processes and a series of personal and environmental influences that researchers and managers ought take into account. This chapter aims to provide an overview of such processes and influences, and to explain the basic theories that underlie tourist behaviour. Such theories borrow from a variety of disciplines, including economics, psychology, sociology and anthropology highlighting the multidisciplinarity of the field. Initially, the focus is on defining and presenting the paradigms that may be used for researching tourist behaviour. The following section theorizes tourist decision-making (DM) and the tourism experience, which constitute the two major dimensions of tourist behaviour. The reader should note that although many principles and theories presented below are relevant whatever the cultural context, this chapter presumes a western European focus as to the general statements and illustrations given.

Definitions and paradigms for researching tourist behaviour

Purchasing, consuming and evaluating tourism services

Tourist behaviour focuses on the activities people undertake for obtaining, consuming, and evaluating tourism and travel services. Drawing from general consumer behaviour frameworks, most tourist behaviour models consist of three stages: pre-purchase, consumption and post-consumption (e.g. Engel and Blackwell 1982; Howard and Sheth 1969; Nicosia 1966). In the first stage, potential tourists recognize the need for, and hence feel some motivation to go on holiday. They search for information about various destinations and evaluate those alternatives in order to choose one destination as a focus for their holiday (Klenosky and Gitelson 1998; Um and Crompton 1990). A variety of supply- and demand-related factors influence a decision to take a holiday as well as the choice of destinations, including: psychological; economic; social; political; geographical and demographic factors (Crompton and Ankomah 1993). The consumer behaviour literature makes a general distinction between individual and environmental influences on tourist behaviour. The former involve determinants that make each of us unique as an individual (including consumers' demographics, personality traits, lifestyles and values, emotions, involvement etc.) whereas the latter pertain to external factors (including social, cultural, business and media variables) that shape one's behaviour and have an impact on decisions and choices.

In the second, consumption stage, tourists experience the destination and the travel products or services. This stage is made up of a series of behaviours or activities (Smith 2003), which help consumers to satisfy their needs but also to give meaning, and convey symbolic value, to their choices and actions (Kim 2001; Uriely 2005). Consumer experience is highly subjective and is based on sensations, emotions, and social interaction to a large extent in tourism. It involves participation in activities and results in learning or knowledge acquisition. Consumer experience is now crucial in creating value and businesses must orchestrate memorable events for their customers, such that the experience itself and the memories created become the product (Pine and Gilmore 1999).

In the last post-consumption stage, after their holiday is over, tourists evaluate their experiences by matching the outcome not only with the information received from various sources such as media and relatives but also with their own expectations (Pizam, Neumann and Reichel 1978). Their evaluation typically results in feelings of dis/satisfaction. Different theories may be used to explain the formation of dis/satisfaction judgments (for a review, see Decrop 2000), i.e. the intervention of emotions, the comparison process of performances with expectations or experience-based norms, the attribution theory, or the distribution of costs/benefits among the different members of the holiday decision-making unit (DMU). Satisfaction often leads to loyalty or at least to intentions to come back, whereas dissatisfaction will make travellers switch to other domestic or international destinations. In certain cases, however, satisfaction results in attitudinal and behavioural change when the holidaymaker is driven by emotions, or by variety/collection seeking. In the same way, a behavioural change is not the only possible consequence of dissatisfaction. A dissatisfied holidaymaker may be urged to repeat his/her purchase because of compensation, resignation or frustration. Both satisfaction and dissatisfaction result in perceptual change and word-of-mouth. Tourists often tell others about favourable or unfavourable aspects of their experiences (Baker and Crompton 2000; Kozak 2001).

Paradigms for researching tourist behaviour

Five major theoretical approaches may be used in order to come to a better understanding of tourist decisions and behaviours, i.e. the micro-economic approach, the motivational perspective, the behaviourist paradigm, the cognitivist approach and the postmodern perspective (Decrop 2010).

The micro-economic approach offers a normative view of a rational consumer who makes decisions in order to maximize his/her utility (satisfaction) within his/her budget constraint. This approach aims at predicting and explaining how the consumer should behave and not how s/he really behaves. This static and purely individual approach presents products as global entities and decisions as being timeless and detached from any environmental influence ('all other things being equal'). Decisions are thought to be governed by price: the lower the price, the higher the volume of demand and vice versa. In addition, any product (holiday alternative) is thought to possess objective characteristics or attributes that are used by consumers in their evaluations. Utility is ultimately derived from these attributes and maximizing utility requires choosing a product alternative that generates the optimum bundle of attributes. The questions of how and why the holidaymaker arrives at actual choices are dismissed.

The motivational perspective is inspired by the psycho-analytic theories developed by Dichter, Freud and/or Jung, which do not focus on the objective results (utilities) of behaviours but on their subjective causes in the individual's inner world. Motivation refers to the process by which a consumer is driven to act/behave in a certain way. It is characterized by a 'state of tension within the individual which arouses, directs and maintains behaviour toward a goal' (Mullen and Johnson 1990: 178). The motivational approach aims to uncover the deep/latent motives that underlie behaviour and consumption. These reasons are often assumed to be either hidden or disclosed, thus researchers have to penetrate the individual's inner world of previously lived experiences in order to discover them.

The behaviourist paradigm is rooted in behavioural psychology (e.g. Pavlov, Skinner). It is similar to the motivational approach in that it strives to understand the reasons of behaviours in order to better motivate consumers to buy products and to stay loyal to the company. However, behaviourism presents a very deterministic view on behaviour, assuming that it is possible to condition consumers and to create automatic responses. The repetition of stimuli is thought necessary to create such conditioning. For example, the repetition of advertising stimuli is likely to produce strong buying habits, through first provoking and then reinforcing positive responses by consumers.

The cognitivist approach today represents the prevailing paradigm for theorizing consumer/tourist behaviour. Drawing from cognitive and social psychology, this approach focuses on the individual's mental (cognitive) world. Its goal is to understand the consumer's processes for solving problems. The cognitive paradigm focuses on the socio-psychological variables and processes involved in DM. The consumer is no longer passive but becomes an actor of his/her choices and behaviours: s/he thinks and develops rules and strategies in order to solve his/her problems, to satisfy his/her needs. Perception and information processing are the core processes for these activities. The consumer is presented as a risk-averse person who never stops collecting and processing information in order to make satisfying choices. Such cognitive principles lie at the core of tourist DM theories presented in the next section.

In addition to the previous approaches, a new perspective on tourist behaviour has emerged in the last 20 years. This perspective is related to the postmodern turn in social sciences and to the emergence of Consumer Culture Theory (CCT; Arnould and Thompson 2005). Postmodern research is characterized by an ontological, epistemological and methodological break; the goal is no longer to explain and predict behaviour but to understand the *how's* and *why's* of behaviour in a complex world. Postmodernism suggests a less normative and more relative perspective than the former paradigms, based on the premise that consumers are often confronted with routine choices and that they let themselves be guided by simple decision rules (e.g. 'I buy the cheapest product'). Context, and more particularly the socio-cultural environment and the consumer's level of involvement, is taken into account in order to better understand behavioural differences between individuals and between choice situations.

The cultural complexity of consumer behaviour and consumption phenomena lies at the core of CCT researchers' interest. CCT does not present culture as a homogeneous system of collectively shared beliefs, meanings, values, and lifestyles. CCT rather tries to account for the heterogeneous distribution of meanings and the plurality of cultural groupings that coexist in the socio-historical framework of globalization and market capitalism. Finally, the postmodern approach explores objects and issues that were neglected by consumer research thus far. Such new interests include the affective dimensions of choices (fun, feelings, fantasies ...) and the experiential aspects of consumption. In the same way, postmodern researchers bring into light the symbolic dimension of many purchases and possessions, and the consumption processes that contribute to consumers' identity positions and broader meanings of existence as human beings. Issues of meaning and sense-making then become central to understanding tourist consumer behaviour.

Theorizing tourist decision-making

Investigating purchase decisions (product, brand, store, mode of payment ...) is worthwhile as this information provides companies with the necessary knowledge about consumers, which enables them to sell their goods and services effectively. The consumer's final purchase is only the visible part of the iceberg, since it is the materialization of a whole DM process thought to start with the recognition of a problem (need). Several theories have been developed to explain consumer DM, borrowing from the general paradigms discussed in the previous section. The holidaymaker's DM process has been investigated in a substantial number of papers and monographs in the last three decades. The great majority of these are restricted in scope since they are limited to some specific aspects of holiday DM, such as motivation (Fodness 1994; Mansfeld 1992), information search (Fesenmaier and Vogt 1992; Fodness and Murray 1997; Mäser and Weiermair 1998), or family DM (Jenkins 1978; Nichols and Snepenger 1988; van Raaij 1986). However, a few general conceptualizations have been proposed. In his review, Decrop (2006) makes a distinction between micro-economic, cognitive and interpretive DM models.

Micro-economic models use traditional demand theory in order to explain tourism behaviour. The rational holidaymaker tries to maximize the utility of his/her choices under the constraint of his/her budget. Tourism demand analysis has benefited from considerable interest (e.g. Rugg 1973; Morley 1992; Papatheodorou 2000; and Seddighi and Theocharous 2002). In contrast, cognitive models do not pay attention to the price-demand relationship but to the mental processes that underlie the DM process. Two types of cognitive models may be identified: structural and process models. Most of those models lean heavily on classical buyer behaviour theory and postulate a (bounded) rational and hierarchical tourist DM.

Structural models focus on relationships between inputs (traveller and marketing variables) and outputs (preferences, intentions, and choices). Most of the time such relationships are presented as an evolution of tourism alternatives in consideration sets (Crompton 1977; Um and Crompton 1990; Woodside and Lysonski 1989). The consideration set (evoked set) comprises all the alternatives the holidaymaker contemplates for his/her holiday in the choice process. It is part of the perceived opportunity set (awareness set), which includes all the alternatives known to the holidaymaker. As the latter is not omniscient, the awareness set is itself only a part of the total opportunity set, which entails all possible alternatives (Woodside and Sherell 1977;

Goodall 1991). Choice then consists in an evaluation and selection process where the different alternatives in the consideration set are compared with each another on an alternative- or an attribute-basis.

Process models (e.g. Mathieson and Wall 1982; Van Raaij and Francken 1984; van Raaij 1986; Moutinho 1987; Goodall 1988; Middleton 1994) do not pay as much attention to the structural relationships between input and output as to the mental processes that underlie DM. In the process approach to DM, the focus is not on decision in itself but rather on the way consumers come to have cognitive and affective judgements, intentions, commitments prior to arriving at a final decision (Abelson and Levi 1985). Most process models are sequential as they suggest an evolution of plans and decisions through different stages. These typically are: problem identification, information search, evaluation of alternatives, choice and post-choice processes.

In contrast with both micro-economic and cognitive models, interpretive frameworks are not concerned with *how holidaymakers should* but on *how they actually make* decisions. The personal, social and cultural context of DM is taken into account to present a more naturalistic and experiential view of the consumer. DM is much more than a formalized multistage process. This results in alternative sets of propositions and frameworks of DM that include variables and hypotheses (such as low involvement or passive information search) that are not taken into account in the conventional models. In addition to the contributions of Woodside and McDonald (1994) and Teare (1994), Decrop (2006) has developed an integrative framework of tourist DM on the basis of a longitudinal qualitative study of Belgian holidaymakers (Figure 19.1). This model first introduces three levels of decisions (generic, modal and specific decisions; see below) and lists a series of 15 items that may be involved in the holiday DM process. A distinction is then made between three types of factors that may influence holiday decisions and the variables involved in the DM process, i.e. personal, interpersonal and environmental factors.

As suggested by Figure 19.1, environmental factors such as culture or the geo-political context are structural conditions on which the holidaymaker has no control. They enclose the other (personal and interpersonal) factors. Primary personal factors include the basic individual demographic and psychological features that may have an impact on secondary personal factors such as the individual resources (money, time, cognition), motives and involvement, and the travel experience. These personal factors then intertwine in the dynamics of group DM as most holiday decisions are made together with other people, rather than on an individual basis. Interpersonal factors such as group interaction, consensus and conflict management, or distribution of roles are likely to direct holiday judgments and decisions.

A multi-level approach to decision-making

Most of the time, DM models are presented horizontally, considering the different steps consumers follow from 'need recognition' to 'purchase' and 'post-purchase' processes. A funnel-like procedure is proposed in which choices are narrowed down among comparable alternatives through cognitive, affective, and behavioural (CAB) stages (Payne, Bettman and Johnson 1997; Shafir, Simonson and Tversky 1997). Such a sequence is typical of the structural and process models described in the previous section. In a conceptual paper, Decrop and Kozak (2006) suggest that in order to investigate consumers' DM processes more thoroughly, a vertical and a transversal perspective to the horizontal dimension should be added (see Figure 19.2 below). The vertical perspective consists of looking at how plans and decisions are made in multiple product levels simultaneously. Indeed it often happens that consumer choices arise within a series of product-related decisions where some decisions condition (or are conditioned by) the others. The transversal perspective is related to how plans and decisions are made socially. This is to take

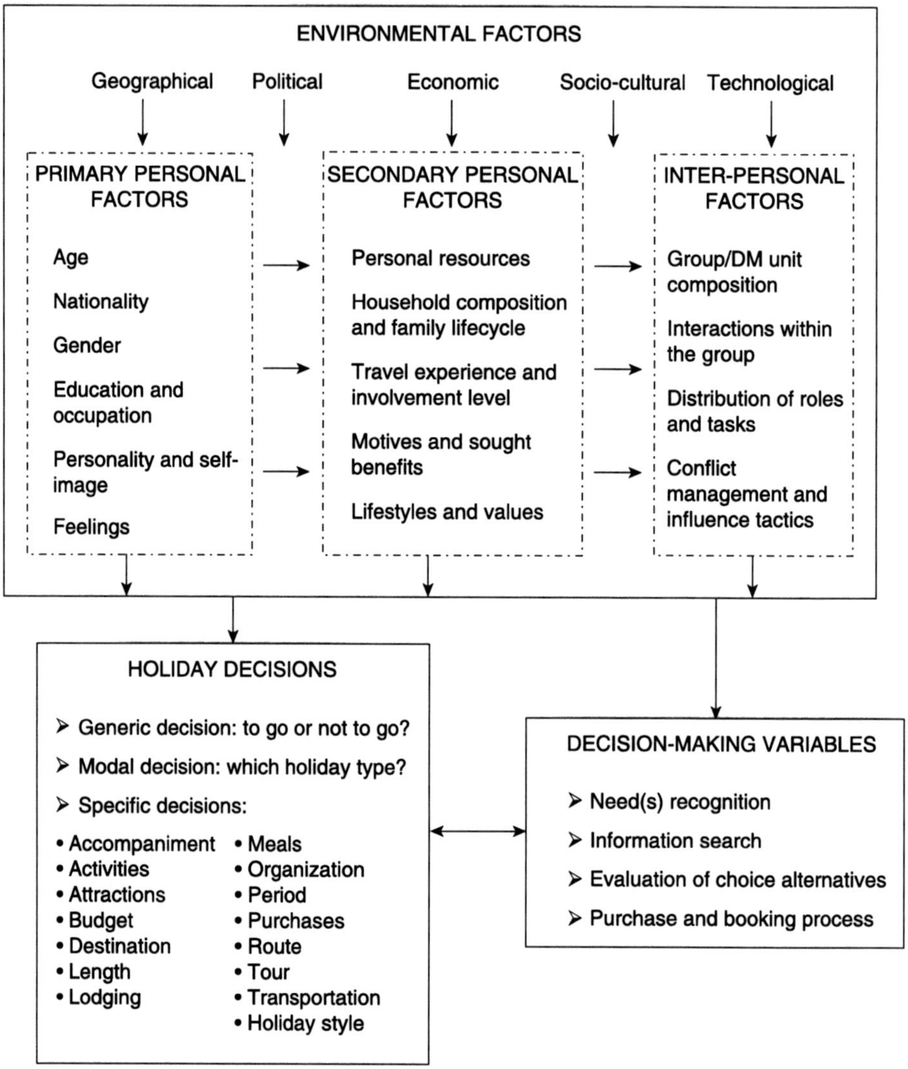

Figure 19.1 An integrative framework of holiday decision-making (Decrop 2010).

account of the predominantly social nature of tourism decision-making, e.g. involving a family or a group of friends. Those two perspectives make DM much more complex than when only one horizontal level is concerned.

Verticality in holiday decision-making

Holiday DM involves a series of decisions and sub-decisions. Switching from a horizontal to a vertical approach, three levels may be distinguished (Figure 19.2):

1 the level of the generic decision to go or not to go on holiday;
2 the level of modal decisions pertaining to the mode or type of holiday; and
3 the level of specific holiday decisions such as destination, accommodation, or transportation.

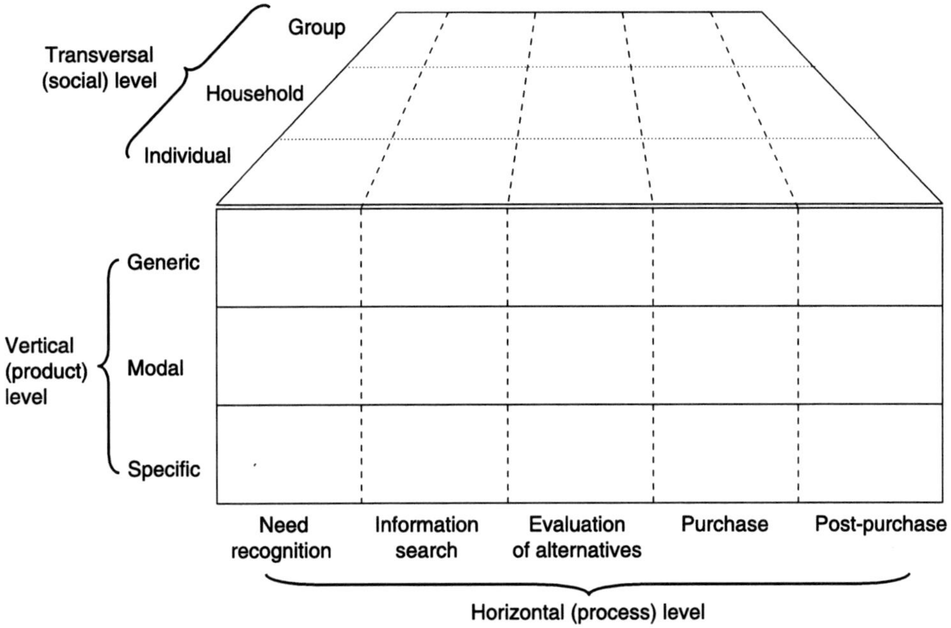

Figure 19.2 Decision levels in consumer decision-making (Decrop and Kozak 2009).

Those levels should be regarded as conceptual levels and not as hierarchical or sequential levels.

The *generic decision* level involves non-comparable choices (Johnson 1984, 1986), e.g. spending time on a holiday or repairing the house, going on holiday or buying new furniture. Some studies have shown that the generic decision to go on holiday is not always considered first, nor is the destination decision considered in the last instance (Decrop and Snelders 2004). For example, the growing phenomenon of last-minute booking means that the generic decision may come after decisions are made on the timing of a holiday/trip. It is of interest to note that tourism products compete not only with each other in terms of attracting potential clients, but also with other products such as buying a new house, a new car or investing for education (Sirakaya, McLellan and Uysal 1996).

In contrast with generic decisions, each holiday item at the level of *specific decisions* entails comparable alternatives. Comparability is defined as the degree to which alternatives are described or represented by the same attributes. Non-comparable alternatives have few attributes in common, while comparable alternatives share the same attribute background. Since visitors are confronted by a wide variety of destinations, more choices of accommodation, a diverse range of activities and tours, it has become increasingly difficult for consumers to decide where to go, how to go and where to stay (Laws 1995). Moreover, the sequence of specific decisions appears to be a key issue, leading to dissonant results. For example, Fesenmaier and Jeng (2000) and Hyde (2004) have found that the choice of travel route (a 'core' decision) often precedes choice of attractions (an 'en route' decision), whereas King and Woodside (2001) suggested the opposite. Of course, these specific choices are affected by a number of personal (e.g. previous experience, position in the family life cycle, educational level, money and time resources), psychological (e.g. motives, beliefs/images, attitudes, intentions, personality and lifestyle) and environmental variables (e.g. product's pull factors).

The level of *modal decisions* lies between generic and specific decisions since some decision items are considered in any holiday type (e.g. destination, accommodation, transportation . . .) whereas other items are particular to one type only and then non-comparable with the other holiday types (e.g. the ski material, tour . . .). Three criteria prevail in modal choices:

1 length of the trip (e.g. short break vs. longer holiday);
2 period of the year (e.g. winter vs. summer holiday); and
3 trip purpose (e.g. leisure, business, or visit friends and relatives).

Those criteria are often used for segmentation (e.g. Etzel and Woodside 1973; Sirakaya and Woodside 2005). Because time and money resources are limited, the consumer is urged to make trade-offs between modal alternatives. In other words, s/he has to decide about the number of trips to make that year. Although alternatives are not fully comparable, visitors weigh up their benefits, assess their cost and the length of stay they can afford to reserve and pay for, by taking into consideration their financial and time constraints (Alegre and Pou 2005). A final remark about this vertical dimension is that generic and modal decisions involve exclusive, substitutable or independent alternatives, while holiday decisions rely on inclusive, complementary or dependent alternatives.

Transversality in holiday decision-making

As previously discussed, holidays and travel are thought to be joint decisions that involve the different members of the household or friends in the group. However, most of the time tourism research relies on individual data when studying holiday decisions and processes. In contrast, Decrop's integrative model includes a consideration of transversality, or the exploration of group factors, in holiday DM. Different types of DM units may be compared, e.g. singles, couples, families with children and larger holidaying groups, such as parties of friends (Figure 19.2). The thrust of extant research on holiday group DM has focused on the family, especially the wife/husband dyad and the parents/children relationship (Darley and Lim 1986; Howard and Madrigal 1990; Nichols and Snepenger 1988; Thornton, Shaw and Williams 1997; for a review, see Decrop 2008). Most of these studies have focused on the distribution of roles and power relationships within the family. For example, Jenkins (1978) found that husbands dominate autonomic decisions such as length of stay, timing and spending (i.e. modal decisions). In contrast, syncretic decisions are typical for choice aspects such as mode of transport, activities, accommodation and destination (i.e. specific decisions).

In contrast with families, parties of friends have not received much attention in the literature (Decrop, Pecheux and Bauvin 2004). Moreover, the question as to what extent individual and group values, preferences and expectations converge/diverge in the DM process has been neglected to date. Indeed, group decisions are not as easy as individual decisions due to interpersonal constraints and conflicts. Finally, the issue of 'mixed' DM units is worthwhile investigating since consumers are often involved in more than one type of holiday decision simultaneously. For example, teenagers may be involved in decisions relating to a holiday project with friends in addition to the family summer trip.

Theorizing tourism consumption

In the current market economy characterized by digital technologies and competitive pressures, consumers are often confronted with a large number of alternatives (brands or even substitutable goods) and are overwhelmed with information coming from many sources (family, friends, advertising, salespeople and so on). Uncertainty about product use and performance, as well as difficult trade-offs (such as price versus quality) result in serious market dilemmas for consumers. 'This multifaceted nature of the consumer DM task has generated a number of important questions' (Bettman, Johnson and Payne 1991: 50), and over the last decade or so, general interpretative frameworks have emerged to account for the hedonic and experiential dimensions of tourist behaviour.

In this perspective, the analytic focus shifts away from the DM process as such and towards consumers' experiences of products and services (Hirschman and Holbrook 1982; Holbrook 1984). Hedonic consumption pertains to 'those facets of consumer behaviour that relate to the multisensory [i.e. tastes, sounds, scents, tactile impression and visual images], fantasy and emotive aspects of one's experience with products' (Hirschman and Holbrook 1982: 92). Consumers seek to make decisions that will maximize their pleasure and emotional arousal. Note that painful hedonic consumption is also possible, since 'consumers can utilize painful knowledge to expend emotions and construct fantasies that enable them to deal with unhappy realities better' (1982: 96). Therefore, Holbrook (1984) suggests there is a need to replace the disenchanting classical C-A-B (cognition, affect, behaviour) sequence by a C-E-V (consciousness, emotion, value) model. This reconceptualization of consumer behaviour focuses on product usage, the consumption experience, and the hedonic and symbolic dimensions of the product. Products are no longer considered as objective entities but as subjective symbols associated with emotional responses, sensory pleasures, daydreams or aesthetic considerations. This hedonic and experiential perspective is particularly relevant for tourism consumption contexts. It is not surprising then that the tourism literature includes a still expanding number of papers investigating the consumption experience itself, most of the time from naturalistic and interpretive perspectives. Contributions have been made as to the consumption of tourism destinations and other cultural places or to the role of ICT in enhancing the tourism experience while others have focused on particular motivations lying at the core of the tourism experience (e.g. sex tourism; dark tourism; volunteering; shopping). Still other authors have explored the consumption related to food, travelling styles and activities such as extreme sports.

Most of the experiential aspects of tourism have been investigated from a socio-anthropological perspective. The major contributions of this perspective may be subsumed under two general themes. The first is concerned with the problem of authenticity and alienation. The second is related to the personal transition from everyday to holiday life. To a certain extent, this dichotomy parallels the motivational distinction between push and pull factors. These two themes are discussed below. Of course, we do not pretend to be exhaustive in such a discussion. We revisit older theorisations that remain pertinent to theorizing tourism consumption today. In addition to these two 'classical' themes, a more recent perspective presenting the tourism experience as the primary source of value will be discussed as well, borrowing from psychology and the services marketing literature.

Authenticity and alienation

After Veblen (1899), one of the earliest formulations of tourism as a social phenomenon comes from Boorstin (1964). He considers tourism as the prime example of 'pseudo-events', i.e. mass tourists insulated in 'environmental bubbles' (i.e. guided groups isolated from the host environment and communities in the familiar American-style hotel) who find pleasure in inauthentic, contrived attractions. Boorstin observes that his contemporary Americans enjoyed these 'pseudo-events' and disregarded the real (strange) world outside. These ideas of alienation and superficiality were elaborated by Turner and Ash (1975). Tourists were restricted by surrogate parents (travel agents, couriers, hotel managers) in strictly circumscribed and fumigated worlds where they were relieved of any responsibility and protected from harsh reality. Those surrogates made sure that tourists only saw 'approved' places and objects, in order to avoid too much contradiction with the home country. Characteristics of local cultures were over-simplified and mass-produced, resulting in 'tourist kitsch'.

Cohen (1972, 1979, 1988) smooths this negative view by maintaining that there is no single tourist as such but rather a variety of tourist types and modes of tourist experiences. 'Experiential', 'experimental' and 'existential' tourists do not rely on and, to varying degrees, even reject conventional organized tourist activity. Moreover, such environmental bubbles 'permit many people to visit places which otherwise they would not, and to have at least some contact with the "strange" places thereby encountered' (in Urry 1990: 8).

The major challenge to Boorstin's position came from MacCannell (1976). He criticizes Boorstin (1964) and Lévi-Strauss (1955) because their accounts are exemplary of an upper-class view, where deriding tourists is 'intellectually chic': 'tourists dislike tourists' to quote MacCannell's own words (1976: 10). He further argues that the so-called 'pseudo-events' stem from the social relations resulting from tourism and not from an individualistic commitment to the lack of authenticity. For MacCannell, all tourists are looking for authenticity. This postmodern quest for authenticity is paralleled with the universal concern with the sacred. The tourist then is a kind of modern pilgrim, seeking authenticity away from everyday life in other historical periods, other cultures as well as in purer, simpler lifestyles. Among these, tourists are particularly fascinated by the 'real lives', that is the daily work lives of others. Since direct observation of these real lives is difficult and ethically unacceptable, tourist attractions (or 'tourist spaces') are constructed backstage in a contrived and artificial manner. These constructions lie at the core of MacCannell's concept of 'staged authenticity'. Other authors have elaborated on this concept (Pearce and Moscardo 1986; Crick 1988). MacCannell also speaks of alienated leisure (since tourism involves a return to the workplace). He notes the extreme diversity of tourist centres of attractions and the regulation of these (tourists' attention cannot be left to chance).

Urry (1990) also neglects authenticity as the basis for the organization of tourism: tourists are not looking for authenticity but 'just' for an escape from everyday life. Another argument comes from Feifer (1985) who points out that some tourists ('post-tourists') almost delight in the inauthenticity of tourist experiences. They know that there is no authentic 'tourist experience' as such but merely a series of games that can be played. Based on Foucault's (1976) idea of the gaze, Urry proposes an alternative explanation of tourism. The tourist gaze arises from a movement (journey) of people to, and their stay in various other destinations, i.e. outside the normal places of residence and work. While tourist gazes may bear on a lot of different places and objects, they share common characteristics, i.e.:

1 Gazes are related to purposes that are not directly connected with paid work.
2 Tourist gazes have a mass character.
3 Features have to be out-of-the-ordinary, in that they separate the tourist from everyday and routine experiences.
4 Tourist satisfaction stems from the anticipation of intense pleasures, especially through daydreaming and fantasy (Campbell 1987). Such anticipation is constructed and sustained by advertising and the media, which generate sets of signs.
5 'The gaze is constructed through signs and tourism involves the collection on such signs' (Urry 1995: 3).

Of course, issues of authenticity and gazes evolve in the present virtual and mobile world, characterized by a time-space compression. As a consequence, multifold gazes emerge which Urry and Larsen (2011: 23) interpret as a 'a shift from a solid, fixed modernity to a more fluid and speeded-up liquid modernity'.

The tourism experience as transition between everyday life and holiday life

The second major theme in the experience literature focuses on tourists and their odysseys, or tourism as a personal *passage* from an ordinary/profane workaday time to an extraordinary/sacred touristic time. Based on the processual model in anthropology (i.e. all societies mark the passage of time through rituals and special events), a holiday is seen as a kind of ritual of renewal in the annual cycle. A holiday marks a seasonal, special and sacred break from the mundane and profane everyday work; it is 'functionally and symbolically equivalent to other institutions that humans use to embellish and add meaning to their lives' (Graburn 1989: 22). Further, particular tourist experiences such as honeymoon trips or retirement cruises are analogous to 'rites de passage' (van Gennep 1909) or intermittent pilgrimages (Turner and Turner 1978; Smith 1992), which may be paralleled with the Muslim 'hajj' to Mecca (Graburn and Moore 1994).

MacCannell (1976) proposes a number of stages involved in tourist rituals: naming the sight, framing and elevation, enshrinement, mechanical reproduction as new sights name themselves after the famous. Turner (1973, 1974) makes a distinction between three ritual stages, which were adapted to tourism by other authors (Cohen 1988; Lett 1983; Shields 1990):

1 The social and spatial separation from the conventional social ties and usual place of residence.
2 Liminality: the direct experience of the sacred (shrines) out of time, place, and conventional social ties. This results in a kind of uplifting experience. This also gives room for 'liminoid situations' (Turner and Turner 1978) where everyday obligations are suspended or even inverted leading to permissive and playful behaviour, and/or unconstrained social togetherness.
3 Reintegration: 'the individual is reintegrated in the previous social group, usually at a higher social status' (in Urry 1990: 10).

Tourism experience is portrayed as a quest for the inversion of the everyday: the upper middle-class tourist seeks to be a 'peasant for a day' while the lower middle-class will seek to be a 'king/queen for a day'. Moreover, in their passages (since tourists are touring), tourists are moving from one experiential state to another, with greater or lesser consequences for them and their home societies (Lett 1983; Nash 1996).

Drawing on Turner, Jafari (1987) uses a springboard metaphor to describe how a tourist temporarily leaves his/her everyday life to jump into the holiday experience before falling back into ordinary life. His conceptualization entails five major steps:

1 corporation: represents the body's aspiration 'to leave the springboard behind' (1987: 151);
2 emancipation: the act of departure from the springboard platform;
3 animation: the tourist enjoying activities in the extraordinary world of tourism;
4 repatriation: the return to the reality of ordinary life;
5 incorporation: getting back to the body and context of ordinary life.

The tourism experience as the primary *source of value*

Holbrook and Hirschmann (1982) were the first to consider the consumption experience as the primary source of value, through the fantasies, feelings and fun it generates. Since then, marketing and tourism scholars have drifted away from utilitarian to more hedonistic and symbolic aspects of consumption. For Palmer (2010), a customer experience is not only made of hedonistic drives but also comprises 'hygiene' factors, that is raw stimuli appearing during the service encounter (e.g. brand relationships, physical evidence, interpersonal contacts). In tourism, Smith (1994) was one of the first authors to include emotional and experiential elements as part of the tourism product. Murphy, Pritchard and Smith (2000: 44) went even further in defining the tourism destination as 'an amalgam of individual products and experience opportunities that combine to form a total experience of the visited area'.

Broadening the scope, Pine and Gilmore (1999) declared the shift from a commodity- and service-based economy to an 'experience economy' in which the consumption experience itself becomes the primary source of value. The key challenge for companies is to produce memorable staged experiences for their customers. A few years later, Vargo and Lusch (2004) introduced a similar shift from the concept of 'value-in-exchange', embedded in the product and captured by price, to that of 'value-in-use', suggesting that value is created when a product or service is actually used. Such a value-in-use is global (it results from the total experience of tangible and intangible elements of the servicescape) and unique to each customer (because it is contextually interpreted by the user).

Later on, Lusch and Vargo (2006) went a step further in contending that consumers should help companies to produce the experience and that 'the customer is always a co-creator.' Since then, co-creation of value has become a focus of the experiential approach and tourists are seen as playing active roles in co-creating their experiences while on vacation. For Fuchs (2004), destination efficiency depends on both the destination's proper allocation of available resources and the tourist's own resource involvement. Such a combination determines the benefits received by tourists and destination operators. Yuksel, Yuksel and Bilim (2010) show that tourists' satisfaction and loyalty can be explained by the emotional associations and symbolic meanings they develop during their destination experience. Chekalina, Fuchs and Lexhagen (2013: 62) suggest that destinations, by their staging of intangible and tangible elements, and tourists, by their direct participation and allocation of own resources, co-create 'experiencescapes', places where the tourist experience occurs. They develop a conceptualization where destination experience is seen as a transformation process of a destination's tangible, intangible resources and human assets into the value-in-use for a customer. They also show that such a value-in-use helps to build customer loyalty.

Conclusion

Theorizing tourist behaviour is not an easy task as tourists may show thousands of facets in their choices and activities. In this chapter the aim was to present diverse perspectives to better understand and conceptualize tourist behaviour. These avenues draw from a series of scientific disciplines, including micro-economics, cognitive and social psychology, anthropology and sociology. Tourism scholars have first drawn on 'Grand Models' taken from the psychological consumer behaviour literature, such as the Engel and Blackwell model, in order to isolate the cognitive steps or 'building blocks' leading to purchase. Other authors have developed models deemed to be more tourist-specific as they encapsulate the well-established characteristics of services such as intangibility, inseparability, heterogeneity and perishability, as well as the emotional and social aspects related to the consumption experience. Finally, postmodern conceptualizations coming from anthropology and sociology have offered a wider view of tourists' behaviour and experience, going beyond the presentation of a material and rational consumer to include symbolism and sense-making.

These different perspectives on tourist behaviour are not in opposition but complement one another to offer a panoramic vision. After all, the study of tourists is the study of human beings in all their complexity: beings who both think and feel, beings who both look to satisfy functional needs and higher-order aspirations, beings who both make decisions and enjoy experiences. This whole process of making decisions and experiencing the holiday can be summarized by the concept of transition, i.e. the passage from one state of affairs to another. Indeed, tourism behaviour may be seen as a transitional activity involving four major dimensions (Figure 19.3).

First, the holidaymaker is motivated toward leaving his/her ordinary (daily-life) time for the extraordinary (holiday) time. The need to break with routine and to get away is the basic push factor. It can be refined into a temporal and a spatial escape. For some holidaymakers, such a transition is connected with leaving the pace and stress of occupational or household everyday life. The holiday means other activities, another time, another pace. There is no need to get away from home for this. In contrast, other holidaymakers need to escape home to really feel as though they are on holiday. Second, holiday DM and the tourism experience is characterized by a

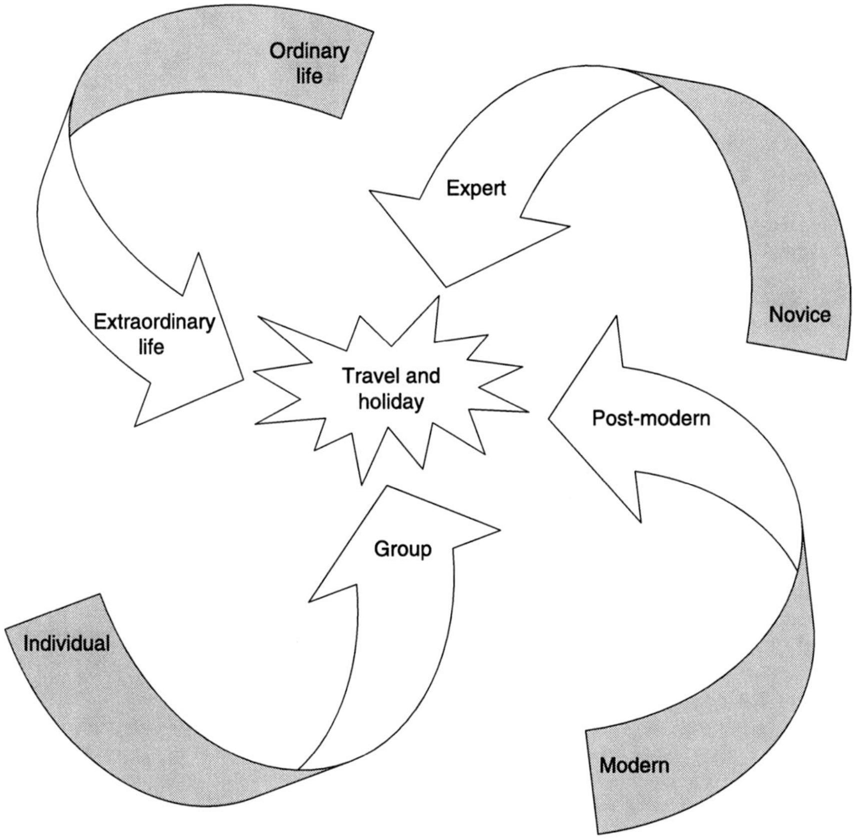

Figure 19.3 The tourist in transition (Decrop 2010).

socialization process through which the holidaymaker is sharing thoughts and emotions, communicating and negotiating individual values and preferences with the other members of the DM unit. Third, the consumer evolves in his/her life cycle and holidaymaker's 'career' (Pearce 1988). As experience and maturity grows, there is a shift in holiday motives, involvement, and expectation level. The novice tourist progressively becomes an expert. Finally, the contemporary holidaymaker clearly fits into postmodernity: eclectic and insatiable, s/he looks continuously for new experiences and to engage the emotions. While looking for authenticity, s/he is not always in a position to perceive the difference between the 'genuine' and the 'fake' in a hyperreal world.

The postmodern holidaymaker shows ever more complex desires, preferences, and behaviours. Such an evolution fits into the socioeconomic changes that affect today's tourism and that will impact on tomorrow's holidaymaking. Tourism practitioners should take inspiration from such transitional changes described in Figure 19.3 in order to propose exciting products to holidaymakers, which allow them to meet the diversity of their needs. Tour-operators should not only care for individual needs but they should also listen more closely to the wishes of the DM unit, be it a couple, a family or a group of friends. Moreover, they should pay attention to the increasing experience and maturity of many contemporary holidaymakers because involvement and motivation spiral upwards as a consequence.

Finally, postmodern tourists no longer satisfy themselves with a passive role of *consumers* but they wish to become *co-producers* of their choices and behaviours. They want to be more involved in the creation of tourism offerings (co-creation of value) or in their travel activities (participatory tourism). Creating value lies thus in the hands of both operators and tourists. Therefore tour-operators should help travellers to develop their tailor-made trips through virtual interaction (Internet, Web 2.0, etc.), but also keep offering 'easy' readymade stays. More broadly, tourism professionals should avoid segmenting and targeting their markets too hermetically since tourists more than ever appear chameleon-like and omnivorous in their tourism behaviour.

References

Abelson, R.P. and Levi, A. (1985) 'Decision making and decision theory' in Lindzey, G. and Aronson, E. (eds) *The Handbook of Social Psychology*. New York: Random House, pp. 231–309.

Alegre, J. and Pou, L. (2006) 'The length of stay in the demand for tourism', *Tourism Management*, 27: 1343–55.

Arnould, E. and Thompson, C. (2005) 'Consumer Culture Theory (CCT): twenty years of research', *Journal of Consumer Research*, 31(March): 868–82.

Bettman, J.R. and Sujan, M. (1987) 'Effects of framing on evaluation of comparable and noncomparable alternatives by expert and novice consumers', *Journal of Consumer Research*, 14: 141–54.

Boorstin, D.J. (1964) *The Image: A Guide to Pseudo-events in America*. New York: Harper.

Campbell, C. (1987) *The Romantic Ethic and the Spirit of Modern Consumerism*. Oxford: Blackwell Publishers.

Chekalina, T., Fuchs, M. and Lexhagen, M. (2011) 'Determinants of the co-created destination experience: an empirical validation from Sweden' in M. Kozak *et al.* (eds), *Transforming Experiences: Tourism Marketing from Both Sides of the Counter*. Cambridge: Scholars Publishing, pp. 57–79.

Cohen, E. (1972) 'Towards a sociology of international tourism', *Social Research*, 39: 164–82.

— (1979) 'A phenomenology of tourist types', *Sociology*, 13: 179–201.

— (1988) 'Traditions in the qualitative sociology of tourism', *Annals of Tourism Research*, 15: 29–46.

Crick, M. (1988) 'Sun, sex, sights, savings and servility', *Criticism, Heresy and Interpretation*, 1: 37–76.

Crompton, J. (1977) 'A systems model of the tourist's destination selection decision process with particular reference to the role of image and perceived constraints', Unpublished Doctoral Dissertation. Texas A and M University.

Darley, W. and Lim, J. (1986) 'Family decision making in leisure-time activities: an exploratory investigation of the impact of locus of control, child age influence factor and parental type on perceived child influence', *Advances in Consumer Research*, 13: 370–4.

Decrop, A. (2000) 'The antecedents and consequences of vacationers dis/satisfaction: tales from the field', *Tourism Analysis*, 5: 203–9.
— (2005) 'Group processes in vacation decision making', *Journal of Travel and Tourism Marketing*, 18(3): 23–36.
— (2006) *Vacation Decision Making*. Wallingford: CABI.
— (2010) *Le touriste consommateur. Comprendre les comportements pour améliorer son efficacité marketing*. Bruxelles: De Boeck.
Decrop, A. and Kozak, M. (2006) 'A multi-level framework for studying vacation decision making', proceedings of the 35th EMAC Conference, Athens, Greece.
— (2009) 'Tourist decision strategies in a multi-level perspective' in A. Fyall, M. Kozak, L. Andreu, J. Gnoth and S. Lebe (eds), *Marketing Innovations for Sustainable Destinations*. Oxford: Goodfellow Publishers, pp. 80–91.
Decrop, A. and Snelders, D. (2004) 'Planning the summer vacation: an adaptable and opportunistic process', *Annals of Tourism Research*, 31: 1008–30.
Decrop, A., Pecheux, C. and Bauvin, G. (2004) 'Let's make a trip together: an exploration into decision making within groups of friends', *Advances in Consumer Research*, 31: 291–7.
Engel, J.F. and Blackwell, R.D. (1982) *Consumer Behavior*. Hinsdale: The Dryden Press.
Etzel, M. J. and Woodside, A.G. (1973) 'Segmentation vacation markets: the case of the distant and near-home travelers', *Journal of Travel Research*, 20(4): 10–14.
Feifer, M. (1985) *Going Places*. London: MacMillan.
Fesenmaier, D. and Vogt, C. (1992) 'Evaluating the utility of touristic information sources for planning Midwest vacation travel', *Journal of Travel and Tourism Marketing*, 1(2): 1–18.
Fesenmaier, D. and Jeng, J. (2000) 'Assessing structure in the pleasure trip planning process', *Tourism Management*, 5: 13–17.
Fodness, D. (1994) 'Measuring tourist motivation', *Annals of Tourism Research*, 21: 555–81.
Fodness, D. and Murray, B. (1997) 'Tourist information search', *Annals of Tourism Research*, 24: 503–23.
Foucault, M. (1976) *The Birth of the Clinic*. London: Tavistock.
Fuchs, M. (2004) 'Strategy development in tourism destinations: a DEA approach', *Poznan University Economics Review*, 4(1): 52–73.
Goodall, B. (1991) 'Understanding holiday choice' in C.P. Cooper (ed.) *Progress in Tourism, Recreation and Hospitality Management*, vol. 3. London: Belhaven Press, pp. 59–77.
Graburn, N.H. (1989) 'Tourism: the sacred journey' in V.L. Smith (ed.) *Hosts and Guests: The Anthropology of Tourism*. Philadelphia: University of Pennsylvania Press, pp. 21–36.
Graburn, N.H. and Moore, R.S. (1994) 'Anthropological research on tourism' in J.R. Brent Ritchie and C.R. Goeldner (eds) *Travel, Tourism, and Hospitality Research: A Handbook for Managers and Researchers*. New York: John Wiley & Sons, pp. 233–42.
Hirschman, E.C. and Holbrook, M.B. (1982) 'Hedonic consumption: emerging concepts, methods and propositions', *Journal of Marketing*, 46(Summer): 92–101.
Holbrook, M.B. (1984) 'Emotion in the consumption experience: toward a new model of the human consumer' in R.A. Peterson, W.D. Hoyer and W.R. Wilson (eds) *The Role of Affect in Consumer Behavior: Emerging Theories and Applications*. Lexington: Lexington Books, pp. 17–52.
Holbrook, M.B. and Hirschman, E.C. (1982) 'The experiential aspects of consumption: consumer fantasies, feelings, and fun', *Journal of Consumer Research*, 132–40.
Howard, D. and Madrigal, R. (1990) 'Who makes the decision: the parent or the child? The perceived influence of parents and children on the purchase of recreation services', *Journal of Leisure Research*, 22: 244–58.
Howard, J.A. and Sheth J.N. (1969) *The Theory of Buyer Behavior*. New York: John Wiley and Sons.
Hyde, K.F. (2004) 'A duality in vacation decision making' in G.I. Crouch, R.R. Purdue, H.J.P. Timmermans and M. Uysal (eds) *Consumer Psychology of Tourism, Hospitality and Leisure*, Vol. 3. Wallingford: CABI, pp. 161–8.
Jafari, J. (1987) 'Tourism models: the socio-cultural aspects', *Tourism Management*, 8(2): 151–9.
Jenkins, R. (1978) 'Family decision making' *Journal of Travel Research*, 16(4): 2–7.
Johnson, M.D. (1984) 'Consumer choice strategies for comparing noncomparable alternatives', *Journal of Consumer Research*, 11: 741–53.
— (1986) 'Modeling choice strategies for noncomparable alternatives', *Marketing Science*, 5: 37–54.
King, R.L. and Woodside, A.G. (2001) 'Qualitative comparative analysis of travel and tourism purchase-consumption systems', in J.A. Mazanec, G.I. Crouch, J.R.B. Ritchie and A.G. Woodside (eds) *Consumer Psychology of Tourism, Hospitality and Leisure*, Vol. 2. Wallingford: CABI, pp. 67–86.

Laws, E. (1995) *Tourist Destination Management: Issues, Analysis and Policies.* NY: Routledge.
Lett, J. (1983) 'Ludic and liminoid aspects of charter yacht tourism in the Caribbean', *Annals of Tourism Research*, 10: 35–56.
Lévi-Strauss, C. (1955) *Tristes tropiques.* Paris: Plon.
Lusch, R.F. and Vargo, S.L. (2006) *The Service-dominant Logic of Marketing: Dialog, Debate, and Directions.* ME Sharpe Inc.
MacCannell, D. (1976) *The Tourist: A New Theory of the Leisure Class.* New York: Schocken Books.
Mansfeld, Y. (1992) 'Tourism: towards a behavioural aproach. The choice of destination and its impact on spatial behaviour', *Progress in Planning*, 38: 1–92.
Mäser, B. and Weiermair K. (1998) 'Travel decision-making: from the vantage point of perceived risk and information preferences', *Journal of Travel and Tourism Marketing*, 7: 107–21.
Mathieson, A. and Wall, G. (1982) *Tourism: Economic, Physical and Social Impacts.* Harlow: Longman.
Middleton, V.T. (1994) *Marketing in Travel and Tourism*, 2nd edn. Oxford: Butterworth-Heinemann.
Morley, C.L. (1992) 'A microeconomic theory of international tourism demand', *Annals of Tourism Research*, 19: 250–67.
Moscardo, G., Morrison, A.M., Pearce, P.L., Lang, C. and O'Leary, J.T. (1993) 'Understanding vacation destination choice through travel motivation and activities', *Journal of Vacation Marketing*, 2: 109–22.
Moutinho, L. (1987) 'Consumer behaviour in tourism', *European Journal of Marketing*, 21(10): 2–44.
Mullen, B. and Johnson, C. (1990) *The Psychology of Consumer Behavior.* Hillsdale, NJ: Lawrence Erlbaum Associates.
Murphy, P., Pritchard, M.P. and Smith, B. (2000) 'The destination product and its impact on traveller perceptions', *Tourism Management*, 21(1): 43–52.
Nash, D. (1996) *Anthropology of Tourism.* Kidlington: Pergamon.
Nichols, C.M. and Snepenger, D.J. (1988) 'Family decision making and tourism behavior and attitudes', *Journal of Travel Research*, 26(Spring): 2–6.
Nicosia, F.M. (1966) *Consumer Decision Processes: Marketing and Advertising Implications.* Englewood Cliffs, NJ: Prentice Hall.
Palmer, A. (2010) 'Customer experience management: a critical review of an emerging idea', *Journal of Services Marketing*, 24(3): 196–208.
Papatheodorou, A. (2001) 'Why people travel to different places', *Annals of Tourism Research*, 28: 164–79.
Payne, J.W., Bettman, J.R. and Johnson, E.J. (1997) 'The adaptive decision maker: effort and accuracy in choice' in W.M. Goldstein and R.M. Hogarth (eds) *Research on Judgment and Decision Making: Currents, Connections and Controversies.* Cambridge: Cambridge University Press, pp. 181–204.
Pearce, P.L. (1988) *The Ulysses Factor: Evaluating Visitors in Tourist Settings.* New York: Springer Verlag.
Pearce, P. and Moscardo, G. (1986) 'The concept of authenticity in tourist experiences', *Australian and New Zealand Journal of Sociology*, 22: 121–32.
Pine, B.J. and Gilmore, J.H. (1999) *The Experience Economy: Work Is Theatre & Every Business a Stage.* Boston, MA: Harvard Business Press.
Pizam, A, Neuman, Y. and Reichel, A. (1978) 'Dimensions of tourist satisfaction with a destination area', *Annals of Tourism Research*, 5: 314–22.
Rugg, D. (1973) 'The choice of journey destination: a theoretical and empirical analysis', *The Review of Economics and Statistics*, 55: 64–72.
Seddighi, H.R. and Theocharous, A.L. (2002) 'A model of tourism destination choice: a theoretical and empirical analysis', *Tourism Management*, 23: 475–87.
Shafir, E., Simonson, I. and Tversky, A. (1997) 'Reason-based choice' in W.M. Goldstein and R.M. Hogarth (eds) *Research on Judgment and Decision Making: Currents, Connections and Controversies.* Cambridge: Cambridge University Press, pp. 69–94.
Shields, R. (1990) *Places on the Margin.* London: Routledge.
Sirakaya, E. and Woodside, A.G. (2005) 'Building and testing theories of decision making by travellers', *Tourism Management*, 26(6): 815–32.
Sirakaya, E., McLellan, R. and Uysal, M. (1996) 'Modeling vacation destination decisions: a behavioral approach', *Journal of Travel and Tourism Marketing*, 5(1/2): 57–75.
Smith, S.L. (1994) 'The tourism product', *Annals of Tourism Research*, 21(3): 582–95.
Smith, V.L. (1992) 'Introduction: the quest in guest', *Annals of Tourism Research*, 19(1): 1–17.
Teare, R. (1994) 'Consumer decision making' in R. Teare, J.A. Mazanec, S. Crawford-Welch and S. Calver (eds) *Marketing in Hospitality and Tourism: A Consumer Focus.* London: Cassell, pp. 1–96.

Thornton, P.R., Shaw, G. and Williams, A.M. (1997) 'Tourist group holiday decision-making and behaviour: the influence of children', *Tourism Management*, 18: 287–97.
Turner, L. and Ash, J. (1975) *The Golden Hordes*. London: Constable.
Turner, V. (1973) 'The center out there: pilgrim's goal', *History of Religions*, 12: 191–230.
— (1974) *The Ritual Process.* Harmondsworth: Penguin.
Turner, V. and Turner, E. (1978) *Image and Pilgrimage in Christian Culture.* New York: Columbia University Press.
Um, S. and Crompton, J.L. (1990) 'Attitude determinants in tourism destination choice', *Annals of Tourism Research*, 17: 432–48.
Urry, J. (1990) *The Tourist Gaze: Leisure and Travel in Contemporary Societies.* London: Sage.
— (1995) *Consuming Places.* London: Routledge.
Urry, J. and Larsen, J. (2011) *The Tourist Gaze 3.0.* London: Sage Publications Limited.
van Gennep, A. (1909) *Les rites de passage: Etude systématique des rites.* Paris: Nourry.
van Raaij, W.F. (1986) 'Consumer research on tourism: mental and behavioral constructs', *Annals of Tourism Research*, 13: 1–9.
van Raaij, W.F. and Francken, D.A. (1984) 'Vacations decisions, activities and satisfaction', *Annals of Tourism Research*, 11: 101–12.
Vargo, S.L. and Lusch, R.F. (2004) 'Evolving to a new dominant logic for marketing', *Journal of Marketing*, 68(1): 1–17.
Veblen, T. (1899) *The Theory of the Leisure Class.* New York: The Viking Press.
Woodside, A.G. and Lysonski, S. (1989) 'A general model of traveler destination choice', *Journal of Travel Research*, 27(Spring): 8–14.
Woodside, A.G. and MacDonald, R. (1994) 'General system framework of customer choice processes of tourism services', in R.V. Gasser and K. Weiermair (eds) *Spoilt for Choice. Decision Making Processes and Preference Change of Tourists: Intertemporal and Intercountry Perspectives.* Thaur: Kulturverlag, pp. 30–59.

20

Fragmenting tourism

Niche tourists

Michael O'Regan

Introduction

Tourism, a global socio-economic phenomenon, is freely used as a broad generic term that covers a broad continuum of tourism and other travel related mobilities, comprising tourist and visitor activities and experiences serviced by a travel and tourism industry as well as host destinations. While always acknowledged as a fragmented industry, increased global tourist arrivals and international tourism expenditure has seen many large commercial and public sector organizations address Western-centric societies through mass undifferentiated marketing; targeting entire marketplaces such as specific countries or regions with 'one size fits all' holidays. Broad-brush marketing often announced the existence of a destination or a packaged tourism product and how they are to be performed, often presenting potential tourists with certain kinds of limited knowledge about tourism spaces, peoples and pasts; a process that often did not distribute the benefits of tourism to a large cross section of those societies. Such marketing approaches can create a cluttered, untargeted environment in which tourists become part of indiscernible 'mass markets', which may overlook other 'niche markets' and ensure that many legitimate businesses fail to meet customer needs in the provision of tourist products and services. While other industries have seen a paradigm shift from 'mass markets' to 'mass niches', reflecting fragmenting industries and niche consumption, this chapter investigates if a paradigm shift or nudge has occurred within tourism. By focusing on changing supply and demand issues, this chapter asks whether tourism marketing has adapted to more demanding specific interests, when such interests coalesce into coherent niche tourism markets determined to be treated as 'special'.

Rigid forms of mass tourism development 'complemented' (Marson 2011) the rigid novelty and climatic motivational properties of the early 'old tourist' (Poon 1989), 'mass tourism' marketing primarily seeking to develop and cultivate high volume, low value and mass market consumptive opportunities. Often, such opportunities are still marketed as normal practice, a purchase signalling acceptance into membership of society, conformity to social convention and rising social mobility. The global tourism-industrial complex, made up of an alliance of large private–public businesses and institutions have, particularly in periods of economic growth, offered limited choices for means to achieve social, political and economic inclusion based on norms, tradition, custom as well as promotional and regulatory discourses. Mass tourism is 'deeply embedded in the organization of life in the more developed world' (Shaw and Williams 1994: 175), hegemonic tourist discourses now firmly etched into many tourist movements and spaces, meaning habits are conditioned by institutionalized configurations that precede tourists and which continue to intensify and reproduce across generations. Pre-disposed to act in certain ways, tourists are often relieved of decision making, standardization meeting limited 'desire for performance' (Soguk 2003: 30) and expectations of participation (Marson 2011), tourism imagery often positioning tourists in distinct social spaces that orchestrated new forms of social life (Sheller and Urry 2006).

Often bereft of market research and customer intelligence, destination managers when facilitating tourists' experience of otherness have done so through a tried and tested network of shopping malls, museums, golf courses, and railway stations, hotels, resorts, airports, museums and beaches. This approach is often successful early in the destination lifecycle (Butler 1980) and emerging markets such as China, helping to manufacture relationships between elements that would otherwise have no connection, while facilitating individual independence from group interests, organic or territorially bounded social relations (Aradau *et al.* 2010). However, many have critiqued the 'mass markets' approach since it often facilitates the expulsion of alterity beyond 'the boundaries of some ethnically, culturally or civilizationally purified homogeneous enclave, at whatever level of social or geographical scale' (Morley 2004: 309). Whilst the positive and negative effects of mass tourism are well documented (Shaw and Williams 1994), the scope of economic power and the scale economics surrounding 'mass markets' may mean the tourism-industrial complex can assert a hegemonic right to regulate and exploit mass undifferentiated markets within homogenized templates, and circulate tourists according to its own desires for profit and capital accumulation. Because of the focus on volume, only limited and tried and tested choices may be available to consumers and while remaining popular for many, since it finds a way to meet the needs of 'old tourists', it can stifle diversity and give consumers the 'lowest common denominator' (Lew 2008: 411). It also ignores those willing and demanding to pay premium prices for more unique, individualized products, services and experiences. While the 'mass markets' approach is product driven, the post-modern and dynamic societies in which individuals now live means a shift in orientation across industries from a product-orientation to a consumer-orientation that customizes products and services for distinct 'niche markets', requiring flexible and responsive practices and a move from mass marketing to niche marketing. The refrain from many industries is that there are no more mass markets. From computing to retail, mass markets have splintered into a myriad of differentiated niche markets, where demanding consumers have pushed firms to offer a greater range of products customized to their needs. Therefore, the implication is that tourism, a complex phenomenon working more as a metaphor than a label in a world where everybody seems to have mobility related aspirations, plans or projects, has seen a similar shift, or at least a nudge.

Fragmenting tourism

Tourism, while complex, suggests and informs the imagination and novel forms of identity making. Bruner (1991) rejects any deterministic position that confines the tourist to a discourse constituted outside their own physicality, outside their own 'selves', as he states that 'of course tourists have agency... There are no persons without agency, without active selves' (Bruner 2005: 12). Tourism, then, can no longer be considered a single phenomenon where the tourist role is pre-arranged and produced by a dedicated tourism industry and consumed by an unreflexive, habitual population, since the most ordinary of people at the most ordinary of times can now 'deploy their imaginations in the practice of their everyday lives' (Appadurai 1996: 5). It is this imagination which 'is now central to all forms of agency, is itself a social fact, and is the key component of the new global order' (Appadurai 1996: 31). In a world in motion, individuals are drawing upon their imagination and access to mobility to cross borders in ever-greater numbers inside and outside of quotidian realities, in pursuit of opportunities and possibilities, provoking 'new concepts, new ways of seeing and being' (Robertson 1994: 2). Connecting 'within and across different societies and regions, transport-systems, accommodation and facilities, resources, environments, technologies, and people and organizations' (Van der Duim 2007: 967–68) enables individuals to explore consumerist post-modern aesthetic and intensified forms of individualized identities (Savage *et al.* 2005) in far greater numbers than was ever before possible.

To suggest that the tourism industry is fragmented is not new with Poon (1989) noting the shift from 'old tourism' (e.g. the standardized holiday package) to 'new tourism' which is segmented, customized and flexible. However, individuals are now able to 'live "in" the world of modernity much more comprehensively than was ever possible before the advent of modern systems of representation, transportation and communication' (Giddens 1991: 211), Cresswell (2006: 45) noting that 'not only does the world appear to be more mobile, but our ways of knowing the world have also become more fluid', which possibility might not just change the world but ways of knowing it. This identity construction encompasses both people's 'sense of who they are (what might be termed personal identity) and their sense of who they are like, and who they are different from (what might be termed social location)' (Skinner and Rosen 2007: 83). This trend has been also been propelled by global competition; economic turbulence; over-familiarity (and defiance) with the concept of 'mass destination' (Holden 2008), uniqueness of new niche products, time squeeze, investment in tourism infrastructure, technology, space contraction, affluence, economics of scope, new marketing and branding strategies (Lew 2008; Marson 2011; Poon 1989).

A 'new age of mobility' (Ki-Moon 2009) and individualism has led to spatio-temporal orderings where 'transitional identities may be sought and performed' (Edensor 2000: 333) and from which narratives can be constructed and new perspectives communicated. It means individuals now seem to be more than ever prone to articulate complex affiliations, allegiances, belongings, attachments and occasioned, intermittent, sustained encounters to multiple issues, pasts, events, people, places, cultures and traditions, opening up the 'possibility of adjusting understandings, relationships and self-actualization' (Crouch 2006: 361). As individuals search for new belongings, changing the way that they conceive of themselves and their perspective on the world, it is often at the expense of older certainties, belongings, solidarities, loyalties and block identities. The acceptance of 'personal choice across a range of tourist activities' (Robinson, Heitmann and Dieke 2011: xii) does not mean the end of mass markets and the systems and structures that organized much of mainstream tourist life by choreographing mobility and social relations. While fragmenting, tourism has not dissipated into shapeless crowds. However, as people rearrange their social relations with regard to the constraints and opportunities that new and innovative tourist products can give when experiencing the world, the fragmentation of tourism products (Marson 2011) means the 'the old stories of group (Communal) belonging' (Bauman 2001: 98) are becoming replaced with 'identity stories' in which 'we tell ourselves about where we came from, what we are now and where we are going' (ibid. 99).

Policy-makers, planners and many in the tourism industry who largely failed to address more unique wants and needs now recognize the demand shift in the niche markets is significantly large, and often made up of consumers willing to pay for meaningful experiences. The late acceptance and identification of those unique wants and needs was often because they lacked specific descriptors. For example, the needs of 'drifters' in the 1970s were not met, and it wasn't until youth independent travel remerged in the early 1990s that the label 'backpacker' came to be produced as a clearly defined discursive category. It was only then, governments and entrepreneurs began to have a practical sense of this world and its inhabitants' needs, their dispositions seen as durable through economic downturns and unforeseen events, making them an attractive long-term investment. Backpackers today are viewed as strategically important by an increasing number of businesses, regions, institutions and governments (O'Regan 2010), their mobility becoming central to many economics and livelihoods.

As it was with backpacking, the paradigm shift may be better described as a nudge with a snowball effect developing as more individuals seeking better control of their social and spatial positioning proved vocal, persistent and motivated in their preferences, undermining the central assumptions of the mass market approach and homogenized templates. The advent of technological forces and the Internet in particular has made many existing and emerging niches visible, encouraging new relationships between consumers, between consumers and small producers and amongst/between producers. Slowly, but with increasing momentum, those who sought to transform themselves into the kinds of people they're supposed and want to be, are influencing the direction of their own moves and experiences and standing out more because, for once, they were not being herded together with the masses or left in the margins. As people share similar habits, practical knowledge, assumptions and routines, and reflexively recognize a shared pattern that is inter-subjectively communicated, so a process is initiated, the 'beginning of institutionisation' (Jenkins 1996: 128). As new social labels emerged (i.e. wine tourist) or such labels become understood with reference to an internal–external dialectic of identification (Jenkins 1996) such as 'backpacker', where 'all identities – individual and collective – are constituted' (Jenkins 1996: 20). The specific nature of the skills, competencies, knowledge and interactions between those who react to such labels has become an interest for academic researchers who see tourism from an 'interior, subjective perspective as well as a positivistic, external objective position' (Novelli 2005: x). As researchers looked behind macro descriptions of tourism and the tourist (which are often value laden) to uncover 'other, socially differentiated realities' (Favell *et al.*, 2006: 2), they are finding individuals explicitly acting to fashion their identities by regulating their bodies, their thoughts and their conduct in new ways from within a fragmenting industry, along with diverse businesses developing and marketing diverse tourism products catering to diverse but specific needs and wants.

Niche tourism

The term 'niche' may be used where a particular social group might occupy a space (Chinatown) or even when a subculture (i.e. urban explorers, environmental activists, artists, free-runners) occupy a specific niche within a larger community by appropriating specific places or infrastructure. As an expression of identity and belonging, these 'niches' often encompass alternative spaces and sites of interaction that work outside mainstream societal codes, regulatory over sight, civic law or rules and may even challenge the habitual and the routine. Over time, a niche might become associated with the language of business and become a specialized market, since niches can be identified with distinct consumption patterns, and demand for specific tailor-made products and services. Such niches may even sustain their own economies that exist under the radar of large Fordist-style firms, since as limited markets, they may be attractive for entrepreneurs as well as smaller and flexibly organized businesses. Entrepreneurs may have been co-participants in a niche before getting involved in developing products and services for that niche; or niche businesses eager to escape competition enter a niche by exploiting some specific and special competence such as firm specialization, product differentiation, customer focus and niche marketing (Dalgic 2006).

When used in the context of tourism, the terms of 'niche tourism' and 'niche tourist', whilst widely used and easily understood descriptors, are borrowed from the term 'niche marketing', which in turn appropriated the niche concept from language used in the discipline of ecology (Robinson and Novelli 2005). As a label or category, 'niche tourism' and 'niche tourist' can generate a surprising amount of debate. From the scholars who contest the conflicting claims to its origin, the entrepreneurs who seek to extend it as a label to the tourists who wish to distance themselves from it, there is little agreement as to the nature of 'niche tourism' or 'niche tourists'. From a demand viewpoint, niche tourists participate in special interest practices, experiences, products and services that distinguish and differentiate them, niche tourism reflecting 'the power, or at least the apparition of power, of the consumer' (Robinson and Novelli 2005: 1). From a supply perspective, specific interests can coalesce into coherent markets or segments within segments which a business can exploit by 'catering to the needs of specific markets by focusing on more diverse tourism products' (Marson 2011: 9). Such 'niches' may often generalize, homogenize and objectify those who participate in a particular practice or experience a similar product, with Robinson, Heitmann and Dieke (2011) noting the tourist product consumption is often misidentified as niche, when in fact, it may be more related to tourist motivation (e.g. wedding tourism, sex tourism). Robinson and Novelli (2005: 7) argue that the usage of the term 'niche' is not without its semantic problems but has 'taken on a common-sense meaning', favoured by policy makers, statisticians, academic researchers and marketing publications. Even if 'niche tourist' when extended to a particular product, experience or practice (i.e. religious tourist) has not become an internal identification for the individuals participating, it does, however, make them legible in a modern society.

Seeking to classify particular interests as a form of mass and/or niche tourism misses the point, since there is always a necessity to understand tourists' unifying constructs, behaviours and interests, and subsequently identify and develop products that suit those interests and motivate them to travel. Rather than opposite, counter-point or left over from 'mass' tourism, these small specialized sectors of tourism labelled 'niche tourism' indicate a quantitative difference in comparison to mass tourism, since niche products only appeal to select smaller groups that geographically span the globe. However, authors such as Novelli (2005) also suggest a qualitative difference, if niche tourists engage in socially responsible and sustainable behaviour.

Niche tourism supply

From a tourism supply perspective, 'differentiated upon patterns of perceived demand segments that in turn are located within social and environmental characteristics, both embracing and attracting the participant' (Trauer 2006: 185), the tourism product range expanded as 'special interests' emerged from personal choices in the early 1980s. While small practitioners have always adopted the notion of differentiation or specialization by catering to niche markets (Weber 2001), the unique needs and wants of many niches remained unseen to many large public and private institutions, their lack of foresight, customer intelligence, resources, capabilities or credibility preventing them from identifying and developing products to meet the needs of smaller groups with similar interests. Coming out of a global recession in the late 1980s and early 1990s, businesses became more responsive to the forces and energy of those with special interests, the fragmentation of tourism products developing into specific niche markets.

Niche tourism creates openings for tourism to be negotiated differently by consumers in the marketplace but also creates openings for flexibility for small- and medium-scale entrepreneurial enterprises and grass roots organizations which, if in physical closeness to niche products, may be in the best position to extend tailored offerings within existing niches. In contrast to mass tourism, businesses need to be flexible and nimble as they develop new products, a bottom-up approach driven by knowledge of the niche's aggregate individual needs (Shani and Chalasani 1992). While not all common 'special interests' groups will become niche markets that can be selected and grouped and made profitable, regulated or managed, specific, innovative and even radical tourism products may be profitably developed for many. While many of these so-called consumers would fail to recognize themselves as niche tourists or as 'belonging' to markets, smaller firms, rather than being driven to control all aspects of a tourist experience can forge customer-centric relationships that fulfill the needs of small groups of customers by innovating to their niche demands and interests.

Given the increased recognition, many trans-border special interest groups, subcultures, and others with similar affiliations, ideas, taste and lifestyle, businesses and destinations may develop products for emerging niches that have yet to take hold. They may initiate and provide new tourist products and customized experiences before a market exists for them so as to promote belief in a niche before it materializes for participants who have money to spend. Businesses that identify a niche before others and develop it by concentrated marketing can create a base of 'early majority' customers, and may hope to build authority and dominance over a niche market. Such an approach, however specialized, supports and grows diversity of choice, since each innovation is according to a diverse idea, taste, lifestyle, preferences and niche interest, with many willing to pay premium prices to have their demands, needs and interests met. This has led to niche tourists being characterized as wealthier, better-educated and more desirable consumers (Robinson and Novelli 2005) because rather than consume a narrow range of high volume, low value, largely standardized products, niche tourist consumption is primarily motivated by very specific activities, peoples, places, events or pasts. However, such conclusions can only be drawn from particular demand segments and the particularities of a supply system in particular locations and times (Trauer 2006).

Classifying niche tourists and tourism

While Robinson and Novelli (2005: 5) argue that there are 'no formal rules for what can, or what cannot, be referred to as niche tourism and there exists considerable variation under this broad term', they do make a division between niche tourism and mass tourism activities, a split, that may be seen as arbitrary, since many of the niches mentioned by the authors may have already gone on to become mass markets. They do make a division between macro-niches and micro-niches, and thereby create sub-divisions. A macro-niche is characterized as a relatively large market sector (i.e. cultural tourism, sport tourism, etc.), with each capable of been broken down as micro-niche activities and practices of a particular parent group (i.e. cultural tourism may include genealogical tourism and faith tourism as micro-niches). Marson (2011) goes on to argue that as this micro-niche tourism grows, it begins to fragment into smaller products and markets (i.e. faith tourism fragments into pilgrimage). Micro-niches are often in danger of being objectified, reduced to economic value; Robinson's and Novelli's (2005) model categorization of niche tourism forming a common-sense meaning spectrum does allow for continued innovation, diversity and research. The authors also argue that niche tourism can be related to one of three approaches. They are a 'geographical or demographic approach' wherein 'place' plays a key role in tourism consumption (i.e. wine growing areas and their related activities in wine tourism), a 'product related approach' when the presence of activities, attractions, settlements, food and other amenities is emphasized, and a 'customer related approach' when tourist requirements and expectations are the focus of the niche tourism marketing approach.

Micro niche tourism markets mentioned in research have included photographic tourism, geotourism, youth tourism, faith tourism, gay tourism, dark tourism, genealogy tourism, gastronomic tourism, wellness tourism, whisky tourism, bicycle tourism, slum tourism, educational tourism, volunteer tourism, battlefield tourism, adventure tourism, gaming tourism, wildlife/safari tourism, agritourism, culinary tourism, diaspora tourism, drug tourism, ecotourism, geotourism, health tourism, literary tourism, pro-poor tourism, rural tourism, social tourism and much more (Novelli 2005; Papathanassis 2011; Robinson *et al.* 2011). Such broad clustering is helpful but often deceiving. It helps with facilitating promotional plans, targeted marketing, estimating numbers and creating appropriate price points. However, many micro-niches remain largely underexplored (usually those that don't promise profitability), while other 'written about' niches go unchallenged, with little in the way of a balanced corpus of research and literature surrounding many, except by those eager to structure them as growth markets, even if such analysis leading to that conclusion is based on derived or short-term demand. Employed labels and typologies that suggest market niche participants share similar different traits can be deceiving, given it is inadequate to label anyone an 'ecotourist' just because they visit a protected area or label anyone who stays in a backpacker hostel a 'backpacker', niches and their participants often engaging in very different practices for very different reasons. A label such as 'adventure tourism' may encompass hundreds of activities, whilst other labels simply overlap so much as to make any understanding of the participants' needs difficult (i.e. war tourism, battlefield tourism, military tourism, disaster tourism). Such labels also do not address whether various 'soft' or more 'serious' participants exist within any given niche, with labels often little more than 'adjectival tourism' (all forms of tourism that have an adjective in front of them). Such labels may also be driven by conceptual research (i.e. existential tourism, experiential tourism). That said, a growing academic corpus investigating niche tourism from demand and supply-side perspectives, and incorporating other variables such as the media, has established niche tourism beyond a list of 'instances, case studies and variations' (Franklin and Crang 2001: 5). Research on demand systems (i.e. level of involvement, interest and financial situation) and the supply system (i.e. tourism places/destinations, tourist products) suggests that when you combine all these different niches, it rivals the mass market in size and span.

Marketing

The persuasive discursive context generated by a tourism-industrial complex is primarily based on scale economies, low prices, branding and saturation mass marketing in traditional tourism markets. It is a top-down approach that may be applied to a society at large or through (large) market segmentation. The more specialized, flexible and customer tailored offerings inherent to niche tourism, however, are dependent on understanding motivations, demographics, buying behaviour, lifestyle characteristics and the psychographics of a particular tightly defined market niche. Niche marketing is 'a method to meet customer needs through tailoring goods and services for small markets' (Stanton *et al.*, 1991). In niche marketing, 'the focus is on the customer and on profit; niche marketers specialize in serving marketing niches. Instead of pursuing the whole market (mass marketing), or large segments of the market, these firms target segments within segments or, for the sake of simplicity, niche' (Dalgic and Leeuw 1994: 44).

Businesses that identify different market niches and meet their needs need a well-developed understanding of its participants, before any decision on promotional planning, marketing messages, communication tools and distribution channels is made. As businesses develop a customer-centric approach so as to assist niche tourists (or those with a more critical form of subjectivity that refuse any label) in becoming self-transformed, they are looking to penetrate niches by understanding motivations and meeting customer needs so as to generate enough profit to make the effort worthwhile. A lack of detailed research or information reduces the effectiveness of marketing campaigns, whilst better intelligence and an understanding of how niche tourists are involved in the 'co-creation' of experience (Binkhorst *et al.* 2009) would allow businesses to develop niche markets and engage in more efficient marketing, contributing to more rapid and evenly based growth.

Since niches are often discovered and cultivated as a market by small businesses owners, often fronted by enthusiastic entrepreneurs, they may be able to identify underserved niches, emerging niches and changing values without the benefit of extensive market research. They are often 'closer' to their product consumers and they may also feel they 'know' their customers better, and therefore they are better placed to gather the 'customer intelligence' needed to create emotional relationships while innovating differentiated products and services. Lifestyle entrepreneurs (run by specialists, hobbyists and enthusiasts) can use reputational or relational capital in their networks and their own experiences to start up a business in a particular niche (Peters *et al.* 2009), but increasingly use online-offline market surveys and data mining to identify potential niche market segments and develop smarter niche-marketing campaigns to explore those niches which are growing. A host of new and often free online tools have emerged to help businesses identify and develop a niche business. Tools such as the Ice Rocket Trend tool (http://trend.icerocket.com/) may, for example, indicate how popular a certain topic or niche is, while other tools may help to investigate the online popularity of a given niche, subculture or interest group. Businesses are also looking to destination marketing organizations (DMOs) and Central Statistics Offices to conduct frequent and more detailed surveys of visitors and their requirements, as well as utilizing national census data and ideas from customers themselves. Such tools, techniques and sources can quickly identify niches driven to the surface because of environmental, political, social, technological and economic changes (i.e. increased urbanization leading to a growth in niche active tourism in the countryside). Large and established tourism institutions in contrast, while armed with market research data, a better understanding of modern technology (i.e. communications, analytical tools) and an inventory of exploitable natural, cultural and historical resources at destinations, will need to tailor individual niche marketing plans to suit particular markets and break with transactional relationships using disruptive marketing. A top-down marketing and segmentation approach will lack the nuance and credibility of a customer-centric, bottom-up approach.

Niche marketing campaigns

As a fragmented industry is recognized, businesses are moving away from mass marketing to niche marketing or even micro marketing (tailoring products and marketing to suit the tastes of specific individuals and geographic locations). A niche's establishment is often linked to a business's, a 'niche marketing' philosophy. Techniques are required to communicate business depth, values, and competencies to niche consumers, through credible claims, testimonials, accreditation, motivational messages and consistent images, so as to cultivate respect and trust while forging closer long term customer relationships. Rather than pursue the whole market (or segments), businesses target niches using bottom-up 'down to earth', 'below the line', 'relationship', Dalgic (2006: 10) noting how 'niche marketers specialise in serving marketing niches' through a bottom-up approach where the marketer starts from the needs of a few customers and gradually builds up a larger customer base (Shani and Chalasani 1992). However, the complexities of developing niche tourism markets and communicating with a possibly widely scattered niche population means niche marketing interactions must be thoughtfully designed. Whilst a niche should promise potential profits and growth, niche marketing is about developing a strong foothold by branding, building awareness and driving long-term demand so as to serve a niche viably and profitably. However, it is a challenge since businesses have to make a profit from relatively low sales. This means marketing costs and other overheads must be kept low, since they can be spread over a high output. As fixed costs per unit are relatively large, high prices have to be charged to be successful in a niche market.

To be sufficiently recognizable or differentiated, communication through websites, engaging niche users through blogs, niche market trade shows, business networking, brochures and personal communications, may require partnering with established retailers, specialized tour operators, niche publications and tourism boards for cutting through a marketplace saturated with competing messages. Due to the high level of sophistication and individualism of many niches, the development of relationships through computer technologies, mobile devices, mobile apps and social media, while fraught with complexity, has both marketing opportunities and challenges. Business owners must also seek out and link the right cluster of activities, peoples, events, partners and cross-sector information that gives enough pull and credibility for target niches in a way in which they can create meaningful tourist experiences. This approach has the benefit of increasing the visibility of niche products as well as creating added value to the overall tourist experience by giving tourists greater variety and diversity. These networks also allow tourists more freedom and independence to pursue their own interests within a niche, resulting in more individualized and customized tourist experiences. Such 'place' networks may also create the impetus for joined up destination marketing. However, such a move depends on creating internal place identification amongst the network participants and a general integration of products into the fabric of a place and destination.

Niche marketing at a destination level

So successfully has niche tourism competed in an increasingly competitive and cluttered tourism environment, that localities, regions and nations have after assessment of their inventory of resources (products, businesses, events, subcultures) used joined up niche marketing campaigns to focus on (economically) prioritized and tightly defined niche markets, making those events, businesses etc. 'market fit' for specific niches. It is an approach that could be aimed at diversifying, differentiating and rejuvenating tourism products, acquiring a competitive edge, maximizing the tourism potential of a destination or using niche tourism to kickstart a tourism industry. By designing a destination to meet the needs of a certain niche, destinations at a national level have successfully diversified their tourism industry, but any city (i.e. Bangkok – medical tourism) or locality may also be marketed where products are identified as 'fitting' within a niche. While Mongolia has sought to promote horse riding, fly-fishing, cultural expeditions and visits to nomad based communities to mid- to upscale niche markets (Gantemur 2012), Newquay in the United Kingdom has promoted itself as a surfing destination, creating a network of specialist shops, training schools and accommodation establishments for surfers (Meethan 2002). Other examples may include archaeological tourism in Sudan and Ethiopia, fishing in The Gambia, trophy-hunting in South Africa, surfing in Côte D'Ivoire and diving tourism in Eritrea (World Bank 2009).

However, some destinations have drawn accusations that they market fictional niche products or market niche environments as 'themes' to facilitate place marketing. These fictional competencies are often unrealistically produced for political and economic reasons. Destinations, for example, may market their distinction and differentiation through their subcultural life (i.e. gay districts in Manchester – Hughes 2003) to tourists as a signal of its uniqueness. Grazian (2003) argues that Chicago, for example, invented and marketed its status as the blues capital of the world by creating commercialized niche tourist attractions for those seeking authentic black blues culture.

Challenges

Certain late twentieth-century niche practices have expanded to impact society at large, having becoming embedded in new processes, spaces and places of regeneration and even post-conflict resolution (i.e. Cambodia), its practitioners often using innovative customer-centric niche marketing strategies to attract tourists, creating both opportunities and challenges. Mass niches remain burdened with the cultural, political, social, economic and environmental baggage of 'tourism' since niche tourism remains linked to a spatial logic and tourist consumption. While smaller businesses, volunteer groups and local communities may offer disassociation from a tourist industrial complex and grant more agency, choice and inventiveness, they too manufacture and trade in experiences and exploit the demand for emotional involvement and authenticity. While often innovative, flexible and responsive to emerging niche market needs, niche businesses are subject to the 'coercive laws of competition' that may eventually force such independent efforts to behave like capitalist enterprises, even when their product is politically, socially, environmentally or culturally sensitive (safari tourism, pro-poor tourism, slum tourism, gay tourism, dark tourism). As niches impact on the centre, they are often subject to the attention of larger firms looking to grow or change and driven by competitive reasons to pursue leadership positions by expanding each niche to its full potential by whatever (exploitative) means. Since small businesses are often under-capitalized and business fragile, when combined with weak regulatory checks, low barriers to entry, competitive intensity and difficulty of supervision, a short-term profit focus may emerge.

New challenges emerge when niche practices and the infrastructure that surrounds them become popular and fundamental to the mainstream tourism industry. They may create their own issues, controversies and challenges, with tourism marketers often struggling to manage the messages around changing processes, spaces and places of transition when 'success' strikes the spaces, systems, processes, communities that originally made development appropriate for a destination. There is also the risk that niche tourism makes fragile communities and destinations visible in a global context, reducing people and places into something only important as marketing attributes appealing to a mid- to upscale niche market interest and taste. The activities and practices that attract tourists may also become magnified, distorted, lost, or refuted in the process of growth and transition. Gallipoli, often associated with battlefield tourism through its Anzac day commemorations, has become associated with backpacker tourism and educational tourism after niche growth and commercial cross sell.

Marketers have also struggled to deal with the fall-out-of niche tourism practices which are found to under-deliver in terms of expected economic benefits (i.e. job creation), sustainability and when niche development and management have adverse impacts on the sustainable development of destinations (e.g. small cruises to Antarctica). While many niches, when developed appropriately, can enhance the local economy, preserve a destination for future generations and cultivate ethnical tourists, certain niche activities may not be suitable for some destinations and their communities. The development of niche tourism in communities is also challenging, since those involved in tourism, while enthusiastic, often lack the professional skills and experience required to successfully attract and satisfy niche tourists. This is especially true if a community seeks familiarity with particular subcultures for marketing and promotion purposes. This may be exacerbated in relation to tourism products and services built around specialist knowledge and training (adventure tourism, safari tourism, photographic tourism). Niche tourism may also not offer a solution to those destinations seeking a form or type that is more sustainable or integrated to the real economy than mass tourism.

Further research

Niche tourism has become a focus for conferences, modules in formal academia and institutions and investigations by academics, practitioners, policy makers, consultants and researchers. However, the focus is usually on a small number of established niches, rather than those in decline, while many others remain unexplored. There is a need to expand beyond the focus of niches as a 'consumption process' (Novelli 2005) with more research required on why certain niches emerge and the specific needs, interests and motivations that sustain them, as well as the different motivations and practices of those within a niche. Such research may create a greater understanding of niche tourist behaviour so as to better aid small businesses to identify a profitable niche and position/target their products. There is also a lack of understanding as to the challenges and complexities businesses face if seeking to attract specific niche tourism markets to specific areas, and whether success can lead to neighbourhood, community, regional and national development. There is also a gap in knowledge as to how supportive linked networks may be developed between niche businesses and the role of regional and national governments in developing, promoting and facilitating niche tourism. Further research is also required in understanding the complexities of the relationships niche tourists form with people, places and pasts as they come to consume and experience them, the impact niche tourism development may have on future destination development and whether forms of niche tourism could be more sustainably developed and managed by businesses and communities.

Conclusions

The stark dichotomy between mass and niche is too simple to capture the development of niche tourism and tourists. Social, economic, political and cultural factors combined with innovations in information, communications and transport technologies, have given impetus to individuals seeking new bonds, social differentiation, distinction and status. These are deep forces, and for many, the economic crises (2007–current) will hasten individuals to rethink aspects of their lives – from where they live, how they work, to how they invest their lives. Rather than consume discourses provided by a tourist-industrial complex, the fullest stretches of the imagination are now sought (and increasingly catered for and met) in the margins. Individuals can now imagine themselves in a countless variety of settings and practices no matter how remote or inaccessible, the imagination envisaging global possibilities often far from their immediate environments. This chapter, in seeking to make sense of this reflexive identity search and longing for unscripted spaces, peoples and cultures, argues that profound societal changes have enabled the development of what is commonly labelled niche tourism. A constant mutual exchange between suppliers and markets has enabled thousands of small to medium enterprises, and, more recently, large firms and destination marketing organizations to serve, co-produce and collaborate so as to develop niche products. These diverse consumption related activities have become woven into the social, political and economic lives of communities, villages, towns and cities across the globe. The development and access to new tourism experiences has helped integrate localities and consumers into the wider tourism economy and helped extend consumer choice, and thereby create a global consumer marketplace that is a major driver in tourism growth.

Business success depends on gathering and analyzing information so as to sense and respond to rapidly changing customer interests and deliver the right niche product, at the right time, at the right price, for the right customer; customer intelligence is required to identify, evaluate and meet the needs of 'niche' markets whose similarity of ideas, taste, lifestyle have led to similar consumption patterns. Products, services, events and destinations offered to niches through niche marketing must offer differentiation and specialization, and the means to support the staging and transformation of the self. Where individuals mobilize themselves to reflexively align with the value or fundamental truths associated with a niche product, an immersive performance can potentially provide power, taste, uniqueness and feelings of 'being someone'. The chapter sought to look at some of the complexities when seeking to identify and meet niche market needs as well as pursue a niche marketing strategy. While as a term, 'niche tourism' remains contestable (vis-à-vis other terms such as special interest tourism), market fragmentation, differentiation and specialization will continue to remain important features of tourism.

References

Appadurai, A. (1996) *Modernity at Large: Cultural Dimensions of Globalization*. Minneapolis, London: University of Minnesota.

Aradau, C., Huysmans, J. and Squire, V. (2010) 'Acts of European Citizenship: A Political Sociology of Mobility', *Journal of Common Market Studies*, 48(4): 945–65.

Ateljevic, I. and Doome, S. (2000) 'Staying within the Fence Lifestyle Entrepreneurship', *Journal of Sustainable Tourism*, 8(5): 378–92.

Bauman, Z. (2001) *Community: Seeking Safety in an Insecure World*. Cambridge: Polity Press.

Binkhorst, E. and Den Dekker, T. (2009) 'Agenda for Co-Creation Tourism Experience Research', *Journal of Hospitality Marketing & Management*, 18(2/3): 311–27.

Boniface, P. (1998) 'Tourist Culture', *Annals of Tourism Research*, 25(3): 746–49.

Bruner, E.M. (1991) 'Transformation of Self in Tourism', *Annals of Tourism Research*, 18(2): 238–50.

— (2005) *Culture on Tour: Ethnographies of Travel*. Chicago: University of Chicago Press.

Butler, R.W. (1980) 'The Concept of the Tourist Area Life-cycle of Evolution: Implications for Management of Resources', *Canadian Geographer*, 24(1): 5–12.

Cresswell, T. (2006) *On the Move*. London: Routledge.

Crouch, D. (2006) 'Tourism, Consumption and Rurality', in P. Cloke, T. Marsden and P.H. Mooney (eds) *Handbook of Rural Studies*. London: Sage, pp. 355–64.

Dalgic, T. (2006) *Handbook of Niche Marketing: Principles and Practice*. New York: The Haworth Press.

Dalgic, T. and Leeuw, M. (1994) 'Niche Marketing Revisited: Concept, Applications and Some European Cases', *European Journal of Marketing*, 28(4): 39–55.

Desforges, L. (2000) 'Travelling the World: Identity and Travel Biography', *Annals of Tourism Research*, 27(4): 926–45.

Edensor, T. (2000) 'Staging Tourism: Tourists as Performers', *Annals of Tourism Research*, 27(2): 322–44.

Favell, A., Feldblum, M. and Smith, M. (2006) 'The Human Face of Global Mobility: A Research Agenda', in E. Smith and A. Favell (eds) *The Human Face of Global Mobility*. New Brunswick, NJ: Transaction Publishers, pp. 1–25.

Franklin, A. and Crang, M. (2001) 'The Trouble with Tourism and Travel Theory', *Tourist Studies*, 1(1): 5–22.

Gantemur, D. (2012) 'Mongol Passion: History and Challenges – Can Tourism Be a Tool to Empower It?', in R. Conrady and M. Buck (eds) *Trends and Issues in Global Tourism*. Berlin: Springer–Verlag, pp. 49–56.

Giddens, A. (1991) *Modernity and Self-Identity: Self and Society in the Late Modern Age*. Cambridge: Polity Press.

Gottdiener, M. (1995) *Postmodern Semiotics: Material Culture and the Forms of Postmodern Life*. Oxford: Blackwell.

Grazian, D. (2003) *Blue Chicago: The Search for Authenticity in Urban Blues Clubs*. Chicago: University of Chicago Press.

Grossberg, L. (1996) 'Identity and Cultural Studies: Is that All There Is?', in S. Hall and P. du Gay (eds) *Questions of Cultural Identity.* London: Sage, pp. 87–107.

Holden, A. (2008) *Environment and Tourism*, 2nd edn. Abingdon, UK: Routledge.

Hughes, H.L. (2003) 'Marketing Gay Tourism in Manchester: New Market for Urban Tourism or Destruction of "Gay Space"?', *Journal of Vacation Marketing*, 9(2): 152–63.

Ki-Moon, B. (2009) Opening address of H.E. Mr. Ban ki–Moon, Secretary General of the United Nations at the third global forum on migration and development. Athens – 4 November 2009. Available: http://www.un.org/esa/population/migration/Opening_remarks_SG_Athens.pdf (accessed 17 July 2012).

Lew, A.A. (2008) 'Long Tail Tourism: New Geographies for Marketing Niche Tourism Products', *Journal of Travel and Tourism Marketing*, 25(3–4): 409–19.

Marson, D. (2011) 'From Mass Tourism to Niche Tourism', in P. Robinson, S. Heitmann and P. Dieke (eds) *Research Themes for Tourism*. Wallingford: CABI Publishing, pp. 1–15.

Meethan, K. (2002) 'Selling the Difference: Tourism Marketing in Devon and Cornwall, South-west England', in R. Voase (ed.) *Tourism in Western Europe: A Collection of Case Histories.* Wallingford: CABI Publishing, pp. 23–42.

Morley. D. (2004) 'At Home with Television', in L. Spigel and J. Olsson (eds) *Television after TV.* Durham, NC: Duke University Press, pp. 303–23.

Novelli, M. (ed) (2005) *Niche Tourism – Contemporary Issues, Trends and Cases.* Oxford: Elsevier Butterworth-Heinemann.

O'Regan, M. (2010) 'Backpacker Mobilities: The Practice and Performance of Travellerscapes in a Global World', unpublished thesis, University of Brighton.

Papathanassis, A. (ed) (2011) *The Long Tail of Tourism: Holiday Niches and their Impact on Mainstream Tourism.* Wiesbaden: Gabler.

Peters, M., Frehse, J. and Buhalis, D. (2009) 'The Importance of Lifestyle Entrepreneurship: A Conceptual Study of the Tourism Industry', *PASOS Journal of Tourism*, 7(3): 393–405.

Poon, A. (1989) 'Competitive Strategies for New Tourism', in C. Cooper (ed.) *Progress in Tourism Recreation and Hospitality Management*, Vol. 1. London: Belhaven Press, pp. 91–102.

Robertson, G. (1994) 'As the World Turns: Introduction', in G. Robertson, M. Mash, L. Tickner, J. Bird, B. Curtis and T. Putnam (eds) *Travellers' Tales: Narratives of Home and Displacement.* London: Routledge, pp. 1–6.

Robinson, M. and Novelli, M. (2005) 'Niche Tourism: An Introduction', in M. Novelli (ed.) *Niche Tourism: Contemporary Issues, Trends and Cases.* Oxford: Butterworth-Heinemann Ltd, pp. 1–14.

Robinson, P., Heitmann, S. and Dieke P. (2011) (eds) *Research Themes for Tourism.* Wallingford, UK: CABI Publishing.

Savage, M., Bagnall, G. and Longhurst, B. (2005) *Globalization and Belonging.* London: Sage.

Shani, D. and Chalasani, S. (1992) 'Exploiting Niches Using Relationship Marketing', *Journal of Consumer Marketing*, 9(3): 33–42.

Shaw, G. and Williams, A.M. (1994) *Critical Issues in Tourism: A Geographical Perspective.* Oxford: Blackwell Publishers Ltd.

Sheller, M. and Urry, J. (2006) 'The New Mobilities Paradigm', *Environment and Planning A*, 38(2): 207–26.

Skinner, D. and Rosen, P. (2007) 'Hell is Other Cyclists: Rethinking Transport and Identity', in D. Horton, P. Cox and P. Rosen (eds) *Cycling and Society*. London: Ashgate, pp. 83–96.

Soguk, N. (2003) 'Incarcerating Travels: Travel Stories, Tourist Orders, and the Politics of the "Hawai'ian Paradise"', *Journal of Tourism and Cultural Change*, 1(1): 29–53.

Stanton, W.E.J., Etzel, M.J. and Walker, B.J. (1991) *Fundamentals of Marketing.* New York, NY: McGraw-Hill.

Van der Duim, R. (2007) 'Tourismscapes: An Actor-network Perspective', *Annals of Tourism Research*, 34(4): 961–76.

Weber, K. (2001) 'Outdoor Adventure Tourism. A Review of Research Approaches', *Annals of Tourism Research*, 28(2), 360–77.

World Bank (2009) *The State of Tourism in Africa.* Available: <http://siteresources.worldbank.org/EXTAIRTRANSPORT/Resources/515180-1262792532589/State_of_Tourism_in_Africa_May_2010.pdf> (accessed 4 March 2013).

21
Searching the travel network

Zheng Xiang, Yeongbae Choe and Daniel R. Fesenmaier

Introduction

Information search is one of the most important features of traveller decision making. This is because the tourism product is intangible, experiential and complex and therefore, travel planning often requires a substantial amount of information (Fodness and Murray 1998; Vogt and Fesenmaier 1998). Travellers often actively seek information to plan a trip, and the information search process itself can be seen as an essential part of the travel experience. As such, information available to individual travellers has significant impact on various aspects of traveller decision making, especially when choosing a particular destination to visit (Fodness and Murray 1998; Vogt and Fesenmaier 1998; Gursoy and McCleary 2004; Jeng and Fesenmaier 2002; Bieger and Laesser 2004).

Research on travel information search is especially relevant for tourism marketing (Jang 2005) in that providing the right information at the right place during the right time holds the key to successfully meeting travellers' needs and wants. Today's information technology enables marketers to identify and develop personalized information for an extremely complex product such as a tourist destination (Hoffman and Novak 1996; Fesenmaier, Wöber and Werthner 2006). It is argued that because of the ubiquity of the Internet both at home and on-the-go, and the growing adoption of mobile devices such as smartphones with high storage and computing capabilities, travel information search behaviour is going through fundamental changes. Within this context, information search for travel products has become more fluid, flexible, fragmented and more likely to be intertwined with other tasks within one's everyday life. As a consequence certain search strategies such as on-going search and *en route* search are becoming increasingly prominent.

This chapter introduces and synthesizes the literature related to travel information search with the goal of providing a new perspective on its role within travel marketing. This chapter is organized into five sections. Specifically, Section 2 summarizes the literature on travel information search including the more traditional views on the search process, types and source of search, search strategies. Section 3 discusses the factors that influence search behaviour including travellers' personal characteristics, situational needs and decision frames. Section 4 reviews recent literature on online travel information search while in Section 5 it is argued that today's information technology fundamentally transforms the conditions of information search and calls for a paradigm shift. Finally, the future of travel information search behaviour and its implications for tourism marketing are discussed.

Travel information search

Understanding the uniqueness of travel and tourism products has always been of primary interest to tourism researchers because they are intangible personal service products which can induce functional, financial, physical, psychological and social risks. Traditional perspectives of travel information search have focused on functional needs. According to this perspective, the search for information enables travellers to reduce the level of uncertainty and to enhance the quality of a trip (Bieger and Laesser 2004; Fesenmaier and Vogt 1992; Fodness and Murray 1997; Vogt and Fesenmaier 1998). Vogt and Fesenmaier (1998) expanded the conventional functional information search perspective by identifying four additional needs: hedonic, innovation, aesthetic and sign needs. This view argues that information needs other than functional needs capture the basic psychological, sociological, aesthetical and symbolic aspects of information searching. Based on this model, it is understood that not everyone who collects information actually intends to travel, and many of the travel information search motivations can be considered as leisure and recreation-based. In a similar vein, Cho and Jang (2008) explored vacation information value structure for the pre-trip information search and identified five information value dimensions, i.e. utilitarian, risk avoidance, hedonic, sensation seeking and social, and empirically validated them.

With its roots in consumer information processing theory, the process-based perspective of travel information search has a long history and a prominent presence in tourism research (Woodside and Lysonski 1989; Um and Crompton 1992). Based on this view, travel decision making consists of several stages of information search and processing: travellers begin the information search process by accessing internal memory sources to list product alternatives after recognizing a purchase need. If this initial list of alternatives is satisfactory, the evaluation phase can begin; however, if the list derived from internal memory is not satisfactory, individuals start searching for information using external sources such as word-of-mouth from friends and social circles, mass media channels, etc. Once a satisfactory amount of information is accumulated, the various alternatives are evaluated and subsequently selected or eliminated.

Considerable research has examined traveller information search strategies where the most widely applied classification distinguishes between pre-purchase and on-going information search (Bloch, Sherrell and Ridgway 1986). Pre-purchase information search efforts are those that aim at increasing product-related knowledge to inform a specific purchase decision. On-going search, on the other hand, provides additional benefits by focusing on the future use of the obtained information as well as satisfaction with the search activity itself. Most research on travel information search considers pre-purchase information search as the key component in decision making (Vogt and Fesenmaier 1998; Bieger and Laesser 2004). Stewart and Vogt (1999) proposed an alternative model that describes the *en route* information search and decision making behaviour. According to this model, travellers develop trip plans before their trip, but these plans are subject to change, especially when they fail to satisfy travellers' timely needs during the course of the trip. Plan failure then initiates plan revision. They further argued that the occurrence of unplanned behaviour, which leads to revision of a travel plan, is likely when travellers are exposed to new information, disparities between expectations and actual experience, unanticipated constraints during a trip. Following from their model, Hwang (2011) proposed a two-phase framework that recognizes a pre-trip phase and an *en route* phase and seems to be an appropriate representation of a decision process that reflects the differences between planned and actual behaviour.

The information search process has also been evaluated within a source-based perspective which argues that travellers use two different information sources to acquire knowledge for decision making, i.e. internal and external. By definition, internal information search involves one's memory and occurs prior to external search. External information search refers to everything but memory when searching for information. Internal information is an individual's personal experiences, past information search results and low-involvement learning. It can be actively or passively acquired. External information is always actively acquired through personal sources, marketer sources, neutral sources and experiential sources (Crotts 1999). The research focusing on the nature of external information sources has been extended in order to understand the level of importance of various information sources (Leiper 1990; Bieger and Laesser 2004) within the overall decision making process. Importantly, this research shows that travel-related decisions are influenced most by prior experience (internal search) and personal friends. However, recent studies by the United States Travel Association (USTA 2011) and others show that the huge majority of US travellers actively use the Internet for vacation planning, where search engines are the "first step" in the travel planning process.

Online travel information search processes

Information and communication technology (ICT) has fundamentally changed the way tourism-related information is distributed and the way people search for travel products (Gretzel, Fesenmaier and O'Leary 2006; Werthner and Klein 1999; Xiang, Wöber and Fesenmaier 2008). Pan and Fesenmaier (2006) conceptualized travel information search on the Internet as the interaction between information searchers and the information space (the part of the Internet related to tourism and travel destinations) in the context of trip planning. As shown by Figure 21.1 the travel information space contains different types of information provided by various parties in the tourism industry who are marketing their tourism products and communicate with travellers. Three components constitute the interaction: a travel information searcher, the interface and the travel information space (Figure 21.1). Travellers' situational factors, knowledge and skills regarding travelling and the travel information space, contribute to effective travel information search; the travel information space refers to all the travel related web pages on the Internet which potential travellers can access; the interface consists of search engines, the information structure of websites, and various metatags and link structures which are used to facilitate the information search. This framework raises a number of interesting questions regarding the growing impact of the Internet on travel information search including: How do we understand today's travellers who are using the Internet as opposed to those using conventional media? And how do we understand the various interfaces that represent the increasingly complex travel information spaces?

Following this framework, Pan and Fesenmaier (2006) devised an experiment to describe the information search process of travel planning in a trip planning exercise in which 15 subjects were asked to plan a weekend trip to destination. This study confirmed that the travel information search follows a hierarchical structure, in which the process can be divided into different "chapters". One chapter denotes one aspect of travel planning, for example, selecting a hotel, an attraction, or a transportation method. Furthermore, one chapter can be divided into different episodes. For example, to make an accommodation choice, the planner may consider several alternatives by visiting different hotel websites. Each alternative considered is one episode of the accommodation chapter. Their mental foci at each chapter and episode are different.

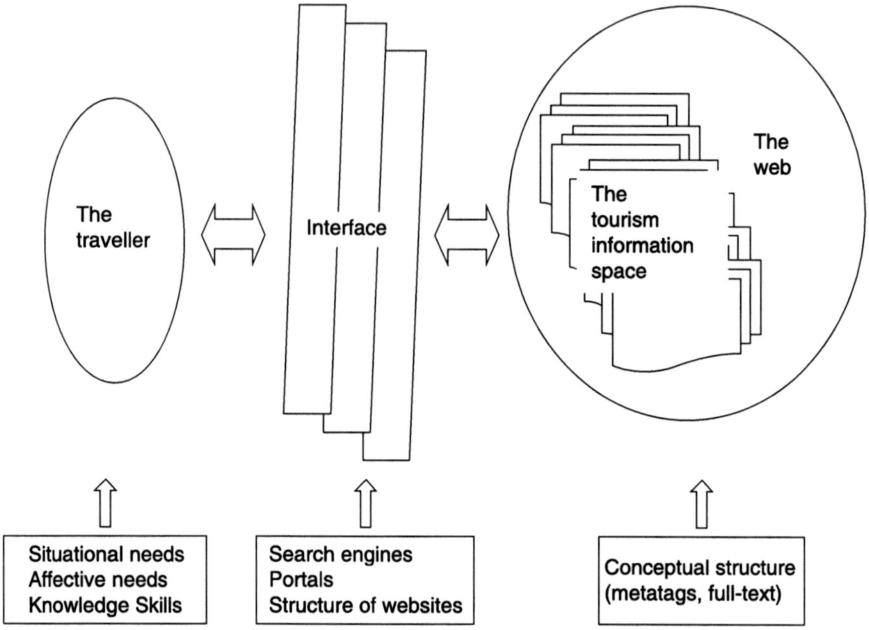

Figure 21.1 Travellers interacting with the Internet when searching information (Pan and Fesenmaier 2006).

However, there are commonalities in the chapter level since results show that more than half of the subjects make their accommodation choice first.

With the amount of travel-related information continuously growing, tools such as search engines have become increasingly important in directing online travel. The impact of the Internet has generated a considerable amount of interest in understanding the use of search engines for travel planning (Xiang *et al.* 2008; Xiang and Gretzel 2010; Fesenmaier *et al.* 2011). For example, Xiang *et al.* (2008) focus attention on understanding the representation of the tourism domain on the Internet. Analyses of search results from a major search engine were conducted in order to assess:

1 the visibility of destination-related information;
2 the visibility of various industry sectors within destinations; and
3 the power structure of websites that represent a specific destination.

The results show that although there is a huge amount of information indexed, travellers can access only a tiny fraction of the domain; also, there are a relatively small number of websites dominating the search results.

Travel information search is increasingly being captured in travellers' 'footprints' online. Recently, Xiang and Pan (2011) studied patterns in travel queries using transaction log files from a number of search engines and show important patterns in the way travel queries are constructed as well as the commonalities and differences in travel queries about different cities in the United States. The ratio of travel queries among all queries about a specific city seems to associate with the 'touristic' level of that city. Also, keywords in travellers' queries reflect their knowledge about the city and its competitors. Fesenmaier *et al.* (2011) suggest that the use of a search engine by travellers can be described in three stages, where the first stage, namely *Pre-Search Conditions*, reflects travellers' use of (or preference for) various types of information as well as the perceived usefulness of the various travel tools (i.e. types of websites) available on the Internet. The second stage, namely *Search Process*, describes the basic strategies travellers use to navigate through the Internet to find relevant information in order to make various travel decisions. These strategies act as 'frames' within which the information accessed through use of search engines is evaluated (Dholakia and Bagozzi 2001; Fesenmaier and Jeng 2000). The third stage, i.e. *Post-Search Evaluation*, focuses on the overall evaluation of search engines. Importantly, this stage of use not only results in overall evaluation (i.e. satisfied vs. not satisfied), but also attitude formation toward search engine use for travel planning (Pan and Fesenmaier 2006). It is argued that an in-depth understanding of these relationships is essential as destination marketers seek to optimize the conversion rate between seeing the search result and actually choosing to visit the destination website.

Another important concept is information overload. As information technology further evolves, a huge amount of information has been made available on the Internet. Besides, each individual has different information processing ability and behaves differently in response to the situation they are facing (Bettman 1979; Eppler and Mengis 2004). These may affect the information seekers' perception of the quantity and the complexity of information (Henry 1980). More specifically, information overload occurs when the information processing requirement (IPR) exceeds the information processing capacity (IPC) of each individual (Bergamaschi, Guerra and Leiba 2010). Consumers suffer from information overload which would cause them to be confused, feel constrained in their abilities to set priorities and struggle to recall every piece of information needed for their decision (Eppler and Mengis 2004). The effect of information overload on decision accuracy is usually referred to as the inverted U-curve.

Once information load goes beyond the optimal point of information processing, people usually try to avoid the overloaded situation using two different strategies, filtering strategy and withdrawal strategy (Savolainen 2007). For example, some people might browse the information selectively or intend to use a recommender system, while the others stop their searching behaviour right away. The concept of information overload is evidential in certain online search behaviours, particularly in the context of using search engines. For example, the majority of online search engine users only review results in the first three search results pages (Spink and Zimmer 2008). Further, social media, online review sites and other new media such as mobile apps are generating enormous amounts of information on a daily basis. While abundance of information is beneficial for users, it may increase the level of information overload at the same time.

The Mind-Set Formation and Influence (MSFI) model proposed by Dholakia and Bagozzi (2001) integrates some of the most relevant factors of consumer search behaviours on the Internet (see Figure 21.2). According to this model, website selection, length of website visit and information obtained depend on one's mind-set. Four different mind-sets of the information seeker have been identified: deliberative, implemental, exploratory and hedonic. A deliberative mind-set represents a cognitive orientation with a focus on collecting and processing information, while an implemental mind-set is defined as the state in which a consumer's focus is oriented toward the smooth action execution for goal achievement. An exploratory mind-set refers to the state of mind in which a consumer focuses on new experiences, and a hedonic mind-set represents a state where the individual pays attention to the sensory elements of the experience. Both deliberative and implemental mind-sets are more goal-oriented whereas exploratory and hedonic mind-sets focus more on the search experience itself (Dholakia and Bagozzi 2001).

Three antecedent factors combine to determine the consumer's mind-set when one starts to use the Internet. For example, a consumer wanting to perform his/her banking activities

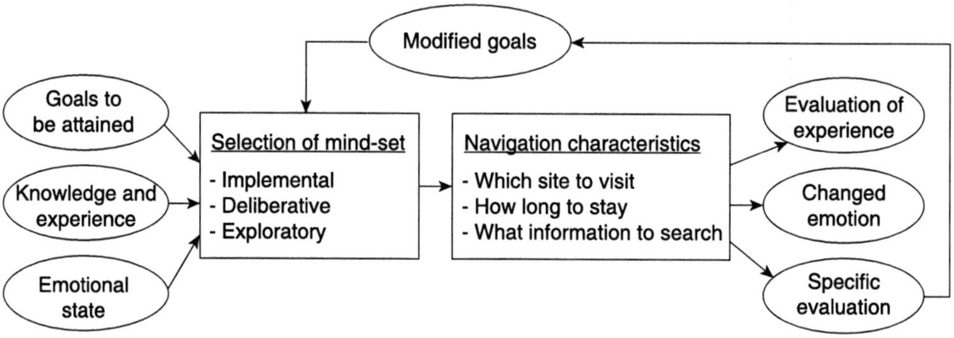

Figure 21.2 Mind-set formation and influence (MSFI) model (adapted from Dholakia and Bagozzi 2001).

online may fall into an implemental, action-focused mind-set, whereas someone wanting to plan for a vacation a few months later may start from an exploratory mind-set, browsing through a number of websites in order to accumulate information for future decision-making. Thus, an individual's mind-set can vary from time to time depending on goals to be attained, relevant knowledge/experience and the emotional state at the time the search process occurs. Also, mind-sets can change during the actual search process as the result of the interaction with the information source and/or the information found. This model of consumer mind-set formation and influence is parsimonious and has the potential to explain a variety of consumer behaviour in digital environments.

From an information seeking standpoint, Marchionini (1999) defines information search in an electronic environment as an interactive process and understanding the information environment, then, is as important as understanding the searcher's cognitive processes, as it is the interaction between the two that establishes and reveals the actual information seeking strategies of the user. Marchionini identifies eight information-seeking components, which can be described as falling into four information entities (or contexts). These contexts are summarized and compared to previous information seeking model contexts in Figure 21.4. The key supposition of Marchionini's model is that information seeking is a relatively linear process, and the information seeker looks at and evaluates one information need at a time. The evaluation either leads to the identification of a whole new information need, or reveals possible problems in the search process, resulting in the searcher re-defining the information need, employing

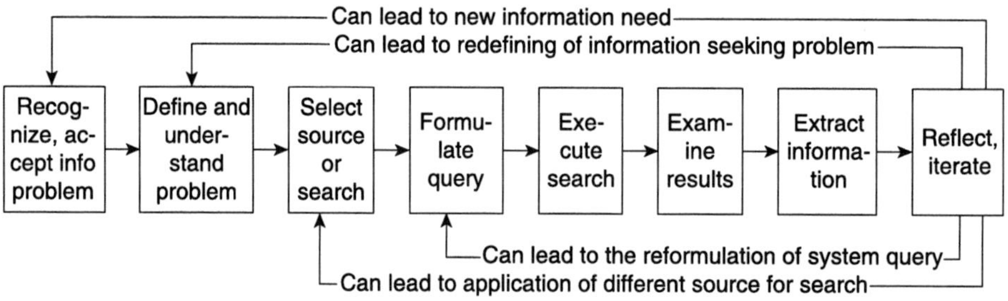

Figure 21.3 Conceptual framework of information search in an electronic environment (Marchionini 1999).

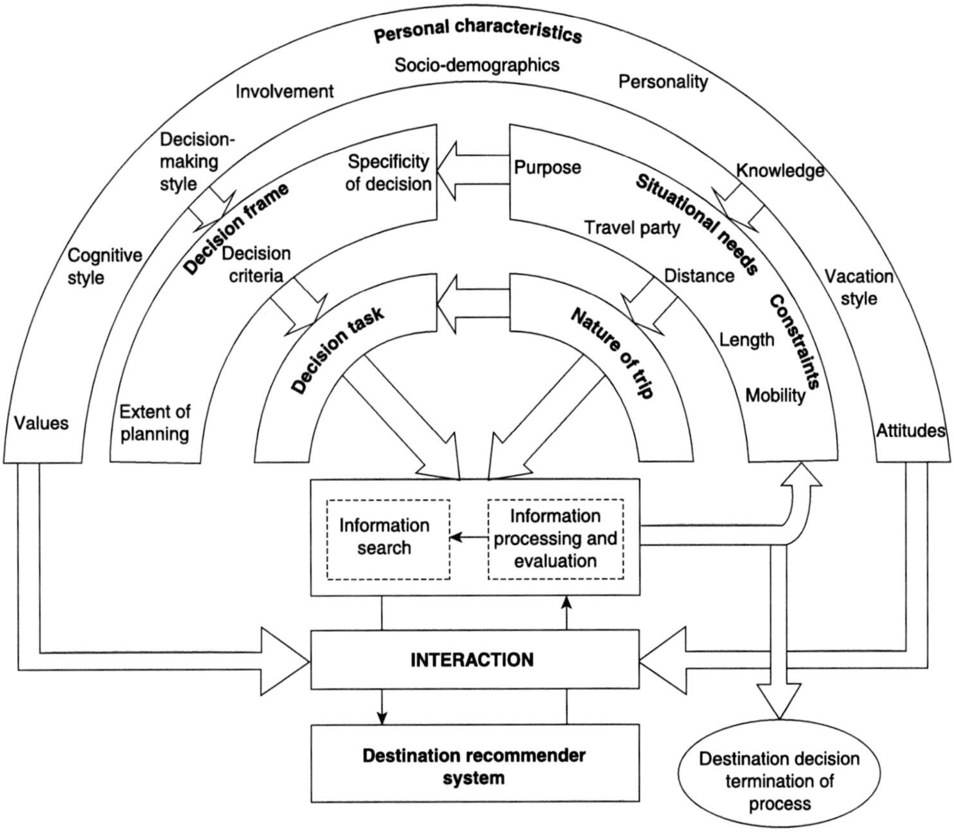

Figure 21.4 A framework of travel decision-making in interaction with an information system (adapted from Gretzel, Hwang and Fesenmaier 2012).

another electronic source, or simply formulating a new query. In reality, though, information seeking and retrieval is often far more ambiguous than this.

Factors influencing travel information search

Based on the travel destination choice and information search and processing literatures, Gretzel, Hwang and Fesenmaier (2012) developed a conceptual framework which integrates various factors that shape travel information search, particularly when one is interacting with an online system (e.g. a destination recommender system). As can be seen from Figure 21.4, the framework assumes that individuals access an online system to learn about alternative destinations and that three essential factors influence travellers' information search:

1 the traveller's personal characteristics;
2 situational needs and constraints (e.g. trip length); and
3 aspects of the decision-making process (e.g. the specificity of the choice task and decision frames used).

Each of these aspects of information search is discussed below.

Personal characteristics

Personal characteristics of the traveller potentially influence travel information search and decision-making. They include socio-demographics, knowledge, personality, involvement, values, attitudes, cognitive style, decision-making style and vacation style. Travellers' socio-demographic characteristics have been extensively studied as explanatory variables for evoked set formation, categorization of alternative destinations and antecedents of information processing (see, for example, Mayo and Jarvis 1981; Woodside and Lysonski 1989; Um and Crompton 1991; Woodside and MacDonald 1994). Characteristics such as age, education, income and marital status are often employed as surrogates for determining the travel decision-maker's resources and constraints. In terms of age, existing research indicates that older travellers tend to rely more on family and past experience as information sources (Capella and Greco 1987) and are more interested in satisfying hedonic, aesthetic and sign needs in the information search process (Vogt and Fesenmaier 1998). Also, more educated travellers with higher levels of income tend to search for more information (Gitelson and Crompton 1983; Etzel and Wahlers 1985). Women are more likely to consider functional aspects in their information search than men (Vogt and Fesenmaier 1998); in general, females are more comprehensive information processors who consider both subjective and objective attributes, and are more likely to respond to subtle cues than males (Darley and Smith 1995). Income influences the constraints within which trips have to be planned and also the extent to which a trip has to be planned to avoid additional cost.

Travellers' knowledge is an important cognitive domain that influences information search and processing behaviour as well as travel decision-making (Brucks 1985). Knowledge influences the range of alternatives considered (Snepenger, Meged, Snelling and Worrall 1990). Further, previous experience with a destination plays an important role in terms of how a destination is categorized during decision-making processes with respect to how well the location could perform when selected as a travel destination (Woodside and Lysonski 1989). Also, differences in the choice of destinations/attractions between first-time visitors and repeat visitors, that is, travellers that have prior experience with the destination, are prevalent. First-time visitors tend to choose destinations that are easily accessible while experienced visitors are more likely to consider destinations with low accessibility (McKercher 1998) and repeat visitors are more selective and less prone to visit multiple destinations (Oppermann 1992; Decrop 1999; Hwang *et al.* 2002). Interestingly, a number of different perspectives have been suggested regarding the relationship between knowledge and information search behaviour (Punj and Staelin 1983; Alba and Hutchinson 1987; Moorthy, Ratchford and Talukdar 1997). Knowledge and previous experience have been included in several studies within the context of travel information search (Manfredo 1989; Snepenger *et al.* 1990; Perdue 1993).

Travel information search and processing also depend to a great extent on individuals' level of involvement (Finn 1983; Celsi and Olsen 1988; Jamrozy, Backman and Backman 1996). For example, as the perceived risk involved in the decision task increases, situational involvement rises accordingly and individuals tend to invest more resources in external information search (Murray 1991). That is, highly involved travellers are likely to use more criteria, search for more information, use more information sources, process relevant information in detail, make more inferences and will form attitudes that are less likely to change (Celsi and Olsen 1988; Fesenmaier and Johnson 1989). In a complex decision and choice situation developing commitment and stronger attitudes is of greater need in order to accomplish the task. On the other hand, simple and routine decisions require relatively low consumer involvement (Reid and Crompton 1993).

Plog (1994) suggests that two fundamental personality dimensions are of importance within the context of tourism: allocentricism and psychocentricism. Allocentric travellers, who exhibit a self-assured and venturesome personality, are more likely to choose exotic destinations while psychocentric travellers, whose centre of attention is focused on self-doubts and anxieties, are thought to prefer familiar destinations (Plog 1994; Ross 1994). Griffith and Albanese (1996) have shown that Plog's model can be used to characterize travellers in terms of their psychographics and suggested practical use of these traits to make destination recommendations. Further, personality traits related to locus of control and risk avoidance, which influence an individual's decision-making style, play an important role in any decision-making process but are of particular importance for destination choice processes because of the high levels of uncertainty involved (Roehl and Fesenmaier 1992). Personality has also been identified as a factor with considerable influence on information search and processing strategies. For example, individuals' differences in the complexity of the causal explanations they reach to make sense of their environments suggest that personality influences the extent and nature of information search and integration patterns (Murphy 1994). Also, individuals with a tendency to postpone decisions when faced with difficult choices or conflicts have been found to engage in search patterns that are different from those used by individuals who are not indecisive (Ferrari and Dovidio 2001).

Finally, Woodside and Lysonski (1989) argue that personal value systems influence travellers' destination awareness. Um and Crompton (1991) describe personal values as an internal input that initiates the formation of an evoked set from an awareness set. Studies by Madrigal (1995) indicate that personal values are a better predictor of choice between group tours and individual tours than personality, and Zins (1998) suggests that personal values are an important antecedent variable for hotels. Attitudes are significant determinants of whether or not a destination is considered as an alternative and how the destination is evaluated in later stages of the destination choice process. The attitude–behaviour model provides explanations for human behaviour based on individual attitudes and the behavioural intentions that can be derived from them (Ajzen and Fishbein 1980). Um and Crompton (1990) argue that destinations with higher attitude scores are more likely to be included in the evoked set and, ultimately, are more likely to be selected as the final destination.

The preferred strategies in which individuals process information are referred to as cognitive style. Cognitive styles affect information gathering, evaluation and selection processes in the context of vacation trip planning (Grabler and Zins 2002). Rumetshofer, Pühretmair and Wöß (2003), and Rosen and Purinton (2004), demonstrate that information presentation needs to match the cognitive style of the traveller in order to be processed effectively. Decision-making styles are mainly viewed as a mental, cognitive orientation towards shopping and purchasing (Sproles and Kendall 1986) or a learned habitual pattern (Scott and Bruce 1995), which dominates the consumer's choice and constitutes a relatively enduring consumer personality. Vacation styles combine psychographic characteristics such as travel motives with behavioural patterns (Zins 1999). They have emerged from earlier tourist type research seeking to identify traveller segments that fundamentally differ in terms of the benefits sought from vacations (Dolnicar and Mazanec 2000). Vacation styles have been found to provide a rather stable criterion for marketing segmentation and can be seen as strong determinants of trip preferences.

Situational needs

Destination-related decisions are highly sensitive to the situation in which they occur. The literature indicates that trip characteristics are the most important determinants and include travel purpose, length of travel, distance between origin and destination, travel group composition, as well as travel mobility. Travel purpose can be generally defined as one's stated needs or motives for travel. Travel purpose is, oftentimes, closely connected to activities and settings (e.g. golf vacation or visit to a cultural heritage site) and, therefore, significantly constrains/defines the range of alternative destinations considered. Travel purpose also influences information search strategies. Fodness and Murray (1998) find that those travelling for vacation purposes are the most likely to rely on their personal experience to plan their trips.

The time available for a trip constrains the geographical range of the trip. Thus, travellers with limited amounts of time available tend to prefer nearby destinations. In contrast, travellers with more time tend to prefer more distant destinations (McKercher 1998). In this sense, length of trip constrains the range of alternatives that will be considered. Length of travel has also been identified as a factor that influences the use of particular information sources (Snepenger *et al.* 1990). Whether a destination will be considered as an alternative is also a function of the distance from home to a destination, a factor which has been included as a key variable in aggregated destination choice models (Kim and Fesenmaier 1990; Lo 1992). Empirical evidence suggests that a relationship between travel distance and information search strategies exists. For example, Pennington-Gray and Vogt (2003), among others, find that out-of-state visitors are more likely to obtain travel information at welcome centres than in-state residents.

Alternative destinations considered by a person who plans to go on a family vacation, for example, are probably different from those considered for a trip with friends. The characteristics of the travel party also impact the geographical range of alternative destinations in respect to the mobility of the travel group. A family with children tends to take short vacations at easily accessible destinations. In contrast, couples without children are more likely to choose destinations with modest accessibility (McKercher 1998). Additionally, the nature of the travel party defines the degree of heterogeneity in the group with respect to interests (Fesenmaier and Lieber 1985, 1988; Lue, Crompton and Fesenmaier 1993). In addition, travel group composition has been found to influence the information search strategy selected (Fodness and Murray 1997). Family groups tend to use media as information sources more than other types of travel parties, and are more likely to be involved in extensive search processes in order to assure satisfaction of all the members (Gitelson and Crompton 1983).

Mobility is not only a function of the nature of the travel group but also depends on the transportation mode a traveller uses during a trip (Tideswell and Faulkner 1999). Alternative destinations, which a traveller with a rental car or personal car can think of, might be unavailable to travellers who use, for instance, only public transportation. Travel mobility has an impact on the flexibility of the travel itinerary and is positively related to not only the number of destinations but also the number of attractions and activities that can be integrated into the trip. Transportation mode used can also explain certain tendencies toward multi-destination travel, as travellers with greater mobility are better equipped for visits to more than one destination (Cooper 1981). Further, Fodness and Murray (1999) find evidence for a relationship between mode of transportation and types of travel information sources used.

Decision frames

Destination decisions can be framed in various ways depending on personal preferences for certain decision-making strategies and the needs or constraints derived from the specific trip planning situation. Specifically, the number and type of decision criteria taken into account will vary based on the nature of the trip to be planned. For instance, trips defined around a specific activity such as golfing will strongly influence the frame in which the decision has to be made.

For such a trip, beach access at the destination might be desired but might not be perceived as being as important as in the case of a typical summer, sun and beach vacation. Also, personal characteristics can be assumed to influence one's need, ability and/or willingness to take certain criteria into consideration. A low annual household income, for instance, will probably encourage the adoption of a decision frame that incorporates price as a main criterion. In addition, personal cognitive styles can greatly influence the amount of information sought to support the decision-making process and especially the number of alternatives considered by the individual decision-maker (Hunt Krzystofiak, Meindl and Yousry 1989; Driver Brousseau and Hunsaker 1990). Similarly, decision-making styles will influence the timing of the decision, the extent of planning and specific criteria taken into account. For instance, an impulsive style will lead to very little planning and a small number of decision criteria while brand consciousness results in a focus on well-established travel product and services brands (Sproles and Kendall 1986). Further, destination decisions can be taken at different levels in the travel planning hierarchy, that is, one can select a main destination, a secondary destination, or places within a destination such as attractions and restaurants (Jeng and Fesenmaier 2002). Given the impact of choosing a main destination on decisions with respect to lower-level facets of a trip, being in the process of selecting the main destination of a trip implies that many characteristics of this trip are still undetermined. In contrast, if the main destination has been chosen and the decision-making process refers to finding one or more secondary destinations, one can assume that many important characteristics of the trip have already been outlined and that the range of destination alternatives in the consideration set will be rather limited. At the most specific level, destination decisions involve choosing places to visit at a destination. This latter form of destination decision can be characterized by a high level of constraint and, consequently, a relatively small number of alternatives to be considered. Depending on the specificity of the destination decision, the amount and type of information taken into account in the decision-making process will vary (Bloch *et al.* 1986). More specific destination decisions require more specific information. If no destination decision has been made, the information sought will be in the general form of destination alternatives and will often be more image-based than functional. If a main destination has been selected, the destination decision will focus on secondary destinations in proximity to the main destination. Such a decision requires image-related information but also more specific details about distances and activity/attraction portfolios to evaluate destination complementarities. Finally, those decisions that involve selecting places/attractions at a specific destination will to a large extent include detailed and more functional information in the form of opening hours, prices, admission restrictions, etc.

The changing nature of travel information search

The Internet is now comprised of a huge amount of information reportedly in the range of hundreds of billions of gigabytes and essentially comprises the 'external memory' for many people (Sparrow, Liu and Wegner 2011). Tools such as Google and other search engines provide instant access to this 'ocean' of information at one's fingertips and, as a result, individuals have now become increasingly reliant upon it for everyday life. In travel and tourism, this unimaginable amount of information has been made available through destination portals and distribution channels such as global distribution systems (GDSs), online travel agencies (OTAs) and travel specific search engines (e.g. Kayak) for promotional and transaction-related purposes. Importantly, the exponential growth of social media including websites such as TripAdvisor and Yelp has changed the dynamics of online communications and, in turn, the composition of the so-called tourism domain (Xiang and Gretzel 2010). Travel-related social media has significant influence on travel information search and sharing behaviour and, consequentially, mediates the way travellers perceive and interact with travel products and tourism destinations. Additionally, recent developments in mobile computing, particularly with the emergence of smartphones and their apps for travel, creates new locales for information search and use on-the-go where travellers' situational needs for information and communication are becoming increasingly prominent (Wang, Park and Fesenmaier 2012). The notion of 'travel in the network' (Gretzel 2010) serves as a convenient metaphor that helps us understand travel behaviour in today's increasingly connected world and which has important implications for travel information search.

It is argued that traditional views of travel information search are static and rigid and focused primarily on the pre-trip stage of decision making. This perspective generally assumes that once a trip planning task is given information search will follow suit to identify the optimal solution to the problem and which is constrained by a number of factors such as the combination of the travel party, time and financial constraints, and other variables which frame the process (Gretzel *et al.* 2006). However in the current environment, travellers do not have to commit to a 'complete' travel plan before they embark on the trip. Instead, knowing that the information is always out there will change the trip planning behaviour in that travellers may postpone some of the decisions to a later stage, resulting in more on-going and *en route* searches. A recent six year longitudinal study conducted by the National Laboratory for Tourism and eCommerce at Temple University on American travellers' trip planning behaviour clearly shows that there are important trends in travellers' search behaviour (Xiang, Wang and Fesenmaier 2013). As can be seen from Table 21.1, searching for 'information about a particular destination' has been one of the top priorities for American travellers in their travel planning activities in the past six years; however, this aspect of search is a declining trend in that there are fewer people searching for this type of information once a destination has been decided, and indicates travellers may look for information about this specific destination at a later stage. Interestingly, this trend contrasts sharply with another indicating that there are an increasing number of people using the Internet to search for 'potential' destinations to visit. Another notable trend is that the use of the Internet for 'printed out maps and/or driving directions' has been decreasing, likely owing to the growing adoption of GPS systems. It is also very interesting to see that many of the search-related activities have remained fairly constant over this time period.

Searching the travel network also suggests that travel information search has become increasingly connected with one's social circles and intertwined with one's everyday life in many different ways. Recently, it has been recognized that the use of information technology in everyday life 'spills over' to other activities including travel (MacKay and Vogt 2012). Today's communication tools such as smartphones and the Internet have been recognized for their capabilities to 'decapsulate' travel experience, which refers to connecting travellers with people, places and issues in their ordinary lives and reminding them of 'reality' in another spatial and temporal context (Jansson 2007). For example, the push alert function available on different smartphone apps instantly informs travellers of incoming emails, friends' posts or comments and even the potential friends nearby. As such, the information in other domains of life 'breaks the boundaries' set up by space and time and spill over into the context of travel. Travellers voluntarily or involuntarily absorb the information flows that are seemingly irrelevant to their trips, and they have reported the willingness to stay 'informed' because those domains are part of their lives (Wang, Park and Fesenmaier 2012).

The growing importance of social media also has attracted much attention and has been well documented in recent tourism research (Xiang and Gretzel 2010; Leung, Law, van Hoof and Buhalis 2013; Sigala, Christou and Gretzel 2012). In the same longitudinal study of American

Table 21.1 Types of information searched by American travellers for trip planning in the past six years

Type of information searched	*2007* N = 2,436 %	*2008* N = 2,166 %	*2009* N = 2,014 %	*2010* N = 1,159 %	*2011* N = 1,032 %	*2012* N = 1,041 %	*Change (2012–2007)*
Info about a particular destination	75.3	73.8	70.0	66.9	71.6	68.8	–6.5
Hotel prices or places to stay	71.6	69.0	66.4	68.4	75.3	69.5	–2.0
Airline fares and schedule/flight times	64.4	66.0	59.2	71.2	69.2	63.3	–1.1
Printed out maps and/or driving directions	50.4	47.4	44.5	36.7	36.7	31.2	–19.2
Things to do at the destination	47.3	49.2	43.9	46.0	52.3	47.2	–0.1
Potential destinations to visit	39.6	44.2	37.4	41.2	47.9	45.7	6.1
Rental car prices and availability	38.8	39.1	33.3	41.0	45.6	41.0	2.2
Any type of travel discount or promotion	37.7	39.7	37.2	37.6	43.2	38.3	0.6
Dining and entertainment	34.8	36.3	32.9	35.5	42.2	37.8	3.0
Event calendars at the destination	27.8	28.6	25.0	26.4	31.8	26.0	–1.8
Travel packages for resorts, etc.	25.5	29.2	23.4	24.0	28.1	25.8	0.3
Cruises	21.1	22.4	19.4	18.6	21.4	20.7	–0.4
Stores or other places to shop	17.8	22.2	17.1	23.0	27.4	25.6	7.9
Sites that distribute free travel brochures	11.8	11.2	10.6	9.3	10.6	10.7	–1.2
800 numbers	6.9	6.2	5.8	3.7	5.0	6.0	–0.9

Source: National Laboratory for Tourism and eCommerce, Temple University (2013)

travellers' trip planning behaviour (Xiang *et al.* 2013), it is found that travellers now extensively use consumer generated information for travel planning purposes. As shown in Table 21.2, the online travel planning activity 'looking at comments/materials posted by other travellers' has overtaken 'print out travel information/online brochures' as the most significant activity (in 2012), representing nearly a 50 per cent increase from year 2007. Similarly, there has been an increase in (from 2007 to 2012) 'read travel-related blogs' which indicates that social media are becoming a dominant source for travel information search.

Owing to the growing use of mobile technologies and the increasing amount of information accessible during the *en route* and on-site phases, new technological conditions significantly alter the context of decision-making (Hwang 2011; March and Woodside 2005). It is argued that, as opposed to the pre-trip planning behaviour, on-the-move travellers need to make decisions that are time-sensitive, immediate, unreflective and spontaneous, and technologies such as smartphones are considered ideal in supporting these decision-making processes (Hwang 2011). Indeed, Wang *et al.* (2011) found that travellers using smartphones are likely to change their plans because they can easily access the Internet in order to get information for decision-making, and that travellers often feel more secure, confident and excited when they use their smartphone. As such, the traveller's spontaneous and unplanned behaviour is likely to increase

Table 21.2 Types of online travel planning activity in the past six years

Online travel planning activity	*2007* N = 2,436 %	*2008* N = 2,166 %	*2009* N = 2,014 %	*2010* N = 1,159 %	*2011* N = 1,032 %	*2012* N = 1,041 %	*Change (2012–2007)*
Print out travel info/online brochures	48.4	46.5	41.8	39.3	38.8	35.0	–13.4
Request printed materials/ brochures	41.5	37.4	35.7	29.9	34.9	33.4	–8.0
Look at comments/materials posted by travellers	28.0	31.7	33.1	39.9	44.6	41.4	13.4
Print out coupons	27.6	28.3	28.7	28.5	26.5	29.9	2.3
Use interactive calendar of events	20.3	19.4	18.3	20.2	25.8	22.9	2.5
Use interactive trip planners	18.5	17.5	15.6	18.1	21.3	21.0	2.6
Read travel-related blogs	16.2	18.4	18.9	22.4	28.4	24.4	8.2
Watch videos	14.6	18.0	15.0	22.0	29.1	29.6	15.0
Download videos	4.5	5.2	3.8	8.0	9.2	8.4	3.8
Use live chat to talk with travel experts	4.3	4.8	3.7	6.9	9.0	8.2	3.9
Listen to travel-related audio files	3.1	3.7	2.8	4.0	5.7	6.4	3.3

Source: National Laboratory for Tourism and eCommerce, Temple University (2013)

due to the use of a device such as a smartphone and the traveller will, over time, become less reliant upon the information search and planning prior to embarking on the actual trip.

Conclusions

Information search is an essential activity that supports travel decision making. The literature reviewed in this chapter reveals the richness of the topic as well as the changing nature of this behavioural aspect of travel and tourism driven by today's information technologies especially the Internet. Knowledge about travel information search behaviour serves as the foundation for tourism marketing. For example, the use of destination recommender systems and search engine marketing has been growing in recent years as the result of deeper knowledge about what travellers need and want within a technological context. While the Internet continues to evolve with new channels for communications and transactions, new conditions for information search are being created; for example, computer algorithms are being developed in order to tap into the wealth of social knowledge embedded in consumer search behaviour as well as through social networks to provide highly personalized and more trustworthy information. Thus, it is anticipated that travel information search will become even more context-based, dynamic and more personalized, and therefore, will be increasingly intertwined within one's everyday life. This, obviously, will raise more important challenges for both the traveller and the industry as they consider how to adjust to this new paradigm in travel and tourism.

References

Ajzen, I. and Fishbein, M. (1980) *Understanding Attitudes and Predicting Social Behaviour.* Englewood Cliffs, NJ: Prentice-Hall.

Alba, J.W. and Hutchinson, J.W. (1987) 'Dimensions of consumer expertise', *Journal of Consumer Research*, 13(4): 411–54.

Bergamaschi, S., Guerra, F. and Leiba, B. (2010) 'Guest editors' introduction: Information overload', *Internet Computing, IEEE*, 14(6): 10–13.

Bettman, J.R. (1979) *An Information Processing Theory of Consumer Choice.* Reading, MA: Addison Wesley.

Bieger, T. and Laesser, C. (2004) 'Information sources for travel decisions: Toward a source process model', *Journal of Travel Research*, 42(4): 357–71.

Bloch, P.H., Sherrell, D.L. and Ridgway, N.M. (1986) 'Consumer search: An extended framework', *Journal of Consumer Research*, 13: 119–26.

Brucks, M. (1985) 'The effects of product class knowledge on information search behavior', *Journal of Consumer Research*, 12: 1–16.

Capella, L.M. and Greco, A.J. (1987) 'Information sources for elderly vacation decisions', *Annals of Tourism Research*, 14: 148–51.

Celsi, R.L. and Olson, J.C. (1988) 'The role of involvement in attention and comprehension processes', *Journal of Consumer Research*, 15(2): 210–24.

Cho, M.H. and Jang, S.C. (2008) 'Information value structure for vacation travel', *Journal of Travel Research*, 47(1): 72–83.

Cooper, C.P. (1981) 'Spatial and temporal patterns of tourist behavior', *Regional Studies*, 15(3): 359–71.

Crotts, J. (1999) 'Consumer decision making and prepurchase information search', in A. Pizam and Y. Mansfeld (eds) *Consumer Behavior in Travel and Tourism.* New York, USA: Psychology Press.

Darley, W.K. and Smith, R.E. (1995) 'Gender differences in information processing strategies: An empirical test of the selectivity model in advertising response', *Journal of Advertising*, 24(1): 41–56.

Decrop, A. (1999) 'Tourists' decision-making and behavior processes', in A. Pizam and Y. Mansfield (eds) *Consumer Behavior in Travel and Tourism.* Binghamton, NY: The Hawthorn Hospitality Press.

Dholakia, U.M. and Bagozzi, R.P. (2001) 'Consumer behavior in digital environments', in J. Wind and V. Mahajan (eds) *Digital Marketing: Global Strategies from the World's Leading Experts.* New York: Wiley, pp. 163–200.

Dolnicar, S. and Mazanec, J.A. (2000) 'Vacation styles and tourist types: Emerging new concepts and methodology', in W. Gartner and D.W. Lime (eds) *Trends in Outdoor Recreation, Leisure and Tourism.* New York: CABI, pp. 245–56.

Driver, B.L., Brousseau, K.R. and Hunsaker, P.L. (1990) *The Dynamic Decision-maker: Five Decision Styles for Executive and Business Success.* New York: Harper and Row.

Eppler, M.J. and Mengis, J. (2004) 'The concept of information overload: A review of literature from organization science, accounting, marketing, MIS, and related disciplines', *The Information Society*, 20(5): 325–44.

Etzel, M.J. and Wahlers, R.G. (1985) 'The use of requested promotional material by pleasure travelers', *Journal of Travel Research*, 23(4): 2–6.

Ferrari, J.R. and Dovidio, J.F. (2001) 'Behavioral information search by indecisives', *Personality and Individual Differences*, 30: 1113–23.

Fesenmaier, D.R. and Jeng, J. (2000) 'Assessing structure in the pleasure trip planning process', *Tourism Analysis*, 5(3): 13–28.

Fesenmaier, D.R. and Johnson, B. (1989) 'Involvement-based segmentation: Implications for travel marketing in Texas', *Tourism Management*, 10(4): 293–300.

Fesenmaier, D.R. and Lieber, S.R. (1985) 'Spatial structure and behavior response in outdoor recreation participation', *Geografiska Annaler B*, 67: 131–8.

— (1988) 'Destination diversification as an indicator of activity compatibility: An exploratory analysis', *Leisure Sciences*, 10(3): 167–8.

Fesenmaier, D.R. and Vogt, C. (1992) 'Evaluating the utility of touristic information sources for planning Midwest vacation travel', *Journal of Travel and Tourism Marketing*, 1(2): 1–18.

Fesenmaier, D.R., Wöber, K.W. and Werthner, H. (eds) (2006) *Destination Recommendation Systems: Behavioural Foundations and Applications.* Oxfordshire, UK: CABI.

Fesenmaier, D.R., Xiang, Z., Pan, B. and Law, R. (2011) 'A framework of search engine use for travel planning', *Journal of Travel Research*, 50(6): 587–601.

Finn, D. (1983) 'Low involvement isn't low involving', in R. Barozzi and A. Tybout (eds) *Advances in Consumer Research*. Ann Arbor, MI: Association for Consumer Research, pp. 419–24.
Fodness, D. and Murray, B. (1997) 'Tourist information search', *Annals of Tourism Research*, 24(3): 503–23.
— (1998) 'A typology of tourist information search strategies', *Journal of Travel Research*, 37(2): 108–19.
— (1999) 'A model of tourist information search behavior', *Journal of Travel Research*, 37: 220–30.
Gitelson, R.J. and Crompton, J.L. (1983) 'The planning horizons and sources of information used by pleasure vacationers', *Journal of Travel Research*, 21(3): 2–7.
Grabler, K. and Zins, A.H. (2002) 'Vacation trip decision styles as basis for an automated recommendation system: Lessons from observational studies', in K. Wöber, A. Frew and M. Hitz (eds) *Information and Communication Technologies in Tourism 2002*. Vienna, Austria: Springer Verlag, pp. 458–69.
Gretzel, U. (2010) 'Travel in the network: redirected gazes, ubiquitous connections and new frontiers', in M. Levina and G. Kien (eds) *Post-global Network and Everyday Life*. New York: Peter Lang, pp. 41–58.
Gretzel, U., Fesenmaier, D.R. and O'Leary, J.T. (2006) 'The transformation of consumer behavior', in D. Buhalis and C. Costa (eds) *Tourism Business Frontier*. Oxford: Elsevier, pp. 9–18.
Gretzel, U., Hwang, Y.H. and Fesenmaier, D.R. (2012) 'Informing destination recommender systems design and evaluation through quantitative research', *International Journal of Culture, Tourism and Hospitality Research*, 6(4): 297–315.
Griffith, D.A. and Albanese, P.J. (1996) 'An examination of Plog's psychographic travel model within a student population', *Journal of Travel Research*, 34(4): 47–51.
Gursoy, D. and McCleary, K.W. (2004) 'An integrative model of tourists' information search behavior', *Annals of Tourism Research*, 31(2): 353–73.
Henry, W.A. (1980) 'The effect of information-processing ability on processing accuracy', *Journal of Consumer Research*, 7(1): 42–8.
Hoffman, D.L. and Novak, T.P. (1996) 'Marketing in hypermedia computer-mediated environments: Conceptual foundations', *Journal of Marketing*, 60: 50–68.
Hunt, R.G., Krzystofiak, F.J., Meindl, J.R. and Yousry, A.M. (1989) 'Cognitive style and decision making', *Organizational Behavior and Human Decision Processes*, 44: 436–53.
Hwang, Y.H. (2011) 'A theory of unplanned travel decisions: Implications for modeling on-the-go travelers', *Information Technology and Tourism*, 12(3): 283–96.
Hwang, Y.H., Gretzel, U. and Fesenmaier, D.R. (2002) 'Behavioural foundations for human-centric travel decision-aid systems', in Proceedings of *Ninth International Conference on Information and Communication Technology in Tourism*. New York/Innsbruck, Austria: Springer, pp. 356–65.
Hwang, Y.H., Xiang, Z., Gretzel, U. and Fesenmaier, D.R. (2009) 'Assessing structure in travel queries', *Anatolia*, 20(1): 223–35.
Jamrozy, U., Backman, S. and Backman, K. (1996) 'Involvement and opinion leadership in tourism', *Annals of Tourism Research*, 23: 908–24.
Jang, S.C. (2005) 'The past, present, and future research of online information search', *Journal of Travel and Tourism Marketing*, 17(2–3): 41–7.
Jansson, A. (2007) 'A sense of tourism: New media and the dialectic of encapsulation/decapsulation', *Tourist Studies*, 7(1): 5–24.
Jeng, J. and Fesenmaier, D.R. (2002) 'Conceptualizing the travel decision-making hierarchy: A review of recent developments', *Tourism Analysis*, 7(1): 15–32.
Kim, S. and Fesenmaier, D.R. (1990) 'Evaluating spatial structure effects in recreational travel', *Leisure Sciences*, 12: 367–81.
Leiper, N. (1990) 'Tourist attraction systems', *Annals of Tourism Research*, 17(3): 367–84.
Leung, D., Law, R., van Hoof, H. and Buhalis, D. (2013) 'Social media in tourism and hospitality: A literature review', *Journal of Travel and Tourism Marketing*, 30(1-2): 3–22.
Lo, L. (1992) 'Destination interdependence and the competing-destinations model', *Environment and Planning A*, 24: 1191–204.
Lue, C.C., Crompton, J.L. and Fesenmaier, D.R. (1993) 'Conceptualization of multi-destination pleasure trip decisions', *Annals of Tourism Research*, 20: 289–301.
MacKay, K. and Vogt, C. (2012) 'Information technology in everyday and vacation contexts', *Annals of Tourism Research*, 39(3): 1380–401.
McKercher B. (1998) 'The effect of market access on destination choice', *Journal of Travel Research*, 37: 39–47.
Madrigal, R. (1995) 'Personal values, traveler personality type, and leisure travel style', *Journal of Leisure Research*, 27(2): 125–42.

Manfredo, M.J. (1989) 'An investigation of the basis for external information search in recreation and tourism', *Leisure Sciences*, 11(1): 29–45.
March, R. and Woodside, A.G. (2005) *Tourism Behaviour: Travellers' Decisions and Actions*. Oxfordshire, UK: CABI.
Marchionini, G. (1997) *Information Seeking in Electronic Environments*. Cambridge, UK: Cambridge University Press.
Mayo, E.J. and Jarvis, L.P. (1981) *The Psychology of Leisure Travel: Effective Marketing and Selling of Travel Services*. Boston, MA: CBI Publishing Company, Inc.
Mazanec, J.A. (2002) 'Introducing learning and adaptivity into web-based recommender systems for tourism and leisure services', *Tourism Review*, 57(4): 8–14.
Moorthy, S., Ratchford, B.T. and Talukdar, D. (1997) 'Consumer information search revisited: Theory and empirical analysis', *Journal of Consumer Research*, 23(4): 263–77.
Murphy, R. (1994) 'The effects of task characteristics on covariation assessment: The impact of accountability and judgment frame', *Organizational Behavior and Human Decision Processes*, 60: 139–55.
Murray, B. (1991) 'A test of services marketing theory: Consumer information acquisition activities', *Journal of Marketing*, 55: 10–23.
Oppermann, M. (1992) 'International tourist flows in Malaysia', *Annals of Tourism Research*, 19(3): 482–500.
Pan, B. and Fesenmaier, D.R. (2006) 'Travel information search on the Internet', in D.R. Fesenmaier, K.W. Wöber and H. Werthner (eds) *Destination Recommendation Systems: Behavioural Foundations and Applications*. Oxfordshire, UK: CABI, pp. 30–44.
Pennington-Gray, L. and Vogt, C. (2003) 'Examining welcome center visitors' travel and information behaviors: Does location of centers or residency matter?', *Journal of Travel Research*, 41(3): 272–80.
Perdue, R.R. (1993) 'External information search in marine recreational fishing', *Leisure Sciences*, 15(1): 169–87.
Plog, S.C. (1994) 'Developing and using psychographics in tourism research', in J.R.B. Ritchie and C.R. Goeldner (eds) *Travel, Tourism and Hospitality Research: A Handbook for Managers and Researchers*. Brisbane: John Wiley.
Punj, G.N. and Staelin, R. (1983) 'A model of consumer information search behavior for new automobiles', *Journal of Consumer Research*, 9(4): 366–80.
Reid, I.S. and Crompton, J.L. (1993) 'A taxonomy of leisure purchase decision paradigms based on level of involvement', *Journal of Leisure Research*, 25(2): 182–202.
Roehl, W.S. and Fesenmaier, D.R. (1992) 'Risk perceptions and pleasure travel: An exploratory analysis', *Journal of Travel Research*, 30(4): 17–26.
Rosen, D.E. and Purinton, P. (2004) 'Web site design: Viewing the Web as a cognitive landscape', *Journal of Business Research*, 57: 787–94.
Ross, G.F. (1994) *The Psychology of Tourism*. Melbourne: Hospitality Press.
Rumetshofer, H., Pühretmair, F. and Wöß, W. (2003) 'Individual information presentation based on cognitive styles for tourism information systems', in A.J. Frew, M. Hitz and P. O'Connor (eds) *Information and Communication Technologies in Tourism 2003*. Vienna: Springer, pp. 440–47.
Savolainen, R. (2007) 'Filtering and withdrawing: Strategies for coping with information overload in everyday contexts', *Journal of Information Science*, 33(5): 611–21.
Scott, S.G. and Bruce, R.A. (1995) 'Decision-making style: The development and assessment of a new measure', *Educational and Psychological Measurement*, 55(5): 818–31.
Sigala, M., Christou, E. and Gretzel, U. (eds) (2012) *Social Media in Travel, Tourism and Hospitality: Theory, Practice and Cases*. Oaks, CA: Sage.
Snepenger, D., Meged, K., Snelling, M. and Worrall, K. (1990) 'Information search strategies by destination-naive tourists', *Journal of Travel Research*, 29(1): 13–6.
Sparrow, B., Liu, J. and Wegner, D.M. (2011) 'Google effects on memory: Cognitive consequences of having information at our fingertips', *Science*, 333(6043): 776–8.
Spink, A. and Zimmer, M. (eds) (2008) *Web Search: Multidisciplinary Perspectives* (Vol. 14). New York: Springer.
Sproles, G.B. and Kendall, E. (1986) 'A methodology for profiling consumers' decision making styles', *The Journal of Consumer Affairs*, 20(2): 268–79.
Stewart, S.I. and Vogt, C.A. (1999) 'A case-based approach to understanding vacation planning', *Leisure Sciences*, 21(2): 79–95.
Tideswell, C. and Faulkner, W. (1999) 'Multidestination travel patterns of international visitors to Queensland', *Journal of Travel Research*, 37: 364–74.

Um, S. and Crompton, J.L. (1992) 'The roles of perceived inhibitors and facilitators in pleasure travel destination decisions', *Journal of Travel Research*, 30(3): 18–25.

USTA (2011) *Travelers' Use of the Internet*. Washington, DC: Travel Industry Association of America.

Vogt, C. and Fesenmaier, D.R. (1998) 'Expanding the functional information search model', *Annals of Tourism Research*, 25(3): 551–78.

Wang, D., Park, S. and Fesenmaier, D.R. (2012) 'The role of smartphones in mediating the touristic experience', *Journal of Travel Research*, 51(4): 371–87.

Werthner, H. and S. Klein (1999) *Information Technology and Tourism – A Challenging Relationship*. Vienna: Springer.

Woodside, A.G. and Lysonski, S. (1989) 'A general model of traveler destination choice', *Journal of Travel Research*, 27(4): 8–14.

Woodside, A.G. and MacDonald, R. (1994) 'General system framework of customer choice processes of tourism services', in R. Gasser and K. Weiermair (eds) *Spoilt for Choice*. Thaur, Austria: Kulturverlag, pp. 31–59.

Xiang, Z. and Gretzel, U. (2010) 'Role of social media in online travel information search', *Tourism Management*, 31(2): 179–88.

Xiang, Z. and Pan, B. (2011) 'Travel queries on cities in the United States: Implications for search engine marketing for tourist destinations', *Tourism Management*, 32(1): 88–97.

Xiang, Z., Wöber, K. and Fesenmaier, D.R. (2008) 'Representation of the online tourism domain in search engines', *Journal of Travel Research*, 47(2): 137–50.

Xiang, Z., Wang, D. and Fesenmaier, D.R. (2013) 'Adapting to technological change: A longitudinal study of travelers' use of Internet for trip planning', working paper. Temple University: National Laboratory for Tourism and eCommerce.

Zins, A. (1998) 'Leisure traveler choice models of theme hotels using psychographics', *Journal of Travel Research*, 36(4): 3–15.

Zins, A. (1999) 'Destination portfolios using a European vacation style typology', *Journal of Travel and Tourism Marketing*, 8(1): 1–23.

22

Dynamics of tourists' decision-making

From theory to practice

Antónia Correia, Metin Kozak and Manuel Tão

Introduction

Tourism marketing is all about tourists. The effects of marketing on tourists start well before the trip, and finish long after, if they end at all. A tourist displays a particular behaviour when purchasing tourism products. First of all, the acquisition of services takes place prior to their consumption. Such a lag between the act of acquisition and consumption can be typified by the fact that a given journey begins long before the act of boarding a plane to reach a certain holiday location. Far from their own domestic environment, the tourist becomes emotionally fragile and to alleviate this they search for more information about destination features. Even when the holiday time is over, the consumption of the tourism product may not have been completed, in the sense that registered emotions are captured and 'frozen' by photos and films, to be shared with relatives and friends. Finally, the decision-making is also constrained by the difficulty of having full information prior to the consumption of tourism products; this constraint arises on information sources available and cognitive processing limitations (Correia 2002). These effects have to be measured throughout the tourist decision-making process.

Although there is not a body of scientific knowledge about tourist behaviour, researchers have adapted the fundamental/seminal theories of consumer behaviour in order to understand tourists. Like consumer behaviour, tourist behaviour is a multidisciplinary field of study, drawing on economics, sociology, psychology and anthropology, supporting the optimization of marketing strategies. Tourist behaviour derives from consumer behaviour research, but distinguishes itself from that major study area due to paradoxical characteristics of the tourist product. To buy a trip or a holiday is both a demanding effort and an enthusiastic pleasure. It both demands and requests a high level of involvement from the individual because it involves decisions about many aspects, in an uncertain context that brings about risk and anxiety. Tourist behaviour presents particularities that derive from and are the result of the specification of the tourism product itself.

Hence, tourism has what March and Woodside (2005) call a purchase-consumption system, a complex and inter-reliant process with multiple phased options to be overcome by the tourist. Despite the number of researchers around the topic, models of tourists' decision-making contain important limitations. To overcome such limitations, conceptual studies have proposed comprehensive models that approach decision-making from different perspectives. From the field of psychology to the vast set of economic models, the only consensus is that decision-making is a complex process that involves a plethora of variables. Such a topic is as complex as it is challenging. This chapter attempts to discuss the tourist decision-making process in a practical sense, highlighting how economics, psychology and marketing should contribute to develop a tourism-based decision model. This chapter, therefore, approaches the heuristics that should be taken into account when modelling tourism decision-making. These are critically discussed, and implications for marketing strategies in a tourism context are outlined.

Seminal theories of consumer behaviour

The study of tourist decision-making is grounded mostly in neoclassical economic theory and discrete choice theory. Neoclassical economic theory (CCB) frames consumption choices as rational and purposeful. Therefore, individuals tend to maximize the utility of the 'basket of assets' they can purchase, bearing in mind the need for diversity and budget restrictions. Following this stream of literature, Lancaster (1966) contends that utility does not derive directly from the product but from the attributes the product has that enable it to fulfil the needs of the consumer. Broadly speaking, a 'technologic constraint' was introduced in terms of optimization problems, which is commonly referred to as a preference function. In the context of tourism decisions another constraint was considered, the availability of time for leisure (Bull 1995). From this perspective (CCB, incorporating Lancaster's extensions [1966]) choice in tourism has been approached by various scholars (e.g. Rugg 1973; Morley 1992; Papatheodorou 2001), who argue that travel decision-making is a rational choice process that emerges from the evaluation of several alternatives constrained by the tourist's pervasive availability of time and money in light of destination attributes (preference function). Utility functions were estimated but these models did not consider interpersonal and intrapersonal variables, which led tourism research to consider discrete choice theory (Jeng and Fesenmaier 1996).

Discrete choice theory arose with contributions from economists and cognitive psychologists. Discrete choice problems involve choices between two or more discrete alternatives, such as going or not going on holiday, or choosing between destinations. Such choices contrast with standard consumption models in which the quantity of each good consumed is assumed to be a continuous variable. In a continuous case, demand can be modelled using regression models. Regression models allow us to answer 'how much' type questions. In discrete choice problems the outcome is discrete and therefore discrete choice models should be applied; hence discrete choice models help us to answer 'which' type questions.

Two streams of discrete choice models could be considered: revealed and stated preferences approaches. Revealed preference theory assumes that the preferences of consumers can be observed, being utility functions derived from their choices, given their budget constraints. For instance, if a tourist chooses Hawaii instead of Fiji islands, both being affordable, it means that this tourist prefers Hawaii. Furthermore, this preference is stable and irreversible, over the observed time period. This theory was widely criticized, since in the real world, when it is observed that a consumer purchases a certain commodity, it is impossible to say what good or set of goods was discarded, and so there is not clear evidence that the commodity bought is necessarily the preferred one. In this sense, preference is not revealed at all in the sense of ordinal utility. Applications of revealed preference rely mostly on destination attributes (Perdue 1986; Morey, Shawand and Rowe 1991; Dubin 1998; Colledge and Timmermans 1990; Siderelis and Moore 1998; Schroeder and Louviere 1999; Haider and Ewing 1990).

Revealed preference experiments considering intrapersonal determinants are less common and, even when applied, generally only include socio-demographic variables (e.g. Morley 1992; Eyamn and Ronning 1997; Riera 2000) whilst an even more limited number include variables such as trip motivations, past experience or holiday experience (Eyamn and Ronning 1997; Fesenmaier 1988; Correia, Santos and Barros 2007). These choice models mostly rely on multinomial logit models which allow researchers to assess how preferences for a certain destination may increase if a certain attribute is improved, despite the importance of assessing the moderator role of destination attributes to redesign tourism marketing strategies. The likelihood of this attribute moderating tourist choice is barely assessed as it is assumed that all the other attributes remain unchangeable. Furthermore, this method estimates preferences at the global sample level, which does not allow representation of individual preferences.

Stated preference approaches assess the ranking or scoring preferences of hypothetical choice alternatives (Timmermans and Golledge 1989; Batsell and Louviere 1991), and have been widely used to assess willingness to choose, mostly in transport research (Balcombe, Fraser and Harris 2009; Dennis 2007). These approaches have been widely criticized as well, due to the fact that they do not reflect reality (real choices). Intentions may not coincide necessarily with tourists' behaviour in the end (Kroes and Sheldon 1988).

Extending tourism destination choice research

Despite the importance of these models, tourist behaviour modelling still suffers from serious drawbacks, especially in terms of the restrictions because none of them include psychological factors. On the other hand, Kahneman and Tversky (1979), based on cognitive psychology, developed the prospect theory that appears to offer a better approach as it develops and extends CCB with psychological factors, namely intuition, emotionality and perception, recognizing the interdisciplinary nature of consumer behaviour.

The interdisciplinary nature of consumer behaviour has given rise to two distinct groups of models (Sirakaya, Uysal and Mclellan 1996): structural models and processional models. The structural models examine the relationship between an input (stimulus) and an output (response) (Abelson and Levi 1985). The processional models examine individuals' decisions, concentrating on the cognitive processes (the transformation processes between the input and the output) that are generated prior to the final decision being taken (Abelson and Levi 1985). In other words, the first set of models focus on determinants of tourists' choice whereas processional models focus on the stages (choice-sets) that the process of choice comprised.

Those models have common propositions: they are based on human rationality. Tourists are rational beings, the Homo-economicus, even if some acknowledge the existence also of psychological and social factors influencing the decision (for example, Mayo and Jarvis 1981; Woodside 2004). Tourists are also perceived as individual decision-makers, and most of these models have been more concerned with the decision of where to travel, that is, destination choice, than with whether or not tourists will have holidays. Only more recently has the primary decision of travelling or not, that is the participation decision, begun to appear in the literature (Woodside 2004), as well as the role of motivations as psychological variables and also the influence of social environment. In fact, tourism is a social activity and some evidence has been found that suggests it is more an interpersonal decision than an individualistic one; and also as tourism is an emotional experience with memorable events, the tourist decision is not only rational but is also affective; last but not least, tourism models so far are parsimonic, meaning that they are very complex and so difficult to test.

In conclusion, tourism decision models anchor widely on CCB assumptions even if in the last few decades there has been recognition of the need to emphasize the role of social and psychological variables in tourist decision-making, such as the dimensions of consumer behaviour covered by prospect theory (Kahneman and Tversky 1979). Prospect theory developed as a psychologically realistic alternative to expected utility theory. It has become a starting point for deeper research into rationalization of the real world decision behaviour of human beings.

Prospect theory

The main contribution of economic theories relies on presuppositions that beyond the optimization problem there is also a perception function. Following Kahneman and Tversky (1979), the structure of cognition (or thinking and deciding) can be explained through two systems, which correspond roughly to everyday concepts of reasoning and intuition. One way to describe reasoning is to say that this is the process involved when an individual uses his/her mind to consider something carefully: like solving some logical problem such as playing chess. Any process of drawing a conclusion from a set of premises with effort can be called a process of reasoning whereas intuition is the instinctive knowledge of some facts without the use of rational processes. Intuitive thought comes to mind spontaneously and without effort.

To better understand how these two systems of cognition can be expressed in tourism research and traveller decision we will adapt the example of the 'bat and ball' (this example stated that a bat and a ball cost $1.10 in total, where the bat cost $1 more than the ball. If asked how much the ball costs, the common or intuitive response is to say 10 cents). Little processing is required for this simple problem. Let's consider the situation when a tourist is searching for the cheapest alternatives to go from city A to city B and finds a promotion to go by a low cost airline for €10. Costs of other alternatives are around €20. The normal reaction of the traveller, without spending additional time to find out all the information about this choice, would be to buy this ticket. But after some time spent reading all the terms and conditions he/she finds out that the price including surcharges and taxes raises the total price for the trip to €30, thus making this choice much less attractive.

This example shows that people are not accustomed to spending a lot of effort or hard thinking, and are often content to trust a plausible judgment that quickly comes to his/her mind. But from the alternative position, intuitive thinking can also be powerful and accurate in the case of an individual having high skills, acquired by prolonged practice. In the example discussed above, if the traveller is used to travelling by plane he/she should know that, in this kind of promotion, the price of some surcharges and taxes may not be included in the initial promotional offer.

The general characteristics of perception and the two types of cognitive systems are labelled by Stanovich and West (2000) as system 1 and system 2. Operations of system 1 (or intuition) are fast, parallel, automatic, effortless, associative and often emotionally charged. Slow-learning is explained as often operations from system 1 are governed by habit and are therefore hard to modify or change over time. Another important factor is that the perception of people is generally based on intuition. Systematic research indicates that most thoughts and actions are normally intuitive in the sense given above. The operations of system 2 (or reasoning) are much slower as they require more time to make a decision, being serial, controlled and effortful. A big difference between this and the previous system is flexibility.

The main key to distinguish whether an operation should be included in system 1 or system 2 is the effort spent on this operation. Effort-key, as an important tool to distinguish between the two systems, can be explained using the capacity of mental activity and its limitation.

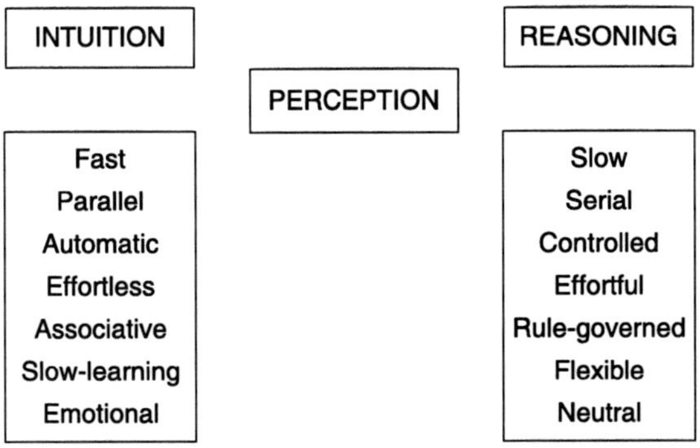

Figure 22.1 Properties of intuition and reasoning (adapted from Kahneman 2002).

Normally effortful operations, which are included in system 2 type processes, tend to interrupt each other, while effortless processes (system 1) can be combined without big losses.

Based on the model of thinking and deciding Kahneman and Tversky proposed their prospect theory. Following it, the choice of the consumer can be made in two phases: an early *phase of editing* and a subsequent *phase of evaluation*. A central feature of prospect theory and a general property of the perceptual system is *reference dependence*. That means that perceptions are not a single-valued function, but also require a parameter for reference value. In other words it is necessary to know current and prior stimulations. The main ideas that guided the research of Kahneman and Tversky (1979) in this field were as follows:

- Perceptual system plus the intuition operations generate impressions of the attributes of objects.
- Intuitive judgment occupies a position between the automatic operations of perception and the deliberate operation of reasoning.
- All characteristics that are attributed to intuition are also properties of perceptual operations.
- Unlike perception, however, the operation of system 1 is not restricted to the processing of the current stimulus.
- The view of scientific knowledge available about perceptual phenomena can be a source of useful hypotheses about the working of intuition.

To draw upon analogies of perception, an explanation is needed of the accessibility of thoughts following Kahneman (2003a). *Accessibility* here is a technical term used to describe the degree to which mental contents are accessible to the mind. Accessibility of thought can serve as another way to understand systems of cognition and the differences between them. Accessibility gives to perceptions a dimension, in particular a visual one. That means that some attributes are more available than others, both in perception and judgment. Furthermore, accessibility is a continuum, not a dichotomy. Some of the determinants of the accessibility are probably genetic, others develop through experience; and accumulation of skills gradually increases the accessibility of useful responses and of productive ways to organize information, until skilled performance becomes almost effortless.

Kahneman and Tversky proposed in their alternative theory of choice that carriers of utility are gain and loss changes rather than states of wealth. This assumption can be explained from the point of view that it is compatible with basic principles of perception and judgment.

This statement was implemented in *value function*, the first central element of prospect theory. The emphasis on changes as the carriers of the value should not be taken to imply that the value of a particular change is independent of an initial position. Value should be treated as a function of two arguments: the asset position that serves as a reference point and the magnitude of the change from the reference point. In other words value function represents the outcomes expected.

Speaking broadly about value function, it has an s-shape characterized by the following features:

- It is defined on deviation from the reference point.
- It is concave in the domain of gains, favouring risk aversion.
- It is convex in the domain of losses, favouring risk seeking.
- It is sharply kinked at the reference point, and loss-averse – steeper for losses than for gains by a factor of about 2–2, 5.

The last point argues that deterioration that an individual expects in losing a sum of money is bigger than the pleasure associated with gaining the same amount. As the evidence shows, most people find a symmetrical situation in which they can lose or gain the same amount with the same probability distinctly unattractive. Another central component of prospect theory is *weighting function* which transforms single probabilities into decision weights. The original version of the theory with transformation in weighted function implies violations of first-order stochastic dominance. That is, one prospect might be preferred to another even if it yielded a worse or equal outcome with the probability prospect. This disadvantage has motivated the development of cumulative prospect theory variants which uses transformation of cumulative probabilities rather than single probabilities. Theoretical results in the field of reference-dependence in cumulative prospect theory are obtained by Schmidt (2004).

The weighting function proposed by Kahneman (1979) satisfies overweighting and subadditivity for small values of p, and subcertainty and subproportionality. As a fact, subproportionality together with the overweighting of small probabilities imply that π is subadditive over all ranges (0, 1).

The basic formula of the theory of choice of Kahneman and Tversky in the simplest form combines value function v and weighting function π in order to determine the overall value. It is assumed for the evaluation phase and given by:

$$V(x_1, p_1; x_2, p_2) = \pi(p_1)v(x_1) + \pi(p_2)v(x_2),$$

where x_1 and x_2 are potential outcomes; p_1 and p_2 their respective probabilities; $(x_1, p_1; x_2, p_2)$ is a regular prospect (either $p_1 + p_2 < 1$ or, $x_1 \geq 0 \geq x_2$ or $x_1 \leq 0 \leq x_2$).

This theory, which constitutes a good complement to CCB, solves some of the main frailties of the original models, offering new paths for tourism research. General reasons for CCB frailty and the advantages of prospect theory are comparatively analyzed in the following section.

New frontiers in tourism research

In order to clearly state the advantages of prospect theory compared with CCB, a number of assumptions, implications and consequences of CCB were recovered in order to compare them with the results of Kahneman and Tversky. They will be the main points of our discussion of differences and possible links between the classical theory of consumer behaviour and prospect theory.

First and the most important unstable fact which raises a lot of discussion on CCB is ***rationality*** of consumer behaviour. The basic postulate of the classical theory is that the consumer maximizes utility, or in other words behaves rationally. Since his/her income is limited, he/she maximizes utility subject to a budget constraint, through an optimization problem.

Second (lack of information, evaluation of alternatives, cognitive ability), it is assumed that consumers enter the marketplace with well-defined preferences and are capable of ranking commodity combinations consistently in order of preference. This ranking is described mathematically by the consumer's ordinal utility function. ***Preference orderings*** are assumed to share four simple properties:

- Completeness: A preference ordering is complete if the consumer is able to rank all possible combinations of goods and services.
- Transitivity: For any three bundles, A, B and C, if an individual prefers A to B and B to C, then he always prefers A to C.
- More is better: This property means simply that, given other things being equal, more goods is preferred to less.
- And last but not least it assumes a diminishing marginal rate of substitution. Along any indifference curve, if a consumer moves in one direction he/she acquires more Q_1 and less Q_2 and the rate at which he/she is willing to sacrifice Q_2 to acquire more Q_1 declines. A preference ordering with a diminishing marginal rate of substitution will thus generate indifference curves that are convex.

Third, the ***amount of labour*** performed by the consumer affects his/her level of utility. This amount of labour can be determined on the basis of the rational-decision criterion of utility maximization. The equilibrium conditions are similar to those which hold for the selection of an optimal commodity combination.

Fourth, the consumer's ***reaction to different changes*** in price and level of income can be analyzed in terms of substitution and income effects (Henderson and Quandt 1980 and others).

CCB has been challenged already by evidence from anthropology, evolutionary biology, neurology and cognitive psychology. A survey of these challenges was undertaken by McFadden (2005) with particular attention to opportunities afforded by new measurement methods coming into economics.

Figure 22.2 shows diagrammatically the representation of the usefulness of prospect theory. Here we emphasize eight main issues which show improvements that Kahneman's and Tversky's theory can bring into tourism modelling and research.

More concretely, it is stated that the agent in economic theory is rational and *selfish*. Nevertheless, selfishness as rationality is also challenged. Briefly, Kahneman (2003b) describes how developments in economics correct and elaborate on this assumption. The tourism context is distinguished by the *sociality* of human beings. Woodside argues that besides economic factors, tourist decision-making is influenced by psychological and social factors. Correia and Pimpão (2008) state that social status is one of the major drivers of travel. As empirical evidence, Silva and Correia (2008) emphasize the need for a travel companion. Also, participation and approval from friends and relatives can be a constraint or a facilitator to travelling.

Modern decision theory traces *unchanged tastes*, which originated in the famous St Petersburg essay in which Bernoulli (1954) formulated the original version of expected-utility theory. Unchanged taste can be also viewed as an aspect of rationality (Kahneman 2003b). Nevertheless, the static nature of the traditional demand theory cannot account for the evolutionary features of the tourism product, especially the emergence of new destinations or withering of others

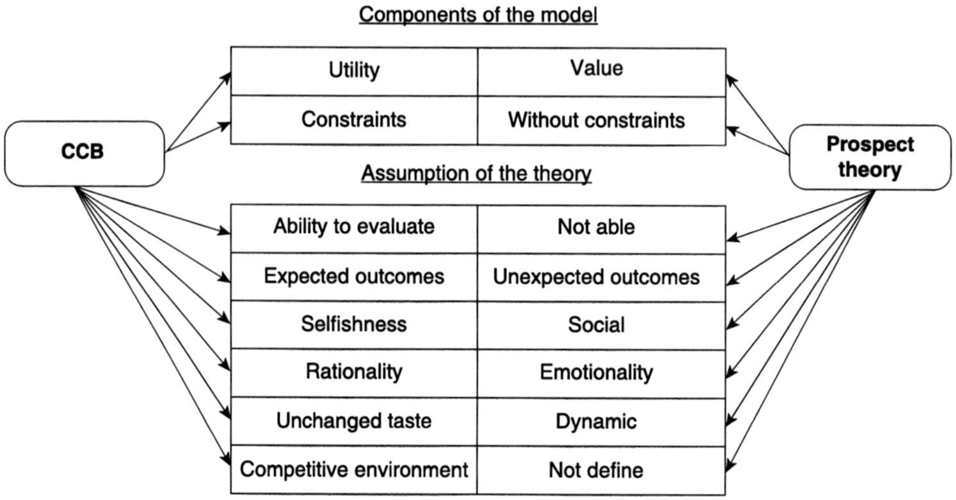

Figure 22.2 Advantages of prospect theory.

(Butler 1980). Another important argument in changing tastes in tourism is analysis derived by Pearce and Lee (2005) based on travelling motivation and experience. Changing tastes in tourism are inherent to Plog's (1974) tourist typologies, which describe a novelty seeking scale (in addition to that of Cohen 1972).

Following the CCB and Characteristic theory (Gorman 1980; Lancaster 1966) economic factors must be explained by basic *constraints* for decision-making, which are money (consumer's budget constraint) and time. However, there is strong evidence that within tourism the product must be regarded as multifaceted (Echtner and Jamal 1997; Gaburn and Jafari 1991; Jafari and Ritchie 1981; Jafari 1990, 2001, 2002; Tribe 1997) and includes not only economic restrictions but also psychological and social constraints. Among research on constraints, Blazey (1987) examined how age (particularly adults over 55 years old), health and presence of a travel companion influence each other and can restrict consumer choices; health and money are also restrictors found by Fleischer and Pizam (2002) among Israeli seniors; Pennington-Gray and Krestter (2002) and Nyaupane, Morais and Graefe (2004) found that personal fears constrain participation in specific activities (such as skiing); Woodside Krauss, Caldwell and Chebat (2006) conclude that the primary decision of travelling, the one that dictates whether a person travels or not, is influenced by a person's context and lifestyle. Silva and Correia's (2008) study, based on southeast Portugal citizens, suggests that besides the structural inhibitors of time and money, intrapersonal motivation and interpersonal factors are determinant in tourism choices.

The classical theory can only function within a *competitive environment* where the producers act as pathetic price takers, who are incapable of coordinating their strategies or of manipulating tourist flows. However, Papatheodorou (2001) argues that suppliers are able to reap the advantages of their oligopolistic power to the detriment of consumers and destinations. As was mentioned above, the main carrier of the consumer *utility* in CCB is stated wealth. Thus, prospect theory brings to us value function which defines individuals' perceptions of gains and losses. At the same time perception can be explained through motivation and its components, namely objective attributes, social motivations and own motivations.

Furthermore, the tourist has *cognitive ability and is able to evaluate all alternatives* (*certainty*). However, Decrop (1999) shows that tourists are incapable of perceiving and evaluating all existing choices. Moreover, tourism cannot be compared to supermarket shopping as the choice of the former should contain perception issues in the context of prospect theory (Correia and Pimpão 2008; Kim and Yoon 2003; Otto 1997; Otto and Ritchie 1995; Vogt, Klenosky and Andereck 2003). Furthermore, the tourist (consumer) in general has limited memory and performs decisions through simplification processes (Bettman and Park 1980). Good evidence in this regard is provided by Nicosia (1966) and Miller (1956). They show that the tourist's decision process tends to narrow down alternatives, and he/she is only capable of choosing between from two to seven different destinations. Another important evidence is Howard (1963) who differentiated the 'awareness set' from the 'unawareness set', stating that the former one is defined by all the destinations of which the individual may be aware, and that might be reduced to form the 'evoked set' (a small number of alternatives between which the buyer chooses), and the latter one is comprised of those destinations of which the individual is not aware. The same basic idea has been developed by various scholars (e.g. Hauser and Wernerfelt 1989; Howard and Sheth 1969; Narayana and Markin 1975; Sibley 1976; Woodside and Lysonski 1989; Woodside and Sherell 1977).

The approach of demand theory states that outcomes are *expected* and clearly defined in their values or taken as an exogenous constant in the model; however, it seems that during any journey the tourist budget can easily fluctuate depending on the taste of the individual and his/her emotionality, thus in this context prospect theory is much more flexible and can provide a more convincing approach.

Rationality states that consumers allocate financial resources among tourist and non-tourist products in ways that maximize his/her utility. Yet within tourism it is already known that decisions are influenced both by emotions and cognition (Kim and Yoon 2003; Vogt, Klenosky and Andereck 2003; Correia, Valle and Moço 2007). In recent years, Woodside (2004) proposed a holistic overview of a person's contexts in order to explain tourist behaviour, which was based on psychology of development and ecological system theory (Bronfenbrenner 1979). A similar suggestion for understanding traveller decisions has been made by Mayo and Jarvis (1981). Thus, a number of determinants of tourist decision choice may be proposed that go beyond the traditional approach of choice models, whether in a quantitative or probabilistic fashion.

Choice-set models

Choice-set models have received substantial attention in the literature of tourism decision-making because of their practical use for destination marketers. The concept of choice sets was first introduced by Howard (1963) in consumer behaviour and adapted by others (e.g. Howard and Sheth 1969; Narayana and Markin 1975; Brisoux and Laroche 1981; Spiggle and Sewall 1987). According to the theory, a potential traveller first develops a set of destinations from their early consideration or awareness set. The destinations are chosen from a large number of alternatives, comprising of all the destinations available, which is also known as the 'total set'. The number of alternatives is then reduced to shape his/her late consideration or evoked set. Finally, one alternative is selected from the evoked set as the final choice. In this sense, one criticism that can be levied against the choice-set theory is that it may tend to be deterministic in nature (Ben-Akiva and Boccara 1995).

Howard (1963) introduces the concepts of awareness, unawareness and evoked sets. He suggests that all brands belong either to the consumer's awareness set or unawareness set. An awareness set is comprised of all brands, or alternatives, that the buyer may be aware of at any given time, while an unawareness set encompasses all the brands that the buyer is unaware of. Howard and Sheth (1969) further refine the evoked set as the brands that the buyer considers acceptable for his next purchase. Narayana and Markin (1975) redefine the evoked set and include all brands that may be in the buyer's awareness set. Narayana and Markin (1975) introduce the concepts of inert and inept sets. An inert set is made up of the brands that the consumer has given neither a positive nor a negative evaluation. The inept set encompasses the brands that the buyer has rejected from their purchase consideration, either because they have had an unpleasant experience or because they have received negative feedback from other sources.

Spiggle and Sewall (1987) also contribute an important extension to the concept of choice-sets. They present a model for retail decision-making that is built upon and extends the evoked-set concept previously investigated by Narayana and Markin (1975). Spiggle and Sewall's (1987) model includes five new choice-sets, which were hypothesized as being the subsets of an evoked-set. The new sets comprise the:

1 action set;
2 interaction set;
3 inaction set;
4 quiet set; and
5 reject set.

Action set is defined as 'all stores towards which a consumer takes some action – she or he goes at least as far as making a visit to the store site' (Spiggle and Sewall 1987: 99). The interaction set includes:

> all of the stores in which a consumer allowed himself/herself to be exposed to personal selling. The inaction set comprises of all the stores in evoked set that a consumer does not visit. Quiet set composes stores that consumers visit and leave before interacting with a sales clerk. The reject set is made up of the stores that are originally in the evoked, action, or interaction sets and towards which a consumer's evaluation is transformed from positive to negative during purchase deliberation.
>
> *(Spiggle and Sewall 1987: 101)*

The choice set approach in the tourist's decision making process is initiated as an alternative and more practical perspective to behavioural approaches, which are generally criticized as being too complex and difficult to test empirically. Rather than being strong theoretical exercises, choice-set research seeks to bring to light results more applicable to destination choice behaviours.

A number of conclusions should be underlined. Tourists seek well-being; thus, the utility of a vacation should be measured by a value function where perceived gains and losses are highly valued. Furthermore, perceptions should be explained through motivation and its components, namely objective attributes, social motivations and psychological motivations.

The human being has cognitive abilities and is not able to evaluate all alternatives (certainty). Thus, decisions arise in a context of uncertainty and that should be taken into account. Furthermore, tourists (consumers) in general have a limited memory and perform decisions through a simplification process that at the very end is likely to be based on trust and intuitive perceptions rather than a reasoning process. Simplification processes and uncertainty give rise to decisions where outcomes may be unexpected. In this sense, touristic decisions are influenced by emotions and cognitions, as well as by psychological and social factors. In the same vein it has been widely assumed that preferences are stable and unchangeable; however, in tourism the evolutionary features of the tourism product and the accumulated experience of tourists dictate that preferences are dynamic.

Generally speaking, models of tourist decision-making should consider that decisions are dynamic and risky, constrained by the individual and social contexts of tourists, from which emotional and cognitive factors play a role in the final choice. It is under this plethora of factors and assumptions that the tourist decision-making arises, thus producers should act within a competitive environment with coordinated strategies to be able to manipulate tourist flows.

Marketing implications

In light of the results of the several authors outlined in this chapter, a number of important findings should be weighed to feed marketing strategies.

First, informative marketing strategies should comprise emotional and cognitive features in order to stimulate an appetite to visit the announced destination. Retention and fidelization, however, rely on the destination attribute's quality. Second, clustering the market through social and demographic characteristics is the first step to derive a tailor-made marketing strategy. Hence, the role of peer groups and the family life cycle would contribute to understanding the target market. Next, understanding the length of the tourist's learning process is critical to defining marketing information campaigns. The more involved the tourists are, the more precise and clear should be the information about the destination. A stepwise decision is expected; as such, destination information should be interrelated with activities, transports, shops, accommodation and areas to visit. As it is not expected that this set of decisions occurs simultaneously, providing dynamic systems of information before, during and after the visit is advisable.

Since tourists do not always decide on all facets simultaneously, it is important to understand how tourists' choices of different aspects of their travel decisions are distributed over time. Different timing for choices would influence the decision; thus, it would be critical to implement more effectively strategic policy and management actions and/or marketing and communications strategies. For example, if tourists decide on their geographical destinations before they decide on their accommodation, information or pricing strategies regarding hotel facilities could be implemented more effectively once market communications on countries and regions were previously implemented. In the same vein, temporal sequence and direction of the influence on a tourist's choice of vacation elements should be depicted. For example, once a choice of destination is made, this will constrain choices of places of accommodation, which in turn may constrain choices of places at which to dine. Categorizing destinations within the consideration sets of tourists will help the competitive positioning that the destination marketers are trying to achieve.

References

Abelson, R.P. and Levi, A. (1985) 'Decision making and decision theory', in G. Lindzey and E. Aronson (eds) *The Handbook of Social Psychology*, 3rd edn, Vol. 1. New York: Random House, pp. 231–309.

Balcombe, K., Fraser, I. and Harris, L. (2009) 'Consumer willingness to pay for in-flight service and comfort levels: a choice experiment', *Journal of Air Transport Management*, 5: 21–30.

Batsel, R.R. and Louviere, J.J. (1991) 'Experimental choice analysis', *Marketing Letters*, 2: 199–214.

Ben-Akiva, M. and Boccara, B. (1995) 'Discrete choice models with latent choice sets', *International Journal of Research in Marketing*, 12(1): 9–24.

Bernoulli, D. (1954) 'Exposition of a new theory on the measurement of risk', *Econometrica*, 22(1): 22–36.

Bettman, J.R. and Park, C.W. (1980) 'Effects of prior knowledge and experience and phase of the choice process on consumer decision processes', *Journal of Consumer Research*, 7: 234–48.

Blazey, M. (1987) 'The differences between participants and non-participants in a senior travel program', *Journal of Travel Research*, 26(1): 7–12.

Brisoux, J.E. and Laroche, M. (1981) 'Evoked set formation and composition: an empirical investigation under a routinized response behaviour situation', *Advances in Consumer Research*, 8(1): 357–61.
Bronfenbrenner, U. (1979) *The Ecology of Human Development: Experiments by Nature and Design*. Cambridge, MA: Harvard University Press.
Bull, A. (1995) *The Economics of Travel and Tourism*, 2nd edn. Melbourne: Longman.
Butler, R.W. (1980) 'The concept of the tourist area life-cycle of evolution: implications for management of resources', *Canadian Geographer*, 24(1): 5–12.
Cohen, E. (1972) 'Towards a sociology of international tourism', *Sociological Research*, 39: 164–82.
Colledge, R.G. and Timmermans, H. (1990) 'Application of behavioural research on spatial problems', *Progress in Human Geography*, 14: 57–99.
Correia, A. (2002) 'How do tourists choose?', *Tourism*, 50(1): 21–9.
Correia, A. and Pimpão, A. (2008) 'Decision-making processes of Portuguese tourists travelling to South America and Africa', *International Journal of Culture, Tourism, and Hospitality Research*, 4(2): 330–73.
Correia, A., Santos, C. and Barros, C. (2007) 'Tourism in Latin America: a choice analysis', *Annals of Tourism Research*, 34(3): 610–29.
Correia, A., Valle, P. and Moço, C. (2007) 'Why people travel to exotic places?', *International Journal of Culture, Tourism, and Hospitality Research*, 1(1): 45–61.
Decrop, A. (1999) 'Tourists' decision-making and behaviour processes', in A. Pizam and Y. Mansfield (eds) *Consumer Behaviour in Travel and Tourism*. Binghamton, NY: The Haworth Press, pp. 103–33.
Dennis, N. (2007) 'End of the free lunch? The responses of traditional European airlines to the low-cost carrier threat', *Journal of Air Transport Management*, 13(5): 311–21.
Dubin, J. (1998). *Studies in Consumer Demand: Econometric Methods Applied To Market Data*. Kluwer Academic Publishers.
Echtner, C.M. and Jamal, T.B. (1997) 'The disciplinary dilemma of tourism studies', *Annals of Tourism Research*, 24(4): 868–83.
Eymann, A. and Ronning, G. (1997) 'Microeconometric models of tourists' destination choice', *Regional Science and Urban Economics*, 27: 735–61.
Fesenmaier, D.R. (1988) 'Integrating activity patterns into destination choice models', *Journal of Leisure Research*, 20: 175–91.
Fleischer, A. and Pizam, A. (2002) 'Tourism constraints among Israeli seniors', *Annals of Tourism Research*, 29(1): 106–23.
Gorman, W.M. (1980) 'A possible procedure for analyzing quality differentials in the egg market', *Review of Economic Studies*, 47: 843–56.
Graburn, N.H.H. and Jafari, J. (1991) 'Introduction: tourism social science', *Annals of Tourism Research*, 18: 1–11.
Haider, W. and Ewing, G.O. (1990) 'A model of tourist choices of hypothetical Caribbean destinations', *Leisure Sciences*, 12(1): 33–47.
Hauser, J.R. and Wernerfelt, B. (1989) 'The competitive implications of relevant-set/response analysis', *Journal of Marketing Research*, 26(4): 391–405.
Henderson, J. and Quandt, R. (1980). *Microeconomic Theory: A Mathematical Approach* (Economics handbook series), 3rd edn. New York: Mcgraw-Hill College.
Howard, J. (1963) *Marketing Management, Analysis and Planning*. New York: McGraw-Hill.
Howard, J.A. and Sheth, J.N. (1969) *The Theory of Buyer Behaviour*. New York: John Wiley.
Jafari, J. (1990) 'Research and scholarship: the basis of tourism education', *Journal of Tourism Studies*, 1(1): 33–41.
— (2001) 'The scientification of tourism', in V. Smith and M. Brent (eds) *Hosts and Guests Revisited: Tourism Issues of the 21st Century*. Elmsford, NY: Cognizant Communication Corporation, pp. 28–41.
— (2002) 'Retracing and mapping tourism's landscape of knowledge', *ReVista – Tourism in the Americas: Harvard Review of Latin America*, Winter.
Jafari, J. and Ritchie, J.R.B. (1981) 'Towards a framework of tourism education: problems and prospects', *Annals of Tourism Research*, 8: 13–34.
Jeng, J. and Fesenmaier, D.R. (1996) 'A neural network approach to discrete choice modelling', *Journal of Travel and Tourism Marketing*, 6(1/2): 119–44.
Kahneman, D. (2002) 'Maps of bounded rationality: a perspective on intuitive judgment and choice', Prize Lecture, 8 December 8 2002, http://www.nobelprize.org/nobel_prizes/economics/laureates/2002/kahnemann-lecture.pdf (last accessed on 14 February 2013).

— (2003a) 'A perspective on judgment and choice: mapping bounded rationality', *American Psychologist*, 58(9): 697–720.

— (2003b) 'A psychological perspective on economics', *American Economic Review*, 93(2): 162–8.

Kahneman, D. and Tversky, A. (1979) 'Prospect theory: an analysis of decision under risk', *Econometrica*, 47(2): 263–91.

Kim, S. and Yoon, Y. (2003) 'The hierarchical effects of affective and cognitive components on tourism destination image', *Journal of Travel and Marketing*, 14(20): 1–22.

Kroes, E.P. and Sheldon, R.J. (1988) 'Stated preference methods: an introduction', *Journal of Transport Economics and Policy*, 22(1): 11–25.

Lancaster, K.J. (1966) 'A new approach to consumer theory', *Journal of Political Economy*, 74: 132–57.

McFadden, D.L. (2005) 'The new science of pleasure: consumer behaviour and the measurement of well-being', Firsch Lecture, Econometric Society World Congress. Available at http://emlab.berkeley.edu/wp/mcfadden0105/ScienceofPleasure.pdf (last accessed on 14 February 2013).

March, R. and Woodside, A. (2005) 'Testing theory of planned versus realized tourist behaviour', *Annals of Tourism Research*, 32(4): 905–24.

Mayo, E. and Jarvis, L. (1981) *The Psychology of Leisure Travel: Effective Marketing and Selling of Travel Services*. Boston: CBI Publishing.

Miller, G.A. (1956) 'The magical number seven, plus or minus two: some limits on our capacity for processing information', *Psychological Review*, 63: 81–97.

Morey, E.R., Shaw, W. and Rowe, R. (1991) 'A discrete choice model of recreational participation, site choice and activity valuation when complete trip data is not available', *Journal of Environmental Economics and Management*, 20: 181–201.

Morley, C.L. (1992) 'A microeconomic theory of international tourism demand', *Annals of Tourism Research*, 19: 250–67.

Narayana, C.L. and Markin, R. (1975) 'Consumer behaviour and product performance: an alternative conceptualization', *Journal of Marketing*, 39: 1–6.

Nicosia, F.M. (1966) *Consumer Decision Process: Marketing and Advertising Implications*. Englewood Cliffs, NJ: Prentice Hall.

Nyaupane, G.P., Morais, D.B. and Graefe, A.R. (2004) 'Nature tourism constraints: a cross-activity comparison', *Annals of Tourism Research*, 31(3): 540–55.

Otto, J.E. (1997) 'The role of the affective experience in the service experience chain'. Unpublished doctoral dissertation. Canada: The University of Calgary.

Otto, J.E. and Ritchie, J.R.B. (1995) 'Exploring the quality of the service experience: a theoretical and empirical analysis', in T. Swartz, D. Bowen and S. Brown (eds) *Advances in Services Marketing and Management: Research and Practice*. Connecticut: JAI Press, pp. 37–62.

Papatheodorou, A. (2001) 'Why people travel to different places', *Annals of Tourism Research*, 28(1): 164–79.

Pearce, P.L. and Lee, U.I. (2005) 'Developing the travel career approach to tourist motivation', *Journal of Travel Research*, 43: 226–37.

Pennington-Gray, L. and Kerstetter, D.L. (2002) 'Testing a constraints model within the context of nature-based tourism', *Journal of Travel Research*, 40(4): 416–23.

Perdue, R.R. (1986) 'Traders and nontraders in recreational destination choice', *Journal of Leisure Research*, 18(1): 12–25.

Plog, S. (1974) 'Why destination areas rise and fall in popularity', *The Cornell Hotel and Restaurant Administration Quarterly*, 14(3): 55–8.

Riera Font, A. (2000) 'Modelización de elección discreta y coste del viaje. Los espacios protegidos en Mallorca', *Revista de Economía Aplicada*, 8(24): 181–201.

Rugg, D. (1973) 'The choice of journey destination: a theoretical and empirical analysis', *Review of Economics and Statistics*, 55: 64–72.

Schmidt, U. (2004) 'Reference dependence in cumulative prospect theory', *Journal of Mathematical Psychology*, 47(2): 122–31.

Schroeder, H.W. and Louviere, J. (1999) 'Research leisure travel participation – the case of the Southeast of Portugal', *Plicada*, 31(3): 300–24.

Sibley, D. (1976) 'On pattern and dispersion', *Area*, 8: 163–5.

Siderelis, C. and Moore, R. (1998) 'Recreation demand and the influence of site preference variables', *Journal of Leisure Research*, 30: 301–18.

Silva, O. and Correia, A. (2008) 'Facilitators and constraints in leisure travel participation – the case of the southeast of Portugal', *International Journal of Culture, Tourism, and Hospitality Research*, 2(1): 25–43.

Sirakaya, E., McLellan, R.W. and Uysal, M. (1996) 'Modelling vacation destination decisions: a behavioural approach', *Journal of Travel and Tourism Marketing*, 5(1/2): 57–75.

Spiggle, S. and Sewall, M. (1987) 'A choice sets model of retail selection', *Journal of Marketing*, 51(April): 97–111.

Stanovich, K.E. and Richard, F.W. (2000) 'Individual differences in reasoning: implications for the rationality debate?', *Behavioural and Brain*, 23(5): 645–65.

Timmermans, H. and Golledge, R.G. (1989) 'Application of behavioural research on spatial problems II: preference and choice', *Progress in Human Geography*, 14: 311–54.

Tribe, J. (1997) 'The indiscipline of tourism', *Annals of Tourism Research*, 24(3): 638–57.

Vogt, C., Klenosky, D.B. and Andereck, K. (2003) 'Place visitation and activity history as predictors of a new park's potential visitation', *Leisure Research Symposium*. Ashburn, VA: National Recreation and Park Association.

Woodside, A.G. (2004) 'Advancing from subjective to confirmatory personal introspection in consumer research', *Psychology and Marketing*, 21: 987–1010.

Woodside, A. and Lysonski, S. (1989) 'General model of traveller destination choice', *Journal of Travel Research*, 27(4): 8–14.

Woodside A.G. and Sherel, D. (1977) 'Traveller evoked, inept, and inert sets of vacation destinations', *Journal of Travel Research*, 16(1): 14–8.

Woodside, A.G., Krauss, E., Caldwell, M. and Chebat, J. (2006) 'Advancing folk theory of behaviour explanation, ecological systems theory, and the fit-like-a-glove model for understanding lifestyle, leisure, and travel behaviour'. Unpublished working paper.

23

Tourist destination choice

A review and critical evaluation of preference estimation methods in tourism marketing research

Chunxiao Li

Since tourists' decision-making is a quite complicated mental process, it has been a challenge for tourism scholars to find out how to investigate this abstract object and to apply research methods satisfactorily. There have been all kinds of quantitative and qualitative research methods adopted to understand tourists' decision-making. As a matter of fact, different perspectives on this interesting topic require different instruments. In order to understand the critical implications of these studies for wider tourism marketing, as well as to understand which method is most appropriate for different circumstances or research questions, it is important for us to have a clear understanding about what kinds of methods are available, what functions these methods serve and what goals can be achieved through each method.

However, there are few reviews of decision-making approaches in tourism that focus on the debates surrounding research approach and methods, either in terms of a critical analysis of the methods used to measure tourists' decision-making behaviour or in terms of propositions for methodological development. This chapter tries to address this gap with a review and analysis of the existing estimation methods applied to tourists' decision-making and a consideration of some possible new estimation methods, which are emerging in recent studies on tourism decision-making. Since other chapters in this handbook deal with theoretical issues in tourist decision-making, the current focus is entirely on the estimation methods of tourists' preferences in destination choice behaviour.

Although the process of tourists' destination choice can be very complex, there is one area of agreement amongst scholars, and that is that destinations are chosen based on certain criteria, which are set by tourists according to their own preferences. Moreover, tourism destinations are different from manufactured products because they consist of a range of intangible and tangible attributes and features, including social, cultural and environmental resources. Thus, the utility perceived by tourists is derived from different parts or attributes of this amalgamation of destination resources. Generally tourists' evaluations of destinations are based on the relative importance they attach to different attributes in their established criteria.

Therefore investigating these evaluation criteria is the key to understanding tourists' preferences and their choice behaviour. There are three important questions that need to be answered regarding the evaluation criteria used during tourists' decision-making:

1 which are the attributes/factors used as evaluation criteria by tourists;
2 how important are each of these attributes in tourists' decision-making; and
3 how are these attributes manipulated by tourists to evaluate alternatives.

This chapter addresses these key questions as a framework in which to discuss and evaluate the research methods that have been or might be used to understand tourists' preferences. The chapter concludes by arguing that combined techniques and emerging methods offer good prospects to future research to understand how tourists make destination choice decisions in different market contexts.

Which attributes/factors are selected as evaluation criteria by tourists?

The simplest way to find out which attributes or factors are important for tourists is to ask them straightforwardly either in the form of questionnaire or interviews. In previous questionnaire based studies, researchers have tended to generate a list of possible attributes that are deemed to be important to tourists such as price, safety or destination weather etc. and then ask respondents to do a Likert-type scale or rating task for each attribute regarding their importance (e.g. Haahti 1986; Um and Crompton 1990; Go and Zhang 1997). For example, Um and Crompton (1990) used a three-point scale questionnaire to classify 20 different attributes into perceived inhibitors, neither perceived inhibitors nor perceived facilitators, or perceived facilitators. They then used a five-point scale to assess the relative strength of each attribute as a facilitator or inhibitor. Using this method, based on the positive or negative role of each attribute, the attitudes of tourists toward each destination can be estimated. In addition, if there are too many relevant attributes which are found to be important during the decision-making, a factor analysis can be conducted to reduce the number of attributes into a fewer dimensions/factors. Additionally, the attributes should be in a form of at least ordinal data, and thus the reliability of each dimension is indicated by Cronbach's alpha which is a coefficient of internal consistency. The study conducted by Beerli and Martin (2004) is an example using factor analysis to classify the attributes that form a positive destination image as well to identify the motivations behind destination selection.

In qualitative interview approaches, open-ended questions such as 'what attributes do you consider when you choose a tourism destination?' are frequently used and the qualitative data provided can be analyzed using content analysis so that frequently used phrases and words can be coded and generalized as common attributes that are considered important (see Klenosky 2002).

As these two methods only ask for tourists' opinions toward each attribute without comparisons and the survey task or interview questions are easily understandable, the respondents only need to use simple judgements to provide answers. Therefore, the response rate should be higher than with more complicated methods containing complex tasks. Normally, for a new market or an unfamiliar market whose preferences are still unknown, qualitative interviews or simple questionnaires with further data analysis are very useful to explore the relevant attributes concerned and how they are used as criteria in tourists' decision-making. However, since respondents don't need to compare different attributes directly and qualitative interview methods cannot provide generalizable descriptions, the relative importance values of each attribute compared to each other cannot be obtained and it is impossible to estimate how much effect on the decision-making would be generated if the selected attributes change in importance. In order to know more about these relevant attributes, it is necessary to quantify their importance, and the most common approach used in tourism studies is a range of regression methods including simple regression, multinomial logistic regression and conditional logistic regression. The following section evaluates these approaches.

How important are these attributes during tourists' decision-making?

Regression analysis can provide more detail about the relative importance of each attribute and how the value of total preference of destinations changes when any one of the relevant attributes varies. The value of total preference can be indicated by the number of tourist arrivals in the destination or by the assigned values of how much tourists prefer this destination. Additionally, the relevant attributes can be derived from the hypothesis of researchers or previous exploratory studies.

Different types of regression have different functions. If the interest is only on testing the specific influence of a single attribute (e.g. price and climate) on the choice, a simple regression can be used. The most common simple regression used in tourism destination choice studies is linear regression which assumes that a change of the independent variable (the attribute) can directly lead to the change of the dependent variable (the preference) and that the pattern of change is linear. For example, if the independent variable is transport price and the dependent variable is the number of annual arrivals of one destination, a simple linear regression may be able to find that transport price is inversely proportional to the annual arrivals and every unit increase of the transport price will generate a 0.6 unit decrease of the number of annual arrivals to this destination. Sometimes the influence of the attribute on the preference is not linear but in a curve shape such as the temperature of the destination. The preference may start to increase from a lower level of temperature until reaching the peak at a certain temperature at which point it starts to decrease. In such situations, when linear regression is not suitable, polynomial regression (e.g. quadric regression and cubic regression) can be used to explore an influence relationship in any level of curvilinearity. And in this case, quadric regression is the correct method for finding the ideal temperature that generates maximum preference.

However, due to the complexity of a destination as a product, it is rare that the final destination selected is only based on a single attribute. Therefore, simple regression is normally used to confirm the influence that a certain attribute plays during the decision-making. But in order to gain a more comprehensive insight on the decision-making process, we may look into the combined effect of a group of attributes together and hence a multi-regression approach is required. Actually multi-regression is an extension of simple regression that incorporates two or more independent variables in a prediction equation for a dependent variable. The study of Sonmez and Graefe (1998) is an example that adopted both simple regression and multi-regression techniques to test the effect of different demographic characteristics on risk perception (multi-regression) and the influence of risk perception on the preference of foreign tourists (simple regression). Other examples include the ordinary least square regression used to explore the impact of personality on perceived destination values (Ekinci and Hosany 2006) and a multi-regression of tourists visiting Australia (Crouch *et al.* 1992). In addition, significance tests such as ANOVA and T-test provide a way of measuring the quality of the findings since they can indicate to what extent the relationship found by the regression can be a product of mere coincidence.

Normally, regressions only deal with ratio data or at least ordinal data that can be regarded as continuous variables. But in circumstances where the dependent variable is dichotomous or categorical, general regressions are not enough. For instance, in situations where the research seeks to investigate how perceived important attributes determine the final choice of the tourists.

The dependent variable here is the final choice of tourists, which can be formulated either in terms of whether or not a certain destination is chosen (dichotomous variable) or, which destination among a few options is chosen (categorical variable). In this situation, it is possible to use logistic regression, also known as a logit model, to find out the possibility of each outcome based on the independent variables (the predictors). There are two types of logistic regressions that are used frequently in tourism destination choice studies, multinomial logit and conditional logit. Basically, multinomial logit is used to identify the influence of individual characteristics (e.g. Morley 1994) such as demographics or attitudes of tourists in decision-making while the conditional logit is used for testing the importance of destination characteristics on final choice (e.g. Seddighi and Theocharous 2002).

One thing to be noted is that importance of the attributes measured by general regression analysis is represented by the coefficient value, which describes the changing ratio between dependent and independent variables. It is not a measure of the absolute importance value assigned to each attribute by tourists but rather a value that indicates the elasticity of each attribute. For example, if we find the coefficient values for price and local temperature on destination choice are 0.4 and 0.2, it does not mean that for tourists price is twice as important as local temperature or tourists would consider price first then local temperature. It only means that every unit of change of price level would generate twice the effects on overall preference than every unit of change in local temperature. Furthermore, regression analysis simplifies the complex mental decision-making process into an input–output relationship between independent variables and dependent variables. The simplification enables statistical calculations for such a complex problem but it does not allow explanatory insights concerning the true process of tourists' decision-making.

In recent years, a more sophisticated method named Analytic Hierarchy Process (AHP) has been widely used in a variety of multi-criteria decision-making fields including government, industry, healthcare and education. The AHP was initially introduced by Saaty (1997) for operations management studies. It is a methodology that provides a systematic problem-solving framework. Specifically, it enables the researcher to estimate the relative priority of elements within the hieratical structure by conducting a series of paired comparisons. Compared with traditional multi-criteria decision-making analysis methods such as the regressions mentioned above, the respondents found the AHP method required less difficult mental processing since it is quite straightforward and due to the systematic guide provided by AHP during the comparisons. The respondents perceived the findings about the importance of each attribute more trustworthy (Schoemaker and Waid 1982). A brief summary of how this method works is presented below.

Firstly, the AHP decomposes the decision-making problem into a hierarchy. A simple hierarchical structure of decision-making from the top to bottom is comprised as follows: choice objective; criteria; sub-criteria; and alternatives (see Figure 23.1). Actually, the criteria can be further divided into many layers of sub-criteria. Secondly, decision makers pair-wise compare the criteria (N = 3 in Figure 23.1) at level 2 by expressing their preference between every 2 criteria. For the example listed in Figure 23.1, criterion 1 is two times more important than criteria 3 but equally important as criterion 2, criterion 2 is two times more important than criteria 3. These paired comparisons can be formed into a (N * N) preference matrix and then by using the eigenvector solution it is possible to convert the preference matrix into the numerical priority values of each criterion. Thus the sum of priority values at each level equals 1.

As can be seen in Figure 23.1, the calculated priority values for the three criteria at level 2 are 0.4, 0.4 and 0.2. Following the same paired comparison and calculation process, the local priority values for the sub-criteria within each criterion at level 3 can be calculated. In order to

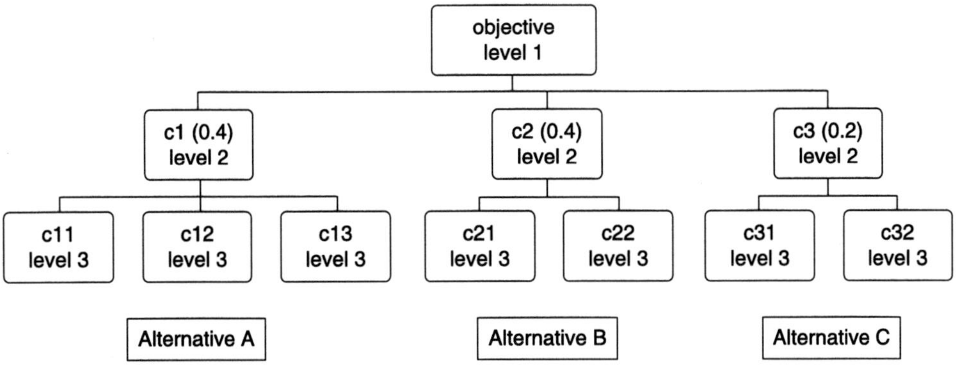

Figure 23.1 Hierarchical structure of decision-making.

compare the importance from c11 to c32, it is necessary to know their global priority values. Their global priority values are their local priority values multiplied by the weight of their superior criterion.

Let's assume that the local priority values for c11, c12 and c13 are 0.2, 0.2 and 0.4, which means within criterion 1, c11 is equally important to c12 and half as important as c13. The global priority values for c11, c12 and c13 are their local values multiplied by the weight of c1 (0.4), which are 0.08, 0.08 and 0.16. Actually the local priority value of each sub-criterion is their preference weight within one criterion while the global priority value is their preference weight that can be used to make a comparison across the whole level.

At last, after having the global priority values for each sub-criterion, the decision maker needs to pair-wise compare all the alternatives regarding their real performance on each sub-criterion and provide a quality score for each sub-criterion of each alternative. For example, there are alternatives A, B and C. As for the performance regarding sub-criterion 1, Alternative A is equally as good as B but twice as good as C, then the quality scores of this sub-criterion for each alternative are 0.4, 0.4 and 0.2 (the calculation process is the same as the calculation for the priority values). So the total preference for each alternative is given by global priority value * quality score of each sub-criterion. Eventually, the ranking of the alternatives and final decision can be made based on these preference values.

In addition, this method uses subjective judgments from respondents. And in order to make sure the judgments of the respondents are consistent with each other through the whole process, the AHP allows a consistency ratio measurement, which is used to check whether the comparisons of respondents are rational in terms of consistency. For example, if one respondent thinks A is twice as important as B and B is equally important as C, then when he compares A and C, he should think A is about twice important than C. However, the method does not require the respondents to be perfectly consistent during the whole paired comparisons. The rule of thumb is that the consistency ratio should be equal to or less than 0.1 to make sure this respondent is rational and consistent enough. Otherwise, the evaluation of this respondent cannot be used as a valid data.

Unlike asking respondents to assign preference values to each sub-criterion directly, this method helps respondents to go through the whole decision-making process step by step, from the comparison between broad criteria to the comparison between the sub-criteria within each broad criteria. This hierarchical process of pair-wise comparison enables respondents to make the judgements easier and more accurate. And this advantage makes the AHP a good method to deal with evaluations among a large number of attributes with different qualities that are difficult to compare directly, which is often the case in destination choice.

An introduction to and empirical research on the application of AHP can be found in some tourism studies (e.g. Deng *et al.* 2002; Crouch and Ritchie 2005; Calantone and di Benedetto 1991). Additionally this method was used by Hsu *et al.* (2009) as an analysis method to investigate tourists' preferences of destination choice. A four-level AHP model with 22 sub-criteria on the fourth level was used in this study. Compared to other tourism decision-making studies using regression methods, it was able to provide the relative weights of a large number (22) of attributes at one time. Furthermore, by clustering attributes into different levels, tourists only need to evaluate the attributes with a similar nature, which makes the comparison easier. The 22 attributes estimated by Hsu *et al.* (2009) were initially divided into internal factors and external factors, where the internal factors were further sub-divided into four categories and external factors were divided into two categories. At each stage, respondents only need to compare two attributes at the same level and within the same superior criterion.

Although the paired comparison for respondents at each stage is quite simple, there would be a huge amount of workload if there were a large number of attributes within one category. If for example there are nine attributes within the same superior criterion, then the respondents need to complete 45 comparisons to make sure all the attributes are compared to each other. Additionally, where there is a large number of alternatives the number of comparisons among alternatives regarding each attribute's quality score would be too complex for respondents. Furthermore, in the traditional AHP method, the pair-wise comparison is made using a nine-point scale (1–9), which converts human preferences between available alternatives as equally, moderately, strongly, very strongly or extremely preferred. In some real situations, respondents might be reluctant or unable to provide exact numerical values to the comparison judgments. Therefore, modification and improvement of the traditional AHP approach concerning these disadvantages are required.

In Hsu *et al.* (2009), the authors combined a fuzzy theory method with the traditional AHP to reduce the workload of respondents, which allowed respondents to provide fuzzy judgements instead of assigning precise comparison values. It is thus clear that a smart combination of methods can be a good way to overcome the disadvantages of a single method and to make estimations more effective.

How are attributes manipulated (choice heuristics) by tourists to evaluate alternatives?

All the methods mentioned above are helpful for use in studies to gain more understanding about which destination attributes are important to tourists and how much they are preferred. As a matter of fact, in order to predict the final choice of tourists' decision-making, we not only need to know what attributes or factors are involved, but it is also necessary to understand the choice heuristics that are applied by decision makers. The choice heuristic, or the evaluation rules, refers to the way tourists use criteria to evaluate alternative destinations. For example, some tourists (type A) may weigh every attribute carefully and select one destination with the highest score whilst others (type B) may look at the most important attribute first and keep the alternative with the best performance. If there is a tie, then they would look at the second important attribute and select the one with the best performance, until there is only one destination left. As a matter of fact, even if the two types of tourists evaluate the same attributes during their decision-making process their choices might be different because of the different choice heuristics they applied.

According to psychologists, choice heuristics can be generally divided into two main categories, compensatory and non-compensatory (Abelson and Levi 1985). In the above example, some tourists (type A) use a compensatory choice heuristic, which allows the low value of one attribute to be compensated by the high value of another attribute. The compensatory heuristic model is also known as utility maximization theory in economics. Whereas other tourists (type B) use a non-compensatory choice heuristic which does not allow for trade-off between attributes, if one alternative does not meet the requirement on the most important attribute, it will not be considered even if its performance on the rest of the attributes is quite attractive. The decisions for type B tourists are made based on non-negotiable principles. Due to the huge influence of economics, most studies assume that tourists are rational and would use a compensatory choice heuristic to maximize the utility of their choice. There are few studies in tourism that focus on exploring the possibility of using a non-compensatory choice heuristic. But actually this is disingenuous since in many contexts, with limited information, time and energy, tourists tend to adopt a non-compensatory choice heuristic, which can simplify the decision-making process.

The following section deals with the issues in the following way. Firstly, a review of the use of conjoint analysis is outlined, which is the dominant estimation method used in marketing and tourism studies to investigate compensatory choice heuristics. And then a new method known as greedoid analysis is introduced, which may provide an alternative method to estimate non-compensatory preference and choice heuristics in tourism decision-making studies.

Conjoint analysis

Conjoint measurement was first introduced by Luce and Tukey in 1964 as a new type of fundamental measurement of extensive quantities in the field of mathematics and statistics. It differs from classic measures because it can compare the effects of combinations formed by quantities of items of different qualities rather than a comparison between combinations of quantities from one single specified kind (Luce and Tukey 1964). For instance, when people want to buy a car, they may consider the colour and the price of the car. However due to certain reasons, the manufacturer can only provide a black car at £20,000 and a red car at £18,000. In such situations, for the buyers who prefer black colour and lower price, they need to compare the combinations of colour and price and then make a decision. In this case, only knowing buyers' preferences for colour or price separately are not enough for researchers to make a prediction here. Instead, there is a need to be able to estimate which combination (black car at £20,000 or red car at £18,000) is more attractive and conjoint measurement is an option here.

Green developed conjoint measurement further as an analysis method and adapted it to the field of marketing (e.g. Green and Rao 1971; Green and Wind 1973; Green and Srinivasan 1978). Consumer researchers used the scaling aspects of conjoint analysis – finding specific numerical scale values under an assumed composition rule, mostly weighted additive (compensatory) composition. To be precise, researchers usually use the conjoint method to determine what combination of attributes is most influential on respondent choice by estimating the values or part-worth of each attribute.

In consumer decision-making research, conjoint analysis has been a very popular method used by scholars for two reasons. Firstly, this method can estimate the contributions of different attributes and the levels of an attribute involved in a product. For example, it can tell us how much the price contributes to the willingness of a consumer to buy a computer and which price level is the best to attract the most potential consumers. Secondly, conjoint analysis can be used to establish a model of consumer judgment which allows us to predict consumers' preferences on any combinations of attributes, even those not included in the original test (Hair *et al.* 1998). In tourism contexts, conjoint analysis has also been widely applied (e.g. Bernoulli 1954; Dellaert *et al.* 1995; Dellaert *et al.* 1997; Basala and Klenosky 2001; Suh and Gartner 2004). Most of these studies use conjoint analysis to estimate the importance of different attributes in order to infer tourists' choice of activity packages or destinations. For example, Suh and Gartner (2004) used conjoint analysis to investigate the preferences of international urban travellers from Seoul, Korea with the aim to identify the relationship between preferences and expenditures for the attributes or activities.

Conjoint analysis can be used to test different models based on relationships between consumers' preferences and the nature of the attributes, which include the vector model, the ideal-point model and the part-worth function model. The vector model describes consumers' monotone preference on some continuous attributes. The most preferred value of an attribute is at infinity such as durability or price, more or less is always regarded better by consumers. The ideal-point model is also known as the quadratic model, which is used to illustrate some attributes like temperature of an environment. Too hot or too cold are both dis-preferred. The ideal amount preferred is always at the moderate level. Some attributes for which the preference pattern on them is uncertain (such as some categorical attributes like the mode of travel), the part-worth function model is more suitable since it only estimates the importance of specific levels within an attribute rather than assuming that any preference shape exists (Orme 2005). Generally speaking, the part-worth function model provides the greatest flexibility in allowing different shapes for the preference function along each of the attributes (Hawkins *et al.* 1989). After deciding a certain type of test module, there are always three essential steps involved in conjoint analysis, which are data collection, questionnaire design and estimation. The common ways used in previous conjoint studies for every stage are summarized below.

There are two main ways to collect the data required by conjoint analysis: the two-factor-at-a-time procedure and the full-profile approach. The two-factor-at-a-time procedure asks respondents to rank the various combinations of each pair of factor levels from most preferred to least preferred (Johnson 1974). This procedure is simple to apply and reduces information overload on the part of the respondent (Hawkins *et al.* 1989). But this decomposition method eliminates the influence of other attributes and it is not able to mimic the real selection situation as much as the full profile approach since respondents are only comparing different combinations of two factors rather than two products.

The full-profile approach (also referred to as the concept evaluation task) utilizes the complete set of factors including product profiles consisting of all relative important product features generalized by previous literature or investigations, which are presented to respondents. Although it will never be perfectly full-profiled and even the omitted attributes may generate bias, this approach gives a more realistic description of stimuli. Additionally, whilst the two-factor-at-a-time procedure provides only a set of rank orders, the full profile approach can employ either a rank order or ratings. However, since respondents need to process the information on every attribute, it might lead to problems of information overload. Under the circumstances of information overload, respondents might try to simplify this task by ignoring variations in the less important factors or even refuse to respond. Therefore, the full-profile procedure is generally confined to, at most, five or six factors in any specific sort (Hawkins *et al.* 1989; Gabbott and Hogg 1994).

In recent years, a choice-based approach was developed based on the traditional full-profile approach. However, unlike the traditional method, respondents are not required to rate or rank each profile directly. By using an online survey, respondents need to select one preferred stimuli among a subset of stimulus until enough information is obtained for sorting all profiles. This new technical way is more similar to what buyers actually do in the marketplace. And it allows respondents to select a 'none' option, which may reveal some non-compensatory preference information about the cut-off point regarded by respondents. For example, I would not choose any option within this set because prices of all offered products are too high. But information overload is a key problem for full-profile choice-based tasks since respondents need to deal with lots of information to select one profile with all attributes described before giving a single answer for each choice set, which is even harder than rating each stimulus. As a result, partial-profile choice-based conjoint studies were adopted later by researchers, which only provide a subset of the total number of attributes in each choice question. Because of attributes' omission, the information gathered by this method is not enough for estimating the part-worth of each individual respondent assigned to attribute levels. Data from groups of respondents are normally aggregated for analysis so that part-worth of a target group can be investigated.

Parameter (attributes) estimation is normally the last step in conjoint analysis. During this step, the part-worth utilities of each attribute are calculated so that the product with maximized utility can be predicted. According to the literature review of Green and Srinivasan (1978) there are three kinds of estimation methods which are:

1 non-metric estimation methods such as MONANOVA and LIMAP, which assume that the dependent variable is, at most, ordinal scaled;
2 metric estimation methods such OLS, which assume that the dependent variable is interval scaled and compute part-worth utilities by minimizing the squared sum of deviations between estimated and observed metric values;
3 methods that relate paired-comparison data to a choice probability model or parametric estimation methods. Methods in this class are the logit and probit models.

Nowadays, conjoint analysis is used as a prevalent tool in marketing research. In a survey among market research institutes, 65 per cent of the institutes indicated having used conjoint analysis within the last 12 months, and growing usage frequency was forecasted (Hartmann and Sattler 2002). Compensatory models with conjoint analysis are so popular because they not only forecast decision-making processes of compensatory preferences but also approximate the outcomes of other kinds of decision rules (Wahab *et al.* 1976). For instance, a weighted additive model can theoretically reproduce a non-compensatory decision process if, in the ordered set of weights, each weight is larger than the sum of all weights to come. Therefore, flexibility in assigning weights is the biggest advantage of conjoint analysis.

However, these methods to measure decision-making processes, which are based on utility maximization, have been questioned by scholars since the 1970s (Payne 1976; Beach and Mitchell 1978; Gigerenzer and Todd 1987; Rieskamp and Otto 2006). Some simple non-compensatory heuristic models such as conjunctive, disconjunctive and lexicographic heuristics were introduced and proved to be more or at least equally accurate in predicting consumer behaviour in some situations (Czerlinski *et al.* 1999). Besides, the time required to complete surveys and information overload for respondents is another disadvantage of conjoint tasks with a relatively large set of attributes. How to increase respondent rate and prevent unreliable answers caused by the complexity of the task remains a key problem to be solved. And this issue takes us to the application of greedy algorithms to these decision-making problems.

Greedoid analysis

Greedoid analysis based on a greedy algorithm was developed by Kohli and Jedidi (2007) and Yee *et al.* (2007) to infer non-compensatory heuristics including: conjunctive heuristic;

disconjunctive heuristic; lexicographic-by-features and lexicographic-by-aspects heuristic types. The concept of greedoid analysis was first proposed by Korte and Lovasz (1981) for proposing the generalization of the matroid concept and referring to a class of optimization problems which can be solved by greedy algorithms (Edmonds 1971). Greedy algorithms aim to solve a combinatorial optimization problem piece by piece and to always select the piece with the most benefit. They are simple and very easy to implement but sometimes they might be shortsighted since they simplify the decision process by always following the problem solving heuristic of making the locally optimal choice at each stage.

The most common example to explain the greedy algorithm is 'Making the change'. If only 50 pence, 20 pence and 1 penny coins are available, the goal is to 'make a change' of 74 pence with the minimum number of coins. In order to achieve this goal, the greedy algorithm is applied so that each time the coin of the highest value, but less than the remaining change owed, is selected until the whole process is finished. Therefore, one 50-pence coin, one 20-pence coin and four 1-penny coins are selected to make the change. The algorithm, however, fails if the available coins are 50 pence, 20 pence and 3 pence since after giving a 50-pence and a 20-pence coin, the algorithm cannot use 3-pence coins for the remaining 4 pence change. But a human would easily use one 50-pence coin and eight 3-pence coins to fulfil the task. Greedy algorithms can be used to mimic non-compensatory preference because sometimes people make decisions just like the process presented by the greedy algorithm. Sometimes, people tend to select the options with the most important attribute they regard and then keep selecting based on the second important attribute and continue on until the final option is selected. They will not go back to review other information on other attributes which makes the decision process simple and quick but in which the decision maker may miss some attractive options that did not meet their requirement on the most important attribute but were very compelling on the other important attributes.

In order to estimate this kind of non-compensatory (lexicographic) choice process for consumers, the greedy algorithm was introduced and developed by Kohli and Jedidi (2007) and Yee *et al.* (2007) independently. Kohli and Jedidi (2007) modified a greedy algorithm to infer lexicographic preference and two variants (conjunctive preference and lexicographic preference by aspect) on purchase decisions of laptop computers. Because in reality there is no perfect match between a certain type of preference function and the observed preference rank order, the authors simply assigned the most fit (statistically) preference model to each individual. For the test of model goodness-of-fit, the Kendall Tau value is used to indicate which preference model has more powerful predictability. During the data collection, each laptop is described by five attributes with 13 aspects in total. After the fractional factorial design, 16 profiles are generated and presented to 69 MBA students using cards. The respondents needed to rate each alternative according to their preference by a scale from 0–100. The results showed two-thirds of the subjects in a study of consumer preference for laptops use non-compensatory heuristics.

Yee *et al.* (2007) tested greedoid-based methods with applications to smartphones and computers. They compared lexicographic preference by aspect (LBA) to two compensatory benchmarks: hierarchical Bayes ranked logit (HBRL) and LINMAP. The greedy algorithm is programmed in Java. A Fractional factorial design generated 32 full profiles and a web-based questionnaire was conducted. The respondents were also students (339), they needed to rank the alternatives either in a full rank manner or select the ones they would consider and then rank these considered smartphones. The conjoint data set for computer choice was obtained from a previous study, which was rating data on a ten-point scale for 16 full profiles. The findings suggested that the lexicographic models predict well.

The details of the greedy algorithm and the mathematics behind the computer programming are presented in the study of Yee *et al.* (2007). A simple example to explain how greedoid-based dynamic programming works can be provided. Let's use the case of car purchasing again. Assume the car buyers are using a lexicographic-by-aspect choice heuristic, which means the buyers will select the cars with their most preferred attribute's aspect and then if there are ties, select the cars with their second preferred attribute's aspect until they find the final choice. There are three attributes with six aspects that are important for car buyers. These are the price (£18,000 and £20,000), the colour of the car (red and black) and the brand of the car (Mercedes Benz and Ford). There are eight combinations of the six aspects. And one respondent's preference ranking on the eight possible combinations presented by stimuli cards is:

1 Price £18,000, Red colour, Benz
2 Price £18,000, Red colour, Ford
3 Price £20,000, Red colour, Benz
4 Price £20,000, Red colour, Ford
5 Price £18,000, Black colour, Benz
6 Price £20,000, Black colour, Benz
7 Price £18,000, Black colour, Ford
8 Price £20,000, Black colour, Ford.

By observing the preference ranking, it is possible to tell that this respondent uses a perfect lexicographic-by-aspect choice heuristic, which means all the cars with red colour are put forward before any other cars and then if there are ties, the ones which are Mercedes Benz are ranked before other cars and then if there are still ties, the ones with lower price are ranked before other cars. When the aspects are very small and the respondents are following a perfect lexicographic heuristic, the lexicographic aspects order can be observed manually. But when there are a relatively larger number of aspects and many respondents, it is too much work for human analysis. The greedoid programme mimics the human observation analysis. Firstly, it starts with one aspect and checks if all the cars with this aspect are ranked before other cars until it finds the right aspect. And then the programme starts to check which aspect is the second preferred aspect until the aspects order can sort all stimuli cards. In addition, most of the time, the respondents are not following a perfect lexicographic heuristic, which means there is no one lexicographic aspects order that can replicate the ranking exactly. In these cases, the greedoid programme is able to find the best-fit aspects order that can replicate the closest ranking.

Although greedoid analysis is not able to provide the estimation of part-worth values of the attributes, there are several advantages that make greedoid analysis a promising method to estimate tourists' preference in destination decision-making. Firstly, it is a method that provides a better insight of non-compensatory choice process by incorporating the principles of non-compensatory factors rather than just adapting weighting schemes to imitate the output of non-compensatory heuristics (Gabbott and Hogg 1994). When there are numerous alternative destinations, tourists may tend to use a simplified non-compensatory choice heuristic. Therefore, the greedoid method can help us to explore the possibility of non-compensatory choice. Secondly, compared with traditional conjoint analysis, the greedoid method requires less in terms of respondent workload since it can deal with full-rank, consider-then-rank and rating tasks. Moreover, the dynamic programming algorithm proposed by Yee (2007) substantially reduces computation time and makes it feasible to identify the best lexicographic ordering for large samples of respondents and moderately large numbers of aspects. Finally, greedoid analysis can also identify the must-have aspect and the aspects that tourists used to eliminate the destinations.

The information is of great help for governments to improve their destinations, for travel agencies and tour operators to more effectively promote their products and for marketers to devise appropriate marketing strategies.

Conclusion

Depending on different objectives, different preference estimation methods can be used in a range of situations. For the tourism market where little or nothing is known about, the more direct methods such as simple questionnaires and interviews are handy to obtain the first impression of what attributes or factors tourists in this group care about. After narrowing down the important attributes into a shortlist, it is possible to test the specific influences of certain attributes or the combined effects of multi-attributes by more sophisticated methods such as regressions or conjoint analysis. If more detailed exploration about the mental processing in tourism decision-making is required, rather than thinking of it as a simple input and output procedure, the AHP method that decomposes decision-making into different stages may be applied. And in some contexts such as limited information available or limited time to make the decision, where tourists do not use utility maximization evaluation, methods that are based on non-compensatory choice heuristic theory such as greedoid method could be useful. However, the methods mentioned in this chapter are not the only options to estimate tourists' preference but just those commonly available and used.

All of these methods are adopted from other disciplines (e.g. economics) or research fields (e.g. marketing research and operations studies). Although these methods are very useful tools to investigate general decision-making, tourism decision-making may have its own features compared to other types of decision-making. Therefore, how to adapt these methods accordingly is a key issue for tourism scholars. A smart methods combination is one option. For example, due to the large number of destinations available, Hsu (2009) combined fuzzy theory with the traditional AHP to reduce the huge workload for tourists to compare the alternatives. Cina (2012) combined game theory with conjoint analysis to identify which combinations of attributes are suitable for different tourism festivals.

Moreover, with the development of tourism decision-making studies, more innovative research methods are desired to further explore tourists' preferences rather than staying at the stage of identifying preferred attributes or assign utility values to different attributes. For instance, do tourists evaluate destinations rationally? How do their preferences change at different stages? How is it possible to distinguish between different preference groups? All of these questions require more sophisticated theory models and estimation methods to answer. Greedoid analysis provides a starting point to explore non-compensatory (irrational) choice heuristics. However, further research needs to be done to apply or modify this method into tourism decision-making studies.

References

Abelson, R.P. and Levi, Y. (1985) 'Decision making and decision theory', in Lindzey, G. and Aronson, E. (eds) *The Handbook of Social Psychology*. New York: Random House.

Basala, S.L. and Klenosky, D.B. (2001) 'Travel-style preferences for visiting a novel destination: a conjoint investigation across the novelty-familiarity continuum', *Journal of Travel Research*, 40: 172–82.

Beach, L. and Mitchell, T. (1978) 'A contingency model for the selection of decision strategies', *The Academy of Management Review*, 3: 439–49.

Beerlt, A. and Martin, J.D. (2004) 'Factors influencing destination image', *Annals of Tourism Research*, 31: 657–81.

Bernoulli, D. (1954) 'Exposition of a new theory on the measurement of risk', *Econometrica*, 22: 23–36.
Calantonbe, R.J. and Di Benedetto, C.A. (1991) 'Knowledge acquisition modeling in tourism', *Annals of Tourism Research*, 18: 202–12.
Crouch, G.I. and Ritchie, J.R.B. (2005) 'Application of the analytic hierarchy process to tourism choice and decision making: a review and illustration applied to destination competitiveness', *Tourism Analysis*, 10: 17–25.
Crouch, G.I., Schultz, L. and Valerio, P. (1992) 'Marketing international tourism to Australia: a regression analysis', *Tourism Management*, 13: 196–208.
Czerlinski, J., Gigerenzer, G., Goldstein, D. and Todd, P. (1999) *How Good Are Simple Heuristics? Simple Heuristics that Make Us Smart*. London: Oxford University Press.
Dellaert, B., Borgers, A. and Timmermans, H. (1995) 'A day in the city: using conjoint choice experiments to model urban tourists' choice of activity package', *Tourism Management*, 16: 347–53.
Dellaert, B.G.C., Borgers, A.W.J. and Timmermans, H.J.P. (1997) 'Conjoint models of tourist portfolio choice: theory and illustration', *Leisure Sciences: An Interdisciplinary Journal*, 19: 31–58.
Deng, J., King, B. and Bauer, T. (2002) 'Evaluating natural attractions for tourism', *Annals of Tourism Research*, 29: 422–38.
Edmonds, J. (1971) 'Matroids and the greedy algorithm', *Mathematical Programming*, 1: 127–36.
Ekinci, Y. and Hosany, S. (2006) 'Destination personality: an application of brand personality to tourism destinations', *Journal of Travel Research*, 45: 127–39.
Gabbott, M. and Hogg, G. (1994) 'Consumer behaviour and services: a review', *Journal of Marketing Management*, 10: 311–24.
Gigerenzer, G. and Todd, P.M. (1987) *Simple Heuristics that Makes Us Smart*. New York: Oxford University Press.
Go, F. and Zhang, W. (1997) 'Applying importance-performance analysis to Beijing as an international meeting destination', *Journal of Travel Research*, 35: 42–9.
Green, P.E. and Rao, V.R. (1971) 'Conjoint measurement for quantifying judgmental data', *Journal of Marketing Research*, 8: 353–63.
Green, P.E. and Srinivasan, V. (1978) 'Conjoint analysis in consumer research: issues and outlook', *Journal of Consumer Research*, 5: 103–23.
Green, P.E. and Wind, Y. (1973) *Multi-attribute Decisions in Marketing*. New York: Holt Rinehart & Winston.
Haahti, A.J. (1986) 'Finland's competitive position as a destination', *Annals of Tourism Research*, 13: 11–35.
Hair, J.F., Anderson, R.E., Tatham, R.L. and Black, W. (1998) *Multivariate Data Analysis*. Upper Saddle River: Prentice Hall.
Hartmann, A. and Sattler, H. (2002) *Commercial Use of Conjoint Analysis in Germany, Austria and Switzerland*, [Online]. Available: http://uni.uni-hamburg.de/fachbereiche-einrichtungen/fb03/ihm/RP6.pdf (Accessed 18 February 2013).
Hawkins, D.I., Best, R.J. and Coney, K.A. (1989) *Consumer Behavior: Implications for Marketing Strategy*. Homewood, EL: Richard D. Irwin.
Johnson, R.M. (1974) 'Trade-off analysis of consumer values', *Journal of Marketing Research*, 11: 121–7.
Klenosky, D.B. (2002) 'The 'pull' of tourism destinations: a means-end investigation', *Journal of Travel Research*, 40: 396–403.
Kohli, R. and Jedidi, K. (2007) 'Representation and inference of lexicographic preference models and their variants', *Marketing Science*, 26: 380–99.
Korte, B. and Lovász, L. (1981) 'Mathematical structures underlying greedy algorithm', in Gecseg, F. (ed.) *Fundamentals of Computation Theory: Proceedings of the International FCT-conference, Szeged, Hungaria, 24–28 August 1981*. Berlin: Springer.
Luce, R.D. and Tukey, J.W. (1964) 'Simultaneous conjoint measurement: a new type of fundamental measurement', *Journal of Mathematical Psychology*, 1: 1–27.
Morley, C.L. (1994) 'Experimental destination choice analysis', *Annals of Tourism Research*, 21: 780–91.
Orme, B.K. (2005) *Getting Started with Conjoint Analysis: Strategies for Product Design and Pricing*. Madison: Research Publishers, LLC.
Payne, J.W. (1976) 'Task complexity and contingent processing in decision making: an information search and protocol analysis', *Organizational Behavior and Human Performance*, 16: 366–87.
Rieskamp, J. and Otto, P.E. (2006) 'SSL: a theory of how people learn to select strategies', *Journal of Experimental Psychology: General*, 135: 207–36.
Saaty, T.L. (1997) 'That is not the analytic hierarchy process: what the AHP is and what it is not', *Journal of Multi-Criteria Decision Analysis*, 6: 324–35.

Schoemaker, P.J.H. and Waid, C.C. (1982) 'An experimental comparison of different approaches to determining weights in additive utility models', *Management Science*, 28: 182–96.
Seddighi, H.R. and Theocharous, A.L. (2002) 'A model of tourism destination choice: a theoretical and empirical analysis', *Tourism Management*, 23: 475–87.
Sonmez, S.F. and Graefe, A.R. (1998) 'Influence of terrorism risk on foreign tourism decisions', *Annals of Tourism Research*, 25: 112–44.
Suh, Y.K. and Gartner, W.C. (2004) 'Preferences and trip expenditures – a conjoint analysis of visitors to Seoul, Korea', *Tourism Management*, 25: 127–37.
Um, S. and Crompton, J.L. (1990) 'Attitude determinants in tourism destination choice', *Annals of Tourism Research*, 17: 432–48.
Wahab, S., Crampon, L.J. and Rothfield, L.M. (1976) *Tourism Marketing: A Destination-Orientated Programme for the Marketing of International Tourism*. London: Tourism International Press.
Yee, M., Dahan, E., Hauser, J.R. and Orlin, J. (2007) 'Greedoid-based noncompensatory inference', *Marketing Science*, 26: 532–49.

Part 6

Micro-marketing issues in tourism

24

Service design

Co-creating meaningful experiences with customers

Marc Stickdorn

Why tourism needs service design

Customer experience is increasingly becoming the decisive success factor of tourism products. The provision of good customer experience cannot be left to chance and, thus, the design of services and the whole service ecosystem is becoming vital in an environment of growing competition for customer experiences. Service design is a user-centred approach to systematically analyze, innovate and improve service processes from a customer's perspective. This first section of this chapter provides an introduction on the increasing importance of customer experiences not only for the tourism industry. The subsequent parts provide an overview on the basics of service design in a tourism context, outline the service design process and present three hands-on tools.

Customer experience

Practitioners and academics – also beyond the tourism field – agree that customer experiences become a decisive factor for the success of brands, products and services. This realization is far from being new, but rather has evolved over more than 40 years (e.g. Toffler 1970; Holbrook and Hirschman 1982; Schulze 1992; Pine and Gilmore 1999). However, only recently have companies become increasingly focused on offering superior experiences as a main source of their competitive advantage (e.g. Hsieh 2010). The evident impact of social media can be seen as one of the main factors driving this change across all industries, since customers increasingly trust more the verdict of other customers than classic corporate communications (Stickdorn and Schneider 2010).

In its early years marketing focused on goods. Services only gained importance in marketing from the 1970s onwards as researchers realized that the economic value of services was beginning to exceed that of other kinds of activity (Kimbell 2010). In this context, Booms and Bitner (1981) expanded the classic marketing mix (product, price, promotion and place) by three additional factors: participants (i.e. people involved in the service encounter), processes (i.e. procedures, mechanisms and flows of activities) and physical evidences (the surroundings and tangible objects).

According to classic definitions, services have been differentiated from products by their particular characteristics of intangibility, heterogeneity, inseparability and perishability (Regan 1963; Rathmell 1966; Shostack 1977; Zeithaml *et al.* 1985). However, current literature criticizes such definitions and understands service rather as 'the whole organization's performance in providing the customer with a good experience' (Edvardsson *et al.* 2005). Vargo and Lusch (2004a, 2004b) argue that products cannot provide a desired benefit unless the customer interacts with them and Pine and Gilmore (1999) realize that products often serve as the hardware for consumption experiences. Hence, customer experience refers to all direct and indirect interactions customers have with products as well as with (tourism) services.

The importance of customer experience in tourism

Most tourism products are booked and paid for in advance. Thus, customers have to rely on the accuracy of accessible information. Besides the information provided by tourism companies, social media and particularly online review websites enable customers to share personal reviews on products and services. Studies show that up to 95 per cent of German tourists consider online customer reviews as trustworthy and 65 per cent would no longer book any travel without previously checking customer reviews on respective websites (IUBH 2011). Since online reviews affect potential customers in their purchase decision, and such reviews ultimately reflect customer satisfaction, customer satisfaction emerges as a crucial success factor for the tourism industry.

Tourism products generally consist of multiple services and are often referred to as a service package or bundle. Characteristically these bundles are built around a main (or core) service, framed by auxiliary (or peripheral) services as add-ons (Grönroos 2001). One single service provider seldom provides these bundles alone, but rather tourism products link together various services offered by different service providers. The fundamental product in tourism is the destination experience and thus competition centres on destinations (Ritchie and Crouch 2000). In this context, Buhalis (2000) defines destinations as 'amalgams of tourism products, which offer an integrated experience to consumers'. The overall customer experience of a destination ultimately depends on the sum of each service experience within a destination, which is provided by various companies. However, the variety of stakeholders involved in this destination experience induces an almost intrinsic conflict of interest. Since service providers within the same branch of business compete with each other within a destination, to compete as a destination on any market, a rather consistent branding and image is required, and, thus, a certain level of coordination between these competitors is needed. One major challenge for successful destination management is to align individual interests of stakeholders into an efficient cooperation.

Although a holistic view on tourism products within complex tourism destination gains importance, the overall customer experience goes far beyond the mere destination experience and it involves even more stakeholders than those within a destination. The overall customer experience of tourists starts long before the destination experience in the so-called pre-service period, when potential customers search information through catalogues, magazines, websites, online reviews or social media. It also includes the booking procedures of tourism products. The destination experience comprises all customer experiences during the stay on site as well as the journey to and from the destination, the so-called service period. The post-service period refers to all customer experiences after the stay, such as customer relationship efforts of involved companies as well as communication by customers via word-of-mouth or electronic word-of-mouth. Such a sequence of customer experiences is always divided into pre-service, service and post-service period and reflects the complexity of customer experiences beyond the tourism product (Stickdorn 2009).

The tourism experience

The overall customer experience of a tourist can be described as a customer journey. Just like a movie portrays the story of a main actor, a customer journey describes the customer experiences of a customer in a similar manner. And just like a movie tells a story as a sequence of scenes, a customer journey consists of a sequence of touchpoints. Thus, a touchpoint describes one single customer experience that can be a direct interaction between a customer and a service provider, such as the check-in process of a hotel, but a touchpoint can be also an indirect interaction, such as when customers recommend a hotel to a friend. Such a customer journey consisting of a sequence of touchpoints can be represented in various forms, e.g. as a story like the script of a movie or as a storyboard with drawings illustrating what happens at each touchpoint somewhat like a comic strip. The Customer Journey Canvas by Stickdorn and Schneider (2010) provides a simple template to envision this concept (Figure 24.1).

Touchpoints within the pre-service period evoke certain expectations about a particular tourism product regardless of whether these touchpoints are directly between customers and a brand (such as advertisements, telephone or email contact, etc.) or indirectly (such as word-of-mouth or electronic word-of-mouth). Also past experiences belong to the pre-service period, e.g. when a loyal customer returns because of positive memories. The sum of all these touchpoints builds up certain customer expectations towards a tourism product.

Touchpoints within the service period refer to the actual destination experience including the in- and outbound journey. The example of a customer journey focusing on only one stakeholder exemplifies the complexity of the customer journey reflecting a whole destination experience with multiple stakeholders. The sequence of touchpoints regarding only the hotel experience could be as follows: the arrival at a hotel, orientation in the lobby, queuing up for the check-in, the check-in process, luggage handling, finding the room, etc. Taking into account the complexity of tourism products and the various services provided by different companies, a single customer journey can consist out of a vast number of touchpoints. Thus, in practice customer journeys are made for different levels of details depending on the focus of interest. At least subconsciously, customers permanently compare their experiences of touchpoints within the service period with their a priori expectations. Theories such as Kano's theory of attractive quality (Kano and Takahashi 1979) or the expectancy-disconfirmation paradigm (Oliver 1977) allow an analysis of why customers are dissatisfied (i.e. negative disconfirmation), satisfied (i.e. confirmation) or even delighted (i.e. positive disconfirmation) with certain touchpoints.

Touchpoints of the post-service period reflect that satisfied guests are not only more likely to return and eventually even become loyal customers, but are also more likely to recommend the respective product through various channels (e.g. face-to-face or online). In consequence, such positive reviews influence the purchase decisions of potential customers in their pre-service period as visualized with the arrows in the Customer Journey Canvas. Likewise, customer relationship efforts can support the establishment of meaningful customer relationships in the post-service period, which increases the probability of repurchases if customers were at least satisfied with the tourism product.

Service design

Service design describes a strategic design process with the aim to deliberately create good customer experiences. Although the colloquial usage of the term design often refers to the look and feel of a physical product, the purpose of design should be rather described as a process 'to change existing situations into preferred ones' (Simon 1996). Therefore, design can be used not only to create better products, but also better services. Service design has a strong

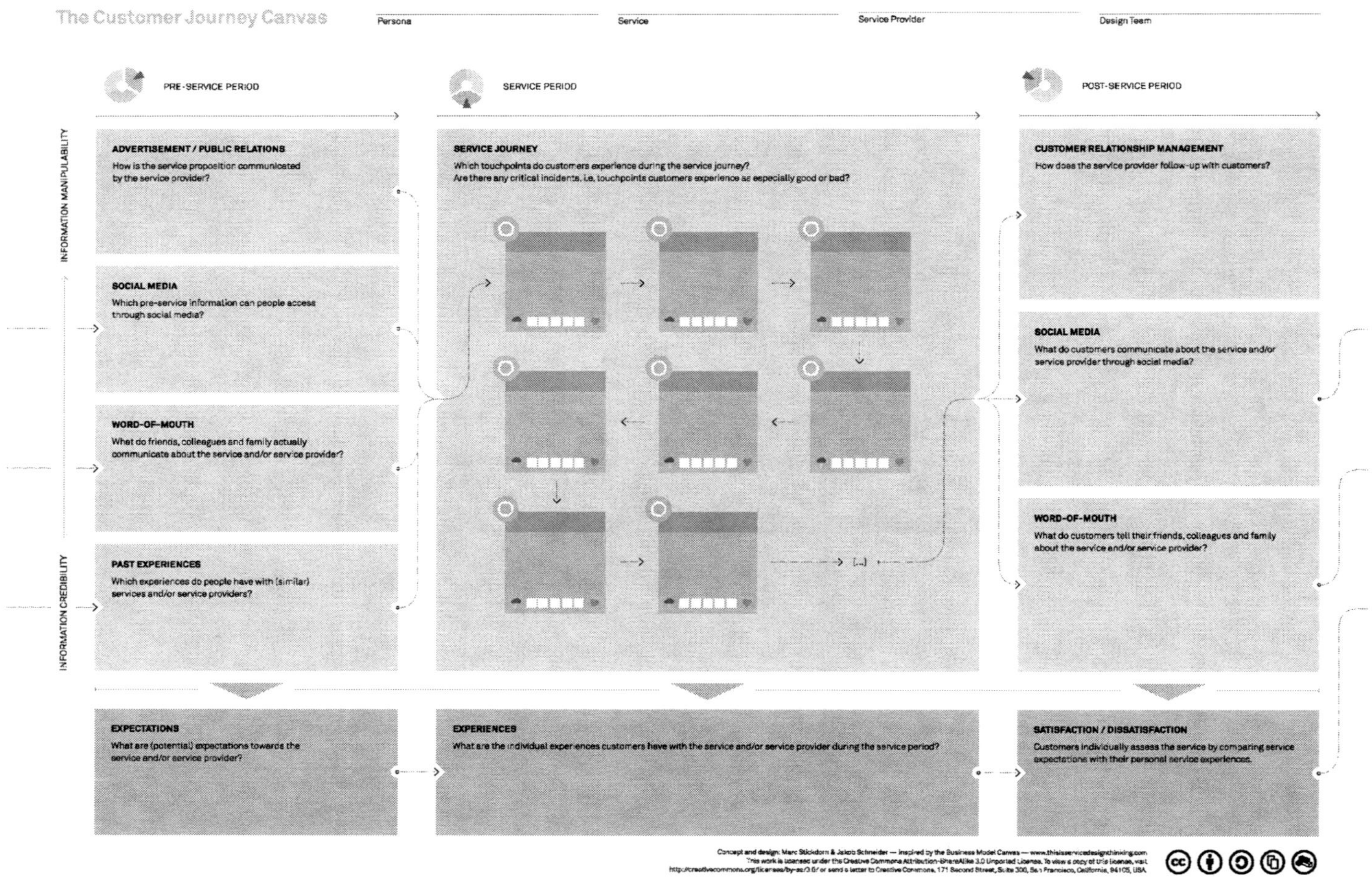

Figure 24.1 The customer journey canvas (Stickdorn and Schneider 2010).

inter-disciplinary character that allows including various perspectives into the design process, such as strategic management and service marketing, but also operations management, psychology, sociology, architecture, information systems, anthropology and many more. Nevertheless, a strong focus always remains on design disciplines, such as product, interaction or communication design. The design of a service includes the design of all relevant touchpoints throughout the customer journey as well as involved organizational processes. Service design can not only be applied in B–C situations, but also in B–B circumstances, organization-internal services and with increasing economic significance also to design C–C service systems.

Although there are various attempts to define service design, there is not yet a commonly accepted definition. However, the one from Moritz (2005) is one of the most-cited: 'Service Design helps to innovate (create new) or improve (existing) services to make them more useful, usable, desirable for clients and efficient as well as effective for organizations. It is a new holistic, multi-disciplinary, integrative field.' In the field of product or industrial design the value of a strategic design process including early concept tests, user feedback and iterative improvement of concepts is widely accepted. Before a product is brought to market it passes through several iterations of concept tests and prototypes to identify failures and thereby reduce the risk to flop on the market. This is not yet common practice for the development or improvement of services. Although some fundamental tools such as service blueprinting date back to service marketing literature from the 1980s (Shostack 1982, 1984), only recently service design with its distinctive process, tools and terminology gains momentum in practice and academia.

Service design is an approach which uses concepts, theories, methods and tools of various disciplines. Although the boundaries between disciplines blur in the context of service design, there are some important differences between the two main disciplines driving service design: service marketing and design. Kimbell (2010) identifies 'some important differences, shaped in part by the influences of the social sciences within marketing and by the educational backgrounds of many service designers in art and design schools' (2010: 51). Table 24.1 outlines this briefly.

Table 24.1 Service design in the context of marketing and design

Marketing	*Design*
Marketing is about organizations creating and building relationships with customers to co-create value.	Design aims to put stakeholders at the centre of designing services and preferably co-design with them.
Marketing scholars and practitioners have developed tools and concepts including blueprints, service evidence and a focus on the service encounter.	Designers use these tools and develop others that often focus on individual users' experiences as a way into designing services.
Marketers define who the customers of a service are or could be and the broad detail of the kinds of relationship an organisation might have with them.	Designers give shape and form to these ideas, and can enrich and challenge assumptions by making visualizations.
Marketing researchers study customers to develop insights into their practices and values.	Designers can use insights as the starting point for design and add a focus to the aesthetics of service experiences.
Marketing has a view of new service development that is shaped by problem-solving.	Design professionals have an understanding of an iterative design process that involves exploring possibilities and being open to serendipity and surprise.

Source: Kimbell (2010): 50–1

The service ecosystem

Customer experiences take place within an often complex system of several services, products and organizations: the so-called service ecosystem. Touchpoints of a customer journey take place on various on- and off-line channels and include other customers, stakeholders and even competitors. All these services, products, stakeholders, places, devices and many others form an ecosystem in which many of these actors depend on each other. An often used example in this context is the customer experience of an iPod. This depends on the look and feel of the device itself, but also on the user experience of the software, the marketing activities by Apple, the shopping experience in the store, the unpacking of the product and so on. However, the service system only works with iTunes as a platform to simply buy music and videos, with other devices like a computer to run the software, and predominantly with numerous people producing and sharing or selling music on this platform as well as intermediaries such as music labels and record companies. A similar – yet even more complex example – would be smartphones (Android, Windows, Apple, etc.) with their respective operating systems, platforms, markets and numerous Apps including their companies, developers, related products and so on. In 2011 an email became known from Nokia CEO Stephen Elop to his employees (various sources, e.g. Ziegler 2011). In his 'Burning Platforms' memo, Elop summarized what he felt was wrong with Nokia's ecosystem:

> The battle of devices has now become a war of ecosystems, where ecosystems include not only the hardware and software of the device, but developers, applications, ecommerce, advertising, search, social applications, location-based services, unified communications and many other things. Our competitors aren't taking our market share with devices; they are taking our market share with an entire ecosystem. This means we're going to have to decide how we either build, catalyse or join an ecosystem.
>
> *(Elop cited in: Ziegler 2011)*

Also tourism destinations can be analyzed as service ecosystems, whereby such an ecosystem goes beyond the mere physical actors within the destination itself – just like the described ecosystem of an iPod or smartphone goes beyond the mere product. A destination incorporates various frontstage services (accommodation, transportation, food and beverage, shops, leisure activities, etc.), backstage services (grocery supply, laundry, maintenance, construction industry, etc.), products (TV, computer, facilities, sport and leisure equipment, etc.), organizations (DMO, government, tour operator, travel agent, etc.) as well as various frontstage platforms (destination websites, hotel review sites, etc.) and backstage platforms (destination information and management software). Tourists seek a seamless experience throughout the whole customer journey within this ecosystem. The overall experience depends on the coordination between all involved stakeholders and their individual customer experience. Only if most single actors within the destination ecosystem provide good customer experiences, the ecosystem as a whole is healthy and stable. Just as an ecosystem can cope with only a limited number of parasites, a destination can cope with only a few stakeholders providing bad customer experiences. Consequently, if there are too many parasites an ecosystem breaks down – and so does a destination.

There is a growing interest in academic research on service ecosystems. Although most of the research focuses on service ecosystems in the context of information systems (e.g. Barros *et al.* 2005; Barros and Dumas 2006; Sawatani 2007), using different terminology, service ecosystems have been researched in other areas as for example 'Service Value Network', 'Business Webs' or 'Internet of Services' (Riedl *et al.* 2009). Such inter-organizational networks are closely linked to the idea of open innovation (Vanhaverbeke and Cloodt 2006; Chesbrough 2003). Beside the academic interest in service ecosystems, the deriving question for tourism is how to manage such a complex system, how to understand it and how to improve or even create service ecosystems. The iterative service design process with its distinctive methods and tools provides a practical approach to analyze, visualize and innovate service ecosystems.

The iterative design process

The process of designing services is similar to any design process, e.g. the design process of a car. The design process of a physical product such as a car might start with market research to discover what kind of car potential customers would prefer. Only if there is a market for a product, is it worth proceeding. Based on these explorations, designers start sketching first ideas and constantly iterate these according to the defined requirements and user or representative feedback. Then, a fundamental idea takes form through virtual 3D or even tangible clay models. Technical components are integrated and various aspects of the concept need to be re-modelled and improved according to feedback from different stakeholders. Prototypes are built and tested in terms of functionality, usability, production feasibility, cost and pricing, market response and so on. Only if these tests remain positive will the new car be produced and brought to market. Any mistakes during such a process may result in enormous costs and may damage the company's image. As this simple example of a design process illustrates, a well-thought-out approach to the design of a new product is crucial for its subsequent success. The same applies for services, although the methods and tools need to reflect the mostly intangible nature of services. Also services need to be tested and prototyped with the intention not to avoid failures, but to identify them as early in the design process as possible following the maxim: fail early, fail cheap, fail safe.

It is important to understand that the structure of any design process is iterative. This means that at every stage of a service design process, it might be necessary to take a step back or even start again from scratch. The single but very important difference is in ensuring that a design process learns from the failure of a previous iteration. A mistake would only be to repeat the same failure twice. Thus, the proposed process should be understood as a rough framework and not as a prescriptive, linear how-to guide. In fact, the very first step of a service design process is to design the process itself, since the process ultimately depends on the context of the service being designed and thus varies from project to project. The iterative four steps of exploration, creation, reflection and implementation are a very basic approach to structure such a complex design process. Literature and practice refer to various other frameworks made up of three to seven or even more steps, but all of them share the iterative practice. Stickdorn and Schneider (2010: 126) mention various examples for service design processes in practice, e.g. 'identify–build–measure' (Engine 2009), 'insight–idea–prototyping–delivery' (live | work 2009) or 'discovering–concepting–designing–building–implementing' (DesignThinkers 2009). The design process should also reflect recurrent leaps between designing in detail and designing holistically, e.g. whilst working on the details of a touchpoint, its position within the whole customer journey should be considered or when working on redesigning employee interactions, the organizational structure as a whole should be considered. This always leads to dilemmas and paradoxes, since decisions have to be made according to budget, resources and client requests (Stickdorn and Schneider 2010)

The five principles of service design thinking

Service design as it is understood today refers to an inter-disciplinary approach that people from diverse disciplines can agree on to co-design services within the ecosystems in which they are embedded with the aim to induce good customer experiences. A designer in this context should not be understood as someone at the end of an innovation process responsible only for the look and feel of products, interfaces or graphical elements involved in a service process. A designer in the context of service design rather acts as a facilitator of workgroups, who supports the workflow between people with diverse backgrounds. Visual design skills as well as facilitation skills and design management skills are key for successful service design processes. A basic prerequisite within such a workgroup is to agree on a common way of thinking, as described by the five basic principles of service design thinking (Stickdorn and Schneider 2010).

User-centred

Services should be experienced through the customer's eyes. The inherent intention of a service is to meet the customer's needs and, as a result, be used frequently and recommended heartily. Thus, the user should be the centre of the design process. This requires a genuine understanding of customers beyond mere quantitative statistics and empirical analyses of their needs. A true understanding of their habits, culture, social context and motivation is crucial. Therefore, design research uses mainly ethnographic methods to slip into the customer's shoes and understand their individual service experience and its wider context. This often results in a different customer segmentation that is based on similar patterns within customer journeys rather than demographic and other classic segmentation criteria. Based on such insights and customer segmentation, the user remains in the centre throughout the whole design process. Often, service design uses Personas as a simple method to describe customer segments with empathic stereotypes.

Co-creative

All stakeholders should be included in the service design process. A customer journey includes many touchpoints that depend on or involve various stakeholders, such as front-line staff, back-office employees and managers, as well as non-human interfaces such as vending machines or websites. A service design process should not only actively involve customers, but also include the most important stakeholders involved in creating and providing a service. Within such a co-creative workgroup, designers often serve as facilitators. They consciously generate an environment that facilitates the creation, communication and evaluation of ideas. Service design provides a toolset to effectively design with customers and not only for them. This includes not only the gathering of genuine user insights, but also the co-creative development of ideas, the prototyping and testing of new service concepts, as well as their implementation in organizations. Following a co-creative approach during the design process leads to a smoother interaction between involved stakeholders during the actual service provision. This is essential for sustainable customer and employee satisfaction.

Sequencing

Experiences should be visualized as a sequence of interrelated touchpoints. Such a customer journey can be visualized in different ways and analysed with various methods according to the design focus. Unlike flowcharts or process maps, customer journey maps emphasize this sequence in a user-centred and empathic manner. They usually include sketched storyboards to visualize touchpoints as almost realistic situations. Often customer journey maps provide additional data such as an emotional journey that demonstrates which touchpoints different customer groups perceive as positive and which ones as negative. Envisioning the dramatic arc of customer journeys helps to understand the rhythm and tension of certain touchpoints. Although concepts of the emotional journey and dramatic arc are often confused, they both refer to different ideas. Customers can perceive touchpoints with high tension as positive (e.g. a roller-coaster ride in an amusement park) and negative (e.g. chaotic security check at an airport) as well as touchpoints with low tension as positive (e.g. window-shopping after the security check in an airport) and negative (e.g. waiting in the roller-coaster queue in an amusement park). It is important to understand the experience of each touchpoint and their sequence within the customer journey. Film and theatre studies provide a rich resource to understand underlying patterns, e.g. the dramatic arc of certain services can be compared with a classic James Bond movie (Lawrence and Hormess 2012). A swimlane diagram or service blueprint visualizes in which channels touchpoints take place and which backstage processes they involve. Again drawing from theatre studies, touchpoints can be classified by whether customers actively interact with a service provider (frontstage), customers see what is happening backstage, but cannot interfere with this (interaction vs. visibility in a service blueprint) or whether touchpoints take place backstage, so without any notice by the customer. Just like actors have to run through many rehearsals to achieve an excellent theatrical performance, services need to run through many prototypes to achieve an excellent customer experience.

Evidencing

Intangible processes should be visualized in terms of physical artefacts. Some touchpoints take place backstage unnoticed by customers, such as housekeeping in a hotel. In fact, such touchpoints are intentionally designed to be inconspicuous. Service evidences can reveal backstage processes and make them visible for customers. Sometimes service evidences can evolve to standard service symbols such as the folded toilet paper in hotels represents that housekeeping took place – even if the room looks unchanged at first sight. Service evidences should be designed according to the service's inherent story, which is told through every touchpoint. Moreover, service evidences can prolong the customer journey far into the post-service period, e.g. when customers take hotel amenities back home and use them later or when they take a look at souvenirs or photos after a holiday. Thus, service evidences can have various forms, such as signs, photos, bills, brochures, mails and emails, souvenirs and other products. Service evidences add a tangible component to what would otherwise have been only an intangible experience. Thereby, they can help to make services more memorable and meaningful for customers.

Holistic

The entire environment of a service should be considered. Although services are intangible, they take place in a physical environment, using physical artefacts and in some cases generate some form of physical outcome. Customers perceive touchpoints with all their senses. The conscious awareness of what customers might perceive only subconsciously can have a profound impact on design process and ultimately influence the experience of the service. Customers can see, hear, smell, touch and taste services. Moreover, at the same time other stakeholders experience the very same touchpoints from a different perspective and thereby they might influence each other's experience. Thus, it is important to map not only the touchpoint sequence of one single customer, but also how different customers and other stakeholders experience their touchpoint sequence throughout the whole service journey. The mere presence of other customers might disturb an important touchpoint. The comparison of the following situations exemplifies this issue: A customer is in a bank (or even worse in a pharmacy) to talk about rather private issues (a) alone or (b) with a queue closely behind. Particularly in tourism, the concurrence of different customer segments in the same locations can lead to conflict situations (e.g. when children use the same spa as romantic couples). Understanding how various involved actors interrelate with each other provides valuable information for the design of holistic services within service ecosystems.

Three basic service design tools

Service design is a young and emerging practice rooted in various disciplines. Therefore, a vast number of methods and tools can be used to understand customers, to identify touchpoints, to map customer journeys, to create ideas, to test and prototype service concepts and to ultimately implement them in organizations. These methods and tools derive from many different disciplines, such as market and design research, ethnography, design thinking, service marketing and management, psychology, sociology, architecture, change management and many more. It depends on the project how a design team is set up and which disciplinary backgrounds the team requires. Depending on the characteristics of the team members involved, the team can draw from a vast toolset. The following three tools only serve as an example of the most common tools of service design: personas, stakeholder maps and customer journey maps (for more tools see: van Dijk *et al.* 2010). These tools should be understood as dynamic tools that a design team can use in various stages of a service design project to improve existing services, to innovate new concepts and to communicate new ideas. Such tools should be iteratively developed in parallel and not be understood as stand-alone approaches. There are various free templates available to start working with the following three basic service design tools.

Personas

Personas visualize stakeholder groups as empathic stereotypes. They are mostly used to exemplify the main customer groups and should be based on both ethnographic fieldwork and quantitative data. Personas represent fictional profiles, described as real characters with which all participants of a service design project can engage. Typically, a persona includes a name, age, gender, educational background, social and family background, hobbies, and other interests. At least a persona should be envisioned by a simple sketch or photo of the person's silhouette.

Effective personas can bring to life abstract statistical data and help a service design team to focus on authentic wants and needs of real people. Mostly, they are developed by assembling research insights of customers and segmenting them into groupings of common interest, the so-called data-driven personas. However, sometimes they are generated the other way around: in a workshop setting, personas are generated based on sheer assumptions of the participants and only later tested and iterated with qualitative and quantitative data, the so-called assumption or ad-hoc personas. Personas can vary from strong visual representations to text-based profiles based on storytelling.

Stakeholder maps

Stakeholder maps visualize all stakeholders involved in the provision of a service and the interrelations between these stakeholders. This might include staff, customers, competitors, partners and other stakeholders, but also involves products, places and whatever might be of interest for customers related to a respective service. In this way, the interrelations between these various groups can be illustrated and analyzed. A stakeholder map thus visualizes the system in

BERT
Short name
32
Age
Sex
BERT
Name
Bertram Miller
Profession
Engineer
Interest
Family, football, hiking
Personal background
Bertram is somehow just the average guy next door. He has got a secure employment at the national railway company; he likes his job. Bertram is a good worker and respected by his colleagues. His working day is over at five and he loves that becaus he always tries to get some sunlight in the large park facilities along his way home. He tries to go by bike everyday; he lives a healthy life.
Family background
Bertram's family is the center of his life. When he is not working he tries to spend every single second with his wife and his two daughters. The family's most favorite events are the long weekend trips to the lake near to their hometown. Travelling far is nothing for the Millers.

Figure 24.2 An exemplary persona of young German tourists (Smaply 2013a).

which customer journeys take place and thereby helps to understand the influence even of those actors which are only indirectly involved.

Such a stakeholder map can represent a single service, such as a hotel or a transportation company, or a whole service ecosystem, such as a tourism destination. Depending on the level of complexity, stakeholder maps are also called stakeholder value maps or service ecosystem maps. To create a stakeholder map, first all potential stakeholders should be collected for example using simple sticky notes. Second, these stakeholders should be prioritized regarding how important they are for the service delivery: some of them are absolutely essential to provide the certain service, several might be beneficial, and others might be only potentially related to the service. Third, the stakeholders should be visualized and arranged on a map according to the prioritization. Fourth, relationships or the exchange of values between the stakeholders are sketched out. Stakeholder maps can vary from abstract visual representations of whole service ecosystems to physical representations based on storytelling.

Customer journey maps

Customer journey maps visualize service processes from a user-centred perspective. A customer journey map provides a vivid but structured visualization of customer experiences as a sequence of touchpoints. Beside stages (e.g. pre-service, service and post-service period) and substages (e.g. planning a trip, booking, travelling, arriving at the destination, etc.), each touchpoint is described and possibly visualized by a simple sketch or photo. The sequence of touchpoints should tell a coherent story just as a storyboard summarizes a movie. Different layers of a customer journey map can refer to various aspects or perspectives of a customer journey.

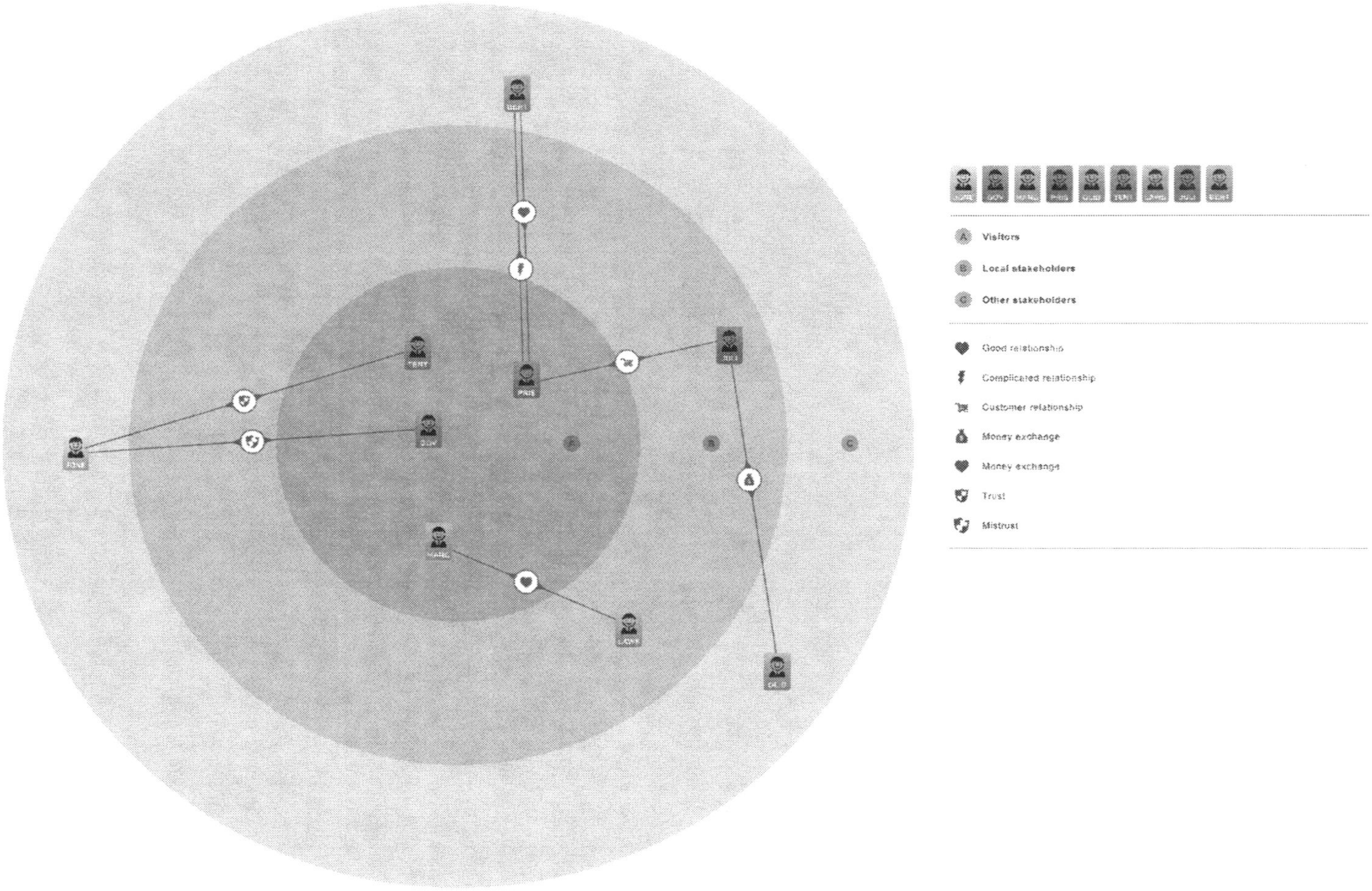

Figure 24.3 An exemplary stakeholder map of a tourism destination (Smaply 2013b).

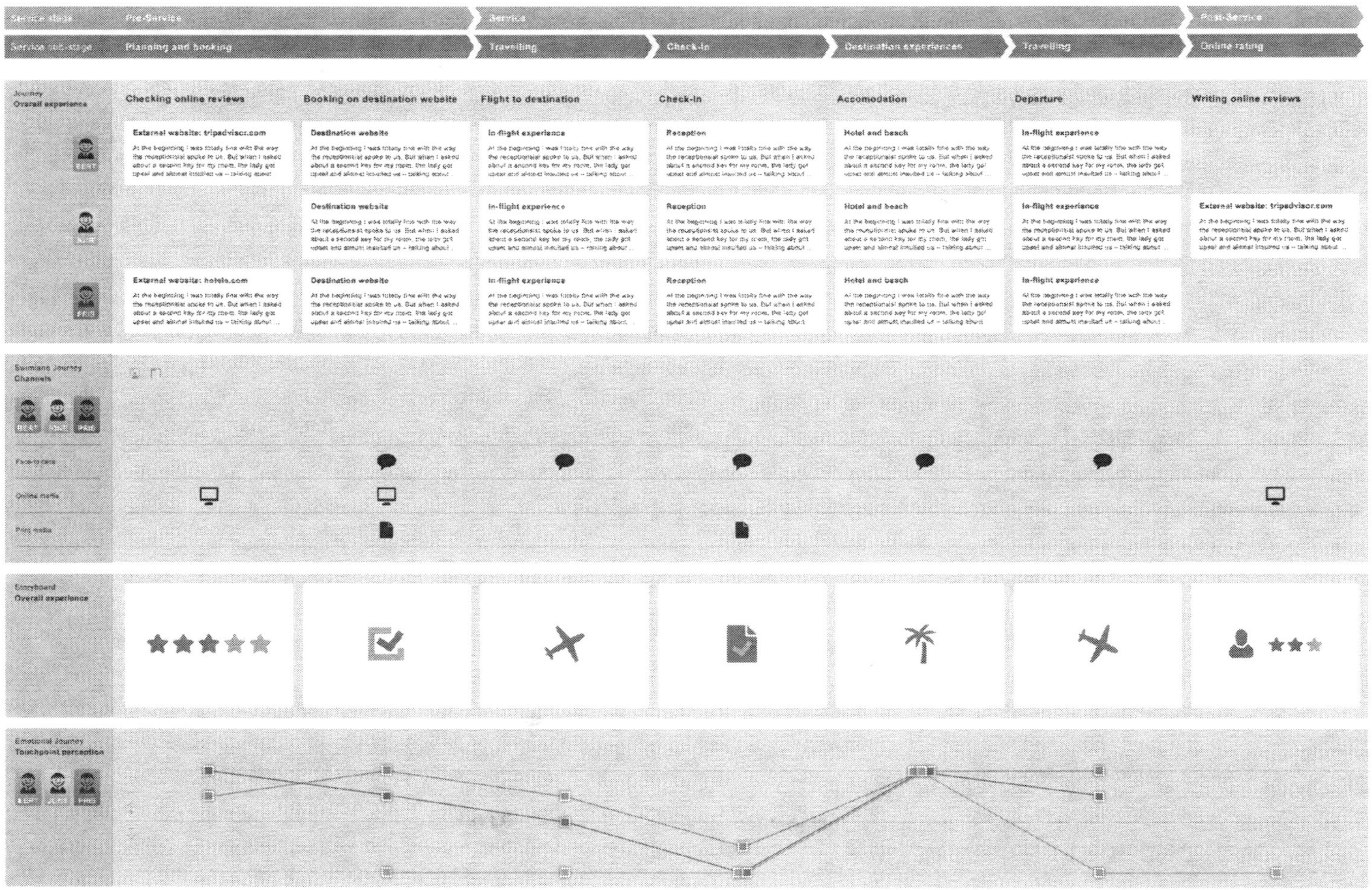

Figure 24.4 An exemplary high-level customer journey map (Smaply 2013c).

An emotional journey can graphically visualize how a positive or negative customer perceives each single touchpoint. Likewise, a dramatic arc can represent how much tension a customer experiences at each touchpoint. A swimlane diagram can exemplify on which communication or distribution channel (e.g. company website, social media, face-2-face, shop, etc.) each touchpoint takes place.

A customer journey map can be quickly done with sticky notes in a workshop setting together with respective customers or by a design team based on prior customer research. Typically, ethnographic methods like observation, shadowing and contextual interviews are used to gather such insights into real customer journeys. Detailed and well-visualized customer journey maps are usually plotted on A0 paper and can be easily several metres long. Such a map provides a high-level overview of factors influencing the customer experience, which enables a design team to identify both strength and weaknesses and thus areas and opportunities for innovation. This structured visual representation makes it possible to compare several customer experiences in the same visual language, and also facilitates quick and easy comparisons between a service and its competitors.

Conclusions

Holidays are of superior value for leisure tourists regarding both the temporarily limited time period per year and the investment of financial resources long before the actual tourism product is consumed. Hence, tourism products are always a matter of trust and the purchase decision highly depends on the expectations raised in the pre-service period. These expectations build on different sources, both directly from tourism companies as well as indirectly from (electronic) word-of-mouth by other customers. Discrepancies between these sources cause mistrust, while convergence evokes trust. The congruence of expectations influenced by both online reviews and corporate communications with the actual experiences increasingly becomes the deciding factor determining the success of tourism products. Great customer experiences and satisfied customers are the best advertisement any brand, product or service can have.

The tourism industry is dominated by small and medium-sized enterprises. Although they are confronted with competitive disadvantages, their offer of authentic customer experiences can lead to positive online reviews. Considering that the purchase decision increasingly depends on online reviews, such small and medium-sized tourism enterprises can even compete with large and even multi-national competitors, as competition increasingly depends on customer experiences and not marketing budgets (Stickdorn and Zehrer 2009). Service design offers an easy-to-grasp toolset which is also applicable by small enterprises. Such companies should adopt and incorporate these tools in their daily work and continuously check and iterate their service concepts from their customer's perspective. An entrepreneurial mindset and motivation is crucial to apply service design methods on this level. Bigger tourism companies and destinations can apply service design to better understand their customers, develop tourism products together with customers and not only for them, and differentiate themselves through unique customer experiences. The methods help to analyse the whole service ecosystem in which they operate and thereby identify potential strategic partnerships (Stickdorn and Frischhut 2012).

There are some tourism-specific factors which can make or break service design projects (Sukowski and Amersdorffer 2012):

1. put the customer in the centre of all reflections;
2. consider everything as a service;
3. increase cooperation and mutual understanding of stakeholders;

4 work in multi-disciplinary teams;
5 be aware of the iterative and co-creative process;
6 service design has to be fun; and
7 do not stop with the concept.

However, the service design process and tools described in this chapter should only serve as an introduction. Service design cannot be learned out of textbooks, as the main key competence is the skill set needed to successfully facilitate co-creative workshops. In fact, service design needs to be based on a holistic management approach and has to be applied throughout the whole organization, which implies the development of respective internal processes and a customer-centred strategy. Organizations are often structured in silos, whereas customers increasingly demand multi-channel structures. Yet also service design tools and methods should be adapted, modified and further developed with regards to specific industries and changing user behaviours.

References

Barros, A. and Dumas, M. (2006) 'The Rise of Web Service Ecosystems', *IEEE IT Professional*, 8(5): 31–7.

Barros, A., Dumas, M. and Bruza, P. (2005) 'The Move to Web Service Ecosystems', *BPTrends*: 1–9.

Booms, B.H. and Bitner, M.J. (1981) 'Marketing Strategies and Organization Structures for Service Firms', in J.H. Donnelly and W.R. George (eds) *Marketing of Services*. Chicago, IL: American Marketing Association.

Buhalis, D. (2000) 'Marketing the Competitive Destination of the Future', *Tourism Management*, 21(1): 97–112.

Chesbrough, H. (2003) 'The era of open innovation', *MIT Sloan Management Review*, 44(3): 35–41.

Designthinkers (2009) *DT 5 Steps Service Innovation Method*, Online. Available: <http://www.designthinkers.nl> (accessed 2 August 2010).

Edvardsson, B., Gustafsson, A. and Roos, I. (2005) 'Service Portraits in Service Research: A Critical Review', *International Journal of Service Industry Management*, 16: 107–21.

Engine (2009) *Engine Service Design – Our Process*, Online. Available: <http://www.enginegroup.co.uk/service_design/v_page/our_process> (accessed 2 August 2010).

Grönroos, C. (2001) 'A Service Quality Model and its Marketing Implications', *European Journal of Marketing*, 18(4): 36–44.

Holbrook, M.B. and Hirschman, E.C. (1982) 'The Experiential Aspects of Consumption: Consumer Fantasies, Feelings, and Fun', *Journal of Consumer Research*, 2(September): 132–40.

Hsieh, T. (2010) *Delivering Happiness: A Path to Profits, Passion, and Purpose*. New York: Business Plus.

IUBH (2011) *Untersuchung der Bedeutung & Glaubwürdigkeit von Bewertungen auf Internetportalen*, Online. Available: <http://www.v-i-r.de/em/dokumente/data/731–908.pdf> (accessed 25 March 2013).

Kano, N. and Takahashi, F. (1979) 'Nippon QC Gakkai', *9th Annual Presentation Meeting*: 21–6.

Kimbell, L. (2010) 'Services Marketing', in M. Stickdorn and J. Schneider (eds) *This is Service Design Thinking*. Amsterdam: BIS Publishers.

Lawrence, A. and Hormess, M. (2012) 'Boom! Wow. Wow! WOW! BOOOOM!!!', *Touchpoint – Journal of Service Design*, 4(2): 24–7.

Livework (2009) *What We Do*, Online. Available: <http://www.livework.co.uk/what-we-do> (accessed 2 August 2010).

Moritz, S. (2005) *Service Design: Practical Access to an Evolving Field*, MA Thesis. Köln International School of Design, Online. Available: <http://www.service-design-network.org/system/files/media/Practical_Access_to_Service_Design.pdf> (accessed 27 March 2013).

Oliver R. (1977) 'Effect of Expectation and Disconfirmation on Postexposure Product Evaluations – An Alternative Interpretation', *Journal of Applied Psychology*, 62(4): 480–6.

Pine, J. and Gilmore, J. (1999) *The Experience Economy*. Boston: Harvard Business School Press.

Rathmell, J.M. (1966) 'What is Meant by Services?', *Journal of Marketing*, 30: 32–6.

Regan W.J. (1963) 'The Service Revolution', *Journal of Marketing*, 47: 57–62.

Riedl, C., Böhmann, T., Leimeister, J.M. and Krcmar, H. (2009) 'A Framework for Analysing Service Ecosystem Capabilities to Innovate', *Proceedings of 17th European Conference on Information Systems 2009*, Online. Available: <http://ssrn.com/abstract=1650662> (accessed 25 March 2013).

Ritchie, J.R.B. and Crouch, G.I. (2000) 'The Competitive Destination: A Sustainable Perspective', *Tourism Management*, 21: 1–7.
Sawatani, Y. (2007) 'Research in Service Ecosystems', *Proceedings of Portland International Center for Management of Engineering and Technology*: 2763–68.
Schulze, G. (1992) *Die Erlebnisgesellschaft: Kultursoziologie der Gegenwart*. Frankfurt a.M.: Campus.
Shostack L. (1977) 'Breaking Free from Product Marketing', *Journal of Marketing*, 41: 73–80.
— (1982) 'How to Design a Service', *European Journal of Marketing*, 16(1): 49–63.
— (1984) 'Designing Services that Deliver', *Harvard Business Review*, 62(1): 133–9.
Simon, H.A. (1996) *The Sciences of the Artificial*, 3rd edn. Cambridge, MA: MIT Press.
Smaply (2013a) *Persona Visualisation with Smaply: An Example from the Tourism Industry*, Online. Available: <http://www.smaply.com/examples/tourism> (accessed 25 March 2013).
— (2013b) *Stakeholder Map Visualisation with Smaply: An Example from the Tourism Industry*, Online. Available: <http://www.smaply.com/examples/tourism> (accessed 25 March 2013).
— (2013c) *Customer Journey Map Visualisation with Smaply: An Example from the Tourism Industry*, Online. Available: <http://www.smaply.com/examples/tourism> (accessed 25 March 2013).
Stickdorn, M. (2009) 'Service Design in Tourism', in S. Miettinen and M. Koivisto (eds) *Designing Services with Innovative Methods*. Helsinki: Taik Publications.
Stickdorn, M. and Frischhut, B. (eds) (2012) *Service Design and Tourism: Case Studies of Applied Research Projects on Mobile Ethnography for Tourism Destinations*. Norderstedt: Books on Demand.
Stickdorn, M. and Schneider, J. (eds) (2010) *This is Service Design Thinking*. Amsterdam: BIS Publishers.
Stickdorn, M. and Zehrer, A. (2009) 'Service Design in Tourism – Customer Experience Driven Destination Management', *Proceedings of the First Nordic Conference on Service Design and Service Innovation*, Online. Available: <http://www.aho.no/PageFiles/6819/Stickdorn_Zehrer.pdf> (accessed 25 March 2013).
Sukowski, D. and Amersdorffer, D. (2012) 'Outlook to the Future', in M. Stickdorn and B. Frischhut (eds) *Service Design and Tourism: Case Studies of Applied Research Projects on Mobile Ethnography for Tourism Destinations*. Norderstedt: Books on Demand.
Toffler, A. (1970) *Future Shock*. New York: Random House.
Van Dijk, G., Raijmakers, B. and Kelly, L. (2010) 'This is a Toolbox – Not a Manual', in M. Stickdorn and J. Schneider (eds) *This is Service Design Thinking*. Amsterdam: BIS Publishers.
Vanhaverbeke, W. and Cloodt, M. (2006) 'Open Innovation in Value Networks', in H. Chesbrough, W. Vanhaverbeke and J. West (eds) *Open Innovation: Researching a New Paradigm*. Oxford: Oxford University Press.
Vargo, S. and Lusch, R. (2004a) 'Evolving to a New Dominant Logic in Marketing', *Journal of Marketing*, 68(1): 1–17.
— (2004b) 'The Four Service Marketing Myths: Remnants of a Goods-based Manufacturing Model', *Journal of Service Research*, 6(4): 324–35.
Zeithaml, V.A., Parasuraman, A. and Berry, L.L. (1985) 'Problems and Strategies in Services Marketing', *Journal of Marketing*, 49: 33–46.
Ziegler, C. (2011) 'Nokia CEO Stephen Elop Rallies Troops in Brutally Honest "Burning Platform" Memo? (Update: It's Real!)', Online. Available: http://www.engadget.com/2011/02/08/nokia-ceo-stephen-elop-rallies-troops-in-brutally-honest-burnin/ (accessed 25 March 2013).

25

Contextualizing the past, conceptualizing the future

Tourism distribution and the impact of ICTs

Andrew J. Spencer and Dimitrios Buhalis

Introduction

This chapter gives an overview of the use of information and communication technologies and their impact on the present and future of tourism distribution. Undoubtedly, ICTs have and are continuing to change the way that most industries operate and function and have evolved from being imaginary futuristic tools to being necessary to competitiveness and efficiency in the marketing of products and daily operation of lucrative businesses. This is no different for the global tourism industry which is now more than ever, dependent on ICTs to provide an ever evolving technologically savvy market with the goods, services and products which it demands. A background to the concept of ICTs in the travel industry is given, with specific focus on the Internet. It will also examine the literature related to distribution strategies while giving practical examples of the way the travel supply chain has evolved over time. Technology Diffusion and Adoption will also be discussed with focus on the *Technology Acceptance Model* of Davis (1989) which has advanced ideas related to adoption drivers with specific emphasis on individual and personal adoption.The concepts of diffusion and adoption will be taken as two semantically different but relevant concepts in this discussion of tourism distribution.Adoption here refers to making use of an innovation within operational practices and processes while diffusion addresses how information about the innovation is transmitted in a group (Rogers 1994).We contend that these two concepts are very interrelated and symbiotic as knowledge transmission may affect the decision to use (adoption) and inversely adoption will necessitate diffusion. Finally, the work will highlight the critical and often overlooked determinant of the adoption and acceptance of ICTs in tourism distribution; that of the leadership of firms and close with a discussion of the trends, future prospects and challenges that may greet this dynamic industry in the areas of distribution and marketing.

The ICT debate: an evolution of perspectives

The concept of using ICTs in the travel industry is not a novel one and stems from the first reservation systems in the 1950s to the tourist information systems like TIS and Gulliver of the

1980s (Werthner 1996; Werthner and Klein 1999) to major global distribution systems like SABRE and Amadeus in the 1990s to the enormous number of current travel activities on the Web. The wider concept of distribution strategies has been defined as 'the process of strategically managing the movement and storage of materials, parts, and finished inventory from suppliers through the firm and onto its customers' (Christopher 1992: 4). Now more than ever the Internet brings a multiplicity of players together with relatively easy access to each other and each other's information base. The implication of this is clearly that a more level playing field has been created with more options available to the creators of products and services and the final consumer. Internet booking brings new independence for suppliers and travellers (Poon 1993).

More than a decade ago it was felt that the international landscape showed Internet readiness in some countries. Canadians and North Americans in general were keen users. According to Law and Leung (2000) Europe lagged behind North America by 14–18 months for Internet penetration. Of particular importance is that the developing world and in particular the Caribbean typically lags behind both. There are obvious implications for countries which are slower on the uptake of ICTs and for businesses operating in those contexts. Intermediaries in Jamaica, which are predominantly travel agencies that focus on the outbound traveller, may therefore not experience some of these global issues at the same rate as more developed economies and as a result become complacent. Studies related to technology adoption may be categorized as pre-Internet or post-Internet phase studies. Dominant works in the pre-Internet phase had their foundations in the work of Rogers (1962) and Davis (1989). Fundamental differences in these schools of thought lie in their approaches to understanding the drivers of adoption. In Rogers' (1962) diffusion of innovations, he focuses on innovation, communication and the role of the social system, while in Davis' (1989) technology acceptance model, the emphasis is on individual perceptions about whether a particular technology innovation is easy to use or meets individual needs (usefulness).

In the post-Internet phase, the debate suggests that technology is now more pervasive and widespread than earlier technologies such as those which enhanced the productivity of farming processes for example those originally studied by Rogers (1962). According to Parker (1988), information, rather than land or capital, will drive the creation of wealth and prosperity over the next several decades. Technology is irreversibly changing the business world and internal organizational operations. Drucker (1990) further argues that there is a transformation in which it is knowledge and not capital, natural resources or labour, which has the greatest impact as a means of production. Technology which facilitates knowledge transfer allows for competitive advantage for businesses (Porter 2001). There is a difficulty, however, in providing a succinct definition of ICT. Buhalis (2002) points out that ICTs include hardware, software, groupware, netware, as well as the intellectual capacity to develop, programme and maintain the equipment. Due to the complexity and breadth of these electronic tools that facilitate the strategic management of organizations, it is important to note that this chapter aims to focus on what is arguably the most pervasive of these tools: the Internet and the impact on retail and distribution firms.

Although conceived in 1969 the Internet never had widespread use as we know it today until 1991. In comparison to other technologies the Internet spread much faster throughout the world and all dimensions of organizations and industries have to be re-examined in the light of the power of this new ICT (Amit and Zott 2001). Other theorists in the *post-Internet phase* argue that the Internet affects every part of the business' operation from internal processes to external relationships and has the ability to permeate multiple economic sectors and industries and transform the business operations internally and externally (Timmers 1998; Wirtz 2001; Tang and Yang 2011).

Distribution strategies

In discussing distribution strategies in the 1990s, Christopher (1992: 4) noted that they involve the much wider consideration of logistics related to inventory levels, materials management and information systems as with transport. While there was an awareness of the need for competitive distribution strategies, there were still major challenges in the implementation of them because there was the need for new management skills (Christopher 1986). These skills involve complete systems management, customer service management and operations coordination.

The literature on distribution strategies shifted focus from internal management of the organization to a greater emphasis on channel strategy. Gattorna (1994) states that the most strategically significant challenge facing organizations is the development of a channel strategy. While the literature in previous decades (Christopher 1986) focused on physical distribution of tangible products, Gattorna highlights that any progressive organization including service organizations such as banks, airlines and insurance companies should attempt to select the right strategy for getting the final product or service to the consumer. However, his definition of distribution channels still reflects a preoccupation with tangible goods. In order for a distribution channel structure to be established, authors (Hatton 1994; Chorn 1994) argue that three determinants emerge. They identify the first as being the requirements of the final customer as measured by an aggregation of customers with similar requirements. The channel strategy will therefore depend on the constituents of the segment and what route will reach them best. This therefore means that e-commerce adoption may be determined by whether the market segment is predisposed to online or offline transactions.

The second determinant is identified as the capabilities of the organization, which supports the resource-based perspective that says that a firm's strategic decisions are in large part influenced by its resources. Capabilities may also refer to management capabilities which were also highlighted in the literature on ownership and leadership. The third determinant is stated as the availability and willingness of intermediaries (if needed) to participate in the channel. The discussion of intermediaries has been limited to their role as a conduit for the supplier; very little is, however, said about the determinants of their own distribution strategies. Discussions of channel strategy, however, moved to a broader debate of managing the entire supply chain. Particularly within the discourse on international distribution it has been posited that there needs to be the careful management of all companies involved in the distribution of goods and services (Chorn 1994). This indicates an emphasis on the needs of the final consumer and also the need for the supplier to use resources in an efficient, cost-effective manner. The literature, however, neglects to discuss that the intermediary must also mange the relationship in two directions within the supply chain.

Schary and Larsen (1998) state that the concept of the supply chain embraces a number of elements. It identifies the complete process of providing goods and services to the final user and brings the actions of supplier and customer into a single system. The main objective of the supply chain is service to customers; however, this must be balanced against costs and assets. Supply chain members, however, do not do this on their own, as individual achievement is dependent on the performance of the chain as a whole. It is the management of a network of interconnected businesses involved in the ultimate provision of product and service packages required by end customers (Harland 1996). The travel supply chain involves the supplier, wholesaler, retailer and consumer. The supplier here represents those creating and providing the service such as airlines, hotels, attractions and car rental companies. The wholesaler refers to tour operators such as Thomas Cook and Thomson Travel who create packages while retailers are travel agencies which sell directly to customers in the marketplace. It is clear that as the customer contact agent, an exploration is needed to determine what factors drive or deter these travel agents' engagement in e-commerce. Suppliers attempting to compete internationally must manage their distribution effectively. This effective management will involve claiming market shares while managing cost and satisfying market share in order to retain and maintain control.

Establishing a presence in particular markets affects the bottom line of organizations. Suppliers however must do cost benefit analyses to ensure that benefits in dollars outweigh the cost of gaining market access and distributing products. Many firms such as Google do this through strategies that enable them to give away the product free of charge. Terpstra (1991) adds from a marketing perspective that there are three distribution tasks: gaining entry into a foreign market, serving many markets at the same time and establishing presence as an insider to each market. It is not acceptable to assume that good products will sell themselves, neither is it advisable to imagine that success today will carry forward into tomorrow (Christopher 1998). On this basis organizations are seeking avenues through which to meet the needs of markets while minimizing their distribution costs. With contemporary theorists (Woodward 2000; Smith 2007) arguing that distribution involves the dissemination of information, the means of booking and purchasing, product bundling and packaging, researchers should no longer merely focus on the distribution strategies of suppliers but pay more keen attention to other firms such as intermediaries who must also make critical decisions about how they reach their markets and transact business.

Reduced transaction cost and commission present a strong case for complete elimination of travel intermediaries (Buhalis and Licata 2002). Hatton (2004) states that the reduction of commissions paid and the competition provided by the Internet present uncertain operating environments. In 2003, British Airways reduced agents' income in the UK to 1 per cent. What is clear from these events is that organizations must do what is necessary to ensure profitability; this may either be done by finding new ways to increase revenues or by reducing costs, or a combination of both. With inflation, competition and rising oil prices, revenue increases in many cases will only be marginal as cheaper prices may not be passed on to the consumers. Due to high fuel costs and competition, the heavy focus is therefore on reducing cost especially those related to distribution.

Pearce (2009) argues that suppliers and their location destinations must seek to develop more effective distribution strategies. He further suggests that the tourism marketing literature has taken a tier-by-tier approach rather than a network approach to understanding distribution design, which has led to channel width considerations being poorly addressed. A network approach, however, while useful in drawing attention to relationships between many players, does not address the deeper operational concerns of specific players. Intermediaries do not operate at either end of the supply chain therefore a look at their buying relationship with suppliers is a critical element of the debate surrounding the strategies which they employ. The concept of strategic purchasing is not a new one and theorists (Eames and Norkus 1988) have long discussed relationships in business to business (B2B) transactions. They have in fact suggested that business buyers should create a strategy that consists of four elements: self-analysis, vendor-analysis, vendor-performance analysis and programme review. The purchaser must conduct detailed research before entering into an agreement. This is vital as the stock or input purchased from another business will affect the final output of the buying company.

ICT strategy and adoption

ICT can change the structure of an industry and alter rules of competition (Porter and Millar 1985; Porter 2001). ICT can be used to create sustainable competitive advantage and provide companies with new competitive instruments. The emphasis of research on the relationship between strategy and ICT in the strategic management literature tends to focus on how ICT influences competitive, distribution and procurement strategies. The symbiotic relationship is largely ignored and recently Beckinsale *et al.* (2011), while recognizing the important role of ICT in strategy, have emphasized the role of strategy in ICT adoption. This re-conceptualization and reassessment of the causal direction is critical to demonstrate how different types of strategies affect levels of adoption for technology-based innovations.

Porter (2001) suggests that technological change, such as ICT, is one of the most important forces that can alter the rule of competition. This is because a majority of activities in an organization create and use information and this will be more powerful for industries where information is the key product. Until recently travel agents have operated with privileged information as their primary stock in trade (Cheyne *et al.* 2006). They argue that the Internet is a major source of information and so the agencies' stock is at risk due to the availability of information to end users in an unprecedented manner. They now need to find new ways to gain and maintain a competitive advantage. David (2007) argues that competitive advantage is essential for the long term success of any organization or industry. It is therefore not sufficient to simply gain competitive advantage but to also achieve a sustained competitive advantage for the economic sustainability of industries and organizations. Firm strategy discourse must, however, consider how strategy decisions are made within firms. Strategy decisions fall within the scope of theories of organizational decision-making, which will also provide a framework within which to discuss technology adoption decision models.

Technology diffusion

The diffusion and adoption paradigm saw growth in the 1940s with research from Ryan and Gross (1943). Almost two decades later the research in this area was limited due to the insularity of the research to the specific field. In 1962 Rogers created a transferable generic theory which allowed for this paradigm to be accepted across disciplines. This therefore led to the theory of diffusion and adoption of innovations being applied extensively. The work of Everett Rogers (1962, 1976, 1983, 1994 and 2003) has provided the foundation for much of the discussion on innovation diffusion. In his text *Diffusion of Innovations* he grapples with why obviously advantageous ideas take such a long time to be adopted. Diffusion is defined by Rogers (2003) as the process in which an innovation is communicated through certain channels over time among the members of a social system. The key variable is that new ideas are being communicated. He therefore describes the four key elements of diffusion as:

1 innovation;
2 communication channels;
3 time; and
4 social system.

Rogers (2003) makes a clear distinction between innovation and technology and refers to innovation as any perceived new idea, practice or object. While this includes technology it is not limited to technological advancement. The critical variable here is 'newness' of anything which is being introduced. In many cases technology is a fairly new introduction into organizations and Latzer (2009) has taken a look at the possibilities of technological innovations being disruptive or sustainable as opposed to the earlier approaches of simply identifying these innovations as positive (see for example Bagozzi *et al.* 1992). Keller (2008) sums the discussion up very well in stating that no single factor will determine the success or failure of technological innovation, but that it is the combination of many factors across disciplines such as social, political and economic, which may explain innovation effectiveness.

Communication channel speaks to how this 'new' idea is exchanged or passed on from one individual to others (Rogers 1994). While diffusion of the innovation is critical to the adoption process it does not guarantee innovation adoption. It is, however, a prerequisite for adoption since the use of an innovation would require previous knowledge of its existence and usefulness. Hoffman and Roman (1984) viewed information flow as having two key dimensions in organizations: the origin of the information and the emphasis on innovation. Although leadership is not explicitly stated it is inherent in their argument. The second dimension in particular is dependent on leadership decisions and may be influenced through organizational culture or strategy. Additionally innovations are likely to be deemed more legitimate if they originate with organizational leadership. Information flow about innovation may have become easier however through the speed of the Internet, which has had a revolutionary impact (Xue 2005). While this may hold partial validity, it does not explain what drives the diffusion of information about the Internet as an innovation itself.

Technology acceptance and adoption

The work of Zhou (2008) categorizes innovation diffusion research as covering three levels: individual, organizational and national. Much of the same drivers of innovation diffusion such as personal, situational, social, socioeconomic, market and infrastructural factors, can be found at these three levels. Zhou further argues that a fourth level known as the intra-organizational level should be introduced which articulated varying levels of adoption within the organization taking into account how persons respond differently to various stimuli. These are termed as voluntary adopters, forced adopters, resistant non-adopters and dormant non-adopters.

In addition to the seminal work of Rogers, however, the *Technology Acceptance Model* by Davis (1989) argues that the degree to which a person feels that the technology will require little or no effort determines perceived ease of use. Therefore if there seems to be added value to a process, individuals are more likely to accept technology. *Lederer et al.* (1998) support the notion that perceived usefulness and perceived ease of use were the primary factors which led to an intention to use and ultimately usage behaviour. A key weakness in the TAM is that it only focuses on cognitive processes of the individual. This essentially places this technology decision model within micro decision-making models. The importance of combining the influence of personal factors as well as social systems which was previously articulated makes the TAM very limited in its approach. Perceptions of usefulness and ease of use are often influenced by attitude (Wöber and Gretzel 2000). The idea of technology attitude is critical to the discussion and forms an important part of the adoption debate. Theorists focusing on attitude and personal behaviour have, however, looked at personal usage intentions without sufficiently considering the impact of macro issues. It may be argued that perceived usefulness, perceived ease of use and attitudes are affected by demographic factors such as age and education. Another important personal factor is the role of learning in adoption. Bagozzi *et al.* (1992) developed a discussion of the importance of the role of 'learning to use' the computer in the overall adoption process. This was an important development in the literature as previous arguments tended to focus in a limited way on the act of using computers.

In contrast to the proponents of the TAM, contemporary researchers such as Dulle and Minishi-Manjanja (2011) found support in their research for the Unified Theory of Acceptance and Use of Technology Model. This model identifies in addition to personal factors such as attitude and expectancy about usefulness and ease of use, that facilitating conditions and social influence are important drivers of usage. Previous theorists (Hooff *et al.* 2005) have added the element of the impact of situational influences on communication technology usage. This indicates that the observation of others using or refusing technology in that environment may shape individual views about its applicability to their needs.

Fuchs *et al.* (2010) further extended the debate and highlight that the environmental context and the availability of ICT infrastructure are important drivers of technology adoption. Lippert and Davis (2006) previously argued that these types of considerations are limited and still do not explain why 50 per cent of implemented systems in the United States for example are considered failures. They therefore introduce trust into a conceptual model and propose that 'technology trust' and 'interpersonal trust' along with 'planned change activities' will influence technology adoption behaviour and enhance the level of adoption and internalization within firms and individuals.

The e-commerce adoption mentioned in the final stage is scarce for firms which were traditionally offline operators at their inception (Lippert and Davis 2006). While in many cases resource constraints are posited as the cause, Gray (2006) highlights that ICT adoption may in fact be used to overcome resource limitations in order to grow the business. The reality however is that some small to medium sized firms are unable to find these resources initially. Many small companies in the developing regions such as the Caribbean, for example, argue that the returns on such an investment are not substantial enough. Nonetheless, it is possible that this reluctance is, however, more an issue of attitude than one of resources. Zappala and Sarchieli (2006) purport that the attitude towards ICT adoption and the climate for innovation, are key determinants in the adoption of e-commerce. Very interestingly they contrast the fact that online selling has stagnated although online purchasing is on the rise. Alternatively Mochrie *et al.* (2006) argue that some firms simply do not have sufficient capacity to develop both the physical and human capital necessary to develop effective adoption strategies. Firms may choose to reject some innovations based on the above constraints. Rogers (1962, 1976, 1983) states that rejection of innovations may take place at any stage in the innovation diffusion process mentioned earlier and discontinuance may also occur.

There is consensus by many theorists (Wirtz 2001; Porter 2001; Rappa 2002) that the rules of competition for established business have been transformed by the Internet in three critical ways:

- information asymmetry reduction;
- disintermediation; and
- reintermediation.

Information asymmetry on markets has been reduced by the web (Wirtz 2001). Collecting information on products such as features and price has become much easier without the need for physical, actual visits to outlets. For the firm, however, the greatest benefit is that the capital requirement to operate in a market is significantly reduced. The Web also minimizes market imperfection and facilitates a larger number of players to compete in cyberspace. The Internet means lower distribution costs, larger market share and higher revenues (Law 2001). Hatton (2004) further argues that given the millions paid globally for commission, pressures from consumers for lower prices and increasing demands for ROI from investors, many seek to remove these payments. This argument identifies the interplay between the firm and the markets, where firms make strategic decisions that enhance profit and consumer behaviour leans towards greater value for money. The Internet offers an effective means of developing a single and sustainable electronic infrastructure for information gathering and business transactions for both travellers and suppliers (Law *et al.* 2004). Opposing theorists argue that it is the acknowledgement and utilization of these benefits that will create what is termed as reintermediation.

In contrast to disintermediation proponents, a counter claim has been made that discussions of complete elimination are premature (Palmer and McCole 1999) and that what is likely to emerge is a new kind of intermediary. The 'info-mediary' will take the new role of brokering relationships between consumers and producers in the world of e-commerce. Goldsmith and Litvin (1999) state that the new info-mediary must gather information on the supplier and consumer and be able to merge these interests online. In addition to having an online presence, agents will still act as counsellors, therefore they should be able to access and process large amounts of information to narrow down choices and match with consumer preferences (Lang 2000). They must be able to access information, assess quality and provide expert advice. Users often get so much information that they cannot use it in a meaningful way. It is the job of intermediaries to eliminate these problems by providing a platform for information exchange between buyers and sellers, which aggregates the relevant information and brings the appropriate trading partners together.

The ongoing debate between disintermediation opponents and proponents has largely been unresolved, which has led to a broadening of the technology adoption debate and has facilitated a strengthening of earlier discussed classical theories of innovation diffusion and technology acceptance. Of particular significance is the fact that the post-Internet discourse has heightened the debate on the global digital divide, which brings into sharp focus issues of information gaps, information inequality and information poverty across and within societies.

The digital divide

The notion of the digital divide addresses the degree to which information technology access provides an advantage and disadvantage to some individuals and directly influences tourism distribution. A review of the literature on the digital divide addresses the research objective which seeks to investigate the influence of external firm factors such as the digital divide in technology adoption in owner-managed small firms. The concept has primarily been framed using four distinct and contrasting approaches (Sassi 2005). He argues that the many different views on the digital divide may be placed in four categories:

- *The Technocratic Approach*, which takes the position that the Internet is an important means of everyday life and an essential tool for the new economy. This approach assumes that new technology will overcome social inequality.
- *The Social Structure Approach*, which emphasizes the unevenness of Internet use across different social structures. Theorists such as Winston (1986), Sparks (2000) and May (2002) argue that the diffusion of the Internet cannot be generalized until societies are able to overcome social inequality.
- *The Information Structure and Exclusion Approach* emphasizes social segregation and the process of marginalization. Lash (1994) and Wacquant (1996) argue that poverty drives the exclusion of some groups from modernization processes such as diffusion and adoption of information technology.
- *The Modernization and Capitalism Approach* argues that capitalism drives modernization processes. Castells (2000) discusses this along the lines of social stratification theory and concludes that what is currently taking place is informational capitalism.

Much of the debate on the digital divide spans the period 1986–2005, however fairly little attention has been given to this concept within tourism. More contemporary work on the digital divide by Minghetti and Buhalis (2010: 278) articulates that 'tourists and destinations within developed countries and between developed and developing countries suffer from a multiplicity of technological divides (motivational, physical, informational, etc.), which lead to different levels of digital exclusion'. It is evident that the digital divide issues are also present in the travel and tourism context and it may even be argued that due to the interaction between countries which is necessitated by tourism, the digital divide may be more resonant in this industry.

While discussions of the digital divide have been active since the 1970s, the debate became more vibrant as theorists such as Castells (2000) argue that the existing inequality and polarization are outcomes of 'informational capitalism' which must be consciously addressed through public policy. Norris (2000) also posits that in the face of world poverty the digital divide is likely to continue in the foreseeable future. What has been consistent throughout decades of research is that there is a knowledge gap which continues to widen with unequal access to information technologies.

The digital divide has been conceptualized in three ways. The first was the access divide and then subsequently the learning and content divides became more resonant. The argument put forward by James (2004) serves to point to a closing of the divide based on access. It, however, does not challenge the position of Rogers (2003) which states that while the access-divide has received most of the attention, it is the learning-divide and content-divide among others which will present a disadvantage for some. This argument provides key insights into issues of matching content to audience needs. Innovators and designers of information technology are likely to create content that suits its own audience in the first instance. Even if this content is later customized for external audiences this ensures a lag as the learning curve for external users is initially higher based on the introduction of content that is not necessarily suited for that environment.

The leadership imperative

The importance of leadership in a discussion of ICT adoption in tourism distribution cannot be overlooked. Kouzes and Posner (1987) define leadership as a reciprocal relationship which clearly separates those who influence from those who are influenced. Hitt *et al.* (2001) describe the leader as a catalyst for strategic change. It is therefore critical to assess dominant leadership categories. In his seminal work more than three decades ago, Burns (1978) introduced the concepts of transformational and transactional leadership. Since then a number of researchers (Bass and Avolio 2003; Singh and Krishnan 2007) have attempted to expand on these concepts in particular in the area of their measurement. Leadership has been found to be a key driver of technology adoption in small owner-managed travel and distribution firms (Spencer 2012) though research which focuses on these leadership classifications in the travel and technology context has been lacking.

Broadly speaking, transformational leaders uplift the morale, motivation, and morals of their followers while transactional leaders cater to their followers' immediate self-interests. Leadership that creates change is an important element of transformational leadership and provides a framework for exploring attributes of change leadership. According to Bass (1999) a considerable amount of empirical research has been completed since the seminal work of Burns (1978), supporting the utility of the distinction between the two forms of leadership. He further articulated that changes in the marketplace and workforce over these decades have resulted in the need for leaders to become more transformational and less transactional if they were to remain effective. Leaders play an important role in determining which innovations to introduce (Victorino *et al.* 2006). This is significant as innovations enable a firm to stay ahead of competitors (Porter 1985; David 2007). Additionally some innovations such as technological ones may assist in providing more efficient operations. Leaders are also resource handlers and their willingness to provide resources will have an impact on quality and performance (Lewis and McCann 2004). The combination of resources and the effective use of these resources as directed by the leadership of the organization may determine competitiveness.

A resonant theme from owners of small travel firms is whether some forms of technology adoption were compatible with their sales and distribution strategy. Of all the variables posited by Wöber and Gretzel (2000) such as speed, convenience, accuracy and security, firm managers have indicated that the markets which they served value personal interaction as the most important variable in conducting travel business. Managers often speak of high-end clients who had 24/7 access to them in much the same way that they would have access to online booking sites. Relationship building forms the cornerstone of their operation. While managers agree that the Internet provided speed and convenience they were less convinced about its strength in terms of personal interaction, accuracy, security and simplicity. They think that these were all areas in which traditional agents had a competitive edge over online sources. Additionally they felt that the market did not think there was sufficient credit card security (Spencer 2012).

Owner-managers have also alluded to the fact that though ICT is changing the face of tourism distribution, many customers still prefer to have someone to blame if things went wrong. If there were someone accountable for errors then that person would be responsible to correct those errors. In online situations they felt that their 'low-tech market' experienced what has been termed as transaction loneliness. Of particular interest was the fact that most managers felt that there is a high level of incompatibility with having a high-tech strategy coupled with a hi-touch one (intense personal interaction) despite compelling arguments by theorists (see for example Buhalis and Licata 2002; Hatton 2004) that a multi-platform approach to distribution will yield sound business models. Owner-managers for example, seem more concerned with what Eastlick and Lotz (1999) refer to as a perceived psychological risk of becoming too dependent on the Internet and losing the essence of their customer interaction. It is clear therefore that if these managers are to engage in greater Internet technology adoption, they will need some form of assurance that online and offline channels of distribution can 'peacefully co-exist'.

Conclusion

In light of the rapid increase in technological platforms for marketing and distribution such as social media and mobile technology applications, which are in many ways experiential, traditional firms will either need to redefine business practices or clearly distinguish between their offerings and those of more contemporary technology-competent firms. This must be balanced against an understanding of the tech-savvy consumer and the value-seeker, which speak to transaction processes but also to the quality of the final output from the service provider.

It is evident that ICTs have and will continue to change the face of tourism distribution (and retail firms in particular) but adoption levels vary based on various issues. The conceptualizations have emphasized drivers such as national culture (Westwood and Low 2003), the global digital divide (Minghetti and Buhalis 2010), resources (Brown *et al.* 2007), strategy (Stonehouse and Snowdon 2007) and leadership (Elenkov and Manev 2005; Peterson *et al.* 2009). The future of travel distribution will hinge more and more on cutting edge technology as the industry evolves to match the expectation of tech-savvy consumers. The industry will clearly need transformational leaders who are willing to co-opt the technology and infuse it in their business models rather than those who remain resistant to change.

In the final analysis this means that suppliers in the tourism industry will need to determine whether the four-tiered traditional distribution channel for their services (to include intermediaries such as tour operators and travel agencies) is still applicable in this new environment, or whether a more flattened supply chain may be substituted or managed concurrently. Ideally multiple platforms allow for meeting a variety of customer needs and preferences; however, supplier firms must now subjectively assess their own distribution needs in the face of rising costs and changing demographics.

References

Amit, R. and Zott, C. (2001) 'Value creation in eBusiness', *Strategic Management Journal*, 22: 493–520.

Applegate, L. (2001) 'Emerging eBusiness models: lessons from the field', *HBS*, 9(801): 172.

Bagozzi, R., Davis, F. and Warshaw, P. (1992) 'Development and test of a theory of technological learning and usage', *Human Relations*, 45(7): 659–86.

Bass, B.M. (1999) 'Two decades of research and development in transformational leadership', *European Journal of Work and Organisational Psychology*, 8(1): 9–32.

Bass, B.M., Avolio, B.J., Jung, D.I. and Berson, Y. (2003) 'Predicting unit performance by assessing transformational and transactional leadership', *Journal of Applied Psychology*, 88: 207–18.

Beckinsale, M., Ram, M. and Theodorakopoulos, N. (2011) 'ICT adoption and ebusiness development: understanding ICT adoption amongst ethnic minority businesses', *International Small Business Journal*, 29: 193–219.

Bigne, J., Aldas, J. and Andrieu, L. (2008) 'B2B services: IT adoption in travel agency supply chains', *Journal of Services Marketing*, 22(6): 454–64.

Brown, J., Hendry, C. and Harborne, P. (2007) 'Developing radical technology for sustainable energy markets: the role of new small firms', *International Small Business Journal*, 25: 603–25.

Buhalis, D. (2002) *eTourism: Information Technologies for Strategic Tourism Management*. Essex: Pearson Education.

Buhalis, D. and Licata. M.C. (2002) 'The future eTourism intermediaries', *Journal of Tourism Management*, 23: 207–20.

Buhalis, D. and Deimezi, O. (2004) 'E-tourism developments in Greece: information communication technologies adoption for strategic management of the Greek tourism industry', *Tourism and Hospitality Research*, 5(2): 1467–3584.

Burns, J.M. (1978) *Leadership*. New York: Harper and Row.

Castells, M. (2000) *End of Millennium*, 2nd edn. Oxford: Blackwell.

Cheyne, J., Downes, M. and Legg. S. (2006) 'Travel agent vs. Internet: what influences travel consumer choices?', *Journal of Vacation Marketing*, 12(1): 41–57.

Childers, T. (1975) *The Information Poor in America*. Lanham, MD: Scarecrow.

Chorn, N. (1994) 'The new logistics organization', in J. Gattorna (ed.) *The Gower Handbook of Logistics and Distribution Management*, 4th edn. Aldershot: Gower Publishing.

Christopher, M. (1986) *The Strategy of Distribution Management*. Oxford: Heinemann Professional Publishing.

— (1992) *Logistics and Supply Chain Management: Strategies for Reducing Cost and Improving Service*. London: Prentice Hall.

— (1998) *Logistics and Supply Chain Management: Strategies for Reducing Cost and Improving Service*. London: Prentice Hall.

Crotts, J., Aziz, A. and Raschid, A. (1998) 'Antecedents of supplier's commitment to wholesale buyers in the international travel trade', *Tourism Management*, 19(2): 127–34.

David, F. (2007) *Strategic Management: Concepts and Cases*. New Jersey: Prentice Hall.

Davis, F.D. (1989) 'Perceived ease of use, and user acceptance of information technology', *MIS Quarterly*, 13(3): 319–39.

Drucker, P. (1990) *Post Capitalist Society*. New York: Harper Business.

Dulle, F.W. and Minishi-Majanja, M.K. (2011) 'The suitability of the unified theory of acceptance and use of technology (UTAUT) model in open access adoption studies', *Information Development*, 27(1): 32–45.

Eames, D. and Norkus, G. (1988) 'Developing your procurement strategy', *Cornell Hotel and Restaurant Administration Quarterly*, 29: 30–3.

Eastlick, M.A. and Lotz, S. (1999) 'Profiling potential adopters and non-adopters of an interactive electronic shopping medium', *International Journal of Retail and Distribution Management*, 27(6): 209–23.

Elenkov, D. and Manev, I. (2005) 'Top management leadership and influence on innovation: the role of socio-cultural context', *Journal of Management*, 31(3): 381–402.

Fuchs, M., Hopken, W., Foger, A. and Kunz, M. (2010) 'E-business readiness, intensity and impact: an Austrian destination management organization study', *Journal of Travel Research*, 49(2): 165–78.

Gattorna, J. (ed.) (1994) *The Gower Handbook of Logistics and Distribution Management*, 4th edn. Aldershot: Gower Publishing.

Goldsmith, R.E. and Litvin, S.W. (1999) 'Heavy users of travel agents: a segmentation analysis of vacation travelers', *Journal of Travel Research*, 38: 127–33.

Gray, C. (2006) 'Stage models of ICT adoption in small firms', in S. Zappala and C. Gray (eds) *Impact of e-commerce on Consumers and Small Firms*. Aldershot: Ashgate.

Hamel, G. and Prahalad, C.K. (1994) *Competing for the Future*. Boston: Harvard Business School Press.

Harland, C.M. (1996) 'Supply chain management, purchasing and supply management, logistics, vertical integration, materials management and supply chain dynamics', in N. Slack (ed.) *Blackwell Encyclopedic Dictionary of Operations Management*. UK: Blackwell.

Hatton, G. (1994) 'Designing a warehouse or distribution centre', in J. Gattorna (ed.) *The Gower Handbook of Logistics and Distribution Management*, 4th edn. Aldershot: Gower Publishing.

Hitt, M.A., Ireland, R.D. and Hoskisson, R.E. (2001) *Strategic Management: Competitiveness and Globalization*, 4th edn. Mason, OH: South Western Publishing.

Hoffman, D. and Novak, T. (1996) 'Marketing in hypermedia computer-mediated environments: conceptual foundations', *Journal of Marketing*, 60: 50–68.

Hooff, B., Groot, J. and Jonge, S.D. (2005) 'Situational influences on the use of communication technologies: a meta-analysis and exploratory study', *Journal of Business Communication*, 4(2): 4–27.

James, J. (2004) 'The global digital divide in the Internet: developed countries constructs and Third World realities', *Journal of Information Science*, 31(2): 114–23.

Keller, K. (2008) 'From here to there in information technology: the complexities of innovation', *American Behavioral Scientist*, 51(1): 97–106.

Kouzes, J.M. and Posner, B.Z. (1987) *The Leadership Challenge: How to Keep Getting Extraordinary Things Done in Organizations*. San Francisco, CA: Jossey Bass.

Lang, T. (2000) 'The effect of the Internet on travel consumer purchasing behaviour and implications for travel agencies', *Journal of Vacation Marketing*, 6: 368–85.

Lash, S. (1994) 'Reflexivity and its doubles: structure, aesthetics, community', in U. Beck, A. Giddens and S. Lash (eds) *Reflexive Modernization*. Cambridge: Polity Press, pp 110–73.

Latzer, M. (2009) 'Information and communication technology innovations: radical and disruptive?', *New Media Society*, 11(4): 599–619.

Law, R. and Leung, R. (2000) 'A study of airlines' online reservation services on the Internet', *Journal of Travel Research*, 39: 202–11.

Law, R., Leung, K. and Wong, J. (2004) 'The impact of the Internet on travel agencies', *International Journal of Contemporary Hospitality Management*, 16(2): 100–7.

Laws, E. (2001) 'Distribution channel analysis for leisure travel', in D. Buhalis and E. Laws (eds) *Tourism Distribution Channels: Practices, Issues and Transformations*. London: Continuum, pp. 53–72.

Lederer, A., Maupin, D., Sena, M. and Zhuang, Y. (1990) 'The role of ease of use, usefulness and attitude in the prediction of World Wide Web usage', *Proceedings of the Hawaii International Conference on Systems Science (HICSS)*, 32: 195–204.

Legris, P., Ingham, J. and Collerette, P. (2003) 'Why do people use information technology? A critical review of the technology acceptance model', *Information & Management*, 40: 191–204.

Lewis, B. and McCann, P. (2004) 'Service failure and recovery: evidence from the hotel industry', *International Journal of Contemporary Hospitality Management*, 16(1): 6–17.

Lippert, S. and Davis, M. (2006) 'A conceptual model integrating trust into planned change activities to enhance technology adoption behaviour', *Journal of Information Science*, 32(5): 434–48.

Loudon, D. and Della Bitta, A. (1993) *Consumer Behaviour: Concepts and Applications*, 4th edn. New York: McGraw-Hill.

Lumsdon, L.M. and Swift, J.S. (1999) 'The role of tour operators in South Africa, Argentina, Chile, Paraguay and Uraguay', *International Journal of Tourism Research*, 4(1): 429–39.

Mansell, R. (2002) 'From digital divides to digital entitlements in knowledge societies', *Current Sociology*, 50(3): 407–26.

May, C. (2002) *Information Society: A Sceptical View.* Cambridge: Polity Press.
Minghetti, V. and Buhalis, D. (2010) 'Digital divide in tourism', *Journal of Travel Research*, 49(3): 267–81.
Mochrie, R., Galloway, L. and Deakins, D. (2006) 'The value of Internet forums to small rural business', in S. Zappala and C. Gray (eds) *Impact of e-Commerce on Consumers and Small Firms.* Aldershot: Ashgate.
Moital, M., Vaughan, D.R. and Edwards, J.R. (2009) 'Using involvement for segmenting the adoption of e-commerce in travel', *Service Industries Journal*, 29(5): 723–39.
Norris, P. (2000) 'Digital divide? Civic engagement, information poverty and the Internet in democratic societies', Online. Available from: web.archive.org/web/20010217154551/http://ksghome.harvard.edu/~.pnor ris.sho renstein.ksg/book1.htm (accessed 9 November 2010).
Palmer, A. and McCole, P. (1999) 'The virtual re-intermediation of travel services: a conceptual framework and empirical investigation', *Journal of Vacation Marketing*, 6(1): 33–47.
Parker, M. (1988) *Information Economics.* London: Prentice-Hall.
Pearce, D.G. (2009) 'Beyond tiers: a network approach to tourism distribution', *Tourism Analysis*, 13: 517–30.
Peterson, S.F. Walumbwa, Byron, K. and Myrowitz, J. (2009) 'CEO positive psychological traits, transformational leadership, and firm performance in high-technology start-up and established firms', *Journal of Management*, 35: 348–68.
Poon, A. (1993) *Tourism, Technology and Competitive Strategies.* Wallingford: CAB International.
Porter, M. (1985) *Competitive Advantage.* New York: The Free Press.
— (2001) 'Bewährte strategien werden mit dem Internet noch wirksamer', *Harvard Business Manager*, 5: 64–81.
Porter, M. and Millar, V. (1985) 'How information gives you competitive advantage', *Harvard Business Review*, 63(4): 149–60.
Rappa, M. (2002) 'Business models on the Web', Online. Available from: http://digitalenterprise.org/models/models.html (accessed 7 February 2010).
Rogers, E. (1962) *Diffusion of Innovations.* New York: The Free Press.
— (1976) 'New product adoption and diffusion', *Journal of Consumer Research*, 2: 290–301.
— (1983) *Diffusion of Innovations.* New York: The Free Press.
— (1986) *Communication Technology: The New Media in Society.* New York: The Free Press.
— (1994) *A History of Communication Study – A Biographical Approach.* New York: The Free Press.
— (2003) *Diffusion of Innovations*, 5th edn. New York: The Free Press.
Ryan, B. and Gross, N. (1943) 'The diffusion of hybrid seed corn in two Iowa communities', *Rural Sociology*, 8: 15–24.
Saffu, K. and Walker, J. (2008) 'Strategic value and electronic commerce adoption among small and medium-sized enterprises in a transactional economy', *Journal of Business and Industrial Marketing*, 23(6): 395–404.
Sassi, S. (2005) 'Cultural differentiation or social segregation? Four approaches to the digital divide', *New Media and Society*, 7(5): 684–700.
Schary, P. and Larsen, T. (1998) *Managing the Global Supply Chain.* Copenhagen: Copenhagen Business School Press.
Singh, N. and Krishnan, V.R. (2007) 'Transformational leadership in India: developing and validating a new scale', *International Journal of Cross Cultural Management*, 7(2): 219–36.
Smith, K. (2007) 'Distribution channels for events: supply and demand-side perspectives', *Journal of Vacation Marketing*, 13: 321–38.
Sparks, C. (2000) 'The distribution of online resources and the democratic potential of the Internet', in J. van Cuilenburg and R. van der Wurff (eds) *Cultural, Economic and Policy Foundations for Media Openness and Diversity in East and West.* Amsterdam: Het Spinhuis, pp. 229–54.
Spencer, A., Buhalis, D. and Moital, M. (2012) 'A hierarchical model of technology adoption for small owner-managed travel firms: an organizational decision-making and leadership perspective', *Tourism Management*, (In Press) DOI: http://dx.doi.org/10.1016/j.tourman.2011.11.011.
Stansfield, M. and Grant, K. (2003) 'An investigation into issues influencing the use of the Internet and electronic commerce among small–medium sized enterprises', *Journal of Electronic Commerce Research*, 4(1): 15–33.
Stonehouse, G. and Snowdon, B. (2007) 'Competitive advantage revisited: Michael Porter on strategy and competitiveness', *Journal of Management Inquiry*, 16(3): 256–73.
Stump, R.L., Gong, W. and Li, Z. (2008) 'Exploring the digital divide in mobile-phone adoption levels across countries: do population socioeconomic traits operate in the same manner as their individual-level demographic counterparts?', *Journal of Macromarketing*, 28: 397–412.

Tang, L. and Yang, P. (2011) 'Symbolic power and the Internet: the power of a "horse"', *Media Culture Society*, 33: 675–91.
Teo, T., Lin, S. and Lai, K. (2009) 'Adopters and non-adopters of e-procurement in Singapore: an empirical study', *Omega*, 37(5): 972–87.
Terpstra, V. and David, K. (1991) *The Cultural Environment of International Business*. Cincinnati, OH: South Western Publishing.
Timmers, P. (1998) 'Business models for electronic markets', *Electronic Markets*, 8: 3–8.
Victorino, L., Verma, V., Plaschka, G. and Dev, C. (2006) 'Service innovation and customer choices in the hospitality industry', *Managing Service Quality*, 15(6): 555–76.
Vrana, V. and Zafiropoulos, C. (2006) 'Tourism agents' attitudes on Internet adoption: an analysis from Greece', *International Journal of Contemporary Hospitality Management*, 18(7): 601–8.
Wacquant, L.J.D. (1996) 'The rise of advanced marginality. notes on its nature and implications', *Acta Sociologica*, 39(2): 121–39.
Werthner, H. (1996) *Design Principles of Tourism Information Systems*. Vienna: Springer Verlag.
Werthner, H. and Klein, S. (1999) *Information Technology and Tourism: A Challenging Relation*. Vienna: Springer Verlag.
Westwood, R. and Low, D.R. (2003) 'The multicultural muse culture, creativity and innovation', *International Journal of Cross Cultural Management*, 3(2): 235–59.
Willis, S. and Tranter, B. (2006) 'Beyond the "digital divide": Internet diffusion and inequality in Australia', *Journal of Sociology*, 42(1): 43–59.
Winston, B. (1986) *Misunderstanding Media*. London: Routledge and Kegan Paul.
Wirtz, B.W. (2001) *Electronic Business*. Wiesbaden: Gabler Verlag.
Wöber, K. and Gretzel, U. (2000) 'Tourism managers' adoption of marketing decision support systems', *Journal of Travel Research*, 39: 172–81.
Woodward, T. (2000) 'Using brand awareness and brand image in tourism channels of distribution', *Journal of Vacation Marketing*, 6: 119–30.
Xue, S. (2005) 'Internet policy and diffusion in China, Malaysia and Singapore', *Journal of Information Science*, 31(3): 238–50.
Zappala, S. and Gray, C. (eds) (2006) *Impact of e-Commerce on Consumers and Small Firms*. Aldershot: Ashgate.
Zappala, S. and Sarchielli, G. (2006) 'Climate for innovation, attitude to Internet and ICT adoption in small firms', in S. Zappala and C. Gray (eds) *Impact of e-Commerce on Consumers and Small Firms*. Aldershot: Ashgate.
Zhou, Y. (2008) 'Voluntary adopters versus forced adopters; integrating the diffusion of innovation theory and the technology acceptance model to study intra-organization adoption', *New Media Society*, 10(3): 475–96.

26

Pricing as a strategic marketing tool

Anita Fernandez-Young

Introduction

We always discuss pricing as one element in the marketing mix, but this is misleading; it is perfectly possible to use pricing in this way, and if you are considering your marketing mix from a strategic point of view you will naturally consider how your pricing strategy contributes to this, but because of the special nature of pricing for all businesses it can be regarded as unique within the mix. If the pricing strategy is not considered within the overall financial strategy of the business there is a possibility that the business will not meet its costs and may not make a profit. When setting prices, the fundamental requirement is to cover costs and then achieve some level of profit which will enable the business to continue and, if possible, proceed to growth. If this is not done, the business will not be viable and however clever the marketing mix might look, it will fail. One of the difficulties for authors of textbooks on tourism marketing is this very primacy of pricing for the business: focusing on marketing collaboratively, for instance, neglects the realities of market price sensitivities (Fyall and Garrod 2005) or suggesting that there are three or four basic approaches to pricing (premium, value for money, 'cheap' pricing, for instance) when the industry crosses many sectors where these concepts are not helpful (Holloway 2004; Cooper 2008) is crude and limiting.

Given this recognition of the importance of pricing, we must consider whether there is anything about tourism businesses which renders them particularly vulnerable to errors in price-setting. Two apparently contradictory influences combine in tourism: on the one hand, nobody enters the tourism industry in any sector with the intention of making a quick profit. Whichever sector we consider, whether it is transport, accommodation, hospitality or attractions, the product or service to be consumed is an experience good and the business providing it must develop and sustain its reputation over a period of time. On the other hand, the industry is very volatile and dynamic; dramatic changes take place in the products available, in the economic, social and political environment in which they are offered, and in the consumption patterns of world-wide consumers. Wars and other sources of political conflict make some previously attractive destinations closed to tourism; outbreaks of disease create temporary problems; once fashionable destinations lose popularity because the smart set have decided to go elsewhere; fluctuations in the exchange rates between currencies influence holiday choices. Given these issues, it is evident that a strategic marketing approach is essential to the majority of tourism businesses because they can use it to reduce their exposure to these dynamic influences to some extent, and pricing is one tool which can be used to this purpose.

A recent study by Masiero and Nicolau (2012) points out that the role of price in determining the response of the market to tourism products is particularly complex, and brings the analysis down to the motivations of individual tourists for the activities they intend to consume during their tourism experience as the main determinants of price sensitivity. They even find that to some extent tourism activities can be treated as a normal good, for pricing purposes. This demonstrates clearly the complexity of the role price plays in the tourism purchase decision and shows the importance to the tourism business of understanding the consumer's requirements as fully as possible. Underlying all the studies of tourism pricing and the perceived relationship between prices and quality lies a substantial literature in consumer research; an interesting example can be found in Kardes *et al.* (2004) using an experimental approach to understanding how consumers process price information.

While tourism marketing research has recently concentrated on the rise of Internet and social marketing (Fleischer and Felsenstein 2004; Garin and Amaral 2011; Rambolinaza 2006), the ease with which prices can be changed and pricing strategies be adapted to changing markets has not been fully recognized in the literature. In addressing first of all the basics of price setting and then by means of examples considering the range of pricing options available in different sectors of the tourism industry, we intend to demonstrate that while the tourism industry is adapting to challenging market conditions and utilizing every conceivable pricing strategy, there are still gaps in the research approach which need to be filled. Sector by sector, different pricing strategies are dominant, essentially because they are driven by different overall business strategies.

Price setting

An understanding of how businesses set prices, and why they use the methods they do, will set the strategic use of pricing in context. The most basic method of setting a price for a product or service is to determine what it costs to produce and then add on a proportion to provide a profit (cost-plus pricing). This sounds like a relatively easy process; unfortunately, it is often difficult to determine exactly what the costs are or are likely to be, especially in a volatile context such as tourism. Costs may also vary greatly among competitors, making price-setting according to what competitors are charging also a risky way to decide prices. Another method is to decide how much profit is required from the operational investment and to design the product or service so that a certain sales volume will deliver this margin at a given cost. Then there is value-based pricing, where the price is determined by the value the product or service gives to the consumer, even if the cost of production is very much lower: this method is unlikely to be relevant to a tourism business, but it is possible to imagine, say, a specialist tour operator using it for an extremely new or different type of holiday.

Whichever of these basic approaches is used, however, there are also the psychological implications of price to be considered within the overall pricing model. Especially in the case of services or experience goods such as tourism products there are psychological as well as monetary prices. Many aspects of time are important to tourism consumers, such as the lead time between booking and taking the holiday (they may be prepared to pay more to book in advance and secure the holiday they want) or the amount of time they must travel between home and the holiday resort (they may want to begin consuming the sand, sea and sun as quickly as possible, so prefer to pay for a short-haul destination rather than a long-haul one). We must also consider issues of convenience: supposing the price of taking a railway train from home to the destination is the same as the price of an airline ticket to the same destination, the choice may be determined by the cost of getting to the railhead or to the airport in terms of money and time. This type of decision may also be influenced by the age and agility of the passenger, by the passenger's preferences for flying or not and many other considerations which do not appear to relate specifically to monetary price. Another type of psychological pricing is what is known as 'point pricing' where the price is held down below a certain threshold in order to make it more attractive to the customer. This is applicable across the tourism industry: aircraft seats, hotel rooms, meals and the courses of which they are composed may all use point pricing in some way. We will examine some of these later in the chapter.

One important aspect of pricing in tourism is the use of prices to indicate quality and value to the potential customer. This may be used in addition to any of the other pricing methods, but again it is a common aspect of the pricing of experience goods; a high price signals superior quality alongside the tangibles which are being used to promote the good. We can clearly see this in action in the case of specialist holiday firms such as Voyages Jules Verne or Page and Moy. The decision to use price as a signal in this way is very much a strategic decision because it has implications for so many other areas of the marketing mix. This is how pricing can relate to position in the market, of course, if the strategy of the firm is to position its brand in a way that requires a particular pricing approach. Although it is possible to see price strategy in terms of three potential price positions (premium pricing, value-for-money pricing and super-low pricing or undercut-pricing, see Holloway (2004) and Cooper (2008), for instance) the approach to pricing differs greatly from sector to sector and from brand to brand; examples later in the chapter will illustrate this issue.

Price discrimination

Whatever strategic approach is taken to price setting in the tourism business, the aim ultimately is to achieve the long-term objectives of the firm. The role of pricing is to extract the maximum amount of consumer surplus from the market so that the firm is in a position to continue in business and, if it is considered desirable, to grow. While a very high proportion of firms in the tourism industry are small (independent hotels, travel agencies, restaurants, local guides, local transport operators) we must not assume that all of them are content to remain small; many will wish to expand, acquire other small businesses or merge with similar businesses up or down the supply chain. Any kind of growth or expansion will require funds, and while large corporations are able to raise funds more easily in the market, even small firms will want to ensure their long-term future and it is impossible to do this if you are not making profits for your proprietors or shareholders.

Extracting the maximum consumer surplus is done by means of price discrimination. The most sophisticated version of price discrimination is seen in yield management systems, but these are most readily understood by means of examples which we will explore below. There are commonly three types or levels of price discrimination which it is useful to grasp because they are all relevant to different aspects or sectors of the tourism industry.

First degree price discrimination, or 'perfect' price discrimination as it is sometimes called, is the situation where the supplier knows what each consumer is prepared to pay for the good and is able to charge every customer the highest possible price. This would capture the maximum consumer surplus, but it is impossible to achieve in the real world, although there are some examples which come close, such as Dutch or reverse auctions and haggling or arguing over prices in informal markets. First degree price discrimination is an ideal to which to aspire, but it is important to remember that it is the PRICE which changes, not the PRODUCT: we are not talking about adapting the product to the market, simply about adjusting the price of the same product to fit what the customer is willing to pay. Increased transparency of prices which has been made possible by the Internet may be providing tourism businesses with another method of reaching their customers but it is difficult to determine whether this is enabling them to access more of the consumer surplus or making them vulnerable to consumer power; examples may help us to understand this (and see, for instance Bock *et al.* 2007; Fleischer and Felsenstein 2004; and Garín and Amaral 2011).

Second degree price discrimination is sometimes known as 'block-pricing' because it describes a situation where different quantities of the good are provided at different prices. Examples of this are bulk-buys of perishable foods, where the price for one unit is held but the price for multiple units is reduced in order to move the goods more quickly, and the sale of block bookings of hotel rooms or aircraft seats to package holiday providers at discounted rates. The release of quantities of seats or rooms to brokers such as Lastminute.com is another example of using second degree price discrimination to move surplus inventory.

Third degree price discrimination is the area in which we begin to see the importance of elasticity in pricing and consumption decisions. Generally speaking, tourists are assumed to be relatively price-elastic because they can choose not to take a holiday or can choose where and when to take their tourism experience depending on how much they want to spend. However, there are circumstances in which this elasticity of demand is reduced: recent changes in the rules for families who want to take their children out of school in the UK have made the school holiday period more rigid and forced many families to take their holidays in periods of high demand. Of course, they can still choose to look for cheaper alternatives but if they wish to take a holiday they will find that prices overall are higher because of the high demand. Students who are constrained by fixed term times may also find that prices are higher in the vacations, but one example of third degree price discrimination is the choice on the part of the supplier to charge different prices to different segments of the market. We can often see this in operation at attractions, where there is a 'student rate' or a 'senior rate' which takes account of the smaller consumer surplus enjoyed by people who are not in employment because they are studying or are retired from work (sometimes referred to as 'unwaged' to include the unemployed but willing to work). Again, it is important to recognize that this is a difference in price rather than a difference in the product or service being offered; there are also specialist tourism products which are focused on the student market or the seniors market, and they may also be cheaper than mainstream products, but in the case of third degree price discrimination the product remains the same, only the price is changed in order to maximize the revenue. A student or senior can choose not to consume the product at all, but may well be attracted by the reduced price, so can be said to have different demand elasticity from the family or couples market.

Any peak period travel is relatively inelastic in demand; off-peak services show much more elasticity. The traditional assumption is that tourism products are highly price-elastic because the tourist can choose between such a wide range of destinations; she can choose to holiday close to home, or may even find that a holiday in an inexpensive destination will cost her less than staying at home, depending on exchange rates and the cost of living in different places. One of the most difficult issues in tourism is how to estimate future demand for a tourism product: some of the best tourism economists have worked on this problem (for example: Sinclair and Stabler; Blake; Papatheodorou; Song) and some are still working on it. There are few destinations which are not subject to some levels of seasonality, and this feeds through to tourism businesses which serve them; the reduction of seasonality is a constant objective for many destinations and their constituent businesses, but often depends on the transport infrastructure which may not be under the destination's control (as when Ryanair, a low-cost carrier, operates some routes seasonally because low season would not be profitable; see Anton *et al.* 2010). The implications of elasticity issues for tourism pricing are: that any technique which makes pricing easier is welcome; that pricing must be taken extremely seriously by any tourism business; and that strategic approaches are essential to help to defend the business from demand fluctuations and consequent falls in revenue. A meta-analytic approach to studying price elasticities of demand for air travel was carried out by Brons *et al.* (2002) but the data was insubstantial and airline pricing has been relatively neglected by researchers; for examples, see below.

Variability, as suggested above, is an important issue for price setting. Determining what the costs of a tourism business will be when planning what prices to set for a forthcoming season is difficult when the business is exposed to foreign exchange rates, to fuel prices in a volatile market, even to fluctuations in food prices responding to changes in weather patterns, disease, transport costs and labour costs.

The tourism industry is also vulnerable to perishability. If a seat on an aircraft remains unsold when the aircraft takes off, or a hotel room is empty for a night, the revenue from these potential sales cannot be recouped because the product (seat or bed-night) cannot be stored for future sale. The fixed costs of operating aircraft and hotels are generally high; often the finance for the business will have to be serviced (aircraft are leased; buildings may be leased and must be maintained, for instance) and the employees paid, whether or not the facility is operating at maximum efficiency and high levels of sales. We assume high fixed costs, but many tourism businesses are also running with high variable costs too, such as fuel consumption. Much of the labour involved in tourism businesses such as hotels is organized as core permanent staff with a pool of casual labour in order to transfer the costs from fixed to variable in order to manage seasonality and fluctuations in demand, but this tends to reduce the quality of service available to the consumer. A very useful study of the influence of price instability on the profitability of hotels in Taiwan has been carried out by Chen and Chang (2012) which also references Qu *et al.* (2002) looking at short-term price changes in Hong Kong; these studies demonstrate the issues of seasonality in hotel price-setting and how they can affect profitability.

Estimating future fixed costs in order to establish cost-based pricing may depend on fluctuations in bank rate, because of the dependence of the business on loans and the need to service them. Scheduled airlines must anticipate possible fluctuations in fuel costs, taxes and landing fees and the exchange rates in the countries in which they operate. Referring to the prices set by their competitors is similarly risky as a pricing strategy because their competitors' costs may well be different; their means of financing themselves, their exposure to foreign exchange rates, their operational models and ability to cross subsidize, may all differ. Global hotel chains can cross-subsidize loss-making operations in destinations which are experiencing difficulties, where local or regional chains cannot; small low cost carriers with tightly defined regional or local markets may be very vulnerable to changes in their markets, such as the low cost specialist business carriers in Europe which have failed during the economic downturn.

Figure 26.1 shows how it is possible to maximize revenue by manipulating prices.

The higher prices charged above the single market price are possible in tourism situations when elasticity is low; the additional revenue when marginal cost is zero can be obtained when all costs have been covered at the single market price but there is spare capacity which can be sold for lower prices as the date of consumption approaches, such as empty hotel rooms or aircraft seats.

The idea of yield management (treated more fully elsewhere) is sometimes conflated with price setting, because the purpose of the practice is to maximize the revenue obtainable from sales. Of course, it is essential that the consumer base is aware of the possibility that different prices may be charged for the same product, depending on the date of purchase (see Ovchinnikov

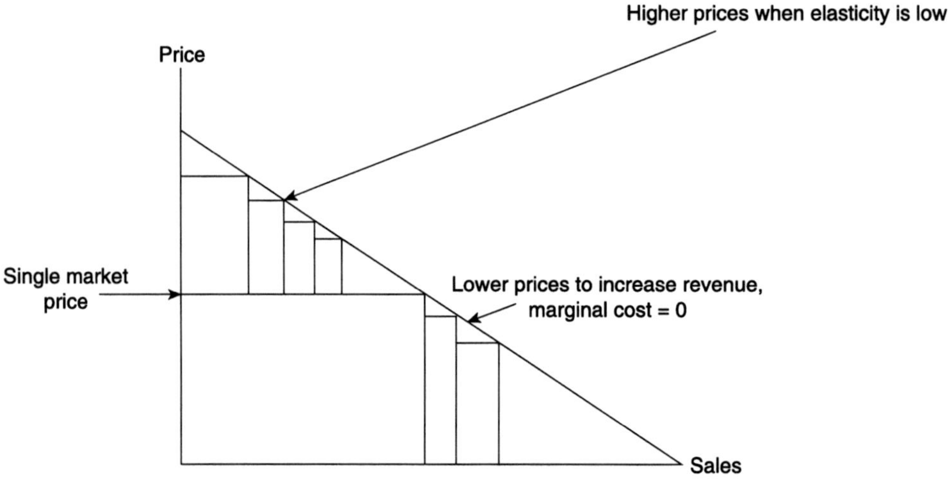

Figure 26.1 Price discrimination.

and Milner 2007) otherwise confusion and dissatisfaction could reduce the benefits of using the technique. The travel and tourism industry has adopted yield management approaches because of their easy application to the fixed availability of inventory: there are only so many seats on a plane and only so many beds or rooms in a hotel, and demand may easily outstrip supply during certain periods, while at others, for seasonal or other reasons, demand may need to be stimulated by promotions. If we consider, for instance, what can happen at the time of mega-events such as the World Cup in soccer or the Olympic Games, and during the periods immediately before and after such events, when demand is relatively inelastic for the event but much more elastic in the peripheral period, we can see how valuable a yield management system can be.

Sector-based examples

Package tours

The issue for package tourism companies is how transparent or opaque their bundling is to be, given that it is now possible for consumers to check the price of comparable independent bookings by means of the Internet. By selecting and reserving their accommodation and transport in advance and in some cases using their own planes and hotels, tour operators (package providers) can ensure that their offer is unique in the market, so that comparable independently booked holidays will generally be more expensive because they cannot take advantage of economies of scale as the package providers can. In addition, the package providers can add value in various ways to ensure that their offer is still more attractive to the cost-conscious purchaser, by providing airport to hotel shuttles, childcare facilities, meal deals or all-inclusive packages (see Aguiló *et al.* 2003). If they had not been able to, or had been unwilling to build in the added value, the package providers might not have weathered the economic downturn as effectively as some of them have. Dynamic packaging (which gives the appearance to customers of providing unique combinations of travel and accommodation options) is just another way of ensuring that prices are kept low to the customer and also opaque – it is difficult for the customer to identify the economies of scale in operation. For a hedonic pricing approach to the topic, see Thrane (2005).

Rosselló and Riera (2012) find that Internet prices appear to be lower than those offered through other channels, irrespective of quality and quantity, for European package tours, whether provided by traditional tour operators or by new Internet retailers. This may reflect the cost reduction in Internet supply as against traditional call centres and brochure sales. The concurrent move in package holiday supply to all-inclusive offerings in traditional and mature destinations has also been examined in European markets, this time by Aguiló and Rosselló (2012) who find that the all-inclusive tourist has a lower level of spending, of repeat visit intention and of satisfaction. Their study suggested that the move to all-inclusive was driven not by consumer demand but by the package tour providers' convenience; this and other similar studies (Anderson 2010; Alegre and Pou 2008) have implications for tour operator pricing strategies.

Airlines

In the case of airlines the most obvious strategic issue is the business model: the introduction of the low cost carrier model from the 1970s onwards has changed the expectations of tourists in two ways. Firstly it has opened up many secondary airports and thus increased the number of destinations available to the independent traveller; secondly it has provided a challenge for the traditional package holiday operators whose profits depended on the bundling of flights with accommodation non-transparently. Calling the operators 'low cost carriers' reminds us that the so-called 'cheap flights' depend on the carrier's costs being kept to the minimum necessary to operate safely and reliably. This is done by using secondary airports where landing costs and taxes are cheaper than those demanded by the big hub airports and by providing far fewer services included in the ticket price, such as baggage handling and food and beverage services. Some LCCs also charge separately for booking, for seat reservations, for priority boarding, online or airport check-in and so on, although in the UK they are no longer allowed to advertise their prices without including taxes and landing charges and there is pressure on them to move to greater transparency.

These carriers, like the full-service or flag-carrying airlines, have adopted yield management systems to help them to maximize their revenue. Automated booking systems mean that there is no need to employ large numbers of call-centre staff, again reducing costs. It is easy to test the way prices rise as the date of take-off gets nearer and more seats have been sold; all you need to do is to identify a specific flight (date and time) to a specific destination with a specific low cost carrier and check the price of unsold seats once (or more) a week from about three months before take-off. The smooth rising curve may be broken by promotions or other tactical changes in price, but if you plot a number of these curves you will find them all very similar in shape. You will also find that they are good examples of point-pricing: glance at any advertisements in your local newspapers and you will see examples such as: 'Fly from £22.95' (Flybe 2012); 'Rome, Warsaw, Venice from £22' (Ryanair 2012). There is a price point at £23 below which flights are clearly 'low cost'. Note that the prices are *from* the price shown; that is to remind the reader that these are not fixed single prices with unlimited dates, but they will increase as soon as the system recognizes that sufficient seats have been sold at those prices. A useful early study of the LCC and Full Service Carriers' pricing strategies can be found in Piga and Bachis (2006), with a more recent study from Pitfield (2008) and a case study of Ryanair (Malighetti *et al.* 2009).

From time to time seats on low cost airlines are sold at extremely low prices, such that it is difficult to imagine how the airline can cover its costs at the prices asked; for instance, there are examples of 'seat sales' where the customer has been able to purchase tickets for very short-haul flights for under £20 sterling. These have largely disappeared even from the most promotion-friendly low cost carriers, but when they were available they tended to be seats on flights which were not very popular but which the airline was obliged to include in its schedule in order to ensure that the plane was in the right place (i.e. at the right airport) for a more popular flight. This type of discounting represents the situation where marginal costs per seat are close to zero – the cost of operating the flight is offset by the reductions in costs attained by maintaining the smallest fleet consonant with the safe operation of the routes chosen by the LCC. The flight must take place, so any revenue obtainable is an extra benefit. A new approach to pricing has emerged very recently: some LCCs are offering the basic seat price, which includes hand baggage only and no seat allocation, and an enhanced price which includes hold (checked) baggage and seat allocation in addition to hand baggage, and even a top-range price which includes additional benefits such as extra hold baggage, priority boarding, executive lounge, onboard food and beverage service and so on. Thus the LCC is moving closer to the full service airline model in which different prices are charged for different classes of seating and facilities per passenger although the basic seat price remains the same throughout the booking period, sometimes being discounted very shortly before take-off (see Granados *et al.* (2012) for a look at the issues, with an interesting discussion on the 'decommoditization' of airline services).

The LCC model has been shown to bring new tourists to mature destinations (Anton *et al.* 2010) and to provide tourists who would have made their visit by other means with a new, more convenient transport option. The role of convenience and speed in the decision to use LCCs rather than full cost airlines, trains, coaches or other transport methods has not been fully explored; this study also found, for instance, that travellers from the UK were happy to pay for taxis to their final destination rather than using shuttle buses, supporting the conclusion that convenience rather than price was driving the decision to use the LCC in the first place.

Pricing will continue to be used as a strategic tool for both low cost and full service carriers. For an interesting discussion of some of the issues, see Koenigsberg *et al.* (2008), although the dynamic nature of the industry in the face of recession may have overtaken some of its conclusions.

Hotels and hospitality

Hotels have been using yield management techniques to improve their revenues for some years. Useful terms to be aware of in the pricing context are REVPAR, which is the short form for 'revenue per available room', and 'rack rate', the advertised price of a room charged to walk-in customers exclusive of any available discounts. The REVPAR is calculated for a given period by identifying the total revenue (without deducting taxes etc.) and dividing it by the actual number of available room-nights during the period. It is a relatively easy calculation to make and can be used to make comparisons with competing hotels or with other hotels in the same chain. Because it takes into account the proportion of rooms that are occupied as well as the prices (which may vary according to the season and size and class of available room) it is a useful base for comparing results from season to season. An alternative measure is GOPPAR, or gross operating profit per available room, which takes into account the additional revenues made from, for instance, food and beverage services. However, although it is a more sophisticated calculation it makes meaningful comparisons with other hotels more difficult because of differences in the facilities available. It is also less widely disclosed than REVPAR which is a long-standing practice in the industry and can often be available (anonymized) from local agencies.

When considering pricing issues, the question of 'rack rates' is often discussed. If the rack rate is seldom used, why does it exist? It is very useful for hotels which have a clientele which varies widely from season to season. For instance, a hotel which serves a racecourse may experience very high levels of occupancy when there is a race meeting and be able to use the rack rate as its normal rate during that period; outside the period of high demand it may use discounts of various kinds to attract new customers who are unconnected with the racing business. Of course, if you decide that you will use discounts of different kinds for different purposes, tactical or strategic, such as group bookings, bookings through agencies, advance bookings and so on, you will need the rack rate as the benchmark from which to make the percentage discounts, otherwise you are in danger of simply picking numbers at random rather than choosing them carefully with revenue levels in mind. As with airline pricing there can be ethical issues where customers become aware that they have been charged different prices from other customers; see, for instance, Mattila and Choi (2006) and Yelkur and Da Costa (2001).

In the case of chain hotels, the trend over the last few decades has been to differentiate classes of hotel and therefore prices by the brand of hotel. For example, Starwood Hotels have (in 2012) a total of nine different brands, each of which has a different offer range and different pricing framework. Accor Hotels have as many as 15 brands, from the Formule 1 economy brand to the Sofitel Legend super luxury brand. Clearly, the pricing of rooms across the range of brands is a complex and sophisticated challenge to management, and must form part of the strategic marketing approach.

As a more thorough consideration of the relationship between hotel prices and satisfaction the US study by Mattila and O'Neill (2003) deserves consideration. Findings include the negative relationship between average daily room rate charged and guest satisfaction, with satisfaction levels being most volatile in the medium price range. Price information was guiding service quality expectations, most strongly in the cheapest and most expensive rates. A significant finding of this study was that the (at that time) current industry approach to reducing the availability of food and beverage services was driven more by the desire to cut operating costs than by customer demand – rather like the situation in all-inclusive package tours. This issue calls for new research in the current difficult operating conditions for hotel and lodging operations; for instance, Saló *et al.* (2012) look at prices for second-home rentals in comparison with hotels and find differences of seasonality between them. It is noticeable that there is a steady flow of research relating to mature destinations in the US and Europe but relatively little has been published analyzing other markets.

Attractions and events

There are almost as many considerations to take into account in attraction and event pricing as there are attractions and events, but the following core considerations apply. As with hotels, the requirement for the infrastructure to support the attraction/event is paramount. In attempting to use price to reduce seasonality for an attraction this must always be taken into consideration, because however cheap the attraction may be (and some attractions do not, or perhaps cannot, charge an entry fee) unless there is readily available transport to it and facilities for food and beverage services and toilets, or in some cases overnight accommodation also, there is no prospect of increasing visitation. One option, discussed by Chalip and McGuirty (2004), is to bundle event elements and/or attractions with the destination in a package, which can take account of the many attractions in the position of being unable to make entrance charges, sometimes because of restrictions imposed by local or national governments or by substantial donors. It may be possible for them to use quasi-pricing strategies such as inviting donations with a minimum suggested sum, or they may prefer to use ancillary services such as hospitality or a shop to raise revenue as an alternative to charging for entry. Loomis and Kindberg (2006) take a useful look at the appropriate pricing principles for both natural and cultural attractions.

Another useful device for attractions is the season ticket: this offers admission to the attraction for multiple visits for a price equivalent to some minimum number of visits, and may be adjusted to admit groups or families. There are several benefits arising from this pricing technique: even though the purchaser may make more than the minimum number of visits, thus apparently reducing potential revenue from each additional visit, the presence of extra visitors on site is more attractive to potential visitors, there is the potential to obtain additional revenue from hospitality and shop sales, and season ticket holders can be contacted for feedback on the operation of the attraction and for cross-selling and loyalty purposes, making them a considerable asset to the attraction. Using discounted prices for this purpose should be part of the attraction's overall pricing strategy. For a study of revenue management practices in theme parks, see Heo and Lee (2009). Lennon (2004) showed in an early study of UK attractions that pricing was a neglected area of management practice in the sector. In the case of Heritage attractions, Leask, Fyall and Garrod (2002) comment on the difficulty of price setting where the offering changes during the year and includes special exhibitions too.

Event pricing is particularly difficult because in the case of a unique event it often appears impossible to estimate attendance numbers in advance. However, the usual considerations apply: costs must be covered and an allowance made for profit, assuming profit is anticipated. Many organizations plan events as part of their operations which are not intended to make a profit but for other strategic purposes, such as publicity, staff bonding, creating public awareness and so on, but price must still be a consideration if losses are to be avoided.

In the case of mega-events and major festivals, setting prices for the component events or for the component aspects such as accommodation, transport and ancillary services is a complex and challenging part of the planning, and will depend on the overall strategic perspective of the organizing group. The decision whether to keep aspects of the pricing transparent or to use bundling to offset potential losses in any one part of the operation is fundamental to the pricing strategy. It must be remembered that customer experience and awareness of the cost inputs can create resistance to price opacity, so when dealing with an experienced and sophisticated consumer base there is less scope for padding prices.

And finally

Price setting is easier to do when you know your market and what it will bear. Knowing what your costs are or at least what they have been and are likely to be in the future will enable you to arrive at a pricing strategy which will maximize your revenues and thereby your profits. The more you know the more effective your pricing strategy will be.

However, as discussed above, the most important influences on tourism pricing strategies are different for each sector. There is a clear trend towards reducing operating costs, in the package and accommodation sectors as well as for LCCs. While LCCs still promote their offerings on the basis of much lower prices than traditional full service carriers, their influence on the industry has also been to offer new destinations and greater convenience to customers, and the research opportunities for the future will lie in a better understanding of the relationships between motivation, price and satisfaction.

References

Aguiló, E. and Rosselló, J. (2012) *Research Note:* 'The new all-inclusive board formula in mature destinations – from motivation to satisfaction', *Tourism Economics*, 18(5): 1117–23.

Aguiló, E.J. Alegre and Sard, M. (2003) 'Examining the market structure of the German and UK tour operating industries through an analysis of package holiday prices', *Tourism Economics*, 9(3) 255–78.

Anton, S., Fernandez-Young, A., Cortes Jimenez, I. and Saladie, O. (2010) 'Destination management and new tourism mobilities' presented to the Government of Catalunya, 31 October.

Bock, G.W., Lee S.Y.T. and Li, H.Y. (2007) 'Price comparison and price dispersion: products and retailers at different maturity stages', *International Journal of Electronic Commerce*, 11: 101–24.
Brons, M., Pels, E., Nijkamp, P. and Rietveld, P. (2002) 'Price elasticities of demand for passenger air travel: a meta-analysis', *Journal of Air Transport Management*, 8: 165–75.
Chalip, L. and McGuirty, J. (2004) 'Bundling sport events with the host destination', *Journal of Sport Tourism*, 9(3): 267–82.
Chen, C.-M. and Chang, K.L. (2012) 'Effect of price instability on hotel profitability', *Tourism Economics*, 18(6): 1351–60.
Cooper, C., Fletcher, J., Fyall, A., Gilbert, D. and Wanhill, S. (2008) *Tourism: Principles and Practice*. Essex: Pearson.
Fleischer, A. and Felsenstein, D. (2004) 'Face-to-face or cyberspace? Choosing the Internet as an intermediary in the Israeli travel market', *Tourism Economics*, 10(3): 345–59.
Fyall, A. and Garrod, B. (2005) *Tourism Marketing: A Collaborative Approach*. Clevedon: Channel View Publications.
Garín, T. and Amaral, T. (2011) 'Internet usage for travel and tourism planning', *Tourism Economics*, 17: 1071–85.
Granados, N., Kauffman, R.J., Lai, H. and Lin, H. (2012) 'À la carte pricing and price elasticity of demand in air travel', *Decision Support Systems*, 53: 381–94.
Heo, C.Y. and Lee, S. (2009) 'Application of revenue management practices to the theme park industry', *International Journal of Hospitality Management*, 28: 446–53.
Holloway, J.C. (2004) *Marketing for Tourism*, 4th edn. Essex: Pearson.
Kardes, F.R., Cronley, M.L., Kellaris, J.J. and Posavac, S.S. (2004) 'The role of selective information processing in price-quality inference', *Journal of Consumer Research*, 31: 368–74.
Koenigsberg, O., Muller, E. and Vilcassim, N.J. (2008) 'EasyJet® pricing strategy: should low-fare airlines offer last minute deals?', *Quantitative Market Economics*, 6: 279–97.
Leask, A., Fyall, A. and Garrod, B. (2012) 'Managing revenue in Scottish visitor attractions', *Current Issues in Tourism*, 15: 1–26.
Lennon, J.J. (2004) 'Revenue management and customer forecasts: a bridge too far for the UK visitor attractions sector?', *Journal of Revenue and Pricing Management*, 2: 338–52.
Loomis, J. and Kindberg, K. (2006) 'Pricing principles for natural and cultural attractions in tourism', in L. Dwyer and P. Forsyth (eds) *International Handbook on the Economics of Tourism*. Cheltenham: Edward Elgar, pp. 173–87.
Malighetti, P., Paleari, S. and Redondi, R. (2009) 'Pricing strategies of low-cost airlines: the Ryanair case study', *Journal of Air Transport Management*, 15: 195–203.
Masiero, L. and Nicolau, J.L. (2012) 'Price sensitivity to tourism activities: looking for determinant factors', *Tourism Economics*, 18(4): 675–89.
Mattila, A. and Choi, S. (2006) 'A cross-cultural comparison of perceived fairness and satisfaction in the context of hotel room pricing', *International Journal of Hospitality Management*, 25(1): 146–53.
Mattila, A. and O'Neill, J. (2003) 'Relationships between hotel room pricing, occupancy, and guest satisfaction: a longitudinal case of a midscale hotel', *Journal of Tourism and Hospitality Research*, 27(3): 328–41.
Ovchinnikov, A. and Milner, J.M. (2007) 'Revenue management with end-of-period discounts in the presence of customer learning', Working paper. Rotman School of Business.
Piga, C.A. and Bachis, E. (2006) 'Pricing strategies by European traditional and low cost airlines. Or, when is it the best time to book online?', Discussion Paper Series 2006 14, revised July 2006. Department of Economics, Loughborough University.
Pitfield, D.E. (2008) 'Some insights into competition between low-cost airlines', *Research in Transportation Economics*, 24: 5–14.
Qu, H., Xu, P. and Tan, A. (2002) 'A simultaneous equations model of the hotel room supply and demand in Hong Kong', *International Journal of Hospitality Management*, 21: 455–62.
Rosselló, J. and Riera, A. (2012) 'Pricing European package tours: the impact of new distribution channels and low-cost airlines', *Tourism Economics*, 18(2): 265–79.
Saló, A., Garriga, A., Rigall-i-Torrent, R., Vila, M. and Sayeras, J.M. (2012) 'Differences in seasonal price patterns among second home rentals and hotels: empirical evidence and practical implications', *Tourism Economics*, 18(4): 731–47.
Thrane, C., (2005) 'Hedonic price models and sun-and-beach package tours: the Norwegian case', *Journal of Travel Research*, 43(3): 302–8.
Yelkur, R. and Da Costa, M.M.N. (2001) 'Differential pricing and segmentation on the Internet: the case of hotels', *Management Decision*, 39(4): 252–62.

27

Revenue management in tourism

Una McMahon-Beattie and Ian Yeoman

Introduction

Revenue Management (RM) has been described as an essential instrument, approach or tool which seeks to use information systems and pricing strategies to sell the right capacity to the right customer at the right price and at the right time (Kimes 1989; Kimes and Wirtz 2003a; Ivanov and Zhechev 2012). At the heart of RM is an understanding of customers' perception of a product's or service's value and an accurate alignment of price, placement and availability within identified customer segments (Cross, Higbie and Cross 2011). Given its focus on the three strategic levers of price, time and space (Kimes and Renaghan 2011) RM therefore encompasses elements of both the operations and marketing functions. Operationally it focuses on capacity allocation given exogenous demand estimates (Gallego and van Ryzin 1997). In marketing management terms it plays a role in managing customer behaviour (Anderson and Xie 2010) and stimulating and managing customer demand (Cross, Higbie and Cross 2009). Here pricing is crucial as it, 'allows a firm to capture rent for the activities that the organization undertakes to create value for the customers' (Sinha and Gazley 2012: 251). This chapter will provide an overview of the rise of and use of RM in tourism. It will examine why RM is widely practised in services where fixed costs are high relative to variable costs, allowing discriminatory prices to appeal to buyers with differing levels of price elasticity. The practice of RM is explored in the context of the economic theory of consumer surplus, which examines consumers' perceived value of a product/service and their willingness to pay. Finally, the key challenges and issues for RM are highlighted such as the potential conflicts between Customer Relationship Management (CRM) and RM, the implications of dynamic pricing and ethical issues relating to trust and fairness.

The definition of RM

The origins of RM (then known as Yield Management) can be seen in the development of a computer reservation system (SABRE) by American Airlines in 1966 which had the capability of controlling reservations inventory. However, its popularity as a capacity management strategy came after the deregulation of the US airline industry in 1978 when airlines 'inadvertently created a revolutionary way for all companies to boost revenue and profits by using data and analytics to predict consumer behavior and optimize price and availability of products' (Cross, Higbie and Cross 2011: 8). Kimes (1989) has aptly described RM as the process of allocating the right type of capacity or inventory unit to the right type of customer at the right place at the right time so as to maximize revenue or yield. The goal of RM can then be seen as the profitable alignment of the product or service, the buyer and the price. In the context of services, RM can be defined as a 'revenue maximization technique which aims to increase net revenue through the predicted allocation of available inventory capacity to predetermined market segments at optimum price' (Donaghy, McMahon-Beattie, Yeoman and Ingold 1998: 188). From a strategic perspective, Jones (2000: 88) extended the definition of RM in the hotel context to indicate that RM is 'a system . . . to maximize profitability through . . . senior management . . . identifying the profitability of market segments, establishing value, setting prices, creating discounts and displacement rules for application to the advances reservation process, and the monitoring of the effectiveness of these rules and their implementation'. This definition helps to highlight both the tactical and strategic role that RM plays in managing capacity. More holistically, Chiang, Chen and Xu (2007: 98) have summarized the nature and purpose of RM as follows:

> Revenue management, or yield management, is concerned with creating and managing service packages to maximize revenue. By thoroughly understanding customers' value functions and behaviour, a firm can design service packages for different market segments using appropriate combinations of attributes such as price, amenities, purchase restrictions, and distributions.

RM does not replace the basic managerial functions and responsibilities such as forecasting, setting appropriate strategies, monitoring and feedback on performance and the establishment of corrective action. Rather it supports not replaces effective managerial decision-making and intellectual human capital (McMahon-Beattie 2009) and functions such as forecasting, setting appropriate strategies, monitoring and feedback on performance and the establishment of corrective action remain the preserve and responsibility of management (Lee-Ross and Johns 1997).

Industry adoption and classification

The three major traditional industries that have adopted RM are airlines (e.g. Ingold and Huyton 2000; van Ryzin and McGill 2000; Talluri 2001; Boyd and Bilegan 2003; Zeni and Lawrence 2004; Zhang and Cooper 2005; Harris and DeB 2006), hotels (e.g. Hadjinicola and Panagi 1997; Baker and Collier 1999; Choi and Cho 2000; Choi and Kimes 2002; Orkin 2003; Chen and Freimer 2004; Okumus 2004; Lai and Ng 2005; Choi and Mattila 2006; Ivanov and Zhechev 2012) and car rental (e.g. Carroll and Grimes 1995; Geraghty and Johnson 1997; Anderson and Blair 2004; Savin, Cohen, Gans and Katalan 2005). However, it is also being applied in a wide range of other service industries such as restaurants (Kimes 1999; Whelyan-Ryan 2000; Susskind, Reynolds and Tsuchiya 2004; Kimes 2005), casinos (Norman and Meyer 1997; Hendler and Hendler 2004; Zheng 2007), golf (Kimes 2000a; Kimes and Wirtz 2003b; Rasekh and Li 2011), cruising (Hoseasons 2000), broadcasting and media (Kimms and Muller-Bungart 2006; Mangani 2006), and even sex and saunas (Yeoman *et al.* 2004b) among others. Indeed, in the international hotel industry, RM practices and procedures are now so well accepted that they are seen as the

Table 27.1 Industry/sector classification

Industry	*Product and customer inventory segmentation*
Passenger transport	Ticket for transport or seat segmented by time of booking, venue of booking, subscriptions, conditions
Car rentals	Right to use car segmented by time of booking, point of sale, return behaviour, conditions
Hotels	Overnight stay segmented by time and duration of booking, venue of booking, conditions
Cruises	Participation in cruise segmented by time and duration, packages
Casinos	Overnight stay. Hotel-like segmentation versus customer value
Freight	Transport or storage segmented by time and venue of booking, conditions, volume versus weight
Advertising	Placement of advertisement or commercial segmented by time of booking, subscription or bulk, placement, frequency
Telecommunication	Bandwidth in time or data segmented by subscription plan, age of customers, business versus private customers
Energy	Transport and usage of energy segmented by bulk buys, seasonality
Retail	Fashion, consumer electronics, groceries segmented by seasonality, product life cycle

Source: Adapted from Cleophas *et al.* (2011)

competitive advantage of the future. One commentator has stated that, 'The mantra "location, location, location" is fast becoming replaced with "revenue management, revenue management, revenue management"' (Hales cited in Chase 2007: 59).

Cleophas, Yeoman, McMahon-Beattie and Veral (2011) have produced a useful classification of industries by the type of product and customer inventory segmentation. For example, they note that in the car rental industry customer segmentation is based on time of booking, point of sale and return of the car whereas in the retail industry it is based on product life cycle and seasonality.

The practice of RM has become widely accepted as a method for maximizing financial returns in service industries where demand is variable, and fixed costs are a high proportion of total costs (Donaghy *et al.* 1995; Kimes 2000b; Chiang *et al.* 2007; McMahon-Beattie 2009). Indeed, a number of empirical studies have claimed significant increases in total revenue when a service business moves from a relatively passive average pricing system to an active system of price discrimination between customers, locations and time of use (e.g. Cross 1997; Boyd 1998; Elliott 2003; Yeoman and McMahon-Beattie 2004; Cross, Higbie and Cross 2011).

Preconditions and key ingredients

RM suits service industries such as tourism where the market can be segmented and the consumer demand is unstable. Combining these features with low marginal costs and the ability to sell a perishable product/service to consumer in advance of consumption are the key characteristics of sectors that can utilize RM effectively. Kimes (2000b) has outlined a number of preconditions for successful RM and has suggested a number of 'ingredients' which are prerequisites for the implementation of RM in services.

Preconditions

The preconditions of successful RM have been categorized by Kimes (2000b) as relatively fixed capacity, predictable demand, perishable inventory, time-variable demand and appropriate cost and pricing structures.

Relatively fixed capacity

Capacity-constrained service industries have no opportunity to inventory their perishable products or services in order to deal with fluctuations in customer demand. However, capacity can be in terms of physical and non-physical units. Physical capacity, for example, is about the number of airline seats, the number of seats at a sporting event, the number of seats in a restaurant or the number of hotel bedrooms. Non-physical capacity can be thought of as time-based. Kimes argues that physical capacity can be used for a specific period of time, for example, seat-hours for restaurants or theatre performances. Therefore time also becomes a constraint on capacity in services. Capacity can be changed in the longer term. For example, airlines can buy or lease larger planes or hotels can add extra bedroom or function space but this may involve considerable financial investment.

Predictable demand

In the RM context, demand consists of both those customers who buy in advance and those who simply 'walk-in' and both forms of demand need to be managed effectively in order to achieve the most profitable mix of customers. As McMahon-Beattie and Yeoman (2004: 205) state, 'It is all about predicting what advance booking will be made at different price levels against walk-in or "on-demand" situations (otherwise known as 'demand forecasting).' To do this, detailed information is required on the percentage of reservations and walk-ins, customer time periods and likely service duration (Kimes 2000b).

Perishable inventory

As stated above, the inventory of a capacity-constrained service should be thought of as a unit of time which is perishable. A unit of time might be a concert ticket, a bed-night in a hotel, a round of golf or the performance of a play. If the opportunity to sell that unit of time or experience is lost, the revenue is lost.

Time-variable demand

Demand in services is well known to vary by the week, by the day, by the time of day and seasonally. Managers must be able to forecast time-variable demand so that effective pricing decisions can be made regarding allocations of available inventory units. Flexible pricing structures allow organizations to maximize pricing opportunities in both off-peak and peak periods.

Appropriate cost and pricing structures

Organizations using RM such as hotels and airlines have a cost structure that has relatively high fixed costs and fairly low variable costs (Edgar 2000). The costs incurred by, for example, selling a concert ticket to a customer in otherwise unused capacity is relatively inexpensive and incurs only minor servicing costs. This allows for a wide range of price discretion allowing service companies the option of reducing prices during low demand times.

Key ingredients

Kimes (2000b: 9) has also categorized the ingredients necessary for an effective YM system:

> . . . a company must possess the ability to segment the market based on its willingness to pay, information on historical demand and booking patterns, good knowledge of pricing, a well-developed overbooking policy, and a good information system.

The necessity of a good information system is apparent when considering the quantity and complexity of information required to produce accurate forecasts per market segment. Also essential is a good understanding of how an organization can segment its users by purpose, time, different points of consumption and price sensitivity. A logical overbooking policy is also important as service companies such as hotels and airlines tend to overbook to protect themselves against the possibility of no-shows. Of particular interest to the revenue management practitioner is the necessity for a good knowledge of pricing. By using multiple rates to optimise revenue, the manager will know (in theory) when to use price discrimination and how. Indeed, beyond the basics of price discrimination between identifiable market segments, research has been investigating dynamic pricing and approaches to applying optimal pricing in real time based on a number of factors including customers' willingness to pay (Westermann 2006; Lu and Mazzarella 2007; Cleophas, Frank and Kliewer 2009).

Strategic levers: price, time and space

Kimes and Chase (1998) and Kimes (2000b) identified two strategic levers at the disposal of the revenue manager: demand-based pricing (price) and customer duration management (time). They argued that whilst many companies already offer price related promotions to manage peaks and troughs in demand (e.g. early bird specials, special promotions), more sophisticated manipulations of price in RM include not only time-of-the-day and day-of-week pricing but also price premiums or discounts for different market segments. Successful RM, they argue, stems from the ability to ascertain optimal balance between price and time. A third strategic lever, space, has been proposed by Kimes and Renaghan (2011). Space can be used directly to generate revenue, by dividing it into units and selling it to customers for a specific period of time (e.g. a hotel bedroom for a night or an airline seat on a flight). However, revenue generation can also be indirect. Here space is divided into units that are used to sell things to customers (e.g. advertisements or retail). An understanding of how these three levers can be used in practice can assist the revenue manager to maximize financial returns.

Revenue management, consumer surplus and price discrimination

For the revenue management professional an understanding of the relationship between price and revenue management decision is essential. McMahon-Beattie, Palmer and Yeoman (2011) have noted that what RM tries to do is to reconcile the supply demand though the price mechanism and exploit consumer surplus. Economists argue that consumer surplus is the difference between the price that a consumer actually pays for a product, and the highest price that they would be prepared to pay for it. A company which charges a uniform price for its products or services will only achieve maximum profits through this pricing method where consumers' evaluation of the product offer is homogenous and there is no consumer surplus. As such, 'price discrimination is at the heart of pricing RM tools' (Ivanov and Zhechev 2012: 181). Simply put, different market segments are charged different prices for the same inventory units (e.g. rooms, airline seats) based on differences in price sensitivity and willingness to pay. For example airline business travellers are less price-sensitive and are willing to pay higher prices compared to leisure travellers. What prevents the migration from high to low products and services is the use of rate fences (Zhang and Bell 2010; Mauri 2012). These are the rules or criteria that companies use to prevent customers migrating from high to low priced services and products. Physical fences can include such things as, for example, the location of a hotel room or view from a room and the provision of add-on amenities. Non-physical fences can include day of the week, length of stay and cancellation terms.

RM and dynamic pricing

Nowadays, developments in technology and the Internet have made dynamic pricing both possible and commercially feasible (Elmaghraby and Keskinocak 2003; Abrate, Fraquelli and Viglia 2012; Mauri 2012). Dynamic pricing has been seen as a new version of price discrimination (Krugmann 2000) where technology permits the continual adjustment of prices in line with customer demand and their willingness and ability to pay. In line with this customers, 'frequently pay different prices even when they have one and the same booking details depending on the moment of the reservation' (Ivanov and Zhechev 2012: 182). Such frequent changes in prices pose a number of challenges for marketers. Service companies that use a relatively simple range of fixed prices can establish a consistent price positioning in the minds of customers. In service industries such as tourism where prior evaluation of quality is difficult, price can be the most important indicator of expected service quality (Chen *et al.* 1994; Palmer and McMahon-Beattie 2008; McMahon-Beattie 2009). However, RM practices can have the apparently perverse effect of reversing the link between service quality and price. At times of peak demand, congestion (such as longer queues to check-in at a hotel or airport) results in lower perceived quality, yet customers are charged more than in off-peak periods when quality of service may be higher. It follows, therefore, that if price changes frequently, consumers may have greater difficulty in assessing the likely quality of a service. Additionally, research has examined how the lack of openness in modern IT based dynamic pricing systems may create conditions of mistrust (McMahon-Beattie 2009) where consumers are unsure as to how and why the price has been set. The following section will examine this in further detail.

Ethical issues: fairness and trust

Given the above, McMahon-Beattie, Palmer and Yeoman (2011) have noted that a number of studies have considered customers' perceptions of fairness within RM (Kimes and Wirtz 2003a, 2003b; Choi and Mattila 2003, 2005, 2006; Hwang and Wen 2009; Heo and Lee 2011). Perceptions of unfairness, it is argued, might lead to loss of customer satisfaction and goodwill and ultimately to loss of business. According to Kimes and Wirtz (2003b), customers may view the price discrimination and demand based pricing as unfair for several reasons. They suggest that if customers consider peak-demand prices as higher than their normal reference price, or see regular prices as higher than their reference price due to benefiting from frequent low-demand prices, then they may perceive the prices charged as unfair. Understandably customers may feel that companies are not providing more 'value' for higher priced offerings at peak-demand times.

To combat this, what is required is the provision of an appropriate level of information on the company's pricing policy and this is believed to have a positive impact on customers' perceived fairness of RM (Choi and Mattila 2003, 2005, 2006; Rohlfs and Kimes 2005). Clear information about booking, cancellation and amendment terms needs to be available and understood by customers (Ivanov and Zhechev 2012).

Other studies (McMahon-Beattie 2009; McMahon-Beattie, Palmer and Yeoman 2011) have considered the impact of variable pricing on the level of consumer trust in a company. They have explored whether variable pricing, and the fact that a company may not be offering a customer the best price available, undermines trust, which many studies have argued to be a central characteristic of long-term buyer–seller relationships (e.g. Ganesan 1994; Morgan and Hunt 1994). It has been noted that trust is a particularly important factor early in a relationship and an essential precondition for the relationship to move to more committed stages of development (Dwyer, Schurr and Oh 1987; Grayson and Ambler 1999). Findings have shown that variable pricing in itself does not cause distrust, but consumers' level of knowledge of the 'rules' in which variable pricing operates does. Indeed, if customers understand how and why the benefits from variable pricing can be obtained, and they have experienced such benefits, they may come to trust a business' use of variable pricing as a legitimate business practice. This re-emphasizes that consumers' familiarity with the rules, terms and conditions associated with variable pricing should be a key consideration for RM professionals.

RM and CRM

The adoption of RM strategies by companies in the tourism industry has often been accompanied by the development of CRM systems. CRM has been seen by many (e.g. Bull 2003; Muther 2002) as a solution for developing a true marketing orientation by a company – that is, providing a differentiated product offer that meets the needs of individual customers, rather than the 'average' customer. However, a number of commentators (Mathies and Gudergan 2007; McMahon-Beattie, Palmer and Yeoman 2011; Mauri 2012) have noted that service companies face a number of challenges when they engage in RM and CRM practices simultaneously. For example, CRM focuses on lifetime values of current and potential customers. RM, however, aims to maximize revenue on a single transaction by allocating perishable inventory to existing demand using price discrimination. As such, the essential difference between RM and CRM is the time horizon for revenue maximization (Mathies and Gudergan 2007). RM does not consider the long-term gains that might be achieved from each customer. Additionally in RM customer segmentation utilizes price elasticities and associated consumer willingness to pay whilst in CRM customers are segmented on their lifetime profitability. As a result some customers with a high lifetime value could fall into a number of different elasticity segments and receive inconsistent treatment and pricing. For example a business traveller who is usually price insensitive in terms of airline and hotel room bookings may be very price conscious when booking the family holiday.

Noone, Kimes and Renaghan (2003) and Mathies and Gudergan (2007) highlight the need to develop a customer-centric value based RM if customer lifetime values are to be realized. Metters, Queenan, Ferguson, Harrison, Higbie, Ward, Barfield, Farley, Kuyumcu and Duggasani (2008) have reported some success in the casino industry which has integrated data from CRM systems and player tracking systems in order to set room rates based on potential spend. However, the integration of RM and CRM systems remains a challenge and requires further development in terms of software development and appropriate managerial decision-making.

RM and distribution channels

Tourism companies can now make use of a wide variety of distribution channels including global distribution systems, central reservation systems, traditional and online travel agents, company websites and mobile applications. E-intermediaries such as Travelocity and Expedia are often the first port of call for travellers in their search for the right hotel, flight or holiday. This leads to challenges for the companies in that they have to simultaneously manage their distribution channels to ensure optimization of revenue. Developments such as dynamic pricing require frequent changes in prices and require an accurate knowledge of inventory availability. In addition the different channels have different characteristics, costs, revenue potential and degree of control (Mauri 2012). Notably tourism companies are actively implementing tactics to direct potential customers to their own website by offering, for example, the best rates available and utilizing multi-variant analysis to customize promotion and marketing.

Conclusion

For tourism marketers operating in capacity constrained organizations an understanding of RM is essential. Of the 4 'P's of marketing, price is the one that generates revenue and hence an understanding how price, time and space interact enables companies to sell their products or services to the right customers at the right price at the right time. As Cross, Higbie and Cross (2011: 9) note, 'The essence of this discipline is in understanding customers' perception of product value and accurately aligning product prices, placement and availability with each customer segment.' Challenges remain in terms of the integration of RM and CRM to enable more customer-centric approaches and in the management of the complexity of distribution channels. Consumers will continue to fly, stay in hotels, hire cars and take cruises but, given the variety of providers, it is inevitable that they will only enter into long-term relationships with those companies who meet effectively meet their needs with fair pricing and in whom they can trust.

References

Abrate, G., Fraquelli, G. and Viglia, G. (2012) 'Dynamic pricing strategies: Evidence from European hotels', *International Journal of Hospitality Management*, 31(1), 160–68.

Anderson, C.K. and Blair, M. (2004) 'Performance monitor: The opportunity cost of revenue management', *Journal of Revenue and Pricing Management*, 2(4), 353–67.

Anderson, C.K. and Xie, X. (2010) 'Improving hospitality industry sales: Twenty-five years of revenue management', *Cornell Hospitality Quarterly*, 51(1): 53–67.

Baker, T.K. and Collier, D.A. (1999) 'A comparative revenue analysis of hotel yield management heuristics', *Decision Sciences*, 30: 239–63.

Boyd, E.A. (1998) 'Airline alliance revenue management', *OR/MS Today*, 25: 28–31.

Boyd, E.A. and Bilegan, I.C. (2003) 'Revenue management and e-commerce', *Management Science*, 49: 1363–386.

Bull, C. (2003) 'Strategic issues in customer relationship management (CRM) implementation', *Business Process Management Journal*, 9(5): 592–602.

Carroll, W.J. and Grimes, R.C. (1995) 'Evolutionary change in product management: Experience in the car rental industry', *Interfaces*, 25: 84–104.

Chase, N. (2007) 'Revenue management redefined', *Hotels*, February: 59–62.

Chen, D. and Freimer, M. (2004) 'Understanding the bid price approach to revenue management: A case of the Revenue Inn', in I. Yeoman and U. McMahon-Beattie (eds) *Revenue Management and Pricing: Case Studies and Applications*. London: Thomson.

Chen, I.J., Gupta, A. and Rom, W. (1994) 'A study of price and quality in service operations', *International Journal of Service Industry Management*, 5(2): 23–33.

Chiang, W.-C., Chen, J.C.H. and Xu, X. (2007) 'An overview of research on revenue management: Current issues and future research', *International Journal of Revenue Management*, 1(1): 97–128.
Choi, S. and Kimes, S.E. (2002) 'Electronic distribution channel's effect on hotel revenue management', *Cornell Hotel and Restaurant Administration Quarterly*, 43: 23–31.
Choi, S. and Mattila, A.S. (2003) 'Hotel revenue management and its impact on customer' perceptions of fairness', *Journal of Revenue and Pricing Management*, 2(4): 303–10.
— (2005) 'Impact of information on customer fairness perceptions of hotel revenue management', *Cornell Hotel and Restaurant Administration Quarterly*, 46(4): 444–51.
— (2006) 'The role of disclosure in variable hotel pricing', *Cornell Hotel and Restaurant Administration Quarterly*, 47(1): 27–35.
Choi, T.Y. and Cho, V. (2000) 'Towards a knowledge discovery framework for yield management in the Hong Kong hotel industry', *International Journal of Hospitality Management*, 19: 17–31.
Cleophas, C., Frank, M. and Kliewer, N. (2009) 'Recent developments in demand forecasting for airline revenue management', *International Journal of Revenue Management*, 3(3): 252–69.
Cleophas, C., Yeoman, I., McMahon-Beattie, U. and Veral, E. (2011) 'The applications of revenue management and pricing', in I. Yeoman and U. McMahon-Beattie *Revenue Management: A Practical Pricing Perspective*. Basingstoke, UK: Palgrave Macmillan.
Cross, R. (1997) *Revenue Management: Hard Core Tactics for Market Domination*. New York: Broadway Books.
Cross, R.G., Higbie, J.A. and Cross, Z.N. (2009) 'Revenue management's renaissance: a rebirth of the art and science of profitable revenue generation', *Cornell Hospitality Quarterly*, 50(1): 56–81.
— (2011) 'Milestones in the application of analytical pricing and revenue management', *Journal of Revenue and Pricing Management*, 10(1): 8–18.
Donaghy, K., McMahon, U. and McDowell, D. (1995) 'Yield management: An overview', *International Journal of Hospitality Management*, 14(2): 139–50.
Donaghy, K., McMahon-Beattie, U., Yeoman, I. and Ingold, A. (1998) 'The realism of yield management', *Progress in Tourism and Hospitality Research*, 4(3): 187–96.
Dwyer, F.R., Schurr, P.H. and Oh, S. (1987) 'Developing buyer–seller relationships', *Journal of Marketing*, 51: 11–27.
Edgar, D.A. (2000) 'Economic theory of pricing for the hospitality and tourism industry', in A. Ingold, U. McMahon-Beattie and I. Yeoman (eds) *Yield Management: Strategies for the Service Industries*, 2nd edn,. London: Thomson.
Elliott, T.L. (2003) 'Maximising revenue production while cutting costs: An airline industry mandate', *Journal of Revenue and Pricing Management*, 1(4): 355–68.
Elmaghraby, W. and Keskinocak, P. (2003) 'Dynamic pricing in the presence of inventory considerations: Research overview, current practices and future directions', *Management Science*, 49(10): 1287–309.
Gallego, G. and Van Ryzin, G. (1997) 'A multiproduct dynamic pricing problem and its application to network revenue management', *Operations Research*, 45(1): 24–41.
Ganesan, S. (1994) 'Determinants of long-term orientation in buyer–seller relationships, *Journal of Marketing*, 58: 1–19.
Geraghty, M.K. and Johnson, E. (1997) 'Revenue management saves national car rental', *Interfaces*, 27: 107–27.
Grayson, K. and Ambler, T. (1999) 'The dark side of long-term relationships in marketing services', *Journal of Marketing Research*, 36(1): 132–41.
Hadjinicola, G.C. and Panayi, C. (1997) 'The overbooking problem in hotels with multiple tour operators', *International Journal of Operations and Production Management*, 17: 874–85.
Harris, F.H. de B. (2006) 'Large scale entry deterrence of a low-cost competitor: An early success of airline revenue management', *International Journal of Revenue Management*, 1(1): 2–27.
Hendler, R. and Hendler, F. (2004) 'Revenue management in fabulous Las Vegas: Combining customer relationship management and revenue management to maximise profitability', *Journal of Revenue and Pricing Management*, 3(1): 73–9.
Heo, C.Y. and Lee, S. (2011) 'Influences of customer characteristics on fairness perceptions of revenue management pricing in the hotel industry', *International Journal of Hospitality Management*, 30(2): 243–51.
Hoseason, J. (2000) 'Capacity management in the cruise industry', in A. Ingold, U. McMahon-Beattie and I. Yeoman (eds.) *Yield Management: Strategies for the Service Industries*, 2nd edn. London: Thomson.
Hwang, J. and Wen, L. (2009) 'The effect of perceived fairness toward hotel overbooking and compensation practices on customer loyalty', *International Journal of Contemporary Hospitality Management*, 21(6): 659–75.

Ingold, A. and Huyton, J.R. (2000) 'Yield management and the airline industry', in A. Ingold and U. McMahon-Beattie and I. Yeoman (eds) *Yield Management: Strategies for the Service Industries*, 2nd edn. London: Thomson.
Ivanov, S. and Zhechev, V. (2012) 'Hotel revenue management – a critical literature review', *Tourism Review*, 60(2): 175–97.
Jones, P. (2000) 'Defining yield management and measuring its impact on hotel performance', in A. Ingold and U. McMahon-Beattie and I. Yeoman (eds) *Yield Management: Strategies for the Service Industries*, 2nd edn. London: Thomson.
Kimes, S.E. (1989) 'The basics of yield management', *Cornell Hotel and Restaurant Administration Quarterly*, 30(3): 14–9.
— (1999) 'Implementing restaurant revenue management', *Cornell Hotel and Restaurant Administration Quarterly*, 40: 16–21.
— (2000a) 'Revenue management on the links: Applying yield management to the golf-course industry', *Cornell Hotel and Restaurant Administration Quarterly*, 41: 120–27.
— (2000b) 'A strategic approach to yield management', in A. Ingold, U. McMahon-Beattie and I. Yeoman (eds) *Yield Management: Strategies for the Service Industries*, 2nd edn. London: Thomson.
— (2005) 'Restaurant revenue management: Could it work?', *Journal of Revenue and Pricing Management*, 4(1): 95–7.
Kimes, S.E. and Chase, R.B. (1998) 'Strategic levers of yield management', *Journal of Service Research*, 1(2): 156–66.
Kimes, S.E. and Renaghan, L.M. (2011) 'The role of space in revenue management', in I. Yeoman, and U. McMahon-Beattie (eds) *Revenue Management: A Practical Pricing Perspective*. Basingstoke, UK: Palgrave Macmillan.
Kimes, S.E. and Wirtz, J. (2003a) 'Has revenue management become acceptable?', *Journal of Service Research*, 6(2): 125–35.
— (2003b) 'Perceived fairness of revenue management in the US golf industry', *Journal of Revenue and Pricing Management*, 1(4): 18–29.
Kimms, A. and Muller-Bungart, M. (2006) 'Revenue management for broadcasting commercials: The channel's problem of selecting and scheduling ads to be aired', *International Journal of Revenue Management*, 1(1): 28–44.
Krugmann, P. (2000) 'What price fairness?', *The New York Times*, 4 October.
Lai, K.-K. and Ng, W.-L. (2005) 'A stochastic approach to hotel revenue optimization', *Computers and Operations Research*, 32: 1059–72.
Lee-Ross, D. and Johns, N. (1997) 'Yield management in hospitality SME's', *International Journal of Contemporary Hospitality Management*, 9(2/3): 66–9.
Lu, J. and Mazzarella, J. (2007) 'Application of modified nested and dynamic class allocations models for cruise line revenue management', *Journal of Revenue and Pricing Management*, 6(1): 19–32.
McMahon-Beattie, U. (2009) 'Variable pricing and consumer trust', unpublished thesis, University of Gloucestershire.
McMahon-Beattie, U., Palmer, A. and Yeoman, I. (2011) 'Does the customer trust you?', in I. Yeoman and U. McMahon-Beattie, *Revenue Management: A Practical Pricing Perspective*, Basingstoke, UK: Palgrave Macmillan.
Mangani, A. (2006) 'The optimal ratio between advertising and sales income', *International Journal of Revenue Management*, 1(1): 65–78.
Mathies, C. and Gudergan, S. (2007) 'Revenue management and customer centric marketing – how do they influence travellers' choices', *Journal of Revenue and Pricing Management*, 6: 331–46.
Mauri, A.G. (2012) *Hotel Revenue Management: Principles and Practices*. Milan: Pearson.
Metters, R., Queenan, C., Ferguson, M., Harrison, L., Higbie, J., Ward, S., Barfield, B., Farley, T., Kuyumcu, H.A. and Duggasani, A. (2011) 'The killer application of revenue management: Harrah's Cherokee casino and hotel', *Interfaces*, 38(3): 161–75.
Morgan, R.M. and Hunt, S.D. (1994) 'The commitment-trust theory of relationship marketing', *Journal of Marketing*, 58: 20–38.
Muther, A. (2002) 'Customer relationship management. Electronic customer care in the new economy', *Journal of Consumer Marketing*, 19(6): 532–33.
Noone, B.M., Kimes, S.E. and Renaghan, L.M. (2003) 'Integrating customer relationship management and revenue management: A hotel perspective', *Journal of Revenue and Pricing Management*, 2(1): 7–21.

Norman, E.D. and Mayer, K.J. (1997) 'Yield management in Las Vegas casino hotel', *Cornell Hotel and Restaurant Administration Quarterly*, 38: 28–35.
Okumus, F. (2004) 'Implementation of yield management practices in service organisations: empirical findings from a major hotel group', *Service Industries Journal*, 24(6): 65–89.
Orkin, E. (2003) 'The emerging role of function space optimisation in hotel revenue management', *Journal of Revenue and Management Pricing*, 1: 172–74.
Palmer, A. and McMahon-Beattie, U. (2008) 'Variable pricing through revenue management – A critical evaluation of affective outcomes', *Management Research News*, 31(3): 189–99.
Rasekh, L. and Li, Y. (2011) 'Golf course revenue management', *Journal of Revenue and Pricing Management*, 10(2): 105–11.
Savin, S.V., Cohen, M.A., Gans, N. and Katalan, Z. (2005) 'Capacity management in rental businesses with two customer bases', *Operations Research*, 53: 617–31.
Sinha, A. and Gazley, A. (2012) 'Guest editorial: Special issue on pricing and revenue management models of marketing', *Journal of Revenue and Pricing Management*, 11(3): 251–52.
Susskind, A.M., Reynolds, D. and Tsuchiya, E. (2004) 'An evaluation of guests' preferred incentives to shift time-variable demand in restaurants', *Cornell Hotel and Restaurant Administration Quarterly*, 45: 68–84.
Talluri, K.T. (2001) 'Airline revenue management with passenger routing control: A new model with solution approaches', *International Journal of Services Technology and Management*, 2: 102–15.
Van Ryzin, G.J. and McGill, J. (2000) 'Revenue management without forecasting or optimization: An adaptive algorithm for determining airline seat protection levels', *Management Science*, 46: 760–75.
Westermann, D. (2006) '(Realtime) Dynamic pricing in an integrated revenue management and pricing environment: An approach to handling undifferentiated fare structures in low-fare markets', *Journal of Revenue and Pricing Management*, 4(4): 389–415.
Whelyan-Ryan, F. (2000) 'Yield management in the restaurant industry', in A. Ingold, U. McMahon-Beattie and I. Yeoman (eds) *Yield Management: Strategies for the Service Industries*, 2nd edn. London: Thomson.
Yeoman, I. and McMahon-Beattie, U. (2004) (eds) *Revenue Management and Pricing: Case Studies and Applications.* London: Thomson.
Yeoman, I., Drudy, C., Robertson, R. and McMahon-Beattie, U. (2004) 'Sex and saunas', in I. Yeoman and U. McMahon-Beattie (2004) (eds) *Revenue Management and Pricing: Case Studies and Applications.* London: Thomson.
Zeni, R.H. and Lawrence, K.D. (2004) 'Unconstraining demand data at US Airways', in I. Yeoman and U. McMahon-Beattie (eds) *Revenue Management and Pricing: Case Studies and Applications.* London: Thomson.
Zhang, D. and Cooper, W.L. (2005) 'Revenue management in parallel flights with customer choice behaviour', *Operations Research*, 53: 415–34.
Zhang, M. and Bell, P.C. (2010) 'Fencing in the context of revenue management', *International Journal of Revenue Management*, 4(1): 42–68.
Zheng, G. (2007) 'Which way to go? Analysis of gaming revenue enhancement approaches for Macau', *International Journal of Revenue and Pricing Management*, 6(1): 33–9.

28

Staying close to the self-service traveller

Managing customer relationships in the era of self-service technologies

Rosemary Stockdale

Introduction

The online environment has brought many challenges to the travel and tourism industry, such as developing new online business models and adjusting to an influx of new entrants to the market. A further challenge is developing strategies for the provision of self-service technologies (SSTs) for travellers. The use of SSTs has increased rapidly as organizations seek to reduce labour costs and raise efficiency in a progressively competitive market (Liu 2012). Consumers can now seek information, plan and book holidays, and check-in for flights online with little direct input or interaction from the organization. This has dramatically changed the role of travel intermediaries by moving the emphasis from selling products to facilitating information searches and supporting booking services (Buhalis and Licata 2002). The developing landscape has seen customers' behaviour change; consumers display lower levels of loyalty to any particular organization, plan shorter but more frequent trips and are motivated to search for bargains (Bos 2004). These customers are relying more on SSTs, but have high expectations in terms of choice, value, customization and convenience (Wynn *et al.* 2001).

Such changes create a dilemma for organizations as they seek to build strong, long lasting relationships with their customers to counteract the effects of an intensely competitive market, while at the same time encouraging consumer autonomy through the use of SSTs. This is particularly evident in the travel and tourism industry that services very diverse needs. Organizations must support travellers' requirements for social interaction, entertainment and rich information and at the same time provide them with the autonomy to search for information and complete transactions.

This chapter examines how the concepts of customer relationship management (CRM) can be related to self-service technologies (SSTs) within the travel and tourism industry. It considers how organizations can benefit from the use of SSTs while maintaining effective CRM strategies. In other words, how they can manage and encourage the independence of self-service behaviour in tourists while constructing strategies to build customer relationships. The constructs related to both SSTs and CRM are examined and used to create a framework that supports the development of effective strategies for the management of customer relationships within the self-service environment of eTourism.

Self-service technologies

SSTs are defined as 'technological interfaces that enable customers to produce a service independent of direct service employee involvement' (Meuter, Ostrom, Roundtree and Bitner 2000: 50). They are extensively used on the Web although not all SSTs are web-based and services offered extend from metro swipe cards and self-checkout machines (e.g. libraries and supermarkets) to ATMs and self-fill petrol pumps (Forbes 2008). The advent of social media tools is extending the range of SSTs by offering broader access to targeted information through applications that for example, enable customers to make price comparisons when shopping or provide real time flight information. SSTs offer a range of benefits to both customers and organizations that encourage adoption, although there are challenges for all stakeholders in the increasing use of such technologies (Lee, Castellanos and Choi 2012).

The customer perspective

From a customer perspective SSTs provide a measure of customer empowerment through promoting a perception of control to the individual (Lee *et al.* 2012). The use of the Web has enabled customers both to service their own information requirements and to facilitate their own online purchasing (Jensen 2012). This dual activity of information search and transaction activity is a distinct feature of Web activity, particularly in the tourism sector, which is information rich and socially orientated and was an early adopter of the Web (Werthner and Klein 1999). Web-based SSTs enable customers to search extensively for information, locate and book flights, hotels and other travel services, and to communicate with other travellers.

Meuter *et al.* (2005) examine customer satisfaction with self-service technologies and identify the concepts of successful use as ease of use and perceived usefulness. They extend their consideration of contributory concepts to discuss the role of customer readiness in terms of three factors: customer knowledge and understanding of what they have to do, motivation to use SSTs and having the necessary skills to complete a task (Meuter *et al.* 2000). Liljander, Gillberg, Gummerus and van Riel (2006) add that customers must see a clear benefit to themselves before they will engage with a SST. For example, when offered extra air miles customers' use of check-in kiosks increased only to decline again when the offer ended. The customers' perception of benefits lay in gaining air miles and not in direct gain from using the kiosks. However, there is some counter-evidence that suggests that once the initial reluctance to use a SST has been overcome, customers become more frequent users and demand more SSTs to speed up service (Lee *et al.* 2012). In other words, as Meuter *et al.* (2000) forecast, customers become more accustomed to using SSTs as they gain the necessary skills and knowledge of how to do so and in turn, may remain loyal to an organization despite the self-service requirements. Lee *et al.* (2012) report that use of airline check-in kiosks has increased substantially in 2012 and only 24 per cent of customers surveyed now abjure kiosks in favour of human interaction at the check-in desk.

The organizational perspective

In the fast moving domain of SSTs, earlier arguments that customers have been a paramount obstacle to organizations' ability to extend the use of SSTs (Meuter *et al.* 2005; Kinard, Capella and Kinard 2009) are fading. However, many consumers remain resistant or slow to accept these technologies and in the very competitive environment of, for example, airline travel, the extent of cost saving has forced the pace of adoption (Liu 2012). For example, Lee *et al.* (2012) report that SSTs reduce the cost of check-in from $3.68 per customer to 16 cents and such benefits make SSTs necessary to a successful business model in such a price-competitive market. Despite the potential savings there are questions as to whether this may be counter-productive if their use results in negative attitudes towards the provider (Liu 2012).

Other studies suggest that notwithstanding difficulties such as customer anxiety (Kinard *et al.* 2009) and failures of service (Forbes 2008), self-service opportunities are attracting more customers who are becoming familiar with the technologies and find them to be convenient and time saving (Lee *et al.* 2012). Organizations are moving to exploit the trend with customized offerings to remain competitive. Airlines are leading the development of SSTs (Frary 2005) and are putting considerable effort into reducing the consequences of forced use by developing additional service offerings including smartphone check-in and the ability to print luggage labels (Lee *et al.* 2012). Reinders, Dabholkar and Framback (2008) further recommend that airlines retain options for customers to choose between modes of interaction, such as retaining some check-in staff, to minimize the effects of anxiety. This choice of delivery options is considered a key management strategy in the use of SSTs (Curran and Meuter 2007).

In other areas of travel and tourism, SSTs are prevalent and significant numbers of tourists now search and book all or some of their travel online (Xiang and Gretzel 2010). Despite earlier speculation regarding the demise of intermediaries, the complexity of travel information counters the arguments for disintermediation and there remains a strong presence of service providers, such as travel agents, who undertake at least part of a consumer's travel arrangements. This very competitive market allows for new entrants who are quick to establish novel offerings and to exploit the consumer's willingness to share travel experiences (Stockdale and Borovicka 2006). The ubiquity and accessibility of social media technologies further support new offerings and new entrants. For example, a smartphone application that handles travel bookings, itinerary planning and integrated expenses management for business travellers (www.concur.com). Hotel chains offer direct booker discounts, passing on a proportion of the commissions saved to the customer (*The Economist* 2002) while budget airlines such as AirAsia operate at very low cost by using high levels of SSTs (Frary 2005).

In this highly complex market, the potential to be gained from investment in SSTs is substantial (Gianforte 2003) although it requires organizations to plan and execute initiatives well. As Forbes (2008) notes, customers will rarely re-purchase after a failure of an SST activity that may result from such events as out of stock, defective products, incomplete information or, most often, customer error in the process. Regaining customer trust requires service recovery procedures, which in Forbes' study were woefully inadequate, equal to a 'Do Nothing' approach. Such indifference to the plight of the self-service customer translates into very low levels of loyalty and little repeat custom. Developing strategies for managing customer relationships within the self-service culture of travel and tourism is therefore both a necessity and a challenge.

Managing customer relationships

The term customer relationship management is used interchangeably with relationship management in an academic context. The former, with its emphasis on technology-based solutions, can be described as 'information-enabled relationship marketing' (Ryals and Payne in Payne and Frow 2005: 167). The term eCRM incorporates marketing activity in the online environment (Luck and Lancaster 2003) and more recently, social CRM (SCRM) is seen as 'the business strategy of engaging customers through social media with the goal of building trust and brand loyalty' (Greenberg in Woodcock, Green and Starkey 2011: 52). While these adjustments accommodate developments in customer offerings across a variety of platforms, the intrinsic need to manage relationships with customers remains constant.

Managing customer relationships is a key strategy for building and enhancing ties with customers that can materially contribute to sustaining competitive advantage. Once ties of loyalty have been established, customers are less likely to be lured away by competitive organizations (Vatanasombut, Stylianou and Igbaria 2004). People prefer familiarity in purchasing and tend to remain loyal to brands and gain a sense of security from recognized and trusted brand names (Reichheld, Markey and Hopton 2000; Vatanasombut *et al.* 2004). Creating and maintaining such trust and loyalty requires organizations to adopt a customer-centric view that involves the customer more as a partner in co-creation and co-production of value (Payne and Frow 2005). The role of 'customer as partner' has become an imperative with the advent of social media technologies. The very social environment of the current networking era encourages the sharing of user generated content (UGC) both between individuals and with organizations, thereby enhancing customer engagement (Morgan and Chan 2011; Woodcock *et al.* 2011). Social media tools have fuelled the ability of individuals to comment and report on their customer experiences to a seemingly limitless audience beyond the control of any organization. Those that cannot adapt to the 'customer as partner' mode of working risk adverse publicity and loss of market share (Kietzmann, Hermkens, McCarthy and Silvestre 2011).

Reichheld *et al.* (2000) argue for the reinvention of the pre-Internet 'golden rule' governing the pursuit of loyal and profitable customers. Its premise is that long-term, loyal customers are of immense value and the level of return rises over time provided the organization properly resources the relationship and customers perceive they are gaining benefits. In the online environment, many have overlooked the value of the golden rule and loyalty has been traded away for 'anonymity, reduced variety and lower prices' (Peppard 2000). This fundamental premise of customer loyalty is potentially more powerful online where customers may feel less confident in the anonymous environment and require the stability of a recognized brand. Trust then becomes more powerful than price as customers are less sensitive to cost as they seek out organizations they perceive as reliable and trustworthy (Vatanasombut *et al.* 2004; Richard and Zhang 2012). Again, the need for trustworthiness is very evident in the trend towards social media where organizations are challenged, in a very visible way, to meet customer demands for good service and to maintain high levels of trust (Kaplan and Haenlein 2010).

There are shortfalls between what organizations think their CRM will deliver and what they actually achieve. Effective strategies are very difficult to determine as organizations struggle to understand the scope and potential of what CRM can or should deliver (Payne and Frow 2005) and as many as 75 per cent of organizations deem their CRM implementations to be failures as they are not seen to increase customer satisfaction or impact on sales (Feinberg and Kadam 2002). However, when organizations use CRM efficiently and create an effective and focused strategy there is evidence that they can gain substantial advantages (Rigby and Ledingham 2004).

CRM in travel and tourism

There are travel and tourism organizations that have been innovative adopters of CRM and recognize the advantages of implementing strategies to more fully understand their customers (Buhalis and Licata 2002). Others struggle to adapt and the primary reasons for non-adoption are poor understanding of CRM, unwillingness to change and lack of long-term vision (Genesys 2002). Some industry players understand the importance of CRM but struggle to integrate customer service strategies with customer service delivery (Gamble, Chalder and Stone 2000).

Luck and Lancaster (2003) report that many hotel groups tend to use their websites for little more than posting information and have failed to achieve any real gains in this area. An Amadeus report on social media (Frary 2005: 4) urges the travel industry to 'recognize that the traveller is "social" and expects brands to be listening to what they want, and to provide informational, supportive, relevant, and valuable communications through their choice of communication channels'. In other words, travel organizations need to communicate, to interact and to understand their customers.

Customers relate to interpersonal elements such as self-image, status, information and money (Morais, Backman and Dorsch 2003; Richard and Zhang 2012) while evidence of reciprocal commitment reinforces customer loyalty (Vatanasombut *et al.* 2004). Reciprocity is judged in terms of contribution matching that of the customer's through evidence of friendship, loyalty and commitment that creates emotional bonds that cannot be substituted by discounts and perks (Morais *et al.* 2003; Richard and Zhang 2012). Customers want accurate and complete information, good access, information searching facilities, prompt system response and reliable service (Hsu, Chiu and Ju 2004). The perception of reciprocity is particularly important for social media users who expect higher levels of interaction. The arrival of new highly visible intermediaries such as TripAdvisor enhances such interaction and gratifies consumers' desire to share travel experiences (Xiang and Gretzel 2010). Tourism marketers therefore need to be careful to integrate social media and develop customer-centric strategies into their planning of relationship marketing.

Developing customer relationships in an SST environment

In the apparently paradoxical themes of pushing customers towards self-service technologies and maintaining good customer relationships, there is a complementary thread of placing customers within a partnership rather than regarding them as marketing targets (Meuter *et al.* 2005; *The Economist* 2002). Meuter *et al.* (2005) argue that such is the value of the customer as a co-producer that truly customer-centric organizations will extend internal practices to include customers with the resulting benefits of increasing services and improving relationships. Customers become stakeholders and their commitment to the relationship is reinforced (Wynne, Berthon, Pitt, Ewing and Napoli 2001). This argument has been strengthened as technologies have developed that facilitate co-production activities and also promote customer-to-customer interaction that affects the way organizations are perceived by their market. This section discusses the constructs of relationship building within the context of a customer-centric business offering SST facilities.

Design factors in building relationships

It has been argued that design and functionality of customer interfaces, together with some evidence of innovativeness, can 'enhance perceptions of quality, encourage repeat patronage, and result in increased loyalty to the firm' (Curran and Meuter 2007: 2830). Therefore, while the technicalities of SSTs or websites are not discussed here, there are design considerations that affect the ability of organizations to maximize their CRM strategies.

The travel industry is very highly Web-based, which is key to supporting many of the SSTs available. Travel customers are known to be prone to site hopping and have been likened to 'empowered fruit flies' with attention spans estimated to be as low as ten seconds (Lueg 2001). This type of behaviour calls for simplicity of website design in preference to an organization's desire for artistry, novelty or fashion. In other words, design priorities should be to enable customers to have a good online experience and find what they need quickly and efficiently

(Frary 2005). Muhtaseb *et al.* (2012) find the two primary factors that influence travellers' confidence and satisfaction in a website are content and personalization. Customers want to find information quickly and easily and they want to be recognized and treated as individuals.

Despite the emphasis on effective design, a lack of appreciation of interactivity and personalization in websites means that many remain in the domain of advertising (Corigliano and Baggio 2004). A study into the importance of good design concludes that travel companies could lift sales by at least one third if they address customer experiences rather than their own perceptions of what is a good website (Gianforte 2003). This organizational focus in design is being replicated in the development of Web 2.0 offerings where there is 'a high propensity of traditional advertisement and limited collaboration with users' (Hvass and Munar 2012: 93). In the airline sector Hvass and Munar (2012) note that a lack of clear strategies and inconsistent use of social media applications has resulted in missed opportunities for relationship building. Such views echo those of Vogt (2011: 360) who argues that organizations should aim to 'delight consumers with more insightful service interactions and ultimately consumption experiences stand to strengthen customer loyalty and commitment'.

Albert, Goes and Gupta (2004) present a framework for the development, design and management of customer-centric websites. Such sites facilitate gathering of data on visitor characteristics and behaviour, understanding where they come from, segmentation, tracking of segment behaviour and development of site content and interactivity to meet the needs of each segment. In essence, to fulfil customers' needs for specific information or transactional capability. Such sites are models of best practice and not within the resources of many smaller organizations within the travel sector, although adherence to basic principles can improve customer experience. Social media do not affect the basic principles of web design, but do call for greater speed and new ways of interacting with customers that should complement, not replace, other marketing activity (Hvass and Munar 2012).

Design considerations also impact on customers' willingness to use SSTs. Perceived control encourages self-efficacy and encourages repeat use by customers and can be enhanced through design features that provide interactivity and comparative information (Zhu, Nakata, Sivakumar and Grewal 2007). Once consumers have engaged with an SST, problems may arise in completion of the transactional or informational process. Early evidence suggests that customers are unwilling to take the blame for failure of an SST process, although nearly 60 per cent of failed procedures result from customer actions (Forbes 2008). Where the problem is held to be the result of design problems, consumers will assume that it is a long-term issue and are likely to discontinue use (Meuter *et al.* 2000; Forbes 2008). Again, simplicity of design is more important than complex offerings that do not meet consumer needs (Zhu *et al.* 2007), supporting arguments for effective relationship marketing to enable organizations to understand customers' needs.

Identifying the customer

Differentiating market segments is a central tenet of marketing and the ability to segment very large markets is a feature of effective Information Systems (Vogt 2011). Market segmentation facilitates targeted marketing and enables organizations to identify the contribution to sales of each segment (Reichheld *et al.* 2000). Not all customers are equally profitable and organizations need to recognize what appeals to the most potentially profitable segment to encourage greater depths of loyalty (Peppard 2000). In other words, organizations should be careful to concentrate appropriate resources on the high value customers (Luck and Lancaster 2003).

In travel and tourism a range of metrics are used to identify valued customers. For example, airlines tend to regard frequency of travel as a measure of a valued customer whereas an online intermediary may calculate value by revenue per head, yet other service providers may give priority to customers booking new tourism destinations. Once identified by the planned criteria, marketing spend can be more specifically targeted and products tailored to meet the different needs of the various groups, with due consideration given to the most profitable segment (Peppers, Rogers and Dorf 1999). Such segmentation identifies the unique characteristics of individual customers and allows for tailoring of products/services to meet their needs. This differentiation allows for current and potential values to be calculated and is a key element of building customer relationship strategies that maximize the potential of the customer base. It is estimated that it takes three years to meet the point of maximum profitability in a customer relationship (Peppers *et al.* 1999) therefore a long-term strategy can maximize profitability.

Market segmentation also raises issues in the use of SSTs. Lee Castellanos and Choi (2012) find that 24 per cent of customers remain resistant to SST use while others may have low levels of IT capabilities (Vatanasombut *et al.* 2004; Reichheld *et al.* 2000). The less technically sophisticated will have different needs from more skilled customers with the former less likely to transact online or use SSTs. Customers with little readiness to use require 'hand holding' features in the form of customer friendly training aids, or a troubleshooting employee, to support their efforts (Meuter, Bitner, Ostrom and Brown 2005; Kinard *et al.* 2009). More skilled customers may become impatient of simple services, complete more complex tasks and require a higher level of service and usability. A further complication is the use of social media, where segmentation of customers allows for very specific targeting, and tools and applications can be more closely targeted to groups that will respond in different ways to different approaches (Hvass and Munar 2012).

Customer information gathering

Customer data supports the analysis of market segments and the identification of valuable customers through accumulation of data on spending habits, preferences and actions (Peppers *et al.* 1999). There are many sources of data including emails, database log files and cookies to clarify customers' histories of visits to a website (Albert *et al.* 2004). Other communication channels such as call centre enquiries and social media platforms also offer data sources, with the latter having the potential to offer 'immediate information' such as likes and dislikes of customers (Morgan and Chan 2011). Effective use of this data requires that strategies can be put in place to determine what information is required for particular purposes (Morgan and Chan 2011). However, the complexity of data gathering has led to many organizations struggling to cope to the extent that even basic information may not be used appropriately. For example, Reichheld *et al.* (2000) found that less than 20 per cent of organizations systematically use logs to track customer behaviour.

For effective customer knowledge, organizations should attempt to collect non-transactional data on customer preferences and behaviour. This is not an easy task in an information rich industry where travellers search for information and post opinions to a wide range of online communities and intermediary sites. In terms of immediate relationship management, existing or transactional customer data can be garnered, but dynamic website design must accommodate interfaces to capture data from the non-transactional customer who also holds value in terms of future business (Albert *et al.* 2004).

Communication with customers

Communication is critical to building relationships with customers. The Internet, although a many-to-many medium, is best considered as one-to-one for company-to-customer communication (Gurau, Ranchhod and Hackney 2003). This view supports the development of individual customer relationships where the company can respond to needs by customizing products and services to fit each customer (Peppers *et al.* 1999). It also supports the recognition of customers as co-producers by engaging with them in an individual way (Meuter *et al.* 2005). The ability to respond to customers in this way is essential for gaining the competitive advantage that comes from establishing and retaining long-term relationships. The communication landscape has become more complicated as new technologies come into use and the number of communication channels increases. While, for example, social media contribute value by enhancing the one-on-one relationships that engage customers, they make communication methods more diverse, more immediate and more complicated (Morgan and Chan 2011). Business sources suggest that organizations are not putting effective strategies in place to deal with a wider range of customer channel interfaces and thereby missing opportunities to communicate effectively (Genesys 2002; Morgan and Chan 2011; Frary 2005).

Multiple communication channels such as e-mail, call centres and personal interaction offer more opportunities for customers to communicate, but require enhanced planning to meet customer needs (Buhalis and Licata 2002). Customers do not distinguish between channels and anticipate that organizations should respond to them whether the interface is offline or online. Delays in responding to customer concerns significantly increase dissatisfaction and complaints and lead to loss of loyalty (Cho Im and Hiltz 2003). Seamless integration across all channel interfaces is therefore a necessity (Reichheld *et al.* 2000), but becomes more of a problem in the age of social networking where instant responses are anticipated (Frary 2005; Hvass and Munar 2012).

Despite the advantages of one-to-one communications in building individual relationships, there are benefits to be gained from the use of one-to-many communication tools (Gurau *et al.* 2003). Significant cost savings in SSTs can be made through the implementation of tools such as FAQs. When well designed and maintained they can reduce call costs by posting answers to customers' most frequent queries and thereby leave specialists to answer more difficult questions (Buhalis and Licata 2002). This has a dual benefit of reducing the load on call centres and motivating staff to deal with more interesting and complex queries.

Maintaining loyalty and trust

Loyalty and trust are seen as essential elements of relationship management. Loyalty is earned by organizations over time through repeated interactions and transactions (Vogt 2011) while trust is identified as the single most important factor in online customer relationships (Luck and Lancaster 2003). Organizations can gain durable advantage if they demonstrate to their customers that they understand the value of trust. Successful trust building can overcome the lack of traditional face-to-face meetings in an online or SST environment, but requires that organizations deliver on promises to sustain customer loyalty through delivering 'a consistently superior customer experience' (Reichheld and Schefter in Luck and Lancaster 2003). An effective method is to develop a trusted brand and, where applicable, to build on an established offline brand (Reichheld *et al.* 2000). Where trust is lacking or lost, commitment to the relationship from the customer is withdrawn (Vatanasombut *et al.* 2004). Loyalty depends initially on trust and then requires that the organization identify the key drivers of customer allegiance. There are several recognized strategies for building customer loyalty as follows.

Branding

The personal involvement of customers increases the opportunities to add value to a brand by enabling identification of features that appeal to the customer base (Buhalis and Licata 2002).

By personalizing the product via recognition of the target market and micro-segmentation, organizations have the opportunity to increase brand recognition on a one-to-one basis, thereby building loyalty (Heldal, Sjovold and Heldal 2004). Customers often attribute anthropomorphic characteristics to brands and identify with them, self-justifying their investment by displaying attachment, telling others of their positive experiences and becoming resistant to change (Reichheld *et al.* 2000). The relationship develops through an investment of resources from both sides, and organizations must freely share information and make evident the special position of loyal customers (Reichheld *et al.* 2000). They must also commit to customer expectations of a high level of overall interaction and service (Hamid 2005). Where service fails to meet expectations, the results can have a negative effect, such as displayed by a disgruntled airline passenger who broadcast a YouTube posting 'United Broke My Guitar', which has had over 12 million views (Kietzmann *et al.* 2011).

Customer loyalty schemes

There is a growing body of literature that suggests while loyalty schemes may promote repeat sales they are not particularly successful in retaining customers. The cost of a loyalty scheme in some cases has been found to exceed the revenues from increased sales. Morais *et al.* (2004) found that the tourism market was 'rushing to establish loyalty programmes' while empirical evidence suggests that such programmes are ineffective. They argue that customers are influenced by more intangible elements such as an environment of trust, status and information. In contrast, Verhoef (2003) found that loyalty programmes using customer incentives increase retention of customers. His findings contradict the literature, but Verhoef suggests that this shows that loyalty schemes have to work in addition to other customer relationship initiatives. Indeed, loyalty programmes such as frequent flyer accounts have become as ubiquitous as the ATM and they are no longer a competitive advantage or CRM tool but a necessity in the eyes of the customer (Gamble *et al.* 2000). The advantage of loyalty programmes will therefore lie in their use as a data collection tool and as an incentive to reward certain consumer actions, such as promoting certain purchases or encouraging SST use. However, with the advent of smart cards finer levels of information gathering on customers, including searches and purchases, will be possible and potentially increase the value of loyalty schemes to organizations (Vogt 2011).

Community sites

A business model that has connotations for building loyalty is that of the business sponsored online community, which is finding favour with more organizations (Preece and Maloney-Krichmar 2003). Although creating an effective community is slow in terms of revenue returns, the contribution to the development of customer relationships can be considerable (Stockdale and Borovicka 2006). Communities allow for businesses to communicate with their customers, but also for participants to exchange ideas with each other (Vatanasombut *et al.* 2004). The tourism industry is well suited to the business community model as the social elements inherent in leisure travel encourage peer-to-peer interaction, the industry is highly information dependent, and it has a diverse customer base (Werthner and Klein 1999). The high level of interaction encourages the sharing of travel information and mutual support between customers and introduces a hedonic element that is often overlooked in the travel industry (Stockdale and Borovicka 2006). More recently, community has become a central element of social media use although Hvass and Munar (2012) found airlines tend towards formality on their social media platforms, using a traditional command and control approach that does not sit well with the content-generation habits of that environment. Travel firms are also using social media for advertising rather than for engagement, thereby seriously underestimating the potential of online communities (Frary 2005; Hvass and Munar 2012).

Developing a framework

The concepts of self-service technologies and customer relationship building are both complex and complementary. Customers tend to prefer face-to-face contacts when dealing with organizations, although this is changing as people become more familiar with the benefits and rewards of SSTs. Those who are reluctant to engage with technology can be supported and encouraged through design features, FAQs and, in the case of physically located SSTs, with helpful staff. Effective action by employees can contribute to the development of long-term relationships despite the seeming disconnect of promoting self-service activity in customers. Benefits for all stakeholders are enhanced when organizations implement strategies to enhance customers' acceptance of SSTs.

The constructs of customer relationship development identified in this chapter are given in Table 28.1 together with a summary of the factors related to those constructs. These are expanded in the suggestions that are included in the table and relate the literature to the development of appropriate strategies for enhancing customer relationships within the context of an organization. The constructs are inter-dependent and all of them influence the ability to develop longer-term relationships. For example, design factors affect both the design of the website and associated social media use as well as the level of technical sophistication required from customers in using the SST. Effective design minimizes errors in self-service and encourages repeat use that allows for relationship building through identification of customer segments and reciprocal communication that will ultimately encourage development of trust and loyalty. Effective design also affects the ability of the organization to gather appropriate and extensive data from customer interactions that can compensate for the lack of face-to-face activity.

Another feature of SSTs that has yet to be fully explored is the change in the role of the customer. Where customers are accepting of their role as active agents in their travel searches and bookings they have a greater perception of empowerment and involvement. This is underpinned by the enhanced levels of interactivity promoted by social media and leads to a shift from passive recipient of service to active participant in meeting customer (i.e. their own) requirements (Morgan and Chan 2011). The role of customer as partner in co-production of value enhances engagement and encourages loyalty and trust (Payne and Frow 2005). Recognition of the customer in co-production is becoming a key attribute for relationship building in the self-service environment.

As a contributor to the organization-customer dynamic, SSTs invoke a co-production role that aligns the customer to an organization's culture. This in turn enhances the relationship, and supports the perception of friendship, loyalty and status, thereby strengthening emotional bonds (Richard and Zhang 2012). Additionally, effective communication practices reinforce customers' identification with the organization and encourage further commitment to the relationship. Figure 28.1 provides a framework to support the management of customer relationships in an SST environment. The combined constructs of customer relationship development and SST provision require an organization to contribute efficient communications, the perception of friendship, loyalty and status to the target customer in order to manage the customer relationship.

Benefits are indicated as part of the contribution to the customer, although it should be noted that these are largely intangible such as increased perception of control, empowerment and self-efficacy. Direct, tangible benefits in the form of discounts or lower prices are less effective than

Table 28.1 Constructs of customer relationship development

Constructs	*Factors to be considered*	*Suggestions to consider*
Design factors in building relationships	The website, social media tools and SSTs should provide good customer experience to all visitors. Design should take into account the targeted market segments and fulfil customer expectations in information seeking and transactional activities.	• Does the design reflect customer service needs or organizational artistry? • Does the website fully support the self-service offerings? • Does the website offer value-added additional facilities to encourage return visits? • Do social media initiatives promote interactivity with and between customers? • Are the website and other applications effectively managed with frequent updates, continuous assessment and on-going innovation? • Are the SSTs designed to accord with target market level of skills and confidence?
Identifying the customer	Improve market segmentation through the identification of each customer segment. • Novice users • Sophisticated • Transactional • Non-transactional • High value customers • Low value customers	• Have the varying levels of IT sophistication of customers been taken into account? • Are non-transactional customers of value to the organization? • Are resources targeted appropriately to high value customers? • Are there mechanisms in place to track customer value over time?
Customer information gathering	Strategies for gathering, analysing and using customer data to provide information on their activities. Information is used to customize products and follow changes in customer trends.	• Are customers' emails, bulletin board postings, social media communications and call centre enquiries monitored and analysed? • Is customer behaviour tracked on the website and the information used to support innovation? • Would the organization benefit from the purchase of consumer behaviour analyses from a third party? • Is a customer database used to register individual customer preferences? • Are monitoring tools used to scrape social media platform sites relevant to the organization? • Are the SSTs monitored for customer behaviour? • Are there strategies for dealing with the wealth of data?
Communication with customers	The web and social media support a one-to-one approach with customers with one-to-many facilities for more simple requirements.	• Are customer enquiries and postings answered correctly and within a specified time? • Is there a co-ordinated response to customers' enquiries through all channel interfaces? • Do employees have access to the right information to satisfy customer queries? • Can FAQs be used to respond to simple, repetitive queries?

(Continued)

Table 28.1 (Continued)

Constructs	*Factors to be considered*	*Suggestions to consider*
Loyalty and trust	Trust is seen as the single most important element in customer relationship building. Loyalty and trust can be developed and nurtured through: Branding Customer loyalty schemes Community sites	• Is brand development based on recognition of attributes of the customer base? • If a loyalty scheme is used, is it cost effective? Is there evidence that it promotes customer loyalty? • Have customer attributes been identified? Is commitment to the customer signalled by appropriate displays of reciprocal measures such as information sharing and indications of status? • Is a community site a considered option for the customer base? Does the organization have the resources to build and maintain such a site? Can a community be created via a social media platform?

status or perceived friendship in maintaining relationships (Morais *et al.* 2003; Richard and Zhang 2012) and are not included. In return for the organizational offerings, engaged customers will commit to friendship, loyalty and reciprocal communication that will contribute to the organization's knowledge of its target market. This in turn will support the on-going development of strategies to maintain relationships with customers while maximising the organizational benefits of SSTs.

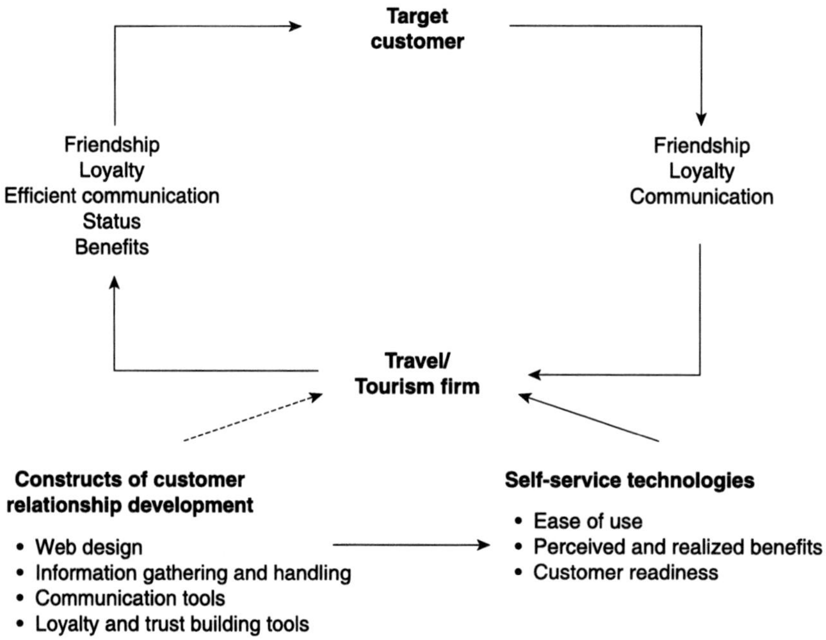

Figure 28.1 Framework to support the management of customer relationships in an SST environment (Stockdale 2007).

Conclusions

In the current environment of the travel and tourism industry a major challenge for organizations is to retain customers by building effective relationship strategies while developing cost effective self-service offerings. The apparent contradiction of encouraging autonomy of action while building close one-on-one relationships can be resolved by using information technology tools to meet customer demands and create loyalty to the organization.

The use of SSTs benefits organizations in terms of cost savings and in drawing the customer into a proactive or co-production role that empowers the customer and encourages relationship development. By developing SSTs that are easily accessible and appropriate to consumer readiness, travel and tourism organizations encourage the creation of loyalty and status to reinforce the mutual commitment between organization and customer. In further considering relationship management constructs organizations can enhance the use of SSTs and underpin the involvement of consumers, thereby creating loyalty and enhancing the role of the self-service offerings. This has the dual benefit of increasing loyalty ties with customers and gaining cost savings from increased use of the SSTs. The provision of a framework as a starting point for improving the management of customer relationship in a self-service environment may contribute towards alleviating the 'small number of adopters, the limitations of usage and the perceived lack of benefits' (Liljander *et al.* 2006: 187) currently prevalent in SSTs in the travel and tourism industry.

The contribution of this research for practitioners is the reconciliation of the seemingly contradictory aspects of encouraging independence in customers through self-service offerings while promoting the call for effective customer relationship management. The implications for practice lie in the identification of the constructs relating to building customer relationship strategies that embrace the SST environment, while also deriving the benefits of SST use. The framework further contributes a view of how managing contributions to the customer result in reciprocation of loyalty, friendship and trust to the organization.

From a research perspective making the link between self-service technologies and customer relationships opens up several avenues for further research. The co-production role of customers is a fruitful area for continuing research, particularly in the development of SSTs. While co-production is largely seen as a positive move, there is little research into how it can be effectively managed in traditional travel industry organizations, beyond the customer-orientated sites such as TripAdvisor. Additionally, as the trend for self-service in the travel sector increases there is a need for greater insights into customer requirements such as the essential touch points of personal service as opposed to areas that can be serviced by SSTs. The fast moving developments in social media technologies also bring research opportunities. For example, how can customer relationships be enhanced by the use of social media and how can the very immediate and personal demands arising from use of these technologies be met by SSTs? Finally, customer relationship management requires analysis of customer data. The wealth of data that can be accumulated from SST interactions brings problems of how to use such data effectively. Research into data management in the travel sector is required to meet the not inconsiderable challenges of the current age of big data.

References

Albert, T.C., Goes, P.B. and Gupta, A. (2004) 'GIST: A model for design and management of content and interactivity of customer-centric web sites', *MIS Quarterly*, 28(2): 161–82.

Bos, H. (2004) *Tourism Trends for Europe*. Brussels: European Travel Commission.

Buhalis, D. and Licata, M.C. (2002) 'The future eTourism intermediaries', *Tourism Management*, 23: 207–20.

Cho, Y., Im, I. and Hiltz, R. (2003) 'The impact of E-services failures and customer complaints on electronic commerce customer relationship management', *Journal of Consumer Satisfaction, Dissatisfaction and Complaining Behaviour*, 16: 106–18.

Corigliano, M.A. and Baggio, R. 'Tourism, technology, information and the relationship with customer'. Paper presented at the International Conference on Leisure Futures, Bolzano, 10–12 November 2004.

Curran, J. and Meuter, M. (2007) 'Encouraging existing customers to switch to self-service technologies: Put a little fun in their lives', *Journal of Marketing Theory and Practice*, 15(4): 283–98.

Economist, The (2002) 'Travel agents. Fit for DIY?', *The Economist*, September: 63. Online. Available: http://www.economist.com/node/1159511 (accessed 14 April 2013).

Feinberg, R. and Kadam, R. (2002) 'E-CRM web service attributes as determinants of customer satisfaction with retail websites', *International Journal of Service Industry Management*, 13(5): 432–51.

Forbes, L. (2008) 'When something goes wrong and no one is around: Non-Internet self-service technology failure and recovery', *Journal of Services Marketing*, 22(4): 316–27.

Frary, M. (2005) *Self-service. Future or fad? An Amadeus Global Travel Report*. Online. Available: http://www.amadeus.com/corporations/documents/corporations/Self-service_white_paper_V3_LowRes.pdf (accessed 14 April 2013).

Gamble, P., Chalder, M. and Stone, M. (2000) 'Customer knowledge management in the travel industry', *Journal of Vacation Marketing*, 7(1): 83–91.

Genesys Travel (2002) *Customer Relationship Management in Travel*. Slough, UK: Genesys Travel Technology Consultants.

Gianforte, G. (2003) 'The world at our fingertips – How online travel companies can turn clicks into bookings', *Journal of Vacation Marketing*, 10(1): 79–86.

Gurau, C., Ranchhod, A. and Hackney, R. (2003) 'Customer-centric strategic planning: Integrating CRM in online business systems', *Information Technology and Management*, 4(2–3): 199–214.

Hamid, N. (2005) 'ECRM: Are we there yet?', *Journal of American Academy of Business*, 6(1): 51–7.

Heldal, F., Sjovold, E. and Heldal, A. (2004) 'Success on the Internet – Optimizing relationships through the corporate site', *International Journal of Information Management*, 24: 115–29.

Hsu, M.H., Chiu, C. and Ju, T.L. (2004) 'Determinants of continued use of the WWW: An integration of two theoretical models', *Industrial Management and Data Systems*, 104(9): 766–75.

Hvass, K. and Munar, A. (2012) 'The takeoff of social media in tourism', *Journal of Vacation Marketing*, 18(2): 93–103.

Jensen, J.M. (2012) 'Shopping orientation and online travel shopping: The role of travel experience international', *Journal of Tourism Research*, 14: 56–70.

Kaplan, A. and Haenlein, M. (2010) 'Users of the world, unite! The challenges and opportunities of social media', *Business Horizons*, 53: 59–68.

Kietzmann, J., Hermkens, K., McCarthy, I.P. and Silvestre, B.S. (2011) 'Social media? Get serious! Understanding the functional building blocks of social media', *Business Horizons*, 54: 241–51.

Kinard, B., Capella, M. and Kinard, J. (2009) 'The impact of social presence on technology based self-service use. The role of familiarity', *Services Marketing Quarterly*, 30: 303–14.

Lee, W., Castellanos, C. and Choi, H.S. (2012) 'The effect of technology readiness on customers' attitudes toward self-service technology and its adoption: The empirical study of U.S. airline self-service check-in kiosks', *Journal of Travel and Tourism Marketing*, 29(8): 731–43.

Liljander, V., Gillberg, F., Gummerus, J. and van Riel, A. (2006) 'Technology readiness and the evaluation and adoption of self-service technologies', *Journal of Retailing and Consumer Services*, 13: 177–91.

Luck, D. and Lancaster, G. (2003) 'E-CRM: Customer relationship marketing in the hotel industry', *Managerial Auditing Journal*, 18(3): 213–31.

Lueg, C. (2001) 'Information dissemination in virtual communities as challenge to real world companies', Proceedings of the first IFIP Conference on E-Commerce, E-Business and E-Government. Zurich: Kluwer Academic Publishing.

Liu, S. (2012) 'The impact of forced use on customer adoption of self-service technologies', *Computers in Human Behavior*, 28: 1194–201.

Meuter, M., Ostrom, A. Roundtree, R. and Bitner, M. (2000) 'Self service technologies: Understanding customer satisfaction with technology-based service encounters', *Journal of Marketing*, 64: 50–64.

Meuter, M., Bitner, M., Ostrom, A. and Brown, S. (2005) 'Choosing among alternative service delivery modes: An investigation of customer trial of self-service technologies', *Journal of Marketing*, 69: 61–83.

Morais, D., Backman, S. and Dorsch, M. (2003) 'Toward the operationalization of resource investments made between customers and providers of a tourism service', *Journal of Travel Research*, 41: 362–74.

Morgan, J. and Chan, C. (2011) *An Introduction to Social CRM for the Travel Industry*. Chess Media Group. Online. Available: http://www.chessmediagroup.com/resources/white-papers/introduction-to-social-crm-for-travel/ (accessed 14 April 2013).

Muhtaseb, R., Lakiotaki, K. and Matsatsini, N. (2012) 'Applying a multi-criteria satisfaction analysis approach based on user preferences to rank usability attributes in E-tourism websites', *Journal of Applied and Theoretical Electronic Commerce Research*, 7(3): 28–48.

Payne, A. and Frow, P. (2005) 'A strategic framework for customer relationship management', *Journal of Marketing*, 69(4): 167–76.

Peppard, J. (2000) 'Customer Relationship Management (CRM) in financial services', *European Management Journal*, 18(3): 312–27.

Peppers, D., Rogers, M. and Dorf, B. (1999) 'Is your company ready for one-to-one marketing?', *Harvard Business Review*, Jan–Feb: 151–60.

Preece, J. and Maloney-Krichmar, D. (2003) 'Online communities: Focusing on sociability and usability', in A Sears (ed.) *Handbook of Human–Computer Interaction*. Mahwah, NJ: Lawrence Erlbaum Assoc. Inc., pp. 586–620.

Reichheld, F., Markey Jr, R. and Hopton, C. (2000) 'E-customer loyalty – Applying the traditional rules of business for online success', *European Business Journal*, 12(4): 173–79.

Reinders, M. Dabholkar, P. and Framback, R. (2008) 'Consequences of forcing consumers to use technology based self-service', *Journal of Service Research*, 11(2): 107–23.

Richard, J. and Zhang, A. (2012) 'Corporate image, loyalty, and commitment in the consumer travel industry', *Journal of Marketing Management*, 28(5–6): 568–93.

Rigby, D. and Ledingham, D. (2004) 'CRM done right', *Harvard Business Review*, November: 118–29.

Ryals, L. and Knox, S. (2001) 'Cross-functional issues in the implementation of relationship marketing through customer relationship management', *European Management Journal*, 19(5): 534–42.

Stockdale, R. (2007) 'Managing customer relationships in the self-service environment of e-tourism', *Journal of Vacation Marketing*, 13(3): 205–19.

Stockdale, R. and Borovicka, M.C. (2006) 'Ghost towns or vibrant villages? Constructing business-sponsored online communities', *International Journal of Communications, Law and Policy*, 11, Autumn. Online. Available: http://ijclp.org/11_2006/ (accessed 14 April 2013).

Vatanasombut, B., Stylianou, A. and Igbaria, M. (2004) 'How to retain online customers', *Communications of the ACM*, 47(6): 65–9.

Verhoef, P. (2003) 'Understanding the effect of customer relationship management efforts on customer retention and customer share development', *Journal of Marketing*, 67(4): 30–44.

Vogt, C. (2011) 'Customer relationship management in tourism: Management needs and research applications', *Journal of Travel Research*, 50(4): 356–64.

Werthner, H. and Klein, S. (1999) *Information Technology and Tourism – A Challenging Relationship*. Vienna: Springer Verlag.

Woodcock, N., Green, A. and Starkey, M. (2011) 'Social CRM as a business strategy', *Journal of Database Marketing and Customer Strategy Management*, 18: 50–64.

Wynne, C., Berthon, P., Pitt, L., Ewing, M. and Napoli, J. (2001) 'The impact of the Internet on the distribution value chain', *International Marketing Review*, 18(4): 420–31.

Xiang, Z. and Gretzel, U. (2010) 'The role of social media in online travel information search', *Tourism Management*, 31: 179–88.

Zhu, Z., Nakata, C., Sivakumar, K. and Grewal, D. (2007) 'Self-service technology effectiveness: the role of design features and individual traits', *Journal of the Academy of Marketing Science*, 35: 492–506.

29

Marketing communications in tourism

A review and assessment of research priorities

Scott McCabe and Clare Foster

Introduction

Despite being touted as one of the largest 'industries' in the world, accounting for millions of jobs, 9.3 per cent of global GDP, and 5 per cent of world exports (World Travel and Tourism Council 2013), it is credible to ask the question whether there is anything more to tourism than mere puffery (exaggerated or false claims in advertising). That tourism exists is undisputable. Yet as an industry it is almost completely dependent on marketing, and marketing communications specifically. Tourism relies on natural or otherwise extant resources in a locality (transport links, attractions, accommodation and hospitality). As an intangible experience, tourism is a confected value proposition, co-created and shared by tourists, without whose complicity in suspending disbelief (in everyday reality) the experience value would surely collapse. *Being a tourist* is perhaps little more than a state of mind.

And yet the industry has been plagued by accusations that it persistently fails to recognize the role of marketing as a strategic business function that adds value to the industry (Fyall and Garrod 2005). Although most tourism industry professionals would acknowledge that marketing is important, there are critical characteristics which have impacted on the perception of marketing's value within the sector. For example, Fyall and Garrod argue that tourism is more product-driven and supply led than other sectors, is largely characterised by short-termism, is susceptible to fixed capacity constraints, is a high involvement/risk purchase for consumers and tourism products are so vulnerable to externalities beyond the control of the organization, leading to an unduly narrow focus on sales and revenue management within marketing.

These characteristics may produce unintended consequences in terms of consumer perceptions of and trust in the veracity of tourism marketing appeals. The industry has consistently faced charges of misrepresentation or negative stereotyping in its advertising (Thurot and Thurot 1983; Sirakaya and Sönmez 2000; Shellhorn and Perkins 2004), a French campaign aimed at the UK market just one recent example of the misappropriation of beach images from different countries to represent Normandy/Brittany (Newling 2012). Regardless of the attribution of blame for individual errors (i.e. it is often the advertising agency that is responsible not the DMO (destination marketing organization), or the fact that the industry increasingly finds itself on the receiving end of negative or biased information generated by consumers and posted on websites such as TripAdvisor, the role of consumer to consumer (C2C) generated communications through social media and other online channels, often referred to as user generated content (UGC), is radically reorienting the power balance in marketing communications in favour of customers. The advent of digitally-accessed, large scale, anonymous information on the Internet has created a new set of questions concerning Electronic Word-of-Mouth (eWOM). The consequences for tourism marketers cannot be underestimated. In fact, the purpose of marketing has recently come into question, prompting industry bodies such as the Chartered Institute of Marketing (CIM) and the Academy of Marketing (annual conference 2013) in the UK to address and highlight marketing's organizational relevance in the global economic downturn.

This situation also begs a number of crucial questions about the role of marketing and the position of tourism marketing research within the academy. Tourism marketing research can be described as at best patchy, with little emphasis on many mainstream marketing topics, especially concerning the field of marketing communications. There has perhaps been too much focus on measuring the efficiency and effectiveness of tourism marketing – and not enough on the consumer's contexts (situational factors, attitudes towards a range of media, prior knowledge, processing goals, processing outcomes) or from the industry perspective on integrated marketing communications strategies, drivers of channel strategy decisions, agency analyses and so on. This chapter provides a review of research in the field of tourism marketing communications. The review demonstrates that the application of marketing communications concepts and practices has received only partial coverage in the tourism marketing literature. The chapter first defines and positions marketing communications, relating to tourism marketing concepts, issues and research. The chapter then outlines issues relating to tourism marketing communications as a basis to identify research avenues and gaps for future research. Five key areas for further research are highlighted: inter and intra-sectoral comparative studies; information search processing; gender and social demographics; WOM; and trust and credibility issues.

Defining marketing communications: contemporary issues

Marketing communications essentially concerns the aspects of marketing strategy dealing with provision of information to the various publics of the organization. Although it can most readily be associated with the micromarketing aspects of the promotional mix, marketing communications essentially brings a strategic approach to *all* information originating from and being received by the firm/organization, including: potential and actual customers, suppliers, shareholders, wider publics, the media. It is more correctly associated by the integration of advertising and public relations functions. Thinking about communications as a strategic function allows firms to focus attention on the longer term and the role that branding plays in representing the values and aims of the organization (McCabe 2009). Communications therefore form a vital part of the marketing strategy of the organization.

In the contemporary environment, dominated by social media engagement and the increased power of consumers as generators of information about destinations as well as other tourism brands, marketing communications has become a focal strategic issue, encompassing not only how the brand is presented to the target audience through advertising, but incorporating reputation management and customer engagement. The speed of change brought about by the influence of social media as a communications channel has meant that the field of marketing communications faces the most dramatic change (Keller 2001). It is now common to think about marketing communications as more concerned with 'communicating with' rather than 'promoting to' audiences.

However, this claim cannot be made of all tourism organizations. The high value, high involvement end of the spectrum is just one type of tourism after all, in which customers need a great deal of emphasis on personal interactions. The low-value, low-involvement business models such as those adopted by low cost airlines often mean that communications is more concerned with promotion, to the extent that it can be difficult to interact personally with any member of the firm, either face to face in the context of service interaction or via social media (Irish low cost airline Ryanair is perfect example – with no social media presence, no customer service department, no means of contacting the organization presented through the website).

The numbers of media channels are increasing at a rapid rate, not only via the Internet, but also via traditional channels (i.e. the range of TV channels carrying advertising, the numbers of print publications – although the numbers of regional and local newspapers may be falling) leading to a highly fragmented and cluttered media environment. However, consumers' engagement with marketing is also changing. Consumers switch TV channels, fast-forward through TV ads (enabled via on demand services), use ad-blockers, spam-blockers and caller ID to block unwanted messages, meaning that the old interruption marketing model has suffered. This has led to a massive increase in the incidence of 'outdoor' as well as the adoption of guerrilla marketing techniques, sponsorship and increasingly sophisticated ways in which to involve customers in the communications process (including games and interactive marketing). Sources of trust are also shifting (Smith and Zook 2011). User-generated travel information posted on websites such as user reviews, video and photo-sharing sites, blogs etc. (Xiang and Gretzel 2010) has gained wide acceptance by consumers such that the information is often seen as more credible than 'authorized' sources of information (i.e. guide books and tourist information publicity material), especially for travel due to the experiential nature of tourism products (Yoo, Lee, Gretzel and Fesenmaier 2009).

As a result of all these changes, modern marketing strategies employ a diverse range of tools and media. Yet marketing evaluation studies are often limited to a focus on one 'communication option' that fails to recognize 'that an integrated marketing communication programme requires that: 1) multiple types of communication options are employed and 2) communication options are designed in a way to reflect the existence and content of other communication options in the program' (Keller 2001: 822). There are practically no studies which focus on the relative effectiveness of a range of tools and media in influencing travel/tourism decisions within the context of one campaign.

Within the field of tourism, the proliferation and fragmentation of media forms and channels has consequences for the nature of and aims for communications. Rather than being directed towards persuasion, because of dramatic changes in the ways people access, share and respond to information about brands, an organization needs to consider listening, informing and reminding types of communications activities (Hughes and Fill 2007). These are just some of the complexities associated with contemporary interpretations and usage of marketing communications. The promotional mix might have provided the basis for firms to communicate with their audiences, however due to the complex communications environment of today, its relevance is questionable for the future, when consumers care little about the terms used to describe the forms of communication.

Hughes and Fill argue that there are two keys developments in marketing which have changed the emphasis away from the promotional mix to the 'Marketing communications mix' (MCM) these being relational theory and the resource based view of the firm. Whilst promotional mix theory emphasised product and price aspects of communication, relational theory influenced marketing in terms of the move towards customer relationship management (CRM) and the need for deeper and more connective relationships with customers as being the focus of communications. The resource based view of the firm argues that sustainable competitive advantage can only be achieved when an organization utilizes all its resources. Hughes and Fill argue that the move to digital marketing has impacted on all promotional media, but the ability of organizations to collect and utilize vast amounts of customer information has allowed them to establish truly connective communications (dialogues) and to customize messages accordingly using direct media channels. This, they argue, is having an impact on the types of messages firms generate, that recognize the shift in power balance typical of the resource based perspective. Where once marketing communications used to be largely about creating messages for a passive audience, where active involvement for consumers was equated with a decision either to notice or ignore an advertisement, 'the once passive audience has been unshackled and empowered by technology' (Smith and Zook 2011: 6).

Communications theories

Fundamental to research are the theories on which understanding are based. These provide the building blocks, or frameworks for the co-ordinated and systematic investigation of phenomena. Marketing communications is no different in this respect. Various scholars have contributed to, and developed our understanding of the communication process, the earliest conceptualizations developed one-way 'transmission models' which depicted the transmission of messages from a source, via specific channels to a receiver (Shannon and Weaver 1962). This simple model has subsequently been refined and developed to reflect the social context in which communications take place along with the influence of specific individuals on the communications process, with each re-iteration aiming to depict a more realistic depiction of how communications works. More recently, the role of the consumer as a 'passive receiver' of marketing communications has begun to be questioned. The traditional models have therefore been extended to reflect the two-way or interactive communications between consumers and companies and to incorporate the concept of 'inbound marketing', whereby social media brings customers' conversations to the organization (Steenburgh, Avery and Naseem 2010). These models also acknowledge the interaction between customers within communication networks facilitated by social media (see Pendleton, Lundstrom and Dixit 2012, for a full discussion).

Similarly, fundamental to all marketing communications is an understanding of the target market. Theoretical ideas borrowed from psychology, sociology, social psychology, economics and cultural anthropology have contributed to the development of frameworks and models which attempt to depict complexities of consumer buyer behaviour and to help marketers understand how consumers respond to marketing communication messages. For example, various linear or hierarchical models have been produced to explain how communications work on consumers through the stages of the decision process, from awareness, evaluation and purchase. These models are useful to assist with the planning of tools and media needed to design and deliver appropriate communications with consumers at each stage of the process. The Elaboration Likelihood Model (Petty and Cacioppo 1983) is a further development of linear models. However, it recognizes both rational and emotional responses from consumers and different levels of involvement with products and hence a need for marketers to provide different types of communication dependent upon the degree of cognitive processing expected. Other scholars point to a need to understand the various personal variables (i.e. beliefs, attitudes, motivations, perceptions and so on) which affect responses to communications whilst an attempt has also been made to draw together hierarchical models with intervening variables into 'complex models' (Howard and Sheth 1969).

Communication issues in tourism

Communication is important for tourism since it is essentially an intangible, experiential, multifaceted product-service bundle, often incorporating numerous brands, and a range of channels and media. Communication in tourism is also important because it involves the concept of a 'destination' as a critical component in the product-service communication mix, for which images may be generated by a wide range of sources. Strategic and integrated communications are required to communicate these intangible and experiential qualities. Furthermore, the Internet offers new opportunities to conduct real-time, i.e. synchronous communication online with many people that can be stored, recorded and kept for future users (asynchronously). This may impact on credibility, and thus influence cognitive, affective or behavioural intentions. These types of communications might be better capable of capturing and communicating emotion experiences, and/or adding rich detail on experiences to help overcome the challenges of communication for tourism services. In the following section attention turns to some key aspects of tourism communications research along with a discussion of gaps in knowledge.

Inter and intra-sectoral comparative studies

The majority of research on marketing communications issues in the tourism domain has focused on destination marketing issues. There are a number of possible reasons for this. Destinations and destination marketing organizations (DMOs) in particular, are often publicly funded (or amalgams of public and privately funded organizations) and as such, they are important providers of tourism information representing a clearly defined, and bounded geographical context. And as such, DMO marketing is characterized by being both the main channel through which destinations are presented to publics/tourist prospects, and constrained by the need to represent a diverse and amorphous industry. The promotional materials developed by DMOs contribute to the formation of destination image, which is an important area of tourism research together with opinions of others, news media and popular culture (films and TV shows featuring the place). However, a recent study undertaken by Govers, Go and Kumar (2007) found that tourism destination marketing was not very effective in influencing formation (pre-visit) of destination image, compared to other sources of information.

This perhaps questions the purpose of destination marketing materials, in terms of generating 'awareness' of the destination. Perhaps the purpose of destination marketing is to convert 'lookers into bookers', and much work has been undertaken to understand the conceptual and methodological foundation for measuring the effectiveness of destination marketing (see Chapter 16 for a review). But there is little evidence in the literature of any evaluation of marketing campaign success or failure in other sectors, either in aviation and transport, lodging and accommodation. In much the same way as previous research has questioned the ability of the web to generate affective responses, we need to know how different types of appeals affect consumers across different channels (including outdoor) in different service contexts.

Loda, Coleman and Backman (2009) is practically the only example found in the literature of a study that compared consumers' reaction to the marketing strategy of one destination in online and offline channels (in an experimental design to examine attitudes towards the destination, message strength, credibility and purchase intention). There is often little credible data available which evaluates strategies on media channels and their literature review found no prior studies comparing the effects of offline vs online media in relation to affect, cognition or buyer behaviour. Their results confirmed early hypotheses that offline advertising was not very persuasive on its own in driving tourist behaviour (in terms of attitude, credibility, message strength and intention), and that a website was critically important in influencing consumers. The study concluded that the best results were obtained when offline advertising and a website are used in conjunction.

Do the results hold true for firms in the private sector? What are the effects of online and offline media for such organizations in terms of buyer behaviour? Do similar sequences in message exposure and media combinations also hold true? These aspects are just a few of the many questions that have yet to be explored across tourism sectors. There is also an emerging research interest in communication processing in destination marketing contexts. Tang and Jang (2012) applied advertising pretesting conceptual models to tourism destination marketing and found that involvement was a high moderator of affect and attitude towards the destination website. Favourable feelings towards the destination led to more positive attitudes, which were transferred to favourable attitudes towards the information on the website. Also destination cognition exerted strong positive influence on attitudes towards the destination which was transferred to travel intention for the highly involved group. The consequence is that DMOs need to consider the level, depth and quality of information on offer about the destination as advocated in the ELM model. More detailed information is likely to have a strong positive effect on intentions amongst more involved travellers. Whilst research on destinations remains popular there is still much to be learnt in terms of specific aspects of marketing communications and destinations. For example, more research is needed on the effectiveness of different types of appeals (rational vs emotional) and on the creative aspects of messages.

Information search processing

In the field of tourist behaviour, information search processing has been a significant area of research. This has been driven from a consumer psychology perspective. However, there is less emphasis on the supply side, or that tries to integrate the consumer perspective with the communications perspective (Kerstetter and Cho 2004). One example of research in this area is Xiang, Gretzel and Fesenmaier (2009), which mapped how tourism was presented on the Web to understand if there was semantic congruence between customers' search queries and the information provided on the web by tourism service providers. They found huge discrepancies between the domain ontologies of tourism websites and that emerging from user queries. The concept of domain ontology is used in the context of computing and information science to refer to the representations used to support online search queries.

Meaning needs to be established and shared between the various components in the system (in its broadest sense) and users, and this has given rise to the concept of the semantic web, whereby search engines have developed technology that can understand the semantic basis of, for example, open questions posed by users, such as 'which are the best restaurants in city X?'. Previous studies have found a marked difference between the information needs of travellers and those provided by tourism service providers on the Internet, as well as the visibility of DMOs and hotel operators on popular search engines, which had found they both suffered from very low rankings amongst search results (Xiang, Wober and Fesenmair 2008). In their later study, Xiang, Gretzel and Fesenmaier found that the tourism domain was very rich, although a small number of words dominated (travel, information, hotel, attractions) (2009: 449), there was an incredibly long and rich 'tail', comprising a huge number of words reflecting a wide range of experiences. The study concluded that most information sought is functional rather than hedonic.

Two key questions arise from this research. Tourists form their destination images from a wide range of media sources including films, TV and other visual media (online such as YouTube) and written media such as books, magazines (eReaders) and so on. We know that these types of information are important. But we do not know if these types of sources service more hedonic information requirements. Perhaps, the traditional role of the glossy holiday brochure was to help tourists fantasize about the outcomes and benefits of travel, thus serving more hedonic information needs. Perhaps video media have replaced these functions, but it is not clear how different media are used by consumers and how different information provided through different online or offline channels meet consumers' range of needs for information about travel.

Furthermore, information search processing is just one aspect in terms of the various stages depicted in hierarchical models. Little is known for example in relation to the impact of marketing communications on post-purchase dissonance and importantly the role played by social media in the reduction of cognitive dissonance. Additionally, it has been noted that there has been a growth in the use of outdoor media and communication tools such as sponsorship. So what role does the use of these tools and media play in the process? Given the range of media sources used by consumers, perhaps one pertinent area of research which remains to be explored is that of the integration of marketing communications. This issue becomes increasingly important with the increasingly widespread use of destination-based TV programmes and films. However, given the ongoing popularity of holiday programmes and the rise in 'reality TV' programmes such as 'Holiday Airport', 'Holidays Uncovered' amongst others, the issue of integrated communications is an important area of research for both destinations and companies alike.

Gender and socio-demographics

Many previous studies have focused on the sexualised gaze in tourism and the power and gender-mediated nature of marketing communications in tourism (Cohen 1982; Cohen 1995; Dann 1996). Morgan and Pritchard have noted that landscapes have been framed from a feminized and sexualized perceptive (1998, see also Crick 1989) and it has been established that much tourism marketing privileges the male gaze, often depicting women as submissive, welcoming and available (Albers and James 1988; Sirakaya and Somnez 2000). Yet Pan and Ryan (2007) assert that the gendered and sexualized representation of people and landscapes in tourism promotional materials is also largely determined by the male-dominated advertising industry.

However, there is limited research on the ways in which consumers process information stimuli. Whilst there have been some studies that have assessed differences in attitude between the genders towards travel websites and preferences for information search (Kim, Lehto and Morrison 2007) there has been less attention on the differences in attitudes towards or behavioural or emotional responses to travel information context or visual stimuli. In a rare exception, Koc (2002) in a study of gender differences in decision making in the context of Turkish travel agencies found that males tended to make travel decisions based on decision heuristics such as credibility of the source and attractiveness of the material, whereas females relied more on the cognitive and affective content of the materials. Pan and Ryan (2007) focused on the differences in the ways in which men and women journalists frame their news reports. They found that men and women were different in their selection and emphasis of the less salient or established themes in soft news items such as travelogues, although the type of news report, the culture of the organization and market demand are stronger determinants of the content of news features. Of course salience of the material is also important to information processing, and gender may be only one source of variance determining how tourism communications are interpreted.

Pan and Ryan (2007) identified that further research is needed in terms of the interactions between national tourism organizations (NTOs) and international advertising agencies. Also, recognizing the role that promotional materials play in influencing travel media content, marketing managers' roles as gatekeepers to media content need to be explored. Further work is required on gender and culture to understand any congruence between thematic reporting and cultural backgrounds. They also highlighted that recent advances in quantitative analysis could be applied to understand framing strategies to generate significant new managerially relevant insights. More research is required on the demographic characteristics driving use of and responses to marketing communications in tourism. Little is known of the differences in responses to tourism communications in terms of age, cultural differences, education and so on, or on the receptiveness of different demographic groups to online or offline stimuli.

WOM communications

Many tourism marketing studies have recognized the important influence that friends and relatives played in travel decision making (Beiger and Laesser 2004). Friends and relatives are an important source of word-of-mouth (WOM) information and organic destination image agents (Murphy, Moscardo and Benendorff 2007). Recommendations from consumers who have prior experience with a tourism product are the most influential sources of information in travel decision making (Pan, MacLaurin and Crotts 2007). However, WOM is often treated in research as a homogenous category, when social media have made this much more complex. Murphy *et al.* 2007 distinguish between WOM from friends and relatives with that of other travellers. Additionally, with the advent of viral marketing campaigns, a further blurring of the lines between what constitutes WOM and commercial messages is also evident (Litvin, Goldsmith and Pan 2008). Murphy *et al.* found significant differences in travel choice and behaviour based on differences in WOM information source usage, but weak links between WOM information source and destination image. WOM is becoming more pervasive and amorphous (Litvin *et al.* 2008) and so there is a need to tease out differences in effectiveness and types of value they provide to tourists.

Word-of-mouth, often referred to as 'recommendations', can be described as 'informal communications directed at other consumers about the ownership, usage or characteristics of particular goods and services or their sellers' (Westbrook 1987: 261). The transition from web 1.0, which was characterized by one-way information publication and distribution with limited opportunities for user involvement, to web 2.0, characterized by websites that encourage users active participation in the provision of information content has created what Scott and Orlikowski (2012) call a *power-charged* environment of accountability and performance measurement. Online reviews are important in tourism as recent research has shown that online reviews are influential in travel information search and decision making, such that reading a review increases the probability that consumers consider making a booking in the reviewed hotel (Vermeulen and Seegers 2009).

Particularly, Scott and Orlikowski were interested in how organizations were being held to account by various constituencies (publics, governments, client groups, lobbyists and interest groups and so on) and the responses of those organizations to this online accountability process. Online review sites such as TripAdvisor are so important because of the profound effect they have on consumer behaviour. Offering to break through the often misleading and hyperbolic public relations-eze of conventional travel guides, through the provision of travel information supposedly legitimated through the collective process of user-generated social media, TripAdvisor claims to present unbiased and true (i.e. based on 'real', lived experiences of travellers, and thus detached and objective) reviews of travel firms. However, Scott and Orlikowski found that by refusing to divulge details of its ranking algorithm, the company '... effectively reinstates the patriarchal dependency from which they claim to have rescued the world of travel' producing, 'material effects on business and management. Indeed for some tourism and hospitality enterprises, such accountability can mean the difference between profit and loss, surviving a season or deciding to close down' (2012: 39).

Indeed it is this very stark, almost brutal set of consequences brought about by the practices of sites such as TripAdvisor which brings about the need for much more detailed and systematic research into the use and consequences of UGC as a communications medium.

Perhaps the most widely cited piece of research on eWOM in the tourism context is Litvin, Goldsmith and Pan (2007), which argued that travellers rely on the experiences of others because of the intangibility aspects and the experiential nature of tourism. In their review of the literature on WOM it became very clear that there is a dearth of research on WOM in the tourism field. Litvin *et al.* noted that WOM originated out of an interest in the role that opinion leaders play in consumer trends and purchase behaviour. Secondly they noted that the main mediating variables were influences on the originator and influences on the receiver of the WOM message. These are evidently changing in the era of eWOM, when the personal characteristics and/or identities of unknown other tourists may exact influences on the behaviour of other travellers who access the reviews for information purposes.

The purpose of viral campaigns and increasingly for many communications is to generate 'buzz', otherwise known as the amplification of marketing efforts through the active or passive involvement of third parties (Carl 2006), and thus there is a need to understand social influences, and how different forms of WOM influence affective, cognitive and behavioural aspects of tourist behaviour (Litvin, Goldsmith and Pan 2008). Policing of blogging and review sites has emerged as a contentious issue, as there is often little regulation and so much at stake for businesses that it prompted Litvin *et al.* to argue that abuse of online communities would take little effort or imagination. This might be in the form of 'stealth' marketing (i.e. employing tactics that engage the prospect without them being aware of the fact that they are being marketed to).

Therefore not only are studies required which critically examine the communications context in which online recommendations are produced and consumed, there is a need for more general and fundamental research on the effects of different sources of information on destination image formation and/or travel decision making. Murphy, Moscardo and Benkendorff (2007) argue that there are very few studies that confirm these linkages.

Trust and credibility in tourism marketing communications

The success or failure of communication is partially determined by the credibility of the message, but also crucially by the credibility (trust and expertise) of the source of the message (Smith and Zook 2011). This has already been raised as a perennial issue for tourism marketers as WOM is often seen as more credible than 'official' sources in tourism marketing. However, there are remarkably few efforts amongst the tourism academy to explore issues of trust and credibility. Trust exists when an individual has confidence in the reliability and integrity of the word of another individual. Therefore individuals expect that the information they receive from a company is honest, responsible, fair, reliable and benign. Whilst the importance of trust has been highlighted early on in the services marketing literature (Morgan and Hunt 1994), and issues of trust, ethics and honesty are implicit in much of the discourse surrounding tourism marketing and particularly in the context of sustainability (Wheeler 1995; Lansing and deVries 2007), and are addressed in relation to price setting and ethics in tourism price and revenue management (see McMahon-Beattie and Yeoman in this volume), it has not been taken up as a distinct aspect of tourism marketing research as noted by Clarke *et al.* in this volume in the context of trust in sustainable tourism marketing. However, with the move to online and user generated content, and the possibilities for abuse, this is an emerging research area for the future (Lee, Law and Murphy 2011; Kusumasondjaja Shanka and Marchegiani 2012).

Yoo, Lee, Gretzel and Fesenmaier (2009) reviewed the literature and found few studies that have looked into issues of trust with UGC (or consumer generated media CGM). Their study generated findings which contradicted the received wisdom about the credibility of online WOM via CGM. They found that users did not overwhelmingly trust CGM, with over 55 per cent only agreeing that they trusted it 'somewhat'. Additionally, consumers found that use of CGM led them to spend more time and effort on their travel information search than non-users. Finally, their findings contradicted general assumptions when they found that users thought that CGM is most credible when it is posted on official tourism bureau websites, or travel agency sites. So-called unbiased third party sites only came in third, and social networking sites had a relatively low credibility rating with only 13 per cent of respondents. They also looked into determinants of trust in travel-related CGM, and found that perceived expertise of people who posted material online and perceived credibility of travellers/websites were important predictors of trust. Clearly this is an important study, but there is more research needed to understand trust and credibility issues. What are the main factors or mediators of trust when it comes to unknown recommendations?

A more recent study published by Dickinger (2011) sought to understand the relationships between type of online content and level of trustworthiness. She selected three main types of online information provider: marketing content from tourism service providers; public relations style content from DMOs, which she calls editorial content; and user generated content. This study differentiated between trust (i.e. the degree to which people have confidence in the integrity and so on of others) and trustworthiness (i.e. the degree that people perceive a third party to have integrity, credibility etc.). The study showed that whereas UGC is perceived to be highly informative, the degree of quality of the information is doubted. The information provided by editorial content was perceived to have a high degree of integrity and to be more trustworthy than service providers and UGC. The study also found important relationships between antecedents of trustworthiness and the different channels. For example, it found that benevolence was dominant for personal channels (UGC), linked to social needs, and the sense of helping each other as part of a personal exchange being an important issue for travellers. However, ability negatively contributes to trust in UGC. For marketing channels, integrity is the main driver of trust, highlighting the perceived sincerity of service providers, whereas for the editorial channels, informative-ness is the main driver of trust, but relatively few travellers consult these channels. Kusumasondjaja *et al.* (2012) found that credibility increased when there was congruence between the identities of the reviewer and valence of the information.

What can be done to improve credibility of key sources of information for tourism? What are the roles of face-to-face communications through WOM compared with eWOM and so on? What are the factors influencing source credibility? Do any factors such as asynchronous or synchronous communication heighten or lessen or otherwise affect trust/credibility of the information? Other user characteristics, such as profile and/or identity of the message source, as well as salience of the review to the user, could influence perceived credibility of the information and so there are many avenues for further research in this area.

Furthermore the issue of trust and credibility relates not only to UGC and the online environment, but also the credibility of sources through traditional media channels. The use of opinion leaders (CEOs, celebrities, experts, consumers) is a well-established tactic to increase the credibility of marketing messages. Whilst these aspects have been explored widely in general marketing, there is a lack of similar studies in relation to the tourism context. Whilst it may be easy to determine experts for certain services (e.g. doctors, dentists), just who are considered 'experts' in the field of tourism? This is just one of many interesting areas of research yet to be explored. The media vehicle selected to carry communication messages also affects credibility. Does the same message have the same degree of impact if carried via upscale media outlets compared to those that are targeted towards the working classes for example? What are the most credible media vehicles for different types of tourism products? Issues of trust, integrity and credibility of information provide a critically important set of contexts for tourism marketing research with many consequences for tourism firms.

Conclusions

This chapter has highlighted the changing communications environment in tourism marketing. Partly, this is connected to a wider change in the consumption context of tourism. Markets are changing in their behaviour and in terms of their engagement with firms and marketing material. As Smith and Zook identify, this offers both challenges and opportunities, 'as marketers stalk rapidly changing markets, they face a brave new world, one that has changed forever, offering new opportunities to those who seize them' (Smith and Zook 2011: 6). Engagement is the new focus for marketing communications, along with the facilitation of communication with and between customers.

Furthermore, whilst tourists have long been recognized as co-producers of the tourism experience, advances in technology mean that they should now also be recognized as co-producers of marketing communications. Yet there is still much to be learnt about this rapidly changing environment. Marketing communications research has traditionally explored the production of messages by companies and interpretation by consumers, but little is known about this process when the roles are reversed. This concept of 'inbound marketing' (Steenburgh *et al.* 2010) opens up a new field of research within the context of tourism.

Consumers are also faced with ever more sophisticated channels of information which creates a paradox, increasing the amount of information available increases choice, and yet there are also real dangers posed by the quantity and quality of information and the sheer array of media channels. Consumers' processing goals and strategies, incorporating strategies to deal with information overload, are critical research issues for tourism marketing in the future.

Similarly, the advent of social media marketing, and the drive to encourage viral marketing through social media campaigns or as a method of customer acquisition and engagement, have challenged the basic assumptions underpinning marketing communications. Trust and credibility are opening up new ways in which tourism marketing research can inter-relate to marketing communications theory and concepts, yet this chapter has argued that this is still at a nascent stage and has tried to suggest further potential avenues for future research based on a marketing communications perspective. Marketing communications concepts offer tourism marketing scholars great opportunities to position and integrate research in the future for both practical and theoretical advances.

References

Albers, P.C. and James, W.R. (1988) 'Travel Photography: A Methodological Approach', *Annals of Tourism Research*, 15(1): 134–58.

Beiger, T. and Laesser, C. (2004) 'Information Sources for Travel Decisions: Towards a Source Process Model', *Journal of Travel Research*, 42: 357–71.

Carl, W.J. (2006) 'What's All the Buzz About? Everyday Communication and the Relational Basis of Word-of-Mouth and Buzz Marketing Practices', *Management Communication Quarterly*, 19(4): 601–34.

Cohen, C.B. (1995) 'Marketing Paradise, Making Nation', *Annals of Tourism Research*, 22: 404–21.

Cohen, E. (1982) 'The Pacific Islands from Utopian Myth to Consumer Product: The Disenchantment of Paradise', *Cahiers du Tourisme* (série B): 27.

Crick, M. (1989) 'Representations of International Tourists in Social Sciences: Sun, Sex, Sights, Savings and Servility', *Annual Review of Anthropology*, 18: 307–44.

Dann, G.M.S. (1996) *The Language of Tourism: A Sociolinguistic Analysis.* Wallingford: CAB International.

Dickinger, A. (2011) 'The Trustworthiness of Online Channels for Experience- and Goal-Directed Search Tasks', *Journal of Travel Research*, 50(4): 378–91.

Fill, C. (2005) *Marketing Communications: Engagement, Strategies and Practice*, 4th edn Harrow, England: Prentice Hall.

Fyall, A. and Garrod, B. (2005) *Tourism Marketing: A Collaborative Approach.* Clevedon: Channel View Publications.

Govers, R., Go, F.M. and Kumar, K. (2007) 'Promoting Tourism Destination Image', *Journal of Travel Research*, 46: 15–23.

Howard, J.A. and Sheth, J.N. (1969) *The Theory of Buyer Behaviour.* New York: Wiley.

Kerstetter, D. and Cho, M.H. (2004) 'Prior Knowledge, Credibility and Information Search', *Annals of Tourism Research*, 31(4): 961–85.

Kim, D.-Y., Lehto, X-Y. and Morrison, A.M. (2007) 'Gender Differences in Online Travel Information Search: Implications for Marketing Communications on the Internet', *Tourism Management*, 28(2): 423–33.

Koc, E. (2002) 'The Impact of Gender in Marketing Communications: The Role of Cognitive and Affective Cues', *Journal of Marketing Communication*, 8(4): 257–75.

Kusumasondjaja, S., Shanka, T. and Marchegiani, C. (2012) 'Credibility of Online Reviews and Initial Trust: The Roles of Reviewers Identity and Review Valence', *Journal of Vacation Marketing*, 18: 185–95.

Lansing, P. and de Vries, P. (2007) 'Sustainable Tourism: Ethical Alternative or Marketing Ploy?', *Journal of Business Ethics*, 72: 77–85.

Lee, H.A., Law, R. and Murphy, J. (2011) 'Helpful Reviewers in TripAdvisor, an Online Travel Community', *Journal of Travel and Tourism Marketing*, 28(8): 675–88.

Litvin, S.W., Goldsmith, R.E. and Pan, B. (2008) 'Electronic Word-of-Mouth in Hospitality and Tourism Management', *Tourism Management*, 29(3): 458–68.

McCabe, S. (2009) *Marketing Communication in Tourism and Hospitality: Concepts, Strategies and Cases.* London: Taylor and Francis.

Morgan, N. and Pritchard, A. (1998) *Tourism Promotion and Power: Creating Images, Creating Identities.* Chichester: John Wiley.

Morgan, R.M. and Hunt, S.D. (1994) 'The Commitment-Trust Theory of Relationship Marketing', *Journal of Marketing*, 58(3): 20–38.

Murphy, L., Moscardo, G. and Benkendorff, P. (2007) 'Exploring Word-of-Mouth Influences on Travel Decisions: Friends and Relatives vs. Other Travellers', *International Journal of Consumer Studies*, 31: 517–27.

Newling, D. (2012) 'French Tourism Campaign Uses Photographs of South African Beach', *Telegraph Online*, available from: http://www.telegraph.co.uk/news/worldnews/europe/france/9170719/French-tourism-campaign-uses-photographs-of-South-African-beach.html (last accessed 14 March 2013).

Pan, S. and Ryan, C. (2007) 'Gender, Framing, and Travelogues', *Journal of Travel Research*, 45: 464–74.

Pan, S., MacLaurin, T. and Crotts, J.C. (2007) 'Travel Blogs and the Implications for Destination Marketing', *Journal of Travel Research*, 46: 35–45.

Pendleton, G., Lundstrom, W. and Dixit, A. (2012) 'Exploring a Paradigm Shift in Marketing Communications: Consumers Changing from Passive to an Active Role', *Journal of Academy of Business and Economics*, 12(1): 151–60.

Petty, R. and Cacioppo, J.T. (1983) 'Central and Peripheral Routes to Persuasion: Application to Advertising', in L. Percy and A. Woodside (eds), *Advertising and Consumer Psychology*. Lexington, MA: Lexington Books, pp. 3–23.

Scott, S.V. and Orlikowski, W.J. (2012) 'Reconfiguring Relations of Accountability: Materialization of Social Media in the Travel Sector', *Accounting, Organizations and Society*, 37: 26–40.

Schellhorn, M. and Perkins, H.C. (2004) 'The Stuff of which Dreams are Made: Representations of the South Sea in German-language Tourist Brochures', *Current Issues in Tourism*, 7(2): 95–133.

Shannon, C. and Weaver, W. (1962) *The Mathematical Theory of Communication*. Urbana, IL: University of Illinois Press.
Sirakaya, E. and Sönmez, S (2000) 'Gender Images in State Tourism Brochures: An Overlooked Area in Socially Responsible Tourism Marketing', *Journal of Travel Research*, 38(4): 353–62.
Smith, P.R. and Zook, Z. (2011) *Marketing Communications. Integrating Offline and Online with Social Media*, 5th edn. London: Kogan Page Ltd.
Steenburgh, T., Avery, J. and Naseem, D. (2010) *Hubspot: Inbound Marketing and Web 2.0*. Boston: Harvard Business School Publishing, pp. 509–49.
Tang, L. and Jang, S. (2012) 'Investigating the Routes of Communication on Destination Websites', *Journal of Travel Research*, 51(1): 94–108.
Thurot, J.M. and Thurot, G. (1983) 'The Ideology of Class and Tourism: Confronting the Discourse of Advertising', *Annals of Tourism Research*, 10: 173–89.
Vermeulen, I. and Seegers, D. (2009) 'Tried and Tested: The Impact of Online Hotel Reviews on Consumer Consideration', *Tourism Management*, 30: 123–27.
Westbrook, R.A. (1987) 'Product/Consumption-based Affective Responses and Post-Purchase Responses', *Journal of Marketing Research*, 24(3): 258–70.
Wheeler, M. (1995) 'Tourism Marketing Ethics: An Introduction', *International Marketing Review*, 12(4): 38–49.
Xiang, Z., Wober, K. and Fesenmaier, D.R. (2008) 'The Representation of the Tourism Domain in Search Engines', *Journal of Travel Research*, 47(2): 137–50.
Xiang, Z., Gretzel, U. and Fesenmaier, D.R. (2009) 'Semantic Representation of Tourism on the Internet', *Journal of Travel Research*, 47(4): 440–53.
Yoo, K.H., Lee, Y., Gretzel, U. and Fesenmaier, D.R. (2009) 'Trust in Travel-related Consumer Generated Media', in W. Höpken, U. Gretzel and R. Law (eds), *Information and Communication Technologies in Tourism*. Vienna: Springer, pp. 49–59.

Part 7

Destination marketing and branding issues

30

Key issues in destination brand management

Nigel Morgan and Annette Pritchard

Introduction

Today there is more imperative than ever for places to manage their reputations as they compete globally in attracting visitors, residents and businesses (Jaffe and Nebenzahl 2006; Yeoman 2008). Put simply, each time the name of a place is mentioned there is an opportunity to add or subtract value to its equity or its brand. And a place with a positive reputation finds it easier to vie for attention, resources, people, jobs and money; a positive place reputation builds place competitiveness and cements a place as somewhere worth visiting (Florida 2002, 2010; Malecki 2004, 2007; Jansson and Power 2006). Today the world has 265 countries and approximately 3,400 large cities – all of which are seeking to improve, reverse, adapt or in some way manage their international image. This means that more and more places looking to build or maintain strong reputations are considering a holistic approach to their brand strategy which incorporates tourism, economic development and a sense of place. A strong place brand is a powerful mediator of culture, communities and peoples and being a powerful and resilient brand is hugely important for any tourism destination in the fight to combat increasing product parity, substitutability and competition. All of which opens up controversial questions of place authenticity, narratives and authorship, performativity and story-telling as destinations are both geo-political systems – often with their own Destination Management Organization or DMO (Buhalis 2000) – and socio-culturally produced spaces, the result of constantly evolving discursive practices (Morgan 2004; Pike 2004; Saarinen 2004).

Place reputation management has a hugely significant but complex relationship with tourism destination development and marketing and the various connectivities between place brands, place images, place reputations and competitive place identities lack critical exploration. What do we even mean by 'destination'? Arguably, destinations are only marked as such through the act of marketing and visiting. In other words, a place only becomes a destination through the narratives, stories and messages attached to it through tourism. It is beyond the scope of this chapter to tackle these questions around the wider aspects of place competitiveness, destinations as symbolic and cultural constructions or to address the important topic of place image. Instead it focuses expressly on how cities, regions and counties develop their competitive identities or brands for tourism markets (see Kavaratzis and Ashworth 2010 and Morgan, Pritchard and Pride 2011a for more detailed analyses). Specifically, this chapter describes the five phases of developing a destination brand strategy and in doing so introduces some of the key challenges in destination brand management: leadership; partnership; authenticity; sense of place; digital platforms; evaluation. First, however, it is essential to delineate the topic of destination brand strategy.

What is a destination brand?

Branding has its origins in pre-history and the word itself is derived from the Old Norse 'brandr' – to burn, referring to the practice of burning producers' marks onto goods. Consumer brands emerged with the advent of packaged goods and the industrial revolution, but the notion of tourism destinations pursuing formalised brand strategies as we understand them today only dates from the 1990s. Whereas earlier 1980s sloganeering such as 'I love New York' and 'Glasgow's miles better' presaged it, a strategic approach to destination brand management was first introduced at a national level in countries such as Spain, Hong Kong and Australia. Later a host of countries, regions and cities – like the US cities of Seattle, Las Vegas and Pittsburgh – embraced it largely as a response to a need to compete more effectively (Morgan and Pritchard 2004). Of course, we need to ask whether a destination can actually be a brand (Hankinson 2010). Certainly countries have equity and there is an extensive literature on the country-of-origin effect which refers to the emotional value resulting from consumers' association of a brand with a country (Kotler and Gertner 2012). Perhaps in strict marketing terms destinations cannot be brands, which is why some commentators talk of reputation management or competitive identity rather than branding (Anholt 2006, 2012). Whilst this is useful, we have elsewhere coined the term 'reputation stewardship' to reflect the reality that destination reputation is derived from a host of sources, of which tourism marketing is but a minor one, that in our disintermediated world dominated by social media DMOs do not control the destination story or its image and that they do not control the destination (Morgan, Pritchard and Pride 2011b).

In other words, a destination has an organic reputation regardless of what marketing its DMO does. In essence, that reputation is the culmination of three factors: firstly, conversation – reputation is something you talk about; secondly, discrimination – reputation is something you critically assess; and thirdly differentiation – reputation is something distinctive (Parjanen, Harmaakorpi and Kari 2012). Of course this organic reputation could be positive or negative and responsible governments, regional administrations and DMOs need to identify that reputation and develop a strategy to manage and, where possible enhance it. A destination's key stakeholders can have a vision of how they want their place to be perceived internally and externally and brand management techniques can enable them to achieve differentiation and to secure a competitive identity and future success for their city, region or country. On the other hand, ignoring or mismanaging the opportunity to engage in strategic branding could result in a lack of visibility, less perceived relevance and low levels of emotional attachment or closeness to a destination – all of which may result in less differentiation and motivational 'pull' for visitors.

In simple terms, a destination brand is a promise to the tourist, an expectation of a set of experiences and a mark of integrity and reputation; it builds up continuously in the minds of the destination's consumers and it is affected by interactions and memories (Travis 2000). Broadly speaking, a destination brand can be derived from:

1. existing assets of the place such as its value offering or organic reputation;
2. created assets, such as sports and cultural events, landmark buildings and facilities or government policies; or
3. abstract concepts associated with the place, such as tolerance or innovation.

Unlike classical subjects of branding like products, services, companies or even people, strategizing a destination brand, particularly a nation or a city is a much more complex process. This complexity is largely the result of the sheer numbers and diversity of the stakeholders in the process. Effective destination brands are therefore the result of both cutting-edge marketing innovation and the successful managing of local, regional and national politics and interest groups. 'In this sense, DMOs are less responsible for the management and more for the stewardship of destination reputations' (Morgan *et al.* 2011b: 6). Nonetheless, theirs is still a key role in supporting and facilitating destination brand management, speaking not only to the consumer but to the whole tourism system, developing and nurturing stakeholder partnerships. Collaborations require encouragement and leadership and here the DMO has a pivotal role as the brand steward, leading, guiding and coordinating the destination's online and offline 'critical promise points': all those interactions when the destination brand promise is encountered and evaluated by its key target markets (Baker 2007). The challenges of such stewardship should not be underestimated in today's rapidly changing world of accelerated and intensified globalization.

Simply desiring a strong reputation will not deliver a powerful and sustainable destination brand. So, regardless of their organic reputations, most countries and cities now have a strategic destination brand, whether it is 100 per cent Pure New Zealand, South Africa it's Possible, YourSingapore, Incredible India or Iamsterdam. Today, over 80 per cent of DMOs have an official brand strategy and a toolkit explaining how to apply the brand (WTO and ETC 2009), whilst the Destination Marketing Association International, the world's largest official organization for DMOs designates a brand strategy as an essential requirement of its Destination Marketing Association Accreditation Programme (Baker 2007). Some countries have achieved very powerful place brand equity. For example, the value of the 100 per cent Pure New Zealand brand is estimated at around US$13.6 billion, ranked just outside the world's top 20 most powerful brands, just behind Samsung but ahead of brands such as Dell (10yearsyoung.tourismnewzealand.com).

Such destinations have achieved high levels of brand saliency – the development of an emotional relationship with the tourist through highly choreographed communications campaigns focused on conveying the spirit of a place (Morgan and Pritchard 2002).

Developing and refreshing strong destination brand strategies

As we have outlined, their lack of management control and the sheer diversity of their stakeholders, audiences and partners pose unique challenges for destination marketers. Yet destination brand saliency – the emotional attachment between a tourist and a place – can hold the key to powerful and sustainable destination differentiation. After all, despite accelerating globalization and commoditization, every place on earth is unique and each one potentially holds special attachments for residents and visitors alike. In our world of social media recommendations, reputation is all important, so DMO staff must establish how their destination's image compares with those of its key competitors, its so-called competitor set. How does their destination rate on 'wish you were here appeal' or 'celebrity value'? Yet, when DMO managers ask themselves, 'what can we do to make our destination more appealing, more famous or more visible?', they are actually asking the wrong question. They would do better to ask 'what can we do to make our destination more relevant, do our brand stories pass the "re-tweet" test and do they have pinterest?' To build a destination brand, which is motivating and appealing for relevant audiences, it has to be meaningful, relevant and – if possible – hold the promise of connection on an emotional level for potential tourists. This is why the recent brand strategies for India and New Zealand have been so successful, since both offer the tourist some meaningful, powerful and even spiritual connection with the destination.

As we outlined above, a destination brand can be derived from:

1 its existing assets such as its value offering or organic reputation;
2 its created assets, such as sports and cultural events, landmark buildings and facilities or government policies; or
3 its association with abstract concepts.

Countries often showcase their history, their culture and their beautiful scenery in their marketing but most destinations can lay claim to some if not all of those attributes. It is critical to build a brand on assets or associations which uniquely connect a destination to the audience now or have the potential to do so in the future. It must also be a proposition which competitors may be able to emulate but which they cannot usurp. For example, other world cities can claim to be spiritual, but only Rome (or more strictly, the Vatican) is The Eternal City – it has that epithet, it had it first and no other place can now claim it. Likewise, Virginia in the USA has had phenomenal success with its long-running Virginia is for Lovers campaign, first launched in 1969 and recently described by Advertising Age as 'one of the most iconic ad campaigns in the past 50 years' (Pakesh 2012). Yet, despite this success, no destination can surpass Paris' organic associations with romance. Whatever proposition is used it must also be sustainable and have the potential to evolve in a long-term branding campaign, so it is essential to get it right. However, the point of differentiation must also reflect a promise which can be delivered and which matches expectations. An effective destination brand is therefore unique and resilient but its originality needs to be sustainable, credible and relevant. One destination which has transcended the substitutable nature of the tourism product and promised this kind of unique and deliverable experience is India. There are many countries with breath-taking scenery and fascinating heritage, yet such is the emotional power of the sub-continent with its poignant history, diverse cultures and varied landscapes that its brand promise to the visitor – that a trip to India can actually change you on a spiritual level – has proved enduring and hugely successful. Indeed, India has been voted one of the top four most memorable destination brands in a survey of DMO professionals (WTO and ETC 2009).

Recognizing that branding is a two-way process done with and not to the consumer, some time ago we suggested (Morgan and Pritchard 2002) that instead of thinking in terms of a traditional or modified Tourist Area Life Cycle model (Butler 1980; Agarwal 2002), tracking visitor volume over time, DMO managers should be thinking of an S-shaped destination brand fashion curve. This instead charts the destination brand's emotional relationship with its visitors, through fashionable, famous, familiar and fatigued phases – each requiring a different communications and marketing strategy. At first the market is small and a place is chic because it is exclusive. Here the destination brand is at the beginning of its fashionable phase and its visitors are early adopters who, although few in numbers, are influential opinion-formers and trendsetters. If the destination becomes famous and less exclusive, its cutting-edge appeal will wane; these tourists will therefore not want to be seen somewhere which they consider rather passé. In the famous phase, a destination brand's consumers are loyal and affluent but at any time, the destination's brand values may lose their currency – hence the continued need to remain relevant and appealing. If the place fails to appear contemporary, it will drift into the familiar zone where everyone knows about it, but no one considers it significant: it has become the antithesis of cool. Becoming familiar can ultimately lead a destination to fatigue – a place which finds it difficult to attract lucrative market segments (there are many examples of such familiar and fatigued resorts on the Mediterranean coast of Spain). Without appropriate strategic intervention or investment in its brand, such a destination will slide further into stagnation, decline and brand decay.

Phase one of a destination brand strategy – discovery research

The first of the five phases in developing or refreshing any destination brand strategy is discovery research to (re)establish the core values of the destination brand – these should be durable, relevant, communicable and hold saliency for potential tourists (Table 30.1). This research phase should consider just how contemporary or relevant the brand is to today's tourism consumer and in broad terms where it sits in the consideration set of relevant audiences. Hildreth (2012: 156) argues that 'trying to measure the overall image of a place is typically folly – and comparing the overall images of a number of places is hopelessly problematic'. As he later comments (2012: 162), if the purpose of developing a brand strategy is to enable a place to become its 'best self', how is comparing the images of, say, Canada and Sweden 'on the whole' of any more use than comparing images of Mohammed Ali and Picasso 'on the whole'? Broadly speaking, discovery research is designed to: develop a comprehensive understanding of the destination brand; explore stakeholder perceptions and requirements of any brand developed; assess existing and potential markets; understand how consumers in those markets interact with marketing communications (see Morgan and Pritchard 2000, 2004). Common approaches include: focus groups, panel interviews, in-depth interviews and questionnaires.

Phase two of a destination brand strategy – brand strategy platform

Once this discovery research phase is complete, the next phase is to develop the brand identity. One of the hardest tasks for a DMO is this translation of the discovery research findings into a brand strategy platform. Often the sheer weight of information collected can overwhelm managers but through the application of concepts such as the brand benefit pyramid and brand architecture a strong and emotionally appealing brand platform can be crafted. Once the brand's core values have been established, they should underpin and imbue every component of the brand identity – from photography, colour, typography and tone of voice to the brand marque – so that the brand values are cohesively communicated. A brand design style guide or toolkit, which ensures consistency of message and approach, should also reinforce the brand values (WTO and ETC 2009). The vision (which must be shared and owned by the key stakeholders) should be clearly expressed in the brand's core values which are consistently reinforced through the product and in all marketing communications – both online and offline – every execution in all media contributes to maintaining brand

Table 30.1 The five phases in developing a destination brand strategy

Phase	*Strategic Task*
Phase one	Discovery research
Phase two	Brand strategy platform
Phase three	Creative development
Phase four	Brand implementation
Phase five	Brand management

presence. To successfully create an emotional attachment the destination brand platform has to be:

- credible;
- deliverable;
- differentiating;
- conveying powerful ideas;
- enthusing for stakeholders and partners;
- resonating with the consumer.

Critical to the success of any destination brand is the extent to which the destination's brand personality appeals to its relevant audiences. Just like people, brands should be complex and rich, yet multifaceted personalities are quite rare in a world where brand attributes are often arbitrarily and superficially constructed. Traits such as 'friendly', 'natural' and 'contemporary' are popular hoped-for descriptors but they hardly help to build an engaging or aspirational brand. Destination brand enhancement is all about developing a rich, relevant brand personality. 'Developing' is the significant word here – successful brands never atrophy – instead they reflect and respond to changes in consumers' lives and whilst the brand's core values remain the same, its personality will continue to evolve. To paraphrase the Chinese proverb, brands should never be afraid to grow gradually, they should only be afraid of standing still.

A brand's personality has both a head and a heart – its head refers to the logical brand features, whilst its heart refers to its emotional benefits and associations. Brand propositions and communications can be based around either a brand's head or its heart: head communications convey a brand's rational values, whilst heart communications reveal its emotional values and associations. Brand benefit pyramids sum up consumers' relationships with a brand and are frequently established during the discovery consumer research phase where consumers are usually asked to describe what features a destination offers and what the place means to them. Using the research, it should then be relatively straightforward to ascertain what particular benefits consumers associate with the destination in question (see Figure 30.1).

The benefit pyramid can be instrumental in helping to distil the essence of a destination brand's unique proposition. This refers to the point at which the tourist's expectations and the destination's benefits and relevancy intersect – any brand communication (online or offline) should then encapsulate the essence of the brand. Whilst many ideas may be initially suggested, the challenge is to develop a proposition which makes the destination brand relevant, contemporary and appealing – establishing the brand's architecture can be critical to this process. Brand architecture is a concept borrowed from mainstream product branding. It refers to how an organization structures and manages a portfolio of brands, providing each brand with purpose, relevance and clarity so that each sub-brand benefits the whole.

There are four types of brand architecture strategy: the house of brands; endorsed brands; sub-brands; branded house strategies (Aaker and Joachimsthaler 2000). The house of brands strategy includes a portfolio of sub-brands that act independently of each other under an umbrella brand. The driver here is the sub-brand, each of which is allowed to differentiate itself. One of the most successful destinations to pursue this house of brands strategy is Spain, geopolitically divided into 17 autonomous regions each with its own tourism destination brand strategy, working independently of TourSpain, the national tourism board umbrella brand. Once a destination with a reputation for poor quality service and facilities, in the early 1980s the Spanish government began what was to become one of the most consistent and successful brand enhancement exercises in destination marketing supported by a significant financial

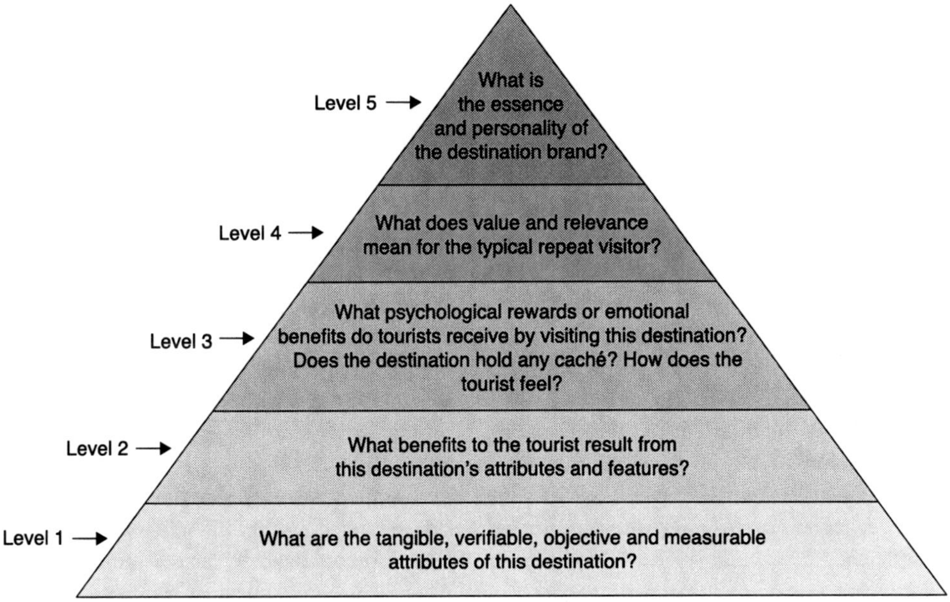

Figure 30.1 The destination brand benefit pyramid (adapted from Morgan and Pritchard 2004).

commitment – which continued right up until the recent economic crisis. The suprabrand of Spain (Espana) attracts over 50 million visitors a year and its cities (such as Barcelona, Madrid, Valencia and Seville) and regions (such as Andalusia and Galicia) are the second-level brands. At the country level Spain has remained remarkably constant in its advertising with each new campaign promoting the diversity and variety of the country, focusing on its heritage and culture, as well as its staple sun and sand product. At the heart of the brand for 30 years has been Joan Miro's logo, designed in 1983 (the year he died) by mixing elements from his own pictures and his own alphabet. As a piece of modern art, this logo both symbolizes Spain's past and looks to the future and incorporates representations of the sun (yellow and red), the stars, and the bullring (black) to portray Spain (see http://www.spain.info/). The shifts in the campaigns from 'Everything Under the Sun' (first used in 1984) through to campaigns including 'Passion for Life', 'Bravo Spain', 'Spain Marks' and 'I Need Spain' have been gradual, well thought out and have never compromised the brand values (see http://www.ineedspain.com/). Whilst Spain is a very successful example of this type of strategy, the disadvantage of the house of brands strategy is that allowing numerous sub-brands to promote themselves individually within a confined geographical space renders each vulnerable to marketing overlap, brand dilution and wasted expenditure. While there is coordination between Spain's national tourism board and its regions, there is considerable duplication of effort and room for more cohesion on a regional sub-brand level.

The second type of brand architecture strategy is that of endorsement brands; these differ from a house of brands in that the umbrella brand and its sub-brands are perceptually linked to transfer general values although the link is not so overt to the extent that the core values of individual destinations are at risk of being diluted. Endorsement brand strategies apply to supranational brands like Britain, Scandinavia and Europe as these are umbrellas for the individual countries within them. Britain is the suprabrand or umbrella brand and its sub-brands are Scotland, Wales, London and the English regions, all of which are both part of, and at the same time, distinct from it (Hall 2004). Similarly, Sweden, Norway, Denmark, Finland and Iceland have a gestalt image and are seen by potential tourists as a single entity, linked by association to general 'Scandinavian values' such as tolerance and innovation. In contrast to these endorsement brands, the third strategy – the sub-brand strategy – involves much stronger links and shared associations so that both the supra or umbrella brand and the sub-brand are strong drivers influencing consumer perceptions. A good example of this is Australia, whereby the country shares similar overall values with its regional brands (such as Western Australia) and its city brands (such as Perth) (see Crockett and Wood 1999; Morgan and Pritchard 2002). This approach has the benefit of creating a flexible brand framework that allows sub-brands to maintain their individuality while complementing the suprabrand and it allows the suprabrand to leverage certain sub-brands to attract niche markets. However, it can be costly and time-consuming as each sub-brand has to be developed in close collaboration with the umbrella brand. There is also an issue of brand fit as sub-brands may have to adapt to suit the suprabrand proposition, in addition attempts to over-stretch the master brand into too many sub-brands may result in brand dilution, overlap and confusion.

The fourth and final strategy is the branded house strategy, characterized by a single brand with a dominant driver role which supports other descriptive brands. This achieves economies of scale and cost savings due to low investment for each successive brand extension and is also effective in creating high brand awareness. A good example is New Zealand, whereby the nation brand essence is 'landscape' which has associations with growth, purity and nature (Morgan and Pritchard 2005, 2006). These qualities are embedded in the silver fern, New Zealand's country-of-origin symbol which functions as an anchor in New Zealand's branding and which plays a crucial driver role in leveraging New Zealand in areas such as tourism, sport, trade and enterprise, film and education, getting high impact from the All Blacks (rugby), the Silver Ferns (Netball) and Team New Zealand (yachting). Whilst New Zealand is perhaps the most successful example of this strategy (and perhaps of any destination brand strategy), it runs the risk that, whilst positive associations impact on all the linked brands, so too do negative images, making them all vulnerable to any 'shocks'.

Decisions about which type of brand architecture strategy a destination should adopt should be made once a brand audit has been completed. This involves analysis of: external and internal factors (including awareness, associations, etc.); the nature of the brand (its essence, symbols, icons, etc.); the key audiences (both internal and external). The answers to the audit determine whether the brand needs to be leveraged and supported, amalgamated to reduce overlap or whether a new brand needs introducing to target new audiences or to broaden the offer. Once a DMO has identified the key elements of the brand strategy platform, i.e. what kind of brand to develop (house of brands, etc.), the next steps are to identify the brand personality and the brand promise. This should reflect all the key components of a destination brand including its positioning, its rational (head) and emotional (heart) benefits and associations. The brand personality should guide brand enhancement, development and marketing and reflect the benefits identified in the destination brand benefit pyramid (Figure 30.1).

Phase three of a destination brand strategy – creative development

This phase shifts the emphasis in the process away from strategic issues and focuses on creating a destination brand's visual and verbal identity – what Pride (2012) calls its tone of voice. This phase of the brand strategy development turns the findings of the discovery research which informed the brand platform into engaging, creative communications and campaigns, all of which share the same tone of voice. Place tone exists in the material, symbolic and virtual worlds but to have impact in destination reputation management it must be consistently and effectively communicated in all these worlds. Places are trying to engage visitors, residents and other stakeholders in a stimulating conversation and place reputations must be communicated with a strong, distinctive and engaging tone of voice in all online and offline interactions with the key target audiences (Pride 2012). A place's tone reflects its ambience, the attitudes of its people, its heritage and narratives and is inseparable from a destination's sense of place. Yet communicating this is no simple undertaking and opens up controversial challenges of place authenticity, brand narratives, leadership and authorship, performativity, story-telling and aesthetics (Dinnie 2008, 2012; Allan 2012; Fyall 2012; Hornskov 2012; Parjanen *et al.* 2012). It is difficult to overstate the emotional power of a destination's tone, its identity and sense of belonging. A destination tells its stories in its everyday fabric, communicating a message to its residents and visitors more powerfully than any marketing campaign. The public management of space is thus a key ingredient in any destination brand strategy. Creative destinations present residents and visitors with opportunities to continually rediscover and enjoy their spaces, which are designed from the bottom-up with an emotional as well as a utilitarian dimension to allow the originality of the local people to shine through in the making of place (Boschma and Fritsch 2009; Vitiellio and Willcocks 2006, 2012).

This phase in the strategy is about creating a buzz around the destination which harnesses word-of-mouth and creates a destination with conversational value. The phase includes the development of a brand tagline and logo, and copy style and brand stories, remembering that a logo and tagline are not the brand. A tagline is a word or short phrase that captures the spirit of the destination promise (e.g. Spain: Everything under the sun); it can be a short descriptor, a call to action or an explanation. It needs to be credible (so tourists believe and value the underlying proposition); differentiating (to make the destination stand apart in a meaningful way); enduring (capable of resilience and evolution); motivating (to inspire and entice); relevant (to each audience); and strategic (so it fits with the destination's vision, strategic objectives and community values). This is also the time to (re)design the destination's web portal. The digital revolution has forced DMOs to finally realize that they never had control of their brands and that they are open to consumer scrutiny. This poses a number of challenges for the DMO (e.g. of content, socialization, integration and measurement, see Weber 2009; Munro and Richards 2012) but when DMOs strike the right note – as with the Queensland Best Job in the World campaigns of 2009 and 2013 (http://www.youtube.com/watch?v=9tNxvKT_z_U) or the Your Singapore portal and living logo (www.yoursingapore.com) – there is conversational social media capital to be made, which extends beyond segment boundaries like tourism, business and studying.

Phase four of a destination brand strategy – implementation

Far too many DMOs commission brand strategies and tourism master plans without due regard for their implementation. The adoption of a destination brand strategy must be about more than using a new logo or adhering to a brand identity kit: the brand must be alive, have resonance with the community and be owned by stakeholders and community partners. This phase in the process concerns how the brand promise must be delivered on the ground, particularly focusing on the role of partnership, on the importance of creating a sense of place and on the role of people in creating the pulse and heart of a destination. While there are many creative tools in a DMO's branding tool-box, it is people who are the credible communicators of brand experiences and in this respect the implementation phase can often be very much about change management as it can call for transformed relationships and partnerships (Baker 2007).

The number one priority in the implementation phase is to encourage understanding and adoption of the brand. There is one brand but it is multifaceted and a composite of stories; it is built on experiences and memories and there are many partners who will deliver those brand experiences. The entire brand strategizing effort can be wasted by one rude taxi driver, unhelpful receptionist or unfriendly resident who ignores a lost tourist asking for directions. Since destinations are really in the business of experience management, a place's stories, ambience and 'feeling' are inseparable from the place itself so DMOs need to consider how they bring the brand to life when visitors arrive. Most of our focus in this chapter has been on bringing people to a place and many destinations do engender loyal and repeat visits. But many more people are in search of new and unique experiences and so will never return, yet they can generate word-of-mouth about a destination – good or bad – and bad news travels faster and further in social media. It is these stories told by tourists, students, residents and businesspeople of a destination, which will add or subtract the real equity to a destination's reputation. If the destination experience is memorable and delivers or exceeds the brand promise then positive testimonies will reinforce and enhance a destination's reputation. Of course, if the opposite happens, then equity flows away from the brand and the reservoir of goodwill is slowly drained. Despite all the marketing opportunities which exist today, word-of-mouth is still the most powerful form of communication and the digital revolution is accentuating its importance.

Digital channels have created an irrevocable change in consumer-brand relationships, evident in the proactive role customers take in shaping the dialogue with the brand and ultimately its reputation (Constantinides and Fountain 2008). This is also transforming how destinations perform online, with participation, openness, conversations, community and connectedness the key words characterizing this digitally-inspired revolution (Spannerworks 2007). As this conversation culture replaces our information culture (Leonhard 2009) much of the social networking sites' content provides a wealth of 'independent' peer-produced dynamic content. Today 'the wisdom of the crowd is embodied in a wiki' and customers are 'lifecasting' their brand experiences on sites such as Wikitravel, TripAdvisor and IgoUgo (Munro and Richards 2012). In this way, every person who has something positive to say about a destination - its culture, the welcome of its people and the quality of its environment and infrastructure - becomes an ambassador for a destination's brand promise.

The brand promise can be endorsed and affirmed in so many ways – through the cuisine of a place, in the use of public art and flagship building projects, at information points, through signage and simply in the cleanliness and safety of a place. A place's culture and history offer the most potential for unique experiences and yet many destinations place so little value on it that they demolish their heritage to make way for sports stadia, shopping malls and the increasingly ubiquitous and anonymous skyscrapers, which are in fact a major turn-off for tourists in search of the 'real' or 'authentic' place (Leiper and Park 2010). Authenticity has become a hugely controversial concept amongst tourism scholars. Some argue that today's emphasis on the post-modern, the hyper-mediated, the global rather than the local, all suggest the redundancy of authenticity. Yet for any destination, heritage and traditions is a vital ingredient of a sense of place; for many destinations it is the well-spring of their reputation and identity premium (Hornskov 2012). Effectively and sympathetically communicated through marketing activities, tradition is the ingredient which distinguishes the bland from the unique. This should not be a static tradition, but one which is being constantly performed, engaged, renewed, reinterpreted and augmented by new narratives which respond to and are engaged with making new socio-cultural forms (Morgan 2012).

Phase five of a destination brand strategy – management

Once strategized, a destination brand requires management and stewardship if it is to thrive and grow. The long-term health of a destination brand depends on how well the DMO manages five things:

- brand leadership and its stakeholders;
- brand management;
- brand communications;
- experience management;
- monitoring and evaluation.

Importantly, the brand strategy must be integrated into the strategic plans of the DMO and should not be an 'add-on'. Most DMOs are publicly funded political organizations dealing with many stakeholder groups such as government departments, industry associations, and retailers (Pike 2004; Fyall and Garrod 2005). One of the hardest tasks in managing the brand is resolving conflicts among competing interests groups as the brand must be owned across the destination and everyone from town-planners and architects to retailers and transport companies must value it (Fyall 2012). However, even when agencies recognize the value of stewarding a successful brand, such a diverse group of actors and stakeholders are involved (with so many competing priorities and resource demands) that bringing them together is a huge task. All of these actors operate with very different values, goals and operating procedures; they may be suspicious of each other and this often becomes a volatile combination (Dredge 2006). Moreover, whilst ownership must be broad-based, decision-making must be focused. The more people and groups involved in decision-making, the more confused the task becomes and the more blurred the brand promise. Baker (2007) cites the examples of Pittsburgh, which had a branding committee of 120 people, and Denver (170 civic and business leaders), as cases of bad practice. Decision-making needs to be focused, involving a small group of leaders who understand the emotional basis of branding and who can act as brand champions to wider communities of interest.

A vital person in the management of any brand is a brand champion or brand steward. It is his or her job to keep the brand development on track. Without a brand steward brand adoption and application may be erratic (Allan 2012). This person must have the authority to bring things back on course. Unlike brand leadership, brand management is tactical and short-term and periodically brand managers have to re-energize partners, stakeholders and consumers. Brand management is about extending the brand to the destination infrastructure, gateways, visitor services, streetscapes and environments (Allan 2012; Vitellio and Willcocks 2012). It could involve designing street furniture, banners, lighting and signage carrying the logo. At every point of communication (in print, electronically or in person) the brand promise must be conveyed and reinforced. Finally, since branding strategies perform three basic functions – to persuade, change or reinforce brand values, and raise the brand's profile – the brand steward must undertake or commission evaluation to measure each. DMOs must monitor the following six indicators to ensure the brand remains relevant and meaningful:

- target audience demographics, behaviour and satisfaction;
- the brand's visual identity and communications;
- brand positioning and destination promise relevancy;
- customer demand and behaviour;

- brand promise points to ensure they align with customer needs and reflect the brand;
- core experiences to ensure quality and meaningfulness.

Conclusions

Destination reputation management is largely concerned with enhancing how the outside world sees tourism places but it begins at home; as part of the wider process of place reputation stewardship it depends upon building a productive coalition between civil society, government and business which can then act as a powerful dynamic for change management (Morgan, Pritchard and Pride 2011). This often requires new ways of working, building partnerships across disparate, competing and even conflicting stakeholder groups with the DMO as an obvious coordinator. Central to the whole process is a place's vision for its future (Anholt 2010, 2009a, 2009b). What kind of place does its leaders, stakeholders and communities want it to be? A place's reputation reflects how others see it and how it sees itself; its enhancement moves its reputation forward to where it wants to be seen. Competitive destinations are those which find bottom-up, inclusive ways of enhancing and sustaining their reputation, taking advantage of the events economy, harnessing popular culture and digital platforms, delivering unique individual experiences and employing the testimonies of residents, tourists, investors and students as place ambassadors (Morgan 2012).

Harnessing tradition, culture, and talent to get where they want to be requires responsible governments, administrations and DMOs to reconcile competing needs, pressures and desires and agree a platform for action. They must also ask fundamental questions about the kind of society and communities they want and the kind of environment they desire for tourists and residents alike (Insch and Florek 2010). When it comes to tourism, communities must ask what kind of tourism industry they want. Do they see tourism as important in their economic, social and cultural development? If so, how will they project their traditions and culture to the outside world? Who will have the authority to tell their stories, whose narratives will be told and whose will be excluded? These and other questions need answers if a place is to enhance its reputation and build equity in its tourism brand (Morgan 2012). Crucially, to be truly effective destination brand management must be a holistic strategy which coheres tourism, economic development, urban planning, major event planning and a host of other activities and sectors. In this chapter we have seen how, in today's competitive globalized tourism marketplace, standing for something and standing out from the crowd has never been more important. Tourism provides us with a unique opportunity to personalize our relationship with places. Just the very act of visiting somewhere makes a place's reputation or image more significant for the visitor; once we are there our experiences will lead us to reappraise that place's reputation – for good or ill. The tourist's voice is a critically important piece of the overall destination brand, but it is only an echo of the destination itself, a looking glass that mirrors reality. The destination brand promise is also a reflection of its stakeholders' belief for what the country, region or city stands for. Or perhaps more accurately, their hopes for what the destination will become. Deliver on that promise and the destination becomes the place its residents want it to be. Exceed that promise for tourists and the destination quickly has a legion of brand advocates, disappoint and no amount of strategizing can enhance its reputation.

References

Aaker D.A. and Joachimsthaler, E. (2000) 'The brand relationship spectrum: Key to the brand architecture challenge', *California Management Review*, 42(4): 8–23.

Agarwal, S. (2002) 'Restructuring seaside tourism: The resort lifecycle', *Annals of Tourism Research*, 29(1), 25–55.
Allan, M. (2011) 'The leadership challenge', in Morgan, N., Pritchard, A. and Pride, R. (eds) *Destination Brands: Managing Place Reputation*. Oxford: Elsevier, pp. 81–90.
Anholt, S. (2006) *Competitive Identity: The New Brand Management for Nations, Cities and Regions*. London: Palgrave.
— (2009a) *Places: Identity, Image and Reputation*. London: Palgrave.
— (2009b) 'Editorial', *Journal of Place Branding and Public Diplomacy*, 5(2): 91–6.
— (2010) 'Towards "governmental social responsibility"', *Journal of Place Branding and Public Diplomacy*, 6(2): 69–75.
— (2011) 'Competitive identity', in Morgan, N., Pritchard, A. and Pride, R. (eds) *Destination Brands: Managing Place Reputation*. Oxford: Elsevier, pp. 21–32.
Baker, B. (2007) *Destination Branding for Small Cities*. Oregon: Creative Leap Books.
Boschma, R. and Fritsch, M. (2009) 'Creative class and regional growth: Empirical evidence from seven european countries', *Economic Geography*, 85(4): 391–423.
Buhalis, D. (2000) 'Marketing the competitive destination of the future', *Tourism Management*, 21: 95–116.
Butler, R.W. (1980) 'The concept of the tourist area life-cycle of evolution: Implications for management of resources', *Canadian Geographer*, 24(1): 5–12
Crockett, S.R. and Wood, L. (1999) 'Brand Western Australia: A totally integrated approach to destination branding', *Journal of Vacation Marketing*, 5(3): 276–89.
Dinnie, K. (2008) *Nation Branding. Concepts, Issues, Practice*. Oxford: Butterworth Heinemann.
— (2011) 'The ethical challenge', in Morgan, N., Pritchard, A. and Pride, R. (eds) *Destination Brands: Managing Place Reputation*. Oxford: Elsevier, pp. 69–80.
Dredge, D. (2006) 'Policy networks and the local organisation of tourism', *Tourism Management*, 27: 269–80.
Florida, R. (2002) *The Rise of Creative Class. And How It Is Transforming Work, Leisure, Community and Everyday Life*. New York, USA: Basic Books.
— (2010) *The Great Reset: How New Ways of Living and Working Drive Post-Crash Prosperity*. New York, USA: Harper.
Fyall, A. (2011) 'The partnership challenge', in Morgan, N., Pritchard, A. and Pride, R. (eds) *Destination Brands: Managing Place Reputation*. Oxford: Elsevier, pp. 91–104.
Fyall, A. and Garrod, B. (2005) *Tourism Marketing: A Collaborative Approach*. Clevedon: Channel View Publications.
Hall, C.M. and Williams, A. (eds) *A Tourism Companion*. Oxford: Blackwell, pp. 438–49.
Hall, J. (2004) 'Branding Britain', *Journal of Vacation Marketing*, 10(2): 171–85.
Hankinson, G. (2010) 'Place branding theory: A cross-domain literature review from a marketing perspective', in Kavaratzis, M. and Ashworth, G. (eds) *Towards Effective Place Brand Management*. Oxford: Edward Elgar, pp. 15–35.
Hildreth, J. (2011) 'The measurement challenge', in Morgan, N., Pritchard, A. and Pride, R. (eds) *Destination Brands: Managing Place Reputation*. Oxford: Elsevier, pp. 155–68.
Hornskov, S. (2011) 'The authenticity challenge', in Morgan, N., Pritchard, A. and Pride, R. (eds) *Destination Brands: Managing Place Reputation*. Oxford: Elsevier, pp. 105–16.
Insch, A. and Florek, M. (2010) 'Place satisfaction of city residents: Findings and implications for city branding', in Kavaratzis, M. and Ashworth, G. (eds) *Towards Effective Place Brand Management*. Oxford: Edward Elgar.
Jaffe, E.D. and Nebenzahl, I.D. (2006) *National Image and Competitive Advantage*. Copenhagen: Copenhagen Business School.
Jansson, J. and Power, D. (2006) 'The image of the city – urban branding as constructed capabilities in Nordic city regions', available at: www.nordicinnovation.net/_img/image_of_the_city_-_web.pdf.
Kavaratzis, M. and Ashworth, G. (eds) (2010) *Towards Effective Place Brand Management*. Oxford: Edward Elgar.
Kotler, P. and Gertner, D. (2011) 'A place marketing and place branding perspective revisited', in Morgan, N., Pritchard, A. and Pride, R. (eds) *Destination Brands: Managing Place Reputation*, Oxford: Elsevier, pp. 33–54.
Leiper, N. and Park, S.Y. (2010) 'Skyscrapers' influence on cities' roles as tourist destinations', *Current Issues in Tourism*, 13(4): 333–49.
Leonhard, G. (2009) *Social Media and the Future of Marketing and Advertising*, www.mediafuturist.com.

Malecki, E.J. (2004) 'Jockeying for position: What it means and why it matters to regional development policy when places compete', *Regional Studies*, 38: 1101–20.

— (2007) 'Cities and regions competing in the global economy: Knowledge and local development policies', *Environment and Planning C*, 25: 638–54.

Morgan, N. (2004) 'Problematising place promotion', in Lew, A., Hall, C.M. and Williams, A. (eds) *A Tourism Companion*. Oxford: Blackwell, pp. 173–83.

— (2012) 'Time for mindful destination marketing and management?', *Journal of Destination Marketing & Management*, 1(1/2): 8–9.

Morgan, N. and Pritchard, A. (2000) *Advertising in Tourism and Leisure*. Oxford: Elsevier.

— (2002) 'Contextualising destination branding', in Morgan, N., Pritchard, A. and Pride, R. (eds) *Destination Branding: Creating the Unique Destination Proposition*. Oxford: Elsevier, pp. 11–41.

— (2005) '(PR)omoting place: The role of PR in building New Zealand's destination brand relationships', *Journal of Hospitality & Leisure Marketing*, 12 (1/2): 157–76.

— (2006) 'Promoting niche tourism destination brands: Case studies of New Zealand and Wales', *Journal of Promotion Management*, 12(1): 17–33.

Morgan, N., Pritchard, A. and Pride, R. (2011a) (eds) *Destination Brands: Managing Place Reputation*. Oxford: Elsevier.

— (2011b) 'Tourism places, brands, and reputation management', in Morgan, N., Pritchard, A. and Pride, R. (eds) *Destination Brands: Managing Place Reputation*. Oxford: Elsevier, pp. 3–21.

Munro, J. and Richards, B. (2011) 'The digital challenge', in Morgan, N., Pritchard, A. and Pride, R. (eds) *Destination Brands: Managing Place Reputation*. Oxford: Elsevier, pp. 141–54.

Online. Available: < 10yearsyoung.tourismnewzealand.com (accessed 25 April 2013).

— Available: <http://www.spain.info/> (accessed 25 April 2013).

— Available: <http://www.ineedspain.com/> (accessed 25 April 2013).

— Available: <www.yoursingapore.com> (accessed 25 April 2013).

— Available: <http://www.youtube.com/watch?v=9tNxvKT_z_U> (accessed 25 April 2013).

Pakesh, R. (2012) Online. Available: <http://adage.com/article/agency-news/martin-agency-founder-dave-martin-passes-82/237554/ > (accessed 24 April 2013).

Parajanen, S., Harmaakorpi, V. and Kari, K. (2011) 'The aesthetics challenge', in Morgan, N., Pritchard, A. and Pride, R. (eds) *Destination Brands: Managing Place Reputation*. Oxford: Elsevier, pp. 117–28.

Pike, S. (2004) *Destination Marketing Organisations*. Oxford: Elsevier.

Pride, R. (2011) 'The tone of voice challenge', in Morgan, N., Pritchard, A. and Pride, R. (eds) *Destination Brands: Managing Place Reputation*. Oxford: Elsevier, pp. 129–40.

Pritchard, A., Morgan, N. and Pride, R. (2011) 'Epilogue: Tourism and place reputation in an uncertain world', in Morgan, N., Pritchard, A. and Pride, R. (eds) *Destination Brands: Managing Place Reputation*. Oxford: Elsevier, pp. 347–56.

Saarinen, J. (2004) 'Tourism and touristic representations of nature', in Lew, A., Hall, C.M. and Williams, A.M. (eds) *A Companion to Tourism*. Malden, MA: Blackwell Publishing, pp. 438–9.

SpannerWorks (2007) 'What is social media', www.spannerworks.com/ebooks, in Constantinides, E. and Fountain, S.J. (2008) 'Web 2.0: Conceptual foundations and marketing issues', *Journal of Direct, Data and Digital Marketing Practice*, 9(3): 231–44.

Travis, D. (2000) *Emotional Branding: How Successful Brands Gain the Irrational Edge*. Roseville, CA: Prima Venture.

Vitellio, R. and Willcocks, M. (2006) 'The difference is in the detail: the potential of detail as a place branding tool and its impact on our perceptions and responses', *Journal of Place Branding*, 3(2): 248–62.

— (2011) 'Destination branding and the urban lexicon: London, New York and Barcelona', in Morgan, N., Pritchard, A. and Pride, R. (eds) *Destination Brands: Managing Place Reputation*. Oxford: Elsevier, pp. 303–20.

Weber, L. (2009) *Marketing to the Social Web: How Digital Customer Communities Build Your Business*. New Jersey: John Wiley & Sons.

WTO and ETC (2009) *Handbook on Tourism Destination Branding*. Brussels: ETC.

Yeoman, I. (2008) *Tomorrow's Tourist*. Oxford: Elsevier.

31

Capacity for co-creation among destination marketing organizations

Iis Tussyadiah and Florian Zach

Introduction

Recently, trends in the market and discussions in marketing literature signal the changing roles of customers. Marketing literature not only emphasizes the importance of devising customer-focused strategies for organizations to stay competitive in the market, but also, to a great extent, makes an attempt to theorize consumers as co-producers and co-creators of value (Lusch and Vargo 2006; Cova and Dalli 2009). Many different terms have been suggested to signal this new role of consumers: prosumers (Toffler 1980), consumeractors, etc., all of which characterize consumers as able and willing to actively engage in the construction of value through experiences and relationships with organizations. Therefore, the concept of co-creation surfaces, suggesting that consumers can enter into and engage in production and innovation processes with companies.

Prahalad and Ramaswamy (2002) assert that companies with a consumer-centric view regard consumers as an integral part of their system for value creation, in that consumers can influence the value generation process, compete with companies in value extraction and collaborate with companies in encounters. This means that consumers are not merely asked to contribute information regarding their needs and wants and satisfaction or dissatisfaction from consumption, but are also invited to contribute their creative insights and problem-solving skills to create, conceptualize and experience new products/services (Prahalad and Ramaswamy 2004). Engaging active, informed, connected and empowered consumers in different stages of the value chain will manifest in the co-creation of value that generates and expands knowledge and strengthens the competitive advantage of organizations (Volberda, Foss and Lyles 2010). Hence, co-creation is a process in which value is co-created jointly by companies and consumers through consumer–company interactions (Payne, Storbacka and Frow 2008; Prahalad and Ramaswamy 2002, 2004).

Cova and Dalli (2009) summarize several streams of research that highlight the active roles of consumers in the co-creation of value with companies. The first stream of literature focuses on the nature of consumption experiences and co-production of value in service encounters. It is suggested that through consumption, consumers immerse in an experiential context (Firat and Dholakia 1998), engage imaginatively and creatively in the construction of contextual values of products and services. Indeed, Lusch and Vargo (2006) argue that consumers co-construct values with companies by co-creating the function and the meanings of consumption experiences. This leads to the definition of co-creation as consumer integration through participation in consumption experiences, where consumers attach meanings and contextual values to products and services.

Consumers' active role in service production and encounter (i.e. co-production) is also believed to provide more value to consumers and companies. For example, researchers have discovered that when consumers are more involved in the process of service production, which leads to positive emotional interactions between consumers and companies during the service encounter, the perceived value of the service increases (Bitner, Brown and Meuter 2000; Pugh 2001). The linkage between value created during consumption stage and value created at the production stage has been discussed in literature (Ritzer and Jurgenson 2010). Lusch and Vargo (2006) suggest that service production activities are connected with consumption activities. Hence, co-production and co-creation are seen as nested concepts (Lusch and Vargo 2006).

Another stream of literature focuses more attention on consumer empowerment and collaborative innovation (von Hippel 1986, 2005) to integrate consumers in the process of new product or service development for companies' productivity gains (Inauen and Schencker-Wicki 2011). It is believed that innovation that starts with and is driven by the needs and requirements of end users, also referred to as consumer-driven innovation, will be successful in the market. In practice, earlier attempts on collaborative innovation typically involve select groups of lead users, who are identified as influential in their respective networks and communities. However, companies have started to involve more general end users to participate in the creation of new products and services. This leads to an interpretation of co-creation as integrating consumers as partners for innovation through participatory activities that support consumer–company collaboration whereby consumers are able to contribute their insights and knowledge to create new or improve products and services (i.e. co-production). These co-creation activities occur at the production stage preceding the consumption stage.

It is suggested that co-creation of value is inherent to tourism due to the experiential nature of tourism products and services. The unique characteristics of tourism, where experiences are produced and consumed simultaneously, make the concept of co-creation of value particularly significant in tourism. Binkhorst (2005) describes that the uniqueness in tourism lies in 'no separation between supply and demand, company and customer, tourist and host . . .' (2005: 3). Rather, tourism should be seen as 'a holistic network of stakeholders connected in experience environments in which everyone operates from different spatiotemporal contexts' (Binkhorst 2005: 3). Furthermore, tourism experience may vary greatly due to contextual details and subjective interpretation given by different types of tourists. Volo (2009) asserts that even the same tourism activity can generate different experiences to people in the same market segment. In line with Prahalad and Ramaswamy (2004), tourism destinations are creating experience environments in which tourists have active dialogue to co-construct their own personalized experiences. Therefore, co-creation between tourists and destinations in the process of experience production and consumption is unmistakable.

Further, the concept of co-creation suggests that, in order to create value, companies and organizations need to go beyond organizational boundaries into the value chain to foster collaborative exchange and integrate resources and skills to gain competitive advantage. Prahalad and Ramaswamy (2004) propose the convergence of companies and consumers by putting multiple points of interaction between consumers and companies at the locus of value creation. This indicates that companies and organizations need to transform their internal processes to be able to accommodate the co-created problems and solutions resulting from their interactions with consumers at different points in the value chain. However, there have been limited studies on how to assess the capability of organizations to successfully co-create values with consumers. To date, most studies on co-creation are conceptual propositions or case studies identifying motivators for consumer participation in new product development (e.g. Ostrom *et al.* 2010; Volberda, Foss and Lyles 2010). Similarly, research in the context of tourism so far has yet to understand how well destinations can identify and extract tourists' knowledge for tourism innovation. Therefore, in order to provide a foundation for successful consumer co-creation in a tourism context, the goal of this chapter is to conceptualize and assess the capacity of tourism destinations to co-create value with the consumers.

Organizational capacity for co-creation

In the business literature, consumer participation and organizational design have been cited as the two critical dimensions for the realization of co-creation. The level of consumer integration in the tourism co-creation process depends on how tourism organizations empower tourists to play a role in new product development. In other words, for tourism organizations, the success of co-creation depends on their ability to identify, locate and empower tourists with the right skills and characteristics, and turn them into collaborators. Tourism organizations need to integrate tourists into the value creation process by interacting with them at multiple points along the value chain. Indeed, Payne, Storbacka and Frow (2008) suggest that consumers need to be strategically integrated at essentially every step along the product and/or service encounter. This provides a series of encounters through which tourism organizations can identify and extract information from tourists. The purposeful setup for learning from consumers not only changes consumers' role, but also alters the relationship between organizations and consumers and, ultimately, the product or service experience (Payne, Storbacka and Frow 2008). Thus, from the dimension of consumer integration, the capacity for co-creation among tourism organizations is represented by their ability to identify creative consumers and facilitate them to become co-creators.

Another dimension of co-creation capacity is the capability to integrate the concept of co-creation in the culture of organizations. It is often related with dynamic capability, which is defined as firms' capability to integrate, build and reconfigure internal and external competence to address changing environments (Benner 2009) and absorptive capacity (Cohen and Levinthal 1990), which is the capability of the firms to value, assimilate and realize new ideas from external sources. For tourism organizations, co-creation capacity is supported by their receptiveness of relevant insights and ideas from consumers and ability to transform these ideas into successful consumer-centric, co-created products and services. The goal of integrating consumer knowledge is the development of new products and services and/or to significantly improve current ones (through increased effectiveness or efficiency) to ultimately create a competitive advantage (Volberda, Foss and Lyles 2010).

Payne, Storbacka and Frow (2008) suggest a conceptual framework of a process-based value co-creation consisting of three components: customer value-creating processes (i.e. the processes, resources and practices used by customers to manage their activities), supplier value-creating processes (i.e. the processes, resources and practices used by the organization to manage their activities and relationships with customers) and interaction processes (i.e. the processes of interaction and exchange between customers and the organization, which can be in the form of communication, use and service interactions). The framework represents an interconnected set of processes with different encounters that occur as a result of their respective value-creating processes. Further, it is suggested that customers engage in a learning process based on their interactions with the organization and, similarly, the organization engages in a learning process, gaining new knowledge from its interactions with customers to better improve their relationship with the customers (Payne, Storbacka and Frow 2008). Hence, from the organizations' point of view, organizational learning facilitates the value-creation processes and interactions with consumers and assists them with the design and delivery of relevant customer experiences.

As organizational learning and consumer learning are integral parts of the value co-creation process, knowledge management within organizational processes becomes important to take advantage of co-creation opportunities. It is suggested that the knowledge regarding consumers' value-creating processes acquired through meaningful encounters with consumers should be managed so that it would be transformed into skills and competence that organizations use to gain competitive advantage (i.e. prescriptive knowledge, techniques) (Payne, Storbacka and Frow 2008; Vargo and Lusch 2008). It is this chapter's interest to elaborate on learning and knowledge management from the organizations' perspectives, as it is consistent with the concept of absorptive capacity in literature on organizational learning. It is suggested that the concept of absorptive capacity can be used to assess the capacity of tourism organizations to co-create value with consumers, specifically because it provides a framework to illustrate how tourism organizations can extract knowledge from the consumers and then manage the knowledge to design better, relevant experiences.

Absorptive capacity is understood as a higher level capacity that consists of several lower level capabilities (Volberda, Foss and Lyles 2010). Dynamic capabilities literature formulated a process-based concept based on the knowledge flow (i.e. the streams of new knowledge that are obtained, transferred and integrated to enrich internal knowledge) during the different organizational learning processes. Zahra and George (2002) suggest four dimensions of absorptive capacity: acquisition, assimilation, transformation and exploitation. Assimilation capability refers to the capacity of tourism organizations to recognize relevant information from consumers. Assimilation is associated with organizational processes that allow analyzing and understanding of extracted information. Transformation capability is organizations' ability to adapt the extracted information into knowledge (i.e. internalizing the knowledge flow). Exploitation refers to the ability to exploit the knowledge for the benefit of the tourism organization. Acquisition and assimilation capabilities are labelled potential absorptive capacity (PAC); while transformation and exploitation capabilities are labelled realized absorptive capacity (RAC). Therefore, according to Zahra and George (2002), the ratio between PAC to RAC reflects the organization's efficiency in leveraging value from the acquired knowledge.

Another stream of literature in organizational learning suggests that PAC corresponds to explorative learning (i.e. knowledge acquisition) and RAC corresponds to exploitative learning (i.e. knowledge exploitation), thereby suggesting transformative learning (i.e. knowledge transformation) as the bridge between PAC and RAC (Lichtenthaler 2009) instead of an element within RAC. In the case of consumer co-creation, PAC describes how organizations are capable of acquiring new ideas from consumers. That is to say, the capability to integrate consumers in the new product development process is part of PAC, whereby organizations are able to acquire and extract consumers' ideas through consumer–company interactions (i.e. co-extraction of value with consumers). On the other hand, RAC reflects the ability of the organizations to leverage the absorbed knowledge into profit generation. In the context of co-creation, it is the capacity of tourism organizations to turn the co-created knowledge into co-created products/services. Transformation is seen as a social integration mechanism to bridge between PAC and RAC, implying that organizations that nurture information sharing and collaboration among employees will be more efficient in transforming knowledge into profit.

The complementarity of the different dimensions of absorptive capacity has been emphasized recently, due to the perceived increase in inter-organizational knowledge exchange. That is to say, tourism organizations increasingly communicate and share their knowledge in exchange of new ideas or practices, typically as a part of networked collaboration. The capacity to explore, transform and exploit knowledge from consumers are not mutually exclusive, but are likely complementary (Lane, Koka and Pathal 2006; Lichtenthaler 2009; Zahra and George 2002), because 'their impact on innovation and performance seems to depend on one another' (Lichtenthaler 2009: 827). Therefore, the synergy from the different dimensions of absorptive capacity would lead to the benefit that is greater than that of single processes. For tourism organizations to be able to successfully co-create value with consumers, it is important to ensure that all lower level capabilities are developed and synergized.

Assessing organizational capacity for co-creation among DMOs

As marketers and major contributors to the development of tourism destinations it is argued that destination marketing organizations (DMOs) need to engage in innovation activities (Hjalager 2002). Due to their central role within their destination DMOs are orchestrators of innovation (Dhanaraj and Parkhe 2006). This role is of particular importance for DMOs as they are merely a hub for information and as such bring together destination businesses that with or without the DMO can engage in the development of new tourism products and services (Wang and Xiang 2007). Indeed, recent studies found that DMOs do engage in the development of tourism products and services that are new to their organization and new to their destination (Sundbo, Orfila-Sintes and Sørensen 2007), whereby this development often takes place in collaboration with destination businesses (Zach 2012). It was found that working with business partners results in tourism products and services that fit with strategic and organizational goals as well as DMOs' market orientation and ultimately lead to innovation success (Zach 2012). This supports research by Wang and Fesenmaier (2007) that argues that collaboration between DMOs and destination tourism service providers is critical for destination success.

Taking it one step further, Zach and Gretzel (2012) identified the relationships that exist between destination organizations due to visitor movements, suggesting that DMOs can exploit business-to-business dyads in this visitor-activated network for new service development. For DMOs it is thus important to better understand and manage information surrounding and passing through them to identify opportunities for new tourism product and service development (Cooper 2006; Hjalager 2002). For the context of online marketing it was found that DMOs' absorptive capacity is a critical success factor (Wang 2007). However, it is yet unclear how exactly DMOs can take advantage of engaging destination visitors beyond a mere observation of visitor behaviour. To measure tourism organizations' capacity for consumer co-creation, measurement items corresponding to Lichtenthaler's (2009) absorptive capacity measures that are relevant to the context of consumer integration were adopted and reworded to fit into the study context of US and Swiss DMOs. After a consultation with four experts in tourism and social media and a back and forth translation from English to German, Italian and French, items with redundant statements in any of the four languages were excluded. As a result, 13 items were retained for this study.

Questionnaires were developed and integrated into a survey on a broader theme of destination innovation and technology targeting destination marketing organizations (DMOs). All items are measured on 7-point Likert scales with 1=Strongly Disagree and 7=Strongly Agree. The survey was made available in English, German, Italian and French, and was distributed to essentially all DMOs in Switzerland (225) and the USA (2,000) in early 2012. This results in a total of 76 (Switzerland) and 183 (USA) complete responses, representing a response rate of 33.7 per cent and 9.1 per cent respectively.

To assess the multidimensionality of capacity for consumer co-creation, this study tested several alternative models using confirmatory factor analysis based on the number of dimensions supported by theory (i.e. one, three and four-dimension models). Further, higher-order factor modelling was employed to assess the complementarity of the dimensions of co-creation capacity. Higher order factor modelling has been considered useful to represent the factor structure of measurement items that assess several highly related domains that are hypothesized to comprise a general construct.

Hierarchical comparison was conducted to identify the model that best estimates DMOs' multidimensionality of the co-creation capacity construct. In Model 1, the base model, items were loaded into a unidimensional factor. In Model 2, items were loaded into three factors, representing explorative, transformative and exploitative capacities (three dimension model) as suggested by Lichtenthaler (2009). In Model 3, items were loaded into four factors: acquisition, assimilation, transformation and exploitation following Zahra and George (2002). Last, Model 4 will be based on the multidimensional model with the better fit indices (either Model 2 or 3) to investigate the complementarity of the dimensions of co-creation capacity as a higher-order construct (see Figure 31.1).

First we evaluated the construct reliability (Table 31.1). We found that for the four construct solutions the coefficient alpha was found to be higher than the suggested cut-off value of 0.7 (Nunnally 1978) and that three of the constructs had a value higher than the more recent and more stringent value of 0.8 (Nunnally and Bernstein 1994). Only assimilation (Zahra and George 2002) did not reach the 0.8 cut-off, but came very close (Table 31.1). In the three construct solution, it was found that Cronbach's alpha was higher for transformation which here includes items from both assimilation and transformation from Zahra and George (2002) (Table 31.2).

Table 31.1 Reliability tests for the Four Construct Model

Items	*Cronbach's alpha*	*Mean scores*
Acquisition	0.82	
1) Scan the environment for visitors' insights, reviews and feedback		5.57
2) Observe visitors' opinion		5.74
3) Collect visitors' ideas		5.30
Assimilation (Zahra and George, 2002)	0.79	
1) Acquire ideas from visitors		4.93
2) Communicate with visitors to acquire new ideas		5.00
Transformation (Zahra and George, 2002)	0.82	
1) Communicate relevant knowledge across the units of our organization		6.03
2) Knowledge management is functioning well in our organization		5.55
3) We are proficient in transforming visitor ideas into new products		4.87
4) Recognize the usefulness of visitor knowledge for existing knowledge		5.42
5) Our employees are capable of sharing their expertise with visitors to develop new products		5.46
Exploitation	0.87	
1) Apply visitor ideas in new visitor services/products		5.10
2) Consider how to better exploit visitor ideas		5.24
3) Implement visitor ideas in new visitor services/products		4.78

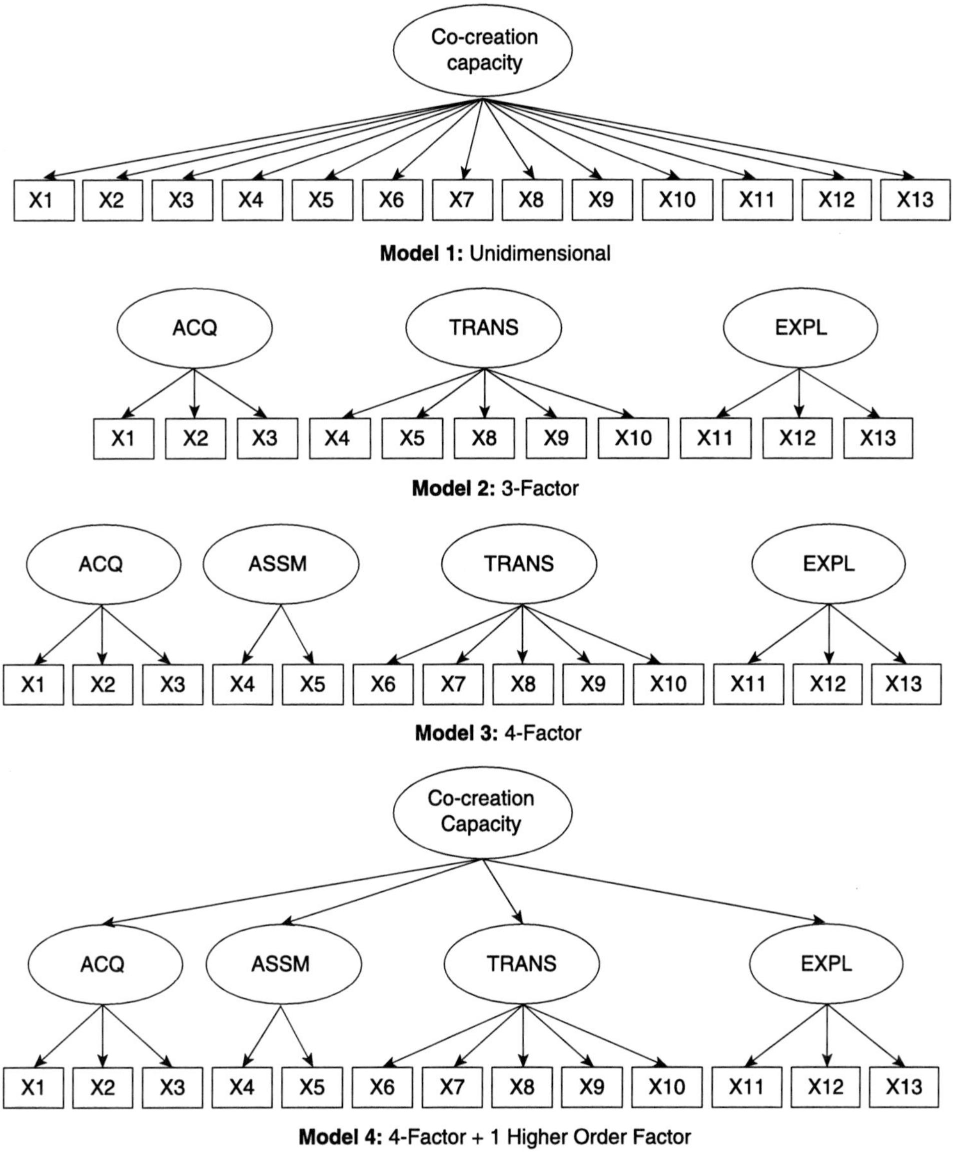

Figure 31.1 Co-creation capacity model comparison (note: *ACQ = Acquistion; ASSM = Assimilation; TRANS = Transformation; EXPL = Exploitation).*

Tests of discriminant and convergent validity were conducted using average variance extracted (AVE) as suggested by Fornell and Larcker (1981) and no problems were found. The hierarchical comparison between Model 1 and Model 2 shows that Model 2 has a better fit due to the lower chi-square relative to the degree of freedom. Only one fit index for Model 1, the standardized root mean square residual (SRMR), was within the acceptable measures for the reported measures, that is $\chi^2/df \leq 2.5$ (Muthén and Muthén 2007), Comparative fit index (CFI) ≥ 0.90 (Muthén and Muthén 2007), Tucker-Lewis index (TLI) > 0.90 (Hair *et al.* 1995) and (SRMR) $\leq .08$ (Kline 1998) (see Table 31.3). While Model 2 achieved better results it is inferior to

Table 31.2 Reliability test for the Transformation Construct in the Three Construct Model

Items	*Cronbach's alpha*	*Mean scores*
Transformation (Lichtenthaler 2009)	0.87	
1) Acquire ideas from visitors		4.93
2) Communicate with visitors to acquire new ideas		5.00
3) Communicate relevant knowledge across the units of our organization *[Omitted]*		6.03
4) Knowledge management is functioning well in our organization *[Omitted]*		5.55
5) We are proficient in transforming visitor ideas into new products		4.87
6) Recognize the usefulness of visitor knowledge for existing knowledge		5.42
7) Our employees are capable of sharing their expertise with visitors to develop new products		5.46

Model 3, the three lower order factor model. Hence, Model 3 is slightly better than Model 2, supporting the multidimensionality of the capacity for co-creation. The data empirically supports that the specific lower level capacities corresponding to different learning processes are distinguishable in the context of consumer co-creation.

With the four lower order factors (Model 3) being superior to the three lower order capacities model (Model 2) we evaluated the co-creation capacity construct by creating Model 4, which is an adaptation of Model 3 as it includes a higher-order construct in addition to the 4 lower order factors. Model 4 achieved a better fit than Model 3. However, while Models 2 to 4 are within the boundaries for CFI and SRMR, they are only close to these measures for TLI and χ^2/df. Having identified that Model 4 (four lower order factors plus one higher order construct) is superior to Model 3 (four lower order factors, but no higher order construct), the existence of the higher order co-creation capacity construct was tested with the target coefficient index. This index is the ratio of the chi-square value of the four lower order factors (Model 3) to the chi-square value of the four lower actors plus one higher order factor (Model 4) (Marsh and Hocevar 1985) and reflects the extent to which the higher order model accounts for covariation among the lower order factors. The target coefficient of 0.898 strongly suggests evidence of a higher order co-creation capacity construct as 89.8 per cent of the variation in the four lower order factors is explained by the higher order construct, namely the co-creation capacity.

Table 31.3 Hierarchical comparison for the Co-Creation Capacity Construct

Model	*χ^2 (df)*	*χ^2/df*	*CFI*	*TLI*	*SRMR*
0: Null model	2,023.51 (78)	25.94	—	—	0.428
1: 1 factor	400.00 (65)	6.15	.828	.793	.071
2: 3 factors	236.89 (62)	3.82	.910	.887	.056
3: 4 factors	223.71 (59)	3.79	.915	.888	.055
4: 4 factors + 1 higher order	249.12 (61)	4.08	.903	.876	.058

Note: N=259. Target coefficient of Model 4 using Model 3 as target model is 0.898.

Of the two alternative models (three versus four lower order factors) it was found that the four lower order factor model is a better fit for the sample data. Furthermore, as theory suggests the existence of an overarching co-creation capacity construct (Model 4) is of great theoretical interest given the high target coefficient of 89.8 per cent which indicates a high explanatory power of co-creation capacity over the variation in acquisition, assimilation, transformation and exploitation capacities.

Several independent two-tailed t-tests were conducted to evaluate differences of the co-creation dimensions between US and Swiss DMOs. The t-tests were conducted based on the four lower order factor models. No statistical significant difference between US and Swiss DMOs was found for acquisition: US $M = 5.57$, $SD = 0.89$ versus Swiss $M = 5.37$, $SD = 1.30$. However, there were statistical significant differences for the remaining three co-creation dimensions: assimilation (US: $M = 5.13$, $SD = 1.00$; Switzerland: $M = 4.56$, $SD = 1.07$; $t_{(247)} = -3.76$, $p = 0.000$), transformation (US: $M = 5.24$, $SD = 1.00$; Switzerland: $M = 4.85$, $SD = 0.86$; $t_{(247)} = -3.03$, $p = 0.003$) and exploitation (US: $M = 5.12$, $SD = 1.08$; Switzerland: $M = 4.73$, $SD = 1.16$; $t_{(255)} = -2.99$, $p = 0.003$). These results suggest that US and Swiss DMOs are to a similar degree capable of harvesting information from destination visitors, but that US DMOs are slightly more efficient in leveraging value from the acquired knowledge from consumers.

Results

Today tourism organizations, such as destination marketing organizations, are continuously challenged to develop new tourism products and services to cater to current and new destination visitors. Including visitors in this innovation development process is critical for DMOs as information provided by those that experience the destination can prove valuable for the DMO if visitors have an opportunity to participate in innovation development. Consumer co-creation in tourism is particularly important because of the experiential nature of tourism products. Hence, conceptualizing the capability of tourism organizations to integrate consumers into co-creation activities has an important theoretical as well as managerial implication.

In this chapter we tested the concept of absorptive capacity, which is the capability of organizations to extract and integrate external knowledge for their benefit, in this case for the development of new tourism products and services. The results show that capacity for co-creation is a multidimensional capacity, which consists of lower order capabilities. Both the three and four lower order factor models (Models 2 and 3) were identified as better models than the unidimensional model (Model 1), indicating that the lower order capacities are distinguishable. Therefore, it can be suggested that DMOs' capacity to work together with consumers in the process of innovation can be measured by DMOs' capacity to acquire knowledge (i.e. explore knowledge from consumers), transform knowledge within their organization and exploit the knowledge for new product/service development.

References

Benner, M.J. (2009) 'Dynamic or static capabilities? Process management practices and response to technological change', *Journal of Product Innovation Management*, 26: 473–86.

Binkhorst, E. (2005) *The Co-creation Tourism Experience.* Sitges: Whitepaper Co-creations.

Bitner, M.J., Brown, S. W. and Meuter, M.L. (2000) 'Technology infusion in service encounters', *Journal of the Academy of Marketing Science*, 28: 138–49.

Cohen, W.M. and Levinthal, D.A. (1990) 'Absorptive capacity: A new perspective on learning and innovation', *Administrative Science Quarterly*, 35: 128–52.

Cooper, C. (2006) 'Knowledge management and tourism', *Annals of Tourism Research*, 33: 47–64.

Cova, B. and Dalli, D. (2009) 'Working consumers: The next step in marketing theory?', *Marketing Theory*, 9: 315–39.
Dhanaraj, C. and Parkhe, A. (2006) 'Orchestrating innovation networks', *Academy of Management Review*, 31: 659–69.
Firat, A.F and Dholakia, N. (2006) 'Theoretical and philosophical implications of postmodern debates: Some challenges to modern marketing', *Marketing Theory*, 6: 123–62.
Fornell, C. and Larcker, D.F. (1981) 'Evaluating structural equation models with unobservable variables and measurement error', *Journal of Marketing Research*, 18: 39–50.
Hair, J.F., Anderson, R.E., Tatham, R.L. and Black, W.C. (1995) *Multivariate Data Analysis with Readings*, 4th edn. Englewood Cliffs, NJ: Prentice Hall.
Hjalager, A.-M. (2002) 'Repairing innovation defectiveness in tourism', *Tourism Management*, 23: 465–74.
Inauen, M. and Schencker-Wicki, A. (2011) 'The impact of outside-in open innovation on innovation performance', *European Journal of Innovation Management*, 14: 496–520.
Kline, R.B. (1998) *Principles and Practices of Structural Equation Modeling*. New York, NY: Guilford Press.
Lane, P., Koka, B. and Pathal, S. (2006) 'The reification of absorptive capacity: A critical review and rejuvenation of the construct', *Academy of Management Review*, 31: 833–63.
Lichtenthaler, U. (2009) 'Absorptive capacity, environmental turbulence, and the complementarity of organizational learning processes', *Academy of Management Journal*, 52: 822–46.
Lusch, R.F. and Vargo, S.L. (2006) 'Service-dominant logic: Reactions, reflections and refinements', *Marketing Theory*, 6: 281–8.
Marsh, H.W. and Hocevar, D. (1985) 'Application of confirmatory factor analysis to the study of self-concept: First- and higher-order factor models and their invariance across groups', *Psychological Bulletin*, 97: 562–82.
Muthén, L.K. and Muthén, B.O. (2007) *Mplus User's Guide* (5th edn). Los Angeles, CA: Muthén & Muthén.
Nunnally, J.C. (1978) *Psychometric Theory*. New York, NY: McGraw-Hill.
Nunnally, J.C., and Bernstein, I.H. (1994). *Psychometric Theory*, 3rd edn. New York, NY: McGraw-Hill.
Ostrom, A.L., Bitner, M.J., Brown, S.W., Burkhard, K.A., Goul, M., Smith-Daniels, V., Demirkan, H. and Rabinovich, E. (2010) 'Moving forward and making a difference: Research priorities for the science of service', *Journal of Service Research*, 13: 4–36.
Payne, A., Storbacka, K. and Frow, P. (2008) 'Managing the co-creation of value', *Journal of the Academy of Marketing Science*, 36: 83–96.
Prahalad, C.K. and Ramaswamy, V. (2002) 'The co-creation connection', *Strategy & Business*, 27: 51–60.
— (2004) 'Co-creating unique value with customers', *Strategy & Leadership*, 32: 4–9.
Pugh, S.D. (2001) 'Service with a smile: Emotional contagion in the service encounter', *Academy of Management Journal*, 44: 1018–27.
Ritzer, G. and Jurgenson, N. (2010) 'Production, consumption, prosumption: The nature of capitalism in the age of the digital "prosumer"', *Journal of Consumer Culture*, 10: 13–36.
Sundbo, J., Orfila-Sintes, F. and Sørensen, F. (2007) 'The innovative behaviour of tourism firms – Comparative studies of Denmark and Spain', *Research Policy*, 36: 88–106.
Toffler, A. (1980) *The Third Wave*. New York: Bantam Books.
Vargo, S.L. and Lusch, R.F. (2008) 'Service-dominant logic: Continuing the evolution', *Journal of the Academy of Marketing Science*, 36: 1–10.
Volberda, H.W., Foss, N.J. and Lyles, M.A. (2010) 'Absorbing the concept of absorptive capacity: How to realize its potential in the organization field', *Organization Science*, 21: 931–51.
Wang, Y. and Fesenmaier, D.R. (2007) 'Collaborative destination marketing: A case study of Elkhart county, Indiana', *Tourism Management*, 28: 863–75.
Wang, Y. and Xiang, Z. (2007) 'Toward a theoretical framework of collaborative destination marketing', *Journal of Travel Research*, 46: 75–85.
Von Hippel, E.A. (1978) 'Successful industrial products from customer ideas', *Journal of Marketing*, 42: 39–49.
— (2005) *Democratizing Innovation*. Cambridge MA: MIT Press.
Volo, S. (2009) 'Conceptualizing experience: A tourist based approach', *Journal of Hospitality, Marketing and Management*, 18: 111–26.
Zach, F. (2012) 'Partners and innovation in American destination marketing organizations', *Journal of Travel Research*, 51: 412–25.
Zach, F. and Gretzel, U. (2012) 'Tourist-activated networks: Implications for dynamic bundling and en route recommendations', *Information Technology & Tourism*, 13: 229–38.
Zahra, S.A. and George, G. (2002) 'Absorptive capacity: A review, reconceptualization, and extension', *The Academy of Management Review*, 27: 185–203.

32

'Living the brand'

The evangelical experiences of seasonal snowsport workers

Shelagh Ferguson and Amy Bourke

Introduction

In this chapter we contribute towards the current debate surrounding destination brand experiences. This research adopts the perspective of the workers as brand authors (Holt 2004) and fleshes out the role they play in the brand experience, in particular how employees represent and co-create brand experiences with and for consumers. The structure of the chapter is as follows: firstly traditional destination brand literature is considered before drawing from Consumer Culture Theory research that illustrates how brand experiences are personally and individually constructed and may differ from the intention of the brand's owners. Services marketing literature is also discussed as the brand experience has been richly explored within that context but dominantly from a consumer perspective.

Thus this chapter aims to understand the cultural richness of a destination brand through the perspectives of seasonal snowsport workers, as the group of employees who predominate in customer interaction at the snowsport destination. Having established a knowledge gap, Holt's (2004) brand authorship model identifies three ways that seasonal snowsport workers contribute to brand experience knowledge; although not brand owners they are the critical customer facing aspects of the destination brand experience; they are also consumers of the destination brand and they both draw upon and reflect popular culture meaning in the process of destination brand culture creation. Utilizing a qualitative approach, this research explores how seasonal workers interact with and reflect upon the destination brand of Cardrona, New Zealand. Holt's model (2004) is used as a framework to discuss the research findings and implications for destination branding.

Destination brand authorship and culture

The concept of destination branding has been subject to growing interest in the Tourism Marketing field with Morgan, Pritchard and Prides' (2002) book and a special issue of the Journal of Brand Management (Hall 2002) demonstrating an emergent body of management orientated research, which has since developed into a significant stream of research and is addressed in other chapters of this book. Destination branding builds upon the traditional approach to branding developed from a marketing management perspective which sees brands as a device to gain competitive advantage by offering added value to its customers (de Chernatony and McDonald 2003). The principles of branding, originally developed to differentiate between fast moving consumer goods, have increasingly been applied to a diverse range of items such as charities, museums, educational institutions, celebrities, countries, regions and towns (both as a place brand and a destination) (Montoya and Vandehey 2005). Current marketing management practice believes that intangible experiences (such as holidays at a destination) can be managed and developed into brands controlled by the organization and valued by consumers, using a set of established marketing principles. Hence the application of branding principles and practices to destination brands at country, region and resort level (Morgan, Pritchard and Pride 2002).

However, recent consumer research has uncovered the complex and incredibly rich symbolic and cultural meaning that brands can represent for a consumer which has a twofold implication for conventional understanding of branding theory (Muniz and O'Guinn 2001; Kozinets 2002; Kates 2004; Bengtsson, Ostberg *et al.* 2005). Firstly, these meanings are personally and individually constructed by consumers and secondly, they may differ from the intention of the brand's owners. This suggests that brands may anarchically career beyond the control of an organization's marketing function driven by divergent and disharmonious meanings that exist within consumers' minds. If we define brand culture as a framework of shared meaning and understanding surrounding the brand and related to practice (Bengtsson, Ostberg *et al.* 2005), consumers creating their own meanings and practices around brands can impact significantly on brand culture.

Holt (2004) extends this thinking to recognize the importance of other actors in the development of brand cultures beyond owners and consumers of the brand. This creates a rich and challenging area for consumer researchers who recognize that a variety of actors engage in and influence the process of brand construction and the subsequent culture surrounding the brand. Typically actors could be employees, investors, local communities and suppliers engaged in an iterative brand culture creation process (Hatch and Schultz 2001). Mapping and understanding such complex brand cultures is desirable not only from a strategic perspective but as an insight into contemporary markets.

Also relevant to this discussion is a body of services marketing literature on brand experience which has to date mainly focused on consumers' perspectives. Nysveen, Pedersen and Skard (2012) summarize that there is agreement that customer value is generated through brand experience rather than functional attributes. More specifically Mosley (2007) proclaims, the ultimate aim of brand management has always been to deliver a consistent and distinctive customer brand experience, he explains that personal interactions in service delivery are the most important part of customer service satisfaction and can be actively influenced by on-brand employee behaviours. He concludes that in providing a robust mechanism for aligning employees' brand experience with the desired customer brand experience, and a common platform for marketing and HR, employer brand management represents a significant evolution in the quest for corporate brand integrity (Mosley 2007: 123). Despite this ringing endorsement, the preceding step of mapping brand experience from an employee perspective and its impact on brand culture has been missing from the literature. Although brand design, communications and environments have been found to be essential to the brand experience for the customers, the interactions with customer facing staff are critical to the customers' experience. Brand experience has been mapped from the consumer perspective (O'Cass and Grace 2004) but not the employee perspective despite their inextricable and central role in service provision.

The practice of branding is gradually changing from the sole premise of the marketing function to an activity that engages the whole organization. Holt (2002) identifies that brand

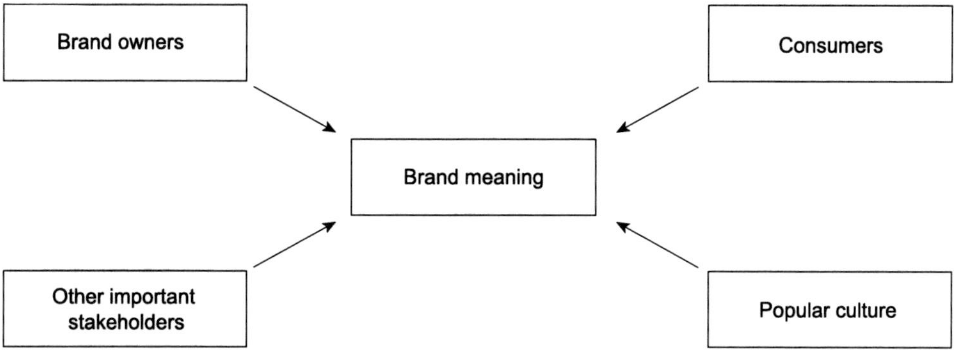

Figure 32.1 Authors of the brand (source: Holt 2004).

culture is dialectically constructed through an iterative and continuous action. Holt (2004) further develops brand meaning as being multi culturally authored by the narratives from brand owners, consumer, stakeholders and popular culture. This research seeks to understand the cultural richness of a destination brand through the eyes of one particularly influential group of employees within an organization, seasonal snowsport workers. We acknowledge that seasonal workers represent only one group of actors out of the many who create brand meaning. Seasonal snowsport workers provide a rich context to study their role in the creation of brand cultures, they are not brand owners but they are part of the organization that owns the brand (normally the lowest status and least remunerated members of staff), they are consumers (with high cultural capital) but not paying consumers, drawing upon and reflecting popular cultural in the process of brand culture creation. Duncan's (2008) research found seasonal snowsport workers commonly used the phrase 'living the dream' to describe their lifestyle. This perception of having 'the ultimate lifestyle, being paid to ski' was shared by them, their family and friends and is strongly rooted in popular culture. Therefore this group represent three of Holt's (2004) four authors of brand meaning merged within one group.

Seasonal snowsport workers

Seasonal snowsport workers interact with brand culture in two specific ways. Firstly they use the existing brand meaning as part of their personal identity projects, which increasingly use highly symbolic consumption forms to create visible and unique identities. These seasonal workers have typically moved many thousands of miles to do very poorly paid work. Interaction with the destination brand must create rich and highly valued meaning for them to offset these negative aspects. They will draw upon the history of the brand and create new meaning and symbolic value based upon their interaction during their engagement with the destination brand. Secondly they are actors engaged in the interpretation and production of the brand culture (Bengtsson and Ostberg 2006).

From the management perspective, these seasonal workers produce most of the human generated brand culture available for consumption by paying guests arriving at the ski area. They will be greeted at the car park, buy lift tickets from, be instructed and served food by seasonal workers. If management are able to facilitate or influence the growth of a brand culture that values interactions with customers, a competitive advantage is obtained as aptly described by Jon Reveal, General Manager of Aspen Snowmass: 'every ski area has lifts, parking lots, restaurants and machinery, yet one is more successful than the next because of the way its management treats its employees and in turn, the way the employee treats the guests' (cited by Ismert and Petrick 2004). However, as discussed earlier, brand culture grows independently of the best efforts of management. Seasonal snowsport workers are the lowest paid, least valued with the greatest job insecurity – the inverse markers of high status work. Limited previous research revealed a negative attitude towards ski area customers by seasonal workers, they were to be tolerated but mocked behind their backs with a variety of derogatory terms used to describe them (such as punter and billy) designed to reinforce the perception of higher status of the seasonal worker (Ismert and Petrick 2004; Purdue 2004). This was contradicted by Duncan's later work which found workers valued customers as without them there would be no lifestyle available for the workers. Both findings presented in the research lack an understanding of the process leading to the attitude and behaviour.

This research seeks an alternative perspective to examine brand culture as understood by these seasonal workers and the role they play in creating current brand culture for a destination brand. The other aspect that makes seasonal ski workers an important group to study is their traversing of traditional work/leisure boundaries. This blurring of boundaries between work and leisure has been well documented in seasonal ski employment (Ismert and Petrick 2004; Boon 2006; Dickson and Huyton 2008; Duncan 2008) but the impact this has on the culture of the brand has not been explored. These workers for the duration of their employment: wear clothing festooned with the resort brand during work and leisure time; willingly spend most of their leisure time at their place of employment; interact almost exclusively with their co-workers in all aspects of their life for the duration of their employment – essentially they are living branded lives.

The sociohistoric patterning of work and leisure as separate entities has been well documented and there is significant interest in the new merging of work and leisure. Specifically, this research investigates how seasonal ski workers understand the brand culture of the place of their employment and how this plays out in the blurring of traditional work/leisure boundaries. Further to the sample justification given earlier, seasonal ski workers were selected as a group to study due to them being a cohesive group with a close relationship to the ski area destination brand (they are employed by the owners of the brand and choose to spend their free time at Cardrona Ski area and live in a small neighbouring village of Wanaka).

Methodology

An inductive approach was utilized, as this method allows for theory to emerge, appropriate to the immaturity of this area of research. According to Patton's (2002) criteria, a qualitative mode of inquiry is most appropriate for this research. Firstly, there is a lack of current empirical research available, thus the constructs or predicted outcomes cannot be predetermined before data collection. In addition personal understanding of brand meaning cannot be fully understood or uncovered through a quantitative means (Guba and Lincoln 2005). A qualitative approach is commensurate with the stated aims of understanding a phenomenon in greater detail to ascertain meaning and depth (Sullivan 2001). The research was conducted at Cardrona Alpine Resort in the South Island of New Zealand. The resort opens from late June to early October. It is relatively small (790 acres of skiable terrain, seven lifts and an hourly lift capacity of 7,800 people per hour) compared to American, Canadian and European resorts. For example, Whistler in Canada has 8,100 acres of skiable terrain, 38 lifts and an hourly lift capacity of 65,507 people per hour.

The management team at Cardrona were prepared to allow us access to their staff to recruit informants during work hours but to hold in-depth interviews away from the work, thus creating an environment more conducive to open and honest revelation of true attitude towards work and reduce social desirability bias. Informants were guaranteed confidentiality in all aspects of discussion and trust was generated by both researchers having personal experience of seasonal work in ski areas. Both researchers also spent time in the ski area before data collection commenced to observe interactions between workers and become a familiar sight to potential informants, thus reducing barriers and assisting with open and honest discussion.

Data was collected six weeks after the start of the season to allow an understanding of working at Cardrona to be established within informants. An open ended questioning technique was used; informants were encouraged to tell their story of how they first came across the name Cardrona and their unfolding experience and interactions. In depth probing was utilized to explore emerging perspective on the relationship they had with the destination of Cardrona and associated meanings thus allowing naturalistic data to emerge without prompting, giving trustworthiness to the resultant following themes. The 15 informants were selected to represent a range of departments and experiences (some returning workers, other first timers); the ages within this sample ranged from 21 to 48 years.

Content analysis is an appropriate tool for this research, as it is a method used to systematically evaluate the symbolic content of all forms of recorded communications (including interviews). Braun and Clarke's (2006) process of performing a thematic content analysis was applied to the interview transcripts, through analysis of whole texts. The method of emergent coding was appropriate given the exploratory nature of the research problem. The themes are produced inductively and not restricted to pre-determined codes (Creswell 2003), hence providing a consistent and insightful interpretation of the data. The coding protocol used was a combination of Thomas' (2006) general inductive coding approach, which is well regarded for similar social science research, and Mayring's (2000) six step model of category development. Following the coding, a thorough reading of the text with the research direction in mind was undertaken (Mayring 2000; Thomas 2006). Through this process of analysis, many rich and interesting themes emerged that related to brand culture. Specific and defined themes emerged which were applied consistently throughout the different documents (transcripts, notes etc.), in order to create congruency of themes and codes. Peer coding was also utilized to ensure trustworthiness of the themes emerging from analysis to support coder reliability. Through these processes the following findings emerged and are subsequently explained.

Findings and discussion

The desired brand culture of Cardrona as described by Nadia Ellis, Cardrona's marketing manager was 'family friendly and fun'. She develops her description of the brand culture in relation to Cardrona's competition, one ski area is much steeper and more extreme, another is very racing orientated and efficient thus Cardrona occupies a middle ground of easy family orientated terrain and staffed by happy and welcoming staff. When asked to describe the culture of Cardona every single informant used the words 'family orientated and friendly'. Clearly the staff have a similar understanding of the core elements of Cardona's brand culture as desired by the management team. The literature describes brand culture as being dialectically constructed through an iterative and continuous action, hence even though the management and staff may hold similar views on Cardrona's brand culture, this does not mean that there is agreement on how that culture is created and maintained. One informant expresses his understanding of the Cardrona brand culture thus,

> We want them (the customers) to come back, they're on holiday, they pay a shit load of cash. So I personally think that the culture here is giving people the best experience that they

> could possibly have. Cause there's a lot of competition. We've got two resorts over in Queenstown and we've got obviously Treble Cone up there. What sets us apart? I personally believe all the decent skiers go to TC and hoon around; whereas people come to Cardies (Cardrona) for a family vacation. And the parents get as much joy out of seeing their kids going down the magic carpet area as dropping off some kind of cliff themselves. So it's just a laid back family kind of resort. I think that's transmitted through all the staff. You try to the best to your ability to *give* the customers what you can. I think it's because so many people take pride in what they do, then it's just self reinforced. It's kind of self-policed. You get so many return staff, that the newbies (new members of staff) that come in, they'll see the way that people act and then they just emulate that.
>
> *(Alex, ski school, a Cardrona veteran of three seasons)*

This quote gives insight into the brand culture, how Cardrona is positioned against its competitors and how the culture is passed from experienced to new members of staff. Central to this understanding of Cardrona brand culture is Alex's integration of himself into the culture and the contribution of his role (he sees himself as having some ownership of the brand), he sees himself *giving* as much as he can (emphasis added). He does not attribute the enculturation of new members of staff as being a management responsibility. He also makes the unspoken assumption that customers would not get that kind of experience without using the conduit of the staff to transmit the destination brand messages. He perceives the seasonal staff facilitate the transfer of brand culture. Underpinning this quote is the recognition that seasonal workers must be at the centre of the brand culture rather than a peripheral underpaid and undervalued figure and the culture has a tangible aspect that can be transmitted to new staff.

This quote serves as an introduction to this analysis of brand culture and we note that Holt's (2004) four authors model of brand meaning implies separate processes for each author. However, this research highlights the interconnectedness of the workers' perception of the work they do, their role in the ski snowsport community and how the popular culture understanding of 'living the dream' seamlessly merges for this informant. These form the three main themes of this analysis which are examined in this section:

1. the workers' perception of their work, specifically, how seasonal workers make sense of the destination brand of Cardrona through their lived experience which blurs traditional work and leisure boundaries;
2. seasonal workers' roles within the snow sport community; and
3. how popular culture relates to the 'living the dream' style of life.

The 'living the dream' concept reflects across all three themes as does the emphasis on the merging of work and leisure in a singular lifestyle where one is inseparable from the other, as discussed in depth by informants. They used traditional socio-historical concepts of work to frame their understanding and formulate their sense making strategy:

Seasonal workers' perceptions of their work at Cardrona

> Honestly the first three weeks of starting at Cardrona, we'd drive up in the van and I'd get out of the van at the top and it was gale force winds and you've got this crazy sunburst

> sunrise in front of you with all this white, it's beautiful. Or you could be in England, you could be walking round your local home town, everything's grey and people are scraping their knuckles on the floor – why would I want to do that? Well you could be sat in a job which you're working your entire life and you get to the top of the job and you've got your flash television and you've got an amazing sofa and stuff but you don't really like your job and once every year you've got a two week holiday where you go away for two weeks to have the time of your life. I'm having it every day.
>
> *(Andrew, ski hire, new this year to Cardrona)*

Andrew uses direct comparison to his possible life back in England to frame his understanding of traditional work concepts such as poor rates of pay, lack of financial security and the financial necessity of working two jobs (one at the ski area and busking). His personal values see these traditionally negative aspects as directly compensated by the beautiful aesthetics of his surroundings and his ability to ride during his lunch break. His analysis concludes that being able to ride for the short duration of his lunch break and his geographical location of living in a holiday resort outweigh any perceived disadvantages. Andrew's appreciation of his style of life can only be made with knowledge of the 'other'; characterized by the 'greyness' of England and recognition that a majority of the population can only stay at Cardrona for a couple of week compared to his three month work contract, despite the work he feels he is on holiday. Andrew's analysis is very simplistic with little inherent tension expressed. This lack of tension between work and style of life was characteristic of many informants. They were almost evangelical in their attitude towards the work aspect of their combined work and leisure lifestyle, despite the hardships that the work entails as described by Iain:

> Even when it's absolutely shitting it down with snow, and it's freezing, and my fingers are cold and I've got my parka off, and my goggles are all skew wiff and I'm getting blown everywhere, still love it, just cause you're teaching, you're helping these people – just being able to do what you are passionate about! I don't know, I can't describe it but, you can see my voice goes different when I talk about something I enjoy. I like ... I love it, yeah I honestly love giving people the poma lift. I've had people say 'you're really good with people' and I say 'ah just doing my job' and it's great. I love it yeah.
>
> *(Iain, lift operator on the beginner slopes, new to Cardrona)*

Iain's love of his work is obvious from this quote; he receives enormous enjoyment and satisfaction from his interaction with customers. He is not alone. The 'love of work' was described by many informants. The 'love' is always framed by the negatives of the work often focusing on poor pay and somehow this is perceived as a positive, representing a more simplified life:

> Every single thing about my job I love and even the salary because when I first left school I stacked shelves in the supermarket, and now I earn less than I did then. And fucking hell it is 23 years later on and I'm still earning less than that. But I still have enough for food; I still have enough for rent. I don't need anything else. And what I've generally found is the more I earn, the more I spent. And I just had bigger and better toys, which were owned by the bank invariably. It was just nuts.
>
> *(Paul, ski school, third year at Cardrona)*

Roles within and membership of the seasonal snow sport community

A sense of knowing who they are in relation to others was reflected in this theme, not just the functional aspect of the role but the identity of the role and the shared consciousness of being similar are reflected in the following two quotes:

> So winter came round and we sort of knew all the important people around the town and we are the locals on the mountain. And we, you know we just owned it. Not really but just knew a lot more about the mountain, we'd spent some time there and everything was really close. It is really small, like real tight knit, so you can't really choose who you do and don't like, you have to deal with everyone.
>
> *(Jake, cleaner)*

> I can be sat next to somebody from the café or patrol on the bus to work, it really brings that community spirit cause you end up just chatting to whoever next to you. And it's awesome because you know the *lifties*, cause you sat next to them in the van, or you've been to a party with them, then they help your kids. This year I've been helping out in rentals on Saturday morning. Which is awesome 'cause rentals know me, and like when you're in the staff room everyone's interacting.
>
> *(Alex, ski school, third year at Cardrona)*

Both informants use similar terms, 'tight knit' and 'community spirit' to describe how they feel about their co-workers. Knowing someone socially is not perceived as being significantly different from knowing them within the context of work, sharing the experience of working at Cardrona creates a merging of spheres of work into a community of seasonal workers. Membership of this community forms a bond of interaction that is not freely chosen, as Jake comments 'you have to deal with everyone'. This description has much in common with Muniz and O'Guinn's (2001) definition of a community, the shared consciousness of being similar with a shared outlook overriding any personal differences.

Inherent in the sense of community is the sense of difference from the customers and the literature implies that as 'locals' the snow sport workers believe they have higher status than customers, however several informants expressed their gratitude towards customers. This underpinned their sense of difference but not necessarily their superiority:

> Every day I come up here and look at all the customers and thank God for them! If they were not here paying lots of money I wouldn't be able to do the job I love. So every single day I want to thank them.
>
> *(Maureen, snowboard instructor)*

Popular culture and 'living the dream'

The underpinning assumption regarding the desirability of the lifestyle of seasonal snowsport workers is evident in the preceding two sections; this final section addresses how the 'living the dream' concept is articulated by seasonal workers. They draw upon resources of the 'other' life and popular culture perceptions of the attractiveness of their chosen style of life. 'Living the dream' was mapped by Duncan (2008) in her work on snowsport employees at Whistler ski resort in Canada. The phrase represented a seamless combination of work practices, community membership and very enjoyable leisure practices. This analysis maps aspects of the destination brand culture drawing heavily on traditional concepts of work and leisure to frame the seasonal experience. Comparison with the 'other' type of life available is always negative compared to the style of life experienced at Cardrona and popular culture understanding of living the dream provides status for traditional low status work experiences such as low pay and physically hard and uncomfortable work. The following quote illustrates how envy is interpreted by seasonal workers as a customer response to the seasonal worker's style of life.

> I guess that people are a bit envious that you are working in the (ski) field that they are spending so much money just to come here and ride at Cardrona, they are *spending* loads of money whereas we're *earning* shit money but we're constantly in the (ski) field and we're part of the lifestyle.
>
> *(Mark, cleaner, new to Cardrona)*

This comment recognizes the divide between customers and seasonal workers as consumers, customers spend money whereas seasonal workers don't spend much because they do not earn much and it is possible for them to maintain their style of life without significant funds. Mark believes that customers envy him for his style of life, not because of the poorly paid work he does but because of his location. He is constantly where he believes customers want to be. Hence the popular cultural understanding of living the dream requires a separation between customers and seasonal worker, if everyone could 'live the dream' it would not hold the same cache.

Work practices relating to destination brands

The previous section mapped three dominant themes that emerged from the data, in order to link these findings to the themes of destination brand experience and how seasonal workers, are actors engaged in the interpretation and production of brand culture, the following discussion focuses firstly on how these themes relate to their work practices. These quotes pertain to work practice but the underpinning appreciation of an enjoyable style of life where being a seasonal worker at Cardrona means being a member of a community where the work/leisure divide is easily traversed:

> If someone comes in and takes a set of skis from us and they're not great, I just want to make sure they have the best ride. And if it's quiet you can maybe say 'oh I'm just gonna run these over the waxer for you' and then they leave being happy, yeah, you're just making things better. I'm passionate about my job. I just love, the way that the company actually treats me, makes me want to treat the company, create the right image for the company.
>
> *(Andrew, ski hire, first season at Cardrona)*

> It's like a big family kind of thing. I know everyone works hard and the people that don't work hard you can kind of pick up on them and try to pull them in. Well, I try to get their attention and get them into it. You get the vibe that you just want to get down to it. Even if you've come into work and you've got a massive hangover, you just get down to it because it's a fun job and you're quite lucky to have a job where you walk out the door and you've just got all this.
>
> *(Paul, ski school)*

During discussion of work practice, informants began to mention management actions and their impact upon the culture of Cardrona. Paul continued on this theme and gave an example that he perceived as a means to maintain the culture:

> I worked in Canada and a lad that I met over in Canada said to me 'what's Cardies like?' and I said 'ah it's awesome' and he said 'can I use you as a reference?' and I said 'yeah if you want, absolutely not a problem'. My supervisor, whose dual-cert means he can teach snowboarding and skiing, he's a trainer and my boss over in Canada said 'oh I'm applying to your place' and I said 'oh well if you want just use my name as a referee, and I've got no problem giving you a reference'. He said 'nah it's alright don't need it'. I said 'okay sweet', my mate got the job, my boss didn't because as long as you do a good job then they (Cardrona management) knows that you are only going to bring likeminded people with you. And it goes on recommendation all the time.

Through these descriptions and articulations of work practices we can see how seasonal workers transfer their understanding of the destination brand culture into their work practices. These seasonal workers have become evangelical brand ambassadors for Cardrona seeking to create a sense of unique customer experience within the destination that actually contributes to the meaning of the destination brand itself.

The three themes mapped in the findings discussion both support and contradict the literature by supporting claims that brand culture for these seasonal workers is tangible, in the sense that they can describe it in depth and are deeply affected by it in both their work and leisure spheres. These seasonal workers are evangelical brand ambassadors who create a sense of unique customer experience within the destination that actually contributes to the meaning of the destination brand itself for their experience and that of the customer. The contradiction is that the workers do not see themselves as *contributing* towards the brand culture but as *key* authors of the brand culture. They see themselves as envied in their lifestyle choice; their perception of work as an inseparable part of their style of life and the enormous enjoyment they derive from interaction with the brand of Cardrona though being part of the seasonal workers' community all contribute towards the responsibility they hold for the brand culture. It would seem that this responsibility is not taken lightly by seasonal workers, counter to earlier literature. As actors engaged in the interpretation and production of brand culture, it seems the management should take care to support their active and self directed culture production as it is an asset that would be hard to value or replace.

Conclusions

In conclusion and supportive of the work of Bengtsson *et al.* (2005), Kates (2004), Kozinets (2002) and Muniz and O'Guinn (2001), seasonal workers take the destination brand of Cardrona and create independent and personally constructed meaning about their related style of life that blends leisure and work seamlessly. They articulate very little work related tension when narrating their experience of the brand culture which recognizes the importance of a sense of community and an evangelical love of the actual work. The brand culture as understood by these seasonal workers may reflect the managerial perspective but does not seem to be derived from them. Brand culture at Cardrona is created through experience and the management are noticeably absent in most of these informants' accounts, whereas comparisons against a 'feared other life', what they could be doing if there were not at Cardrona, seems to inspire a great appreciation of the fun and family friendly experience available at Cardrona. This 'other' life that these seasonal workers could be living must exist as a viable option in their minds and is a dominant theme in these accounts. The only reference to management practice as having a strong influence on the brand culture was related to work practice. This research modifies Holt's (2004) brand meaning model by concluding that the brand authors are not separate entities as his model indicates but can be blended seamlessly into a single group of seasonal workers who draw upon popular culture of the living the dream lifestyle, comparisons against 'other' life working practices and almost obligatory community membership to create brand meaning.

Finally this research does recognize that this methodology captured Cardrona's brand culture at a single moment in time and subsequently investigation may exhibit different findings. This research does not aim to represent a comprehensive picture of all seasonal ski workers or be generalisable in any way but to understand in depth a contested and commonly misrepresented phenomenon; seasonal snowsport workers as key meaning creators for destination brands and passionate enthusiasts for their lifestyle. This research is an exemplar of interpretive pre understanding that should underpin strategic analysis informing enlightened business strategy. This work moves beyond descriptive qualitative accounts by digging through the layers of meaning to show how cultural experience is both personally and socio-historically located. It shows how these cultural practices work in complicated and unintended ways to both re-create and maintain a brand culture in a dynamic process.

References

Bengtsson, A. and Ostberg, J. (2006) 'Researching the cultures of brands'(ed.) in R.W. Belk, *Handbook of Qualitative Research Methods in Marketing*. Northampton, MA: Edward Elgar, pp. 83–93.

Bengtsson, A., Ostberg, J. and Kjeldgaard, D. (2005) 'Prisoners in paradise: subcultural resisitance to the marketization of tatooing', *Consumption Markets & Culture*, 8(3): 261–74.

Boon, B. (2006) 'When leisure and work are allies: the case of skiers and tourist resort hotels', *Career Development International*, 11(7): 594–608.

Braun, V. and Clarke, V. (2006) 'Using thematic analysis in psychology', *Qualitative Research in Psychology*, 3(1): 77–101.

Creswell, J. (2003) *Research Design: Qualitative, Quantitative and Mixed Methods Approaches*. London: Sage.

de Chernatony, L. and McDonald, M.H.B. (2003) *Creating Powerful Brands*. Oxford: Butterworth-Heinemann.

Dickson, T. and Huyton, J. (2008) 'Customer service, employee welfare and snowsports tourism in Australia', *International Journal of Contemporary Hospitality Management*, 20: 199–214.

Duncan, T. (2008) 'The internationalisation of tourism labour markets: working and playing in a ski resort', in C.M. Hall and T. Coles (eds) *International Business and Tourism: Global issues, Contemporary Interactions*. London: Routledge, pp. 181–94.

Guba, E.G. and Lincoln, Y.S. (2005) 'Paradigmatic controversies, contradictions, and emerging influences', in N.K. Denzin and Y.S. Lincoln (eds) *The Sage Handbook of Qualitative Research*. Thousand Oaks, CA: Sage, pp. 191–215.

Hall, D. (2002) 'Brand development, tourism and national identity: the re-imaging of former Yugoslavia', *Journal of Brand Management*, 9(4/5): 323–34.

Hatch, M.J. and Schultz, M. (2001) 'Are the strategic stars aligned for your corporate brand?', *Harvard Business Review*, February: 128–34.

Holt, D.B. (2004) *How Brands Become Icons: The Principles of Cultural Branding*. Boston, MA: Harvard Business School Press.

Ismert, M. and Petrick, F. (2004) 'Indicators and standards of quality related to seasonal employment in the ski industry', *Journal of Travel Research*, 43: 46–56.

Kates, S.M. (2004) 'The dynamics of brand legitimacy: an interpretive study in the gay men's community', *Journal of Consumer Research*, 31(September): 455–64.

Kozinets, R.V. (2002) 'Can consumers escape the market? Emancipatory illuminations from burning man', *Journal of Consumer Research*, 29(June): 20–38.

Mayring, P. (2000) 'Qualitative content analysis', *Forum: Qualitative Social Research*, 1(2), Art. 20, Online: Available at: http://nbn-resolving.de/urn:nbn:de:0114-fqs0002204 (last accessed 1 May 2013).

Montoya, P. and Vandehey, T. (2005) *The Brand Called You: The Ultimate Brand-Building and Business Development Handbook to Transform Anyone into an Indispensable Personal Brand*. Tustin, CA: Peter Montoya Publishing.
Morgan, N., Pritchard, A. and Pride, R. (eds) (2002) *Destination Branding: Creating the Unique Destination Proposition*. Oxford, UK: Butterworth-Heinemann.
Mosley, R.W. (2007) 'Customer experience, organisational culture and the employer brand', *Journal of Brand Management*, 15(2): 123–34.
Muniz, A. and O'Guinn, T. (2001) 'Brand communities', *Journal of Consumer Research*, 27 (March): 412–32.
Nysveen, H., Pedersen, Per. E. and Skard, S. (2012) 'Brand experiences in service organizations: exploring the individual effects of brand experience dimensions', *Journal of Brand Management*, 20: 404–2.
O'Cass, A. and Grace, D. (2004) 'Exploring consumer experiences with a service brand', *Journal of Product & Brand Management*, 13(4): 257–68.
Patton, M. (2002) *Qualitative Research and Evaluation Method*. Thousand Oaks, CA: Sage.
Sullivan, M. (2001) 'Researcher and researched – community perspectives: toward bridging the gap', *Health Education and Behavior*, 28(2): 130–49.
Thomas, D. (2006) 'A general inductive approach for qualitative data analysis', *American Journal of Evaluation*, 27(2): 237–46.

33

Determinants and outcomes of tourists' emotional responses

Towards an integrative model for destination brands

Sameer Hosany and Girish Prayag

Introduction

In recent years, academics and practitioners have garnered increased interest in understanding affective dimensions of tourists' experiences and the meanings of places/destinations (e.g. Ekinci and Hosany 2006; Hosany *et al.* 2006; Gretzel *et al.* 2006). Intensifying competition among regions, countries and cities requires marketers to appreciate the symbolic value and experiential qualities of the tourism offerings (Gretzel *et al.* 2006). Tourist experiences often include satisfying and pleasurable emotions (Gnoth 1997; Aho 2001; Coghlan, Buckley and Weaver 2012). Tourist emotional reactions are fundamental determinants of satisfaction, behavioural intentions and attitudes (Gnoth 1997). Prior studies also establish that people develop relationships with places (e.g. Hidalgo and Hernandez 2001) and elicit emotions toward their immediate physical and social environment (Farber and Hall 2007). Despite the significance of emotions in tourism, empirical studies investigating the emotional associations or meanings tourist attached to places/destinations remain limited (Yuksel, Yuksel and Bilim 2010).

Realizing the lack of research, Hosany and Gilbert (2010) develop the destination emotion scale (DES) to measure tourists' emotional responses toward holiday destinations. Hosany (2012), building on cognitive appraisal theories, further investigates the conditions under which tourists elicit the emotions of joy, love and positive surprise. This chapter extends Hosany and Gilbert (2010) and Hosany's (2012) conceptualizations to propose an integrative model linking determinants and consequences of tourists' emotional responses toward destinations, drawing from a cross-disciplinary review of the literature. Tourist destinations are characterized here as brands (Boo, Busser and Baloglu 2009; Qu, Kim and Im 2011; García, Gómez and Molina 2012) representing an amalgam of several components (e.g. hotels, visitor attractions) that combine to create a holistic experience (Murphy, Pritchard and Smith 2000).

The chapter aims to provide an overview of the extant literature addressing the role of emotion in consumer and tourism research. Next, drawing on research in psychology, marketing and tourism, the chapter discusses the measurement of tourists' emotional responses. The chapter then identifies the determinants and consequences of tourists' emotional responses.

Thereafter, the chapter advances an integrated conceptual model linking determinants and consequences of tourist emotional responses. Finally, the chapter discusses implications for marketing practices and highlights directions for future research.

Role of emotion in consumer and tourism research

A rich body of research establishes emotion's relevance in marketing. Emotions are defined as states characterised by episodes of intense feelings associated with a specific referent and instigate specific response behaviours (Cohen and Areni 1991). Emotions play an important function in defining consumption experiences and influencing consumer reactions. Early studies mainly focus on consumers' emotional responses to advertising (e.g. Aaker, Stayman and Hagerty 1986; Edell and Burke 1987). Other research examines emotions generated by specific product use (e.g. Holbrook, Chesnut, Oliva and Greenleaf 1984), services (e.g. Liljander and Strandvik 1997), or in general consumption situations (e.g. Derbaix and Pham 1991). Scholars also investigate the impact of consumption emotions on global evaluative measures such as satisfaction (Ladhari 2007a) and behavioural intentions (Zeelenberg and Pieters 2004). Some studies demonstrate the appropriateness of emotions as a segmentation variable (e.g. Westbrook and Oliver 1991; Oliver and Westbrook 1993; Maute and Dubé 1999; Schoefer and Diamantopoulos 2009). For example, Westbrook and Oliver (1991) identify five patterns of emotional response to product experiences – happy/content, pleasant (positive) surprise, unemotional, unpleasant (negative) surprise and angry/upset. Schoefer and Diamantopoulos (2009) uncover four distinct emotional response styles during service recovery encounters – negatives, positives, concerned and unemotionals. Each cluster systematically corresponds to different perceptions of satisfaction, trust and commitment.

Similarly, in recent years, the role of emotion in tourism research has received unprecedented recognition (Gnoth 1997; Goossens 2000). For example, previous studies show emotions affect tourists' satisfaction (e.g. del Bosque and San Martin 2008) and behavioural intentions (e.g. Bigne, Andreu and Gnoth 2005). Emotions also influence decisions to purchase tourism and leisure services (Goossens 2000; Kwortnik and Ross 2007). For example Goossens (2000) shows that emotion affects tourist destination choice. Kwortnik and Ross (2007) note that tourists experience a variety of positive emotions, such as comfort and pleasure, as they plan their vacation. In addition, Bigné and Andreu (2004) demonstrate emotion's suitability as a segmentation variable for tourism and leisure services. Bigné and Andreu's (2004) findings bifurcate tourists into less versus greater emotion segments. Tourists with greater positive emotions display favourable behavioural intentions (loyalty and willingness to pay more).

Measurement of tourists' emotional responses

The psychology literature offers two main approaches to describe and categorize emotions: dimensional and categorical. The first approach conceptualizes emotions using few dimensions such as positive and negative (Watson *et al.* 1988), or pleasantness and arousal (Russell 1980). The dimensional approach does not require distinguishing between distinct negative (e.g. anger, fear or sadness) and positive (e.g. contentment, happiness or excitement) emotions (Rucker and Petty 2004). The second approach conceptualises emotion as a set of idiosyncratic affective states (e.g. joy, anger, sadness, surprise). Research shows that discrete emotions of the same valence (e.g. regret and disappointment) independently affect satisfaction (Machleit and Eroglu 2000), judgement (Lerner and Keltner 2000) and behaviour (Zeelenberg and Pieters 2004).

Research in marketing measures emotions via two broad methods: self-report (verbal measures) and psychophysiological indices (non-verbal measures). In consumer studies, self-reports remain the most popular method to capture emotional experiences (Diener 2000). Typically, respondents rate their emotional reactions to a stimulus. Marketing scholars often adapt psychology-based self-report measures to fit the consumption context. Four common psychological scales include Plutchik's (1980) eight primary emotions, Izard's (1977) Differential Emotion Scales (DES), Mehrabian and Russell's (1974) Pleasure, Arousal and Dominance (PAD) scale and Watson *et al.* (1988) Positive Affect and Negative Affect Scale (PANAS).

In recent years, concerns are surfacing about the applicability, reliability and validity of adapting psychological emotion scales in consumer studies (e.g. Richins 1997; Laros and Steenkamp 2005; Schoefer and Diamantopoulos 2008). Since these scales were not developed purposely for consumer research, they are unlikely to capture the entire domain of consumption related emotions, suggesting important shortcomings. Realizing the need for sound measures, some marketing scholars have developed context-specific emotion scales. For example, Richins' (1997) Consumption Emotion Set (CES) captures emotions encountered during consumption experiences. Honea and Dahl's (2005) Promotion Affect Scale (PAS) assesses consumers' emotional reactions to sale promotion offers. More recently, Schoefer and Diamantopoulos (2008) developed a scale to measure experienced emotions during service recovery encounters.

Hosany and Gilbert (2010) note existing taxonomies from psychology and marketing do not take into account tourism and destination-specific characteristics. Adapting existing scales fails to achieve content validity, leading to erroneous conclusions (see Haynes *et al.* 1995). To measure tourists' emotional responses toward destinations, by means of two empirical studies, Hosany and Gilbert (2010) follow a rigorous process, consistent with conventional guidelines in developing the destination emotion scale (DES). The DES captures the diversity and intensity of tourists' emotional responses toward destinations. Hosany and Gilbert's (2010) study reveal a parsimonious three-dimensional (joy, love and positive surprise) 15-item scale, displaying solid psychometric properties in terms of unidimensionality, reliability and validity (see Table 33.1).

The scale dimensions are theoretically consistent with past and more recent conceptualizations of emotion in consumer research. Five items measure Joy (cheerful, pleasure, joy, enthusiasm and delight). Joy is an intrinsic component of peak experiences (e.g. Mathes *et al.* 1982) that is often

Table 33.1 The destination emotion scale: initial and final scale statistics

Items	*Study 1 (S1): N=200*		*Study 2 (S2): N=520*		*S1*	*S2*	*S1*	*S2*	*S1*	*S2*
	Factor loading[a]	*Item-total correlation*	*Factor loading[b]*	*Item-total correlation*	*Coefficient alpha (α)*		*Composite reliability*		*Average variance extracted*	
Joy					.87	.89	.83	.86	.50	.55
Cheerful[c]	.83	.76	.71	.72						
Pleasure[c]	.70	.73	.71	.77						
Joy[c]	.69	.73	.79	.74						
Enthusiasm[c]	.69	.69	.69	.71						
Delight[c]	.60	.70	.79	.76						
Enjoyment	.73	.70								
Happiness	.71	.75								
Entertained	.71	.69								
Comfortable	.69	.61								

(Continued)

Table 33.1 (Continued)

Items	*Study 1 (S1): N=200*		*Study 2 (S2): N=520*		*S1*	*S2*	*S1*	*S2*	*S1*	*S2*
	Factor loading[a]	*Item-total correlation*	*Factor loading[b]*	*Item-total correlation*	*Coefficient alpha (α)*		*Composite reliability*		*Average variance extracted*	
Love					.85	.87	.84	.88	.51	.59
Tenderness[c]	.83	.71	.78	.70						
Love[c]	.70	.73	.82	.76						
Caring[c]	.70	.67	.80	.71						
Affection[c]	.66	.64	.74	.68						
Warm-hearted[c]	.66	.69	.71	.66						
Sentimental	.74	.61								
Romantic	.64	.60								
Compassionate	.58	.60								
Passionate	.55	.61								
Positive surprise					.84	.85	.84	.89	.52	.62
Amazement[c]	.84	.78	.90	.77						
Astonishment[c]	.80	.70	.86	.74						
Fascinated[c]	.77	.71	.72	.65						
Inspired[c]	.61	.58	.74	.55						
Surprise[c]	.56	.50	.61	.57						

Source: Adapted from Hosany and Gilbert (2010)

Notes: [a] From principal components factor analysis; [b] From confirmatory factor analysis; [c] Items comprise the final destination emotion scale.

associated with playfulness (Frijda 1986), and affirms the meaningfulness of life (de Rivera, Verette and Weiner 1989). Hosany and Gilbert (2010) demonstrate that joy is a key aspect of tourists' emotional responses. Past research (e.g. Currie 1997; Goossens 2000) shows the pursuit of pleasurable experiences is a key motivational factor in tourism. Carr (2002) further notes that tourists have a higher propensity for pleasure seeking experiences while on holidays.

The love dimension includes items such as tenderness, caring and affection. Love is defined as 'an attitude held by a person toward a particular person, involving predispositions to think, feel, and behave in certain ways toward that other person' (Rubin 1970: 265). Prior research has established the relevance of love as a marketing construct (e.g. Ahuvia 2005; Carroll and Ahuvia 2006; Albert, Merunka and Valette-Florence 2008; Batra, Ahuvia and Bagozzi 2012). All of these studies show that consumers can experience the feelings of love toward products and brands. Similarly, destination marketing organizations (DMOs) emphasise 'love' in their marketing and branding strategies. Some examples include the 'I Love New York' seminal campaign, Taiwan 'Touch your Heart' slogan and Hong Kong 'Live it. Love it' media campaign.

The DES last dimension includes items such as amazement, inspired and astonishment. Surprise is often characterized as a neutrally valenced and short-lived emotion that arises as a result of unexpected occurrences (Meyer, Reisenzein and Schutzwohl 1997). Surprise can also be accompanied by other emotions to elicit either positive surprise (e.g. surprise and joy) or negative surprise (e.g. surprise and anger). Over the years, consumer research has been mostly interested in positive surprise and its relationship with consumption related outcome variables such as satisfaction, loyalty and word-of-mouth. For example, Westbrook and Oliver (1991) note that positively surprised customers are usually more satisfied and exhibit higher levels of loyalty. Likewise, destination marketers, incorporate 'surprise' in their branding campaigns (e.g. 'Amazing Thailand, Amazing Value'). Other examples include: Germany 'Simply Inspiring'; Netherlands 'Surprising Cities'; 'Fascinating' Malaysia; and Edinburgh 'Inspiring Capital'.

The DES dimensions represent positive valence emotions. A plausible explanation for the absence of negative emotions in tourists' evaluations is that vacations are characterized as a set of positive experiential processes (Mannell and Iso-Ahola 1987; Nawijn 2011). Vacations are usually positively anticipated (Mitchell *et al.* 1997) and are primarily consumed for hedonic purposes (Otto and Ritchie 1996). Tourists seek pleasurable and memorable experiences through the consumption of their vacation (Currie 1997). In addition, people tend to reconstruct their holistic experiences by forgetting unsatisfactory occurrences (Klaaren, Hodges and Wilson 1994) in order to reduce their cognitive dissonance (Cooper and Fazio 1984).

Nevertheless, some destinations around the world are judged risky, elicit negative emotions such as fear and tourists worry about visiting them (Larsen, Brun and Ogaard, 2009). Other studies on dark tourism show that some places evoke negative emotions including fear, sadness, depression and empathy (Miles, 2002; Kang *et al.* 2012). Realizing the need for a balanced sampling of tourists' emotional responses, Hosany and Prayag's (2013) study adapted the DES, adding a negative emotion dimension – unpleasantness (unhappiness, displeasure, regret, sadness and disappointment). Hosany and Prayag (2013) uncover a small segment of tourists exhibiting high levels of negative emotions toward destination brands.

Appraisal dimensions as determinants of tourists' emotional responses

Evolution in psychology research unifies the study of emotions into cognitive appraisal theories. Arnold (1960) first coins the term appraisal referring to the cognitive process involved in emotion elicitation. Appraisal theories consider cognition as antecedent of emotion '[E]valuation and interpretations of events, rather than events per se determine whether an emotion will be felt and which emotion it will be' (Roseman, Spindel and Jose 1990: 899). For example, joy is elicited by the appraisal of an event as beneficial and within reach, anger by appraising an event as goal obstructive (Frijda 1986). The psychology literature is replete with many independently developed, yet highly convergent appraisal theories (Scherer 1988). Following Arnold's (1960) classical view, four independent appraisal theories appeared in the 1980s (i.e. Scherer 1984; Roseman 1984, 1991; Smith and Ellsworth 1985; Frijda 1986). All four theories suggest emotions are derived as a result of an individual's subjective evaluations of a situation or event on a number of appraisal dimensions. The four theories differ in terms of the number of appraisal dimensions but there is a high degree of convergence with regard to the nature of appraisal dimensions. Pleasantness, goal congruence, unexpectedness, certainty and compatibility with social or personal standards are common across the proposed models.

Recent consumer research highlights the merits of appraisal theories to understand the determinants of consumption emotions (Ruth and Otnes 2002; Johnson and Stewart 2005; Soscia 2007; Watson and Spence 2007). For example, Watson and Spence (2005) propose an integrative theory of consumer behaviour linking appraisals, consumption emotions and post-consumption evaluations such as satisfaction and behavioural intentions. However, with the notable exception of Hosany's (2012) study, applications of appraisal theories in tourism research remain largely underexplored. Hosany (2012) further extended Hosany and Gilbert's (2010) conceptualization and investigates the determinants of tourists' emotional responses toward destination brands. Consistent with cognitive appraisal theories, canonical correlation analysis supports an emotion-appraisal model in the tourism context. Results indicate that appraisals of pleasantness, goal congruence and internal self-compatibility elicit the emotional responses of love, joy and surprise toward destinations.

Pleasantness refers to the appraisal of whether the outcome of a situation is good or bad (positive or negative) (Watson and Spence 2007). The appraisal of pleasantness is a fundamental dimension and accounts for the majority of variance explained in attempts to categorise emotions (Smith and Ellsworth 1985; Ruth, Brunel and Otnes 2002). Furthermore, goal congruence, referred to as motive consistency (Roseman *et al.* 1990), desirability (Ortony, Clore and Collins 1988) or goal significance (Scherer 1984) involves an assessment of the degree to which a situation is or is not conducive to goal fulfilment. A close link exists between people's goals and the emotions they experience (Carver and Scheier 1990). Goal-congruent situations lead to positive emotions and goal-incongruent situations generate negative emotions. Holidaying is a form of leisure in which tourists anticipate to have fun, pleasurable, satisfying and memorable experiences (Sirgy 2010). If tourists, at the end of their holiday, achieve their desired goals, positive emotions are elicited toward the destination.

Internal self-compatibility involves assessing the degree to which an event is compatible with one's self-concept (Scherer 1984, 1988). Hosany's (2012) results indicate that when tourists perceive the destination experience as compatible with their internal self, such a situation elicits joy, love and positive surprise. Prior studies recognize the relevance of self-image congruence in understanding tourist behaviours (e.g. Beerli, Meneses and Gil 2007; Hosany and Martin 2012). For example, Beerli *et al.* (2007) found the greater the match between a destination's image and one self-concept, the greater the tendency for tourists to visit that place.

In addition to pleasantness, goal congruence and self-compatibility, Hosany's (2012) study revealed that novelty and uncertainty elicits surprise. Novelty is an assessment of whether a stimulus event deviates from one's expectations. The appraisal of novelty is connected to the familiarity and predictability of an occurrence (Scherer 1988). Certainty involves assessing the perceived likelihood of particular outcome (Roseman 1984; Smith and Ellsworth 1985). Certainty about a situation or outcomes arises from experience or knowledge as a result of prior exposure (Johnson and Stewart 2005). The certainty dimensions differentiate emotions with a known outcome, such as joy and anticipatory emotions with unknown outcomes, such as hope and surprise (Roseman 1984; Smith and Ellsworth 1985). Hosany's (2012) findings demonstrate the importance for destination marketers to manage tourists' expectations in order to engender positively surprising experiences. In turn, pleasant surprise is associated with higher levels of satisfaction (Oliver and Westbrook 1993) and favourable word-of-mouth (Derbaix and Vanhamme 2003).

Cognitive appraisal theorists propose a range of dimensions as determinants of emotional responses. However, Hosany's (2012) study only focuses on key appraisal dimensions (as discussed above) that elicit positive emotions of joy, love and surprise. Future research could investigate the underlying conditions that cause negative emotions such as regret and disappointment toward destination brands. Three key appraisal dimensions are relevant to understand negative emotions: fairness, coping potential and agency. The appraisal of fairness refers to the extent one perceives an event to be appropriate and fair (Frijda 1986; Scherer 1988; Smith and Ellsworth 1985). Prior studies in the context of service failure and recovery establish the fairness-emotion relationship (e.g. McColl-Kennedy and Sparks 2003). Coping potential reflects an individual's evaluation of the potential to cope with a situation to attain a desired outcome or avoid an undesired one (Lazarus 1991). Finally, appraising agency involves the attribution of cause (oneself, someone else or circumstance) to an outcome (Ortony *et al.* 1988; Roseman 1991). Consumer research shows that agency is linked to different coping strategies in response to product failures (Yi and Baumgartner 2004).

Major outcomes on tourists' emotional responses

Investigating the effects of emotions on post-consumption behaviours is an important development in consumer and tourism research (Mano and Oliver 1993; Gnoth 1997; Liljander and Strandvik 1997; Bagozzi *et al.* 1999). Prior studies demonstrate emotions influence satisfaction (e.g. del Bosque and San Martin 2008) and behavioural intentions (e.g. Ladhari 2007b). The next section reviews the effects of emotion on satisfaction and loyalty intentions.

Effects of emotion on satisfaction

Emotions arising from consumption experiences deposit affective memory traces which consumers process to form post-consumption evaluations of satisfaction (Westbrook and Oliver 1997). Satisfaction is a positive reaction resulting from a favourable appraisal of a consumption experience (Babin and Griffin 1998). The direct link between positive emotion and satisfaction is well documented in the marketing literature (e.g. Mano and Oliver 1993; Liljander and Strandvik 1997; Ladhari 2007a). Satisfaction is a key outcome of positive emotional responses such as pleasure, interest and joy (Oliver 1997). However, mixed evidence exists about the relationship between negative emotions and satisfaction. Previous research found a significant influence of negative emotion on customer satisfaction (e.g. Westbrook 1987). Other studies establish that negative emotion has no effect on satisfaction (e.g. Westbrook and Oliver 1991; van Dolen *et al.* 2004). A plausible explanation could be that satisfaction is an affective state and shares common variance with positive emotions (Bagozzi *et al.* 1999). Consequently, compared to negative emotions, a stronger link is expected between satisfaction and positive emotion (Dubé, Bélanger and Trudeau 1996). Research in tourism also confirms the direct influence of emotions on satisfaction (e.g. Bigné *et al.* 2005; Yuksel and Yuksel 2007; Faullant *et al.* 2011).

Effects of emotion on behavioural intentions

Modelling customer loyalty remains an important area of research in marketing and tourism literatures. Loyalty is conceptualized as a commitment to repurchase a brand or re-patronize a preferred product/service (Dick and Basu 1994). Prior studies operationalize loyalty in terms of three behavioural variables: intention to return, willingness to recommend and word-of-mouth (e.g. Cronin *et al.* 2000; Soscia 2007). Research confirms the relationship between positive emotions and intention to return (e.g. Bloemer and de Ruyter 1999), willingness to recommend (Lee *et al.* 2008; Jang and Namkung 2009); and word-of-mouth (Ladhari 2007b). In contrast, a relatively small number of studies (e.g. Zeelenberg and Pieters 2004; Soscia 2007; Romani, Grappi and Dali 2012) investigate the effects of negative emotions on behavioural outcomes. For example, Zeelenberg and Pieters (2004) establish that regret and disappointment is related to negative word-of-mouth. Soscia (2007) study further reveals that guilt inhibits negative word-of-mouth.

Conclusions and future research

This chapter establishes the relevance of emotion in tourism research. Based on a cross-disciplinary review of the literature, determinants and outcomes of tourist emotional responses toward destination brands are identified and summarized in Figure 33.1.

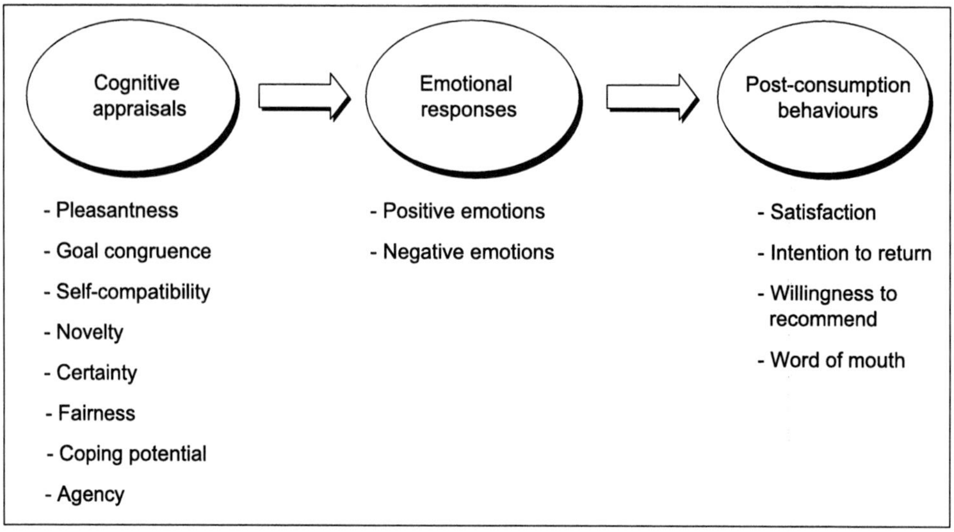

Figure 33.1 Destination brand emotion model: appraisals, emotional responses and post-consumption behaviours.

To further theoretical developments, researchers can adapt the proposed model to study both positive and negative tourist emotional responses towards destination brands. For example, in modelling positive emotional experiences, key appraisal determinants are pleasantness, goal congruence, self-compatibility and relevant outcomes variables are satisfaction, intention to return, willingness to recommend and word-of-mouth. However, prior studies tend to focus on the positive experiential aspects of tourism and research on dissatisfying vacation experiences is often neglected. For researchers interested in studying tourists' negative emotional responses (e.g. regret and disappointment), the relevant cognitive appraisal dimensions are fairness, coping potential, agency and the outcome variables are dissatisfaction, complaining behaviour and behavioural intentions.

From a pragmatic point of view, the proposed model offers implications for marketing destination brands. It is important for destination marketers to monitor the nature of tourists' emotional responses. Such knowledge will enable destination brands to better meet the expectations of tourists, resulting in favourable attentions and behavioural intentions. Tourism providers should engineer positive emotions to create enjoyable and memorable experiences. To instigate an emotional appeal, many tourist destinations have successfully employed imagery, visual effects and music in their advertising. Examples of latest promotional media campaigns emphasizing positive emotions include Australia's 'There's Nothing Like Australia' and Cyprus' 'In Your Heart'.

In addition, the appraisals of pleasantness, goal congruence and internal self-compatibility are identified as the main determinants of joy, love and positive surprise. The various players involved in shaping the holistic destination brand experience should strive to understand tourists' specific goals and create pleasant experiences in order to consistently elicit positive emotional responses. Marketers can develop segmentation strategies based on tourists' goals. Different tourists at the same destination have different travel goals and will appraise their experiences differently. In addition, destination marketers could manipulate their advertising message to prospective tourists' self-concept. Previous research establishes that advertising appeals congruent with one's self-concept are superior to incongruent appeals in enhancing advertising effectiveness (Graef,1996; Hong and Zinkhan 1995).

Future research

Mixed emotions

Tourists can display distinct positive and negative emotional responses toward destinations. However, no studies can be identified investigating the effects of mixed emotions in tourism. Mixed emotions are the experience of multiple positive and/or negative emotions (Otnes *et al.* 1997). Research in marketing (e.g. Williams and Aaker 2002; Olsen *et al.* 2005; Lau-Gesk 2005) and psychology (e.g. Larsen, McGraw and Cacioppo 2001; Schmmack 2001) establishes it is common for individuals to experience mixed emotions. Increases in positive emotions do not come necessarily at the expense of negative emotions (Andrale and Cohen 2007). Future research should investigate the conditions eliciting mixed emotional responses toward destinations and the resulting effects on tourist post-travel behaviour.

Discriminant validity of the destination emotion scale

The DES display sound measurement properties but further research is needed to establish its discriminant validity with other related constructs, such as place attachment. Place attachment is the emotional bond between an individual and a particular spatial setting (Williams *et al.* 1992). Two distinct dimensions represent the place attachment construct: place dependence (functional attachment) and place identity (emotional attachment). Place dependence reflects the importance of a place in providing features and conditions that support a person's goals or desired activities (Stokols and Shumaker 1981). Place identity refers to the symbolic importance of a place as a repository for emotions that give meaning and purpose to life (Guiliani and Feldman 1993).

Cross-cultural studies

The proposed model builds on Hosany and Gilbert (2010) and Hosany (2012) earlier works on tourist emotional experiences. The two studies are specific to one culture (British nationals). People of different cultures and languages categorise emotions differently (Russell 1991). Previous research also concludes that appraisal patterns are culture specific (Stipek, Weiner and Li 1989) and some appraisal dimensions (e.g. self-compatibility) are cross-culturally different. To further advance knowledge, Steenkamp and Burgess (2002) emphasize the need for researchers to test measures in different countries. Future studies need to validate the proposed model using tourists from different nationalities/cultures and across various destination brands of different geographical sizes (e.g. cities versus countries). Such research can further our understanding of the complex relationship between culture, emotions and tourist behaviour.

On-site versus retrospective evaluations of tourists' emotions

Studies in tourism mostly measure emotions retrospectively using post-visit surveys (e.g. Hosany and Gilbert 2010). However, relying on retrospective evaluations can be problematic in capturing tourists' emotional responses (Cutler, Larsen and Bruce 1996). Retrospective reports are vulnerable to memory reconstructions (Kahneman 1999). In addition, emotions are dynamic and time-dependent (Kuppens, Stouten and Mesquita 2009). Over the duration of a visit, tourists' self-reported emotions vary in type and intensity (Lee and Kyle 2012). Future research should attempt to capture in-situ (on-site) tourists' emotional responses using, for example, the experience sampling procedure. In experience sampling methodology (ESM), respondents complete repeated assessments over the course of time (Scollon, Kim-Prieto and Diener 2003). ESM minimizes biases associated with retrospective recall (Vogt and Stewart 1998).

References

Aaker, D.A., Stayman, D.M. and Hagerty, M.R. (1986) 'Warmth in advertising: Measurement, impact and sequence effects', *Journal of Consumer Research*, 12(4): 365–81.

Aho, S.K. (2001) 'Towards a general theory of touristic experiences: Modelling experience process in tourism', *Tourism Review*, 56(3): 33–7.

Ahuvia, A.C. (2005) 'Beyond the extended self: Love objects and consumers' identity narratives', *Journal of Consumer Research*, 32(1): 171–84.

Albert, N., Merunka, D. and Valette–Florence, P. (2008) 'When consumers love their brands: Exploring the concept and its dimensions', *Journal of Business Research*, 61(10): 1062–75.

Andrade, E.B. and Cohen, J.B. (2007) 'On the consumption of negative feelings', *Journal of Consumer Research*, 34(3): 283–300.

Arnold, M.B. (1960) *Emotion and Personality*. New York: Columbia University Press.

Babin, B.J. and Griffin, M. (1998) 'The nature of satisfaction: An updated examination and analysis', *Journal of Business Research*, 41(2): 127–36.

Bagozzi, R.P., Gopinath, M. and Nyer, P.U. (1999) 'The role of emotions in marketing', *Journal of the Academy of Marketing Science*, 27(2): 184–206.

Batra, R., Ahuvia, A. and Bagozzi, P. (2012) 'Brand love', *Journal of Marketing*, 76(2): 1–16.

Bigné, J. E. and Andreu, L. (2004) 'Emotions in segmentation', *Annals of Tourism Research*, 31(3): 682–96.

Bigné, J.E., Andreu, L. and Gnoth, J. (2005) 'The theme park experience: an analysis of pleasure, arousal and satisfaction', *Tourism Management*, 26(6): 833–44.

Bloemer, J. and de Ruyter, K. (1999) 'Customer loyalty in high and low involvement service settings: The moderating impact of positive emotions', *Journal of Marketing Management*, 15(4): 315–30.

Boo, S., Busser, J. and Baloglu, S. (2009) 'A model of customer–based brand equity and its application to multiple destinations', *Tourism Management*, 30(2): 219–31.

Carr, N. (2002) 'The tourism-leisure behavioural continuum', *Annals of Tourism Research*, 29(4): 972–86.

Carver, C.S. and Scheier, M.F. (1990) 'Origins and functions of positive and negative affect: A control-process view', *Psychological Review*, 97(1): 19–35.

Coghlan, A., Buckley, R. and Weaver, D. (2012) 'A framework for analysing awe in tourism experiences', *Annals of Tourism Research*, 39(3): 1710–14.

Cohen, J.B. and Areni, C. (1991) 'Affect and consumer behaviour', in Robertson, S.T. and Kassarjian, H.H. (eds) *Handbook of Consumer Behaviour.* Englewood Cliffs, NJ: Prentice Hall, pp. 188–240.

Cooper, J. and Fazio, R.H. (1984) 'A new look at dissonance theory', in Berkowitz, L. (ed.) *Advances in Experimental Social Psychology.* New York: Academic Press, pp. 229–66.

Cronin, J., Brady, M. and Hult, G. (2000) 'Assessing the effects of quality, value and customer satisfaction on consumer behavioral intentions in service environments', *Journal of Retailing*, 76(2): 193–218.

Currie, R.R. (1997) 'A pleasure-tourism behaviors framework', *Annals of Tourism Research*, 24(4): 884–97.

Cutler, S.E., Larsen, R.J. and Bruce, S.C. (1996) 'Repressive coping style and the experience and recall of emotion: A naturalistic study of daily affect', *Journal of Personality*, 64(2): 379–405.

de Rivera, J., Verette, J.A. and Weiner, B. (1989) 'Distinguishing elation, gladness, and joy', *Journal of Personality and Social Psychology*, 57(6): 1015–23.

del Bosque, I.R. and San Martin, H. (2008) 'Tourist satisfaction: A cognitive-affective model', *Annals of Tourism Research*, 35(2): 551–73.

Derbaix, C. and Pham, M.T. (1991) 'Affective reactions to consumption situations: A pilot investigation', *Journal of Economic Psychology*, 12(2): 325–55.

Derbaix, C. and Vanhamme, J. (2003) 'Inducing word-of-mouth by eliciting surprise: A pilot investigation', *Journal of Economic Psychology*, 24(1): 99–116.

Dick, A.S. and Basu, K. (1994) 'Customer loyalty towards an integrated framework', *Journal of Academy of Marketing Science*, 22(2): 99–113.

Diener, E. (2000) 'Subjective well-being: The science of happiness and a proposal for a national index', *American Psychologist*, 55(1): 34–43.
Dubé, L., Bélanger, M.C. and Trudeau, E. (1996) 'The role of emotions in healthcare satisfaction', *Journal of Healthcare Marketing*, 16(2): 45–51.
Edell, J.A. and Burke, M.C. (1987) 'The power of feelings in understanding advertising effects', *Journal of Consumer Research*, 14(3): 421–33.
Ekinci, Y. and Hosany, S. (2006) 'Destination personality: An application of brand personality to tourism destinations', *Journal of Travel Research*, 45(2): 127–39.
Farber, M.E. and Hall, T.E. (2007) 'Emotion and environment: Visitors' extraordinary experiences along the Dalton highway in Alaska', *Journal of Leisure Research*, 39(2): 248–70.
Faullant, R., Matzler, K. and Mooradian, T.A. (2001) 'Personality, basic emotions, and satisfaction: Primary emotions in the mountaineering experience', *Tourism Management*, 32(6): 1423–30.
Frijda, N.H. (1986) *The Emotions*. Cambridge: Cambridge University Press.
García, J.A., Gómez, M. and Molina, A. (2012) 'A destination-branding model: An empirical analysis based on stakeholders', *Tourism Management*, 33(3): 646–61.
Giuliani, M.V. and Feldman, R. (1993) 'Place attachment in a developmental and cultural context', *Journal of Environmental Psychology*, 13(3): 267–74.
Gnoth, J. (1997) 'Motivation and expectation formation', *Annals of Tourism Research*, 24(2): 283–304.
Goossens, C. (2000) 'Tourism information and pleasure motivation', *Annals of Tourism Research*, 27(2): 301–21.
Graeff, R. (1996) 'Image congruence effects of product evaluation: The role of self-monitoring and public/private consumption', *Psychology & Marketing*, 13(5): 481–99.
Gretzel, U., Fesenmaier, D.R., Formica, S. and O'Leary, J.T. (2006) 'Searching for the future: Challenges faced by destination marketing organisations', *Journal of Travel Research*, 45(2): 116–26.
Haynes, S.N., Richard, D.C.S. and Kubany, E.S. (1995) 'Content validity in psychological assessment: A functional approach to concepts and methods', *Psychological Assessment*, 7(3): 238–47.
Hidalgo, M.C. and Hernandez, B. (2001) 'Place attachment: Conceptual and empirical questions', *Journal of Environmental Psychology*, 21(3): 273–81.
Holbrook, M.B., Chesnut, R.W., Oliva, T.A. and Greenleaf, E.A. (1984) 'Play as a consumption experience: The roles of emotions, performance and personality in the enjoyment of games', *Journal of Consumer Research*, 11(2): 728–39.
Honea, H. and Dahl, D.W. (2005) 'The promotion affect scale: Defining the affective dimensions of promotion', *Journal of Business Research*, 58(4): 543–51.
Hong, J.W. and Zinkhan, G.M. (1995) 'Self concept and advertising effectiveness: The influences of congruency, conspicuousness and response modes', *Psychology & Marketing*, 12(1): 53–77.
Hosany, S. (2012) 'Appraisal determinants of tourist emotional responses', *Journal of Travel Research*, 51(3): 303–14.
Hosany, S. and Gilbert, D. (2010) 'Measuring tourists' emotional experiences toward hedonic holiday destinations', *Journal of Travel Research*, 49(4): 513–26.
Hosany, S. and Martin, D. (2012) 'Self-image congruence in consumer behaviour', *Journal of Business Research*, 65(5): 685–91.
Hosany, S. and Prayag, G. (2013) 'Patterns of tourists' emotional responses, satisfaction, and intention to recommend', *Journal of Business Research*, 66(6): 730–7.
Hosany, S., Ekinci, Y. and Uysal, M. (2006) 'Destination image and destination personality: An application of branding theories to tourism places', *Journal of Business Research*, 59(5): 638–42.
Izard, E.E. (1977) *Human Emotions*. New York: Plenum Press.
Jang, S.C. and Namkung, Y. (2009) 'Perceived quality, emotions, and behavioral intentions: Application of an extended Mehrabian–Russell model to restaurant', *Journal of Business Research*, 62(4): 451–60.
Johnson, A.R. and Stewart, D.W. (2005) 'A reappraisal of the role of emotion in consumer behavior: Traditional and contemporary approaches', in Malhotra, N.K. (ed.) *Review of Marketing Research*. Armonk, NJ: M.E Sharpe, pp. 3–33.
Kahneman, D. (1999) 'Objective happiness', in Kahneman, D., Diener, E. and Schwarz, N. (eds) *Well-being: The Foundations of Hedonic Psychology*. New York: Russell Sage Foundation, pp. 85–105.
Kang, E.-J., Scott, N., Lee, T.J.and Ballantyne, R. (2012) 'Benefits of visiting a "dark tourism" site: The case of the Jeju April 3rd Peace Park, Korea', *Tourism Management*, 33(2): 257–65.
Klaaren, K.J., Hodges, S.D. and Wilson, T.D. (1994) 'The role of affective expectations in subjective experience and decision-making', *Social Cognition*, 12(2): 77–101.

Kuppen, P., Stouten, J. and Mesquita, B. (2009) 'Individual differences in emotion components and dynamics: Introduction to the special issue', *Cognition and Emotion*, 23(7): 1249–258.
Kwortnik, R.J. and Ross, W.T. (2007) 'The role of positive emotions in experiential decisions', *International Journal of Research in Marketing*, 24(4): 324–35.
Ladhari, R. (2007a) 'The movie experience: A revised approach to determinants of satisfaction', *Journal of Business Research*, 60(5): 454–62.
— (2007b) 'The effect of consumption emotions on satisfaction and word-of-mouth communications', *Psychology & Marketing*, 24(12): 1085–108.
Laros, F.J.M. and Steenkamp, J.-B.E.M. (2005) 'Emotions in consumer behavior: A hierarchical approach', *Journal of Business Research*, 58(10): 1437–45.
Larsen, J.T., McGraw, P. and Cacioppo, J.T. (2001) 'Can people feel happy and sad at the same time?', *Journal of Personality and Social Psychology*, 81(4): 684–96.
Larsen, S., Brun, W. and Øgaard, T. (2009) 'What tourists worry about – Construction of a scale measuring tourist worries', *Tourism Management*, 30(2): 260–5.
Lau-Gesk, L. (2005) 'Understanding consumer evaluations of mixed affective experiences', *Journal of Consumer Research*, 32(1): 23–8.
Lazarus, R.S. (1991) *Emotion and Adaptation*. New York: Oxford University Press.
Lazarus, R.S. and Smith, C.A. (1988) 'Knowledge and appraisal in the cognition-emotion relationship', *Cognition and Emotion*, 2(4): 281–300.
Lee, J. and Kyle, G.T. (2012) 'Recollection consistency of festival consumption emotions', *Journal of Travel Research*, 51(2): 178–90.
Lee, Y.K., Lee, C.K., Lee, S.K. and Babin, B.J. (2008) 'Festivalscapes and patrons' emotions, satisfaction, and loyalty', *Journal of Business Research*, 61(1): 56–64.
Lerner, J.S. and Keltner, D. (2000) 'Beyond valence: Toward a model of emotion-specific influences on judgement and choice', *Cognition & Emotion*, 14(4): 473–93.
Liljander, V. and Strandvik, T. (1997) 'Emotions in service satisfaction', *International Journal of Service Industry Management*, 8(2): 148–69.
Machleit, K.A. and Eroglu, S.A. (2000) 'Describing and measuring emotional response to shopping experience', *Journal of Business Research*, 49(2): 101–11.
McColl-Kennedy, J. R. and Sparks, B.A. (2003) 'Application of fairness theory to service failures and service recovery', *Journal of Service Research*, 5(3): 251–66.
Mannell, R.C. and Iso-Ahola, S.E. (1987) 'Psychological nature of leisure and tourism experience', *Annals of Tourism Research*, 14(3): 314–31.
Mano, H. and Oliver, R.L. (1993) 'Assessing the dimensionality and structure of the consumption experience: Evaluation, feeling and satisfaction', *Journal of Consumer Research*, 20(3): 451–66.
Mathes, E.W., Zevon, M.A., Roter, P.M. and Joerger, S.M. (1982) 'Peak experience tendencies: Scale development and theory testing', *Journal of Humanistic Psychology*, 22(3): 92–108.
Maute, M.F. and Dubé, L. (1999) 'Patterns of emotional responses and behavioural consequences of dissatisfaction', *Applied Psychology: An International Review*, 48(3): 349–66.
Mehrabian, A. and Russell, J.A. (1974) *An Approach to Environmental Psychology*. Cambridge, MA: MIT Press.
Meyer, W.-U., Reisenzein, R. and Schutzwohl, A. (1997) 'Toward a process analysis of emotions: The case of surprise', *Motivation and Emotion*, 21(3): 251–74.
Miles, W.F.S. (2002) 'Auschwitz: Museum interpretation and darker tourism', *Annals of Tourism Research*, 29(4): 1175–178.
Mitchell, T.R., Thompson, L., Peterson, E. and Cronk, R. (1997) 'Temporal adjustments in the evaluation of events: The "Rosy View"', *Journal of Experimental Social Psychology*, 33(4): 421–8.
Murphy, P., Pritchard, M.P. and Smith, B. (2000) 'The destination product and its impact on traveller perceptions', *Tourism Management*, 21(1): 43–52.
Nawjin, J. (2011) 'Determinants of daily happiness on vacation', *Journal of Travel Research*, 50(5): 559–66.
Oliver, R.L. (1997) *Satisfaction: A Behavioral Perspective on the Consumer*. New: McGraw-Hill.
Oliver, R. L. and Westbrook, R.A. (1993) 'Profiles of consumer emotions and satisfaction in ownership and usage', *Journal of Consumer Satisfaction, Dissatisfaction & Complaining Behavior*, 6: 12–27.
Olsen, S.O., Wilcox, J. and Olsson, U. (2005) 'Consequences of ambivalence on satisfaction and loyalty', *Psychology & Marketing*, 22(3): 247–69.
Ortony, A., Clore, G.L. and Collins, A. (1988) *The Cognitive Structure of Emotions*. New York: Cambridge University Press.
Otnes, C.C., Lowrey, T.M. and Shrum, L.J. (1997) 'Toward an understanding of consumer ambivalence', *Journal of Consumer Research*, 24(1): 80–93.

Otto, J.E. and Ritchie, B.R. (1996) 'The service experience in tourism', *Tourism Management*, 17(3): 165–74.
Plutchik, R. (1980) *Emotion: A Psychoevolutionary Synthesis*. New York: Harper and Row.
Qu, H., Kim, L.H. and Im, H.H. (2011) 'A model of destination branding: Integrating the concepts of the branding and destination image', *Tourism Management*, 32(3): 465–76.
Richins, M.L. (1997) 'Measuring emotions in the consumption experience', *Journal of Consumer Research*, 24(2): 127–46.
Romani, S., Grappi, S. and Dalli, D. (2012) 'Emotions that drive consumers away from brands: Measuring negative emotions toward brands and their behavioral effects', *International Journal of Research in Marketing*, 29(1): 55–67.
Roseman, I.J. (1984) 'Cognitive determinants of emotions: A structural theory', in Shaver, P. (ed.) *Emotions, Relationships and Health*, Vol. 5. Beverley Hills, CA: Sage, pp. 11–36.
— (1991) 'Appraisal determinants of discrete emotions', *Cognition and Emotion*, 5(3): 161–200.
Roseman, I.J., Spindel, M.S. and Jose, P.E. (1990) 'Appraisals of emotion-eliciting events: Testing a theory of discrete emotions', *Journal of Personality and Social Psychology*, 59(5): 899–915.
Rubin, Z. (1970) 'Measurement of romantic love', *Journal of Personality and Social Psychology*, 16(2): 265–73.
Rucker, D.D. and Petty, R.E. (2004) 'Emotion specificity and consumer behavior: Anger, sadness, and preference for activity', *Motivation and Emotion*, 28(1): 3–21.
Russell, J.A. (1980) 'A circumplex model of affect', *Journal of Personality and Social Psychology*, 39(6): 1161–78.
— (1991) 'Culture and the categorisation of emotions', *Psychological Bulletin*, 110(3): 426–50.
Ruth, J.A., Brunel, F.F. and Otnes, C.C. (2002) 'Linking thoughts to feelings: Investigating cognitive appraisals and consumption emotions in a mixed-emotions context', *Journal of the Academy of Marketing Science*, 30(2): 44–58.
Scherer, K.R. (1984) 'On the nature and function of emotion: A component process approach', in Scherer, K.R. and Ekman, P. (eds) *Approaches to Emotion*. Hillsdale, NJ: Lawrence Erlbaum, pp. 293–317.
— (1988) 'Criteria for emotion-antecedent appraisal: A review', in Hamilton, V., Bower, G.H. and Frijda, N.H. (eds) *Cognitive Perspectives on Emotion and Motivation*. Dordrecht, Netherlands: Kluwer Academic, pp. 89–126.
Schimmack, U. (2001) 'Pleasure, displeasure, and mixed feelings: Are semantic opposites mutually exclusive?', *Cognition and Emotion*, 15(1): 81–97.
Schoefer, K. and Ennew, C. (2005) 'The impact of perceived justice on consumers' emotional responses to service complaint experiences', *Journal of Services Marketing*, 19(5): 261–70.
Schoefer, K. and Diamantopoulos, A. (2008) 'Measuring experienced emotions during service recovery encounters: Construction and assessment of the ESRE scale', *Service Business*, 2(1): 65–81.
— (2009) 'A typology of consumers' emotional response styles during service recovery encounters', *British Journal of Management*, 20(3): 292–308.
Scollon, C.N., Kim-Prieto, C. and Diener, E. (2003) 'Experience sampling: Promises and pitfalls, strengths and weaknesses', *Journal of Happiness Studies*, 4(1): 5–34.
Sirgy, M.J. (2010) 'Toward a quality-of-life theory of leisure travel satisfaction', *Journal of Travel Research*, 49(2): 246–60.
Smith, C.A. and Ellsworth, P.C. (1985) 'Patterns of cognitive appraisal in emotion', *Journal of Personality and Social Psychology*, 48(4): 813–38.
Socia, I. (2007) 'Gratitude, delight, or guilt: The role of consumers' emotions in predicting postconsumption behaviors', *Psychology & Marketing*, 24(10): 871–94.
Steenkamp, J.-B.E.M. and Burgess, S.M. (2002) 'Optimum stimulation level and exploratory consumer behavior in an emerging consumer market', *International Journal of Research in Marketing*, 19(2): 131–50.
Stipek, D., Weiner, B. and Li, K. (1989) 'Testing some attribution-emotion relations in the people's republic of China', *Journal of Personality and Social Psychology*, 56(1): 109–16.
Stokols, D. and Shumaker, S.A. (1981) 'People in places: A transactional view of settings', in Harvey, J.H. (ed.) *Cognition, Social Behavior and the Environment*. Hillsdale, NJ: Erlbaum, pp. 441–88.
van Dolen, W., de Ruyter, K. and Lemmink, J. (2004) 'An empirical assessment of the influence of customer emotions and contact employee performance on encounter and relationship satisfaction', *Journal of Business Research*, 57(4): 437–44.
Vogt, C.A. and Stewart, S.I. (1998) 'Affective and cognitive effects of information use over the course of a vacation', *Journal of Leisure Research*, 30(4): 498–520.
Watson, D., Clark, L.A. and Tellegen, A. (1988) 'Development and validation of brief measures of positive and negative affect: The PANAS scales', *Journal of Personality and Social Psychology*, 54(6): 1063–70.

Watson, L. and Spence, M.Y. (2007) 'Causes and consequences of emotions on consumer behavior: A review and integrative cognitive appraisal theory', *European Journal of Marketing*, 41(5/6): 487–511.
Westbrook, R.A. (1987) 'Product/consumption-based affective responses and postpurchase processes', *Journal of Marketing Research*, 24(3): 258–70.
Westbrook, R.A. and Oliver, R.L. (1991) 'The dimensionality of consumption emotion patterns and consumer satisfaction', *Journal of Consumer Research*, 8(1): 84–91.
Williams, P. and Aaker, J.L. (2002) 'Can mixed emotions coexist?', *Journal of Consumer Research*, 28(4): 636–49.
Willians, D.R., Patterson, M.E., Roggenbuck, J.W. and Watson, A.E. (1992) 'Beyond the commodity metaphor: Examining the emotional and symbolic attachment to places', *Leisure Sciences*, 14(1): 29–46.
Yi, S. and Baumgartner, H. (2004) 'Coping with negative emotions in purchase-related situations', *Journal of Consumer Psychology*, 14(3): 303–17.
Yuksel, A. and Yuksel, F. (2007) 'Shopping risk perceptions: effects on tourists' emotions, satisfaction and expressed loyalty intentions', *Tourism Management*, 28(3): 703–13.
Yuksel, A., Yuksel, F. and Bilim, Y. (2010) 'Destination attachment: Effects on customer satisfaction and cognitive, affective and conative loyalty', *Tourism Management*, 31(2): 274–84.
Zeelenberg, M. and Pieters, R. (2004) 'Beyond valence in customer dissatisfaction: A review and new findings on behavioural responses to regret and disappointment in failed services', *Journal of Business Research*, 57(4): 445–55.

34

Post-disaster recovery marketing for tourist destinations

Gabby Walters and Judith Mair

Introduction

Climate change, terrorist attacks and natural disasters are all potentially devastating for tourist destinations. Some of the climate change impacts that are projected to increase over the next 50–100 years include more frequent severe weather events (for example, hurricanes, cyclones and typhoons), the increased risk of bush fire in some areas of the world, brought on by reduced rainfall, and conversely, the increased risk of flooding in other areas (IPCC 2007). Terrorist attacks such as 9/11, the Bali bombings and the attacks in London on 7/7 are rare, but nonetheless cause significant and long lasting problems. Finally, natural disasters such as earthquakes and volcanoes, while not necessarily more common than previously, have the potential to damage or destroy ever-growing towns, cities and infrastructure around the world.

The terms 'crisis' and 'disaster' are often used interchangeably, but it is important to note that they refer to slightly different situations, and that each has its own definition. The most commonly cited definition is that coined by Faulkner (2001: 136), who stated that a disaster is 'a situation where an enterprise or destination is confronted with sudden unpredictable catastrophic changes over which it has little control'. A crisis on the other hand is 'a situation where the root cause of the event is, to some extent, self-inflicted through such problems as inept management structures or practices, or a failure to adapt to change' (Faulkner 2001: 136). This chapter examines natural disasters, and while there may be some elements of poor planning and management that reveal themselves during a disaster, the chapter will not examine crises.

It is important for tourist destinations to be aware of their vulnerability to disasters, whether man-made or not. Disaster management plans should be integrated into all tourism business and operating plans at both a national and operational level. Yet, despite the obvious risks, many tourism organizations and businesses have not been well prepared when a disaster strikes, and have relied instead on ad hoc responses (Ritchie 2008; Walters and Mair 2012). Research to help tourism destinations assess how best to recover has been relatively scarce, and in many cases very descriptive (Carlsen and Liburd 2008). However, literature is building in this area (Prideaux, Coghlan and Falco-Mammone 2008), and research is beginning to demonstrate that such ad hoc measures, especially in marketing, may be ineffective and in some cases do more damage than good.

Sadly, there have been many disasters around the world which have affected tourist destinations, and therefore there have been plenty of opportunities to witness recovery efforts and to assess the effectiveness of marketing communications following such disasters. We know that it is vital for destinations and operators to have disaster management plans, yet we also know that many do not. However, research has not kept pace with the number of disasters that have occurred, and while we have some ideas how to help a destination recover from a disaster, we are not yet in the position to make any substantive claims about the best way to do this. This chapter examines visitor responses and post-disaster marketing communications in two case studies – the Brisbane and Queensland floods of 2011 and the Black Saturday Victorian Bushfires in 2009. In doing so, this chapter reviews a number of marketing techniques and messages that have been used in disaster-struck regions, and identifies those messages that appear to have been effective, and those that should not, perhaps, have been employed.

Disastrous events and the tourism market

The importance of the destination image perceived by potential tourists is universally acknowledged, given its influence on the tourist's decision-making process and ultimate destination choice (Gartner 1993; Pearlman and Melnik 2008; Lehto, Douglas and Park 2007; Armstrong and Ritchie 2008; Pearlman and Melnik 2008; Machado 2010; Dolnicar and Huybers 2007; Beirman 2006; Faulkner 2001; Walters and Clulow 2010). The downturn in visitor numbers following a disastrous event provides increasing evidence of this. Following the 2004 Tsunami, tourist arrivals to Phuket decreased by 50.4 per cent (Tourism Authority of Thailand 2005a); visitor numbers to Victoria declined significantly following the Black Saturday bushfires (DRET 2009); whilst Christchurch, NZ, experienced a loss of one million guest nights in the year following the 2011 earthquake (Carlville 2012). The global and often sensationalized coverage by the media can rapidly lead to negative perceptions, and it is these perceptions (which may not reflect reality) that have the potential to dissuade tourists from visiting the destination (Cavlek 2002; McKercher and Pine 2005; Kozak, Crotts and Law 2007). The management of such perceptions represents the biggest challenge for tourism destination marketers (DMOs), and one possible explanation for this is that little is known or understood of the precise reasons why tourists choose to stay away from disaster prone areas (even after the immediate danger has long passed), and what motivates those who choose to visit regardless. The following case study presents a snapshot of behavioural responses to a destination struck by disaster, and subsequent motivations behind a tourist's decision to travel to the destination.

Case study 1: The tourism market's response to the Queensland floods

Between December 2010 and January 2011, a series of floods hit the Australian state of Queensland and over 75 per cent of the state was underwater. Prolonged rainfall, accompanied by the mismanagement of Queensland's waterways and storage resources (Queensland Floods Commission 2012), led to the loss of 33 lives and the inundation of 29,000 homes and businesses. Over 2.5 million people were affected by the disaster, which was estimated to have cost the state in excess of 5 billion dollars. Much of the state was officially declared a disaster zone, and the majority of the state's main thoroughfares remained closed for up to seven days, leading to a significant shortage of food and water supplies in the short term. The tourism industry expected to lose up to 590 million dollars (IBISworld 2011) for the year following the event, and saw as its most immediate challenge the extensive damage to the image of its tourist product (Tourism Queensland 2011).

Critical to a DMO's success in managing consumer perceptions following an event such as this is an understanding of the intervening effect that disasters have on the tourist's behaviour. The aim of this project was to gain an understanding of the tourist's psychological and behavioural responses to the 2011 Queensland floods. An online survey was distributed to members of Queensland's interstate travel market. A database comprising 12,000 members of this population was purchased from a commercial database provider and a total of 2110 usable responses were obtained.

To gain some idea of the impact of the flood on the travel behaviour of visitors who had intended to visit Queensland at the time, respondents who did have plans to travel to the region were asked whether they had cancelled, postponed or gone ahead with their trip. Of those who had travel plans, only 14 per cent cancelled their trip, 40 per cent postponed their arrangements until a later date and 46 per cent of respondents were not deterred by the flood events and went ahead with their trip as originally planned. Respondents were also asked to provide an open-ended explanation of their decision. Accessibility to and within the state was the most common deterrent for those who had cancelled their existing travel plans. The fear of being in the way or hindering recovery efforts was also a common reason given by respondents. Many open-ended comments also presented a collection of words and phrases such as 'scared' and 'fear of the unknown', which suggested that those who had cancelled their trip may have done so out of fear. A review of the qualitative responses also suggested that those who had cancelled or postponed their trip did so out of concerns for their safety. Perceptions regarding the weather in Queensland at the time of the floods also led to the cancellation of travel plans.

Those respondents who stated they would be prepared to visit Queensland despite the floods were asked to rate their motivations or reasons behind their decision. These are listed in Table 34.1.

Two of the three primary motivations of those willing to visit the state at the time of or immediately following the floods appeared to be a sense of compassion and empathy for the Queensland community and a keenness to assist in the recovery process. The third motivation is testament to the good news stories presented via the media regarding the local community spirit and camaraderie that evidently appealed to the visitor market. On examination of the least motivating factors, it appears that curiosity or the need to witness the extent of the damage first-hand, perhaps a type of thanatourism (Lennon and Foley 2000), was not a motivating factor for

Table 34.1 Primary motivations behind willingness to visit Queensland at the time of the floods

Rank	*Motivation*	*Mean*
1	I would like to help the Queensland tourism industry recover	5.5
2	I feel sorry for the Queensland people	5.3
3	I would like to witness the community spirit seen on the media	5.0
4	I believe I could offer some assistance	4.1
4	I believe Queensland would be much the same	4.1
5	I believe it would be quieter	3.8
5	I would like to see how things have changed	3.8
6	I would feel guilty if I did nothing to help the industry recover	3.7
7	I believe it would be cheaper at this time	3.5
8	I would like to see for myself	3.3
8	I would like to see the extent of damage and destruction	3.3

the Australian visitor market. The prospect of accessing a cheaper holiday as a result of the disaster was also found to be unlikely to motivate the tourist.

Marketing implications

Based on the results, the following recommendations were put forward.

Given that access is clearly a consideration, DMOs and those responsible for the dissemination of disaster related information were advised to avoid 'regionalizing' the affected areas and to refer to each specific affected area individually when communicating to a national audience. Tourists' awareness of those areas not affected by the floods would enable them to consider alternative Queensland destinations, should they need to re-evaluate their current travel plans. DMOs were also advised to work closely with the media and other organizations likely to relay disaster related information to ensure tourists are adequately informed about the safety status of the destination. Honest and factual information from a trusted source appeared to be essential to the eradication of unnecessary fears and other negative perceptions resulting from sensationalized media coverage.

Those responsible for the management of the State's natural resources, i.e. beaches and national parks, should also take steps to ensure that regular information regarding their safety and accessibility is available to the interstate tourism market. One of the main reasons interstate visitors chose not to visit Queensland at the time of or immediately after the floods was their expectation of bad weather. In the case of flood activity, it seems logical to assume that it is accompanied by consistent rainfall, when in fact this was not the case in Queensland. To counter these perceptions, the research suggested that regular updates should also be provided regarding the weather conditions – particularly if they are favourable.

Since the two primary motivations of those willing to visit Queensland at the time of floods were firstly their desire to assist the tourism industry to recover, and secondly their sympathy for Queensland people, it was recommended that DMOs employ empathetic themes when compiling their advertising messages, themes that are likely to tap into this psychological disposition of wanting to help. Media should also be encouraged to present a more balanced approach to their coverage of the event, with emphasis on the 'good news' stories that are based on the community spirit and camaraderie that have developed as a result of the disaster.

The role of marketing post-disaster

Clearly, first thoughts and actions after a disaster are directed towards the immediate recovery efforts – rescuing people, assessing damage, stabilizing buildings and infrastructure, and caring for those injured and displaced. During this time, communication generally takes place between the relevant authorities, the victims of the disaster and the media (Henderson 2003). However, once the dust has settled, so to speak, it is not long before governments and agencies begin to consider how to help the affected area recover economically. Tourism is often seen as a good way to boost the economic recovery efforts, and as Carslen and Hughes (2008) point out, an operator's first concern is to restore visitor numbers to normal. This can be problematic on a number of levels. In the first place, the disaster may have destroyed or badly affected existing basic infrastructure such as roads, communications and power supplies. Further, the disaster may have reduced the destination's capacity to cater for visitors. Hotels, shops and restaurants may be damaged or limited in their operations (Sanders *et al.* 2008). Finally, it is likely that the disaster would have had some impact on the tourism product itself – beaches, scenery, attractions and activities (Cioccio and Michael 2007). Nonetheless, the role of marketing communications in restoring visitation to the destination is undeniable (Lehto, Douglas and Park 2008). Communicating with the tourism market may have a number of different goals, from correcting misperceptions about the scale of the disaster, to restoring confidence in the destination, reducing perceptions of risk to repairing the destination image. In each case, it is important to craft a marketing message that is likely to achieve the goal of the destination marketer.

In a review of the existing literature on post-disaster marketing for tourist destinations, Walters and Mair (2012) identified nine major themes that have been used in the past as marketing messages to encourage tourists following a disaster. Examples of the types of messages DMOs are likely to use when employing such themes are demonstrated in case study 2. Research has shown that some of these messages are more successful than others, but it is worth remembering that each disaster is unique and therefore there is unlikely to be any one message or strategy that will work on every occasion. Nonetheless, the most commonly used message types are discussed below.

Open and ready for business

This type of message is one of the most commonly used following disasters, and reflects the keenness of DMOs to see their destination's visitor numbers return to normal as soon as possible. 'Business as usual', or 'open and ready for business' messages have been used in a number of settings, including New Orleans post-Hurricane Katrina (Pearlman and Melnik 2008), Far North Queensland following Cyclone Larry (Prideaux *et al.* 2008), in the Maldives after the Boxing Day Tsunami (Carlsen and Hughes 2008) and in Canberra following the 2006 bushfires (Armstrong and Ritchie 2008). More recently, Queensland's destination marketing organization employed this message in their bid to prevent tourists cancelling their Queensland holiday plans at the time of and immediately following the 2011 floods (Walters, Mair and Ritchie 2011). There have been some criticisms of such messages, particularly where it seems clear that the destination is far from ready to cater for visitors. In the case of Queensland for example, their 'open for business' marketing attempts were being transmitted at the same time as requests from the State's Premier for charity aid and assistance to help the region to recover. This mixing of messages is not good for the overall destination, and touches on an important point, that of the identified lack of communication between various stakeholders that govern a destination (Xu and Grunewald 2009).

Solidarity messages

As demonstrated in the previous case study, in the aftermath of a disaster it is normal for adults to experience numerous powerful emotional reactions (Vastfjall, Peters and Slovic 2008; Lazarus 1991; Raholm, Arman and Rehnsfeldt 2004; Walters and Clulow 2010). These feelings may also have an impact on everyday decisions (Vastfjall *et al.* 2008; Schwarz, Zuma and Clore 1988) and the impact of emotions on the tourist's decision-making process is well documented (Crouch and Louviere 2001; Kahneman 1995; Otto and Ritchie 1996; Tuan Pham, Pracejus and Hughes 2001). Several destinations have used messages intended to evoke an emotional reaction among potential visitors. Examples are 'Canberra needs your support' and 'By visiting the Maldives you are helping us'. These types of messages are also intended to counteract any guilt on the part of visitors associated with the thought of getting in the way of recovery efforts. Such beliefs were identified by Walters and Clulow (2010) in their study of Victoria, Australia, following the Black Saturday bushfires in 2009. Lehto *et al.* (2008) also suggested that visitors anticipated an intensive recovery process which put them off visiting a disaster-struck destination.

Community readiness

It is important to remember that when a disaster strikes, the local community has to endure not only the initial physical impact, but also the prospect of ongoing economic hardship due to loss of businesses and income (Pearlman and Melnik 2008; Walters and Clulow 2010). Therefore, it may seem that getting tourists to return as quickly as possible would be the main aim. However, as noted above, tourists may feel that they would be intruding on locals at a bad time or imposing on people in difficult situations. One way to counteract this is to design marketing messages that reassure potential visitors that the community wants them to come. Promoting community readiness in this way is potentially an effective message. 'We are ready to welcome you' was used in Sri Lanka following the Boxing Day Tsunami (Robinson and Jarvie 2008).

Messages to restore confidence

One of the key problems with marketing a tourist destination post-disaster is that the market may have lost a degree of confidence in the affected destination. This is often based on the reports that they have seen in the media, which may be misleading and are often accused of being sensationalized (Hystad and Keller 2008) or perpetuating disaster myths (Faulkner 2001). On some occasions, media coverage has led to confusion regarding the extent of the disaster by exaggerating the extent of damage or the size of the affected area (Walters and Clulow 2010). Lehto *et al.* (2008) suggest that the first marketing message should aim to restore confidence in the minds of potential visitors. The central theme of this message type focuses on reassuring visitors that the effect of the disaster is less than they think. Examples of messages used in this context include 'Our heart's still going strong' (Armstrong and Ritchie 2008), used to promote Canberra after bushfires in 2004; 'New Orleans – never better' (Pearlman and Melnik 2008), following Hurricane Katrina; and 'Never Better' (Prideaux *et al.* 2008), used in Far North Queensland following Tropical Cyclone Larry. It is important, however, that this message approach be considered only if destination marketers are confident that the majority of spaces tourists are likely to occupy remain relatively unaffected.

Curiosity enhancement

Sanders *et al.* (2008) highlight the importance of portraying a good news story, with less focus on the destination's need for help, and more focus on encouraging people to return to it and see it 'with fresh eyes', or to see its condition for themselves. Research suggests that messages related to curiosity enhancement are likely to be effective in post-disaster marketing. Ashworth and Hartmann (2005), for example, claim that unusual natural phenomena, such as hurricanes and floods, draw tourists to experience the unusual event and satisfy human curiosity – which, according to Mayo and Jarvis (1981), is simply a need humans are born with. Also of relevance to this approach is the concept of 'thanatourism' or 'dark tourism'. Seaton and Lennon (2004) propose that the motivation to participate in this type of tourism is driven by a fascination with death and or misfortunes of others. While the majority of tourists who engage in this form of tourism are normally attracted to sites of mass or individual death, internment sites and memorials or places that offer symbolic representations of death, one of the main driving forces is curiosity (Lennon and Foley 2000). Rittichainuwat (2008), in her study that investigated tourist motivations to visit the island of Phuket following the Boxing Day Tsunami, provides support for this proposition, revealing that curiosity was one of the primary motivations among Thai and Scandinavian tourists to visit the destination.

Messages using visitor testimonials or celebrity endorsement

Testimonials have been used successfully by a number of destinations. These can be a celebrity endorsement, or testimonials from guests who have recently visited the destination. Guest testimonials have been seen as particularly credible by potential tourists (Carlsen and Hughes 2008), and as such may be of considerable value to destinations. However, in our celebrity-obsessed society, an endorsement from a well-known figure may capture the viewer's attention, increase public awareness of the destination and encourage consumers to purchase the product, or visit the destination (Avraham and Ketter 2008). Swerdlow and Swerdlow (2003) suggest that celebrity association, bought or contrived, has certain advantages and risks. A celebrity product association can capture a viewer's attention, increase the public's awareness of the product, and cause consumers to purchase the product endorsed. In contrast, celebrity product associations can be very costly and risky based on the potentially volatile image, nature and credibility of the spokesperson used. Examples of celebrity use in endorsing destinations struck by disaster include Olympian Grant Hackett's endorsement of Queensland's Sunshine Coast following the 2009 oil spill (Koopman 2009) and Hollywood actor Brad Pitt's advocacy following Hurricane Katrina (Moore 2010).

As well as designing marketing messages to encourage tourists to visit the destination, there may be occasions when the disaster forces a destination to make changes to its overall tourism strategy, perhaps in light of changes to the built and natural environment, or perhaps in response to low numbers of visitors following a disaster. There are a number of strategies that destinations could consider, and the most common of these are pricing strategies and product diversification strategies.

Short term discounts

A number of disaster-affected destinations have used a pricing strategy to help them to recover. In some cases this may take the form of short term price reductions, while in others it may be more about adding value to the existing product. As Lehto *et al.* (2008) point out, on occasions the product may be damaged or operating below capacity or below standard, and for this reason a discount may be offered to reflect the changed circumstances. However, in most cases short term discounting is generally considered to be a last resort. Operators are already suffering from financial difficulties due to loss of business, and discounting new business will not help them to recover (Beirman 2006). Adding value with offers such as four nights for the price of three, or two entrance tickets for the price of one, may be a better option. Research has not yet identified the long term impacts of post-disaster discounting on tourism business, but it may be that operators find it difficult to resume full prices.

Product diversification

Another option open to operators and destinations is product diversification. It has been suggested that festivals and events might encourage visitation and be a drawcard for those who have not visited the destination before (Lehto *et al.* 2008; Sanders et al. 2008). For example, Victoria's key destination marketing organization, Tourism Victoria, took this approach following the Black Saturday Bushfires and provided financial and other incentives to fire-affected destinations to organize and host an array of community festivals and events, with the expectation that intrastate tourists in particular would be drawn to these regions (Walters and Mair 2012). Other options might utilize existing attractions in a different way, for example offering special interest tours to disaster-affected areas. Biologists, for example, might be interested to see the re-growth and recovery of a burnt out forest, architects and town planners to see the results of an earthquake. However, these are likely to be small-scale and short term options, and research has not yet fully engaged with the evaluation of such strategies.

The following case study provides some insight into the effectiveness of these post-disaster marketing messages, the tourists' attitudes towards post-disaster marketing communications and the timeframe in which tourists are likely to return.

Case study 2: How and when to market a post-disaster destination: the case of Gippsland, Victoria

A study by Walters and Mair (2012) tested the effectiveness of the nine post-disaster marketing messages in encouraging visitation to a disaster-affected destination. Using Gippsland, Victoria, and the 2009 Black Saturday Bushfires as the context, the study employed an experimental design to test the effectiveness of nine mock print advertisements (see Table 34.2). The messages in these advertisements were designed by the authors for demonstrative purposes in consultation with a DMO from the region of Gippsland, one of several Victorian regions to be affected by the Black Saturday Bushfires in 2009.

The study's results indicated strong support for the use of celebrity endorsement to persuade tourists to visit a disaster-affected region. The authors stress, however, that it is important that the chosen celebrity is recognized by the target market as having some affiliation with the

Table 34.2 Common disaster recovery marketing messages

Ad number	*Theme*	*Message*
1	Open and ready for business	Gippsland, open and ready for business – come, be inspired!
2	Solidarity/ empathy	Gippsland needs you now more than ever, come and visit, support our tourism industry and let us inspire you.
3	Community readiness	Gippsland, ready to inspire you. . . . . . we wouldn't invite you if we weren't ready.
4	Restoring confidence and changing misperceptions	Gippsland, still going strong. Less than 5% of Gippsland was affected by the Victorian bushfires. In fact, some of our most inspiring national parks and destinations remain untouched. All our roads are open and for 99% of our operators it's business as usual.
5	Curiosity enhancement	Gippsland, come and see for yourself . . . Gippsland's stunning natural attractions are regenerating faster than ever. Visit now and be inspired by the fascinating landscape mosaic of fire-recovery mixed with the usual Gippsland splendour . . . don't miss this opportunity to experience the resilience of nature.
6	Short term discounts/price reductions	Gippsland is on sale! Visit our website now to take advantage of our special promotional offers and save up to 50% on accommodation, attractions and food and wine produce. Find a variety of inspiring packages starting from just $200 per couple.

Ad number	*Theme*	*Message*
7	Visitor testimonial	'. . . If you want a peaceful country or coastal break at one of our most precious destinations, now is the time to go . . .' 'My family and I visited Gippsland immediately after the fires. While it is right that there has been some fire damage in Gippsland, this has only affected a very small part of the region and most of the areas and attractions that we love remain untouched. We were able to go swimming, boating, hiking and participate in all the things we love. Basically, it was like nothing ever happened and the local tourism operators were so happy to see us.' Darrell Jones, Bayswater
8	Celebrity endorsement	Denise Drysdale . . . one of our biggest fans 'I'm a great fan of Gippsland and I was so saddened by the news of the bushfires in the region. However, having just spent a number of weeks travelling throughout Gippsland I was surprised to see that many of Gippsland's fascinating landscapes remain relatively untouched and it's pretty much business as usual as far as the tourism industry goes. I strongly urge the Victorian people to come and see for themselves just how resilient Gippsland's wondrous natural landscape is . . .' Denise Drysdale
9	Product diversification – *Festivals and Events*	Look what's happening in Gippsland in February. Our events calendar is full of fantastic reasons why you should let yourself be inspired by Gippsland this February. Whether you're a racegoer, a music lover or a fan of fiery foods we have it all going on in Gippsland this summer (events calendar included).

region so potential tourists can see a clear relationship between the region and the celebrity. An advertisement communicating community readiness also proved effective in evoking an emotional response among tourists, which, according to previous research, can often lead to a travel decision (Walters, Sparks and Herington 2010).

In contrast to the existing literature, the study found that messages appealing to curiosity, as used for example in the case of the Victorian bushfires in 2006 (Sanders *et al.* 2008), were not well received by respondents. In addition, one of the most commonly used messages – 'open for business' also performed relatively badly in this study, with responses indicating that the messages lacked credibility. The study also found that price discounting is unlikely to capture the tourist's attention and consequently generate interest in the destination.

The timeframe within which tourists will return to a disaster-struck destination is often one of the biggest concerns for DMOs and operators alike. This study revealed that in the case of a bushfire event, tourists generally are likely to return within 12–24 months following a disaster, and it would therefore be difficult for this particular destination to encourage new visitors within 12 months. Nevertheless, the study did suggest that regular visitors (who have visited five or more times in the past) are more likely to return within six months of the disaster than irregular visitors (i.e. those who have visited only once).

Finally, the study addressed the question raised by Beirman (2006), that is, whether it is in fact appropriate for a destination to continue promotional activities during and immediately following a disaster. Surprisingly, the study indicated that tourists believe that it is not inappropriate for destinations to continue their marketing and promotional activities in the wake of a disaster, and that destinations should carry on with their efforts to attract visitors.

Lessons learnt

This study has several valuable implications for those responsible for disaster recovery communications. Evidence has been provided to support the continuation of marketing and promotional activities over the course of the disaster recovery period. In particular, the fact that frequent visitors are more likely to return in the short term strongly suggests that relationship marketing should be the focus of the initial promotional activity. Operators need to be encouraged to maintain visitor databases, identify their loyal consumer base and within the initial six month period make contact with their regular clientele and encourage their patronage. When marketing a destination struck by disaster, destination marketers should consider integrating in their post-disaster recovery campaigns celebrity-endorsed messages that communicate community readiness. Not only should the chosen celebrity be recognizable by the target market as having some connection with the region, the advertising campaign should be accompanied by public relations activity in the early stages of development to educate the market about the celebrity/product association. It was strongly recommended that post-disaster communications messages be factual in nature and provide an honest representation of the region's status in its attempts to reassure tourists that the destination is ready to host them. Finally, 'open for business' campaigns should not be employed until the community is ready and willing to receive tourists. When this time arises, the 'open for business' message should be exchanged for a promotional message that communicates community readiness, and short term discounting strategies should not be employed at any time throughout the disaster-recovery phase as a means of encouraging visitation.

Conclusions

This chapter has highlighted a range of recommendations for consideration by DMOs that seek to restore their destination image following a disastrous event. In the case of the 2009 Queensland floods, research showed that tourists who felt that they might be able to assist the destination is some way would still consider visiting immediately after the disastrous event. Tourists also showed a reluctance to cancel or postpone their travel, particularly if they were reassured the destination was accessible and/or they were planning to visit family and friends. To this end, open communication between the destination and the tourism market is encouraged, and it is imperative that the information communicated at this time is perceived as both factual and honest.

The chapter discussed a range of different message options DMOs could employ in their attempts to encourage visitation and prevent unnecessary cancellations. In the case of the 2009 Black Saturday Bushfires, a celebrity-endorsed message appeared to be the most effective means of communicating with the post-disaster market. It was noted, however, that the chosen celebrity must have some affiliation with the destination and be widely recognized as doing so. Messages communicating community readiness were also given some credibility. However, DMOs are advised against the dissemination of such messages too prematurely to avoid instilling a sense of distrust in the market.

Finally it is worth noting that all disasters are different, with different contexts, on different scales, and involving different destinations and participants. Therefore, planning how to respond to a disaster must be somewhat generic as it may not be able to predict the exact consequences of any given event. Future research into post-disaster response is badly needed, with a focus not just on the best and most persuasive messages to use in any given circumstance, but also on the roles and responsibilities of various stakeholders such as DMOs, local authorities, emergency managers and the media. In addition, there is an immediate need for a framework that incorporates appropriate timelines for a destination's recovery marketing strategies to ensure the effectiveness of its marketing messages. As noted, good communication is of vital importance in the event of a disaster, and while the best marketing response may vary with context, a well planned and executed disaster management plan will produce a considered and suitable marketing response.

References

Armstrong, E.K. and Ritchie, B.W. (2008) 'The Heart Recovery Marketing Campaign – Destination Recovery After a Major Bushfire in Australia's National Capital', *Journal of Travel & Tourism Marketing*, 23(2): 175–89.

Avraham, E. and Ketter E. (2008) *Media Strategies for Marketing Places in Crisis*. Oxford: Butterworth-Heinemann.

Beirman, D. (2006) 'Best Education Network Think Tank v Keynote Address: "Marketing Tourism Destinations from Crisis to Recovery"', *Tourism Review International*, 10: 7–16.

Carlsen, J.C. and Hughes, M. (2008) 'Tourism Market Recovery in the Maldives after the 2004 Indian Ocean Tsunami', *Journal of Travel & Tourism Marketing*, 23(2): 139–49.

Carlsen, J.C. and Liburd, J.J. (2008) 'Developing a Research Agenda for Tourism Crisis Management, Market Recovery and Communications', *Journal of Travel & Tourism Marketing*, 23(2): 265–76.

Carlville, O. (2012) *Desparate Times for Tourism Operators*. Fairfax New Zealand Ltd, http://www.stuff.co.nz/national/christchurch-earthquake/7433732 (accessed 14 August 2012).

Cavlek, N. (2002) 'Tour Operators and Destination Safety', *Annals of Tourism Research*, 29(2): 478–96.

Cioccio, L. and Michael, E.J. (2007) 'Hazard or Disaster: Tourism Management for the Inevitable in Northeast Victoria', *Tourism Management*, 28(1): 1–11.

Crouch, G.I. and Louviere, J.J. (2001) 'A Review of Choice Modeling Research in Tourism, Hospitality and Leisure', in J.A. Mazanec, G.I. Crouch, J.R. Ritchie and A.G. Woodside (eds), *Consumer Psychology in Tourism, Hospitality and Leisure* (Vol. 2). Oxford: CABI, pp. 67–83.

DRET (Department of Resources, Energy and Tourism) (2009) '$10 Million for Tourism Victoria Recovery', Press Release issued 28 August, http://minister.ret.gov.au/MediaCentre/Speeches/Pages/$10MillionforTourismVictoriaRecovery.aspx (accessed 14 August 2012.)

Dolnicar. S. and Huybers, T. (2007) 'Different Tourists – Different Perceptions of Different Places: Accounting for Tourists' Perceptual Heterogeneity in Destination Image Measurement', *Tourism Analysis*, 12(5–6): 447–61.

Faulkner, B. (2001) 'Towards a Framework for Tourism Disaster Management', *Tourism Management*, 22(2): 135–47.

Gartner, W. (1993) 'Image Formation Process', *Journal of Travel and Tourism Marketing*, 2(2/3): 191–215.

Henderson, J.C. (2003) 'Communicating in a Crisis: Flight SQ006', *Tourism Management*, 24: 279–87.

Hystad, P.W. and Keller, P.C. (2008) 'Towards a Destination Tourism Disaster Management Framework: Long-term Lessons from a Forest Fire Disaster', *Tourism Management*, 29: 151–62.

IBIS World Pty Ltd (2011) *Queensland Floods: The Economic Impact*. Special Report, January, http://www.ibisworld.com.au/common/pdf/QLD%20floods%20special%20report.pdf (accessed 1 July 2012).

IPCC (2007) *Summary for Policymakers. In Climate Change 2007: Impacts, Adaptation and Vulnerability. Contribution of Working Group II to the Fourth Assessment Report of the Intergovernmental Panel on Climate Change*. Cambridge: Cambridge University Press.

Kahneman, D. (1995) 'Reference Points, Anchors, Norms and Mixed Feelings', *Organizational Behavior and Decision Processes*, 51: 296–312.

Koopman, D. (2009) 'Grant Hackett Filming Open for Business Tourism', *Brisbane City News*, http://www.bnecity.com.au/News/News-article.aspx?id=631&returnurl=~/News/Default.aspx (accessed 1 July 2012).

Kozak, M., Crotts, J.C. and Law, R. (2007) 'The Impact of the Perception of Risk on International Travellers', *International Journal of Tourism Research*, 9(4): 233–42.

Lazurus, R.S. (1991) 'Progress on a Cognitive–Motivational–Relational Theory of Emotion', *American Psychologist*, 46(8): 819–34.
Lehto, X., Douglas, A.C. and Park, K. (2008) 'Mediating the Effects of Natural Disasters on Travel Intention', *Journal of Travel & Tourism Marketing*, 23(2): 29–43.
Lennon, J. and Foley, M. (1999) 'Interpretation of the Unimaginable: The U.S. Holocaust Memorial Museum, Washington, DC, and Dark Tourism', *Journal of Travel Research*, 38(August): 46–50.
Machado, L.P. (2010) 'Does Destination Image Influence the Length of Stay in a Tourism Destination?', *Tourism Economics*, 16(2): 443–56.
McKercher, B. and Pine, R. (2005) 'Privation as a Stimulus to Travel Demand?', *Journal of Travel & Tourism Marketing*, 19(2–3): 107–16.
Moore, O. (2010) 'Brad the Builder in New Orleans', *The Observer*, 14 March, http://www.guardian.co.uk/artanddesign/2010/mar/14/brad-pitt-architecture-new-orleans (accessed 14 August 2012).
Otto, J.E. and Ritchie, J.R.B. (1996) 'The Service Experience in Tourism', *Tourism Management*, 17(3): 165–74.
Pearlman, D. and Melnik, O. (2008) 'Hurricane Katrina's Effect on the Perceptions of New Orleans Leisure Tourists', *Journal of Travel & Tourism Marketing*, 25(1): 58–67.
Pforr, C. and P.J. Hosie (2008) 'Crisis Management in Tourism – Preparing for Recovery', *Journal of Travel & Tourism Marketing*, 23(2): 249–64.
Prideaux, B., Coghlan, A. and Falco-Mammone, F. (2008) 'Post Crisis Recovery – The Case of After Cyclone Larry', *Journal of Travel & Tourism Marketing*, 23(2): 163–74.
Queensland Floods Commission of Inquiry (2012) *Queensland Floods Commission Final Report*, http://www.floodcommission.qld.gov.au/_data/assets/pdf_file/0007/11698/QFCI-Final-Report-March-2012.pdf (accessed 14 August 2012).
Raholm, M., Arman, M. and Rehnsfeldt, A. (2008) 'The Immediate Lived Experience of the 2004 Tsunami Disaster by Swedish Tourists', *Journal of Advanced Nursing*, 63(6): 597–606.
Ritchie, B.W. (2008) 'Tourism Disaster Planning and Management: From Response to Recovery Reduction and Readiness', *Current Issues in Tourism*, 11(4): 315–48.
Robinson, L. and Jarvie, J. (2008) 'Post-Disaster Community Tourism Recovery: The Tsunami and Arugam Bay, Sri Lanka', *Disasters*, 32(4): 631–45.
Sanders, D., Laing, J. and Houghton, M. (2008) *Impact of Bushfires on Tourism Visitation in Alpine National Parks*. Technical Report prepared for the Sustainable Tourism Cooperative Research Centre, Australia.
Schwarz, N., Zuma, M. and Clore, G.L. (1988) 'How Do I Feel About it? The Information Function of Affective States', in K. Fiedler and J. Forgas (eds), *Affect, Cognition and Social Behavior*. New York: C.J. Hogrefe, pp. 44–62.
Scott, N., Laws, E. and Prideaux, B. (2008) 'Tourism Crises and Marketing Recovery Strategies', *Journal of Travel & Tourism Marketing*, 23(2): 1–13.
Swerdlow, R.A. and Swerdlow, M.R. (2003) 'Celebrity Endorsers: Spokesperson Selection Criteria and Case Examples of FREDD', *Academy of Marketing Studies Journal*, 7(2): 13–26.
Tourism Authority of Thailand (2005a) *International Tourist Arrivals to Thailand by Nationality at International Airport*, January–December. Bangkok: Tourism Authority of Thailand.
Tourism Queensland (2011) *Cyclone and Flood Recovery Update*, June, http://www.townsvilleenterprise.com.au/Libraries/Tourism_Document_Library/Microsoft_PowerPoint_-_RecoveryForum_Mission_Beach_12th_April.sflb.ashx (accessed 14 August 2012).
Tuan Pham, M., Cohen, J.B., Pracejus, J.W. and Hughes, G.D. (2001) 'Affect Monitoring and the Primacy of Feelings in Judgment', *Journal of Consumer Research*, 28(2): 167–89.
Vastfjall, D., Peters, E. and Slovic, P. (2008) 'Affect, Risk Perception and Future Optimism After the Tsunami Disaster', *Judgment and Decision Making*, 3(1): 64–72.
Walters, G. and Clulow, V. (2010) 'The Tourism Market's Response to the 2009 Black Saturday Bushfires: The Case of Gippsland', *Journal of Travel & Tourism Marketing*, 27: 844–57.
Walters, G.A. and Mair, J.A. (2011) 'The Effectiveness of Post Disaster Marketing Messages: The Case of the 2009 Victorian Bushfires', *Journal of Travel and Tourism Marketing*, 29: 87–103, available online.
Walters, G.A., Sparks, B.A. and Herington, C. (2010) 'The Impact of Consumption Vision and Emotion on the Tourism Consumer's Decision Behavior', *The Journal of Hospitality and Tourism Research*, 36(3): 336–89.
Walters, G.A., Mair, J.A. and Ritchie, B. (2011) *The Australian Tourism Market's Response to the 2011 Queensland Floods*. Australia: University of Queensland.
Xu, J. and Grunewald, A. (2009) 'What Have we Learned? A Critical Review of Tourism Disaster Management', *Journal of China Tourism Research*, 5(1): 102–30.

Part 8

Social and digital media marketing issues in tourism

35

Challenges of tourism marketing in the digital, global economy

Simon Hudson

Introduction

In 1999, Steven Spielberg convened a three-day think tank to gather insights from 23 top futurists for the making of his sci-fi thriller *Minority Report* which depicted the world of 2054. The goal was to create a realistic view of a plausible future. Projecting out from the present day's marketing and media technologies – barcode scanners, GPS devices, Bluetooth-enabled cell phones and TiVo personal video recorders – the filmmakers gave shape to an advertising-saturated society where billboards call out to you on a first-name basis, cereal boxes broadcast animated commercials, newspapers deliver news instantly over a broadband wireless network, holographic hosts greet you by name at retail stores and where biometric retina scans deduct the cost of goods instantly from your bank account.

The technologies portrayed in the film were far from science fiction, and today many are in use or are in development – an indication of the rapid pace of technological development. Wireless newspapers and magazines that stream news updates – like the *USA Today* seen in the film – are extensions of 'digital paper' technologies currently being developed. Meanwhile, today's GPS and wireless network technologies are close to the place-based, personalized advertising that provides a backdrop for the film's city scenes. GPS-based technologies are used by wireless carriers to target ads to users in specific locations; and new Wi-Fi based Location Enabled Networks (LENs) carve up a wireless network into discrete segments that target users passing through a specified location. As users pass access points, content can be served up based on their position. Of course, for all their commercial potential, these technologies are not free of ethical considerations – a point the movie drives home with a heavy hand (Mathieson 2002). However, what we are witnessing is a rapidly changing communications environment dominated by digital technology – and Spielberg's futuristic world is already upon us.

This chapter looks at this new digital era of marketing communications as it applies to tourism, a digital era dominated by social media. The chapter begins with an introduction to today's digital marketing environment, and is followed by an analysis of the consumer decision process in the new digital world. The third section takes a close look at social media and shows how tourism marketers are embracing social media because of its potential for engagement and collaboration with consumers. The next part of the chapter outlines the challenges facing tourism marketers in the digital, global economy, and a final section speculates on the future of digital marketing communications, making suggestions for further research in this area.

Today's digital marketing environment

The marketing communications environment has changed enormously in the last decade. Technology and the Internet have fundamentally altered the way the world interacts and communicates. Traditional approaches to branding that put emphasis on mass media techniques are less and less effective in a marketplace where customers have access to massive amounts of information about brands, products and companies and in which social networks have, in some cases, supplanted brand networks (Keller 2009).

In the new media environment, consumers are increasingly in control. Not only do they have more choices of media to use, they also have a choice about whether and how they want to receive commercial content. In response marketers are employing more varied marketing communications techniques than ever before. To communicate effectively and efficiently, tourism marketers have to go where the consumers are – and this is increasingly online. There were over two billion Internet users in 2011, up from one billion in 2005, 420 million in 2000 and 45 million in 1995. Two-thirds of the population in North America and Europe regularly go online. Much of current and future Internet user growth is coming from populous countries such as China, India, Brazil, Russia and Indonesia. The travel sector itself boasted annual online sales of almost $100 billion in 2012, around a third of all global e-commerce activity (Carey, Kang and Zea 2012).

The Internet is moving marketers much closer to one-to-one marketing. The web not only offers merchants the ability to communicate instantly with each customer, but it also allows the customer to talk back, and that makes it possible for companies to customize offers and services. The Internet also allows organizations to provide 7-day, 24-hour service response. In fact, the main reason consumers have adopted the Internet is that it enables them to shop 24/7 in the comfort of their home with no time zone worries. Ease of navigation is then the primary reason for variations in purchase decisions between different online products.

Many consumers, too, are looking to build relationships on the web. Godin introduced the concept of permission marketing (Godin 1999), in which consumers volunteer to be marketed to on the Internet in return for some kind of reward. This type of marketing uses the interactivity offered by the web to engage customers in a dialogue and, as a consequence, in a long-term interactive relationship. Permission marketing is based on the premise that the attention of the consumer is a scarce commodity that needs to be managed carefully. Its emphasis is on building relationships with consumers instead of interrupting their lives with mass marketing messages.

The Internet has also upended how consumers engage with brands to the extent that consumers are promiscuous in their brand relationships (Edelman 2010). They connect with myriad brands through new media channels often beyond the marketer's familiarity or control. In the past, marketing strategies emphasized brand awareness and ultimate purchase. However, after purchase, consumers may remain aggressively engaged, actively promoting or assailing the products they have bought and collaborating in the brand's development. The touch points when consumers are most open to influence have changed, requiring a major adjustment to realign marketers' strategy and budgets with where consumers are actually spending their time. Table 35.1 summarizes some of the interactive marketing communication options that are now available.

Table 35.1 Digital marketing communications options

• Website	Companies must design websites that express their purpose, vision, products and history. A key challenge is to design a site that is attractive enough on first viewing and continue to raise people's interest to repeat visit. Dedicated websites for mobile devices are on the increase.
• Mobile marketing	Mobile marketing will become increasingly important. Particularly, smartphone use is growing amongst travellers.
• Social media	Companies are embracing social media because of its potential for collaboration and engagement with consumers. Social media advertising will yield relatively stronger results due to its ability to tightly target audiences based on social media activity.
• Display ads	Display ads are small, rectangular boxes with text and perhaps a picture that companies pay to place on certain websites. The larger the readership, the more the placement costs.
• Internet-specific ads and videos	With user generated content sites (i.e. YouTube, Google Video, MySpace Video), consumers and marketers can upload ads and videos to be shared virally by millions of people.
• E-mail	Email uses only a fraction of the cost of a 'd-mail', or direct mail campaign.
• Blogs	Blogs are commonly maintained by an individual with regular entries of commentary, description of events, or other material such as graphics or video. Most blogs with high quality are interactive, which allows visitors to leave comments and even message each other.
• Microsites	A microsite is a limited area on the web managed and paid for by an external advertiser. A microsite is an Internet web design term referring to an individual web page or a small cluster (around 1 to 7) of pages which are meant to function as a discrete entity within an existing website or to complement an offline activity.
• Search ads	Paid-search or pay-per-click ads, represent 40% of all online ads. 35% of all searches are reportedly for products or services. The search terms serve as a proxy for the consumer's consumption interests and trigger relevant links to product or service offerings alongside search results from Google, MSN and Yahoo! Advertisers pay only if people click on the links.
• Interstitials	Interstitials are advertisements, often with video or animation, that pop up between changes on a website.
• Online brand communities	Many firms sponsor online communities whose members communicate via postings, chat discussions and instant messaging about special interests related to the firm's products and brands.

Source: Adapted from Keller (2009): 147

The consumer decision process in today's digital world

The Internet has fundamentally changed the consumer decision process. In the past, marketers assumed that consumers started with a large number of potential brands in mind and methodically narrowed their choices until they had decided which one to buy (Edelman 2010). This was known as the funnel metaphor. After purchase, their relationship with the brand typically focused on the use of the product or service itself. But this decision process has changed. Court, Elzinger, Mulder and Vetvik (2009) have introduced a more nuanced view of how consumers engage with brands called the Consumer Decision Journey (see Figure 35.1).

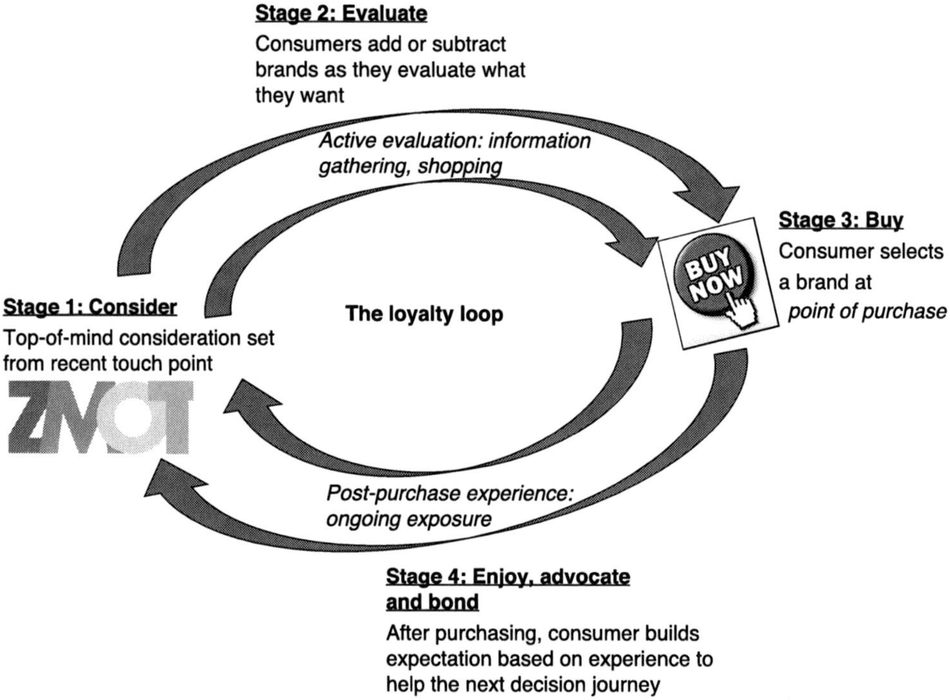
Stage 2: Evaluate
Consumers add or subtract brands as they evaluate what they want
Active evaluation: information gathering, shopping
Stage 3: Buy
Consumer selects a brand at point of purchase
BUY NOW
Stage 1: Consider
Top-of-mind consideration set from recent touch point
ZMOT
The loyalty loop
Post-purchase experience: ongoing exposure
Stage 4: Enjoy, advocate and bond
After purchasing, consumer builds expectation based on experience to help the next decision journey

Figure 35.1 The consumer decision journey today (adapted from Court *et al.* 2009).

They developed their model from a study of the purchase decisions of nearly 20,000 consumers across five industries and three continents. Their research revealed that rather than systematically narrowing their choices until they had decided what to buy, consumers add and subtract brands from a group under consideration during an extended evaluation stage. After purchase, they often enter into an open-ended relationship with the brand, sharing their experience with it online through social media.

The four stages of the consumer decision journey are:

1 consider;
2 evaluate;
3 buy; and
4 enjoy, advocate and bond.

New media make the 'evaluate' and 'advocate' stages increasingly relevant. Consumers' outreach to marketers and other sources of information is much more likely to shape their ensuing choices than marketers' efforts to persuade them. An addition to the original model is the 'Zero Moment of Truth' (ZMOT). Online marketers have coined this term to describe the new reality where marketers have to compete for shoppers' attention online long before a purchase decision is made (Lecinski 2011).

After purchase, a deeper connection begins as the consumer interacts with the product and with new online touch points. A good example of that 'enjoy, advocate and bond' stage would be the evolution of the skiing experience. In decades past, a skier at Vail Colorado would purchase a ski ticket at the hill, enjoy his or her days' skiing and then have no further contact with the resort (apart from perhaps a direct marketing piece) until the next visit. Now, a skier can purchase a ski ticket online, and have their card (with a built in chip) delivered to the door. When a skier arrives at Vail, he or she can then engage with Vail's EpicMix social media campaign. The idea of EpicMix is to track activity on and around the mountain via radio frequency scanners installed at the 89 lifts across Vail, Beaver Creek, Breckenridge, Keystone and Heavenly. The scanners interact with the RF-enabled chip embedded in lift tickets, listing lift rides, vertical feet skied and days on hill. Special accomplishments – like clocking up 10,000 vertical feet – are recognized with collectible digital pins which can be instantly flaunted on Facebook after downloading the EpicMix app. Users can also create colourful collages, mixing professional photos with their own snapshots, any pins they have won and snow reports or resort stats – effectively designing their own promotional postcard to commemorate their holiday. This gaming option won Vail a Webby award in 2011.

Leveraging social media

Social media platforms like those employed by Vail are emerging as the dominant digital communications channel, particularly for people under 34 years of age (McKinsey 2011). In 2011, 33 per cent of consumers in the US used social networks to navigate content on the Web, up from 13 per cent in 2008, and the same year social network use doubled among those over 55. As consumers spend more time on these networks, decisions about what to purchase often reflect interactions with friends and other influencers. Figure 35.2 shows recent consumer research related to how social media is changing travellers' experiences. A large percentage of consumers read reviews of hotels, attractions and restaurants prior to vacation, and over half 'Liked' Facebook pages or posted Facebook updates before their holiday. Whilst on vacation over 70 per cent post vacation photos on a social network or update their Facebook status, and nearly half check-in to a social media location. The same research found that 85 per cent of travellers are using smartphones during their vacation. After returning home travellers are still active on social media networks, posting reviews or photos, or 'Liking' Facebook pages related to a specific destination.

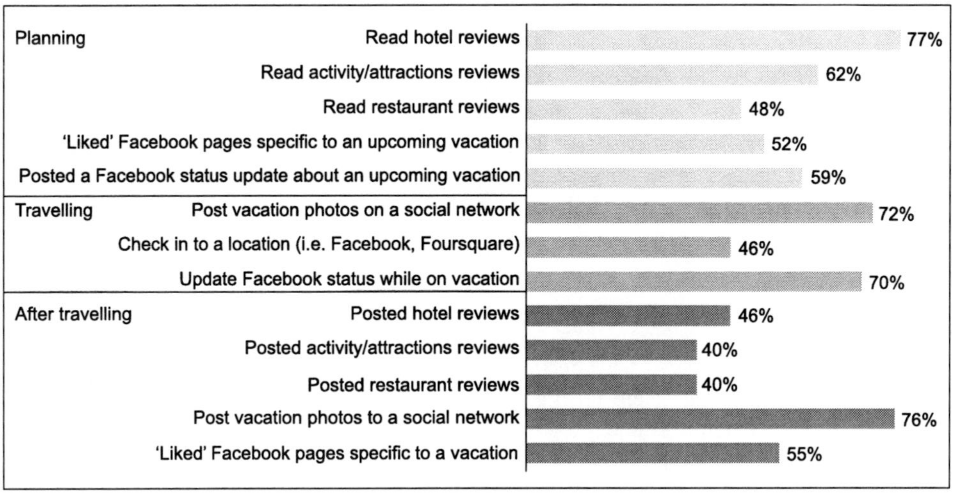

Figure 35.2 The behaviour of today's networked traveller (source: Lab42 2012).

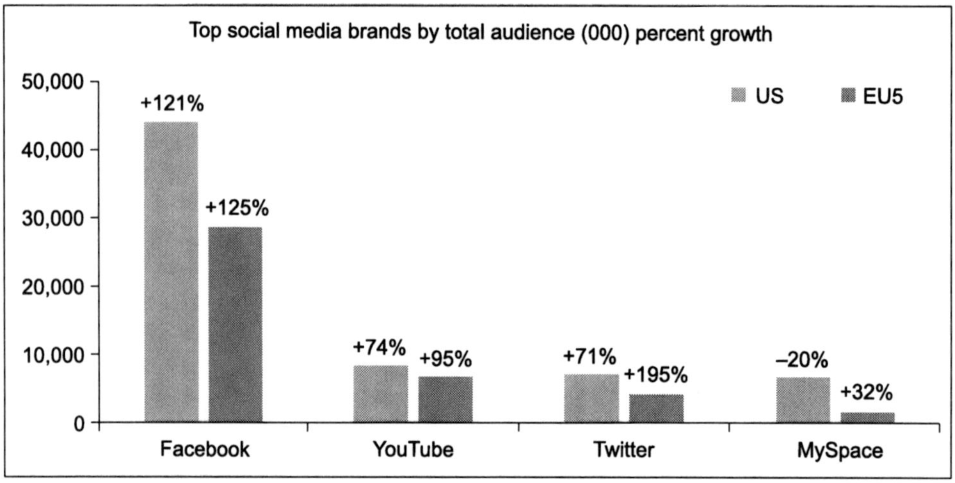

Figure 35.3 Top social media brands by total audience (000) per cent growth (source: comScore 2011).

Many companies like Vail Resorts have embraced social media because of its potential for engagement and collaboration with these networked consumers. Through social media marketers can gain rich, unmediated consumer insights, faster than ever before. Others see the value of social media in its networking. According to Facebook, the average user has 130 friends on the social network, and when people hear about a product or service from a friend, they become a customer at a 15 per cent higher rate than when they find out about it through other means. The growth of social networking is mainly driven by Facebook, which reached 90 per cent of US social media users and 85 per cent of European users in 2010, and grew more than 120 per cent that year. YouTube and Twitter hold second and third position in the US and Europe, but the European market shows much stronger growth (see Figure 35.3).

For travel and tourism marketers, the use of social media is commonplace, but there is still potential for growth. AirPlus (2009) surveyed 174 travel professionals on the subject of social media marketing and found that LinkedIn (58%) and Facebook (45%) were the most popular, followed by Blogs (12%). Interestingly, 28 per cent were using no social media platforms at all. Figure 35.4 shows the views of travel professionals on the effectiveness of social media marketing efforts.

For destination marketing organizations (DMOs), the most influential social media tools are Facebook (64%), Twitter (26%), TripAdvisor (4%), YouTube (3%) and Foursquare (1%) (Sparkloft Media 2011). The two most common objectives for social media efforts for destinations are to increase awareness for the destination and to build engagement with consumers (see Figure 35.5).

Social media tools employed by tourism marketers

User generated video contests have become an increasingly popular communication tool for many destinations who use them to engage consumers and prompt them to become digital ambassadors for their brands. Users are encouraged to submit a personal video to the competition's website, from which they can be selected to win a free dream holiday, such as those offered in reality television programmes. In the return, the lucky winners are expected to share their impressions on Facebook, Twitter, YouTube, Flickr and blogs, serving as the place's ambassadors.

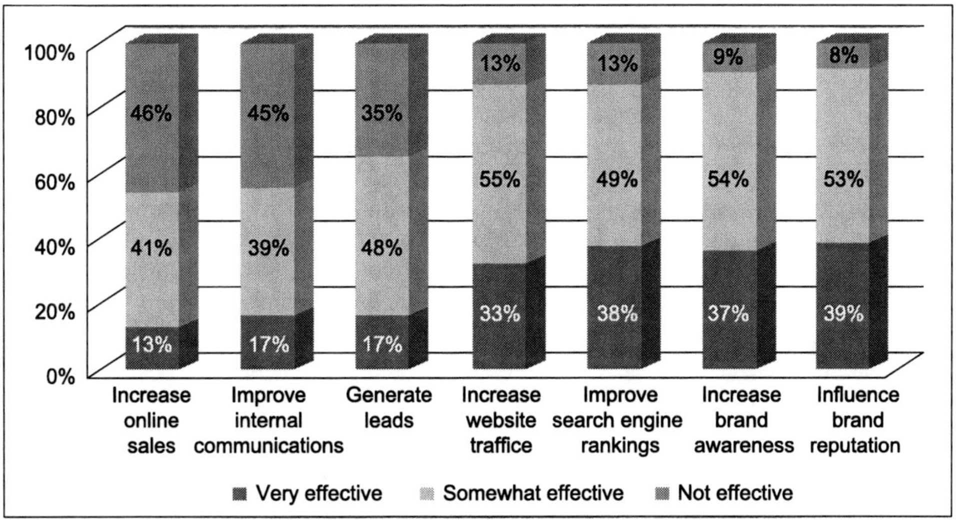

Figure 35.4 Effectiveness of social media marketing efforts (adapted from Air Plus 2009).

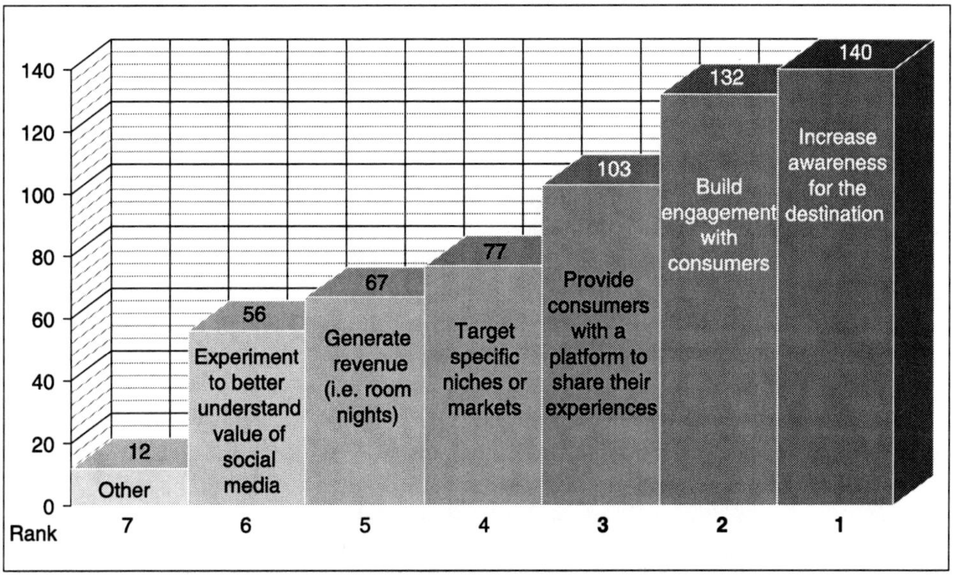

Figure 35.5 DMO objectives of social media efforts (adapted from Sparkloft Media 2011).

Perhaps one of the most successful campaigns of this type was the 'Best Job in the World' Queensland campaign. In January 2009 Tourism Queensland embarked on a global search to find an Island Caretaker to explore the Islands of the Great Barrier Reef in Queensland Australia and report back to the world about their experiences. The campaign was called the 'Best Job in the World'. On offer was a salary of AUD $150,000 for a six month position with live-in luxury accommodation on Hamilton Island and the opportunity to explore all that the region has to offer. Over 34,000 would-be caretakers from all over the world uploaded a 60-second video showing their creativity and skills. From celebrities, writers, tour guides, environmentalists, students, to mums, dads and retirees everyone was vying for the Best Job in the World. A shortlist of 50 applicants from 22 countries was narrowed down to a final 16, 15 of whom were chosen by Tourism Queensland, and the 16th a 'wild card' applicant Claire Wang from Taiwan chosen by popular vote. The job went to 'ostrich-riding, bungee-jumping' charity worker Ben Southall from Hampshire in England, who was still in 2011 reporting via blogs on his adventures. Tourism Queensland claims that the campaign generated more than $80m of equivalent media advertising space – for an investment of just $1m (Sweney 2009). The campaign, developed by the Brisbane-based agency of Nitro, won two top awards at the Cannes Lions International Advertising Festival.

By offering an opportunity to win a free vacation, marketers involved with these types of campaigns create excitement, interest and commitment among competitors and hope to raise awareness of their destination by generating free media coverage. In 2009, the Orlando Convention and Visitor's Bureau initiated a 67 Days of Smiles contest, promising two lucky winners the chance to visit Orlando for 67 days. The idea was that it would take a tourist 67 days to experience everything the Orlando area has to offer. Kyle and Stacey were chosen for the job and recorded their trip on a 67 Days of Smiles blog. By the end of their experience, the Days of Smiles website had recorded over 67,000 hits and their Twitter account had almost 1,000 followers. The travelling duo was also featured by several media outlets including the *New York Times*.

Twitter is increasingly being used as a stand-alone marketing tool to generate awareness for a tourism product or service. The Virginia Tourism Corporation (VTC) won a marketing award in 2009 for a wine tourism promotion called 'Vintage Tweets' – a cutting-edge public relations effort that utilized social media to promote wine tourism in Virginia. VTC organized Vintage Tweets in September of 2009 in Arlington to kick off October Virginia Wine Month. The state tourism agency used Twitter to target media, bloggers and consumers who were passionate about wine travel, live in and around Washington, DC, and had a significant number of Twitter followers. VTC used Twitter to invite 40 of those consumers to a wine reception, featuring six different wineries from across the state. The guests tweeted about their wine tastings and also took part in Virginia Wine Travel Twitter trivia. In total, Vintage Tweets was able to reach over 43,000 consumers in just 24 hours, providing key facts and travel ideas to potential visitors from across the country.

One relatively new social media platform that is helping tourism and hospitality businesses is the emergence of geo-location sites such as Foursquare, Gowalla and Loopt. Foursquare encourages consumers to broadcast their whereabouts (or 'check-in') in exchange for discounts or coupons etc. Foursquare recently hit one billion check-ins (Mogg 2011). People use the Foursquare app on their smartphones to check in to places like restaurants, pubs and hotels, and just about any other type of physical and even nonphysical location. Once they check in, users often share that information with friends, families and followers on Facebook and Twitter. Foursquare users compete for badges points and 'mayorships', awarded to those who check in to a place most frequently. Business owners claim their venue on Foursquare (for free) and reward people simply for checking in, for checking in a certain number of times, for checking in with friends, or reward the person who checks in the most (the 'mayor'). For example, Chili's Grill and Bar, a national restaurant chain in the US, rewards its customers with free chips and salsa every time they check in. Chili's makes money on the deal because customers don't walk into Chili's just for free chips and salsa and leave. They order appetizers, entrees and drinks.

Dutch Airline KLM used Foursquare as part of an innovative social media campaign that focused on random acts of kindness. An effective way to emotionally connect with consumers is through random acts of kindness designed to produce customer gratitude. Gratitude is a powerful, and potentially quite profitable, emotion to inspire (Palmatier, Burke, Bechkoff and Kardes 2009). The airline's 'How Happiness Spreads' campaign of 2010 employed a 'Surprise Team' to give passengers tailored, unexpected gifts at the airport (Trendwatching 2011). When passengers checked in at KLM's Foursquare locations, the KLM Surprise team used social networks such as LinkedIn, Twitter and Facebook to find out information about the passenger. The KLM Surprise team then used this information to come up with a personalized gift to surprise the passenger with. The team followed up after surprising a passenger by monitoring the conversation generated on social networks by that person and their friends. They also took photos of the people they had surprised and posted them to the KLM Facebook page. KLM has previously proven its social media savvy with a popular Facebook application allowing users to create luggage tags using their Facebook photos. In 2006 the company had another success with an award winning viral video for its Fly for Fortune game.

Virgin Atlantic Airways (VAA) is another airline that is leveraging the power of social media to reinforce its brand (Barwise and Meehan 2010). The VAA customer promise is innovation, fun, informality, honesty, value and a caring attitude. VAA uses social media to support these brand values. For example, the most-read section of its Facebook page includes travel tips from crew members – communication that comes across as honest, informal and caring. VAA builds trust by delivering on that promise. Trust is mainly about service delivery, but when things go wrong, keeping customers informed can prevent that trust from eroding. During the volcanic-ash crisis in 2010, VAA's website couldn't keep pace with the rapidly changing situation, so it used Facebook and Twitter to communicate with customers.

Another type of social media is the online brand community. Brand communities are defined as 'specialized, non-geographically bound communities, based on a structured set of social relationships among admirers of a brand' (Bagozzi and Dholakie 2006: 45). The emergence of brand communities has coincided with the growth in consumer empowerment. They are venues where intense brand loyalty is expressed and fostered, and emotional connection with the brand forged in customers. Research on such communities has found that commitment to a brand can be influenced (positively) by encouraging interactions with groups of like-minded customers and identification with the group in social context offered (and sponsored) by the firm and the brand, but controlled and managed primarily by the consumers themselves.

As use of the Internet becomes more pervasive, so too have online brand communities become effective tools for influencing sales. One study of online brand communities (Adjei, Noble and Noble 2010) found that the quality of the communication exchanged between customers reduces the level of uncertainty about the firm and its products, which relates to increased profits for the firm in terms of immediate purchase intentions, and the number of products purchased. It also found that the impact of negative information is not as strong as the benefits of positive information. So maintaining a brand community that allows customers to know the firm more intimately through peer-to-peer conversations will work in the firm's favour, even if negative information is shared.

A challenge in building and managing online brand communities is that consumers can easily associate marketers' efforts with extrinsic motives of profit exploitation and thus become less likely to engage with, and contribute to, such a community (Algesheimer, Dholakia and Herrmann 2005; Lee, Kim and Kim 2011). One possible solution is to develop a platform of online brand communities encouraging consumers to voluntarily share and exchange their ideas rather than imposing the organization's own ideas, such as sales coupons or sweepstakes. This implies that marketers should employ a passive role when facilitating brand communities.

A good example of this passive engagement in a brand community is the Walt Disney World Moms Panel. This is a forum where online 'Moms' answer questions and offer advice about family vacations to Disney. The 'Moms' are selected to be panellists because they have demonstrated an excellent knowledge of Disney products. Being familiar with the Parks, Resort hotels, dining and entertainment, shopping, and recreational activities, they can offer the help and tips consumers need when planning their vacations. As Leanne Jakubowski, who oversees the programme, says 'It is important that the Moms Panel is made up of real guests and represents a diverse spectrum of thoughts and perspectives so we can offer honest, heartfelt and useful information' (Walt Disney World 2011). Panellists receive a trip to the Walt Disney World Resort for their participation and in 2012 the Panel boasted 43 panellists whose expertise spanned Walt Disney World Resort, Disney Cruise Line, Disney Vacation Club, Adventures by Disney and Disneyland Resort offerings. The Moms Panel offers guests vacation insights on a variety of platforms including exclusive 'How-To' videos from panellists and celebrities, dedicated Facebook content, personal Disney Parks Blog posts and in-park meet-ups.

Because brand community members have a strong interest in the product and in the brand, they can also be a valuable source of innovation. In a study of brand community members, research found that the stronger the identification with the brand, and the higher the brand trust, the more likely a consumer was willing to contribute to open innovation projects initiated by a brand. This activity has been called 'crowdsourcing', a term coined in 2006 by *Wired* magazine Contributing Editor Jeff Howe (Sullivan 2010). Crowdsourcing-led innovation means opening the door to allow customers, employees, or the general public at large into the innovation process to help improve products, services or marketing efforts. Consumers get a direct line to the company and the opportunity to steer offerings to better reflect their needs, while companies benefit from getting more insights, opinions and wisdom that can be translated into actionable innovation ideas for less money than a typical RandD initiative. Dell for example created an online venue called IdeaStorm to give customers a central location where they could share ideas with the company. In the first three years, IdeaStorm crossed the 10,000 idea mark and implemented nearly 400 ideas.

For Virgin Atlantic Airways the greatest social media opportunity lies in gathering insights to drive continual incremental improvements (Barwise and Meehan 2010). For example, in response to online-community suggestions, it launched a system to arrange taxi sharing on arrival with passengers from the same flight. Fresh insights from social media also reinforce the innovation aspect of the brand. Facebook interactions helped the company appreciate the extensive planning that goes into a big trip, so they launched Vtravelled, a site dedicated to inspirational journeys. Customers moderate the conversation and exchange information, stories and advice. The site leads to some sales, but its main benefit to VAA comes from brand reinforcement and new customer insights.

Challenges

As more aspects of everyday life converge toward digital, opportunities for tourism organizations to interact with consumers expand dramatically. But Mulhern (2009) suggests that the digital revolution poses a serious challenge for media companies, agencies and brand marketers who have constructed a sophisticated infrastructure to send messages to target audiences through media channels, but do not have the mindset or the technical expertise to master the data analysis and modelling of the digital media world. The data analysis (or data mining) is both a challenge and an opportunity for tourism marketers in the digital era. Travel companies have access to mind-boggling data: everything from basic personal information to preferred airline seats, in-flight entertainment preferences, favoured television channels in hotels, meals in restaurants and credit card usage. They have the means to paint detailed pictures of consumers that will drive marketing initiatives to deeply engage them. Yet few of them truly maximize the potential of the data at their disposal (Carey et al., 2012). Those in the travel sector could follow the example of Amazon, who became the thorn in the side of every bookseller by mining data to craft individualized customer experiences full of conversion-ready streams of recommendations.

But mining such data does not come without a price. One related challenge facing marketers is that social media websites remain one of the lowest-scoring categories of websites when it comes to customer satisfaction. User concerns about privacy, including being targeted for advertising, continues to be problematic for social media websites (ACSI 2011). In 2011, the social media category earned a score of 70 on the American Consumer Satisfaction Index's (ASCI) 0 to 100 scale. Wikipedia topped the social media category with 78, benefiting from its non-profit position that allows users to surf, create and edit content without intrusion from commercial messages. Google-owned YouTube came in second place with 74, while Facebook scored a low 66. Facebook is facing intense scrutiny from consumers, courts and regulators worldwide about how it handles the data it collects from its 845 million users (Sengupta 2012). The scrutiny is at its most intense in Europe; a proposed Europe-wide law requires Facebook, along with every online business, to expunge every bit of personal data at a consumer's request.

One more downside to the proliferation of online social networking for tourism and hospitality companies is the loss of control over the consumer evaluation process (Kim and Hardin 2010). While reasonable criticisms taken from social networking sites could lead to further improvements in services, consumers can easily distribute damaging information using social media, without the opportunity for companies to resolve consumer complaints. A good example was Oliver Beale's letter to Virgin Atlantic chairman Richard Branson which is generally acknowledged to be the best customer service complaint letter ever (*Daily Telegraph* 2009). The complainant contacted Branson after a flight from Mumbai to Heathrow, to convey his disappointment with the food served on board the airline. In his 2008 missive, Beale, an ad agency employee, deconstructs a flight from London to Mumbai. His tirade mocks the food ('a crime against bloody cooking'), the in-flight movie ('Is that Ray Liotta?') and pokes fun at Branson (I can't imagine what dinner round your house is like, it must be like something out of a nature documentary'), all in 1,070 hugely entertaining words. The letter also included five photographs of the 'offending' dishes. At the time of writing, the YouTube version of the complaint letter had been viewed by over 17,000 people.

Another challenge with social media is measuring the return on investment and its impact on the bottom line. Brands that conduct social media interactions with consumers in a meaningful way are beginning to see a positive return (Cruz and Mendelsohn 2010), but there are too few research studies that can support this claim. One study by Dholakia and Durham (2010) did show a clear relationship between social media engagement and the bottom line. The experiment set up a company's Facebook page and measured the effect on customer behavior. The partner in this experiment was Dessert Gallery (DG), a popular Houston-based bakery and café chain. The researchers launched a Facebook page and invited everyone on a DG customer mailing list to become a fan. DG updated its page several times a week with pictures of goodies, news about contests and promotions, links to favourable reviews, and introductions to DG employees. Three months later, they resurveyed customers, this time receiving 1,067 responses from DG's Facebook fans, Facebook users who did not become fans and customers not on Facebook. They analyzed the data sets separately and then compared participants in the first survey with those in the second who had become DG fans.

Facebook changed customer behaviour for the better. People who had replied to both surveys and had become fans ended up being DG's best customers. Though they spent about the same amount of money per visit, they increased their store visits per month after becoming Facebook fans and generated more positive word-of-mouth than nonfans. They went to DG 20 per cent more often than nonfans and gave the store the highest share of their overall dining-out dollars. They were the most likely to recommend DG to friends and had the highest average Net Promoter Score – 75, compared with 53 for Facebook users who were not fans and 66 for customers not on Facebook. DG fans also reported significantly greater emotional attachment to DG. Additionally, fans were the most likely to say they chose DG over other establishments whenever possible.

Finally, another challenge for marketers is measuring the power of online word-of-mouth. Some organizations though are beginning to use tools that show them the influence that online consumers wield with their words. In fact, a recent survey of US, European and Asian companies found that 23 per cent used social media analytics tools in order to identify and reward key influencers (Birkner 2011). Palms Hotel and Casino in Las Vegas, for example, mines online data to give amenities and discounts to customers with the best social media footprint. Quasar Expeditions, a luxury cruise operator, similarly studies its Facebook page to find fans who have posted the most photos and positive comments, and then offers them discounts on future trips.

The future

While the author does not purport to predict the future as well as Steven Spielberg, some obvious trends can guide tourism marketers in the evolving digital era. The latest evolution on the consumer technology front is the widespread use of smartphones, and Google CEO Eric Schmidt recently said that the future will be 'mobile first'. Mobile devices are used 24/7 by consumers for many functions in addition to phone calling. Figure 35.6 shows the most common mobile phone uses in the US in 2011. While Europeans took the lead with their early and widespread adoption of text messaging and higher smartphone penetration compared to the US, the US has now eclipsed Europe in terms of penetration of mobile media, with 47 per cent of American mobile audiences using connected media in 2010 compared to 34 per cent of Europeans (comScore 2011). The pervasiveness of mobile technology is creating what MTN, the South African-based telecommunications and mobile finance brand, calls a whole mobile lifestyle (Roberti 2011). Providing accessibility to banking and credit facilities, travel itineraries, insurance, utilities services, as well as voice and Internet connectivity, is revolutionizing where, when and how we communicate personally and with businesses.

Certainly smartphone use is growing amongst travellers; by the middle of 2010, 20 per cent of US travellers had downloaded one or more travel-related applications to their smartphones (Reed 2010). Of those that had, 47 per cent used GPS functionality to find their way to a destination, and 46 per cent searched for flight updates. Another 29 per cent compared airfares or hotel rates and 18 per cent booked air travel or lodging. Another 15 per cent viewed virtual visitor guides, and a number of guidebook companies including Lonely Planet, Fodor's and Frommer's have released apps for major destinations. Travellers are increasingly using apps to create digital itineraries based on their specific interests. The SpotWorld app for example encourages travellers to post itineraries on Facebook with the idea that friends can share the information and make suggestions on alternative places to visit.

At airports, travellers can download iPhone apps to receive location-specific information on their devices such as where to find the shortest security line, or special deals being offered by nearby stores. At Copenhagen Airport a new programme tracks travellers' movements based on

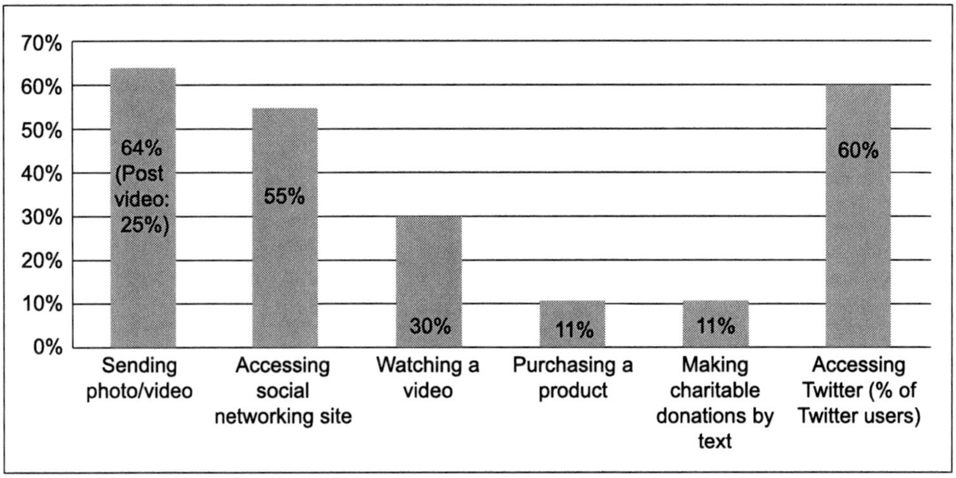

Figure 35.6 Common mobile phone uses (US) (adapted from Rainie 2011).

the Wi-Fi-emitting devices they carry (Negroni 2011). Airport officials can get a real-time picture of where travellers go and what they do, and can use this information to improve the design of the airport, direct the flow of passengers or shift employees to improve the efficiency of security or immigration checkpoints.

In 2011, about 20 per cent of air travellers had a device that emitted Wi-Fi signals, but this number is expected to increase with the growing appetite for smartphones, which also allow users to pay for purchases and display barcodes to board the airplane. In fact, smartphones are emerging as the device of choice for email, Web browsing and product research. More than 60 per cent of smartphone users surveyed in 2010 would consider buying goods with it or have already done so (McKinsey 2011). As the power and functionality of devices grow, the possibilities for making money from mobile platforms will continue to improve. McKinsey (2011) have found that smart phone users already are more accustomed to paying for digital content than traditional online users are, and Forrester predict that 75 per cent of marketers will include mobile in their marketing mix.

Smartphone technology is continually evolving presenting tremendous opportunities to tourism marketers. A 2011 campaign in Poland brought art to a whole new generation thanks to smartphones and QR codes. People visiting the Sukiennice National Museum in Krakow could use their phones to scan the paintings and when they did so it used augmented reality to act out scenes from the paintings and bring the whole museum to life. The application for use on an iphone provides eight 2D video films depicting the most interesting painting masterpieces which are presented at the exhibition. It can often be hard to relate to art work that is hundreds of years old but the stories told through video brought a whole new understanding of the art work and made people appreciate it more. The campaign itself was a huge success with the tour booked months in advance, and the initiative picked up mainstream attention on television, media, blogs and online in general.

The use of augmented reality has spread to other sectors of travel and tourism. In 2012, destination marketers in Hawaii and Mexico were experimenting with Aurasma to lead the future of tourism marketing with their cross-media creative campaigns. Aurasma is a visual browser – a new platform technology that merges the physical world with the virtual. Available as a free app for iPhone 4, iPad 2 and high-powered Android devices or as a free kernel for developers, Aurasma uses advanced image and pattern recognition to recognize and understand real-world images and objects in much in way the human brain does. It then seamlessly blends the real-world with rich interactive content such as videos and animations called 'Auras'. Auras can be created for printed images, product packaging, clothing, physical places and users can even use the app to create and share their own.

To capture the public's attention and further entice travel to Hawaii and Mexico, these destinations used Aurasma's ability to visually transport their vacation hotspots to potential travellers. In Chicago and San Francisco, pedestrians could position their mobile devices over outdoor print ads of Hawaii, and use Aurasma to see the printed ads dissolve into videos of Hawaii. Those interested in getting more information could then tap on their mobile touch screen and were automatically directed to gohawaii.com. Mexico used Aurasma to offer exclusive content to media and key influencers in North America via postcards. When the Aurasma viewer saw the front of the postcard, the image triggered a series of video testimonials from recent trips to Mexico. To incentivize recipients to unlock the digital content and watch the video, marketers also included a nice prize. One lucky viewer could win an iPad 2.

Conclusion

In retrospect, the marketing landscape has clearly changed in the last decade for tourism marketers. The ability to choose the most effective mix of online and offline marketing channels has become a critical issue, but the integration of online marketing within overall marketing strategy is complicated by diversity in current and emerging online applications. In addition, the challenges with new media, such as user concerns about privacy, the loss of control for marketers over the consumer evaluation process and the problems of measuring the return on investment and its impact on the bottom line are yet to be resolved. Marketers are aware that traditional communications channels have retained their historically favoured attributes, especially trust and reliability of information (Danaher and Rossiter 2011). But they are unsure if existing marketing communications models such as advertising persuasion, consumer behaviour, and 'reach, frequency, and impact' apply in online media (Valos, Ewing and Powell 2010). To accommodate a digital world, more research is needed to guide tourism marketers, and research must adopt new approaches to theory and method. Most of the research about digital media deals with small behavioural questions about online behaviour and, even then, the work is often quickly outdated (Mulhern 2009). Research on a deeper level, exploring consumer emotional and behavioural responses to digital media for example is needed (Page and Mapstone 2010). One fruitful avenue of further research could be the examination of social media's influence on brand relationship quality (BRQ), described as a customer-based indicator of the strength and depth of the person-brand relationship (Fournier 1998). Future research could also address which social media applications have the most success across different customer age groups. If researchers can identify exactly how, when and where social media influences consumers, it will help marketers craft marketing strategies that take advantage of social media's unique ability to engage with consumers (Divol, Edelman and Sarrazin 2012).

The digital revolution has upended business as usual in almost all industries, and travel is not an exception (Carey *et al.* 2012). Consumers are empowered by information. They have near-access to their flight, hotel and car-rental options; virtual price-transparency; and the ability to play suppliers off against one another. The game, according to many, is delivering a superior customer experience. As we have seen in this chapter, some companies are using technology to shape this experience, and we can expect more to come. KLM Royal Dutch Airlines for example, are launching a service that allows its passengers to use their Facebook or LinkedIn profiles to choose seatmates on upcoming flights. So the next time you get on a flight, look at the person next to you; they may have chosen you as their best next buddy!

References

ACSI (2011) 'Social media websites struggle with customer satisfaction', *ACSI Commentary*, July 2011. Press Release. Available: <http://www.theacsi.org/> (accessed 6 September 2011).

Adjei, M., Noble, S. and Noble, C. (2010) 'The influence of C2C communications in online brand communities on customer purchase behavior', *Journal of the Academy of Marketing Science*, 38(5): 634–53.

AirPlus (2009) 'Harnessing social media', *The Wire*, May 2009. Available: <http://www.airpluscommunity.com/wp-content/uploads/2009/05/airplus_thewire_may092.pdf> (accessed 25 January 2012).

Algesheimer, R., Dholakia, U.M. and Herrmann, A. (2005) 'The social influence of brand community', *Journal of Marketing*, 69: 19–34.

Bagozzi, R. and Dholakia, U. (2006) 'Antecedents and purchase consequences of customer participation in small group brand communities', *International Journal of Research in Marketing*, 23(1): 45–61.

Barwise, P. and Meehan, S. (2010) 'The one thing you must get right when building a brand', *Harvard Business Review*, 88(12): 80–4.

Birkner, C. (2011) 'Sharing the LOVE', *Marketing News*, 45(3): 20–1.

Carey, R., Kang, D. and Zea, M. (2012) 'The trouble with travel distribution', *McKinsey Quarterly*, February.

comScore (2011) *The comScore 2010 Mobile Year in Review*. Available: <http://www.comscore.com/Press_Events/Presentations_Whitepapers/2011/2010_Mobile_Year_in_Review> (accessed 7 January 2012).

Court D., Elzinga, D. Mulder, S. and Vetvik, O.J. (2009) 'The consumer journey', *McKinsey Quarterly*, June 2009. Available: <https://www.mckinseyquarterly.com/The_consumer_decision_journey_2373> (accessed 17 November 2011).

Cruz, B. and Mendelsohn J. (2010) *Why Social Media Matters to Your Business*. Chadwick Martin Bailey. Available: <http://www.cmbinfo.com/cmb-cms/wp-content/uploads/2010/04/Why_Social_Media_Matters_2010.pdf> (accessed 7 January 2012).

Daily Telegraph (2009) 'Virgin: the world's best passenger complaint letter?', *Daily Telegraph Travel*, 26 January 2009. Available: <http://www.telegraph.co.uk/travel/travelnews/4344890/Virgin-the-worlds-best-passenger-complaint-letter.html> (accessed 11 September 2011).

Danaher, P.J. and Rossiter, J.R. (2011) 'Comparing perceptions of marketing communication channels', *European Journal of Marketing*, 45(1/2): 6–42.

Dholakia, U.M. and Durham. E. (2010) 'One café chain's Facebook experiment', *Harvard Business Review*, 88(3): 26.

Divol, R., Edelman, D. and Sarrazin, H. (2012) 'Demystifying social media', *McKinsey Quarterly*, April 2012. Available: <http://www.mckinseyquarterly.com> (accessed 25 April 2012).

Edelman, D. (2010) 'Branding in the digital age', *Harvard Business Review*, 88(12): 62–9.

Fournier, S. (1998) 'Consumers and their brands: developing relationship theory on consumer research', *Journal of Consumer Research*, 24: 343–73.

Godin, S. (1999) *Permission Marketing*. New York: Simon and Schuster.

Keller, K. (2009) 'Building strong brands in a modern marketing communications environment', *Journal of Marketing Communications*, 15(2/3): 139–55.

Kim, J. and Hardin, A. (2010) 'The impact of virtual worlds on word-of-mouth: improving social networking and servicescape in the hospitality industry', *Journal of Hospitality Marketing and Management*, 19(7): 735–53.

Lab42 (2012) 'Techie traveler. the behavior of today's tech-based travel aficionado'. Available: <http://blog.lab42.com/techie-traveler> (accessed 25 March 2012).

Lecinski, L. (2011) 'Winning the zero moment of truth', *Knowledge@Wharton*, 11 May 2011. Available: <http://knowledge.wharton.upenn.edu/article.cfm?articleid=2825> (accessed 23 November 2011).

Lee, D., Kim, H. and Kim, J. (2011) 'The impact of online brand community type on consumer's community engagement behaviors: consumer-created vs. marketer-created online brand community in online social-networking web sites', *CyberPsychology, Behavior and Social Networking*, 14(1/2): 59–63.

McKinsey (2011) 'Are your customers becoming digital junkies?', *McKinsey Quarterly*, July.

Mathieson, R. (2002) 'The future according to Spielberg: *Minority Report* and the world of ubiquitous computing', *Mpulse Magazine*, August 2002. Available: <http://www.rickmathieson.com/articles/0802-minorityreport.html> (accessed 5 October 2011).

Mogg, T. (2011) 'Foursquare hits a billion check-ins, looking forward to "the next quadrillion"', *Digital Trends*, 20 September 2011. Available: <http://www.digitaltrends.com/mobile/foursquare-hits-a-billion-check-ins-looking-forward-to-the-next-quadrillion/> (accessed 5 March 2012).

Mulhern, F. (2009) 'Integrated marketing communications: from media channels to digital connectivity', *Journal of Marketing Communications*, 15(2–3): 85–101.

Negroni, C. (2011) 'Tracking your Wi-Fi trail', *The New York Times*, 22 March: B5.

Page, K. and Mapstone, M. (2010) 'How does the web make youth feel? Exploring the positive digital native rhetoric', *Journal of Marketing Management*, 26(13–14): 1345–366.

Palmatier, R.W., Burke, C.B., Bechkoff, J.R. and Kardes, F.R. (2009) 'The role of gratitude in relationship marketing', *Journal of Marketing*, 73: 1547–7185.

Rainie, L. (2011) 'The social media landscape', Pew Research Center's Internet and American Life Project, 20 September 2011. Available: <http://www.pewinternet.org/Presentations/2011/Sept/Social-Media-Landscape.aspx> (accessed 13 November 2011).

Reed, D. (2010) 'Smartphone use grows among travellers', *USA Today*, 30 August.

Roberti, J. (2011) 'QandA', *Marketing Week*, 2 June: 29.

Sengupta, S. (2012) 'Risk and riches in user data. Scrutiny of Facebook threatens its top asset', *New York Times*, 27 February: B1.

Sparkloft Media (2011) 'State of the travel and tourism industry: social media 2011'. Available: <http://sparkloftmedia.com/blog/resources/state-of-the-travel-and-tourism-industry-in-social-media-2011/> (accessed 25 January 2012).

Sullivan, E. (2010) 'A group effort', *Marketing News*, 28 February: 22–8.

Sweney, M. (2009) '"Best job in the world" campaign storms Cannes Lions advertising awards', *The Guardian*, 23 June 2009. Available: <http://www.guardian.co.uk/media/2009/jun/23/best-job-advertising-awards> (accessed 25 March 2012).

Trendwatching (2011) '11 Crucial Trends for 2011'. Available: <http://www.trendwatching.com/trends/11trends2011/> (accessed 2 May 2011).

Valos, M.J., Ewing, M.T. and Powell, I.H. (2010) 'Practitioner prognostications on the future of online marketing', *Journal of Marketing Management*, 26(3–4): 361–76.

Walt Disney World (2011) 'Love sharing your knowledge of Mickey's California crib? Raced around every attraction at Walt Disney World Resort?', *PRNewswire*, 12 September 2011. Available: <http://multivu.prnewswire.com/mnr/disneyparks/48532 /> (accessed 2 March 2012).

36

Premises and promises of social media marketing in tourism

Ulrike Gretzel and Kyung-Hyan Yoo

Introduction

The term social media refers to a collection of technological applications and platforms that were originally designed to support social interactions among individuals. While some of them (e.g. virtual communities) have been available for quite some time, there has been a recent surge in development of such applications, which has prompted a need to create a summary term and to better understand their use. Enticed by the large numbers of prospective customers reachable through these media and encouraged by the technology developers who integrated advertising-based business models to attract funding, it did not take long for companies to discover the commercial potential of social media. The viral component of social media makes them especially attractive as messages can achieve enormous reach without big marketing investments. However, due to the infancy and ongoing development of most of these social media, companies have yet to determine how to best use social media for marketing purposes. It is therefore important to look at the fundamental principles of social media and related consumer behaviours, and to infer theoretical foundations in order to identify marketing opportunities and inform marketing practice.

Interactive media, i.e. computer-based media that are able to respond to individual consumer inputs with specific content, offer unique possibilities for marketers to promote products and services but also require adjustments of marketing strategies (Schlosser and Kanfer 2000). Interactive media call for interactive marketing, which is essentially built on information *from* the customer, not just *about* the customer (Day 1998). Parsons, Zeisser and Waitman (1998) stress that successful interactive marketing includes:

1 attracting users;
2 engaging users' interest and participation;
3 retaining users on sites;
4 learning about user preferences; and
5 relating back to users in the form of customized interactions.

Gretzel, Yuan and Fesenmaier (2000) already described the essential outcomes of such marketing approaches in the early days of online tourism marketing as deeper relationships and greater customization. Both are essential for survival in the increasingly competitive tourism domain.

Social media marketing builds on these assumptions of interactive marketing, but the interactive media it takes advantage of are fundamentally different from the websites available when the first interactive marketing strategies were developed. Social media marketing is essentially interactive marketing 'on steroids', with a much greater focus on relationships and a more active role of consumers in creating and distributing marketing messages than in traditional forms of marketing. It is fuelled by an increasing number of interactive media that support social interactions such as co-creation and content sharing and a growing number of users worldwide. For example, eMarketer (2012) predicted that in 2012 about one in every five people worldwide will use social networking sites, with the largest populations of users residing in China and the United States and growth rates being the highest in India and Indonesia. Given this massive adoption of social media around the globe, social media marketing will soon become a standard way for marketers to interact with consumers. This means that a fundamental shift in communication approaches across all media and in the structure of company–customer relationships is to be expected. To anticipate this change, it is important to understand the basic social media marketing principles.

This chapter will give a basic overview of social marketing principles and strategies, discussing its premises and promises specifically in the context of tourism, where the nature of the product and the context of interactions create unique opportunities but also lead to enormous challenges for social media marketers.

Social media marketing defined

Social media marketing discourse is full of acronyms that are often used interchangeably but sometimes refer to slightly different things or perspectives. Also, while in-depth knowledge of the technology that drives social media marketing is not necessary, it is important to recognize the technological basis of these marketing initiatives and how the marketing approaches are intertwined with the developments and resulting cultures of the Internet and its specific applications. This section of the chapter provides definitions and presents fundamental assumptions that shape social media marketing philosophies.

Web 2.0, the Social Web, social media, CGM and UGC

Web 2.0 refers to Internet technology and applications that allow users to be actively engaged in creating and distributing Web content (Gillin 2007). While the Internet and the Web have always emphasized content creation and sharing, Web 2.0 technologies (e.g. XML, Ajax, API, RSS, mash-ups, etc.) make it a lot easier for data to be exchanged. Contents are much more moveable and interactions more visible, giving rise to what is often referred to as the Writable or Social Web (Gillin 2009). As such, the term Social Web describes the totality of the phenomenon, including technologies, contents and connections. Safko and Brake (2009: 6) describe the Social Web as 'activities, practices, and behaviours among communities of people who gather online to share information, knowledge, and opinions'. The notion of the Social Web therefore emphasizes aspects of the Web that make it a networked conversation space in which social dynamics play an important role.

While Web 2.0 refers to the technological base including programming languages and protocols that support the participatory nature of the Web, social media represent the platforms and channels through which content is created and shared. Thus, social media are Web-based applications built on the philosophical and technical foundations of the Web 2.0 that make it possible to create and easily transmit content (Safko and Brake 2009; Kaplan and Haenlein 2010). The text, pictures, videos, audio files, etc. created and shared through social media are called user-generated contents (UGC) (Gillin 2007) or consumer-generated media (CGM). The latter term is somewhat problematic in that it does not recognize the growing amount of content generated by corporate users. Both terms however stress that, in contrast to websites based on Web 1.0 technologies, social media contain contents produced by individuals other than the immediate owner/publisher of the site. Social media are all about people sharing opinions, experiences, expertise, interesting links, etc. (Gillin 2009).

It is important to recognize that the term social media encompasses a large array of specific types of media such as blogs, message boards, review sites, social networking sites, etc. Safko and Brake (2009) describe the phenomenon as a social media eco-system. This recognizes that social media do not represent a uniform species of technology applications but rather a multitude of channels and platforms that are interlinked and perform different functions. According to Constantinides and Fountain (2008), there are five main categories of social media, which include:

1. blogs;
2. social networks;
3. content communities;
4. forums/bulletin boards; and
5. content aggregators.

Kaplan and Haenlein (2010) classified social media into six types based on the degree of social presence/media richness and the degree of self presentation/disclosure. Their classification of social media includes blogs/microblogs (e.g. Twitter), social networking sites (e.g. Facebook), virtual social worlds (e.g. Second Life), collaborative projects (e.g. Wikipedia), content communities (e.g. YouTube) and virtual game worlds (e.g. World of Warcraft). The social media ecosystem is dynamic in that new social media types constantly emerge (e.g. Pinterest), some types become extinct (e.g. Friendster) and the prominence of a specific medium can change (e.g. MySpace evolving from a dominant social networking platform to a niche medium). Some of them even live in symbiosis, e.g. tweets can be displayed on Facebook pages.

The various social media types provide unique affordances in terms of the type of content that can be created and shared as well as the way of sharing. They have also developed their own conventions of what is appropriate and desirable. The different social media attract very different users (Gretzel, Fesenmaier, Lee and Tussyadiah 2011) and are characterized by specific cultures. Moreover, they provide marketers with varying options in terms of presenting and promoting content, interacting and forming relationships with existing and potential customers, and obtaining market intelligence.

The social media marketing paradigm

Social media marketing can be defined as using social media channels to promote a company and its products (Barefoot and Szabo 2010). The main difference is that the audience of the marketing messages not only consumes but also actively creates marketing contents (Evans 2008). Step 2 of the interactive marketing process (engaging users' interest and participation) (Parsons *et al.* 1998) is therefore critical in social media marketing campaigns. Engagement is indeed one of the buzzwords often used in social media marketing. Evans (2008) sees it as one of three pillars:

engagement, action and loyalty. It assumes an active audience of prosumers (Toffler 1980) who want to interact with marketers beyond the immediate sales transaction. It further acknowledges that loyalty in social media cannot be assumed, but must be actively assured (Kozinets 1999). Social media marketing thus falls within the new marketing logic described by Vargo and Lusch (2004), which, instead of focusing on tangible resources, embedded value and transactions, fully embraces intangible resources, co-creation of value and relationships.

Social media marketing is essentially about building relationships (Barefoot and Szabo 2010). In order to build those relationships, it needs to enable and shape conversations (Safko and Brake 2009). Social media marketers are therefore conversation managers who develop methods to strategically influence conversations (Mangold and Faulds 2009). Consequently, social media marketing is concerned with how conversations can be prompted, promoted and monetized (Safko and Brake 2009). Consumers are active participants and equal partners in these conversations who co-create value together with marketers by exchanging resources and information (Vargo and Lusch 2004). It is important to note that this means marketers cannot control these conversations but can only try to influence them. User generated contents can either reinforce marketing efforts or beat marketers at their own games (Evans 2008). It also implies that marketers need to obtain an intricate understanding of how meaning creation happens in a particular social media type and what use conventions have emerged so that they can manage conversations in a way that is appreciated rather than seen as intrusive by the consumers.

Social media marketing is based on traditional marketing but adopts a fundamentally different philosophy in terms of the way interactions with potential and actual customers are structured. Birch (2011) describes social media marketing as being focused on 4 Rs rather than the traditional 4Ps (Table 36.1). Similarly, Gunelius (2011) calls for well-planned, active and continuous engagement with influential consumers. This requires intricate knowledge of the social media types and their users, a long-haul commitment and continuous engagement through interesting content.

Reputation management is an important aspect of social media marketing as much of the consumer-generated content consists of opinions/reviews. Given the focus on conversations and reputation, social media marketing has a lot of similarities with public relations. However, it would be naive to narrow it down to just that. As illustrated by Yoo and Gretzel (2010), social media marketing functions span across all elements of marketing (Table 36.2). Therefore, social media marketing efforts should be seen as all-encompassing and as complementary extensions of other marketing efforts instead of a replacement (Evans 2008). It is important to note the much greater emphasis on research. This is the case not only because of the participatory culture and high trackability of interactions on social media but also the greater need to inform targeting to cut through the clutter and encourage viral spread.

Table 36.1 Marketing paradigm shift

Classic marketing	*Twenty-first-century marketing*	*Social media marketing*
Product	Experience	Relationship
Price	Exchange	Return on engagement
Place	Everyplace	Reach based on relevance
Promotion	Evangelism	Reputation

Source: Adapted from Birch (2011)

Table 36.2 Social media marketing functions

Traditional marketing	*Marketing functions*	*Social media marketing*
– One-way communication – Offline customer service center – Limited customer data – B2C communication – Prescribed solutions; scripted responses – Delayed response – One-off interaction	Customer relations	– Interaction – Online customer service – Customer identification with data mining – Virtual customer communities – Crowd sourcing – Real-time communication – Relationship
– Limited product information – Mass products for mainstream markets – Company-created products	Product	– Value added info on products: pictures, video, catalogue, consumer reviews etc. – Product customization – Co-creation with consumers – Digital/virtual product
– One-price pricing – Limited payment options	Price	– Flexible pricing (price transparency) – Online payment – Social buying
– Offline promotions – One promotion message – Partnerships with traditional partners – Targeting customers – Mediated through mass media	Promotion	– Online promotions – Customized promotion messages – Non-traditional partnerships – Customer participation – Viral spread facilitated by Web 2.0 tools
– Intermediaries – Required time to process order/ booking – Offline distribution of products	Place	– Dis-/re-intermediation – Real-time ordering and processing – Online distribution of products
– Delayed results – Push – Encouraged through incentives – No follow-up – Mediated – Sporadic – Costly – Response limited to numbers and text	Research	– Real-time info through RSS or email alerts – Pull – Based on altruistic motivations – Immediate reaction – Unmediated – Continuous – Free data – Multiple formats
– Leads – Discrete times – Hard sales/visitor numbers	Performance measurement	– Conversations – Continuous – Consumer sentiment

Source: Adapted from Yoo and Gretzel (2010)

Both Table 36.1 and Table 36.2 clearly illustrate the focus on customer relationships. Diller (2000) identifies the building blocks of relationship marketing as encompassing '6is' (Figure 36.1):

1 information about customers;
2 investments in customers;

3 individuality for customers;
4 interaction with customers;
5 integration of customers; and
6 intention of a unique relationship.

These principles still hold true for social media marketing but the way they are defined and implemented is fundamentally different. Information about customers is a fundamental component but now not only includes basic demographic and transactional data but a massive amount of opinions and social data that is readily available to companies. Marketers still need to decide in which customers to invest but customer value needs to be redefined and customer expectations of what an 'investment' in them looks like have changed. Also, the enormous amounts of data available allow for different segmentation approaches and the nature of social media allows for extensive behavioural targeting not possible before. Individuality through personalization creating an aura of exclusivity is essential for traditional relationship marketing while in a social media context customers are more concerned with relevance and social sharing of offers. Interaction with customers and their integration into value-creation processes have reached new levels in social media marketing with interaction being continuous and customers being more than willing to provide inputs in a variety of ways (Sigala 2012). Both build fundamentally on the data, segmenting, targeting and personalizing that represent the base of the relationship marketing pyramid. Also, in addition to customer–company interactions, social media marketing is about stimulating and supporting customer–customer interactions, a tactic often referred to as tribal marketing (Pace, Fratocchi and Cocciola 2007). There is still an intention to build a lasting relationship but companies cannot expect that this means customers will not form similar relationships with competitors. Also, these relationships are now visible to other customers and competitors (e.g. customers' 'liking' of a company is visible on their Facebook timeline).

In order to design and implement successful social media marketing campaigns, it is essential to understand the culture on which social media-based interactions are formed. The Social Web

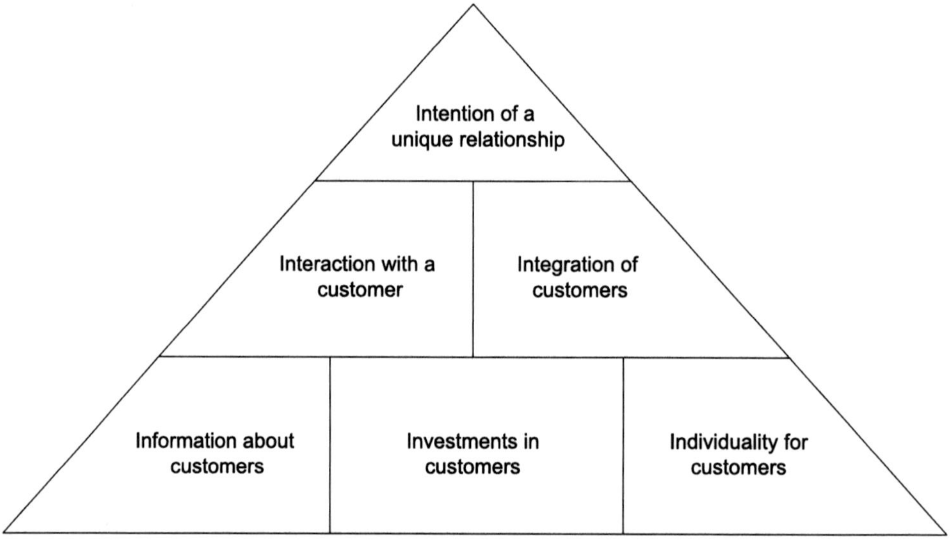

Figure 36.1 Relationship marketing pyramid (adapted from Diller 2000).

is all about democracy, community, collaboration, authenticity and transparency (Barefoot and Szabo 2010). Social media contents contribute to informed consumption choices by aggregating and making available the collective experience and resultant conversations of consumers (Evans 2008). Social media of the pre-marketing days were platforms where consumers turned to each other for unbiased information, avoiding ads and sales pitches. Kaplan and Haenlein (2010) stress the importance of acknowledging that social media marketing is fundamentally about participation, sharing and collaboration rather than straightforward advertising and selling. This puts marketers into an unfamiliar and somewhat awkward situation and has prompted some to pose as consumers in a desperate attempt to fit in with the rest of the social media users and their conversations. Many of these efforts backfired as they violate the transparency principle. Marketers need to be genuine partners in the social media conversations in order to be respected and listened to.

Trust is essential to any form of conversation on the Social Web (Evans 2008), and such trust needs to be earned. While consumer-based word-of-mouth is typically seen as trustworthy, marketers have to work hard in order to establish credibility in the social media space. This can only be done through open and authentic communication that aims at generating genuine connections. Meerman Scott (2007) summarizes the social media marketing paradigm as follows:

- authenticity instead of spin;
- participation instead of propaganda; and
- close the sale, continue the conversation.

Thus, it becomes clear that social media marketing is still very much based on basic marketing principles aiming at profit maximization, but that the focus and the tools are fundamentally different.

Social media marketing strategies

The paradigm shift in underlying assumptions implies a need for innovative strategies to achieve marketing success in the new conversation space. Strategic marketing questions to be asked are how social media can be used to create additional business value and how they can help in the realms of customer acquisition and retention (Constantinides and Fountain 2008). Unfortunately, there is not much academic literature available that has specifically looked at marketing strategy in the context of social media. This section of the chapter therefore summarizes strategy insights mostly derived from social media marketing practice.

One fundamental strategic decision to make relates to channel presence. Hamill, Stevenson and Attard (2012) distinguish between 'high' (present in two-thirds or more of the available channels), 'medium' (present in half to two-thirds) and 'low' (presence in less than half). Many of the channels can now be linked (e.g. Twitter updates and Pinterest posts appear on Facebook, and videos posted on YouTube can be inserted into other social media postings), allowing for important synergies. The channel presence strategy decision is a function of the target markets and their specific preferences for certain social media. It is important to stress that the social media landscape is dynamic and that the channel presence needs to be continuously adjusted.

The other element is the engagement profile. It describes the depth and level of engagement within a specific social medium (Hamill *et al.* 2012). Indeed, Hamill *et al.* (2012) convincingly argue that mere presence is not enough for achieving social media success. Rather it requires interesting conversations to be held with the right audience. Taken together, channel presence and engagement profile lead to four generic types of social media strategy (Elowitz and Li 2009):

1 Mavens (high level of engagement across a range of social media);
2 Butterflies (use of a large number of social media but only low to medium engagement);
3 Selectives (high engagement in a small number of media); and
4 Wallflowers (small number of channels and only low to medium engagement).

Overall, social media marketing strategy has to tackle two big issues:

1 which social media among the plethora of available types to select; and
2 how to communicate within a specific medium.

The diversity of social media makes it impossible to be present in all and requires selection based on relevance for specific marketing goals (Gunelius 2011). Kaplan and Haenlein (2010) also stress the importance of choosing social media outlets carefully and taking advantage of already existing applications instead of re-inventing the wheel. They also strongly argue for ensuring activity alignment across social media, as well as making certain that employees stand fully behind the company's social media engagement. This suggests that internal marketing takes on a significant role in the context of social media marketing.

It is important to note that social media marketing and search engine marketing are closely intertwined strategies. Social media provide increased online visibility (Barefoot and Szabo 2010). The structure of social media makes them attractive for search engine spiders, increasing the likelihood of social media to be frequently indexed and to appear on top of search listings (Xiang and Gretzel 2010). Providing interesting contents on a website or blog encourages users to link to the content through their social media platforms, which increases the incoming links for the page on which the content resides. On the other hand, marketers have to assure that their social media content can be found. For messages to effectively diffuse a social network, they have to reach central (influential) nodes (Pan and Crotts 2012). This, in turn, requires an understanding of who the influencers are in a social network and how they can be best reached using social media channels.

Social media marketing strategies need to be culturally sensitive. First, the availability, penetration and popularity of certain social media types differ significantly across countries (Gretzel, Kang and Lee 2008). Second, the very same social media are used differently by different cultures. For instance, Lee, Yoo and Gretzel (2009) found significant differences in the way US and Korean travellers use blogs to communicate their tourism experiences, with US blogs being more focused on recording and sharing one's personal experience while Korean bloggers focus on giving recommendations to influence the experiences of others. Third, specific social media platforms emphasize specific modes of communication, including recreational, informational, transformational and relational modes (Kozinets 1999). This leads to the creation of social media type-specific interaction cultures. Gunelius (2011) points out that social media marketing requires learning how consumers engage in a specific social media type and what value they want to derive from their engagement.

Whatever the specific strategy is, its execution needs to reflect what the company stands for. Given the value placed on trust and authenticity by most social media users, approaches have to be genuine and backed by the necessary resources. Hiring a PR firm or advertising agency to implement the overall strategy appears to be inherently counter-productive. However, certain aspects of social media marketing might have to be outsourced given the resource constraints of smaller organizations and the intense and continuous level of engagement required by some social media initiatives.

Measuring social media marketing outcomes

Relevance can only be assured if social media are continuously monitored and effects of marketing campaigns are effectively tracked. Fortunately, interactions in the social media space leave digital traces that can be tracked and measured. The issue is what should be tracked and how it can be translated into measures that can directly inform strategic marketing decisions. This section offers a brief overview of social media monitoring as a way to inform social media marketing strategies.

Based on the definition of social media as conversation spaces, monitoring involves trying to understand who is talking to whom and what they are saying (Evans 2008). One of the problems to consider when monitoring social media-based conversations is that there are different levels of user engagement (Tedjamulia, Olsen, Dean and Albrecht 2005). The majority of users are lurkers and only a small percentage of users are active content creators (Yoo and Gretzel 2011; Gillin 2009). These content creators have specific demographic characteristics and personalities and might not be representative of the company's typical target market. Another challenge lies in most content posted being positive (Gillin 2009; De Ascaniis and Gretzel 2012). Overall ratings of experiences such as in the case of travel reviews, for example, do often not reflect the actual content of the review (Jiang, Gretzel and Law 2010). This means that superficial measures can be very misleading and general brand sentiment might not be a very insightful measure. It is very important to include not only the conversations these consumers have with the marketers but also those they have among themselves. This requires knowing where such conversations take place.

The currency of social media marketing is influence. This means that the effectiveness of social media marketing campaigns should be measured in terms of influence. This is not only a question of what kind of influence is exercised but also on whom. The goal is to reach those who will likely help spread the message. Influencers in the social media space are a new breed of opinion leaders and should not be confused with traditional influencers (e.g. celebrities, etc.). Influencers can be described based on their level and type of engagement with the brand as well as their desire and ability to influence others (Gillin 2009). Influencers play a critical role in shaping conversations. There are increasing efforts in the social media space to identify those with greater influence than others. Klout.com is an example of such an initiative.

Success in social media marketing is not about return on investment but rather return on engagement (Frick 2010). Harden and Heyman (2009) describe the 'mathematics of engagement' as requiring a focus on click depth rather than just clicks, loyalty (number of visits), recency (return visits within a certain time frame), visit duration, interactivity (consumer actions such as comments, retweets, etc.) and commitment (e.g. subscription). These outputs have to be related to the engagement inputs on the marketer side, e.g. the number of posts, types of contents posted, frequency of posts, etc.

The relationship focus of social media marketing implies that its value is the network, i.e. the connections established with consumers and other stakeholders (Gillin 2009). However, not all connections are equal. Thousands of 'likes' on Facebook and 'followers' on Twitter are only of value if they represent genuine connections. While research exists on motivations of consumers to contribute contents in virtual communities (Yoo and Gretzel 2009), very little information exists on why consumers would want to connect with companies. Gretzel (2010) found that most consumers define their relationships with companies on Facebook as functional and benefit-based rather than emotional. Understanding what drives consumers to connect with marketers is critical in being able to provide value.

The strategic need for social media monitoring has led to the emergence of social media monitoring tools, which are applications that facilitate monitoring across multiple social media channels by indexing relevant information, providing mechanisms for marketers to search the information (e.g. by keyword, date, etc.) and allowing for further analysis and data visualisation (Stevenson and Hamill 2012). Stevenson and Hamill (2012) have identified over 200 of such tools currently available. Their main uses lie in supporting active listening to consumer-driven conversations and measuring the effectiveness of social media marketing campaigns. Social media monitoring tools are supported by general Web analytics tool.

In summary, new marketing assumptions demand new ways to measure performance. The above suggests that social media monitoring is an emerging field that has yet to establish sound measures and measurement approaches but at the same time relies heavily on the ability to determine success beyond established marketing effectiveness measures such as impressions and conversion. Thus, it can be assumed that social media monitoring will continue to receive increased attention from researchers and practitioners.

Challenges and opportunities for social media marketing in tourism

Conversations are fundamental elements of tourism information search and decision-making. The sharing of experiences through personal narratives, pictures, etc. is also an integral part of tourism experiences (Gretzel *et al.* 2011). The personal experience accounts of others serve as input for those planning vacations or as inspiration for the future. Therefore, it is not surprising that social media have become heavily used by travellers to document and communicate their experiences and to inform their decisions (Yoo and Gretzel 2008; Fotis, Buhalis and Rossides 2012). Tourism content is inherently experiential and very engaging and, therefore, a seemingly natural fit for social media. There is also often a strong feeling of solidarity among fellow travellers and an acknowledgement that experiential tourism information should be shared with others to help improve their tourism experiences and promote those providers that offer exceptional service. Some of the early virtual communities were actually tourism-related (e.g. the Lonelyplanet thorn tree forum) and simply mimicked the sharing behaviours that were already occurring through other media (e.g. comments left on bulletin boards in hostels). This can make one assume that tourism is a perfect match for social media marketing endeavours. However, marketers have to recognize that many of the platforms emerged for the very purpose of avoiding conversations with marketers and a clear distrust in information coming from travel companies. Couchsurfing.com is the ultimate negation of the commercial travel industry, trying to cut companies completely out of the picture. On the other hand, tourism products are often seen as status symbols and important elements of identity construction (Lee *et al.* 2009). Associating with a travel company or destination through social media can be an important part of establishing a social traveller identity. Yet, travellers will probably be very careful in choosing companies and destinations they want to openly associate with.

Another aspect of tourism that needs to be recognized is variety seeking and low purchase incidences. The main question is whether tourists want to commit to long-term relationships with travel companies or destinations if they really only consume their products once in a while or actually only once in a lifetime. While a deep relationship might be useful in the planning phases, during the trip and immediately after a vacation, the value of a relationship beyond that has to be questioned. While there is a lot of focus on the 'rules of engagement' in social media, there is clearly also a need to discuss 'rules of disengagement', especially in tourism. The need for such disengagement from a consumer perspective will of course largely depend on the type of social medium used and the kinds of interactions it fosters, with some media being more 'pushy' than others. The question is whether content continuously pushed toward users who no longer have an immediate interest in the company can actually lead to negative effects. Social media marketers in tourism need to carefully think about opportunities to engage with users who might no longer have a desire to travel to a specific destination or use specific services. Social media marketing in tourism thus requires a very holistic view of the customer lifecycle.

Much has been said about different social media types requiring different strategic approaches. Given the complexity and diversity of players in the tourism industry, one has to also consider that strategies have to be adjusted based on the specific type of provider. Empirical research conducted by Gretzel and colleagues (Gretzel 2010; Gretzel and Fesenmaier 2012) indicates that relationships formed with destinations on Facebook are fundamentally different from those formed with travel companies such as hotels, airlines and restaurants. While relationships with travel companies are formed to obtain exclusive deals, relationships with destinations are more focused on information and expressing emotional attachment. Such differences have to be acknowledged and taken into account when deciding on strategies.

There are many small tourism providers and destination marketing organizations (DMOs) who do not have the organizational capacities to engage in labour-intense social media campaigns. While social media provide immense opportunities to level the playing field by offering marketing opportunities with low entry costs and potentially immense reach, there are barriers to adoption based on lack of knowledge and lack of human resources. Continuous conversations require someone to actually engage with potential and actual consumers. Hamill *et al.* (2012) applied the Elowitz and Li typology presented above to national DMOs in Europe and found that only one DMO was actually a maven, engaging deeply across a wide range of social media. Shao, Davila Rodriguez and Gretzel (2012) illustrate how some DMOs have taken advantage of social media (e.g. through hosting polls on Facebook that introduce potential travellers to the various attractions at a destination) and have experimented with different approaches (e.g. linking the destination's YouTube channel to Google Maps and encouraging sharing through a variety of social media platforms). However, the research also recognizes that in general, social media are not used to their full potential in the destination marketing realm.

Conclusion

Social media marketing requires understanding the social dynamics of the Web as a vast networked space and further demands adjustments of marketing strategies to embrace the technological capabilities as well as the interaction cultures that have emerged in various social media types. Social media marketing campaigns are often perceived as cheap and therefore not carefully executed. The hidden costs lie in having to engage with consumers in much deeper, more authentic, more personal and continuous manners than through traditional media. Consumer expectations are high in the social media space and negative word can spread fast. Deciding on where to establish a presence and how to enable and shape conversations are important strategic decisions. Social media marketing can also not happen in a vacuum but, rather, needs to complement the overall marketing mix strategies. For tourism marketers, social media open up a new world of possibilities to form meaningful connections with actual and potential customers. However, social media engagement has to be carefully designed and continuously managed in order to be successful. This requires not only commitment of resources but often also a complete change in organizational culture, especially with respect to how the tourism organization manages customer relationships.

Social media marketing is a dynamic field with new technologies and new advertising models constantly emerging. This means that the social media landscape keeps changing and that social media marketing strategies have to be continuously adjusted to new and often fleeting realities. This makes it incredibly difficult to prescribe rules on how success can and should be achieved. The dynamic nature also stresses the need for research in this area and strong theoretical bases so that new phenomena can be described comprehensively, explained in detail and maybe even anticipated. While general use of social media by travellers and motivations to create contents are receiving growing attention by researchers (Yoo and Gretzel 2012; Cox, Burgess, Sellitto and Buultjens 2009), very little is currently known about how travellers perceive and react to specific marketing tactics implemented online and how they would prefer to relate and engage with travel companies and destinations through social media. Also, while there are considerable research efforts in the sentiment analysis space, these are often driven by computer scientists who have very little understanding of the intricate nature of tourism. Further, the theory–practice gap is especially large in social media marketing in tourism as many of the tourism businesses have yet to make the shift towards the data-driven approaches that form the basis of successful social media marketing. Therefore, there is a great need to build theory in this area and also to develop the appropriate methodologies that will allow for obtaining the insights needed from a theoretical as well as marketing practice point of view.

References

Barefoot, D. and Szabo, J. (2010) *Friends with Benefits: A Social Media Marketing Handbook*. San Francisco, CA: No Starch Press.

Birch, D. (2011) 'Travel and Tourism is a Mature Business – Nothing Much Changes or Does It?', proceedings of the ENTER 2011 International Conference on Information and Communication Technologies in Tourism. Innsbruck, Austria, 26 January 2011.

Constantinides, E. and Fountain, S.J. (2008) 'Web 2.0: Conceptual Foundations and Marketing Issues', *Journal of Direct, Data and Digital Marketing Practice*, 9(3): 231–44.

Cox, C., Burgess, S., Sellitto, C. and Buultjens, J. (2009) 'The Role of User-generated Content in Tourists' Travel Planning Behaviour', *Journal of Hospitality Marketing and Management*, 18(8): 743–64.

Day, G.S. (1998) 'Organizing for Interactivity', *Journal of Interactive Marketing*, 12(1): 47–53.

De Ascaniis, S. and Gretzel, U. (2012). 'What's in a Travel Review Title?', in M. Fuchs, F. Ricci, and L. Cantoni (eds) *Information and Communication Technologies in Tourism*. Vienna, Austria: Springer, pp. 494–505.

Diller, H. (2000) 'Customer Loyalty: Fata Morgana or Realistic Goal?', in T. Hennig-Thurau and U. Hansen (eds) *Relationship Marketing. Gaining Competitive Advantage Through Customer Satisfaction and Customer Retention*. Berlin: Springer, pp. 29–48.

Elowitz, B. and Li, C. (2009) 'The World's Most Valuable Brands. Who's Most Engaged?' Online. Available http://www.engagementdb.com (accessed 10 April 2012).

eMarketer (2012). 'Where in the World are the Hottest Social Networking Countries?', Online. Available http://www.emarketer.com/Article.aspx?id=1008870andR=1008870 (accessed 17 April 2012).

Evans, D. (2008) *Social Media Marketing: An Hour a Day*. Indianapolis, IN: John Wiley and Sons.

Fotis, J., Buhalis, D. and Rossides, N. (2012) 'Social Media Use and Impact During the Holiday Travel Planning Process', in M. Fuchs, F. Ricci and L. Cantoni (eds) *Information and Communication Technologies in Tourism*. Vienna, Austria: Springer, pp. 13–24.

Frick, T. (2010) *Return on Engagement: Content, Strategy, and Design Techniques for Digital Marketing*. Burlington, MA: Focal Press.

Gillin, P. (2007) *The New Influencers: A Marketer's Guide to New Social Media*. Fresno, CA: Quill Driver Books.

— (2009) *Secrets of Social Media Marketing: How to Use Online Conversations and Customer Communities to Turbo-Charge Your Business!* Fresno, CA: Quill Driver Books.

Gretzel, U. (2010) 'Social Media and Travel', paper presented at the 41st Travel and Tourism Research Association Annual Conference. San Antonio, TX, 20–22 June 2010.

Gretzel, U. and Fesenmaier, D.R. (2012) 'Customer Relations 2.0 – Implications for Destination Marketing', paper presented at the TTRA Annual International Conference, 17–19 June 2012. Virginia Beach, VA.

Gretzel, U., Yuan, Y. and Fesenmaier, D.R. (2000) 'Preparing for the New Economy: Advertising Strategies and Change in Destination Marketing Organizations', *Journal of Travel Research*, 39(2): 146–56.

Gretzel, U., Kang, M. and Lee, W. (2008) 'Differences in Consumer-generated Media Adoption and Use: A Cross-national Perspective', *Journal of Hospitality Marketing and Management*, 17(1/2): 99–120.

Gretzel, U., Fesenmaier, D. R., Lee, Y.-J. and Tussyadiah, I. (2011) 'Narrating Travel Experiences: The Role of New Media', in R. Sharpley and P. Stone (eds), *Tourist Experiences: Contemporary Perspectives*. New York: Routledge, pp. 171–82.

Gunelius, S. (2011) *10 Laws of Social Media Marketing*. Online. Available at http://www.entrepreneur.com/article/218160 (accessed 18 April 2012).

Hamill, J., Stevenson, A. and Attard, D. (2012) 'National DMOs and Web 2.0', in M. Sigala, E. Christou, and Gretzel, U. (eds) *Social Media in Travel, Tourism and Hospitality: Theory, Practice and Cases*. Surrey, UK: Ashgate, pp. 99–120.

Harden, L. and Heyman, B. (2009) *Digital Engagement: Internet Marketing that Captures Customers and Builds Intense Brand Loyalty*. New York: AMACOM.

Jiang, J., Gretzel, U. and Law, R. (2010) 'Do Negative Experiences Always Lead to Dissatisfaction? – Testing Attribution Theory in the Context of Online Travel Reviews', in U. Gretzel, R. Law, and M. Fuchs (eds) *Information and Communication Technologies in Tourism*. Vienna, Austria: Springer Verlag, pp. 297–308.

Kaplan, A.M. and Haenlein, M. (2010) 'Users of the World, Unite! The Challenges and Opportunities of Social Media', *Business Horizons*, 52(1): 59–68.

Kozinets, R.V. (1999) 'E-Tribalized Marketing? The Strategic Implications of Virtual Communities of Consumption', *European Management Journal*, 17(3): 252–64.

Lee, Y.-J., Yoo, K.-H. and Gretzel, U. (2009) 'Social Identity Formation Through Blogging: Comparison of U.S. and Korean Travel Blogs', in *Proceedings of the 14th Annual Graduate Student Research Conference in Hospitality and Tourism*. Las Vegas, 4–6 January 2009.

Mangold, W.G. and Faulds, D.J. (2009) 'Social Media: The New Hybrid Element of the Promotion Mix', *Business Horizons*, 52(3): 357–65.

Meerman Scott, D. (2007) *The New Rules of Marketing and PR: How to Use News Releases, Blogs, Podcasting, Viral Marketing and Online Media to Reach Buyers Directly*. Hoboken, NJ: John Wiley and Sons.

Pace, S., Fratocchi, L. and Cocciola, F. (2007) 'Internationalization of a Craft Enterprise through a Virtual Tribe: 'Le Nuvole' and the Pipe-smoker Tribe', in B. Cova, R.V. Kozinets, and A. Shankar (eds) *Consumer Tribes*. Burlington, MA: Elsevier, pp. 312–28.

Pan, B. and Crotts, J.C. (2012) 'Theoretical Models of Social Media, Marketing Implications, and Future Research Directions', in M. Sigala, E. Christou, and U. Gretzel (eds) *Social Media in Travel, Tourism and Hospitality: Theory, Practice and Cases*. Surrey, UK: Ashgate, pp. 73–85.

Parsons, A., Zeisser, M. and Waitman, R. (1998) 'Organizing Today for the Digital Marketing of Tomorrow', *Journal of Interactive Marketing*, 12(1): 31–46.

Safko, L. and Brake, D.K. (2009) *The Social Media Bible: Tactics, Tools and Strategies for Business Success*. Hoboken, NJ: John Wiley and Sons.

Schlosser, A. and Kanfer, A. (2000) 'Culture Clash in Internet Marketing', in M.J. Shaw, R. Blanning, T. Strader, and A. Whinston (eds) *Handbook on Electronic Commerce*. New York: Springer Verlag, pp. 195–211.

Shao, J., Davila Rodriguez, M. and Gretzel, U. (2012) 'Riding the Social Media Wave: Strategies of DMOs Who Successfully Engage in Social Media Marketing', in M. Sigala, E. Christou, and U. Gretzel (eds) *Social Media in Travel, Tourism and Hospitality: Theory, Practice and Cases*. Surrey, UK: Ashgate, pp. 87–97.

Sigala, M. (2012) 'Web 2.0 and Customer Involvement in New Service Development: A Framework, Cases and Implications in Tourism', in M. Sigala, E. Christou, and U. Gretzel (eds) *Social Media in Travel, Tourism and Hospitality: Theory, Practice and Cases*. Surrey, UK: Ashgate, pp. 25–38.

Stevenson, A. and Hamill, J. (2012) 'Social Media Monitoring: A Practical Case Example of City Destinations', in M. Sigala, E. Christou, and Gretzel, U. (eds) *Social Media in Travel, Tourism and Hospitality: Theory, Practice and Cases*. Surrey, UK: Ashgate, pp. 293–311.

Tedjamulia, S.J.J., Olsen, D.R., Dean, D.L. and Albrecht, C.C. (2005) 'Motivating Content Contributions to Online Communities: Toward a More Comprehensive Theory', in *Proceedings of the 38th Hawaii International Conference on System Sciences (HICSS)*.

Toffler, A. (1980) *The Third Wave*. New York: Bantam Books.

Vargo, S.L. and Lusch, R.F. (2004) 'Evolving to a New Dominant Logic for Marketing', *Journal of Marketing*, 68(January): 1–17.

Xiang, Z. and Gretzel, U. (2010) 'Role of Social Media in Online Travel Information Search', *Tourism Management*, 31(2): 179–88.

Yoo, K.H. and Gretzel, U. (2008) 'Use and Impact of Online Travel Reviews', in P. O'Connor, W. Höpken, and U. Gretzel (eds) *Information and Communication Technologies in Tourism*. Vienna: Springer, pp. 35–46.

— (2009) 'What Motivates Consumers to Write Online Travel Reviews?', *Journal of Information Technology and Tourism*, Special Issue on Virtual Communities, 10(4): 283–96.

— (2010) 'Web 2.0: New Rules for Tourism Marketing', in *41st Annual Proceedings of the Travel and Tourism Research Association Conference*. San Antonio, TX, 20–22 June 2010. Travel and Tourism Research Association.

— (2011) 'Influence of Personality on Travel-Related Consumer Generated Media Creation', *Computers in Human Behavior*, 27(2): 609–21.

— (2012) 'Use and Creation of Social Media by Travellers', in M. Sigala, E. Christou, and U. Gretzel (eds) *Social Media in Travel, Tourism and Hospitality: Theory, Practice and Cases*. Surrey, UK: Ashgate, pp. 189–205.

37

Foundations of search engine marketing for tourist destinations

Zheng Xiang, Bing Pan and Daniel R. Fesenmaier

Introduction

The Internet has redefined the tourism industry in a number of important ways (Werthner and Klein 1999). On the demand side, most travellers rely on the Internet to look for information as part of the trip planning effort (USTA 2011), whereas on the supply side, tourism businesses and organizations have adopted the Internet as one of the primary communication channels for gaining and retaining visitors (Buhalis and Law 2008; Gretzel and Fesenmaier 2000). Indeed, reports by the US Travel Association indicate that search engines are becoming one of the most important channels used by a huge majority of online US travellers for vacation planning (USTA 2011). Additionally, studies indicate that the generation of online traffic to hospitality websites has led to a substantial number of direct bookings (Hopkins 2008; Prescott 2006). It was estimated that the value of the North America search engine marketing industry was worth US$16.6 billion in 2010 (eConsultancy 2010). Thus, search engine marketing has emerged as one of the most important strategic tools for marketing tourism destinations.

Search engines not only provide opportunities for tourism destinations and businesses to engage their potential visitors, but also pose many challenges. However, research on SEM is limited in both the marketing and tourism literature (Beckwith 2003; Ho and Liu 2005; Moran and Hunt 2005; Pan, Litvin and O'Donnell 2007; Sen 2005; Xiang, Gretzel and Fesenmaier 2009). Existing studies of search engines are mostly conducted within the computer science and information science fields, and focus primarily on the technical designs of search engines as information retrieval systems. Perhaps most important, it is argued that dynamic relationships exist between the search engine, tourism and other businesses, and the traveller as the search engine user. And, these dynamics of online search have not been well documented, let alone incorporated into SEM practices. From the destination marketing perspective, a series of important questions remain unanswered such as: How can a destination compete with other similar businesses knowing that they will probably adopt similar online marketing strategies? And how does a destination marketing organization (DMO) compete on search engine visibility given that search engines are constantly changing their algorithms?

With these questions in mind, the goal of this chapter is to synthesize the recent literature related to search engine marketing in general and for tourism specifically. This chapter is organized as follows. The following section is based upon an article by Pan, Xiang, Law and Fesenmaier (2011) which critically reviews the literature related to the three key 'actors' and their dynamic relationships in SEM, namely search engines, online travellers as search engine users and the online tourism domain. In the next section, a model is discussed to look at SEM at the behavioural level by outlining the process wherein travellers use a search engine for trip planning. Based upon these studies six key lessons for successful SEM practice as well as implications for research and development are discussed.

The structure of search engine marketing

Search engines are developed to provide access to the huge amount of information on the Internet by crawling, indexing, retrieving and representing relevant information for users based upon unique algorithms. Generally, Search Engine Marketing (SEM) is defined as a form of marketing on the Internet whereby businesses and organizations seek to gain visibility on search engine results pages (SERPs) through paid or non-paid means (Moran and Hunt 2005). There are several forms of SEM, including (see Table 37.1):

1. organic search-based techniques, i.e. search engine optimization, which involves employing methods that help improve the ranking of a website when a user types in relevant keywords in a search engine. These techniques include creating an efficient website structure, providing appropriate web content, and managing inbound and outbound links to other sites;
2. paid inclusion, which means paying search engine companies for inclusion of the site in their organic listings; and
3. search engine advertising, or paid placement, which implies buying display positions at the paid listing area of a search engine or its content network. Google AdWords and Microsoft AdCenter are the two most popular programs wherein paid placement listings are shown as 'Sponsored Links'.

The phenomenon of searching on the Internet has attracted numerous studies in computer science, information sciences and human computer interaction with the focus on the technological aspects

Table 37.1 Forms of search engine marketing

Type	*Form*	*Explanation*	*Payment scheme*	*Examples*
Nonpaid	Search Engine Optimization (SEO)	The process of improving the quality or quantity of traffic from search engines to a website	None paid to search engines	SEO practices
	Paid placement	Bidding on keywords on SERPs	Pay-per-click	Google AdWords Yahoo! Precision March
Paid	Contextual advertising	Pay to appear on relevant websites or web pages	Pay-per-click or Pay-per-thousand-impressions	Google AdSense
	Paid inclusion	Annual subscription fee to search engines to be included in their indices	Pay	Yahoo

Source: Sen (2005)

as well as user behaviors of searching (Brin and Page 1998; Jansen and Molina 2006; Jansen and Spink 2005a). The existing literature related to SEM can be organized according to the 'actors' that define the components of search engine marketing:

1 the search engine, defined as the online tools which algorithmically index, organize and retrieve relevant web documents and, according to user queries, present those documents in a pre-defined format (Gendler, Ellis, Chang and Davis 2005; Sen 2005);
2 the travel information searcher, defined as those travellers who are planning trips or gathering travel-related information on the Internet (Pan and Fesenmaier 2006); and
3 the online tourism domain, defined as the collection of links, domain names and web pages that contain texts, images and audio/video files related to travel and tourism (Pan and Fesenmaier 2006; Xiang, Wöber and Fesenmaier 2008).

The following three sections review this research with the goal of identifying the underlying structure and dynamics of search engine marketing.

The search engine

Metaphorically, search engines can be thought of as the 'Hubble Telescope of the Internet' in that they enable travellers to gain access to billions of web pages that comprise the online tourism domain (Xiang, Gretzel and Fesenmaier 2009; Xiang, Wöber and Fesenmaier 2008). The major part of the search engine interface is used to display those results based on the internal ranking (i.e. organic listing). In addition, major search engines such as Google, display paid advertisements on the top and right side of major result page, ranked by businesses' bidding price on clicks and the quality of pages, which is termed a 'Paid Listing.' Paid listings can also appear blended with organic listings for certain search engines, as they do in Baidu.com (the most popular search engine in mainland China) and Bing.com. However, the two companies separated the two types of results under pressure from the public in recent years (Back 2009; Schwartz 2009).

In 2012, Google had 66 per cent of online search volumes, followed by Bing and Yahoo! (comScore 2012). Among the components of search engines, the algorithm a search engine uses to rank web pages in organic listings is most important in determining which web pages to display and in what order. The rank of a web page for certain queries on most popular search engines determines their online visibility to a large extent (Pan, Hembrooke, Joachims, Lorigo, Gay and Granka 2007). Given a query, almost all search engines use certain characteristics of web pages and link structure to rank the web pages (Levine 2000). The characteristics of web pages include:

1 whether or not the keywords are in the Uniform Resource Locator (URL) of that page;
2 the frequency and size of the keywords on a web page;
3 the keywords in the link anchor text, i.e. pieces of text which contain a link. Usually web authors imbed meaningful link anchors to provide the user indications of the content on the linked page. Search engines view link anchors as good summaries of linked pages;
4 alternative text for images, i.e. the text associated with images; and
5 meta-tags, keywords in Titles and Descriptions embedded on a given web page (Cai, Feng and Breiter 2004).

Some search engines further incorporate the link structure of the web to determine the importance of web pages (Brin and Page 1998). A web page with many inbound links will be considered more valuable and important and, thus, having a higher importance compared to the ones with fewer inbound links. In addition, search engines use an iterative process to determine the quality of links (Brin and Page 1998; Langville and Meyer 2006; Levene 2006). Other criteria affecting page ranking include age of the site and the frequency of updating (Malaga 2007; Sullivan 2006), page loading time and the popularity of the page (Fish 2009).

In general, link structures, web page content, frequency of updating, the loading time and the implicit feedbacks in the form of click behavior from users are all determining factors in the ranking of search results. Still, indexing, ranking and representing the enormous amount of information on the Internet is a huge challenge for search engines. While the most popular search engine, Google, currently claims to index more than one trillion web pages (Google 2008), the entire information space on the Internet can only be covered in small parts by a single search engine (Levene 2006). The 'deep web' pages such as those buried in the databases and dynamic pages are not indexable by many search engines and, thus, are inaccessible to users who query a search engine (Bergman 2001; Lawrence and Giles 1999).

The travel information searcher

While travellers may use search engines at different stages of their trip, a majority of them find search engines particularly helpful in serving their trip planning purposes (TIA 2008; USTA 2011). Studies have shown that the process of using a search engine consists of two major cognitive steps including query formulation and search results evaluation. Search queries have been studied extensively in fields such as information sciences as well as travel and tourism (Jansen and Pooch 2001; Jansen and Spink 2005b; Jansen, Spink and Saracevic 2000; Pan *et al.* 2007; Pan, Litvin and O'Donnell 2007; Xiang and Pan 2011).

Search queries are short strings of words or terms that reflect a user's goals, information needs, search intent, as well as his/her search strategies. Studies in information science, consumer behavior and tourism have explored the characteristics of search engine queries such as the length and depth of search, types of search and changes of search characteristics over time. For example, a typical web session is around 15 minutes; 47 per cent of users only search once during a session; about 20 to 29 per cent of queries only contain one term; in the United States, around 11 to 20 per cent of user queries contained logical operators; users only view a few result pages, mostly the first page (73 per cent of users) (Jansen and Spink 2005b; Jansen, Spink and Saracevic 2000). Search queries reflect users' goals including navigational goals (looking for a specific web page), informational goals (trying to obtain a piece of information) and transactional goals (carrying out certain action) (Jansen and Molina 2006). Recently, Jansen *et al.* (2008) found that users' queries in general are largely informational (81 per cent), followed by navigational tasks (10 per cent) and transactional tasks (9 per cent).

In travel and tourism, recent studies indicate that travellers' questions tend to be short, consisting of less than four keywords; and, most travellers do not go beyond the results provided on the second page. As a result, only a relatively small number of websites are visible to the traveller though millions of potential web pages were found (Xiang, Wöber and Fesenmaier 2008). Pan *et al.*'s (2007) study also indicates that searchers in the US usually focus on cities as the geographical boundary instead of states or countries; and, travellers often combine their searches for accommodations with other aspects of the trip, including dining, attractions, destinations, or transportation. In addition, this study indicates that there are strong associations between place names (particularly city names) and a specific hotel and a hotel brand. Xiang *et al.* (2009) found that there are relatively few distinct words in travel queries beyond 'hotel' and 'attractions', indicating that there is a 'long tail' of words that represent travellers' heterogeneous information needs and their own mental images of the tourism experience and the idiosyncratic nature of place.

Researchers have also studied users' interaction with the search engine interface and it was found that the interface of search engines and the rank of web pages significantly influence which search results are chosen. For example, Henzinger (2007) found that the majority of search engine users do not look beyond the first three pages of search results. Pan *et al.* (2007) found that the position of organic search results influences users' perception of relevance in a non-linear way. Some studies also show that users are more likely to trust organic listings and organic listings have a higher conversion rate (Jansen and Resnick 2005; Marketing Sherpa 2005). Last, Kim and Fesenmaier (2008) found that the words included in search engines results have the potential to significantly affect one's overall evaluation of a destination website.

The online tourism domain

A domain can be defined as a collection of all informational entities about a specific subject (Pan and Fesenmaier 2006; Wöber 2006; Xiang, Wöber and Fesenmaier 2008). In the context of the Internet, a domain is the collection of links, domain names and Web pages that contain texts, images and audio/video files stored in hypertext formats. Therefore, the online tourism domain is comprised of all informational entities that are related to travel. Werthner and Klein (1999) proposed a conceptual framework to delineate the interaction between the consumer and the industry suppliers with the Internet playing a facilitating and mediating role. From an information search perspective, Pan and Fesenmaier (2006) used the term 'online tourism information space' to describe the collection of hypertextual content available for travel information searchers. More recently, Xiang *et al.* (2008) conceptualized the online tourism domain based upon the integration of a number of theoretical perspectives in tourism studies including:

1 the industry perspective with the focus on the composition of the supply of tourism on the Internet (Leiper 1979, 2008; Smith 1994);
2 the symbolic representation perspective describing the representation of tourism products and related experiences provided by the industry in various forms (Cohen and Cooper 1986; Dann 1997; Leiper 1990);
3 the travel behavior perspective including the activities and the supporting systems at different stages of the travel experience (Crompton 1992; Pearce 1982; Woodside and Dubelaar 2002); and
4 the travel information search perspective emphasizing the information sought to support travel experiences (e.g. Fodness and Murray 1998; Gursoy and McLeary 2004; Vogt and Fesenmaier 1998).

Wöber (2006) examined one very important aspect of the tourism domain, i.e. the visibility of tourism enterprises, particularly destination marketing organizations and individual hotel operations in Europe. His study indicates that many tourism websites suffer from very low rankings, which makes it extremely difficult for online travellers to directly access individual tourism websites. Xiang *et al.*'s (2008) analysis of the tourism domain suggests that the representation of the tourism industry through one of the most important interfaces, i.e. a search engine, is extremely rich, reflecting the idiosyncratic nature of destinations and travellers' heterogeneous information needs. In addition, their study demonstrated that popular search engines largely define the representation of the domain and, thus, shape the way online travellers and tourism suppliers use the Internet.

The online tourism domain was traditionally seen as primarily comprised of the so-called 'tourism industries'. However, with the growth of consumer/user generated content, travellers are now playing an increasingly important role as information providers on the Internet. A recent study conducted by Xiang and Gretzel (2010) shows that social media constitute a substantial part of the search results in search engines, indicating that search engines likely direct travellers to social media sites. Their study confirms the growing importance of social media in online tourism wherein tourism businesses have little control.

The dynamics of the search triad

The search triad, as shown in Figure 37.1, describes the interactions among the three parties that may have different goals, objectives, expectations, as well as their specific behaviors. They form a dialectic structure in which the behavior of each 'actor' is determined by the strategies and behavior of other 'actors', and their behavior will potentially change the strategies of others and, ultimately will lead to changes in the structure and balance of the system (Giddens 1976). Specifically, from the standpoint of the search engines, their role is to provide users relevant information on a given query in order to gain and retain loyal users to their company. They continue to modify the algorithms and interfaces based on a better understanding of users' search behavior and online tourism information. They also need to continuously explore ways to attract businesses to market with them, and at the same time, combat those businesses that misuse SEO and paid listings. From the perspective of the information searcher, travellers seek the most relevant information in order to plan their trips and as such, their search behavior is affected by their understanding, learning and overall trust toward search engines, knowledge of online tourism domain, image of the destination and the goals for their trip planning activities. These aspects of search behavior adapt to changing search engine algorithms and related

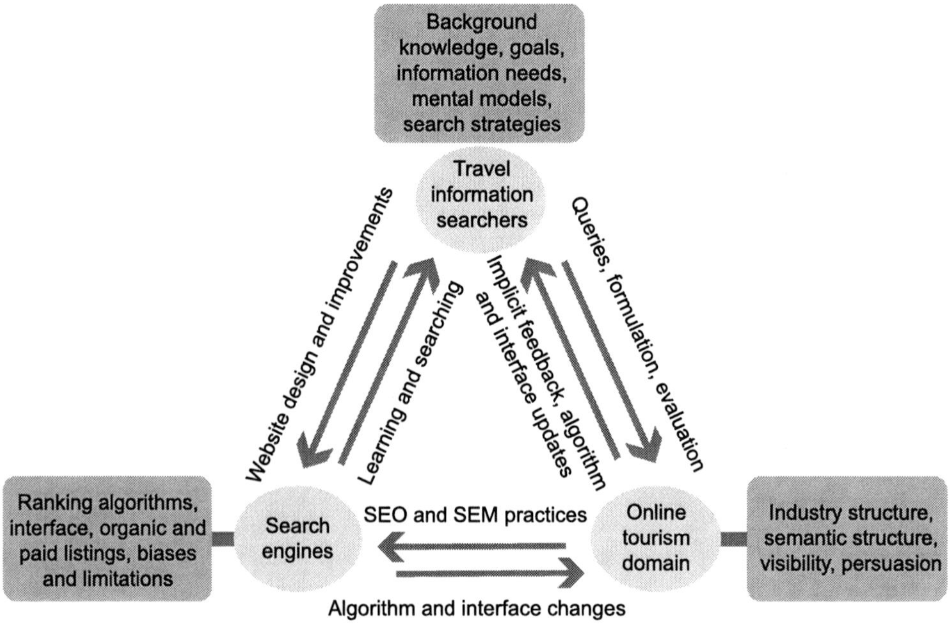

Figure 37.1 The search engine marketing triad.

technologies, the representation of relevant search results and increasing amount of travel information. Finally, from the perspective of the tourism businesses and organizations, they have to adapt to the changes brought about by both evolving technology and travellers as they seek to gain visibility and further customers on search engines. They must adopt a series of search engine practices as part of their strategy to gain a competitive advantage online.

Various studies have demonstrated this dynamic and co-evolving relationship. Users are adapting to changing search engines with their changing behavior. For example, from 1997 to 2001, an analysis on search engine transaction logs from Excite showed that there were significant decreases in the percentages of searches on topics such as entertainment and pornography, and significant increases in searches for commerce and people (Jansen, Spink and Pedersen 2005). Another study (Jansen and Spink 2005b) analyzed nine transaction log data from various search engines; their results showed that recent search engine users used simpler queries and viewed fewer result pages. They explain this phenomenon by search engines' algorithmic enhancements. A similar study (Malaga 2007) analyzed AltaVista search engine log from 1998 to 2002, and showed that recent users spent more time in one search session, typed in more keywords in a query, viewed more result pages and had broader search topics in 2002. The differences might be due to the different search engines analyzed. These studies indicated that users are changing their search behavior in relation to available information on the Web and the different and enhanced search algorithms.

From the information provider's perspective, tourism businesses and organizations have been taking advantage of the knowledge of ranking algorithms and trying to reach to the top on SERPs. They are in the forms of either legitimate format of SEM, endorsed by major search engines, or more malevolent types, in the form of search engine spamming or Google bombing (Bar-Ilan 2007). On one hand, industry cases have shown the successful SEM practices by destinations and tourism businesses (Brusha 2009; Google 2007). On the other hand, knowledgeable information providers, including common users and businesses, have been trying to use a variety of techniques for their own advantage, which might be against search engine use policies (Chaffey 2009). For example, Google bombing is a collective behavior by Internet users to change the positions of their web pages on Google by malicious hyperlinking (Sen 2005). For example, the home page of the previous president George W. Bush of the United States used to be the top Google result for the query 'miserable failure' due to the collective behavior of a number of right-wing bloggers when they hyperlinked his homepage with those keywords as text anchors (Bar-Ilan 2007). In addition, one common mistake businesses and organizations make relates to keyword stuffing, which is placing too many keywords in the tags (Bar-Ilan 2004).

Search engines are also tweaking their algorithms to combat businesses' misuses and adapt to changing user behavior. For example, Google adjusts their algorithms to stop search engine 'bombs' (eMarketer 2007). Search engines fought keyword spamming by decreasing the weight applied to each keyword (Bar-Ilan 2004). When facing more sophisticated users, Google have altered their interfaces, such as introducing Universal Search (blending images, blogs, videos and other formats of results together in SERP) and search filters, allowing users to slice and dice results (Google 2007a, 2009). The emerging Web 2.0 in terms of social media places a more and more important role, since search engines have granted those sites more weight (Xiang and Gretzel 2010). Recently, Google made a landmark change on their algorithm, termed Google Panda, in which PageRank was downgraded in importance while it gave more weights to new websites and social media sites (McCullagh 2011).

In general, dynamic and co-evolving relationships exist among travel information searchers, tourism businesses and the search engines, as three actors in this search system. However, search engines are only the technology which facilitates and mediates the connection between travellers and tourism businesses; travel information searchers, as users, are the central actor. Thus, discovering information needs of travellers and the way they express them in queries, and representing the tourism products honestly online and building the trust will be the unchanging communication philosophy for destination marketing organizations and other tourism businesses (Urban, Sultan and Qualls 2000). This philosophy should be the guiding principle to survive in the dynamic and evolving search engine world.

A framework for the use of search engines for travel planning

Search engine results provide essential clues about the traveller, the destination website and the destination itself. Recent research by Fesenmaier, Xiang, Pan and Law (2011) suggests that the use of a search engine by travellers can be described in three stages, where the first stage, namely Pre-Search Conditions, reflect travellers' use of (or preference for) various types of information as well as the perceived usefulness of the various travel tools (i.e. types of websites) available on the Internet. The second stage, namely Search Process, describes the basic strategies travellers use to navigate through the Internet to find relevant information in order to make various travel decisions. These strategies act as 'frames' within which the information accessed through use of search engines is evaluated (Dholakia and Bagozzi 2001; Fesenmaier and Jeng 2000). The third stage, i.e. Post-Search Evaluation, focuses on the overall evaluation of search engines. Importantly, this stage of use not only results in overall evaluation (i.e. satisfied vs. not satisfied), but also attitude formation toward search engine use for travel planning (Pan and Fesenmaier 2006). Finally, this third stage prepares one for future use of search engine for trip planning, and is therefore linked to the first stage in the overall process. It is argued that an in-depth understanding of these relationships is essential as destination marketers seek to optimize the conversion rate between seeing the search result and actually choosing to visit the destination website. The following provides a brief summary of the three stages of search.

Pre-search conditions

Figure 37.2 suggests that two constructs in Stage 1 determine, to a large extent, whether or not the traveller regularly uses a search engine as part of the online travel planning process. These constructs are the various types of information used (Fodness and Murray 1998; Vogt and Fesenmaier 1998; Vogt, Fesenmaier and MacKay 1993) and the perceived usefulness of the various tools/websites (Jansen and Molina 2006). Information search tasks can be measured by

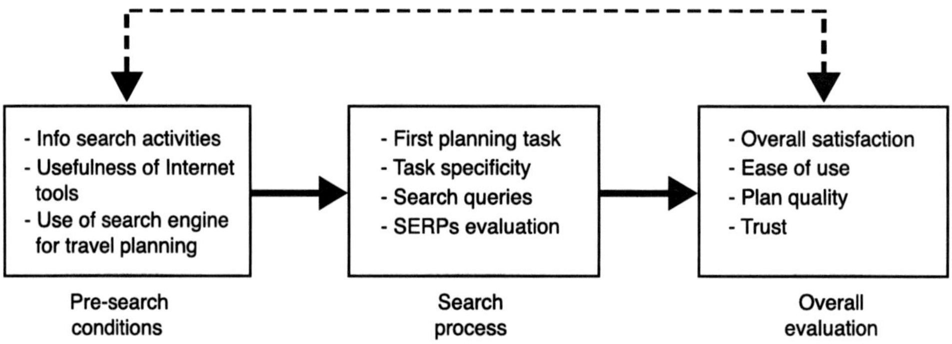

Figure 37.2 A general framework of the use of a search engine for travel planning.

the types of information travellers typically use when planning a pleasure trip including information about destinations, attractions, accommodations, car rental information and/or choosing routes. The perceived usefulness of various travel tools/websites, including travel agency sites, travel company sites, travel magazines, virtual communities, focuses on the ability of the Internet to support the travel planning effort. IT can be measured by the perceived usefulness of the various types of online tools/websites. Thus, one might expect that travellers with different information needs and their assessment of the various Internet travel planning tools would differ significantly in their use of search engines. Further, the interaction of these two constructs, search for travel information and use of various types of websites, enables one to gain experience, knowledge and the understanding necessary to evaluate the relative usefulness of search engines in helping find the information necessary.

The search process

The process of search within the context of travel planning shapes the strategies used in evaluating search engine results (Fesenmaier and Jeng 2000; Pan and Fesenmaier 2006). Also, following Jeng and Fesenmaier (2002), Pan and Fesenmaier (2000) and Hwang *et al.* (2009), the degree of specificity (i.e. general vs. specific) of the planning task also affects the way one evaluates search engine results. For example, a person having already decided to visit a particular destination might use an online travel agency in order to arrange the flight or use a company hotel website to book accommodations (i.e. a very specific task). However, if a person is undecided about a specific destination and is seeking information about alternative destinations, that person might use a travel community website or an online magazine to learn about potentially interesting places to visit.

Thus, an online search engine user (i.e. travel planner) will differ significantly in terms of the keywords entered into the search engine as well as the number of search results considered. Recent studies by Pan *et al.* (2006), Pan, Litvin and O'Donnell (2007) and Xiang *et al.* (2008) indicate that search strategies (i.e. keywords and number of search results) differ significantly depending upon the nature of the task (i.e. facet of the trip being considered and level of specificity) and user goals. For example, when a traveller has already decided the destination and seeks information about attractions to visit or a hotel to stay in, he/she would use the name of the destination as the keyword within a search engine; the number of search results he/she would evaluate would be limited. However, if the person perceives greater flexibility in the places to visit or the activities to participate in, he/she might search much further among the search engine results.

Post-search evaluation

Four constructs define the third stage of a search process, the evaluation stage. First, the online travel planner forms an overall evaluation of search engines use for travel planning, reflected in a general satisfaction measure (Pan and Fesenmaier 2006). Also, the experience is translated into attitudes towards search engines in terms of trust, ease of use and their efficacy in supporting the travel planning process (Gefen, Karahanna and Straub 2003; Gretzel, Fesenmaier and O'Leary 2006; Pan and Fesenmaier 2006). Thus, a person who is very satisfied with her/his use of search engines would consider search engines as trustworthy, easy to use and the search results enable the traveller to make better decisions. On the other hand, dissatisfied users might see search engines as untrustworthy, difficult to use and/or not very effective in helping them plan a trip. Finally, studies suggest that these evaluations and resulting attitudes shape the perceptions that travellers have of the Internet and travel planning tools as well as the use of search engines.

Closing the circle: linking post-search evaluation and pre-search conditions

The results of Fesenmaier *et al.* (2010) indicate that extremely satisfied users of general search engines are more likely to search for information about a particular destination (83 per cent), hotel prices or places to stay (72 per cent) and things to do at the destination (61 per cent); beyond this, no correlation exists between information search strategies for travel planning and satisfaction with general search engines. Interestingly, the extremely satisfied search engine users consistently perceived other types of online planning tools to be significantly more useful in finding online travel information than those who were not satisfied. These differences were consistent for most of the tools/websites considered. However, the reverse was true for those using travel guidebook sites such as Fodors or Lonely Planet; in this case, extremely unsatisfied search engine users were more likely to consider these tools essential and/or very useful.

Six key lessons for effective search engine marketing in tourism

With the increasing importance of search in travellers' access to information, tourist destinations and businesses must find better ways to adapt to the fast paced change in the environment. Search engine marketing comes to the fore to serve this purpose. However, a successful SEM program requires a deep understanding of the dynamics in SEM in tourism. This section synthesizes existing literature related to this topic. The proposed search triad model provides a comprehensive understanding of the foundations of SEM and offers important managerial implications for online tourism marketing as well as the construction of theories that describe the relationships between the three parties.

As described in the model, the three parties in the search triad all have different goals and perspectives; that is, they may compete and co-operate with each other at the same time. This system's perspective requires destination marketing organizations to adopt new ways of thinking. However, certain rules stay unchanged, i.e. the need to understand the traveller, the way travellers express their needs in queries and honestly representing one's products and making the connections with travellers' needs. Based on this understanding, the following key lessons are considered essential for a destination marketing organization to be competitive in search engine marketing. These are:

1 understanding user queries;
2 SERP design;
3 keyword targeting;
4 micro targeting;
5 competitive analysis; and
6 monitoring.

Each of these lessons is discussed as follows.

Key lesson #1: Understanding user queries

To merely study and understand the information needs of potential customers is not sufficient; one also needs to understand how travellers translate these needs into queries. Additionally, it is important to recognize the fact that queries vary depending on many factors including an individual's knowledge and experience, decision making stage, Internet use experience, etc. With a good understanding of how travellers develop queries, online marketers can link the words used by tourists with product offerings, and even alter or design new products.

Key lesson #2: SERP design

Search results (i.e. snippets) are short advertisements that represent 'first contact' with a potential visitor on a search engine, and establish a first impression of the destination. Thus, the snippets should be deliberately designed to fit within the strategic communication goals of the tourism organization. Additionally, one would expect that the words/terms used within the queries should relate directly (i.e. be included within) to the SERPs as they serve to reinforce the relevance of the website. Importantly, the way search engines create snippets from a site vary substantially; therefore, carefully monitoring the results of the search engine is crucial to effectively control the messages conveyed by it.

Key lesson #3: Keyword targeting

Search queries for a destination follow a long tail shape: a few keywords have tremendous search volumes while a large amount of niche keywords are searched infrequently. For popular keywords in the 'head' of the distribution curve such as the word 'hotels' or the name of a destination, the cost for both organic results and paid listing will be very high. Thus, DMOs should focus on complementing and/or strengthening the range of opportunities within the destination. For example in most American cities, 'hotels' is the most frequently used tourism-related search word associated with a destination and many top results for these queries are from major online travel agencies or online review sites such as expedia.com, hotels.com, or tripadvisor.com; many searches for a destination will also have a Wikipedia entry as one of the top results. In order to be effective, a sensible approach for a tourism destination is to provide additional resources beyond hotel reservations including offering opportunities to visit local attractions, alternative routes to the city etc.

Key lesson #4: Micro targeting

DMOs also need to be flexible in targeting the long tail because the niche keywords offer potentially substantial opportunities for tourism organizations to more effectively market to their target customer community. The long tail is represented by those niche geographic keywords more specific to a certain destination (such as 'DuPont Circle Washington DC') or seasonal keywords (such as 'Cherry Blossom Washington DC' in the spring). Studies indicate that these words offer DMOs the opportunity to gain premier positions in SERPs given their limited resources and huge competitions from the accommodation sector.

Key lesson #5: Competitive analysis

Given the dynamic relationships between the three actors, it is essential to anticipate similar approaches one's competitors might adopt. Those competitors are likely to bid on relevant keywords and adopt link campaigns targeting same organizations and bloggers. Indeed, a study conducted by Sen (2005) has shown that, when everyone is adopting search engine optimization on the same keywords, paid listing will give the businesses a competitive advantage. As such, destination marketing organizations need to differentiate themselves by adopting diverse SEM tactics or targeting different keywords. Organizations should avoid those keywords the dominating competitors in the marketplace will target and thus, avoid a heads-on rivalry for top positions. This strategy includes not only search engine optimization (SEO) to increase visibility in organic listings, but also the use of paid listings.

Key lesson #6: Monitoring

It is essential for DMOs to keep track of the dynamics of the search engine triad: the changing popularity and algorithms of search engines, the changing competitors on various tourism domains, and the changing behavior of travellers. Monitoring systems should be adopted to track these changes by assessing the ranking of each site, the changes in search volumes and the sudden drop or increase of conversion rates. Thus, search engine marketing is a continuous effort, requiring constant evaluation after the initial SEO and paid listing campaign. The tools for monitoring the rankings and tracking website performance include analytics tools such as Google Analytics and Google AdWords. With these tools, every user who clicked on a paid listing or website can be tracked and the DMOs or businesses could precisely monitor Return on Investment (ROI). Accurate data can reveal where visitors are visiting and what they are clicking on, which provides a wealth of information about businesses' web pages and online advertising. In addition, tourism businesses need to better monitor the information sources from the third-party and social media websites such as tripadvisor.com and take advantage of them.

Future developments in search engine marketing

Online marketing has been a focus of much research since the Internet became an important information source for travel marketing (Buhalis and Law 2008; Gretzel and Fesenmaier 2000; Wang and Fesenmaier 2003; Wang and Fesenmaier 2006; Werthner and Klein 1999; Werthner and Ricci 2004). The increasing importance of search and dominance of search engines gives rise to the need for fresh thinking because the focus for online marketing has shifted from improving the usability of a website toward utilizing search engines to attract and influence online travellers. In addition, the continuous struggle between different players on the Internet has been evidenced by the threat posed by websites such as Facebook in that social media are gaining important ground since their enormous amount of information that is not readily available for the search engines to index. This requires a paradigm shift that embraces a new set of notions including the social media for travel, the so-called Web 2.0, as well as the 'search economy' and the 'link economy'. Also, these trends demand a shift of marketing paradigm from delivering messages to influencing conversations between consumers and business partners and stakeholders. More studies are crucial in exploring the third-party information sources created by the consumers and other information resources.

Additionally, the conception of the dynamic relationships in the search engine triad indicates that there is a need to develop new metrics that can be used to evaluate the effectiveness of SEM programmes. For example, how should marketers define and measure the competitive space for a destination in the search context? How should the effectiveness of a tourism organization or business on search engines be measured? The metrics should include search volume for certain keywords, the ranking of a site or page on those keywords and the conversion rates. The benchmarking metrics might be different from one business to another, depending on the goals and strategies of the DMO or businesses. For example, if transactions are one of the goals, the revenue generated from clicks directly from search engines will be one metric; if the goal is to forward clicks to the web pages of other local tourism businesses, then outbound links should be monitored and reported frequently.

Last, the performance of the businesses, the performance of competitor websites and changes on the search engine algorithms should be monitored, tracked and studied continuously. Since user behaviour, information on the web and search engine algorithms change constantly, the online experiment at one time might not hold or be relevant over a longer time period. Obviously, within the changing technology field any study of search engines is bound to be a snapshot of the current landscape. Many technological developments will continue to change. For example, the search engine Bing.com claims to be a 'decision engine' by providing a search function specifically for travel and the boundaries between general search and specific travel search are blurred. Furthermore, the popularity of social media sites and mobile applications has the potential to dramatically change this landscape. However, it seems that we are still far away from the day when technologies are sophisticated enough that they can adequately anticipate our information needs based on locations, preferences and learned behavior, thus making search obsolete. As such, it is argued that search engines will continue to play a crucial, even dominant, role in helping travellers find information and connecting potential customers with the tourism industry.

References

Back, A. (2009) 'Baidu may be set for costly changes', *Wall Street Journal*, 8 January.

Bar-Ilan, J. (2007) 'Google bombing from a time perspective', *Journal of Computer-Mediated Communication*, 12(3): 910–38.

Beckwith, K. (2003) 'Googled: the quest for visibility on the Internet', *Learned Publishing*, 16(4): 277–83.

Bergman, M.K. (2001) 'The deep web: surfacing hidden value', *Journal of Electronic Publishing*, 7(1): 1–7.

Brin, S. and Page, L. (1998) 'The anatomy of a large-scale hypertextual Web search engine', Paper presented at the *7th International Conference on World Wide Web*, pp. 107–17.

Brusha, P. (2009) *Case Study 2009*. Retrieved November 2009, from http://www.acoupleofchicks.com/casestudies_vcmbc.html.

Buhalis, D. and Law, R. (2008) 'Progress in information technology and tourism management: 20 years on and 10 years after the Internet – the state of eTourism research', *Tourism Management*, 29(4): 609–23.

Cai, L.A., Feng, R. and Breiter, D. (2004) 'Tourist purchase decision involvement and information preferences', *Journal of Vacation Marketing*, 10(2): 138–48.

Chaffey, D. (2009) *Google Adwords – Brand-Bidding Changes – Impact in UK*. Retrieved October 2010, from http://www.davechaffey.com/Paid-Search-Best-Practice/category-5-alert-for-all-uk-companies-using-google-adwords.

Cohen, E. and Cooper, R. (1986) 'Language and tourism', *Annals of Tourism Research*, 13(4): 533–63.

comScore (2012) *comScore Releases July 2012 U.S. Search Engine Rankings*. Retrieved November 2012 from http://www.comscore.com/Insights/Press_Releases/2012/8/comScore_Releases_July_2012_US_Search_Engine_Rankings.

Crompton, J.L. (1992) 'Structure of vacation destination choice sets', *Annals of Tourism Research*, 19(3): 420–34.

Dann, G.M.S. (1997) *The Language of Tourism: A Sociolinguistic Perspective*. Wallingford, UK: CAB International.

Dholakia, U.P. and Bagozzi, R.P. (2001) 'Consumer behavior in digitial environments', in J. Wind and V. Mahajan (eds) *Digital Marketing: Global Strategies from the World's Leading Experts*. New York: John Wiley and Sons, pp. 163–200.

eConsultancy (2010) *State of Search Engine Marketing Report 2010*. Retrieved November 2012 from http://c.ymcdn.com/sites/www.sempo.org/resource/resmgr/Docs/State-of-Search-Engine-Market.pdf.

Fesenmaier, D.R. and Jeng, J. (2000) 'Assessing structure in the pleasure trip planning process', *Tourism Analysis*, 5: 13–27.

Fesenmaier, D.R. Xiang, Z., Pan, B. and Law, R. (2010) 'A framework of search engine use for travel planning', *Journal of Travel Research*, 50(6): 587–601.

Fish, R. (2009) *New and Interesting Insights Into Google Rankings and Spam from Pubcon*. Retrieved November 2009 from http://www.seomoz.org/blog/new-interesting-insights-into-google-rankings-spam-from-pubcon.

Fodness, D. and Murray, B. (1998) 'A typology of tourist information search strategies', *Journal of Travel Research*, 37(2): 108–19.

Gefen, D., Karahanna, E. and Straub, D.W. (2003) 'Trust and TAM in online shopping: An integrated model', *MIS Quarterly*, 27(1): 51–90.

Gendler, S., Ellis, J., Chang, S. and Davis, D.J. (2005) *System and Method for Search Advertising*. Google Patents.

Giddens, A. (1976) *New Rules of Sociological Method: A Positive Critique of Interpretive Sociologies*. London: Hutchinson.

Google (2007) *Life's a Beach*. Retrieved November 2009 from https://www.google.com/intl/en_us/adwords/select/success/stories/twiddy.pdf.
— (2008) *We Knew the Web was Big*. Retrieved March 2009 from http://googleblog.blogspot.com/2008/07/we-knew-web-was-big.html.
Gretzel, U. and Fesenmaier, D.R. (2000) 'Preparing for the new economy: advertising and change in destination marketing organizations', *Journal of Travel Research*, 39(2): 146–56.
Gretzel, U., Fesenmaier, D.R. and O'Leary, J.T. (2006) 'The transformation of consumer behaviour', in D. Buhalis and C. Costa (eds) *Tourism Business Frontiers*. Oxford, UK: Butterworth-Heinemann, pp. 9–18.
Gursoy, D. and McLeary, K.W. (2004) 'An integrated model of tourists' information search behavior', *Annals of Tourism Research*, 31(2): 343–73.
Henzinger, M. (2007) 'Search technologies for the Internet', *Science*, 317(5837): 468–71.
Ho, C.-I. and Liu, Y.-P. (2005) 'An exploratory investigation of web-based tourist information search behavior', *Asia Pacific Journal of Tourism Research*, 10(4): 351–60.
Hopkins, H. (2008) *Hitwise US Travel Trends: How Consumer Search Behavior is Changing*. Retrieved 26 April 2009 from http://www.hitwise.com/registration-page/hitwise-report-travel-trends.php.
Hwang, Y.H., Xiang, Z., Gretzel, U. and Fesenmaier, D.R. (2009) 'Assessing structure in travel queries', *Anatolia: An International Journal of Tourism and Hospitality Research*, 20(1): 223–35.
Jansen, B.J. and Pooch, U. (2001) 'A review of web searching studies and a framework for future research', *Journal of the American Society for Information Science and Technology*, 52(3): 235–46.
Jansen, B.J. and Resnick, M. (2005) 'Examining searcher perceptions of and interactions with sponsored results', Paper presented at *the Workshop on Sponsored Search Auctions at ACM Conference on Electronic Commerce*, 5 June, Vancouver, BC, Canada.
Jansen, B.J. and Spink, A. (2005a) 'An analysis of Web searching by European AlltheWeb.com users', *Information Processing and Management*, 41(2): 361–81.
Jansen, B.J. and Spink, A. (2005b) 'How are we searching the World Wide Web? A comparison of nine search engine transaction logs', *Information Processing and Management*, 42(1): 248–63.
Jansen, B.J. and Molina, P.R. (2006) 'The effectiveness of Web search engines for retrieving relevant ecommerce links', *Information Processing and Management*, 42(4): 1075–98.
Jansen, B.J., Spink, A. and Saracevic, T. (2000) 'Real life, real users, and real needs: a study and analysis of user queries on the web', *Information Processing and Management*, 36(2): 207–27.
Jansen, B.J., Spink, A. and Pedersen, J. (2005) 'A temporal comparison of AltaVista Web searching', *Journal of the American Society for Information Science and Technology*, 56(6): 559–70.
Jansen, B.J., Booth, D.L. and Spink, A. (2008) 'Determining the informational, navigational, and transactional intent of Web queries', *Information Processing and Management*, 44: 1251–66.
Jeng, J. and Fesenmaier, D.R. (2002) 'Conceptualizing the travel decision-making hierarchy: a review of recent developments', *Tourism Analysis*, 7: 15–32.
Kim, H., and Fesenmaier, D.R. (2008) 'Persuasive design of destination Websites: an analysis of first impression', *Journal of Travel Research*, 47(1): 3–13.
Langville, A.N. and Meyer, C.D. (2006) *Google's PageRank and Beyond: The Science of Search Engine Rankings*. Princeton, NJ: Princeton University Press.
Lawrence, S. and Giles, C.L. (1999) 'Accessibility and distribution of information on the Web', *Nature*, 400: 107–9.
Leiper, N. (1979) 'The framework of tourism: towards a definition of tourism, tourist, and the tourist industry', *Annals of Tourism Research*, 6(4): 390–407.
— (1990) 'Partial industrialization of tourism systems', *Annals of Tourism Research*, 17: 600–5.
— (2008) 'Why "the tourism industry" is misleading as a generic expression: the case for the plural variation, "tourism industries"', *Tourism Management*, 29(2): 237–51.
Levene, M. (2006) *An Introduction to Search Engines and Web Navigation*. New York: Addison-Wesley.
Levine, R. (2000) *The Cluetrain Manifesto: The End of Business as Usual*. Cambridge, MA: Perseus Books.
Malaga, R.A. (2007) 'The value of search engine optimization: an action research project at a new e-commerce site', *Journal of Electronic Commerce in Organizations*, 5(3): 68–82.
McCullagh, D. (2011) *Testing Google's Panda Algorithm: CNET Analysis*. Available at: http://news.cnet.com/8301-31921_3-20054797-281.html.
MarketingSherpa (2005) *MarketingSherpa Study Results: 3,271 Marketers Reveal Search Marketing Costs, Clicks and Conversions Review of Reviewed Item*. Available at: http://www.marketingsherpa.com/sample.cfm?contentID=3078#.

Moran, M. and Hunt, B. (2005) *Search Engine Marketing, Inc.: Driving Search Traffic to Your Company's Web Site*. Upper Saddle River, NJ: IBM Press.
Pan, B. and Fesenmaier, D.R. (2000) 'A typology of tourism related web sites: its theoretical foundation and implications', *Information Technology and Tourism*, 3(3/4): 155–76.
— (2006) 'Online information search: vacation planning process', *Annals of Tourism Research*, 33(3): 809–32.
Pan, B., Litvin, S.W. and Goldman, H. (2006) 'Real users, real trips, and real queries: an analysis of destination search on a search engine', Paper presented at *the Annual Conference of Travel and Tourism Research Association (TTRA 2006)*, Dublin, Ireland.
Pan, B., Hembrooke, H., Joachims, T., Lorigo, L., Gay, G. and Granka, L. (2007) 'In Google we trust: users' decisions on rank, position and relevancy', *Journal of Computer-Mediated Communication*, 12(3): 801–23.
Pan, B., Litvin, S.W. and O'Donnell, T.E. (2007) 'Understanding accommodation search query formulation: the first step in putting "heads in beds"', *Journal of Vacation Marketing*, 13(4): 371–81.
Pan, B., Xiang, Z., Fesenmaier, D.R. and Law, R. (2011) 'The dynamics of search engine marketing for tourist destinations', *Journal of Travel Research*, 47(4): 440–53.
Pearce, P. (1982) *The Social Psychology of Tourist Behavior*. Oxford: Pergamon Press.
Prescott, L. (2006) *Hitwise US Travel Report*. Retrieved 12 August 2008 from http://www.hitwise.com/registration-page/hitwise-us-travel-report.php.
Schwartz, B. (2009) *Yahoo to Drop Paid Inclusion Program*. Retrieved November 2009 from http://searchengineland.com/yahoo-to-drop-paid-inclusion-program-27852.
Sen, R. (2005) 'Optimal search engine marketing strategy', *International Journal of Electronic Commerce*, 10(1): 9–25.
Smith, S.L.J. (1994) 'The tourism product', *Annals of Tourism Research*, 21(3): 582–95.
Sullivan, D. (2006) *Search Engine Ratings*. Nielson NetRatings.
TIA (2008) *Travelers' Use of the Internet*. Washington DC: Travel Industry Association of America.
Urban, G.L., Sultan, F. and Qualls, W.J. (2000) 'Placing trust at the center of your Internet strategy', *Sloan Management Review*, 42(1): 39–48.
USTA (2011) *Travelers' Use of the Internet*. Washington DC: United States Travel Association.
Vogt, C.A. and Fesenmaier, D.R. (1998) 'Expanding the functional information search model', *Annals of Tourism Research*, 25(3): 551–78.
Vogt, C.A., Fesenmaier, D.R. and MacKay, K. (1993) 'Functional and aesthetic information needs underlying the pleasure travel experience', *Journal of Travel and Tourism Marketing*, 2(2): 133–46.
Wang, Y. and Fesenmaier, D.R. (2003) 'Assessing motivation of contribution in online communities: an empirical investigation of an online travel community', *Electronic Markets*, 13(1): 33–45.
— (2006) 'Identifying the success factors of Web-based marketing strategy: an investigation of convention and visitors bureaus in the United States', *Journal of Travel Research*, 44: 239–49.
Werthner, H. and Klein, S. (1999) *Information Technology and Tourism: A Challenging Relationship*. Vienna: Springer.
Werthner, H. and Ricci, F. (2004) 'E-commerce and tourism', *Communications of the ACM*, 17(12): 101–9.
Wöber, K. (2006) 'Domain specific search engines', in D.R. Fesenmaier, K. Wöber and H. Werthner (eds) *Destination Recommendation Systems: Behavioral Foundations and Applications*. Wallingford, UK: CABI.
Woodside, A.G. and Dubelaar, C. (2002) 'A general theory of tourism consumption systems: a conceptual framework and an empirical exploration', *Journal of Travel Research*, 41(2): 120–32.
Xiang, Z. and Gretzel, U. (2010) 'Role of social media in online travel information search', *Tourism Management*, 31(2): 179–88.
Xiang, Z. and Pan, B. (2011) 'Travel queries on cities in the United States: implications for search engine marketing for tourist destinations', *Tourism Management*, 32(1): 88–97.
Xiang, Z., Wöber, K. and Fesenmaier, D.R. (2008) 'Representation of the online tourism domain in search engines', *Journal of Travel Research*, 47(2): 137–50.
Xiang, Z., Gretzel, U. and Fesenmaier, D.R. (2009) 'Semantic representation of the online tourism domain', *Journal of Travel Research*, 47(4): 440–53.
Xiang, Z., Fesenmaier, D.R., Pan, B. and Law, R. (2010) 'Assessing the visibility of destination marketing organizations in Google: a case study of convention and visitors bureau websites in the United States', *Journal of Travel and Tourism Marketing*, 27(7): 519–32.

38

Virtual communities

Online blogs as a marketing tool

Carmela Bosangit

Introduction

The Internet has affected the travel and tourism industry in various ways such as marketing, distribution channel and information search for tourism products and services, to name a few. With developments in web technology particularly that of virtual communities, blogs, e-review sites and photo sharing websites, the industry is again challenged to cope with the changes they bring into tourism consumption as well as the delivery of tourism products. According to Stepchenkova, Mills and Jiang (2007), virtual communities revolutionised the way people socialize, exchange information, access resources and perform transactions. Inevitably, these communities have also penetrated tourist's and travellers' practices. Virtual travel communities have empowered tourists in many ways but not limited to:

1 building a community of consumers with shared goals and interests;
2 connecting with other travellers;
3 exchanging of information;
4 holistic evaluation of their travel experiences; and
5 more convenient communication tool.

These developments further enhance the tourist experiences and tourist practices and hence require the attention of the industry as it presents them with opportunities to reach their customers as well as gain deeper understanding of their behaviour which can offer insights to their services and destinations. These web applications are helping more and more users in all the three phases of the tourism consumption process (pre-consumption, consumption and post-consumption) suggesting places to go, proposing hotel reviews and so on (Cantoni, Tardinin, Inversini and Marchiori 2009: 16).

Blogging is an innovation in personal publishing and has become a new form of social interaction on the web, massively distributed but completely connected conversation on every imaginable topic of interest (Marlow 2004). The phenomenal growth of blogging has turned it into a key part of online culture (Hsu and Lin 2008). Blogs, also referred to as consumer- or user generated content, create a vast pool of unbiased information generated by consumers without commercial interest that are used by other consumers in their information search and decision making process. Sweeney, Soutar and Mazzarol (2008) noted how blogs have gained much credibility in the eyes of the consumer as a relevant and unbiased input into their decision making process. Blogging reality is entering tourism as a tool widely used to read and write reviews on accommodation and travel services (Munar 2009: 27). Blogs are seen as being particularly important for travel where bloggers are often seen as authorities or experts and are more influential among their own regular readers and casual surfers lead to their blogs by more efficient search engines (O'Connor, Wang and Li 2011). Travel blogs as one of the attributes of a virtual travel community represent the experiences of travellers that are easily accessible as research data. Destinations should acknowledge that travellers in this networked world are expected to increasingly take advantage or contribute to consumer-generated content sharing experiences or advice with others across the Internet's global community which greatly empowers the consumers and forces travel product suppliers to strive for excellence (Jamal and Robinson 2009).

This chapter focusses on virtual travel communities and the blogging phenomenon and their marketing implications.Virtual communities and blogs are platforms for word-of-mouth communication and sources of information on tourist behaviour and experiences which may affect consumer decisions and tourist behaviour. A general overview on virtual communities starts off the chapter, followed by a discussion on virtual travel communities and its characteristics. Travel blogs as records of travel experiences are highlighted as tourist practices and have become part of tourist experiences. Lastly, the theoretical and marketing implications of travel blogs are outlined.

Virtual communities

Virtual community (VC) is a new form of communication whereby community members share information and knowledge for mutual learning or problem solving (Lechner and Hummel 2002). It is also referred to as community networks and online community which has become a broad term to describe any collection of people who communicate online (Wang, Yu and Fesenmaier 2002). For Fernback and Thompson (1995), it is a set of social relationships forged in cyberspace through repeated contacts within a specified boundary. A VC has the following characteristics (Balasubramanian and Mahajan 2001):

1. aggregation of people;
2. rational members;
3. interaction in cyberspace without physical collocation;
4. process of social exchange; and
5. an objective, property/identity or interests shared by members.

Koh and Kim (2004) simply define a virtual community to be a group of people with common interests or goals, interacting predominantly in cyberspace. Similarly, Dholakia and Bagozzi (2004) also recognized these communities as consumer groups of varying sizes that connect and interact online for the purpose of meeting personal and shared goals.

Koh and Kim (2004) posited that there is 'a sense of community' in a virtual community. A sense of community refers to an individual's feeling of relationship to a community or personal knowledge about belonging to a collective that includes others (Heller, Price, Reinharz, Riger, Wandersman and D'Aunno 1984; Newbrough and Chavis 1986). Wang *et al.* (2002) argued that VC is not an entity but rather a process defined by its members and that it possesses many

Table 38.1 Criteria for typologies of virtual communities

Authors	*Criteria for typologies of virtual communities*
Armstrong and Hagel (1995); Krishnamurthy (2003)	Community's purpose (revenue generation, fulfil consumer needs for fantasy, interaction or transaction)
Jones and Rafaeli (2000)	Social tie strength and public versus private nature of membership/interaction
Preece (2000); Stanoevska-Slabeva (2002)	Supporting communication technology design (chat, bulletin board system or user functional requirements)
Bagozzi and Dholakia (2002)	Structure of interaction (small group or network)
Markus (2002)	Orientation (social, professional and commercial; and relationship building or entertainment communities)
Porter (2004)	Who established the virtual community (member-initiated or sponsored by organization) and relationship orientation (social or professional for member initiated and commercial, non-profit and government for organization-sponsored)

essential traits as physical communities and the substance that allows for common experience and meaning among members. However, Bromberg (1996) warned that some online discussion groups and chat rooms should only be considered as a means of communication among people with common interests if they are lacking in the personal investment, intimacy and commitment that characterize the ideal sense of community.

There is no single accepted definition of the virtual community. Inevitably, this is the same for the typologies of VC. Existing typologies of virtual communities proposed by researchers are based on various criteria as presented in Table 38.1.

Porter (2004) claimed that the proposed typology is an improvement to existing typologies as it recognizes that virtual communities can either be established by their members or sponsored by organizations and that there is the dimension of the relationship orientation of those communities. This particular dimension of who initiated the VC is crucial for researchers and marketers if they aim to use virtual communities in fulfilling business goals and establishing stronger relationships with customers. For example, communities that were initiated by customers independent of any company control or association are not necessarily advantageous to an organization as pointed out by Catterall and Maclaran (2001). Examples of those communities are Harley Davidson motorcycles, Saab Cars, MacIntosh computers and the Mini car (Schouten and McAlexander 1995; Muniz and O'Guinn 1998; Pei-ya 2000). A strong brand community organized by its members can be a threat as they can reject particular marketing activities and changes to a product and multiply one unsatisfied customer to thousands in a nanosecond (Muniz and O'Guinn 1998).

Another important aspect that firms should be familiar with about virtual communities is their multiple functions to the users. As functions of VCs can fulfil some needs of the members in their online activities, this can provide insights to the users' motivations for joining the community and most probably their continuous use of it. According to Wang *et al.* (2002), there are three fundamental needs of the members in their online activities:

1 functional needs;
2 social needs; and
3 psychological needs.

Functional needs include transactions (buying and selling between members), information gathering and entertainment or convenience of access to information limited by time and geographical limits; social needs include relationship and interactivity among members and communication; and psychological needs refer to the need for identification, involvement, unity/belonging and relatedness. Wang *et al.* (2002) point out that a successful community must meet multiple needs of the member.

However, the focus of these needs may differ based on the purpose of the community and member characteristics. Their work confirmed that proper development and management of an online community based on the members' needs can enhance customer relationships and promote understanding of consumer behaviour in achieving the goals of relationship marketing. Tracking how consumers make use of the community and understanding the drivers and effects of their participation are crucial to the cultivation of the community as a marketing tool (de Valck, Bruggen and Wierenga 2009: 96–7). Likewise, firms with an intention to establish communities for their own brands should design in accordance to consumers' needs, and their expectations of joining and actively participating in the community to maximize this strategy in reaching out to their consumers.

User groups within a virtual community have also been identified as crucial for their marketing implications. For example, de Valck, Bruggen and Wierenga (2009) identified five member types according to participation patterns and background variables:

1 core members (frequent visitors who make extensive use of the community's knowledge as well as add to that knowledge, actively participate in forum discussion and chats);
2 hobbyists (users with low level of information retrieved and supplied and low level of participation but engaging in updating and maintain personal page and playing around with techniques in the website);
3 conversationalists (users who have frequent and short visits to the site but a high degree of participation in supplying and discussing information);
4 functionalists (users who have fewer and shorter visits but high level and profound interest in retrieving information);
5 informationalists (users who have less frequent visits, more time online, low participation in forum and chats but high level in retrieving and supplying information); and
6 opportunists (least frequent visitors and less time online, no participation in forum and chats and only focus is retrieving information).

According to the authors, these user groups will allow marketers to distinguish the community's true influentials from other contributors to the community's content and who are really interested in increasing their knowledge about the community's topic of interest apart from those lurkers that pass by without a real motivation to do so. This can inform the firm on whom to target or pay attention to among its members and to whom it should direct its marketing communications. Firms have to recognize that not all content is of high quality and that community members contribute differently. Hence, the traditional approach of targeting specific members who produce quality content would be more efficient and effective for gathering insights on their behaviour.

Virtual travel communities

The travel industry, one of the first industries to go online, has long recognized the potential of virtual travel communities (VTCs) for destination and production promotion (Stepchenkova,

Mills and Jiang 2007: 163). Niininen, March and Buhalis (2006) noted that numerous tourists from around the world are connected via virtual communities and a variety of experience-based information on tourism places and service are exchanged in these communities. Markus (2002) classified travel related online communities as relationship building communities as they are formed around a shared interest as the result of geographical proximity, demographic similarity or a common hobby. She suggests that commitment to the group is strongest in this kind of community. Online travel communities changed communications among a large number of people for travel related activities such as: obtaining travel information, maintaining connections, finding travel companions, providing travel tips and suggestions, or just for the fun of telling each other interesting travel experiences and stories without restrictions of time and distance (Wang *et al.* 2002). Aside from the functional use of virtual communities for tourists, they also offer opportunities for members' sense of belonging, fun and self-identification and serve as an extension of travel/tourism-related experiences beyond the actual travel (Jamal and Robinson 2009).

VTCs are also becoming an important channel for spreading word-of-mouth to other travellers (Niininen, March and Buhalis 2006). For example, travel reviews in TripAdvisor.com, raveable.com and tripwolf.com had become a sphere of social interaction for bloggers to post evaluations and communicate with other bloggers through posts that provide a rich source of marketing intelligence (Crotts, Davis and Mason 2012). VTCs have become platforms for electronic word-of-mouth that are perceived as credible even if the readers do not know the blogger personally. Several studies had pointed out that consumers have generally accepted reviews from other consumers as more credible than marketers' communications (Allsop, Bassett and Hoskins 2007; Gunter, Campbell, Touri and Gibson 2009; Pan, McLaurin and Crotts 2007). Like any virtual communities, VTCs were observed to have several groups within the blogging community as identified by Fun and Wagner (2008) and Wang and Fesenmaier (2004) based on the level of use of blogs and perceived benefits and incentives. These user groups are very similar to de Valck, Bruggen and Wierenga's (2009) member types. However, the authors used different labels: habitual or enthusiastic, active uses, personal bloggers and blogging lurkers (Fun and Wagner 2008); tourist, mingler, devotee and insider (Wang and Fessenmaier 2004) which are all self-explanatory. These groups will allow marketers to maximize the advantage of VTCs through word-of-mouth communication and identify the most influential bloggers or opinion leaders to monitor more regularly.

Blogs in virtual communities, according to Diaz-Loque (2009), pose new possibilities and challenges for tourism marketers as they are considered to be more persuasive than advertising. Schmallegger and Carson (2008) identified the following VTCs that are most prominent for their travel blogs: travelblog.org, travelpod.com, blog.realtravel.com, youtraveljournal.com, travelpost.com, igougo.com and virtualtourist.com. Blogs on these VTC are now recognized by some destination marketing organizations who have started to incorporate them in their websites as promotional tools. Most city websites have special links to blogs which gives the organization some control on the positive messages of a personal experience of the city (Diaz-Loque 2009).

Travel blogs

Blogs are usually presented in reverse chronological order via a web page interface (Wenger 2008). A blog has the following structure: header (with information about the author, title and date of entry); body of the blog (may contain texts, images and other media files); footer (tools for readers to comment and enter into a dialogue with the blog author and other readers); and links (connecting to other sources of information available in the web). Technology such as blogs makes the process of story-telling especially easy as pictures can be manipulated, contents can be assembled from one's own materials or integrated from other sites, narration and sounds can be easily added, and posted materials can be assigned with different meanings through tags (Jamal and Robinson 2009). Podcast and videos add an auditory and visual dimension to story-telling while tagging provides an opportunity to add relevance to consumer-generated stories and make them even more searchable (Jamal and Robinson 2009). Most blogs allow readers to comment or respond to postings which is an important part of the feeling of community that typifies Web 2.0 (O'Connor, Wang and Li 2011: 233).

Puhringer and Taylor (2008) defined travels blogs as those forums and individual entries which relate to planned, current or past travel. They are the equivalent of personal online diaries and are made up from one or more individual entries strung together by a common theme (for example, a round-the-world trip) (Puhringer and Taylor 2008: 179). These blogs generally cover general description of destinations such as climate, cuisine, transport, attractions or region-specific stereotypes (Carson 2008; Pan, Crotts, McLaurin 2007; Wenger 2008). Blogs are also comprised of pictures and videos uploaded by tourists for their readers to view. Used as digital substitutes for traditional photo albums, the digital images uploaded onto community web pages and discussion boards help recall aspects of trips and assist consumers in constructing memories of vacations (Jamal and Robinson 2009: 569). An important feature of blogs is the functions that allow tourists to share their experiences with others easily by updating their blogs directly even from mobile phones (moblogging), or capture a moment or scenery and upload it directly to their blogs (Tussyadiah and Fesenmaier 2009). Micro-blogs is a form of blogging that allows users to write brief text updates (usually 140 characters) and publish them from text messages from a mobile phone, instant messaging by email or from a website (O'Connor, Wang and Li 2011). Examples of these are updates from Twitter, Jaiku, Tumblr and Facebook. Consequently, this blurs the lines between enroute activities and post consumption behaviours which Jamal and Robinson (2009) predict will increasingly happen while still on a trip. For example, bloggers, particularly backpackers and long-haul and multiple destination travellers, are seen to be blogging while they are travelling instead of doing it upon returning home (Bosangit 2012).

Travel blogs are considered by tourists as records of their travel experiences. Blogs are rich narratives that contain details of experiences from multiple guests and provide a great deal of useful information to the blog reader (Zehrer, Crotts and Magnini 2011). Jansson (2007) pointed out how blogs have provided opportunities to compose a personal script based on very specific sources of knowledge and, most importantly, have reduced the risk of cultural shock or alienation. The travel stories can mimic real-world storytelling activities typical of the last stage of the tourism consumption process (Jamal and Robinson 2009). In a blog, narratives and images can be reworked, rearranged and idealized into a framework for a touristic memoryscape in a website, photo-sharing sites and weblogs that are consumed by a wider audience (Jansson 2007). Blogs are comprised of images, videos and films that Tussyadiah and Fessenmaier (2009) refer to as technology-assisted mediators which represent destinations. This mediation of experiences covers the various stages of tourist experiences as shown in Figure 38.1.

Tussayadiah and Fesenmaier (2009) emphasized that shared images help tourists at the post-visit stage in the recollection process and the remembrance of past experiences. In this case, blogs can also be considered something for the tourist when they get home; as Crang (1997) observed, tourist events are not so much experienced in themselves but rather for their future memory. Blogs can reinforce the magic of a leisure trip and prolong the creation of ideal ensembles of representation through the immediate sharing of extraordinary multisensory experiences (Jansson 2007). This medium offers new levels of interactivity and immediacy in broadcasting a story that were not conceivable in the past and has the advantage of closely resembling traditional travel journals which used to be kept by many travellers (Jamal and

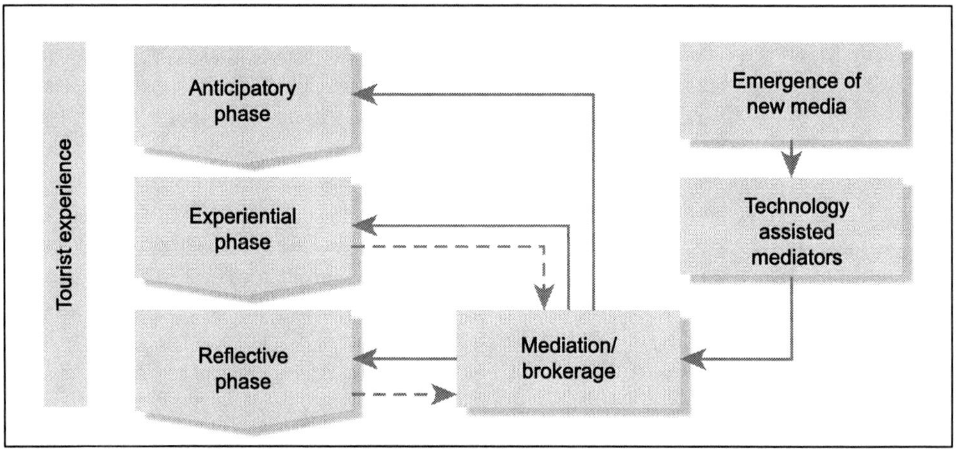

Figure 38.1 Mediation of tourist experience with technology-assisted mediators (source: Tussyadiah and Fesenmaier 2009: 27).

Robinson 2009: 570). Volo (2012) noted that several researchers have pointed out that blogs published on VCs are growing in popularity because of their perceived credibility of consumer opinions which are seen as more authoritative word-of-mouth communications than traditional tourist information sources.

Travel blogs are also being used for travel advertisements. Huang, Cho and Lin (2010) attested that travel blogs carry many Internet ads and attract a wide range of bloggers. These included target advertisements (built in by the blog service providers to lead bloggers to click through more information) and placement advertisements (which are posted inside the content of blogs by blog hosts or respondents). In this context, blogs were also suggested to play a positive role in the processing of ad messages which are an influential factor in the purchase intention.

Theoretial and marketing implications of travel blogs

Theoretical implications

Travel blogging has become part of tourist practices and tourist experiences; hence an in-depth understanding of blogs can contribute to theories on tourist experiences. Few researchers had started using blogs to gain deeper understanding of tourist experiences as told by bloggers. Volo (2010) explored how bloggers write about the essence of experience; Bosangit (2012) demonstrated how tourist experiences were constituted in and through discourses generated in travel blogs; and Bosangit, Dulnuan and Mena (2012) put forward travel blogging as part of the post-consumption stage of the tourist experience.

Blogs as naturally occurring, vast and diverse data of travel experiences can reveal aspects on tourist experiences that have remained elusive to researchers and marketers. A discourse analysis of travel blogs showed that tourist experiences are retold by bloggers to their readers as experiences which elicited responses (emotional, intellectual physical) from them and whose value and meaning to them adds to their memories, self-identity and evolved self which became part of their life story (Bosangit 2012). Tourist experiences as told in travel blogs are seen to be reflecting also the individual's life goals and projects throughout the whole duration of the trip. Travel blogging was observed to be used by tourists to share various stories of challenges

Table 38.2 Focus of research and possible insights to theories and marketing practices

Focus of research	*Possible insights to marketing*
Travel blogs (text, photos, videos and links)	Travel experiences as narrated (types of experiences, emotional responses, thoughts and reflections) Perceived and represented destination images
Travel bloggers (the tourists/travellers)	Bloggers segmentation (opinion leaders vs. lurkers) Travel blogging as tourist practice and part of tourist experience (motivation)
Travel blog website (virtual travel communities)	Possible distribution channel or advertising platform Travel bloggers as a community of consumers Uses of virtual travel communities
Blog readers (other blog members, family and friends and the general public)	Effectiveness as a word-of-mouth communication Influence to purchase decision making

and risks, learning and reflections, novelty and differences, self-expansion and escape to their audiences. The presentation of self and development of self was observed as an underlying theme of these stories. It is clear that travel blogging allows bloggers to maximize the benefits of travel beyond the trip itself.

Travel blogging becoming part of tourist practices implies that stages of the tourist experience are blurred. Bosangit (2012) and Tussyadiah and Fesenmaier (2009) have emphasized how bloggers blog while they are travelling and instantly capture moments through their mobile phones and share them. Therefore, tourism researchers need to consider the implications for theories of tourist experiences proposed to have stages of a linear nature (pre-travel, the travel itself and post-travel). For example, evaluation, storing and enrichment of memories on travel (Aho 2001) and remembering events (Larsen 2007) are said to be post-trip stage activities but with blogging tourists are doing it during the travel itself and sharing it with their readers. Tourism researchers should consider how this blogging phenomenon among tourists challenges extant theories on tourist experience and its stages.

Travel blogs are valuable research data on tourists and their experiences. Table 38.2 provides more examples of possible research areas and their insights to theories which may carry marketing implications as well.

Marketing implications

Extant literature on travel blogging provides adequate empirical evidences of the use of travel blogs as sources of information on tourists' behaviours, activities, perceptions and evaluations of destinations and as word-of-mouth communication. The use of blogs for marketing and management was highlighted by Lin and Huang (2006), Pan, Crotts and McLaurin (2007), Akenhurst (2008), Schmalleger and Carson (2008), Mack and Blose (2008), Puhringer and Taylor (2008), Volo (2010) and Xiang and Gretzel (2010), to name a few. Puhringer and Taylor (2008) identified a range of possible applications for consumer-generated content found in travel blogs that would be useful for destination marketing organizations. These include:

1 identifying and monitoring trends in travellers' movement to and from the destination such as previous and future stopover locations;
2 specific product evaluations and reviews of service standards;

3 event evaluations;
4 identifications of product or infrastructure gaps;
5 performance reviews of associated products or collaborators; and
6 competitor analysis.

Table 38.3 provides evidence on how travel blogs have been used to examine various areas of tourism marketing and management.

To maximize the use of travel blogs for tourism marketing, it is crucial for researchers and marketers to have a good understanding of the blogging phenomenon and to approach it in a systematic and efficient manner. For example, an examination of travel bloggers' profiles, their practices and motivations can provide rich information about this specific group of tourists who spend time and effort in blogging about their travels. The value of understanding travel bloggers is demonstrated in the empirical work of Bosangit (2012) based on a survey participated in by 1,214 travel bloggers from travelblog.org, one of the top travel blogging websites. The survey offered several insights to marketers and researchers on travellers' practices, for example:

1 the socio-demographic profile of the travel bloggers (mostly between 25 to 44 years old, educated to college level and some with postgraduate degrees, and the majority of the bloggers coming from the USA, the United Kingdom, Australia and Canada) provides an overview on who would be valuable promoters or critiques of destinations;

Table 38.3 Diverse focus of research on travel blogs

Authors	*Focus of research*
Kurashima *et al.* (2005, 2006)	Geographically mapped tourists' behaviour in urban settings at a specific time and location by extracting tourist experience from blogs
Douglas and Mills (2006)	Brand images communicated by bloggers who had visited the Middle East and North Africa
Pan *et al.* (2007)	Visitor opinions posted on leading travel blog sites via semantic network analysis to gain an understanding of the destination experience
Carson (2008)	Different sources of consumer-generated web content about travel to Australia's Northern Territory; evaluated the authorship, readership and the nature of the content itself
Schmallager and Carson (2008)	Web 2.0 applications and how increasing number of travel blogs may influence the key functions of new media such as promotion, product distribution, communication, management and research
Wenger (2008)	Insights into the use of blogs about travel to Austria for travel recommendations (consumer to consumer) and market research (by destinations and tourism operators)
Tussyadiah and Fessenmaier (2008)	Understanding tourist experiences in their temporal and spatial dimensions
Keng and Ting (2009)	Interactivity and perceived similarities between blog readers and others, and incorporates the concept of customer experiential value of blog users
Volo (2010)	Looked at the space and time continuum and distinguishing experience essence and experience as offering

Source: Summarized from Zehrer, Crotts and Magnini (2011); Volo (2010); Tussyadiah and Fessenmaier (2008); Kurashima *et al.* (2005, 2006)

2 most bloggers are blogging about their longer trips, indicating increasing long-term and multiple-destination travellers, and this points to opportunities among destination marketers for possible joint marketing communication strategies to capture this market;
3 the top three most important motivations for blogging:
   a updating family and friends about their whereabouts;
   b keeping a record of travels; and
   c sharing experiences
   indicate management and marketing implications such as providing travellers with access to the Internet to share immediate memories of their experiences which includes holistic evaluation of the place as they update their family and friends.

According to King (2002), tourism marketing is very much focussed on destination and calls for a focus on tourist experiences. The use of travel blogs as a research data can facilitate efforts to shift marketing from destination-based to experience-based. As demonstrated above, travel blogs provide in-depth understanding of tourist experiences, particularly in terms of how tourists constitute these experiences through and in travel blogs, which reveals aspects of tourist experiences that are worth blogging about. This information can provide key insights to marketers on how to market the destination based on tourist experiences as told by tourists rather than the destination features. This can also aid in the formulation of marketing communication strategies, improving and reinventing destination images. From stories in the travel blogs, a consistent mix of brand elements can be identified to assist in defining a distinct destination image (Prebensen 2007). Destination marketers should be able to determine aspects of a tourist experience through blogs that have rich emotional meaning, great conversation value and provide high anticipation for their potential tourists (Morgan, Pritchard and Piggott 2002; Tasci and Kozak 2006). In addition, marketers should bear in mind that as bloggers write about the destination, images are reshaped; therefore blogs should be monitored as brand images are communicated by bloggers (Douglas and Mills 2006).

There are, however, several challenges and issues that tourism marketers should recognize and address in using travel blogs as research data. It is noted that the use of blogs for research is hindered by several weaknesses that were highlighted by a number of researchers:

1 issues and problems in blog sampling (Volo 2010) which may be attributed to the lack of profile of the blogger;
2 blogs may have few insights in understanding destination image (Wegner 2008);
3 vastness and diversity of blogs and their idiosyncratic or disorganized style of writing (Bosangit 2010); and
4 locating and analyzing relevant content is time consuming and requires a lot of effort (Carson 2008; Schmalleger and Carso, 2008).

Volo (2010) outlined that investigators have identified five weaknesses in using blogs which are:

1 shortness of text in blogs;
2 the difficulty of generalizing findings due to the small sample size;
3 the issues and problems encountered in blog 'sampling';
4 little opportunity for destination marketing organizations to gather important insights from visitors' narratives; and
5 the need for further study to assess how potential visitors interpret these stories.

Carson (2008) suggested that an alternative – and perhaps more successful – approach to using travel blogs would be to have a more specific set of questions to ask of the data. In addition, he pointed out that strategies in reducing noise, in locating blogs and analyzing the profiles of the authors and the content will reduce the cost of blog analysis. Wenger (2008), on the other hand, suggested identifying important blog authors who may have more valuable insights of marketing; in other words, being selective of which blogs to use for research. Blog Visualer, a system reducing the amount of searching and collating the user has to do to get the required destination information from relevant blogs had been proposed by Sharda and Ponnada (2008) to tackle this issue. This system is capable of creating a virtual tour of the destination for the traveller based on the extracted information from current blogs. Magnini, Crotts and Zehrer (2011) noted that the amount of consumer research invested in blog analysis appears to fall short of what is invested in other consumer research initiatives such as comment cards and satisfaction surveys; they thus suggest that blogs can be considered as another utility for this traditional practice. There is also much scope for exploring various methods for extracting desired information out of the naturally occurring, vast and diverse rich narratives of travel blogs. Banyai and Glover (2012) call for investigating current research methods appropriate for analyzing blog content. Alternative methods for analyzing travel blogs, such as netnography, collaborative ethnography and technobiography can provide a deeper analysis than content and narrative analyses which are currently the most used methods.

Conclusion

Despite the growth in research on travel blogs over the years, there are still many areas left unexplored in the blogging phenomenon and virtual online communities of tourists. There are possibly more theoretical and marketing implications not outlined here; however, it is hoped that this chapter has encouraged future research on travel blogs. Blogs are Internet content created, owned, managed and consumed by individuals (Huang, Shen, Lin and Chang 2007) and they represent the voices and opinions of tourists that are found be a more powerful form of traditional word-of-mouth communication. Hence, their importance as a research data and marketing tool cannot be over-emphasized. To maximize the use of travel blogs as research data, challenges and issues should be turned into opportunities for a more in-depth analysis of tourists and their experiences. Tourism marketers and researchers have to focus on the advantages of blogs such as those outlined by Hookway (2008: 92–3):

1. they provide a publicly available, low-cost and instantaneous technique for collecting substantial amounts of data;
2. they are naturalistic data in textual form, allowing the creation of immediate text without the resource intensiveness of tape recorders and transcriptions;
3. they enable access to populations otherwise geographically or socially removed from the researcher; and
4. the archived nature of blogs makes them amenable to examining social processes across space and time, particularly trend and panel type longitudinal research.

Blogs and virtual communities along with other social media should be recognized for their significant practical, theoretical and methodological contributions to the development of tourism studies.

References

Aho, S. (2001) 'Towards a general theory of touristic experiences: modelling experience process in tourism', *Tourism Review*, 56 (3/4): 33–7.

Akenhurst, G. (2008) 'User generated content: the use of blogs for tourism organisations and tourism consumers', *Service Business*, 3(1): 51–61.

Allsop, D.T., Bassett, B. and Hoskins, J. (2007) 'Word-of-mouth research: principles and applications', *Journal of Advertising Research*, 47: 388–411.

Armstrong, A. and Hagel III, J. (1995) 'Real profits from virtual communities', *The Mckinsey Quarterly*, 3: 126–41.

Bagozzi, R.P. and Dholakia, U.M. (2002) 'Intentional social action in virtual communities', *Journal of Interactive Marketing*, 16(2): 2–21.

Balasubramanian, S. and Mahajan, V. (2001) 'The economic leverage of the virtual community', *International Journal of Electronic Commerce*, 5(3): 103–38.

Banyai, M. and Glover, T. (2012) 'Evaluating research methods on travel blogs', *Journal of Travel Research*, 51(3): 267–77.

Bosangit, C. (2010) 'Understanding how consumers remember and relive their experiences and their marketing implications', paper presented at *Academy of Marketing Conference 2010: Transformational Marketing*, Coventry, July 2010.

— (2012) 'Understanding consumption experiences: a discourse analysis of travel blogs', unpublished thesis, University of Nottingham.

Bosangit, C., Dulnuan, J. and Mena, M. (2012) 'Using travel blogs to examine the post-consumption behaviour of tourists', *Journal of Vacation Marketing*, 18(3): 207–19.

Bromberg, H. (1996) 'Are MUDs communities? Identity, belonging and consciousness in virtual worlds', in R. Shields (ed) *Cultures of Internet: Virtual Spaces, Real Histories, Living Bodies*. London: Sage.

Cantoni, L, Tardinin, S., Inversini, A. and Marchiori, E. (2009) 'From paradigmatic to syntagmatic communities: a socio-semiotic approach to the evolution pattern of online travel communities', paper presented at the *ENTER 2009*, Amsterdam, January 2009.

Carson, D. (2008) 'The "blogosphere" as a market research tool for tourism destinations: a case study of Australia's Northern Territory', *Journal of Vacation Marketing*, 14(2): 111–19.

Catterall, M. and Maclaran, P. (2001) 'Researching consumers in virtual worlds: a cyberspace odyssey', *Journal of Consumer Behavior*, 1(3): 228–37.

Crang, M. (1997) 'Picturing practices: research through the tourist gaze', *Progress in Human Geography*, 21(3): 359–73.

Crotts, J., Davis, B. and Mason, P. (2012) 'Analysing blog content for competitive advantage: lessons learned in the application of software aided linguistic analysis', in M. Sigala, E. Christou and U. Gretzel (eds) *Social Media in Travel, Tourism and Hospitality: Theory Practice and Cases*. Surrey: Ashgate Publishing Ltd.

De Valk, K., Bruggen, G. and Wierenga, B. (2009) 'Virtual communities: a marketing perspective', *Decision Support Systems*, 47: 185–203.

Dholakia, U.M. and Bagozzi, R.P. (2004) 'Motivational antecedents, constituents and consequents of virtual community identity', in S. Godar and S. Pixie-Ferris (eds) *Virtual and Collaborative Teams: Process, Technologies, and Practice*. London: IDEA Group.

Diaz-Luque, P. (2009) 'Official tourism web sites and city marketing', in M. Gasco-Hernandez and T. Torres-Coronas (eds) *Information Communication Technologies and Marketing: Digital Opportunities Around the World*. London: Information Science Reference.

Douglas, A. and Mills, J. (2006) 'Logging brand personality online: Website content analysis of Middle Easterna and North African destinations', *Information and Communication Techologies in Tourism*, DOI:1007/3-211-32710-X.

Fernback, J. and Thompson, B. (1995) 'Virtual communities: abort, retry, failure?', *Computer Mediated Communication and the American Collectivity*. Available: http://www.ewll.com/user/hlr/texts/Vccivil.html.

Fun, R. and Wagner, C. (2008) 'Weblogging: a study of social computing and its impact on organizations', *Decision Support Systems*, 45: 242–50.

Gunter, B., Campbell, V., Touri, M. and Gibson, R. (2009) 'Blogs, news and credibility', *Aslib Proceedings*, 61(2): 184–204.

Heller, K., Price, R.H., Reinharz, S., Riger, S., Wandersman, A. and D'Aunno, T. (1984) *Psychology and Community Change: Challenges of the Future*. Monterey, CA: Brooks/Cole Publishing Company.

Hookway, N. (2008) 'Entering the blogosphere: some strategies for using blogs in social research', *Qualitative Research*, 8(1): 91–101.
Hsu, C.L. and Lin, C. (2008) 'Acceptance of blog usage: the roles of technology acceptance, social influence and knowledge sharing motivation', *Information and Management*, 45(1): 65–74.
Huang, C., Shen, Y., Lin, H. and Chang. S. (2007) 'Bloggers' motivations and behaviours: a model', *Journal of Advertising Research*, 47(4): 472–84.
Huang, C.Y., Chou, C.J. and Lin, P.C. (2010) 'Involvement theory in constructing bloggers' intention to purchase travel products', *Tourism Management*, 31(4): 513–26.
Jamal, T. and Robinson, M. (2009) *The Sage Handbook of Tourism Studies*. London: Sage Publications.
Jansson, A. (2007) 'A sense of tourism: new media and the dialectic of encapsulation/decapsulation', *Tourist Studies*, 7(1): 5–24.
Jones, Q. and Rafaeli, S. (2000) 'Time to split, virtually: discourse architecture and community building create vibrant virtual publics', *Electronic Markets*, 10(4): 214–23.
Keng, C.-J., and Ting, H.-Y. (2009) 'The acceptance of blogs: using a customer experiential value perspective', *Internet Research*, 19(5): 479–95.
King, J. (2002) 'Destination marketing organisations: connecting the experience rather than promoting the place', *Journal of Vacation Marketing*, 8(2): 105–8.
Koh, J. and Kim, Y. (2004) 'Sense of virtual community: a conceptual framework and empirical validation', *International Journal of Electronic Commerce*, 8(2): 75–93.
Krishnamurthy, S. (2003) *E-commerce Management: Text and Cases*. Australia: South-Western.
Kurashima, T., Tezuka, T. and Tanaka, K. (2005) 'Blog map of experiences: extracting and geographically mapping visitor experiences from Urban blogs', *WISE*, 2005 LNC: 3806.
— (2006) 'Mining and visualizing local experiences from blog entries', *DEXA*, 2006 LNCS: 4080.
Larsen, S. (2007) 'Aspects of a psychology of the tourist experience', *Scandinavian Journal of Hospitality and Tourism*, 7(7): 7–18.
Lechner, U. and Hummel, J. (2002) 'Business models and system architectures of virual communities: from a sociological phenomenon to peer-to-peer architectures', *International Journal of Electronic Commerce*, 6(3): 41–53.
Lin, Y. and Huang, J. (2006) 'Internet blogs as a tourism marketing medium: a case study', *Journal of Business Research*, 59: 1201–5.
Mack, R., Blose, J. and Pan, B. (2008) 'Believe it or not: credibility of blogs in tourism', *Journal of Vacation Marketing*, 14(2): 133–44.
Magnini, V., Crotts, J. and Zehrer, A. (2011) 'Understanding customer delight: an application of travel blog analysis', *Journal of Travel Research*, 50(5): 535–45.
Markus, U. (2002) *Characterizing the Virtual Community* (5th edn). SAP Design Guild. Available from: http://www.sapdesignguild.org/editions/edition5/communities.asp.
Marlow, C. (2004) 'Audience, structure and authority in weblog community', *54th Annual Conference of the International Communication Association*. Available at: http://www.researchmethods.org/ICA2004.pdf.
Morgan, N., Pritchard, A. and Piggott, R. (2002) 'New Zealand, 100% Pure: the creation of a powerful niche destination brand', *Journal of Brand Management*, 9(4/5): 335–54.
Munar, A.M. (2009) 'Challenging the brand', in L. Cai, W. Gartner and A.M. Munar (eds) *Tourism Branding: Communities in Action*. Bingley, UK: Emerald Group Publishing Limited.
Muniz, A. and O'Guinn, T.C. (1998) 'Brand community', Working paper. Urbana-Champaign, IL, USA: University of Illinois.
Newbrough, J.R. and Chavis D.M. (eds) (1986) 'Psychological sense of community', *American Journal of Community Psychology*, 14(1): 3–5.
Niininen, O., March, R. and Buhalis, D. (2006) 'Consumer centric tourism marketing', in D. Buhalis and C. Costa (eds) *Tourism Management Dynamics: Trends, Management and Tools*. London: Butterworth Heinemann, pp. xxiii, 279.
O'Connor, P., Wang, Y. and Li, X. (2011) 'Web 2.0, the online community and destination marketing', in Y. Wang and A. Pizam (eds) *Destination Marketing and Management: Theories and Applications*. Oxfordshire: CAB International, pp. 225–43.
Pan, B., Maclaurin, T. and Crotts, J. (2007) 'Travel blogs and the implications for destination marketing', *Journal of Travel Research*, 46: 35–45.
Pei-Ya, C. (2000) 'The exploration of brand community: a case study of the Mini car community', unpublished MSc dissertation, De Montfort University, Leicester.

Porter, C.E. (2004) 'A typology of virtual communities: a multi-disciplinary foundation for future research', *Journal of Computer-Mediated Communication*, 10(1): Article 3.
Prebensen, N. (2007) 'Exploring tourists' images of a distant destination', *Tourism Management*, 28(3): 747–56.
Preece, J. (2000) *Online Communities: Designing Usability, Supporting Sociability*. Chichester: John Wiley and Sons Ltd.
Puhringer, S. and Taylor, A. (2008) 'A practitioner's report on blogs as a potential source of destination marketing intelligence', *Journal of Vacation Marketing*, 14(2): 177–87.
Schmallegger, D. and Carson, D. (2008) 'Blogs in tourism: changing approaches to information exchange', *Journal of Vacation Marketing*, 14(2): 99–110.
Schouten, J.W. and McAlexander, J.H. (1995) 'Subcultures of consumption: an ethnography of the new bikers', *Journal of Consumer Research*, 22: 43–61.
Sharda, N. and Ponnada, M. (2007) 'Tourism blog visualiser for better tour planning', paper presented at *First Annual Conference on Blogs in Tourism*, Kitzbuhel, July 2007.
Stanoevska-Slabeva, K. (2002) 'Toward a community-oriented design of Internet platforms', *International Journal of Electronic Commerce*, 6(3): 71–95.
Stepchenkova, S., Mills, J.E. and Jiang, H. (2007) 'Virtual travel communities: self-reported experiences and satisfaction', in M. Sigala, L. Mich and J. Murphy (eds) *The 14th International Conference on Information Technology and Travel and Tourism (ENTER)*, Slovenia, January 2007.
Sweeney, J., Soutar, G. and Mazzarol, T. (2008) 'Factors influencing word-of-mouth effectiveness: receiver perspectives', *European Journal of Marketing*, 42: 344–64.
Tasci, A. and Kozak, M. (2006) 'Destination brands vs destination images: do we know what we mean?' *Journal of Vacation Marketing*, 12(4): 299–317.
Tussyadiah, I. and Fesenmaier, D. (2008) 'Marketing places through first-person stories: an analysis of Pennsylvania roadtripper blog', *Journal of Travel and Tourism Marketing*, 24(3–4): 299–311.
— (2009) 'Mediating tourist experiences: access to places via shared videos', *Annals of Tourism Research*, 36(1): 24–40.
Volo, S. (2010) 'Bloggers' reported tourist experiences: their utility as a tourism data source and their effect on prospective tourists', *Journal of Vacation Marketing*, 16(4): 297–311.
— (2012) 'Re-inventing tourism communication', in M. Sigala, E. Christou and U. Gretzel (eds) *Social Media in Travel, Tourism and Hospitality: Theory, Practice and Cases*. Surrey: Ashgate Publishing Ltd.
Wang, Y. and Fesenmaier, D. (2004) 'Modeling participation in an online travel community', *Journal of Travel Research*, 42: 261–70.
Wang, Y., Yu, Q. and Fesenmaier, D. (2002) 'Defining the virtual tourist community: Implications for tourism marketing', *Tourism Management*, 23: 407–17.
Wenger, A. (2008) 'Analysis of travel bloggers' characteristics and their communication about Austria as a tourism destination', *Journal of Vacation Marketing*, 14(2): 169–76.
Xiang, Z. and Gretzel, U. (2010) 'Role of social media in online travel information search', *Tourism Management*, 31(2): 179–88.
Zehrer, A., Crotts, J.C. and Magnini, V.P. (2011) 'The perceived usefulness of blog postings: an extension of the expectancy-disconfirmation paradigm', *Tourism Management*, 32(1): 106–13.

39

Tourism marketing goes mobile

Smartphones and the consequences for tourist experiences

Scott McCabe, Clare Foster, Chunxiao Li and Bhanu Nanda

Introduction

Tourism is going mobile. This statement might seem grammatically tautological but until relatively recently, many of the online aspects of travel and tourism that are beyond the trip experience, including: search for ideas and inspiration, recommendations and relevant information, reflection and sharing stories and photos and so on, were characterized by their spatial fixity. Society's increasing dependence on the Internet and digital social media in particular pretty much dictated a fixed location, in that consumers needed to be at their desktops or within access of an Internet connection via a laptop in order to engage and communicate online with their social networks and tourism businesses and destinations. However, as other authors in this volume have alluded to, recent developments in smartphone technology, adoption and use are changing the rules of the game in which all businesses, including tourism businesses and destinations, operate.

Social media giants such as Facebook and Twitter as well as travel-related websites, such as TripAdvisor have had to readjust the basis for their business models, as they come to terms with the fact that many of their customers access their sites from mobile devices, which in turn affects advertising capabilities. Smartphone adoption globally heralds a paradigm shift in m-commerce with consequent marketing impacts. For example, one of the authors of this chapter attended a UK travel industry briefing on mobile applications in 2010, at which travel industry executives around the room argued they were holding off investment decisions in mobile applications and business development because at the time they complained that they could not see the revenue potential. That situation has rapidly evolved. According to a recent report, marketing research analysts Forrester noted that mobile paid advertising and search surpassed email *and even* social media in 2011 for the first time (in the US), and forecast a 38 per cent compound annualised growth rate until 2016, to over $8 billion, far outstripping all other areas of interactive marketing spend (VanBoskirk 2011).

However, it is the way in which consumers have embraced smart mobile technology since the launch of Apple's iPhone in 2007 (although smartphones had been in existence since around 2000, largely spearheaded by Nokia), that is really driving business development and marketing issues. TripAdvisor launched its mobile site in 2010 and has reached over 26 million downloads of its mobile app subsequently (*Forbes Magazine* 2013), whilst recent research for toonz using Google Analytics found that 20 per cent of destination marketing organization web traffic comes from tourists using mobile devices to find out things to do within the destination, despite roaming charges (Fox 2013). There is compelling evidence emerging to suggest that smartphones have the potential to alter information search and planning processes, through the provision of convenient, contextually-relevant information, in real time (Brown and Chalmers 2003). A range of studies have assessed the influence of smartphones on tourist behaviour in different ways: within particular visitor contexts, such as museums (e.g. Kramer, Modsching, Hagen and Gretzel 2007), provision of destination based services that open the way to unplanned experiences (Tussyadiah and Fesenmaier 2009), mediation of psychological as well as behavioural dimensions through the facilitation of social activities, such as learning about the destination and sharing information at any time during the trip (Wang, Park and Fesenmaier 2011). It is the ubiquitous and pervasive qualities of smartphone access to 3G/4G or wifi-enabled location-based applications and services that consumers appear to really value in their tourism experiences.

However, empirical studies on smartphone use of the Internet and travel-related applications for tourism are still few in number. This chapter outlines findings from a study undertaken in the UK that aimed to establish how consumers accessed the Internet for travel related information in their daily lives and at different stages in their last tourism trip. The purpose of the study was to understand if and how consumers used smartphones to access travel-related information and services now and to ascertain potential future uses, to compare users with non-users' patterns of behaviour and to their activity on the Internet, and to identify implications for managing and marketing tourism. The chapter begins with a short review of the literature on the pivotal role of technology in tourism and a discussion of the emerging literature on smartphone and mobile applications and their effects on tourist experience. The methods and results of the study are then outlined, and the chapter concludes with a discussion of the implications for tourism marketing.

Technology, m-commerce and smartphones in tourism

Developments in information and communication technology (ICT) have heralded a paradigm shift over the last 20 years in both consumers' practices and commercial applications for the tourism industry (Buhalis and Law 2008). Information has long been recognized as fundamental in overcoming problems associated with the communication of quality and value for intangible services (Sheldon 1997). The Internet has played a pivotal role in transforming tourist decision making, impacting for example on: destination image formation processes compared to conventional channels (Frías, Rodríguez and Castañeda 2008); attitudinal differences between men and women in their engagement with online tourism information (Kim, Lehto and Morrison 2007); perceptions of loyalty and purchase decisions (Kim, Lee and Hiemstra 2004); and the role of online social groups/communities via social media to inform information processing through e-word-of-mouth and tourist behaviour through modifications to tourist activity schedules (e.g. Pan and Fesenmaier 2006; Litvin, Goldsmith and Pan 2008; Xiang and Gretzel 2010).

Greater and wider access to information, has led to an enhanced role for the consumer, who has become empowered through the availability and usability of information resources via Internet technology (Pires, Stanton and Rita 2006), demanding more personalized and relevant engagement with tourism service providers and destinations (Stamboulis and Skyannis 2003). In broad terms, until recently the majority of research in this area has tended to assess the commercial impacts of technology with relatively less focus on understanding how technology has influenced or shaped tourist experiences. However, recent research has noted the potential implications of smartphone adoption and contextually aware 3G/4G-enabled Internet applications on tourist experiences, which is discussed later in this section.

In terms of m-commerce in tourism, Kim, Park and Morrison (2008) identified how important interactive mobile technology would be for tourism and hospitality services in the future, in that:

> M-commerce not only extends the benefits of the Web, but also allows for unique services enabled by the convergence of the Internet with mobile technologies. Travel service providers will find new ways to increase customer loyalty, generate supplemental revenue streams and reduce operating costs.
>
> *(Kim, Park and Morrison 2008: 394)*

They identified that perceived usefulness and ease of use were important factors affecting respondents' intentions towards mobile technology, and that usefulness was perceived as being more important.

Watson *et al.* (2004) had earlier identified that mobile phones would revolutionise access to Internet technology and consequently services, and thus create new commercial applications (*u-commerce* opportunities). In terms of the impact on marketing, they argued that mobile commerce would add value in four main ways: through: *Amplification*: creating value by extending or enhancing the conscious interaction with the phenomena; *Attenuation*: creating value by reducing the necessity of consciously interacting with the phenomena; *Contextual*: processes that are time-space specific and add value through their specificity; and *Transcension*: processes that create value by transcending or enabling transcension, of the conventional constraints of time and space (Watson *et al.* 2004: 320).

The ability of the tourism and travel industries to harness these opportunities for contextual and ubiquitous business development has yet to be realized, however. Lee and Mills remind us that quality and relevance are still paramount to commercial applications of mobile technologies for service development. They found that tourists were more likely to repeat purchase and use mobile Internet services when they were satisfied with the product and service offered via the mobile platform and consumers found there was room for improvement before m-commerce could be fully optimized in the tourism industry (Lee and Mills 2010).

However, the current situation is very dynamic. Marentakis and Emiris (2010) proposed a conceptual model of the potential for location aware auctions of tourism services, recognizing that the ability of tourism service providers to offer last minute, locationally-relevant discounted products and services could help manage yields more effectively. There is currently a great deal of activity in developing effective marketing that harnesses social media networks. A number of studies have proposed useful technological solutions to enhance the tourism marketing value of user-generated online information about destinations, such as photographs and descriptions of places in order to reduce 'noise' and enhance the usability of the information for a range of purposes (see Hao, Cai, Wang, Xiao, Yang, Pang and Zhang 2010 for example). In terms of opportunities for advertisers, compared with traditional broadcast advertising channels, mobile advertising offers businesses the opportunity to deliver personalized and interactive messages according to a consumer's unique location and environment (Chen and Hsieh 2011).

Mobile applications and the tourist experience

Early research in this field focused on the development, user-testing and application of mobile devices such as PDA's applied to interactivity within learning and visiting experiences of museums. Beyond the museum context, early prototypes of mobile tourist applications developed models for tourist-related information with maps and positioning (GPS) technology (e.g. Laakso, Gjesdal and Sulebak 2003) in mobile tour guide systems. Abowd, Atkeson, Hong, Long, Kooper and Pinkerton (1997) in one of the earliest studies detailing a prototype 'Cyberguide' recognized the critical elements of any mobile tourism application as being: a cartographer–map component, to display geographic information on the device; an information component, to provide relevant tourist information on what is available; a positioning component so that users can locate themselves within the destination context; and a communications component to allow tourists to communicate with each other or to contact relevant service personnel.

Another early example was the CRUMPET prototype, which developed a user-friendly, context-aware tourism service, designed for travellers who did not have the time to plan all the elements of their trip (Poslad, Laamanen, Malaka, Nick, Buckle and Zipl 2001). CRUMPET proposed services which would integrate 'four key emerging technology domains and applying to the tourism domain: personalised services, smart component-based middleware or "smartware" that uses multi-agent technology, location-aware services and transparent mobile data communication' (2001: 28). The CRUMPET project not only encapsulated the core problems facing visitors within the context of their being in-the-destination, but also established the major technological components required to meet these needs. Until recently it was accepted that the main commercial applications of telephone-based 'mobile tourism' applications were in three areas:

> tourist or museum guides with pre-installed applications, namely rigidly defined content (in text, visual and auditory format) that cannot be customized according to user preferences; mobile devices used to access mobile web portals and browse tourist information of interest; mobile electronic guides devices that use either wireless or mobile network connections to access context-aware services.
>
> *(Kenteris, Gavalas and Economou 2009: 104)*

Other early examples of mobile services aimed at enhancing tourist experiences through service development. Schöning, Hecht and Starosielski (2008) developed a demonstrator application entitled 'Wikear', that aimed to overcome the problems of scale of tourism information (that information is either, very generic, or is very detailed but only at the small scale, micro-level) by generating locationally relevant stories based on data mined from Wikipedia. The resulting stories were then organised according to principles derived from narrative theory and built into educational audio tours. Ballagas and Walsh (2007) first built a gaming experience into a tourism destination context with the development of a 'spell-casting' game available for tourists to play in a destination (Rasenberg in Germany) which connected historical information about the destination to users' mobile devices in an interactive gaming format. Therefore in a range of contexts and disciplines, tourist experiences have become the focus for the development of new mobile services that have attempted to address challenges to the visitor experience beyond the confines of visitor attractions.

However, more recently, the focus of research seems to have shifted towards an understanding and critical evaluation of the potential implications of smartphone use in transforming the inherently social nature of tourist experiences. Firstly, in the context of increasing orientation generally to mobility, increased travel for all types of purposes, coupled with a more disparate social network, all social life has become mediated by personal, digital and mobile technology. Travel has become increasingly necessary in order to sustain social relations (Larsen, Urry and Axhausen 2007). Equally, tourism can be experienced vicariously through the Internet, through the process of mediatization, in which images of destinations and narratives of travel experiences can be accessed anywhere anytime, which can be extended to mobile devices (Jansson 2002). Increased connectivity through mobile phones and the Internet has the potential to disrupt the possibility for 'escape', blurring the distinctions between what it means to be away from home (White and White 2007). Tourists are now always connected to people and work back home through their devices, problematizing the meaning of being away (Gretzel 2010).

Gretzel argues that such technologies not only enable travel but fundamentally structure tourism experiences (2010). Web-enabled mobile devices are beginning to re-direct the tourist gaze, becoming the mediator between people and tourism destinations. The tourist can double-check information about places through their phones, but also more crucially, these technologies can help tourists rely less on tourist guidebooks and perhaps open up new spaces in which to sightsee. Additionally, Gretzel argues that the typical direction of the tourist gaze was predominantly social, shared events. Yet the smartphone allows for or perhaps encourages a more individualized experience, as the mobile device becomes the main focal point through which the tourist experience is mediated, the screen becomes the object of the gaze. This may leave little scope to explore the unknown or to access serendipitous or unpredictable experiences that often contribute to successful travel outcomes. Gretzel argues that the applications available for tourists to experience places, are perhaps designed for fairly basic, surface level experiences of culture and landscapes, thus limiting the opportunity for deeper engagement with tourism destinations. This may dictate a more spurious and fleeting level of experience, such that the social fabric of travel is changed, to either heighten or discourage emotional engagement with what is actually experienced (Gretzel 2010).

Gretzel (2012) has gone on to argue that the academic discourse on technology development and the implications for tourism have been coloured by a level of thinking that assumes all progress is good. This has presented an unbalanced focus on greater efficiencies, increased accessibility and transparency of information, enhanced services, greater connectivity, positive impacts on mobility, the levelling of playing fields and power shifts in favour of tourism consumers. Thus, an incomplete picture emerges that negates the fact that tourism and technology exist within broader environmental, political, economic and social contexts that will impact on the type and direction of technological advances. Technological progress can also lead to issues of dependency, an inability to cope without access to the Internet through mobile phones (Gretzel 2010), power imbalances and opportunities for inequalities to be exacerbated and for abuse of power (Gretzel 2012).

Although at an early stage of development, there are a range of studies emerging that have sought to explore consumers' perspectives on the mediating role of mobile digital technology on tourist experience. For example, Tussyadiah and Fesenmaier (2009) assessed the role played by shared videos in mediating the touristic experience. Although the focus of this study was on the broader online sphere, they recognized the increasing importance of mobile platforms for capturing and sharing video online. Shared videos provided pleasure by stimulating daydreams and by bringing foreign landscapes and cultures to life through narrative. Such videos enhanced cognitive and emotional involvement in tourist destinations.

There are a wide range of software applications that have been designed for use on smartphone operating systems. Wang, Park and Fesenmaier (2011) conducted a study based on reviews of travel-related smartphone applications. First they identified 12 categories of mobile apps, and performed a content analysis on a large sample of detailed reviews to understand the possible mediating roles. They found that smartphone apps allowed tourists to change their plans due to the ease of access to the Internet, that they found them a source of useful information for decision-making, and critically that tourists often felt more secure, confident and excited when they used their smartphone. This study went on to outline five scenarios that exemplified the mediating role of smartphones on tourist experience: to provide good value and efficiency; to enhance and enrich visiting experiences; to provide delight and novelty in the experience; to enable sharing, either as a form of status enhancement or for happiness and peace of mind; and to inspire future travel. Further studies have sought to understand the types of uses of smartphones in particular for: travel planning and reservations; information search in the destination, location based services, such as tour guiding and maps, and sharing tourist experiences, largely through social media (Wang and Xiang 2012). Finally, Tussyadiah (2013) found that tourists tended to anthropormorphize their interactions with their mobile phones, treating them as social companions, depending on the perceived intelligence, socialness and positive social characteristics, as well as frequency of use in travel. This study demonstrates the important potential of mobile phones to affect opportunities for social interaction in travel.

Generally there is a limited amount of empirical evidence on the influences of smartphone use on tourism experiences. The rates of adoption are very fast and new business models are emerging to take account of the opportunities that smartphones might offer to tourism suppliers, but little is known about how a shift towards mobile advertising might impact on consumers in the future. The present study sought to understand what types of mobile applications are currently used in tourists' experiences, and at which stages in the experience. The research consisted of an online survey, which was sent out to a large database of UK consumers. The survey sought to understand the current level of smartphone ownership amongst consumers (in 2010), their use of social media and Internet technology at different points in tourism planning and trip/post-trip experiences in order to compare users with non-users. The survey also asked which types of smartphone applications tourists used in different types of trips to understand how tourists' use of these types of applications holds implications for tourism business and marketing.

Types of mobile digital applications in tourism

As with previous studies (Wang *et al.* 2011; Wang and Xiang 2012) this study began with a search of the available applications by trawling Apple's 'Appstore' and Android's marketplace. Applications on the 'Appstore' are already categorized, although we did not limit our search to the travel section, but included navigation, lifestyle and social networking categories. A simple evaluation of the types of applications enabled an evaluation of the range of mobile applications currently available in the market. These categories of applications informed the survey development in terms of the types of applications used.

- *Transport planning apps* (e.g. Trainline, Flight track). These applications allow users to track flight information in many locations in real time, helping them to share information on travel disruptions with other users and to make alternative arrangements.
- *What's on guide/event listing apps* (e.g. buzzd). These applications allow users to up(down)load information on events and activities in their current location and to rate/recommend places and events. These types of applications could increase tourists' sense of spontaneity, encourage new forms of sociality through recommendations and word-of-mouth.
- *Travel planner applications* (e.g. TripIT, Tripcase, TripDeck). Different to the transport planning applications described above, these apps perform integrated itinerary management functions including flights and car hire, hotel and restaurant reservations, and meetings, which are synchronized to the user's i-calendar. These types of applications mirror the function of the tour operator and allow users to manage their itinerary on the move.

- *Accommodation planning applications* (e.g. hotels.com, hotelpal). These applications function as a location-based tourist information centre service for accommodation services. Users are able to find hotels within their current location and compare prices, quality levels and other features, as well as book accommodation. These assist users' information search processes, enabling shorter planning times and increased flexibility and choice.
- *Tour guide applications* (e.g. UK Travel guide, NY Travel guide). These applications generally consist of city guides providing recommendations for restaurants, shopping, attractions, nightlife and possibly some augmented reality services. These applications add value since the information is constantly updated, often includes the reviewers of other visitors as well as sponsored information, which is easy to use and relatively cost-effective.
- *Directional services* (e.g. Google maps, Navmii). Can offer complete satellite navigation software designed for a mobile platform, or a simple map service to help users find their way through and about their location. These types of applications offer simple solutions to tourists seeking to find their way around a city or tourism destination and offer search functions, distances and other information.
- *Location based social-networking applications* (e.g. Gowalla, Foursquare). These applications have the potential to offer important social opportunities for tourists, helping them to identify friends and contacts in their location and to discover opportunities to experience different aspects of a destination. This could enhance the feeling of connection with a place, and lead to more authentic visitor experiences (off the beaten track). Users receive rewards and can play games, adding value to the visitor experience.
- *Attraction applications* (e.g. ThrillSeeker). These types of applications have often been developed to deliver an enhanced visitor experience at a particular site or attraction. Some include an augmented reality feature, which allows users to point their camera phone at a location and additional information is overlaid onto the viewfinder to create a more interactive user experience and add additional quality to the interpretation of an artefact or location.
- *Company specific applications* (e.g. British Airways, Lufthansa). These applications allow users to view and manage their bookings and other information that the company may hold about them. Airlines provide customers with scannable QR codes as boarding passes to mobiles, and these applications are very useful for companies to manage their customer relationships.
- *Tourist assistance applications* (e.g. eCurrency, language translator). These types of applications provide supporting services for travellers including spoken language translation and translation services using the camera function. These services can facilitate tourist experiences and enable new types of tourist interactions.
- *Social-networking applications* (e.g. Facebook, Twitter). These types of applications are also available on mobile platforms, which allow users to share information, photographs and experiences about places with their friends.

These apps were classified according to their relevance within different stages of the tourist experience. Some apps are more relevant to the planning and information gathering stages, whereas others are specific to the activities during travel. Others, such as social networking apps are generic and applicable to all stages.

Methodology

For this study an online survey methodology was adopted, which has proven useful in tourism and hospitality research (Hung and Law 2011). The study aimed to understand if and how consumers used smartphone applications in their tourism activities and the possible effects on tourist experience. Initial questions sought to ascertain respondents' use of the Internet for a range of activities in their daily lives (information search, email, social networking, downloading music or movies, financial work [banking etc.], checking news, sports, weather reports, purchase travel related services, or purchasing tickets for events). Next, we asked if respondents shared travel experiences online using a range of channels (social networking, writing travel blogs, writing travel reviews, participating in travel forums, or uploading photographs). The survey went on to ask about the frequencies of trips for business and leisure undertaken in the last year, as well as the most recent trip and sought to understand whether respondents had accessed the Internet during their most recent trip, for specific types of activity and through which channels, including their smartphones, but also via their hotel, Internet cafes and so on. Final questions asked about smartphone ownership, whether non-users intended to buy a smartphone in the near future, whether users had accessed the different types of applications identified earlier, and which of them they thought they were likely to use in the future.

An email link was sent to a representative sample of UK residents, via a commercial partner, Experian UK, a leading global information service. Experian are the UK's leading supplier of consumer email databases for market research purposes, with a UK consumer database of 45 million people. The sample consisted of around 105,000 UK consumers and was distributed in September 2010. A total of 3,503 respondents opened the email of which 780 clicked through to the survey link. This yielded a total response of 635 respondents completing the survey, of which 611 completed all sections including the demographic profile questions. There are limitations with this response set, as the profile of respondents was skewed towards the older demographic profile, however the study yielded interesting results particularly in comparing smartphone users with non-users in terms of their user characteristics and secondly, the smaller response set of smartphone users did broadly correspond to smartphone ownership rates in the UK at the time and the demographic profiles for users.

Descriptive analysis such as frequencies was run firstly to obtain basic information for each variable. Crosstabulation was then used to compare the difference between groups on nominal variables such as the use of each travel related smartphone application for leisure and business trips. In order to understand if there were any differences between smartphone users and non-users, the Mann-Whitney test was performed on how often people used the Internet for each activity and how likely they would use the ten smartphone applications in the future. Both questions are ordinal data which required a non-parametric test. In addition, a factor analysis was run on the ten travel-related smartphone applications.

Sample

There was a fairly even proportion of males (56 per cent n=340) to females (44 per cent n= 271). The demographic was skewed towards the older age groups with around 85 per cent (523) people over 45, with 32 per cent (195) of those over 65. A high percentage of respondents classified themselves as retired (47 per cent). This may account for the finding that leisure trips are taken much more often than business trips. Around 70 per cent respondents take a few leisure trips per year (27 per cent stated between one to two, and 43 per cent between three to five leisure trips per year). Compared with leisure trips, only 14 per cent of respondents take one or two business trips and 7 per cent take three to five business trips.

Results

Comparing smartphone users with non-users

When we compared the responses for smartphone users with non-users, our findings suggested that in general, smartphone users are heavier Internet users. There was a significantly higher propensity for smartphone users to use the Internet for information search, emailing and reading news on a daily basis. Smartphone users were more frequent users of financial services, purchasing travel related service and purchasing tickets for events based on weekly basis. It is worth noting that more than half non-smartphone users never use the Internet for social networking (52.7 per cent) or downloading music (59.5 per cent), which is much greater compared with smartphone users (social network 27.2 per cent, download music 25.2 per cent). This finding is interesting although this large discrepancy could be attributed to the higher age profile of respondents to this survey.

In order to understand in further detail the differences between the two groups in their use of different types of Internet activities we undertook a factor analysis of the different activities and looked for patterns between users and non-users. We used a standard Principal Component Analysis using Varimax method and Kaiser normalization. The data were stable over four iterations. Three factors were identified, which we labelled:

- travel related activity (including: information search, purchase travel services and purchase tickets for events);
- leisure related activity (including: social networking and downloading music);
- work related activity (including: emailing, financial services, news).

In terms of the whole range of activities, items in the travel related factor were used less frequently amongst all respondents. However, smartphone owners were more likely to use the Internet for these items on a weekly–monthly basis than non-users. As noted in the crosstab, in the leisure category, the interesting issue was the lack of likeliness that non-users would engage in these activities on the Internet, and finally in the work-related category, smartphone users' activity levels in the various associated activities are more prevalent on the daily to weekly basis than non-users.

How are smartphones used in tourism?

The survey asked smartphone users if they used any of the types of mobile digital applications on different types of trips (business or leisure). The highest use of any application by respondents is for domestic trips whether for business or leisure. Our assumption is that international roaming charges prohibit the use of application services when abroad for many leisure users. In terms of domestic leisure trips, directional services (n=71) received the highest number of responses, followed by transport applications such as train line, flight track etc. Many respondents use directional service applications on domestic business trips as well. Smartphones are much less used during international trips. But accessing applications containing company specific services (n=18) such as British Airways or Hilton, together with applications offering tourist assistance (n=23) (e.g. currency rate, language translation), are the two types of applications most used through smartphones.

In general, for business trips, the smartphone is mostly used for transport planning followed by directional services. For leisure trips, the most popular applications are directional services, finding out what's on and social networking.

A final observation from the comparison was that smartphone users take more trips per year for both business and leisure purposes. More than 20 per cent of smartphone users take more than 12 business trips per year while less than 10 per cent of non-users do. However, in the leisure category, where we might expect a higher incidence of travel amongst the older age group, we also noted a higher frequency of leisure trips amongst smartphone owners. Around 25 per cent of smartphone users take more than nine trips for leisure compared to only 5 per cent of non-users. Therefore, whilst the limitations concerning the skewed dataset towards older people amongst non-users may have an impact on the findings, it does appear that in general smartphone users can be characterized as more frequent travellers with a greater reliance on online services and who use the Internet more frequently for all types of activity including travel-related information and purchases.

This finding has some correspondence with previous studies. Chircu, Keskey and Kauffman's (2001) work for example revealed that frequent travellers use online booking features with less cognitive effort than infrequent travellers. They reported differences in usage preferences, for example they found that frequent travellers are more likely to use online booking services. Similarly, Tan, Fu, Goh and Theng (2007) found that less frequent travellers felt that information about the destination was more important than frequent travellers, whereas frequent travellers felt that maps and directional guides were more important. This suggests there are differences in the types of information and online experiences sought between smartphone users and non-users, or perhaps that the drivers of behaviour associated with different types of trips (business or leisure) lead to different levels of engagement with Internet technology and mobile applications.

Smartphone use in tourism now and in the future

In order to find out what kinds of activities are undertaken in general in tourism related contexts, respondents were asked to select amongst a range of activities (search for information, purchase tours, transport and accommodation, purchase tickets for events, find out what's on, get live reports on traffic, get live information on the weather forecast and E check-in). The most cited activities were *search for information* (n=164), *purchase tours, transport and accommodation* (n=164) and *find out what's on* (n=146). And among different channels (tourist information centre, smartphone, Internet via a hotel or café and other), most respondents accessed the Internet for these activities from their hotel or café (but note that 22 per cent of the respondents owned a smartphone). For those who own a smartphone, the most common activities were *to get live information on the weather forecast* (n=46) followed by *to get live reports on traffic* (n=38) and *search for information for planning* (n=24). Therefore smartphones (as well as the wider Internet) are used most frequently to serve functional, information needs, rather than to enrich the experience of travel itself.

Finally, non-smartphone users were asked if they were considering purchasing a smartphone in the future (in a range of time categories). The respondents who confirmed that they were considering a purchase, together with current users, were asked how likely they would be to use the range of smartphone applications as for the previous question, in the future. A total of 253 respondents answered this question. Again, the most likely useful types of applications were (n=number ticking very likely and somewhat likely) *directional services* (n=198), followed by *transport planning* (n=148), *accommodation planning* (n=137) and *tourist assistance applications* (n=130). However, future users (those considering a smartphone purchase) also highlighted the potential for behaviourally relevant applications such as *travel planning, tour guide* and *attraction applications,* in the future, which were all significant in tests of significance ($p<0.05$).

Conclusions

Smartphones are very rapidly becoming the preferred choice for consumers amongst mobile platforms. In addition, tablet and mini-tablet computers create an enhanced sense of mobility for all forms of human-computer interactions for the future. Their enhanced mobile functionality based on 3/4G WAP protocols, wifi and GPS make their potential to impact on tourist experiences in situ very powerful. However, research on smartphone use (and types of applications) in tourism is still emerging, and has largely focused either on the technical aspects of their use (Abowd *et al.* 1997), the development of prototypes (Poslad *et al.* 2001) and enhancement of experiences through service development (Schoning *et al.* 2008). However, more recent analyses have applied a sociological lens to address how smartphones may impact on the essential qualities of tourist experiences (White and White 2007; Tussyadiah and Fesenmaier 2009; Gretzel 2010).

A number of studies such as the one outlined here have sought to understand the implications of smartphone applications on the tourist experience (Wang, Park and Fesenmaier 2011) and their uses at different stages of the experience (Wang and Xiang 2012). These studies concur that, presently mobile applications seem to have most relevance to users for information provision during the trip. Mobile applications increase the opportunity for spontaneity, decrease the need for forward planning and improve service delivery through information that is contextually relevant, in real time. However, in terms of information provision, this is not necessarily all positive. Tourists may become dependent on their phones and social interaction may decrease, leading to more superficial experiences within destinations and local cultures (Gretzel 2012). Guidebooks written by 'authoritative' voices may disappear in favour of superficial, user-generated evaluations. Information will remain a key need to enrich tourist experiences, but there is a need for quality information, that is impartial and reliable as well as merely convenient.

Additionally, there are potentially important implications for destination marketing organisations (DMOs). These include a better understanding of how, what types and when tourists access information and services within the destination. Survey respondents highlighted that they relied on the Internet for information in the destination via a range of channels, which suggests a diminishing role of Tourism Information centres as key contact points for tourists during their trips compared to online information. Smartphones will radically change the ways in which tourists access information, book tickets for events and/or accommodation in destinations, including the timing of bookings. DMOs need to develop strategies to manage their inventories effectively and develop business models accordingly.

This study found that future users found that applications which were related more to behavioural aspects of experience potentially more appealing than current users. Some applications, such as location-based gaming and social networking applications offer the opportunity for new value creation in destinations, which could alter tourists' behaviour and emotional experience. Mobile applications potentially enable new authentic experiences of destinations through recommendations provided by local people and/or other tourists. They open up possibilities for interactions, for serendipitous experiences which take tourists 'off the beaten track', by providing content-rich recommendations delivered through crowd-sourced online information (Gretzel 2010). Yet for tourism marketers, more research is required about what tourists' needs are from smartphones, whether it is for functional (information), social or experiential applications. It may be possible to identify different segments based on smartphone use, and services can be developed accordingly.

Tan *et al.* (2007) warn that mobile services need to be user-oriented and based on what customers need otherwise there is a risk of them being overwhelmed. There may be great opportunities but currently there is little evidence of appetite in the market for making big-ticket purchases through a mobile phone. This may indicate high risk perceptions amongst users about the security of purchasing online through a mobile device. The opportunities for u-commerce identified by Watson *et al.* (2004) are rapidly becoming a reality. However, there is limited evidence on users' reactions to mobile marketing, and privacy is a key issue. More research is required to assess the implications of this shift to a mobile commerce arena particularly on tourist experiences, and to understand the business and destination marketing opportunities and challenges arising out of it.

References

Abowd, G.D., Atkeson, C.G. Hong, J., Long, S., Kooper, R. and Pinkerton. M. (1997) 'Cyberguide: a mobile context-aware tour guide', *Wireless Networks*, 3(1): 421–33.

Ballagas, R. and Walz, S. (2007) 'REXplorer: using iterative design techniques for pervasive games', in C. Magerkurth and C. Röcker (eds) *Pervasive Gaming Applications – A Reader for Pervasive Gaming Research*, volume 2. Aachen: Shaker Verlag.

Brown, B. and Chalmers, M. (2003) 'Tourism and mobile technology', in K. Kuutti and E.H. Karsten (eds) *Proceedings of the Eighth European Conference on Computer Supported Cooperative Work, Helsinki, Finland, 14–18 September 2003*. Boston: Kluwer Academic Press.

Buhalis, D. and Law, R. (2008) 'Progress in information technology and tourism management: 20 years on and 10 years after the Internet – the state of eTourism research', *Tourism Management*, 29(4): 609–23.

Chen, P.–T. and Hsieh, H.–P. (2011) 'Personalized mobile advertising: Its key attributes, trends, and social impact', *Technological Forecasting and Social Change*, 79: 543–57.

Chircu, A.R., Keskey, D. and Kauffman, R.J. (2001) 'Maximizing the value of Internet-based corporate travel reservation systems', *Communications of the ACM*, 44(11): 57–63.

Forbes Magazine (2013) 'TripAdvisor is ready to post another quarter of strong growth'. Online. Available: http://www.forbes.com/sites/greatspeculations/2013/02/12/tripadvisor-is-ready-to-post-another-quarter-of-strong-growth/ (accessed 17 May 2013).

Fox, L. (2013) 'How destinations are consumed on mobile'. Online. Available: <http://www.tnooz.com/2013/01/31/mobile/how-destinations-are-consumed-on-mobile/?utm_source=Tnooz+Mailing+Listandutm_medium=emailandutm_campaign=d249d1c4f9-RSS_EMAIL_CAMPAIGN> (accessed 17 May 2013).

Frías, D.M., Rodríguez, M. and Castañeda, J.A. (2008) 'Internet vs travel agencies on pre-visit destination image formation: an information processing view', *Tourism Management*, 29: 163–79.

Gretzel, U. (2010) 'Travel in the network: redirected gazes, ubiquitous connections and new frontiers', in M. Levina and G. Kien (eds) *Post-global Network and Everyday Life*. New York: Peter Lang, pp 41–58.

— (2012) 'Tourism in a technology-dependent world', working paper published by Laboratory for Intelligent Systems in Tourism, University of Wollongong, Wollongong, Australia.

Hao, Q., Cai, R., Wang, C., Xiao, R., Yang, J.-M., Pang, Y. and Zhang, L. (2010) 'Equip tourists with knowledge mined from travelogues', in *Proceedings of the International World Wide Web Conference (IW3C2), WWW 2010*, 26–30 April 2010, Raleigh, North Carolina, USA.

Hung, K. and Law, R. (2011) 'An overview of Internet-based surveys in hospitality and tourism journals', *Tourism Management*, 32: 717–24.

Jansson, A. (2002) 'Spatial phantasmagoria: the mediatization of tourism experience', *European Journal of Communication*, 17(4): 429–43.

Kenteris, M., Gavalas, D. and Economou, E. (2009) 'An innovative mobile electronic tourist guide application', *Personal Ubiquitous Computing*, 13: 103–18.

Kim, D.-Y., Lehto, X.-Y. and Morrison, A.M. (2007) 'Gender differences in online travel information search: implications for marketing communications on the Internet', *Tourism Management*, 28(2): 423–33.

Kim, D.-Y., Park, J. and Morrison, A.M. (2008) 'A model of traveller acceptance of mobile technology', *International Journal of Tourism Research*, 10: 393–407.

Kim, W., Lee, C. and Hiemstra, S. (2004) 'Effects of an online virtual community on customer loyalty and travel product purchases', *Tourism Management*, 25(3): 343–55.

Kramer, R., Modsching, M., Hagen, K. and Gretzel, U. (2007) 'Behavioural impacts of mobile tour guides', in M. Sigala, L. Mich and J. Murphy (eds) *Information and Communication Technologies in Tourism 2007*. Vienna: Springer, pp. 109–18.

Laakso, K., Gjesdal, O. and Sulebak, J.R. 'Tourist information and navigation support by using 3D maps displayed on mobile devices', paper presented at the workshop HCI in mobile Guides, Udine (Italy), 8 September 2003.

Larsen, J., Urry, J. and Axhausen, K.W. (2007) 'Networks and tourism: mobile social life', *Annals of Tourism Research*, 34(1): 244–62.

Lee, J.-K. and Mills, J.E. (2010) 'Exploring tourist satisfaction with mobile experience technology', *International Management Review*, 6(1): 91–110.

Litvin, S.W., Goldsmith, R.E. and Pan, B. (2008) 'Electronic word-of-mouth in hospitality and tourism management', *Tourism Management*, 29: 458–68.

Marentakis, C. and Emiris, D. (2010) 'Location aware auctions for tourism services', *Journal of Hospitality and Tourism Technology*, 1(2): 121–43.

Pan, B. and Fesenmaier, D.R. (2006). 'Online information search: vacation planning process', *Annals of Tourism Research*, 33(3): 809–32.

Pires, G.D., Stanton, J. and Rita, P. (2006) 'The Internet, consumer empowerment and marketing strategies', *European Journal of Marketing*, 40(9–10): 936–49.

Poslad, S., Laamanen, H., Malaka, R., Nick, A., Buckle, P. and Zipl, A. (2001) 'CRUMPET: creation of user-friendly mobile services personalised for tourism', in *Second International Conference on 3G Mobile Communication Technologies* (CP477) London, UK, 26–28 March 2001, pp. 28–32. ISBN: 0 85296 731 4. DOI:10.1049/cp:20010006.

Schöning, J., Hecht, B. and Starosielski, N. (2008) 'Evaluating automatically generated location-based stories for tourists', in *Proceedings of the CHI 2008 Conference*, 5–10 April, Florence, Italy, pp. 2937–942.

Sheldon P.J. (1997) *Tourism Information Technology*. Wallingford: CAB International.

Stamboulis, Y. and Skayannis, P. (2003) 'Innovation strategies and technology for experience-based tourism', *Tourism Management*, 24(1): 35–43.

Tan, E.M.Y., Foo, S., Goh.D. and Theng, Y.L. (2007) 'An analysis of services for the mobile tourist', in *Proceedings of The International Conference on Mobile Technology, Applications and Systems*, Singapore, 10–12 September 2007.

Tussyadiah, I. (2013) 'When cell phones become travel buddies: social attribution to mobile phones in travel', in L. Cantoni and Z. Xiang (eds) *Information and Communication Technologies in Tourism: 2013 Proceedings of the International Conference in Innsbruck, Austria, 23–25 January*. New York: Springer, pp. 82–93.

Tussyadiah, I. and Fesenmaier, D.R. (2009) 'Mediating tourist experiences: access to places via shared videos', *Annals of Tourism Research*, 36(1): 24–40.

VanBoskirk, S. (2011) *US Interactive Marketing Forecast, 2011–2016*. Cambridge, MA: Forrester Research Inc.

Wang, D. and Xiang, Z. (2012) 'The new landscape of travel: a comprehensive analysis of smartphone apps', in M. Fuchs, F. Ricci and L. Cantoni (eds), *Information and Communication Technologies in Tourism 2012*. New York: Springer, pp. 308–19.

Wang, D., Park, S. and Fesenmaier, D.R. (2011) 'The role of smartphones in mediating the touristic experience', *Journal of Travel Research*, 51(4): 371–87.

Watson, R., Akselsen, S., Monod, E. and Pitt, E. (2004) 'The open tourism consortium: laying the foundations for the future of tourism', *European Management Journal*, 22(3): 315–26.

White, R.N. and White, P.B. (2007) 'Home and away: tourists in a connected world', *Annals of Tourism Research*, 34(1): 88–104.

Xiang, Z. and Gretzel, U. (2010) 'The role of social media in online travel information search', *Tourism Management*, 31: 179–88.

Part 9
Reflections

40

Tourism marketing from 1990–2010

Two decades and a new paradigm

Daniel R. Fesenmaier and Zheng Xiang

Introduction

Tourism marketing has gone through a substantial evolution over the past two decades as the tourism industry struggled to respond to the dramatic shocks brought about by an increasingly connected world. The goal of this chapter is to identify and describe some of the leading forces of change and their impacts on tourism marketing during this time. This chapter takes the perspective that the last two decades represent a time whereby most of the original foundations of tourism marketing were first dismantled, but then rebuilt and replaced by a new paradigm such that they are now much better equipped to meet the enduring forces of change. The discussion is organized into three sections. The first briefly discusses the global forces that have buffeted the travel and tourism industry; the second section describes three important responses from the industry, particularly through the lens of destination marketing organizations, to these challenges. The last section outlines an emergent paradigm for tourism marketing based upon our understanding of changes in response to these changes in society.

Tourism marketing and the foundations of change

One way to characterize tourism marketing over the past two decades is 'paradigm shift'. Driven by the development of the Internet, the world changed during this time to such a remarkable degree that one would not be able to understand nor predict the extent to which the tourism industry would be transformed. Perhaps the most important work that set the foundation for this transformation is Michael Porter's book *The Competitive Advantage* (1985), whereby he explained how information technology could be used to 'deconstruct' the value chain in order to more effectively compete in traditional and non-traditional marketplaces. Further, the early books such as *Paradigm Shift* (Tapscott and Caston 1993), *Digital Capital* (Tapscott, Ticoll and Lowy 2000) and *Being Digital* (Negroponte 1995), followed by Michael Dertouzos' (2001) *The Unfinished Revolution* and *The Cluetrain Manifesto* by Levine, Locke and Searls (2001) provided a complex vision of how firms including destination marketing organizations could realize the promises of this new technology. Also in an important political essay, *The World is Flat: A Brief History of the Twenty-First Century* (2005), Thomas Friedman argued that the Internet had enabled the world economy to become so intertwined that seemingly unrelated events in one country now have huge implications in another. Parallel to this work, a few books and articles focusing on the role of the Internet in marketing and tourism were written; most important were Poon's *Tourism, Technology and Competitive Strategies* (1993), *Sheldon's Tourism Information Technology* (1997) and Werthner and Klein's *Information Technology and Tourism – A Challenging Relationship* (1999); early marketing articles by Hoffman and Novak (1996), Novak and Hoffman (1996), and in tourism by Buhalis (1998, 2000), Gretzel, Yuan and Fesenmaier (2000) and Yuan, Gretzel and Fesenmaier (2003) are examples that reflect the 'new' thinking regarding the nature and impact of the Internet.

During this first decade of the Internet (roughly 1991–2002), the tourism industry became one of the leaders in the use of the Internet whereby industry leaders began to realize that they were largely information arbitrators, and that the Internet enabled them to communicate easily and effectively with their existing and potential customers. Also, importantly, many envisioned new ways of meeting the information needs of this market where websites replaced travel brochures for essentially every destination and attraction, and for every travel-related service worldwide. In the United States, for example, virtually every tourism organization had developed a website by the early 2000s, and many had gone through the evolution from a simple 'electronic brochure' to highly interactive systems that supported reservations, search and even virtual tours; importantly, the website had become the primary (and in many circumstances, the only) source of contact with potential visitors (Zach, Gretzel and Xiang 2010). In retrospect, this transformation is easily understood as the computer framework already existed through the various global distribution systems (GDSs) linking travel agencies to the airlines. Also during this time, many innovative destination marketing organizations (DMOs) began to realize their new role as partners within the 'tourism system' wherein they became 'information brokers' as they sought to develop and coordinate a range of new systems that would be used by their stakeholders (Gretzel and Fesenmaier 2002; Wang and Xiang 2007).

The decade of the 1990s was also a time where the leaders of the tourism industry began to understand and appreciate that travel experiences are 'products' that can be bundled and sold. Exemplified by the success of *The Experience Economy* by Pine and Gilmore (1999), the core business model of many/most tourism organizations changed. With this new perspective on the core product, the tourism industry is challenged to recognize that the 'new consumer' demands highly personalized experiences, that competition for visitors would now be waged in global markets, and that the traveller somehow was in the position to 'control' this new marketplace. Traditional travel agencies were decimated by newly formed online firms such as Expedia and Travelocity; the large travel suppliers such as airlines and hotels could connect directly with potential customers; search engines such as Google became dominant as they provided instant access to websites, and therefore could be indexed, advertised and managed; on top of all this, meta search engines such as Kayak further made the distribution of travel products more accessible and more transparent. In response, DMOs were forced to recalibrate again their role to become a different kind of intermediary whereby they largely focused on building the capacity necessary to assist small and medium tourism firms in adapting to this new and very challenging environment. And, as a result, they became destination managers. In effect, they had to change their business model to focus on creating new forms of value within the tourism chain (Wilson, Fesenmaier, Fesenmaier and van Es 2001).

Interestingly, the second decade (2001–present) was a time of even greater change for tourism marketing where the focus of technology change emerged from development (i.e. growth in the number of websites) and usability to one of persuasion and customer empowerment, and more recently to ubiquity through mobile systems. That is, while many of the core industry changes were realized in the first decade, the introduction of Web 2.0 signalled a new round of adaptation which required another new and even more transformational framework for tourism marketing. The first part of this second decade of the Internet saw the expansion of high speed Internet where the richness of the new interactive medium could be exploited, and this enabled the development of brochures which largely realized the interactive and personalized vision of the early developers. The more important feature of this decade was the development of new 'social' systems which began to emerge as an 'Army of Davids' (Reynolds 2006). TripAdvisor, for example, was launched in 2000 and now handles over 50 million inquiries monthly; Wikipedia was launched in 2001 and now hosts over 250 million articles in 285 different languages; and Facebook, launched in 2004, now services over one billion users annually. Importantly, at about the same time, mobile phone systems began to penetrate the marketplace to enable travellers to communicate more easily and from essentially anywhere on the planet. Finally in the later part of the decade, the introduction of smartphones enriched the social environment further such that the embedded technology in them empowers users to substantially control their travel experience. Within the tourism literature, Buhalis (2003) provided the leading book which discussed in practical terms how the tourism industry could successfully navigate through this new world. More recently, Sigala, Christou and Gretzel (2012) offer a different vision which is situated within this new rich socially networked environment whereby the 'army of travellers' is now the central player within the value chain, and Wang, Park and Fesenmaier (2012) describe the increasing influences that smartphones have in mediating the travel experience.

This emergence of the Internet over the past 20 plus years was not an isolated event that changed the tourism industry. Concomitant with the introduction of the Internet, the world experienced significant social, economic and environmental traumas, all of which somehow facilitated transformation in all aspects of life. These events are not discussed in detail in this chapter, but rather briefly acknowledged as to their vital role in shaping the various systems that provide the foundation for the travel industry, and in particular, tourism marketing. Arguably, the most important was the emergence of China as a leader in the world's economic and political systems. Much has been written that documents the importance of China including the size of its markets and the growth of the middle class, its dominance within the region and its growing competition with the United States for global leadership (Friedman 2005). Along with the growth in China, India, Brazil and Russia (BRIC countries) and the emergence of South Korea, Indonesia and Venezuela have reshaped the geography of world travel.

While seismic population and economic shifts were taking place, the world was also buffeted by the war on terrorism. September 11, 2001 will be remembered as the start of the 'war on terror' but it is clear that the terrorism had caused many problems for tourism long before that event. However, the worldwide response to the dangers posed by al-Qaeda was radical; many governments passed new laws to combat terrorism. In particular, Germany enacted two important laws to limit the ability of organizations to fund terrorist organizations while another law focused on enabling intelligence to be gathered. In the United States, the Department of Homeland Security was created and the USA Patriot Act provided additional powers to fight terrorism. Worldwide, the response to this 'new' threat was immediate having realized the new and threats posed by terrorism – both economically and politically – most countries created many new barriers to the 'open skies' arrangements sought by the travel industry.

The changes in social, economic and political structures were not only recognized along geographic borders but also in terms of consumer demographics (Benckendorff, Moscardo and Pendergast 2009). Importantly, baby-boomers finally began to retire while the younger generations seemed to simply watch as the markets adjusted. Cruise ships were built and retirement communities developed. However, with the changing economic realities, many of the 'older generation' decided not to retire while many of the younger generation decided that they did not want a world dominated by work. Indeed, research suggests that the children of Generation Y have distinctly different values, attitudes and behaviours from previous generations as a response to the technological and economic implications of the Internet such that the nature of travel differs substantially between generations as the younger generation is more interested in highly individualized and more 'authentic' experiences (Benckendorf *et al.* 2009).

Many other important social and political events occurred during these two decades which will have an enduring impact on the world. The emergence of the European Union and a common currency is one factor, the Great Recession and the financial restructuring of many countries is another. However, a more important and lasting force of change is that of environmental change. Although there are some leaders that doubt the 'reality' of climate change, many organizations within the tourism industry have begun to recognize the need for the industry to adopt sustainable tourism practices (Erkuş-Öztürk and Eraydın 2012; Tao and Wall 2009).

Leading tourism marketing efforts: the case of DMOs

The Internet fundamentally changed the nature of destination marketing (Gretzel, Fesenmaier and O'Leary 2006). Indeed, early statements by marketing gurus regarding the impact of technology went so far as to assert that if businesses did not adapt to technology change, they would not survive. Interestingly, many of the businesses that did NOT adopt the new technology are still around, just different (Gretzel and Fesenmaier 2001a). In April 2002, the National Laboratory for Tourism and eCommerce held a workshop at the University of Illinois which focused on the challenges facing DMOs. In essence the workshop focused on the question of the future of destination marketing in the United States. The results of this meeting were summarized in a paper by Gretzel, Fesenmaier, Formica and O'Leary (2006). The group identified six key challenges:

1 adapting to technological change;
2 managing expectations as part of the community leadership;
3 moving from destination marketing to destination management;
4 confronting new levels of competition;
5 recognizing creative partnering as the new way of life; and
6 finding new measures of success – increased need to demonstrate accountability.

It appears that American destination marketing organizations have addressed these six challenges in three important ways:

1 by shifting their focus toward the individual and away from mass markets;
2 by seeking to control their markets through strong brands; and
3 by adopting a renewed focus on measurement and efficiency.

Each of these activities is briefly discussed below.

A shift in focus toward the individual and away from mass markets

As discussed above, there was a sea change within tourism marketing led by the publication of *The Experience Economy*. Interestingly, it is easily argued that the tourism industry recognized the importance of 'experience' much before this publication as represented by the work of Jakle (1985), Gunn (1988, 1994) and Urry (1990), among others. Indeed, Arnould and Price (1993) in their article 'River Magic: Extraordinary service and the extended service encounter' clearly documented the role of experience within what they later characterized as the 'servicescape'. However, the emergence of the Internet enabled destination marketing organizations to now realize the catchphrase 'markets of one'. In large part this was accomplished by a systematic restructuring of DMOs whereby they changed from focusing on external marketing to building capacity within the organization and the destination necessary to support visitors in very different ways. Importantly, these changes mirrored the emerging conversation within the marketing literature that examined the nature of places, the nature of the tourism experience, the role of the visitor within the experience, the role of various forms of communications and, more recently, the role of social settings (both immediate and further away) in creating the visitor experience.

Parallel to this evolution in destination marketing, our understanding of services emerged within the general marketing literature under the rubric 'services dominant logic', whereby Vargo and Lusch (2004, 2008) compellingly argued that services are essentially different than goods and therefore the economic models of exchange and marketing should differ. This meant that service businesses including tourism marketing organizations can (and should) use a variety of business models in order to create value, communicate with and ultimately realize revenue from the visitor. Further, this new paradigm has led to a new area called 'service design' or within tourism, 'experience design', which now unifies the basic concepts proposed by Gunn (1988) in Vacationscape, the concepts of servicescape and the basic principles of event design. Examples of the emergence of S-D logic within tourism and hospitality setting include the initial success of themed restaurants such as the Rain Forest Café and the Hard Rock Café, the growth of highly niche marketed hotels and resorts, the dominance of systems such as TripAdvisor whereby the experiences of the travellers provide the core product, and, finally, epitomized by the success of Disney in that they have designed 'mass market products' which are now highly individualized. As such, these products support and therefore derive value from their customers across the entire range of tourism experiences.

Based upon the success of these organizations, tourism marketing has also shifted in focus from a traditional 'marketing' and 'advertising' approach characterized by simple promotion of the destination to a variety of forms such as permission marketing and customer relationship management (CRM). This shift toward 'markets of one' has been exemplified by the sophistication in the second and third generation design of destination websites, the use of search engine optimization strategies and destination recommendation systems, and the realization that success is led by the innovativeness of organizations' partnerships and their efforts in 'long tail' marketing (Anderson 2008). Importantly, the foundations created by investing heavily in adapting to the new 'experience marketing' paradigm have enabled destination marketing organizations to respond to the challenges of social media. That is, they have 'emerged' from the last two decades better able to exploit a range of business models which ultimately create value for the destination.

Efforts in market control by destinations through branding

Over the past two decades 'destination branding' has become the logic *de jour* as destination marketing organizations tried to model the success of consumer products such as Nike and Coca Cola, hotels such as Hilton, Marriott, Holiday Inn and the Ritz-Carleton, and cities such as Las Vegas, New York and Paris. Initiated early in the 1990s when Aaker (1991) wrote

Managing Brand Equity and quickly followed by *Building Strong Brands* (1995), it was argued that destinations should promote their 'brand' in order to define themselves with respect to their competitors and to break through overwhelming clutters of information available through the many channels. Essentially, the goal of branding was to exert some kind of 'control' over the market place which was increasingly NOT 'controlled' by the destination marketing organizations. Importantly, a new form of branding was achieved when tourism organizations began defining a vital organizational structure within the destination as well as a 'place' within the minds of existing and potential visitors. Unfortunately, it seems that many destination branding efforts stopped short as they focused more on the slogan which could be used to best represent the essential place (i.e. 'I love New York', 'Incredible India', 'Italy Much More', 'I feel sLOVEnia') and less on creating the internal architecture needed to support the branded destination.

Many recent studies suggest that destinations and their liaison – destination marketers – are losing their ability to communicate effectively with travellers as a variety of online systems (e.g. GDSs and CRSs) which exert control over a huge portion of the hotel, airline, cruise ship and events markets. Search engines, including Google and Kayak, have increased their impact within the online search market, and travel community websites and other forms of consumer generated content such as TripAdvisor and Facebook become even more popular as travellers can overcome the control that marketers seek to effect over traveller decisions. Indeed, many destination marketing organizations have adjusted their focus to include managing their online reputations based upon the assumption that brands can be hurt or even destroyed by the complaints of a small number of visitors and 'Black Swan' events such as floods, hurricanes, wars and atomic plant explosions. For example, The Greek National Tourism Organization (GNTO) recently introduced 'True Greece', an Internet-based reputation management initiative which aims to clarify any existing 'inaccuracies or speculations' regarding Greek tourism destinations (http://www.aboutourism.com/online-reputation-management-destination-marketing-the-case-of-greece/). It is argued that destination reputations should be a central focus as they are more dynamic and therefore more easily managed across the various online platforms (Marchiori and Cantoni 2012).

Focus on measurement and efficiency

The new economic and political environment of the 1990s also forced destination marketing organizations to examine their core functions and to consider alternative strategies for allocation of budgets according to new measures of performance. The old strategies based upon 'intuition' gave way to a variety of new paradigms based upon measurement and benchmarking. Perhaps the most predominant of these efforts focused on advertising evaluation; led by Burke and Gitelson (1990), Woodside (1990), Woodside, McDonald and Trappey (1997) and others (McWilliams and Crompton 1997; Messmer and Johnson 1993) many destination marketing organizations adopted a series of practices which enabled them to better rationalize their advertising efforts. Beginning in the early to mid-1990s, however, DMOs began to recognize the importance of evaluation in other areas of the marketplace such as destination competitiveness, organization structure and service quality through benchmarking.

Perhaps the most widely recognized article (and later turned into a book) on destination competitiveness was written by Crouch and Ritchie (1999), wherein they identified a number of dimensions which should be used to assess the competitiveness of the destination and the destination organization. Zeithaml, Berry and Parasuraman (1990), on the other hand, outlined the foundations for measuring service quality (through SERVQUAL), and offered a five stage

GAP model which identified the areas where tourism organizations can focus (and rationalize) their efforts. Importantly, Kaplan and Norton (1992) developed The Balanced Scorecard, which stands as one of the most influential models for benchmarking organizations and which identifies a process to evaluate performance based upon a series of inputs, processes and outputs. Additionally, Wöber (2002) wrote *Benchmarking in Tourism and Hospitality Industries*, which offered new conceptual and analytical tools for defining and evaluating hospitality and tourism organizations including DMOs.

During this time, leading tourism organizations such as Destination Marketing Association International (DMAI), Tourism Canada (now called The Canadian Tourism Commission), Tourism Australia, the European Travel Commission and European Cities Marketing (ECM) began developing guidelines and tools needed to support destination evaluation. For example, DMAI has developed a series of measure that can be used by DMOs to assess (and benchmark) performance across a range of activities within the organization. Tourism Canada offers the Canadian tourism industry a variety of cutting-edge tools to support knowledge creation including an online library, interactive tools to access online marketing data, and to facilitate connections between and among travel firms/organizations located throughout the country (see, for example, http://en-corporate.canada.travel/resources-industry/tools); similarly, the Australian tourism office has developed a toolbox enabling destinations to conduct research and to evaluate alternative marketing strategies (see http://www.tourism.australia.com/en-au/industry/toolkits.aspx). The Laboratory for Community and Economic Development and the National Laboratory for Tourism and eCommerce, the University of Illinois (now located at Temple University), developed a series of online tools which enable destination marketing organizations to assess their competitiveness, their capacity to develop as a tourism destination and to benchmark themselves against other convention and visitor bureaux within the state (http://community development.uiuc.edu/). Last, the European Travel Commission, along with the Austrian Tourism Organization and MODUL University, Vienna supports the development of TourMIS, which was implemented in 2000 and is used by many European DMOs as a primary tool for assessing European travel trends (http://www.tourmis.info) (Wöber 2003).

Emergence of a new marketing paradigm

As suggested above, the many forces of change have heavily impacted all facets of the tourism industry – they have fundamentally changed how travellers experience travel, how destinations market themselves and, in turn, how the tourism industry develops and measures its success. Evidence of this restructuring is manifest in many ways, none more so that in an article by Gretzel (2012) entitled *Travel in the Network: Redirected gazes, ubiquitous connections and new frontiers* wherein she used, like Castells (1996), the 'network' as a metaphor to describe the various systems that have fundamentally change the travel experience; and in articles by McCabe and Stokoe (2010) and MacKay and Vogt (2012), who suggest that there is a huge 'spillover effect' which links our daily lives, both in terms of how we behave and our use of technology, and the way we experience travel. These articles are essential in that they clearly explain the formation of new models of travel behaviour, new models for product design and new models for research and evaluation which, in turn, establishes a new paradigm of tourism marketing.

As suggested by Gretzel (2012) and others (see for example, Gretzel *et al.* 2006; Wang and Fesenmaier 2012), travel today differs substantially from travel 50 years ago when mass tourism began in earnest. Indeed, it appears that the change in travel follows in parallel to the 'stages of change' model proposed by Contractor, Wasserman and Faust (2006) and Gretzel, Yuan and Fesenmaier (2000) regarding the impact of technology on organizations (Gretzel and Fesenmaier

2001b). In particular, the first two stages of technology use create an 'expansion' in activity, but not any fundamental change in behaviour and that it is only in the third stage that we see real structural changes in the nature of use – that is, travel behaviour. A recent book by Turkle (2012) is mirrored by Gretzel and her colleagues (2012, 2006), MacKay and Vogt (2012), Tussyadiah and her colleagues (2013a, 2013b) and Wang and Fesenmaier (2012), who suggest that there are now important structural changes in travel behaviour whereby travellers tend to 'extend' daily life into travel, become much more involved in creating/controlling the tourism experience by sharing with others, are more involved and creative as they seek authentic experiences, and today's travellers tend to adapt much better to local settings by using various forms of mobile technology.

These new ideas to describe change in travel behaviour require a new paradigm of tourism marketing. In particular, the metaphor of 'travel in the network' suggests there are a number of new conditions for tourism marketing as the result of behavioural change in travel. First, it has already been well documented that, in general, today's marketing practice, from political campaigns to selling groceries, is primarily driven by information technology as the penetration rate of the Internet in the United States has reached to a maximum level of saturation (see http://www.pewinternet.org/). Also in travel and tourism, the Internet is the predominant information source for travel planning (TIA 2011). Within this context, the notion of 'travel in the network' offers a new lens for understanding today's travellers. That is, instead of simply seeing travellers as users of technology, today's travellers can be considered an active partner in technology-supported networks, which further consist of numerous information spaces (e.g. DMO websites) and channels (e.g. OTAs and travel search engines) that support the basic information activities of the traveller. Thus, the Internet is no longer a monolithic eCommerce platform; instead, it offers countless networks and platforms vying for the traveller's attention and spending power by supporting information seeking and transactions (Xiang, Wöber and Fesenmaier 2008). And from a marketing standpoint, creating and delivering the right message to the right person at the right moment is fundamentally important. Indeed, it may be of primary importance for marketers to focus on understanding how travellers navigate these information spaces and channels within the network structure in order to build and anticipate their upcoming travel plans and experiences.

Second, technology-supported networks are social and community-based. Indeed, tourism information on the Internet has taken this perspective from the very moment when the Internet became a public and commercial infrastructure; examples include VirtualTourist and IGoUGo whereas virtual places travellers congregate to share their experiences (Wang and Fesenmaier 2004). However, the explosive growth of Web 2.0 with a variety of tools and platforms that support consumer-generated content has further transformed the Internet into the networks for social interactions (Xiang and Gretzel 2010). Facebook, Twitter, Youtube and Pinterest are quintessential Web 2.0 applications in that they were developed as novel ways to facilitate exchange of information and social networking. Particularly in travel and tourism, websites such as TripAdvisor and Yelp are social spaces wherein word-of-mouth is created, distributed and shared among peer travellers and consumers. As a result, tourism marketing is no longer a practice of advertising and promotion; rather, the focus now has shifted to participating in and being part of the online conversations. Therefore, social media marketing has emerged as a new strategic area for tourism marketing, and there is a growing body of literature documenting this paradigm shift (Gretzel *et al.* 2006; Leung *et al.* 2013; Sigala, Christou and Gretzel 2012).

Third, another important aspect of the travel in the network metaphor is that technology-supported networks are mobile, where today's cutting-edge apps offer all kinds of tools for travellers to search for information and to make decisions on-the-go thereby creating what are described as 'Tourism Activated Networks' (Zack and Gretzel 2011; Wang and Xiang 2012). It is argued that mobile technology such as smartphones (and iPads) can be used to strengthen travellers' social ties and interactions. For many people, a mobile phone is far beyond a communication tool or an accessory of daily lives, and it has become an inseparable part of his/her life or even body (Turkle 2011; Wang and Fesenmaier 2012). As such, the ubiquitous presence of these devices in people's lives potentially intensifies and encourages the participation in mobile social networking. According to a report by comScore, in the United States (2011), 36 per cent of smartphone users use smartphone's browser to access social networks and approximately 42 per cent of smartphone users access social networks through smartphone applications. As a result, the users of social networks and messengers have become one of the major components in terms of mobile Internet traffic (comScore 2012). Therefore, the notion of 'travel in the network' implies that tourism marketing must be built upon a solid understanding of social connectivity and dynamic decision making within mobile contexts.

These radical changes in travel behaviour are mirrored by a host of new tools in research methodology including text analysis, netnography, social network analysis and a variety of customer driven forecasting systems. These new approaches have been developed to take advantage of the inherent quality of travel – they are huge creators of data through the multitude of 'touch points' within the trip whereby travellers leave 'traces' based upon product searches, reviews and purchases, the sharing of experiences with family and friends, and from reports in the news (Gretzel *et al.* 2012). Particularly, the networks that surround travellers in trip planning and their mobility encompass systems that capture and generate an enormous amount of consumer data, and the so-called 'Big Data' offer numerous opportunities and pose new challenges for tourism marketing. For example, destinations and tourism businesses are now engaged in brand and reputation management by tracking and monitoring consumer sentiments about their products and brands in social media and search queries and clickstream data can be used to make inferences about the visitor volume to a destination and even hotel revenues. Also, the emergence of 'geo-location' data enables businesses to identify movement patterns, preferences and levels of loyalty within a destination. Thus, the new systems supporting a variety of destination metrics (typified by Google Analytics) enable marketers in tourism to better understand where and how potential and existing visitors live, the nature of information used to plan a trip, as well as with whom travellers share their experiences before, during and after the trip. These business analytic applications support this new paradigm by offering enhanced customer intelligence, improving business processes and, ultimately, enabling the development of new strategies for navigating an increasingly competitive environment.

Conclusions

The tourism industry has responded to the various forces of change by adopting a new paradigm that embraces innovation which is led by travellers' co-creation activities. Once thought of as a 'problem' which could not be controlled, it appears that many leaders within the industry now recognize the 'brilliance' of this strategy through the extensive use of customer relationship management (CRM) programs, the use of social media/user generated media such as Facebook and TripAdvisor, videos, blogs and tweets, and customer driven innovation (CDI) which are used to create new travel products such as the Quilt Gardens Tour in Northern Indiana (Lee, Tussyadiah and Zach 2010). The revolution over the past two decades appears to have taken hold, and now offers the means for both the traveller and the industry to realize a future just imagined a few years ago.

References

Aaker, D.A. (1991) *Managing Brand Equity: Capitalizing on the Value of a Brand Name.* New York: The Free Press.

— (1995) *Building Strong Brands.* New York: The Free Press.

Anderson, C. (2008) *Long Tail: Why the Future of Business is Selling Less of More.* New York: Hyperion.

Arnould, E.J. and Price, L. (1993) 'River magic: Extraordinary experience and the extended service encounter', *Journal of Consumer Research*, 20(1): 24–45.

Benckendorff, P., Moscardo, G. and Pendergast, D. (2009) *Tourism and Generation Y.* Wallingford, UK: CAB International.

Buhalis, D. (1998) 'Strategic use of information technologies in the tourism industry', *Tourism Management*, 19(5): 409–21.

— (2000) 'Marketing the competitive destination', *Tourism Management*, 21(1): 97–116.

— (2003) *eTourism: Information Technology for Strategic Tourism Management.* New York: Prentice Hall.

Burke, J.F. and Gitelson, R. (1990) 'Conversion studies: Assumptions, applications, accuracy and abuse', *Journal of Travel Research*, 28(3): 46–51.

Castells, M. (1996) *The Rise of the Network Society* (Vol. 1). Oxford: Blackwell Publishers.

Contractor, N.S., Wasserman, S. and Faust, K. (2006) 'Testing multi-level, multi-theoretical hypotheses about networks in 21st century organizational forms: An analytic framework and empirical example', *Academy of Management Review*, 31(3): 681–703.

Crouch, G.I. and Ritchie, J.R.B. (1999) 'Tourism, competitiveness and societal prosperity', *Journal of Business Research*, 44(3): 137–52.

Dertouzos, M. (2001) *The Unfinished Revolution.* New York: HarperCollins Publishers.

Erkuş-Öztürk, H. and Eraydın, A. (2010) 'Environmental governance for sustainable tourism development: Collaborative networks and organisation building in the Antalya tourism region', *Tourism Management*, 31(1): 113–24.

Friedman, T. (2005) *The World is Flat: A Brief History of the Twenty-First Century.* New York: Farrar, Straus and Giroux.

Gretzel, U. (2010) 'Travel in the network: Redirected gazes, ubiquitous connections and new frontiers', in M. Levina and G. Kien (eds) *Post-global Network and Everyday Life.* New York: Peter Lang, pp. 41–58.

Gretzel, U. and Fesenmaier, D.R. (2001a) 'Measuring effective IT use among American convention and visitors bureaus', in P. Sheldon, K. Wöber and D.R. Fesenmaier (eds) *Information and Communication Technologies in Tourism 2001.* Vienna: Springer-Verlag, pp. 52–61.

— (2001b) 'Defining Internet readiness for the tourism industry: Concepts and case study', in H. Werthner (ed.) *Readings in E-Commerce.* Vienna: Springer, pp. 77–101.

— (2002) 'Implementing knowledge-based interfirm networks in heterogeneous B2B environments: A case study of the Illinois tourism network', in K. Wöber, A.J. Frew and M. Hitz (ed) *Information and Communication Technologies in Tourism 2002.* Vienna: Springer-Verlag, pp 39–48.

Gretzel, U., Yuan, Y.L. and Fesenmaier, D.R. (2000) 'Preparing for the new economy: Advertising strategies and change in destination marketing organizations', *Journal of Travel Research*, 39(2): 146–56.

Gretzel, U., Fesenmaier, D.R., Formica, S. and O'Leary, J.T. (2006) 'Searching for the future: Challenges faced by destination marketing organizations', *Journal of Travel Research*, 45(2): 116–26.

Gunn, C.A. (1988) *Vacationscape: Designing Tourist Regions*, 2nd edn. New York: Van Nostrand Reinhold.

— (1994) *Tourism Planning: Basics, Concepts, Cases*, 3rd edn. London: Taylor and Francis.

Hoffman, D.L. and Novak, T.P. (1996) 'Marketing in hypermedia computer-mediated environments: Conceptual foundations', *The Journal of Marketing*, 60: 50–68.

Jakle, J. (1985) *The Tourist: Travel in the Twentieth Century North America.* Lincoln: The University of Nebraska Press.

Kaplan, R.S. and Norton, D.P. (1992) 'The balanced scorecard: Measures that drive performance', *Harvard Business Review*, January–February: 71–80.

Lee, G., Tussyadiah, I.J. and Zach, F. (2010) 'A visitor-focused assessment of new product launch: The case of Quilt Gardens tourism in Northern Indiana's Amish Country', *Journal of Travel and Tourism Marketing*, 27: 723–35.

Leung, D., Law, R., van Hoof, H. and Buhalis, D. (2013) 'Social media in tourism and hospitality: A literature review', *Journal of Travel and Tourism Marketing*, 30(1–2): 3–22.

Levine, R., Locke, C., Searls, D. and Weinberger, D. (2001) *The Cluetrain Manifesto: The End of Business as Usual.* Cambridge, MA: Perseus Publishing.

McCabe, S. and Stokoe, E.H. (2010) 'Have you been away? Holiday talk in everyday interaction', *Annals of Tourism Research*, 37(4): 1117–40.

MacKay, K. and Vogt, C. (2012) 'Information technology in everyday and vacation contexts', *Annals of Tourism Research*, 39(3): 1380–401.

McWilliams, E.G. and Crompton, J.L. (1997) 'An expanded framework for measuring the effectiveness of destination advertising', *Tourism Management*, 18(3): 127–37.

Marchiori, E. and Cantoni, L. (2012) 'The online reputation construct: Does it matter for the tourism domain? A literature review on destinations' online reputation', *Information Technology and Tourism*, 13: 139–59.

Messmer, D.J. and Johnson, R.R. (1993) 'Inquiry conversion and travel advertising effectiveness', *Journal of Travel Research*, 31(4): 14–21.

Negroponte, N. (1995) *Being Digital*. New York: Knopf.

Novak, T.P. and Hoffman, D.L. (1996) 'New metrics for new media: Toward the development of Web measurement standards'. Online as <http://ecommerce.vanderbilt.edu/novak/web.standards/webstand.html>; reprinted in *World Wide Web Journal*, 2(1): 213–46.

Pine II, B.J. and Gilmore, J.H. (2011) *The Experience Economy*. Cambridge, MA: Harvard Business Press.

Poon, A. (1993) *Tourism, Technology and Competitive Strategies*. Wallingford, UK: CAB International.

Porter, M. (1985) *The Competitive Advantage: Creating and Sustaining Superior Performance*. New York: Free Press.

Reynolds, G. (2006) *An Army of Davids: How Markets and Technology Empower Ordinary People to Beat Big Media, Big Government and Other Goliaths*. Nashville, TN: Thomas Nelson Inc.

Ritchie, J.R. and Crouch, G.I. (2000) 'The competitive destination: A sustainability perspective', *Tourism Management*, 21(1): 1–7.

Sheldon, P. (1997) *Tourism Information Technology*. Wallingford, UK: CAB International.

Sigala, M., Christou, E. and Gretzel, U. (2012) *Social Media in Travel, Tourism and Hospitality: Theory, Practice and Cases*. Thousand Oaks, CA: Sage.

Tao, T.C. and Wall, G. (2009) 'Tourism as a sustainable livelihood strategy', *Tourism Management*, 30(1): 90–8.

Tapscott, D. (1997) *The Digital Economy: Promise and Peril In The Age of Networked Intelligence*. East Windsor, NJ: McGraw-Hill.

Tapscott, D. and Caston, A. (1993) *Paradigm Shift: The New Promise of Information Technology*. New York: McGraw-Hill.

Tapscott, D., Ticoll, D. and Lowy, A. (2000) *Digital Capital: Harnessing the Power of Business Webs*. Boston: Harvard Business Press.

TIA (2011) *Travellers' Use of the Internet*. Washington, DC: Travel Industry Association of America.

Turkle, S. (2011) *Alone Together: Why We Expect More From Technology And Less From Each Other*. New York: Basic Books.

Tussyadiah, I.P. (2012) 'A concept of location-based social network marketing', *Journal of Travel and Tourism Marketing*, 29(3): 205–20.

Tussyadiah, I.P. and Fesenmaier, D.R. (2008) 'Marketing places through first person stories – An analysis of Pennsylvania roadtripper blog', *Journal of Travel and Tourism Marketing*, 25(3/4): 299–311.

— (2009) 'Mediating tourist experiences: Access to places via shared videos', *Annals of Tourism Research*, 36(1): 24–40.

Tussyadiah, I.P. and Zach, F. (2012) 'The role of geo-based technology in place experiences', *Annals of Tourism Research*, 39(2): 780–800.

Urry, J. (1990) *The Tourist Gaze*. Thousand Oaks, CA: Sage.

Vargo, S.L. and Lusch, R.F. (2004) 'Evolving to a new dominant logic for marketing', *Journal of Marketing*, 68(1): 1–17.

— (2008) 'Service-dominant logic: Continuing the evolution', *Journal of the Academy of Marketing Science*, 36(1): 1–10.

Wang, D. and Xiang, Z. (2012) 'The new landscape of travel: A comprehensive analysis of smartphone apps', in M. Fuchs, F. Ricci and L. Cantoni (eds) *Information and Communication Technologies in Tourism 2012*. Vienna: Springer-Verlag.

Wang, D., Park, S. and Fesenmaier, D.R. (2012) 'The role of smartphones in mediating the touristic experience', *Journal of Travel Research*, 51(4): 371–87.

Wang, Y. and Fesenmaier, D.R. (2004) 'Towards understanding members' general participation in and active contribution to an online travel community', *Tourism Management*, 25(6): 709–22.

Wang, Y. and Xiang, Z. (2007) 'Toward a theoretical framework of collaborative destination marketing', *Journal of Travel Research*, 46(1): 75–85.

Werthner, H. and Klein, S. (1999) *Information Technology and Tourism – A Challenging Relationship*. Vienna: Springer-Verlag.

Wilson, S., Fesenmaier, D.R., Fesenmaier, J. and Van Es, J.C. (2001) 'Factors for success in rural tourism development', *Journal of Travel Research*, 40(2): 132–8.

Woodside, A.G. (1990) 'Measuring advertising effectiveness in destination marketing strategies', *Journal of Travel Research*, 29(2): 3–8.

Woodside, A.G., McDonald, R.M. and Trappey, R.J. (1997) 'Measuring linkage advertising effects on customer behavior and net revenue', *Canadian Journal of Administrative Sciences*, 14(2): 214–28.

Wöber, K.W. (2002) *Benchmarking in Tourism and Hospitality Industries*. Wallingford, UK: CAB International.

— (2003) 'Information supply in tourism management by marketing decision support systems', *Tourism Management*, 24(3): 241–55.

Xiang, Z. and Gretzel, U. (2010) 'Role of social media in online travel information search', *Tourism Management*, 31(2): 179–88.

Xiang, Z., Wöber, K. and Fesenmaier, D.R. (2008) 'Representation of the online tourism domain in search engines', *Journal of Travel Research*, 47(2): 137–50.

Yuan, Y.L., Gretzel, U. and Fesenmaier, D.R. (2003) 'Internet technology use by American convention and visitors bureaus', *Journal of Travel Research*, 41(3): 240–55.

Zach, F. and Gretzel, U. (2011) 'Tourist-activated networks: implications for dynamic bundling and en route recommendations', *Information Technology and Tourism*, 13(3): 229–38.

Zach, F., Gretzel, U. and Xiang, Z. (2010) 'Innovation in the Web marketing programs of American convention and visitor bureaus', *Information Technology and Tourism*, 12(1): 47–63.

Zeithaml, V.A., Parasuraman, A. and Berry, L.L. (1990) *Delivering Quality Service: Balancing Customer Perceptions and Expectations*. New York: The Free Press.

41

Futurecasting the tourism marketplace

Luiz Moutinho, Ronnie Ballantyne and Shirley Rate

Introduction

The tourism industry is by nature a dynamic one, but recent years have witnessed turbulent and chaotic change from dramatic demographic shifts, climate change, technological revolutions, two major terrorist incidents and a global economic crisis, all of which have momentous implications for tourist trade. Yet tourism remains one of the most valuable economic sectors in the world and the European Travel Commission (2012) indicates that even with a backdrop of on-going government austerity limiting and slowing economic growth, tourism demand in Europe has not significantly dropped. Holidays remain an important aspect of annual expenditure – an emotional and protected purchase. Thus, tourism marketers face unique opportunities in a global context that is stifling other industries. But with opportunities come considerable challenges. This environment of unprecedented worldwide flux and uncertainty makes for extremely difficult and risky business decision making. Analyzing future trends or 'futurecasting' in the tourism sector has become a critical success factor for marketing managers.

The aim of this chapter is to apply futurecasting to a tourism marketing context. The purpose is to highlight the key emerging trends in the tourism environment with implications for future tourist motivations and behaviours and thus the effective marketing of tourism products and services. Futurecasting involves the identification not only of megatrends in the operating environment but also those 'weak signals' in environmental scanning terms that are likely to dictate the nature of the tourist consumer and dominate the make-up of competitive arenas in the tourism sector of the future. These are the developments which if on the 'tourism radar' will allow marketers both an intelligence and time-advantage over their competitors. It is these developments which will drive change in the traditional approaches to tourism marketing. New paradigms of marketing thought must emerge as the implications of future trends produce novel and unparalleled consumer contexts.

As the tourism environment shifts and evolves at an increasingly rapid rate, the challenges for marketers become particularly steep – markets emerge and disappear, new technologies shape the way people seek and share information, consumers become more inquisitive, sophisticated, changeable and demanding, core values which influence motivations, interests, activities have been reinvented as generations evolve. Thus, the traditional concept of meeting consumer needs as the backbone of marketing practice has taken on an entirely different meaning. Old models of marketing become outdated in the face of such revolutions. Consumer-centricity has become one of the fundamental laws. Paradigms of marketing must change and be driven by the outcomes of this business orientation. No longer can the old frameworks of bygone marketing be applied as standard, marketers must sense and respond to their unique markets, their unique relationships, their unique understanding of the changing customer.

Increasingly then, the flexibility and the degree of reactivity to the changing tourism environment are becoming pivotal to competing successfully in this sector. Marketers must have a grasp not only of their immediate and current environment and its impact on consumers, but more importantly, on the landscape of tomorrow, the next day and the more distant future. The ability to predict new key emerging trends will allow fluidity and flexibility of marketing initiatives, accuracy of consumer communication and innovation of delivery.

This chapter will consider some of the developments and trends which pose the most substantial challenges for the marketing of tourism products and the marketing responses which might best address them. First, *The Unknown Tourism Consumer* which considers the new emergent demands of today's and tomorrow's consumer which are influencing the nature of the market; second, *The Tourist as a 'Prosumer'* which focuses on the future implications of more empowered consumers; third, *The New e-Tourist Generation* which explores how new technologies are influencing all aspects of marketing delivery as well as consumer behaviour; fourth, *Evolutions and Revolutions in Branding* which considers a new branding paradigm based upon these consumer shifts. Finally, the chapter outlines *Vectors of Future Success* – a summary of those paradigm shifts necessary for tourism marketers to successfully engage with the new tourist.

The unknown tourism consumer

Few organizations in any sector genuinely know their customers. Today's consumer is very difficult to truly understand. All markets in all sectors are fragmenting, behaviours are becoming more fluid, changeable and individual. Conceptualizing consumers using outmoded techniques and variables no longer helps to forecast behaviour. Inconsistencies in behaviour are persistent across age, gender, geographic as well as many other vectors which now lack power in discriminating between consumers. People are simply more difficult to predict. As tourists become more sophisticated in their behaviour, tourism marketers must in turn become more sophisticated with regards to understanding them and, subsequently, developing marketing strategies and tactics that they use to interact with them. Futurecasting key trends in the tourist environment, some obvious, some currently less distinct, can lead marketers to a better understanding of motives and how to predict and fulfil them. The rise of the '*prosumer*' in the tourist sector, discussed in detail in the following section, is an outcome of some of the more noteworthy developments in the tourist marketplace.

There are some critical shifts in our economic, demographic and global competitive arena in tourism which will cause momentous change in the way we approach market tourist goods and services. Perhaps one of the most obvious and dramatic changes in the consumer marketplace is the ageing population. In the USA the 'baby boomer' generation, now aged between 47 and 65, accounts for the largest share in sales in most product categories (Dickie 2012). By 2050, 22 per cent of the world's population will be 60 years or over (UN 2011). The UK, Italy, Germany and Japan represent 70 per cent of the world's tourism expenditure and these countries have the fastest growing ageing populations (Yeoman 2012). Yet marketers have been slow to respond to such changes in their marketplaces. Where they have, an indifferent and stereotypically-driven set of initiatives has prevailed. The 'older tourist' has to be redefined. Assumptions of infirmity and frailty in body and mind are outdated notions that prevent a true understanding of a market which will eventually dominate the tourist sector. Older consumers are living longer and healthier lives thanks to advances in medicine. While retirement ages may shift and continued contribution to the workforce may be the norm, they still have more time, money and inclination to travel (Deloitte LLP 2010). Younger at heart with materialism behind them, this group are experienced travellers ready to try new things as well as repeat experiences of their youth – the new wave of 'rich-packers', returning to the places they backpacked as penniless tourists, is just one of the many trends the industry is likely to witness (Dwyer *et al.* 2008).

Another critical driver of the new global tourist is wealth. While the economic balance of power is shifting rapidly towards developing countries, the growth of Brazil, Russia, India and China (BRIC countries) is such that the average 'international tourist' of the future will look very different to today. Already these countries are seeing rapid growth in personal spending power as their economies expand (Yeoman 2012). Tourism marketers must recognize in all their efforts to brand their products and services that a new wave of middle class tourist, eager to spend their newly acquired wealth on hitherto unavailable experiences, is likely to think differently, respond uniquely and want entirely different relationships with their brands. The more affluent people become across the globe, the more complex life and product decisions become and a new disillusionment with the marketplace is beginning to spread – 'affluenza' is the result of a growing tension between wealth and the desire for a simpler, less materialistic life (Hamilton and Denis 2006). Increasingly, consumers are seeking personal fulfilment through experiential consumption. This bodes well for the tourism sector but only if marketers can get behind the motives of this new social movement.

Authenticity of experience is becoming a key goal in tourism purchasing (Yeoman, Brass and McMahon-Beattie 2007). The concept of mass tourism dominated by standard packaged products and service is fast in decline. Touristic consumers want to participate, not spectate. Social and environmental consciousness continues to grow and with that more emphasis is being placed on provenance and sustainability but also tourist consumption is more about discovery and learning – it is no longer where you go that matters but what you do when you are there (Forum for the Future 2009). Dwyer *et al.* (2008) go as far as to predict that the barrier between education and leisure will blur such that it will eventually disappear. Within this, there is more demand for multi-experience holidays – interacting with the community, buying local produce, getting close to nature; volunteering and conservationism are niche, but growing requirements of some markets (Dickie 2012).

With all this, the tourist consumer is becoming especially discerning. More priority is placed upon value. New technologies which have opened up access to information about holidays from independent reviewers, marketers and fellow tourists, providing visualizations of e-destinations, accommodations and services have 'tangibilized the intangible'. Risk is reduced as consumers feel they can effectively try before they buy. Price is no longer the only way to define quality – quality can be seen and thus assured and price becomes secondary. The shift is already evident. As consumers can be more certain of quality of product, the emphasis is moving to quality of personal service (Dickie 2012). This is a differentiator that tourism marketers must harness in a field so competitive that, often, few differences can be found between providers.

Perhaps most striking about all these trends is the level of individualism demanded by the new tourist – holidays must fit specific requirements. Choice abounds and tourists have the desire to create their own package of experiences suiting their desires and needs. They are more experienced, more marketing-savvy with higher expectations, greater access to information and a better eye for truthfulness and authenticity. Evolutions in technology have given them more control and more ability to discriminate accurately and quickly between tourist operators and their offerings. This new '*Prosumer*' is enabled and empowered and takes command in designing unique and customised travel experiences. The smart tourist marketer will listen, provide platforms for this new desire for control and take a new role of facilitator of dreams and memory-creation.

The tourist as a 'prosumer'

The new emergent empowered tourist consumer enabled by the Internet – no longer alone, digitally connected and well informed – will seek out authentic, customized, environmentally aware and friendly tourism experiences; specialist niche interest activities and independently customized tourism will flourish. As such, tourism providers must become truly customer centric – they must listen to the 'voice of the consumer'. The rise of prosumption begins to challenge classic top-down or 'outbound' marketing and management philosophies of 'we market to you' or 'telling and selling', to a 'bottom up' experience whereby the consumer can become a more active participant in the overall brand experience as opposed to a passive receiver of information and products. As such the 'New Tourist' is no longer content in terms of simply waiting for new products and services to arrive and will continue to demonstrate a more active behaviour in consumption thus blurring the traditional boundaries of producer and consumer and importantly allowing for shifts in business thinking, thus facilitating new paradigms of marketing and importantly branding.

Prosumption presents real opportunities for tourism providers and is viewed as a megatrend that the Tourism industry must respect and turn to its advantage. The very nature of tourism determines a degree of inseparability between production and consumption of the tourist experience. Historically, however, consumers had little ability or power to truly customize and shape their tourism experience to best suit their needs, wants, desires and indeed their dreams. Customer-produced experiences will continue to accelerate in the twenty-first century. The phenomenon of corporations creating goods, services and experiences in close cooperation with experienced and creative consumers, tapping into their intellectual capital, and in exchange giving them a direct say in (and rewarding them for) what actually gets produced, manufactured, developed, designed, serviced, processed or experienced will increasingly become the norm across many business sectors including the tourism arena. The web has given rise to a more powerful consumer – liberating and empowering them but at a deeper level there is a new consciousness paradigm. The new consumer is searching for real value and needs to know what is behind the brand name and promise. By encouraging and facilitating co-creation, the dimensions of the brand become more transparent to the consumer and indeed the consumers themselves become the lead authors of the brand experience – thus leading to greater trust and more involved, stronger relationships between organizations and individuals. In summary the continued growth of prosumers challenges traditional business logic where:

- firms create value unilaterally;
- consumers are passive;
- products and services represent the value.

Prosumption brings new frame of reference by:

- focusing on the customer–company interaction as a new value creation;
- co-creating value through customer and company collaboration;

- taking into consideration that value is unique to each customer and is associated to personalized experiences;
- products and services are only means to an end.

Prosumption is then transforming the customer–company relationship by allowing consumers to co-construct their own unique value. This new type of operation is turning the 'supply chain' into a 'demand value chain', by reversing the flow of marketing from 'company to customer' to 'customer to company'. Enlightened tourism marketers will collaborate with consumers to build a dialogue and exchange process that creates value for both parties. This shift in thinking moves the emphasis from what marketers do to consumers to what consumers want from marketing.

New e-tourist generation

Technology continues to play a massive part in changing entire business models in almost every sector. The impacts are obvious – the way products are designed, created and marketed has altered immeasurably. For marketers, technology can be a threat or an opportunity. The potential that new technologies present for meeting and exceeding the needs of the new tourist are immense. With an understanding of the need for consumer-centricity, marketers must harness the Internet and other new media as a means of gaining consumer intelligence. Those tourist operators which have managed this have developed a competitive edge which cannot be rivalled. With big data, comes the ability to tailor and customize communications, develop brand relationships which have strength and endurance and build bonds with consumers which shut out the competitive voice.

Nonetheless, repeatedly, studies show that technology investment in the tourism industry significantly lags behind other sectors – the sector has simply not taken an active role in developing or adapting new technology (Dwyer *et al.* 2008). It has been argued that this is due to the structure of the industry made up largely of small and medium sized enterprises. Yet findings from Dwyer *et al.* (2009) indicate that practitioners are aware that technology actually offers the platform to compete with larger organizations on a more level playing field. Opportunities to develop, maintain and maximize competitive advantage remain significant.

For tourist consumers, the world of products and services will never be the same and is in constant flux. The current fragmented world in which we all live, part-physical, part-virtual, with what seems like infinite touch points available to us is the new reality. A new 'marketsphere' has emerged – a technology-driven, borderless world with fragmenting media and diverse customers resistant to traditional push marketing is now upon us. In particular, we have witnessed the rise of social media. Social media has become a ubiquitous feature of online life – given the greater accessibility and reduced cost of broadband, coupled with the accelerated development of communication tools such as microblogs and video sharing websites are of much interest to the industry as these are increasingly viewed as a relevant metric of brand value. Consumers' engagement with social media in the tourism arena has evolved beyond anyone's expectations (Buhalis and Law 2008) providing a forum for '*twinsumers*' – our taste twins, fellow consumers somewhere in the world who think, react, enjoy and consume the same way we do and on whose advice/information we rely to make purchase decisions. Tourism marketers must focus not only on customer service as a means of harnessing these forums (Dickie 2012) but also take advantage of this propensity to engage online. Consumers want to interact, but expectations of the quality of these interactions are very high.

Yet the tourism industry is in danger of missing opportunities. Focusing primarily on an e-commerce model that centres on reducing channel costs, where price has become the primary mode of product differentiation is no longer sustainable. New emergent models must realign to consider how best to maximize returns by serving consumers' technological needs. At a minimum, marketers must deliver distribution systems which are fast, reliable and open the doors for consumers to flex their individual muscles, facilitating the 'self-designed' holiday. Hilton is among those operators who place this as high priority having devised an app for the iPhone which allows guests to manage their bookings in their increasingly mobile worlds. But some marketers are being more technologically adventurous than others, examples include hotels which use in-room technology to enhance the consumer experience, such as windows that turn into televisions, beds that rock guests to sleep and floors that light up when walked on in the dark. Also, Virtual Reality technology is being used by some destinations to beam destination images direct to the home, providing sustainable and cheap ways of seeing protected destinations (Guttentag 2010).

These are perhaps visions of a more distant future but for now a tourist industry that lags behind others in wooing their markets digitally must focus on harnessing the immense opportunities to build lasting relationships. Bonds can be now created and maintained with large customer bases at a fraction of the cost and labour-intensity. As such companies are beginning to utilize search-based advertising via the online platform and are also initiating 'word-of-mouth' or indeed 'word-of-net' based presence to stimulate buzz, interest and hyperbole via blogs, discussion forums and tourist communities as new and more relevant ways to replace mass advertising. Consumers can then become advocates, true ambassadors and endorsers of the brand.

The concept of the influential consumer has taken on a whole new level of importance. It can be argued that influential consumers have become the true gatekeepers of success for firms. The biggest shift powered by the digital lever is that the average consumer has become the new storyteller, and digital experiences are becoming more important to an empowered consumer, who now has more options than ever before. Consumer generated marketing via blogs, discussion forums or indeed Youtube reviews and testimonials reviewed in previous chapters of this volume is the most revolutionary concept in marketing for a long time. As the role of trust and source credibility becomes heightened in consumer decision making, bias free reviews and recommendations will carry great influence in generating awareness and facilitating consumer choice of tourism choice alternatives. Consumer generated marketing is a fact of life to which all of us will have to adapt. Consumers are then gaining more and more control, brand 'authority' is diminished and consumers are becoming increasingly empowered to create and tailor the product themselves, such that it is the consumer who now owns the brand (Deloitte LLP 2010).

Evolutions and revolutions in tourism branding

Brands have become omnipresent in today's marketplace. Consumers have become accustomed to using brands as essential guides to help navigate an over-cluttered multiple-choice, multiple-destination, multiple-experience world in which we live. Brands have historically facilitated short cuts in consumer decision making, allowing consumers to develop decision making heuristics, reducing time and effort by identifying reputable and trusted sources of consumer value. Within the tourism arena, destinations, travel companies, accommodation, food and entertainment providers alike have all adopted traditional product-based approaches to brand development and marketing, with particular brand dimensions and personality traits highlighted and exaggerated in advertising claims.

Tourism operators have sought to position their brands distinctively in the hearts and minds of their target audiences, thus facilitating the development and maintenance of the brand tribe or brand community. Nevertheless the classic branding paradigm is becoming tired and may now be beginning to lose its edge. As consumers grow less and less passive and are increasingly more savvy about marketing and commercial realism, brands must modify their approach. Reading consumers is becoming more complex and multidimensional in nature. In the future the most successful brands will be those that abandon the traditional top-down approach in favour of bottom up strategies whereby the consumer is an active participant in the design of the overall brand experience – in effect tomorrow's megabrands will be the consumer's agents as opposed to producers', thus pioneering a transformation from trademarks to trust marks using trust-based marketing.

The challenge for marketers is that consumers in the future will want less not more, sense not nonsense and above all they want companies to inject simplicity into marketing. The time when brands preached and consumers listened is no longer as dominant as it once was. This means repositioning tourism brands to survive in an environment of knowledgeable and cynical, marketing literate consumers who no longer seek solace in false brand gods, hype and spin. In a society where brands are now becoming 'mental pollutants' and the traditional 'Marketing Medicine' (e.g. I buy therefore I am and to buy is to be perceived) is increasingly diagnosed more as a 'disease', we are now witnessing the era of *demarketing* chic.

Brands can become negative baggage as they are undermined by the very values they own in the mind of the consumer. The deferential consumer, conditioned to 'salivate' and desire upon being 'buzzed' by brands, has been buried along with the golden era of marketing. Consumers are already becoming increasingly brand immune and in some cases they are developing 'brand allergies'. Consumers are no longer willing to be forced to absorb brand messages. As a consequence brands may lose control of their own image. Nonetheless they can turn this to an advantage of content creation via prosumption and associated buzz generated by consumers themselves. Brands must move from a marketing model that says, 'I'm going to talk to you and you better listen up' to an experiential model.

The new realities of branding are upon us and innovative companies are dispensing with the mass economy tactics of the twentieth century and replacing them with tactics more suited to the new consumer economy. Tourism marketers must then recognize that markets consist of human beings and not segmentation typologies. Markets can no longer be treated as pure demographics, geo-demographics or psychographics in terms of segmentation bases with brands to fit each neat category. Markets actually consist of human beings each with unique needs and desires. This awareness, coupled with less passive consumers, prompts the need for a new model of brand relations – the 'Brain to Brain' model. Companies must adopt an intelligent and integrated marketing and management approach that seeks to establish and nurture 'intelligent dialogue' with customers, which ironically may mean for some brands a return to classical marketing: solving people's problems at a profit period.

As brands evolve to ensure an intelligent dialogue with customers, ever greater demand for (emotional) authenticity and value will be desired by consumers. The emotional value *is* the economic value or momentary worth of feelings when consumers positively (or negatively) experience branded products and services. Emotional value, as much as quality or any other product attribute or dimension of a tourism brands worth can make or break a business. We live in a world where the 'little things' really do matter – each encounter be it physical or virtual and no matter how brief, is a micro interaction which makes a deposit or withdrawal from our rational and emotional subconscious. As such if companies do not handle consumers' emotional needs and wants satisfactorily, brands are at risk. Incorporating emotional design into the development and branding of the tourism product is becoming a necessity for tourism and travel providers. We will see an increased move towards branding as a form of immersive experience whereby the consumer is an active participant in generating and manifesting that experience. The experience now has to be something more than simply the act of searching and buying products in a pleasing physical environment or virtual environment. Brands must deliver a unique immersive themed sensory experience and importantly an emotional one; it must make the consumer feel good. Moreover a brand experience platform that allows for flexibility and reactivity is desirable, change will be necessary as consumers get bored very quickly and as such the 'experience' must continue to evolve and change so as to allow on-going new experiences, thus the experience is always new and therefore desired.

Today and in the future, marketers want to extend their contact with customers through time. In effect the brand must change from being thought of not as a product or a service but an invitation, specifically to an emotionally satisfying and enduring relationship. The brand promise should connote the quality of that relationship. Branding must then become more than seduction and emotional manipulation or indeed the construction of artificial needs and desires – it becomes the fostering and promotion of trusting relationships and demonstrating intelligence, caring and human common sense to satisfy real existing human needs. As such marketers must get back to creating and telling compelling brand stories based on substance and not spin. Brands are beginning to seek to build platforms which enable them to engage their customers. Increasingly, these platforms get people to be part of the narrative or story and to contribute to it. It is a totally different approach to the traditional brand building and advertising strategy based around intervention.

Concluding remarks – vectors of future success

In summary, perhaps more than most sectors, the tourism industry is experiencing unprecedented change at an extraordinary pace. Trends and changes in the environment are converging to create an entirely new tourist consumer. This consumer represents a new geo-demographic, shirking the materialistic values of previous generations, placing new importance on people, societies and environments and expecting businesses to follow suit. New consumers will not accept mass marketing communications or the one-product-fits-all approach; they want personalized treatment, real, true and authentic experiences and expect products and services to function as a gateway to authentic living. Consumers live in a 24 hour information society where new technologies play a bigger role than that of the mighty television. They have education, knowledge and understanding of the tourism sector and all it offers and are savvier about product portfolios than operators themselves.

The new breed of consumer will only respond to trustworthy, truer brands – brands that understand their personal needs and fit into their lifestyles. In terms of a 'world view' clearly not all states and consumers are at the same stage with regards to consumption practices and technology – global disparities still exist at present, nonetheless as technology becomes ever more affordable and accessible and as consumers share more experiences via social networking sites, it is evident that this consumer attitude will become dominant. Customer-centricity is then crucial – customers must become the pivotal strategic focus for firms. As such we are at the beginning of a journey from 'brand building' and 'customer relationship management' to the new standard of consumer agency.

New business and marketing models must emerge. The era of brands dictating through annoying and disruptive advertising is now being replaced by interactive community-orientated engagement marketing. Tourism marketers in conjunction with their consumers must move towards creating immersive brand experiences that provide the best end-to-end experience whilst delivering both sales and on-going loyalty. This new vision of tourism marketing is driven less by knowing about consumers and more by an ability to develop an understanding with them. Consumers are now beginning to view themselves as citizens not only of countries but of corporations and as citizens they expect to have an input in how that organization behaves.

The implications for Tourism Marketing practice are clear: the savvy tourism marketer is one that accepts these new developments and trends as challenges rather than threats and considers the many opportunities that can be harnessed in a bid to engage with their consumers. Indeed, advances in technology have enhanced the desire to travel (Forum for the Future 2009); the challenge is keeping up with changeable needs and increasing demands. At a very minimum, tourism providers must deliver distribution systems that allow seamlessness and immediacy in the booking process as well as control in packaging and personalizing the product. The key is in understanding what adds real value and delivering services to match.

References

Buhalis, D. and Law, R. (2008) 'Progress in Information Technology and Tourism Management: 20 Years on and 10 Years after the Internet – the State of eTourism Research', *Tourism Management*, 29: 609–23.

Deloitte LLP (2010) *Hospitality 2015: Game Changers or Spectators?* London: Deloitte LLP.

Dickie, S. (2012) *Trends and Markets Research Report: Research for Tourism Leadership Group*. Edinburgh: Visit Scotland.

Dwyer, L., Edwards, D., Mistilis, N., Roman, C., Scott, N. and Cooper, C. (2008) *Megatrends Underpinning Tourism to 2020: Analysis of Key Drivers for Change*. Gold Coast, Queensland, Australia: Cooperative Research Centre for Sustainable Tourism.

Dwyer, L., Edwards, E., Mistills, N., Roman, C. and Scott, N. (2009) 'Destination and Enterprise Management for a Tourism Future', *Tourism Management*, 30: 63–74.

European Travel Commission (2012) *European Tourism 2012: Trends and Prospects*. Brussels: European Travel Commission.

Forum for the Future (2009) *Tourism 2023: Four Scenarios, a Vision and a Strategy for UK Outbound Travel and Tourism*. London: Forum for the Future.

Guttentag, D.A. (2010) 'Virtual Reality: Applications and Implications for Tourism', *Tourism Management*, 31: 637–51.

Hamilton, C. and Deniss, R. (2006) *Affluenza: When too Much is Never Enough*. Sidney: Allen and Unwin.

Yeoman, I. (2012) *2050 Tomorrow's Tourism*. Bristol: Channel View Publications.

Yeoman, I., Brass, D. and McMahon-Beattie, U. (2007) 'Current Issue in Tourism: The Authentic Tourist', *Tourism Management*, 28: 1128–38.

Index